Weiss Ratings'
Guide to
Health Insurers

Weiss Ratings
4400 Northcorp Parkway
Palm Beach Gardens, FL 33410
561-627-3300

Published by Grey House Publishing, Inc., located at 4919 Route 22, Amenia, NY 12501; telephone 518-789-8700. Grey House Publishing neither guarantees the accuracy of the data contained herein nor assumes any responsibility for errors, omissions or discrepancies. Grey House Publishing accepts no payment for listing; inclusion in the publication of any organization, agency, institution, publication, service or individual does not imply endorsement of the publisher.

4919 Route 22
PO Box 56
Amenia, NY 12501-0056

Edition No. 80, Spring 2015

ISBN: 978-1-61925-589-0
ISSN: 2158-5938

Contents

Terms and Conditions

This Document is prepared strictly for the confidential use of our customer(s). It has been provided to you at your specific request. It is not directed to, or intended for distribution to or use by, any person or entity who is a citizen or resident of or located in any locality, state, country or other jurisdiction where such distribution, publication, availability or use would be contrary to law or regulation or which would subject Weiss Ratings or its affiliates to any registration or licensing requirement within such jurisdiction.

No part of the analysts' compensation was, is, or will be, directly or indirectly, related to the specific recommendations or views expressed in this research report.

This Document is not intended for the direct or indirect solicitation of business. Weiss Ratings, LLC and its affiliates disclaims any and all liability to any person or entity for any loss or damage caused, in whole or in part, by any error (negligent or otherwise) or other circumstances involved in, resulting from or relating to the procurement, compilation, analysis, interpretation, editing, transcribing, publishing and/or dissemination or transmittal of any information contained herein.

Weiss Ratings has not taken any steps to ensure that the securities or investment vehicle referred to in this report are suitable for any particular investor. The investment or services contained or referred to in this report may not be suitable for you and it is recommended that you consult an independent investment advisor if you are in doubt about such investments or investment services. Nothing in this report constitutes investment, legal, accounting or tax advice or a representation that any investment or strategy is suitable or appropriate to your individual circumstances or otherwise constitutes a personal recommendation to you.

The ratings and other opinions contained in this Document must be construed solely as statements of opinion from Weiss Ratings, LLC, and not statements of fact. Each rating or opinion must be weighed solely as a factor in your choice of an institution and should not be construed as a recommendation to buy, sell or otherwise act with respect to the particular product or company involved.

Past performance should not be taken as an indication or guarantee of future performance, and no representation or warranty, expressed or implied, is made regarding future performance. Information, opinions and estimates contained in this report reflect a judgment at its original date of publication and are subject to change without notice. Weiss Ratings offers a notification service for rating changes on companies you specify. For more information visit WeissRatings.com or call 1-877-934-7778. The price, value and income from any of the securities or financial instruments mentioned in this report can fall as well as rise.

This Document and the information contained herein is copyrighted by Weiss Ratings, LLC. Any copying, displaying, selling, distributing or otherwise reproducing or delivering this information or any part of this Document to any other person or entity is prohibited without the express written consent of Weiss Ratings, LLC, with the exception of a reviewer or editor who may quote brief passages in connection with a review or a news story.

Message To Insurers

All data on insurers filing a Health financial statement received on or before November 4, 2014 has been considered or incorporated into this edition of the Directory. If there are particular circumstances which you believe could affect your rating, please use the online survey (http://weissratings.com/survey/) or e-mail Weiss Ratings (insurancesurvey@weissinc.com) with documentation to support your request. If warranted, we will make every effort to incorporate the changes in our next edition.

Guide to Health Insurers

Most people automatically assume their insurance company will survive, year after year. However, prudent consumers and professionals realize that in this world of shifting risks, the solvency of insurance companies can't be taken for granted.

If you are looking for accurate, unbiased ratings and data to help you choose health insurance for yourself, your family, your company, or your clients, *Weiss Ratings Guide to Health Insurers* gives you precisely what you need.

In fact, it's the only source that currently provides ratings and analyses on over 1,200 health insurers, including all Blue Cross/Blue Shield plans and over 500 health maintenance organizations.

Weiss Ratings' Mission Statement

Weiss Ratings' mission is to empower consumers, professionals, and institutions with high quality advisory information for selecting or monitoring a financial services company or financial investment.

In doing so, Weiss Ratings will adhere to the highest ethical standards by maintaining our independent, unbiased outlook and approach to advising our customers.

Why rely on Weiss Ratings?

Weiss Ratings provides fair, objective ratings to help professionals and consumers alike make educated purchasing decisions.

At Weiss Ratings, integrity is number one. Weiss Ratings never takes a penny from insurance companies for its ratings. And, we publish Weiss Financial Strength Ratings without regard for insurers' preferences. However, other rating agencies like A.M. Best, Fitch, Moody's, and Standard & Poor's are paid by insurance companies for their ratings and may even suppress unfavorable ratings at an insurer's request.

Our ratings are more frequently reviewed and updated than any other ratings. You can be sure that the information you receive is accurate and current – providing you with advance warning of financial vulnerability early enough to do something about it.

Other rating agencies focus primarily on a company's current claims paying ability and consider only mild economic adversity. Weiss Ratings also considers these issues, but in addition, our analysis covers a company's ability to deal with severe economic adversity and a sharp increase in claims.

Our use of more rigorous standards stems from the viewpoint that an insurance company's obligations to its policyholders should not depend on favorable business conditions. An insurer must be able to honor its policy commitments in bad times as well as good.

Our rating scale, from A to F, is easy to understand. Only a few outstanding companies receive an A (Excellent) rating, although there are many to choose from within the B (Good) category. An even larger group falls into the broad average range which receives C (Fair) ratings. Companies that demonstrate marked vulnerabilities receive either D (Weak) or E (Very Weak) ratings.

How to Use This Guide

The purpose of the *Guide to Health Insurers* is to provide policyholders and prospective policy purchasers with a reliable source of insurance company ratings and analyses on a timely basis. We realize that the financial strength of an insurer is an important factor to consider when making the decision to purchase a policy or change companies. The ratings and analyses in this Guide can make that evaluation easier when you are considering:

- Medical reimbursement insurance
- Managed health care (PPOs and HMOs)
- Disability income
- Long-term care (nursing home) insurance

This Guide includes ratings for health insurers such as commercial for-profit insurers, mutual insurers, Blue Cross/Blue Shield plans, and for-profit and not-for-profit insurers. This is the only source of ratings on many of these companies.

In addition, many companies that offer health insurance also offer life, property or liability insurance. If you are shopping for any of those types of coverage, please refer to either our *Guide to Life and Annuity Insurers* or our *Guide to Property and Casualty Insurers*.

The rating for a particular company indicates our opinion regarding that company's ability to meet its commitments to the policyholder – not only under current economic conditions, but also during a declining economy or in the event of a sharp increase in claims. Such an increase in claims and related expenses may be triggered by any number of occurrences including rising medical costs, malpractice lawsuits, out-of-control administrative expenses, or the unexpected spread of a disease such as AIDS. The safest companies, however, should be prepared to deal with harsh and unforeseen circumstances.

To use this Guide most effectively, we recommend you follow the steps outlined below:

Step 1   To ensure you evaluate the correct company, verify the company's exact name and state of domicile as it was given to you or appears on your policy. Many companies have similar names but are not related to one another, so you want to make sure the company you look up is really the one you are interested in evaluating.

Step 2   Turn to Section I, the Index of Companies, and locate the company you are evaluating. This section contains all health insurance companies analyzed by Weiss Ratings including those that did not receive a Financial Strength Rating. It is sorted alphabetically by the name of the company and shows the state of domicile following the name for additional verification.

Step 3   Once you have located your specific company, the first column after the state of domicile shows its Weiss Financial Strength Rating. See *About Weiss Financial Strength Ratings* for information about what this rating means. If the rating has changed since the last issue of this Guide, a downgrade will be indicated with a down triangle ▼ to the left of the company name; an upgrade will be indicated with an up triangle ▲.

Step 4   Following Weiss Financial Strength Rating is some additional information about the company such as its type, size and capital level. Refer to the introduction of Section I, to see what each of these factors measures.

Step 5   Some insurers have a bullet • following the domicile state in Section I. This means that more detailed information about the company is available in Section II.

If the company you are evaluating is identified with a bullet, turn to Section II, the Analysis of Largest Companies , and locate it there (otherwise skip to step 9). Section II contains all health insurers and Blue Cross/Blue Shield plans plus the largest property & casualty and life & annutiy insurers offering health insurance rated by Weiss, regardless of rating. It too is sorted alphabetically by the name of the company.

Step 6   Once you have identified your company in Section II, you will find its Financial Strength Rating and a description of the rating immediately to the right of the company name. Then, below the company name is a description of the various rating factors that were considered in assigning the company's rating. These factors and the information below them are designed to give you a better feel for the company and its strengths and weaknesses. Refer to the introduction of Section II to get a better understanding of what each of these factors means.

Step 7   To the right, you will find a five-year summary of the company's Financial Strength Rating, capitalization and income. Look for positive or negative trends in these data. Below the five-year summary, we have included a graphic illustration of the most crucial factor or factors impacting the company's rating. Again, the Section II introduction provides an overview of the content of each graph or table.

Step 8   If the company you are evaluating is a Medicare HMO, you can also look it up in Section VII to get some idea of the quality of service being offered. Here you can see the number of complaints against a company that have reached the federal review level based on the most recent data available.

Step 9   If you are interested in long-term care insurance, you can turn to Section V and get a listing of long-term care insurers. To compare long-term care policies see the Long-Term Care Insurance Planner within the Appendix.

Step 10   If the company you are evaluating is not highly rated and you want to find an insurer with a higher rating, turn to the page in Section IV that has your state's name at the top. This section contains those Recommended Companies (rating of A+, A, A- or B+) that are licensed to underwrite health insurance in your state, sorted by rating. From here you can select a company and then refer back to Sections I and II to analyze it.

Step 11   If you decide that you would like to contact one of Weiss Recommended Companies about obtaining a policy or for additional information, refer to Section III where you will find all of Weiss recommended companies listed alphabetically by name. Following each company's name is its address and phone number to assist you in making contact.

Step 12 Many consumers have reported to us the difficulties they have encountered in finding a Recommended Company that offers the best pricing and benefits. Therefore, when considering medical reimbursement or managed care coverage, you may want to consider other companies that have received a good (B or B-) rating even though they did not make Weiss Recommended List. However, for long-term policies such as nursing home care or disability income, we recommend sticking to companies with a rating of B+ or higher.

Step 13 In order to use Weiss Financial Strength Ratings most effectively, we strongly recommend you consult the Important Warnings and Cautions. These are more than just "standard disclaimers." They are very important factors you should be aware of before using this Guide. If you have any questions regarding the precise meaning of specific terms used in the Guide, refer to the Glossary.

Step 14 Make sure you stay up to date with the latest information available since the publication of this Guide. For information on how to set up a rating change notification service, acquire follow-up reports, or receive a more in-depth analysis of an individual company, visit www.weissratings.com or call 1-877-934-7778.

Data Sources: Annual and quarterly statutory statements filed with state insurance commissioners and data provided by the insurance companies being rated. Medicare HMO complaint data were provided by the Centers for Medicare and Medicaid Services: The Center for Health Dispute Resolution, (formerly known as Health Care Financing Administration), and is reprinted here. The National Association of Insurance Commissioners has provided some of the raw data. Any analyses or conclusions are not provided or endorsed by the NAIC.

Date of data analyzed: June 30, 2014 unless otherwise noted

About Weiss Financial Strength Ratings

Weiss Financial Strength Ratings represent a completely independent, unbiased opinion of an insurance company's financial strength. The ratings are derived, for the most part, from annual and quarterly financial statements obtained from state insurance commissioners. These data are supplemented by information that we request from the insurance companies themselves. Although we seek to maintain an open line of communication with the companies being rated, we do not grant them the right to influence the ratings or stop their publication.

Weiss Financial Strength Ratings are assigned by our analysts based on a complex analysis of hundreds of factors that are synthesized into a series of indexes: risk-adjusted capital, capitalization (L&H and HMDI companies only), reserve adequacy (P&C companies only), profitability, investment safety (L&H and HMDI companies only), liquidity, and stability. These indexes are then used to arrive at a letter grade rating. A good rating requires consistency across all indexes. A weak score on any one index can result in a low rating, as insolvency can be caused by any one of a number of factors, such as inadequate capital, unpredictable claims experience, poor liquidity, speculative investments, or operating losses.

Following is an outline of the primary components of Weiss Financial Strength Rating.

Risk-Adjusted Capital Indexes gauge capital adequacy in terms of each insurer's risk profile under both *moderate* and *severe* loss scenarios. For more information please see Section I and the Appendix.

Capitalization Index combines the two Risk-Adjusted Capital ratios with a leverage test that examines pricing risk.

Reserve Adequacy Index measures the adequacy of the company's reserves and its ability to accurately anticipate the level of claims it will receive.

Profitability Index measures the soundness of the company's operations and the contribution of profits to the company's financial strength.

Investment Safety Index measures the exposure of the company's investment portfolio to loss of principal and /or income due to default and market risks.

Liquidity Index values a company's ability to raise the necessary cash to settle claims. We model various cash flow scenarios, applying liquidity tests to determine how the company might fare in the event of an unexpected spike in claims and/or a run on policy surrenders.

Stability Index integrates a number of sub-factors that affect consistency (or lack thereof) in maintaining financial strength over time. These sub-factors will vary depending on the type of insurance company being evaluated but may include such things as 1) risk diversification in terms of company and group size, number of policies in force, patient and provider enrollment, use of reinsurance; 2) deterioration of operations as reported in critical asset, liability, income and expense items; 3) years in operation; 4) former problem areas where, despite recent improvement, the company has yet to establish a record of stable performance over a suitable period of time; 5) a substantial shift in the company's operations; 6) potential instabilities such as reinsurance quality, asset/liability matching, and source of capital; and 7) relationships with holding companies and affiliates.

Each of these indexes is measured according to the following range of values.

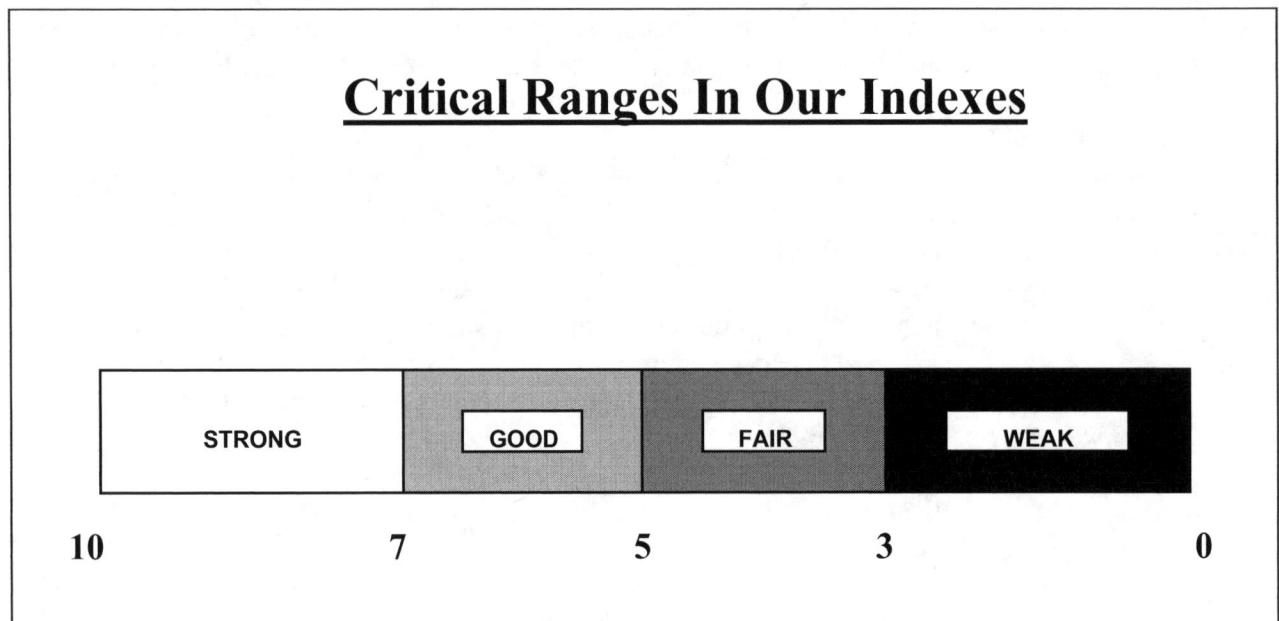

What Our Ratings Mean

A   **Excellent.**   The company offers excellent financial security. It has maintained a conservative stance in its investment strategies, business operations and underwriting commitments. While the financial position of any company is subject to change, we believe that this company has the resources necessary to deal with severe economic conditions.

B   **Good.**   The company offers good financial security and has the resources to deal with a variety of adverse economic conditions. It comfortably exceeds the minimum levels for all of our rating criteria, and is likely to remain healthy for the near future. However, in the event of a *severe* recession or major financial crisis, we feel that this assessment should be reviewed to make sure that the firm is still maintaining adequate financial strength.

C   **Fair.**   The company offers fair financial security and is currently stable. But during an economic downturn or other financial pressures, we feel it may encounter difficulties in maintaining its financial stability.

D   **Weak.**   The company currently demonstrates what we consider to be significant weaknesses which could negatively impact policyholders. In an unfavorable economic environment, these weaknesses could be magnified.

E   **Very Weak.**   The company currently demonstrates what we consider to be significant weaknesses and has also failed some of the basic tests that we use to identify fiscal stability. Therefore, even in a favorable economic environment, it is our opinion that policyholders could incur significant risks.

F   **Failed.**   The company is deemed failed if it is either 1) under supervision of an insurance regulatory authority; 2) in the process of rehabilitation; 3) in the process of liquidation; or 4) voluntarily dissolved after disciplinary or other regulatory action by an insurance regulatory authority.

+   **The plus sign** is an indication that the company is at the upper end of the letter grade rating.

-   **The minus sign** is an indication that the company is at the lower end of the letter grade rating.

U   **Unrated Companies.**   The company is unrated for one or more of the following reasons: 1) total assets are less than $1 million; 2) premium income for the current year is less than $100,000; 3) the company functions almost exclusively as a holding company rather than as an underwriter; or 4) we do not have enough information to reliably issue a rating.

How Our Ratings Differ From Those of Other Services

Weiss Financial Strength Ratings are conservative and consumer oriented. We use tougher standards than other rating agencies because our system is specifically designed to inform risk-averse consumers about the financial strength of health insurers.

Our rating scale (A to F) is easy to understand by the general public. Users can intuitively understand that an A+ rating is at the top of the scale rather than in the middle like some of the other rating agencies.

Other rating agencies give top ratings more generously so that most companies receive excellent ratings.

More importantly, other rating agencies focus primarily on a company's *current* claims paying ability or consider only relatively mild economic adversity. We also consider these scenarios but extend our analysis to cover a company's ability to deal with severe economic adversity and potential liquidity problems. This stems from the viewpoint that an insurance company's obligations to its policyholders should not be contingent upon a healthy economy. The company must be capable of honoring its policy commitments in bad times as well.

Looking at the insurance industry as a whole, we note that several major rating firms have poor historical track records in identifying troubled companies. The 1980s saw a persistent decline in capital ratios, increased holdings of risky investments in the life and health industry as well as recurring long-term claims liabilities in the property and casualty industry. Despite these clear signs that insolvency risk was rising, other rating firms failed to downgrade at-risk insurance companies. Instead, they often rated companies by shades of excellence, understating the gravity of potential problems.

They have not issued clear warnings that the ordinary consumer can understand. Few, if any, companies receive "weak" or "poor" ratings. Surely, weak companies do exist. However, the other rating agencies apparently do not view themselves as consumer advocates with the responsibility of warning the public about the risks involved in doing business with such companies.

Additionally, these firms will at times agree *not* to issue a rating if a company denies them permission to do so. In short, too often insurance rating agencies work hand-in-glove with the companies they rate.

At Weiss Ratings, although we seek to maintain good relationships with the firms, we owe our primary obligation to the consumer, not the industry. We reserve the right to rate companies based on publicly-available data and make the necessary conservative assumptions when companies choose not to provide the additional data we request.

Comparison of Insurance Company Rating Agency Scales				
Weiss Ratings [a]	**Best** [a,b]	**S&P** [c]	**Moody's**	**Fitch** [d]
A+, A, A-	A++, A+	AAA	Aaa	AAA
B+, B, B-	A, A-	AA+, AA AA-	Aa1, Aa2, Aa3	AA+, AA, AA-
C+, C, C-	B++, B+,	A+, A, A-, BBB+, BBB, BBB-	A1, A2, A3, Baa1, Baa2, Baa3	A+, A, A-, BBB+, BBB, BBB-
D+, D, D-	B, B- C++, C+, C, C-	BB+, BB, BB-, B+, B, B-	Ba1, Ba2, Ba3, B1, B2, B3	BB+, BB, BB-, B+, B, B-
E+, E, E- F	D E, F	CCC R	Caa, Ca, C	CCC+, CCC, CCC- DD

[a] Weiss Ratings and Best use additional symbols to designate that they recognize an insurer's existence but do not provide a rating. These symbols are not included in this table.

[b] Best added the A++, B++ and C++ ratings in 1992. In 1994, Best classified its ratings into "secure" and "vulnerable" categories, changed the definition of its "B" and "B-" ratings from "good" to "adequate" and assigned these ratings to the "vulnerable" category. This table contains GAO's assignment of Best's ratings to bands based on our interpretation of their rating descriptions prior to 1994.

[c] S&P discontinued CCC "+" and "-" signs, CC, C and D ratings and added the R rating in 1992.
Source: 1994 GAO *Insurance Ratings* study.

[d] Duff & Phelps Credit Rating Co. merged with Fitch IBCA in 2000, and minor changes were made to the rating scale at that time. These changes were not reflected in the GAO's 1994 study, but *are* reflected in this chart.

Rate of Insurance Company Failures

Weiss Ratings provides quarterly financial strength ratings for thousands of insurance companies each year. Weiss Ratings strives for fairness and objectivity in its ratings and analyses, ensuring that each company receives the rating that most accurately depicts its current financial status, and more importantly, its ability to deal with severe economic adversity and a sharp increase in claims. Weiss Ratings has every confidence that its financial strength ratings provide an accurate representation of a company's stability.

In order for these ratings to be of any true value, it is important that they prove accurate over time. One way to determine the accuracy of a rating is to examine those insurance companies that have failed, and their respective Financial Strength Ratings. A high percentage of failed companies with "A" ratings would indicate that Weiss Ratings is not being conservative enough with its "secure" ratings, while conversely, a low percentage of failures with "vulnerable" ratings would show that Weiss Ratings is overly conservative.

Over the past 25 years (1989–2013) Weiss Ratings has rated 580 insurance companies, for all industries, that subsequently failed. The chart below shows the number of failed companies in each rating category, the average number of companies rated in each category per year, and the percentage of annual failures for each letter grade.

	Financial Strength Rating	Number of Failed Companies	Average Number of Companies Rated per year	Percentage of Failed companies per year (by ratings category)*
Secure	A	1	154	0.03%
	B	6	1095	0.02%
	C	71	1619	0.18%
Vulnerable	D	253	753	1.34%
	E	249	213	4.68%

A=Excellent, B=Good, C=Fair, D=Weak, E=Very Weak

On average, only 0.11% of the companies Weiss rates as "secure" fail each year. On the other hand, an average of 2.08% of the companies Weiss rates as "vulnerable" fail annually. That means that a company rated by Weiss Ratings as "Vulnerable" is almost 19 times more likely to fail than a company rated as "Secure".

When considering a Weiss financial strength rating, one can be sure that they are getting the most fair, objective, and accurate financial rating available anywhere.

*Percentage of Failed companies per year = (Number of Failed Companies) / [(Average Number of Companies Rated per year) x (years in study)]

Data as of December 31, 2013 for Life and Annuity Insurers, Property and Casualty Insurers, and Health Insurers.

What Does Average Mean?

At Weiss Ratings, we consider the words average and fair to mean just that – average and fair. So when we assign our ratings to insurers, a large percentage of companies receive an average C rating. That way, you can be sure that a company receiving Weiss B or A rating is truly above average. Likewise, you can feel confident that companies with D or E ratings are truly below average.

Percentage of Health Insurers in Each Rating Category

2014 Weiss Ratings Distribution

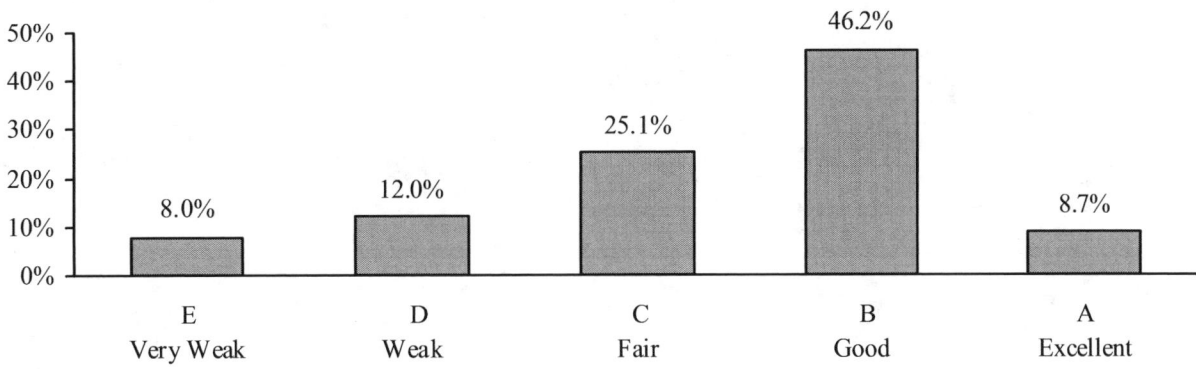

Important Warnings and Cautions

1. A rating alone cannot tell the whole story. Please read the explanatory information contained in this publication. It is provided in order to give you an understanding of our rating philosophy, as well as paint a more complete picture of how we arrive at our opinion of a company's strengths and weaknesses.

2. Weiss Financial Strength Ratings represent our opinion of a company's insolvency risk. As such, a high rating means we feel that the company has less chance of running into financial difficulties. A high rating is not a guarantee of solvency nor is a low rating a prediction of insolvency. Weiss Financial Strength Ratings are not deemed to be a recommendation concerning the purchase or sale of the securities of any insurance company that is publicly owned.

3. Company performance is only one factor in determining a rating. Conditions in the marketplace and overall economic conditions are additional factors that may affect the company's financial strength. Therefore, a rating upgrade or downgrade does not necessarily reflect changes in the company's profits, capital or other financial measures, but may be due to external factors. Likewise, changes in Weiss indexes may reflect changes in our risk assessment of business or economic conditions as well as changes in company performance.

4. All firms that have the same Financial Strength Rating should be considered to be essentially equal in strength. This is true regardless of any differences in the underlying numbers which might appear to indicate greater strengths. Weiss Financial Strength Rating already takes into account a number of lesser factors which, due to space limitations, cannot be included in this publication.

5. A good rating requires consistency. If a company is excellent on four indicators and fair on one, the company may receive a fair rating. This requirement is necessary due to the fact that fiscal problems can arise from any *one* of several causes including speculative investments, inadequate capital resources or operating losses.

6. We are an independent rating agency and do not depend on the cooperation of the companies we rate. Our data are derived, for the most part, from annual and quarterly financial statements that we obtain from federal banking regulators and state insurance commissioners. The latter may be supplemented by information insurance companies voluntarily provide upon request. Although we seek to maintain an open line of communication with the companies, we do not grant them the right to stop or influence publication of the ratings. This policy stems from the fact that this publication is designed for the protection of the consumer.

7. Affiliated companies do not automatically receive the same rating. We recognize that a troubled company may expect financial support from its parent or affiliates. Weiss Financial Strength Ratings reflect our opinion of the measure of support that may become available to a subsidiary , if the subsidiary were to experience serious financial difficulties. In the case of a strong parent and a weaker subsidiary, the affiliate relationship will generally result in a higher rating for the subsidiary than it would have on a stand-alone basis. Seldom, however, would the rating be brought up to the level of the parent. This treatment is appropriate because we do not assume the parent would have either the resources or the will to "bail out" a troubled subsidiary during a severe economic crisis. Even when there is a binding legal obligation for a parent corporation to honor the policy obligations of its subsidiaries, the possibility exists that the subsidiary could be sold and lose its parental support. Therefore, it is quite common for one affiliate to have a higher rating than another. This is another reason why it is especially important that you have the precise name of the company you are evaluating.

Section I

Index of Companies

An analysis of 1,772 rated and unrated

U.S. Health Insurers

Companies are listed in alphabetical order.

Section I Contents

This section contains the information about company type, size and capital level for all rated and unrated health insurers analyzed by Weiss Ratings.

1. Insurance Company Name — The legally-registered name, which can sometimes differ from the name that the company uses for advertising. If you cannot find the company you are interested in, or if you have any doubts regarding the precise name, verify the information with the company before looking the name up in this Guide. Also, determine the domicile state for confirmation. (See column 2.)

2. Domicile State — The state which has primary regulatory responsibility for the company. It may differ from the location of the company's corporate headquarters. You do not have to be living in the domicile state to purchase insurance from this firm, provided it is licensed to do business in your state.

Also use this column to confirm that you have located the correct company. It is possible for two unrelated companies to have the same name if they are domiciled in different states.

3. Financial Strength Rating — Our rating is measured on a scale from A to F and considers a wide range of factors. Please see *What Our Ratings Mean* for specific descriptions of each letter grade and the following pages for information on how our ratings differ from those of other rating agencies. Most important, when using this rating, please be sure to consider the Important Warnings and Cautions regarding the ratings' limitations and the underlying assumptions.

4. Data Date — The latest quarter-end for which we have received the company's financial statement.

5. Total Assets — All assets admitted by state insurance regulators in millions of dollars as of the most recent quarter end. This includes investments and current business assets such as receivables from agents, reinsurers and subscribers.

The overall size is an important factor which affects the ability of a company to manage risk. Mortality, morbidity (sickness) and investment risks can be more effectively diversified by large companies. Because the insurance business is based on probability, the number of policies must be large enough so that actuarial statistics are valid. The larger the number of policyholders, the more reliable the actuarial projections will be. A large company with a correspondingly large policy base can spread its risk and minimize the effects of claims experience that exceeds actuarial expectations.

6. Total Premiums — The amount of insurance premiums received from policyholders as of the most recent year end. If the company issues life insurance or property insurance, those premiums are included in this figure as well.

Generally speaking, companies with large premium volume generally have more predictable claims experience.

7. Health Premiums

The amount of insurance premiums received from policyholders for health policies only as of the most recent year end.

Compare this figure with Total Premiums in the previous column to see how much of the company's business relates to health coverage.

8. Capital and Surplus

The company's statutory net worth in millions of dollars as of the most recent quarter end. Consumers may wish to limit the size of any policy so that the policyholder's maximum benefits do not exceed approximately 1% of the company's capital and surplus. For example, when buying a policy from a company with capital and surplus of $10,000,000, the 1% limit would be $100,000. (When performing this calculation, do not forget that figures in this column are expressed in millions of dollars.)

Critical Ranges In Our Ratios

Indicators	*Strong*	*Good*	*Fair*	*Weak*
Risk-Adjusted Capital Ratio #1	—	1.0 or more	0.75 - 0.99	0.74 or less
Risk-Adjusted Capital Ratio #2	1.0 or more	0.75 - 0.99	0.5 - 0.74	0.49 or less

---

9. Risk-Adjusted Capital Ratio #1

This ratio examines the adequacy of the company's capital base and whether the company has sufficient capital resources to cover potential losses which might occur in an average recession or other moderate loss scenario. Specifically, the figure cited in this column answers the question: For every dollar of capital that we feel would be needed, how many dollars in capital resources does the company actually have? (See the table above for the levels which we believe are critical.) You may find that some companies have unusually high levels of capital. This often reflects special circumstances related to the small size or unusual operations of the company.

10. Risk-Adjusted Capital Ratio #2

This is similar to item 9. But in this case, the question relates to whether the company has enough capital cushion to withstand a *severe* recession or other severe loss scenario. For more details on risk-adjusted capital, see the Appendix.

INSURANCE COMPANY NAME	DOM. STATE	RATING	DATA DATE	TOTAL ASSETS ($MIL)	TOTAL PREMIUMS ($MIL)	HEALTH PREMIUMS ($MIL)	CAPITAL & SURPLUS ($MIL)	RISK ADJUSTED CAPITAL RATIO 1	RATIO 2
21ST CENTURY CENTENNIAL INS CO	PA	B	2q 2014	563.3	698.2	0.0	550.1	1.87	1.85
21ST CENTURY PREMIER INS CO	PA	B-	2q 2014	268.4	48.5	0.5	264.3	4.65	4.50
4 EVER LIFE INS CO	IL	● A	2q 2014	202.8	206.2	191.7	91.6	4.31	3.07
AAA LIFE INS CO	MI	B	2q 2014	550.5	529.0	66.0	111.3	2.36	1.43
ABILITY INS CO	NE	● D	2q 2014	854.3	75.7	75.0	34.4	1.34	0.70
ABSOLUTE TOTAL CARE INC	SC	● C-	2q 2014	86.4	329.4	329.4	36.7	1.78	1.48
ACCENDO INS CO	UT	U	--	--	--	--	--	--	--
ACCESS (See COVENTRY HEALTH CARE OF MISSOURI INC)									
ACCESS CARE II (See HOSPITAL SERV ASSN OF NORTH EAST PA)									
ACCESS DENTAL PLAN	CA	U		--	--	--	--	--	--
ACCESS DENTAL PLAN OF NEVADA INC	NV	U		--	--	--	--	--	--
ACCESS INS CO	TX	C-	2q 2014	134.4	209.8	0.1	29.0	0.64	0.58
ACCESS MANAGED HEALTH CARE	NY	U		--	--	--	--	--	--
ACCESS PLUS (See COVENTRY HEALTH CARE OF MISSOURI INC)									
ACCESSCARE GENERAL INC	IL	U		--	--	--	--	--	--
ACCESSCARE GENERAL LLC	KS	U		--	--	--	--	--	--
ACCESSCARE GENERAL OKLAHOMA LLC	OK	U		--	--	--	--	--	--
ACCOUNTABLE HEALTH PLANS OF AMERICA	TX	U		--	--	--	--	--	--
ACE AMERICAN INS CO	PA	B-	2q 2014	11,795.8	4,030.3	555.1	2,997.7	1.52	1.25
ACE INS CO	PR	B-	2q 2014	146.2	70.5	10.0	48.9	1.56	1.08
ACE PROPERTY & CASUALTY INS CO	PA	C	2q 2014	7,001.3	2,047.9	21.3	1,995.3	2.96	2.00
ACN GROUP OF CALIFORNIA INC	CA	U		--	--	--	--	--	--
ADMAR MED NETWORK	CA	U		--	--	--	--	--	--
ADVANCE INS CO OF KS	KS	● B+	2q 2014	52.2	10.4	3.4	42.3	3.47	2.29
ADVANTAGE BLUE (See LA HEALTH SERVICE & INDEMNITY CO)									
ADVANTAGE CARE NETWORK INC	TX	U		--	--	--	--	--	--
ADVANTAGE HEALTH SOLUTIONS INC	IN	● C	2q 2014	75.1	403.8	403.8	24.5	0.87	0.72
ADVANTICA INS CO	MO	U		--	--	--	--	--	--
ADVANTRA (See COVENTRY HEALTH CARE OF MISSOURI INC)									
ADVICARE CORP	SC	U		--	--	--	--	--	--
AECC TOTAL VISION HEALTH PLAN OF TX	TX	U		--	--	--	--	--	--
AEGIS SECURITY INS CO	PA	B-	2q 2014	103.8	85.9	9.9	52.9	2.24	1.71
AETNA BETTER HEALTH (AN OHIO CORP)	OH	U		--	--	--	--	--	--
AETNA BETTER HEALTH INC	IL	● B	2q 2014	143.9	308.2	308.2	35.8	2.37	1.97
AETNA BETTER HEALTH INC (A CT CORP)	CT	U		--	--	--	--	--	--
AETNA BETTER HEALTH INC (A FLORIDA)	FL	U		--					
AETNA BETTER HEALTH INC (A GA CORP)	GA	U		--	--	--	--	--	--
AETNA BETTER HEALTH INC (A NEW YORK)	NY	U		--	--	--	--	--	--
AETNA BETTER HEALTH INC (A PA CORP)	PA	● D-	2q 2014	183.8	305.9	305.9	33.2	2.14	1.78
AETNA DENTAL INC. (A NJ CORP)	NJ	U		--	--	--	--	--	--
AETNA DENTAL OF CALIFORNIA INC	CA	U		--	--	--	--	--	--
AETNA HEALTH & LIFE INS CO	CT	● B+	2q 2014	2,193.0	0.3	0.3	292.5	3.02	1.79
AETNA HEALTH INC (A CT CORP)	CT	● C	2q 2014	114.0	350.2	350.2	47.3	2.18	1.82
AETNA HEALTH INC (A FLORIDA CORP)	FL	● A-	2q 2014	324.6	1,220.0	1,220.0	142.8	2.23	1.85
AETNA HEALTH INC (A GEORGIA CORP)	GA	● B	2q 2014	101.4	343.2	343.2	51.5	2.80	2.34
AETNA HEALTH INC (A MAINE CORP)	ME	● B-	2q 2014	31.6	98.3	98.3	13.1	2.10	1.75
AETNA HEALTH INC (A MICHIGAN CORP)	MI	U		--	--	--	--	--	--
AETNA HEALTH INC (A NEW JERSEY CORP)	NJ	● B	2q 2014	337.6	1,355.1	1,355.1	165.6	2.32	1.93
AETNA HEALTH INC (A NEW YORK CORP)	NY	● B+	2q 2014	377.2	575.1	575.1	251.2	6.86	5.71
AETNA HEALTH INC (A PA CORP)	PA	● B	2q 2014	866.6	3,019.9	3,019.9	341.2	2.62	2.18
AETNA HEALTH INC (A TEXAS CORP)	TX	● B	2q 2014	211.2	703.9	703.9	91.5	2.32	1.94
AETNA HEALTH INS CO	PA	● B	2q 2014	70.5	86.9	86.9	38.0	5.87	4.89

www.weissratings.com

Arrows denote recent upgrades ▲ or downgrades▼

23

● Bullets denote a more detailed analysis is available in Section II.

INSURANCE COMPANY NAME	DOM. STATE	RATING	DATA DATE	TOTAL ASSETS ($MIL)	TOTAL PREMIUMS ($MIL)	HEALTH PREMIUMS ($MIL)	CAPITAL & SURPLUS ($MIL)	RISK ADJUSTED CAPITAL RATIO 1	RATIO 2
AETNA HEALTH INS CO OF NY	NY	• B	2q 2014	11.3	2.2	2.2	10.1	7.60	6.33
AETNA HEALTH OF CALIFORNIA INC	CA	• B	2q 2014	450.7	1,910.1	1,910.1	144.0	1.29	0.85
AETNA LIFE INS CO	CT	• B+	2q 2014	22,226.6	19,814.4	18,556.1	3,168.5	1.59	1.14
AETNA U.S. HEALTHCARE (See AETNA HEALTH INC (A PA CORP))									
AF&L INS CO	PA	E	2q 2014	160.1	25.0	25.0	0.0	0.00	0.00
AFFINITY DENTAL HEALTH PLAN	CA	U		--	--	--	--	--	--
AHC	WI	U		--	--	--	--	--	--
AHL SELECT PROVIDER NETWORK (See AMERICAN HERITAGE LIFE INS CO)									
AHP PREFERRED PROVIDER NETWORK	PA	U		--	--	--	--	--	--
AIDS HEALTHCARE FOUNDATION MCO OF FL	FL	U		--	--	--	--	--	--
AIG INS CO - PUERTO RICO	PR	B	2q 2014	193.3	89.0	6.8	135.5	9.85	6.28
AIG SPECIALTY INS CO	IL	C	2q 2014	333.3	834.8	0.7	239.8	2.66	1.77
AIU INS CO	NY	C	2q 2014	238.9	-2,286.2	0.0	232.3	2.76	2.71
ALAMEDA ALLIANCE FOR HEALTH	CA	F	2q 2014	117.6	449.7	449.7	13.6	0.30	0.19
ALFA LIFE INS CORP	AL	B-	2q 2014	1,373.2	141.2	0.8	219.3	2.75	1.56
ALIGNIS INC	GA	U		--	--	--	--	--	--
ALL FLORIDA PPO INC	FL	U		--	--	--	--	--	--
ALL SAVERS INS CO	IN	B-	2q 2014	34.0	76.3	76.3	19.3	1.25	1.04
ALLEGIAN INS CO	TX	• C	2q 2014	20.9	42.4	42.4	8.8	1.66	1.38
ALLEGIANCE LIFE & HEALTH INS CO INC	MT	• C	2q 2014	16.5	53.0	53.0	7.3	1.49	1.24
ALLIANCE HEALTH & LIFE INS CO	MI	• B+	2q 2014	66.3	209.3	209.3	26.8	1.74	1.45
ALLIANCE REGIONAL HEALTH NETWORK	TX	U		--	--	--	--	--	--
ALLIANCE SELECT (See WELLMARK INC)									
ALLIANT HEALTH PLANS INC	GA	• C	2q 2014	34.9	94.1	94.1	17.1	1.57	1.31
ALLIANZ GLOBAL RISKS US INS CO	IL	C-	2q 2014	3,493.7	823.1	43.0	924.5	0.68	0.48
ALLIANZ LIFE INS CO OF NORTH AMERICA	MN	C+	2q 2014	112,131.9	9,377.3	177.5	4,844.6	1.75	1.04
ALLIANZ LIFE INS CO OF NY	NY	B	2q 2014	2,813.4	318.9	3.5	129.5	3.99	2.08
ALLIED NETWORK INC	TX	U		--	--	--	--	--	--
ALLSTATE LIFE INS CO	IL	B	2q 2014	35,158.7	1,180.1	29.1	2,565.9	1.32	0.82
ALLSTATE LIFE INS CO OF NEW YORK	NY	B-	2q 2014	6,677.3	178.1	14.4	575.5	2.29	1.21
ALOHACARE	HI	• B	3q 2013	114.5	232.7	232.7	70.3	3.13	2.61
ALPHA DENTAL OF NEW MEXICO INC	NM	U		--	--	--	--	--	--
ALPHACARE OF NEW YORK INC	NY	U		--	--	--	--	--	--
ALTIUS HEALTH PLANS	UT	• B	2q 2014	124.6	489.9	489.9	50.4	1.82	1.52
AMALGAMATED CASUALTY INS CO	DC	C	2q 2014	45.1	5.0	0.0	38.6	15.62	9.42
AMALGAMATED LIFE & HEALTH INS CO	IL	C-	2q 2014	5.7	6.0	6.0	3.8	2.25	2.03
AMALGAMATED LIFE INS CO	NY	• A-	2q 2014	107.0	39.8	12.9	48.6	3.53	2.78
AMCARE HEALTH PLANS OF TEXAS INC	TX	U		--	--	--	--	--	--
AMERICAN ALTERNATIVE INS CORP	DE	C	2q 2014	503.0	802.6	70.5	178.1	16.16	14.54
AMERICAN BANKERS INS CO OF FL	FL	B	2q 2014	1,970.3	1,739.9	156.8	570.2	2.60	1.49
AMERICAN BANKERS LIFE ASR CO OF FL	FL	• B	2q 2014	526.3	425.4	202.9	48.1	4.15	2.32
AMERICAN CASUALTY CO OF READING	PA	C	2q 2014	143.9	568.6	0.0	143.8	2.20	2.15
AMERICAN COMMERCE INS CO	OH	C+	2q 2014	320.1	281.5	0.1	112.8	2.98	2.30
AMERICAN COMMUNITY MUT INS CO	MI	F	4q 2010	46.6	150.3	147.5	17.9	0.36	0.29
AMERICAN CONTINENTAL INS CO	TN	• B	2q 2014	136.4	300.6	271.1	52.5	1.22	0.95
AMERICAN DENTAL PLAN OF WI INC	WI	U		--	--	--	--	--	--
AMERICAN FAMILY CARE OF UTAH (See MOLINA HEALTHCARE OF UTAH INC)									
AMERICAN FAMILY CARE/MOLINA MEDICAL CENTER (See MOLINA HEALTHCARE OF CALIFORNIA)									
AMERICAN FAMILY INS CO	OH	B	2q 2014	23.3	221.7	0.7	16.8	9.30	8.37
AMERICAN FAMILY LIFE ASR CO OF COLUM	NE	• B+	2q 2014	111,249.2	20,528.6	14,804.4	10,245.4	3.46	2.22
AMERICAN FAMILY LIFE ASR CO OF NY	NY	• A-	2q 2014	706.5	285.6	276.3	227.9	5.00	3.50
AMERICAN FAMILY MUT INS CO	WI	B+	2q 2014	13,709.4	5,180.1	92.9	5,822.8	2.13	1.67

www.weissratings.com

Arrows denote recent upgrades ▲ or downgrades▼

• Bullets denote a more detailed analysis is available in Section II.

INSURANCE COMPANY NAME	DOM. STATE	RATING	DATA DATE	TOTAL ASSETS ($MIL)	TOTAL PREMIUMS ($MIL)	HEALTH PREMIUMS ($MIL)	CAPITAL & SURPLUS ($MIL)	RISK ADJUSTED CAPITAL RATIO 1	RATIO 2
AMERICAN FEDERATED LIFE INS CO	MS	C	2q 2014	26.8	13.3	6.6	9.2	2.20	1.98
AMERICAN FIDELITY ASR CO	OK	● B+	2q 2014	4,848.9	1,001.5	719.2	347.3	1.81	1.05
AMERICAN FINANCIAL SECURITY L I C	MO	D	2q 2014	5.3	2.1	2.1	4.2	2.67	2.40
AMERICAN GENERAL LIFE INS CO	TX	B	2q 2014	161,065.9	14,408.7	219.2	11,615.5	3.71	1.88
AMERICAN GUARANTEE & LIABILITY INS	NY	C	2q 2014	277.4	1,032.0	0.0	178.2	19.87	17.89
AMERICAN HALLMARK INS CO OF TX	TX	C	2q 2014	312.3	121.5	4.9	118.3	1.60	1.31
AMERICAN HEALTH & LIFE INS CO	TX	● B-	2q 2014	969.9	157.2	78.8	251.3	3.68	2.50
▲ AMERICAN HEALTH INC	PR	● B	2q 2014	178.5	519.9	519.9	58.2	1.24	1.04
AMERICAN HEALTH NETWORK OF IN LLC	IN	U		--	--	--	--	--	--
AMERICAN HEALTHGUARD CORP	CA	U		--	--	--	--	--	--
AMERICAN HERITAGE LIFE INS CO	FL	● B	2q 2014	1,852.6	831.6	693.0	424.1	1.36	1.12
AMERICAN HOME ASR CO	NY	● C	2q 2014	26,478.6	928.6	649.3	6,978.8	2.29	1.51
AMERICAN HOME LIFE INS CO	KS	C-	2q 2014	239.3	22.5	0.0	19.8	2.16	1.18
AMERICAN IMAGING MANAGEMENT EAST LLC	NJ	U		--	--	--	--	--	--
AMERICAN INCOME LIFE INS CO	IN	B-	2q 2014	2,837.4	762.0	72.9	219.8	1.30	0.82
AMERICAN INDEPENDENT NETWORK INS CO	NY	E	2q 2014	27.4	3.1	3.1	2.5	0.60	0.54
AMERICAN LABOR LIFE INS CO	AZ	D	2q 2014	8.5	0.8	0.8	6.3	3.08	2.77
▼ AMERICAN LIFE & SECURITY CORP	AZ	E	2q 2014	14.4	4.7	0.0	0.5	0.11	0.09
AMERICAN LIFE INS CO	DE	● C	2q 2014	7,218.3	1,082.6	292.0	2,485.1	0.74	0.70
AMERICAN LIFECARE NETWORKS LLC	LA	U		--	--	--	--	--	--
▼ AMERICAN MEDICAL & LIFE INS CO	NY	E-	2q 2014	8.0	17.5	17.1	-1.0	0.03	0.03
AMERICAN MEMORIAL LIFE INS CO	SD	B-	2q 2014	2,579.8	483.5	0.0	108.8	1.52	0.77
AMERICAN MODERN HOME INS CO	OH	C+	2q 2014	1,245.2	574.8	0.3	379.5	2.09	1.57
AMERICAN MODERN LIFE INS CO	OH	● B	2q 2014	49.9	15.8	6.5	26.6	1.91	1.78
AMERICAN NATIONAL INS CO	TX	B	2q 2014	17,985.5	1,231.4	73.9	2,780.3	1.31	1.06
AMERICAN NATIONAL LIFE INS CO OF TX	TX	● B-	2q 2014	138.5	62.9	59.5	39.1	4.32	3.07
AMERICAN PACIFIC INS COMPANY	HI	B	2q 2014	11.5	4.2	3.8	11.2	80.24	72.21
AMERICAN PIONEER LIFE INS CO	FL	D+	2q 2014	78.6	73.3	67.0	11.9	1.25	0.89
AMERICAN PREFERRED PROVIDER PLAN MID	DC	U		--	--	--	--	--	--
AMERICAN PROGRESSIVE L&H I C OF NY	NY	● B	2q 2014	238.9	485.5	471.1	120.3	1.45	1.14
AMERICAN PUBLIC LIFE INS CO	OK	B	2q 2014	83.3	45.8	44.6	22.6	2.04	1.48
AMERICAN REPUBLIC CORP INS CO	NE	B	2q 2014	26.4	64.2	64.0	8.4	1.96	1.77
AMERICAN REPUBLIC INS CO	IA	● A-	2q 2014	799.7	187.1	169.3	457.3	5.08	3.79
AMERICAN RETIREMENT LIFE INS CO	OH	B-	2q 2014	45.5	16.8	16.7	26.2	1.82	1.62
AMERICAN SECURITY INS CO	DE	B	2q 2014	2,023.8	1,637.0	3.1	802.4	2.56	1.80
AMERICAN SENTINEL INS CO	PA	C	2q 2014	34.0	20.7	12.0	15.6	2.49	1.72
▲ AMERICAN SPECIALTY HEALTH INS CO	IL	● D-	2q 2014	8.2	5.2	5.2	7.3	9.01	7.51
AMERICAN SPECIALTY HEALTH ODS OF NJ	NJ	U	4q 2013	0.8	2.7	2.7	0.4	--	--
AMERICAN SPECIALTY HEALTH PLANS INC	CA	U		--	--	--	--	--	--
AMERICAN STATES INS CO	IN	C	2q 2014	133.6	479.2	0.3	120.9	49.34	44.40
AMERICAN UNDERWRITERS LIFE INS CO	AZ	D+	2q 2014	82.2	7.0	1.0	10.6	0.63	0.44
AMERICAN UNITED LIFE INS CO	IN	B+	2q 2014	22,972.9	3,104.0	74.5	1,009.3	3.30	1.67
AMERICAS 1ST CHOICE HEALTH PLANS INC	SC	● E	2q 2014	16.5	80.9	80.9	8.9	0.77	0.64
AMERICAS 1ST CHOICE INS CO OF NC INC	NC	● C	2q 2014	11.7	41.7	41.7	8.1	0.91	0.76
AMERICAS PPO	MN	U		--	--	--	--	--	--
AMERICASHEALTH PLAN INC	CA	U	1q 2014	1.5	0.0	0.0	1.5	--	--
AMERICHOICE OF CONNECTICUT INC	CT	U		--	--	--	--	--	--
AMERICHOICE OF GEORGIA INC	GA	U		--	--	--	--	--	--
AMERICHOICE OF NEW JERSEY INC	NJ	● B	2q 2014	511.8	1,726.7	1,726.7	225.0	2.40	2.00
AMERICO FINANCIAL LIFE & ANNUITY INS	TX	B-	2q 2014	3,809.8	196.2	0.1	431.0	1.79	1.06
AMERIGROUP COMMUNITY CARE (See AMERIGROUP OHIO INC)									
AMERIGROUP COMMUNITY CARE NM	NM	● B-	2q 2014	89.8	492.9	492.9	70.6	2.76	2.30

www.weissratings.com   25

Arrows denote recent upgrades ▲ or downgrades▼   ● Bullets denote a more detailed analysis is available in Section II.

INSURANCE COMPANY NAME	DOM. STATE	RATING	DATA DATE	TOTAL ASSETS ($MIL)	TOTAL PREMIUMS ($MIL)	HEALTH PREMIUMS ($MIL)	CAPITAL & SURPLUS ($MIL)	RISK ADJUSTED CAPITAL RATIO 1	RATIO 2
▼ AMERIGROUP FLORIDA INC	FL	• B	2q 2014	155.9	599.5	599.5	60.6	1.96	1.63
AMERIGROUP INS CO	TX	• B-	2q 2014	131.4	394.1	394.1	91.9	4.28	3.57
AMERIGROUP KANSAS INC	KS	• B-	2q 2014	193.9	720.6	720.6	66.7	1.22	1.02
AMERIGROUP LOUISIANA INC	LA	• B-	2q 2014	95.9	411.0	411.0	46.5	1.89	1.57
AMERIGROUP MARYLAND INC	MD	• B	2q 2014	325.7	764.2	764.2	113.4	2.85	2.38
AMERIGROUP NEVADA INC	NV	• B-	2q 2014	70.0	188.1	188.1	34.7	3.78	3.15
AMERIGROUP NEW JERSEY INC	NJ	• A-	2q 2014	235.0	645.5	645.5	139.9	4.07	3.39
AMERIGROUP OHIO INC	OH	• B	2q 2013	48.1	169.6	169.6	31.0	4.31	3.59
AMERIGROUP TENNESSEE INC	TN	• B	2q 2014	256.9	917.0	917.0	116.1	2.57	2.14
▼ AMERIGROUP TEXAS INC	TX	• B+	2q 2014	645.6	2,627.5	2,627.5	273.3	1.96	1.63
▲ AMERIGROUP WASHINGTON INC	WA	• B	2q 2014	222.4	133.9	133.9	96.8	12.11	10.09
AMERIHEALTH CARITAS OF LOUISIANA INC	LA	• C	2q 2014	96.5	490.6	490.6	35.0	1.37	1.14
AMERIHEALTH DISTRICT OF COLUMBIA INC	DC	• C	2q 2014	92.4	255.5	255.5	26.3	1.57	1.31
AMERIHEALTH HMO INC	PA	• B	2q 2014	1,350.2	391.7	391.7	1,243.3	4.66	3.88
AMERIHEALTH INSURANCE CO OF NJ	NJ	• C-	4q 2013	169.1	415.8	415.8	83.7	3.44	2.87
AMERIHEALTH MICHIGAN INC	MI	U	--	--	--	--	--	--	--
AMERIHEALTH NEBRASKA INC	NE	• E	2q 2014	16.8	57.0	57.0	7.9	2.34	1.95
AMERITAS LIFE INS CORP	NE	• B	2q 2014	9,678.1	1,600.9	607.6	1,557.0	1.33	1.15
AMERITAS LIFE INS CORP OF NY	NY	• B-	2q 2014	1,131.3	92.8	27.1	75.4	2.04	1.11
AMEX ASSURANCE CO	IL	• B	2q 2014	317.6	181.2	56.8	221.3	9.99	5.82
AMFIRST INS CO	OK	• B	2q 2014	40.2	11.5	11.5	32.7	4.16	3.46
AMFIRST INS CO	OK	• B	2q 2014	40.2	11.5	11.5	32.7	4.16	3.46
AMGP GEORGIA MANAGED CARE CO INC	GA	• B	2q 2014	261.7	795.0	795.0	123.5	3.18	2.65
AMGUARD INS CO	PA	C+	2q 2014	401.1	230.5	0.2	107.1	1.66	1.27
ANTHEM BLUE CROSS (See BLUE CROSS OF CALIFORNIA)									
ANTHEM BLUE CROSS BLUE SHIELD OF CONNECTICUT (See ANTHEM HEALTH PLANS INC)									
ANTHEM BLUE CROSS LIFE & HEALTH INS	CA	• B	2q 2014	2,584.3	5,348.0	5,348.0	1,408.2	4.39	3.66
ANTHEM HEALTH NETWORK	NY	U	--	--	--	--	--	--	--
ANTHEM HEALTH PLANS INC	CT	• B	2q 2014	778.4	1,808.9	1,808.9	364.9	3.81	3.18
ANTHEM HEALTH PLANS OF KENTUCKY INC	KY	• A-	2q 2014	1,023.5	2,205.0	2,205.0	430.9	3.97	3.31
ANTHEM HEALTH PLANS OF MAINE INC	ME	• B-	2q 2014	395.6	1,030.8	1,030.8	163.3	4.55	3.79
ANTHEM HEALTH PLANS OF NEW HAMPSHIRE	NH	• B+	2q 2014	343.1	521.3	521.3	166.0	3.27	2.72
ANTHEM HEALTH PLANS OF VIRGINIA	VA	• B	2q 2014	2,165.4	4,010.5	4,010.5	829.6	4.46	3.72
ANTHEM INS COMPANIES INC	IN	• B	2q 2014	3,012.6	5,008.5	5,008.5	1,131.6	3.93	3.28
ANTHEM LIFE & DISABILITY INS CO	NY	A-	2q 2014	23.0	5.4	1.5	19.5	5.18	4.67
ANTHEM LIFE INS CO	IN	• A-	2q 2014	571.2	203.7	86.0	89.2	1.95	1.35
ANTHEM SENIOR ADVANTAGE (See ANTHEM INS COMPANIES INC)									
ANTILLES INS CO	PR	B	2q 2014	103.8	61.6	0.0	68.0	0.84	0.65
ARAZ GREAT PLAINS	SD	U	--	--	--	--	--	--	--
▼ ARCADIAN HEALTH PLAN INC	WA	• C+	2q 2014	70.5	227.5	227.5	55.0	3.85	3.21
ARCADIAN HEALTH PLAN INC	CA	• D	2q 2014	83.3	227.6	227.6	63.9	2.00	1.34
ARCH INS CO	MO	C	2q 2014	3,111.4	1,416.3	42.3	757.1	1.37	1.03
ARCHES MUTUAL INS CO	UT	U	--	--	--	--	--	--	--
ARIZONA FOUNDATION FOR MEDICAL CARE	AZ	U	--	--	--	--	--	--	--
ARKANSAS BANKERS LIFE INS CO	AR	D+	2q 2014	3.3	1.2	0.1	1.7	1.53	1.38
ARKANSAS BLUE CROSS BLUE SHIELD (See USABLE MUTUAL INS CO)									
ARKANSAS FIRST SOURCE	AR	U	--	--	--	--	--	--	--
ARKANSAS PREFERRED PROVIDER ORG	AR	U	--	--	--	--	--	--	--
ARKANSAS SUPERIOR SELECT INC	AR	U	--	--	--	--	--	--	--
ARROWOOD INDEMNITY CO	DE	U	2q 2014	1,542.1	0.0	0.0	261.3	--	--
ASPIRE HEALTH PLAN	CA	U	2q 2014	3.7	0.0	0.0	-1.0	--	--
ASSOCIATED MUTUAL	MI	D	2q 2014	11.7	11.1	10.7	8.5	2.65	2.32

Arrows denote recent upgrades ▲ or downgrades▼

www.weissratings.com
• Bullets denote a more detailed analysis is available in Section II.

INSURANCE COMPANY NAME	DOM. STATE	RATING	DATA DATE	TOTAL ASSETS ($MIL)	TOTAL PREMIUMS ($MIL)	HEALTH PREMIUMS ($MIL)	CAPITAL & SURPLUS ($MIL)	RISK ADJUSTED CAPITAL RATIO 1	RATIO 2
ASSURANCEAMERICA INS CO	SC	D	2q 2014	51.2	72.0	0.8	12.2	1.06	0.90
ASSURITY LIFE INS CO	NE	● B+	2q 2014	2,436.6	249.6	97.3	304.3	3.17	1.69
ASURIS NORTHWEST HEALTH	WA	● B-	2q 2014	97.0	241.2	241.2	57.8	3.64	3.03
ATHENE ANNUITY & LIFE ASR CO	DE	C-	2q 2014	11,120.7	961.4	31.2	1,136.4	0.91	0.69
ATHENE ANNUITY & LIFE ASR CO OF NY	NY	C	2q 2014	3,467.6	84.1	0.8	178.0	1.42	0.65
ATHENE ANNUITY & LIFE CO	IA	C+	2q 2014	43,901.2	3,025.9	3.5	1,013.4	1.09	0.59
ATHENE LIFE INS CO OF NEW YORK	NY	C	2q 2014	1,733.3	124.0	1.0	77.8	2.01	0.95
ATHENS AREA HEALTH PLAN SELECT INC	GA	● C-	2q 2014	17.5	36.4	36.4	11.1	1.75	1.45
ATLANTA LIFE INS CO	GA	D	2q 2014	55.5	2.0	0.1	14.2	1.38	0.98
ATLANTIC COAST LIFE INS CO	SC	C+	2q 2014	123.8	24.0	0.1	12.1	1.53	1.37
ATLANTIC SOUTHERN DENTAL FOUNDATION	NJ	U	--	--	--	--	--	--	--
ATLANTIC SPECIALTY INS CO	NY	C	2q 2014	2,365.0	868.4	94.0	697.2	1.42	1.01
ATLANTIS HEALTH PLAN	NY	● E-	2q 2014	18.9	70.8	70.8	0.1	0.00	0.00
ATRIO HEALTH PLANS INC	OR	● C-	2q 2014	42.3	148.1	148.1	20.0	1.85	1.54
AULTCARE INS CO	OH	● C-	2q 2014	118.6	454.1	454.1	60.5	1.54	1.28
AURIGEN REINS CO OF AMERICA	AR	D	2q 2014	25.2	0.7	0.7	21.0	5.75	5.18
AUTO CLUB LIFE INS CO	MI	C+	2q 2014	526.1	10.3	0.9	61.2	1.15	0.80
AUTO CLUB PROPERTY & CASUALTY INS CO	MI	C	2q 2014	80.2	79.1	0.7	27.5	2.17	1.67
AUTO-OWNERS LIFE INS CO	MI	A	2q 2014	3,557.4	250.2	15.1	342.1	2.33	1.24
AUXILIO PLATINO INC	PR	U	--	--	--	--	--	--	--
AVALON INS CO	PA	● C	2q 2014	34.8	46.0	46.0	18.3	4.01	3.34
AVANTE BEHAVIORAL HEALTH PLAN	CA	U	--	--	--	--	--	--	--
AVEMCO INS CO	MD	B	2q 2014	112.2	31.3	0.4	71.7	3.53	3.18
AVERA HEALTH PLANS INC	SD	● C-	2q 2014	30.7	81.7	81.7	8.0	0.62	0.52
AVMED HEALTH PLANS (See AVMED INC)									
AVMED INC	FL	● B+	2q 2014	291.3	778.3	778.3	156.2	2.60	2.17
AWARE (See BLUE CROSS BLUE SHIELD OF MINNESOTA)									
AXA EQUITABLE LIFE INS CO	NY	B	2q 2014	163,402.2	12,592.2	78.1	5,419.8	2.13	1.29
AXIS INS CO	IL	C+	2q 2014	1,443.8	762.9	33.9	540.2	1.75	1.16
BALBOA LIFE INS CO	CA	● A-	2q 2014	58.9	7.9	6.5	48.9	2.37	2.26
BALBOA LIFE INS CO OF NY	NY	B	2q 2014	19.3	0.2	0.0	18.8	5.47	4.92
BALTAS VISION LLC	KY	U	--	--	--	--	--	--	--
BALTIMORE LIFE INS CO	MD	B	2q 2014	1,111.7	141.1	1.6	74.6	2.05	1.07
BANKERS CONSECO LIFE INS CO	NY	● D	2q 2014	201.4	49.7	14.2	50.7	4.49	3.50
BANKERS FIDELITY LIFE INS CO	GA	● B	2q 2014	143.2	99.6	88.4	35.3	1.58	1.12
BANKERS LIFE & CAS CO	IL	● D+	2q 2014	16,044.7	2,202.7	1,042.1	1,057.8	1.97	1.02
BANKERS LIFE INS CO	FL	C+	2q 2014	300.3	68.3	0.0	21.7	1.33	0.60
BANKERS LIFE OF LOUISIANA	LA	C	2q 2014	13.4	32.8	22.3	4.3	1.39	1.06
BANKERS RESERVE LIFE INS CO OF WI	WI	● C-	2q 2014	481.2	2,322.6	2,322.6	250.7	1.90	1.58
BANKERS STANDARD FIRE & MARINE CO	PA	C	2q 2014	183.3	0.0	0.0	76.8	4.50	2.98
BANNER LIFE INS CO	MD	D	2q 2014	1,703.4	848.7	0.0	362.4	1.41	1.07
BAPTIST HEALTH SERVICES GROUP	TN	U	--	--	--	--	--	--	--
BASIC CHIROPRACTIC HEALTH PLAN INC	CA	U	--	--	--	--	--	--	--
BAYCARE HEALTH NETWORK INC	FL	U	--	--	--	--	--	--	--
BCS INS CO	OH	● B	2q 2014	293.7	341.8	288.2	157.1	6.93	3.93
BEAZLEY INS CO INC	CT	C+	2q 2014	260.4	163.5	0.3	124.0	5.13	3.80
BEHEALTHY AMERICA INC	FL	U	--	--	--	--	--	--	--
BENEFICIAL LIFE INS CO	UT	B	2q 2014	2,970.4	81.0	0.0	614.2	6.14	3.26
BERKLEY INS CO	DE	C	2q 2014	16,216.4	193.2	1.6	4,851.3	1.33	1.05
BERKLEY LIFE & HEALTH INS CO	IA	● B-	2q 2014	178.2	130.8	130.6	103.2	6.56	5.04
BERKSHIRE HEALTH PARTNERS	PA	U	--	--	--	--	--	--	--
BERKSHIRE LIFE INS CO OF AMERICA	MA	● A	2q 2014	3,589.9	460.6	449.6	599.1	8.67	4.25

www.weissratings.com

27

Arrows denote recent upgrades ▲ or downgrades▼   ● Bullets denote a more detailed analysis is available in Section II.

INSURANCE COMPANY NAME	DOM. STATE	RATING	DATA DATE	TOTAL ASSETS ($MIL)	TOTAL PREMIUMS ($MIL)	HEALTH PREMIUMS ($MIL)	CAPITAL & SURPLUS ($MIL)	RISK ADJUSTED CAPITAL RATIO 1	RATIO 2
BEST CHOICE PLUS	FL	U	--	--	--	--	--	--	--
BEST LIFE & HEALTH INS CO	TX	C	2q 2014	14.8	33.7	33.1	10.0	1.46	1.19
BEST MERIDIAN INS CO	FL	● B-	2q 2014	263.8	79.3	50.2	49.5	1.92	1.25
BLOCK VISION OF NEW JERSEY INC	NJ	U	--	--	--	--	--	--	--
BLOCK VISION OF TEXAS INC	TX	U	--	--	--	--	--	--	--
BLUE ACCESS (See ANTHEM HEALTH PLANS OF KENTUCKY INC)									
BLUE ADVANTAGE PLUS OF KANSAS CITY	MO	U	--	--	--	--	--	--	--
BLUE CARE ELECT (See BLUE CROSS BLUE SHIELD OF MA)									
BLUE CARE INC (See GOOD HEALTH HMO INC)									
BLUE CARE NETWORK OF MICHIGAN	MI	● B+	2q 2014	1,719.3	2,613.3	2,613.3	1,008.1	6.68	5.57
BLUE CARE OF MICHIGAN INC	MI	● C+	2q 2014	6.6	2.4	2.4	6.6	9.85	8.21
BLUE CHIP COORDINATED HEALTH PARTNERS (See BLUE CROSS BLUE SHIELD OF RI)									
BLUE CHOICE	NY	U	--	--	--	--	--	--	--
BLUE CHOICE (See BLUE CARE NETWORK OF MICHIGAN)									
BLUE CHOICE (See ANTHEM HEALTH PLANS OF MAINE INC)									
BLUE CHOICE (See BLUE CROSS BLUE SHIELD OF MA)									
BLUE CHOICE (See HIGHMARK BCBSD INC)									
BLUE CHOICE (See ANTHEM HEALTH PLANS OF NEW HAMPSHIRE)									
BLUE CHOICE (See BLUE CROSS BLUE SHIELD OF KANSAS INC)									
BLUE CHOICE HEALTH CARE (See BLUE CROSS BLUE SHIELD OF GEORGIA)									
BLUE CHOICE PLATINUM (See BLUE CROSS BLUE SHIELD OF GEORGIA)									
BLUE CHOICE SENIOR PLAN (See EMPIRE HEALTHCHOICE ASSURANCE INC)									
BLUE CLASSIC (See BLUECROSS BLUESHIELD OF TENNESSEE)									
BLUE CROSS & BLUE SHIELD MA HMO BLUE	MA	● B	2q 2014	1,881.8	3,952.9	3,952.9	1,109.4	4.03	3.36
▼ BLUE CROSS & BLUE SHIELD OF FLORIDA	FL	● B	2q 2014	4,891.3	6,812.5	6,812.5	1,211.1	2.86	2.38
BLUE CROSS BLUE SHIELD HEALTHCARE GA	GA	● A-	2q 2014	657.4	1,445.8	1,445.8	254.8	3.23	2.69
BLUE CROSS BLUE SHIELD OF ALABAMA	AL	● A-	2q 2014	2,987.4	4,114.1	4,114.1	1,228.9	6.87	5.72
BLUE CROSS BLUE SHIELD OF ARIZONA	AZ	● A+	2q 2014	1,642.2	1,531.9	1,531.9	1,059.1	7.23	6.02
BLUE CROSS BLUE SHIELD OF CENTRAL NEW YORK (See EXCELLUS HEALTH PLAN INC)									
BLUE CROSS BLUE SHIELD OF GEORGIA	GA	● B	2q 2014	1,260.2	2,007.5	2,007.5	378.0	3.77	3.14
BLUE CROSS BLUE SHIELD OF HAWAII (See HAWAII MEDICAL SERVICE ASSOCIATION)									
BLUE CROSS BLUE SHIELD OF ILLINOIS (See HEALTH CARE SVC CORP A MUT LEG RES)									
BLUE CROSS BLUE SHIELD OF INDIANA (See ANTHEM INS COMPANIES INC)									
BLUE CROSS BLUE SHIELD OF IOWA (See WELLMARK INC)									
BLUE CROSS BLUE SHIELD OF KANSAS INC	KS	● B	2q 2014	1,611.9	1,725.3	1,725.3	802.7	2.24	1.61
▼ BLUE CROSS BLUE SHIELD OF KC	MO	● B-	2q 2014	1,031.5	1,255.4	1,255.4	605.2	4.85	4.04
BLUE CROSS BLUE SHIELD OF LOUISIANA (See LA HEALTH SERVICE & INDEMNITY CO)									
BLUE CROSS BLUE SHIELD OF MA	MA	● B	2q 2014	2,051.5	2,331.1	2,331.1	785.1	3.58	2.98
BLUE CROSS BLUE SHIELD OF MARYLAND (See CAREFIRST OF MARYLAND INC)									
BLUE CROSS BLUE SHIELD OF MICHIGAN	MI	● B	2q 2014	7,904.8	6,688.4	6,688.4	3,573.8	4.57	3.81
BLUE CROSS BLUE SHIELD OF MINNESOTA	MN	● A	2q 2014	2,106.6	3,082.6	3,082.6	816.3	3.96	3.30
BLUE CROSS BLUE SHIELD OF MS, MUTUAL	MS	● B+	2q 2014	855.7	1,190.4	1,190.4	575.1	7.84	6.53
BLUE CROSS BLUE SHIELD OF NC	NC	● A	2q 2014	4,159.1	5,819.3	5,819.3	2,452.6	6.09	5.08
BLUE CROSS BLUE SHIELD OF NEBRASKA	NE	● A-	2q 2014	945.9	1,578.1	1,578.1	442.8	5.89	4.91
BLUE CROSS BLUE SHIELD OF NEW HAMPSHIRE (See ANTHEM HEALTH PLANS OF NEW HAMPSHIRE)									
BLUE CROSS BLUE SHIELD OF NEW MEXICO (See HEALTH CARE SVC CORP A MUT LEG RES)									
BLUE CROSS BLUE SHIELD OF NORTH DAKOTA (See NORIDIAN MUTUAL INS CO)									
BLUE CROSS BLUE SHIELD OF OHIO (See COMMUNITY INS CO)									
BLUE CROSS BLUE SHIELD OF OKLAHOMA (See HEALTH CARE SVC CORP A MUT LEG RES)									
BLUE CROSS BLUE SHIELD OF RI	RI	● C	2q 2014	630.7	1,537.7	1,537.7	266.8	2.04	1.70
BLUE CROSS BLUE SHIELD OF SC INC	SC	● A-	2q 2014	3,141.3	2,116.7	2,116.7	2,176.1	5.06	4.22
BLUE CROSS BLUE SHIELD OF TEXAS (See HEALTH CARE SVC CORP A MUT LEG RES)									

Arrows denote recent upgrades ▲ or downgrades ▼

www.weissratings.com

● Bullets denote a more detailed analysis is available in Section II.

INSURANCE COMPANY NAME	DOM. STATE	RATING	DATA DATE	TOTAL ASSETS ($MIL)	TOTAL PREMIUMS ($MIL)	HEALTH PREMIUMS ($MIL)	CAPITAL & SURPLUS ($MIL)	RISK ADJUSTED CAPITAL RATIO 1	RATIO 2
BLUE CROSS BLUE SHIELD OF VERMONT	VT	● B+	2q 2014	248.8	420.8	420.8	140.5	2.58	2.15
BLUE CROSS BLUE SHIELD OF VIRGINIA (See ANTHEM HEALTH PLANS OF VIRGINIA)									
BLUE CROSS BLUE SHIELD OF WASHINGTON & ALASKA (See PREMERA BLUE CROSS)									
BLUE CROSS BLUE SHIELD OF WESTERN NEW YORK (See HEALTHNOW NY INC)									
BLUE CROSS BLUE SHIELD OF WISCONSIN	WI	● B-	2q 2014	520.0	672.8	672.8	277.3	3.98	3.32
BLUE CROSS BLUE SHIELD OF WYOMING	WY	● B+	2q 2014	406.0	270.5	270.5	251.3	6.32	5.27
BLUE CROSS COMPLETE OF MICHIGAN	MI	● E	2q 2014	85.6	123.2	123.2	29.6	2.49	2.07
BLUE CROSS OF CALIFORNIA	CA	● A+	2q 2014	5,235.8	10,762.3	10,762.3	1,560.8	2.66	1.67
BLUE CROSS OF IDAHO CARE PLUS INC	ID	U		--	--	--	--	--	--
BLUE CROSS OF IDAHO HEALTH SERVICE	ID	● A-	2q 2014	844.0	1,245.2	1,245.2	542.5	5.69	4.75
BLUE CROSS OF NORTHEASTERN PENNSYLVANIA (See HOSPITAL SERV ASSN OF NORTH EAST PA)									
BLUE CROSS PREFERRED CARE (See BLUE CROSS BLUE SHIELD OF ALABAMA)									
BLUE CROSS SENIOR SELECT (See BLUE CROSS OF CALIFORNIA)									
BLUE PLUS (See HMO MINNESOTA)									
BLUE PLUS (See BLUE CROSS BLUE SHIELD OF MINNESOTA)									
BLUE PREFERRED (See BLUE CARE NETWORK OF MICHIGAN)									
BLUE PREFERRED (See BLUECROSS BLUESHIELD OF TENNESSEE)									
BLUE PREFERRED CARE (See GROUP HOSP & MEDICAL SERVICES INC)									
BLUE PREFERRED PRIMARY (See ANTHEM HEALTH PLANS OF KENTUCKY INC)									
BLUE PREFERRED PRIMARY RISK (See ANTHEM HEALTH PLANS OF KENTUCKY INC)									
BLUE RIDGE HEALTH NETWORK	PA	U		--	--	--	--	--	--
BLUE SELECT (See BLUECROSS BLUESHIELD OF TENNESSEE)									
BLUE SELECT (See BLUE CROSS BLUE SHIELD OF KANSAS INC)									
BLUE SHIELD OF CALIFORNIA (See CALIFORNIA PHYSICIANS SERVICE)									
BLUE SHIELD OF CALIFORNIA L&H INS CO	CA	● A-	2q 2014	838.0	2,408.0	2,399.4	429.9	1.57	1.25
BLUE SHIELD OF CALIFORNIA PREFERRED PLAN (See CALIFORNIA PHYSICIANS SERVICE)									
BLUE SHIELD OF NORTHEASTERN NEW YORK (See HEALTHNOW NY INC)									
BLUEBONNET LIFE INS CO	MS	B+	2q 2014	53.6	6.1	0.0	48.7	7.14	6.43
BLUECARE HEALTH PLAN (See ANTHEM HEALTH PLANS INC)									
BLUECHOICE (See HMO MISSOURI INC)									
BLUECHOICE (See BLUE CROSS BLUE SHIELD OF GEORGIA)									
BLUECHOICE HEALTHPLAN OF SC INC	SC	● A	2q 2014	309.1	494.7	494.7	214.2	6.91	5.76
BLUECHOICE OPTION (See BLUE CROSS BLUE SHIELD OF GEORGIA)									
BLUECROSS BLUESHIELD OF TENNESSEE	TN	● A	2q 2014	2,450.7	3,658.7	3,658.7	1,712.5	7.59	6.33
BLUEGRASS ACCESS (See BLUEGRASS FAMILY HEALTH INC)									
BLUEGRASS FAMILY HEALTH INC	KY	● B+	2q 2014	105.4	144.8	144.8	74.6	4.39	3.66
BLUELINCS HMO (See GHS HEALTH MAINTENANCE ORGANIZATION)									
BOSTON MEDICAL CENTER HEALTH PLAN	MA	● B-	2q 2014	334.0	1,406.5	1,406.5	193.6	1.67	1.39
BOSTON MUTUAL LIFE INS CO	MA	B+	2q 2014	1,222.3	224.7	55.0	152.6	2.13	1.40
BOULDER VALLEY INDIV PRACTICE ASSN	CO	U		--	--	--	--	--	--
BRAVO HEALTH MID-ATLANTIC INC	MD	● C	2q 2014	82.2	329.2	329.2	29.3	1.48	1.24
BRAVO HEALTH PENNSYLVANIA INC	PA	● B	2q 2014	250.6	1,066.0	1,066.0	109.2	1.95	1.62
BRAZOS VALLEY HEALTH NETWORK	TX	U		--	--	--	--	--	--
BRIDGESPAN HEALTH CO	UT	● B	2q 2014	15.0	0.9	0.9	10.5	57.21	47.68
BROWN & TOLAND HEALTH SERVICES	CA	● E	2q 2014	1.8	1.4	1.4	0.2	0.89	0.56
BUCKEYE COMMUNITY HEALTH PLAN INC	OH	● C+	2q 2014	263.1	795.0	795.0	103.5	2.75	2.29
BUPA INS CO	FL	● D+	2q 2014	395.6	439.8	439.8	118.8	2.60	2.16
CALIFORNIA BENEFITS DENTAL PLAN	CA	U		--	--	--	--	--	--
CALIFORNIA DENTAL NETWORK INC	CA	U		--	--	--	--	--	--
CALIFORNIA HEALTH & WELLNESS PLAN	CA	● D+	2q 2014	85.4	27.3	27.3	23.4	7.16	4.53
CALIFORNIA PHYSICIANS SERVICE	CA	● A+	2q 2014	6,941.7	8,316.4	8,316.4	4,409.3	5.58	3.86
CALOPTIMA (See ORANGE PREVENTION & TREATMENT INTEGR)									

▲

Arrows denote recent upgrades ▲ or downgrades▼   ● Bullets denote a more detailed analysis is available in Section II.

INSURANCE COMPANY NAME	DOM. STATE	RATING	DATA DATE	TOTAL ASSETS ($MIL)	TOTAL PREMIUMS ($MIL)	HEALTH PREMIUMS ($MIL)	CAPITAL & SURPLUS ($MIL)	RISK ADJUSTED CAPITAL RATIO 1	RATIO 2
CALVIVA (See FRESNO-KINGS-MADERA REGIONAL HEALTH)									
CAMBRIDGE LIFE INS CO	MO	• B	2q 2014	68.9	22.3	22.3	49.8	14.04	11.70
CAMBRIDGE NETWORK PROVIDER SERV LLC	NY	U		--	--			--	--
CANADA LIFE ASSURANCE CO-US BRANCH	MI	C	2q 2014	4,426.0	124.0	3.7	145.2	1.21	0.64
CAPITAL ADVANTAGE ASR CO	PA	• C-	2q 2014	347.3	735.1	735.1	161.8	1.86	1.55
CAPITAL ADVANTAGE INS CO	PA	• C	2q 2014	485.3	573.1	573.1	317.5	2.17	1.81
CAPITAL BLUE CROSS	PA	• B-	2q 2014	1,128.9	289.4	289.4	845.7	4.21	3.50
▼ CAPITAL DISTRICT PHYSICIANS HEALTH P	NY	• B	2q 2014	440.2	1,302.2	1,302.2	242.3	2.05	1.71
CAPITAL HEALTH PLAN INC	FL	• A-	2q 2014	468.6	640.2	640.2	371.4	8.80	7.34
CAPITALCHOICE (See GROUP HOSP & MEDICAL SERVICES INC)									
CAPITOL INDEMNITY CORP	WI	C	2q 2014	454.8	81.4	0.4	218.6	1.86	1.28
CARE - PLUS DENTAL PLANS INC	WI	U		--	--	--	--	--	--
CARE 1ST HEALTH PLAN	CA	U		--	--	--	--	--	--
CARE 1ST HEALTH PLAN	CA	• D+	2q 2014	504.0	1,130.8	1,130.8	156.0	1.66	1.03
CARE IMPROVEMENT PLUS OF MARYLAND	MD	U		--	--	--	--	--	--
CARE IMPROVEMENT PLUS OF TEXAS INS	TX	• B	2q 2014	264.9	990.3	990.3	132.3	2.77	2.31
CARE IMPROVEMENT PLUS SOUTH CENTRAL	AR	• C	2q 2014	630.4	2,464.4	2,464.4	329.1	2.75	2.29
CARE IMPROVEMENT PLUS WI INS	WI	• C	2q 2014	16.5	24.6	24.6	9.5	17.96	14.97
CARE N CARE INS CO INC	TX	• D	2q 2014	19.7	74.2	74.2	12.2	1.38	1.15
CARE RESOURCES INC	CA	U		--	--	--	--	--	--
CARE WISCONSIN HEALTH PLAN INC	WI	• B	2q 2014	28.7	92.7	92.7	19.7	1.82	1.52
CAREAMERICA LIFE INS CO	CA	B	2q 2014	28.5	2.1	0.1	25.5	6.40	5.76
CARECENTRIX OF NEW JERSEY INC	NJ	U		--	--	--	--	--	--
CARECHOICE (See NORIDIAN MUTUAL INS CO)									
CARECORE NJ LLC	NJ	U		--	--	--	--	--	--
CAREFIRST BLUECHOICE INC	DC	• A+	2q 2014	1,140.8	2,401.3	2,401.3	739.7	6.28	5.24
CAREFIRST BLUECROSS BLUESHIELD (See GROUP HOSP & MEDICAL SERVICES INC)									
CAREFIRST INC	MD	U		--	--	--	--	--	--
CAREFIRST OF MARYLAND INC	MD	• B	2q 2014	1,389.2	1,867.3	1,867.3	543.3	4.11	3.42
CARELINK (See COVENTRY HEALTH CARE OF WEST VA INC)									
▼ CAREMORE HEALTH PLAN	CA	• B+	2q 2014	298.1	836.7	836.7	87.2	2.79	1.75
CAREMORE HEALTH PLAN OF ARIZONA INC	AZ	• B-	2q 2014	73.9	204.0	204.0	29.6	3.06	2.55
CAREMORE HEALTH PLAN OF COLORADO INC	CO	U		--	--	--	--	--	--
CAREMORE HEALTH PLAN OF NEVADA	NV	• D	2q 2014	30.3	68.2	68.2	14.0	3.19	2.66
CAREPLUS HEALTH PLANS INC	FL	• C	2q 2014	320.7	1,204.3	1,204.3	72.1	2.83	2.36
CAREPOINT INS CO	NJ	U		--	--	--	--	--	--
CARESOURCE	OH	• A	2q 2014	1,491.7	4,161.9	4,161.9	634.0	2.58	2.15
CARESOURCE INDIANA	IN	U		--	--	--	--	--	--
CARESYS PREFERRED PROVIDER NETWORK	CT	U		--	--	--	--	--	--
CARIBBEAN AMERICAN LIFE ASR CO	PR	B	2q 2014	41.3	26.6	10.4	11.9	2.02	1.72
CARIBBEAN AMERICAN PROPERTY INS CO	PR	C+	2q 2014	45.6	52.4	0.1	21.6	0.91	0.59
CARILION CLINIC MEDICARE RESOURCES	VA	• E+	2q 2014	21.8	76.2	76.2	13.3	0.51	0.43
CARITEN HEALTH PLAN INC	TN	• B	2q 2014	277.7	1,044.6	1,044.6	149.7	3.22	2.69
CAROLINA CARE PLAN INC	SC	• B	1q 2014	37.0	109.3	109.3	35.1	5.05	4.21
CATAMARAN INS OF OHIO	OH	C+	2q 2014	34.8	1.2	0.0	10.9	5.03	4.53
CATHOLIC SPECIAL NEEDS PLAN LLC	NY	• D	2q 2014	11.6	39.1	39.1	4.1	0.46	0.38
CATLIN INS CO	TX	C+	2q 2014	254.4	288.5	4.8	58.8	1.61	1.02
CBHNP SERVICES INC	PA	• C+	2q 2014	14.6	48.2	48.2	10.4	2.74	2.28
CCN MANAGED CARE	CA	U		--	--	--	--	--	--
CDPHP UNIVERSAL BENEFITS (See CAPITAL DISTRICT PHYSICIANS HEALTH P)									
CDPHP UNIVERSAL BENEFITS INC	NY	• E	2q 2014	136.5	687.6	687.6	35.4	0.67	0.56
CELTIC INS CO	IL	• C	2q 2014	96.7	140.4	140.3	28.5	1.22	0.96

Arrows denote recent upgrades ▲ or downgrades▼

www.weissratings.com
• Bullets denote a more detailed analysis is available in Section II.

INSURANCE COMPANY NAME	DOM. STATE	RATING	DATA DATE	TOTAL ASSETS ($MIL)	TOTAL PREMIUMS ($MIL)	HEALTH PREMIUMS ($MIL)	CAPITAL & SURPLUS ($MIL)	RISK ADJUSTED CAPITAL RATIO 1	RATIO 2
CELTICARE HEALTH PLAN OF MA INC	MA	• C+	2q 2014	49.4	54.4	54.4	18.1	4.45	3.71
CENCAL HEALTH (See SANTA BARBARA SAN LUIS OBISPO REGION)									
CENPATICO BEHAVIORAL HEALTH OF TEXAS	TX	U		--	--	--	--	--	--
CENTENNIAL CASUALTY CO	AL	B	2q 2014	109.3	17.0	1.2	64.9	2.79	1.63
CENTRAL COAST ALLIANCE FOR HEALTH (See SANTA CRUZ-MONTEREY-MERCED MGD MED)									
CENTRAL HEALTH PLAN OF CALIFORNIA	CA	• E+	2q 2014	19.7	128.6	128.6	7.9	0.11	0.07
CENTRAL RESERVE LIFE INS CO	OH	C+	2q 2014	24.4	10.1	9.4	22.2	1.47	1.39
CENTRAL SECURITY LIFE INS CO	TX	B-	2q 2014	72.0	3.4	0.2	7.8	1.02	0.92
CENTRAL STATES H & L CO OF OMAHA	NE	• A-	2q 2014	405.9	141.6	66.9	121.2	3.97	2.83
CENTRAL STATES INDEMNITY CO OF OMAHA	NE	• B+	2q 2014	424.9	109.6	52.8	355.6	4.28	2.75
CENTRAL SUSQUEHANNA HC PROVIDERS	PA	U		--	--	--	--	--	--
CENTRAL UNITED LIFE INS CO	AR	• C	2q 2014	303.5	80.3	76.4	79.1	0.61	0.56
CENTRE LIFE INS CO	MA	• B-	2q 2014	1,928.5	25.8	25.8	100.2	4.11	2.67
CENTURION LIFE INS CO	IA	• D	1q 2014	1,211.1	1.2	0.4	406.3	4.98	2.92
CENTURY HEALTH SOLUTIONS INC	KS	U		--	--	--	--	--	--
CENTURY INS CO GUAM LTD	GU	B	2q 2014	20.8	12.3	0.0	10.7	2.13	1.26
CENTURY LIFE ASR CO	OK	D+	2q 2014	12.4	1.4	0.3	6.4	2.56	2.31
CENTURY PREFERRED (See ANTHEM HEALTH PLANS INC)									
CHA HMO INC	KY	• C	2q 2014	34.0	25.8	25.8	29.0	9.56	7.96
CHAMPIONS LIFE INS CO	TX	D+	2q 2014	35.7	0.8	0.1	4.2	0.38	0.32
CHEROKEE INS CO	MI	C-	2q 2014	415.8	167.7	30.6	161.7	2.53	1.47
CHEROKEE NATIONAL LIFE INS CO	GA	B	2q 2014	21.3	4.1	1.5	15.9	4.51	4.06
CHESAPEAKE LIFE INS CO	OK	C+	2q 2014	51.0	124.9	80.1	25.5	0.90	0.71
CHILD HEALTH PLUS (See HEALTHNOW NY INC)									
CHILDRENS COMMUNITY HEALTH PLAN INC	WI	• C-	2q 2014	58.9	274.9	274.9	25.2	1.17	0.97
CHINESE COMMUNITY HEALTH PLAN	CA	• B-	2q 2014	61.0	128.1	128.1	32.9	2.58	1.69
CHOICE PHYSICIANS NETWORK	CA	• D+	2q 2014	8.4	50.0	50.0	3.3	0.64	0.39
CHOICE PLUS (See PACIFICARE OF NEVADA INC)									
CHRISTIAN FIDELITY LIFE INS CO	TX	• B-	2q 2014	78.6	49.1	47.8	32.8	2.60	1.92
CHRISTUS HEALTH PLAN	TX	• B-	2q 2014	18.9	29.7	29.7	15.0	3.07	2.56
CICA LIFE INS CO OF AMERICA	CO	C-	2q 2014	738.3	138.1	0.9	56.9	0.71	0.57
CIGNA BEHAVIORAL HEALTH OF CA	CA	U		--	--	--	--	--	--
CIGNA DENTAL HEALTH OF CALIFORNIA	CA	U		--	--	--	--	--	--
CIGNA HEALTH & LIFE INS CO	CT	• B	2q 2014	5,195.8	7,220.3	7,219.7	2,103.0	1.84	1.44
CIGNA HEALTHCARE OF ARIZONA INC	AZ	• C	2q 2014	114.3	505.4	505.4	45.0	1.79	1.49
CIGNA HEALTHCARE OF CALIFORNIA INC	CA	• B	2q 2014	180.3	944.4	944.4	47.2	1.36	0.83
CIGNA HEALTHCARE OF COLORADO INC	CO	• C	2q 2014	5.8	9.8	9.8	4.4	7.10	5.92
CIGNA HEALTHCARE OF CONNECTICUT INC	CT	• C-	2q 2014	32.9	11.0	11.0	32.0	34.73	28.94
CIGNA HEALTHCARE OF FLORIDA INC	FL	• C	2q 2014	4.5	1.2	1.2	4.1	9.02	7.51
CIGNA HEALTHCARE OF GEORGIA INC	GA	• B-	2q 2014	7.7	3.9	3.9	5.2	9.78	8.15
CIGNA HEALTHCARE OF ILLINOIS INC	IL	• C	2q 2014	2.7	1.0	1.0	2.6	4.70	3.91
CIGNA HEALTHCARE OF INDIANA INC	IN	• C+	2q 2014	1.7	0.8	0.8	1.4	2.61	2.18
CIGNA HEALTHCARE OF NEW JERSEY INC	NJ	• C	2q 2014	5.4	3.2	3.2	2.6	4.86	4.05
CIGNA HEALTHCARE OF NORTH CAROLINA	NC	• C	2q 2014	13.5	15.3	15.3	10.3	7.91	6.59
CIGNA HEALTHCARE OF SOUTH CAROLINA	SC	• D+	2q 2014	8.8	1.5	1.5	0.7	1.82	1.52
CIGNA HEALTHCARE OF ST LOUIS	MO	• D+	2q 2014	5.5	5.5	5.5	0.6	1.33	1.10
CIGNA HEALTHCARE OF TENNESSEE INC	TN	• C	2q 2014	12.1	35.4	35.4	7.7	3.56	2.97
CIGNA HEALTHCARE OF TEXAS INC	TX	• B-	2q 2014	26.6	100.8	100.8	13.2	2.38	1.98
CIGNA LIFE INS CO OF NEW YORK	NY	• A-	2q 2014	376.2	124.0	82.6	106.5	3.68	2.31
CIGNA WORLDWIDE INS CO	DE	B	2q 2014	46.6	2.6	2.5	7.2	1.03	0.92
CINCINNATI EQUITABLE LIFE INS CO	OH	C-	2q 2014	79.3	27.9	0.1	9.1	1.16	0.84
CINCINNATI INS CO	OH	A	2q 2014	10,807.9	3,297.2	0.0	4,332.0	2.35	1.71

Arrows denote recent upgrades ▲ or downgrades▼   • Bullets denote a more detailed analysis is available in Section II.

INSURANCE COMPANY NAME	DOM. STATE	RATING	DATA DATE	TOTAL ASSETS ($MIL)	TOTAL PREMIUMS ($MIL)	HEALTH PREMIUMS ($MIL)	CAPITAL & SURPLUS ($MIL)	RISK ADJUSTED CAPITAL RATIO 1	RATIO 2
CINCINNATI LIFE INS CO	OH	B	2q 2014	3,819.1	294.5	6.8	224.4	1.83	1.00
CITIZENS CHOICE HEALTHPLAN (See HONORED CITIZENS CHOICE HEALTH PLAN)									
CITIZENS FIDELITY INS CO	AR	C+	2q 2014	65.5	4.1	0.0	10.9	1.62	1.36
CITIZENS NATIONAL LIFE INS CO	TX	C	2q 2014	12.4	1.3	0.0	2.2	3.04	2.74
CITIZENS SECURITY LIFE INS CO	KY	C	2q 2014	23.3	34.0	21.7	13.8	1.24	0.77
CITRUS HEALTH CARE INC	FL	U	--	--	--	--	--	--	--
CLARIA LIFE & HEALTH INS CO	DE	D+	3q 2013	6.8	7.1	7.1	1.1	0.60	0.54
CLEAR-CARE CORP	PA	U	--	--	--	--	--	--	--
CLOISTER MUTUAL CASUALTY INS CO	PA	U	2q 2014	4.7	0.0	0.0	4.7	--	--
CLUB INS CO	OH	C	2q 2014	13.9	1.3	1.3	12.9	8.00	4.76
CMD HEALTH INC	KY	U	--	--	--	--	--	--	--
CMFG LIFE INS CO	IA	B-	2q 2014	15,754.1	2,317.8	525.9	1,587.2	1.36	1.06
CNA MANAGED CARE	IL	U	--	--	--	--	--	--	--
COASTAL HEALTHCARE ADMINISTRATORS	CA	U	--	--	--	--	--	--	--
COLONIAL LIFE & ACCIDENT INS CO	SC	• C+	2q 2014	2,869.7	1,246.1	985.5	574.1	2.85	1.76
COLONIAL LIFE INS CO OF TX	TX	C-	2q 2014	17.5	1.2	0.3	13.8	4.27	3.84
COLONIAL PENN LIFE INS CO	PA	• D+	2q 2014	750.9	487.7	273.6	92.5	1.41	0.81
COLORADO ACCESS	CO	U	--	--	--	--	--	--	--
COLORADO BANKERS LIFE INS CO	CO	B+	2q 2014	272.7	88.6	3.5	29.7	2.52	1.46
COLORADO CHOICE HEALTH PLANS	CO	• C	2q 2014	16.3	24.6	24.6	4.6	0.97	0.81
COLORADO HEALTH INS COOPERATIVE INC	CO	U	--	--	--	--	--	--	--
COLUMBIA UNITED PROVIDERS INC	WA	• B	2q 2014	37.4	95.3	95.3	20.8	1.87	1.56
COLUMBIAN LIFE INS CO	IL	C+	2q 2014	294.2	212.2	14.0	22.5	1.36	0.90
COLUMBIAN MUTUAL LIFE INS CO	NY	B	2q 2014	1,359.4	92.9	2.9	98.8	1.65	1.06
▼ COLUMBUS LIFE INS CO	OH	B-	2q 2014	3,320.0	270.0	0.1	248.5	2.02	1.07
COMBINED INS CO OF AMERICA	IL	• C+	2q 2014	1,642.8	866.1	788.4	373.5	2.24	1.71
COMBINED LIFE INS CO OF NEW YORK	NY	• B	2q 2014	416.4	126.4	106.8	62.4	2.05	1.43
COMMERCIAL TRAVELERS MUTUAL INS CO	NY	E+	2q 2014	13.9	8.9	8.9	7.1	1.30	1.17
COMMON GROUND HEALTHCARE COOPERATIVE	WI	U	--	--	--	--	--	--	--
▲ COMMONWEALTH ANNUITY & LIFE INS CO	MA	B-	2q 2014	10,614.4	528.0	0.6	1,266.2	1.30	0.95
COMMONWEALTH DEALERS LIFE INS CO	VA	U	4q 2013	6.8	0.0	0.0	5.4	--	--
COMMONWEALTH MUTUAL INS CO	MD	U	1q 2014	0.5	1.0	0.1	0.2	--	--
COMMUNITY BLUE HMO OF BL CROSS W NY	NY	U	--	--	--	--	--	--	--
COMMUNITY CARE ALLIANCE OF ILLINOIS	IL	U	--	--	--	--	--	--	--
COMMUNITY CARE BEHAVIORAL HEALTH	PA	• C	2q 2014	250.7	735.6	735.6	165.9	3.21	2.68
COMMUNITY CARE HEALTH PLAN	CA	U	2q 2014	6.0	0.0	0.0	3.8	--	--
▼ COMMUNITY CARE HEALTH PLAN INC	WI	• B-	2q 2014	17.3	94.8	94.8	11.4	1.27	1.06
COMMUNITY CARE OF OREGON INC	OR	U	--	--	--	--	--	--	--
COMMUNITY CHOICE (See ANTHEM INS COMPANIES INC)									
COMMUNITY DENTAL ASSOC INC	NJ	U	--	--	--	--	--	--	--
COMMUNITY DENTAL SERVICES INC	CA	U	--	--	--	--	--	--	--
COMMUNITY FIRST GROUP HOSPITAL SERV	TX	U	2q 2014	0.8	0.0	0.0	0.7	--	--
COMMUNITY FIRST HEALTH PLANS INC	TX	• B+	1q 2014	85.9	265.0	265.0	46.9	1.88	1.57
COMMUNITY HEALTH ALLIANCE MUTUAL INS	TN	U	--	--	--	--	--	--	--
COMMUNITY HEALTH CHOICE INC	TX	• B-	2q 2014	174.6	663.4	663.4	96.8	1.73	1.44
COMMUNITY HEALTH GROUP	CA	• C	2q 2014	138.7	340.7	340.7	38.9	1.03	0.65
COMMUNITY HEALTH PLAN (See COUNTY OF LOS ANGELES DEPT HEALTH)									
COMMUNITY HEALTH PLAN INS CO	MO	U	--	--	--	--	--	--	--
COMMUNITY HEALTH PLAN OF WASHINGTON	WA	• A-	2q 2014	363.5	901.9	901.9	131.3	1.94	1.62
COMMUNITY INS CO	OH	• B+	2q 2014	2,036.0	5,102.2	5,102.2	747.1	2.62	2.18
COMMUNITY PREFERRED HEALTH PLAN (See ANTHEM INS COMPANIES INC)									
COMMUNITYCARE HMO INC	OK	• A	2q 2014	207.2	661.6	661.6	112.0	2.82	2.35

Arrows denote recent upgrades ▲ or downgrades▼

• Bullets denote a more detailed analysis is available in Section II.

INSURANCE COMPANY NAME	DOM. STATE	RATING	DATA DATE	TOTAL ASSETS ($MIL)	TOTAL PREMIUMS ($MIL)	HEALTH PREMIUMS ($MIL)	CAPITAL & SURPLUS ($MIL)	RISK ADJUSTED CAPITAL RATIO 1	RATIO 2
COMMUNITYCARE LIFE AND HEALTH INS CO	OK	● B-	2q 2014	24.7	73.9	73.9	12.1	1.94	1.61
COMPANION HEALTHCARE (See BLUE CROSS BLUE SHIELD OF SC INC)									
COMPANION LIFE INS CO	NY	B-	2q 2014	929.0	115.1	0.0	61.1	2.01	1.05
COMPANION LIFE INS CO	SC	● A-	2q 2014	278.1	643.3	611.9	134.8	2.76	2.16
COMPANION PROPERTY & CASUALTY INS CO	SC	B	2q 2014	1,001.6	506.2	6.0	253.3	1.65	1.18
COMPBENEFITS INS CO	TX	● B	2q 2014	50.1	119.0	118.9	40.2	1.96	1.59
COMPCARE HEALTH SERVICES INS CORP	WI	● A-	2q 2014	233.6	599.3	599.3	121.0	3.64	3.03
COMPCHOICE (See NORIDIAN MUTUAL INS CO)									
COMPREHENSIVE MOBILE INS ARIZONA INC	AZ	U		--	--	--	--	--	--
CONCENTRAL MANAGED CARE INC	MA	U		--	--	--	--	--	--
CONCERN: EMPLOYEE ASSISTANCE PROGRAM	CA	U		--	--	--	--	--	--
CONCERT HEALTH PLAN (See EMPLOYER CHOICE INS CO)									
CONNECTICARE BENEFITS INC	CT	U		--	--	--	--	--	--
CONNECTICARE INC	CT	● B	2q 2014	265.5	834.3	834.3	127.4	2.85	2.37
CONNECTICARE INS CO INC	CT	● C	2q 2014	116.3	404.9	404.9	44.4	2.09	1.74
CONNECTICARE OF MASSACHUSETTS INC	MA	● C	2q 2014	5.4	14.8	14.8	3.4	2.68	2.23
CONNECTICUT GENERAL LIFE INS CO	CT	● B-	2q 2014	18,669.3	4,028.5	3,433.2	3,248.7	1.61	1.31
CONSECO LIFE INS CO	IN	D+	2q 2014	3,761.1	227.9	32.4	203.2	1.43	0.77
CONSOLIDATED INS ASN	TX	D+	2q 2014	5.4	1.0	0.0	2.8	1.24	1.15
CONSTELLATION HEALTH LLC	PR	U		--	--	--	--	--	--
CONSTITUTION LIFE INS CO	TX	● C+	2q 2014	319.1	71.6	59.5	36.7	1.76	1.17
CONSUMER HEALTH NETWORK	NJ	U		--	--	--	--	--	--
CONSUMERHEALTH INC	CA	U		--	--	--	--	--	--
CONSUMERS CHOICE HEALTH INS CO	SC	U		--	--	--	--	--	--
CONSUMERS LIFE INS CO	OH	C	2q 2014	36.8	130.8	108.7	20.2	1.52	1.19
CONSUMERS MUTUAL INS OF MICHIGAN	MI	U	2q 2014	33.4	0.1	0.1	13.2	--	--
CONTINENTAL AMERICAN INS CO	SC	● B	2q 2014	404.2	350.8	335.7	139.8	3.41	2.45
CONTINENTAL ASSURANCE CO	IL	C	2q 2014	2,509.8	50.3	1.1	247.4	4.11	2.03
CONTINENTAL CASUALTY CO	IL	C+	2q 2014	42,972.3	5,413.2	505.6	11,234.3	2.04	1.57
CONTINENTAL GENERAL INS CO	OH	C	2q 2014	243.3	105.1	93.1	25.0	2.74	1.52
CONTINENTAL LIFE INS CO	PA	D+	2q 2014	21.2	4.7	0.1	2.2	0.62	0.56
CONTINENTAL LIFE INS CO OF BRENTWOOD	TN	● B	2q 2014	211.8	257.5	252.9	96.6	1.05	0.93
CONTRA COSTA HEALTH PLAN	CA	● D	2q 2014	59.1	356.1	356.1	14.8	0.57	0.38
COOK CHILDRENS HEALTH PLAN	TX	● E+	2q 2014	71.2	265.2	265.2	33.5	1.07	0.89
COOPERATIVA DE SEGUROS DE VIDA DE PR	PR	C-	2q 2014	423.6	86.2	19.7	13.9	1.22	0.65
COOPERATIVE HEALTH NETWORK INC	OH	U		--	--	--	--	--	--
COOPORTUNITY HEALTH	IA	U		--	--	--	--	--	--
COORDINATED CARE CORP	IN	● C+	2q 2014	319.9	570.0	570.0	69.0	2.41	2.01
COORDINATED CARE OF WASHINGTON INC	WA	U		--	--	--	--	--	--
COORDINATED HEALTH MUTUAL INC	OH	U		--	--	--	--	--	--
COPIC INS CO	CO	A-	2q 2014	523.3	88.0	1.7	258.2	4.50	3.04
CORVESTA LIFE INS CO	AZ	U	4q 2013	9.2	0.0	0.0	7.7	--	--
COTTON STATES LIFE INS CO	GA	A-	2q 2014	331.7	34.1	0.0	60.5	3.86	2.17
COUNTRY LIFE INS CO	IL	A+	2q 2014	10,519.0	498.0	100.7	1,103.0	2.12	1.39
COUNTRYWAY INS CO	NY	C	2q 2014	26.4	36.9	0.0	22.5	18.89	17.00
COUNTY OF LOS ANGELES DEPT HEALTH	CA	● D	1q 2014	14.3	2.1	2.1	12.8	32.41	21.55
COVENTRY HEALTH & LIFE INS CO	MO	● B+	2q 2014	1,547.4	3,441.1	3,441.1	654.0	3.41	2.84
COVENTRY HEALTH CARE CAROLINAS INC	NC	● B	2q 2014	144.8	307.7	307.7	44.7	2.68	2.24
COVENTRY HEALTH CARE OF DELAWARE INC	DE	● B	2q 2014	67.0	189.1	189.1	40.7	4.56	3.80
COVENTRY HEALTH CARE OF FLORIDA INC	FL	● B	2q 2014	311.3	523.1	523.1	54.2	2.02	1.68
COVENTRY HEALTH CARE OF GEORGIA	GA	● B	2q 2014	167.6	534.1	534.1	73.7	2.59	2.16
COVENTRY HEALTH CARE OF ILLINOIS INC	IL	● B+	2q 2014	104.8	263.5	263.5	44.6	3.58	2.98

Arrows denote recent upgrades ▲ or downgrades▼   ● Bullets denote a more detailed analysis is available in Section II.

INSURANCE COMPANY NAME	DOM. STATE	RATING	DATA DATE	TOTAL ASSETS ($MIL)	TOTAL PREMIUMS ($MIL)	HEALTH PREMIUMS ($MIL)	CAPITAL & SURPLUS ($MIL)	RISK ADJUSTED CAPITAL RATIO 1	RATIO 2
COVENTRY HEALTH CARE OF IOWA INC	IA	● B	2q 2014	59.2	118.6	118.6	24.0	3.40	2.84
COVENTRY HEALTH CARE OF KANSAS INC	KS	● B	2q 2014	270.2	699.7	699.7	128.3	3.60	3.00
COVENTRY HEALTH CARE OF LOUISIANA	LA	● B	2q 2014	50.3	171.1	171.1	24.1	2.77	2.31
COVENTRY HEALTH CARE OF MISSOURI INC	MO	● B	2q 2014	248.8	456.8	456.8	92.6	4.51	3.76
COVENTRY HEALTH CARE OF NEBRASKA INC	NE	● B+	2q 2014	142.3	375.4	375.4	55.4	3.00	2.50
COVENTRY HEALTH CARE OF PENNSYLVANIA	PA	U	--	--	--	--	--	--	--
COVENTRY HEALTH CARE OF TEXAS INC	TX	● B	2q 2014	13.6	1.0	1.0	11.7	16.50	13.75
COVENTRY HEALTH CARE OF VIRGINIA INC	VA	● B	2q 2014	88.6	315.4	315.4	33.3	1.96	1.63
▼ COVENTRY HEALTH CARE OF WEST VA INC	WV	● B+	2q 2014	90.8	235.1	235.1	36.7	2.99	2.49
COVENTRY HEALTH PLAN OF FLORIDA INC	FL	● A-	2q 2014	215.5	268.0	268.0	97.1	6.14	5.11
COVENTRYCARES OF MICHIGAN INC	MI	● B	2q 2014	50.1	163.7	163.7	23.8	3.07	2.55
COX HEALTH SYSTEMS HMO INC	MO	● C	2q 2014	25.7	4.9	4.9	23.7	1.66	1.38
COX HEALTH SYSTEMS INS CO	MO	● B-	2q 2014	39.0	109.8	109.8	14.8	1.07	0.89
CREATIVE HEALTH PLANS INC	OH	U	--	--	--	--	--	--	--
CRESTPOINT HEALTH INS CO	TN	● D	2q 2014	10.7	2.2	2.2	5.2	4.84	4.03
CSAA AFFINITY INS CO	PA	C+	2q 2014	204.5	162.9	4.5	151.2	3.30	3.13
CSAA INS EXCHANGE	CA	A-	2q 2014	6,888.9	1,802.8	0.5	3,961.0	3.77	2.61
▲ CUATRO LLC	NY	● E	2q 2014	4.5	38.4	38.4	2.3	0.36	0.30
DAILY UNDERWRITERS OF AMERICA	PA	C	2q 2014	38.8	10.7	0.0	26.7	2.25	1.54
DAKOTACARE (See SD STATE MEDICAL HOLDING CO)									
DC CHARTERED HEALTH PLAN INC	DC	F	4q 2012	56.1	398.3	398.3	-9.6	0.00	0.00
DEACONESS HEALTH PLANS	IN	U		--	--	--	--	--	--
DEAN HEALTH INS INC	WI	U		--	--	--	--	--	--
DEAN HEALTH PLAN INC	WI	● B	2q 2014	263.5	1,076.7	1,076.7	79.2	1.38	1.15
DEARBORN NATIONAL LIFE INS CO	IL	● A-	2q 2014	2,193.1	528.0	225.3	476.7	2.50	1.68
DEARBORN NATIONAL LIFE INS CO OF NY	NY	B+	2q 2014	41.2	4.7	3.0	21.2	3.45	3.11
DEDICATED DENTAL SYSTEMS INC	CA	U		--	--	--	--	--	--
DELAWARE AMERICAN LIFE INS CO	DE	● B	2q 2014	145.7	65.4	50.8	82.0	5.18	3.71
DELAWARE LIFE INS CO OF NEW YORK	NY	● C	2q 2014	3,113.3	180.1	103.1	405.9	8.36	4.10
DELTA DENTAL OF CALIFORNIA	CA	U		--	--	--	--	--	--
DELTA DENTAL OF IOWA	IA	U		--	--	--	--	--	--
DELTA DENTAL OF PENNSYLVANIA	PA	U		--	--	--	--	--	--
DELTA DENTAL PLAN OF IDAHO INC	ID	U		--	--	--	--	--	--
DELTA DENTAL PLAN OF MAINE (See MAINE DENTAL SERVICE CORP)									
DELTA DENTAL PLAN OF OKLAHOMA	OK	U		--	--	--	--	--	--
DELTA DENTAL PLAN OF PUERTO RICO	PR	U		--	--	--	--	--	--
DELTA DENTAL PLAN OF VERMONT	VT	● C-	4q 2013	23.8	26.2	26.2	20.8	6.20	5.16
DELTA LIFE INS CO	GA	E+	2q 2014	61.9	14.9	1.3	8.7	0.56	0.35
DENTA-CHEK OF MARYLAND INC	MD	U		--	--	--	--	--	--
DENTAL BENEFIT PROVIDERS OF CA INC	CA	U		--	--	--	--	--	--
DENTAL DELIVERY SYSTEMS INC	NJ	U							
DENTAL GROUP OF NEW JERSEY INC	NJ	U		--	--	--	--	--	--
DENTAL HEALTH SERVICES	CA	U		--	--	--	--	--	--
DENTAL NETWORK INC	MD	U		--	--	--	--	--	--
DENTAL SERVICE OF MASSACHUSETTS INC	MA	U		--	--	--	--	--	--
DENTAL SERVICES ORG INC	NJ	U		--	--	--	--	--	--
DENTAQUEST USA INS CO INC	TX	U		--	--	--	--	--	--
DENTEGRA INS CO OF NEW ENGLAND	MA	U		--	--	--	--	--	--
DENTISTS BENEFITS INS CO	OR	C	2q 2014	19.0	5.0	0.5	12.2	3.18	2.20
DENVER HEALTH MEDICAL PLAN INC	CO	● B	2q 2014	45.7	108.9	108.9	31.4	3.04	2.54
▲ DESERET MUTUAL INS CO	UT	B	2q 2014	39.7	12.4	11.5	8.1	1.95	1.76
DEVON HEALTH SERVICES INC	PA	U		--	--	--	--	--	--

Arrows denote recent upgrades ▲ or downgrades▼

● Bullets denote a more detailed analysis is available in Section II.

INSURANCE COMPANY NAME	DOM. STATE	RATING	DATA DATE	TOTAL ASSETS ($MIL)	TOTAL PREMIUMS ($MIL)	HEALTH PREMIUMS ($MIL)	CAPITAL & SURPLUS ($MIL)	RISK ADJUSTED CAPITAL RATIO 1	RATIO 2
DIRECTCARE (See SELECTHEALTH INC)									
DIRECTCARE AMERICA INC	OH	U		--	--	--	--	--	--
DIRECTCARE PLUS (See SELECTHEALTH INC)									
DMC CARE	MI	U		--	--	--	--	--	--
DONGBU INS CO LTD US GUAM BRANCH	GU	B-	2q 2014	55.8	34.7	0.0	30.7	3.02	1.88
DRISCOLL CHILDRENS HEALTH PLAN	TX	• D	2q 2014	57.7	315.6	315.6	21.8	0.68	0.57
DSM USA INS CO INC	PA	U	2q 2014	7.5	0.0	0.0	7.4	--	--
DYNAMIC HEALTH INS CO	DE	U		--	--	--	--	--	--
EASTERN PENNSYLVANIA HEALTH NETWORK	PA	U		--	--	--	--	--	--
EASY CHOICE HEALTH PLAN	CA	• E+	2q 2014	127.7	567.3	567.3	25.2	0.45	0.28
EASY CHOICE HEALTH PLAN OF NY (See ATLANTIS HEALTH PLAN)									
EDUCATORS HEALTH PARTNERS	PA	U		--	--	--	--	--	--
EDUCATORS HEALTH PLANS LIFE ACCIDENT	UT	U		--	--	--	--	--	--
EL PASO FIRST HEALTH PLANS INC	TX	• B	2q 2014	40.7	125.6	125.6	29.1	2.15	1.79
ELDERPLAN INC	NY	• C-	2q 2014	240.3	645.9	645.9	110.0	2.02	1.69
EMC NATIONAL LIFE CO	IA	B-	2q 2014	1,017.8	72.7	1.8	92.2	2.25	1.30
EMERALD HEALTH NETWORK	OH	U		--	--	--	--	--	--
▲ EMI HEALTH	UT	• B-	2q 2014	86.2	34.7	34.7	54.4	4.35	3.63
EMPHESYS INS CO	TX	U	4q 2013	4.4	0.0	0.0	4.3	--	--
EMPIRE BL CROSS BL SHIELD HEALTHNET	NY	U		--	--	--	--	--	--
EMPIRE BLUE CROSS BLUE SHIELD (See EMPIRE HEALTHCHOICE ASSURANCE INC)									
EMPIRE FIRE & MARINE INS CO	NE	C	2q 2014	97.0	339.3	14.4	48.5	7.37	6.63
▼ EMPIRE HEALTHCHOICE ASSURANCE INC	NY	• B-	2q 2014	3,006.6	4,591.4	4,591.4	1,367.8	4.14	3.45
▼ EMPIRE HEALTHCHOICE HMO INC	NY	• B	2q 2014	873.6	1,539.6	1,539.6	311.5	3.78	3.15
EMPIRE PPO (See EMPIRE HEALTHCHOICE ASSURANCE INC)									
EMPLOYER CHOICE INS CO	FL	• E	2q 2014	2.9	2.2	2.2	2.4	3.07	2.56
EMPLOYERS FIRE INS CO	PA	C	2q 2014	19.4	5.6	0.0	19.4	153.30	76.66
EMPLOYERS INS OF WAUSAU	WI	B-	2q 2014	5,426.7	258.6	0.0	1,309.1	1.85	1.26
ENCORE HEALTH NETWORK	IN	U		--	--	--	--	--	--
ENTERPRISE LIFE INS CO	TX	C	2q 2014	18.0	2.7	2.8	15.4	1.13	1.05
▲ ENVISION INS CO	OH	• C	2q 2014	465.7	134.7	134.7	25.2	1.27	1.06
EPIC HEALTH PLAN	CA	• D+	2q 2014	17.3	65.4	65.4	5.6	0.78	0.47
EPIC LIFE INSURANCE CO	WI	• B	2q 2014	61.0	26.9	19.3	31.5	3.56	2.40
▲ EQUITABLE LIFE & CASUALTY INS CO	UT	• C+	2q 2014	284.9	153.9	139.1	41.6	2.49	1.71
ERIE FAMILY LIFE INS CO	PA	A-	2q 2014	2,058.7	178.7	0.3	296.3	3.40	1.89
ESSENCE HEALTHCARE INC	MO	• B	2q 2014	109.3	411.8	411.8	50.9	1.44	1.20
ESSEX INS CO	DE	C	2q 2014	1,305.2	434.8	4.5	433.7	1.41	0.93
ETHIX SOUTHEAST INC	NC	U		--	--	--	--	--	--
EVERENCE INS CO	IN	C	2q 2014	22.9	9.9	9.8	13.7	3.38	3.04
EVERGREEN HEALTH COOPERATIVE INC	MD	U		--	--	--	--	--	--
EVERGREEN MEDICAL GROUP LLC	GA	U		--	--	--	--	--	--
EVOLUTIONS HEALTHCARE SYSTEMS INC	FL	U		--	--	--	--	--	--
▼ EXCELLUS HEALTH PLAN INC	NY	• A	2q 2014	3,060.6	6,290.4	6,290.4	1,290.5	3.33	2.78
EXCLUSICARE (See MUTUAL OF OMAHA INS CO)									
EXCLUSIVE (See COVENTRY HEALTH CARE OF MISSOURI INC)									
EXCLUSIVE PLUS (See COVENTRY HEALTH CARE OF MISSOURI INC)									
▼ EXPRESS SCRIPTS INS CO	AZ	• B	2q 2014	108.0	172.3	172.3	49.5	2.22	1.85
EYEMED INC	CA	U		--	--	--	--	--	--
EYEMED VISION CARE HMO OF TEXAS	TX	U		--	--	--	--	--	--
FALLON COMMUNITY HEALTH PLAN	MA	• B-	2q 2014	407.4	1,195.4	1,195.4	173.8	1.86	1.55
FALLON FLEX (See FALLON COMMUNITY HEALTH PLAN)									
FALLON HEALTH & LIFE ASR CO	MA	• E	2q 2014	29.7	35.2	35.2	5.4	1.05	0.87

Arrows denote recent upgrades ▲ or downgrades▼　　　　　• Bullets denote a more detailed analysis is available in Section II.

INSURANCE COMPANY NAME	DOM. STATE	RATING	DATA DATE	TOTAL ASSETS ($MIL)	TOTAL PREMIUMS ($MIL)	HEALTH PREMIUMS ($MIL)	CAPITAL & SURPLUS ($MIL)	RISK ADJUSTED CAPITAL RATIO 1	RATIO 2
FAMILY BENEFIT LIFE INS CO	MO	C	2q 2014	64.3	1.4	0.0	11.9	1.69	1.52
FAMILY CHOICE HEALTH ALLIANCE	NJ	U		--	--	--	--	--	--
FAMILY HEALTH HAWAII MBS	HI	● D+	2q 2014	3.2	0.2	0.2	2.0	2.33	1.94
FAMILY HERITAGE LIFE INS CO OF AMER	OH	● A-	2q 2014	706.7	194.1	192.9	67.1	1.84	1.30
FAMILY LIFE INS CO	TX	● C	2q 2014	146.9	110.0	78.2	32.9	3.51	2.71
FAMILYCARE HEALTH PLANS INC	OR	● C-	2q 2014	14.4	31.1	31.1	7.1	1.49	1.24
FARA PPO NETWORK	LA	U		--	--	--	--	--	--
FARM BUREAU LIFE INS CO	IA	B+	2q 2014	7,987.7	657.5	8.5	540.2	2.14	1.10
FARM BUREAU LIFE INS CO OF MISSOURI	MO	A-	2q 2014	520.1	48.7	0.3	57.1	2.06	1.30
FARM BUREAU MUTUAL INS CO OF AR	AR	C+	2q 2014	347.0	246.4	0.1	171.4	3.89	2.65
FARM BUREAU MUTUAL INS CO OF MI	MI	B-	2q 2014	645.6	163.6	0.1	274.6	3.93	2.59
FARM FAMILY LIFE INS CO	NY	B	2q 2014	1,268.0	78.6	5.2	152.1	2.11	1.20
FARMERS MUTUAL HAIL INS CO OF IA	IA	B-	2q 2014	630.0	664.6	0.0	350.4	2.32	1.45
FARMERS NEW WORLD LIFE INS CO	WA	B-	2q 2014	7,266.8	922.8	15.2	574.7	2.15	1.20
FARMLAND MUTUAL INS CO	IA	B	2q 2014	506.2	176.1	0.0	164.8	4.02	2.81
FEDERAL INS CO	IN	B+	2q 2014	32,182.2	5,862.1	163.1	14,854.5	1.41	1.29
FEDERAL LIFE INS CO (MUTUAL)	IL	C	2q 2014	231.1	18.2	0.2	17.6	1.34	0.90
FEDERATED LIFE INS CO	MN	A	2q 2014	1,483.1	188.6	23.7	300.2	4.53	2.52
FEDERATED MUTUAL INS CO	MN	● A-	2q 2014	4,667.2	1,042.5	349.6	2,616.8	3.70	2.99
FIDELIO INS CO	PA	U		--	--	--	--	--	--
FIDELIS SECURECARE OF MICHIGAN INC	MI	● C	2q 2014	7.3	20.5	20.5	4.7	1.55	1.29
FIDELIS SECURECARE OF NORTH CAROLINA	NC	● D+	4q 2013	2.3	2.6	2.6	2.0	3.92	3.26
FIDELIS SECURECARE OF TEXAS INC	TX	U		--	--	--	--	--	--
FIDELITY LIFE ASSN A LEGAL RESERVE	IL	C	1q 2014	413.7	124.4	1.2	125.9	5.35	3.06
FIDELITY SECURITY LIFE INS CO	MO	● B-	2q 2014	824.9	699.3	657.9	141.6	3.21	1.98
FIDELITY SECURITY LIFE INS CO OF NY	NY	B	2q 2014	40.7	6.7	6.7	9.2	1.98	1.78
FIDUCIARY INS CO OF AMERICA	NY	E	2q 2014	107.8	61.7	0.2	1.4	-0.02	-0.02
FINANCIAL AMERICAN LIFE INS CO	KS	D+	2q 2014	25.2	8.4	3.3	9.1	2.09	1.88
▲ FIRST ALLMERICA FINANCIAL LIFE INS	MA	C-	2q 2014	4,201.2	21.4	0.3	178.6	3.84	1.82
FIRST ASR LIFE OF AMERICA	LA	● B	2q 2014	37.4	13.4	3.5	32.0	3.17	3.01
FIRST CARE INC	MD	U	2q 2014	22.0	0.0	0.0	5.0	--	--
FIRST CHOICE HEALTH PLAN INC (See LA HEALTH SERVICE & INDEMNITY CO)									
FIRST CHOICE HEATLHPLAN OF MS	MS	U		--	--	--	--	--	--
FIRST CHOICE OF THE MIDWEST INC	SD	U		--	--	--	--	--	--
FIRST COMMUNITY HEALTH PLAN INC	AL	● B	2q 2014	6.4	6.8	6.8	5.3	8.29	6.91
FIRST CONTINENTAL LIFE & ACC INS CO	TX	D	2q 2014	6.0	5.7	5.6	4.5	1.31	1.21
FIRST DENTAL HEALTH	CA	U		--	--	--	--	--	--
FIRST HEALTH GROUP CORP	IL	U		--	--	--	--	--	--
FIRST HEALTH LIFE & HEALTH INS CO	TX	● B	2q 2014	501.4	1,442.9	1,441.9	216.1	1.04	0.87
FIRST INS CO OF HI LTD	HI	C	2q 2014	643.0	68.6	1.2	297.5	5.30	3.68
FIRST INVESTORS LIFE INS CO	NY	B	2q 2014	1,774.9	187.3	0.0	54.3	2.21	1.16
FIRST MEDICAL HEALTH PLAN INC	PR	● E	2q 2014	127.1	643.4	643.4	21.8	0.16	0.14
FIRST NATIONAL LIFE INS CO OF USA	NE	C-	2q 2014	6.0	1.5	0.7	1.9	1.31	0.94
FIRST NET INS CO	GU	E+	2q 2014	18.4	10.4	0.3	12.3	5.45	3.55
FIRST PENN-PACIFIC LIFE INS CO	IN	B	2q 2014	1,749.2	139.2	0.0	221.1	2.80	1.52
FIRST PRIORITY HEALTH (See HMO OF NORTHEASTERN PENNSYLVANIA INC)									
FIRST PRIORITY HEALTH (See HOSPITAL SERV ASSN OF NORTH EAST PA)									
▼ FIRST PRIORITY LIFE INS CO	PA	● C	2q 2014	253.7	416.5	416.5	125.9	3.44	2.87
FIRST RELIANCE STANDARD LIFE INS CO	NY	● A	2q 2014	188.3	78.7	45.4	67.7	6.02	3.89
FIRST SYMETRA NATL LIFE INS CO OF NY	NY	A-	2q 2014	869.5	155.0	8.9	101.2	4.01	1.99
FIRST UNITED AMERICAN LIFE INS CO	NY	● B+	2q 2014	187.3	78.8	48.3	35.6	2.25	1.46
FIRST UNUM LIFE INS CO	NY	● C+	2q 2014	2,768.6	400.7	323.3	265.2	2.67	1.36

36

Arrows denote recent upgrades ▲ or downgrades▼

● Bullets denote a more detailed analysis is available in Section II.

INSURANCE COMPANY NAME	DOM. STATE	RATING	DATA DATE	TOTAL ASSETS ($MIL)	TOTAL PREMIUMS ($MIL)	HEALTH PREMIUMS ($MIL)	CAPITAL & SURPLUS ($MIL)	RISK ADJUSTED CAPITAL RATIO 1	RATIO 2
FIRSTCARE (See SHA LLC)									
FIRSTCAROLINACARE INS CO INC	NC	● B	2q 2014	21.2	65.2	65.2	11.4	1.38	1.15
FIRSTSIGHT VISION SERVICES INC	CA	U		--	--	--	--	--	--
FIVE STAR LIFE INS CO	LA	C+	2q 2014	253.0	124.4	0.3	37.5	2.77	1.74
FLAGSHIP HEALTH SYSTEMS INC	NJ	U		--	--	--	--	--	--
FLORA HEALTH NETWORK	OH	U		--	--	--	--	--	--
FLORIDA COMBINED LIFE INS CO INC	FL	B	2q 2014	46.3	131.7	102.2	24.4	4.64	3.76
FLORIDA HEALTH CARE PLAN INC	FL	● A-	2q 2014	122.1	310.8	310.8	82.3	5.18	4.31
FLORIDA HEALTHCARE PLUS INC	FL	U		--	--	--	--	--	--
FLORIDA MHS INC	FL	U		--	--	--	--	--	--
FLORIDA TRUE HEALTH INC	FL	● E	2q 2014	21.8	10.4	10.4	11.2	6.75	5.62
FOCUS HEALTHCARE MANAGEMENT	TN	U		--	--	--	--	--	--
FOR EYES VISION PLAN INC	CA	U		--	--	--	--	--	--
FORETHOUGHT LIFE INS CO	IN	B-	2q 2014	10,161.2	2,139.6	64.4	569.5	2.70	1.34
FOUNDATION LIFE INS CO OF AR	AR	D+	2q 2014	5.6	1.1	0.1	1.7	1.26	1.13
FREEDOM HEALTH INC	FL	U		--	--	--	--	--	--
FREEDOM LIFE INS CO OF AMERICA	TX	C	2q 2014	53.4	125.3	117.8	26.4	0.78	0.67
FREELANCERS CO-OP OF OREGON INC	OR	U		--	--	--	--	--	--
FREELANCERS CONSUMER OPERATED	NJ	U		--	--	--	--	--	--
FREELANCERS HEALTH SERVICE CORP	NY	U		--	--	--	--	--	--
FREELANCERS INS CO	NY	● B	2q 2014	53.8	112.2	112.2	24.5	2.22	1.85
FREESTONE INS CO	DE	F	3q 2013	327.7	64.7	0.1	57.6	0.44	0.26
FRESNO-KINGS-MADERA REGIONAL HEALTH	CA	● E	2q 2014	70.6	454.5	454.5	11.3	0.37	0.23
GALAXY HEALTH NETWORK	TX	U		--	--	--	--	--	--
GARDEN STATE LIFE INS CO	TX	A-	2q 2014	120.1	30.9	0.0	50.6	5.64	5.08
GATEWAY HEALTH PLAN INC	PA	● B	2q 2014	540.6	1,809.5	1,809.5	220.8	2.37	1.97
GATEWAY HEALTH PLAN OF OHIO INC	OH	U		--	--	--	--	--	--
GEISINGER HEALTH PLAN	PA	● B	2q 2014	406.2	1,466.3	1,466.3	174.5	1.52	1.27
GEISINGER INDEMNITY INS CO	PA	● C	2q 2014	62.0	158.1	158.1	24.0	1.65	1.38
GEISINGER QUALITY OPTIONS INC	PA	● C	2q 2014	94.2	341.5	341.5	40.2	1.46	1.22
GEMCARE HEALTH PLAN INC	CA	● E	2q 2014	16.7	140.0	140.0	6.3	0.08	0.05
GENERAL AMERICAN LIFE INS CO	MO	B	2q 2014	12,079.5	515.9	9.1	815.1	2.79	1.26
GENERAL FIDELITY LIFE INS CO	SC	C+	2q 2014	89.8	0.3	0.0	75.9	9.14	8.22
GENESIS INS CO	CT	C	2q 2014	186.3	22.3	0.3	128.9	7.23	5.60
GENWORTH LIFE & ANNUITY INS CO	VA	B-	2q 2014	24,483.9	2,346.1	73.8	2,242.5	1.51	1.10
GENWORTH LIFE INS CO	DE	● B-	2q 2014	36,940.5	3,263.2	2,309.6	3,610.0	1.10	0.87
GENWORTH LIFE INS CO OF NEW YORK	NY	● B	2q 2014	8,216.0	683.7	200.4	550.7	2.39	1.20
GEORGIA HEALTH PLUS+	GA	U		--	--	--	--	--	--
GERBER LIFE INS CO	NY	● A-	2q 2014	2,680.4	758.5	430.3	269.0	1.97	1.19
GERMANIA LIFE INS CO	TX	C-	2q 2014	68.5	9.6	0.0	9.2	1.27	1.14
GHS HEALTH MAINTENANCE ORGANIZATION	OK	U	2q 2014	37.7	0.0	0.0	32.6	--	--
GHS INS CO	OK	E	2q 2014	20.8	4.1	3.7	8.8	0.61	0.50
GHS MANAGED HEALTH CARE PLANS INC	OK	● B-	2q 2014	14.7	12.9	12.9	2.8	1.82	1.52
GLOBALHEALTH INC	OK	● C+	2q 2014	20.4	156.0	156.0	9.0	0.96	0.80
GLOBE LIFE & ACCIDENT INS CO	NE	B	2q 2014	3,478.3	710.8	30.0	277.7	1.92	1.04
GOLDEN CROSS HEALTH PLAN CORP	PR	U	2q 2010	1.1	0.0	0.0	0.3	--	--
GOLDEN RULE INS CO	IN	● B	2q 2014	772.3	2,063.6	2,018.7	297.5	1.24	0.98
GOLDEN SECURITY LIFE INS CO	TN	● B	2q 2014	22.1	24.0	24.0	9.1	1.99	1.66
GOLDEN STATE MEDICARE HEALTH PLAN	CA	● C-	2q 2014	14.2	8.7	8.7	12.2	12.66	8.08
GOLDEN WEST HEALTH PLAN INC	CA	U		--	--	--	--	--	--
GOOD HEALTH HMO INC	MO	● C	2q 2014	88.3	252.0	252.0	64.4	3.82	3.18
GOVERNMENT EMPLOYEES HOSP ASSOC	MO	U		--	--	--	--	--	--

Arrows denote recent upgrades ▲ or downgrades▼

● Bullets denote a more detailed analysis is available in Section II.

INSURANCE COMPANY NAME	DOM. STATE	RATING	DATA DATE	TOTAL ASSETS ($MIL)	TOTAL PREMIUMS ($MIL)	HEALTH PREMIUMS ($MIL)	CAPITAL & SURPLUS ($MIL)	RISK ADJUSTED CAPITAL RATIO 1	RATIO 2
GOVERNMENT EMPLOYEES INS CO	MD	B+	2q 2014	21,998.7	4,657.5	0.1	13,069.5	3.41	2.11
GOVERNMENT PERSONNEL MUTUAL L I C	TX	• B+	2q 2014	833.6	77.6	28.7	108.4	2.65	1.69
GRAND VALLEY HEALTH PLAN INC	MI	• D+	2q 2014	5.3	22.0	22.0	2.2	0.88	0.73
GRANGE LIFE INS CO	OH	B-	2q 2014	359.5	80.5	0.3	52.9	2.53	1.61
GRANGE MUTUAL CAS CO	OH	B+	2q 2014	2,061.4	541.0	0.1	1,044.3	3.11	2.25
GRANITE ALLIANCE INS CO	UT	U		--	--	--	--	--	--
GRANITE CARE-MERIDIAN HEALTH PLAN NH	NH	U		--	--	--	--	--	--
GRANITE STATE HEALTH PLAN INC	NH	U		--	--	--	--	--	--
GREAT AMERICAN INS CO	OH	B-	2q 2014	5,165.9	1,915.4	46.9	1,394.1	1.73	1.27
GREAT AMERICAN LIFE INS CO	OH	B-	2q 2014	21,681.2	3,840.5	10.3	1,573.5	1.83	1.04
GREAT CENTRAL LIFE INS CO	LA	C	4q 2013	21.4	2.2	0.4	6.5	1.32	0.87
GREAT FIDELITY LIFE INS CO	IN	D+	2q 2014	4.0	0.7	0.7	2.8	1.94	1.75
GREAT REPUBLIC LIFE INS CO	WA	F	1q 2011	16.8	2.0	1.9	0.3	0.13	0.12
GREAT RIVERS NETWORK	MO	U		--	--	--	--	--	--
GREAT SOUTHERN LIFE INS CO	TX	B	2q 2014	225.8	64.5	2.0	42.0	4.58	2.44
GREAT WEST LIFE ASR CO	MI	B-	2q 2014	79.9	14.3	2.3	17.1	2.16	1.65
GREAT-WEST LIFE & ANNUITY INS CO	CO	B-	2q 2014	56,584.7	5,698.9	54.6	1,176.7	1.26	0.70
GREAT-WEST LIFE & ANNUITY INS OF NY	NY	B	2q 2014	1,532.8	209.3	0.0	80.2	2.89	1.52
GREATER GEORGIA LIFE INS CO	GA	B+	2q 2014	50.8	29.3	10.3	17.9	1.37	1.02
GREENVILLE CASUALTY INS CO INC	SC	D-	2q 2014	17.3	23.4	2.1	6.1	0.73	0.61
GROUP DENTAL HEALTH ADMIN INC	NJ	U		--	--	--	--	--	--
GROUP HEALTH COOP OF EAU CLAIRE	WI	• E+	2q 2014	43.9	168.3	168.3	22.1	1.13	0.94
GROUP HEALTH COOP OF S CENTRAL WI	WI	• D+	2q 2014	90.0	316.9	316.9	50.0	1.58	1.32
GROUP HEALTH COOPERATIVE	WA	• A-	2q 2014	1,617.8	2,245.9	2,245.9	912.8	5.34	4.45
GROUP HEALTH INCORPORATED	NY	• D	2q 2014	1,100.4	3,614.6	3,614.6	284.1	1.10	0.91
GROUP HEALTH OPTIONS INC	WA	• B-	2q 2014	224.9	893.6	893.6	103.6	2.55	2.12
GROUP HEALTH PLAN INC	MN	• A+	2q 2014	693.0	1,040.2	1,040.2	170.1	4.68	3.90
▼ GROUP HOSP & MEDICAL SERVICES INC	DC	• B-	2q 2014	2,279.9	3,158.1	3,158.1	894.3	5.13	4.28
GROUP INS ADMINISTRATION INC	DC	U		--	--	--	--	--	--
GUARANTEE TRUST LIFE INS CO	IL	• B	2q 2014	382.3	242.1	215.3	55.8	1.52	1.04
GUARANTY INCOME LIFE INS CO	LA	C-	2q 2014	480.3	29.0	3.8	33.9	2.42	1.19
GUARDIAN INS CO INC	VI	C	2q 2014	35.2	27.7	0.0	16.2	1.68	1.48
GUARDIAN LIFE INS CO OF AMERICA	NY	• A	2q 2014	44,344.6	6,712.2	2,611.1	5,693.7	2.75	1.79
GUGGENHEIM LIFE & ANNUITY CO	DE	B-	2q 2014	11,655.2	736.1	0.0	563.4	1.32	0.73
GULF COAST REGIONAL PPO	AL	U		--	--	--	--	--	--
GULF GUARANTY LIFE INS CO	MS	D	2q 2014	15.3	6.5	2.5	8.3	1.46	1.14
GULF HEALTH PLANS PPO INC	AL	U		--	--	--	--	--	--
GULF STATES LIFE INS CO INC	LA	U	4q 2013	2.9	-0.1	0.0	2.6	--	--
GUNDERSEN HEALTH PLAN INC	WI	• B	2q 2014	45.3	283.9	283.9	18.2	1.13	0.94
GUNDERSEN HEALTH PLAN MN	MN	• B-	2q 2014	1.7	2.2	2.2	1.4	0.72	0.60
HALLMARK SPECIALTY INS CO	OK	C	2q 2014	218.1	95.4	3.2	57.1	2.15	1.29
HAP MIDWEST HEALTH PLAN INC	MI	• B-	2q 2014	103.4	294.6	294.6	38.3	1.96	1.63
HARBOR HEALTH PLAN INC	MI	• E-	2q 2014	10.5	8.9	8.9	7.5	5.33	4.44
HARLEYSVILLE LIFE INS CO	PA	B	2q 2014	415.3	62.5	11.6	30.0	1.60	0.93
▼ HARMONY HEALTH PLAN OF ILLINOIS INC	IL	• B-	2q 2014	106.1	368.1	368.1	46.6	3.52	2.93
HARTFORD FIRE INS CO	CT	B	2q 2014	26,359.5	1,704.2	5.3	14,583.9	2.20	1.51
HARTFORD LIFE & ACCIDENT INS CO	CT	• C-	2q 2014	9,108.6	2,932.0	1,757.3	1,478.8	0.30	0.29
HARTFORD LIFE & ANNUITY INS CO	CT	B-	2q 2014	51,634.7	2,264.0	0.6	3,412.3	7.06	3.87
HARTFORD LIFE INS CO	CT	C+	2q 2014	127,722.5	2,914.7	245.1	5,532.1	1.40	1.09
HARVARD PILGRIM (See HARVARD PILGRIM HEALTH CARE INC)									
HARVARD PILGRIM HC OF NEW ENGLAND	MA	• B	2q 2014	94.5	230.8	230.8	62.1	4.21	3.51
HARVARD PILGRIM HEALTH CARE INC	MA	• B+	2q 2014	837.3	1,786.0	1,786.0	450.9	2.78	2.32

Arrows denote recent upgrades ▲ or downgrades▼

• Bullets denote a more detailed analysis is available in Section II.

INSURANCE COMPANY NAME	DOM. STATE	RATING	DATA DATE	TOTAL ASSETS ($MIL)	TOTAL PREMIUMS ($MIL)	HEALTH PREMIUMS ($MIL)	CAPITAL & SURPLUS ($MIL)	RISK ADJUSTED CAPITAL RATIO 1	RATIO 2
HAWAII MANAGEMENT ALLIANCE ASSOC	HI	● C	2q 2014	37.0	82.0	82.0	13.0	1.21	1.01
HAWAII MEDICAL SERVICE ASSOCIATION	HI	● C	2q 2014	933.2	2,640.0	2,640.0	391.7	1.87	1.56
HCC LIFE INS CO	IN	● B	2q 2014	841.1	894.2	889.6	487.9	3.87	3.16
HCC SPECIALTY INS CO	OK	C+	2q 2014	21.0	18.3	0.0	15.9	10.41	9.37
▼ HCSC INS SERVICES CO	IL	● B	2q 2014	405.2	442.8	442.8	160.9	6.17	5.14
HEALTH & HUMAN RESOURCE CENTER INC	CA	U	--	--	--	--	--	--	--
HEALTH ADMINISTRATIVE SERVICES	TX	U	--	--	--	--	--	--	--
HEALTH ADVANTAGE (See HMO PARTNERS INC)									
HEALTH ALLIANCE (See HEALTH ALLIANCE MEDICAL PLANS)									
HEALTH ALLIANCE MEDICAL PLANS	IL	● A	2q 2014	521.4	1,119.0	1,119.0	191.2	2.62	2.18
HEALTH ALLIANCE NORTHWEST HEALTH PL	WA	U	--	--	--	--	--	--	--
HEALTH ALLIANCE PLAN OF MICHIGAN	MI	● B	2q 2014	483.1	1,869.0	1,869.0	208.6	1.44	1.20
HEALTH ALLIANCE PLUS (See HEALTH ALLIANCE MEDICAL PLANS)									
HEALTH ALLIANCE PREMIER CHOICE (See HEALTH ALLIANCE MEDICAL PLANS)									
HEALTH ALLIANCE SOLUTIONS (See HEALTH ALLIANCE MEDICAL PLANS)									
HEALTH ALLIANCE-MIDWEST INC	IL	● E	2q 2014	10.4	11.8	11.8	6.1	3.42	2.85
HEALTH CARE FOUNDATION OF SAN MATEO	CA	U		--	--	--	--	--	--
HEALTH CARE NETWORK OF WISCONSIN	WI	U		--	--	--	--	--	--
HEALTH CARE REVIEW	TX	U		--	--	--	--	--	--
HEALTH CARE SAVINGS INC	NC	U		--	--	--	--	--	--
HEALTH CARE SVC CORP A MUT LEG RES	IL	● A+	2q 2014	18,206.4	22,686.7	22,686.7	10,353.6	7.18	5.98
HEALTH CHOICE INS CO	AZ	U		--	--	--	--	--	--
HEALTH CHOICE LLC	TN	U		--	--	--	--	--	--
HEALTH CHOICE OF ALABAMA	AL	U		--	--	--	--	--	--
HEALTH CHOICE UTAH INC	UT	● D+	2q 2014	4.4	6.2	6.2	2.8	2.17	1.81
HEALTH FIRST HEALTH PLANS	FL	● C-	2q 2014	112.5	353.1	353.1	61.5	1.96	1.63
HEALTH FIRST INS INC	FL	● D+	2q 2014	8.1	1.0	1.0	3.6	4.64	3.86
HEALTH FIRST NEW YORK (See MANAGED HEALTH INC)									
HEALTH INS CO OF AMERICA INC	NY	U		--	--	--	--	--	--
▼ HEALTH INSURANCE PLAN OF GREATER NY	NY	● B	2q 2014	2,126.2	4,988.5	4,988.5	1,334.5	3.83	3.19
HEALTH LINK PPO	MS	U		--	--	--	--	--	--
HEALTH MAINTENANCE PLAN (HMP) (See ANTHEM INS COMPANIES INC)									
HEALTH MANAGEMENT ASSOCIATES INC	AZ	U		--	--	--	--	--	--
HEALTH MARKETING INC	IL	U		--	--	--	--	--	--
HEALTH MEDICARE ULTRA INC	PR	U		--	--	--	--	--	--
▲ HEALTH NET COMMUNITY SOLUTIONS INC	CA	● B-	2q 2014	871.0	2,158.4	2,158.4	293.2	2.90	1.80
HEALTH NET HEALTH PLAN OF OREGON INC	OR	● E	2q 2014	105.6	294.1	294.1	47.8	1.86	1.55
HEALTH NET INS OF NEW YORK INC	NY	U		--	--	--	--	--	--
HEALTH NET LIFE INS CO	CA	● B	2q 2014	554.9	1,521.0	1,517.9	218.9	1.59	1.29
▼ HEALTH NET OF ARIZONA INC	AZ	● D+	2q 2014	419.2	721.0	721.0	43.9	0.97	0.81
HEALTH NET OF CALIFORNIA INC	CA	● C+	2q 2014	2,315.3	7,078.8	7,078.8	955.5	2.57	1.59
HEALTH NEW ENGLAND INC	MA	● B	2q 2014	144.3	546.6	546.6	55.3	1.07	0.89
HEALTH NOW FLEX (See HEALTHNOW NY INC)									
HEALTH OPTIONS INC	FL	U		--	--	--	--	--	--
HEALTH PARTNERS OF KANSAS	KS	U		--	--	--	--	--	--
HEALTH PARTNERS PLANS INC	PA	● B	2q 2014	332.9	1,000.3	1,000.3	90.4	1.31	1.09
HEALTH PAYORS ORGANIZATION LTD	OH	U		--	--	--	--	--	--
HEALTH PLAN HAWAII (See HAWAII MEDICAL SERVICE ASSOCIATION)									
HEALTH PLAN OF CAREOREGON INC	OR	● B	2q 2014	65.7	115.5	115.5	38.6	3.01	2.51
HEALTH PLAN OF NEVADA INC	NV	● B	2q 2014	423.1	1,564.2	1,564.2	159.5	2.66	2.21
HEALTH PLAN OF SAN JOAQUIN	CA	● B	2q 2014	127.9	301.5	301.5	51.3	2.14	1.32
HEALTH PLAN OF SAN MATEO (See SAN MATEO HEALTH COMMISSION)									

Arrows denote recent upgrades ▲ or downgrades ▼   ● Bullets denote a more detailed analysis is available in Section II.

INSURANCE COMPANY NAME	DOM. STATE	RATING	DATA DATE	TOTAL ASSETS ($MIL)	TOTAL PREMIUMS ($MIL)	HEALTH PREMIUMS ($MIL)	CAPITAL & SURPLUS ($MIL)	RISK ADJUSTED CAPITAL RATIO 1	RATIO 2
HEALTH PLAN OF THE UPPER OHIO VALLEY	WV	• B+	2q 2014	253.1	364.6	364.6	196.4	3.58	2.98
HEALTH TRADITION HEALTH PLAN	WI	• B	2q 2014	25.3	151.3	151.3	12.5	1.07	0.89
HEALTH VENTURES CORP[(See BLUE CROSS OF IDAHO HEALTH SERVICE)									
HEALTH VENTURES NETWORK	MN	U		--	--	--	--	--	--
HEALTHAMERICA PENNSYLVANIA INC	PA	• B	2q 2014	307.0	809.5	809.5	76.3	1.98	1.65
HEALTHASSURANCE (See HEALTHAMERICA PENNSYLVANIA INC)									
HEALTHASSURANCE PENNSYLVANIA INC	PA	• B	2q 2014	341.5	1,065.1	1,065.1	185.1	3.26	2.71
HEALTHCARE OPTIONS INC (See ROCKY MOUNTAIN HEALTHCARE OPTIONS)									
HEALTHCARE USA OF MISSOURI LLC	MO	• A-	2q 2014	203.4	669.4	669.4	102.7	3.61	3.01
HEALTHCARE VALUE MANAGEMENT	MA	U		--	--	--	--	--	--
HEALTHCHOICE (See SELECTHEALTH INC)									
HEALTHCHOICE MANAGED SYSTEMS	FL	U		--	--	--	--	--	--
HEALTHFIRST HEALTH PLAN NEW JERSEY	NJ	• E	2q 2014	82.6	265.3	265.3	23.1	0.69	0.58
HEALTHFIRST PPO	OK	U		--	--	--	--	--	--
HEALTHKEEPERS INC	VA	• A-	2q 2014	650.1	1,658.7	1,658.7	271.9	2.88	2.40
HEALTHLINK HMO INC	MO	U		--	--	--	--	--	--
HEALTHMARKETS INS CO	OK	B-	2q 2014	20.2	16.3	16.3	12.0	3.38	2.62
▼ HEALTHNOW NY INC	NY	• B+	2q 2014	1,063.7	2,463.2	2,463.2	573.4	3.15	2.62
HEALTHPARTNERS	MN	• B+	2q 2014	1,138.9	1,279.2	1,279.2	899.0	3.94	3.28
HEALTHPARTNERS INS CO	MN	• A-	2q 2014	325.5	892.7	892.7	166.5	3.05	2.54
HEALTHPASS INC (See HEALTHAMERICA PENNSYLVANIA INC)									
HEALTHPLEX OF NJ INC	NJ	U		--	--	--	--	--	--
HEALTHPLUS INS CO	MI	• C	2q 2014	46.8	200.1	200.1	22.2	1.15	0.96
▼ HEALTHPLUS OF MICHIGAN	MI	• B-	2q 2014	145.2	490.4	490.4	81.1	1.12	0.93
HEALTHPLUS PARTNERS INC	MI	• B	2q 2014	60.1	226.3	226.3	28.7	1.83	1.52
HEALTHREACH PPO INC	OH	U		--	--	--	--	--	--
HEALTHSENSE (See REGENCE BLUESHIELD OF IDAHO INC)									
HEALTHSMART PREFERRED CARE INC	TX	U		--	--	--	--	--	--
HEALTHSOURCE PROVIDENT (See CIGNA HEALTHCARE OF SOUTH CAROLINA)									
HEALTHSPAN INC	OH	U		--	--	--	--	--	--
HEALTHSPAN INC	OH	U		--	--	--	--	--	--
HEALTHSPAN INTEGRATED CARE	OH	• D	2q 2014	194.8	476.8	476.8	80.0	3.28	2.73
▼ HEALTHSPRING LIFE & HLTH INS CO INC	TX	• B-	2q 2014	627.9	2,124.3	2,124.3	301.6	3.33	2.77
HEALTHSPRING OF ALABAMA INC	AL	• B	2q 2014	148.9	502.9	502.9	63.9	2.60	2.17
HEALTHSPRING OF FLORIDA INC	FL	• B	2q 2014	127.4	752.5	752.5	47.8	1.52	1.27
HEALTHSPRING OF TENNESSEE INC	TN	• C+	2q 2014	303.9	1,170.1	1,170.1	114.8	1.62	1.35
HEALTHSTAR INC	IL	U		--	--	--	--	--	--
▲ HEALTHSUN HEALTH PLANS	FL	• C	2q 2014	73.4	414.0	414.0	20.4	0.76	0.63
HEALTHY ALLIANCE LIFE INS CO	MO	• A-	2q 2014	954.2	1,883.4	1,883.4	428.2	4.60	3.83
HEALTHY FAMILIES (See SAN FRANCISCO HEALTH AUTHORITY)									
HEALTHY PALM BEACHES INC	FL	• D	2q 2014	19.5	51.2	51.2	11.2	1.93	1.61
HEALTHYCT INC	CT	U		--	--	--	--	--	--
HEALTHYWORKERS (See SAN FRANCISCO HEALTH AUTHORITY)									
HEARTLAND NATIONAL LIFE INS CO	IN	C	2q 2014	8.6	30.0	29.9	4.1	1.83	1.64
HERITAGE PROVIDER NETWORK INC	CA	• D	2q 2014	378.3	1,857.4	1,857.4	109.2	0.70	0.43
HFN INC	IL	U		--	--	--	--	--	--
HIGHMARK BCBSD INC	DE	• B	2q 2014	376.5	512.1	512.1	164.6	5.68	4.73
HIGHMARK CASUALTY INS CO	PA	• C	2q 2014	413.1	146.1	98.5	162.7	1.59	1.10
HIGHMARK INC	PA	• B-	2q 2014	7,553.8	6,204.9	6,204.9	4,365.3	3.73	3.11
HIGHMARK SELECT RESOURCES INC	PA	U		--	--	--	--	--	--
HIGHMARK WEST VIRGINIA INC	WV	• B+	2q 2014	623.7	894.3	894.3	311.3	6.22	5.19
HIP INS CO OF NEW YORK	NY	• D-	2q 2014	64.6	146.8	146.8	42.2	4.36	3.64

www.weissratings.com

Arrows denote recent upgrades ▲ or downgrades▼   • Bullets denote a more detailed analysis is available in Section II.

INSURANCE COMPANY NAME	DOM. STATE	RATING	DATA DATE	TOTAL ASSETS ($MIL)	TOTAL PREMIUMS ($MIL)	HEALTH PREMIUMS ($MIL)	CAPITAL & SURPLUS ($MIL)	RISK ADJUSTED CAPITAL RATIO 1	RATIO 2
HM HEALTH INS CO	PA	• C-	2q 2014	291.9	1,143.8	1,143.8	31.1	0.40	0.33
HM LIFE INS CO	PA	• B	2q 2014	570.6	703.7	703.3	291.7	3.10	2.36
HM LIFE INS CO OF NEW YORK	NY	• B+	2q 2014	72.5	87.1	87.1	32.3	2.55	2.01
HMO BLUE	MA	U		--	--	--	--	--	--
HMO BLUE (See BLUE CROSS OF IDAHO HEALTH SERVICE)									
HMO CALIFORNIA (See UNIVERSAL CARE)									
HMO CHOICE (See ANTHEM HEALTH PLANS OF MAINE INC)									
HMO COLORADO	CO	• B-	2q 2014	87.9	145.1	145.1	45.8	4.77	3.97
HMO LOUISIANA INC	LA	• A+	2q 2014	497.8	472.4	472.4	361.6	12.40	10.34
HMO MINNESOTA	MN	• A-	2q 2014	715.0	1,016.7	1,016.7	510.4	7.75	6.46
HMO MISSOURI INC	MO	• B-	2q 2014	72.9	169.1	169.1	44.7	6.00	5.00
HMO MONTANA	MT	U		--	--	--	--	--	--
HMO OF DELAWARE INC	DE	U		--	--	--	--	--	--
HMO OF MISSISSIPPI INC	MS	U		--	--	--	--	--	--
HMO OF NORTHEASTERN PENNSYLVANIA INC	PA	• C	2q 2014	85.0	79.9	79.9	72.9	7.59	6.33
HMO PARTNERS INC	AR	• A+	2q 2014	171.0	153.8	153.8	119.0	11.37	9.47
HN1 THERAPY NETWORK NEW JERSEY LLC	NJ	U		--	--	--	--	--	--
HNE INS CO INC	MA	U	2q 2014	4.9	0.1	0.1	4.9	--	--
HOLMAN PROFESSIONAL COUNSELING CTRS	CA	U		--	--	--	--	--	--
HOME STATE HEALTH PLAN INC	MO	• C-	2q 2014	45.7	185.2	185.2	18.5	2.55	2.12
HOMELAND INS CO OF DE	DE	B	2q 2014	50.7	28.5	0.0	50.5	136.00	67.98
HOMELAND INS CO OF NEW YORK	NY	C	2q 2014	112.2	195.3	8.7	108.6	2.46	2.42
HOMETOWN HEALTH PLAN	OH	U		--	--	--	--	--	--
HOMETOWN HEALTH PLAN INC	NV	• C	2q 2014	75.3	237.4	237.4	25.2	1.00	0.83
HOMETOWN HEALTH PROVIDERS INS CO	NV	• B	2q 2014	40.8	53.6	53.6	29.9	4.18	3.49
HOMETOWN HEALTH PROVIDERS INS CO (See HOMETOWN HEALTH PLAN INC)									
HONORED CITIZENS CHOICE HEALTH PLAN	CA	• E	2q 2014	43.7	161.2	161.2	15.4	0.61	0.38
HOOSIER MOTOR MUTUAL INS CO	IN	C+	2q 2014	12.4	0.6	0.6	11.8	5.71	3.04
HORACE MANN INS CO	IL	B	2q 2014	459.2	215.2	0.0	181.5	1.83	1.17
HORACE MANN LIFE INS CO	IL	B	2q 2014	7,624.9	527.1	3.9	383.9	1.91	0.97
HORIZON BLUE CROSS BLUE SHIELD OF NEW JERSEY (See HORIZON HEALTHCARE SERVICES INC)									
HORIZON HEALTHCARE DENTAL INC	NJ	U		--	--	--	--	--	--
HORIZON HEALTHCARE OF NEW JERSEY INC	NJ	• A-	2q 2014	1,300.1	4,115.5	4,115.5	558.0	2.36	1.97
HORIZON HEALTHCARE SERVICES INC	NJ	• B+	4q 2013	3,679.0	5,243.6	5,243.6	2,212.0	4.11	3.42
HORIZON HMO (See HORIZON HEALTHCARE OF NEW JERSEY INC)									
HORIZON INS CO	NJ	• B	4q 2013	68.0	122.6	122.6	9.9	1.40	1.16
HORIZON POS (See HORIZON HEALTHCARE SERVICES INC)									
HORIZON PPO (See HORIZON HEALTHCARE SERVICES INC)									
HOSPITAL SERV ASSN OF NORTH EAST PA	PA	• C	2q 2014	493.0	215.6	215.6	348.3	4.94	4.12
HOUSTON CASUALTY CO	TX	B-	2q 2014	3,176.9	392.9	26.9	2,072.2	1.97	1.76
HPHC INS CO INC	MA	• B-	2q 2014	164.3	616.1	616.1	38.0	0.91	0.76
HUMAN AFFAIRS INTERNATIONAL OF CA	CA	U		--	--	--	--	--	--
HUMANA BENEFIT PLAN OF ILLINOIS	IL	• B	2q 2014	98.9	172.3	172.3	51.8	5.60	4.67
HUMANA EMPLOYERS HEALTH PLAN OF GA	GA	• D	2q 2014	416.5	628.6	628.6	115.9	3.45	2.87
HUMANA HEALTH BENEFIT PLAN LA	LA	• B	2q 2014	414.2	1,464.8	1,464.8	200.6	3.21	2.68
HUMANA HEALTH CO OF NEW YORK INC	NY	• E	2q 2014	29.4	4.5	4.5	26.9	19.40	16.17
HUMANA HEALTH INS CO OF FL INC	FL	• C	2q 2014	131.9	323.2	323.2	57.3	3.22	2.68
HUMANA HEALTH PLAN INC	KY	• C	2q 2014	1,031.3	3,694.2	3,694.2	352.6	2.14	1.78
HUMANA HEALTH PLAN OF CALIFORNIA INC	CA	• C-	2q 2014	81.9	205.0	205.0	27.8	1.28	0.87
HUMANA HEALTH PLAN OF OHIO INC	OH	• C	2q 2014	116.3	367.0	367.0	45.5	2.27	1.89
HUMANA HEALTH PLAN OF TEXAS INC	TX	• B	2q 2014	494.7	1,362.4	1,362.4	229.1	4.16	3.46
HUMANA HEALTH PLANS OF PUERTO RICO	PR	• B	2q 2014	189.1	907.2	907.2	82.9	1.68	1.40

Arrows denote recent upgrades ▲ or downgrades▼

• Bullets denote a more detailed analysis is available in Section II.

INSURANCE COMPANY NAME	DOM. STATE	RATING	DATA DATE	TOTAL ASSETS ($MIL)	TOTAL PREMIUMS ($MIL)	HEALTH PREMIUMS ($MIL)	CAPITAL & SURPLUS ($MIL)	RISK ADJUSTED CAPITAL RATIO 1	RATIO 2
HUMANA INS CO	WI	U		--	--	--	--	--	--
HUMANA INS CO OF KENTUCKY	KY	● B-	2q 2014	115.2	44.7	25.6	66.7	2.18	1.67
HUMANA INS CO OF NEW YORK	NY	● B	2q 2014	96.7	185.5	185.5	58.3	6.15	5.13
HUMANA INS CO OF PUERTO RICO INC	PR	● B-	2q 2014	73.6	93.2	92.8	55.0	3.12	2.46
HUMANA MEDICAL PLAN INC	FL	● B	2q 2014	1,670.8	5,391.4	5,391.4	380.0	2.92	2.43
▲ HUMANA MEDICAL PLAN OF MICHIGAN INC	MI	● B	2q 2014	35.9	1.8	1.8	17.8	12.07	10.06
HUMANA MEDICAL PLAN OF PENNSYLVANIA	PA	U		--	--	--	--	--	--
HUMANA MEDICAL PLAN OF UTAH INC	UT	● D	2q 2014	38.7	37.3	37.3	27.8	10.09	8.41
HUMANA PRIME HEALTH	MO	U		--	--	--	--	--	--
HUMANA REGIONAL HEALTH PLAN INC	AR	U		--	--	--	--	--	--
HUMANA WISCONSIN HEALTH ORGANIZATION	WI	● B	2q 2014	81.8	241.8	241.8	41.7	2.79	2.33
HUMANADENTAL INS CO	WI	U		--	--	--	--	--	--
▲ IA AMERICAN LIFE INS CO	TX	C	2q 2014	226.1	10.1	0.6	131.5	1.19	1.10
IBA PHP HEALTH PLAN	MI	U		--	--	--	--	--	--
IDEALIFE INS CO	CT	C+	2q 2014	19.8	3.4	2.1	14.8	4.12	3.71
IDS PROPERTY CASUALTY INS CO	WI	B	2q 2014	1,396.4	867.3	0.0	574.5	2.73	2.19
IEHP (See INLAND EMPIRE HEALTH PLAN)									
IHC ACCESS (See SELECTHEALTH INC)									
IHC CARE (See SELECTHEALTH INC)									
IHC CARE PLUS (See SELECTHEALTH INC)									
IHC MED (See SELECTHEALTH INC)									
IHC MED PLUS (See SELECTHEALTH INC)									
ILLINICARE HEALTH PLAN INC	IL	● C+	2q 2014	124.8	309.4	309.4	32.5	2.15	1.79
ILLINOIS MUTUAL LIFE INS CO	IL	● A-	2q 2014	1,354.0	119.5	62.1	181.8	3.20	1.81
ILLINOIS UNION INS CO	IL	C	2q 2014	411.6	454.7	0.3	157.8	15.20	9.67
IMPERIUM INS CO	TX	C-	2q 2014	372.9	98.7	7.0	143.5	1.36	0.86
INDEMNITY INS CO OF NORTH AMERICA	PA	C	2q 2014	375.7	902.1	1.1	108.6	2.87	1.90
INDEPENDENCE AMERICAN INS CO	DE	● C	2q 2014	103.4	56.6	36.9	58.9	2.54	1.49
INDEPENDENCE BLUE CROSS	PA	● C	2q 2014	2,773.2	363.5	363.5	2,125.0	3.80	3.16
INDEPENDENT CARE HEALTH PLAN	WI	● B	2q 2014	51.8	174.3	174.3	18.5	2.44	2.03
▼ INDEPENDENT HEALTH ASSOC INC	NY	● B	2q 2014	646.2	1,356.1	1,356.1	436.4	4.72	3.93
INDEPENDENT HEALTH BENEFITS CORP	NY	● C+	2q 2014	173.6	485.9	485.9	103.6	2.69	2.24
INDIANA UNIVERSITY HEALTH PLANS INC	IN	● D-	2q 2014	10.0	98.2	98.2	7.7	1.27	1.05
INDIVIDUAL ASR CO LIFE HEALTH & ACC	OK	D	2q 2014	18.9	29.7	3.7	7.6	2.28	1.74
INITIAL GROUP INC	TN	U		--	--	--	--	--	--
INLAND EMPIRE HEALTH PLAN	CA	● B	2q 2014	347.0	1,240.9	1,240.9	99.3	1.08	0.68
INNOVATION HEALTH INS CO	VA	● B	2q 2014	42.0	4.3	4.3	14.6	4.63	3.86
INNOVATION HEALTH PLAN INC	VA	● B	2q 2014	15.4	8.8	8.8	7.4	4.69	3.91
INS CO OF NORTH AMERICA	PA	● C	2q 2014	758.6	114.3	39.2	167.4	1.66	1.11
▼ INS CO OF SCOTT AND WHITE	TX	● D+	2q 2014	9.6	14.2	14.2	2.4	1.35	1.13
INS CO OF THE STATE OF PA	PA	D	2q 2014	374.2	1,027.8	10.6	108.0	0.79	0.56
INSTIL HEALTH INS CO	SC	● B	2q 2013	108.7	235.9	235.9	74.0	14.24	11.87
INSURANCE CO OF THE SOUTH	GA	C	2q 2014	22.5	89.2	0.1	10.8	1.84	1.48
INSUREMAX INS CO	IN	D+	2q 2014	14.1	13.5	0.2	5.3	0.78	0.71
INTEGRAND ASR CO	PR	C+	2q 2014	154.5	74.5	1.7	85.4	3.87	2.38
INTEGRATED HEALTH NETWORKS & SERVICE	OH	U		--	--	--	--	--	--
INTER-COUNTY HEALTH PLAN INC	PA	U	2q 2014	4.7	0.0	0.0	2.6	--	--
INTER-COUNTY HOSPITALIZATION PLAN	PA	U	2q 2014	11.6	0.0	0.0	5.3	--	--
INTERBORO MUTUAL INDEMNITY INS CO	NY	D-	2q 2014	85.1	48.1	0.2	29.3	1.84	1.47
INTERGROUP OF ARIZONA (See HEALTH NET OF ARIZONA INC)									
INTERGROUP SERVICES CORP	PA	U		--	--	--	--	--	--
INTERPLAN CORP	CA	U		--	--	--	--	--	--

www.weissratings.com

Arrows denote recent upgrades ▲ or downgrades▼

● Bullets denote a more detailed analysis is available in Section II.

INSURANCE COMPANY NAME	DOM. STATE	RATING	DATA DATE	TOTAL ASSETS ($MIL)	TOTAL PREMIUMS ($MIL)	HEALTH PREMIUMS ($MIL)	CAPITAL & SURPLUS ($MIL)	RISK ADJUSTED CAPITAL RATIO 1	RATIO 2
INTERSTATE BANKERS CASUALTY CO	IL	F	4q 2013	18.9	12.9	0.1	2.7	0.24	0.19
INTERVALLEY HEALTH PLAN	CA	• D	2q 2014	27.9	225.2	225.2	22.1	1.10	0.70
INTERWEST HEALTH	MT	U		--	--	--	--	--	--
INTL HEALTH INS DANMARK FSG	FL	U		--	--	--	--	--	--
INTOTAL HEALTH LLC	VA	• B+	2q 2014	55.3	178.2	178.2	29.1	3.39	2.83
INTRAMERICA LIFE INS CO	NY	B	2q 2014	35.5	1.1	0.0	9.7	1.92	1.73
INVESTORS HERITAGE LIFE INS CO	KY	C	2q 2014	475.7	64.6	3.4	19.7	1.00	0.60
INVESTORS LIFE INS CO NORTH AMERICA	TX	B	2q 2014	692.2	22.6	0.0	51.9	2.60	1.38
IRONSHORE INDEMNITY INC	MN	B-	2q 2014	312.9	183.2	8.6	155.6	3.36	2.26
ISLAND GROUP ADMINISTRATION INC	NY	U		--	--	--	--	--	--
ISLAND HOME INS CO	GU	E+	2q 2014	25.2	28.8	27.6	14.2	2.76	1.50
JACKSON NATIONAL LIFE INS CO	MI	B+	2q 2014	176,569.5	23,059.4	69.9	4,236.9	1.92	1.01
JAIMINI HEALTH INC	CA	U		--	--	--	--	--	--
JEFFERSON INS CO	NY	C	2q 2014	67.2	313.8	5.3	41.5	1.41	1.16
JEFFERSON LIFE INS CO	TX	D	2q 2014	2.7	1.0	0.9	1.7	1.87	1.68
JEFFERSON NATIONAL LIFE INS CO	TX	C-	2q 2014	3,475.7	768.6	3.4	39.0	1.44	0.72
JJ NEWMAN PREFERRED PROVIDER NETWORK	NY	U		--	--	--	--	--	--
JOHN ALDEN LIFE INS CO	WI	• B	2q 2014	349.9	335.8	325.0	64.7	2.28	1.63
JOHN D KERNAN DMD PA	NJ	U		--	--	--	--	--	--
JOHN HANCOCK LIFE & HEALTH INS CO	MA	• B	2q 2014	10,136.3	605.3	595.6	690.5	3.00	1.80
JOHN HANCOCK LIFE INS CO (USA)	MI	B	2q 2014	245,283.4	20,309.9	1,532.4	5,489.4	0.98	0.63
JOHN HANCOCK LIFE INS CO OF NY	NY	A-	2q 2014	17,549.0	992.5	4.0	1,316.0	2.84	1.69
K S PLAN ADMINISTRATORS LLC	TX	• B	2q 2014	67.4	266.9	266.9	38.1	1.68	1.40
KAISER FOUNDATION HEALTH PLAN INC	CA	• A	2q 2014	60,291.5	49,772.6	49,772.6	25,427.0	3.91	2.80
KAISER FOUNDATION HP INC HI	HI	• B	2q 2014	362.8	1,159.0	1,159.0	120.3	3.57	2.98
KAISER FOUNDATION HP MID-ATL STATES	MD	• B	2q 2014	1,128.9	2,409.1	2,409.1	202.1	1.43	1.19
KAISER FOUNDATION HP NORTHWEST	OR	• B	2q 2014	1,257.7	3,008.0	3,008.0	454.4	5.07	4.23
KAISER FOUNDATION HP OF CO	CO	• B+	2q 2014	1,274.6	2,958.0	2,958.0	468.0	3.38	2.82
KAISER FOUNDATION HP OF GA	GA	• D	2q 2014	505.3	1,099.4	1,099.4	119.4	1.38	1.15
KAISER PERMANENTE INS CO	CA	• B+	2q 2014	179.4	245.8	245.8	84.8	5.75	4.79
KAISER PERMANENTE OF THE MID-ATLANTIC (See KAISER FOUNDATION HP MID-ATL STATES)									
KANAWHA HEALTHCARE SOLUTIONS INC	SC	U		--	--	--	--	--	--
KANAWHA INS CO	SC	• C	2q 2014	1,638.6	246.1	174.7	133.2	2.20	1.35
KANSAS CITY LIFE INS CO	MO	B	2q 2014	3,404.6	343.1	54.4	348.4	1.81	1.12
KELSEYCARE ADVANTAGE (See K S PLAN ADMINISTRATORS LLC)									
KENTUCKY HEALTH COOPERATIVE INC	KY	U		--	--	--	--	--	--
KENTUCKY HOME LIFE INS CO	KY	E+	2q 2014	5.8	2.2	0.8	3.5	2.95	2.65
KENTUCKY SPIRIT HEALTH PLAN INC	KY	• C-	2q 2013	176.2	555.5	555.5	79.0	1.82	1.51
KEOKUK AREA HOSP ORG DELIVERY SYSTEM	IA	U		--	--	--	--	--	--
KERN HEALTH SYSTEMS	CA	• C	2q 2014	131.9	232.1	232.1	75.7	3.87	2.37
KEYSTONE HEALTH PLAN CENTRAL INC	PA	• B	2q 2014	135.2	258.1	258.1	88.0	6.02	5.01
KEYSTONE HEALTH PLAN EAST INC	PA	• B+	2q 2014	1,543.2	2,685.7	2,685.7	924.3	5.83	4.85
KEYSTONE HEALTH PLAN WEST INC	PA	• D+	2q 2014	321.7	1,791.3	1,791.3	34.9	0.27	0.23
KEYSTONE POS (See INDEPENDENCE BLUE CROSS)									
KILPATRICK LIFE INS CO	LA	E+	2q 2014	180.2	17.5	0.2	5.8	0.51	0.30
KP CAL	CA	U		--	--	--	--	--	--
KPS HEALTH PLANS	WA	• C	2q 2014	47.6	115.0	115.0	18.8	5.16	4.30
LA CARE HEALTH PLAN (See LOCAL INITIATIVE HEALTH AUTH LA)									
LA HEALTH SERVICE & INDEMNITY CO	LA	• A+	2q 2014	1,813.5	2,181.0	2,181.0	1,169.3	7.40	6.17
LABOR HEALTH (See HEALTHNOW NY INC)									
LAFAYETTE LIFE INS CO	OH	B	2q 2014	3,952.7	625.8	0.3	203.3	1.71	0.88
LAKESIDE COMPREHENSIVE HEALTH CARE	CA	U		--	--	--	--	--	--

Arrows denote recent upgrades ▲ or downgrades▼   • Bullets denote a more detailed analysis is available in Section II.

INSURANCE COMPANY NAME	DOM. STATE	RATING	DATA DATE	TOTAL ASSETS ($MIL)	TOTAL PREMIUMS ($MIL)	HEALTH PREMIUMS ($MIL)	CAPITAL & SURPLUS ($MIL)	RISK ADJUSTED CAPITAL RATIO 1	RATIO 2
LAND OF LINCOLN MUTUAL HEALTH INS CO	IL	U		--	--	--	--	--	--
LANDCAR LIFE INS CO	UT	C+	2q 2014	22.6	1.4	0.8	12.7	1.39	1.15
LANDMARK HEALTHPLAN OF CALIFORNIA	CA	U		--	--	--	--	--	--
LAPORTE HOSP-LAKELAND AREA HEALTH SV	IN	U		--	--	--	--	--	--
▼ LEADERS LIFE INS CO	OK	C+	2q 2014	5.6	10.1	0.9	2.8	1.61	1.42
LEON MEDICAL CENTERS HEALTH PLANS (See HEALTHSPRING OF FLORIDA INC)									
LEXINGTON INS CO	DE	C+	2q 2014	26,838.0	4,024.5	0.2	7,235.9	2.38	1.60
LIBERTY DENTAL PLAN OF CALIFORNIA	CA	U		--	--	--	--	--	--
LIBERTY DENTAL PLAN OF MISSOURI INC	MO	U		--	--	--	--	--	--
LIBERTY DENTAL PLAN OF NEVADA INC	NV	U		--	--	--	--	--	--
LIBERTY DENTAL PLAN OF NEW JERSEY	NJ	U		--	--	--	--	--	--
LIBERTY LIFE ASR CO OF BOSTON	NH	● B	2q 2014	14,171.0	2,186.3	674.6	896.1	2.21	1.29
LIBERTY MUTUAL INS CO	MA	B	2q 2014	42,911.2	4,507.4	1.1	15,034.9	1.60	1.36
LIBERTY NATIONAL LIFE INS CO	NE	B	2q 2014	7,370.4	570.5	125.2	613.4	2.33	1.22
LIBERTY UNION LIFE ASR CO	MI	● C-	2q 2014	11.8	21.1	21.1	4.1	1.94	1.61
LIFE ASSURANCE CO INC	OK	C-	2q 2014	5.2	3.1	0.8	2.2	1.37	1.23
LIFE INS CO OF ALABAMA	AL	● A-	2q 2014	112.7	37.6	31.2	35.8	2.96	1.96
LIFE INS CO OF BOSTON & NEW YORK	NY	A-	2q 2014	120.6	30.9	15.7	22.5	2.50	2.03
LIFE INS CO OF LOUISIANA	LA	C-	4q 2013	8.4	0.6	0.2	3.9	2.14	1.60
LIFE INS CO OF NORTH AMERICA	PA	● B	2q 2014	6,882.4	3,089.8	1,752.2	1,238.8	2.46	1.55
LIFE INS CO OF THE SOUTHWEST	TX	B	2q 2014	12,742.3	1,345.0	0.1	748.5	2.14	1.04
LIFE OF AMERICA INS CO	TX	C	2q 2014	11.6	0.2	0.2	2.0	0.74	0.67
LIFE OF THE SOUTH INS CO	GA	C	2q 2014	75.7	95.2	66.8	20.1	0.88	0.71
LIFECARE MANAGEMENT SYSTEMS INC	NJ	U		--	--	--	--	--	--
LIFEGUARD HEALTH NETWORK	CA	U		--	--	--	--	--	--
LIFEMAP ASR CO	OR	● B	2q 2014	91.5	87.4	61.2	43.3	1.83	1.32
LIFESECURE INS CO	MI	● D-	2q 2014	209.5	19.7	10.6	27.7	2.63	1.70
LIFESHIELD NATIONAL INS CO	OK	B-	2q 2014	67.1	1.7	0.0	22.9	2.15	1.25
LIFEWISE ASR CO	WA	● A	2q 2014	129.7	94.5	88.3	83.9	6.52	4.94
LIFEWISE HEALTH PLAN OF OREGON	OR	● B	2q 2014	106.7	151.3	151.3	62.4	7.12	5.93
LIFEWISE HEALTH PLAN OF WASHINGTON	WA	● B+	2q 2014	150.0	345.0	345.0	59.1	3.50	2.92
LINCOLN BENEFIT LIFE CO	NE	B+	2q 2014	13,279.3	1,641.3	79.5	748.8	1.76	0.80
LINCOLN HERITAGE LIFE INS CO	IL	B-	2q 2014	776.8	346.9	22.8	112.3	3.94	2.05
▲ LINCOLN LIFE & ANNUITY CO OF NY	NY	B	2q 2014	12,459.8	1,267.0	57.2	633.8	2.46	1.27
LINCOLN NATIONAL LIFE INS CO	IN	B	2q 2014	207,935.9	24,310.5	1,338.7	6,996.4	1.45	0.96
LINCOLN REPUBLIC INS CO	ND	B	2q 2014	30.2	1.1	0.2	13.4	2.93	2.64
LITTLE HAVANA CENTERS OF DADE COUNTY	FL	U		--	--	--	--	--	--
LOCAL INITIATIVE HEALTH AUTH LA	CA	● C	2q 2014	1,194.7	2,687.4	2,687.4	190.2	1.00	0.61
LONDON LIFE REINSURANCE CO	PA	● C+	2q 2014	330.2	0.0	0.0	54.4	4.46	2.26
LONGEVITY INS CO	TX	D+	2q 2014	9.1	0.4	0.1	7.7	3.41	3.07
LOUISIANA FARM BUREAU MUTUAL INS CO	LA	B	2q 2014	193.8	146.5	0.1	101.3	4.60	4.10
LOUISIANA HEALTH COOPERATIVE INC	LA	U		--	--	--	--	--	--
LOUISIANA HEALTHCARE CONNECTIONS INC	LA	● C-	2q 2014	91.3	456.7	456.7	47.1	1.90	1.58
LOVELACE HEALTH SYSTEMS INC	NM	● C+	1q 2014	325.1	704.3	704.3	183.8	3.27	2.73
LOVELACE INS CO INC	NM	● D	1q 2014	29.2	101.1	101.1	10.9	0.50	0.42
LOYAL AMERICAN LIFE INS CO	OH	● C	2q 2014	242.4	129.6	122.2	68.0	1.35	1.01
LUTHERAN PREFERRED	IN	U		--	--	--	--	--	--
MADISON NATIONAL LIFE INS CO INC	WI	● C+	2q 2014	496.5	207.6	151.0	77.6	1.23	1.02
MAGELLAN BEHAVIORAL CARE OF IOWA	IA	U		--	--	--	--	--	--
MAGELLAN BEHAVIORAL HEALTH OF NE	NE	● D+	2q 2014	22.7	33.2	33.2	3.1	1.37	1.14
MAGELLAN BEHAVIORAL HEALTH OF NJ LLC	NJ	U		--	--	--	--	--	--
▲ MAGELLAN BEHAVIORAL HEALTH OF PA INC	PA	● D+	2q 2014	93.8	358.5	358.5	42.3	18.17	15.14

Arrows denote recent upgrades ▲ or downgrades▼

www.weissratings.com
● Bullets denote a more detailed analysis is available in Section II.

INSURANCE COMPANY NAME	DOM. STATE	RATING	DATA DATE	TOTAL ASSETS ($MIL)	TOTAL PREMIUMS ($MIL)	HEALTH PREMIUMS ($MIL)	CAPITAL & SURPLUS ($MIL)	RISK ADJUSTED CAPITAL RATIO 1	RATIO 2
MAGELLAN COMPLETE CARE OF ARIZONA	AZ	U		--	--	--	--	--	--
MAGELLAN HEALTH SERVICES OF CA	CA	U		--	--	--	--	--	--
MAGNACARE	NY	U		--	--	--	--	--	--
MAGNET/MAGNACARE	NJ	U		--	--	--	--	--	--
MAGNOLIA HEALTH PLAN INC	MS	● D	2q 2014	98.0	406.6	406.6	31.2	1.54	1.28
MAINE COMMUNITY HEALTH OPTIONS	ME	U		--	--	--	--	--	--
MAINE DENTAL SERVICE CORP	ME	● C-	4q 2013	44.4	53.8	53.8	39.9	5.35	4.46
MAMSI LIFE & HEALTH INS CO	MD	● B-	2q 2014	25.0	73.3	73.3	15.9	4.04	3.37
MANAGED DENTAL CARE	CA	U		--	--	--	--	--	--
MANAGED DENTALGUARD INC (OHIO)	OH	U		--	--	--	--	--	--
MANAGED HEALTH INC	NY	● B-	2q 2014	485.4	1,613.4	1,613.4	177.7	1.45	1.21
MANAGED HEALTH NETWORK	CA	U		--	--	--	--	--	--
MANAGED HEALTH SERVICES INS CORP	WI	● C+	2q 2014	56.7	203.7	203.7	26.8	3.12	2.60
MANAGED HEALTHCARE NORTHWEST INC	OR	U		--	--	--	--	--	--
MANHATTAN LIFE INS CO	NY	B	2q 2014	321.3	17.5	2.6	39.0	1.26	1.04
MANHATTAN NATIONAL LIFE INS CO	OH	B	2q 2014	182.0	21.8	0.1	12.9	1.46	1.31
MAPFRE LIFE INS CO	DE	C+	2q 2014	26.8	0.2	0.2	24.7	6.84	6.16
MAPFRE LIFE INS CO OF PR	PR	● C+	2q 2014	69.5	90.6	85.5	31.8	1.72	1.37
MAPFRE PAN AMERICAN INS CO	PR	C	2q 2014	15.0	3.2	0.0	10.2	6.98	6.28
MAPFRE PRAICO INS CO	PR	D+	2q 2014	393.8	234.2	0.0	153.5	1.49	1.00
MARCH VISION CARE INC	CA	U		--	--	--	--	--	--
MARKEL INS CO	IL	C	2q 2014	1,320.6	504.2	27.5	375.9	1.73	1.05
MARQUETTE GENERAL HOSPITAL	MI	U		--	--	--	--	--	--
MARQUETTE INDEMNITY & LIFE INS CO	AZ	C	2q 2014	7.2	1.2	0.8	3.3	1.75	1.57
MARQUETTE NATIONAL LIFE INS CO	TX	C	2q 2014	6.8	17.5	17.0	5.7	3.05	2.75
MARTINS POINT GENERATIONS LLC	ME	● D	2q 2014	49.7	171.0	171.0	17.5	0.77	0.64
MASSACHUSETTS MUTUAL LIFE INS CO	MA	A-	2q 2014	189,173.1	19,238.3	666.7	13,565.0	1.89	1.32
MASTER HEALTH PLUS (See HEALTHNOW NY INC)									
MASTERCARE COMPANIES INC	NJ	U		--	--	--	--	--	--
MATTHEW THORNTON HEALTH PLAN	NH	● A-	2q 2014	220.6	492.1	492.1	105.4	3.44	2.87
MAX VISION CARE INC	CA	U		--	--	--	--	--	--
MAYAN HEALTH PPO	NY	U		--	--	--	--	--	--
MCLAREN HEALTH PLAN COMMUNITY	MI	U		--	--	--	--	--	--
MCLAREN HEALTH PLAN INC	MI	● B-	2q 2014	143.4	532.6	532.6	46.5	0.96	0.80
MCNA INS CO	TX	U		--	--	--	--	--	--
MCS ADVANTAGE INC	PR	● E	2q 2014	234.8	1,173.8	1,173.8	25.8	0.32	0.27
MCS LIFE INS CO	PR	E+	2q 2014	72.5	253.1	250.3	19.8	0.41	0.35
MD CARE INC	CA	● C	2q 2014	50.8	0.5	0.5	44.9	9.16	7.24
MD INDIVIDUAL PRACTICE ASSOC INC	MD	● B-	2q 2014	115.6	417.3	417.3	67.4	10.49	8.74
MDNY PREFERRED NETWORK INC	NY	U		--	--	--	--	--	--
MDWISE INC	IN	● C+	2q 2014	76.8	449.9	449.9	28.7	1.15	0.96
MEDAMERICA INS CO	PA	● B	2q 2014	860.2	82.2	82.2	39.4	1.60	0.86
MEDAMERICA INS CO OF FL	FL	C+	2q 2014	25.2	4.2	4.2	2.2	0.61	0.54
MEDAMERICA INS CO OF NEW YORK	NY	B	2q 2014	559.6	43.7	43.7	21.5	1.81	1.14
MEDCO CONTAINMENT INS CO OF NY	NY	● B+	2q 2014	69.9	77.2	77.2	48.6	16.24	13.53
MEDCO CONTAINMENT LIFE INS CO	PA	● B+	2q 2014	507.6	513.3	513.3	279.1	9.17	7.64
MEDCOST LLC	NC	U		--	--	--	--	--	--
MEDI-CAL (See SAN FRANCISCO HEALTH AUTHORITY)									
MEDICA CHOICE (See MEDICA HEALTH PLANS)									
MEDICA ELECT (See MEDICA HEALTH PLANS)									
MEDICA HEALTH PLANS	MN	● B+	2q 2014	760.3	1,778.6	1,778.6	414.5	3.30	2.75
MEDICA HEALTH PLANS OF FLORIDA INC	FL	● E	2q 2014	11.4	35.9	35.9	6.1	1.46	1.21

Arrows denote recent upgrades ▲ or downgrades▼

● Bullets denote a more detailed analysis is available in Section II.

INSURANCE COMPANY NAME	DOM. STATE	RATING	DATA DATE	TOTAL ASSETS ($MIL)	TOTAL PREMIUMS ($MIL)	HEALTH PREMIUMS ($MIL)	CAPITAL & SURPLUS ($MIL)	RISK ADJUSTED CAPITAL RATIO 1	RATIO 2
MEDICA HEALTH PLANS OF WI	WI	U		--	--	--	--	--	--
MEDICA HEALTHCARE PLANS INC	FL	• E-	2q 2014	113.4	513.4	513.4	31.2	1.02	0.85
MEDICA INS CO	MN	• C+	2q 2014	626.0	1,463.9	1,463.9	275.6	2.89	2.41
MEDICA PREMIER (See MEDICA HEALTH PLANS)									
MEDICA PRIMARY (See MEDICA HEALTH PLANS)									
MEDICAL ASSOC CLINIC HEALTH PLAN	WI	• B-	2q 2014	3.8	30.9	30.9	3.3	1.26	1.05
MEDICAL ASSOCIATES HEALTH PLAN INC	IA	• B	2q 2014	31.3	115.3	115.3	20.6	1.94	1.62
MEDICAL BENEFITS MUTUAL LIFE INS CO	OH	D	2q 2014	19.5	22.3	21.9	11.1	1.88	1.32
MEDICAL CARE REFERRAL GROUP	TX	U		--	--	--	--	--	--
MEDICAL CONTROL NETWORK SOLUTIONS	TX	U		--	--	--	--	--	--
MEDICAL EYE SERVICES INC	CA	U		--	--	--	--	--	--
MEDICAL HEALTH INS CORP OF OHIO	OH	• B+	2q 2014	114.5	12.3	12.3	77.0	56.24	46.87
MEDICAL MUTUAL OF OHIO	OH	• A-	2q 2014	1,798.4	2,473.5	2,473.5	1,271.5	6.08	5.07
MEDICAL RESOURCES NETWORK LLC	GA	U		--	--	--	--	--	--
MEDICHOICE NETWORK INC	NJ	U		--	--	--	--	--	--
MEDICO CORP LIFE INS CO	NE	B+	2q 2014	25.7	0.6	0.6	24.7	6.09	5.48
MEDICO INS CO	NE	• B	2q 2014	69.5	96.6	94.3	31.2	4.26	3.83
MEDISUN INC	AZ	• B	2q 2014	51.2	238.1	238.1	25.0	0.96	0.80
MEDPLUS INC	PR	U		--	--	--	--	--	--
MEDPOINT (See BLUE CROSS BLUE SHIELD OF NC)									
MEDSTAR FAMILY CHOICE INC	MD	• C-	2q 2014	124.1	224.8	224.8	27.8	1.01	0.84
MEGA LIFE & HEALTH INS CO	OK	• B-	2q 2014	268.9	247.8	238.7	113.0	2.34	1.87
MEMBERS HEALTH INS CO	AZ	• C	2q 2014	33.0	0.7	0.7	31.3	17.45	14.54
MEMBERS LIFE INS CO	IA	C	2q 2014	26.1	92.5	0.0	18.3	4.77	4.30
MEMORIAL HERMANN HEALTH INS CO	TX	• C-	2q 2014	22.4	20.9	20.9	11.8	2.33	1.94
MERCHANTS MUTUAL INS CO	NY	B-	2q 2014	462.8	175.8	0.0	156.6	2.79	2.09
MERCY MARICOPA INTEGRATED CARE	AZ	U		--	--	--	--	--	--
MERCYCARE HMO	WI	• C	2q 2014	34.6	109.0	109.0	19.0	1.71	1.42
MERCYCARE INS CO	WI	• C-	2q 2014	21.2	0.7	0.7	21.0	1.69	1.41
MERIDIAN GEISINGER HLTH NETWORK LLC	NJ	U		--	--	--	--	--	--
▲ MERIDIAN HEALTH PLAN OF ILLINOIS INC	IL	• B	2q 2014	43.0	40.9	40.9	6.2	1.19	0.99
MERIDIAN HEALTH PLAN OF IOWA INC	IA	• E	2q 2014	23.1	57.0	57.0	4.8	0.56	0.46
▲ MERIDIAN HEALTH PLAN OF MICHIGAN INC	MI	• B+	2q 2014	263.1	1,058.6	1,058.6	91.5	1.20	1.00
MERIT HEALTH INS CO	IL	• C	2q 2014	71.8	128.6	128.6	32.7	5.50	4.58
MERIT LIFE INS CO	IN	• B+	2q 2014	560.2	128.0	64.9	190.2	6.31	4.06
MERITUS HEALTH PARTNERS	AZ	U		--	--	--	--	--	--
MERITUS MUTUAL HEALTH PARTNERS	AZ	U		--	--	--	--	--	--
METLIFE HEALTH PLANS INC	NJ	U		--	--	--	--	--	--
METLIFE INS CO OF CT (LIFE DEPT)	CT	B	2q 2014	57,230.5	1,659.8	234.6	4,610.4	1.48	1.07
METLIFE INVESTORS INS CO	MO	B-	2q 2014	14,911.3	97.8	0.0	742.8	4.94	2.38
METROPOLITAN HEALTH PLAN	MN	• C-	2q 2014	69.8	154.5	154.5	29.3	2.01	1.68
METROPOLITAN LIFE INS CO	NY	B-	2q 2014	390,638.9	35,618.4	6,690.8	13,574.1	1.33	0.87
METROPOLITAN PROPERTY & CAS INS CO	RI	B	2q 2014	5,664.7	1,367.6	14.9	2,359.2	2.18	1.71
MHNET LIFE & HEALTH INS CO	TX	• B-	2q 2014	4.3	0.7	0.7	4.0	87.79	73.16
MICHIGAN EYECARE ASSN INC	MI	U		--	--	--	--	--	--
MID AMERICA HEALTH NETWORK INC	MO	U		--	--	--	--	--	--
MID AMERICA HEALTH PARTNERS INC (See COVENTRY HEALTH CARE OF KANSAS INC)									
MID ROGUE HEALTH PLAN	OR	• E	2q 2014	12.2	43.5	43.5	6.0	0.65	0.54
MID VALLEY IPA EMPLOYEE BENEFIT TR	OR	U		--	--	--	--	--	--
MID-WEST NATIONAL LIFE INS CO OF TN	TX	• B-	2q 2014	92.7	85.6	80.4	52.3	5.72	4.47
MIDLAND NATIONAL LIFE INS CO	IA	B+	2q 2014	39,622.6	3,974.3	0.1	2,709.0	2.20	1.14
MIDLANDS CHOICE	NE	U		--	--	--	--	--	--

www.weissratings.com

Arrows denote recent upgrades ▲ or downgrades▼

• Bullets denote a more detailed analysis is available in Section II.

INSURANCE COMPANY NAME	DOM. STATE	RATING	DATA DATE	TOTAL ASSETS ($MIL)	TOTAL PREMIUMS ($MIL)	HEALTH PREMIUMS ($MIL)	CAPITAL & SURPLUS ($MIL)	RISK ADJUSTED CAPITAL RATIO 1	RATIO 2
MIDWESTERN UNITED LIFE INS CO	IN	A-	2q 2014	237.0	3.8	0.0	123.3	12.37	11.13
MII LIFE INC	MN	• B	2q 2014	490.7	0.5	0.5	28.2	2.33	1.94
MINNESOTA LIFE INS CO	MN	B+	2q 2014	34,732.2	5,857.7	280.3	2,491.8	2.40	1.50
MINUTEMAN HEALTH INC	MA	U		--	--	--	--	--	--
MISSISSIPPI PHYSICIANS CARE NETWORK	MS	U		--	--	--	--	--	--
MISSOURI CARE INC	MO	• E	2q 2014	96.2	305.2	305.2	44.6	2.52	2.10
MMM HEALTHCARE INC	PR	• C	2q 2014	305.4	1,733.0	1,733.0	113.8	0.80	0.66
MMM MULTI HEALTH INC	PR	U		--	--	--	--	--	--
MODA HEALTH PLAN INC	OR	• B-	2q 2014	273.2	293.0	293.0	73.9	2.13	1.78
MOHR HEALTH SYSTEMS INC	IL	U		--	--	--	--	--	--
MOLINA HEALTHCARE OF CALIFORNIA	CA	• C-	2q 2014	323.8	770.4	770.4	83.8	1.36	0.88
MOLINA HEALTHCARE OF FLORIDA INC	FL	• D	2q 2014	62.0	264.9	264.9	18.0	0.83	0.69
MOLINA HEALTHCARE OF ILLINOIS INC	IL	• E	2q 2014	22.1	8.3	8.3	3.7	1.39	1.16
MOLINA HEALTHCARE OF MICHIGAN INC	MI	• B	2q 2014	229.7	883.4	883.4	107.0	2.09	1.74
MOLINA HEALTHCARE OF NEW MEXICO	NM	• B	2q 2014	203.0	499.7	499.7	36.0	1.38	1.15
MOLINA HEALTHCARE OF OHIO INC	OH	• B	2q 2014	351.1	1,248.2	1,248.2	151.7	2.26	1.88
MOLINA HEALTHCARE OF SOUTH CAROLINA	SC	U		--	--	--	--	--	--
MOLINA HEALTHCARE OF TEXAS INC	TX	• C	2q 2014	257.2	1,312.4	1,312.4	89.2	1.06	0.88
MOLINA HEALTHCARE OF TEXAS INS CO	TX	C	2q 2014	4.6	87.2	87.2	3.3	1.37	0.90
MOLINA HEALTHCARE OF UTAH INC	UT	• B	2q 2014	90.3	347.3	347.3	53.0	2.34	1.95
MOLINA HEALTHCARE OF WASHINGTON INC	WA	• B+	2q 2014	386.8	1,201.2	1,201.2	149.4	1.88	1.56
MOLINA HEALTHCARE OF WISCONSIN INC	WI	• D	2q 2014	46.3	195.1	195.1	25.2	1.84	1.54
MONARCH HEALTH PLAN	CA	• E-	2q 2014	34.5	133.1	133.1	1.4	0.00	0.00
MONARCH LIFE INS CO	MA	F	4q 2013	755.0	19.7	18.2	6.6	0.50	0.26
MONITOR LIFE INS CO OF NEW YORK	NY	B	2q 2014	17.5	15.8	13.4	9.3	1.67	1.31
MONTANA HEALTH COOPERATIVE	MT	U		--	--	--	--	--	--
MONY LIFE INS CO	NY	B-	2q 2014	7,702.7	348.7	37.4	417.9	2.16	1.15
MOTORISTS COMMERCIAL MUTUAL INS CO	OH	B	2q 2014	344.5	33.4	0.0	143.3	3.14	2.25
MOUNT CARMEL HEALTH INS CO	OH	• D	2q 2014	8.1	9.3	9.3	6.8	3.99	3.33
MOUNT CARMEL HEALTH PLAN INC	OH	• A	2q 2014	336.9	424.8	424.8	305.8	7.37	6.15
MOUNTAIN LIFE INS CO	TN	C-	2q 2014	11.5	4.0	1.1	5.1	1.92	1.73
MOUNTAIN MEDICAL AFFILIATES INC	CO	U		--	--	--	--	--	--
MOUNTAIN STATE BLUE CROSS BLUE SHIELD (See HIGHMARK WEST VIRGINIA INC)									
MTL INS CO	IL	B	2q 2014	1,936.2	242.0	0.4	132.4	2.07	1.11
MULTINATIONAL LIFE INS CO	PR	D-	2q 2014	129.5	39.2	21.2	13.9	1.38	0.76
MULTIPLAN INC	NY	U		--	--	--	--	--	--
MUTUAL ALLIANCE PLAN	MA	U		--	--	--	--	--	--
MUTUAL BENEFIT ASSN OF HAWAII	HI	U	3q 2010	4.1	0.0	0.0	3.8	--	--
MUTUAL OF AMERICA LIFE INS CO	NY	A-	2q 2014	17,180.5	1,772.6	3.7	961.5	3.42	1.62
MUTUAL OF OMAHA INS CO	NE	• B+	2q 2014	6,375.2	988.2	988.2	2,850.2	1.16	1.07
MUTUAL SAVINGS LIFE INS CO	AL	A-	2q 2014	473.8	40.7	5.7	60.7	2.95	1.87
MUTUALLY PREFERRED PPO (See MUTUAL OF OMAHA INS CO)									
MVP HEALTH INS CO	NY	• E	2q 2014	133.1	527.1	527.1	58.2	1.05	0.87
MVP HEALTH INS CO OF NEW HAMPSHIRE	NH	• D	2q 2014	7.9	41.0	41.0	5.0	1.58	1.32
MVP HEALTH PLAN INC	NY	• B-	2q 2014	491.0	1,678.6	1,678.6	289.1	2.93	2.44
MVP HEALTH PLAN OF NEW HAMPSHIRE INC	NH	U		--	--	--	--	--	--
MVPPO	FL	U		--	--	--	--	--	--
NATIONAL ASSOC PREFERRED PROVIDERS	TX	U		--	--	--	--	--	--
NATIONAL BENEFIT LIFE INS CO	NY	B+	2q 2014	475.2	177.4	35.2	165.6	6.98	3.90
NATIONAL CAPITAL PPO	VA	U		--	--	--	--	--	--
NATIONAL CASUALTY CO	WI	B+	2q 2014	287.3	795.3	1.3	127.8	13.40	12.06
NATIONAL DENTAL CARE INC	IL	U		--	--	--	--	--	--

Arrows denote recent upgrades ▲ or downgrades▼   • Bullets denote a more detailed analysis is available in Section II.

INSURANCE COMPANY NAME	DOM. STATE	RATING	DATA DATE	TOTAL ASSETS ($MIL)	TOTAL PREMIUMS ($MIL)	HEALTH PREMIUMS ($MIL)	CAPITAL & SURPLUS ($MIL)	RISK ADJUSTED CAPITAL RATIO 1	RATIO 2
NATIONAL FAMILY CARE LIFE INS CO	TX	C	2q 2014	15.9	7.7	6.4	9.1	2.95	2.66
NATIONAL FARMERS UNION LIFE INS CO	TX	B	2q 2014	219.9	7.0	0.0	45.2	4.24	2.23
NATIONAL FOUNDATION LIFE INS CO	TX	C	2q 2014	25.7	34.7	34.2	11.3	1.28	0.99
NATIONAL GUARDIAN LIFE INS CO	WI	● B	2q 2014	2,823.3	716.4	286.1	255.2	1.56	1.02
NATIONAL HEALTH INS CO	TX	C	2q 2014	12.9	0.2	0.2	10.7	6.30	5.67
NATIONAL HEALTH PLAN CORP	NY	U		--	--	--	--	--	--
NATIONAL HEALTHCARE ALLIANCE INC	TX	U		--	--	--	--	--	--
NATIONAL INCOME LIFE INS CO	NY	B+	2q 2014	137.0	53.9	6.8	31.6	3.46	2.40
NATIONAL INS CO OF WISCONSIN INC	WI	C	2q 2014	45.5	4.5	4.5	20.5	2.21	1.36
NATIONAL INTERSTATE INS CO	OH	C+	2q 2014	1,121.3	442.1	0.8	280.6	1.47	1.20
NATIONAL LIFE INS CO	VT	B	2q 2014	9,099.3	496.3	29.2	1,437.0	1.54	1.19
NATIONAL LLOYDS INS CO	TX	B-	2q 2014	213.3	151.0	0.2	100.5	3.14	2.69
NATIONAL PREFERRED PROVIDER NETWORK	NY	U		--	--	--	--	--	--
NATIONAL SECURITY INS CO	AL	B	2q 2014	51.4	6.7	1.9	12.0	1.94	1.54
NATIONAL TEACHERS ASSOCIATES L I C	TX	● B	2q 2014	401.6	108.4	105.7	77.1	2.62	1.88
NATIONAL UNION FIRE INS CO OF PITTSB	PA	C	2q 2014	26,252.7	6,731.6	1,192.7	6,306.1	2.03	1.37
NATIONAL WESTERN LIFE INS CO	CO	B+	2q 2014	10,001.6	1,124.1	1.8	1,159.3	4.40	2.40
NATIONWIDE LIFE & ANNUITY INS CO	OH	B-	2q 2014	7,177.2	978.7	0.0	518.9	2.98	1.51
NATIONWIDE LIFE INS CO	OH	B	2q 2014	125,009.9	11,737.2	254.3	3,787.5	2.41	1.40
NATIONWIDE MUTUAL FIRE INS CO	OH	B+	2q 2014	5,596.1	1,607.1	0.0	2,489.8	4.87	3.41
NATIONWIDE MUTUAL INS CO	OH	B	2q 2014	33,616.0	3,596.7	8.3	12,193.6	1.53	1.34
NEIGHBORHOOD HEALTH PARTNERSHIP INC	FL	● B-	2q 2014	109.3	477.4	477.4	39.4	1.81	1.50
NEIGHBORHOOD HEALTH PLAN	MA	● C+	2q 2014	412.0	1,363.0	1,363.0	170.7	1.48	1.23
NEIGHBORHOOD HEALTH PLAN OF RI INC	RI	● B-	2q 2014	170.6	428.2	428.2	38.0	0.88	0.74
NET PRO	IN	U		--	--	--	--	--	--
NETCARE LIFE & HEALTH INS CO	GU	E+	2q 2014	24.5	12.3	8.7	3.5	0.67	0.61
NETWORK H (See BLUECROSS BLUESHIELD OF TENNESSEE)									
NETWORK HEALTH INS CORP	WI	● C-	2q 2014	117.8	474.2	474.2	58.4	1.45	1.21
NETWORK HEALTH LLC	MA	● C+	2q 2014	312.6	1,072.8	1,072.8	148.3	2.00	1.67
▼ NETWORK HEALTH PLAN	WI	● D	2q 2014	95.8	418.0	418.0	46.8	1.49	1.25
NEVADA DENTAL BENEFITS LTD	NV	U		--	--	--	--	--	--
NEVADA HEALTH CO-OP	NV	U		--	--	--	--	--	--
NEVADA PREFERRED PROFESSIONALS	NV	U		--	--	--	--	--	--
NEW ENGLAND LIFE INS CO	MA	B	2q 2014	11,648.6	375.4	8.9	643.4	4.05	2.17
NEW ERA LIFE INS CO	TX	● C	2q 2014	390.8	142.2	89.0	61.1	0.92	0.70
NEW ERA LIFE INS CO OF THE MIDWEST	TX	C	2q 2014	78.3	57.4	45.1	11.0	0.70	0.48
NEW HAMPSHIRE INS CO	PA	C	2q 2014	560.1	1,591.7	0.5	233.4	0.90	0.82
NEW HEALTH VENTURES INC	CO	U		--	--	--	--	--	--
NEW MEXICO HEALTH CONNECTIONS	NM	U		--	--	--	--	--	--
NEW WEST HEALTH SERVICES	MT	● E+	2q 2014	45.4	155.2	155.2	9.9	0.26	0.21
NEW YORK LIFE INS CO	NY	A-	2q 2014	142,089.9	12,833.3	550.4	18,839.9	1.62	1.26
NEXDENT DENTAL PLANS INC	WA	U		--	--	--	--	--	--
NHP OF INDIANA LLC	IN	U		--	--	--	--	--	--
NIAGARA LIFE & HEALTH INS CO	NY	B	2q 2014	10.2	6.5	6.5	6.6	2.94	2.64
NIPPON LIFE INS CO OF AMERICA	IA	● A-	2q 2014	222.1	353.3	348.5	133.6	3.10	2.48
NORIDIAN MUTUAL INS CO	ND	● C+	4q 2013	458.2	1,195.6	1,195.6	199.1	1.58	1.31
NORTH ALABAMA MANAGED CARE INC	AL	U		--	--	--	--	--	--
NORTH AMERICA LIFE INS CO OF TX	TX	E-	2q 2014	54.5	0.4	0.0	-13.6	-0.84	-0.56
NORTH AMERICAN CAPACITY INS CO	NH	C	2q 2014	112.5	117.0	0.0	50.9	7.00	6.30
NORTH AMERICAN CO FOR LIFE & H INS	IA	B	2q 2014	16,347.9	2,074.3	0.1	1,126.6	2.43	1.12
NORTH AMERICAN INS CO	WI	C	2q 2014	21.5	26.9	26.9	10.5	1.31	1.02
NORTH CAROLINA CHOICE (See UNITED HEALTHCARE OF NC INC)									

www.weissratings.com

Arrows denote recent upgrades ▲ or downgrades▼   ● Bullets denote a more detailed analysis is available in Section II.

INSURANCE COMPANY NAME	DOM. STATE	RATING	DATA DATE	TOTAL ASSETS ($MIL)	TOTAL PREMIUMS ($MIL)	HEALTH PREMIUMS ($MIL)	CAPITAL & SURPLUS ($MIL)	RISK ADJUSTED CAPITAL RATIO 1	RATIO 2
NORTH CAROLINA FARM BU MUTUAL INS CO	NC	B-	2q 2014	1,691.2	930.8	0.1	966.9	4.23	2.82
NORTH CAROLINA MUTUAL LIFE INS CO	NC	D-	2q 2014	143.8	16.7	3.0	3.2	0.41	0.34
NORTH COAST LIFE INS CO	WA	B	2q 2014	146.1	7.6	0.0	8.0	0.93	0.82
NORTH SHORE-LIJ CARECONNECT INS CO	NY	U		--	--	--	--	--	--
NORTH TEXAS HEALTHCARE NETWORK	TX	U		--	--	--	--	--	--
NORTHCARE	CO	U		--	--	--	--	--	--
NORTHEAST HEALTH DIRECT LLC	CT	U		--	--	--	--	--	--
NORTHWESTERN LONG TERM CARE INS CO	WI	● B	2q 2014	2,475.9	468.6	468.6	261.5	1.91	1.06
NORTHWESTERN MUTUAL LIFE INS CO	WI	A-	2q 2014	222,040.6	16,865.6	1,127.5	17,821.2	3.63	1.85
NORTHWESTERN NATL INS CO SEG ACCNT	WI	D-	2q 2014	32.5	0.5	0.5	6.9	0.52	0.42
NOVA CASUALTY CO	NY	C	2q 2014	99.3	246.2	0.0	93.9	1.99	1.96
OBI NATIONAL INS CO	PA	C	2q 2014	13.0	3.7	0.0	13.0	134.40	67.21
OCCIDENTAL LIFE INS CO OF NC	TX	C	2q 2014	270.7	47.8	0.1	34.4	3.45	1.96
OHIO CASUALTY INS CO	NH	C	2q 2014	5,587.2	376.3	0.0	1,433.9	2.39	1.54
OHIO COMP NETWORK INC	OH	U		--	--	--	--	--	--
OHIO HEALTH CHOICE	OH	U		--	--	--	--	--	--
OHIO MOTORISTS LIFE INSURANCE CO	OH	B-	2q 2014	10.0	0.2	0.1	9.9	4.10	3.69
OHIO NATIONAL LIFE ASR CORP	OH	B+	2q 2014	3,450.3	581.8	17.8	316.6	2.80	1.44
OHIO NATIONAL LIFE INS CO	OH	B	2q 2014	26,841.3	2,834.3	15.2	1,022.9	1.38	0.96
OHIO STATE LIFE INS CO	TX	B-	2q 2014	13.7	35.4	0.0	10.2	18.99	9.41
OKLAHOMA FARM BUREAU MUTUAL INS CO	OK	C	2q 2014	291.7	227.6	0.1	90.7	1.67	1.22
OLD AMERICAN INS CO	MO	B	2q 2014	248.3	69.4	0.8	22.3	2.40	1.31
OLD REPUBLIC INS CO	PA	A-	2q 2014	2,591.0	872.1	10.7	935.1	3.85	2.38
OLD REPUBLIC LIFE INS CO	IL	● B-	2q 2014	132.3	30.5	15.0	33.4	3.28	2.06
OLD SPARTAN LIFE INS CO INC	SC	C	2q 2014	23.3	9.1	6.7	15.9	1.91	1.22
OLD SURETY LIFE INS CO	OK	C	2q 2014	24.7	37.7	37.5	10.6	0.87	0.66
OLD UNITED LIFE INS CO	AZ	● B	2q 2014	89.7	11.1	5.4	45.7	5.92	3.44
OMAHA INS CO	NE	B-	2q 2014	23.6	51.2	51.2	14.3	3.04	1.67
ON LOK SENIOR HEALTH SERVICES	CA	● B	2q 2014	126.1	97.0	97.0	94.0	3.72	2.72
ONEBEACON AMERICA INS CO	PA	C	2q 2014	93.7	1.3	0.0	88.7	64.26	57.84
ONENATION INS CO	IN	U	3q 2011	79.0	0.0	0.0	78.5	--	--
OPEN ACCESS (See AETNA HEALTH INC (A NEW YORK CORP))									
OPTIMA HEALTH GROUP INC	VA	U		--	--	--	--	--	--
OPTIMA HEALTH INS CO	VA	● C	2q 2014	38.9	113.6	113.6	22.5	2.12	1.77
OPTIMA HEALTH PLAN	VA	● B+	2q 2014	320.8	1,302.4	1,302.4	165.7	1.74	1.45
OPTIMUM CHOICE INC	MD	● C+	2q 2014	88.4	233.5	233.5	53.6	5.65	4.71
OPTIMUM HEALTH NETWORK	SC	U		--	--	--	--	--	--
OPTIMUM HEALTHCARE INC	FL	U		--	--	--	--	--	--
ORANGE CTY FOUNDATION FOR MED CARE	CA	U		--	--	--	--	--	--
ORANGE PREVENTION & TREATMENT INTEGR	CA	● B	2q 2014	610.1	1,743.2	1,743.2	224.7	1.66	1.07
ORTHONET OF THE MID-ATLANTIC	NJ	U		--	--	--	--	--	--
OSCAR INS CORP	NY	U		--	--	--	--	--	--
OXFORD HEALTH INS INC	NY	● C+	2q 2014	1,963.7	2,862.9	2,862.9	895.4	5.90	4.92
OXFORD HEALTH PLANS (CT) INC	CT	● B	2q 2014	232.1	653.1	653.1	110.8	3.14	2.61
OXFORD HEALTH PLANS (NJ) INC	NJ	● B	2q 2014	342.5	1,143.7	1,143.7	134.0	2.23	1.85
OXFORD HEALTH PLANS (NY) INC	NY	● A+	2q 2014	817.8	2,524.6	2,524.6	407.2	1.40	1.17
OXFORD LIFE INS CO	AZ	B-	2q 2014	1,161.3	182.5	19.9	152.9	2.01	1.36
OZARK NATIONAL LIFE INS CO	MO	B-	2q 2014	740.8	85.4	0.3	122.7	5.04	3.01
PACIFIC CENTURY LIFE INS CORP	AZ	B	2q 2014	340.5	0.2	0.0	336.2	30.32	18.99
PACIFIC FOUNDATION FOR MEDICAL CARE	CA	U		--	--	--	--	--	--
PACIFIC GUARDIAN LIFE INS CO LTD	HI	● A-	2q 2014	518.1	78.3	32.9	105.2	4.81	2.75
PACIFIC HEALTH ALLIANCE	CA	U		--	--	--	--	--	--

www.weissratings.com

49

Arrows denote recent upgrades ▲ or downgrades▼   ● Bullets denote a more detailed analysis is available in Section II.

INSURANCE COMPANY NAME	DOM. STATE	RATING	DATA DATE	TOTAL ASSETS ($MIL)	TOTAL PREMIUMS ($MIL)	HEALTH PREMIUMS ($MIL)	CAPITAL & SURPLUS ($MIL)	RISK ADJUSTED CAPITAL RATIO 1	RATIO 2
PACIFIC UNION DENTAL	CA	U		--	--	--	--	--	--
PACIFICARE LIFE & HEALTH INS CO	IN	• C+	2q 2014	554.9	104.7	104.7	538.2	34.61	22.36
PACIFICARE LIFE ASR CO	CO	U		--	--	--	--	--	--
PACIFICARE OF ARIZONA INC	AZ	• B	2q 2014	255.6	986.4	986.4	98.0	2.68	2.23
▼ PACIFICARE OF COLORADO INC	CO	• B-	2q 2014	249.8	849.8	849.8	102.4	2.80	2.33
PACIFICARE OF NEVADA INC	NV	• E	2q 2014	27.5	86.6	86.6	13.9	2.88	2.40
PACIFICARE OF OKLAHOMA INC	OK	• B	2q 2014	119.0	362.3	362.3	65.8	3.32	2.77
PACIFICARE OF WASHINGTON INC	WA	U		--	--	--	--	--	--
PACIFICARE PREFERRED (See PACIFICARE OF COLORADO INC)									
PACIFICSOURCE COMMUNITY HEALTH PLANS	OR	• C	2q 2014	92.4	300.4	300.4	46.2	1.48	1.24
PACIFICSOURCE HEALTH PLANS	OR	• B-	2q 2014	237.9	722.2	722.2	152.0	1.58	1.32
PAN AMERICAN LIFE INS CO OF PR	PR	B	2q 2014	9.7	17.3	17.0	6.7	2.21	1.70
PAN-AMERICAN LIFE INS CO	LA	• B	2q 2014	1,420.2	321.2	253.3	253.7	2.34	1.45
▲ PARAMOUNT ADVANTAGE	OH	• A-	2q 2014	172.9	390.0	390.0	65.1	2.12	1.77
▲ PARAMOUNT CARE OF MI INC	MI	• B-	2q 2014	10.3	23.1	23.1	6.8	1.88	1.57
PARAMOUNT HEALTH CARE	OH	• C	2q 2014	97.9	212.8	212.8	65.1	3.17	2.64
▲ PARAMOUNT INS CO	OH	• B-	2q 2014	53.7	79.2	79.2	16.7	2.12	1.76
PARKLAND COMMUNITY HEALTH PLAN INC	TX	• B	2q 2014	188.4	518.6	518.6	125.6	3.09	2.58
PARTNERRE AMERICA INS CO	DE	• C	2q 2014	270.4	1.3	0.4	132.3	14.93	13.43
PARTNERSHIP HEALTHPLAN OF CALIFORNIA	CA	• A-	2q 2014	502.0	928.9	928.9	286.3	7.26	4.45
PASSPORT HEALTH PLAN (See UNIVERSITY HEALTH CARE INC)									
PATRIOT INS CO	ME	C	2q 2014	101.1	49.1	0.0	28.5	2.63	1.94
PAUL REVERE LIFE INS CO	MA	• C+	2q 2014	4,273.4	315.5	303.1	360.8	1.89	1.20
PAVONIA LIFE INS CO OF MICHIGAN	MI	C	2q 2014	397.2	95.1	19.4	73.1	1.73	1.27
PAVONIA LIFE INS CO OF NEW YORK	NY	D	2q 2014	35.0	7.1	0.4	14.0	2.71	2.44
PCC SELECT (See COMMUNITYCARE HMO INC)									
PEACH STATE HEALTH PLAN INC	GA	• C	2q 2014	213.4	799.0	799.0	93.8	2.33	1.94
PEARLE VISIONCARE INC	CA	U		--	--	--	--	--	--
PEKIN LIFE INS CO	IL	• B	2q 2014	1,304.1	235.9	88.0	125.4	2.30	1.40
PENN HIGHLANDS HEALTH PLAN	PA	U		--	--	--	--	--	--
PENN MUTUAL LIFE INS CO	PA	B	2q 2014	16,718.4	1,652.4	12.4	1,547.4	2.24	1.50
PENNSYLVANIA BLUE SHIELD (See HIGHMARK INC)									
PENNSYLVANIA LIFE INS CO	PA	• C	2q 2014	613.1	20.7	20.7	420.5	204.37	170.31
PEOPLES HEALTH INC	LA	• D	2q 2014	62.1	699.7	699.7	31.7	0.71	0.59
PERSONAL CARE PLAN (See BLUE CROSS BLUE SHIELD OF NC)									
PERSONAL CHOICE (See INDEPENDENCE BLUE CROSS)									
PHARMACY INS CORP OF AMERICA INC	PR	• C-	4q 2013	8.2	9.5	9.5	5.2	4.30	3.58
PHILADELPHIA AMERICAN LIFE INS CO	TX	• B-	2q 2014	210.8	121.0	106.6	30.2	1.33	0.86
PHOEBE HEALTH PARTNERS INC	GA	U		--	--	--	--	--	--
▼ PHOENIX HEALTH PLANS INC	AZ	• D+	2q 2014	30.7	68.7	68.7	7.5	0.70	0.58
PHOENIX LIFE INS CO	NY	C	2q 2014	13,456.8	518.6	1.7	592.9	1.14	0.70
PHOENIX PREFERRED PPO	CT	U		--	--	--	--	--	--
PHP FAMILYCARE	MI	• C+	2q 2014	19.7	54.3	54.3	8.2	1.30	1.08
PHP INS CO	MI	• C	2q 2014	16.5	41.2	41.2	7.6	1.42	1.19
PHP INS CO OF INDIANA INC	IN	• C+	4q 2013	2.5	0.8	0.8	2.4	14.18	11.82
PHYSICIANS BENEFITS TRUST LIFE INS	IL	B-	2q 2014	14.4	24.9	24.9	9.2	2.37	1.91
PHYSICIANS CARE NETWORK	SC	U		--	--	--	--	--	--
PHYSICIANS GROUP INC	GA	U		--	--	--	--	--	--
PHYSICIANS HEALTH CHOICE (See PHYSICIANS HEALTH CHOICE OF TEXAS)									
PHYSICIANS HEALTH CHOICE OF TEXAS	TX	• B-	2q 2014	88.3	404.1	404.1	52.1	2.78	2.31
PHYSICIANS HEALTH PLAN OF NO IN	IN	• B	2q 2014	90.1	167.1	167.1	50.5	2.52	2.10
PHYSICIANS HP OF MID-MICHIGAN	MI	• B	2q 2014	85.7	195.3	195.3	58.4	1.92	1.60

www.weissratings.com

Arrows denote recent upgrades ▲ or downgrades▼

• Bullets denote a more detailed analysis is available in Section II.

INSURANCE COMPANY NAME	DOM. STATE	RATING	DATA DATE	TOTAL ASSETS ($MIL)	TOTAL PREMIUMS ($MIL)	HEALTH PREMIUMS ($MIL)	CAPITAL & SURPLUS ($MIL)	RISK ADJUSTED CAPITAL RATIO 1	RATIO 2
PHYSICIANS LIFE INS CO	NE	• A-	2q 2014	1,406.1	332.6	84.9	123.4	2.89	1.41
PHYSICIANS MUTUAL INS CO	NE	• A+	2q 2014	1,968.0	295.4	295.4	953.3	4.26	3.22
PHYSICIANS PLUS INS CORP	WI	• D	2q 2014	81.7	352.4	352.4	32.1	0.51	0.43
PHYSICIANS UNITED PLAN INC	FL	F	1q 2014	110.7	375.0	375.0	14.5	0.20	0.17
PHYSICIANSPLUS BAPTIST & ST DOMINIC	MS	U	--	--	--	--	--	--	--
PIEDMONT COMMUNITY HEALTHCARE	VA	• B	2q 2014	14.3	57.8	57.8	7.7	0.96	0.80
PIEDMONT WELLSTAR HEALTHPLANS INC	GA	U		--	--	--	--	--	--
PIONEER EDUCATORS HEALTH TRUST	OR	U		--	--	--	--	--	--
PIONEER HEALTH	MA	U		--	--	--	--	--	--
PIONEER MUTUAL LIFE INS CO	ND	B+	2q 2014	507.2	31.5	0.0	41.9	2.86	1.52
PL MEDICO SERV DE SALUD BELLA VISTA	PR	U		--	--	--	--	--	--
PLAN DE SALUD HOSP DE LA CONCEPCION	PR	U		--	--	--	--	--	--
PLATEAU INS CO	TN	B-	2q 2014	29.3	32.2	17.0	12.1	2.51	1.95
PLATTE RIVER INS CO	NE	C	2q 2014	128.0	42.3	0.0	40.9	3.07	1.78
PMC MEDICARE CHOICE INC	PR	• B-	2q 2014	84.9	402.7	402.7	31.9	0.93	0.78
POMCO PLUS	NY	U		--	--	--	--	--	--
POS NEW MEXICO (See HEALTH CARE SVC CORP A MUT LEG RES)									
PPO NEBRASKA (See BLUE CROSS BLUE SHIELD OF NEBRASKA)									
PPO NEW MEXICO (See HEALTH CARE SVC CORP A MUT LEG RES)									
PPO OKLAHOMA	OK	U		--	--	--	--	--	--
PPOM	MI	U		--	--	--	--	--	--
PPONEXT - CALIFORNIA	CA	U		--	--	--	--	--	--
PRE-PAID DENTAL SERVICES INC	OK	U		--	--	--	--	--	--
PREFER ONE (See SEECHANGE HEALTH INS CO INC)									
PREFERRED BLUE (See BLUE CROSS BLUE SHIELD OF SC INC)									
PREFERRED BLUE (See HIGHMARK INC)									
PREFERRED BLUE (See BLUE CROSS OF IDAHO HEALTH SERVICE)									
PREFERRED CARE (See BLUE CROSS BLUE SHIELD OF NC)									
PREFERRED CARE BLUE (See BLUE CROSS BLUE SHIELD OF KC)									
PREFERRED CARE INC	PA	U		--	--	--	--	--	--
PREFERRED CARE PARTNERS INC	FL	• E-	2q 2014	108.8	566.5	566.5	26.5	0.76	0.63
PREFERRED CARE SELECT (See BLUE CROSS BLUE SHIELD OF NC)									
PREFERRED COMMUNITYCHOICE PPO INC	OK	U		--	--	--	--	--	--
PREFERRED HEALTH CARE	PA	U		--	--	--	--	--	--
PREFERRED HEALTH PLAN INC	KY	U		--	--	--	--	--	--
PREFERRED HEALTH PROFESSIONALS	KS	U		--	--	--	--	--	--
PREFERRED HEALTHCARE SYSTEM INC	PA	U		--	--	--	--	--	--
PREFERRED INS SERVICES INC	IL	U		--	--	--	--	--	--
PREFERRED MEDICAL PLAN (PMP) (See ANTHEM INS COMPANIES INC)									
PREFERRED MEDICAL PLAN INC	FL	• D+	2q 2014	136.4	108.5	108.5	19.5	2.19	1.83
PREFERRED PATIENT CARE (See BLUE CROSS & BLUE SHIELD OF FLORIDA)									
PREFERRED PLAN	GA	U		--	--	--	--	--	--
PREFERRED PLAN (See REGENCE BLUESHIELD)									
PREFERRED PLAN INC	IL	U		--	--	--	--	--	--
PREFERRED-BLUE (See ANTHEM HEALTH PLANS OF NEW HAMPSHIRE)									
PREFERREDONE COMMUNITY HEALTH PLAN	MN	• D	2q 2014	16.6	59.6	59.6	8.1	1.07	0.89
PREFERREDONE INS CO	MN	• B	2q 2014	107.0	165.7	165.7	36.6	1.66	1.38
PREFERREDONE PREFERRED PROVIDER ORG	MN	U		--	--	--	--	--	--
PREMERA BLUE CROSS	WA	• A-	2q 2014	2,178.3	2,556.1	2,556.1	1,367.6	6.49	5.41
PREMIER BEHAVIORAL SYSTEMS OF TN LLC	TN	U		--	--	--	--	--	--
PREMIER BLUE (See BLUE CROSS BLUE SHIELD OF KANSAS INC)									
PREMIER HEALTH PLAN SERVICES INC	CA	• C-	2q 2014	17.4	17.9	17.9	5.2	6.89	4.58

www.weissratings.com

51

Arrows denote recent upgrades ▲ or downgrades▼   • Bullets denote a more detailed analysis is available in Section II.

INSURANCE COMPANY NAME	DOM. STATE	RATING	DATA DATE	TOTAL ASSETS ($MIL)	TOTAL PREMIUMS ($MIL)	HEALTH PREMIUMS ($MIL)	CAPITAL & SURPLUS ($MIL)	RISK ADJUSTED CAPITAL RATIO 1	RATIO 2
PREMIER HEALTH SYSTEMS	SC	U		--	--	--	--	--	--
PREMIUM PREFERRED NETWORK (See ANTHEM INS COMPANIES INC)									
PRESBYTERIAN HEALTH PLAN INC	NM	• B+	2q 2014	415.3	1,142.5	1,142.5	198.1	2.88	2.40
PRESBYTERIAN INS CO INC	NM	• B	2q 2014	63.8	150.8	150.8	32.7	2.47	2.06
PRESIDENTIAL LIFE INS CO	TX	C	2q 2014	4.5	1.5	1.4	3.1	2.43	1.93
PRIMARY HEALTH SERVICES INC	OH	U		--	--	--	--	--	--
PRIMECARE MEDICAL NETWORK INC	CA	• C	2q 2014	167.1	620.8	620.8	53.7	1.49	0.93
PRIMERICA LIFE INS CO	MA	B	2q 2014	1,481.0	1,873.1	0.6	542.5	1.49	1.22
PRINCIPAL LIFE INS CO	IA	B+	2q 2014	150,015.7	5,467.7	1,296.7	4,045.6	2.04	1.07
PRIORITY HEALTH	MI	• B	2q 2014	670.3	1,878.2	1,878.2	431.9	2.47	2.06
PRIORITY HEALTH CHOICE INC	MI	• B+	2q 2014	76.2	231.5	231.5	28.0	1.90	1.58
PRIORITY HEALTH INS CO	MI	• C	2q 2014	107.2	197.3	197.3	44.9	2.88	2.40
PRISM HEALTH NETWORKS OF NEW JERSEY	NJ	U		--	--	--	--	--	--
PRIVATE HEALTHCARE SYSTEMS	MA	U		--	--	--	--	--	--
PROFESSIONAL INS CO	TX	• C-	2q 2014	106.1	37.1	35.2	33.0	3.68	2.55
PROMINENCE HEALTHFIRST	NV	• D+	2q 2014	37.6	83.7	83.7	11.3	0.62	0.52
PROMINENCE PREFERRED HEALTH INS CO	NV	• D	2q 2014	27.8	69.2	69.2	6.1	0.74	0.62
PRONET	TX	U		--	--	--	--	--	--
PROTECTIVE INS CO	IN	A-	2q 2014	770.4	316.5	7.9	396.2	1.47	1.06
PROTECTIVE LIFE & ANNUITY INS CO	AL	B	2q 2014	2,138.6	170.4	0.4	168.0	2.43	1.25
PROTECTIVE LIFE INS CO	TN	B	2q 2014	41,733.1	4,160.7	34.8	3,246.6	1.39	1.03
PROVIDENCE HEALTH ASR	OR	U		--	--	--	--	--	--
PROVIDENCE HEALTH NETWORK	CA	U	2q 2014	3.9	0.0	0.0	1.6	--	--
PROVIDENCE HEALTH PLAN	OR	• A+	2q 2014	738.7	1,076.2	1,076.2	522.3	6.06	5.05
PROVIDENT AMER LIFE & HEALTH INS CO	OH	B-	2q 2014	15.8	17.5	16.7	13.6	1.86	1.60
▲ PROVIDENT AMERICAN INS CO	TX	D+	2q 2014	20.6	1.4	0.9	10.0	0.60	0.53
PROVIDENT LIFE & ACCIDENT INS CO	TN	• C+	2q 2014	8,355.4	1,157.6	826.0	700.5	2.60	1.31
PROVIDENT LIFE & CAS INS CO	TN	• B-	2q 2014	765.1	84.3	81.3	154.5	4.69	2.50
PRUDENT BUYER PLAN (See PREMERA BLUE CROSS)									
PRUDENTIAL INS CO OF AMERICA	NJ	B	2q 2014	303,214.1	17,384.6	1,433.5	11,187.9	1.47	1.00
PUBLIC HEALTH TRUST OF DADE COUNTY	FL	U		--	--	--	--	--	--
PUBLIC SERVICE INS CO	IL	D+	2q 2014	530.1	144.2	0.0	135.3	1.84	1.17
PUPIL BENEFITS PLAN INC	NY	• C-	2q 2014	7.0	8.3	8.3	2.6	1.71	1.43
PURITAN LIFE INS CO OF AMERICA	TX	D+	2q 2014	38.4	23.6	16.1	5.0	0.99	0.81
PYRAMID LIFE INS CO	KS	• C	2q 2014	196.1	434.1	428.0	105.6	1.73	1.37
QBE INS CORP	PA	C	2q 2014	2,166.9	1,281.0	160.7	688.5	1.89	1.43
QBE SPECIALTY INS CO	ND	D	2q 2014	806.3	777.0	0.0	215.2	1.99	1.34
QCA HEALTH PLAN INC	AR	• C-	2q 2014	47.9	141.3	141.3	19.7	1.21	1.01
QCC INS CO	PA	• B	2q 2014	1,334.2	2,002.2	2,002.2	690.4	4.68	3.90
QUALCHOICE LIFE & HEALTH INS CO	AR	• C	2q 2014	3.1	6.1	6.1	2.2	1.15	0.95
QUALITY HEALTH PLANS OF NEW YORK INC	NY	• E	2q 2014	1.7	1.2	1.2	0.7	1.10	0.92
QUALITY HEALTHCARE PARTNERSHIP	GA	U		--	--	--	--	--	--
QUINCY HEALTH CARE MANAGEMENT INC	IL	U		--	--	--	--	--	--
▼ RED ROCK INS CO	OK	F	1q 2014	57.1	0.6	0.2	16.8	1.71	0.81
REGAL LIFE OF AMERICA INS CO	TX	D-	2q 2014	10.7	1.7	1.2	6.8	1.00	0.98
REGENCE BL CROSS BL SHIELD OREGON	OR	• B+	2q 2014	1,047.9	1,891.2	1,891.2	636.5	5.95	4.96
REGENCE BLUE CROSS BLUE SHIELD OF UT	UT	• B	2q 2014	550.8	1,086.4	1,086.4	273.5	5.18	4.32
▼ REGENCE BLUESHIELD	WA	• B	2q 2014	1,684.2	2,190.6	2,190.6	1,106.2	6.78	5.65
REGENCE BLUESHIELD OF IDAHO INC	ID	• B	2q 2014	275.4	479.6	479.6	149.9	6.00	5.00
REGENCE CHOICE (See REGENCE BLUESHIELD OF IDAHO INC)									
REGENCE HEALTH MAINTENANCE OF OREGON	OR	U		--	--	--	--	--	--
REGENCE HMO OREGON	OR	U		--	--	--	--	--	--

Arrows denote recent upgrades ▲ or downgrades▼

• Bullets denote a more detailed analysis is available in Section II.

INSURANCE COMPANY NAME	DOM. STATE	RATING	DATA DATE	TOTAL ASSETS ($MIL)	TOTAL PREMIUMS ($MIL)	HEALTH PREMIUMS ($MIL)	CAPITAL & SURPLUS ($MIL)	RISK ADJUSTED CAPITAL RATIO 1	RATIO 2
REGION 6 RX CORP	PA	U		--	--	--	--	--	--
RELIABLE LIFE INS CO	MO	B-	2q 2014	23.8	109.3	7.5	13.5	2.56	1.28
RELIANCE STANDARD LIFE INS CO	IL	● B	2q 2014	7,240.6	1,909.4	740.6	671.9	1.69	0.96
RELIANCE STANDARD LIFE INS CO OF TX	TX	U	4q 2013	746.4	0.0	0.0	687.0	--	--
RELIASTAR LIFE INS CO	MN	C+	2q 2014	21,248.9	2,773.8	639.6	1,849.9	2.18	1.31
RELIASTAR LIFE INS CO OF NEW YORK	NY	B	2q 2014	3,203.8	275.9	37.2	346.9	4.02	2.13
RESERVE NATIONAL INS CO	OK	● A	2q 2014	112.3	144.2	132.1	51.6	2.38	1.83
RESOURCE LIFE INS CO	IL	C+	2q 2014	16.5	0.0	0.0	10.5	3.31	2.98
RETAILERS MUTUAL INS CO	MI	D-	2q 2014	20.1	5.8	0.6	9.4	1.86	0.83
RGA REINSURANCE CO	MO	● B	2q 2014	23,561.5	12.6	3.4	1,506.8	1.67	0.88
RIVERSIDE CTY FOUNDATION MED CARE	CA	U		--	--	--	--	--	--
RIVERSOURCE LIFE INS CO	MN	C-	2q 2014	105,461.7	6,478.8	362.1	3,029.7	1.79	1.07
RIVERSOURCE LIFE INS CO OF NY	NY	C	2q 2014	6,517.8	443.7	19.2	271.9	2.88	1.45
ROBERT T DORRIS & ASSOC INC	CA	U		--	--	--	--	--	--
ROCKY MOUNTAIN HEALTH MAINT ORG	CO	● A-	2q 2014	147.0	159.4	159.4	80.8	5.05	4.20
ROCKY MOUNTAIN HEALTHCARE OPTIONS	CO	● E	2q 2014	42.2	170.4	170.4	16.6	0.53	0.44
ROCKY MOUNTAIN HOSPITAL & MEDICAL	CO	● B+	2q 2014	889.3	1,921.6	1,921.6	449.7	3.83	3.19
ROYAL STATE NATIONAL INS CO LTD	HI	● B-	2q 2014	46.2	10.8	2.9	29.3	3.12	2.20
RURAL MUTUAL INS CO	WI	C+	2q 2014	381.6	165.5	0.6	182.3	5.61	3.90
RYDER HEALTH PLAN INC	PR	● D	2q 2014	1.4	2.6	2.6	0.6	0.48	0.40
S BAY IND PHYSICIANS MED GROUP INC	CA	U		--	--	--	--	--	--
S USA LIFE INS CO INC	AZ	C	2q 2014	13.5	1.8	0.0	8.0	2.85	2.57
SAFEGUARD HEALTH PLANS INC	CA	U		--	--	--	--	--	--
SAFEGUARD HEALTH PLANS INC	TX	U		--	--	--	--	--	--
SAFEGUARD HEALTH PLANS INC A FL CORP	FL	U		--	--	--	--	--	--
SAFEHEALTH LIFE INS CO	CA	U		--	--	--	--	--	--
SAGICOR LIFE INS CO	TX	C-	2q 2014	1,193.6	362.4	0.2	77.1	1.48	0.78
SAMARITAN ADVANTAGE HEALTH PLAN (See SAMARITAN HEALTH PLANS INC)									
SAMARITAN HEALTH PLANS INC	OR	● B-	2q 2014	17.5	55.4	55.4	7.5	0.90	0.75
SAN FRANCISCO COMMUNITY HEALTH AUTHORITY (See SAN FRANCISCO HEALTH AUTHORITY)									
SAN FRANCISCO HEALTH AUTHORITY	CA	● C+	2q 2014	174.9	250.1	250.1	40.4	1.66	1.08
SAN FRANCISCO HEALTH PLAN (See SAN FRANCISCO HEALTH AUTHORITY)									
SAN LUIS VALLEY HMO (See COLORADO CHOICE HEALTH PLANS)									
SAN MATEO HEALTH COMMISSION	CA	● B+	2q 2014	298.4	503.9	503.9	158.7	5.56	3.40
SANFORD HEALTH PLAN	SD	● B	2q 2014	62.7	143.3	143.3	28.7	1.73	1.45
SANFORD HEALTH PLAN OF MINNESOTA	MN	● E	2q 2014	1.8	3.0	3.0	1.1	1.22	1.02
SANFORD HEART OF AMERICA HEALTH PLAN	ND	● D+	2q 2014	2.1	3.8	3.8	1.1	0.75	0.63
SANTA BARBARA SAN LUIS OBISPO REGION	CA	● E+	2q 2014	109.7	343.9	343.9	39.7	0.29	0.18
SANTA CLARA COUNTY HEALTH AUTHORITY	CA	● C-	2q 2014	69.7	384.2	384.2	32.9	1.41	0.86
SANTA CLARA FAMILY HEALTH PLAN (See SANTA CLARA COUNTY HEALTH AUTHORITY)									
SANTA CLARA VALLEY	CA	● C	2q 2014	42.8	212.1	212.1	20.8	1.44	0.88
SANTA CRUZ-MONTEREY-MERCED MGD MED	CA	● B-	2q 2014	492.8	684.4	684.4	346.6	11.16	6.88
SATELLITE HEALTH PLAN INC	CA	U		--	--	--	--	--	--
SAVINGS BANK LIFE INS CO OF MA	MA	B+	2q 2014	2,531.7	342.0	0.0	195.3	2.70	1.49
SBLI USA MUT LIFE INS CO INC	NY	B-	2q 2014	1,476.9	71.3	0.6	92.2	1.52	0.84
SCAN HEALTH PLAN	CA	● C	2q 2014	668.0	1,862.2	1,862.2	461.0	5.01	3.11
SCAN HEALTH PLAN ARIZONA	AZ	● E	2q 2014	31.5	116.8	116.8	20.8	1.43	1.19
SCOTT & WHITE HEALTH PLAN	TX	● B	2q 2014	174.6	589.6	589.6	72.7	1.79	1.49
SCRIPPS CLINIC HEALTH PLAN SERVICES	CA	● D	2q 2014	77.5	249.8	249.8	14.9	0.76	0.46
SD STATE MEDICAL HOLDING CO	SD	● B	2q 2014	39.9	113.9	113.9	19.1	1.37	1.14
SEABRIGHT INS CO	IL	D+	2q 2014	521.1	44.8	0.1	106.6	1.55	0.93
SEARS LIFE INS CO	TX	B	2q 2014	50.8	31.6	19.4	23.2	3.52	3.17

www.weissratings.com

Arrows denote recent upgrades ▲ or downgrades▼

53

● Bullets denote a more detailed analysis is available in Section II.

INSURANCE COMPANY NAME	DOM. STATE	RATING	DATA DATE	TOTAL ASSETS ($MIL)	TOTAL PREMIUMS ($MIL)	HEALTH PREMIUMS ($MIL)	CAPITAL & SURPLUS ($MIL)	RISK ADJUSTED CAPITAL RATIO 1	RATIO 2
SEASIDE HEALTH PLAN	CA	U	2q 2014	7.6	0.0	0.0	5.2	--	--
SECURE BLUE PREFERRED (See HEALTHNOW NY INC)									
SECURE HEALTH PLANS OF GEORGIA	GA	U		--	--	--	--	--	--
SECURIAN LIFE INS CO	MN	• B	2q 2014	225.6	82.6	34.1	133.6	6.50	4.56
SECURITY HEALTH PLAN OF WI INC	WI	• A-	2q 2014	322.0	1,001.8	1,001.8	163.9	1.85	1.54
SECURITY LIFE INS CO OF AMERICA	MN	B	2q 2014	73.5	81.1	72.6	19.3	1.19	0.89
SECURITY LIFE OF DENVER INS CO	CO	C+	2q 2014	14,544.0	682.1	0.2	1,110.0	1.82	1.03
SECURITY MUTUAL LIFE INS CO OF NY	NY	B	2q 2014	2,682.9	347.1	12.6	130.6	1.48	0.80
SECURITY NATIONAL LIFE INS CO	UT	D-	2q 2014	495.0	56.0	0.1	30.2	0.46	0.32
SECURITY PLAN LIFE INS CO	LA	C+	2q 2014	326.1	41.1	0.6	53.8	2.77	1.73
SECURITYCARE OF TENNESSEE INC	TN	U		--	--	--	--	--	--
SEECHANGE HEALTH INS CO INC	CA	• D	2q 2014	33.2	116.3	116.3	9.1	0.55	0.45
SELECT BLUE (See HIGHMARK INC)									
SELECT CARE OF MAINE INC	ME	U		--	--	--	--	--	--
SELECT HEALTH OF SOUTH CAROLINA INC	SC	• B	2q 2014	236.2	848.7	848.7	88.8	1.72	1.44
SELECT MED (See SELECTHEALTH INC)									
SELECT MED PLUS (See SELECTHEALTH INC)									
SELECT PROVIDERS INC	NY	U		--	--	--	--	--	--
SELECTCARE (See MEDICA HEALTH PLANS)									
SELECTCARE ACCESS CORP	PA	U		--	--	--	--	--	--
SELECTCARE HEALTH PLANS INC	TX	• C	2q 2014	22.2	56.0	56.0	14.8	2.75	2.29
SELECTCARE OF OKLAHOMA INC	OK	• B-	2q 2014	2.9	3.2	3.2	1.9	2.68	2.23
SELECTCARE OF TEXAS LLC	TX	• C-	2q 2014	153.2	652.0	652.0	64.7	1.82	1.52
SELECTCHOICE (See NORIDIAN MUTUAL INS CO)									
SELECTHEALTH BENEFIT ASR CO INC	UT	• B	2q 2014	21.3	7.3	7.3	12.4	6.45	5.38
SELECTHEALTH INC	UT	• A	2q 2014	849.6	1,458.0	1,458.0	493.7	4.06	3.38
SELECTIONS (See REGENCE BLUESHIELD)									
SELECTIVE INS CO OF AMERICA	NJ	B-	2q 2014	2,003.3	427.9	0.1	484.1	2.43	1.56
SELECTNET PLUS	WV	U		--	--	--	--	--	--
SENDERO HEALTH PLANS INC	TX	U		--	--	--	--	--	--
SENIOR AMERICAN INS CO	PA	E-	2q 2014	18.3	2.9	2.9	0.0	0.00	0.00
SENIOR BLUE (See HEALTHNOW NY INC)									
SENIOR HEALTH INS CO OF PENNSYLVANIA	PA	• D+	2q 2014	2,932.4	162.1	162.1	88.6	1.21	0.60
SENIOR LIFE INS CO	GA	C-	2q 2014	45.8	29.8	0.0	11.7	2.06	1.00
SENIOR SMART CHOICE (See INDIANA UNIVERSITY HEALTH PLANS INC)									
SENIOR WHOLE HEALTH OF NEW YORK INC	NY	• E	2q 2014	19.5	17.8	17.8	5.6	1.33	1.11
SENIORDENT DENTAL PLAN INC	WI	U		--	--	--	--	--	--
SENSICARE (See COVENTRY HEALTH CARE OF MISSOURI INC)									
SENSICARE PLUS (See COVENTRY HEALTH CARE OF MISSOURI INC)									
SENTINEL SECURITY LIFE INS CO	UT	D	2q 2014	422.0	169.2	51.8	22.3	1.23	0.59
SENTRY INS A MUTUAL CO	WI	A	2q 2014	6,832.1	469.4	2.8	4,224.1	2.39	2.04
SENTRY LIFE INS CO	WI	A	2q 2014	5,167.7	515.7	6.8	284.6	3.91	2.25
SENTRY LIFE INS CO OF NEW YORK	NY	B+	2q 2014	77.0	6.0	0.1	10.6	1.38	1.24
SENTRY SELECT INS CO	WI	B+	2q 2014	672.6	398.7	2.8	236.4	4.17	2.79
SERVCO LIFE INS CO	TX	C+	2q 2014	8.9	-0.1	0.0	5.6	2.56	2.31
SERVICE LIFE & CAS INS CO	TX	C	2q 2014	41.9	-0.3	0.0	31.9	4.54	1.92
SETON HEALTH PLAN INC	TX	• B-	2q 2014	34.0	54.0	54.0	24.1	2.28	1.90
SETTLERS LIFE INS CO	WI	B	2q 2014	392.4	44.7	0.4	54.7	3.55	1.91
SHA LLC	TX	• E	2q 2014	105.3	478.0	478.0	31.4	0.58	0.48
SHARED HEALTH NETWORK	NY	U		--	--	--	--	--	--
SHARP HEALTH PLAN	CA	• B	2q 2014	77.6	320.4	320.4	51.1	1.52	0.99
SHELTER LIFE INS CO	MO	A-	2q 2014	1,097.7	127.1	7.2	187.6	3.71	2.44

www.weissratings.com

Arrows denote recent upgrades ▲ or downgrades▼

• Bullets denote a more detailed analysis is available in Section II.

INSURANCE COMPANY NAME	DOM. STATE	RATING	DATA DATE	TOTAL ASSETS ($MIL)	TOTAL PREMIUMS ($MIL)	HEALTH PREMIUMS ($MIL)	CAPITAL & SURPLUS ($MIL)	RISK ADJUSTED CAPITAL RATIO 1	RATIO 2
SHELTERPOINT INS CO	FL	U	4q 2013	7.9	0.0	0.0	7.8	--	--
SHELTERPOINT LIFE INS CO	NY	● A	2q 2014	103.8	82.8	81.4	50.1	3.00	2.18
SHENANDOAH LIFE INS CO	VA	C	2q 2014	1,238.6	76.7	9.6	78.0	1.68	0.89
SHERIDAN LIFE INS CO	OK	C	2q 2014	2.2	0.0	0.0	2.0	2.54	2.29
SIDNEY HILLMAN HEALTH CENTRE	IL	U		--	--	--	--	--	--
SIERRA HEALTH AND LIFE INS CO INC	NV	● C+	2q 2014	155.4	257.1	257.1	77.8	6.16	5.13
SIERRA HEALTHCARE OPTIONS INC	NV	U		--	--	--	--	--	--
SILVERSCRIPT INS CO	TN	● D	2q 2014	2,788.6	2,994.3	2,994.3	270.3	2.04	1.70
SIMNSA HEALTH CARE (See SISTEMAS MEDICOS NACIONALES SA DE CV)									
SIMPLY HEALTHCARE PLANS INC	FL	U		--	--	--	--	--	--
SIRIUS AMERICA INS CO	NY	● C+	2q 2014	1,556.0	30.0	21.4	597.4	2.37	1.35
SISTEMAS MEDICOS NACIONALES SA DE CV	CA	● C+	2q 2014	21.7	52.8	52.8	11.2	2.17	1.44
SMART INS CO	AZ	U		--	--	--	--	--	--
SOLSTICE BENEFITS INC	FL	● D	1q 2014	5.3	25.7	25.7	2.2	0.65	0.54
SOLSTICE HEALTH INS CO	NY	U	4q 2013	0.5	0.2	0.2	0.5	--	--
SOUNDPATH HEALTH	WA	● C	2q 2014	33.7	150.0	150.0	16.3	1.39	1.15
SOUTH CAROLINA FARM BU MUTUAL INS CO	SC	C	2q 2014	113.0	193.5	0.1	49.6	2.22	1.87
SOUTH CENTRAL PREFERRED	PA	U		--	--	--	--	--	--
SOUTHEASTERN INDIANA HEALTH OPER INC	IN	U		--	--	--	--	--	--
SOUTHEASTERN INDIANA HEALTH ORG INC	IN	● B	2q 2014	17.6	50.1	50.1	9.6	1.63	1.35
SOUTHERN FARM BUREAU LIFE INS CO	MS	A	2q 2014	12,921.4	842.0	53.0	2,434.1	4.41	2.40
SOUTHERN FINANCIAL LIFE INS CO	KY	C	2q 2014	4.0	10.3	4.2	3.4	2.77	2.49
SOUTHERN NATL LIFE INS CO INC	LA	C	2q 2014	14.7	16.3	8.8	10.5	1.62	1.30
SOUTHERN PIONEER LIFE INS CO	AR	B	2q 2014	19.2	1.9	0.6	12.2	3.43	3.09
SOUTHLAND NATIONAL INS CORP	AL	C	2q 2014	161.4	8.1	2.8	9.3	0.94	0.82
SOUTHWEST LIFE & HEALTH INS CO	TX	● C	2q 2014	9.9	21.7	21.7	6.3	1.80	1.50
SOUTHWEST MEDICAL PROVIDER NETWORK	TX	U		--	--	--	--	--	--
SOUTHWEST SERVICE LIFE INS CO	TX	D	2q 2014	12.5	12.2	9.1	5.8	1.02	0.91
SPARKS PREMIERCARE LLC	AR	U		--	--	--	--	--	--
ST PAUL FIRE & MARINE INS CO	CT	B	2q 2014	18,609.4	959.3	0.0	5,935.7	1.54	1.26
STANDARD GUARANTY INS CO	DE	B-	2q 2014	404.4	596.8	0.3	154.5	4.96	2.84
STANDARD INS CO	OR	● B+	2q 2014	19,996.4	3,755.8	1,272.0	1,287.9	2.23	1.24
STANDARD LIFE & ACCIDENT INS CO	TX	● A-	2q 2014	525.1	146.6	131.9	250.0	5.02	3.08
STANDARD LIFE & CAS INS CO	UT	D+	2q 2014	30.2	8.6	4.1	5.8	1.33	1.20
STANDARD LIFE INS CO OF NY	NY	● A-	2q 2014	269.3	99.2	56.0	71.0	3.27	2.17
STANDARD SECURITY LIFE INS CO OF NY	NY	● B	2q 2014	249.3	277.6	276.0	112.7	3.25	2.62
STARMOUNT LIFE INS CO	LA	B	2q 2014	55.7	50.2	40.8	23.6	1.43	1.07
STARNET INS CO	DE	C	2q 2014	216.6	347.7	14.7	110.7	12.21	10.99
STARR INDEMNITY & LIABILITY CO	TX	B-	2q 2014	3,541.3	1,372.5	35.4	1,851.3	1.40	1.17
STARR SURPLUS LINES INS CO	IL	B-	2q 2014	280.0	304.9	0.0	96.4	3.09	1.85
STATE AUTOMOBILE MUTUAL INS CO	OH	C+	2q 2014	2,305.3	444.7	0.0	857.8	1.32	1.19
STATE FARM FIRE & CAS CO	IL	B-	2q 2014	32,504.9	17,971.1	1.4	11,079.3	1.95	1.21
STATE FARM MUTUAL AUTOMOBILE INS CO	IL	B+	2q 2014	135,478.4	32,236.2	1,047.3	79,844.0	2.25	1.89
STATE LIFE INS CO	IN	B	2q 2014	5,195.8	528.8	28.1	339.2	2.04	1.06
STATE MUTUAL INS CO	GA	● C	2q 2014	296.3	40.8	14.7	29.3	1.66	1.00
STEADFAST INS CO	DE	C	2q 2014	556.6	1,088.6	0.0	434.3	3.08	3.01
STERLING INVESTORS LIFE INS CO	GA	C-	2q 2014	15.2	37.3	27.9	6.4	1.93	1.46
STERLING LIFE INS CO	IL	● D	2q 2014	99.4	203.7	203.7	40.7	5.42	4.52
STONEBRIDGE LIFE INS CO	VT	● B-	2q 2014	1,753.9	478.2	287.6	159.8	2.03	1.11
SUMMA INS CO	OH	● D	2q 2014	64.3	219.6	219.6	26.2	0.61	0.51
SUMMACARE HEALTH PLAN PPO (See SUMMACARE INC)									
SUMMACARE INC	OH	● C-	2q 2014	81.9	277.6	277.6	34.8	1.46	1.22

www.weissratings.com

55

Arrows denote recent upgrades ▲ or downgrades▼

● Bullets denote a more detailed analysis is available in Section II.

INSURANCE COMPANY NAME	DOM. STATE	RATING	DATA DATE	TOTAL ASSETS ($MIL)	TOTAL PREMIUMS ($MIL)	HEALTH PREMIUMS ($MIL)	CAPITAL & SURPLUS ($MIL)	RISK ADJUSTED CAPITAL RATIO 1	RATIO 2
SUN LIFE & HEALTH INS CO	CT	• C-	2q 2014	366.3	145.9	86.7	187.4	5.25	3.48
SUN LIFE ASR CO OF CANADA	MI	• D	2q 2014	15,974.7	2,583.1	1,361.4	892.4	0.90	0.47
SUNFLOWER STATE HEALTH PLAN INC	KS	• D+	2q 2014	201.6	801.7	801.7	81.6	1.46	1.21
SUNSET LIFE INS CO OF AMERICA	MO	B-	2q 2014	361.6	26.2	0.0	35.6	2.89	1.47
SUNSHINE HEALTH	FL	• E	2q 2014	264.1	771.3	771.3	54.3	1.28	1.07
SUPER BLUE PLUS (See HIGHMARK WEST VIRGINIA INC)									
SUPER BLUE SELECT (See HIGHMARK WEST VIRGINIA INC)									
SUPERIEN HEALTH NETWORK INC	OH	U		--	--	--	--	--	--
SUPERIOR CALIFORNIA PPO	CA	U		--	--	--	--	--	--
SUPERIOR HEALTHPLAN INC	TX	• C	2q 2014	371.7	1,703.5	1,703.5	189.4	1.97	1.64
SUPERIOR VISION INS INC	AZ	U		--	--	--	--	--	--
SUPERMED PLUS (See MEDICAL MUTUAL OF OHIO)									
SUPERMED SELECT (See MEDICAL MUTUAL OF OHIO)									
SURENCY LIFE & HEALTH INS CO	KS	C	2q 2014	7.3	3.2	3.2	6.4	3.21	2.89
SURETY LIFE & CASUALTY INS CO	ND	C-	2q 2014	10.5	1.4	0.4	4.1	1.80	1.62
SURETY LIFE INS CO	NE	B+	2q 2014	14.3	40.6	0.1	12.5	2.13	1.07
SUSQUEHANNA HEALTH CARE INC	PA	U		--	--	--	--	--	--
SUTTER HEALTH PLAN	CA	U	2q 2014	41.8	0.0	0.0	30.7	--	--
SWBC LIFE INS CO	TX	B	2q 2014	22.9	1.5	0.9	16.2	3.79	2.37
SWISS RE LIFE & HEALTH AMER INC	CT	• C+	2q 2014	10,140.4	0.5	0.5	1,658.0	1.90	1.32
SYMETRA LIFE INS CO	WA	B+	2q 2014	28,322.5	3,068.7	592.9	1,944.7	2.22	1.20
TAKECARE INS CO INC	GU	U		--	--	--	--	--	--
TEACHERS INS & ANNUITY ASN OF AM	NY	A+	2q 2014	256,932.8	12,594.8	14.3	31,979.4	5.77	3.05
TEACHERS PROTV MUTUAL LIFE INS CO	PA	D	2q 2014	62.4	19.0	18.6	2.8	0.44	0.40
TEAM DENTAL INC	TX	U		--	--	--	--	--	--
TEXAS CHILDRENS HEALTH PLAN INC	TX	• B-	2q 2014	136.2	792.7	792.7	80.6	1.07	0.89
TEXAS FARM BUREAU MUTUAL INS CO	TX	D	2q 2014	664.9	403.3	0.7	268.7	2.54	2.28
TEXAS LIFE INS CO	TX	B	2q 2014	999.8	200.3	0.0	96.6	2.25	1.23
TEXAS TRUE CHOICE	TX	U		--	--	--	--	--	--
THERAMATRIX PHYSICAL THERAPY	MI	U		--	--	--	--	--	--
THP INS CO	WV	• D	2q 2014	25.1	53.2	53.2	7.4	0.86	0.72
THRIVENT LIFE INS CO	MN	B+	2q 2014	3,560.4	148.1	0.0	170.8	2.44	1.17
TIAA-CREF LIFE INS CO	NY	B	2q 2014	8,640.9	599.0	6.5	367.5	2.39	1.26
TIMBER PRODUCTS MANUFACTURERS TRUST	WA	• C+	2q 2014	13.0	35.3	35.3	7.4	1.28	1.06
TIME INS CO	WI	• B-	2q 2014	740.1	1,378.2	1,336.4	255.5	1.26	0.98
TODAYS OPTIONS OF OKLAHOMA INC	OK	• C	2q 2014	18.5	63.3	63.3	11.1	1.90	1.58
TODAYS OPTIONS OF PENNSYLVANIA INC	PA	U		--	--	--	--	--	--
TOKIO MARINE PACIFIC INS LTD	GU	• B-	2q 2014	107.1	126.8	112.4	65.0	3.75	2.11
TOTAL HEALTH 65 (See HUMANA HEALTH BENEFIT PLAN LA)									
TOTAL HEALTH CARE INC	MD	U		--	--	--	--	--	--
TOTAL HEALTH CARE INC	MI	• D+	2q 2014	50.7	224.0	224.0	23.3	0.73	0.61
TOTAL HEALTH CARE USA INC	MI	• C+	2q 2014	40.3	114.8	114.8	15.2	1.36	1.13
TOTAL HEALTH CHOICE (See HUMANA HEALTH BENEFIT PLAN LA)									
TOTAL HEALTH CHOICE-INDIVIDUAL (See HUMANA HEALTH BENEFIT PLAN LA)									
TOTAL HEALTH PLAN (See TUFTS ASSOCIATED HEALTH MAINT ORG)									
TOUCHSTONE HEALTH HMO INC	NY	• E	2q 2014	21.9	152.9	152.9	9.2	0.32	0.27
TOWER LIFE INS CO	TX	D+	2q 2014	55.5	0.8	0.0	29.3	4.36	2.54
TOWN & COUNTRY LIFE INS CO	UT	C-	2q 2014	5.9	3.3	3.3	3.4	2.10	1.89
TRANS CITY LIFE INS CO	AZ	C-	2q 2014	19.2	2.2	0.4	9.0	3.27	2.95
TRANS OCEANIC LIFE INS CO	PR	• A	2q 2014	61.6	30.1	27.6	30.7	2.71	1.81
TRANSAMERICA CASUALTY INS CO	OH	B-	2q 2014	319.1	291.8	0.6	118.5	2.48	1.60
TRANSAMERICA FINANCIAL LIFE INS CO	NY	B	2q 2014	30,565.9	5,262.1	97.7	1,029.5	2.93	1.43

www.weissratings.com

Arrows denote recent upgrades ▲ or downgrades▼

• Bullets denote a more detailed analysis is available in Section II.

INSURANCE COMPANY NAME	DOM. STATE	RATING	DATA DATE	TOTAL ASSETS ($MIL)	TOTAL PREMIUMS ($MIL)	HEALTH PREMIUMS ($MIL)	CAPITAL & SURPLUS ($MIL)	RISK ADJUSTED CAPITAL RATIO 1	RATIO 2
TRANSAMERICA LIFE INS CO	IA	B-	2q 2014	117,195.4	16,821.9	890.3	5,439.3	1.82	1.16
TRANSAMERICA PREMIER LIFE INS CO	IA	• C+	2q 2014	32,077.6	1,948.2	528.0	921.4	1.54	0.77
TRAVELERS PROPERTY CAS OF AMERICA	CT	B	2q 2014	846.9	4,561.6	1.2	495.8	16.17	10.12
TRH HEALTH INS CO	TN	• C+	2q 2014	86.0	175.9	175.9	56.7	2.96	2.46
TRIAD HEALTHCARE OF NJ IPA INC	NJ	U	--	--	--	--	--	--	--
TRILLIUM COMMUNITY HEALTH PLAN INC	OR	• C+	2q 2014	102.4	244.5	244.5	25.7	0.96	0.80
TRILOGY HEALTH INS INC	WI	U	--	--	--	--	--	--	--
TRINITY LIFE INS CO	OK	D-	2q 2014	121.8	28.2	0.0	8.1	0.49	0.37
TRINITY PHYSICIAN HOSPITAL ORG LTD	IL	U	--	--	--	--	--	--	--
TRIPLE S VIDA INC	PR	• B-	2q 2014	529.2	155.6	57.2	62.2	1.04	0.71
TRIPLE-S BLUE INC	PR	D-	2q 2014	17.9	11.5	8.7	4.5	1.56	1.14
TRIPLE-S SALUD INC	PR	• B+	2q 2014	713.6	1,455.1	1,455.1	398.9	3.11	2.59
TRITON INS CO	TX	• C+	2q 2014	548.8	97.0	28.6	238.2	11.16	6.11
TRUASSURE INS CO	IL	C-	2q 2014	5.8	2.8	0.1	5.5	3.02	2.72
TRUSTED HEALTH PLAN INC	DC	• C-	2q 2014	17.4	50.5	50.5	6.6	0.88	0.73
TRUSTMARK INS CO	IL	• B+	2q 2014	1,404.7	306.4	150.0	310.3	2.94	1.71
TRUSTMARK LIFE INS CO	IL	• B+	2q 2014	380.8	272.1	260.5	167.4	4.31	2.96
TUFTS ASSOCIATED HEALTH MAINT ORG	MA	• B	2q 2014	1,054.7	2,509.4	2,509.4	712.3	3.13	2.61
TUFTS BENEFIT ADMINISTRATORS (See TUFTS ASSOCIATED HEALTH MAINT ORG)									
TUFTS INS CO	MA	• D+	2q 2014	87.9	233.9	233.9	38.5	2.43	2.02
TULANE REGIONAL HEALTH NETWORK	LA	U	--	--	--	--	--	--	--
TVHP-NC	NC	U	--	--	--	--	--	--	--
U S HEALTH & LIFE INS CO INC	MI	• C-	2q 2014	28.0	67.8	67.8	7.8	1.45	1.21
UAHC HEALTH PLAN OF TENNESSEE	TN	U	--	--	--	--	--	--	--
UCARE HEALTH INC	WI	• D	2q 2014	19.9	59.0	59.0	7.5	0.66	0.55
UCARE MINNESOTA	MN	• A-	2q 2014	969.6	2,413.2	2,413.2	480.9	2.68	2.23
UDC DENTAL CALIFORNIA INC	CA	U	--	--	--	--	--	--	--
UHC OF CALIFORNIA INC	CA	• C+	2q 2014	971.2	6,487.2	6,487.2	322.5	1.31	0.81
ULTIMATE HEALTH PLAN INC	FL	• E	2q 2014	5.6	4.5	4.5	2.0	1.14	0.95
UNDERWRITERS AT LLOYDS	KY	D	2q 2014	198.9	62.2	12.3	33.4	0.41	0.26
UNICARE HEALTH PLAN OF KANSAS INC	KS	U	--	--	--	--	--	--	--
UNICARE HEALTH PLAN OF WEST VIRGINIA	WV	• B+	2q 2014	82.1	215.5	215.5	52.7	4.23	3.53
UNICARE HEALTH PLANS OF TEXAS INC	TX	U	--	--	--	--	--	--	--
UNICARE LIFE & HEALTH INS CO	IN	• B	2q 2014	402.8	347.3	182.7	76.5	1.85	1.37
UNIFIED LIFE INS CO	TX	B	2q 2014	177.8	29.3	22.9	22.9	2.35	1.32
UNIMERICA INS CO	WI	• B	2q 2014	444.3	280.6	268.6	213.6	3.20	2.54
UNIMERICA LIFE INS CO OF NY	NY	B	2q 2014	35.9	5.1	3.2	19.4	4.12	3.71
UNION FIDELITY LIFE INS CO	KS	• D+	2q 2014	19,518.2	42.2	23.0	536.2	1.05	0.54
UNION HEALTH SERVICE INC	IL	• B	2q 2014	23.6	63.9	63.9	14.9	1.30	1.08
UNION LABOR LIFE INS CO	MD	• B-	2q 2014	3,117.1	139.4	79.1	78.2	1.48	1.05
UNION MEDICAL CENTER	IL	U	--	--	--	--	--	--	--
UNION NATIONAL LIFE INS CO	LA	B	2q 2014	18.9	82.4	5.9	14.6	4.84	2.54
UNION PACIFIC RR EMPLOYEES HEALTH	UT	U	--	--	--	--	--	--	--
UNION SECURITY INS CO	KS	• B	2q 2014	5,018.5	1,014.2	738.5	419.4	1.83	1.19
UNION SECURITY LIFE INS CO OF NY	NY	• B+	2q 2014	142.5	32.4	26.4	40.6	4.41	3.97
UNITED AMERICAN INS CO	NE	• B	2q 2014	1,731.7	772.3	708.0	207.9	1.19	0.86
UNITED CONCORDIA DENTAL PLANS OF CA	CA	U	--	--	--	--	--	--	--
UNITED FARM FAMILY LIFE INS CO	IN	A	2q 2014	2,116.5	157.0	1.0	281.9	3.10	1.85
UNITED FIDELITY LIFE INS CO	TX	C	2q 2014	756.9	8.9	0.3	437.2	0.72	0.70
UNITED HEALTHCARE ALABAMA CHOICE (See UNITED HEALTHCARE OF ALABAMA INC)									
UNITED HEALTHCARE ALABAMA SELECT (See UNITED HEALTHCARE OF ALABAMA INC)									
UNITED HEALTHCARE ALBANY (See UNITED HEALTHCARE INS CO OF NY)									

Arrows denote recent upgrades ▲ or downgrades▼

• Bullets denote a more detailed analysis is available in Section II.

INSURANCE COMPANY NAME	DOM. STATE	RATING	DATA DATE	TOTAL ASSETS ($MIL)	TOTAL PREMIUMS ($MIL)	HEALTH PREMIUMS ($MIL)	CAPITAL & SURPLUS ($MIL)	RISK ADJUSTED CAPITAL RATIO 1	RATIO 2

UNITED HEALTHCARE ALBANY CHOICE (See UNITED HEALTHCARE OF NY INC)
UNITED HEALTHCARE ALBUQUERQUE (See UNITED HEALTHCARE INS CO)
UNITED HEALTHCARE ALEXANDRIA CHOICE (See UNITED HEALTHCARE OF LOUISIANA INC)
UNITED HEALTHCARE ALEXANDRIA SELECT (See UNITED HEALTHCARE OF LOUISIANA INC)

UNITED HEALTHCARE ARIZONA CHOICE (See UNITED HEALTHCARE OF ARIZONA INC)
UNITED HEALTHCARE ARKANSAS CHOICE (See UNITED HEALTHCARE OF ARKANSAS INC)
UNITED HEALTHCARE ARKANSAS SELECT (See UNITED HEALTHCARE OF ARKANSAS INC)
UNITED HEALTHCARE ASHEVILLE/WESTERN (See UNITED HEALTHCARE INS CO)

UNITED HEALTHCARE ATHENS (See UNITED HEALTHCARE INS CO)
UNITED HEALTHCARE ATHENS CHOICE (See UNITED HEALTHCARE OF GEORGIA INC)
UNITED HEALTHCARE ATHENS SELECT (See UNITED HEALTHCARE OF GEORGIA INC)
UNITED HEALTHCARE ATLANTA (See UNITED HEALTHCARE INS CO)

UNITED HEALTHCARE ATLANTA CHOICE (See UNITED HEALTHCARE OF GEORGIA INC)
UNITED HEALTHCARE ATLANTA SELECT (See UNITED HEALTHCARE OF GEORGIA INC)
UNITED HEALTHCARE AUGUSTA (See UNITED HEALTHCARE INS CO)
UNITED HEALTHCARE AUSTIN (See UNITED HEALTHCARE INS CO)

UNITED HEALTHCARE AUSTIN CHOICE (See UNITED HEALTHCARE OF TX INC)
UNITED HEALTHCARE AUSTIN SELECT (See UNITED HEALTHCARE OF TX INC)
UNITED HEALTHCARE BALTIMORE AREA (See UNITED HEALTHCARE INS CO)
UNITED HEALTHCARE BALTIMORE AREA CHOICE (See UNITED HEALTHCARE OF MID-ATLANTIC)

UNITED HEALTHCARE BALTIMORE AREA SELECT (See UNITED HEALTHCARE OF MID-ATLANTIC)
UNITED HEALTHCARE BATON ROUGE CHOICE (See UNITED HEALTHCARE OF LOUISIANA INC)
UNITED HEALTHCARE BATON ROUGE SELECT (See UNITED HEALTHCARE OF LOUISIANA INC)
UNITED HEALTHCARE BAYOU CHOICE (See UNITED HEALTHCARE OF LOUISIANA INC)

UNITED HEALTHCARE BAYOU SELECT (See UNITED HEALTHCARE OF LOUISIANA INC)
UNITED HEALTHCARE BEAUMONT (See UNITED HEALTHCARE INS CO)
UNITED HEALTHCARE BOSTON (See UNITED HEALTHCARE INS CO)
UNITED HEALTHCARE BUFFALO/ROCHESTER (See UNITED HEALTHCARE INS CO OF NY)

UNITED HEALTHCARE BUFFALO/ROCHESTER CHOICE (See UNITED HEALTHCARE OF NY INC)
UNITED HEALTHCARE CAMBRIA (See UNITED HEALTHCARE INS CO)
UNITED HEALTHCARE CENTRAL ALABAMA (See UNITED HEALTHCARE INS CO)
UNITED HEALTHCARE CENTRAL ALABAMA CHOICE (See UNITED HEALTHCARE OF ALABAMA INC)

UNITED HEALTHCARE CENTRAL ALABAMA SELECT (See UNITED HEALTHCARE OF ALABAMA INC)
UNITED HEALTHCARE CENTRAL COAST CALIFORNIA (See UNITED HEALTHCARE INS CO)
UNITED HEALTHCARE CENTRAL ILLINOIS (See UNITED HEALTHCARE INS CO)
UNITED HEALTHCARE CENTRAL INDIANA (See UNITED HEALTHCARE INS CO)

UNITED HEALTHCARE CENTRAL PENNSYLVANIA (See UNITED HEALTHCARE INS CO)
UNITED HEALTHCARE CHARLESTON (See UNITED HEALTHCARE INS CO)
UNITED HEALTHCARE CHARLOTTE (See UNITED HEALTHCARE INS CO)
UNITED HEALTHCARE CHATTANOOGA (See UNITED HEALTHCARE INS CO)

UNITED HEALTHCARE CHICAGO (See UNITED HEALTHCARE INS CO)
UNITED HEALTHCARE CHICAGO CHOICE (See UNITED HEALTHCARE OF ILLINOIS INC)
UNITED HEALTHCARE CHICAGO SELECT (See UNITED HEALTHCARE OF ILLINOIS INC)
UNITED HEALTHCARE CINCINNATI (See UNITED HEALTHCARE INS CO)

UNITED HEALTHCARE CINCINNATI, OH & PARTS OF NORTHERN KY CHOICE (See UNITED HEALTHCARE OF OHIO INC)
UNITED HEALTHCARE CINCINNATI, OH; COVINGTON, KY (See UNITED HEALTHCARE INS CO)
UNITED HEALTHCARE CINCINNATI, OH; COVINGTON, KY CHOICE (See UNITED HEALTHCARE OF OHIO INC)
UNITED HEALTHCARE CINCINNATI, OH; COVINGTON, KY SELECT (See UNITED HEALTHCARE OF OHIO INC)

UNITED HEALTHCARE CLARK COUNTY (See UNITED HEALTHCARE INS CO)
UNITED HEALTHCARE CLARK COUNTY (VANCOUVER) (See UNITED HEALTHCARE INS CO)
UNITED HEALTHCARE CLEVELAND, OH (See UNITED HEALTHCARE OF OHIO INC)
UNITED HEALTHCARE CLEVELAND, OH CHOICE (See UNITED HEALTHCARE OF OHIO INC)

Arrows denote recent upgrades ▲ or downgrades▼

● Bullets denote a more detailed analysis is available in Section II.

INSURANCE COMPANY NAME	DOM. STATE	RATING	DATA DATE	TOTAL ASSETS ($MIL)	TOTAL PREMIUMS ($MIL)	HEALTH PREMIUMS ($MIL)	CAPITAL & SURPLUS ($MIL)	RISK ADJUSTED CAPITAL RATIO 1	RATIO 2

UNITED HEALTHCARE CLEVELAND, OH; AKRON, OH; YOUNGSTOWN, OH (See UNITED HEALTHCARE INS CO)
UNITED HEALTHCARE COLUMBIA (See UNITED HEALTHCARE INS CO)
UNITED HEALTHCARE COLUMBUS (See UNITED HEALTHCARE INS CO)
UNITED HEALTHCARE COLUMBUS CHOICE (See UNITED HEALTHCARE OF GEORGIA INC)

UNITED HEALTHCARE COLUMBUS, OH (See UNITED HEALTHCARE INS CO)
UNITED HEALTHCARE COLUMBUS, OH AND SURROUNDING COUNTIES CHOICE (See UNITED HEALTHCARE OF OHIO INC)
UNITED HEALTHCARE COLUMBUS, OH CHOICE (See UNITED HEALTHCARE OF OHIO INC)
UNITED HEALTHCARE COLUMBUS, OH SELECT (See UNITED HEALTHCARE OF OHIO INC)

UNITED HEALTHCARE CORPUS CHRISTI (HOUSTON MARKET) (See UNITED HEALTHCARE INS CO)
UNITED HEALTHCARE CORPUS CHRISTI CHOICE (HOUSTON MARKET) (See UNITED HEALTHCARE OF TX INC)
UNITED HEALTHCARE CORPUS CHRISTI SELECT (HOUSTON MARKET) (See UNITED HEALTHCARE OF TX INC)
UNITED HEALTHCARE DALLAS & NORTHEAST TX CHOICE (See UNITED HEALTHCARE OF TX INC)

UNITED HEALTHCARE DALLAS/FORT WORTH, TX (See UNITED HEALTHCARE INS CO)
UNITED HEALTHCARE DALLAS/FORT WORTH, TX CHOICE (See UNITED HEALTHCARE OF TX INC)
UNITED HEALTHCARE DALLAS/FORT WORTH, TX SELECT (See UNITED HEALTHCARE OF TX INC)
UNITED HEALTHCARE DAYTON, OH (See UNITED HEALTHCARE INS CO)

UNITED HEALTHCARE DAYTON, OH CHOICE (See UNITED HEALTHCARE OF OHIO INC)
UNITED HEALTHCARE DAYTON, OH SELECT (See UNITED HEALTHCARE OF OHIO INC)
UNITED HEALTHCARE DAYTON/CINCINNATI & SPRINGFIELD (See UNITED HEALTHCARE OF OHIO INC)
UNITED HEALTHCARE DAYTON/CINCINNATI & SPRINGFIELD CHOICE (See UNITED HEALTHCARE OF OHIO INC)

UNITED HEALTHCARE DELAWARE (See UNITED HEALTHCARE INS CO)
UNITED HEALTHCARE DENVER/COLORADO SPRINGS (See UNITED HEALTHCARE INS CO)
UNITED HEALTHCARE DES MOINES (See UNITED HEALTHCARE INS CO)
UNITED HEALTHCARE DETROIT (See UNITED HEALTHCARE INS CO)

UNITED HEALTHCARE EAST CENTRAL MISSISSIPPI (See UNITED HEALTHCARE INS CO)
UNITED HEALTHCARE EAST CENTRAL MISSISSIPPI CHOICE (See UNITED HEALTHCARE OF MISSISSIPPI INC)
UNITED HEALTHCARE EAST CENTRAL MISSISSIPPI SELECT (See UNITED HEALTHCARE OF MISSISSIPPI INC)
UNITED HEALTHCARE EAST TEXAS (See UNITED HEALTHCARE INS CO)

UNITED HEALTHCARE EAST TEXAS (DALLAS MARKET) (See UNITED HEALTHCARE INS CO)
UNITED HEALTHCARE EASTERN IOWA (See UNITED HEALTHCARE INS CO)
UNITED HEALTHCARE EASTERN KENTUCKY (See UNITED HEALTHCARE INS CO)
UNITED HEALTHCARE EASTERN KENTUCKY CHOICE (See UNITED HEALTHCARE OF KENTUCKY LTD)

UNITED HEALTHCARE EASTERN KENTUCKY SELECT (See UNITED HEALTHCARE OF KENTUCKY LTD)
UNITED HEALTHCARE EASTERN PENNSYLVANIA (See UNITED HEALTHCARE INS CO)
UNITED HEALTHCARE EL PASO (DALLAS MARKET) (See UNITED HEALTHCARE INS CO)
UNITED HEALTHCARE FAIRFIELD (NYC MARKET) (See UNITED HEALTHCARE INS CO OF NY)

UNITED HEALTHCARE FAYETTEVILLE/UPPER CAPE FEAR (See UNITED HEALTHCARE INS CO)
UNITED HEALTHCARE FORT WAYNE (See UNITED HEALTHCARE INS CO)
UNITED HEALTHCARE FRESNO (See UNITED HEALTHCARE INS CO)
UNITED HEALTHCARE GARDEN CITY (See UNITED HEALTHCARE INS CO)

UNITED HEALTHCARE GEORGIA CHOICE (See UNITED HEALTHCARE OF GEORGIA INC)
UNITED HEALTHCARE GRANT COUNTY (See UNITED HEALTHCARE OF KENTUCKY LTD)
UNITED HEALTHCARE GRANT COUNTY (See UNITED HEALTHCARE INS CO)
UNITED HEALTHCARE GRANT COUNTY CHOICE (See UNITED HEALTHCARE OF KENTUCKY LTD)

UNITED HEALTHCARE GREENSBORO/PIEDMONT (See UNITED HEALTHCARE INS CO)
UNITED HEALTHCARE GREENVILLE (See UNITED HEALTHCARE INS CO)
UNITED HEALTHCARE HARTFORD (See UNITED HEALTHCARE INS CO)
UNITED HEALTHCARE HAWAII (See UNITED HEALTHCARE INS CO)

UNITED HEALTHCARE HOUSTON (See UNITED HEALTHCARE INS CO)
UNITED HEALTHCARE HOUSTON CHOICE (See UNITED HEALTHCARE OF TX INC)
UNITED HEALTHCARE HOUSTON SELECT (See UNITED HEALTHCARE OF TX INC)
UNITED HEALTHCARE INDIANAPOLIS (See UNITED HEALTHCARE INS CO)

www.weissratings.com

59

Arrows denote recent upgrades ▲ or downgrades▼

• Bullets denote a more detailed analysis is available in Section II.

INSURANCE COMPANY NAME	DOM. STATE	RATING	DATA DATE	TOTAL ASSETS ($MIL)	TOTAL PREMIUMS ($MIL)	HEALTH PREMIUMS ($MIL)	CAPITAL & SURPLUS ($MIL)	RISK ADJUSTED CAPITAL RATIO 1	RISK ADJUSTED CAPITAL RATIO 2
UNITED HEALTHCARE INS CO	CT	● C	2q 2014	13,754.9	39,802.8	39,681.2	4,085.6	0.74	0.62
UNITED HEALTHCARE INS CO OF IL	IL	● B	2q 2014	228.6	890.6	890.6	89.4	1.87	1.55
UNITED HEALTHCARE INS CO OF NY	NY	● B-	2q 2014	1,442.2	1,536.2	1,536.2	564.3	50.51	42.09

UNITED HEALTHCARE JACKSONVILLE (See UNITED HEALTHCARE INS CO)

UNITED HEALTHCARE JACKSONVILLE CHOICE (See UNITED HEALTHCARE OF FLORIDA INC)
UNITED HEALTHCARE JACKSONVILLE SELECT (See UNITED HEALTHCARE OF FLORIDA INC)
UNITED HEALTHCARE JEFERSON CITY (See UNITED HEALTHCARE INS CO)
UNITED HEALTHCARE JEFFERSON CITY (See UNITED HEALTHCARE INS CO)

UNITED HEALTHCARE JEFFERSON CITY CHOICE (See UNITED HEALTHCARE OF THE MIDWEST INC)
UNITED HEALTHCARE JEFFERSON CITY SELECT (See UNITED HEALTHCARE OF THE MIDWEST INC)
UNITED HEALTHCARE KANSAS CITY (See UNITED HEALTHCARE INS CO)
UNITED HEALTHCARE KANSAS CITY CHOICE (See UNITED HEALTHCARE OF THE MIDWEST INC)

UNITED HEALTHCARE KANSAS CITY SELECT (See UNITED HEALTHCARE OF THE MIDWEST INC)
UNITED HEALTHCARE KENTUCKY CHOICE (See UNITED HEALTHCARE OF KENTUCKY LTD)
UNITED HEALTHCARE KENTUCKY SELECT (See UNITED HEALTHCARE OF KENTUCKY LTD)
UNITED HEALTHCARE KERN COUNTY (See UNITED HEALTHCARE INS CO)

UNITED HEALTHCARE KNOXVILLE (See UNITED HEALTHCARE INS CO)
UNITED HEALTHCARE LAFAYETTE CHOICE (See UNITED HEALTHCARE OF LOUISIANA INC)
UNITED HEALTHCARE LAFAYETTE SELECT (See UNITED HEALTHCARE OF LOUISIANA INC)
UNITED HEALTHCARE LAS VEGAS (See UNITED HEALTHCARE INS CO)

UNITED HEALTHCARE LITTLE ROCK (See UNITED HEALTHCARE INS CO)
UNITED HEALTHCARE LITTLE ROCK CHOICE (See UNITED HEALTHCARE OF ARKANSAS INC)
UNITED HEALTHCARE LITTLE ROCK SELECT (See UNITED HEALTHCARE OF ARKANSAS INC)
UNITED HEALTHCARE LONG ISLAND (PART OF NYC MARKET) (See UNITED HEALTHCARE INS CO OF NY)

UNITED HEALTHCARE LOS ANGELES (See UNITED HEALTHCARE INS CO)
UNITED HEALTHCARE LOUISIANA CHOICE (See UNITED HEALTHCARE OF LOUISIANA INC)
UNITED HEALTHCARE LOUISIANA SELECT (See UNITED HEALTHCARE OF LOUISIANA INC)
UNITED HEALTHCARE MACON (See UNITED HEALTHCARE INS CO)

UNITED HEALTHCARE MACON CHOICE (See UNITED HEALTHCARE OF GEORGIA INC)
UNITED HEALTHCARE MAINE (See UNITED HEALTHCARE INS CO)
UNITED HEALTHCARE MARYLAND CHOICE (See UNITED HEALTHCARE OF MID-ATLANTIC)
UNITED HEALTHCARE MARYLAND SELECT (See UNITED HEALTHCARE OF MID-ATLANTIC)

UNITED HEALTHCARE MEMPHIS (See UNITED HEALTHCARE INS CO)
UNITED HEALTHCARE MIAMI (See UNITED HEALTHCARE INS CO)
UNITED HEALTHCARE MIAMI CHOICE (See UNITED HEALTHCARE OF FLORIDA INC)
UNITED HEALTHCARE MIAMI SELECT (See UNITED HEALTHCARE OF FLORIDA INC)

UNITED HEALTHCARE MIDLANDS (See UNITED HEALTHCARE INS CO)
UNITED HEALTHCARE MIDLANDS CHOICE (See UNITED HEALTHCARE OF THE MIDLANDS)
UNITED HEALTHCARE MIDLANDS SELECT (See UNITED HEALTHCARE OF THE MIDLANDS)
UNITED HEALTHCARE MILWAUKEE (See UNITED HEALTHCARE INS CO)

UNITED HEALTHCARE MINNEAPOLIS (See UNITED HEALTHCARE INS CO)
UNITED HEALTHCARE MISSISSIPPI CHOICE (See UNITED HEALTHCARE OF MISSISSIPPI INC)
UNITED HEALTHCARE MONROE (See UNITED HEALTHCARE INS CO)
UNITED HEALTHCARE MONTANA (See UNITED HEALTHCARE INS CO)

UNITED HEALTHCARE NASHVILLE (See UNITED HEALTHCARE INS CO)
UNITED HEALTHCARE NEBRASKA/WESTERN IOWA (See UNITED HEALTHCARE INS CO)
UNITED HEALTHCARE NEW ENGLAND CHOICE (See UNITED HEALTHCARE OF NEW ENGLAND INC)
UNITED HEALTHCARE NEW ENGLAND SELECT (See UNITED HEALTHCARE OF NEW ENGLAND INC)

UNITED HEALTHCARE NEW HAMPSHIRE (See UNITED HEALTHCARE INS CO)
UNITED HEALTHCARE NEW ORLEANS CHOICE (See UNITED HEALTHCARE OF LOUISIANA INC)
UNITED HEALTHCARE NEW ORLEANS SELECT (See UNITED HEALTHCARE OF LOUISIANA INC)
UNITED HEALTHCARE NEW YORK CITY (See UNITED HEALTHCARE INS CO OF NY)

Arrows denote recent upgrades ▲ or downgrades▼

www.weissratings.com
● Bullets denote a more detailed analysis is available in Section II.

INSURANCE COMPANY NAME	DOM. STATE	RATING	DATA DATE	TOTAL ASSETS ($MIL)	TOTAL PREMIUMS ($MIL)	HEALTH PREMIUMS ($MIL)	CAPITAL & SURPLUS ($MIL)	RISK ADJUSTED CAPITAL RATIO 1	RATIO 2
UNITED HEALTHCARE NORFOLK (See UNITED HEALTHCARE INS CO)									
UNITED HEALTHCARE NORFOLK CHOICE (See UNITED HEALTHCARE OF MID-ATLANTIC)									
UNITED HEALTHCARE NORFOLK SELECT (See UNITED HEALTHCARE OF MID-ATLANTIC)									
UNITED HEALTHCARE NORTH MISSISSIPPI (See UNITED HEALTHCARE INS CO)									
UNITED HEALTHCARE NORTH ALABAMA (See UNITED HEALTHCARE INS CO)									
UNITED HEALTHCARE NORTH ALABAMA CHOICE (See UNITED HEALTHCARE OF ALABAMA INC)									
UNITED HEALTHCARE NORTH ALABAMA SELECT (See UNITED HEALTHCARE OF ALABAMA INC)									
UNITED HEALTHCARE NORTH CENTRAL ALABAMA (See UNITED HEALTHCARE INS CO)									
UNITED HEALTHCARE NORTH CENTRAL ALABAMA CHOICE (See UNITED HEALTHCARE OF ALABAMA INC)									
UNITED HEALTHCARE NORTH CENTRAL ALABAMA SELECT (See UNITED HEALTHCARE OF ALABAMA INC)									
UNITED HEALTHCARE NORTH GEORGIA (See UNITED HEALTHCARE INS CO)									
UNITED HEALTHCARE NORTH GEORGIA CHOICE (See UNITED HEALTHCARE OF GEORGIA INC)									
UNITED HEALTHCARE NORTH GEORGIA SELECT (See UNITED HEALTHCARE OF GEORGIA INC)									
UNITED HEALTHCARE NORTH KENTUCKY BORDER CHOICE (See UNITED HEALTHCARE OF KENTUCKY LTD)									
UNITED HEALTHCARE NORTH MISSISSIPPI (See UNITED HEALTHCARE INS CO)									
UNITED HEALTHCARE NORTH MISSISSIPPI CHOICE (See UNITED HEALTHCARE OF MISSISSIPPI INC)									
UNITED HEALTHCARE NORTH MISSISSIPPI SELECT (See UNITED HEALTHCARE OF MISSISSIPPI INC)									
UNITED HEALTHCARE NORTHERN INDIANA (See UNITED HEALTHCARE INS CO)									
UNITED HEALTHCARE NORTHERN KENTUCKY BORDER (See UNITED HEALTHCARE INS CO)									
UNITED HEALTHCARE NORTHERN NEW JERSEY (NYC MARKET) (See UNITED HEALTHCARE INS CO)									
UNITED HEALTHCARE NORTHERN NEW YORK (NYC MARKET) (See UNITED HEALTHCARE INS CO OF NY)									
UNITED HEALTHCARE NORTHERN VIRGINIA (MD MARKET) (See UNITED HEALTHCARE INS CO)									
UNITED HEALTHCARE NORTHERN VIRGINIA CHOICE (MD MARKET) (See UNITED HEALTHCARE OF MID-ATLANTIC)									
UNITED HEALTHCARE NORTHERN VIRGINIA SELECT (MD MARKET) (See UNITED HEALTHCARE OF MID-ATLANTIC)									
UNITED HEALTHCARE NORTHWEST INDIANA (WITH CHICAGO) (See UNITED HEALTHCARE OF ILLINOIS INC)									
UNITED HEALTHCARE NORTHWEST INDIANA (WITH CHICAGO) (See UNITED HEALTHCARE INS CO)									
UNITED HEALTHCARE OF ALABAMA INC	AL	● B	2q 2014	168.8	406.2	406.2	76.2	3.67	3.06
UNITED HEALTHCARE OF ARIZONA INC	AZ	● B	2q 2014	89.1	338.9	338.9	45.0	2.48	2.06
UNITED HEALTHCARE OF ARKANSAS INC	AR	● B	2q 2014	12.1	44.9	44.9	9.6	3.32	2.77
UNITED HEALTHCARE OF COLORADO INC	CO	● B	2q 2014	14.0	19.5	19.5	9.3	6.35	5.29
UNITED HEALTHCARE OF FLORIDA INC	FL	● C	2q 2014	429.1	1,668.5	1,668.5	54.1	0.74	0.62
UNITED HEALTHCARE OF GEORGIA INC	GA	● B-	2q 2014	43.6	138.1	138.1	26.3	3.43	2.86
UNITED HEALTHCARE OF ILLINOIS INC	IL	● C	2q 2014	31.6	76.5	76.5	15.6	3.68	3.07
UNITED HEALTHCARE OF KENTUCKY LTD	KY	● B	2q 2014	22.8	95.8	95.8	11.4	2.13	1.78
UNITED HEALTHCARE OF LOUISIANA INC	LA	● D	2q 2014	15.1	5.1	5.1	13.4	11.11	9.26
UNITED HEALTHCARE OF MID-ATLANTIC	MD	● B	2q 2014	347.9	737.0	737.0	110.4	2.83	2.36
UNITED HEALTHCARE OF MISSISSIPPI INC	MS	● C	2q 2014	116.4	362.2	362.2	44.3	2.01	1.67
UNITED HEALTHCARE OF NC INC	NC	● B	2q 2014	287.3	969.0	969.0	146.5	2.90	2.42
UNITED HEALTHCARE OF NEW ENGLAND INC	RI	● B	2q 2014	258.8	587.5	587.5	135.0	3.96	3.30
UNITED HEALTHCARE OF NY INC	NY	● B+	2q 2014	564.2	1,879.0	1,879.0	271.6	2.91	2.43
UNITED HEALTHCARE OF OHIO INC	OH	● B	2q 2014	289.1	1,041.1	1,041.1	117.0	2.06	1.72
UNITED HEALTHCARE OF THE MIDLANDS	NE	● B+	2q 2014	75.7	207.0	207.0	32.4	3.12	2.60
UNITED HEALTHCARE OF THE MIDWEST INC	MO	● C+	2q 2014	336.6	827.7	827.7	113.7	2.74	2.29
UNITED HEALTHCARE OF TX INC	TX	● C	2q 2014	6.2	0.8	0.8	6.0	5.05	4.21
UNITED HEALTHCARE OF UTAH	UT	● B	2q 2014	124.1	360.5	360.5	46.3	2.44	2.04
UNITED HEALTHCARE OF WISCONSIN INC	WI	● B	2q 2014	370.1	1,328.8	1,328.8	147.3	2.38	1.98
UNITED HEALTHCARE OKLAHOMA CITY (See UNITED HEALTHCARE INS CO)									
UNITED HEALTHCARE ORLANDO (See UNITED HEALTHCARE OF FLORIDA INC)									
UNITED HEALTHCARE ORLANDO (See UNITED HEALTHCARE INS CO)									
UNITED HEALTHCARE ORLANDO CHOICE (See UNITED HEALTHCARE OF FLORIDA INC)									
UNITED HEALTHCARE ORLANDO SELECT (See UNITED HEALTHCARE OF FLORIDA INC)									
UNITED HEALTHCARE PANHANDLE CHOICE (See UNITED HEALTHCARE OF FLORIDA INC)									

www.weissratings.com

61

Arrows denote recent upgrades ▲ or downgrades▼   ● Bullets denote a more detailed analysis is available in Section II.

INSURANCE COMPANY NAME	DOM. STATE	RATING	DATA DATE	TOTAL ASSETS ($MIL)	TOTAL PREMIUMS ($MIL)	HEALTH PREMIUMS ($MIL)	CAPITAL & SURPLUS ($MIL)	RISK ADJUSTED CAPITAL RATIO 1	RATIO 2

UNITED HEALTHCARE PENSACOLA (See UNITED HEALTHCARE INS CO)
UNITED HEALTHCARE PHILADELPHIA (See UNITED HEALTHCARE INS CO)
UNITED HEALTHCARE PHOENIX (See UNITED HEALTHCARE INS CO)
UNITED HEALTHCARE PHOENIX CHOICE (See UNITED HEALTHCARE OF ARIZONA INC)

UNITED HEALTHCARE PHOENIX SELECT (See UNITED HEALTHCARE OF ARIZONA INC)
UNITED HEALTHCARE PITTSBURGH (See UNITED HEALTHCARE INS CO)
UNITED HEALTHCARE PORTLAND (See UNITED HEALTHCARE INS CO)
UNITED HEALTHCARE QUAD CITIES (See UNITED HEALTHCARE INS CO)

UNITED HEALTHCARE QUAD COUNTY (See UNITED HEALTHCARE INS CO)
UNITED HEALTHCARE RALEIGH/TRIANGLE (See UNITED HEALTHCARE INS CO)
UNITED HEALTHCARE RENO (See UNITED HEALTHCARE INS CO)
UNITED HEALTHCARE RHODE ISLAND (See UNITED HEALTHCARE INS CO)

UNITED HEALTHCARE RICHMOND (See UNITED HEALTHCARE INS CO)
UNITED HEALTHCARE RICHMOND CHOICE (See UNITED HEALTHCARE OF MID-ATLANTIC)
UNITED HEALTHCARE RICHMOND SELECT (See UNITED HEALTHCARE OF MID-ATLANTIC)
UNITED HEALTHCARE RIO GRANDE VALLEY (See UNITED HEALTHCARE INS CO)

UNITED HEALTHCARE RIO GRANDE VALLEY CHOICE (See UNITED HEALTHCARE OF TX INC)
UNITED HEALTHCARE RIO GRANDE VALLEY SELECT (See UNITED HEALTHCARE OF TX INC)
UNITED HEALTHCARE RIVERSIDE & SAN BERNARDINO (See UNITED HEALTHCARE INS CO)
UNITED HEALTHCARE ROANOKE (See UNITED HEALTHCARE INS CO)

UNITED HEALTHCARE ROANOKE CHOICE (See UNITED HEALTHCARE OF MID-ATLANTIC)
UNITED HEALTHCARE ROCKFORD (See UNITED HEALTHCARE INS CO)
UNITED HEALTHCARE ROME (See UNITED HEALTHCARE INS CO)
UNITED HEALTHCARE ROME CHOICE (See UNITED HEALTHCARE OF GEORGIA INC)

UNITED HEALTHCARE RURAL ARIZONA (See UNITED HEALTHCARE INS CO)
UNITED HEALTHCARE RURAL ARIZONA CHOICE (See UNITED HEALTHCARE OF ARIZONA INC)
UNITED HEALTHCARE RURAL ARIZONA SELECT (See UNITED HEALTHCARE OF ARIZONA INC)
UNITED HEALTHCARE SACRAMENTO (See UNITED HEALTHCARE INS CO)

UNITED HEALTHCARE SALT LAKE CITY (See UNITED HEALTHCARE INS CO)
UNITED HEALTHCARE SAN ANTONIO (AUSTIN MARKET) (See UNITED HEALTHCARE INS CO)
UNITED HEALTHCARE SAN ANTONIO CHOICE (AUSTIN MARKET) (See UNITED HEALTHCARE OF TX INC)
UNITED HEALTHCARE SAN ANTONIO SELECT (AUSTIN MARKET) (See UNITED HEALTHCARE OF TX INC)

UNITED HEALTHCARE SAN DIEGO (See UNITED HEALTHCARE INS CO)
UNITED HEALTHCARE SAN FRANCISCO (See UNITED HEALTHCARE INS CO)
UNITED HEALTHCARE SANTA BARBARA/SAN LUIS OBISPO (See UNITED HEALTHCARE INS CO)
UNITED HEALTHCARE SAVANNAH (See UNITED HEALTHCARE INS CO)

UNITED HEALTHCARE SAVANNAH CHOICE (See UNITED HEALTHCARE OF GEORGIA INC)
UNITED HEALTHCARE SHREVEPORT CHOICE (See UNITED HEALTHCARE OF LOUISIANA INC)
UNITED HEALTHCARE SHREVEPORT SELECT (See UNITED HEALTHCARE OF LOUISIANA INC)
UNITED HEALTHCARE SOUTH ALABAMA (See UNITED HEALTHCARE INS CO)

UNITED HEALTHCARE SOUTH ALABAMA CHOICE (See UNITED HEALTHCARE OF ALABAMA INC)
UNITED HEALTHCARE SOUTH ALABAMA SELECT (See UNITED HEALTHCARE OF ALABAMA INC)
UNITED HEALTHCARE SOUTH FLORIDA CHOICE (See UNITED HEALTHCARE OF FLORIDA INC)
UNITED HEALTHCARE SOUTH FLORIDA SELECT (See UNITED HEALTHCARE OF FLORIDA INC)

UNITED HEALTHCARE SOUTH GEORGIA (See UNITED HEALTHCARE INS CO)
UNITED HEALTHCARE SOUTH GEORGIA CHOICE (See UNITED HEALTHCARE OF GEORGIA INC)
UNITED HEALTHCARE SOUTH TEXAS (See UNITED HEALTHCARE INS CO)
UNITED HEALTHCARE SOUTHEAST INDIANA (See UNITED HEALTHCARE INS CO)

UNITED HEALTHCARE SOUTHEAST INDIANA CHOICE (See UNITED HEALTHCARE OF ILLINOIS INC)
UNITED HEALTHCARE SOUTHEAST INDIANA SELECT (See UNITED HEALTHCARE OF ILLINOIS INC)
UNITED HEALTHCARE SOUTHERN INDIANA (See UNITED HEALTHCARE INS CO)
UNITED HEALTHCARE SOUTHERN MISSISSIPPI (See UNITED HEALTHCARE INS CO)

Arrows denote recent upgrades ▲ or downgrades▼

• Bullets denote a more detailed analysis is available in Section II.

INSURANCE COMPANY NAME	DOM. STATE	RATING	DATA DATE	TOTAL ASSETS ($MIL)	TOTAL PREMIUMS ($MIL)	HEALTH PREMIUMS ($MIL)	CAPITAL & SURPLUS ($MIL)	RISK ADJUSTED CAPITAL RATIO 1 RATIO 2

UNITED HEALTHCARE SOUTHERN MISSISSIPPI CHOICE (See UNITED HEALTHCARE OF MISSISSIPPI INC)
UNITED HEALTHCARE SOUTHERN MISSISSIPPI SELECT (See UNITED HEALTHCARE OF MISSISSIPPI INC)
UNITED HEALTHCARE SOUTHERN NEW JERSEY (See UNITED HEALTHCARE INS CO OF NY)
UNITED HEALTHCARE SOUTHERN NEW JERSEY (See UNITED HEALTHCARE INS CO)

UNITED HEALTHCARE SOUTHWEST INDIANA (See UNITED HEALTHCARE INS CO)
UNITED HEALTHCARE SPRINGFIELD (See UNITED HEALTHCARE INS CO)
UNITED HEALTHCARE SPRINGFIELD, MO (See UNITED HEALTHCARE INS CO)
UNITED HEALTHCARE SPRINGFIELD, MO CHOICE (See UNITED HEALTHCARE OF THE MIDWEST INC)

UNITED HEALTHCARE SPRINGFIELD, MO SELECT (See UNITED HEALTHCARE OF THE MIDWEST INC)
UNITED HEALTHCARE SPRINGFIELD/DECATUR (See UNITED HEALTHCARE INS CO)
UNITED HEALTHCARE ST LOUIS AREA (See UNITED HEALTHCARE INS CO)
UNITED HEALTHCARE ST LOUIS CHOICE (See UNITED HEALTHCARE OF THE MIDWEST INC)

UNITED HEALTHCARE ST LOUIS SELECT (See UNITED HEALTHCARE OF THE MIDWEST INC)
UNITED HEALTHCARE ST LOUIS, MO; SPRINGFIELD, MO CHOICE (See UNITED HEALTHCARE OF THE MIDWEST INC)
UNITED HEALTHCARE ST LOUIS, MO; SPRINGFIELD, MO SELECT (See UNITED HEALTHCARE OF THE MIDWEST INC)
UNITED HEALTHCARE SUBURBAN MARYLAND (See UNITED HEALTHCARE INS CO)

UNITED HEALTHCARE SUBURBAN MARYLAND CHOICE (See UNITED HEALTHCARE OF MID-ATLANTIC)
UNITED HEALTHCARE SUBURBAN MARYLAND SELECT (See UNITED HEALTHCARE OF MID-ATLANTIC)
UNITED HEALTHCARE SYRACUSE (See UNITED HEALTHCARE INS CO OF NY)
UNITED HEALTHCARE SYRACUSE CHOICE (See UNITED HEALTHCARE OF NY INC)

UNITED HEALTHCARE SYRACUSE SELECT (See UNITED HEALTHCARE OF NY INC)
UNITED HEALTHCARE TAMPA CHOICE (See UNITED HEALTHCARE OF FLORIDA INC)
UNITED HEALTHCARE TAMPA SELECT (See UNITED HEALTHCARE OF FLORIDA INC)
UNITED HEALTHCARE TAMPA.GULF COAST REGION CHOICE (See UNITED HEALTHCARE OF FLORIDA INC)

UNITED HEALTHCARE TOLEDO (See UNITED HEALTHCARE INS CO)
UNITED HEALTHCARE TOLEDO CHOICE (See UNITED HEALTHCARE OF OHIO INC)
UNITED HEALTHCARE TOLEDO SELECT (See UNITED HEALTHCARE OF OHIO INC)
UNITED HEALTHCARE TOPEKA (See UNITED HEALTHCARE INS CO)

UNITED HEALTHCARE TOPEKA CHOICE (See UNITED HEALTHCARE OF THE MIDWEST INC)
UNITED HEALTHCARE TOPEKA SELECT (See UNITED HEALTHCARE OF THE MIDWEST INC)
UNITED HEALTHCARE TRI-STATE (MARTINSBURG) (See UNITED HEALTHCARE INS CO)
UNITED HEALTHCARE TUCSON (See UNITED HEALTHCARE INS CO)

UNITED HEALTHCARE TUCSON CHOICE (See UNITED HEALTHCARE OF ARIZONA INC)
UNITED HEALTHCARE TUCSON SELECT (See UNITED HEALTHCARE OF ARIZONA INC)
UNITED HEALTHCARE TULSA (See UNITED HEALTHCARE INS CO)
UNITED HEALTHCARE UTAH (See UNITED HEALTHCARE INS CO)

UNITED HEALTHCARE UTAH CHOICE (See UNITED HEALTHCARE OF UTAH)
UNITED HEALTHCARE UTAH SELECT (See UNITED HEALTHCARE OF UTAH)
UNITED HEALTHCARE VICTORIA (See UNITED HEALTHCARE OF TX INC)
UNITED HEALTHCARE VICTORIA (See UNITED HEALTHCARE INS CO)

UNITED HEALTHCARE WACO (AUSTIN MARKET) (See UNITED HEALTHCARE INS CO)
UNITED HEALTHCARE WACO SELECT (AUSTIN MARKET) (See UNITED HEALTHCARE OF TX INC)
UNITED HEALTHCARE WASHINGTON STATE/SEATTLE (See UNITED HEALTHCARE INS CO)
UNITED HEALTHCARE WASHINGTON, DC (MARYLAND MARKET) (See UNITED HEALTHCARE INS CO)

UNITED HEALTHCARE WASHINGTON, DC CHOICE (MARYLAND MARKET) (See UNITED HEALTHCARE INS CO)
UNITED HEALTHCARE WASHINGTON, DC SELECT (MARYLAND MARKET) (See UNITED HEALTHCARE OF MID-ATLANTIC)
UNITED HEALTHCARE WEST CENTRAL MISSISSIPPI (See UNITED HEALTHCARE INS CO)
UNITED HEALTHCARE WEST CENTRAL MISSISSIPPI CHOICE (See UNITED HEALTHCARE OF MISSISSIPPI INC)

UNITED HEALTHCARE WEST CENTRAL MISSISSIPPI SELECT (See UNITED HEALTHCARE OF MISSISSIPPI INC)
UNITED HEALTHCARE WEST TEXAS (See UNITED HEALTHCARE INS CO)
UNITED HEALTHCARE WEST/CENTRAL TEXAS (See UNITED HEALTHCARE INS CO)
UNITED HEALTHCARE WESTERN KENTUCKY (See UNITED HEALTHCARE INS CO)

INSURANCE COMPANY NAME	DOM. STATE	RATING	DATA DATE	TOTAL ASSETS ($MIL)	TOTAL PREMIUMS ($MIL)	HEALTH PREMIUMS ($MIL)	CAPITAL & SURPLUS ($MIL)	RISK ADJUSTED CAPITAL RATIO 1	RATIO 2
UNITED HEALTHCARE WESTERN KENTUCKY CHOICE (See UNITED HEALTHCARE OF KENTUCKY LTD)									
UNITED HEALTHCARE WESTERN KENTUCKY SELECT (See UNITED HEALTHCARE OF KENTUCKY LTD)									
UNITED HEALTHCARE WESTERN MARYLAND (See UNITED HEALTHCARE INS CO)									
UNITED HEALTHCARE WESTERN MARYLAND CHOICE (See UNITED HEALTHCARE OF MID-ATLANTIC)									
UNITED HEALTHCARE WESTERN MARYLAND SELECT (See UNITED HEALTHCARE OF MID-ATLANTIC)									
UNITED HEALTHCARE WESTERN MASSACHUSETTS (See UNITED HEALTHCARE INS CO)									
UNITED HEALTHCARE WESTERN MICHIGAN (See UNITED HEALTHCARE INS CO)									
UNITED HEALTHCARE WICHITA (See UNITED HEALTHCARE INS CO)									
UNITED HEALTHCARE WILMINGTON/LOWER CAPE FEAR (See UNITED HEALTHCARE INS CO)									
UNITED HERITAGE LIFE INS CO	ID	B-	2q 2014	523.1	73.0	2.9	56.3	2.67	1.38
UNITED HOME LIFE INS CO	IN	B	2q 2014	76.1	32.0	0.0	18.8	2.50	2.25
UNITED INS CO OF AMERICA	IL	B-	2q 2014	3,677.1	187.1	9.9	466.8	1.62	1.01
UNITED LIFE INS CO	IA	B	2q 2014	1,653.9	167.5	1.4	163.6	2.82	1.47
UNITED NATIONAL LIFE INS CO OF AM	IL	C	2q 2014	14.4	15.3	13.4	3.6	0.83	0.63
UNITED OF OMAHA LIFE INS CO	NE	• B	2q 2014	18,410.0	3,708.4	1,664.7	1,378.2	1.95	1.13
UNITED OHIO INS CO	OH	B-	2q 2014	276.1	137.8	0.0	133.7	6.81	4.82
UNITED PAYORS & UNITED PROVIDERS	MD	U		--	--	--	--	--	--
▼ UNITED SECURITY ASR CO OF PA	PA	D+	2q 2014	149.9	30.0	29.7	15.0	1.65	1.29
UNITED SECURITY LIFE & HEALTH INS CO	IL	D	2q 2014	4.7	23.0	20.7	3.2	1.31	1.05
UNITED STATES FIRE INS CO	DE	• C	2q 2014	3,271.1	666.3	201.1	955.1	1.26	0.95
UNITED STATES LIFE INS CO IN NYC	NY	B-	2q 2014	25,775.8	1,974.9	265.0	1,936.4	2.60	1.28
UNITED SURETY & INDEMNITY CO	PR	B	2q 2014	100.9	35.9	0.9	55.3	1.80	1.18
UNITED TEACHER ASSOCIATES INS CO	TX	• C	2q 2014	977.5	183.5	173.2	85.4	2.14	1.18
UNITED WORLD LIFE INS CO	NE	• B+	2q 2014	107.9	455.9	454.3	48.1	3.99	1.67
UNITEDHEALTHCARE BENEFITS OF TEXAS	TX	• B+	2q 2014	703.3	2,412.0	2,412.0	297.2	2.93	2.44
UNITEDHEALTHCARE COMMUNITY PLAN INC	MI	• B	2q 2014	242.2	897.8	897.8	81.9	1.83	1.53
UNITEDHEALTHCARE COMMUNITY PLAN TX	TX	• B+	2q 2014	394.8	1,454.2	1,454.2	166.8	2.32	1.93
UNITEDHEALTHCARE COMMUNITYPLAN OHIO	OH	• B	2q 2014	335.0	667.4	667.4	145.8	4.62	3.85
UNITEDHEALTHCARE INS CO RIVER VALLEY	IL	• B	2q 2014	146.6	443.3	443.3	61.7	2.58	2.15
UNITEDHEALTHCARE LIFE INS CO	WI	• B	2q 2014	81.0	84.9	84.2	35.6	1.50	1.20
UNITEDHEALTHCARE OF CALIFORNIA (See UHC OF CALIFORNIA INC)									
UNITEDHEALTHCARE OF NEW MEXICO INC	NM	• E	2q 2014	255.5	457.1	457.1	107.3	4.49	3.74
UNITEDHEALTHCARE OF OREGON	OR	• B-	2q 2014	69.0	202.0	202.0	37.4	3.75	3.13
UNITEDHEALTHCARE OF PENNSYLVANIA INC	PA	• B	2q 2014	314.7	1,101.8	1,101.8	138.0	2.41	2.01
UNITEDHEALTHCARE OF WASHINGTON INC	WA	• B	2q 2014	476.2	783.7	783.7	197.7	4.50	3.75
UNITEDHEALTHCARE PLAN RIVER VALLEY	IL	• B+	2q 2014	1,172.5	4,071.6	4,071.6	517.3	2.44	2.04
UNITY HEALTH PLANS INS CORP	WI	• B-	2q 2014	137.4	636.1	636.1	52.8	1.52	1.27
UNITY/PRECISION HEALTH PLANS	IN	U		--	--	--	--	--	--
UNIVERSAL CARE	CA	• E-	2q 2014	24.6	50.1	50.1	-1.6	0.00	0.00
UNIVERSAL FIDELITY LIFE INS CO	OK	D	2q 2014	11.5	9.8	9.1	3.9	1.33	1.20
UNIVERSAL GUARANTY LIFE INS CO	OH	C	2q 2014	342.2	11.2	0.0	34.7	1.18	0.75
UNIVERSAL HEALTH NETWORK	NV	U		--	--	--	--	--	--
UNIVERSAL LIFE INS CO	PR	B	2q 2014	710.1	204.2	7.1	39.7	1.81	0.98
UNIVERSAL PREFRRED HEALTH NETWORK	OH	U		--	--	--	--	--	--
UNIVERSAL UNDERWRITERS LIFE INS CO	KS	B-	2q 2014	157.6	10.3	0.0	22.9	2.45	2.20
UNIVERSITY HEALTH ALLIANCE	HI	• C+	2q 2014	82.9	214.1	214.1	49.2	1.78	1.48
UNIVERSITY HEALTH CARE INC	KY	• B+	2q 2014	261.3	685.4	685.4	124.7	2.21	1.84
UNIVERSITY OF ARIZONA HEALTH PLANS	AZ	U		--	--	--	--	--	--
UNUM LIFE INS CO OF AMERICA	ME	• C+	2q 2014	19,334.6	3,972.2	2,788.8	1,517.4	2.41	1.30
UPMC FOR YOU INC	PA	• B+	2q 2014	421.0	1,553.3	1,553.3	175.7	1.56	1.30
UPMC HEALTH BENEFITS (See UPMC HEALTH PLAN INC)									
▼ UPMC HEALTH NETWORK INC	PA	• D+	2q 2014	79.1	1,208.2	1,208.2	35.4	0.17	0.15

www.weissratings.com

Arrows denote recent upgrades ▲ or downgrades▼   • Bullets denote a more detailed analysis is available in Section II.

INSURANCE COMPANY NAME	DOM. STATE	RATING	DATA DATE	TOTAL ASSETS ($MIL)	TOTAL PREMIUMS ($MIL)	HEALTH PREMIUMS ($MIL)	CAPITAL & SURPLUS ($MIL)	RISK ADJUSTED CAPITAL RATIO 1	RATIO 2
UPMC HEALTH OPTIONS INC	PA	U		--	--	--	--	--	--
UPMC HEALTH PLAN INC	PA	● B	2q 2014	322.1	1,036.1	1,036.1	121.9	1.28	1.07
UPPER CHESAPEAKE HEALTH SYSTEMS	MD	U		--	--	--	--	--	--
UPPER PENINSULA HEALTH PLAN INC	MI	● B-	2q 2014	38.0	107.1	107.1	21.3	1.95	1.63
US BEHAVIORAL HEALTH PLAN CALIFORNIA	CA	U		--	--	--	--	--	--
US SPECIALTY INS CO	TX	B-	2q 2014	1,998.7	615.1	8.1	636.1	2.75	1.77
USA INS CO	MS	C-	2q 2014	3.1	0.4	0.3	2.2	2.37	2.14
USA MANAGED CARE ORGANIZATION	AZ	U		--	--	--	--	--	--
USAA LIFE INS CO	TX	A	2q 2014	21,633.7	2,264.8	196.0	2,078.4	4.00	2.13
USABLE LIFE	AR	● B+	2q 2014	426.8	274.8	151.8	182.9	1.72	1.26
USABLE MUTUAL INS CO	AR	● A+	2q 2014	1,521.6	1,393.0	1,393.0	794.6	6.95	5.79
USIC LIFE INS CO	PR	B	2q 2014	7.6	3.7	2.7	6.1	2.38	1.42
UTMB HEALTH PLANS INC	TX	● B-	2q 2014	7.3	0.8	0.8	6.6	46.39	38.66
VALLEY HEALTH PLAN (See SANTA CLARA VALLEY)									
VALLEY PREFERRED	PA	U		--	--	--	--	--	--
VALUE BEHAVIORAL HEALTH OF PA	PA	● E	2q 2014	34.1	97.8	97.8	13.3	1.40	1.17
VALUECARE (See REGENCE BLUE CROSS BLUE SHIELD OF UT)									
VALUEOPTIONS OF CALIFORNIA INC	CA	U		--	--	--	--	--	--
VALUEOPTIONS OF KANSAS INC	KS	U		--	--	--	--	--	--
VANTAGE HEALTH PLAN INC	LA	● B-	2q 2014	52.9	183.7	183.7	17.2	0.87	0.73
VANTAGE HEALTH PLAN OF ARKANSAS INC	AR	U		--	--	--	--	--	--
VANTIS LIFE INS CO	CT	B-	2q 2014	880.9	42.6	0.0	72.5	1.92	1.06
VENTURA COUNTY HEALTH CARE PLAN	CA	● B	2q 2014	24.8	57.5	57.5	10.4	1.85	1.16
VERMONT FREEDOM PLAN (See BLUE CROSS BLUE SHIELD OF VERMONT)									
VERMONT HEALTH PLAN LLC	VT	● B	2q 2014	51.2	173.0	173.0	34.8	2.10	1.75
VERSANT LIFE INS CO	MS	B-	2q 2014	5.3	0.6	0.1	4.4	2.78	2.51
VIAHEALTH PPO INC	NY	U		--	--	--	--	--	--
VIRGINIA FARM BUREAU MUTUAL INS CO	VA	C	2q 2014	353.5	152.4	0.0	151.2	1.95	1.57
VIRGINIA HEALTH NETWORK INC	VA	U		--	--	--	--	--	--
VIRGINIA PREMIER HEALTH PLAN INC	VA	● A-	2q 2014	184.9	715.4	715.4	96.5	1.52	1.27
VISION BENEFITS OF AMERICA II INC	PA	U		--	--	--	--	--	--
VISION FIRST EYE CARE INC	CA	U		--	--	--	--	--	--
VISION PLAN OF AMERICA	CA	U		--	--	--	--	--	--
VISION SERVICE PLAN	CA	U		--	--	--	--	--	--
VISION SERVICE PLAN INS CO	CT	U		--	--	--	--	--	--
VISION SERVICE PLAN OF ILLINOIS NFP	IL	U		--	--	--	--	--	--
VISIONCARE OF CALIFORNIA	CA	U		--	--	--	--	--	--
▼ VISTA HEALTH PLAN INC	PA	● B-	2q 2014	877.1	2,573.7	2,573.7	168.2	2.08	1.73
VIVA HEALTH INC	AL	● B+	2q 2014	156.2	554.8	554.8	82.3	1.99	1.66
VIVA MEDICARE PLUS (See VIVA HEALTH INC)									
VMC BEHAVIORAL HEALTHCARE SERVICES	CA	U		--	--	--	--	--	--
VOLUNTARY EMPLOYEES BENEFIT	HI	● D+	2q 2014	8.4	0.1	0.1	8.3	31.57	26.31
▲ VOLUNTEER STATE HEALTH PLAN INC	TN	● A-	2q 2014	546.3	1,673.1	1,673.1	294.6	3.33	2.78
VOLUSIA HEALTH NETWORK	FL	U		--	--	--	--	--	--
VOYA INS & ANNUITY CO	IA	B	2q 2014	68,284.5	6,390.8	0.1	1,971.7	1.88	0.94
VOYA RETIREMENT INS & ANNUITY CO	CT	B	2q 2014	90,076.8	9,747.9	0.2	1,920.3	2.45	1.20
WASHINGTON NATIONAL INS CO	IN	● D+	2q 2014	4,849.8	648.8	574.0	386.6	1.95	1.04
WATTS HEALTH FOUNDATION INC	CA	U		--	--	--	--	--	--
WEA INS CORP	WI	● C	2q 2014	691.0	597.2	597.2	212.5	1.99	1.40
WELLCARE HEALTH INS OF ARIZONA INC	AZ	● B-	2q 2014	189.0	519.4	519.4	80.9	3.22	2.68
▲ WELLCARE HEALTH INS OF KENTUCKY INC	KY	● C+	2q 2014	434.5	1,403.7	1,403.7	151.8	1.97	1.65
WELLCARE HEALTH PLANS OF NEW JERSEY	NJ	● C	2q 2014	18.4	12.0	12.0	4.4	4.18	3.48

Arrows denote recent upgrades ▲ or downgrades▼

● Bullets denote a more detailed analysis is available in Section II.

INSURANCE COMPANY NAME	DOM. STATE	RATING	DATA DATE	TOTAL ASSETS ($MIL)	TOTAL PREMIUMS ($MIL)	HEALTH PREMIUMS ($MIL)	CAPITAL & SURPLUS ($MIL)	RISK ADJUSTED CAPITAL RATIO 1	RATIO 2
▼ WELLCARE OF CONNECTICUT INC	CT	• C-	2q 2014	33.9	83.2	83.2	20.1	3.69	3.07
▼ WELLCARE OF FLORIDA INC	FL	• B	2q 2014	510.7	2,021.8	2,021.8	102.9	1.23	1.03
▼ WELLCARE OF GEORGIA INC	GA	• B-	2q 2014	390.6	1,805.8	1,805.8	153.2	1.72	1.43
WELLCARE OF KANSAS INC	KS	U	--	--	--	--	--	--	--
▼ WELLCARE OF LOUISIANA INC	LA	• B-	2q 2014	27.7	81.3	81.3	14.4	3.32	2.77
WELLCARE OF NEW YORK INC	NY	U	--	--	--	--	--	--	--
WELLCARE OF OHIO INC	OH	• C	2q 2014	61.0	199.6	199.6	44.9	4.60	3.83
▼ WELLCARE OF SOUTH CAROLINA INC	SC	• B-	2q 2014	71.9	162.9	162.9	33.5	3.58	2.98
▼ WELLCARE OF TEXAS INC	TX	• B-	2q 2014	73.8	271.9	271.9	20.2	1.47	1.22
WELLCARE PRESCRIPTION INS INC	CA	U	--	--	--	--	--	--	--
WELLCARE PRESCRIPTION INS INC	FL	• D	2q 2014	427.8	715.8	715.8	90.9	4.58	3.82
WELLCHOICE HMO OF NEW JERSEY (See EMPIRE HEALTHCHOICE HMO INC)									
WELLINGTON LIFE INS CO	AZ	• D	2q 2014	6.2	0.2	0.2	6.1	53.93	44.94
WELLMARK BLUE CROSS BLUE SHIELD OF SOUTH DAKOTA (See WELLMARK OF SOUTH DAKOTA INC)									
WELLMARK HEALTH PLAN OF IOWA	IA	• B+	2q 2014	233.7	338.0	338.0	158.6	7.30	6.08
WELLMARK HEALTHNETWORK INC	IL	U	--	--	--	--	--	--	--
WELLMARK INC	IA	• B+	2q 2014	2,143.2	2,335.8	2,335.8	1,433.3	6.62	5.52
WELLMARK OF SOUTH DAKOTA INC	SD	• B+	2q 2014	445.3	639.7	639.7	244.8	7.19	5.99
WELLMARK SELECT (See WELLMARK INC)									
WESCO INS CO	DE	C+	2q 2014	900.9	965.2	8.6	174.4	3.96	2.30
WEST COAST LIFE INS CO	NE	C+	2q 2014	4,657.1	660.6	0.0	348.1	2.39	1.19
WESTERN & SOUTHERN LIFE INS CO	OH	B	2q 2014	9,730.6	268.2	29.3	4,363.0	1.76	1.47
WESTERN AMERICAN LIFE INS CO	TX	C	2q 2014	32.0	2.8	0.0	3.3	0.68	0.62
WESTERN DENTAL SERVICES INC	CA	U	--	--	--	--	--	--	--
WESTERN GROCERS EMPLOYEE BENEFITS	OR	U	--	--	--	--	--	--	--
WESTERN HEALTH ADVANTAGE	CA	• D	2q 2014	55.7	444.6	444.6	20.3	0.61	0.37
WESTERN RESERVE LIFE ASR CO OF OHIO	OH	B	2q 2014	9,540.1	727.3	17.6	435.3	2.39	1.39
WESTERN UNITED LIFE ASR CO	WA	B-	4q 2013	14.8	0.6	0.3	7.4	2.59	2.33
WESTPORT INS CORP	MO	C+	2q 2014	5,373.6	797.9	115.5	1,570.2	1.20	0.82
WICHITA NATIONAL LIFE INS CO	OK	C	2q 2014	17.5	5.9	1.1	7.8	2.38	2.15
WILLAMETTE DENTAL INS INC	OR	U	--	--	--	--	--	--	--
WILLAMETTE DENTAL OF IDAHO INC	ID	U	--	--	--	--	--	--	--
WILLAMETTE DENTAL OF WASHINGTON INC	WA	U	--	--	--	--	--	--	--
WILLAMETTE HEALTH SERVICE INC	OR	U	--	--	--	--	--	--	--
WILLIAM PENN LIFE INS CO OF NEW YORK	NY	C-	2q 2014	1,156.0	195.6	0.0	173.8	3.81	1.83
WILLIS-KNIGHTON HEALTH PLAN	LA	U	--	--	--	--	--	--	--
▲ WILTON REASSURANCE LIFE CO OF NY	NY	B	2q 2014	933.5	62.2	0.2	118.8	3.32	1.66
WINDSOR HEALTH PLAN OF GEORGIA INC	GA	U	--	--	--	--	--	--	--
WINDSOR HEALTH PLAN OF LOUISIANA INC	LA	U	--	--	--	--	--	--	--
WINDSOR HEALTH PLAN OF TN INC	TN	• D+	2q 2014	217.2	689.0	689.0	123.2	2.97	2.48
WINDSOR LIFE INS CO	TX	B-	2q 2014	3.2	0.3	0.3	2.8	2.78	2.50
WINHEALTH PARTNERS	WY	• C-	2q 2014	17.8	29.6	29.6	6.1	1.27	1.06
WINHEALTH PPO (See WINHEALTH PARTNERS)									
WISCONSIN PHYSICIANS SERVICE INS	WI	• C+	2q 2014	323.1	499.0	499.0	164.6	2.42	2.02
WISHARD ADVANTAGE (See MDWISE INC)									
WMI MUTUAL INS CO	UT	C	2q 2014	13.8	20.7	20.6	7.4	1.43	1.08
WPPA INC	KS	U	--	--	--	--	--	--	--
WPS HEALTH PLAN INC	WI	• C	2q 2014	33.1	78.8	78.8	8.9	1.19	0.99
WYSSTA INS CO	WI	U	--	--	--	--	--	--	--
XL LIFE INS & ANNUITY CO	IL	U	4q 2013	13.9	0.0	0.0	13.7	--	--
YALE PREFERRED HEALTH INC	CT	U	--	--	--	--	--	--	--
ZALE INDEMNITY CO	TX	C+	2q 2014	41.9	22.1	0.5	13.9	1.45	1.23

www.weissratings.com

Arrows denote recent upgrades ▲ or downgrades▼

• Bullets denote a more detailed analysis is available in Section II.

INSURANCE COMPANY NAME	DOM. STATE	RATING	DATA DATE	TOTAL ASSETS ($MIL)	TOTAL PREMIUMS ($MIL)	HEALTH PREMIUMS ($MIL)	CAPITAL & SURPLUS ($MIL)	RISK ADJUSTED CAPITAL RATIO 1	RATIO 2
ZALE LIFE INS CO	AZ	B-	2q 2014	11.3	2.6	0.8	9.0	3.56	3.21
ZURICH AMERICAN INS CO	NY	C+	2q 2014	30,801.1	5,351.2	290.8	7,494.6	2.50	1.71
ZURICH AMERICAN LIFE INS CO	IL	C	2q 2014	12,958.1	280.7	3.4	143.2	1.95	1.11
ZURICH AMERICAN LIFE INS CO OF NY	NY	C+	2q 2014	42.1	0.4	0.2	19.9	5.42	4.88

www.weissratings.com

Arrows denote recent upgrades ▲ or downgrades▼

67

• Bullets denote a more detailed analysis is available in Section II.

Section II

Analysis of Largest Companies

A summary analysis of all rated

U.S. Health Plans and Blue Cross Blue Shield Plans

plus other **U.S. Insurers**
with capital in excess of $25 million and health insurance
premiums equaling at least 25% of total premiums.

Companies are listed in alphabetical order.

Section II Contents

This section contains rating factors, historical data, and general information on all rated health insurers and Blue Cross/Blue Shield plans plus other insurers with capital in excess of $25 million and health insurance premiums equaling at least 25% of total premiums.

A number of the contents listed below will only apply to health insurers filing the NAIC Health insurance financial statement.

1. **Financial Strength Rating**

    The current Weiss rating appears to the right of the company name. Our ratings are designed to distinguish levels of insolvency risk and are measured on a scale from A (Excellent) to F (Failed). Highly rated companies are, in our opinion, less likely to experience financial difficulties than lower rated firms. See *About Weiss Financial Strength Ratings* for more information.

2. **Major Rating Factors**

    A synopsis of the key indexes and sub-factors that have most influenced the rating of a particular insurer. Items are presented in the approximate order of their importance to the rating. There may be additional factors which have influenced the rating but do not appear due to space limitations or confidentiality agreements with insurers.

3. **Other Rating Factors**

    A summary of those Weiss Ratings indexes that were not included as Major Rating Factors, but nevertheless may have had some impact on the final grade.

4. **Principal Business**

    The major types of policies written by an insurer along with the percentages for each line in relation to the entire book of business, including direct premium, reinsurance assumed and deposit funds. Lines of business for health insurers include comprehensive medical, medical only, medicare supplemental, administrative service contracts, point of service, dental, vision, stop-loss, long-term care, disability, Federal Employee Health Benefits (FEHB), medicare, and medicaid.

5. **Member Physicians**

    The number of physicians who participated in the insurer's network of providers during the current and prior year.

6. **MLR (Medical Loss Ratio)**

    The percentage of total premium income paid out as benefits to members.

7. **Administrative Expense Ratio**

    The percentage of total premium income paid out for administrative expenses.

8. **Enrollment**

    The total number of members (policyholders) as of the current quarter, current year end and prior year end. The letter Q followed by a number represents the quarter (first, second, or third) from which the enrollment numbers were last available.

9. **Medical Expenses Per Member Per Month**

The average dollar amount the insurer spends on a per member per month basis. Calculated as total medical expenses divided by the reported member months.

10. **Principal Investments**

The major investments in an insurer's portfolio. These include investment grade bonds, noninvestment grade bonds, collateralized mortgage obligations (CMOs) and other structured securities, which consist primarily of mortgage-backed bonds, real estate, mortgages in good standing, nonperforming mortgages, common and preferred stocks, contract loans and other investments.

11. **Provider Compensation**

The total annual amount the health insurer pays its providers (e.g., physicians, hospitals, etc.) and manner in which they are paid, including:

- fee-for-service (FFS) – amount paid for the services provided where the payment base is not fixed by contract

- contractual fees – amount paid for services whereby the amount is fixed by contract, e.g., hospital per diems, DRGs, etc.

- salary – amount paid providers who are direct employees of the HMO

- capitation – amount paid to providers on a per member basis as defined by contract

- other – amount paid under various contracts including bonus arrangements, stop-loss arrangements, etc.

12. **Total Member Encounters**

The number of contacts members of the health insurer who are not confined to a health care facility have with the providers during the current year.

13. **Investments in Affiliates**

The percentage of bonds, common and preferred stocks, and other financial instruments an insurer has invested with affiliated companies. This is not a subcategory of "Principal Investments."

14. **Group Affiliation**

The name of the group of companies to which a particular insurer belongs.

15. **Licensed in**

List of the states in which an insurer is licensed to conduct business.

16. **Address**

The address of an insurer's corporate headquarters. This location may differ from the company's state of domicile.

17. **Phone**

The telephone number of an insurer's corporate headquarters.

18. **Domicile State**

The state that has primary regulatory responsibility for this company. You do not have to live in the domicile state to do business with this firm, provided it is registered to do business in your state.

19. Commenced Business   The month and year the insurer started its operations

20. NAIC Code   The identification number assigned to an insurer by the National Association of Insurance Commissioners (NAIC).

21. Historical Data   Five years of background data for Weiss Financial Strength Rating, risk-adjusted capital ratios (moderate and severe loss scenarios), total assets, capital (including capital stock and retained earnings), net premium, and net income. See the next page for more details on how to read the historical data table.

22. Customized Graph (or Table)   A graph or table depicting one of the company's major strengths or weaknesses.

How to Read the Historical Data Table

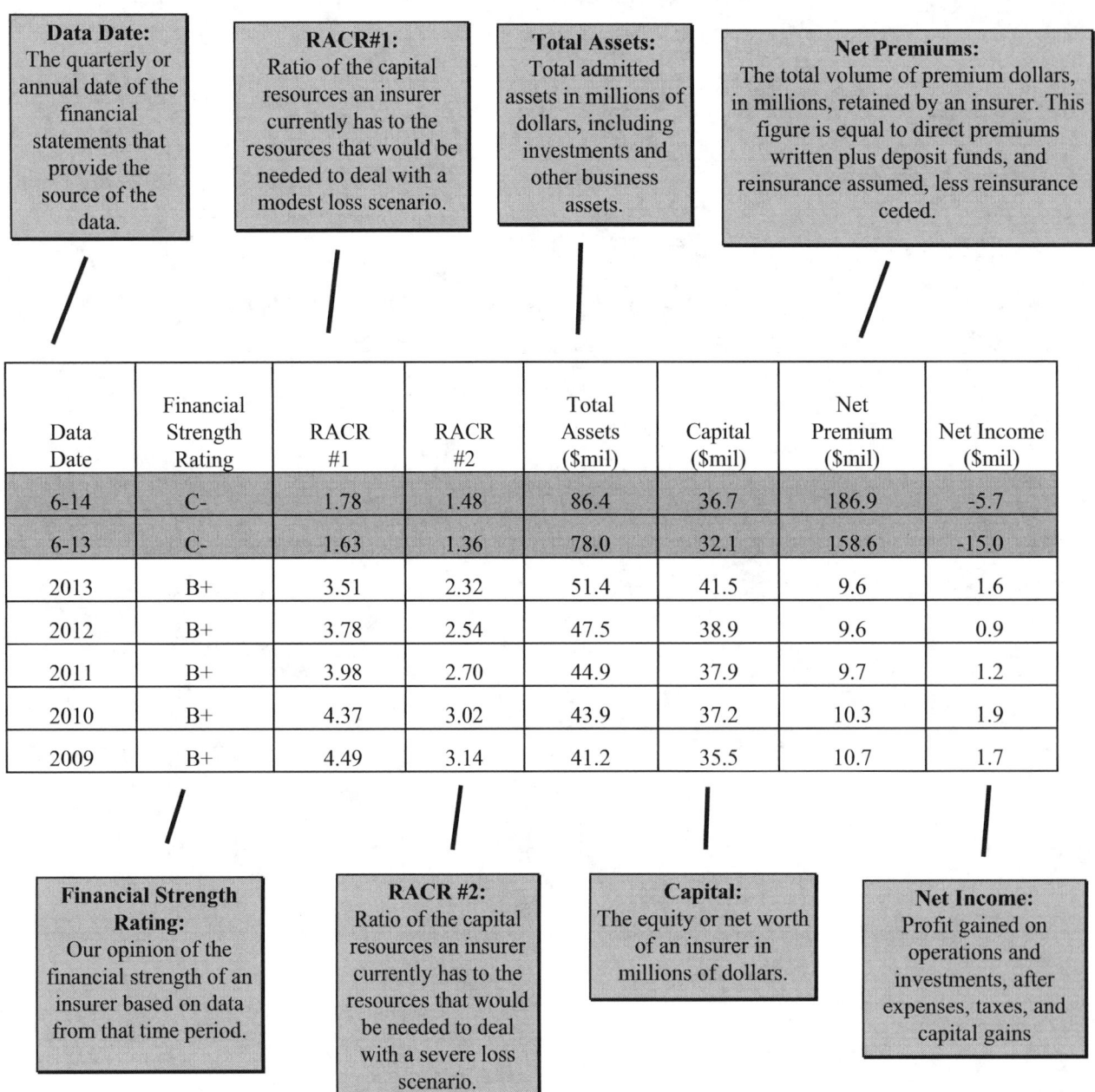

Data Date:
The quarterly or annual date of the financial statements that provide the source of the data.

RACR#1:
Ratio of the capital resources an insurer currently has to the resources that would be needed to deal with a modest loss scenario.

Total Assets:
Total admitted assets in millions of dollars, including investments and other business assets.

Net Premiums:
The total volume of premium dollars, in millions, retained by an insurer. This figure is equal to direct premiums written plus deposit funds, and reinsurance assumed, less reinsurance ceded.

Data Date	Financial Strength Rating	RACR #1	RACR #2	Total Assets ($mil)	Capital ($mil)	Net Premium ($mil)	Net Income ($mil)
6-14	C-	1.78	1.48	86.4	36.7	186.9	-5.7
6-13	C-	1.63	1.36	78.0	32.1	158.6	-15.0
2013	B+	3.51	2.32	51.4	41.5	9.6	1.6
2012	B+	3.78	2.54	47.5	38.9	9.6	0.9
2011	B+	3.98	2.70	44.9	37.9	9.7	1.2
2010	B+	4.37	3.02	43.9	37.2	10.3	1.9
2009	B+	4.49	3.14	41.2	35.5	10.7	1.7

Financial Strength Rating:
Our opinion of the financial strength of an insurer based on data from that time period.

RACR #2:
Ratio of the capital resources an insurer currently has to the resources that would be needed to deal with a severe loss scenario.

Capital:
The equity or net worth of an insurer in millions of dollars.

Net Income:
Profit gained on operations and investments, after expenses, taxes, and capital gains

Row Descriptions:

Row 1 contains the most recent quarterly data as filed with state regulators and is presented on a year-to-date basis. For example, the figure for third quarter premiums includes premiums received through the third quarter. **Row 2** consists of data from the same quarter of the prior year. Compare current quarterly results to those of a year ago.

Row 3 contains data from the most recent annual statutory filing. **Rows 4-7** includes data from year-end statements going back four years from the most recent annual filing. Compare current year-end results to those of the previous four years. With the exception of Total Assets and Capital, quarterly data are not comparable with annual data.

Customized Graphs

In the lower right-hand corner of each company section, a customized graph or text block highlights a key factor affecting that company's financial strength. One of 15 types of information is found, identified by one of the following headings:

# of Months of Claims and Expenses in Capital illustrates the number of months' worth of medical and administrative expenses the company could cover by drawing solely on its current capital position.

Adverse Trends in Operations lists changes in key balance sheet and income statement items which may be leading indicators of deteriorating business performance.

Allocation of Premium Income shows what portion of the company's premium income is being spent on medical benefits and administrative expenses. Any income left after the payment of these two types of expense, is used to pay taxes and extraordinary expenditures; the remainder is profit.

Capital History plots the company's reported capital and surplus in millions of dollars over the last five years. Volatile changes in capital levels may indicate unstable operations.

Detail of Risk-Adjusted Capital Ratio provides a percentage breakdown of target capital components based on lines of business and investments in a moderate or severe loss scenario. Target capital is our opinion of the level of capital the company should have, based on the risk it assumes. For example, if the percentage of target capital for individual life is 33%, this means that 33% of the company's target capital relates to individual life.   C2 refers to the pricing risk element of the risk-adjusted capital formula. C3 refers to disintermediation (interest rate) risk.

Enrollment Trend charts an insurer's year-end membership levels over the last five years.

Exposure to Withdrawals Without Penalty answers the question: For each dollar of capital and surplus, how much does the company have in annuity and deposit funds that can be withdrawn by policyholders with minimal or no penalty? The figures do not include the effects of reinsurance or funds subject to withdrawals from cash value life insurance policies.

Group Ratings shows the group name, a composite Weiss Financial Strength Rating for the group, and a list of the largest members with their ratings. The composite Weiss Financial Strength Rating is made up of the weighted average, by assets, of the individual ratings of each company in the group (including life/health companies, property/casualty companies, or HMOs) plus a factor for the financial strength of the holding company, where applicable.

High Risk Assets as a % of Capital answers the question: For each dollar of capital and surplus, how much does the company have in junk bonds, nonperforming mortgages and repossessed real estate? Accumulations in the Asset Valuation Reserve or AVR, which provide some protection against investment losses, have not been included in the figure for capital. These figures are based on year-end data.

Income Trends shows underwriting and net income results over the last five years.

Investment Income Compared to Needs of Reserves answers the question: Is the company earning enough investment income to meet the expectations of actuaries when they priced their policies and set reserve levels? According to state insurance regulators, it would be "unusual" if an insurer were to have less than $1.25 in actual investment income for each dollar of investment income that it projected in its actuarial forecasts. This provides an excess margin of at least 25 cents on the dollar to cover any unexpected decline in income or increase in claims. This graph shows whether or not the company is maintaining the appropriate 25% margin and is based on year-end data.

Junk Bonds as a % of Capital answers the question: For each dollar of capital and surplus, how much does the company have in junk bonds? In addition, it shows a breakdown of the junk bond portfolio by bond rating – BB, B, CCC or in default. Accumulations in the Asset Valuation Reserve or AVR, which provide some protection against investment losses, have not been included in the figure for capital. These figures are based on year-end data.

Largest Net Exposure Per Risk shows the ratio of the largest net aggregate amount insured in any one risk (excluding workers' compensation) as a percent of capital.

Liquidity Index evaluates a company's ability to raise the cash necessary to pay claims. Various cash flow scenarios are modeled to determine how the company might fare in the event of an unexpected spike in claims costs.

Net Income History plots operating gains and losses over the most recent five-year period.

Nonperforming Mortgages (plus repossessed real estate) as a % of Capital answers the question: For each dollar of capital and surplus, how much does the company have in nonperforming mortgages and repossessed real estate? Nonperforming mortgages include those overdue more than 90 days and mortgages currently in process of foreclosure. Accumulations in the Asset Valuation Reserve or AVR, which provide some protection against investment losses, have not been included in the figure for capital. These figures are based on year-end data.

Policy Leverage answers the question: To what degree is this insurer capable of handling an unexpected spike in claims? Low leverage indicates low exposure; high leverage is high exposure.

Target leverage represents the maximum exposure we feel would be appropriate for a top-rated company.

Premium Growth History depicts the change in the insurer's net premiums written. Such changes may be the result of issuing more policies or changes in reinsurance arrangements. In either case, growth rates above 20% per year are considered excessive. "Standard" growth is under 20%; "shrinkage" refers to net declines.

Rating Indexes illustrate the score and range – strong, good, fair, or weak – on each of Weiss indexes.

Reserve Deficiency shows whether the company has set aside sufficient funds to pay claims. A positive number indicates insufficient reserving and a negative number adequate reserving.

Reserves to Capital analyzes the relationship between loss and loss expense reserves to capital. Operating results and capital levels for companies with a high ratio are more susceptible to fluctuations than those with lower ratios.

Risk-Adjusted Capital Ratio #1 answers the question: In each of the past five years, does the insurer have sufficient capital to cover potential losses in its investments and business operations in a *moderate* loss scenario?

Risk-Adjusted Capital Ratio #2 answers the question: In each of the past five years, does the insurer have sufficient capital to cover potential losses in its investments and business operations in a *severe* loss scenario?

Risk-Adjusted Capital Ratios answers these questions for both a moderate loss scenario (RACR #1 shown by the dark bar), and a severe loss scenario (RACR #2, light bar).

4 EVER LIFE INSURANCE COMPANY *

A **Excellent**

Major Rating Factors: Good quality investment portfolio (6.7 on a scale of 0 to 10) despite mixed results such as: no exposure to mortgages and substantial holdings of BBB bonds but minimal holdings in junk bonds. Good liquidity (6.7) with sufficient resources to handle a spike in claims. Excellent overall results on stability tests (7.1) excellent operational trends and excellent risk diversification.

Other Rating Factors: Strong capitalization (10.0) based on excellent risk adjusted capital (severe loss scenario). Excellent profitability (8.3) with operating gains in each of the last five years.

Principal Business: Group health insurance (82%), reinsurance (12%), and group life insurance (6%).

Principal Investments: NonCMO investment grade bonds (46%), CMOs and structured securities (35%), common & preferred stock (7%), noninv. grade bonds (5%), and cash (3%).

Investments in Affiliates: None

Group Affiliation: BCS Financial Corp

Licensed in: All states, the District of Columbia and Puerto Rico

Commenced Business: November 1949

Address: 2 Mid America Plaza Suite 200, Oakbrook Terrace, IL 60181

Phone: (312) 951-7700 **Domicile State:** IL **NAIC Code:** 80985

Data Date	Rating	RACR #1	RACR #2	Total Assets ($mil)	Capital ($mil)	Net Premium ($mil)	Net Income ($mil)
6-14	A	4.31	3.07	202.8	91.6	86.4	3.5
6-13	A	4.54	3.23	194.2	85.3	66.8	3.4
2013	A	3.92	2.79	186.9	89.9	148.4	6.4
2012	A-	3.43	2.51	187.2	84.4	170.1	6.2
2011	A-	3.49	2.61	174.6	79.7	171.5	6.9
2010	B	3.49	2.63	174.5	77.8	167.5	4.4
2009	B	3.27	2.50	181.4	80.6	188.6	2.4

Adverse Trends in Operations

Decrease in premium volume from 2012 to 2013 (13%)
Increase in policy surrenders from 2011 to 2012 (33%)
Decrease in asset base during 2010 (4%)
Decrease in premium volume from 2009 to 2010 (11%)
Increase in policy surrenders from 2009 to 2010 (268%)

ABILITY INSURANCE COMPANY

D **Weak**

Major Rating Factors: Weak profitability (1.1 on a scale of 0 to 10) with operating losses during the first six months of 2014. Return on equity has been low, averaging -29.9%. Weak overall results on stability tests (1.7) including negative cash flow from operations for 2013. Fair quality investment portfolio (4.1).

Other Rating Factors: Good capitalization (5.5) based on good risk adjusted capital (moderate loss scenario). Excellent liquidity (9.3).

Principal Business: Individual health insurance (85%), reinsurance (14%), and individual life insurance (1%).

Principal Investments: NonCMO investment grade bonds (71%), CMOs and structured securities (15%), noninv. grade bonds (2%), common & preferred stock (2%), and mortgages in good standing (2%).

Investments in Affiliates: None

Group Affiliation: Advantage Capital Partners LLC

Licensed in: All states except CT, ME, NH, NJ, NY, RI, VT, PR

Commenced Business: June 1968

Address: 222 S 15th St Suite 1202S, Omaha, NE 68102

Phone: (402) 218-4069 **Domicile State:** NE **NAIC Code:** 71471

Data Date	Rating	RACR #1	RACR #2	Total Assets ($mil)	Capital ($mil)	Net Premium ($mil)	Net Income ($mil)
6-14	D	1.34	0.70	854.3	34.4	8.8	-1.4
6-13	D	1.31	0.77	828.0	39.1	1.3	-8.9
2013	D	1.81	0.89	827.1	35.2	4.6	-9.6
2012	D	1.11	0.75	805.3	49.0	247.4	-15.7
2011	D	2.40	1.47	840.1	47.2	67.3	2.5
2010	D	2.93	2.04	214.1	33.0	46.0	-9.5
2009	D	2.36	1.76	195.3	21.7	22.9	-7.5

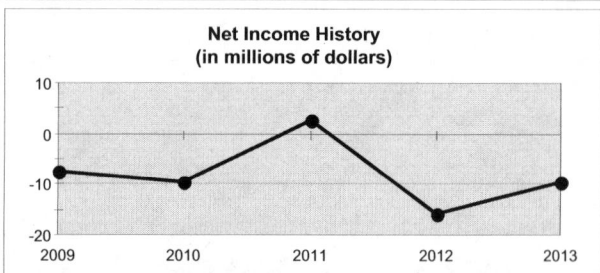

Net Income History
(in millions of dollars)

ABSOLUTE TOTAL CARE INC

C- **Fair**

Major Rating Factors: Weak profitability index (0.9 on a scale of 0 to 10). Good liquidity (5.5) with sufficient resources (cash flows and marketable investments) to handle a spike in claims. Strong capitalization (7.5) based on excellent current risk-adjusted capital (severe loss scenario).

Other Rating Factors: High quality investment portfolio (9.6).

Principal Business: Medicaid (100%)

Mem Phys: 13: 9,962 **12:** 7,535 **13 MLR** 96.7% **/ 13 Admin Exp** N/A

Enroll(000): Q2 14: 102 **13:** 92 **12:** 90 **Med Exp PMPM:** $294

Principal Investments: Long-term bonds (69%), cash and equiv (29%), affiliate common stock (1%), other (1%)

Provider Compensation ($000): Contr fee ($280,600), capitation ($18,017), salary ($16,898), bonus arrang ($557)

Total Member Encounters: Phys (581,496), non-phys (356,167)

Group Affiliation: Centene Corp

Licensed in: SC

Address: 1441 Main St Suite 950, Columbia, SC 29201

Phone: (314) 725-4477 **Dom State:** SC **Commenced Bus:** April 2007

Data Date	Rating	RACR #1	RACR #2	Total Assets ($mil)	Capital ($mil)	Net Premium ($mil)	Net Income ($mil)
6-14	C-	1.78	1.48	86.4	36.7	186.9	-5.7
6-13	C-	1.63	1.36	78.0	32.1	158.6	-15.0
2013	C-	1.99	1.66	83.8	41.0	329.4	-20.2
2012	C-	1.73	1.44	74.4	35.5	319.7	-16.9
2011	C-	1.60	1.33	69.5	34.0	300.0	-2.4
2010	C	1.68	1.40	97.8	34.8	269.5	-6.2
2009	C	1.20	1.00	50.9	14.4	139.0	1.4

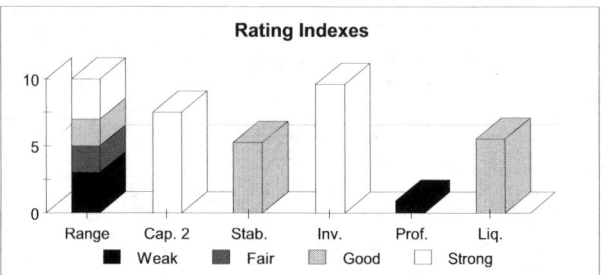

Rating Indexes

Range | Cap. 2 | Stab. | Inv. | Prof. | Liq.

■ Weak ▨ Fair ▨ Good ☐ Strong

ADVANCE INSURANCE COMPANY OF KANSAS *   B+   Good

Major Rating Factors: Good overall results on stability tests (6.8 on a scale of 0 to 10). Stability strengths include excellent operational trends and excellent risk diversification. Fair quality investment portfolio (4.4). Strong capitalization (8.9) based on excellent risk adjusted capital (severe loss scenario). Moreover, capital levels have been consistently high over the last five years.

Other Rating Factors: Excellent profitability (8.3) with operating gains in each of the last five years. Excellent liquidity (7.2).

Principal Business: Group life insurance (53%), group health insurance (33%), and individual life insurance (14%).

Principal Investments: NonCMO investment grade bonds (42%), common & preferred stock (33%), CMOs and structured securities (23%), and cash (1%).

Investments in Affiliates: 2%

Group Affiliation: Blue Cross Blue Shield Kansas

Licensed in: KS

Commenced Business: July 2004

Address: 1133 SW Topeka Blvd, Topeka, KS 66629-0001

Phone: (785) 291-7052 **Domicile State:** KS **NAIC Code:** 12143

Data Date	Rating	RACR #1	RACR #2	Total Assets ($mil)	Capital ($mil)	Net Premium ($mil)	Net Income ($mil)
6-14	B+	3.47	2.29	52.2	42.3	4.8	1.1
6-13	B+	3.66	2.44	48.8	40.0	4.8	0.8
2013	B+	3.51	2.32	51.4	41.5	9.6	1.6
2012	B+	3.78	2.54	47.5	38.9	9.6	0.9
2011	B+	3.98	2.70	44.9	37.9	9.7	1.2
2010	B+	4.37	3.02	43.9	37.2	10.3	1.9
2009	B+	4.49	3.14	41.2	35.5	10.7	1.7

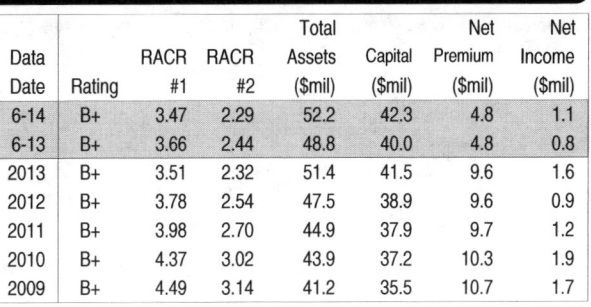

Rating Indexes (Ranges, Cap., Stab., Inv., Prof., Liq.) — Weak, Fair, Good, Strong

ADVANTAGE HEALTH SOLUTIONS INC   C   Fair

Major Rating Factors: Fair profitability index (3.7 on a scale of 0 to 10). Fair capitalization index (4.6) based on fair current risk-adjusted capital (moderate loss scenario). Fair overall results on stability tests (4.8).

Other Rating Factors: High quality investment portfolio (9.9). Excellent liquidity (7.0) with sufficient resources (cash flows and marketable investments) to handle a spike in claims.

Principal Business: Comp med (60%), Medicare (37%), other (3%)

Mem Phys: 13: 8,427 **12:** 8,910 **13 MLR** 88.5% **/ 13 Admin Exp** N/A

Enroll(000): Q2 14: 66 **13:** 66 **12:** 65 **Med Exp PMPM:** $456

Principal Investments: Cash and equiv (100%)

Provider Compensation ($000): Capitation ($227,695), FFS ($129,361), contr fee ($166)

Total Member Encounters: Phys (6,758), non-phys (1,062)

Group Affiliation: None

Licensed in: IN

Address: 9045 River Rd Suite 200, Indianapolis, IN 46240

Phone: (317) 573-2700 **Dom State:** IN **Commenced Bus:** May 2000

Data Date	Rating	RACR #1	RACR #2	Total Assets ($mil)	Capital ($mil)	Net Premium ($mil)	Net Income ($mil)
6-14	C	0.87	0.72	75.1	24.5	196.8	0.6
6-13	C	0.83	0.69	64.9	22.8	198.8	3.5
2013	C	0.88	0.73	68.7	24.7	403.8	4.5
2012	C-	0.71	0.59	54.7	19.4	378.6	-9.0
2011	C	0.84	0.70	56.9	23.1	353.3	1.5
2010	C	0.89	0.74	49.0	22.7	352.5	1.7
2009	C	0.72	0.60	43.8	20.6	373.5	3.2

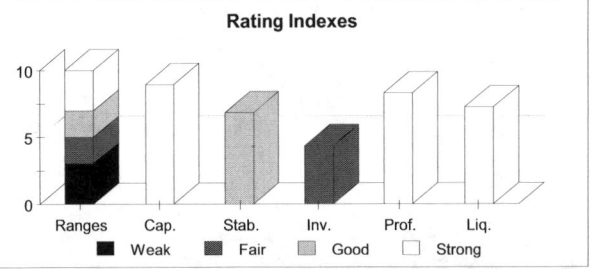

Rating Indexes (Range, Cap. 2, Stab., Inv., Prof., Liq.) — Weak, Fair, Good, Strong

AETNA BETTER HEALTH INC   B   Good

Major Rating Factors: Good overall profitability index (5.7 on a scale of 0 to 10). Good liquidity (5.3) with sufficient resources (cash flows and marketable investments) to handle a spike in claims. Strong capitalization (8.3) based on excellent current risk-adjusted capital (severe loss scenario).

Other Rating Factors: High quality investment portfolio (9.9).

Principal Business: Medicaid (100%)

Mem Phys: 13: 11,413 **12:** 6,762 **13 MLR** 87.7% **/ 13 Admin Exp** N/A

Enroll(000): Q2 14: 31 **13:** 18 **12:** 18 **Med Exp PMPM:** $1,233

Principal Investments: Long-term bonds (101%), other (5%)

Provider Compensation ($000): Contr fee ($206,633), FFS ($22,124), capitation ($9,646)

Total Member Encounters: Phys (402,491), non-phys (328,373)

Group Affiliation: Aetna Inc

Licensed in: (No states)

Address: One South Wacker Dr Suite 1200, Chicago, IL 60606

Phone: (312) 928-3000 **Dom State:** IL **Commenced Bus:** May 2011

Data Date	Rating	RACR #1	RACR #2	Total Assets ($mil)	Capital ($mil)	Net Premium ($mil)	Net Income ($mil)
6-14	B	2.37	1.97	143.9	35.8	205.6	0.4
6-13	A-	3.52	2.93	124.5	39.1	135.8	2.0
2013	B	2.35	1.96	146.4	35.5	308.2	6.5
2012	A-	3.79	3.16	91.6	42.8	230.2	13.9
2011	B	1.18	0.98	55.5	8.7	85.9	-1.3
2010	N/A	N/A	N/A	N/A	N/A	N/A	N/A
2009	N/A	N/A	N/A	N/A	N/A	N/A	N/A

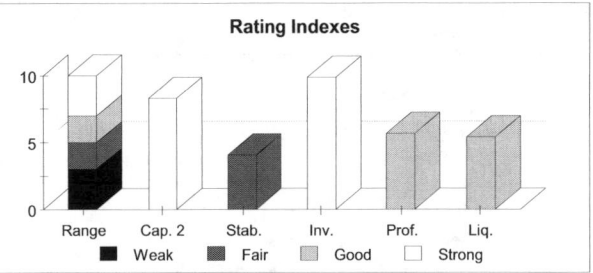

Rating Indexes (Range, Cap. 2, Stab., Inv., Prof., Liq.) — Weak, Fair, Good, Strong

AETNA BETTER HEALTH INC (A PA CORP)   D-   Weak

Major Rating Factors: Weak profitability index (0.9 on a scale of 0 to 10). Fair liquidity (3.5) as cash resources may not be adequate to cover a spike in claims. Strong capitalization (8.0) based on excellent current risk-adjusted capital (severe loss scenario).
Other Rating Factors: High quality investment portfolio (8.3).
Principal Business: Medicaid (100%)
Mem Phys: 13: 18,824 **12:** 13,456 **13 MLR** 96.4% **/ 13 Admin Exp** N/A
Enroll(000): Q2 14: 77 **13:** 72 **12:** 59 **Med Exp PMPM:** $383
Principal Investments: Long-term bonds (89%), cash and equiv (8%), other (3%)
Provider Compensation ($000): Contr fee ($255,989), FFS ($19,847), capitation ($10,284)
Total Member Encounters: Phys (324,302), non-phys (376,945)
Group Affiliation: Aetna Inc
Licensed in: PA
Address: 980 Jolly Rd, Blue Bell, PA 19422-1904
Phone: (800) 872-3862 **Dom State:** PA **Commenced Bus:** April 2010

Data Date	Rating	RACR #1	RACR #2	Total Assets ($mil)	Capital ($mil)	Net Premium ($mil)	Net Income ($mil)
6-14	D-	2.14	1.78	183.8	33.2	189.2	-9.5
6-13	D-	2.29	1.91	140.9	38.5	137.5	-0.9
2013	D-	2.06	1.72	133.6	31.6	305.9	-7.0
2012	D-	2.33	1.94	115.9	39.3	289.5	-13.1
2011	D-	2.46	2.05	98.0	35.7	250.9	-4.1
2010	C+	1.28	1.07	50.5	10.2	99.0	-3.6
2009	N/A	N/A	N/A	N/A	N/A	N/A	N/A

Rating Indexes

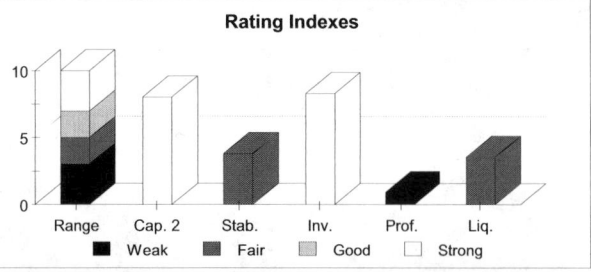

Range Cap. 2 Stab. Inv. Prof. Liq.
■ Weak ■ Fair ▨ Good □ Strong

AETNA HEALTH & LIFE INSURANCE COMPANY *   B+   Good

Major Rating Factors: Good overall results on stability tests (6.8 on a scale of 0 to 10). Stability strengths include excellent operational trends and excellent risk diversification. Good quality investment portfolio (6.3) despite substantial holdings of BBB bonds in addition to moderate junk bond exposure. Exposure to mortgages is significant, but the mortgage default rate has been low. Strong capitalization (8.2) based on excellent risk adjusted capital (severe loss scenario).
Other Rating Factors: Excellent profitability (7.4) with operating gains in each of the last five years. Excellent liquidity (7.4).
Principal Business: Reinsurance (100%).
Principal Investments: NonCMO investment grade bonds (62%), CMOs and structured securities (12%), mortgages in good standing (11%), and noninv. grade bonds (6%).
Investments in Affiliates: 5%
Group Affiliation: Aetna Inc
Licensed in: All states except FL, MO, NH, PR
Commenced Business: October 1971
Address: 151 Farmington Avenue, Hartford, IL 06156-0417
Phone: (708) 245-4001 **Domicile State:** CT **NAIC Code:** 78700

Data Date	Rating	RACR #1	RACR #2	Total Assets ($mil)	Capital ($mil)	Net Premium ($mil)	Net Income ($mil)
6-14	B+	3.02	1.79	2,193.0	292.5	278.9	56.7
6-13	B+	2.89	1.67	2,119.4	257.6	246.2	16.5
2013	B+	3.04	1.80	2,148.2	280.6	501.0	71.2
2012	B+	3.11	1.77	1,988.1	256.3	420.1	53.4
2011	B+	3.21	1.77	1,913.0	248.8	369.5	56.3
2010	B	3.31	1.89	1,906.1	251.7	383.1	58.5
2009	B	2.52	1.54	1,773.0	205.8	396.1	23.1

Adverse Trends in Operations

Decrease in capital during 2011 (1%)
Decrease in premium volume from 2010 to 2011 (4%)
Decrease in premium volume from 2009 to 2010 (3%)

AETNA HEALTH INC (A CT CORP)   C   Fair

Major Rating Factors: Weak profitability index (0.9 on a scale of 0 to 10). Good overall results on stability tests (5.2) despite a decline in enrollment during 2013. Rating is significantly influenced by the good financial results of Aetna Inc. Good liquidity (5.8) with sufficient resources (cash flows and marketable investments) to handle a spike in claims.
Other Rating Factors: Strong capitalization index (8.0) based on excellent current risk-adjusted capital (severe loss scenario). High quality investment portfolio (8.9).
Principal Business: Comp med (68%), Medicare (32%).
Mem Phys: 13: 21,339 **12:** 20,008 **13 MLR** 91.9% **/ 13 Admin Exp** N/A
Enroll(000): Q2 14: 40 **13:** 55 **12:** 63 **Med Exp PMPM:** $440
Principal Investments: Long-term bonds (73%), cash and equiv (27%)
Provider Compensation ($000): Contr fee ($303,250), FFS ($11,105), bonus arrang ($1,564), capitation ($942)
Total Member Encounters: Phys (435,464), non-phys (490,964)
Group Affiliation: Aetna Inc
Licensed in: CT
Address: 1000 Middle St, Middletown, CT 06457
Phone: (800) 872-3862 **Dom State:** CT **Commenced Bus:** June 1987

Data Date	Rating	RACR #1	RACR #2	Total Assets ($mil)	Capital ($mil)	Net Premium ($mil)	Net Income ($mil)
6-14	C	2.18	1.82	114.0	47.3	164.1	-12.8
6-13	B	1.77	1.47	92.9	34.3	180.5	-0.7
2013	B	2.31	1.93	98.8	50.2	350.2	-12.7
2012	B	1.22	1.02	75.4	23.5	314.3	-5.5
2011	B	1.73	1.44	63.1	23.9	246.7	9.3
2010	A-	3.05	2.54	70.4	42.9	252.8	14.1
2009	B	1.83	1.53	59.6	27.7	245.3	-0.2

Rating Indexes

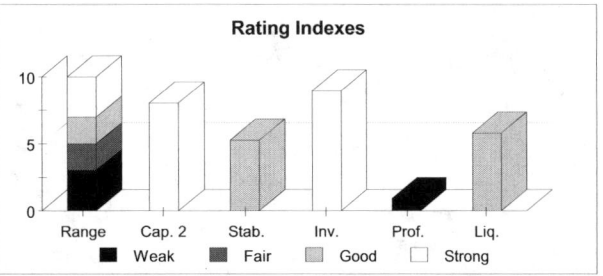

Range Cap. 2 Stab. Inv. Prof. Liq.
■ Weak ■ Fair ▨ Good □ Strong

AETNA HEALTH INC (A FLORIDA CORP) *   A-   Excellent

Major Rating Factors: Excellent profitability (7.9 on a scale of 0 to 10). Strong capitalization index (8.1) based on excellent current risk-adjusted capital (severe loss scenario). High quality investment portfolio (8.4).
Other Rating Factors: Good liquidity (6.3) with sufficient resources (cash flows and marketable investments) to handle a spike in claims. Fair overall results on stability tests (4.6). Rating is significantly influenced by the good financial results of Aetna Inc.
Principal Business: Comp med (95%), Medicare (5%)
Mem Phys: 13: 50,587 **12:** 48,348 **13 MLR** 82.4% **/ 13 Admin Exp** N/A
Enroll(000): Q2 14: 231 **13:** 266 **12:** 302 **Med Exp PMPM:** $306
Principal Investments: Long-term bonds (94%), cash and equiv (6%)
Provider Compensation ($000): Contr fee ($980,663), FFS ($51,172), bonus arrang ($2,620), capitation ($1,624)
Total Member Encounters: Phys (1,012,136), non-phys (1,965,810)
Group Affiliation: Aetna Inc
Licensed in: FL
Address: 4630 Woodland Corporate Blvd, Tampa, FL 33614-2415
Phone: (813) 775-0000 **Dom State:** FL **Commenced Bus:** July 1985

Data Date	Rating	RACR #1	RACR #2	Total Assets ($mil)	Capital ($mil)	Net Premium ($mil)	Net Income ($mil)
6-14	A-	2.23	1.85	324.6	142.8	555.7	25.1
6-13	A-	2.03	1.69	322.6	151.8	620.5	46.2
2013	A-	1.84	1.53	273.7	116.4	1,220.0	77.7
2012	A-	1.42	1.18	310.4	103.2	1,374.2	59.8
2011	A-	2.21	1.84	341.6	165.7	1,477.8	91.4
2010	B+	1.78	1.48	342.0	147.1	1,641.4	75.8
2009	B	1.39	1.16	372.4	148.1	1,988.1	43.9

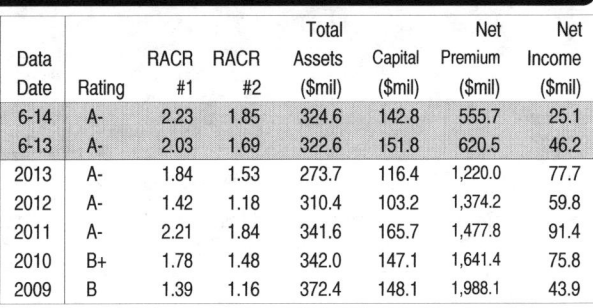

AETNA HEALTH INC (A GEORGIA CORP)   B   Good

Major Rating Factors: Good overall results on stability tests (5.9 on a scale of 0 to 10). Rating is significantly influenced by the good financial results of Aetna Inc. Good liquidity (6.1) with sufficient resources (cash flows and marketable investments) to handle a spike in claims. Excellent profitability (8.5).
Other Rating Factors: Strong capitalization index (8.8) based on excellent current risk-adjusted capital (severe loss scenario). High quality investment portfolio (9.4).
Principal Business: Comp med (75%), FEHB (13%), Medicare (10%)
Mem Phys: 13: 20,314 **12:** 18,765 **13 MLR** 84.6% **/ 13 Admin Exp** N/A
Enroll(000): Q2 14: 98 **13:** 115 **12:** 127 **Med Exp PMPM:** $204
Principal Investments: Long-term bonds (97%), cash and equiv (3%)
Provider Compensation ($000): Contr fee ($269,013), FFS ($13,843), capitation ($1,443), bonus arrang ($238)
Total Member Encounters: Phys (558,629), non-phys (330,367)
Group Affiliation: Aetna Inc
Licensed in: GA
Address: 11675 Great Oaks Way, Apharetta, GA 30022
Phone: (800) 872-3862 **Dom State:** GA **Commenced Bus:** February 1986

Data Date	Rating	RACR #1	RACR #2	Total Assets ($mil)	Capital ($mil)	Net Premium ($mil)	Net Income ($mil)
6-14	B	2.80	2.34	101.4	51.5	148.0	5.8
6-13	B	2.51	2.09	93.9	44.3	176.6	8.0
2013	B	2.79	2.33	102.5	51.3	343.2	14.3
2012	B	2.14	1.78	79.7	37.6	351.6	17.7
2011	B	2.42	2.02	78.1	39.4	340.4	22.6
2010	B-	1.78	1.49	75.4	31.1	351.6	13.3
2009	C+	2.04	1.70	87.4	38.0	359.2	11.3

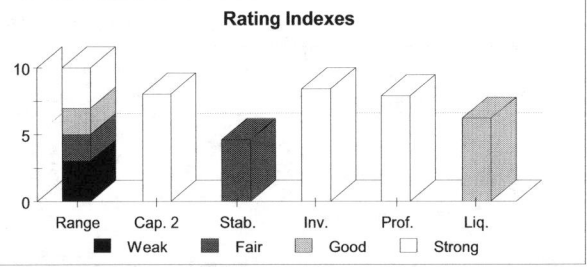

AETNA HEALTH INC (A MAINE CORP)   B-   Good

Major Rating Factors: Fair profitability index (4.7 on a scale of 0 to 10). Good overall results on stability tests (5.0). Rating is significantly influenced by the good financial results of Aetna Inc. Good liquidity (6.6) with sufficient resources (cash flows and marketable investments) to handle a spike in claims.
Other Rating Factors: Strong capitalization index (7.9) based on excellent current risk-adjusted capital (severe loss scenario). High quality investment portfolio (9.9).
Principal Business: Comp med (58%), Medicare (42%)
Mem Phys: 13: 9,415 **12:** 9,010 **13 MLR** 85.9% **/ 13 Admin Exp** N/A
Enroll(000): Q2 14: 18 **13:** 19 **12:** 17 **Med Exp PMPM:** $400
Principal Investments: Long-term bonds (85%), cash and equiv (15%)
Provider Compensation ($000): Contr fee ($79,173), FFS ($2,923), bonus arrang ($396), capitation ($252)
Total Member Encounters: Phys (122,757), non-phys (123,324)
Group Affiliation: Aetna Inc
Licensed in: ME
Address: 175 Running Hill Rd Suite 301, S Portland, ME 04106-3220
Phone: (800) 872-3862 **Dom State:** ME **Commenced Bus:** April 1996

Data Date	Rating	RACR #1	RACR #2	Total Assets ($mil)	Capital ($mil)	Net Premium ($mil)	Net Income ($mil)
6-14	B-	2.10	1.75	31.6	13.1	54.8	-0.5
6-13	B-	2.62	2.19	24.8	13.9	46.4	-0.9
2013	B-	2.23	1.86	34.2	13.9	98.3	-1.4
2012	B-	2.78	2.32	27.6	14.8	93.2	7.4
2011	B-	2.58	2.15	19.4	11.4	72.7	5.6
2010	B-	2.74	2.28	24.2	14.9	81.7	4.2
2009	B	2.44	2.03	32.4	19.4	133.2	3.9

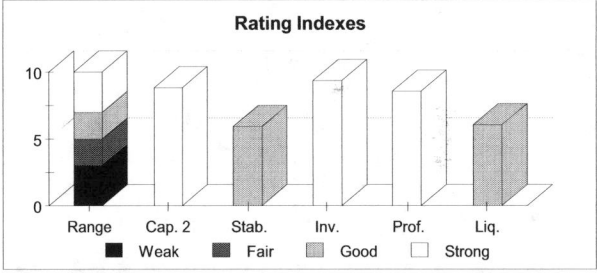

AETNA HEALTH INC (A NEW JERSEY CORP)　　　B　　Good

Major Rating Factors: Good liquidity (6.2 on a scale of 0 to 10) with sufficient resources (cash flows and marketable investments) to handle a spike in claims. Fair profitability index (4.5). Fair overall results on stability tests (4.4) based on a significant 29% decrease in enrollment during the period. Rating is significantly influenced by the good financial results of Aetna Inc.

Other Rating Factors: Strong capitalization index (8.2) based on excellent current risk-adjusted capital (severe loss scenario). High quality investment portfolio (9.3).

Principal Business: Comp med (58%), Medicare (36%), FEHB (6%)

Mem Phys: 13: 31,551　**12:** 29,535　**13 MLR** 87.4%　**/ 13 Admin Exp** N/A

Enroll(000): Q2 14: 164　**13:** 175　**12:** 246　**Med Exp PMPM:** $487

Principal Investments: Long-term bonds (95%), cash and equiv (4%), other (1%)

Provider Compensation ($000): Contr fee ($1,064,617), FFS ($102,957), capitation ($37,615), bonus arrang ($3,649)

Total Member Encounters: Phys (3,451,820), non-phys (1,431,300)

Group Affiliation: Aetna Inc

Licensed in: NJ

Address: 55 Lane Rd, Fairfield, NJ 07004-1011

Phone: (800) 872-3862　**Dom State:** NJ　**Commenced Bus:** March 1983

Data Date	Rating	RACR #1	RACR #2	Total Assets ($mil)	Capital ($mil)	Net Premium ($mil)	Net Income ($mil)
6-14	B	2.32	1.93	337.6	165.6	582.6	8.4
6-13	B	2.05	1.71	353.5	171.1	725.9	24.8
2013	B	2.11	1.76	341.3	149.2	1,355.1	21.7
2012	B	1.83	1.53	368.0	151.1	1,627.9	47.2
2011	B	2.28	1.90	409.2	184.4	1,643.0	48.1
2010	B+	2.65	2.21	447.8	227.8	1,677.6	10.0
2009	B+	2.56	2.13	510.0	258.3	1,877.6	-5.2

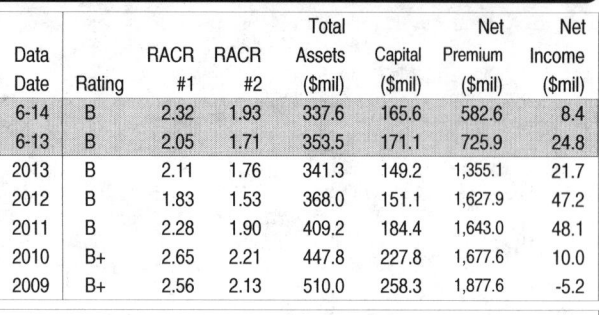

Rating Indexes

AETNA HEALTH INC (A NEW YORK CORP) *　　B+　　Good

Major Rating Factors: Good overall results on stability tests (5.3 on a scale of 0 to 10). Rating is significantly influenced by the good financial results of Aetna Inc. Good liquidity (6.9) with sufficient resources (cash flows and marketable investments) to handle a spike in claims. Excellent profitability (8.9).

Other Rating Factors: Strong capitalization index (10.0) based on excellent current risk-adjusted capital (severe loss scenario). High quality investment portfolio (8.8).

Principal Business: Comp med (54%), Medicare (30%), FEHB (16%)

Mem Phys: 13: 66,708　**12:** 62,915　**13 MLR** 81.6%　**/ 13 Admin Exp** N/A

Enroll(000): Q2 14: 61　**13:** 75　**12:** 79　**Med Exp PMPM:** $538

Principal Investments: Long-term bonds (90%), cash and equiv (5%), affiliate common stock (3%), other (2%)

Provider Compensation ($000): Contr fee ($424,569), FFS ($35,764), capitation ($14,498), bonus arrang ($1,907)

Total Member Encounters: Phys (1,137,973), non-phys (220,332)

Group Affiliation: Aetna Inc

Licensed in: NY

Address: 100 Park Ave 12th Floor, New York, NY 10017-5516

Phone: (800) 872-3862　**Dom State:** NY　**Commenced Bus:** May 1986

Data Date	Rating	RACR #1	RACR #2	Total Assets ($mil)	Capital ($mil)	Net Premium ($mil)	Net Income ($mil)
6-14	B+	6.86	5.71	377.2	251.2	262.2	7.0
6-13	B+	8.23	6.86	356.9	233.8	290.5	40.0
2013	B+	6.63	5.52	362.3	242.4	575.1	42.6
2012	A-	8.67	7.23	363.9	247.1	626.8	73.6
2011	A	7.86	6.55	394.7	208.6	616.5	29.0
2010	B	5.45	4.54	310.5	176.0	702.8	50.1
2009	B-	5.47	4.56	338.8	183.1	801.7	47.4

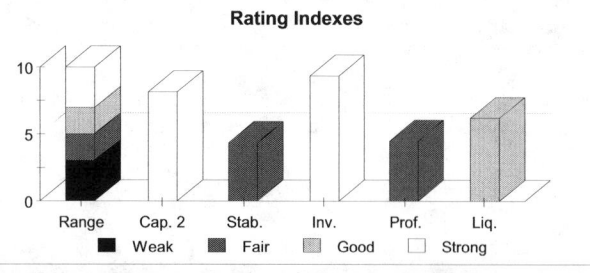

Rating Indexes

AETNA HEALTH INC (A PA CORP)　　B　　Good

Major Rating Factors: Good quality investment portfolio (6.7 on a scale of 0 to 10). Fair overall results on stability tests (4.9). Rating is significantly influenced by the good financial results of Aetna Inc. Fair liquidity (3.7) as cash resources may not be adequate to cover a spike in claims.

Other Rating Factors: Excellent profitability (7.4). Strong capitalization index (8.6) based on excellent current risk-adjusted capital (severe loss scenario).

Principal Business: Comp med (51%), Medicare (25%), FEHB (24%)

Mem Phys: 13: 345,738　**12:** 324,207　**13 MLR** 99.3%　**/ 13 Admin Exp** N/A

Enroll(000): Q2 14: 619　**13:** 701　**12:** 773　**Med Exp PMPM:** $343

Principal Investments: Long-term bonds (91%), cash and equiv (5%), other (4%)

Provider Compensation ($000): Contr fee ($2,824,165), FFS ($99,455), capitation ($75,314), bonus arrang ($9,297)

Total Member Encounters: Phys (5,982,165), non-phys (2,605,237)

Group Affiliation: Aetna Inc

Licensed in: AZ, CO, DC, DE, IL, IN, KS, KY, MD, MA, MO, NV, NC, OH, OK, PA, SC, TN, VA

Address: 980 Jolly Rd, Blue Bell, PA 19422-1904

Phone: (800) 872-3862　**Dom State:** PA　**Commenced Bus:** September 1981

Data Date	Rating	RACR #1	RACR #2	Total Assets ($mil)	Capital ($mil)	Net Premium ($mil)	Net Income ($mil)
6-14	B	2.62	2.18	866.6	341.2	1,486.6	18.5
6-13	B+	2.14	1.78	814.6	358.8	1,540.0	62.7
2013	B	2.54	2.12	813.6	329.3	3,019.9	101.0
2012	A-	2.15	1.79	776.4	360.2	3,703.0	159.3
2011	A-	2.31	1.92	767.1	369.6	3,767.4	213.5
2010	A-	2.29	1.90	806.8	400.5	3,897.7	161.7
2009	B+	2.41	2.01	984.9	474.6	4,228.2	160.7

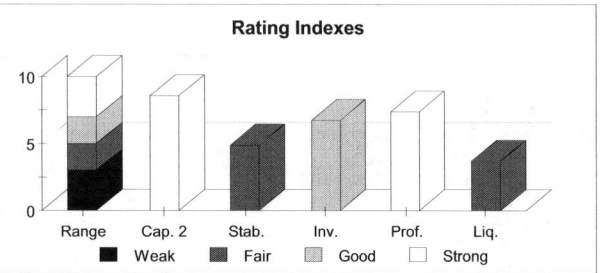

Rating Indexes

AETNA HEALTH INC (A TEXAS CORP)   B   Good

Major Rating Factors: Good overall profitability index (5.4 on a scale of 0 to 10). Good liquidity (5.7) with sufficient resources (cash flows and marketable investments) to handle a spike in claims. Fair overall results on stability tests (3.9). Rating is significantly influenced by the good financial results of Aetna Inc.
Other Rating Factors: Strong capitalization index (8.2) based on excellent current risk-adjusted capital (severe loss scenario). High quality investment portfolio (9.9).
Principal Business: Comp med (49%), Medicaid (26%), Medicare (22%), FEHB (2%)
Mem Phys: 13: 47,973   **12:** 44,220   **13 MLR** 87.6%   **/ 13 Admin Exp** N/A
Enroll(000): Q2 14: 146   **13:** 151   **12:** 171   **Med Exp PMPM:** $321
Principal Investments: Long-term bonds (95%), cash and equiv (5%)
Provider Compensation ($000): Contr fee ($556,769), FFS ($52,484), capitation ($2,492), bonus arrang ($988)
Total Member Encounters: Phys (1,945,675), non-phys (572,631)
Group Affiliation: Aetna Inc
Licensed in: TX
Address: 2777 Stemmons Freeway, Ste 400, Dallas, TX 75207
Phone: (800) 872-3862   **Dom State:** TX   **Commenced Bus:** November 1987

Data Date	Rating	RACR #1	RACR #2	Total Assets ($mil)	Capital ($mil)	Net Premium ($mil)	Net Income ($mil)
6-14	B	2.32	1.94	211.2	91.5	346.8	1.1
6-13	B+	2.49	2.08	196.7	102.2	358.1	2.1
2013	B	2.28	1.90	187.9	89.6	703.9	6.5
2012	B+	2.69	2.24	194.4	110.5	711.6	9.6
2011	B	2.86	2.38	191.8	105.8	714.5	29.1
2010	B	2.71	2.26	221.3	110.4	756.3	37.3
2009	B	2.04	1.70	202.3	93.4	850.0	18.9

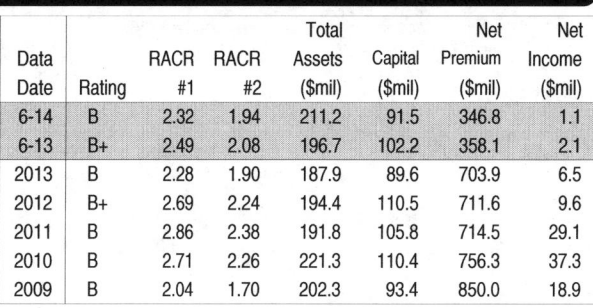

Rating Indexes

AETNA HEALTH INS CO   B   Good

Major Rating Factors: Good quality investment portfolio (6.6 on a scale of 0 to 10). Good liquidity (6.9) with sufficient resources (cash flows and marketable investments) to handle a spike in claims. Fair profitability index (4.9).
Other Rating Factors: Strong capitalization (10.0) based on excellent current risk-adjusted capital (severe loss scenario).
Principal Business: Comp med (100%)
Mem Phys: 13: N/A   **12:** N/A   **13 MLR** 72.0%   **/ 13 Admin Exp** N/A
Enroll(000): Q2 14: 301   **13:** 390   **12:** 498   **Med Exp PMPM:** $12
Principal Investments: Long-term bonds (96%), cash and equiv (4%)
Provider Compensation ($000): FFS ($63,162)
Total Member Encounters: N/A
Group Affiliation: Aetna Inc
Licensed in: All states except CA, CT, MS, NY, PR
Address: 980 Jolly Rd, Blue Bell, PA 19422
Phone: (800) 872-3862   **Dom State:** PA   **Commenced Bus:** December 1956

Data Date	Rating	RACR #1	RACR #2	Total Assets ($mil)	Capital ($mil)	Net Premium ($mil)	Net Income ($mil)
6-14	B	5.87	4.89	70.5	38.0	23.3	-2.1
6-13	B	4.37	3.64	48.3	30.6	30.8	-3.8
2013	B	6.23	5.20	61.6	40.3	86.9	5.6
2012	B	4.98	4.15	52.4	34.8	67.7	-8.6
2011	B	4.30	3.58	46.2	28.2	102.6	13.1
2010	B	3.34	2.78	52.2	26.1	109.3	8.0
2009	C+	1.90	1.59	40.8	17.2	109.6	1.9

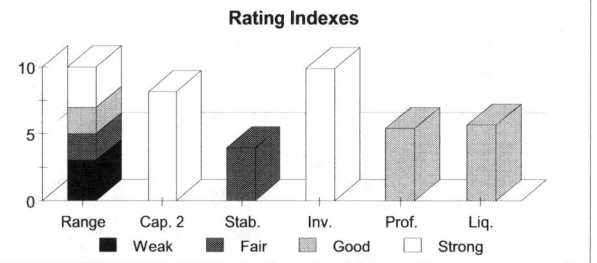

Rating Indexes

AETNA HEALTH INS CO OF NY   B   Good

Major Rating Factors: Fair profitability index (3.5 on a scale of 0 to 10). Strong capitalization (10.0) based on excellent current risk-adjusted capital (severe loss scenario). High quality investment portfolio (9.9).
Other Rating Factors: Excellent liquidity (9.2) with ample operational cash flow and liquid investments.
Principal Business: Comp med (100%)
Mem Phys: 13: N/A   **12:** N/A   **13 MLR** 100.9%   **/ 13 Admin Exp** N/A
Enroll(000): Q2 14: 13   **13:** 24   **12:** 19   **Med Exp PMPM:** $9
Principal Investments: Cash and equiv (63%), long-term bonds (37%)
Provider Compensation ($000): FFS ($1,377), contr fee ($748)
Total Member Encounters: N/A
Group Affiliation: Aetna Inc
Licensed in: NY
Address: 333 Earle Ovington Blvd, Uniondale, NY 11553
Phone: (800) 872-3862   **Dom State:** NY   **Commenced Bus:** August 1986

Data Date	Rating	RACR #1	RACR #2	Total Assets ($mil)	Capital ($mil)	Net Premium ($mil)	Net Income ($mil)
6-14	B	7.60	6.33	11.3	10.1	0.9	0.0
6-13	B	7.65	6.37	10.9	10.1	0.7	-0.6
2013	B	7.71	6.42	11.5	10.2	2.2	-0.5
2012	B	8.04	6.70	12.0	10.6	3.6	0.5
2011	B	7.64	6.37	11.6	10.1	7.1	1.2
2010	B	6.86	5.72	11.7	8.9	8.8	0.5
2009	B-	7.35	6.12	10.3	8.4	9.8	-0.3

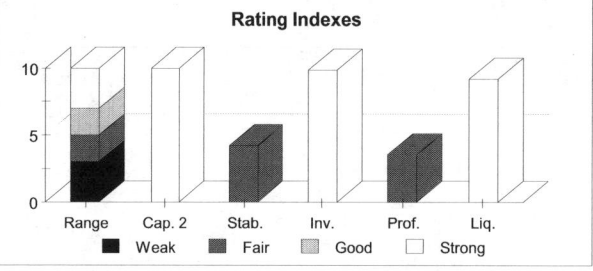

Rating Indexes

AETNA HEALTH OF CALIFORNIA INC | B | Good

Major Rating Factors: Good overall profitability index (6.2 on a scale of 0 to 10). Good capitalization index (5.6) based on good current risk-adjusted capital (severe loss scenario). Fair overall results on stability tests (3.9) based on a significant 32% decrease in enrollment during the period. Rating is significantly influenced by the good financial results of Aetna Inc.

Other Rating Factors: Excellent liquidity (6.9) with sufficient resources (cash flows and marketable investments) to handle a spike in claims.

Principal Business: Medicare (16%)

Mem Phys: 13: N/A **12:** N/A **13 MLR** 85.1% **/ 13 Admin Exp** N/A

Enroll(000): Q2 14: 500 **13:** 577 **12:** 854 **Med Exp PMPM:** $234

Principal Investments ($000): Cash and equiv ($21,486)

Provider Compensation ($000): None

Total Member Encounters: N/A

Group Affiliation: Aetna Inc

Licensed in: CA

Address: 2625 Shadelands Dr, Walnut Creek, CA 94598

Phone: (925) 948-4244 **Dom State:** CA **Commenced Bus:** October 1981

Data Date	Rating	RACR #1	RACR #2	Total Assets ($mil)	Capital ($mil)	Net Premium ($mil)	Net Income ($mil)
6-14	B	1.29	0.85	450.7	144.0	988.1	24.5
6-13	B	1.41	0.93	407.6	158.3	941.1	27.1
2013	B	1.25	0.83	431.4	143.8	1,910.1	53.4
2012	B	1.53	1.02	422.8	177.7	1,893.8	80.3
2011	B	1.73	1.16	446.1	195.2	1,779.8	101.2
2010	B-	1.30	0.86	414.0	146.5	1,798.6	55.5
2009	B-	1.18	0.77	355.7	137.8	1,895.4	48.2

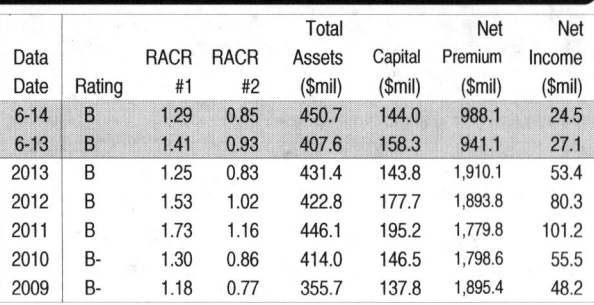

Rating Indexes — Range, Cap. 2, Stab., Inv., Prof., Liq. — Weak, Fair, Good, Strong

AETNA LIFE INSURANCE COMPANY * | B+ | Good

Major Rating Factors: Good quality investment portfolio (6.2 on a scale of 0 to 10) despite large holdings of BBB rated bonds in addition to moderate junk bond exposure. Exposure to mortgages is significant, but the mortgage default rate has been low. Good liquidity (6.4) with sufficient resources to handle a spike in claims as well as a significant increase in policy surrenders. Good overall results on stability tests (6.7) despite excessive premium growth excellent operational trends and excellent risk diversification.

Other Rating Factors: Strong capitalization (7.2) based on excellent risk adjusted capital (severe loss scenario). Excellent profitability (7.1) with operating gains in each of the last five years.

Principal Business: Group health insurance (61%), individual health insurance (32%), group life insurance (5%), group retirement contracts (1%), and reinsurance (1%).

Principal Investments: NonCMO investment grade bonds (57%), CMOs and structured securities (12%), mortgages in good standing (10%), noninv. grade bonds (7%), and real estate (3%).

Investments in Affiliates: 4%

Group Affiliation: Aetna Inc

Licensed in: All states, the District of Columbia and Puerto Rico

Commenced Business: December 1850

Address: 151 Farmington Ave, Hartford, CT 06156

Phone: (860) 273-0123 **Domicile State:** CT **NAIC Code:** 60054

Data Date	Rating	RACR #1	RACR #2	Total Assets ($mil)	Capital ($mil)	Net Premium ($mil)	Net Income ($mil)
6-14	B+	1.59	1.14	22,226.6	3,168.5	7,846.6	506.1
6-13	B+	2.02	1.42	21,804.4	3,485.0	5,948.4	574.1
2013	B+	1.76	1.25	21,793.1	3,199.9	12,142.0	911.1
2012	B+	1.89	1.33	21,175.5	3,332.3	12,689.8	1,020.0
2011	B+	1.73	1.22	20,894.4	3,047.1	11,199.3	1,001.2
2010	B	2.05	1.48	21,237.4	4,182.4	13,868.7	1,193.1
2009	B	2.19	1.58	22,490.3	4,858.2	15,428.6	882.6

Adverse Trends in Operations

Increase in policy surrenders from 2012 to 2013 (336%)
Decrease in capital during 2011 (27%)
Decrease in premium volume from 2010 to 2011 (19%)
Decrease in capital during 2010 (14%)
Decrease in premium volume from 2009 to 2010 (10%)

ALLEGIAN INS CO | C | Fair

Major Rating Factors: Weak profitability index (1.7 on a scale of 0 to 10). Strong capitalization (7.4) based on excellent current risk-adjusted capital (severe loss scenario). High quality investment portfolio (9.9).

Other Rating Factors: Excellent liquidity (7.3) with ample operational cash flow and liquid investments.

Principal Business: Comp med (100%)

Mem Phys: 13: 17,609 **12:** 2,061 **13 MLR** 82.6% **/ 13 Admin Exp** N/A

Enroll(000): Q2 14: 14 **13:** 13 **12:** 12 **Med Exp PMPM:** $229

Principal Investments: Cash and equiv (99%), long-term bonds (1%)

Provider Compensation ($000): Contr fee ($23,902), FFS ($9,471), capitation ($138)

Total Member Encounters: Phys (15,314), non-phys (107,427)

Group Affiliation: Vanguard Health Systems Inc

Licensed in: TX

Address: 2005 Ed Carey Dr, Harlingen, TX 78550

Phone: (956) 389-2273 **Dom State:** TX **Commenced Bus:** March 2006

Data Date	Rating	RACR #1	RACR #2	Total Assets ($mil)	Capital ($mil)	Net Premium ($mil)	Net Income ($mil)
6-14	C	1.66	1.38	20.9	8.8	30.1	0.6
6-13	C	2.29	1.91	22.3	9.7	20.9	-1.2
2013	C	2.48	2.07	21.7	13.4	42.4	-2.5
2012	C	3.51	2.92	21.7	15.4	35.6	2.6
2011	D	1.58	1.31	17.8	8.8	41.3	0.8
2010	D	0.58	0.48	11.8	4.4	58.2	-1.5
2009	D	0.72	0.60	14.6	6.0	65.0	-2.9

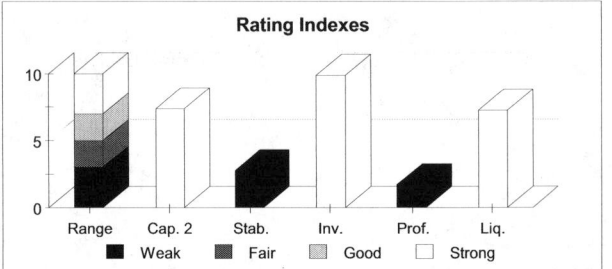

Rating Indexes — Range, Cap. 2, Stab., Inv., Prof., Liq. — Weak, Fair, Good, Strong

ALLEGIANCE LIFE & HEALTH INS CO INC   C   Fair

Major Rating Factors: Fair liquidity (3.0 on a scale of 0 to 10) as a spike in claims may stretch capacity. Weak profitability index (0.7). Strong capitalization (7.2) based on excellent current risk-adjusted capital (severe loss scenario).
Other Rating Factors: High quality investment portfolio (9.3).
Principal Business: Comp med (97%), dental (3%)
Mem Phys: 13: N/A **12:** N/A **13 MLR** 104.1% **/ 13 Admin Exp** N/A
Enroll(000): Q2 14: 9 **13:** 15 **12:** 19 **Med Exp PMPM:** $265
Principal Investments: Long-term bonds (84%), cash and equiv (16%)
Provider Compensation ($000): FFS ($59,035)
Total Member Encounters: Phys (78,812), non-phys (224,696)
Group Affiliation: CIGNA Corp
Licensed in: MT
Address: 2806 S Garfield St, Missoula, MT 59801
Phone: (406) 721-2222 **Dom State:** MT **Commenced Bus:** November 2006

Data Date	Rating	RACR #1	RACR #2	Total Assets ($mil)	Capital ($mil)	Net Premium ($mil)	Net Income ($mil)
6-14	C	1.49	1.24	16.5	7.3	20.5	-0.6
6-13	C	1.54	1.28	22.3	10.4	27.5	0.1
2013	C	1.51	1.26	19.3	7.4	53.0	-3.0
2012	C	1.53	1.28	23.1	10.4	79.4	-2.2
2011	C	1.66	1.38	21.6	10.4	71.6	-2.1
2010	C	2.41	2.01	20.2	12.3	56.5	0.1
2009	C	2.59	2.16	18.8	12.1	43.6	-3.6

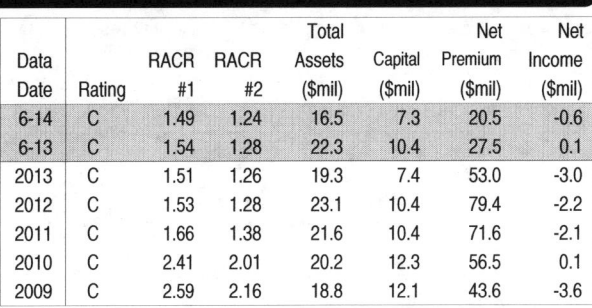

Rating Indexes

ALLIANCE HEALTH & LIFE INS CO *   B+   Good

Major Rating Factors: Good overall profitability index (5.2 on a scale of 0 to 10). Strong capitalization (7.5) based on excellent current risk-adjusted capital (severe loss scenario). High quality investment portfolio (9.9).
Other Rating Factors: Excellent liquidity (7.0) with ample operational cash flow and liquid investments.
Principal Business: Comp med (73%), Medicare (22%), other (5%)
Mem Phys: 13: 9,430 **12:** 10,250 **13 MLR** 81.4% **/ 13 Admin Exp** N/A
Enroll(000): Q2 14: 58 **13:** 59 **12:** 53 **Med Exp PMPM:** $249
Principal Investments: Cash and equiv (76%), nonaffiliate common stock (19%), long-term bonds (1%), other (4%)
Provider Compensation ($000): Contr fee ($157,662), FFS ($9,510), other ($1,724)
Total Member Encounters: Phys (234,852), non-phys (19,531)
Group Affiliation: Henry Ford Health System
Licensed in: MI
Address: 2850 W Grand Blvd,5th Floor, Detroit, MI 48202-2692
Phone: (313) 872-8100 **Dom State:** MI **Commenced Bus:** September 1996

Data Date	Rating	RACR #1	RACR #2	Total Assets ($mil)	Capital ($mil)	Net Premium ($mil)	Net Income ($mil)
6-14	B+	1.74	1.45	66.3	26.8	116.6	-1.4
6-13	A-	2.12	1.77	66.7	30.3	103.0	1.2
2013	A-	1.81	1.50	64.2	27.9	209.3	0.6
2012	B+	2.08	1.73	62.8	29.2	181.2	1.6
2011	B	2.05	1.71	55.7	27.3	170.9	4.7
2010	N/A	N/A	N/A	47.1	22.1	154.7	N/A
2009	N/A	N/A	N/A	39.4	20.5	121.6	N/A

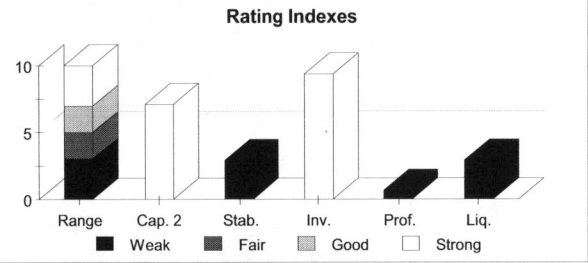

Rating Indexes

ALLIANT HEALTH PLANS INC   C   Fair

Major Rating Factors: Fair quality investment portfolio (3.6 on a scale of 0 to 10). Fair overall results on stability tests (4.3). Weak profitability index (2.3).
Other Rating Factors: Good liquidity (5.4) with sufficient resources (cash flows and marketable investments) to handle a spike in claims. Strong capitalization index (7.3) based on excellent current risk-adjusted capital (severe loss scenario).
Principal Business: Comp med (100%)
Mem Phys: 13: 14,839 **12:** N/A **13 MLR** 85.8% **/ 13 Admin Exp** N/A
Enroll(000): Q2 14: 25 **13:** 21 **12:** 21 **Med Exp PMPM:** $313
Principal Investments: Long-term bonds (87%), nonaffiliate common stock (11%), real estate (2%)
Provider Compensation ($000): Contr fee ($79,304)
Total Member Encounters: Phys (46,767), non-phys (6,600)
Group Affiliation: Health One Alliance LLC
Licensed in: GA
Address: 401 S Wall St Ste 201, Calhoun, GA 30701
Phone: (706) 629-8848 **Dom State:** GA **Commenced Bus:** December 1998

Data Date	Rating	RACR #1	RACR #2	Total Assets ($mil)	Capital ($mil)	Net Premium ($mil)	Net Income ($mil)
6-14	C	1.57	1.31	34.9	17.1	58.9	1.2
6-13	B	2.20	1.83	30.4	19.4	46.8	0.2
2013	C+	1.52	1.27	29.1	16.5	94.1	-4.3
2012	B	2.19	1.82	31.0	19.3	79.5	0.5
2011	B	2.41	2.01	28.9	18.8	71.7	0.7
2010	B	2.85	2.38	27.6	18.0	56.0	1.0
2009	B	3.18	2.65	25.5	17.1	45.4	1.0

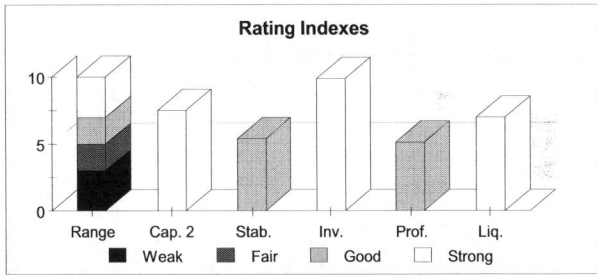

Rating Indexes

ALOHACARE
B   Good

Major Rating Factors: Fair overall results on stability tests (4.8 on a scale of 0 to 10). Strong capitalization index (9.2) based on excellent current risk-adjusted capital (severe loss scenario). High quality investment portfolio (9.7).
Other Rating Factors: Excellent liquidity (7.3) with ample operational cash flow and liquid investments. Weak profitability index (1.9).
Principal Business: Medicaid (92%), Medicare (8%)
Mem Phys: 12: 4,117 **11:** 4,244 **12 MLR** 89.2% **/ 12 Admin Exp** N/A
Enroll(000): Q3 13: 68 **12:** 75 **11:** 82 **Med Exp PMPM:** $218
Principal Investments: Cash and equiv (69%), long-term bonds (25%), other (6%)
Provider Compensation ($000): Contr fee ($105,860), FFS ($90,734), capitation ($4,418)
Total Member Encounters: Phys (395,872), non-phys (217,822)
Group Affiliation: None
Licensed in: HI
Address: 1357 Kapiolani Blvd #1250, Honolulu, HI 96814
Phone: (808) 973-1650 **Dom State:** HI **Commenced Bus:** August 1994

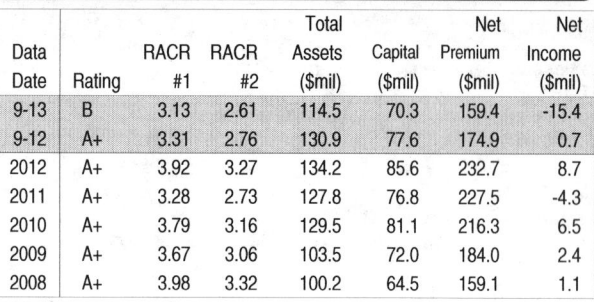

Data Date	Rating	RACR #1	RACR #2	Total Assets ($mil)	Capital ($mil)	Net Premium ($mil)	Net Income ($mil)
9-13	B	3.13	2.61	114.5	70.3	159.4	-15.4
9-12	A+	3.31	2.76	130.9	77.6	174.9	0.7
2012	A+	3.92	3.27	134.2	85.6	232.7	8.7
2011	A+	3.28	2.73	127.8	76.8	227.5	-4.3
2010	A+	3.79	3.16	129.5	81.1	216.3	6.5
2009	A+	3.67	3.06	103.5	72.0	184.0	2.4
2008	A+	3.98	3.32	100.2	64.5	159.1	1.1

Rating Indexes

Range / Cap. 2 / Stab. / Inv. / Prof. / Liq.
Weak Fair Good Strong

ALTIUS HEALTH PLANS
B   Good

Major Rating Factors: Good overall profitability index (6.0 on a scale of 0 to 10). Good quality investment portfolio (6.4). Good liquidity (5.7) with sufficient resources (cash flows and marketable investments) to handle a spike in claims.
Other Rating Factors: Fair overall results on stability tests (4.7) based on inconsistent enrollment growth in the past five years due to declines in 2010, 2011 and 2012. Rating is significantly influenced by the good financial results of Aetna Inc. Strong capitalization index (7.6) based on excellent current risk-adjusted capital (severe loss scenario).
Principal Business: Comp med (81%), Medicare (19%)
Mem Phys: 13: 13,663 **12:** 12,965 **13 MLR** 87.2% **/ 13 Admin Exp** N/A
Enroll(000): Q2 14: 131 **13:** 138 **12:** 126 **Med Exp PMPM:** $261
Principal Investments: Long-term bonds (91%), cash and equiv (5%), other (4%)
Provider Compensation ($000): Contr fee ($326,205), FFS ($83,139), capitation ($6,431), bonus arrang ($91)
Total Member Encounters: Phys (831,580), non-phys (328,668)
Group Affiliation: Aetna Inc
Licensed in: ID, NV, UT, WY
Address: 10421 S Jordan Gateway Ste 400, South Jordan, UT 84095
Phone: (801) 933-3500 **Dom State:** UT **Commenced Bus:** March 1976

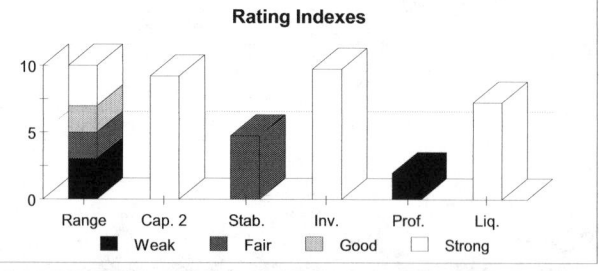

Data Date	Rating	RACR #1	RACR #2	Total Assets ($mil)	Capital ($mil)	Net Premium ($mil)	Net Income ($mil)
6-14	B	1.82	1.52	124.6	50.4	247.9	3.3
6-13	A-	2.06	1.72	101.1	48.6	245.3	4.1
2013	B	1.65	1.37	106.4	45.2	489.9	1.1
2012	A-	2.15	1.79	97.8	50.7	409.9	8.9
2011	A-	2.22	1.85	101.7	54.9	429.3	9.6
2010	A-	2.52	2.10	107.6	59.2	418.3	14.1
2009	B+	2.04	1.70	95.1	50.1	427.5	5.2

Rating Indexes

Range / Cap. 2 / Stab. / Inv. / Prof. / Liq.
Weak Fair Good Strong

AMALGAMATED LIFE INSURANCE COMPANY *
A-   Excellent

Major Rating Factors: Good liquidity (6.3 on a scale of 0 to 10) with sufficient resources to handle a spike in claims. Good overall results on stability tests (6.9). Strengths that enhance stability include excellent operational trends and good risk diversification. Strong capitalization (9.7) based on excellent risk adjusted capital (severe loss scenario). Moreover, capital levels have been consistently high over the last five years.
Other Rating Factors: High quality investment portfolio (8.1). Excellent profitability (8.1) with operating gains in each of the last five years.
Principal Business: Reinsurance (42%), group life insurance (39%), and group health insurance (18%).
Principal Investments: NonCMO investment grade bonds (72%), CMOs and structured securities (26%), and cash (2%).
Investments in Affiliates: None
Group Affiliation: ALICO Services Corp
Licensed in: All states except AL, FL, WY, PR
Commenced Business: February 1944
Address: 333 Westchester Ave, White Plains, NY 10604
Phone: (914) 367-5000 **Domicile State:** NY **NAIC Code:** 60216

Data Date	Rating	RACR #1	RACR #2	Total Assets ($mil)	Capital ($mil)	Net Premium ($mil)	Net Income ($mil)
6-14	A-	3.53	2.78	107.0	48.6	35.2	1.3
6-13	A-	3.33	2.62	93.3	43.0	30.2	1.7
2013	A-	3.45	2.72	99.9	47.2	64.3	3.5
2012	A-	3.31	2.64	88.6	42.2	56.3	3.7
2011	A-	2.99	2.36	78.9	38.3	55.7	1.9
2010	A-	3.13	2.49	72.2	36.3	46.3	2.8
2009	A-	2.89	2.26	65.8	33.5	44.5	2.5

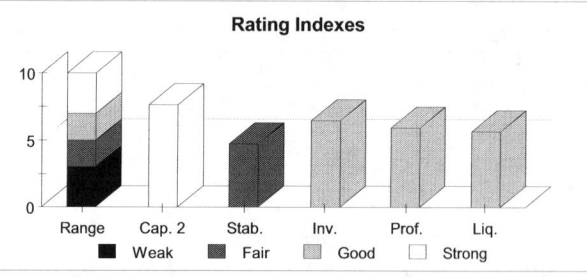

Adverse Trends in Operations

Increase in policy surrenders from 2012 to 2013 (90%)
Increase in policy surrenders from 2011 to 2012 (42%)
Increase in policy surrenders from 2009 to 2010 (28%)

AMERICAN BANKERS LIFE ASSURANCE COMPANY OF FLORID,   B   Good

Major Rating Factors: Good overall results on stability tests (5.4 on a scale of 0 to 10) despite negative cash flow from operations for 2013. Other stability subfactors include good operational trends and excellent risk diversification. Good quality investment portfolio (6.8) despite mixed results such as: minimal exposure to mortgages and large holdings of BBB rated bonds but small junk bond holdings. Good overall profitability (5.9).

Other Rating Factors: Strong capitalization (9.0) based on excellent risk adjusted capital (severe loss scenario). Excellent liquidity (7.6).

Principal Business: Credit life insurance (40%), credit health insurance (37%), reinsurance (17%), individual life insurance (2%), and other lines (4%).

Principal Investments: NonCMO investment grade bonds (64%), CMOs and structured securities (9%), real estate (9%), mortgages in good standing (8%), and misc. investments (9%).

Investments in Affiliates: None

Group Affiliation: Assurant Inc

Licensed in: All states except NY

Commenced Business: April 1952

Address: 11222 Quail Roost Dr, Miami, FL 33157

Phone: (305) 253-2244   **Domicile State:** FL   **NAIC Code:** 60275

Data Date	Rating	RACR #1	RACR #2	Total Assets ($mil)	Capital ($mil)	Net Premium ($mil)	Net Income ($mil)
6-14	B	4.15	2.32	526.3	48.1	44.0	2.5
6-13	B	3.69	2.19	538.8	63.5	55.7	6.0
2013	B	4.07	2.32	521.6	50.4	114.9	11.0
2012	B	3.76	2.25	553.8	67.3	127.7	13.4
2011	B	4.20	2.48	588.1	73.8	118.9	15.4
2010	B	5.75	3.19	626.5	88.1	89.1	23.9
2009	B	6.16	3.43	671.1	116.6	100.9	27.0

Adverse Trends in Operations

Decrease in premium volume from 2012 to 2013 (10%)
Decrease in capital during 2013 (25%)
Decrease in capital during 2011 (16%)
Decrease in capital during 2010 (24%)
Decrease in premium volume from 2009 to 2010 (12%)

AMERICAN CONTINENTAL INSURANCE COMPANY   B   Good

Major Rating Factors: Good current capitalization (5.4 on a scale of 0 to 10) based on mixed results -- excessive policy leverage mitigated by good risk adjusted capital (severe loss scenario), although results have slipped from the excellent range during the last year. Good liquidity (5.4) with sufficient resources to handle a spike in claims. Good overall results on stability tests (5.5) despite excessive premium growth and fair risk adjusted capital in prior years good operational trends and excellent risk diversification.

Other Rating Factors: Weak profitability (1.8) with operating losses during the first six months of 2014. High quality investment portfolio (8.2).

Principal Business: Individual health insurance (90%) and individual life insurance (10%).

Principal Investments: NonCMO investment grade bonds (96%), CMOs and structured securities (11%), and noninv. grade bonds (1%).

Investments in Affiliates: None

Group Affiliation: Aetna Inc

Licensed in: AL, AZ, AR, CO, FL, GA, IL, IN, IA, KS, KY, LA, MI, MN, MS, MO, MT, NE, NV, NM, NC, ND, OH, OK, PA, SC, SD, TN, TX, VA, WV, WI, WY

Commenced Business: September 2005

Address: 800 Crescent Centre Dr, Franklin, TN 37067

Phone: (800) 264-4000   **Domicile State:** TN   **NAIC Code:** 12321

Data Date	Rating	RACR #1	RACR #2	Total Assets ($mil)	Capital ($mil)	Net Premium ($mil)	Net Income ($mil)
6-14	B	1.22	0.95	136.4	52.5	184.6	-11.6
6-13	B	1.24	0.97	101.9	45.3	141.3	-11.6
2013	B	1.32	1.03	127.2	51.3	300.6	-13.5
2012	B	2.02	1.56	98.2	57.5	178.7	-6.0
2011	C	2.01	1.56	84.7	49.7	133.0	-12.0
2010	C	1.53	1.16	61.3	38.6	107.1	-10.9
2009	C+	0.89	0.70	36.7	16.4	66.5	-11.6

Policy Leverage

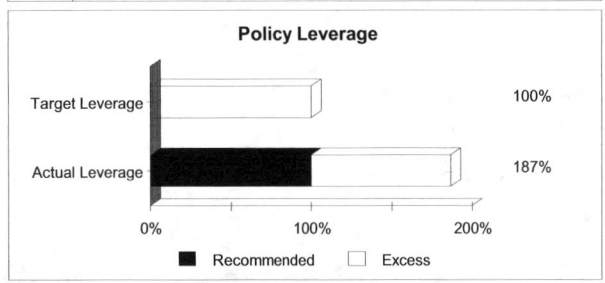

Target Leverage   100%
Actual Leverage   187%

0%   100%   200%

■ Recommended   ☐ Excess

AMERICAN FAMILY LIFE ASSUR COMPANY OF NEW YORK *   A-   Excellent

Major Rating Factors: Excellent overall results on stability tests (7.3 on a scale of 0 to 10). Strengths that enhance stability include excellent operational trends and excellent risk diversification. Strong capitalization (10.0) based on excellent risk adjusted capital (severe loss scenario). Furthermore, this high level of risk adjusted capital has been consistently maintained over the last five years. High quality investment portfolio (8.0).

Other Rating Factors: Excellent profitability (9.3) with operating gains in each of the last five years. Excellent liquidity (7.7).

Principal Business: Individual health insurance (95%), individual life insurance (3%), and group health insurance (2%).

Principal Investments: NonCMO investment grade bonds (98%), CMOs and structured securities (1%), and noninv. grade bonds (1%).

Investments in Affiliates: None

Group Affiliation: AFLAC Inc

Licensed in: CT, MA, NJ, NY, ND, VT

Commenced Business: December 1964

Address: 22 Corporate Woods Blvd #2, Albany, NY 12211

Phone: (706) 660-7208   **Domicile State:** NY   **NAIC Code:** 60526

Data Date	Rating	RACR #1	RACR #2	Total Assets ($mil)	Capital ($mil)	Net Premium ($mil)	Net Income ($mil)
6-14	A-	5.00	3.50	706.5	227.9	146.2	1.8
6-13	A-	4.56	3.23	609.3	199.9	143.7	23.4
2013	A-	4.96	3.49	645.3	221.8	285.5	45.4
2012	A-	4.18	2.99	555.9	176.2	271.1	40.0
2011	A-	3.17	2.29	454.0	123.4	251.8	26.5
2010	A-	2.66	1.94	383.1	95.7	232.8	20.2
2009	A-	2.32	1.71	322.6	77.0	211.9	12.9

Adverse Trends in Operations

Increase in policy surrenders from 2012 to 2013 (34%)
Increase in policy surrenders from 2011 to 2012 (92%)

AMERICAN FAMILY LIFE ASSURANCE COMPANY OF COLUMBU B+ Good

Major Rating Factors: Good overall profitability (6.2 on a scale of 0 to 10) although investment income, in comparison to reserve requirements, is below regulatory standards. Good overall results on stability tests (6.7). Stability strengths include excellent operational trends and excellent risk diversification. Strong capitalization (8.8) based on excellent risk adjusted capital (severe loss scenario).

Other Rating Factors: High quality investment portfolio (7.1). Excellent liquidity (7.6).

Principal Business: Individual health insurance (72%), individual life insurance (24%), individual annuities (4%), and reinsurance (1%).

Principal Investments: NonCMO investment grade bonds (89%), CMOs and structured securities (5%), noninv. grade bonds (3%), and common & preferred stock (1%).

Investments in Affiliates: 1%
Group Affiliation: AFLAC Inc
Licensed in: All states except NY
Commenced Business: April 1956
Address: 1932 Wynnton Rd, Columbus, GA 31999
Phone: (706) 323-3431 **Domicile State:** NE **NAIC Code:** 60380

Data Date	Rating	RACR #1	RACR #2	Total Assets ($mil)	Capital ($mil)	Net Premium ($mil)	Net Income ($mil)
6-14	B+	3.46	2.22	111,249	10,245.4	9,914.1	1,346.0
6-13	B+	3.06	1.93	104,174	9,308.4	10,402.5	1,584.2
2013	B+	3.23	2.09	107,913	9,630.1	20,550.2	2,360.6
2012	B+	2.77	1.74	115,347	8,891.8	23,102.5	2,337.3
2011	B+	2.45	1.44	103,582	6,371.1	20,945.0	443.6
2010	B+	2.78	1.62	89,723.3	6,739.8	18,324.8	1,468.1
2009	B+	2.44	1.40	75,798.4	5,767.9	16,829.9	1,414.1

Net Income History
(in millions of dollars)

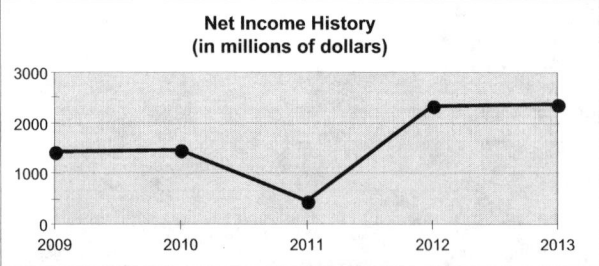

AMERICAN FIDELITY ASSURANCE COMPANY * B+ Good

Major Rating Factors: Good quality investment portfolio (6.1 on a scale of 0 to 10) despite mixed results such as: minimal exposure to mortgages and large holdings of BBB rated bonds but small junk bond holdings. Good liquidity (6.6) with sufficient resources to cover a large increase in policy surrenders. Good overall results on stability tests (6.8) excellent operational trends, good risk adjusted capital for prior years and excellent risk diversification.

Other Rating Factors: Strong capitalization (7.1) based on excellent risk adjusted capital (severe loss scenario). Excellent profitability (8.3) with operating gains in each of the last five years.

Principal Business: Group health insurance (45%), individual health insurance (23%), individual life insurance (13%), individual annuities (13%), and reinsurance (5%).

Principal Investments: NonCMO investment grade bonds (62%), CMOs and structured securities (23%), mortgages in good standing (9%), cash (3%), and misc. investments (4%).

Investments in Affiliates: None
Group Affiliation: Cameron Associates Inc
Licensed in: All states except NY
Commenced Business: December 1960
Address: 2000 N Classen Blvd, Oklahoma City, OK 73106
Phone: (405) 523-2000 **Domicile State:** OK **NAIC Code:** 60410

Data Date	Rating	RACR #1	RACR #2	Total Assets ($mil)	Capital ($mil)	Net Premium ($mil)	Net Income ($mil)
6-14	B+	1.81	1.05	4,848.9	347.3	418.9	32.3
6-13	B+	1.66	0.99	4,533.9	326.8	390.4	33.6
2013	B+	1.82	1.05	4,709.9	342.7	780.9	71.7
2012	B+	1.60	0.95	4,358.1	308.9	765.7	58.5
2011	B+	1.74	1.01	3,994.1	295.0	712.8	55.6
2010	A	1.82	1.06	3,780.9	287.2	681.2	55.9
2009	A	1.92	1.13	3,567.6	282.1	619.7	49.5

Adverse Trends in Operations

Increase in policy surrenders from 2009 to 2010 (28%)

AMERICAN HEALTH & LIFE INSURANCE COMPANY B- Good

Major Rating Factors: Good quality investment portfolio (5.9 on a scale of 0 to 10) despite mixed results such as: no exposure to mortgages and large holdings of BBB rated bonds but small junk bond holdings. Good overall profitability (6.2). Excellent expense controls. Return on equity has been excellent over the last five years averaging 27.9%. Good overall results on stability tests (5.1) good operational trends and excellent risk diversification.

Other Rating Factors: Strong capitalization (9.3) based on excellent risk adjusted capital (severe loss scenario). Excellent liquidity (8.3).

Principal Business: Credit health insurance (34%), credit life insurance (32%), reinsurance (30%), group life insurance (2%), and group health insurance (2%).

Principal Investments: NonCMO investment grade bonds (72%), CMOs and structured securities (17%), common & preferred stock (4%), noninv. grade bonds (3%), and cash (3%).

Investments in Affiliates: 2%
Group Affiliation: Citigroup Inc
Licensed in: All states except NY, PR
Commenced Business: June 1954
Address: 307 West 7th Street, Ste 400, Fort Worth, TX 76102
Phone: (817) 348-7500 **Domicile State:** TX **NAIC Code:** 60518

Data Date	Rating	RACR #1	RACR #2	Total Assets ($mil)	Capital ($mil)	Net Premium ($mil)	Net Income ($mil)
6-14	B-	3.68	2.50	969.9	251.3	102.4	40.5
6-13	B-	4.03	2.72	996.8	274.2	101.2	44.3
2013	B-	3.08	2.11	941.1	208.6	221.8	84.1
2012	B-	3.52	2.39	972.0	234.7	213.5	110.0
2011	B-	2.52	2.05	1,153.2	371.7	214.8	123.8
2010	B	1.99	1.59	1,129.3	278.4	354.5	15.4
2009	B+	4.63	3.56	1,360.5	623.7	148.5	100.0

Adverse Trends in Operations

Decrease in asset base during 2012 (16%)
Decrease in capital during 2012 (37%)
Decrease in premium volume from 2010 to 2011 (39%)
Decrease in capital during 2010 (55%)
Decrease in asset base during 2010 (17%)

AMERICAN HEALTH INC
B Good

Major Rating Factors: Good overall profitability index (6.5 on a scale of 0 to 10). Good capitalization (6.9) based on excellent current risk-adjusted capital (severe loss scenario). Good liquidity (6.4) with sufficient resources (cash flows and marketable investments) to handle a spike in claims.

Other Rating Factors: High quality investment portfolio (9.5).

Principal Business: Medicare (100%)

Mem Phys: 13: 6,253 **12:** 6,253 **13 MLR** 82.0% **/ 13 Admin Exp** N/A

Enroll(000): Q2 14: 51 **13:** 43 **12:** 51 **Med Exp PMPM:** $800

Principal Investments: Long-term bonds (95%), cash and equiv (5%)

Provider Compensation ($000): FFS ($380,948), capitation ($29,828)

Total Member Encounters: Phys (385,209), non-phys (47,558)

Group Affiliation: Triple-S Management Corp

Licensed in: PR

Address: Metro Office Park Microsoft Bl, Guaynabo, PR 00922

Phone: (787) 620-1919 **Dom State:** PR **Commenced Bus:** May 2001

Data Date	Rating	RACR #1	RACR #2	Total Assets ($mil)	Capital ($mil)	Net Premium ($mil)	Net Income ($mil)
6-14	B	1.24	1.04	178.5	58.2	272.8	3.9
6-13	D	0.60	0.50	154.5	42.6	261.8	9.5
2013	C	0.86	0.72	153.5	55.8	519.9	19.7
2012	D-	0.37	0.31	121.3	30.7	539.3	-11.8
2011	C-	0.43	0.36	103.1	17.8	473.8	1.5
2010	C+	0.97	0.81	69.1	17.2	380.7	8.9
2009	E	0.32	0.27	50.9	8.6	265.8	5.2

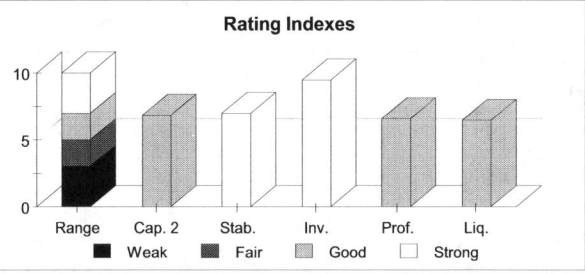

Rating Indexes

AMERICAN HERITAGE LIFE INSURANCE COMPANY
B Good

Major Rating Factors: Good quality investment portfolio (6.3 on a scale of 0 to 10) despite mixed results such as: minimal exposure to mortgages and large holdings of BBB rated bonds but minimal holdings in junk bonds. Good liquidity (6.6) with sufficient resources to handle a spike in claims as well as a significant increase in policy surrenders. Good overall results on stability tests (6.1) excellent operational trends, good risk adjusted capital for prior years and excellent risk diversification.

Other Rating Factors: Strong capitalization (7.2) based on excellent risk adjusted capital (severe loss scenario). Excellent profitability (7.2) with operating gains in each of the last five years.

Principal Business: Group health insurance (49%), individual health insurance (33%), individual life insurance (12%), group life insurance (5%), and reinsurance (2%).

Principal Investments: NonCMO investment grade bonds (50%), policy loans (19%), common & preferred stock (16%), mortgages in good standing (7%), and misc. investments (8%).

Investments in Affiliates: 12%

Group Affiliation: Allstate Group

Licensed in: All states except NY

Commenced Business: December 1956

Address: 1776 American Heritage Life Dr, Jacksonville, FL 32224-6688

Phone: (904) 992-1776 **Domicile State:** FL **NAIC Code:** 60534

Data Date	Rating	RACR #1	RACR #2	Total Assets ($mil)	Capital ($mil)	Net Premium ($mil)	Net Income ($mil)
6-14	B	1.36	1.12	1,852.6	424.1	379.0	83.9
6-13	B	1.35	1.11	1,786.2	371.6	349.5	21.2
2013	B	1.18	0.97	1,770.2	337.7	707.7	57.0
2012	B	1.26	1.05	1,710.7	335.8	649.7	74.7
2011	B	1.24	1.02	1,650.1	293.7	639.9	41.5
2010	B	1.15	0.93	1,518.4	255.0	617.6	26.3
2009	B	1.31	1.06	1,404.5	240.9	458.3	18.2

Adverse Trends in Operations

Increase in policy surrenders from 2009 to 2010 (72%)

AMERICAN HOME ASR CO
C Fair

Major Rating Factors: Fair profitability index (3.3 on a scale of 0 to 10) with operating losses during 2010. Return on equity has been low, averaging 4.4% over the past five years. Fair overall results on stability tests (4.2). The largest net exposure for one risk is excessive at 5.4% of capital.

Other Rating Factors: A history of deficient reserves (2.5). Underreserving can have an adverse impact on capital and profits. In 2011 and 2010 the two year reserve development was 33% and 50% deficient respectively. Good liquidity (6.5) with sufficient resources (cash flows and marketable investments) to handle a spike in claims. Strong long-term capitalization index (7.5) based on excellent current risk adjusted capital (severe and moderate loss scenarios), despite some fluctuation in capital levels.

Principal Business: Other accident & health (70%), auto liability (11%), other liability (6%), auto physical damage (4%), inland marine (4%), homeowners multiple peril (2%), and other lines (4%).

Principal Investments: Investment grade bonds (71%), misc. investments (23%), non investment grade bonds (5%), and cash (1%).

Investments in Affiliates: 0%

Group Affiliation: American International Group

Licensed in: All states except PR

Commenced Business: February 1899

Address: 175 Water St 18th Floor, New York, NY 10038

Phone: (212) 770-7000 **Domicile State:** NY **NAIC Code:** 19380

Data Date	Rating	RACR #1	RACR #2	Loss Ratio %	Total Assets ($mil)	Capital ($mil)	Net Premium ($mil)	Net Income ($mil)
6-14	C	2.29	1.51	N/A	26,478.6	6,978.8	2,797.2	286.9
6-13	C	2.10	1.41	N/A	24,260.4	5,844.0	2,628.9	192.1
2013	C	1.77	1.17	70.0	23,671.1	5,091.7	5,852.4	703.0
2012	C	2.16	1.46	79.5	23,972.2	6,004.3	5,204.4	285.5
2011	C	2.02	1.37	80.0	23,900.3	5,667.3	5,308.9	494.6
2010	C	2.05	1.20	105.9	26,416.6	6,673.1	5,195.4	-776.5
2009	C	1.80	1.06	86.1	24,981.1	5,872.3	6,062.4	249.8

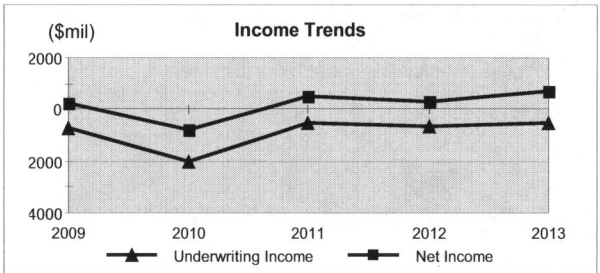

Income Trends

AMERICAN LIFE INSURANCE COMPANY
C   Fair

Major Rating Factors: Fair current capitalization (4.6 on a scale of 0 to 10) based on fair risk adjusted capital (severe loss scenario), although results have slipped from the good range during the last year. Fair quality investment portfolio (3.3). Fair profitability (3.4) with operating losses during the first six months of 2014.

Other Rating Factors: Weak overall results on stability tests (2.8) including weak results on operational trends and negative cash flow from operations for 2013. Excellent liquidity (7.0).

Principal Business: Individual life insurance (42%), reinsurance (22%), group health insurance (15%), group retirement contracts (7%), and other lines (14%).

Principal Investments: Common & preferred stock (54%), nonCMO investment grade bonds (17%), noninv. grade bonds (16%), cash (9%), and policy loans (2%).

Investments in Affiliates: 56%

Group Affiliation: MetLife Inc

Licensed in: DE

Commenced Business: August 1921

Address: One ALICO Plaza, Wilmington, DE 19801

Phone: (302) 594-2000 **Domicile State:** DE **NAIC Code:** 60690

Data Date	Rating	RACR #1	RACR #2	Total Assets ($mil)	Capital ($mil)	Net Premium ($mil)	Net Income ($mil)
6-14	C	0.74	0.70	7,218.3	2,485.1	700.1	-131.9
6-13	C	1.07	0.96	7,949.0	2,929.6	590.3	929.1
2013	C	0.92	0.88	7,296.4	2,711.2	1,140.4	630.5
2012	C	1.01	0.93	8,224.8	3,043.6	8,991.4	317.1
2011	C-	0.80	0.57	102,198	3,309.9	15,495.3	333.8
2010	C-	1.11	0.82	94,591.6	4,320.7	16,504.5	803.4
2009	C-	N/A	N/A	91,042.8	4,146.5	12,861.0	668.6

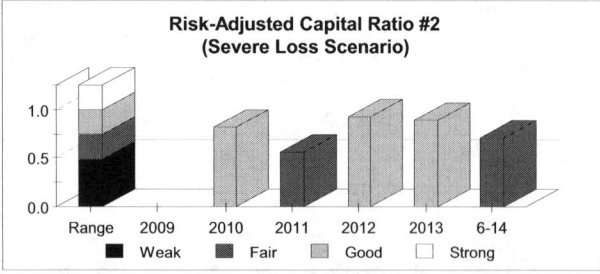

Risk-Adjusted Capital Ratio #2
(Severe Loss Scenario)

AMERICAN MODERN LIFE INSURANCE COMPANY
B   Good

Major Rating Factors: Fair overall results on stability tests (4.2 on a scale of 0 to 10) including negative cash flow from operations for 2013. Weak profitability (2.6) with investment income below regulatory standards in relation to interest assumptions of reserves. Strong capitalization (8.2) based on excellent risk adjusted capital (severe loss scenario).

Other Rating Factors: High quality investment portfolio (8.0). Excellent liquidity (8.4).

Principal Business: Credit life insurance (58%), credit health insurance (40%), and reinsurance (2%).

Principal Investments: NonCMO investment grade bonds (66%), common & preferred stock (25%), CMOs and structured securities (7%), and cash (1%).

Investments in Affiliates: 25%

Group Affiliation: Securian Financial Group

Licensed in: All states except NH, NJ, PR

Commenced Business: January 1957

Address: 400 Robert St N, St Paul, MN 55101-2098

Phone: (800) 543-2644 **Domicile State:** OH **NAIC Code:** 65811

Data Date	Rating	RACR #1	RACR #2	Total Assets ($mil)	Capital ($mil)	Net Premium ($mil)	Net Income ($mil)
6-14	B	1.91	1.78	49.9	26.6	2.3	0.9
6-13	B	1.65	1.53	55.2	24.3	2.3	1.6
2013	B	1.89	1.76	52.1	26.4	4.7	3.9
2012	B	1.55	1.43	58.8	23.1	8.1	1.9
2011	B	1.37	1.21	60.0	20.3	14.2	-3.6
2010	B	1.32	1.25	62.6	21.1	9.7	0.6
2009	B	1.23	1.19	63.4	20.8	11.1	2.8

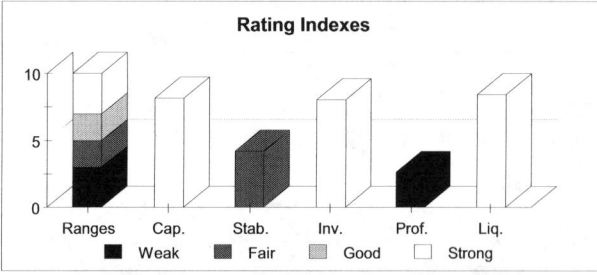

Rating Indexes

AMERICAN NATIONAL LIFE INSURANCE COMPANY OF TEXAS
B-   Good

Major Rating Factors: Good liquidity (6.8 on a scale of 0 to 10) with sufficient resources to handle a spike in claims. Good overall results on stability tests (5.1). Strengths include good financial support from affiliation with American National Group Inc, good operational trends and excellent risk diversification. Weak profitability (2.4). Return on equity has been low, averaging -13.1%.

Other Rating Factors: Strong capitalization (10.0) based on excellent risk adjusted capital (severe loss scenario). High quality investment portfolio (7.1).

Principal Business: Group health insurance (59%), reinsurance (31%), individual health insurance (6%), and individual life insurance (4%).

Principal Investments: NonCMO investment grade bonds (93%), CMOs and structured securities (3%), policy loans (3%), and noninv. grade bonds (2%).

Investments in Affiliates: None

Group Affiliation: American National Group Inc

Licensed in: All states except ME, NJ, NY, VT, PR

Commenced Business: December 1954

Address: One Moody Plaza, Galveston, TX 77550

Phone: (409) 763-4661 **Domicile State:** TX **NAIC Code:** 71773

Data Date	Rating	RACR #1	RACR #2	Total Assets ($mil)	Capital ($mil)	Net Premium ($mil)	Net Income ($mil)
6-14	B-	4.32	3.07	138.5	39.1	20.2	1.8
6-13	B-	3.85	2.66	134.6	36.4	23.3	0.7
2013	B-	4.55	3.17	135.1	41.4	45.1	2.1
2012	B-	4.01	2.80	133.5	39.2	52.8	-2.0
2011	B-	2.51	1.80	115.1	27.5	64.2	-0.8
2010	B-	1.87	1.36	124.5	28.5	92.5	-5.5
2009	B-	1.58	1.16	125.4	26.7	105.1	-14.5

American National Group Inc Composite Group Rating: B Largest Group Members	Assets ($mil)	Rating
AMERICAN NATIONAL INS CO	18036	B
FARM FAMILY LIFE INS CO	1248	B
AMERICAN NATIONAL PROPERTY CAS CO	1156	B
FARM FAMILY CASUALTY INS CO	1037	B+
STANDARD LIFE ACCIDENT INS CO	528	A-

AMERICAN PROGRESSIVE L&H INSURANCE COMPANY OF NY   B   Good

Major Rating Factors: Good overall results on stability tests (5.3 on a scale of 0 to 10) despite fair financial strength of affiliated Universal American Corp and negative cash flow from operations for 2013. Other stability subfactors include good operational trends and excellent risk diversification. Good current capitalization (6.8) based on excellent risk adjusted capital (severe loss scenario) reflecting improvement over results in 2010. Good overall profitability (5.8) despite operating losses during the first six months of 2014.
Other Rating Factors: Good liquidity (5.0). High quality investment portfolio (7.4).
Principal Business: Individual health insurance (97%) and individual life insurance (3%).
Principal Investments: NonCMO investment grade bonds (63%), CMOs and structured securities (32%), common & preferred stock (2%), and noninv. grade bonds (1%).
Investments in Affiliates: None
Group Affiliation: Universal American Corp
Licensed in: AL, CO, CT, DC, DE, HI, IL, IN, LA, ME, MD, MA, MN, MO, NH, NJ, NY, OH, OR, PA, RI, VT, VA, WV
Commenced Business: March 1946
Address: 6 International Dr Suite 190, Rye Brook, NY 10573
Phone: (914) 934-8300 **Domicile State:** NY **NAIC Code:** 80624

Data Date	Rating	RACR #1	RACR #2	Total Assets ($mil)	Capital ($mil)	Net Premium ($mil)	Net Income ($mil)
6-14	B	1.45	1.14	238.9	120.3	207.4	-2.1
6-13	B	1.65	1.31	259.8	136.3	232.3	4.3
2013	B	1.39	1.10	235.7	122.3	469.8	13.5
2012	B	1.84	1.46	263.8	145.4	419.3	14.8
2011	C+	1.39	1.11	252.1	132.0	507.7	4.8
2010	C	1.02	0.83	288.9	140.5	744.3	35.2
2009	C	1.04	0.85	244.8	129.5	557.3	25.1

Universal American Corp Composite Group Rating: C Largest Group Members	Assets ($mil)	Rating
CONSTITUTION LIFE INS CO	317	C+
AMERICAN PROGRESSIVE LH I C OF NY	236	B
PYRAMID LIFE INS CO	212	C
SELECTCARE OF TEXAS LLC	133	C
AMERICAN PIONEER LIFE INS CO	77	D+

AMERICAN REPUBLIC INSURANCE COMPANY *   A-   Excellent

Major Rating Factors: Good liquidity (6.9 on a scale of 0 to 10) with sufficient resources to handle a spike in claims as well as a significant increase in policy surrenders. Strong capitalization (10.0) based on excellent risk adjusted capital (severe loss scenario). Furthermore, this high level of risk adjusted capital has been consistently maintained over the last five years. High quality investment portfolio (7.4).
Other Rating Factors: Excellent profitability (9.2) with operating gains in each of the last five years. Excellent overall results on stability tests (7.0) excellent operational trends and excellent risk diversification.
Principal Business: Reinsurance (46%), individual health insurance (27%), group health insurance (21%), individual life insurance (4%), and credit life insurance (1%).
Principal Investments: NonCMO investment grade bonds (63%), CMOs and structured securities (26%), common & preferred stock (6%), noninv. grade bonds (2%), and misc. investments (3%).
Investments in Affiliates: 5%
Group Affiliation: American Enterprise Mutual Holding
Licensed in: All states except NY, PR
Commenced Business: May 1929
Address: 601 Sixth Ave, Des Moines, IA 50309
Phone: (515) 245-2000 **Domicile State:** IA **NAIC Code:** 60836

Data Date	Rating	RACR #1	RACR #2	Total Assets ($mil)	Capital ($mil)	Net Premium ($mil)	Net Income ($mil)
6-14	A-	5.08	3.79	799.7	457.3	150.3	19.7
6-13	A-	N/A	N/A	804.8	416.6	163.0	11.5
2013	A-	4.85	3.67	801.4	437.5	325.1	40.5
2012	A-	6.09	4.36	522.7	286.4	224.0	44.2
2011	A	4.60	3.35	538.6	259.3	294.5	17.1
2010	A	4.10	3.06	537.8	264.9	362.8	32.6
2009	A-	3.44	2.58	521.5	241.0	399.8	19.0

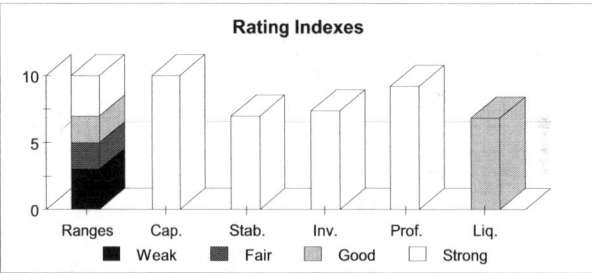

Rating Indexes

Ranges Cap. Stab. Inv. Prof. Liq.
■ Weak ▨ Fair ▧ Good □ Strong

AMERICAN SPECIALTY HEALTH INS CO   D-   Weak

Major Rating Factors: Weak profitability index (2.6 on a scale of 0 to 10). Strong capitalization (10.0) based on excellent current risk-adjusted capital (severe loss scenario). High quality investment portfolio (9.9).
Other Rating Factors: Excellent liquidity (8.9) with ample operational cash flow and liquid investments.
Principal Business: Other (100%)
Mem Phys: 13: 26,836 **12:** 24,528 **13 MLR** 57.8% **/ 13 Admin Exp** N/A
Enroll(000): Q2 14: 263 **13:** 328 **12:** 257 **Med Exp PMPM:** $0
Principal Investments: Cash and equiv (100%)
Provider Compensation ($000): FFS ($1,885)
Total Member Encounters: Non-phys (111,169)
Group Affiliation: American Specialty Health Inc
Licensed in: All states except AK, CT, ME, NJ, NY, NC, RI, PR
Address: 5600 River Rd Suite 800, Rosemont, IL 60018
Phone: (858) 754-2000 **Dom State:** IL **Commenced Bus:** August 1974

Data Date	Rating	RACR #1	RACR #2	Total Assets ($mil)	Capital ($mil)	Net Premium ($mil)	Net Income ($mil)
6-14	D-	9.01	7.51	8.2	7.3	1.7	0.2
6-13	N/A	N/A	N/A	9.3	7.2	2.6	-0.3
2013	E-	8.98	7.49	8.1	7.3	5.2	-0.3
2012	N/A	N/A	N/A	9.2	7.6	4.9	-0.7
2011	N/A	N/A	N/A	9.1	8.3	7.3	0.7
2010	N/A	N/A	N/A	8.4	7.7	6.4	0.2
2009	D-	N/A	N/A	8.2	7.5	6.2	0.2

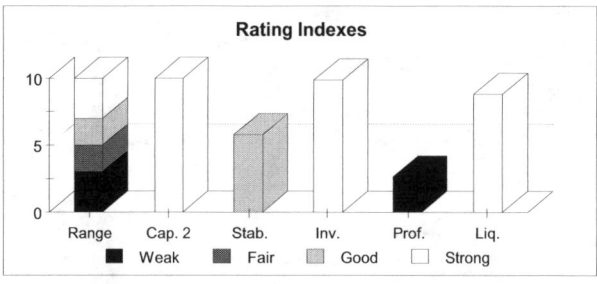

Rating Indexes

Range Cap. 2 Stab. Inv. Prof. Liq.
■ Weak ▨ Fair ▧ Good □ Strong

AMERICAS 1ST CHOICE HEALTH PLANS INC E Very Weak

Major Rating Factors: Weak profitability index (2.0 on a scale of 0 to 10). Fair capitalization (3.9) based on fair current risk-adjusted capital (moderate loss scenario). High quality investment portfolio (9.9).

Other Rating Factors: Excellent liquidity (7.1) with ample operational cash flow and liquid investments.

Principal Business: Medicare (100%)

Mem Phys: 13: 4,564 **12:** 4,113 **13 MLR** 89.9% **/ 13 Admin Exp** N/A

Enroll(000): Q2 14: 5 **13:** 8 **12:** 11 **Med Exp PMPM:** $701

Principal Investments: Cash and equiv (100%)

Provider Compensation ($000): FFS ($76,703), capitation ($631)

Total Member Encounters: Phys (16,244), non-phys (20,408)

Group Affiliation: Americas 1st Choice

Licensed in: AZ, GA, SC

Address: 250 Berryhill Rd Suite 311, Columbia, SC 29210

Phone: (866) 321-3947 **Dom State:** SC **Commenced Bus:** March 2007

Data Date	Rating	RACR #1	RACR #2	Total Assets ($mil)	Capital ($mil)	Net Premium ($mil)	Net Income ($mil)
6-14	E	0.77	0.64	16.5	8.9	25.8	-0.6
6-13	E	0.47	0.39	18.8	6.5	40.1	1.4
2013	E	0.87	0.72	19.7	9.7	80.9	4.4
2012	E	0.37	0.31	19.2	5.1	99.6	3.3
2011	E-	0.03	0.02	12.1	0.1	64.5	-5.4
2010	D+	0.44	0.37	12.7	3.8	55.7	-0.1
2009	D+	0.77	0.64	7.8	3.3	20.2	0.4

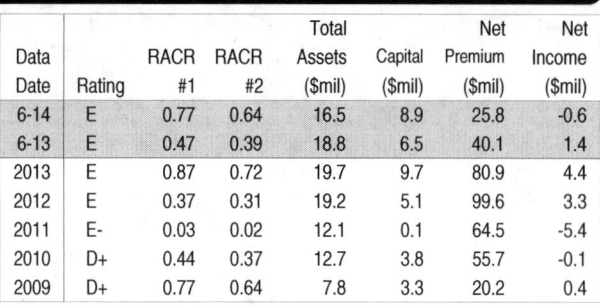

Rating Indexes

AMERICAS 1ST CHOICE INS CO OF NC INC C Fair

Major Rating Factors: Fair capitalization (4.9 on a scale of 0 to 10) based on good current risk-adjusted capital (severe loss scenario). Weak profitability index (1.8). High quality investment portfolio (9.9).

Other Rating Factors: Excellent liquidity (7.2) with ample operational cash flow and liquid investments.

Principal Business: Medicare (100%)

Mem Phys: 13: 9,117 **12:** 24,468 **13 MLR** 84.1% **/ 13 Admin Exp** N/A

Enroll(000): Q2 14: 2 **13:** 4 **12:** 6 **Med Exp PMPM:** $671

Principal Investments: Cash and equiv (77%), long-term bonds (23%)

Provider Compensation ($000): FFS ($37,948), capitation ($246)

Total Member Encounters: Phys (9,039), non-phys (9,699)

Group Affiliation: Americas 1st Choice

Licensed in: NC

Address: One Medical Dr, Benson, NC 27504

Phone: (813) 506-6000 **Dom State:** NC **Commenced Bus:** October 2007

Data Date	Rating	RACR #1	RACR #2	Total Assets ($mil)	Capital ($mil)	Net Premium ($mil)	Net Income ($mil)
6-14	C	0.91	0.76	11.7	8.1	11.1	-1.5
6-13	D+	0.62	0.52	14.0	7.7	20.7	1.3
2013	C	1.19	0.99	15.1	9.8	41.7	3.2
2012	D	0.44	0.37	14.5	6.1	57.1	-1.4
2011	D	0.52	0.43	17.3	7.6	64.2	0.4
2010	D	0.33	0.27	17.9	5.0	72.6	-1.1
2009	D	0.51	0.42	7.9	3.0	25.5	-0.4

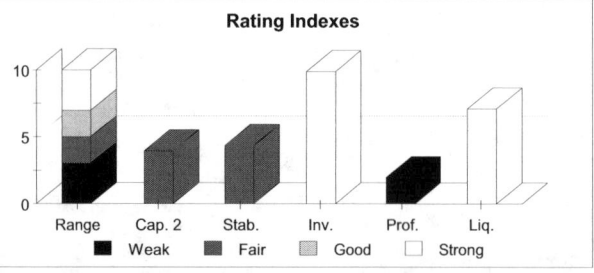

Rating Indexes

AMERICHOICE OF NEW JERSEY INC B Good

Major Rating Factors: Good overall profitability index (6.2 on a scale of 0 to 10). Good liquidity (6.7) with sufficient resources (cash flows and marketable investments) to handle a spike in claims. Strong capitalization index (8.3) based on excellent current risk-adjusted capital (severe loss scenario).

Other Rating Factors: High quality investment portfolio (9.6). Excellent overall results on stability tests (7.3). Rating is significantly influenced by the fair financial results of UnitedHealth Group Inc.

Principal Business: Medicaid (89%), Medicare (8%), comp med (3%)

Mem Phys: 13: 11,614 **12:** 11,521 **13 MLR** 84.6% **/ 13 Admin Exp** N/A

Enroll(000): Q2 14: 437 **13:** 388 **12:** 426 **Med Exp PMPM:** $297

Principal Investments: Long-term bonds (87%), cash and equiv (13%)

Provider Compensation ($000): Contr fee ($1,334,960), FFS ($147,058), capitation ($64,293), bonus arrang ($736)

Total Member Encounters: Phys (3,580,630), non-phys (2,479,123)

Group Affiliation: UnitedHealth Group Inc

Licensed in: NJ

Address: Four Gateway Center, Newark, NJ 07102-4062

Phone: (973) 297-5500 **Dom State:** NJ **Commenced Bus:** February 1996

Data Date	Rating	RACR #1	RACR #2	Total Assets ($mil)	Capital ($mil)	Net Premium ($mil)	Net Income ($mil)
6-14	B	2.40	2.00	511.8	225.0	887.5	21.4
6-13	B	1.52	1.26	391.1	147.1	867.6	3.7
2013	B	2.19	1.83	460.6	204.1	1,726.7	62.3
2012	B	1.43	1.19	440.4	137.8	1,714.3	-15.7
2011	B	1.90	1.58	374.6	142.4	1,345.8	40.4
2010	B	2.04	1.70	264.0	118.7	1,009.5	32.2
2009	B	1.64	1.37	205.8	79.5	786.3	-13.7

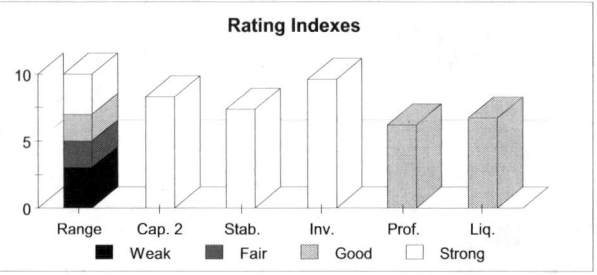

Rating Indexes

AMERIGROUP COMMUNITY CARE NM   B-   Good

Major Rating Factors: Good overall profitability index (5.4 on a scale of 0 to 10). Good quality investment portfolio (5.3). Good liquidity (6.7) with sufficient resources (cash flows and marketable investments) to handle a spike in claims.
Other Rating Factors: Strong capitalization (8.8) based on excellent current risk-adjusted capital (severe loss scenario).
Principal Business: Medicaid (91%), Medicare (9%)
Mem Phys: 13: 6,796 **12:** 6,430 **13 MLR** 83.0% **/ 13 Admin Exp** N/A
Enroll(000): Q2 14: 4 **13:** 24 **12:** 24 **Med Exp PMPM:** $1,409
Principal Investments: Long-term bonds (86%), cash and equiv (7%), other (7%)
Provider Compensation ($000): Contr fee ($406,881), FFS ($4,329), capitation ($342), bonus arrang ($21)
Total Member Encounters: Phys (283,312), non-phys (1,375,698)
Group Affiliation: WellPoint Inc
Licensed in: NM
Address: 2132-A Central Ave SE #150, Albuquerque, NM 87106-4004
Phone: (757) 490-6900 **Dom State:** NM **Commenced Bus:** January 2008

Data Date	Rating	RACR #1	RACR #2	Total Assets ($mil)	Capital ($mil)	Net Premium ($mil)	Net Income ($mil)
6-14	B-	2.76	2.30	89.8	70.6	21.0	2.4
6-13	B-	2.50	2.09	133.3	64.9	252.7	2.9
2013	B-	2.71	2.26	123.2	69.3	492.9	6.5
2012	C+	2.37	1.98	108.7	62.3	494.1	7.4
2011	C+	2.02	1.68	103.2	54.5	459.5	2.0
2010	C	2.07	1.72	99.6	52.6	436.0	7.1
2009	C	1.59	1.32	105.5	42.5	378.2	-7.2

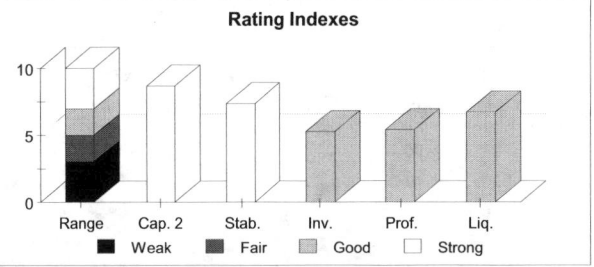

AMERIGROUP FLORIDA INC   B   Good

Major Rating Factors: Good liquidity (5.9 on a scale of 0 to 10) with sufficient resources (cash flows and marketable investments) to handle a spike in claims. Fair overall results on stability tests (4.9) based on inconsistent enrollment growth in the past five years due to declines in 2011, 2012 and 2013. Rating is significantly influenced by the good financial results of WellPoint Inc. Strong capitalization index (7.8) based on excellent current risk-adjusted capital (severe loss scenario).
Other Rating Factors: High quality investment portfolio (8.3). Weak profitability index (2.5).
Principal Business: Medicaid (73%), comp med (13%), Medicare (5%), other (9%)
Mem Phys: 13: 13,323 **12:** 12,945 **13 MLR** 87.3% **/ 13 Admin Exp** N/A
Enroll(000): Q2 14: 294 **13:** 239 **12:** 256 **Med Exp PMPM:** $177
Principal Investments: Long-term bonds (82%), nonaffiliate common stock (9%), cash and equiv (8%), other (2%)
Provider Compensation ($000): Contr fee ($459,597), capitation ($28,937), FFS ($18,704)
Total Member Encounters: Phys (1,362,416), non-phys (905,851)
Group Affiliation: WellPoint Inc
Licensed in: FL
Address: 4200 W Cypress St, Tampa, FL 33607
Phone: (757) 490-6900 **Dom State:** FL **Commenced Bus:** October 1993

Data Date	Rating	RACR #1	RACR #2	Total Assets ($mil)	Capital ($mil)	Net Premium ($mil)	Net Income ($mil)
6-14	B	1.96	1.63	155.9	60.6	365.6	-12.8
6-13	A-	2.64	2.20	133.5	84.8	302.9	5.9
2013	A-	2.35	1.96	155.7	73.4	599.5	6.8
2012	B+	2.42	2.01	118.4	77.5	601.7	11.5
2011	B+	1.85	1.54	113.1	63.9	578.0	-3.1
2010	B+	2.11	1.76	154.0	65.1	562.8	15.7
2009	B	1.50	1.25	148.0	48.6	559.5	7.8

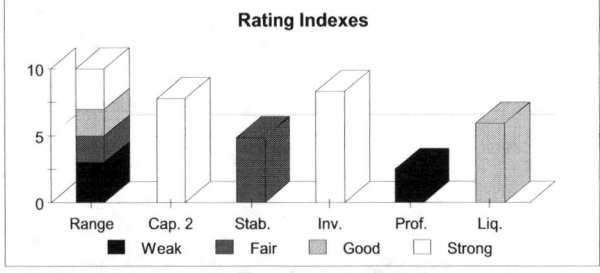

AMERIGROUP INS CO   B-   Good

Major Rating Factors: Good quality investment portfolio (5.4 on a scale of 0 to 10). Good liquidity (6.7) with sufficient resources (cash flows and marketable investments) to handle a spike in claims. Strong capitalization (10.0) based on excellent current risk-adjusted capital (severe loss scenario).
Other Rating Factors: Weak profitability index (1.2).
Principal Business: Medicaid (100%)
Mem Phys: 13: 7,199 **12:** 6,522 **13 MLR** 86.1% **/ 13 Admin Exp** N/A
Enroll(000): Q2 14: 110 **13:** 107 **12:** 119 **Med Exp PMPM:** $251
Principal Investments: Long-term bonds (87%), nonaffiliate common stock (9%), other (4%)
Provider Compensation ($000): Contr fee ($298,027), FFS ($46,380), capitation ($6,356)
Total Member Encounters: Phys (588,165), non-phys (526,127)
Group Affiliation: WellPoint Inc
Licensed in: TX
Address: 3800 Buffalo Speedway Ste 400, Houston, TX 77098
Phone: (757) 490-6900 **Dom State:** TX **Commenced Bus:** March 2012

Data Date	Rating	RACR #1	RACR #2	Total Assets ($mil)	Capital ($mil)	Net Premium ($mil)	Net Income ($mil)
6-14	B-	4.28	3.57	131.4	91.9	190.7	-3.8
6-13	B-	3.28	2.73	118.8	84.1	193.8	5.1
2013	B-	4.46	3.72	136.8	96.3	394.1	16.3
2012	B-	3.11	2.59	119.7	79.6	325.9	-21.4
2011	N/A	N/A	N/A	7.2	7.2	N/A	N/A
2010	N/A	N/A	N/A	N/A	N/A	N/A	N/A
2009	N/A	N/A	N/A	N/A	N/A	N/A	N/A

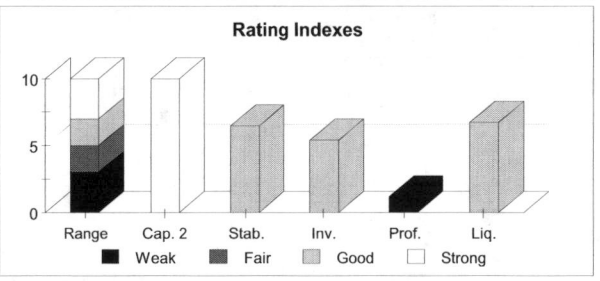

AMERIGROUP KANSAS INC   B-   Good

Major Rating Factors: Good capitalization (6.8 on a scale of 0 to 10) based on excellent current risk-adjusted capital (severe loss scenario). Good liquidity (6.8) with sufficient resources (cash flows and marketable investments) to handle a spike in claims. High quality investment portfolio (7.5).
Other Rating Factors: Weak profitability index (0.9).
Principal Business: Medicaid (96%), comp med (4%)
Mem Phys: 13: 12,994 **12:** 7,315 **13 MLR** 96.8% **/ 13 Admin Exp** N/A
Enroll(000): Q2 14: 130 **13:** 123 **12:** N/A **Med Exp PMPM:** $475
Principal Investments: Cash and equiv (57%), nonaffiliate common stock (24%), long-term bonds (16%), other (2%)
Provider Compensation ($000): Contr fee ($598,701), FFS ($14,719), capitation ($4,092)
Total Member Encounters: Phys (737,477), non-phys (1,747,823)
Group Affiliation: WellPoint Inc
Licensed in: KS
Address: 9393 W 110th Suite 500, Overland Park, KS 66210
Phone: (757) 490-6900 **Dom State:** KS **Commenced Bus:** January 2013

Data Date	Rating	RACR #1	RACR #2	Total Assets ($mil)	Capital ($mil)	Net Premium ($mil)	Net Income ($mil)
6-14	B-	1.22	1.02	193.9	66.7	424.9	-38.0
6-13	N/A	N/A	N/A	87.2	2.5	338.6	-23.6
2013	B-	1.53	1.28	181.9	83.7	720.6	-34.2
2012	N/A	N/A	N/A	7.7	2.4	N/A	-3.5
2011	N/A	N/A	N/A	N/A	N/A	N/A	N/A
2010	N/A	N/A	N/A	N/A	N/A	N/A	N/A
2009	N/A	N/A	N/A	N/A	N/A	N/A	N/A

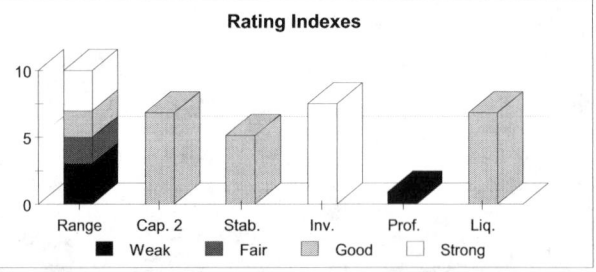

Rating Indexes

AMERIGROUP LOUISIANA INC   B-   Good

Major Rating Factors: Fair quality investment portfolio (4.1 on a scale of 0 to 10). Good liquidity (6.2) with sufficient resources (cash flows and marketable investments) to handle a spike in claims. Strong capitalization (7.7) based on excellent current risk-adjusted capital (severe loss scenario).
Other Rating Factors: Weak profitability index (0.9).
Principal Business: Medicaid (94%), comp med (6%)
Mem Phys: 13: 11,251 **12:** 9,839 **13 MLR** 86.4% **/ 13 Admin Exp** N/A
Enroll(000): Q2 14: 127 **13:** 129 **12:** 139 **Med Exp PMPM:** $224
Principal Investments: Long-term bonds (77%), nonaffiliate common stock (17%), other (7%)
Provider Compensation ($000): Contr fee ($344,449), FFS ($2,806), capitation ($2,615)
Total Member Encounters: Phys (727,012), non-phys (541,177)
Group Affiliation: WellPoint Inc
Licensed in: (No states)
Address: 3501 N Causeway Blvd Ste 307, Metairie, LA 70002
Phone: (757) 490-6900 **Dom State:** LA **Commenced Bus:** February 2012

Data Date	Rating	RACR #1	RACR #2	Total Assets ($mil)	Capital ($mil)	Net Premium ($mil)	Net Income ($mil)
6-14	B-	1.89	1.57	95.9	46.5	198.3	-1.3
6-13	B-	2.44	2.03	83.0	46.4	211.9	9.7
2013	B-	1.92	1.60	94.8	47.4	411.0	9.9
2012	B-	1.97	1.64	69.0	37.5	247.1	-20.4
2011	N/A	N/A	N/A	5.5	4.4	N/A	-0.9
2010	N/A	N/A	N/A	3.0	3.0	N/A	N/A
2009	N/A	N/A	N/A	N/A	N/A	N/A	N/A

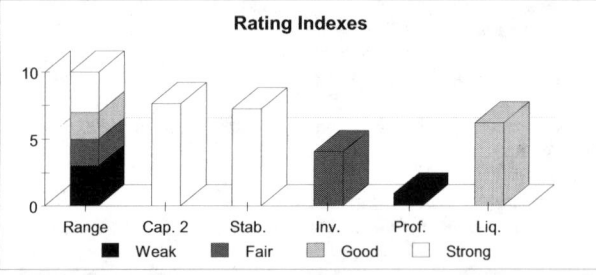

Rating Indexes

AMERIGROUP MARYLAND INC   B   Good

Major Rating Factors: Good quality investment portfolio (6.4 on a scale of 0 to 10). Good liquidity (6.8) with sufficient resources (cash flows and marketable investments) to handle a spike in claims. Excellent profitability (8.5).
Other Rating Factors: Strong capitalization (8.9) based on excellent current risk-adjusted capital (severe loss scenario).
Principal Business: Medicaid (92%), comp med (7%)
Mem Phys: 13: 15,149 **12:** 14,321 **13 MLR** 83.2% **/ 13 Admin Exp** N/A
Enroll(000): Q2 14: 284 **13:** 256 **12:** 218 **Med Exp PMPM:** $223
Principal Investments: Long-term bonds (93%), nonaffiliate common stock (10%), other (2%)
Provider Compensation ($000): Contr fee ($561,282), FFS ($60,072), capitation ($5,629), other ($977)
Total Member Encounters: Phys (1,218,893), non-phys (797,363)
Group Affiliation: WellPoint Inc
Licensed in: MD
Address: 7550 Teague Rd Suite 500, Hanover, MD 21076
Phone: (757) 490-6900 **Dom State:** MD **Commenced Bus:** June 1999

Data Date	Rating	RACR #1	RACR #2	Total Assets ($mil)	Capital ($mil)	Net Premium ($mil)	Net Income ($mil)
6-14	B	2.85	2.38	325.7	113.4	539.8	18.4
6-13	A-	2.97	2.48	283.7	101.2	369.4	16.1
2013	B	2.30	1.91	180.1	88.8	764.2	31.4
2012	A-	3.30	2.75	191.9	114.1	684.2	34.2
2011	A-	3.09	2.57	206.3	117.9	702.9	40.3
2010	A-	3.31	2.76	199.5	125.1	694.8	52.5
2009	B	1.85	1.54	196.4	75.0	657.4	19.5

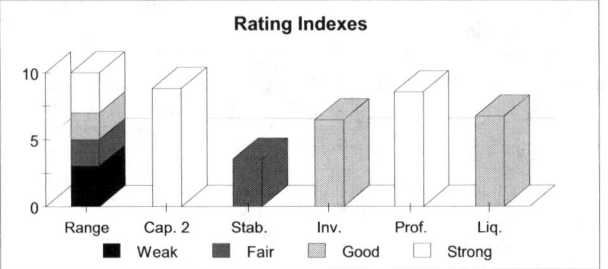

Rating Indexes

AMERIGROUP NEVADA INC
B- Good

Major Rating Factors: Good overall profitability index (6.0 on a scale of 0 to 10). Good liquidity (6.9) with sufficient resources (cash flows and marketable investments) to handle a spike in claims. Strong capitalization (10.0) based on excellent current risk-adjusted capital (severe loss scenario).
Other Rating Factors: High quality investment portfolio (9.4).
Principal Business: Medicaid (95%), comp med (5%)
Mem Phys: 13: 3,462 **12:** 3,053 **13 MLR** 77.1% **/ 13 Admin Exp** N/A
Enroll(000): Q2 14: 153 **13:** 98 **12:** 86 **Med Exp PMPM:** $136
Principal Investments: Long-term bonds (72%), cash and equiv (27%), other (1%)
Provider Compensation ($000): Contr fee ($123,055), capitation ($18,767), FFS ($1,293), bonus arrang ($405)
Total Member Encounters: Phys (430,434), non-phys (160,552)
Group Affiliation: WellPoint Inc
Licensed in: NV
Address: 4426 Corporation Ln, Virginia Beach, VA 23462
Phone: (757) 490-6900 **Dom State:** NV **Commenced Bus:** February 2009

Data Date	Rating	RACR #1	RACR #2	Total Assets ($mil)	Capital ($mil)	Net Premium ($mil)	Net Income ($mil)
6-14	B-	3.78	3.15	70.0	34.7	160.1	6.7
6-13	B	2.61	2.18	37.4	22.7	89.6	1.8
2013	B-	3.12	2.60	45.1	28.0	188.1	7.0
2012	B	3.95	3.29	48.9	35.8	185.4	7.0
2011	B-	2.80	2.33	42.0	28.3	176.3	2.4
2010	B-	2.94	2.45	40.1	26.2	161.5	4.2
2009	C	2.11	1.76	39.4	21.6	110.1	-4.2

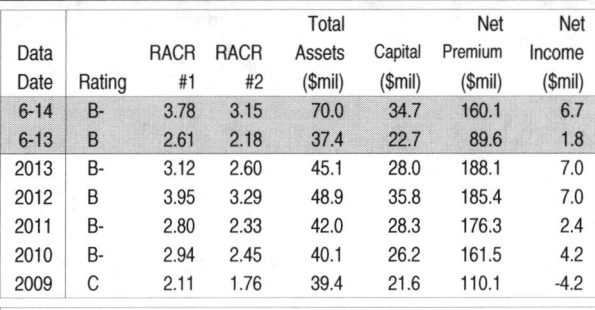

Rating Indexes

Range Cap. 2 Stab. Inv. Prof. Liq.
■ Weak ■ Fair ▨ Good □ Strong

AMERIGROUP NEW JERSEY INC *
A- Excellent

Major Rating Factors: Excellent profitability (7.8 on a scale of 0 to 10). Strong capitalization index (10.0) based on excellent current risk-adjusted capital (severe loss scenario). High quality investment portfolio (8.7).
Other Rating Factors: Excellent overall results on stability tests (8.2). Rating is significantly influenced by the good financial results of WellPoint Inc. Good liquidity (6.7) with sufficient resources (cash flows and marketable investments) to handle a spike in claims.
Principal Business: Medicaid (86%), Medicare (11%), comp med (3%)
Mem Phys: 13: 9,578 **12:** 9,216 **13 MLR** 81.6% **/ 13 Admin Exp** N/A
Enroll(000): Q2 14: 194 **13:** 153 **12:** 152 **Med Exp PMPM:** $286
Principal Investments: Long-term bonds (90%), nonaffiliate common stock (6%), cash and equiv (3%), other (1%)
Provider Compensation ($000): Contr fee ($487,311), capitation ($25,065), FFS ($21,707), bonus arrang ($94)
Total Member Encounters: Phys (871,377), non-phys (1,372,412)
Group Affiliation: WellPoint Inc
Licensed in: NJ
Address: 101 Wood Ave S 8th Floor, Iselin, NJ 08830
Phone: (757) 490-6900 **Dom State:** NJ **Commenced Bus:** February 1996

Data Date	Rating	RACR #1	RACR #2	Total Assets ($mil)	Capital ($mil)	Net Premium ($mil)	Net Income ($mil)
6-14	A-	4.07	3.39	235.0	139.9	423.5	29.1
6-13	A-	2.57	2.15	160.5	89.4	312.1	4.2
2013	A-	3.26	2.72	178.3	110.3	645.5	25.0
2012	A-	2.46	2.05	153.9	85.0	631.2	11.6
2011	A-	2.48	2.06	141.8	69.9	501.9	25.7
2010	A-	3.11	2.59	110.7	68.5	402.7	25.2
2009	B	2.27	1.89	95.2	49.9	316.1	-2.9

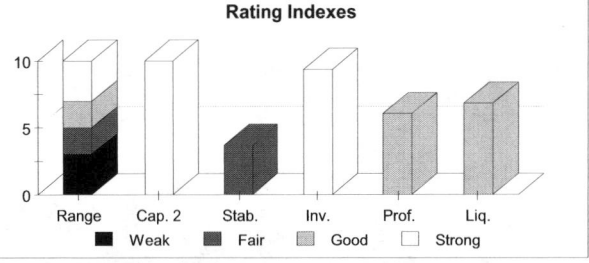

Rating Indexes

Range Cap. 2 Stab. Inv. Prof. Liq.
■ Weak ■ Fair ▨ Good □ Strong

AMERIGROUP OHIO INC
B Good

Major Rating Factors: Good overall profitability index (6.4 on a scale of 0 to 10). Strong capitalization (10.0) based on excellent current risk-adjusted capital (severe loss scenario). High quality investment portfolio (9.9).
Other Rating Factors: Excellent liquidity (7.2) with ample operational cash flow and liquid investments.
Principal Business: Medicaid (100%)
Mem Phys: 12: 6,034 **11:** 4,832 **12 MLR** 67.7% **/ 12 Admin Exp** N/A
Enroll(000): Q2 13: 50 **12:** 54 **11:** 55 **Med Exp PMPM:** $168
Principal Investments: Cash and equiv (51%), long-term bonds (49%)
Provider Compensation ($000): Contr fee ($115,072), FFS ($3,660), capitation ($807)
Total Member Encounters: Phys (127,953), non-phys (93,872)
Group Affiliation: WellPoint Inc
Licensed in: OH
Address: 10123 Alliance Rd, Cincinnati, OH 45242
Phone: (757) 490-6900 **Dom State:** OH **Commenced Bus:** September 2005

Data Date	Rating	RACR #1	RACR #2	Total Assets ($mil)	Capital ($mil)	Net Premium ($mil)	Net Income ($mil)
6-13	B	4.31	3.59	48.1	31.0	80.6	5.6
6-12	B	4.51	3.76	51.4	34.6	83.4	7.4
2012	B	5.61	4.67	58.3	42.0	169.6	13.5
2011	B	4.32	3.60	56.0	32.7	148.0	6.8
2010	B	4.26	3.55	53.4	35.7	154.0	9.2
2009	C	2.06	1.72	80.9	35.8	264.8	3.2
2008	C	1.92	1.60	67.0	32.8	233.3	-2.3

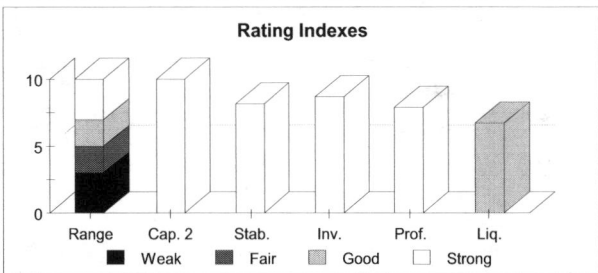

Rating Indexes

Range Cap. 2 Stab. Inv. Prof. Liq.
■ Weak ■ Fair ▨ Good □ Strong

AMERIGROUP TENNESSEE INC

B   **Good**

Major Rating Factors: Good liquidity (6.5 on a scale of 0 to 10) with sufficient resources (cash flows and marketable investments) to handle a spike in claims. Excellent profitability (8.4). Strong capitalization (8.5) based on excellent current risk-adjusted capital (severe loss scenario).
Other Rating Factors: High quality investment portfolio (8.2).
Principal Business: Medicaid (94%), Medicare (6%)
Mem Phys: 13: 8,320   **12:** 8,038   **13 MLR** 82.6%   / **13 Admin Exp** N/A
Enroll(000): Q2 14: 217   **13:** 204   **12:** 206   **Med Exp PMPM:** $311
Principal Investments: Long-term bonds (85%), nonaffiliate common stock (10%), cash and equiv (2%), other (3%)
Provider Compensation ($000): Contr fee ($729,059), capitation ($21,695), FFS ($5,237), bonus arrang ($231)
Total Member Encounters: Phys (1,354,260), non-phys (1,763,727)
Group Affiliation: WellPoint Inc
Licensed in: TN
Address: 22 Century Blvd Suite 310, Nashville, TN 37214
Phone: (757) 490-6900   **Dom State:** TN   **Commenced Bus:** April 2007

Data Date	Rating	RACR #1	RACR #2	Total Assets ($mil)	Capital ($mil)	Net Premium ($mil)	Net Income ($mil)
6-14	B	2.57	2.14	256.9	116.1	475.3	8.6
6-13	B	2.13	1.78	195.0	95.2	451.9	12.4
2013	B	2.42	2.01	236.7	108.1	917.0	23.8
2012	B	2.35	1.96	212.2	106.1	904.9	25.8
2011	B+	2.99	2.49	257.6	144.2	920.1	67.6
2010	B-	3.21	2.67	340.3	150.6	888.6	71.6
2009	C	1.96	1.63	163.4	80.9	626.1	22.5

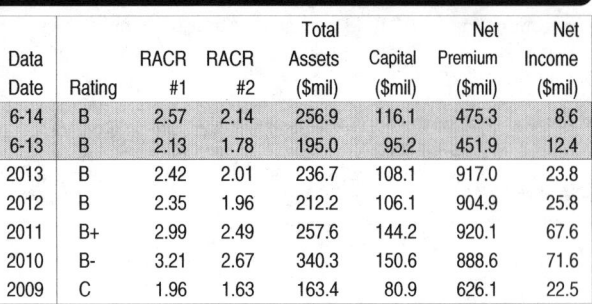

AMERIGROUP TEXAS INC *

B+   **Good**

Major Rating Factors: Good quality investment portfolio (6.6 on a scale of 0 to 10). Good overall results on stability tests (5.2). Rating is significantly influenced by the good financial results of WellPoint Inc. Good liquidity (6.3) with sufficient resources (cash flows and marketable investments) to handle a spike in claims.
Other Rating Factors: Excellent profitability (7.4). Strong capitalization index (7.8) based on excellent current risk-adjusted capital (severe loss scenario).
Principal Business: Medicaid (83%), Medicare (11%), comp med (5%)
Mem Phys: 13: 50,074   **12:** 44,959   **13 MLR** 82.9%   / **13 Admin Exp** N/A
Enroll(000): Q2 14: 635   **13:** 624   **12:** 661   **Med Exp PMPM:** $279
Principal Investments: Long-term bonds (79%), nonaffiliate common stock (14%), cash and equiv (3%), other (4%)
Provider Compensation ($000): Contr fee ($1,928,693), FFS ($244,240), capitation ($19,100), bonus arrang ($1,547)
Total Member Encounters: Phys (3,658,651), non-phys (3,134,065)
Group Affiliation: WellPoint Inc
Licensed in: TX
Address: 3800 Buffalo Speedway Ste 400, Houston, TX 77098
Phone: (757) 490-6900   **Dom State:** TX   **Commenced Bus:** October 1996

Data Date	Rating	RACR #1	RACR #2	Total Assets ($mil)	Capital ($mil)	Net Premium ($mil)	Net Income ($mil)
6-14	B+	1.96	1.63	645.6	273.3	1,318.6	-4.0
6-13	A-	2.34	1.95	518.7	312.7	1,309.4	36.2
2013	A-	2.45	2.04	666.8	348.3	2,627.5	69.3
2012	A-	2.08	1.73	500.7	275.3	2,373.1	23.5
2011	A-	2.14	1.79	382.1	190.2	1,612.2	23.5
2010	A-	2.26	1.88	326.4	167.6	1,397.5	42.5
2009	B	2.08	1.73	316.9	156.7	1,300.0	31.4

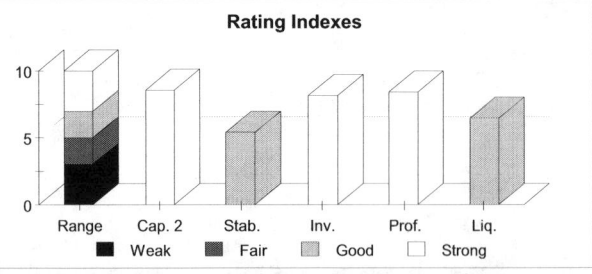

AMERIGROUP WASHINGTON INC

B   **Good**

Major Rating Factors: Good quality investment portfolio (6.7 on a scale of 0 to 10). Fair profitability index (4.2). Strong capitalization (10.0) based on excellent current risk-adjusted capital (severe loss scenario).
Other Rating Factors: Excellent liquidity (6.9) with sufficient resources (cash flows and marketable investments) to handle a spike in claims.
Principal Business: Medicaid (99%)
Mem Phys: 13: 14,018   **12:** 9,167   **13 MLR** 82.1%   / **13 Admin Exp** N/A
Enroll(000): Q2 14: 114   **13:** 35   **12:** 25   **Med Exp PMPM:** $310
Principal Investments: Long-term bonds (59%), cash and equiv (30%), nonaffiliate common stock (10%)
Provider Compensation ($000): Contr fee ($104,280), FFS ($3,330), capitation ($387), bonus arrang ($193)
Total Member Encounters: Phys (165,471), non-phys (101,511)
Group Affiliation: WellPoint Inc
Licensed in: (No states)
Address: 705 Fifth Ave South Suite 100, Seattle, WA 98104
Phone: (757) 490-6900   **Dom State:** WA   **Commenced Bus:** July 2012

Data Date	Rating	RACR #1	RACR #2	Total Assets ($mil)	Capital ($mil)	Net Premium ($mil)	Net Income ($mil)
6-14	B	12.11	10.09	222.4	96.8	205.4	6.8
6-13	B-	8.49	7.08	70.5	38.6	57.4	8.4
2013	B-	5.38	4.48	105.1	35.7	133.9	2.5
2012	B-	6.65	5.54	65.8	30.2	45.5	-4.9
2011	N/A	N/A	N/A	3.1	3.1	N/A	N/A
2010	N/A	N/A	N/A	3.0	3.0	N/A	N/A
2009	N/A	N/A	N/A	N/A	N/A	N/A	N/A

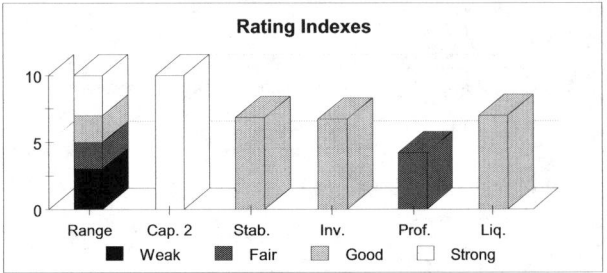

AMERIHEALTH CARITAS OF LOUISIANA INC   C   Fair

Major Rating Factors: Weak profitability index (1.1 on a scale of 0 to 10). Strong capitalization (7.0) based on excellent current risk-adjusted capital (severe loss scenario). High quality investment portfolio (9.9).
Other Rating Factors: Excellent liquidity (7.0) with ample operational cash flow and liquid investments.
Principal Business: Medicaid (100%)
Mem Phys: 13: 17,081 **12:** 13,202 **13 MLR** 85.9% **/ 13 Admin Exp** N/A
Enroll(000): Q2 14: 141 **13:** 145 **12:** 155 **Med Exp PMPM:** $237
Principal Investments: Cash and equiv (100%)
Provider Compensation ($000): Contr fee ($414,923), capitation ($2,786), bonus arrang ($537)
Total Member Encounters: Phys (1,136,361), non-phys (193,097)
Group Affiliation: Independence Blue Cross Inc
Licensed in: LA
Address: 10000 Perkins Rowe Block G 400, Baton Rouge, LA 70810
Phone: (215) 937-8000 **Dom State:** LA **Commenced Bus:** July 2011

Data Date	Rating	RACR #1	RACR #2	Total Assets ($mil)	Capital ($mil)	Net Premium ($mil)	Net Income ($mil)
6-14	C	1.37	1.14	96.5	35.0	232.2	-3.0
6-13	C	1.27	1.06	90.1	26.5	246.1	6.4
2013	C	1.56	1.30	105.7	40.3	490.6	12.4
2012	C	1.45	1.21	85.7	23.4	272.4	-15.3
2011	N/A	N/A	N/A	12.3	5.7	N/A	-6.2
2010	N/A	N/A	N/A	N/A	N/A	N/A	N/A
2009	N/A	N/A	N/A	N/A	N/A	N/A	N/A

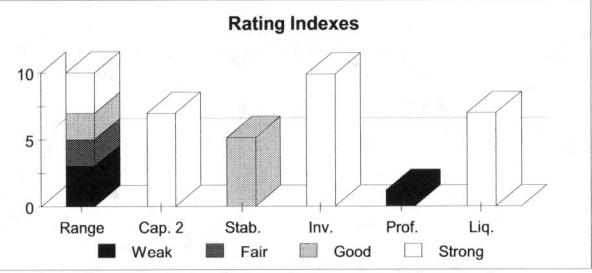

AMERIHEALTH DISTRICT OF COLUMBIA INC   C   Fair

Major Rating Factors: Weak profitability index (0.9 on a scale of 0 to 10). Strong capitalization (7.3) based on excellent current risk-adjusted capital (severe loss scenario). High quality investment portfolio (9.9).
Other Rating Factors: Excellent liquidity (7.0) with ample operational cash flow and liquid investments.
Principal Business: Medicaid (100%)
Mem Phys: 13: 3,815 **12:** N/A **13 MLR** 85.4% **/ 13 Admin Exp** N/A
Enroll(000): Q2 14: 109 **13:** 105 **12:** N/A **Med Exp PMPM:** $267
Principal Investments: Cash and equiv (100%)
Provider Compensation ($000): Contr fee ($146,605), capitation ($27,450)
Total Member Encounters: Phys (405,275), non-phys (35,910)
Group Affiliation: Independence Blue Cross Inc
Licensed in: DC
Address: N/A
Phone: (215) 937-8000 **Dom State:** DC **Commenced Bus:** March 2013

Data Date	Rating	RACR #1	RACR #2	Total Assets ($mil)	Capital ($mil)	Net Premium ($mil)	Net Income ($mil)
6-14	C	1.57	1.31	92.4	26.3	209.3	-0.2
6-13	N/A	N/A	N/A	82.9	26.6	64.8	-1.8
2013	C	1.48	1.24	83.8	24.8	255.5	-6.0
2012	N/A	N/A	N/A	N/A	N/A	N/A	N/A
2011	N/A	N/A	N/A	N/A	N/A	N/A	N/A
2010	N/A	N/A	N/A	N/A	N/A	N/A	N/A
2009	N/A	N/A	N/A	N/A	N/A	N/A	N/A

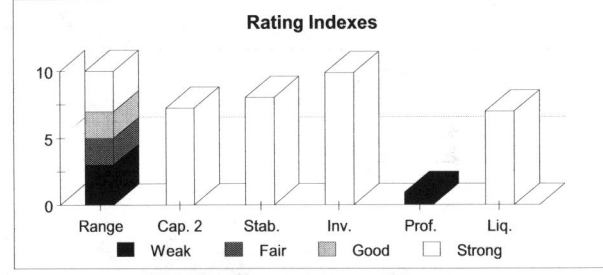

AMERIHEALTH HMO INC   B   Good

Major Rating Factors: Good overall profitability index (5.7 on a scale of 0 to 10). Fair quality investment portfolio (3.4). Strong capitalization index (10.0) based on excellent current risk-adjusted capital (severe loss scenario).
Other Rating Factors: Excellent overall results on stability tests (7.1). Excellent liquidity (7.3) with ample operational cash flow and liquid investments
Principal Business: Comp med (97%), Medicare (3%)
Mem Phys: 13: 48,260 **12:** 47,981 **13 MLR** 81.5% **/ 13 Admin Exp** N/A
Enroll(000): Q2 14: 112 **13:** 84 **12:** 70 **Med Exp PMPM:** $339
Principal Investments: Affiliate common stock (83%), cash and equiv (10%), long-term bonds (7%)
Provider Compensation ($000): Contr fee ($287,712), FFS ($19,170), capitation ($10,138)
Total Member Encounters: Phys (997,424), non-phys (117,501)
Group Affiliation: Independence Blue Cross Inc
Licensed in: DE, NJ, PA
Address: 1901 Market St, Philadelphia, PA 19103
Phone: (215) 241-2400 **Dom State:** PA **Commenced Bus:** April 1978

Data Date	Rating	RACR #1	RACR #2	Total Assets ($mil)	Capital ($mil)	Net Premium ($mil)	Net Income ($mil)
6-14	B	4.66	3.88	1,350.2	1,243.3	321.4	-4.0
6-13	B	4.45	3.71	1,224.9	1,164.9	184.3	3.2
2013	B	4.71	3.93	1,326.7	1,258.9	391.7	5.7
2012	B	4.19	3.49	1,151.2	1,094.7	337.4	215.2
2011	B	3.81	3.18	1,073.2	1,003.4	358.3	110.8
2010	B	3.09	2.57	936.2	878.8	353.6	78.1
2009	B	2.28	1.90	887.9	725.1	334.6	-11.2

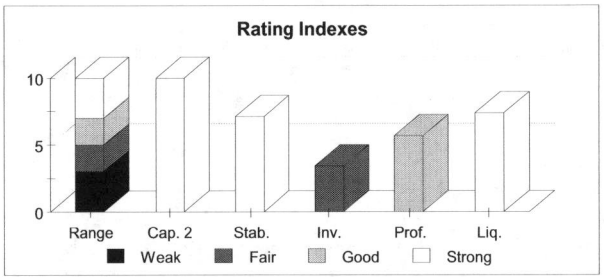

AMERIHEALTH INSURANCE CO OF NJ   C-   Fair

Major Rating Factors: Fair profitability index (4.4 on a scale of 0 to 10). Good liquidity (6.2) with sufficient resources (cash flows and marketable investments) to handle a spike in claims. Strong capitalization (9.6) based on excellent current risk-adjusted capital (severe loss scenario).
Other Rating Factors: High quality investment portfolio (9.9).
Principal Business: Comp med (100%)
Mem Phys: 13: 49,263   **12:** 49,041   **13 MLR** 84.5%   **/ 13 Admin Exp** N/A
Enroll(000):   13: 84   **12:** 63   **Med Exp PMPM:** $396
Principal Investments: Long-term bonds (93%), cash and equiv (7%)
Provider Compensation ($000): Contr fee ($275,485), FFS ($62,663), capitation ($5,464), bonus arrang ($158)
Total Member Encounters: Phys (1,379,927), non-phys (148,178)
Group Affiliation: Independence Blue Cross Inc
Licensed in: NJ
Address: 8000 Midlantic Dr Ste 333, Mount Laurel, NJ 08054-1560
Phone: (609) 662-2400   **Dom State:** NJ   **Commenced Bus:** June 1995

Data Date	Rating	RACR #1	RACR #2	Total Assets ($mil)	Capital ($mil)	Net Premium ($mil)	Net Income ($mil)
2013	C-	3.44	2.87	169.1	83.7	415.8	2.7
2012	C-	4.02	3.35	143.0	79.9	332.6	-2.5
2011	C-	4.60	3.83	136.4	80.3	310.4	18.0
2010	C-	3.00	2.50	122.8	63.7	359.9	18.2
2009	C-	2.57	2.14	127.4	49.8	327.6	-28.0

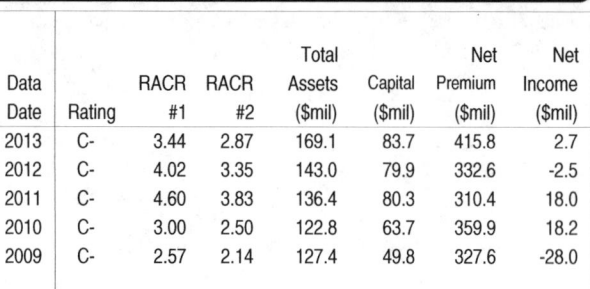

Rating Indexes

AMERIHEALTH NEBRASKA INC   E   Very Weak

Major Rating Factors: Weak profitability index (0.9 on a scale of 0 to 10). Strong capitalization (8.2) based on excellent current risk-adjusted capital (severe loss scenario). High quality investment portfolio (9.9).
Other Rating Factors: Excellent liquidity (7.0) with ample operational cash flow and liquid investments.
Principal Business: Medicaid (100%)
Mem Phys: 13: 7,300   **12:** 6,539   **13 MLR** 84.5%   **/ 13 Admin Exp** N/A
Enroll(000): Q2 14: 23   **13:** 21   **12:** 19   **Med Exp PMPM:** $183
Principal Investments: Cash and equiv (100%)
Provider Compensation ($000): Contr fee ($48,395), bonus arrang ($132)
Total Member Encounters: Phys (156,479), non-phys (48,828)
Group Affiliation: Independence Blue Cross Inc
Licensed in: NE
Address: 2120 S 72nd St, Omaha, NE 68124
Phone: (215) 937-8000   **Dom State:** NE   **Commenced Bus:** February 2012

Data Date	Rating	RACR #1	RACR #2	Total Assets ($mil)	Capital ($mil)	Net Premium ($mil)	Net Income ($mil)
6-14	E	2.34	1.95	16.8	7.9	31.0	-3.1
6-13	C	1.96	1.63	18.5	5.9	27.7	-0.5
2013	C	2.18	1.82	16.2	7.2	57.0	0.7
2012	C	2.39	1.99	21.9	7.2	25.0	-3.7
2011	N/A	N/A	N/A	N/A	N/A	N/A	N/A
2010	N/A	N/A	N/A	N/A	N/A	N/A	N/A
2009	N/A	N/A	N/A	N/A	N/A	N/A	N/A

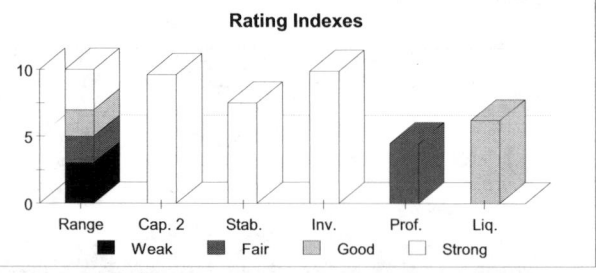

Rating Indexes

AMERITAS LIFE INSURANCE CORP OF NEW YORK   B-   Good

Major Rating Factors: Good quality investment portfolio (6.1 on a scale of 0 to 10) despite significant exposure to mortgages . Mortgage default rate has been low. large holdings of BBB rated bonds in addition to small junk bond holdings. Fair liquidity (4.2) due, in part, to cash value policies that are subject to withdrawals with minimal or no penalty. Fair overall results on stability tests (3.5) including negative cash flow from operations for 2013, weak results on operational trends and excessive premium growth.
Other Rating Factors: Weak profitability (1.8) with operating losses during the first six months of 2014. Strong capitalization (7.2) based on excellent risk adjusted capital (severe loss scenario).
Principal Business: Reinsurance (74%), individual life insurance (16%), group health insurance (7%), group retirement contracts (2%), and individual health insurance (1%).
Principal Investments: NonCMO investment grade bonds (68%), CMOs and structured securities (17%), mortgages in good standing (12%), policy loans (2%), and noninv. grade bonds (1%).
Investments in Affiliates: None
Group Affiliation: UNIFI Mutual Holding Co
Licensed in: NY
Commenced Business: May 1994
Address: 400 Rella Blvd Suite 214, Suffern, NY 10901
Phone: (914) 357-3816   **Domicile State:** NY **NAIC Code:** 60033

Data Date	Rating	RACR #1	RACR #2	Total Assets ($mil)	Capital ($mil)	Net Premium ($mil)	Net Income ($mil)
6-14	B-	2.04	1.11	1,131.3	75.4	46.0	-3.2
6-13	B-	4.03	1.96	974.1	73.6	34.1	-29.7
2013	B-	2.12	1.17	1,113.0	81.8	285.0	-45.8
2012	B-	3.72	3.07	122.3	33.5	71.4	-4.2
2011	B	4.09	3.50	104.6	36.6	71.6	-9.8
2010	B	6.13	5.52	71.0	46.9	29.9	-1.7
2009	B	3.42	2.62	40.5	19.3	30.2	-0.4

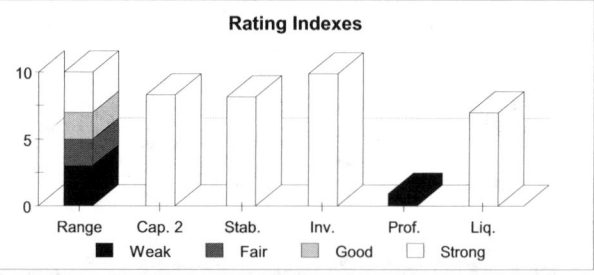

Adverse Trends in Operations

Increase in policy surrenders from 2012 to 2013 (76%)
Increase in policy surrenders from 2011 to 2012 (741%)
Decrease in capital during 2011 (22%)
Increase in policy surrenders from 2010 to 2011 (109%)
Increase in policy surrenders from 2009 to 2010 (54%)

AMERITAS LIFE INSURANCE CORPORATION | B | Good

Major Rating Factors: Good liquidity (6.9 on a scale of 0 to 10) with sufficient resources to handle a spike in claims as well as a significant increase in policy surrenders. Good overall results on stability tests (6.1). Stability strengths include excellent operational trends and excellent risk diversification. Fair quality investment portfolio (3.8).

Other Rating Factors: Strong capitalization (7.2) based on excellent risk adjusted capital (severe loss scenario). Excellent profitability (7.1) with operating gains in each of the last five years.

Principal Business: Group health insurance (35%), group retirement contracts (27%), individual annuities (18%), individual life insurance (15%), and other lines (5%).

Principal Investments: NonCMO investment grade bonds (40%), common & preferred stock (31%), mortgages in good standing (13%), CMOs and structured securities (9%), and misc. investments (7%).

Investments in Affiliates: 24%

Group Affiliation: UNIFI Mutual Holding Co

Licensed in: All states except NY, PR

Commenced Business: May 1887

Address: 5900 O Street, Lincoln, NE 68510

Phone: (402) 467-1122 **Domicile State:** NE **NAIC Code:** 61301

Data Date	Rating	RACR #1	RACR #2	Total Assets ($mil)	Capital ($mil)	Net Premium ($mil)	Net Income ($mil)
6-14	B	1.33	1.15	9,678.1	1,557.0	858.6	32.5
6-13	B	1.32	1.13	8,363.9	1,305.5	791.1	47.7
2013	B	1.30	1.13	9,187.8	1,501.8	1,622.4	64.9
2012	B	1.31	1.13	7,997.9	1,298.4	1,494.5	0.0
2011	B	1.41	1.23	7,278.3	1,349.1	1,265.0	26.2
2010	B+	1.51	1.30	7,124.6	1,330.9	1,154.1	77.9
2009	B+	1.46	1.26	6,529.5	1,249.0	1,227.6	49.9

Adverse Trends in Operations

Decrease in capital during 2012 (4%)
Decrease in premium volume from 2009 to 2010 (6%)

AMEX ASSURANCE CO | B | Good

Major Rating Factors: Good liquidity (6.8 on a scale of 0 to 10) with sufficient resources (cash flows and marketable investments) to handle a spike in claims. Good overall results on stability tests (5.9) despite excessive premium growth. Stability strengths include good operational trends and excellent risk diversification. The largest net exposure for one risk is acceptable at 2.7% of capital.

Other Rating Factors: Fair profitability index (4.9). Excellent expense controls. Return on equity has been fair, averaging 40.6% over the past five years. Strong long-term capitalization index (10.0) based on excellent current risk adjusted capital (severe and moderate loss scenarios), despite some fluctuation in capital levels. Ample reserve history (8.3) that helps to protect the company against sharp claims increases.

Principal Business: (Not applicable due to unusual reinsurance transactions.)

Principal Investments: Investment grade bonds (91%), misc. investments (8%), and non investment grade bonds (1%).

Investments in Affiliates: None

Group Affiliation: American Express Company

Licensed in: All states, the District of Columbia and Puerto Rico

Commenced Business: February 1973

Address: 227 W Monroe St Ste 3600, Chicago, IL 60606

Phone: (623) 492-3094 **Domicile State:** IL **NAIC Code:** 27928

Data Date	Rating	RACR #1	RACR #2	Loss Ratio %	Total Assets ($mil)	Capital ($mil)	Net Premium ($mil)	Net Income ($mil)
6-14	B	9.99	5.82	N/A	317.6	221.3	95.0	35.2
6-13	B	9.89	5.81	N/A	327.5	228.3	70.2	42.5
2013	B	9.10	5.40	49.3	296.5	196.9	177.5	78.9
2012	B	7.41	4.31	42.8	269.2	196.7	244.3	78.9
2011	B	8.91	5.09	35.8	257.6	203.9	233.8	86.2
2010	B	8.55	4.94	32.6	266.9	206.5	227.0	88.7
2009	B-	7.93	4.62	35.0	268.5	205.1	228.2	86.6

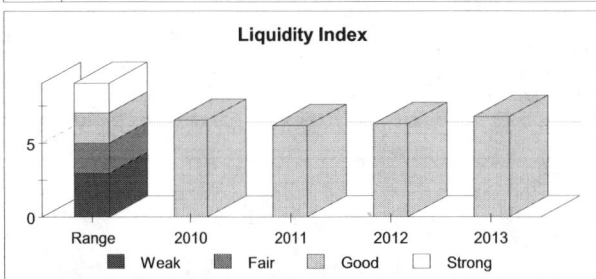

Liquidity Index

AMFIRST INS CO | B | Good

Major Rating Factors: Excellent profitability (7.4 on a scale of 0 to 10). Strong capitalization (10.0) based on excellent current risk-adjusted capital (severe loss scenario). High quality investment portfolio (7.3).

Other Rating Factors: Excellent liquidity (7.3) with ample operational cash flow and liquid investments.

Principal Business: Dental (17%), other (82%)

Mem Phys: 13: N/A **12:** N/A **13 MLR** 115.6% **/ 13 Admin Exp** N/A

Enroll(000): Q2 14: 37 **13:** 28 **12:** 42 **Med Exp PMPM:** $31

Principal Investments: Affiliate common stock (37%), cash and equiv (26%), pref stock (14%), long-term bonds (12%), nonaffiliate common stock (3%), real estate (1%), other (7%)

Provider Compensation ($000): FFS ($13,367)

Total Member Encounters: Phys (34,731), non-phys (98,232)

Group Affiliation: AmFirst Holdings Inc

Licensed in: AL, AZ, AR, FL, GA, LA, MD, MS, NC, OH, OK, PA, SC, TN, TX, VA, WV

Address: 201 Robert S Kerr Ave Ste 600, Oklahoma City, OK 73102

Phone: (800) 800-1397 **Dom State:** OK **Commenced Bus:** January 1999

Data Date	Rating	RACR #1	RACR #2	Total Assets ($mil)	Capital ($mil)	Net Premium ($mil)	Net Income ($mil)
6-14	B	4.16	3.46	40.2	32.7	24.2	2.9
6-13	B	3.27	2.72	27.5	19.8	5.7	1.5
2013	B	2.92	2.43	32.4	23.3	11.6	2.7
2012	B	2.78	2.32	23.3	16.9	29.8	2.4
2011	B	3.97	3.31	19.5	13.3	26.2	1.6
2010	B	3.90	3.25	15.5	10.5	29.9	1.7
2009	C-	2.76	2.30	10.8	6.7	21.7	0.8

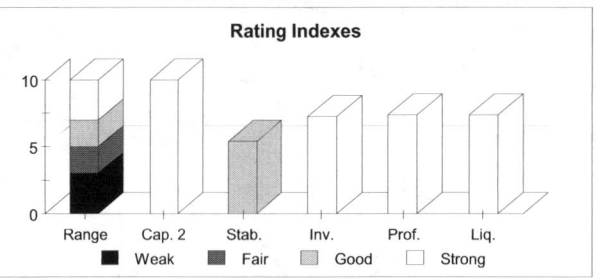

Rating Indexes

AMGP GEORGIA MANAGED CARE CO INC | B | Good

Major Rating Factors: Good liquidity (6.9 on a scale of 0 to 10) with sufficient resources (cash flows and marketable investments) to handle a spike in claims. Excellent profitability (8.3). Strong capitalization (9.3) based on excellent current risk-adjusted capital (severe loss scenario).
Other Rating Factors: High quality investment portfolio (7.8).
Principal Business: Medicaid (88%), comp med (12%)
Mem Phys: 13: 21,650 **12:** 19,536 **13 MLR** 79.2% **/ 13 Admin Exp** N/A
Enroll(000): Q2 14: 356 **13:** 296 **12:** 288 **Med Exp PMPM:** $180
Principal Investments: Long-term bonds (87%), cash and equiv (10%), other (3%)
Provider Compensation ($000): Contr fee ($571,117), capitation ($10,830), FFS ($9,303), bonus arrang ($698)
Total Member Encounters: Phys (1,745,470), non-phys (676,995)
Group Affiliation: WellPoint Inc
Licensed in: GA
Address: 303 Perimeter Center N # 400, Atlanta, GA 30346
Phone: (757) 490-6900 **Dom State:** GA **Commenced Bus:** June 2006

Data Date	Rating	RACR #1	RACR #2	Total Assets ($mil)	Capital ($mil)	Net Premium ($mil)	Net Income ($mil)
6-14	B	3.18	2.65	261.7	123.5	508.2	13.1
6-13	B+	2.83	2.36	168.3	101.9	371.2	19.1
2013	B	2.85	2.37	223.5	109.2	795.0	25.7
2012	A-	3.35	2.80	183.1	123.3	734.4	13.9
2011	A-	2.89	2.41	178.7	108.1	728.7	36.4
2010	B	2.38	1.98	157.7	84.3	690.5	15.3
2009	C	2.12	1.77	118.1	71.5	580.9	9.6

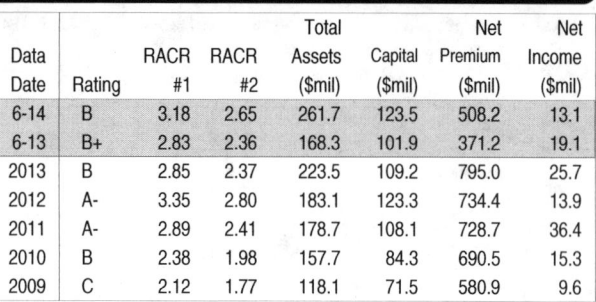

Rating Indexes

ANTHEM BLUE CROSS LIFE & HEALTH INS | B | Good

Major Rating Factors: Good liquidity (6.8 on a scale of 0 to 10) with sufficient resources (cash flows and marketable investments) to handle a spike in claims. Fair quality investment portfolio (3.8). Excellent profitability (8.3).
Other Rating Factors: Strong capitalization (10.0) based on excellent current risk-adjusted capital (severe loss scenario).
Principal Business: Comp med (81%), Medicare (7%), dental (5%), other (6%)
Mem Phys: 13: 59,713 **12:** 59,103 **13 MLR** 80.5% **/ 13 Admin Exp** N/A
Enroll(000): Q2 14: 2,839 **13:** 3,351 **12:** 3,405 **Med Exp PMPM:** $107
Principal Investments: Long-term bonds (84%), cash and equiv (8%), nonaffiliate common stock (3%), pref stock (1%), other (3%)
Provider Compensation ($000): Contr fee ($3,039,173), FFS ($1,242,123), bonus arrang ($1,339), other ($46,143)
Total Member Encounters: Phys (7,028,841), non-phys (4,288,100)
Group Affiliation: WellPoint Inc
Licensed in: CA
Address: 21555 Oxnard St, Woodland Hills, CA 91367
Phone: (818) 234-2345 **Dom State:** CA **Commenced Bus:** August 1991

Data Date	Rating	RACR #1	RACR #2	Total Assets ($mil)	Capital ($mil)	Net Premium ($mil)	Net Income ($mil)
6-14	B	4.39	3.66	2,584.3	1,408.2	2,075.1	210.7
6-13	B	4.81	4.01	2,965.7	1,503.5	2,656.1	156.6
2013	B	3.81	3.17	2,838.2	1,216.8	5,393.8	168.9
2012	B	4.37	3.64	2,739.1	1,361.0	5,231.2	342.4
2011	B	3.43	2.86	2,609.9	1,145.4	5,753.0	203.5
2010	B	3.40	2.84	2,393.9	973.8	4,939.2	205.9
2009	B-	3.50	2.91	2,181.4	813.8	4,250.2	170.5

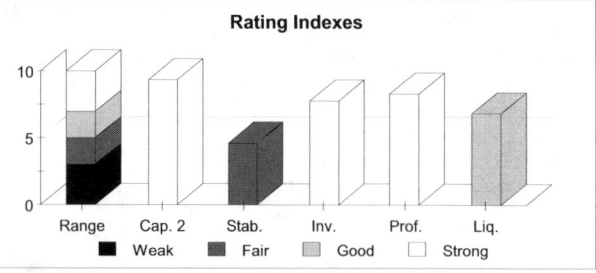

Rating Indexes

ANTHEM HEALTH PLANS INC | B | Good

Major Rating Factors: Good liquidity (6.8 on a scale of 0 to 10) with sufficient resources (cash flows and marketable investments) to handle a spike in claims. Fair quality investment portfolio (3.8). Excellent profitability (8.7).
Other Rating Factors: Strong capitalization (10.0) based on excellent current risk-adjusted capital (severe loss scenario).
Principal Business: Comp med (72%), FEHB (13%), med supp (7%), Medicare (2%), dental (2%), other (3%)
Mem Phys: 13: 22,973 **12:** 22,402 **13 MLR** 84.0% **/ 13 Admin Exp** N/A
Enroll(000): Q2 14: 738 **13:** 743 **12:** 849 **Med Exp PMPM:** $167
Principal Investments: Long-term bonds (125%), nonaffiliate common stock (2%), other (11%)
Provider Compensation ($000): Contr fee ($1,150,942), FFS ($342,321), capitation ($5,294), other ($52,805)
Total Member Encounters: Phys (1,744,414), non-phys (2,661,461)
Group Affiliation: WellPoint Inc
Licensed in: CT
Address: 108 Leigus Rd, Wallingford, CT 06492-2518
Phone: (203) 677-4000 **Dom State:** CT **Commenced Bus:** August 1997

Data Date	Rating	RACR #1	RACR #2	Total Assets ($mil)	Capital ($mil)	Net Premium ($mil)	Net Income ($mil)
6-14	B	3.81	3.18	778.4	364.9	912.7	43.3
6-13	B+	3.87	3.22	765.0	390.5	911.0	58.0
2013	B	3.38	2.81	683.4	320.3	1,811.0	117.8
2012	B+	3.30	2.75	720.7	328.9	1,891.0	133.3
2011	B+	3.00	2.50	730.8	294.1	1,881.1	161.9
2010	B+	3.70	3.08	881.7	444.9	2,295.3	203.6
2009	B+	2.61	2.18	907.0	387.3	2,636.2	135.5

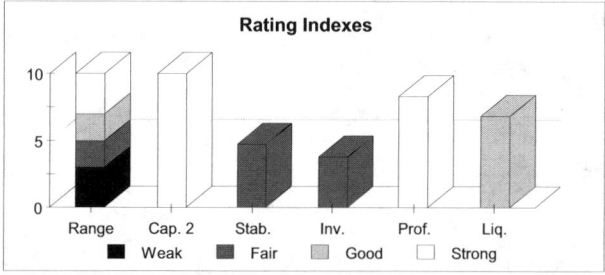

Rating Indexes

ANTHEM HEALTH PLANS OF KENTUCKY INC *   A-   Excellent

Major Rating Factors: Excellent profitability (9.3 on a scale of 0 to 10). Strong capitalization index (10.0) based on excellent current risk-adjusted capital (severe loss scenario). High quality investment portfolio (7.6).

Other Rating Factors: Excellent overall results on stability tests (7.3) based on steady enrollment growth, averaging 6% over the past five years. Rating is significantly influenced by the good financial results of WellPoint Inc. Good liquidity (6.1) with sufficient resources (cash flows and marketable investments) to handle a spike in claims.

Principal Business: Comp med (66%), FEHB (18%), med supp (8%), Medicare (7%).

Mem Phys: 13: 26,598   **12:** 26,229   **13 MLR** 81.6%   **/ 13 Admin Exp** N/A

Enroll(000): Q2 14: 887   **13:** 839   **12:** 796   **Med Exp PMPM:** $179

Principal Investments: Long-term bonds (106%), real estate (4%), other (4%)

Provider Compensation ($000): Contr fee ($1,028,335), FFS ($770,038), bonus arrang ($1,135), capitation ($882)

Total Member Encounters: Phys (3,499,398), non-phys (2,714,477)

Group Affiliation: WellPoint Inc

Licensed in: KY

Address: 13550 Triton Park Blvd, Louisville, KY 40223

Phone: (888) 641-5224   **Dom State:** KY   **Commenced Bus:** July 1993

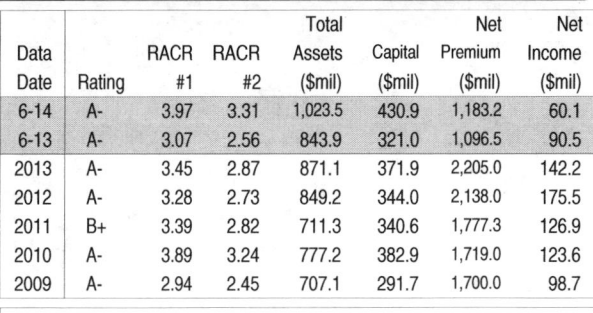

Data Date	Rating	RACR #1	RACR #2	Total Assets ($mil)	Capital ($mil)	Net Premium ($mil)	Net Income ($mil)
6-14	A-	3.97	3.31	1,023.5	430.9	1,183.2	60.1
6-13	A-	3.07	2.56	843.9	321.0	1,096.5	90.5
2013	A-	3.45	2.87	871.1	371.9	2,205.0	142.2
2012	A-	3.28	2.73	849.2	344.0	2,138.0	175.5
2011	B+	3.39	2.82	711.3	340.6	1,777.3	126.9
2010	A-	3.89	3.24	777.2	382.9	1,719.0	123.6
2009	A-	2.94	2.45	707.1	291.7	1,700.0	98.7

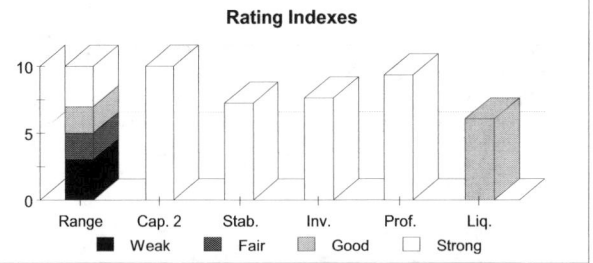

Rating Indexes

ANTHEM HEALTH PLANS OF MAINE INC   B-   Good

Major Rating Factors: Fair quality investment portfolio (4.5 on a scale of 0 to 10). Good liquidity (6.9) with sufficient resources (cash flows and marketable investments) to handle a spike in claims. Excellent profitability (7.2).

Other Rating Factors: Strong capitalization (10.0) based on excellent current risk-adjusted capital (severe loss scenario).

Principal Business: Comp med (75%), FEHB (17%), med supp (4%), Medicare (3%)

Mem Phys: 13: 4,772   **12:** 4,345   **13 MLR** 87.7%   **/ 13 Admin Exp** N/A

Enroll(000): Q2 14: 318   **13:** 323   **12:** 333   **Med Exp PMPM:** $229

Principal Investments: Long-term bonds (109%), real estate (4%)

Provider Compensation ($000): Contr fee ($543,898), FFS ($362,599), other ($1,067)

Total Member Encounters: Phys (1,182,369), non-phys (1,383,745)

Group Affiliation: WellPoint Inc

Licensed in: ME

Address: 2 Gannett Cr, S Portland, ME 04106-6911

Phone: (207) 822-7000   **Dom State:** ME   **Commenced Bus:** June 2000

Data Date	Rating	RACR #1	RACR #2	Total Assets ($mil)	Capital ($mil)	Net Premium ($mil)	Net Income ($mil)
6-14	B-	4.55	3.79	395.6	163.3	507.6	1.1
6-13	B-	4.04	3.37	429.5	181.4	519.1	28.2
2013	B-	4.55	3.79	417.6	163.1	1,030.8	48.4
2012	B-	3.22	2.69	414.9	142.8	1,019.2	39.9
2011	A-	4.55	3.79	480.9	224.6	1,025.4	45.0
2010	B+	4.56	3.80	451.6	229.2	1,010.0	48.8
2009	A	4.15	3.46	412.8	209.5	993.2	20.8

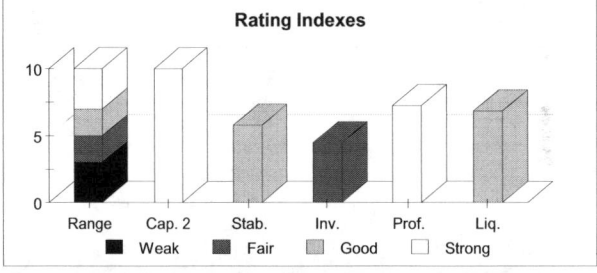

Rating Indexes

ANTHEM HEALTH PLANS OF NEW HAMPSHIRE *   B+   Good

Major Rating Factors: Good quality investment portfolio (4.9 on a scale of 0 to 10). Excellent profitability (8.6). Strong capitalization (9.4) based on excellent current risk-adjusted capital (severe loss scenario).

Other Rating Factors: Excellent liquidity (6.9) with sufficient resources (cash flows and marketable investments) to handle a spike in claims.

Principal Business: FEHB (44%), comp med (37%), med supp (14%), Medicare (4%)

Mem Phys: 13: 13,136   **12:** 12,510   **13 MLR** 83.6%   **/ 13 Admin Exp** N/A

Enroll(000): Q2 14: 137   **13:** 139   **12:** 153   **Med Exp PMPM:** $262

Principal Investments: Long-term bonds (53%), affiliate common stock (47%)

Provider Compensation ($000): FFS ($303,536), contr fee ($127,623), other ($889)

Total Member Encounters: Phys (468,184), non-phys (862,565)

Group Affiliation: WellPoint Inc

Licensed in: NH

Address: 3000 Goffs Falls Rd, Mancheter, NH 03111-0001

Phone: (603) 695-7000   **Dom State:** NH   **Commenced Bus:** October 1999

Data Date	Rating	RACR #1	RACR #2	Total Assets ($mil)	Capital ($mil)	Net Premium ($mil)	Net Income ($mil)
6-14	B+	3.27	2.72	343.1	166.0	248.5	3.8
6-13	B+	3.70	3.08	316.1	186.8	257.4	13.5
2013	B+	3.05	2.54	297.5	154.5	521.3	37.7
2012	B+	3.31	2.75	297.9	166.5	507.1	44.0
2011	B+	2.88	2.40	281.6	134.0	494.9	56.1
2010	B+	2.96	2.47	256.3	128.7	505.2	46.2
2009	B+	3.02	2.52	258.2	140.8	502.2	43.6

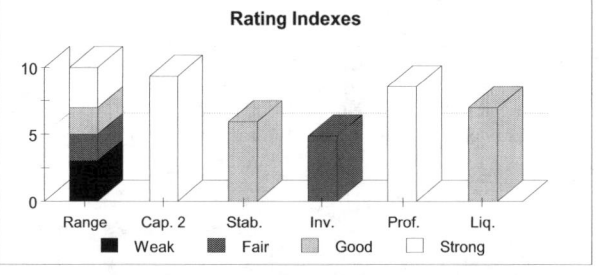

Rating Indexes

ANTHEM HEALTH PLANS OF VIRGINIA — B — Good

Major Rating Factors: Good quality investment portfolio (5.3 on a scale of 0 to 10). Good liquidity (6.9) with sufficient resources (cash flows and marketable investments) to handle a spike in claims. Excellent profitability (8.8).
Other Rating Factors: Strong capitalization (10.0) based on excellent current risk-adjusted capital (severe loss scenario).
Principal Business: Comp med (53%), FEHB (37%), med supp (6%), Medicare (1%), other (3%)
Mem Phys: 13: 25,162 **12:** 25,937 **13 MLR** 82.6% **/ 13 Admin Exp** N/A
Enroll(000): Q2 14: 1,384 **13:** 1,387 **12:** 1,390 **Med Exp PMPM:** $200
Principal Investments: Long-term bonds (52%), nonaffiliate common stock (24%), cash and equiv (4%), real estate (2%), affiliate common stock (1%), other (16%)
Provider Compensation ($000): Contr fee ($3,190,981), FFS ($102,764), bonus arrang ($1,122), other ($76,330)
Total Member Encounters: Phys (328,678), non-phys (34,011)
Group Affiliation: WellPoint Inc
Licensed in: VA
Address: 2015 Staples Mill Rd, Richmond, VA 23230
Phone: (804) 354-7000 **Dom State:** VA **Commenced Bus:** October 1935

Data Date	Rating	RACR #1	RACR #2	Total Assets ($mil)	Capital ($mil)	Net Premium ($mil)	Net Income ($mil)
6-14	B	4.46	3.72	2,165.4	829.6	1,989.8	98.0
6-13	B	4.75	3.96	2,200.4	926.1	1,991.3	166.9
2013	B	3.51	2.92	1,970.0	643.2	4,011.2	269.5
2012	B	3.76	3.13	1,986.9	724.0	4,156.9	345.1
2011	B-	2.92	2.43	1,830.5	534.6	3,996.3	250.7
2010	B+	4.48	3.73	1,872.6	677.4	3,826.2	393.2
2009	B+	4.10	3.41	1,608.5	625.7	3,773.4	334.0

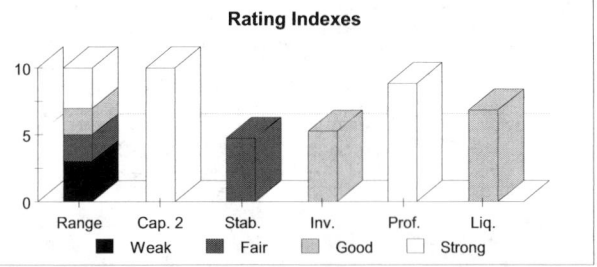

Rating Indexes

ANTHEM INS COMPANIES INC — B — Good

Major Rating Factors: Good liquidity (6.8 on a scale of 0 to 10) with sufficient resources (cash flows and marketable investments) to handle a spike in claims. Fair quality investment portfolio (3.7). Excellent profitability (10.0).
Other Rating Factors: Strong capitalization (10.0) based on excellent current risk-adjusted capital (severe loss scenario).
Principal Business: Comp med (33%), Medicare (32%), FEHB (11%), Medicaid (8%), med supp (3%), other (11%)
Mem Phys: 13: 28,735 **12:** 33,216 **13 MLR** 80.9% **/ 13 Admin Exp** N/A
Enroll(000): Q2 14: 2,364 **13:** 2,425 **12:** 2,650 **Med Exp PMPM:** $139
Principal Investments: Long-term bonds (82%), affiliate common stock (3%), pref stock (2%), other (17%)
Provider Compensation ($000): Contr fee ($2,372,364), FFS ($1,306,619), capitation ($61,741), bonus arrang ($915), other ($390,692)
Total Member Encounters: Phys (2,454,371), non-phys (1,844,365)
Group Affiliation: WellPoint Inc
Licensed in: AL, AZ, AR, CO, CT, GA, ID, IL, IN, IA, KS, KY, LA, ME, MS, MO, MT, NE, NV, NH, NM, NC, ND, OH, OK, OR, SC, SD, TN, TX, UT, VA, WA, WI, WY
Address: 120 Monument Circle, Indianapolis, IN 46204-4903
Phone: (317) 488-6000 **Dom State:** IN **Commenced Bus:** November 1944

Data Date	Rating	RACR #1	RACR #2	Total Assets ($mil)	Capital ($mil)	Net Premium ($mil)	Net Income ($mil)
6-14	B	3.93	3.28	3,012.6	1,131.6	2,373.8	162.3
6-13	B	3.74	3.12	2,831.1	1,131.1	2,510.7	191.1
2013	B	3.51	2.93	2,781.5	1,004.8	5,008.5	374.4
2012	B	3.00	2.50	2,638.3	898.1	5,128.4	327.5
2011	B	2.61	2.18	2,701.3	770.5	5,878.5	279.4
2010	B	2.54	2.11	2,804.4	736.6	5,573.1	344.4
2009	B	2.95	2.46	2,158.3	710.9	4,902.3	267.2

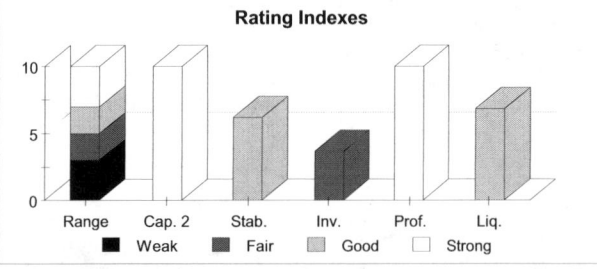

Rating Indexes

ANTHEM LIFE INSURANCE COMPANY * — A- — Excellent

Major Rating Factors: Good liquidity (6.3 on a scale of 0 to 10) with sufficient resources to handle a spike in claims. Excellent overall results on stability tests (7.1). Strengths that enhance stability include excellent operational trends and excellent risk diversification. Strong capitalization (7.5) based on excellent risk adjusted capital (severe loss scenario). Furthermore, this high level of risk adjusted capital has been consistently maintained over the last five years.
Other Rating Factors: High quality investment portfolio (7.6). Excellent profitability (7.4) with operating gains in each of the last five years.
Principal Business: Reinsurance (45%), group life insurance (31%), group health insurance (23%), and individual life insurance (1%).
Principal Investments: NonCMO investment grade bonds (63%), CMOs and structured securities (23%), and cash (3%).
Investments in Affiliates: None
Group Affiliation: WellPoint Inc
Licensed in: All states except NY, RI, VT, PR
Commenced Business: June 1956
Address: 6740 N High St Suite 200, Worthington, OH 43085
Phone: (614) 438-3959 **Domicile State:** IN **NAIC Code:** 61069

Data Date	Rating	RACR #1	RACR #2	Total Assets ($mil)	Capital ($mil)	Net Premium ($mil)	Net Income ($mil)
6-14	A-	1.95	1.35	571.2	89.2	177.3	16.9
6-13	A-	1.93	1.35	556.6	94.4	173.3	15.9
2013	A-	2.17	1.51	575.3	120.4	345.1	47.1
2012	A-	1.60	1.12	565.4	87.4	336.1	13.8
2011	A-	1.46	1.03	542.7	77.8	206.6	6.4
2010	A-	1.98	1.41	326.1	71.5	168.7	24.3
2009	A-	1.70	1.24	285.2	60.8	165.1	18.3

Adverse Trends in Operations

Increase in policy surrenders from 2011 to 2012 (129%)

ARCADIAN HEALTH PLAN INC   D   Weak

Major Rating Factors: Weak profitability index (1.0 on a scale of 0 to 10). Weak overall results on stability tests (2.5) based on a significant 38% decrease in enrollment during the period. Good liquidity (6.7) with sufficient resources (cash flows and marketable investments) to handle a spike in claims. **Other Rating Factors:** Strong capitalization index (7.3) based on excellent current risk-adjusted capital (severe loss scenario).
Principal Business: Medicare (100%)
Mem Phys: 13: N/A **12:** N/A **13 MLR** 96.1% **/ 13 Admin Exp** N/A
Enroll(000): Q2 14: 7 **13:** 26 **12:** 42 **Med Exp PMPM:** $710
Principal Investments ($000): Cash and equiv ($7,007)
Provider Compensation ($000): None
Total Member Encounters: N/A
Group Affiliation: Arcadian Management Services Inc
Licensed in: CA
Address: 500 12th St Suite 350, Oakland, CA 94607
Phone: (510) 817-1036 **Dom State:** CA **Commenced Bus:** May 2008

Data Date	Rating	RACR #1	RACR #2	Total Assets ($mil)	Capital ($mil)	Net Premium ($mil)	Net Income ($mil)
6-14	D	2.00	1.34	83.3	63.9	36.4	4.2
6-13	D	1.76	1.21	145.8	97.6	113.4	4.4
2013	D	2.07	1.43	118.5	79.0	227.6	-12.0
2012	D	1.64	1.12	170.0	91.0	407.5	-38.5
2011	C+	1.31	0.87	99.0	44.9	408.2	-5.3
2010	C+	1.34	0.90	97.0	50.2	381.7	5.9
2009	C-	1.78	1.18	84.8	48.7	275.8	15.8

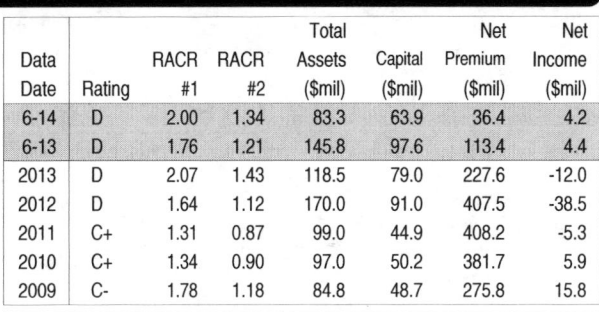

Rating Indexes

ARCADIAN HEALTH PLAN INC   C+   Fair

Major Rating Factors: Good liquidity (5.8 on a scale of 0 to 10) with sufficient resources (cash flows and marketable investments) to handle a spike in claims. Weak profitability index (2.6). Strong capitalization (10.0) based on excellent current risk-adjusted capital (severe loss scenario).
Other Rating Factors: High quality investment portfolio (9.6).
Principal Business: Medicare (100%)
Mem Phys: 13: 150,447 **12:** 19,380 **13 MLR** 91.2% **/ 13 Admin Exp** N/A
Enroll(000): Q2 14: 7 **13:** 26 **12:** 42 **Med Exp PMPM:** $674
Principal Investments: Long-term bonds (91%), affiliate common stock (10%)
Provider Compensation ($000): Contr fee ($212,027), capitation ($5,027), FFS ($2,863)
Total Member Encounters: Phys (449,395), non-phys (279,330)
Group Affiliation: Humana Inc
Licensed in: AZ, CA, IN, KY, ME, MO, NH, SC, TX, VA, WA, WV
Address: 300 Deschutes Way SW #304, Tumwater, WA 98501
Phone: (502) 580-1000 **Dom State:** WA **Commenced Bus:** January 2005

Data Date	Rating	RACR #1	RACR #2	Total Assets ($mil)	Capital ($mil)	Net Premium ($mil)	Net Income ($mil)
6-14	C+	3.85	3.21	70.5	55.0	36.4	4.9
6-13	B	2.95	2.46	125.8	79.9	113.1	4.2
2013	B	4.87	4.06	103.6	70.3	227.5	-4.9
2012	B	1.78	1.48	143.3	72.1	399.8	0.3
2011	C+	1.07	0.89	93.4	38.5	406.0	-2.3
2010	B	1.42	1.18	92.4	44.7	379.7	9.8
2009	C+	1.72	1.43	81.0	45.2	272.8	14.3

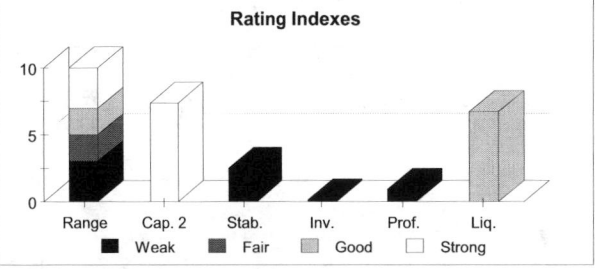

Rating Indexes

ASSURITY LIFE INSURANCE COMPANY *   B+   Good

Major Rating Factors: Good quality investment portfolio (5.5 on a scale of 0 to 10) despite significant exposure to mortgages . Mortgage default rate has been low. large holdings of BBB rated bonds in addition to minimal holdings in junk bonds. Good overall profitability (6.9). Return on equity has been low, averaging 4.4%. Good liquidity (5.8).
Other Rating Factors: Good overall results on stability tests (6.6) excellent operational trends and excellent risk diversification. Strong capitalization (8.0) based on excellent risk adjusted capital (severe loss scenario).
Principal Business: Individual life insurance (52%), individual health insurance (28%), group health insurance (10%), reinsurance (4%), and other lines (7%).
Principal Investments: NonCMO investment grade bonds (58%), CMOs and structured securities (16%), mortgages in good standing (13%), policy loans (5%), and misc. investments (7%).
Investments in Affiliates: None
Group Affiliation: Assurity Security Group Inc
Licensed in: All states except NY, PR
Commenced Business: March 1964
Address: 2000 Q Street, Lincoln, NE 68503
Phone: (402) 476-6500 **Domicile State:** NE **NAIC Code:** 71439

Data Date	Rating	RACR #1	RACR #2	Total Assets ($mil)	Capital ($mil)	Net Premium ($mil)	Net Income ($mil)
6-14	B+	3.17	1.69	2,436.6	304.3	93.3	8.3
6-13	B+	3.11	1.63	2,426.6	272.0	94.9	7.6
2013	B+	3.17	1.69	2,449.3	306.4	191.2	14.6
2012	B+	3.00	1.57	2,419.2	262.7	225.0	21.9
2011	B+	2.77	1.45	2,403.2	257.8	240.6	23.0
2010	B+	2.09	1.21	2,326.3	256.9	254.4	15.0
2009	B+	2.52	1.44	2,237.6	248.7	266.9	-5.8

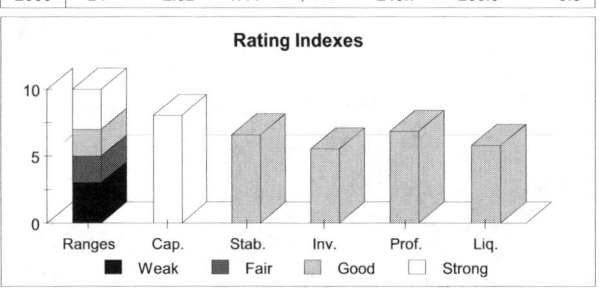

Rating Indexes

ASURIS NORTHWEST HEALTH

B-   **Good**

Major Rating Factors: Good liquidity (6.5 on a scale of 0 to 10) with sufficient resources (cash flows and marketable investments) to handle a spike in claims. Strong capitalization (10.0) based on excellent current risk-adjusted capital (severe loss scenario). High quality investment portfolio (9.9).
Other Rating Factors: Weak profitability index (2.6).
Principal Business: Comp med (84%), Medicare (10%), med supp (1%), other (4%)
Mem Phys: 13: 6,430   **12:** 6,150   **13 MLR** 88.8%   **/ 13 Admin Exp** N/A
Enroll(000): Q2 14: 47   **13:** 63   **12:** 63   **Med Exp PMPM:** $284
Principal Investments: Long-term bonds (89%), cash and equiv (11%)
Provider Compensation ($000): Contr fee ($126,844), FFS ($83,936), bonus arrang ($1,157), capitation ($18)
Total Member Encounters: Phys (615,699), non-phys (669,809)
Group Affiliation: Regence Group
Licensed in: OR, WA
Address: 1800 9th Ave, Seattle, WA 98101
Phone: (206) 464-3600   **Dom State:** WA   **Commenced Bus:** July 1933

Data Date	Rating	RACR #1	RACR #2	Total Assets ($mil)	Capital ($mil)	Net Premium ($mil)	Net Income ($mil)
6-14	B-	3.64	3.03	97.0	57.8	89.7	-5.3
6-13	B+	4.74	3.95	106.7	69.8	119.5	3.5
2013	B	3.98	3.32	100.0	63.3	241.2	-3.4
2012	B	4.50	3.75	100.9	66.2	240.8	11.9
2011	B-	3.27	2.73	98.0	53.5	259.7	2.8
2010	B-	3.26	2.72	89.7	50.5	246.6	4.1
2009	C+	2.92	2.44	85.4	43.8	219.4	-9.4

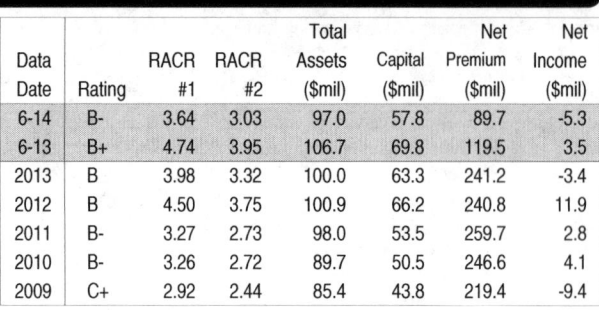

ATHENS AREA HEALTH PLAN SELECT INC

C-   **Fair**

Major Rating Factors: Fair overall results on stability tests (4.7 on a scale of 0 to 10). Weak profitability index (0.6). Strong capitalization index (7.5) based on excellent current risk-adjusted capital (severe loss scenario).
Other Rating Factors: High quality investment portfolio (9.9). Excellent liquidity (7.1) with ample operational cash flow and liquid investments.
Principal Business: Comp med (100%)
Mem Phys: 13: 750   **12:** 750   **13 MLR** 91.3%   **/ 13 Admin Exp** N/A
Enroll(000): Q2 14: 9   **13:** 9   **12:** 8   **Med Exp PMPM:** $334
Principal Investments: Cash and equiv (72%), long-term bonds (29%)
Provider Compensation ($000): FFS ($31,344), capitation ($458)
Total Member Encounters: Phys (52,407), non-phys (14,414)
Group Affiliation: Athens Regional Health Services
Licensed in: GA
Address: 295 W Clayton St, Athens, GA 30601
Phone: (706) 549-0549   **Dom State:** GA   **Commenced Bus:** October 1997

Data Date	Rating	RACR #1	RACR #2	Total Assets ($mil)	Capital ($mil)	Net Premium ($mil)	Net Income ($mil)
6-14	C-	1.75	1.45	17.5	11.1	20.2	-1.1
6-13	C-	2.05	1.71	17.4	12.7	18.0	-0.4
2013	C-	1.92	1.60	17.1	12.2	36.4	-1.6
2012	C	2.11	1.76	17.6	13.0	35.4	-0.9
2011	C	1.96	1.64	18.0	13.0	44.2	0.7
2010	C	1.58	1.32	17.5	11.9	45.6	-2.5
2009	C	1.87	1.56	19.0	13.7	43.7	-2.3

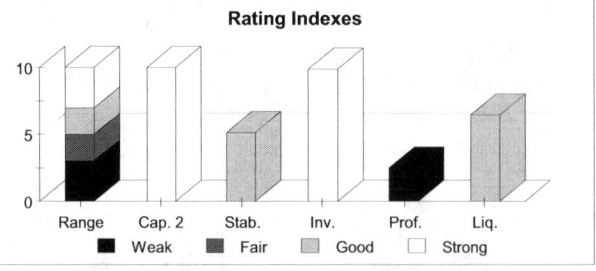

ATLANTIS HEALTH PLAN

E-   **Very Weak**

Major Rating Factors: Weak profitability index (0.9 on a scale of 0 to 10). Poor capitalization index (0.0) based on weak current risk-adjusted capital (severe loss scenario). Weak overall results on stability tests (1.4) based on a decline in the number of member physicians during 2014.
Other Rating Factors: Weak liquidity (0.0) as a spike in claims may stretch capacity. High quality investment portfolio (9.9).
Principal Business: Comp med (93%), Medicare (7%)
Mem Phys: 13: 3,700   **12:** 8,818   **13 MLR** 81.0%   **/ 13 Admin Exp** N/A
Enroll(000): Q2 14: 8   **13:** 13   **12:** 13   **Med Exp PMPM:** $373
Principal Investments: Cash and equiv (100%)
Provider Compensation ($000): Contr fee ($43,846), FFS ($15,667)
Total Member Encounters: Phys (65,913), non-phys (6,424)
Group Affiliation: Atlantis Health Systems Inc
Licensed in: NY
Address: 45 Broadway Suite 1240, New York, NY 10004
Phone: (212) 747-0877   **Dom State:** NY   **Commenced Bus:** September 2000

Data Date	Rating	RACR #1	RACR #2	Total Assets ($mil)	Capital ($mil)	Net Premium ($mil)	Net Income ($mil)
6-14	E-	N/A	N/A	18.9	0.1	26.3	N/A
6-13	E-	N/A	N/A	19.5	0.6	35.3	N/A
2013	E-	N/A	N/A	18.9	0.6	70.8	N/A
2012	E-	N/A	N/A	23.2	0.6	75.5	0.9
2011	N/A	N/A	N/A	26.6	-4.3	96.6	-2.2
2010	E-	N/A	N/A	24.3	-18.3	112.8	-0.2
2009	N/A	N/A	N/A	20.4	-18.2	92.6	N/A

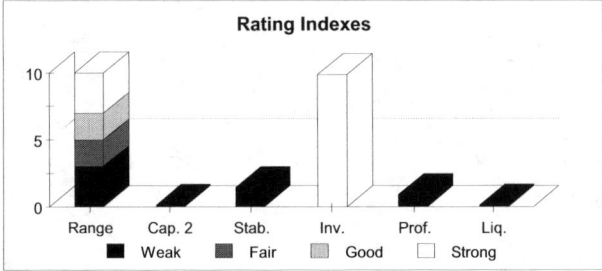

ATRIO HEALTH PLANS INC   C-   Fair

Major Rating Factors: Good overall profitability index (6.9 on a scale of 0 to 10). Strong capitalization (7.6) based on excellent current risk-adjusted capital (severe loss scenario). High quality investment portfolio (9.2).
Other Rating Factors: Excellent liquidity (7.0) with sufficient resources (cash flows and marketable investments) to handle a spike in claims.
Principal Business: Medicare (100%)
Mem Phys: 13: 2,084 **12:** 2,002 **13 MLR** 85.2% / **13 Admin Exp** N/A
Enroll(000): Q2 14: 14 **13:** 13 **12:** 12 **Med Exp PMPM:** $811
Principal Investments: Long-term bonds (64%), cash and equiv (34%), other (1%)
Provider Compensation ($000): Capitation ($124,530), contr fee ($930)
Total Member Encounters: Phys (483,586), non-phys (147,210)
Group Affiliation: None
Licensed in: OR
Address: 2270 NW Aviation Dr Suite 3, Roseburg, OR 97470
Phone: (541) 672-8620 **Dom State:** OR **Commenced Bus:** January 2005

Data Date	Rating	RACR #1	RACR #2	Total Assets ($mil)	Capital ($mil)	Net Premium ($mil)	Net Income ($mil)
6-14	C-	1.85	1.54	42.3	20.0	78.0	1.2
6-13	C-	2.00	1.67	40.0	20.3	70.2	1.7
2013	C-	1.96	1.63	38.6	21.1	148.1	2.0
2012	C-	1.91	1.59	31.0	18.3	135.5	2.7
2011	N/A	N/A	N/A	28.4	17.0	77.9	1.2
2010	N/A	N/A	N/A	14.8	5.9	50.0	0.4
2009	C-	N/A	N/A	13.8	5.6	45.0	0.1

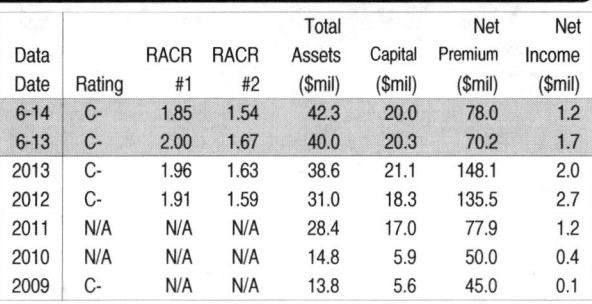

Rating Indexes

AULTCARE INS CO   C-   Fair

Major Rating Factors: Fair profitability index (3.7 on a scale of 0 to 10). Good liquidity (6.6) with sufficient resources (cash flows and marketable investments) to handle a spike in claims. Strong capitalization (7.2) based on excellent current risk-adjusted capital (severe loss scenario).
Other Rating Factors: High quality investment portfolio (9.4).
Principal Business: Medicare (51%), comp med (43%), FEHB (4%), other (1%)
Mem Phys: 13: 1,902 **12:** 2,485 **13 MLR** 88.4% / **13 Admin Exp** N/A
Enroll(000): Q2 14: 115 **13:** 114 **12:** 120 **Med Exp PMPM:** $289
Principal Investments: Long-term bonds (49%), cash and equiv (21%), nonaffiliate common stock (16%), other (13%)
Provider Compensation ($000): Contr fee ($228,172), capitation ($100,133), FFS ($64,043)
Total Member Encounters: Phys (382,723), non-phys (1,192,666)
Group Affiliation: Aultman Health Foundation
Licensed in: OH
Address: 2600 Sixth St NW, Canton, OH 44710
Phone: (330) 363-4057 **Dom State:** OH **Commenced Bus:** November 1989

Data Date	Rating	RACR #1	RACR #2	Total Assets ($mil)	Capital ($mil)	Net Premium ($mil)	Net Income ($mil)
6-14	C-	1.54	1.28	118.6	60.5	230.4	0.1
6-13	U	1.38	1.15	112.9	60.2	222.9	1.7
2013	C-	1.57	1.31	115.2	61.7	454.1	4.7
2012	U	1.33	1.11	112.8	58.4	468.5	-0.3
2011	B	1.29	1.08	122.1	57.4	438.1	-3.1
2010	B	1.44	1.20	118.8	59.6	417.4	2.5
2009	B-	0.97	0.81	103.5	49.2	429.5	5.2

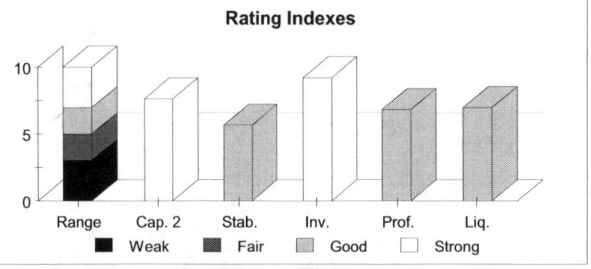

Rating Indexes

AVALON INS CO   C   Fair

Major Rating Factors: Good overall profitability index (5.0 on a scale of 0 to 10). Strong capitalization (10.0) based on excellent current risk-adjusted capital (severe loss scenario). High quality investment portfolio (9.9).
Other Rating Factors: Excellent liquidity (7.1) with ample operational cash flow and liquid investments.
Principal Business: Med supp (9%), other (91%)
Mem Phys: 13: 749 **12:** 664 **13 MLR** 67.8% / **13 Admin Exp** N/A
Enroll(000): Q2 14: 271 **13:** 216 **12:** 192 **Med Exp PMPM:** $12
Principal Investments: Long-term bonds (58%), cash and equiv (37%), nonaffiliate common stock (4%)
Provider Compensation ($000): Contr fee ($16,325), other ($15,549)
Total Member Encounters: N/A
Group Affiliation: Capital Blue Cross Group
Licensed in: PA, WV
Address: 2500 Elmerton Ave, Harrisburg, PA 17110
Phone: (717) 541-7000 **Dom State:** PA **Commenced Bus:** January 2006

Data Date	Rating	RACR #1	RACR #2	Total Assets ($mil)	Capital ($mil)	Net Premium ($mil)	Net Income ($mil)
6-14	C	4.01	3.34	34.8	18.3	27.1	-1.5
6-13	C	4.06	3.38	34.1	19.5	24.0	2.0
2013	C	4.32	3.60	33.5	19.8	46.0	3.0
2012	C	3.65	3.04	31.8	17.5	41.5	1.1
2011	N/A	N/A	N/A	30.4	15.9	35.4	-0.2
2010	C-	3.51	2.93	25.0	15.7	30.8	0.3
2009	C	2.35	1.96	20.4	10.4	30.7	3.2

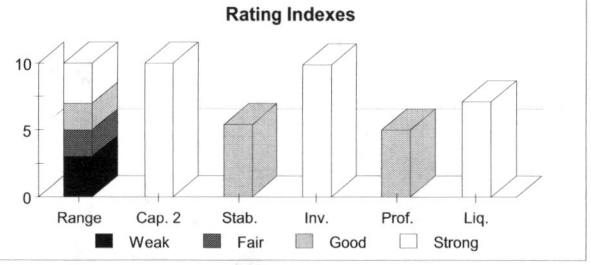

Rating Indexes

AVERA HEALTH PLANS INC

C-   Fair

Major Rating Factors: Fair capitalization index (3.0 on a scale of 0 to 10) based on weak current risk-adjusted capital (moderate loss scenario). Fair overall results on stability tests (3.8). Weak profitability index (1.4).
Other Rating Factors: Weak liquidity (1.9) as a spike in claims may stretch capacity. Good quality investment portfolio (6.4).
Principal Business: Comp med (81%), med supp (18%)
Mem Phys: 13: N/A **12:** 4,529 **13 MLR** 94.8% / **13 Admin Exp** N/A
Enroll(000): Q2 14: 37 **13:** 29 **12:** 28 **Med Exp PMPM:** $235
Principal Investments: Long-term bonds (67%), nonaffiliate common stock (21%), cash and equiv (12%)
Provider Compensation ($000): FFS ($40,072), contr fee ($37,629)
Total Member Encounters: Phys (42,153), non-phys (16,861)
Group Affiliation: Avera Health
Licensed in: IA, NE, SD
Address: 3816 S Elmwood Ave Suite 100, Sioux Falls, SD 57105
Phone: (605) 322-4500 **Dom State:** SD **Commenced Bus:** October 1999

Data Date	Rating	RACR #1	RACR #2	Total Assets ($mil)	Capital ($mil)	Net Premium ($mil)	Net Income ($mil)
6-14	C-	0.62	0.52	30.7	8.0	51.6	-0.7
6-13	C+	0.97	0.81	25.7	11.0	40.5	-0.6
2013	C	0.75	0.62	24.2	9.4	84.3	-2.5
2012	C+	1.03	0.86	25.4	11.7	75.9	0.9
2011	C	0.82	0.68	22.8	9.2	74.1	0.4
2010	C	0.94	0.78	22.2	8.9	66.2	1.5
2009	C-	0.78	0.65	17.0	6.8	48.3	-3.2

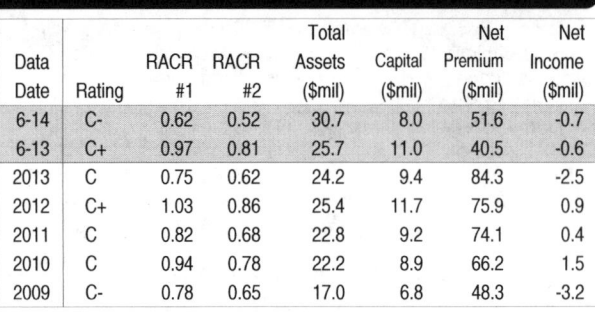

Rating Indexes

Range | Cap. 2 | Stab. | Inv. | Prof. | Liq.
■ Weak ▨ Fair ▨ Good □ Strong

AVMED INC *

B+   Good

Major Rating Factors: Good liquidity (6.8 on a scale of 0 to 10) with sufficient resources (cash flows and marketable investments) to handle a spike in claims. Strong capitalization index (8.6) based on excellent current risk-adjusted capital (severe loss scenario). High quality investment portfolio (7.6).
Other Rating Factors: Fair overall results on stability tests (4.5) based on a significant 15% decrease in enrollment during the period. Weak profitability index (2.9).
Principal Business: Medicare (54%), comp med (43%), FEHB (3%)
Mem Phys: 13: 34,303 **12:** 32,833 **13 MLR** 83.9% / **13 Admin Exp** N/A
Enroll(000): Q2 14: 101 **13:** 109 **12:** 129 **Med Exp PMPM:** $491
Principal Investments: Long-term bonds (61%), cash and equiv (17%), nonaffiliate common stock (16%), real estate (6%)
Provider Compensation ($000): Contr fee ($461,967), FFS ($173,427), capitation ($34,403), bonus arrang ($394)
Total Member Encounters: N/A
Group Affiliation: SantaFe HealthCare Inc
Licensed in: FL
Address: 9400 S Dadeland Blvd, Miami, FL 33156
Phone: (352) 372-8400 **Dom State:** FL **Commenced Bus:** October 1977

Data Date	Rating	RACR #1	RACR #2	Total Assets ($mil)	Capital ($mil)	Net Premium ($mil)	Net Income ($mil)
6-14	B+	2.60	2.17	291.3	156.2	366.0	-1.2
6-13	B+	2.19	1.83	286.1	157.9	397.3	15.6
2013	B+	2.70	2.25	289.6	162.0	782.1	20.4
2012	B+	2.03	1.69	292.4	146.2	908.8	25.4
2011	B+	1.16	0.97	327.0	123.6	1,282.9	-61.6
2010	A-	1.87	1.56	371.1	188.6	1,245.6	8.3
2009	A	2.25	1.87	372.0	190.0	1,065.7	8.6

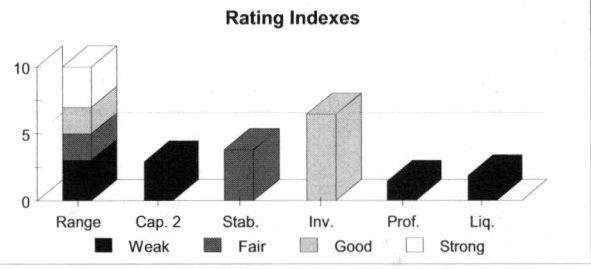

Rating Indexes

Range | Cap. 2 | Stab. | Inv. | Prof. | Liq.
■ Weak ▨ Fair ▨ Good □ Strong

BALBOA LIFE INSURANCE COMPANY *

A-   Excellent

Major Rating Factors: Good overall results on stability tests (5.5 on a scale of 0 to 10). Strengths that enhance stability include good operational trends and excellent risk diversification. Strong capitalization (8.9) based on excellent risk adjusted capital (severe loss scenario). Moreover, capital levels have been consistently high over the last five years. High quality investment portfolio (7.9).
Other Rating Factors: Excellent profitability (8.2) with operating gains in each of the last five years. Excellent liquidity (9.6).
Principal Business: Group health insurance (81%), individual life insurance (17%), and group life insurance (1%).
Principal Investments: NonCMO investment grade bonds (43%), common & preferred stock (33%), cash (16%), and CMOs and structured securities (8%).
Investments in Affiliates: 33%
Group Affiliation: Securian Financial Group
Licensed in: All states except PR
Commenced Business: January 1969
Address: 400 Robert Street North, St Paul, MN 55101-2098
Phone: (651) 665-3500 **Domicile State:** CA **NAIC Code:** 68160

Data Date	Rating	RACR #1	RACR #2	Total Assets ($mil)	Capital ($mil)	Net Premium ($mil)	Net Income ($mil)
6-14	A-	2.37	2.26	58.9	48.9	3.2	1.2
6-13	A-	2.15	2.04	57.8	45.5	4.0	1.3
2013	A-	2.31	2.21	57.7	47.8	7.3	3.4
2012	A-	2.06	1.95	56.8	44.1	11.7	4.2
2011	B+	1.83	1.73	53.0	39.9	14.5	3.5
2010	B+	1.74	1.64	47.7	36.7	13.1	1.3
2009	B+	1.67	1.57	48.1	37.1	14.8	5.6

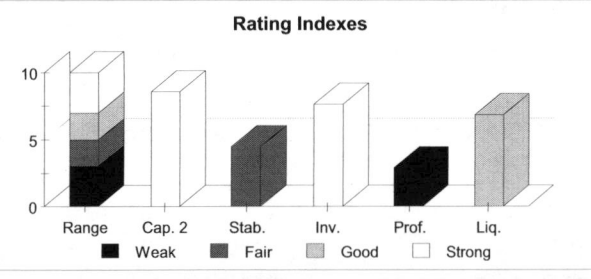

Adverse Trends in Operations

Decrease in premium volume from 2012 to 2013 (38%)
Decrease in premium volume from 2011 to 2012 (19%)
Decrease in premium volume from 2009 to 2010 (12%)
Change in premium mix from 2009 to 2010 (6.4%)

BANKERS CONSECO LIFE INSURANCE COMPANY   D   Weak

Major Rating Factors: Weak overall results on stability tests (1.8 on a scale of 0 to 10). Good quality investment portfolio (6.5) despite mixed results such as: no exposure to mortgages and large holdings of BBB rated bonds but small junk bond holdings. Good overall profitability (6.1). Excellent expense controls. Return on equity has been fair, averaging 6.4%.

Other Rating Factors: Good liquidity (6.4). Strong capitalization (10.0) based on excellent risk adjusted capital (severe loss scenario).

Principal Business: Individual life insurance (59%), individual health insurance (28%), individual annuities (11%), and reinsurance (2%).

Principal Investments: NonCMO investment grade bonds (88%), CMOs and structured securities (6%), cash (3%), noninv. grade bonds (2%), and policy loans (1%).

Investments in Affiliates: None
Group Affiliation: CNO Financial Group Inc
Licensed in: NY
Commenced Business: July 1987
Address: 11815 N Pennsylvania St, Carmel, IN 46032
Phone: (215) 244-1600 **Domicile State:** NY **NAIC Code:** 68560

Data Date	Rating	RACR #1	RACR #2	Total Assets ($mil)	Capital ($mil)	Net Premium ($mil)	Net Income ($mil)
6-14	D	4.49	3.50	201.4	50.7	23.9	3.1
6-13	D	2.76	1.56	358.5	29.0	26.5	1.1
2013	D	4.11	2.30	383.2	45.5	49.2	21.7
2012	D	2.16	1.29	343.6	22.6	48.7	-2.0
2011	D	2.49	1.59	323.4	26.0	44.8	0.0
2010	D	2.54	1.76	301.2	26.4	37.5	2.2
2009	D	2.36	1.80	277.1	25.0	34.8	-4.1

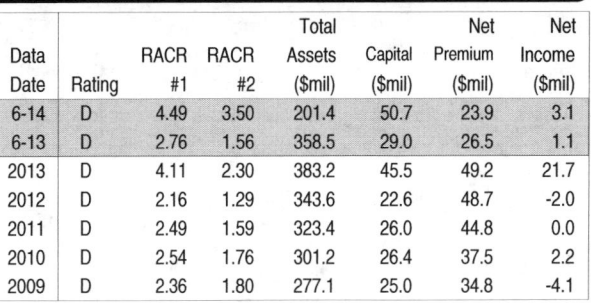

Rating Indexes

BANKERS FIDELITY LIFE INSURANCE COMPANY   B   Good

Major Rating Factors: Good quality investment portfolio (6.4 on a scale of 0 to 10) despite mixed results such as: large holdings of BBB rated bonds but moderate junk bond exposure. Good liquidity (5.6) with sufficient resources to handle a spike in claims. Good overall results on stability tests (5.7) excellent operational trends and good risk diversification.

Other Rating Factors: Strong capitalization (7.2) based on excellent risk adjusted capital (severe loss scenario). Excellent profitability (8.8) with operating gains in each of the last five years.

Principal Business: Individual health insurance (89%) and individual life insurance (11%).

Principal Investments: NonCMO investment grade bonds (78%), common & preferred stock (8%), noninv. grade bonds (8%), policy loans (2%), and misc. investments (3%).

Investments in Affiliates: 3%
Group Affiliation: Atlantic American Corp
Licensed in: All states except CA, CT, NY, VT, PR
Commenced Business: November 1955
Address: 4370 Peachtree Rd NE, Atlanta, GA 30319
Phone: (404) 266-5500 **Domicile State:** GA **NAIC Code:** 61239

Data Date	Rating	RACR #1	RACR #2	Total Assets ($mil)	Capital ($mil)	Net Premium ($mil)	Net Income ($mil)
6-14	B	1.58	1.12	143.2	35.3	51.6	1.8
6-13	B	1.98	1.41	134.0	34.7	50.2	1.5
2013	B	1.58	1.14	138.8	34.5	99.6	3.0
2012	B	2.03	1.48	128.7	33.1	89.6	2.3
2011	B	2.32	1.67	122.1	32.1	70.7	3.6
2010	B	2.44	1.75	117.9	31.9	62.8	3.0
2009	B	2.73	2.01	116.0	31.5	57.2	2.5

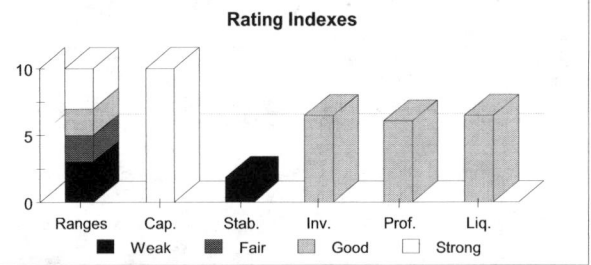

Rating Indexes

BANKERS LIFE & CASUALTY COMPANY   D+   Weak

Major Rating Factors: Weak overall results on stability tests (2.7 on a scale of 0 to 10). Fair quality investment portfolio (3.9) with large holdings of BBB rated bonds in addition to junk bond exposure equal to 86% of capital. Good liquidity (5.4) with sufficient resources to cover a large increase in policy surrenders.

Other Rating Factors: Strong capitalization (7.0) based on excellent risk adjusted capital (severe loss scenario). Excellent profitability (9.3) with operating gains in each of the last five years.

Principal Business: Individual health insurance (41%), individual annuities (30%), individual life insurance (18%), reinsurance (9%), and group health insurance (2%).

Principal Investments: NonCMO investment grade bonds (64%), CMOs and structured securities (21%), noninv. grade bonds (6%), mortgages in good standing (5%), and misc. investments (3%).

Investments in Affiliates: 1%
Group Affiliation: CNO Financial Group Inc
Licensed in: All states except NY, PR
Commenced Business: January 1879
Address: 222 Merchandise Mart Plaza, Chicago, IL 60654
Phone: (312) 396-6000 **Domicile State:** IL **NAIC Code:** 61263

Data Date	Rating	RACR #1	RACR #2	Total Assets ($mil)	Capital ($mil)	Net Premium ($mil)	Net Income ($mil)
6-14	D+	1.97	1.02	16,044.7	1,057.8	1,188.6	117.2
6-13	D+	1.81	0.94	15,397.0	945.0	1,138.8	125.2
2013	D+	2.04	1.06	15,839.5	1,057.0	2,323.5	161.9
2012	D+	1.83	0.96	14,941.3	914.6	2,282.5	231.3
2011	D+	1.60	0.86	14,515.9	816.8	2,518.6	212.0
2010	D+	1.55	0.82	13,753.7	774.7	2,329.0	166.4
2009	D+	1.41	0.80	12,318.8	730.2	2,601.5	86.7

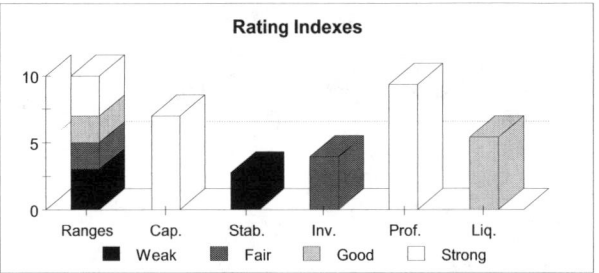

Rating Indexes

BANKERS RESERVE LIFE INS CO OF WI   C-   Fair

Major Rating Factors: Weak profitability index (0.9 on a scale of 0 to 10). Good liquidity (6.9) with sufficient resources (cash flows and marketable investments) to handle a spike in claims. Strong capitalization (7.7) based on excellent current risk-adjusted capital (severe loss scenario).
Other Rating Factors: High quality investment portfolio (9.9).
Principal Business: Medicaid (79%), comp med (21%)
Mem Phys: 13: N/A **12:** N/A **13 MLR** 89.6% **/ 13 Admin Exp** N/A
Enroll(000): Q2 14: 520 **13:** 524 **12:** 527 **Med Exp PMPM:** $323
Principal Investments: Cash and equiv (54%), long-term bonds (44%), affiliate common stock (2%)
Provider Compensation ($000): Contr fee ($1,908,606), capitation ($185,550), salary ($18,471)
Total Member Encounters: Phys (3,324,931), non-phys (3,996,589)
Group Affiliation: Centene Corp
Licensed in: All states except AK, CA, CT, HI, MA, MN, NH, NY, VT, WA, PR
Address: 7700 Forsyth Blvd, St Louis, MO 63105
Phone: (314) 505-6143 **Dom State:** WI **Commenced Bus:** July 1964

Data Date	Rating	RACR #1	RACR #2	Total Assets ($mil)	Capital ($mil)	Net Premium ($mil)	Net Income ($mil)
6-14	C-	1.90	1.58	481.2	250.7	1,169.7	-11.7
6-13	C-	2.11	1.76	389.8	219.5	1,133.4	-5.8
2013	C-	1.80	1.50	434.6	238.1	2,322.6	-4.6
2012	C-	1.84	1.53	409.4	198.6	1,719.3	-126.4
2011	B-	2.61	2.17	110.1	61.6	437.5	15.0
2010	B-	2.60	2.17	116.9	70.6	476.4	13.5
2009	C	1.89	1.58	114.8	56.4	459.4	6.6

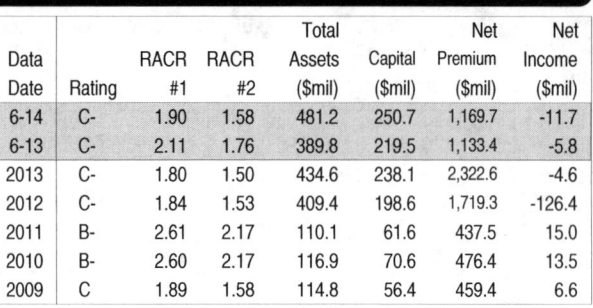

Rating Indexes

Range, Cap. 2, Stab., Inv., Prof., Liq.
■ Weak ▨ Fair ▨ Good □ Strong

BCS INS CO   B   Good

Major Rating Factors: Good overall results on stability tests (5.4 on a scale of 0 to 10) despite potential drain of affiliation with BCS Financial Corp. History of adequate reserve strength (6.0) as reserves have been consistently at an acceptable level.
Other Rating Factors: Good overall profitability index (6.9). Fair expense controls. Return on equity has been low, averaging 4.1% over the past five years. Good liquidity (6.6) with sufficient resources (cash flows and marketable investments) to handle a spike in claims. Strong long-term capitalization index (10.0) based on excellent current risk adjusted capital (severe and moderate loss scenarios), despite some fluctuation in capital levels.
Principal Business: Group accident & health (84%), other liability (11%), and inland marine (4%).
Principal Investments: Investment grade bonds (78%), misc. investments (13%), cash (8%), and non investment grade bonds (1%).
Investments in Affiliates: 1%
Group Affiliation: BCS Financial Corp
Licensed in: All states, the District of Columbia and Puerto Rico
Commenced Business: November 1952
Address: 676 N St Clair St 16th floor, Chicago, IL 60611
Phone: (630) 472-7700 **Domicile State:** OH **NAIC Code:** 38245

Data Date	Rating	RACR #1	RACR #2	Loss Ratio %	Total Assets ($mil)	Capital ($mil)	Net Premium ($mil)	Net Income ($mil)
6-14	B	6.93	3.93	N/A	293.7	157.1	67.2	3.7
6-13	B	9.31	5.27	N/A	259.2	156.6	59.7	5.0
2013	B	7.43	4.22	70.2	267.9	152.9	131.9	6.4
2012	B	10.06	5.70	63.4	254.5	151.9	111.6	8.2
2011	B	8.78	5.36	62.6	230.6	146.6	113.4	7.3
2010	B-	8.80	5.37	65.8	217.9	142.0	107.2	5.1
2009	B-	8.76	5.13	73.4	220.2	140.4	107.0	3.1

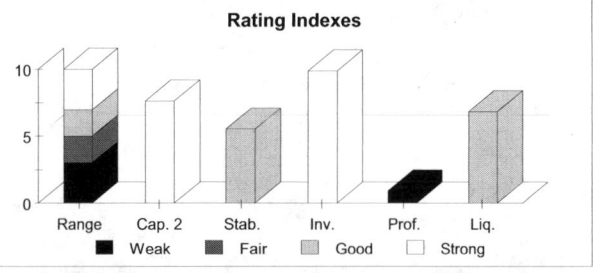

Rating Indexes

Ranges, Cap. 2, Stab., Res., Prof., Liq.
■ Weak ▨ Fair ▨ Good □ Strong

BERKLEY LIFE & HEALTH INSURANCE COMPANY   B-   Good

Major Rating Factors: Good overall results on stability tests (5.2 on a scale of 0 to 10) despite fair financial strength of affiliated W R Berkley Corp and excessive premium growth. Other stability subfactors include excellent operational trends and excellent risk diversification. Strong capitalization (10.0) based on excellent risk adjusted capital (severe loss scenario). Moreover, capital levels have been consistently high over the last five years. High quality investment portfolio (8.6).
Other Rating Factors: Excellent profitability (8.3) despite modest operating losses during 2011. Excellent liquidity (7.5).
Principal Business: Group health insurance (100%).
Principal Investments: NonCMO investment grade bonds (67%), CMOs and structured securities (25%), and cash (8%).
Investments in Affiliates: None
Group Affiliation: W R Berkley Corp
Licensed in: All states except CT, NY, PR
Commenced Business: July 1963
Address: 200 Clarendon St, Boston, MA 02117
Phone: (203) 851-1755 **Domicile State:** IA **NAIC Code:** 64890

Data Date	Rating	RACR #1	RACR #2	Total Assets ($mil)	Capital ($mil)	Net Premium ($mil)	Net Income ($mil)
6-14	B-	6.56	5.04	178.2	103.2	62.6	9.4
6-13	B	6.23	4.79	150.9	90.5	49.4	7.1
2013	B-	6.16	4.73	166.3	94.2	117.1	11.3
2012	B	5.25	4.11	148.7	83.3	123.9	7.7
2011	B	4.59	3.60	112.0	59.5	101.1	-0.6
2010	B	5.64	5.08	31.5	26.4	4.8	0.3
2009	B	6.28	5.65	26.6	26.2	0.0	0.6

W R Berkley Corp **Composite Group Rating:** C **Largest Group Members**	Assets ($mil)	Rating
BERKLEY INS CO	16123	C
BERKLEY REGIONAL INS CO	681	C+
ADMIRAL INS CO	667	C-
NAUTILUS INS CO	246	C-
STARNET INS CO	203	C

BERKSHIRE LIFE INSURANCE COMPANY OF AMERICA *   A   Excellent

Major Rating Factors: Good overall results on stability tests (6.4 on a scale of 0 to 10). Strengths that enhance stability include good operational trends and excellent risk diversification. Good quality investment portfolio (6.5) despite mixed results such as: minimal exposure to mortgages and large holdings of BBB rated bonds but small junk bond holdings. Strong capitalization (10.0) based on excellent risk adjusted capital (severe loss scenario).

Other Rating Factors: Excellent profitability (8.4) with operating gains in each of the last five years. Excellent liquidity (8.9).

Principal Business: Individual health insurance (66%), reinsurance (32%), and individual life insurance (2%).

Principal Investments: NonCMO investment grade bonds (89%), mortgages in good standing (7%), noninv. grade bonds (3%), and CMOs and structured securities (1%).

Investments in Affiliates: None

Group Affiliation: Guardian Group

Licensed in: All states except PR

Commenced Business: July 2001

Address: 700 South St, Pittsfield, MA 01201

Phone: (413) 499-4321   **Domicile State:** MA   **NAIC Code:** 71714

Data Date	Rating	RACR #1	RACR #2	Total Assets ($mil)	Capital ($mil)	Net Premium ($mil)	Net Income ($mil)
6-14	A	8.67	4.25	3,589.9	599.1	57.0	15.8
6-13	A	6.94	3.66	3,345.7	577.8	54.8	51.6
2013	A	8.68	4.24	3,461.4	583.0	115.9	60.0
2012	A	5.30	3.03	3,209.2	543.4	493.9	43.9
2011	A	5.44	3.14	3,034.7	530.9	477.9	29.3
2010	A	5.33	3.11	2,814.7	493.8	458.1	50.7
2009	A	5.02	2.91	2,626.9	452.3	445.6	34.0

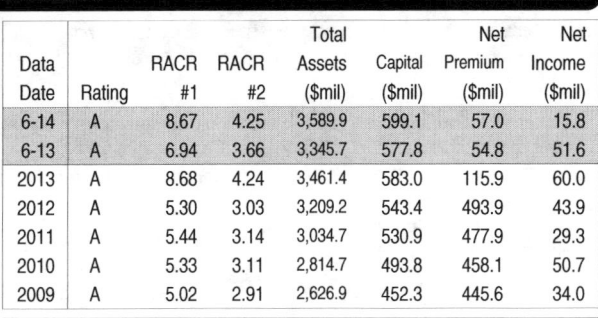

Rating Indexes

BEST MERIDIAN INSURANCE COMPANY   B-   Good

Major Rating Factors: Good quality investment portfolio (6.7 on a scale of 0 to 10) despite significant exposure to mortgages . Mortgage default rate has been low. minimal holdings in junk bonds. Good overall profitability (5.3) although investment income, in comparison to reserve requirements, is below regulatory standards. Good overall results on stability tests (5.3) despite excessive premium growth good operational trends, good risk adjusted capital for prior years and good risk diversification.

Other Rating Factors: Strong capitalization (7.4) based on excellent risk adjusted capital (severe loss scenario). Excellent liquidity (7.2).

Principal Business: Individual health insurance (46%), individual life insurance (27%), reinsurance (25%), and group health insurance (1%).

Principal Investments: NonCMO investment grade bonds (39%), CMOs and structured securities (19%), cash (15%), mortgages in good standing (13%), and misc. investments (12%).

Investments in Affiliates: None

Group Affiliation: BMI Financial Group

Licensed in: FL

Commenced Business: August 1987

Address: 1320 S.Dixie Hwy, 6th Floor, Coral Gables, FL 33146

Phone: (305) 443-2898   **Domicile State:** FL   **NAIC Code:** 63886

Data Date	Rating	RACR #1	RACR #2	Total Assets ($mil)	Capital ($mil)	Net Premium ($mil)	Net Income ($mil)
6-14	B-	1.92	1.25	263.8	49.5	60.6	2.5
6-13	B-	1.42	1.00	247.7	48.8	47.6	3.3
2013	B-	2.02	1.33	254.5	47.9	100.8	7.0
2012	B-	1.08	0.78	239.2	45.9	202.5	7.8
2011	B	2.00	1.25	216.8	41.3	69.5	3.6
2010	B	2.30	1.37	200.1	39.0	63.9	6.4
2009	B	2.16	1.36	181.8	32.9	60.7	5.8

Adverse Trends in Operations

Increase in policy surrenders from 2012 to 2013 (67%)
Decrease in premium volume from 2012 to 2013 (50%)
Change in asset mix during 2012 (4%)
Change in premium mix from 2011 to 2012 (5%)

BLUE CARE NETWORK OF MICHIGAN *   B+   Good

Major Rating Factors: Excellent profitability (8.8 on a scale of 0 to 10). Strong capitalization index (10.0) based on excellent current risk-adjusted capital (severe loss scenario). High quality investment portfolio (9.4).

Other Rating Factors: Excellent overall results on stability tests (7.9). Good financial strength from affiliates. Excellent liquidity (7.2) with ample operational cash flow and liquid investments.

Principal Business: Comp med (74%), Medicare (22%), FEHB (3%)

Mem Phys: 13: 41,018   **12:** 35,887   **13 MLR** 83.8%   **/ 13 Admin Exp** N/A

Enroll(000): Q2 14: 655   **13:** 532   **12:** 545   **Med Exp PMPM:** $347

Principal Investments: Long-term bonds (47%), cash and equiv (42%), affiliate common stock (2%), nonaffiliate common stock (1%), other (8%)

Provider Compensation ($000): Contr fee ($1,622,266), FFS ($260,200), capitation ($204,154), bonus arrang ($102,561)

Total Member Encounters: Phys (3,543,013), non-phys (943,992)

Group Affiliation: Blue Cross Blue Shield of Michigan

Licensed in: MI

Address: 20500 Civic Center Drive, Southfield, MI 48076-4115

Phone: (248) 799-6400   **Dom State:** MI   **Commenced Bus:** May 1981

Data Date	Rating	RACR #1	RACR #2	Total Assets ($mil)	Capital ($mil)	Net Premium ($mil)	Net Income ($mil)
6-14	B+	6.68	5.57	1,719.3	1,008.1	1,490.0	22.5
6-13	A-	6.37	5.31	1,592.7	945.4	1,312.8	57.0
2013	B+	6.62	5.52	1,593.6	999.8	2,613.3	118.6
2012	A-	6.02	5.02	1,567.9	892.5	2,632.8	167.2
2011	A-	4.96	4.14	1,290.2	708.6	2,573.2	163.5
2010	A-	4.07	3.39	1,028.7	530.6	2,330.7	103.9
2009	A-	3.46	2.88	885.0	416.6	2,208.9	62.8

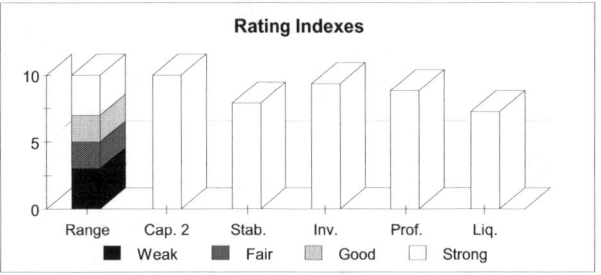

Rating Indexes

BLUE CARE OF MICHIGAN INC   C+   Fair

Major Rating Factors: Fair overall results on stability tests (4.4 on a scale of 0 to 10) based on a significant 21% decrease in enrollment during the period. Rating is significantly influenced by the good financial results of Blue Cross Blue Shield of Michigan. Weak profitability index (1.7). Strong capitalization index (10.0) based on excellent current risk-adjusted capital (severe loss scenario).

Other Rating Factors: High quality investment portfolio (9.9). Excellent liquidity (9.0) with ample operational cash flow and liquid investments.

Principal Business: Comp med (100%)

Mem Phys: 13: N/A **12:** N/A **13 MLR** 91.1% **/ 13 Admin Exp** N/A

Enroll(000): Q2 14: 0 **13:** 0 **12:** 1 **Med Exp PMPM:** $419

Principal Investments: Cash and equiv (61%), long-term bonds (7%), other (32%)

Provider Compensation ($000): Capitation ($2,221)

Total Member Encounters: N/A

Group Affiliation: Blue Cross Blue Shield of Michigan

Licensed in: MI

Address: 20500 Civic Center Dr, Southfield, MI 48076

Phone: (248) 799-6400 **Dom State:** MI **Commenced Bus:** July 1984

Data Date	Rating	RACR #1	RACR #2	Total Assets ($mil)	Capital ($mil)	Net Premium ($mil)	Net Income ($mil)
6-14	C+	9.85	8.21	6.6	6.6	0.9	-0.1
6-13	N/A	N/A	N/A	6.7	6.7	1.3	-0.1
2013	C+	9.90	8.25	6.6	6.6	2.4	-0.1
2012	N/A	N/A	N/A	6.7	6.6	3.0	-0.1
2011	N/A	N/A	N/A	6.7	6.6	3.7	-0.2
2010	N/A	N/A	N/A	6.8	6.8	4.5	-0.2
2009	B-	11.52	9.60	6.9	6.8	4.9	0.2

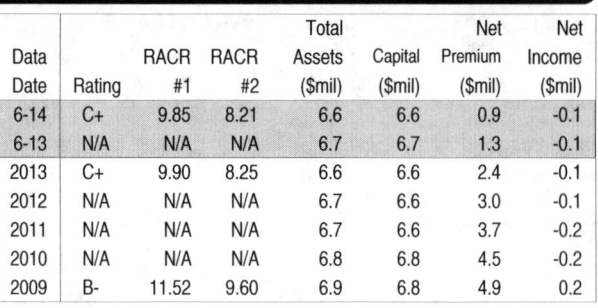

Rating Indexes

BLUE CROSS & BLUE SHIELD MA HMO BLUE   B   Good

Major Rating Factors: Good quality investment portfolio (6.1 on a scale of 0 to 10). Good liquidity (6.4) with sufficient resources (cash flows and marketable investments) to handle a spike in claims. Fair profitability index (3.8).

Other Rating Factors: Strong capitalization (10.0) based on excellent current risk-adjusted capital (severe loss scenario).

Principal Business: Comp med (91%), Medicare (9%)

Mem Phys: 13: 21,503 **12:** 21,331 **13 MLR** 89.8% **/ 13 Admin Exp** N/A

Enroll(000): Q2 14: 750 **13:** 739 **12:** 709 **Med Exp PMPM:** $409

Principal Investments: Long-term bonds (41%), nonaffiliate common stock (15%), real estate (6%), cash and equiv (3%), other (35%)

Provider Compensation ($000): Bonus arrang ($2,256,923), contr fee ($1,057,481), capitation ($158,239), FFS ($69,503)

Total Member Encounters: Phys (2,966,003), non-phys (1,671,314)

Group Affiliation: Bl Cross Bl Shield of Massachusetts

Licensed in: MA

Address: 401 Park Dr, Boston, MA 02215

Phone: (617) 246-5000 **Dom State:** MA **Commenced Bus:** January 2005

Data Date	Rating	RACR #1	RACR #2	Total Assets ($mil)	Capital ($mil)	Net Premium ($mil)	Net Income ($mil)
6-14	B	4.03	3.36	1,881.8	1,109.4	2,056.1	-47.5
6-13	B	4.22	3.51	1,807.2	1,112.2	1,963.0	42.6
2013	B	4.18	3.48	1,855.0	1,151.8	3,952.9	40.6
2012	B	4.09	3.41	1,780.7	1,077.1	3,895.2	117.8
2011	B-	3.57	2.98	1,539.9	915.1	3,980.6	119.5
2010	B-	2.91	2.42	1,363.2	758.6	4,019.3	7.9
2009	B-	2.52	2.10	1,258.0	705.8	4,399.7	-127.9

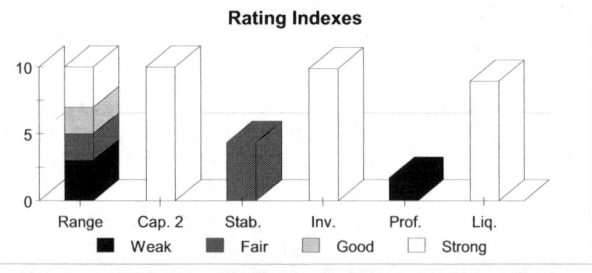

Rating Indexes

BLUE CROSS & BLUE SHIELD OF FLORIDA   B   Good

Major Rating Factors: Good quality investment portfolio (5.6 on a scale of 0 to 10). Fair profitability index (3.6). Strong capitalization (8.9) based on excellent current risk-adjusted capital (severe loss scenario).

Other Rating Factors: Excellent liquidity (6.9) with sufficient resources (cash flows and marketable investments) to handle a spike in claims.

Principal Business: Comp med (57%), FEHB (28%), Medicare (7%), med supp (5%), other (2%)

Mem Phys: 13: 28,531 **12:** 28,276 **13 MLR** 84.2% **/ 13 Admin Exp** N/A

Enroll(000): Q2 14: 1,809 **13:** 1,664 **12:** 1,660 **Med Exp PMPM:** $284

Principal Investments: Long-term bonds (59%), affiliate common stock (15%), nonaffiliate common stock (12%), real estate (4%), pref stock (3%), cash and equiv (1%), other (5%)

Provider Compensation ($000): Contr fee ($5,512,800), FFS ($241,764), capitation ($16,168), bonus arrang ($535)

Total Member Encounters: Phys (13,832,985), non-phys (5,115,025)

Group Affiliation: Blue Cross & Blue Shield Of Florida

Licensed in: FL, PA

Address: 4800 Deerwood Campus Pkwy, Jacksonville, FL 32246

Phone: (904) 791-6111 **Dom State:** FL **Commenced Bus:** January 1980

Data Date	Rating	RACR #1	RACR #2	Total Assets ($mil)	Capital ($mil)	Net Premium ($mil)	Net Income ($mil)
6-14	B	2.86	2.38	4,891.3	1,211.1	3,840.7	-100.0
6-13	B+	7.35	6.12	5,959.5	2,899.8	3,352.2	117.6
2013	B+	7.09	5.91	6,225.0	3,086.8	6,842.0	204.5
2012	B+	7.08	5.90	5,583.0	2,789.9	6,564.7	159.1
2011	B+	7.32	6.10	5,548.5	2,609.0	6,129.2	204.2
2010	B+	7.60	6.34	5,402.6	2,644.7	6,074.2	395.0
2009	B+	5.38	4.48	4,743.5	2,091.9	6,178.8	16.8

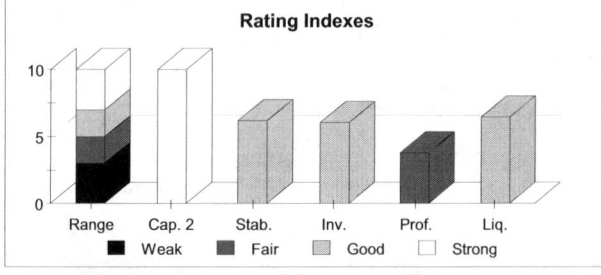

Rating Indexes

BLUE CROSS BLUE SHIELD HEALTHCARE GA *   A-   Excellent

Major Rating Factors: Excellent profitability (8.7 on a scale of 0 to 10). Strong capitalization index (9.3) based on excellent current risk-adjusted capital (severe loss scenario). High quality investment portfolio (9.1).
Other Rating Factors: Excellent overall results on stability tests (7.4). Rating is significantly influenced by the good financial results of WellPoint Inc. Good liquidity (6.9) with sufficient resources (cash flows and marketable investments) to handle a spike in claims.
Principal Business: Comp med (97%), Medicare (1%), other (1%)
Mem Phys: 13: 16,728 **12:** 15,772 **13 MLR** 78.9% **/ 13 Admin Exp** N/A
Enroll(000): Q2 14: 461 **13:** 446 **12:** 447 **Med Exp PMPM:** $218
Principal Investments: Long-term bonds (92%), cash and equiv (5%), other (3%)
Provider Compensation ($000): Contr fee ($1,112,420), capitation ($12,356), other ($11,837)
Total Member Encounters: Phys (2,136,966), non-phys (717,413)
Group Affiliation: WellPoint Inc
Licensed in: GA
Address: 3350 Peachtree Rd NE, Atlanta, GA 30326
Phone: (404) 842-8000 **Dom State:** GA **Commenced Bus:** September 1986

Data Date	Rating	RACR #1	RACR #2	Total Assets ($mil)	Capital ($mil)	Net Premium ($mil)	Net Income ($mil)
6-14	A-	3.23	2.69	657.4	254.8	791.9	31.6
6-13	A-	2.94	2.45	467.1	232.5	708.0	48.8
2013	A-	3.19	2.66	486.2	251.6	1,445.8	70.5
2012	A-	3.01	2.51	449.0	238.8	1,465.7	57.2
2011	B+	2.58	2.15	371.2	191.7	1,428.8	52.7
2010	B+	2.92	2.44	354.3	205.5	1,382.7	66.8
2009	A-	3.04	2.54	378.4	207.9	1,345.5	61.4

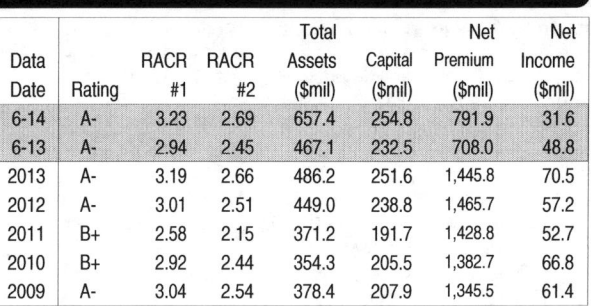

Rating Indexes

BLUE CROSS BLUE SHIELD OF ALABAMA *   A-   Excellent

Major Rating Factors: Strong capitalization (10.0 on a scale of 0 to 10) based on excellent current risk-adjusted capital (severe loss scenario). High quality investment portfolio (8.4). Excellent liquidity (7.1) with ample operational cash flow and liquid investments.
Other Rating Factors: Good overall profitability index (5.1).
Principal Business: Comp med (65%), FEHB (17%), Medicare (9%), med supp (5%), dental (3%)
Mem Phys: 13: 38,661 **12:** 37,985 **13 MLR** 89.3% **/ 13 Admin Exp** N/A
Enroll(000): Q2 14: 1,662 **13:** 1,628 **12:** 1,634 **Med Exp PMPM:** $186
Principal Investments: Long-term bonds (46%), cash and equiv (25%), nonaffiliate common stock (18%), real estate (6%), affiliate common stock (3%), other (1%)
Provider Compensation ($000): Contr fee ($3,655,731), capitation ($36,875), FFS ($3,875), bonus arrang ($2,631)
Total Member Encounters: Phys (20,532,287), non-phys (6,912,463)
Group Affiliation: Bl Cross & Bl Shield of AL Group
Licensed in: AL
Address: 450 Riverchase Parkway E, Birmingham, AL 35298
Phone: (205) 220-2100 **Dom State:** AL **Commenced Bus:** January 1936

Data Date	Rating	RACR #1	RACR #2	Total Assets ($mil)	Capital ($mil)	Net Premium ($mil)	Net Income ($mil)
6-14	A-	6.87	5.72	2,987.4	1,228.9	2,241.9	32.4
6-13	A-	6.48	5.40	2,664.6	1,131.9	2,035.3	43.5
2013	A-	6.95	5.79	2,839.5	1,243.6	4,114.1	69.1
2012	A-	6.41	5.34	2,630.4	1,118.9	4,077.6	114.6
2011	B+	5.71	4.76	2,381.2	991.1	4,105.6	256.9
2010	B	4.04	3.37	2,188.9	855.8	4,273.3	163.0
2009	B	2.62	2.19	1,990.5	649.0	4,283.6	-52.6

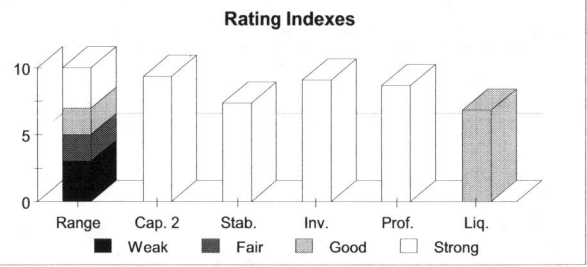

Rating Indexes

BLUE CROSS BLUE SHIELD OF ARIZONA *   A+   Excellent

Major Rating Factors: Excellent profitability (8.3 on a scale of 0 to 10). Strong capitalization (10.0) based on excellent current risk-adjusted capital (severe loss scenario). Excellent liquidity (7.0) with ample operational cash flow and liquid investments.
Other Rating Factors: Fair quality investment portfolio (3.7).
Principal Business: Comp med (61%), FEHB (32%), med supp (4%), other (3%)
Mem Phys: 13: 22,223 **12:** 21,467 **13 MLR** 81.5% **/ 13 Admin Exp** N/A
Enroll(000): Q2 14: 1,405 **13:** 1,310 **12:** 1,284 **Med Exp PMPM:** $79
Principal Investments: Long-term bonds (38%), nonaffiliate common stock (36%), affiliate common stock (6%), real estate (5%), cash and equiv (3%), other (13%)
Provider Compensation ($000): Contr fee ($1,018,857), FFS ($215,078), capitation ($17,571), bonus arrang ($30)
Total Member Encounters: Phys (2,771,094), non-phys (1,463,095)
Group Affiliation: None
Licensed in: AZ
Address: 2444 W Las Palmaritas Dr, Phoenix, AZ 85021
Phone: (602) 864-4100 **Dom State:** AZ **Commenced Bus:** February 1939

Data Date	Rating	RACR #1	RACR #2	Total Assets ($mil)	Capital ($mil)	Net Premium ($mil)	Net Income ($mil)
6-14	A+	7.23	6.02	1,642.2	1,059.1	846.7	9.2
6-13	A+	7.43	6.19	1,526.8	969.4	749.6	60.1
2013	A+	7.08	5.90	1,578.9	1,036.3	1,531.9	85.0
2012	A+	6.78	5.65	1,456.7	908.5	1,448.4	67.7
2011	A+	8.16	6.80	1,324.0	891.0	1,441.9	74.9
2010	A+	7.81	6.51	1,161.8	790.0	1,494.8	75.3
2009	A+	7.44	6.20	1,059.5	717.1	1,472.5	64.6

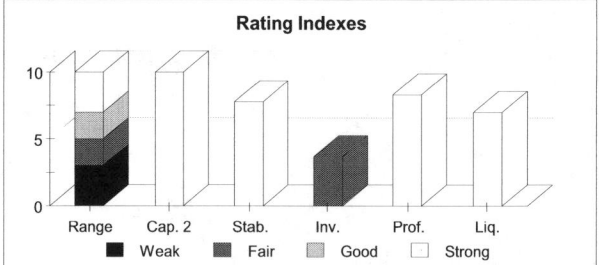

Rating Indexes

BLUE CROSS BLUE SHIELD OF GEORGIA | B | Good

Major Rating Factors: Good liquidity (6.2 on a scale of 0 to 10) with sufficient resources (cash flows and marketable investments) to handle a spike in claims. Excellent overall profitability index (6.9). Strong capitalization (10.0) based on excellent current risk-adjusted capital (severe loss scenario).

Other Rating Factors: Low quality investment portfolio (0.0).

Principal Business: FEHB (51%), comp med (34%), med supp (7%), dental (4%), Medicare (3%), other (2%)

Mem Phys: 13: 19,103 **12:** 18,486 **13 MLR** 89.0% **/ 13 Admin Exp** N/A

Enroll(000): Q2 14: 736 **13:** 660 **12:** 661 **Med Exp PMPM:** $218

Principal Investments: Long-term bonds (76%), nonaffiliate common stock (68%), affiliate common stock (5%), real estate (2%), other (14%)

Provider Compensation ($000): Contr fee ($1,543,387), FFS ($244,525), other ($20,506)

Total Member Encounters: Phys (3,504,121), non-phys (1,935,454)

Group Affiliation: WellPoint Inc

Licensed in: GA

Address: 3350 Peachtree Rd NE, Atlanta, GA 30326

Phone: (404) 842-8000 **Dom State:** GA **Commenced Bus:** November 1937

Data Date	Rating	RACR #1	RACR #2	Total Assets ($mil)	Capital ($mil)	Net Premium ($mil)	Net Income ($mil)
6-14	B	3.77	3.14	1,260.2	378.0	1,534.2	-4.9
6-13	B	2.55	2.12	988.1	272.8	1,006.8	29.7
2013	B	2.79	2.32	928.7	273.0	2,007.5	73.1
2012	B	2.83	2.36	985.9	306.0	2,197.1	79.5
2011	B	2.81	2.34	956.1	305.0	2,281.2	90.5
2010	B	3.69	3.07	1,089.1	428.4	2,444.1	145.3
2009	B+	3.56	2.97	1,071.9	416.5	2,524.1	132.2

Rating Indexes

Range Cap. 2 Stab. Inv. Prof. Liq.
■ Weak ■ Fair ▨ Good ☐ Strong

BLUE CROSS BLUE SHIELD OF KANSAS INCORPORATED | B | Good

Major Rating Factors: Good liquidity (6.6 on a scale of 0 to 10) with sufficient resources to handle a spike in claims. Good overall results on stability tests (6.3). Stability strengths include excellent operational trends and excellent risk diversification. Fair quality investment portfolio (4.1).

Other Rating Factors: Strong capitalization (7.9) based on excellent risk adjusted capital (severe loss scenario). Excellent profitability (7.9).

Principal Business: Group health insurance (76%) and individual health insurance (24%).

Principal Investments: NonCMO investment grade bonds (43%), common & preferred stock (35%), CMOs and structured securities (16%), real estate (2%), and misc. investments (1%).

Investments in Affiliates: 3%

Group Affiliation: Blue Cross Blue Shield Kansas

Licensed in: KS

Commenced Business: July 1942

Address: 1133 SW Topeka Blvd, Topeka, KS 66629-0001

Phone: (785) 291-7000 **Domicile State:** KS **NAIC Code:** 70729

Data Date	Rating	RACR #1	RACR #2	Total Assets ($mil)	Capital ($mil)	Net Premium ($mil)	Net Income ($mil)
6-14	B	2.24	1.61	1,611.9	802.7	890.9	4.1
6-13	B	2.24	1.61	1,492.2	764.4	839.0	28.9
2013	B	2.26	1.62	1,541.9	800.8	1,689.2	78.6
2012	B	2.23	1.62	1,433.2	762.3	1,680.3	55.9
2011	B	2.09	1.55	1,285.8	666.9	1,683.1	77.5
2010	B	2.09	1.56	1,203.4	657.1	1,712.3	72.0
2009	B	2.12	1.63	1,073.1	589.9	1,620.4	19.9

Adverse Trends in Operations

Decrease in premium volume from 2010 to 2011 (2%)

BLUE CROSS BLUE SHIELD OF KC | B- | Good

Major Rating Factors: Fair quality investment portfolio (4.5 on a scale of 0 to 10). Good liquidity (6.7) with sufficient resources (cash flows and marketable investments) to handle a spike in claims. Strong capitalization (10.0) based on excellent current risk-adjusted capital (severe loss scenario).

Other Rating Factors: Weak profitability index (2.4).

Principal Business: Comp med (70%), FEHB (20%), med supp (5%), dental (2%), other (4%)

Mem Phys: 13: 5,966 **12:** 5,799 **13 MLR** 86.1% **/ 13 Admin Exp** N/A

Enroll(000): Q2 14: 366 **13:** 370 **12:** 372 **Med Exp PMPM:** $249

Principal Investments: Long-term bonds (44%), nonaffiliate common stock (31%), affiliate common stock (13%), cash and equiv (4%), real estate (3%), other (6%)

Provider Compensation ($000): Contr fee ($926,551), FFS ($162,176), capitation ($2,126)

Total Member Encounters: Phys (1,384,024), non-phys (282,744)

Group Affiliation: RightCHOICE Managed Care Inc

Licensed in: KS, MO

Address: 2301 Main St, Kansas City, MO 64108-2428

Phone: (816) 395-2222 **Dom State:** MO **Commenced Bus:** May 1982

Data Date	Rating	RACR #1	RACR #2	Total Assets ($mil)	Capital ($mil)	Net Premium ($mil)	Net Income ($mil)
6-14	B-	4.85	4.04	1,031.5	605.2	679.7	-27.0
6-13	A	5.12	4.26	1,003.9	592.6	620.1	6.3
2013	B	4.89	4.08	988.8	610.2	1,255.4	-19.4
2012	A+	5.77	4.81	1,039.5	651.9	1,226.1	26.8
2011	A+	6.05	5.04	1,007.4	649.6	1,128.6	29.3
2010	A+	5.45	4.54	933.3	593.6	1,040.4	29.2
2009	A+	5.80	4.83	829.3	554.5	938.4	49.7

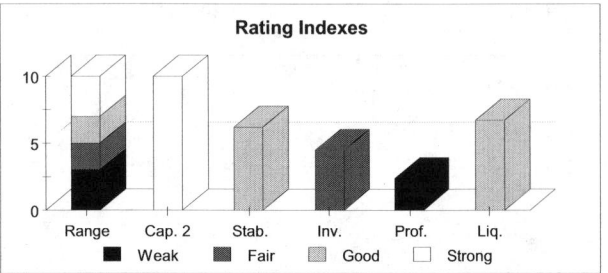

Rating Indexes

Range Cap. 2 Stab. Inv. Prof. Liq.
■ Weak ■ Fair ▨ Good ☐ Strong

BLUE CROSS BLUE SHIELD OF MA   B   Good

Major Rating Factors: Good quality investment portfolio (5.6 on a scale of 0 to 10). Good liquidity (6.5) with sufficient resources (cash flows and marketable investments) to handle a spike in claims. Fair profitability index (3.1).

Other Rating Factors: Strong capitalization (9.8) based on excellent current risk-adjusted capital (severe loss scenario).

Principal Business: Comp med (40%), FEHB (28%), med supp (19%), dental (5%), other (8%)

Mem Phys: 13: 21,503   **12:** 21,331   **13 MLR** 94.7%   **/ 13 Admin Exp** N/A

Enroll(000): Q2 14: 1,220   **13:** 1,192   **12:** 1,115   **Med Exp PMPM:** $157

Principal Investments: Long-term bonds (39%), nonaffiliate common stock (22%), real estate (7%), cash and equiv (4%), other (29%)

Provider Compensation ($000): Contr fee ($1,641,178), FFS ($539,849)

Total Member Encounters: Phys (3,174,672), non-phys (2,011,347)

Group Affiliation: Bl Cross Bl Shield of Massachusetts

Licensed in: MA

Address: 401 Park Dr, Boston, MA 02215-3326

Phone: (617) 246-5000   **Dom State:** MA   **Commenced Bus:** October 1937

Data Date	Rating	RACR #1	RACR #2	Total Assets ($mil)	Capital ($mil)	Net Premium ($mil)	Net Income ($mil)
6-14	B	3.58	2.98	2,051.5	785.1	1,195.2	-43.9
6-13	B	3.05	2.54	2,014.7	615.4	1,150.8	-2.8
2013	B	3.74	3.11	2,096.6	820.1	2,331.1	28.5
2012	B+	3.67	3.05	2,018.4	740.8	2,401.6	46.1
2011	B+	3.74	3.12	1,874.7	711.2	2,365.6	16.6
2010	B+	3.97	3.31	1,672.8	732.7	2,294.4	5.5
2009	B+	4.22	3.52	1,576.8	723.9	2,319.2	-21.3

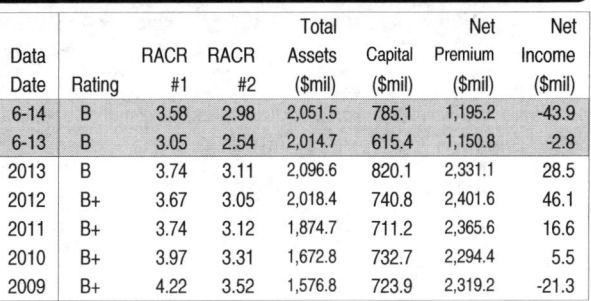

Rating Indexes

Range | Cap. 2 | Stab. | Inv. | Prof. | Liq.

■ Weak   ▨ Fair   ▤ Good   ☐ Strong

BLUE CROSS BLUE SHIELD OF MICHIGAN   B   Good

Major Rating Factors: Good quality investment portfolio (6.8 on a scale of 0 to 10). Good liquidity (6.7) with sufficient resources (cash flows and marketable investments) to handle a spike in claims. Fair profitability index (4.8).

Other Rating Factors: Strong capitalization (10.0) based on excellent current risk-adjusted capital (severe loss scenario).

Principal Business: Comp med (66%), Medicare (17%), FEHB (6%), med supp (5%), dental (1%), other (5%)

Mem Phys: 13: 49,153   **12:** 46,803   **13 MLR** 86.7%   **/ 13 Admin Exp** N/A

Enroll(000): Q2 14: 1,472   **13:** 1,485   **12:** 1,488   **Med Exp PMPM:** $321

Principal Investments: Long-term bonds (49%), affiliate common stock (26%), nonaffiliate common stock (11%), cash and equiv (6%), real estate (2%), other (5%)

Provider Compensation ($000): Contr fee ($5,773,844), bonus arrang ($48,042), capitation ($1,693)

Total Member Encounters: N/A

Group Affiliation: Blue Cross Blue Shield of Michigan

Licensed in: MI

Address: 600 Lafayette East, Detroit, MI 48226

Phone: (313) 225-9000   **Dom State:** MI   **Commenced Bus:** January 1975

Data Date	Rating	RACR #1	RACR #2	Total Assets ($mil)	Capital ($mil)	Net Premium ($mil)	Net Income ($mil)
6-14	B	4.57	3.81	7,904.8	3,573.8	3,642.8	276.3
6-13	B+	4.27	3.56	8,011.2	3,129.2	3,325.1	17.1
2013	B	4.21	3.51	7,715.2	3,288.7	6,688.4	-85.9
2012	B+	4.18	3.49	7,469.4	3,060.6	6,412.7	-2.5
2011	B+	3.97	3.31	6,961.6	2,789.7	6,395.4	40.0
2010	B+	4.08	3.40	6,797.6	2,759.5	6,574.7	205.2
2009	B+	3.79	3.16	6,182.5	2,562.2	6,986.4	12.6

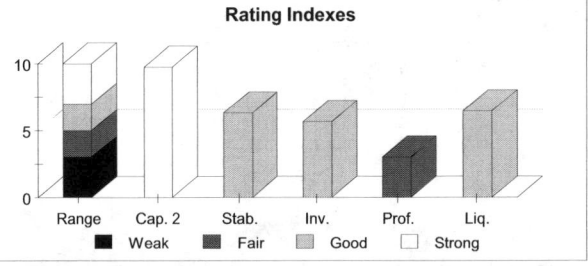

Rating Indexes

Range | Cap. 2 | Stab. | Inv. | Prof. | Liq.

■ Weak   ▨ Fair   ▤ Good   ☐ Strong

BLUE CROSS BLUE SHIELD OF MINNESOTA *   A   Excellent

Major Rating Factors: Strong capitalization (10.0 on a scale of 0 to 10) based on excellent current risk-adjusted capital (severe loss scenario). Good overall profitability index (5.5). Good quality investment portfolio (6.2).

Other Rating Factors: Good liquidity (6.7) with sufficient resources (cash flows and marketable investments) to handle a spike in claims.

Principal Business: Comp med (53%), FEHB (15%), Medicare (14%), med supp (9%), other (10%)

Mem Phys: 13: 43,011   **12:** 42,577   **13 MLR** 84.5%   **/ 13 Admin Exp** N/A

Enroll(000): Q2 14: 687   **13:** 682   **12:** 683   **Med Exp PMPM:** $319

Principal Investments: Long-term bonds (68%), nonaffiliate common stock (28%), affiliate common stock (2%), cash and equiv (1%), other (1%)

Provider Compensation ($000): Bonus arrang ($1,122,131), contr fee ($852,150), FFS ($641,409), other ($105,210)

Total Member Encounters: Phys (3,347,532), non-phys (1,173,125)

Group Affiliation: Aware Integrated Inc

Licensed in: MN

Address: 3535 Blue Cross Rd, Eagan, MN 55122

Phone: (651) 662-8000   **Dom State:** MN   **Commenced Bus:** June 1972

Data Date	Rating	RACR #1	RACR #2	Total Assets ($mil)	Capital ($mil)	Net Premium ($mil)	Net Income ($mil)
6-14	A	3.96	3.30	2,106.6	816.3	1,607.8	30.5
6-13	A+	4.30	3.58	2,171.6	864.9	1,530.7	96.1
2013	A	3.92	3.27	1,996.8	808.0	3,082.6	25.7
2012	A+	4.12	3.43	2,114.8	827.5	3,069.5	50.4
2011	A+	4.45	3.71	2,032.8	793.7	2,919.6	155.4
2010	A-	4.28	3.56	1,996.7	762.8	2,818.9	100.1
2009	B+	3.21	2.68	1,880.0	628.8	2,794.9	33.5

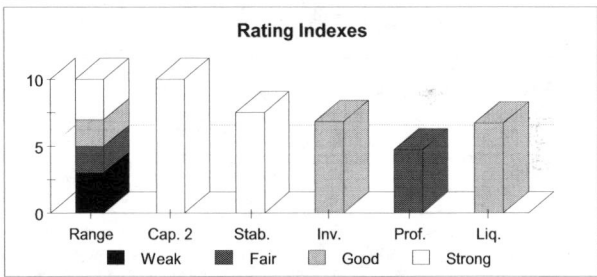

Rating Indexes

Range | Cap. 2 | Stab. | Inv. | Prof. | Liq.

■ Weak   ▨ Fair   ▤ Good   ☐ Strong

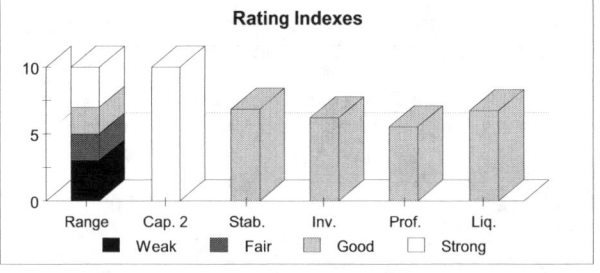

BLUE CROSS BLUE SHIELD OF MS, MUTUAL *

B+   **Good**

Major Rating Factors: Good liquidity (6.8 on a scale of 0 to 10) with sufficient resources (cash flows and marketable investments) to handle a spike in claims. Strong capitalization (10.0) based on excellent current risk-adjusted capital (severe loss scenario). High quality investment portfolio (7.9).
Other Rating Factors: Fair profitability index (4.5).
Principal Business: Comp med (71%), FEHB (26%), med supp (3%)
Mem Phys: 13: 10,453 **12:** 9,543 **13 MLR** 89.3% **/ 13 Admin Exp** N/A
Enroll(000): Q2 14: 606 **13:** 616 **12:** 618 **Med Exp PMPM:** $141
Principal Investments: Long-term bonds (71%), cash and equiv (11%), affiliate common stock (8%), real estate (6%), nonaffiliate common stock (4%)
Provider Compensation ($000): Contr fee ($1,036,667), FFS ($26,581), capitation ($115)
Total Member Encounters: Phys (2,139,998), non-phys (1,366,650)
Group Affiliation: Bl Cross & Bl Shield of Mississippi
Licensed in: MS
Address: 3545 Lakeland Dr, Flowood, MS 39208
Phone: (601) 932-3704 **Dom State:** MS **Commenced Bus:** January 1948

Data Date	Rating	RACR #1	RACR #2	Total Assets ($mil)	Capital ($mil)	Net Premium ($mil)	Net Income ($mil)
6-14	B+	7.84	6.53	855.7	575.1	590.6	14.7
6-13	B+	7.36	6.14	808.1	540.0	578.6	9.0
2013	B+	7.52	6.26	811.9	555.5	1,190.4	4.1
2012	A-	7.80	6.50	788.2	566.0	1,143.2	-1.7
2011	A-	8.18	6.82	778.7	561.1	1,108.2	28.4
2010	B+	8.04	6.70	739.5	534.8	1,072.7	29.6
2009	B	6.06	5.05	741.3	502.4	1,247.5	19.2

Rating Indexes

BLUE CROSS BLUE SHIELD OF NC *

A   **Excellent**

Major Rating Factors: Strong capitalization (10.0 on a scale of 0 to 10) based on excellent current risk-adjusted capital (severe loss scenario). Good overall profitability index (6.7). Good quality investment portfolio (5.1).
Other Rating Factors: Good liquidity (6.7) with sufficient resources (cash flows and marketable investments) to handle a spike in claims.
Principal Business: Comp med (57%), Medicare (18%), FEHB (15%), med supp (5%), dental (2%), other (2%)
Mem Phys: 13: 44,476 **12:** 42,253 **13 MLR** 86.7% **/ 13 Admin Exp** N/A
Enroll(000): Q2 14: 1,919 **13:** 1,723 **12:** 1,584 **Med Exp PMPM:** $250
Principal Investments: Long-term bonds (52%), nonaffiliate common stock (38%), real estate (2%), affiliate common stock (2%), cash and equiv (1%), other (6%)
Provider Compensation ($000): Contr fee ($3,573,941), FFS ($1,420,634), capitation ($11,692)
Total Member Encounters: Phys (8,779,390)
Group Affiliation: Bl Cross & Bl Shield of N Carolina
Licensed in: NC
Address: 5901 Chapel Hill Blvd, Durham, NC 27707-3346
Phone: (919) 489-7431 **Dom State:** NC **Commenced Bus:** January 1968

Data Date	Rating	RACR #1	RACR #2	Total Assets ($mil)	Capital ($mil)	Net Premium ($mil)	Net Income ($mil)
6-14	A	6.09	5.08	4,159.1	2,452.6	3,549.4	66.9
6-13	A+	6.12	5.10	3,509.2	2,111.2	2,801.9	46.9
2013	A	5.94	4.95	3,786.8	2,388.5	5,816.1	180.1
2012	A+	6.03	5.02	3,498.6	2,081.0	5,252.3	89.1
2011	A+	6.16	5.13	3,110.0	1,816.2	4,967.3	201.0
2010	A+	6.36	5.30	2,978.0	1,751.6	4,682.8	94.2
2009	A+	5.28	4.40	2,818.7	1,421.8	4,716.1	59.0

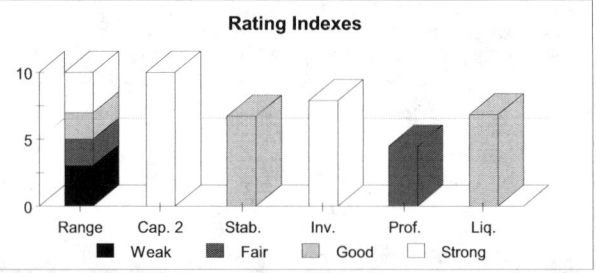

Rating Indexes

BLUE CROSS BLUE SHIELD OF NEBRASKA *

A-   **Excellent**

Major Rating Factors: Strong capitalization (10.0 on a scale of 0 to 10) based on excellent current risk-adjusted capital (severe loss scenario). High quality investment portfolio (7.5). Good liquidity (6.7) with sufficient resources (cash flows and marketable investments) to handle a spike in claims.
Other Rating Factors: Fair profitability index (3.9).
Principal Business: Comp med (73%), FEHB (14%), med supp (10%), other (4%)
Mem Phys: 13: 15,519 **12:** 14,372 **13 MLR** 87.1% **/ 13 Admin Exp** N/A
Enroll(000): Q2 14: 407 **13:** 414 **12:** 408 **Med Exp PMPM:** $279
Principal Investments: Long-term bonds (67%), nonaffiliate common stock (25%), affiliate common stock (2%), real estate (2%), cash and equiv (1%), other (3%)
Provider Compensation ($000): Contr fee ($1,393,598), other ($30,387)
Total Member Encounters: Phys (2,167,206), non-phys (83,451)
Group Affiliation: Blue Cross Blue Shield of Nebraska
Licensed in: NE
Address: 1919 Aksarben Dr, Omaha, NE 68180
Phone: (402) 982-7000 **Dom State:** NE **Commenced Bus:** January 1939

Data Date	Rating	RACR #1	RACR #2	Total Assets ($mil)	Capital ($mil)	Net Premium ($mil)	Net Income ($mil)
6-14	A-	5.89	4.91	945.9	442.8	789.8	22.6
6-13	A-	6.00	5.00	891.8	422.7	764.1	35.8
2013	A-	5.83	4.86	871.3	439.0	1,578.1	24.5
2012	A-	5.47	4.56	831.6	390.3	1,510.6	8.3
2011	A-	5.61	4.68	829.4	380.3	1,448.1	11.4
2010	A-	7.07	5.89	844.8	397.4	1,334.0	29.1
2009	A-	5.23	4.36	775.6	372.4	1,279.1	-39.6

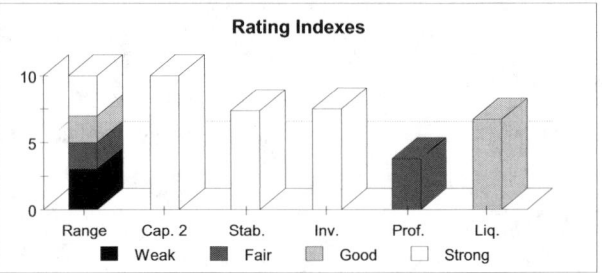

Rating Indexes

BLUE CROSS BLUE SHIELD OF RI   C   Fair

Major Rating Factors: Weak profitability index (2.1 on a scale of 0 to 10). Good liquidity (6.5) with sufficient resources (cash flows and marketable investments) to handle a spike in claims. Strong capitalization (7.9) based on excellent current risk-adjusted capital (severe loss scenario).
Other Rating Factors: High quality investment portfolio (7.5).
Principal Business: Comp med (62%), Medicare (24%), FEHB (6%), med supp (4%), dental (2%), other (1%)
Mem Phys: 13: 4,234 **12:** 3,855 **13 MLR** 86.0% **/ 13 Admin Exp** N/A
Enroll(000): Q2 14: 353 **13:** 344 **12:** 355 **Med Exp PMPM:** $319
Principal Investments: Long-term bonds (49%), nonaffiliate common stock (16%), cash and equiv (8%), real estate (7%), other (20%)
Provider Compensation ($000): Contr fee ($1,324,311), capitation ($987)
Total Member Encounters: Phys (1,471,362), non-phys (775,694)
Group Affiliation: Bl Cross & Bl Shield of Rhode Island
Licensed in: RI
Address: 444 Westminster St, Providence, RI 02903
Phone: (401) 459-1000 **Dom State:** RI **Commenced Bus:** September 1939

Data Date	Rating	RACR #1	RACR #2	Total Assets ($mil)	Capital ($mil)	Net Premium ($mil)	Net Income ($mil)
6-14	C	2.04	1.70	630.7	266.8	816.7	-8.5
6-13	C	2.14	1.78	591.3	269.9	775.4	24.4
2013	C	2.21	1.84	601.5	287.6	1,537.7	21.7
2012	C	2.05	1.71	583.7	260.2	1,558.1	-41.5
2011	B	2.72	2.26	605.5	323.4	1,568.9	72.7
2010	C	1.83	1.53	606.8	249.0	1,631.1	-14.1
2009	B	2.42	2.02	678.8	298.7	1,703.4	-99.9

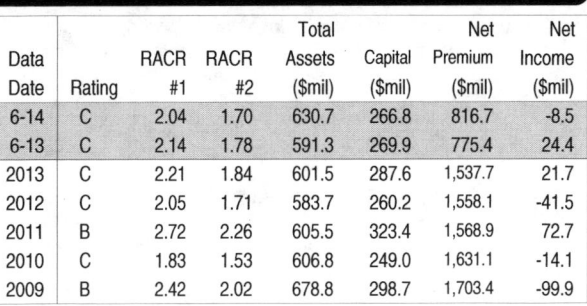

Rating Indexes

Range | Cap. 2 | Stab. | Inv. | Prof. | Liq.
■ Weak ■ Fair ▨ Good ☐ Strong

BLUE CROSS BLUE SHIELD OF SC INC *   A-   Excellent

Major Rating Factors: Excellent profitability (7.9 on a scale of 0 to 10). Strong capitalization (10.0) based on excellent current risk-adjusted capital (severe loss scenario). Excellent liquidity (6.9) with sufficient resources (cash flows and marketable investments) to handle a spike in claims.
Other Rating Factors: Fair quality investment portfolio (3.7).
Principal Business: Comp med (59%), FEHB (20%), med supp (6%), Medicare (5%), dental (3%), other (3%)
Mem Phys: 13: 18,768 **12:** 17,558 **13 MLR** 76.6% **/ 13 Admin Exp** N/A
Enroll(000): Q2 14: 1,243 **13:** 1,223 **12:** 1,205 **Med Exp PMPM:** $115
Principal Investments: Affiliate common stock (30%), long-term bonds (23%), nonaffiliate common stock (11%), real estate (6%), cash and equiv (6%), other (25%)
Provider Compensation ($000): FFS ($627,271), contr fee ($432,919), capitation ($1,311), bonus arrang ($302), other ($608,905)
Total Member Encounters: Phys (3,534,819), non-phys (1,399,555)
Group Affiliation: Blue Cross Blue Shield of S Carolina
Licensed in: SC
Address: 2501 Faraway Dr, Columbia, SC 29219-0001
Phone: (803) 788-3860 **Dom State:** SC **Commenced Bus:** April 1947

Data Date	Rating	RACR #1	RACR #2	Total Assets ($mil)	Capital ($mil)	Net Premium ($mil)	Net Income ($mil)
6-14	A-	5.06	4.22	3,141.3	2,176.1	1,139.6	48.1
6-13	A-	5.08	4.24	2,799.5	2,074.3	1,047.3	46.3
2013	A-	5.01	4.17	2,983.1	2,153.3	2,178.1	82.2
2012	A-	4.81	4.01	2,744.8	1,961.6	2,185.1	77.0
2011	A-	4.84	4.03	2,641.6	1,780.8	2,082.9	60.7
2010	A-	5.52	4.60	2,438.3	1,696.0	1,952.9	96.2
2009	A-	5.33	4.44	2,328.1	1,500.1	1,783.3	66.1

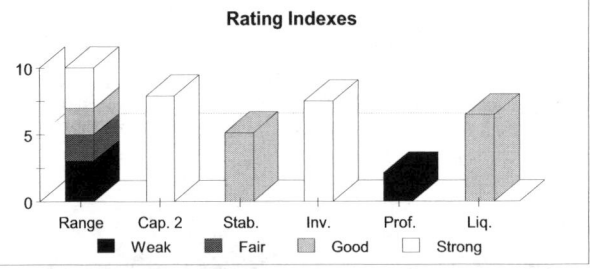

Rating Indexes

Range | Cap. 2 | Stab. | Inv. | Prof. | Liq.
■ Weak ■ Fair ▨ Good ☐ Strong

BLUE CROSS BLUE SHIELD OF VERMONT *   B+   Good

Major Rating Factors: Good overall profitability index (5.3 on a scale of 0 to 10). Good liquidity (6.7) with sufficient resources (cash flows and marketable investments) to handle a spike in claims. Strong capitalization (8.5) based on excellent current risk-adjusted capital (severe loss scenario).
Other Rating Factors: Fair quality investment portfolio (4.7).
Principal Business: Comp med (79%), FEHB (16%), med supp (3%), other (2%)
Mem Phys: 13: 7,091 **12:** 6,829 **13 MLR** 94.4% **/ 13 Admin Exp** N/A
Enroll(000): Q2 14: 205 **13:** 157 **12:** 142 **Med Exp PMPM:** $212
Principal Investments: Long-term bonds (49%), affiliate common stock (35%), nonaffiliate common stock (7%), real estate (5%), cash and equiv (4%)
Provider Compensation ($000): FFS ($172,027), contr fee ($142,451), capitation ($8,613), other ($71,919)
Total Member Encounters: Phys (353,032), non-phys (189,375)
Group Affiliation: Blue Cross Blue Shield of Vermont
Licensed in: VT
Address: 445 Industrial Ln, Montpelier, VT 05602
Phone: (802) 223-6131 **Dom State:** VT **Commenced Bus:** December 1980

Data Date	Rating	RACR #1	RACR #2	Total Assets ($mil)	Capital ($mil)	Net Premium ($mil)	Net Income ($mil)
6-14	B+	2.58	2.15	248.8	140.5	220.8	6.3
6-13	A-	2.58	2.15	206.1	131.4	204.6	0.8
2013	B+	2.42	2.02	214.1	132.4	420.8	3.8
2012	A-	2.47	2.06	208.2	126.0	382.5	-4.7
2011	A-	2.85	2.38	186.6	113.9	290.6	5.9
2010	A-	2.82	2.35	164.0	98.8	278.6	11.8
2009	B+	2.22	1.85	135.9	81.0	286.6	3.6

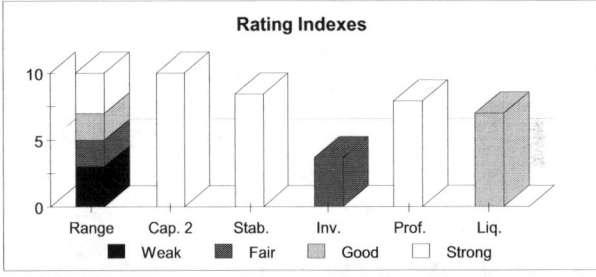

Rating Indexes

Range | Cap. 2 | Stab. | Inv. | Prof. | Liq.
■ Weak ■ Fair ▨ Good ☐ Strong

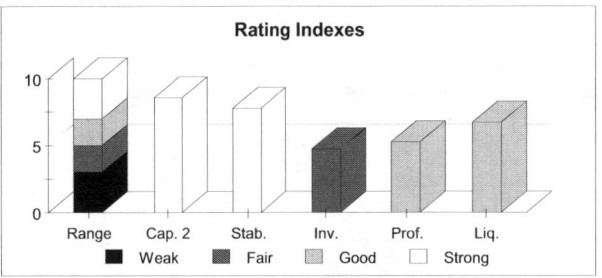

BLUE CROSS BLUE SHIELD OF WISCONSIN
B- **Good**

Major Rating Factors: Fair quality investment portfolio (3.5 on a scale of 0 to 10). Excellent profitability (9.0). Strong capitalization (10.0) based on excellent current risk-adjusted capital (severe loss scenario).
Other Rating Factors: Excellent liquidity (6.9) with sufficient resources (cash flows and marketable investments) to handle a spike in claims.
Principal Business: FEHB (58%), comp med (22%), med supp (12%), dental (3%), other (4%)
Mem Phys: 13: 34,664 **12:** 31,152 **13 MLR** 87.2% **/ 13 Admin Exp** N/A
Enroll(000): Q2 14: 384 **13:** 344 **12:** 301 **Med Exp PMPM:** $141
Principal Investments: Long-term bonds (67%), affiliate common stock (41%), real estate (2%)
Provider Compensation ($000): Contr fee ($322,658), FFS ($232,021), bonus arrang ($174), other ($21,995)
Total Member Encounters: Phys (568,871), non-phys (441,836)
Group Affiliation: WellPoint Inc
Licensed in: WI
Address: 6775 W Washington St, Milwaukee, WI 53214-5644
Phone: (414) 459-5000 **Dom State:** WI **Commenced Bus:** October 1939

Data Date	Rating	RACR #1	RACR #2	Total Assets ($mil)	Capital ($mil)	Net Premium ($mil)	Net Income ($mil)
6-14	B-	3.98	3.32	520.0	277.3	344.4	26.1
6-13	B-	4.15	3.46	485.8	234.1	329.1	25.5
2013	B-	3.40	2.83	474.6	235.2	672.8	69.6
2012	B-	3.40	2.83	418.3	189.9	570.8	86.9
2011	B-	3.09	2.58	417.3	179.4	575.1	81.1
2010	B-	3.10	2.59	513.7	215.2	725.3	43.4
2009	B	3.08	2.57	503.5	218.4	867.6	85.3

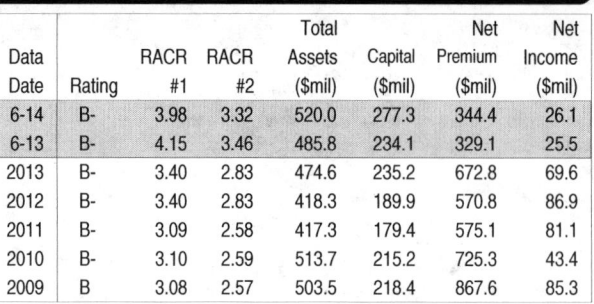

BLUE CROSS BLUE SHIELD OF WYOMING *
B+ **Good**

Major Rating Factors: Excellent profitability (9.0 on a scale of 0 to 10). Strong capitalization (10.0) based on excellent current risk-adjusted capital (severe loss scenario). Excellent liquidity (7.0) with sufficient resources (cash flows and marketable investments) to handle a spike in claims.
Other Rating Factors: Fair quality investment portfolio (3.4).
Principal Business: Comp med (60%), FEHB (31%), med supp (6%), dental (1%), other (2%)
Mem Phys: 13: 3,460 **12:** 3,412 **13 MLR** 87.8% **/ 13 Admin Exp** N/A
Enroll(000): Q2 14: 67 **13:** 67 **12:** 66 **Med Exp PMPM:** $296
Principal Investments: Nonaffiliate common stock (51%), long-term bonds (43%), cash and equiv (1%), real estate (1%), other (5%)
Provider Compensation ($000): FFS ($220,701), contr fee ($20,743), other ($102)
Total Member Encounters: Phys (616,621), non-phys (604,377)
Group Affiliation: None
Licensed in: WY
Address: 4000 House Ave, Cheyenne, WY 82001
Phone: (307) 634-1393 **Dom State:** WY **Commenced Bus:** August 1976

Data Date	Rating	RACR #1	RACR #2	Total Assets ($mil)	Capital ($mil)	Net Premium ($mil)	Net Income ($mil)
6-14	B+	6.32	5.27	406.0	251.3	138.4	2.4
6-13	B+	6.67	5.55	354.5	214.5	130.5	7.2
2013	B+	6.08	5.06	384.6	242.3	270.5	11.8
2012	B+	6.19	5.16	335.0	199.9	275.7	29.6
2011	B+	6.77	5.64	274.2	179.0	254.0	19.1
2010	B+	6.10	5.08	262.1	168.1	233.4	16.1
2009	A-	5.85	4.88	219.3	144.0	228.8	21.3

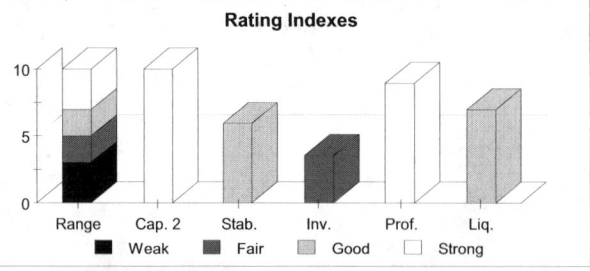

BLUE CROSS COMPLETE OF MICHIGAN
E **Very Weak**

Major Rating Factors: Weak profitability index (0.9 on a scale of 0 to 10). Fair capitalization (2.9) based on good current risk-adjusted capital (moderate loss scenario). High quality investment portfolio (9.9).
Other Rating Factors: Excellent liquidity (7.0) with ample operational cash flow and liquid investments.
Principal Business: Medicaid (100%)
Mem Phys: 13: 14,212 **12:** 6,753 **13 MLR** 97.5% **/ 13 Admin Exp** N/A
Enroll(000): Q2 14: 64 **13:** 43 **12:** 27 **Med Exp PMPM:** $280
Principal Investments: Cash and equiv (93%), long-term bonds (6%), other (2%)
Provider Compensation ($000): Capitation ($72,900), contr fee ($38,205)
Total Member Encounters: Phys (202,101), non-phys (63,190)
Group Affiliation: Blue Cross Blue Shield of Michigan
Licensed in: MI
Address: 20500 Civic Center Dr, Southfield, MI 48076
Phone: (313) 225-9000 **Dom State:** MI **Commenced Bus:** January 2003

Data Date	Rating	RACR #1	RACR #2	Total Assets ($mil)	Capital ($mil)	Net Premium ($mil)	Net Income ($mil)
6-14	E	2.49	2.07	85.6	29.6	95.7	-12.1
6-13	E	0.88	0.73	17.9	2.4	52.5	-2.5
2013	E	2.16	1.80	38.2	12.8	123.2	-9.0
2012	B	1.77	1.47	13.1	4.8	65.9	0.2
2011	B	2.06	1.71	8.4	4.6	59.4	0.3
2010	B-	1.83	1.52	7.8	4.2	60.8	0.3
2009	B-	1.71	1.43	6.9	3.8	58.6	0.5

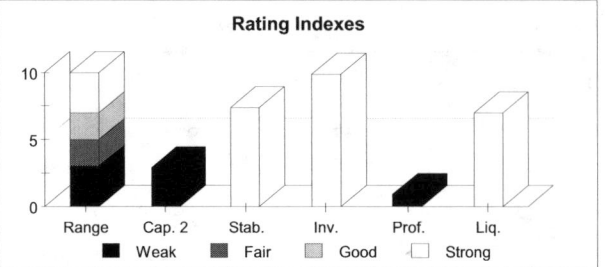

BLUE CROSS OF CALIFORNIA * A+ Excellent

Major Rating Factors: Excellent profitability (7.9 on a scale of 0 to 10). Strong capitalization index (7.8) based on excellent current risk-adjusted capital (severe loss scenario). Excellent liquidity (7.2) with ample operational cash flow and liquid investments.
Other Rating Factors: Good overall results on stability tests (6.8).
Principal Business: Medicaid (17%), Medicare (1%)
Mem Phys: 13: N/A **12:** N/A **13 MLR** 89.3% / **13 Admin Exp** N/A
Enroll(000): Q2 14: 3,686 **13:** 3,122 **12:** 3,233 **Med Exp PMPM:** $275
Principal Investments ($000): Cash and equiv ($2,208,740)
Provider Compensation ($000): None
Total Member Encounters: N/A
Group Affiliation: WellPoint Inc
Licensed in: CA
Address: 1 Wellpoint Way, Thousand Oaks, CA 91362
Phone: (805) 557-6655 **Dom State:** CA **Commenced Bus:** July 1982

Data Date	Rating	RACR #1	RACR #2	Total Assets ($mil)	Capital ($mil)	Net Premium ($mil)	Net Income ($mil)
6-14	A+	2.66	1.67	5,235.8	1,560.8	6,208.1	178.9
6-13	A+	2.37	1.47	4,015.7	1,289.8	5,704.5	284.2
2013	A+	2.37	1.49	4,372.2	1,349.4	10,762.3	453.2
2012	A+	2.26	1.40	3,717.9	1,210.3	11,231.5	407.4
2011	A+	2.45	1.52	3,703.9	1,225.6	10,999.5	507.7
2010	A+	2.48	1.54	3,630.7	1,258.8	10,987.4	413.6
2009	A+	2.60	1.63	3,693.0	1,377.3	11,079.1	450.5

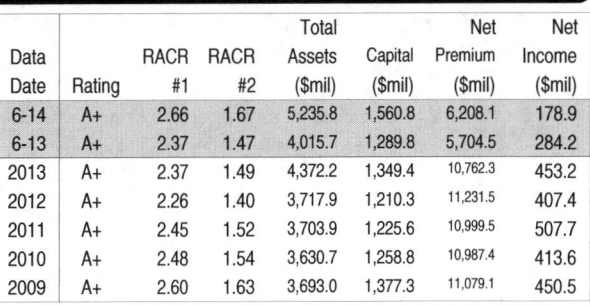

Rating Indexes

BLUE CROSS OF IDAHO HEALTH SERVICE * A- Excellent

Major Rating Factors: Excellent profitability (7.0 on a scale of 0 to 10). Strong capitalization (10.0) based on excellent current risk-adjusted capital (severe loss scenario). Good quality investment portfolio (5.7).
Other Rating Factors: Good liquidity (6.8) with sufficient resources (cash flows and marketable investments) to handle a spike in claims.
Principal Business: Comp med (60%), Medicare (21%), FEHB (9%), dental (6%), med supp (1%), other (2%)
Mem Phys: 13: 10,681 **12:** 5,024 **13 MLR** 86.9% / **13 Admin Exp** N/A
Enroll(000): Q2 14: 627 **13:** 566 **12:** 558 **Med Exp PMPM:** $161
Principal Investments: Long-term bonds (55%), nonaffiliate common stock (37%), cash and equiv (4%), real estate (3%), other (1%)
Provider Compensation ($000): Contr fee ($834,544), bonus arrang ($246,683), capitation ($599)
Total Member Encounters: Phys (1,417,354), non-phys (1,435,730)
Group Affiliation: Blue Cross of Idaho Group
Licensed in: ID
Address: 3000 E Pine Ave, Meridian, ID 83642
Phone: (208) 345-4550 **Dom State:** ID **Commenced Bus:** January 1978

Data Date	Rating	RACR #1	RACR #2	Total Assets ($mil)	Capital ($mil)	Net Premium ($mil)	Net Income ($mil)
6-14	A-	5.69	4.75	844.0	542.5	699.3	-11.2
6-13	A+	5.48	4.56	756.9	517.8	627.8	27.5
2013	A	5.68	4.73	794.3	541.0	1,244.2	39.3
2012	A+	5.09	4.24	718.7	485.7	1,260.4	46.7
2011	A+	4.87	4.06	653.7	443.8	1,230.6	56.6
2010	A+	4.66	3.89	600.3	415.5	1,146.7	45.0
2009	A+	4.48	3.73	534.3	355.6	1,055.3	49.7

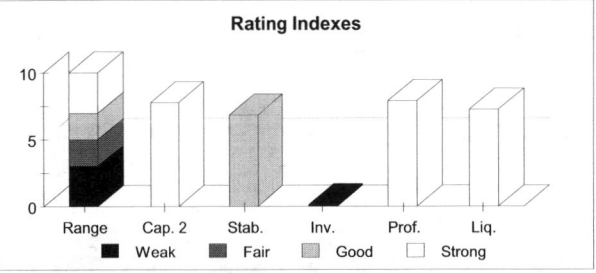

Rating Indexes

BLUE SHIELD OF CALIFORNIA LIFE & HEALTH INS COMPANY * A- Excellent

Major Rating Factors: Good current capitalization (5.1 on a scale of 0 to 10) based on excellent risk adjusted capital (severe loss scenario) reflecting improvement over results in 2012. Good overall profitability (5.2). Excellent expense controls. Return on equity has been low, averaging -5.3%. Good overall results on stability tests (5.5) despite negative cash flow from operations for 2013 good operational trends and excellent risk diversification.
Other Rating Factors: Weak liquidity (1.1). High quality investment portfolio (8.0).
Principal Business: Group health insurance (75%) and individual health insurance (25%).
Principal Investments: CMOs and structured securities (53%) and nonCMO investment grade bonds (47%).
Investments in Affiliates: None
Group Affiliation: Blue Shield of California
Licensed in: CA
Commenced Business: July 1954
Address: 50 Beale St, San Francisco, CA 94105
Phone: (800) 642-5599 **Domicile State:** CA **NAIC Code:** 61557

Data Date	Rating	RACR #1	RACR #2	Total Assets ($mil)	Capital ($mil)	Net Premium ($mil)	Net Income ($mil)
6-14	A-	1.57	1.25	838.0	429.9	988.0	63.8
6-13	A-	1.51	1.19	881.6	399.9	1,173.3	74.0
2013	A-	1.22	0.97	890.7	367.1	2,381.3	12.3
2012	A-	1.20	0.95	802.7	297.3	1,937.3	-19.1
2011	A-	1.31	1.03	637.2	229.9	1,370.8	-41.4
2010	A-	1.58	1.25	578.8	275.5	1,348.0	6.7
2009	A-	1.57	1.25	521.0	247.9	1,214.2	-63.2

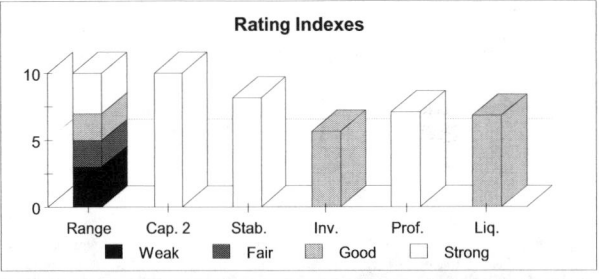

Risk-Adjusted Capital Ratio #2
(Severe Loss Scenario)

BLUECHOICE HEALTHPLAN OF SC INC *

A   Excellent

Major Rating Factors: Excellent profitability (8.5 on a scale of 0 to 10). Strong capitalization index (10.0) based on excellent current risk-adjusted capital (severe loss scenario). High quality investment portfolio (8.4).
Other Rating Factors: Excellent overall results on stability tests (8.4). Good financial strength from affiliates. Good liquidity (6.4) with sufficient resources (cash flows and marketable investments) to handle a spike in claims.
Principal Business: Comp med (86%), Medicaid (14%)
Mem Phys: 13: 18,721 **12:** 17,573 **13 MLR** 113.5% **/ 13 Admin Exp** N/A
Enroll(000): Q2 14: 167 **13:** 165 **12:** 148 **Med Exp PMPM:** $292
Principal Investments: Long-term bonds (50%), cash and equiv (24%), nonaffiliate common stock (17%), affiliate common stock (9%)
Provider Compensation ($000): Contr fee ($554,953), capitation ($3,781), FFS ($3,117)
Total Member Encounters: Phys (1,104,512), non-phys (202,725)
Group Affiliation: Blue Cross Blue Shield of S Carolina
Licensed in: SC
Address: I-20 at Alpine Rd, Columbia, SC 29219
Phone: (803) 786-8466 **Dom State:** SC **Commenced Bus:** October 1984

Data Date	Rating	RACR #1	RACR #2	Total Assets ($mil)	Capital ($mil)	Net Premium ($mil)	Net Income ($mil)
6-14	A	6.91	5.76	309.1	214.2	242.9	5.2
6-13	A	7.75	6.46	268.5	201.2	244.0	6.9
2013	A	6.76	5.64	284.7	209.5	494.7	14.9
2012	A	7.41	6.18	257.9	192.1	403.5	21.3
2011	A	6.86	5.72	238.1	167.9	401.4	17.5
2010	A	6.17	5.14	223.5	138.9	357.7	6.6
2009	A	6.24	5.20	206.8	131.3	342.0	7.9

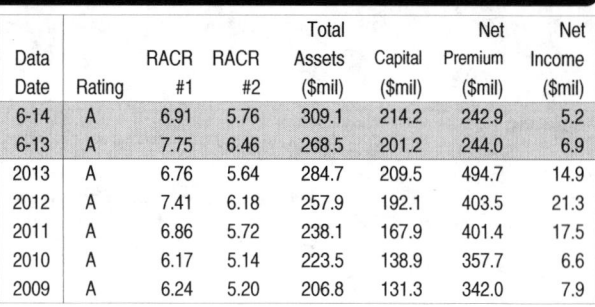

Rating Indexes

Range Cap. 2 Stab. Inv. Prof. Liq.
■ Weak ■ Fair ▨ Good □ Strong

BLUECROSS BLUESHIELD OF TENNESSEE *

A   Excellent

Major Rating Factors: Excellent profitability (8.6 on a scale of 0 to 10). Strong capitalization (10.0) based on excellent current risk-adjusted capital (severe loss scenario). Good quality investment portfolio (6.7).
Other Rating Factors: Good liquidity (6.9) with sufficient resources (cash flows and marketable investments) to handle a spike in claims.
Principal Business: Comp med (62%), FEHB (17%), Medicare (13%), med supp (4%), dental (3%)
Mem Phys: 13: 25,292 **12:** 25,811 **13 MLR** 82.2% **/ 13 Admin Exp** N/A
Enroll(000): Q2 14: 1,746 **13:** 1,487 **12:** 1,359 **Med Exp PMPM:** $171
Principal Investments: Long-term bonds (65%), affiliate common stock (14%), cash and equiv (6%), real estate (5%), other (10%)
Provider Compensation ($000): Contr fee ($2,263,031), FFS ($759,537), capitation ($7,296), bonus arrang ($145)
Total Member Encounters: Phys (10,346,906), non-phys (2,556,894)
Group Affiliation: BlueCross BlueShield of Tennessee
Licensed in: TN
Address: 1 Cameron Hill Cir, Chattanooga, TN 37402
Phone: (423) 535-5600 **Dom State:** TN **Commenced Bus:** October 1945

Data Date	Rating	RACR #1	RACR #2	Total Assets ($mil)	Capital ($mil)	Net Premium ($mil)	Net Income ($mil)
6-14	A	7.59	6.33	2,450.7	1,712.5	2,092.1	52.5
6-13	A	7.70	6.42	2,201.4	1,620.7	1,803.2	119.4
2013	A	7.32	6.10	2,226.9	1,651.4	3,658.7	188.9
2012	A	7.21	6.00	2,090.4	1,514.9	3,368.4	142.3
2011	A-	6.36	5.30	1,927.0	1,313.5	3,432.1	138.0
2010	A-	5.96	4.96	1,809.9	1,243.2	3,351.6	154.7
2009	A-	5.96	4.96	1,741.4	1,137.1	3,152.6	80.9

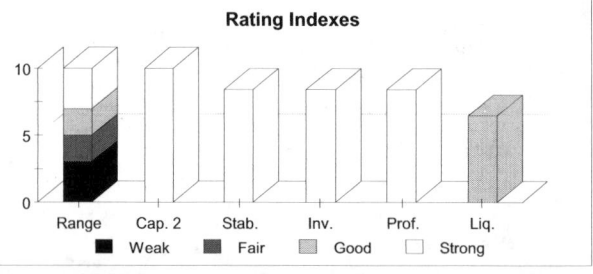

Rating Indexes

Range Cap. 2 Stab. Inv. Prof. Liq.
■ Weak ■ Fair ▨ Good □ Strong

BLUEGRASS FAMILY HEALTH INC *

B+   Good

Major Rating Factors: Good quality investment portfolio (6.6 on a scale of 0 to 10). Good overall results on stability tests (5.2) despite a decline in enrollment during 2013. Good liquidity (6.8) with sufficient resources (cash flows and marketable investments) to handle a spike in claims.
Other Rating Factors: Strong capitalization index (10.0) based on excellent current risk-adjusted capital (severe loss scenario). Fair profitability index (4.7).
Principal Business: Comp med (100%)
Mem Phys: 13: 33,709 **12:** 31,817 **13 MLR** 87.8% **/ 13 Admin Exp** N/A
Enroll(000): Q2 14: 34 **13:** 35 **12:** 43 **Med Exp PMPM:** $296
Principal Investments: Long-term bonds (47%), nonaffiliate common stock (41%), cash and equiv (12%)
Provider Compensation ($000): Contr fee ($125,611), FFS ($2,173), capitation ($1,131)
Total Member Encounters: Phys (284,185), non-phys (62,844)
Group Affiliation: Baptist Healthcare System Inc
Licensed in: IN, KY, TN
Address: 651 Perimeter Park, Ste 300, Lexington, KY 40517
Phone: (859) 269-4475 **Dom State:** KY **Commenced Bus:** April 1993

Data Date	Rating	RACR #1	RACR #2	Total Assets ($mil)	Capital ($mil)	Net Premium ($mil)	Net Income ($mil)
6-14	B+	4.39	3.66	105.4	74.6	72.7	-3.1
6-13	A	3.84	3.20	100.1	72.6	73.4	3.0
2013	A-	4.46	3.72	99.5	75.6	144.8	2.7
2012	A-	3.56	2.97	93.7	67.9	169.6	12.9
2011	B	2.61	2.18	79.7	51.4	182.6	2.8
2010	B	2.64	2.20	77.2	50.5	181.8	0.0
2009	B+	2.40	2.00	75.8	46.6	183.7	4.9

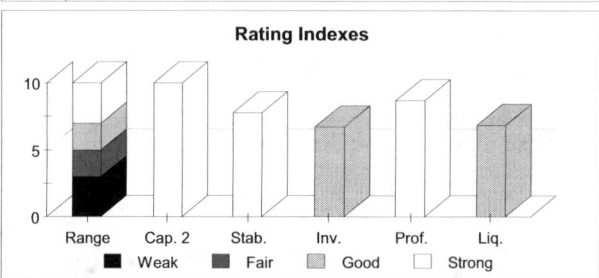

Rating Indexes

Range Cap. 2 Stab. Inv. Prof. Liq.
■ Weak ■ Fair ▨ Good □ Strong

BOSTON MEDICAL CENTER HEALTH PLAN — B- — Good

Major Rating Factors: Good liquidity (6.8 on a scale of 0 to 10) with sufficient resources (cash flows and marketable investments) to handle a spike in claims. Strong capitalization (7.4) based on excellent current risk-adjusted capital (severe loss scenario). High quality investment portfolio (8.3).
Other Rating Factors: Weak profitability index (2.6).
Principal Business: Medicaid (74%), comp med (26%)
Mem Phys: 13: 18,574 **12:** 18,497 **13 MLR** 95.3% **/ 13 Admin Exp** N/A
Enroll(000): Q2 14: 360 **13:** 333 **12:** 264 **Med Exp PMPM:** $396
Principal Investments: Long-term bonds (44%), cash and equiv (39%), nonaffiliate common stock (16%)
Provider Compensation ($000): Contr fee ($1,209,106), capitation ($129,548), bonus arrang ($784)
Total Member Encounters: Phys (2,892,877), non-phys (4,496,399)
Group Affiliation: None
Licensed in: MA
Address: Two Copley Place Suite 600, Boston, MA 02116-6568
Phone: (617) 748-6000 **Dom State:** MA **Commenced Bus:** July 1997

Data Date	Rating	RACR #1	RACR #2	Total Assets ($mil)	Capital ($mil)	Net Premium ($mil)	Net Income ($mil)
6-14	B-	1.67	1.39	334.0	193.6	876.0	-22.6
6-13	C+	2.43	2.03	346.7	236.5	672.3	-0.9
2013	B-	1.86	1.55	341.3	215.4	1,406.5	-0.8
2012	B-	2.43	2.03	360.6	236.4	1,219.5	-7.5
2011	B	3.05	2.54	391.5	293.3	1,293.8	82.9
2010	B-	2.53	2.11	348.1	230.2	1,219.8	81.2
2009	D+	1.45	1.21	272.0	139.6	1,173.9	-44.3

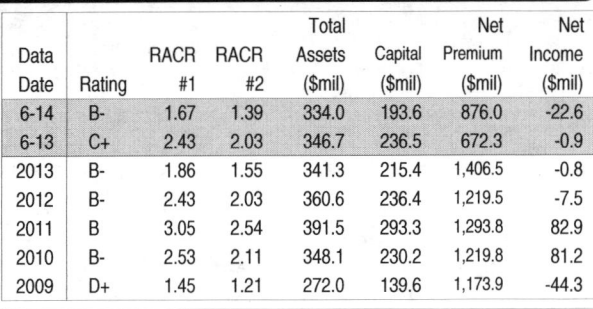

Rating Indexes

BRAVO HEALTH MID-ATLANTIC INC — C — Fair

Major Rating Factors: Fair overall results on stability tests (4.5 on a scale of 0 to 10). Rating is significantly influenced by the good financial results of CIGNA Corp. Weak profitability index (2.9). Good liquidity (5.1) with sufficient resources (cash flows and marketable investments) to handle a spike in claims.
Other Rating Factors: Strong capitalization index (7.2) based on excellent current risk-adjusted capital (severe loss scenario). High quality investment portfolio (8.6).
Principal Business: Medicare (100%)
Mem Phys: 13: 29,285 **12:** 28,463 **13 MLR** 93.0% **/ 13 Admin Exp** N/A
Enroll(000): Q2 14: 21 **13:** 25 **12:** 26 **Med Exp PMPM:** $1,030
Principal Investments: Long-term bonds (86%), cash and equiv (14%)
Provider Compensation ($000): Contr fee ($291,426), capitation ($10,917), salary ($3,969), bonus arrang ($1,512)
Total Member Encounters: Phys (346,101), non-phys (340,753)
Group Affiliation: CIGNA Corp
Licensed in: DC, DE, MD
Address: 3601 ODonnell, Baltimore, MD 21224-5238
Phone: (800) 235-9188 **Dom State:** MD **Commenced Bus:** January 2001

Data Date	Rating	RACR #1	RACR #2	Total Assets ($mil)	Capital ($mil)	Net Premium ($mil)	Net Income ($mil)
6-14	C	1.48	1.24	82.2	29.3	158.9	4.3
6-13	C	1.14	0.95	76.7	23.0	167.4	-5.5
2013	C	1.28	1.07	72.9	25.0	329.2	-4.1
2012	C	1.41	1.18	80.2	28.8	348.7	3.8
2011	C	1.01	0.84	74.4	24.5	320.0	-9.7
2010	C+	1.14	0.95	52.0	19.3	238.8	-1.4
2009	B-	1.01	0.85	47.9	14.9	185.9	1.5

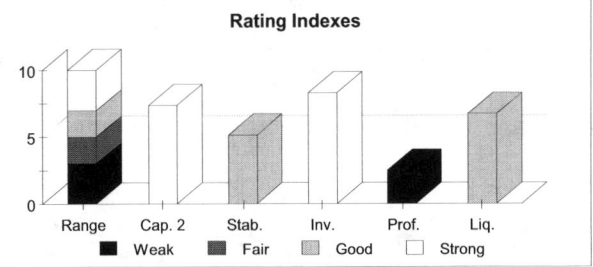

Rating Indexes

BRAVO HEALTH PENNSYLVANIA INC — B — Good

Major Rating Factors: Good liquidity (5.9 on a scale of 0 to 10) with sufficient resources (cash flows and marketable investments) to handle a spike in claims. Fair profitability index (3.1). Strong capitalization (7.7) based on excellent current risk-adjusted capital (severe loss scenario).
Other Rating Factors: High quality investment portfolio (8.5).
Principal Business: Medicare (100%)
Mem Phys: 13: 43,224 **12:** 33,133 **13 MLR** 86.7% **/ 13 Admin Exp** N/A
Enroll(000): Q2 14: 67 **13:** 83 **12:** 80 **Med Exp PMPM:** $940
Principal Investments: Long-term bonds (90%), cash and equiv (9%), other (1%)
Provider Compensation ($000): Contr fee ($844,400), capitation ($51,589), bonus arrang ($8,948), salary ($7,321)
Total Member Encounters: Phys (1,216,845), non-phys (1,219,994)
Group Affiliation: CIGNA Corp
Licensed in: NJ, PA
Address: 1500 Spring Garden St Ste 80, Philadelphia, PA 19130-4071
Phone: (800) 235-9188 **Dom State:** PA **Commenced Bus:** December 2002

Data Date	Rating	RACR #1	RACR #2	Total Assets ($mil)	Capital ($mil)	Net Premium ($mil)	Net Income ($mil)
6-14	B	1.95	1.62	250.6	109.2	480.0	1.3
6-13	A-	2.02	1.69	248.3	109.4	542.2	-10.0
2013	B	1.77	1.48	260.7	98.7	1,066.0	-19.3
2012	A-	2.48	2.07	257.6	136.0	1,069.5	18.8
2011	A-	1.64	1.36	214.9	104.3	1,021.1	14.3
2010	A-	1.55	1.29	183.0	80.3	848.7	19.3
2009	B	1.65	1.37	154.1	71.6	624.5	9.6

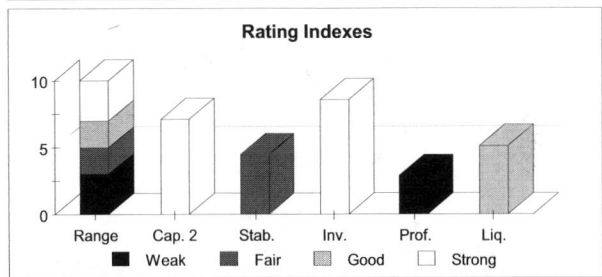
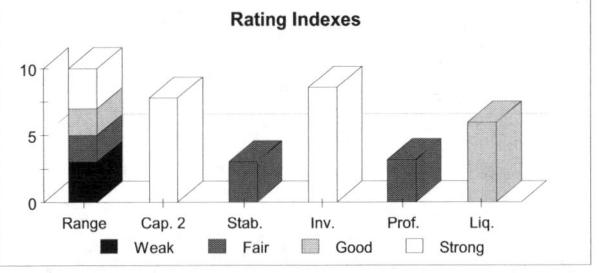

Rating Indexes

BRIDGESPAN HEALTH CO   B   Good

Major Rating Factors: Strong capitalization index (10.0 on a scale of 0 to 10) based on excellent current risk-adjusted capital (severe loss scenario). High quality investment portfolio (9.9). Excellent liquidity (7.5) with ample operational cash flow and liquid investments.
Other Rating Factors: Weak profitability index (0.7). Weak overall results on stability tests (1.9) based on a significant 17% decrease in enrollment during the period. Rating is significantly influenced by the good financial results of Regence Group.
Principal Business: Med supp (100%)
Mem Phys: 13: N/A **12:** N/A **13 MLR** 64.3% **/ 13 Admin Exp** N/A
Enroll(000): Q2 14: 6 **13:** 0 **12:** 0 **Med Exp PMPM:** $135
Principal Investments: Long-term bonds (80%), cash and equiv (20%)
Provider Compensation ($000): Contr fee ($457), FFS ($93)
Total Member Encounters: Phys (6,678), non-phys (12,593)
Group Affiliation: Regence Group
Licensed in: UT
Address: 2890 E Cottonwood Pkwy, Salt Lake City, UT 84121-7035
Phone: (801) 333-2000 **Dom State:** UT **Commenced Bus:** September 1982

Data Date	Rating	RACR #1	RACR #2	Total Assets ($mil)	Capital ($mil)	Net Premium ($mil)	Net Income ($mil)
6-14	B	57.21	47.68	15.0	10.5	9.3	-0.3
6-13	B	86.78	72.32	15.5	13.1	0.4	0.0
2013	B	58.91	49.09	14.3	10.9	0.9	-1.8
2012	A-	86.85	72.37	15.5	13.1	1.2	4.1
2011	A-	231.50	192.90	84.9	83.9	1.3	1.6
2010	A-	50.68	42.23	86.1	82.3	16.7	7.3
2009	A-	15.78	13.15	91.5	77.3	60.7	5.6

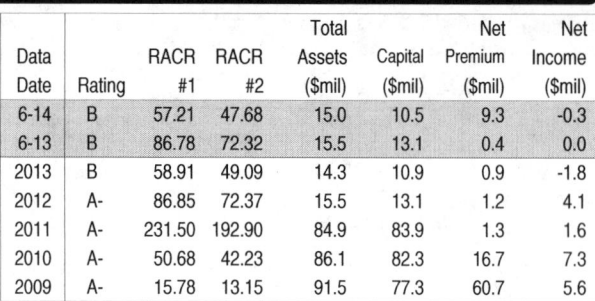

BROWN & TOLAND HEALTH SERVICES   E   Very Weak

Major Rating Factors: Weak profitability index (0.8 on a scale of 0 to 10). Weak overall results on stability tests (1.7). Good capitalization index (5.9) based on fair current risk-adjusted capital (moderate loss scenario).
Other Rating Factors: Excellent liquidity (7.6) with ample operational cash flow and liquid investments.
Principal Business: Managed care (100%)
Mem Phys: 13: N/A **12:** N/A **13 MLR** 100.5% **/ 13 Admin Exp** N/A
Enroll(000): Q2 14: 1 **13:** 1 **12:** N/A **Med Exp PMPM:** N/A
Principal Investments ($000): Cash and equiv ($1,504)
Provider Compensation ($000): None
Total Member Encounters: N/A
Group Affiliation: None
Licensed in: CA
Address: 153 Townsend St Suite 700, San Francisco, CA 94107
Phone: (415) 322-9897 **Dom State:** CA **Commenced Bus:** April 2013

Data Date	Rating	RACR #1	RACR #2	Total Assets ($mil)	Capital ($mil)	Net Premium ($mil)	Net Income ($mil)
6-14	E	0.89	0.56	1.8	0.2	2.7	0.0
6-13	N/A	N/A	N/A	N/A	N/A	N/A	N/A
2013	E	1.01	0.63	1.9	0.2	1.4	-0.1
2012	N/A	N/A	N/A	N/A	N/A	N/A	N/A
2011	N/A	N/A	N/A	N/A	N/A	N/A	N/A
2010	N/A	N/A	N/A	N/A	N/A	N/A	N/A
2009	N/A	N/A	N/A	N/A	N/A	N/A	N/A

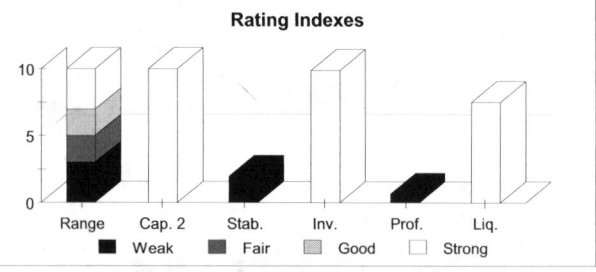

BUCKEYE COMMUNITY HEALTH PLAN INC   C+   Fair

Major Rating Factors: Good liquidity (6.8 on a scale of 0 to 10) with sufficient resources (cash flows and marketable investments) to handle a spike in claims. Excellent profitability (7.3). Strong capitalization (8.7) based on excellent current risk-adjusted capital (severe loss scenario).
Other Rating Factors: High quality investment portfolio (9.5).
Principal Business: Medicaid (98%), Medicare (2%)
Mem Phys: 13: 31,448 **12:** 21,547 **13 MLR** 78.7% **/ 13 Admin Exp** N/A
Enroll(000): Q2 14: 225 **13:** 172 **12:** 157 **Med Exp PMPM:** $318
Principal Investments: Long-term bonds (62%), cash and equiv (34%), affiliate common stock (3%), other (1%)
Provider Compensation ($000): Contr fee ($541,932), capitation ($37,856), salary ($13,730)
Total Member Encounters: Phys (1,078,878), non-phys (1,045,828)
Group Affiliation: Centene Corp
Licensed in: OH
Address: 175 S Third St Suite 520, Columbus, OH 43215
Phone: (314) 725-4477 **Dom State:** OH **Commenced Bus:** January 2004

Data Date	Rating	RACR #1	RACR #2	Total Assets ($mil)	Capital ($mil)	Net Premium ($mil)	Net Income ($mil)
6-14	C+	2.75	2.29	263.1	103.5	484.5	-4.0
6-13	B-	2.98	2.48	167.5	103.5	361.6	11.0
2013	C+	2.80	2.34	199.3	105.7	795.0	13.1
2012	B-	2.54	2.11	161.1	90.7	728.3	13.0
2011	B-	2.42	2.01	159.6	85.5	606.8	15.6
2010	C	2.45	2.05	136.9	80.4	546.8	21.0
2009	C	1.91	1.59	187.4	71.1	558.8	3.5

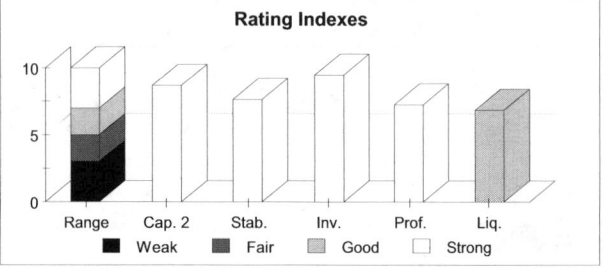

BUPA INS CO   **D+**   **Weak**

Major Rating Factors: Weak profitability index (1.0 on a scale of 0 to 10). Strong capitalization (8.5) based on excellent current risk-adjusted capital (severe loss scenario). High quality investment portfolio (9.7).
Other Rating Factors: Excellent liquidity (8.5) with ample operational cash flow and liquid investments.
Principal Business: Comp med (100%)
Mem Phys: 13: N/A   **12:** N/A   **13 MLR** 27.0%   **/ 13 Admin Exp** N/A
Enroll(000): Q2 14: 112   **13:** 105   **12:** 95   **Med Exp PMPM:** $98
Principal Investments: Cash and equiv (74%), long-term bonds (22%), affiliate common stock (3%)
Provider Compensation ($000): FFS ($117,537)
Total Member Encounters: Phys (32,721), non-phys (17,783)
Group Affiliation: British United Provident Assoc Ltd
Licensed in: FL, PR
Address: 7001 S.W.97th Avenue, Miami, FL 33173
Phone: (305) 275-1400   **Dom State:** FL   **Commenced Bus:** July 1973

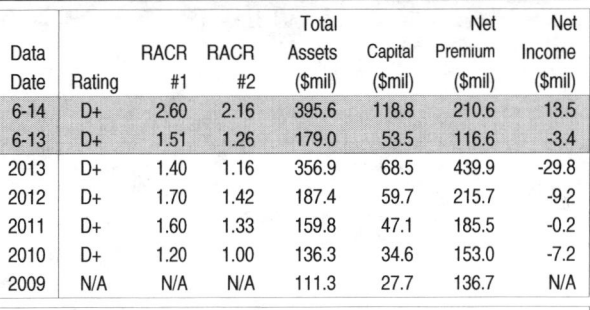

Data Date	Rating	RACR #1	RACR #2	Total Assets ($mil)	Capital ($mil)	Net Premium ($mil)	Net Income ($mil)
6-14	D+	2.60	2.16	395.6	118.8	210.6	13.5
6-13	D+	1.51	1.26	179.0	53.5	116.6	-3.4
2013	D+	1.40	1.16	356.9	68.5	439.9	-29.8
2012	D+	1.70	1.42	187.4	59.7	215.7	-9.2
2011	D+	1.60	1.33	159.8	47.1	185.5	-0.2
2010	D+	1.20	1.00	136.3	34.6	153.0	-7.2
2009	N/A	N/A	N/A	111.3	27.7	136.7	N/A

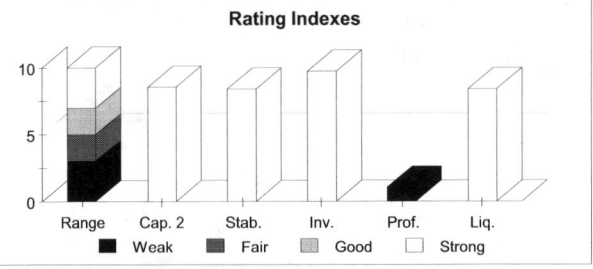

Rating Indexes

Range   Cap. 2   Stab.   Inv.   Prof.   Liq.
■ Weak   ▨ Fair   ▦ Good   □ Strong

CALIFORNIA HEALTH & WELLNESS PLAN   **D+**   **Weak**

Major Rating Factors: Weak overall results on stability tests (2.0 on a scale of 0 to 10). Good overall profitability index (5.1). Strong capitalization index (10.0) based on excellent current risk-adjusted capital (severe loss scenario).
Other Rating Factors: Excellent liquidity (7.2) with ample operational cash flow and liquid investments.
Principal Business: Medicaid (100%)
Mem Phys: 13: N/A   **12:** N/A   **13 MLR** 101.1%   **/ 13 Admin Exp** N/A
Enroll(000): Q2 14: 131   **13:** 93   **12:** N/A   **Med Exp PMPM:** $148
Principal Investments ($000): Cash and equiv ($14,482)
Provider Compensation ($000): None
Total Member Encounters: N/A
Group Affiliation: None
Licensed in: CA
Address: 1740 Creekside Oaks Dr, Sacramento, CA 95833
Phone: (916) 246-3753   **Dom State:** CA   **Commenced Bus:** October 2013

Data Date	Rating	RACR #1	RACR #2	Total Assets ($mil)	Capital ($mil)	Net Premium ($mil)	Net Income ($mil)
6-14	D+	7.16	4.53	85.4	23.4	149.7	3.0
6-13	N/A	N/A	N/A	N/A	N/A	N/A	N/A
2013	D+	3.83	2.42	32.5	12.8	27.3	-3.2
2012	N/A	N/A	N/A	N/A	N/A	N/A	N/A
2011	N/A	N/A	N/A	N/A	N/A	N/A	N/A
2010	N/A	N/A	N/A	N/A	N/A	N/A	N/A
2009	N/A	N/A	N/A	N/A	N/A	N/A	N/A

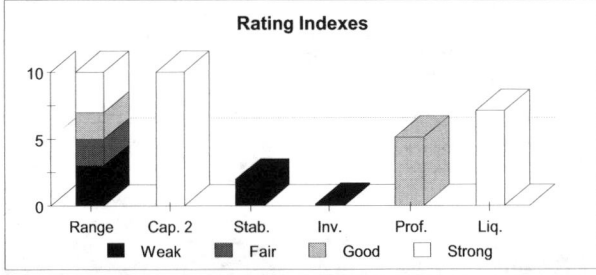

Rating Indexes

Range   Cap. 2   Stab.   Inv.   Prof.   Liq.
■ Weak   ▨ Fair   ▦ Good   □ Strong

CALIFORNIA PHYSICIANS SERVICE *   **A+**   **Excellent**

Major Rating Factors: Excellent profitability (7.0 on a scale of 0 to 10). Strong capitalization index (10.0) based on excellent current risk-adjusted capital (severe loss scenario). Excellent overall results on stability tests (7.9).
Other Rating Factors: Excellent liquidity (7.2) with ample operational cash flow and liquid investments.
Principal Business: Medicare (10%)
Mem Phys: 13: N/A   **12:** N/A   **13 MLR** 87.8%   **/ 13 Admin Exp** N/A
Enroll(000): Q2 14: 3,150   **13:** 2,425   **12:** 2,340   **Med Exp PMPM:** $350
Principal Investments ($000): Cash and equiv ($1,602,932)
Provider Compensation ($000): None
Total Member Encounters: N/A
Group Affiliation: Blue Shield of California
Licensed in: CA
Address: Fifty Beale St, San Francisco, CA 94105
Phone: (415) 229-5821   **Dom State:** CA   **Commenced Bus:** February 1939

Data Date	Rating	RACR #1	RACR #2	Total Assets ($mil)	Capital ($mil)	Net Premium ($mil)	Net Income ($mil)
6-14	A+	5.58	3.86	6,941.7	4,409.3	5,428.2	288.8
6-13	A	4.99	3.46	5,893.2	4,020.6	4,084.4	201.4
2013	A	5.41	3.72	6,028.0	4,143.3	8,316.4	170.6
2012	A	4.89	3.38	5,654.4	3,857.6	8,182.1	204.2
2011	A	4.52	3.12	5,393.5	3,579.6	8,050.6	78.0
2010	A	4.80	3.29	5,108.6	3,580.8	8,403.1	314.8
2009	A	3.57	2.50	4,977.9	3,189.7	8,369.6	148.5

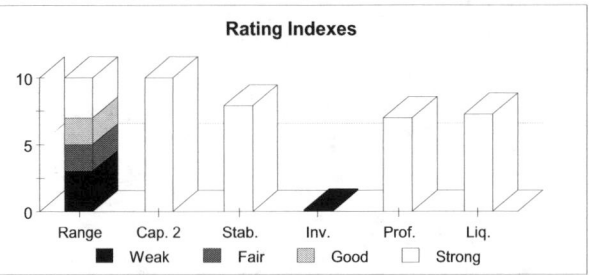

Rating Indexes

Range   Cap. 2   Stab.   Inv.   Prof.   Liq.
■ Weak   ▨ Fair   ▦ Good   □ Strong

CAMBRIDGE LIFE INS CO   B   Good

Major Rating Factors: Strong capitalization (10.0 on a scale of 0 to 10) based on excellent current risk-adjusted capital (severe loss scenario). High quality investment portfolio (9.1). Excellent liquidity (8.0) with ample operational cash flow and liquid investments.

Other Rating Factors: Weak profitability index (2.8).

Principal Business: Dental (1%), other (98%)

Mem Phys: 13: N/A   **12:** N/A   **13 MLR** 81.4%   **/ 13 Admin Exp** N/A

Enroll(000): Q2 14: 17   **13:** 22   **12:** 19   **Med Exp PMPM:** $69

Principal Investments: Long-term bonds (66%), cash and equiv (34%)

Provider Compensation ($000): Contr fee ($21,770), FFS ($140)

Total Member Encounters: N/A

Group Affiliation: Aetna Inc

Licensed in: AZ, AR, CO, IN, KS, LA, MD, MS, MO, MT, NE, NV, NM, NY, NC, OK, SC, SD, TN, TX, UT, WV

Address: 237 E High St, Jefferson City, MO 65102

Phone: (630) 737-7900   **Dom State:** MO   **Commenced Bus:** January 1974

Data Date	Rating	RACR #1	RACR #2	Total Assets ($mil)	Capital ($mil)	Net Premium ($mil)	Net Income ($mil)
6-14	B	14.04	11.70	68.9	49.8	9.5	-0.8
6-13	B	13.87	11.56	77.2	47.9	13.1	-1.3
2013	B	14.31	11.93	84.6	50.6	22.3	1.4
2012	B-	14.35	11.96	75.2	49.3	22.0	2.6
2011	C+	16.73	13.94	72.3	47.2	17.6	-0.7
2010	B-	15.21	12.68	71.2	47.8	22.4	-0.5
2009	N/A	N/A	N/A	74.7	48.0	56.6	N/A

Rating Indexes

CAPITAL ADVANTAGE ASR CO   C-   Fair

Major Rating Factors: Weak profitability index (0.9 on a scale of 0 to 10). Good liquidity (6.4) with sufficient resources (cash flows and marketable investments) to handle a spike in claims. Strong capitalization (7.6) based on excellent current risk-adjusted capital (severe loss scenario).

Other Rating Factors: High quality investment portfolio (7.8).

Principal Business: Comp med (84%), other (15%)

Mem Phys: 13: 19,489   **12:** 17,263   **13 MLR** 86.9%   **/ 13 Admin Exp** N/A

Enroll(000): Q2 14: 203   **13:** 215   **12:** N/A   **Med Exp PMPM:** $348

Principal Investments: Long-term bonds (93%), cash and equiv (7%)

Provider Compensation ($000): Contr fee ($549,094)

Total Member Encounters: Phys (1,323,928), non-phys (1,729,038)

Group Affiliation: Capital Blue Cross Group

Licensed in: (No states)

Address: 2500 Elmerton Ave, Harrisburg, PA 17177-9799

Phone: (717) 541-7000   **Dom State:** PA   **Commenced Bus:** January 2013

Data Date	Rating	RACR #1	RACR #2	Total Assets ($mil)	Capital ($mil)	Net Premium ($mil)	Net Income ($mil)
6-14	C-	1.86	1.55	347.3	161.8	521.7	-16.9
6-13	N/A	N/A	N/A	188.5	106.6	272.2	6.5
2013	C-	2.18	1.81	336.0	181.0	735.1	-13.8
2012	N/A	N/A	N/A	100.7	99.8	N/A	-0.1
2011	N/A	N/A	N/A	N/A	N/A	N/A	N/A
2010	N/A	N/A	N/A	N/A	N/A	N/A	N/A
2009	N/A	N/A	N/A	N/A	N/A	N/A	N/A

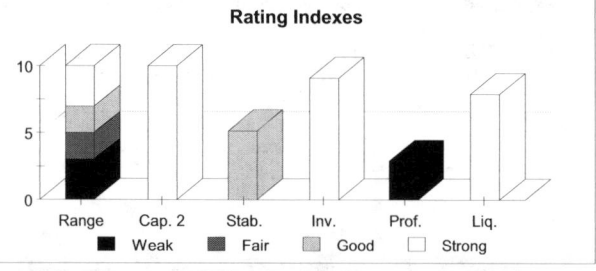

Rating Indexes

CAPITAL ADVANTAGE INS CO   C   Fair

Major Rating Factors: Fair profitability index (3.7 on a scale of 0 to 10). Fair quality investment portfolio (3.8). Strong capitalization (8.0) based on excellent current risk-adjusted capital (severe loss scenario).

Other Rating Factors: Excellent liquidity (6.9) with sufficient resources (cash flows and marketable investments) to handle a spike in claims.

Principal Business: Comp med (51%), Medicare (33%), med supp (5%), dental (3%), other (8%)

Mem Phys: 13: 19,489   **12:** 17,263   **13 MLR** 89.2%   **/ 13 Admin Exp** N/A

Enroll(000): Q2 14: 47   **13:** 63   **12:** 313   **Med Exp PMPM:** $331

Principal Investments: Affiliate common stock (47%), long-term bonds (21%), cash and equiv (5%), nonaffiliate common stock (3%), other (23%)

Provider Compensation ($000): Contr fee ($598,294)

Total Member Encounters: Phys (2,321,931), non-phys (1,328,581)

Group Affiliation: Capital Blue Cross Group

Licensed in: PA

Address: 2500 Elmerton Avenue, Harrisburg, PA 17110

Phone: (717) 541-7000   **Dom State:** PA   **Commenced Bus:** May 1982

Data Date	Rating	RACR #1	RACR #2	Total Assets ($mil)	Capital ($mil)	Net Premium ($mil)	Net Income ($mil)
6-14	C	2.17	1.81	485.3	317.5	133.2	0.9
6-13	C+	2.50	2.08	548.3	353.6	386.2	-10.8
2013	C	2.35	1.96	503.8	340.5	573.1	1.1
2012	C+	2.61	2.17	610.2	366.2	1,409.9	-0.6
2011	C+	2.89	2.41	585.2	370.9	1,369.5	39.1
2010	C	2.63	2.19	548.4	346.2	1,254.9	22.3
2009	C+	2.27	1.89	546.7	349.4	1,359.3	-2.3

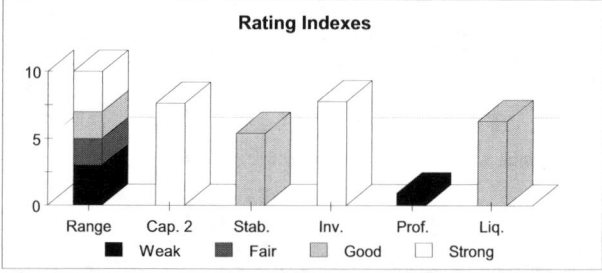

Rating Indexes

CAPITAL BLUE CROSS | B- | Good

Major Rating Factors: Fair profitability index (3.0 on a scale of 0 to 10). Fair quality investment portfolio (3.1). Strong capitalization (10.0) based on excellent current risk-adjusted capital (severe loss scenario).
Other Rating Factors: Excellent liquidity (7.6) with ample operational cash flow and liquid investments.
Principal Business: FEHB (74%), comp med (15%), med supp (10%), other (2%)
Mem Phys: 13: 749 **12:** 664 **13 MLR** 96.5% **/ 13 Admin Exp** N/A
Enroll(000): Q2 14: 98 **13:** 107 **12:** 117 **Med Exp PMPM:** $204
Principal Investments: Long-term bonds (30%), affiliate common stock (25%), nonaffiliate common stock (22%), cash and equiv (5%), real estate (3%), other (15%)
Provider Compensation ($000): Contr fee ($275,090)
Total Member Encounters: Phys (486), non-phys (521,333)
Group Affiliation: Capital Blue Cross Group
Licensed in: PA
Address: 2500 Elmerton Ave, Harrisburg, PA 17110
Phone: (717) 541-7000 **Dom State:** PA **Commenced Bus:** March 1938

Data Date	Rating	RACR #1	RACR #2	Total Assets ($mil)	Capital ($mil)	Net Premium ($mil)	Net Income ($mil)
6-14	B-	4.21	3.50	1,128.9	845.7	129.8	4.1
6-13	B-	4.31	3.60	1,093.9	830.8	146.9	5.6
2013	B-	4.26	3.55	1,119.1	857.7	289.4	10.2
2012	B-	4.28	3.57	1,061.1	824.8	270.0	3.6
2011	B-	4.58	3.81	1,035.7	810.3	265.3	27.9
2010	N/A	N/A	N/A	971.3	767.5	257.7	54.2
2009	B-	3.46	2.88	871.9	654.3	213.0	-44.2

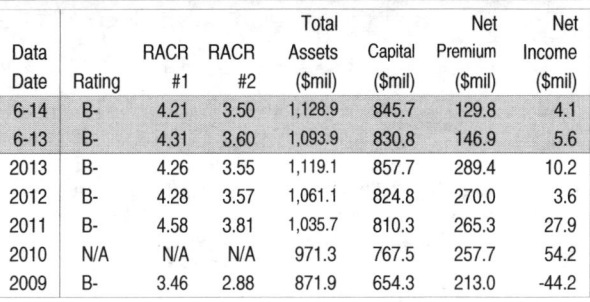

Rating Indexes

CAPITAL DISTRICT PHYSICIANS HEALTH P | B | Good

Major Rating Factors: Good overall profitability index (5.5 on a scale of 0 to 10). Good liquidity (6.8) with sufficient resources (cash flows and marketable investments) to handle a spike in claims. Fair overall results on stability tests (4.7).
Other Rating Factors: Strong capitalization index (7.9) based on excellent current risk-adjusted capital (severe loss scenario). High quality investment portfolio (7.7).
Principal Business: Comp med (42%), Medicaid (26%), Medicare (25%), other (7%)
Mem Phys: 13: 16,523 **12:** 15,125 **13 MLR** 89.2% **/ 13 Admin Exp** N/A
Enroll(000): Q2 14: 240 **13:** 233 **12:** 235 **Med Exp PMPM:** $418
Principal Investments: Long-term bonds (55%), cash and equiv (15%), nonaffiliate common stock (9%), affiliate common stock (2%), other (19%)
Provider Compensation ($000): Contr fee ($684,548), FFS ($369,687), capitation ($38,877), bonus arrang ($31,257), other ($33,909)
Total Member Encounters: Phys (1,948,651), non-phys (631,540)
Group Affiliation: CDPHP Universal Benefits Inc
Licensed in: NY
Address: 500 Patroon Creek Blvd, Albany, NY 12206-1057
Phone: (518) 641-3000 **Dom State:** NY **Commenced Bus:** July 1984

Data Date	Rating	RACR #1	RACR #2	Total Assets ($mil)	Capital ($mil)	Net Premium ($mil)	Net Income ($mil)
6-14	B	2.05	1.71	440.2	242.3	688.5	-11.0
6-13	A+	3.18	2.65	504.7	344.1	639.0	24.1
2013	B+	2.61	2.18	489.4	300.5	1,302.2	23.0
2012	A+	2.97	2.48	529.4	325.0	1,237.9	41.7
2011	A+	3.37	2.81	514.8	316.0	1,085.5	44.3
2010	A+	3.08	2.56	443.3	270.3	1,018.4	43.0
2009	A-	2.59	2.16	404.5	230.3	1,025.1	30.7

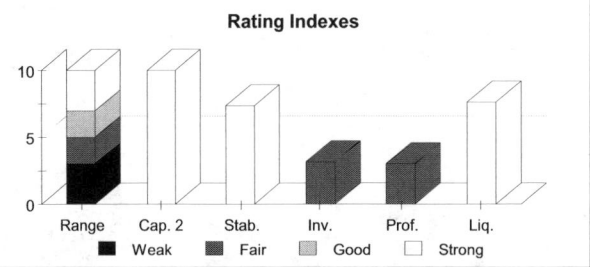

Rating Indexes

CAPITAL HEALTH PLAN INC * | A- | Excellent

Major Rating Factors: Strong capitalization index (10.0 on a scale of 0 to 10) based on excellent current risk-adjusted capital (severe loss scenario). High quality investment portfolio (8.4). Excellent overall results on stability tests (7.6) based on steady enrollment growth, averaging 3% over the past five years. Good financial strength from affiliates.
Other Rating Factors: Good overall profitability index (6.4). Good liquidity (6.7) with sufficient resources (cash flows and marketable investments) to handle a spike in claims.
Principal Business: Comp med (74%), Medicare (24%), FEHB (2%)
Mem Phys: 13: 577 **12:** 583 **13 MLR** 94.4% **/ 13 Admin Exp** N/A
Enroll(000): Q2 14: 128 **13:** 126 **12:** 125 **Med Exp PMPM:** $400
Principal Investments: Long-term bonds (71%), nonaffiliate common stock (19%), real estate (6%), cash and equiv (2%), other (2%)
Provider Compensation ($000): Contr fee ($326,828), FFS ($213,419), salary ($38,088), capitation ($28,821)
Total Member Encounters: Phys (688,756), non-phys (831,103)
Group Affiliation: Blue Cross Blue Shield Of Florida
Licensed in: FL
Address: 2140 Centerville Place, Tallahassee, FL 32308
Phone: (850) 383-3333 **Dom State:** FL **Commenced Bus:** June 1982

Data Date	Rating	RACR #1	RACR #2	Total Assets ($mil)	Capital ($mil)	Net Premium ($mil)	Net Income ($mil)
6-14	A-	8.80	7.34	468.6	371.4	336.8	-0.1
6-13	A	9.01	7.50	437.1	352.9	319.1	6.0
2013	A	8.67	7.23	450.7	365.9	640.2	13.8
2012	A	8.73	7.28	428.4	342.2	617.2	23.0
2011	A	8.25	6.88	396.0	313.1	628.1	52.6
2010	A	7.58	6.32	351.7	266.2	580.2	33.5
2009	A-	7.04	5.86	319.5	220.5	536.4	14.6

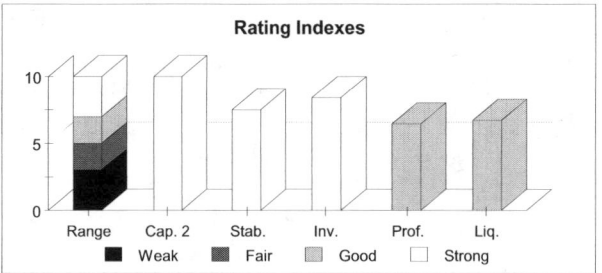

Rating Indexes

CARE 1ST HEALTH PLAN   D+   Weak

Major Rating Factors: Weak liquidity (0.0 on a scale of 0 to 10) as a spike in claims may stretch capacity. Good capitalization index (6.9) based on excellent current risk-adjusted capital (severe loss scenario). Excellent profitability (7.3).
Other Rating Factors: Excellent overall results on stability tests (7.5) based on steady enrollment growth, averaging 8% over the past five years.
Principal Business: Medicaid (66%), Medicare (34%)
Mem Phys: 13: N/A **12:** N/A **13 MLR** 88.1% **/ 13 Admin Exp** N/A
Enroll(000): Q2 14: 476 **13:** 421 **12:** 405 **Med Exp PMPM:** $205
Principal Investments ($000): Cash and equiv ($175,921)
Provider Compensation ($000): None
Total Member Encounters: N/A
Group Affiliation: None
Licensed in: CA
Address: 1000 S Fremont Ave Bldg A11 22, Alhambra, CA 91755
Phone: (323) 889-6638 **Dom State:** CA **Commenced Bus:** July 1996

Data Date	Rating	RACR #1	RACR #2	Total Assets ($mil)	Capital ($mil)	Net Premium ($mil)	Net Income ($mil)
6-14	D+	1.66	1.03	504.0	156.0	747.8	20.7
6-13	D+	1.35	0.84	303.9	132.8	527.0	2.5
2013	D+	1.43	0.89	335.2	143.3	1,130.8	13.3
2012	C-	1.29	0.80	301.1	130.4	889.4	2.5
2011	B-	1.69	1.05	304.5	129.8	726.2	12.3
2010	B-	1.23	0.76	277.3	117.6	628.6	14.8
2009	B-	1.48	0.92	261.3	102.6	665.4	11.6

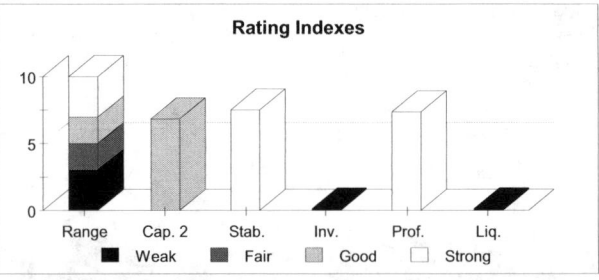

Rating Indexes

CARE IMPROVEMENT PLUS OF TEXAS INS   B   Good

Major Rating Factors: Good liquidity (6.8 on a scale of 0 to 10) with sufficient resources (cash flows and marketable investments) to handle a spike in claims. Excellent profitability (8.8). Strong capitalization (8.8) based on excellent current risk-adjusted capital (severe loss scenario).
Other Rating Factors: High quality investment portfolio (9.9).
Principal Business: Medicare (100%)
Mem Phys: 13: 29,515 **12:** 26,273 **13 MLR** 79.9% **/ 13 Admin Exp** N/A
Enroll(000): Q2 14: 90 **13:** 82 **12:** 39 **Med Exp PMPM:** $880
Principal Investments: Long-term bonds (87%), cash and equiv (13%)
Provider Compensation ($000): Contr fee ($782,763), capitation ($12,377), bonus arrang ($1,545)
Total Member Encounters: Phys (2,044,664), non-phys (482,691)
Group Affiliation: UnitedHealth Group Inc
Licensed in: IL, IN, IA, NM, NY, PA, TX
Address: 540 Oak Center Dr, San Antonio, TX 78258
Phone: (410) 625-2200 **Dom State:** TX **Commenced Bus:** April 2006

Data Date	Rating	RACR #1	RACR #2	Total Assets ($mil)	Capital ($mil)	Net Premium ($mil)	Net Income ($mil)
6-14	B	2.77	2.31	264.9	132.3	560.3	9.9
6-13	B	3.87	3.22	263.8	117.3	471.7	24.0
2013	B	2.79	2.33	230.3	133.3	990.3	42.8
2012	B	3.34	2.78	184.1	100.9	643.4	62.1
2011	B-	2.02	1.69	155.6	75.8	513.6	42.2
2010	C	1.00	0.83	90.9	33.1	361.2	2.7
2009	C-	1.14	0.95	81.4	29.2	316.6	-1.1

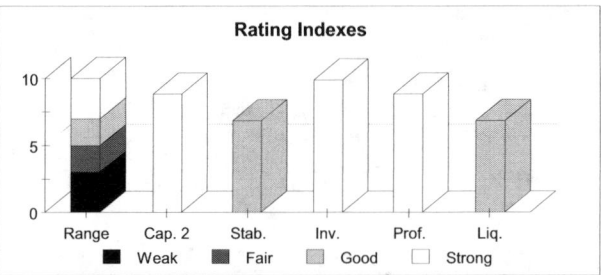

Rating Indexes

CARE IMPROVEMENT PLUS SOUTH CENTRAL   C   Fair

Major Rating Factors: Good liquidity (6.8 on a scale of 0 to 10) with sufficient resources (cash flows and marketable investments) to handle a spike in claims. Excellent profitability (7.3). Strong capitalization (8.7) based on excellent current risk-adjusted capital (severe loss scenario).
Other Rating Factors: High quality investment portfolio (9.9).
Principal Business: Medicare (100%)
Mem Phys: 13: 23,589 **12:** 22,463 **13 MLR** 81.7% **/ 13 Admin Exp** N/A
Enroll(000): Q2 14: 238 **13:** 211 **12:** 100 **Med Exp PMPM:** $888
Principal Investments: Long-term bonds (86%), cash and equiv (14%)
Provider Compensation ($000): Contr fee ($1,974,694), capitation ($40,802), bonus arrang ($3,748)
Total Member Encounters: Phys (5,242,944), non-phys (1,201,548)
Group Affiliation: UnitedHealth Group Inc
Licensed in: AR, GA, MO, SC
Address: 400 W Capitol Suite 2000, Little Rock, AR 72201
Phone: (410) 625-2200 **Dom State:** AR **Commenced Bus:** January 2007

Data Date	Rating	RACR #1	RACR #2	Total Assets ($mil)	Capital ($mil)	Net Premium ($mil)	Net Income ($mil)
6-14	C	2.75	2.29	630.4	329.1	1,444.5	16.5
6-13	C	3.85	3.21	588.2	295.4	1,168.3	30.0
2013	C	2.84	2.37	565.9	340.5	2,464.4	81.5
2012	C	4.22	3.52	502.4	324.6	1,649.2	162.3
2011	N/A	N/A	N/A	369.6	175.8	1,350.7	98.7
2010	N/A	N/A	N/A	231.2	102.0	924.0	-4.9
2009	C	N/A	N/A	183.1	72.0	745.3	-11.2

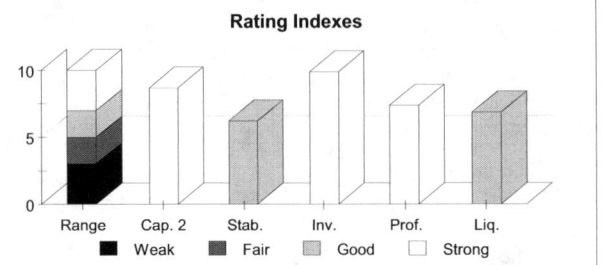

Rating Indexes

CARE IMPROVEMENT PLUS WI INS   C   Fair

Major Rating Factors: Weak profitability index (0.9 on a scale of 0 to 10). Strong capitalization (10.0) based on excellent current risk-adjusted capital (severe loss scenario). High quality investment portfolio (9.9).

Other Rating Factors: Excellent liquidity (7.5) with ample operational cash flow and liquid investments.

Principal Business: Medicare (100%)

Mem Phys: 13: 4,632 **12:** 4,428 **13 MLR** 96.9% **/ 13 Admin Exp** N/A

Enroll(000): Q2 14: 5 **13:** 4 **12:** 0 **Med Exp PMPM:** $630

Principal Investments: Cash and equiv (100%)

Provider Compensation ($000): Contr fee ($21,820), capitation ($507), bonus arrang ($22)

Total Member Encounters: Phys (66,087), non-phys (17,838)

Group Affiliation: UnitedHealth Group Inc

Licensed in: WI

Address: 411 E Wisconsin Ave Suite 2040, Milwaukee, WI 53202-4497

Phone: (410) 625-2200 **Dom State:** WI **Commenced Bus:** January 2012

Data Date	Rating	RACR #1	RACR #2	Total Assets ($mil)	Capital ($mil)	Net Premium ($mil)	Net Income ($mil)
6-14	C	17.96	14.97	16.5	9.5	21.9	1.7
6-13	C	10.40	8.66	14.4	7.9	11.4	-0.8
2013	C	14.70	12.25	16.7	7.7	24.6	-4.8
2012	C	11.53	9.61	11.9	8.8	2.0	-2.6
2011	N/A	N/A	N/A	4.6	4.4	N/A	-0.2
2010	N/A	N/A	N/A	N/A	N/A	N/A	N/A
2009	N/A	N/A	N/A	N/A	N/A	N/A	N/A

Rating Indexes

CARE N CARE INS CO INC   D   Weak

Major Rating Factors: Weak profitability index (0.9 on a scale of 0 to 10). Strong capitalization (7.0) based on excellent current risk-adjusted capital (severe loss scenario). High quality investment portfolio (9.9).

Other Rating Factors: Excellent liquidity (7.2) with ample operational cash flow and liquid investments.

Principal Business: Medicare (100%)

Mem Phys: 13: 1,770 **12:** 839 **13 MLR** 86.1% **/ 13 Admin Exp** N/A

Enroll(000): Q2 14: 9 **13:** 8 **12:** 5 **Med Exp PMPM:** $733

Principal Investments: Cash and equiv (100%)

Provider Compensation ($000): FFS ($46,240), capitation ($17,268)

Total Member Encounters: Phys (16,309)

Group Affiliation: North Texas Specialty Physicians

Licensed in: TX

Address: 1701 River Run Rd Suite 210, Fort Worth, TX 76107

Phone: (817) 810-5213 **Dom State:** TX **Commenced Bus:** May 2008

Data Date	Rating	RACR #1	RACR #2	Total Assets ($mil)	Capital ($mil)	Net Premium ($mil)	Net Income ($mil)
6-14	D	1.38	1.15	19.7	12.2	43.3	-2.6
6-13	D-	1.78	1.49	17.9	10.8	35.9	-0.8
2013	D	1.61	1.34	18.4	14.3	74.2	0.5
2012	D-	1.92	1.60	16.1	11.6	50.2	0.5
2011	D-	2.35	1.96	12.7	10.2	34.7	2.1
2010	D-	2.65	2.21	10.2	7.8	18.4	-2.8
2009	E	1.58	1.32	6.1	5.0	4.1	-3.4

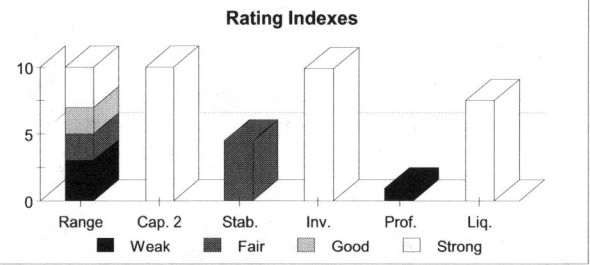

Rating Indexes

CARE WISCONSIN HEALTH PLAN INC   B   Good

Major Rating Factors: Good overall profitability index (5.9 on a scale of 0 to 10). Strong capitalization (7.6) based on excellent current risk-adjusted capital (severe loss scenario). High quality investment portfolio (9.9).

Other Rating Factors: Excellent liquidity (7.0) with sufficient resources (cash flows and marketable investments) to handle a spike in claims.

Principal Business: Medicaid (60%), Medicare (40%)

Mem Phys: 13: 6,470 **12:** N/A **13 MLR** 82.0% **/ 13 Admin Exp** N/A

Enroll(000): Q2 14: 3 **13:** 1 **12:** 1 **Med Exp PMPM:** $4,624

Principal Investments: Long-term bonds (47%), cash and equiv (47%), nonaffiliate common stock (6%)

Provider Compensation ($000): Contr fee ($61,127), FFS ($13,924), other ($570)

Total Member Encounters: Phys (83,410), non-phys (2,903,758)

Group Affiliation: Care Wisconsin First Inc

Licensed in: WI

Address: 2802 International Ln, Madison, WI 53704

Phone: (608) 240-0020 **Dom State:** WI **Commenced Bus:** January 2005

Data Date	Rating	RACR #1	RACR #2	Total Assets ($mil)	Capital ($mil)	Net Premium ($mil)	Net Income ($mil)
6-14	B	1.82	1.52	28.7	19.7	48.2	-0.5
6-13	C	2.03	1.69	27.4	19.1	45.4	3.1
2013	B	1.90	1.59	30.1	20.5	92.7	4.5
2012	C	1.63	1.36	24.6	15.4	87.4	6.6
2011	C	0.89	0.74	19.5	9.1	78.9	-3.0
2010	B	1.83	1.52	39.0	15.2	73.5	3.3
2009	B-	1.44	1.20	23.0	12.1	69.2	1.3

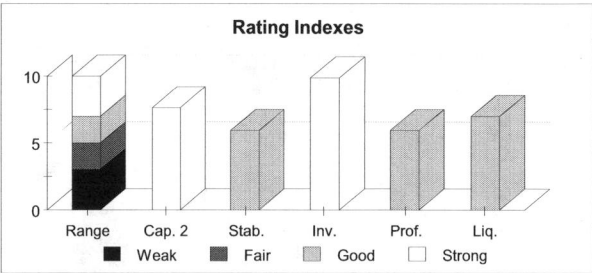

Rating Indexes

CAREFIRST BLUECHOICE INC * A+ Excellent

Major Rating Factors: Strong capitalization index (10.0 on a scale of 0 to 10) based on excellent current risk-adjusted capital (severe loss scenario). High quality investment portfolio (9.3). Excellent overall results on stability tests (7.7). **Other Rating Factors:** Excellent liquidity (6.9) with sufficient resources (cash flows and marketable investments) to handle a spike in claims. Good overall profitability index (6.8).

Principal Business: Comp med (88%), FEHB (11%)

Mem Phys: 13: 40,573 **12:** 36,747 **13 MLR** 79.3% **/ 13 Admin Exp** N/A

Enroll(000): Q2 14: 659 **13:** 570 **12:** 553 **Med Exp PMPM:** $281

Principal Investments: Long-term bonds (76%), nonaffiliate common stock (16%), cash and equiv (8%)

Provider Compensation ($000): Contr fee ($1,893,025), FFS ($19,663), capitation ($2,110)

Total Member Encounters: Phys (3,504,187), non-phys (1,897,537)

Group Affiliation: CareFirst Inc

Licensed in: DC, MD, VA

Address: 840 First Street NE, Washington, DC 20065

Phone: (410) 581-3000 **Dom State:** DC **Commenced Bus:** March 1985

Data Date	Rating	RACR #1	RACR #2	Total Assets ($mil)	Capital ($mil)	Net Premium ($mil)	Net Income ($mil)
6-14	A+	6.28	5.24	1,140.8	739.7	1,353.1	7.3
6-13	A+	6.28	5.23	1,007.1	701.2	1,183.5	34.3
2013	A+	6.23	5.19	1,043.2	733.4	2,401.3	69.2
2012	A+	6.01	5.01	992.4	671.2	2,163.6	25.9
2011	A+	6.59	5.50	1,013.9	673.1	2,006.7	40.4
2010	A+	7.02	5.85	900.1	641.1	1,992.5	166.5
2009	A+	4.94	4.11	709.2	470.7	1,876.8	48.4

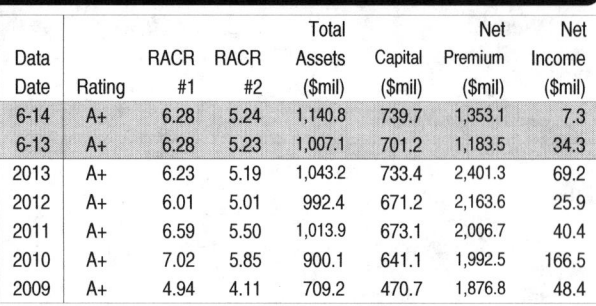

Rating Indexes

CAREFIRST OF MARYLAND INC B Good

Major Rating Factors: Good quality investment portfolio (4.9 on a scale of 0 to 10). Fair profitability index (4.5). Strong capitalization (10.0) based on excellent current risk-adjusted capital (severe loss scenario). **Other Rating Factors:** Excellent liquidity (7.0) with ample operational cash flow and liquid investments.

Principal Business: FEHB (59%), comp med (27%), med supp (7%), dental (3%), other (3%)

Mem Phys: 13: 46,263 **12:** 46,896 **13 MLR** 77.8% **/ 13 Admin Exp** N/A

Enroll(000): Q2 14: 604 **13:** 567 **12:** 563 **Med Exp PMPM:** $214

Principal Investments: Long-term bonds (32%), nonaffiliate common stock (8%), cash and equiv (4%), other (55%)

Provider Compensation ($000): Contr fee ($1,430,016), FFS ($28,104), capitation ($2,005)

Total Member Encounters: Phys (5,990,460), non-phys (2,951,684)

Group Affiliation: CareFirst Inc

Licensed in: DC, MD

Address: 10455 Mill Run Circle, Owings Mills, MD 21117

Phone: (410) 581-3000 **Dom State:** MD **Commenced Bus:** January 1985

Data Date	Rating	RACR #1	RACR #2	Total Assets ($mil)	Capital ($mil)	Net Premium ($mil)	Net Income ($mil)
6-14	B	4.11	3.42	1,389.2	543.3	964.3	-12.7
6-13	B	4.00	3.34	1,341.0	535.4	922.1	11.4
2013	B	4.21	3.51	1,387.1	556.5	1,867.3	22.2
2012	B	3.95	3.29	1,336.2	528.4	1,872.1	8.1
2011	B	3.95	3.29	1,330.4	512.0	1,891.3	39.4
2010	B	3.89	3.24	1,271.0	488.7	1,888.5	-3.6
2009	B	3.02	2.52	1,155.4	407.9	1,830.3	-1.8

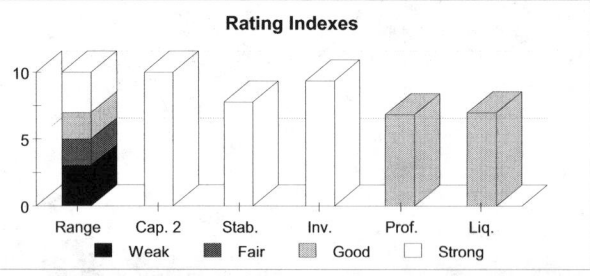

Rating Indexes

CAREMORE HEALTH PLAN * B+ Good

Major Rating Factors: Good overall results on stability tests (5.5 on a scale of 0 to 10). Rating is significantly influenced by the good financial results of WellPoint Inc. Excellent profitability (8.4). Strong capitalization index (7.9) based on excellent current risk-adjusted capital (severe loss scenario). **Other Rating Factors:** Excellent liquidity (7.2) with ample operational cash flow and liquid investments.

Principal Business: Medicare (100%)

Mem Phys: 13: N/A **12:** N/A **13 MLR** 79.1% **/ 13 Admin Exp** N/A

Enroll(000): Q2 14: 52 **13:** 53 **12:** 51 **Med Exp PMPM:** $4,193

Principal Investments ($000): Cash and equiv ($200,157)

Provider Compensation ($000): None

Total Member Encounters: N/A

Group Affiliation: WellPoint Inc

Licensed in: CA

Address: 12900 Park Plaza Dr Suite 150, Cerritos, CA 90703

Phone: (562) 741-4340 **Dom State:** CA **Commenced Bus:** November 2002

Data Date	Rating	RACR #1	RACR #2	Total Assets ($mil)	Capital ($mil)	Net Premium ($mil)	Net Income ($mil)
6-14	B+	2.79	1.75	298.1	87.2	402.8	13.7
6-13	A-	3.24	2.02	254.5	101.3	424.5	24.3
2013	A-	2.85	1.79	248.5	90.1	836.7	35.7
2012	A-	2.04	1.37	215.1	91.2	810.4	61.2
2011	C+	1.53	0.96	229.1	69.7	716.4	35.3
2010	C+	1.43	0.90	140.0	57.4	587.9	45.0
2009	C+	1.40	0.89	123.3	49.1	483.1	47.6

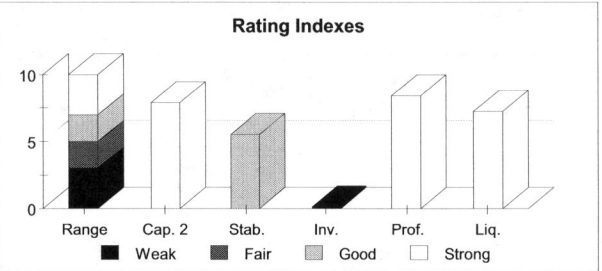

Rating Indexes

CAREMORE HEALTH PLAN OF ARIZONA INC   B-   Good

Major Rating Factors: Good liquidity (5.8 on a scale of 0 to 10) with sufficient resources (cash flows and marketable investments) to handle a spike in claims. Strong capitalization (9.1) based on excellent current risk-adjusted capital (severe loss scenario). High quality investment portfolio (9.3).
Other Rating Factors: Weak profitability index (1.9).
Principal Business: Medicare (100%)
Mem Phys: 13: N/A **12:** 1,390 **13 MLR** 82.0% **/ 13 Admin Exp** N/A
Enroll(000): Q2 14: 16 **13:** 17 **12:** 15 **Med Exp PMPM:** $845
Principal Investments: Long-term bonds (93%), cash and equiv (7%)
Provider Compensation ($000): Contr fee ($122,062), salary ($19,886), capitation ($10,273), other ($11,581)
Total Member Encounters: Phys (92,969), non-phys (33,960)
Group Affiliation: WellPoint Inc
Licensed in: (No states)
Address: 322 West Roosevelt, Phoenix, AZ 85003
Phone: (562) 622-2900 **Dom State:** AZ **Commenced Bus:** January 2010

Data Date	Rating	RACR #1	RACR #2	Total Assets ($mil)	Capital ($mil)	Net Premium ($mil)	Net Income ($mil)
6-14	B-	3.06	2.55	73.9	29.6	94.6	-2.5
6-13	B-	3.61	3.01	75.7	33.4	102.4	-3.3
2013	B-	3.22	2.69	74.6	31.4	204.0	-6.6
2012	B-	3.48	2.90	64.3	32.2	164.7	-7.4
2011	B-	2.86	2.38	42.0	18.0	97.1	-14.8
2010	U	1.21	1.01	15.6	7.6	30.4	-10.8
2009	B-	N/A	N/A	3.6	3.6	N/A	-0.1

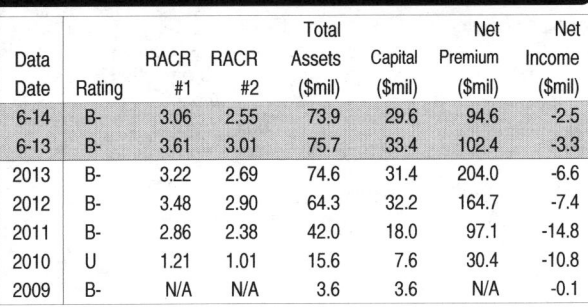

Rating Indexes
Range, Cap. 2, Stab., Inv., Prof., Liq.
■ Weak ▨ Fair ▨ Good ☐ Strong

CAREMORE HEALTH PLAN OF NEVADA   D   Weak

Major Rating Factors: Weak profitability index (0.9 on a scale of 0 to 10). Good quality investment portfolio (5.4). Good liquidity (6.8) with sufficient resources (cash flows and marketable investments) to handle a spike in claims.
Other Rating Factors: Strong capitalization (9.3) based on excellent current risk-adjusted capital (severe loss scenario).
Principal Business: Medicare (100%)
Mem Phys: 13: N/A **12:** 435 **13 MLR** 89.8% **/ 13 Admin Exp** N/A
Enroll(000): Q2 14: 6 **13:** 6 **12:** 5 **Med Exp PMPM:** $933
Principal Investments: Long-term bonds (57%), cash and equiv (43%)
Provider Compensation ($000): Contr fee ($47,812), salary ($5,280), capitation ($2,549), bonus arrang ($520), other ($4,587)
Total Member Encounters: Phys (32,392), non-phys (10,465)
Group Affiliation: WellPoint Inc
Licensed in: (No states)
Address: 12900 Park Plaza Dr Suite 150, Cerritos, CA 90703
Phone: (562) 622-2900 **Dom State:** NV **Commenced Bus:** January 2010

Data Date	Rating	RACR #1	RACR #2	Total Assets ($mil)	Capital ($mil)	Net Premium ($mil)	Net Income ($mil)
6-14	D	3.19	2.66	30.3	14.0	34.6	1.9
6-13	D	3.16	2.63	27.4	11.9	34.1	-4.2
2013	D	2.58	2.15	32.5	11.1	68.2	-11.5
2012	B-	3.49	2.91	24.7	13.2	54.5	-2.6
2011	C-	1.63	1.36	17.2	8.6	38.8	-1.4
2010	U	1.41	1.18	9.6	5.4	17.3	-7.0
2009	D	N/A	N/A	3.7	3.7	N/A	-0.1

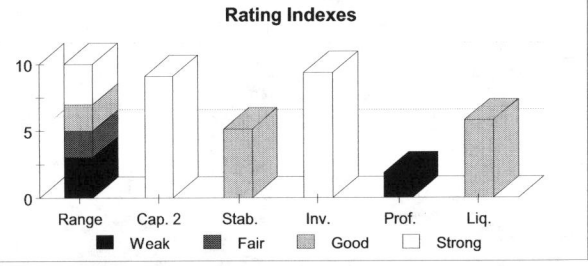

Rating Indexes
Range, Cap. 2, Stab., Inv., Prof., Liq.
■ Weak ▨ Fair ▨ Good ☐ Strong

CAREPLUS HEALTH PLANS INC   C   Fair

Major Rating Factors: Fair overall results on stability tests (2.9 on a scale of 0 to 10) based on a steep decline in capital during 2013 but steady enrollment growth, averaging 2% over the past five years. Rating is significantly influenced by the fair financial results of Humana Inc. Fair liquidity (4.9) as cash resources may not be adequate to cover a spike in claims. Excellent profitability (8.0).
Other Rating Factors: Strong capitalization index (8.8) based on excellent current risk-adjusted capital (severe loss scenario). High quality investment portfolio (8.7).
Principal Business: Medicare (100%)
Mem Phys: 13: 32,531 **12:** N/A **13 MLR** 81.8% **/ 13 Admin Exp** N/A
Enroll(000): Q2 14: 82 **13:** 70 **12:** 66 **Med Exp PMPM:** $1,213
Principal Investments: Long-term bonds (92%), cash and equiv (8%)
Provider Compensation ($000): Capitation ($387,416), contr fee ($301,828), salary ($297,849)
Total Member Encounters: Phys (1,070,074), non-phys (846,639)
Group Affiliation: Humana Inc
Licensed in: FL
Address: 11430 NW 20th St Suite 300, Doral, FL 33172
Phone: (305) 441-9400 **Dom State:** FL **Commenced Bus:** November 1986

Data Date	Rating	RACR #1	RACR #2	Total Assets ($mil)	Capital ($mil)	Net Premium ($mil)	Net Income ($mil)
6-14	C	2.83	2.36	320.7	72.1	652.1	18.6
6-13	B	1.21	1.01	324.0	45.2	604.3	26.1
2013	C+	3.78	3.15	315.9	109.5	1,204.3	66.5
2012	B	3.00	2.50	370.7	153.5	1,186.4	108.0
2011	B	1.98	1.65	351.1	110.6	1,185.2	65.5
2010	B	1.96	1.63	303.5	91.3	1,032.8	50.5
2009	B	2.05	1.70	252.1	99.8	992.5	67.5

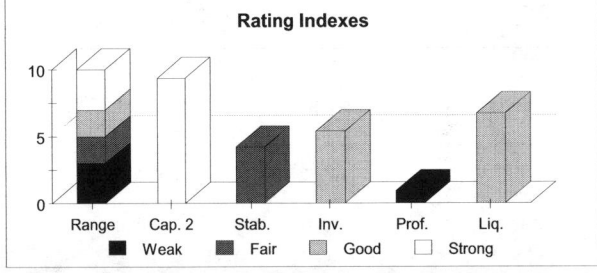

Rating Indexes
Range, Cap. 2, Stab., Inv., Prof., Liq.
■ Weak ▨ Fair ▨ Good ☐ Strong

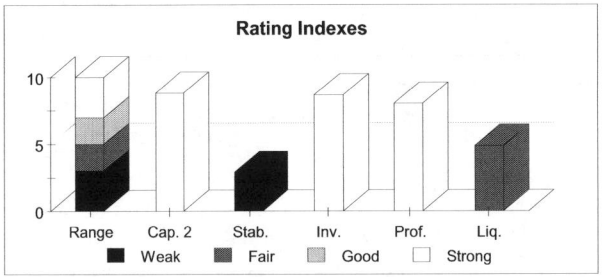

CARESOURCE *   A   Excellent

Major Rating Factors: Excellent profitability (9.1 on a scale of 0 to 10). Strong capitalization index (8.5) based on excellent current risk-adjusted capital (severe loss scenario). High quality investment portfolio (7.3).
Other Rating Factors: Excellent overall results on stability tests (8.5) based on steady enrollment growth, averaging 7% over the past five years. Good liquidity (6.9) with sufficient resources (cash flows and marketable investments) to handle a spike in claims.
Principal Business: Medicaid (99%)
Mem Phys: 13: 27,827   **12:** 26,475   **13 MLR** 84.1%   / **13 Admin Exp** N/A
Enroll(000): Q2 14: 1,114   **13:** 977   **12:** 892   **Med Exp PMPM:** $312
Principal Investments: Long-term bonds (58%), cash and equiv (35%), nonaffiliate common stock (8%)
Provider Compensation ($000): Contr fee ($2,850,369), capitation ($561,857)
Total Member Encounters: Phys (6,206,432), non-phys (3,571,601)
Group Affiliation: CareSource USA
Licensed in: OH
Address: 230 N Main St, Dayton, OH 45402
Phone: (937) 531-3300   **Dom State:** OH   **Commenced Bus:** October 1988

Data Date	Rating	RACR #1	RACR #2	Total Assets ($mil)	Capital ($mil)	Net Premium ($mil)	Net Income ($mil)
6-14	A	2.58	2.15	1,491.7	634.0	2,514.0	28.1
6-13	A-	2.83	2.36	991.1	634.1	1,918.5	99.3
2013	A	2.43	2.03	1,129.1	604.9	4,161.9	134.9
2012	A-	2.30	1.92	935.9	534.5	3,703.5	119.8
2011	A-	2.17	1.81	859.4	414.7	2,965.6	131.2
2010	A-	1.69	1.41	591.1	293.3	2,558.1	112.4
2009	B	1.00	0.84	673.4	180.8	2,440.7	34.9

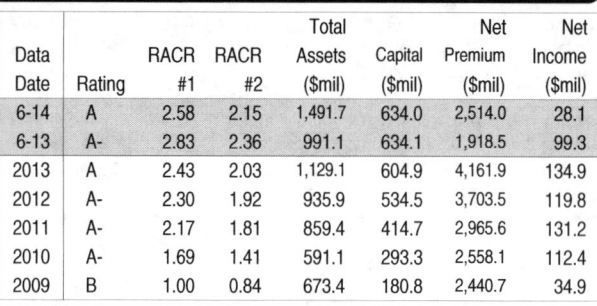

Rating Indexes

CARILION CLINIC MEDICARE RESOURCES   E+   Very Weak

Major Rating Factors: Weak profitability index (0.6 on a scale of 0 to 10). Poor capitalization (2.2) based on weak current risk-adjusted capital (moderate loss scenario). Good liquidity (6.9) with sufficient resources (cash flows and marketable investments) to handle a spike in claims.
Other Rating Factors: High quality investment portfolio (9.9).
Principal Business: Medicaid (67%), Medicare (33%)
Mem Phys: 13: 6,409   **12:** 5,485   **13 MLR** 101.8%   / **13 Admin Exp** N/A
Enroll(000): Q2 14: 11   **13:** 14   **12:** 13   **Med Exp PMPM:** $448
Principal Investments: Cash and equiv (100%)
Provider Compensation ($000): FFS ($73,728), capitation ($1,169)
Total Member Encounters: Phys (141,289), non-phys (105,848)
Group Affiliation: Carilion Clinic
Licensed in: VA
Address: 213 S Jefferson St Suite 720, Roanoke, VA 24011
Phone: (540) 224-5062   **Dom State:** VA   **Commenced Bus:** January 2010

Data Date	Rating	RACR #1	RACR #2	Total Assets ($mil)	Capital ($mil)	Net Premium ($mil)	Net Income ($mil)
6-14	E+	0.51	0.43	21.8	13.3	26.0	1.5
6-13	E	0.48	0.40	21.4	8.4	37.4	-1.6
2013	E+	0.49	0.41	28.5	12.7	76.2	-10.5
2012	E	0.32	0.27	18.0	5.9	48.9	-11.2
2011	D+	3.72	3.10	11.9	9.4	5.1	-2.0
2010	U	1.91	1.60	10.9	5.7	1.9	-10.1
2009	E+	N/A	N/A	4.1	-2.8	N/A	-6.5

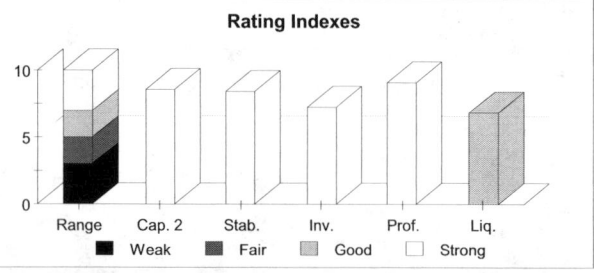

Rating Indexes

CARITEN HEALTH PLAN INC   B   Good

Major Rating Factors: Good overall results on stability tests (5.1 on a scale of 0 to 10). Rating is significantly influenced by the fair financial results of Humana Inc. Good liquidity (6.8) with sufficient resources (cash flows and marketable investments) to handle a spike in claims. Fair profitability index (4.6).
Other Rating Factors: Strong capitalization index (9.3) based on excellent current risk-adjusted capital (severe loss scenario). High quality investment portfolio (8.7).
Principal Business: Medicare (100%)
Mem Phys: 13: 60,014   **12:** N/A   **13 MLR** 79.7%   / **13 Admin Exp** N/A
Enroll(000): Q2 14: 106   **13:** 97   **12:** 90   **Med Exp PMPM:** $724
Principal Investments: Long-term bonds (100%)
Provider Compensation ($000): Contr fee ($595,266), capitation ($223,730), FFS ($4,106)
Total Member Encounters: Phys (2,027,337), non-phys (922,710)
Group Affiliation: Humana Inc
Licensed in: TN
Address: 2160 Lakeside Center Way #200, Knoxville, TN 37922
Phone: (865) 470-3993   **Dom State:** TN   **Commenced Bus:** December 1995

Data Date	Rating	RACR #1	RACR #2	Total Assets ($mil)	Capital ($mil)	Net Premium ($mil)	Net Income ($mil)
6-14	B	3.22	2.69	277.7	149.7	558.8	0.0
6-13	B-	2.83	2.36	302.8	141.0	518.0	25.9
2013	B	3.82	3.18	286.0	178.8	1,044.6	64.9
2012	B-	2.34	1.95	238.7	115.2	857.5	-18.3
2011	B-	1.44	1.20	133.2	53.7	730.7	-5.3
2010	C+	1.68	1.40	111.8	53.3	593.8	2.3
2009	B	2.59	2.16	125.2	79.0	589.0	22.9

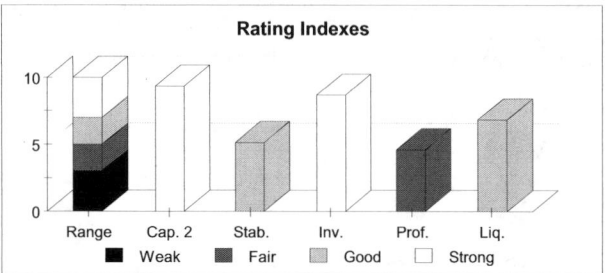

Rating Indexes

CAROLINA CARE PLAN INC B Good

Major Rating Factors: Good overall profitability index (5.6 on a scale of 0 to 10). Fair overall results on stability tests (4.2) based on a significant 82% decrease in enrollment during the period. Rating is significantly influenced by the strong financial results of Medical Mutual of Ohio Group. Strong capitalization index (10.0) based on excellent current risk-adjusted capital (severe loss scenario).

Other Rating Factors: High quality investment portfolio (9.9). Excellent liquidity (7.0) with ample operational cash flow and liquid investments.

Principal Business: Comp med (100%)

Mem Phys: 13: 30,727 **12:** 29,980 **13 MLR** 83.9% **/ 13 Admin Exp** N/A

Enroll(000): Q1 14: 0 **13:** 6 **12:** 32 **Med Exp PMPM:** $332

Principal Investments: Long-term bonds (67%), cash and equiv (33%)

Provider Compensation ($000): Contr fee ($100,868), FFS ($3,380), bonus arrang ($20)

Total Member Encounters: Phys (148,045), non-phys (121,453)

Group Affiliation: Medical Mutual of Ohio Group

Licensed in: SC

Address: 201 Executive Ctr Dr Ste 300, Columbia, SC 29210-8438

Phone: (803) 750-7400 **Dom State:** SC **Commenced Bus:** March 1985

Data Date	Rating	RACR #1	RACR #2	Total Assets ($mil)	Capital ($mil)	Net Premium ($mil)	Net Income ($mil)
3-14	B	5.05	4.21	37.0	35.1	0.0	0.6
3-13	B	3.15	2.63	53.7	29.0	35.7	2.0
2013	B	4.95	4.13	41.3	34.4	109.3	7.3
2012	B	2.95	2.46	53.1	27.1	144.8	3.1
2011	B	2.41	2.01	51.2	23.5	152.3	0.8
2010	B-	2.08	1.73	45.6	22.3	168.9	-0.3
2009	C+	1.87	1.56	50.1	21.9	179.6	-3.0

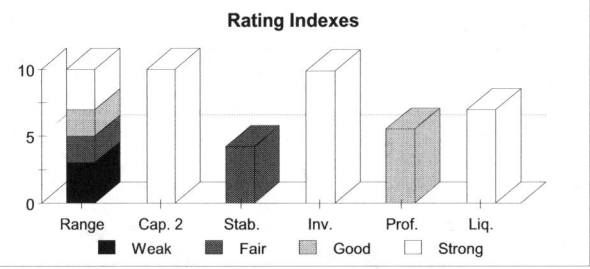

CATHOLIC SPECIAL NEEDS PLAN LLC D Weak

Major Rating Factors: Weak profitability index (2.9 on a scale of 0 to 10). Poor capitalization (1.6) based on weak current risk-adjusted capital (moderate loss scenario). Good liquidity (6.8) with sufficient resources (cash flows and marketable investments) to handle a spike in claims.

Other Rating Factors: High quality investment portfolio (9.9).

Principal Business: Medicare (100%)

Mem Phys: 13: N/A **12:** N/A **13 MLR** 87.8% **/ 13 Admin Exp** N/A

Enroll(000): Q2 14: 1 **13:** 1 **12:** 1 **Med Exp PMPM:** $2,134

Principal Investments: Cash and equiv (100%)

Provider Compensation ($000): Contr fee ($28,678), capitation ($3,912), bonus arrang ($453)

Total Member Encounters: N/A

Group Affiliation: Catholic Health Care System

Licensed in: NY

Address: 155 E 56th St, New York, NY 10022

Phone: (646) 633-4702 **Dom State:** NY **Commenced Bus:** January 2008

Data Date	Rating	RACR #1	RACR #2	Total Assets ($mil)	Capital ($mil)	Net Premium ($mil)	Net Income ($mil)
6-14	D	0.46	0.38	11.6	4.1	19.3	0.1
6-13	D	0.46	0.38	10.8	3.4	19.2	-1.6
2013	D	0.46	0.39	10.6	4.1	39.1	-0.9
2012	B	1.07	0.89	13.2	7.1	37.1	0.2
2011	C+	1.15	0.96	13.2	6.9	32.9	3.4
2010	D	0.49	0.41	11.3	4.3	28.2	1.5
2009	E+	0.31	0.26	8.5	2.7	20.1	-0.1

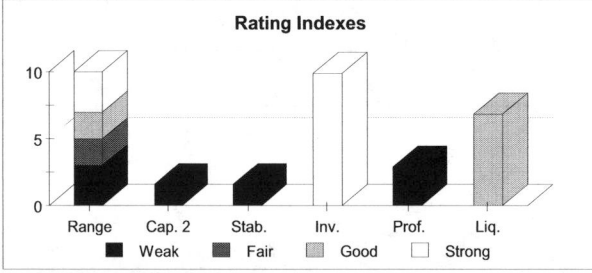

CBHNP SERVICES INC C+ Fair

Major Rating Factors: Weak profitability index (2.5 on a scale of 0 to 10). Strong capitalization (8.7) based on excellent current risk-adjusted capital (severe loss scenario). High quality investment portfolio (9.9).

Other Rating Factors: Excellent liquidity (7.1) with ample operational cash flow and liquid investments.

Principal Business: Medicaid (100%)

Mem Phys: 13: 441 **12:** 2,014 **13 MLR** 91.8% **/ 13 Admin Exp** N/A

Enroll(000): Q2 14: 18 **13:** 17 **12:** 61 **Med Exp PMPM:** $92

Principal Investments: Cash and equiv (65%), long-term bonds (35%)

Provider Compensation ($000): Contr fee ($49,115)

Total Member Encounters: Phys (8,670), non-phys (90,814)

Group Affiliation: Independence Blue Cross Inc

Licensed in: PA

Address: 8040 Carlson Rd, Harrisburg, PA 17112

Phone: (717) 671-6553 **Dom State:** PA **Commenced Bus:** June 2009

Data Date	Rating	RACR #1	RACR #2	Total Assets ($mil)	Capital ($mil)	Net Premium ($mil)	Net Income ($mil)
6-14	C+	2.74	2.28	14.6	10.4	10.3	-0.4
6-13	C	1.99	1.66	21.7	11.0	39.0	-0.2
2013	C+	2.85	2.37	14.9	10.8	48.2	-0.3
2012	C	2.03	1.69	21.0	11.2	76.2	-0.1
2011	C	1.96	1.63	23.7	11.2	82.7	0.2
2010	C	1.86	1.55	26.0	11.1	88.5	0.7
2009	U	1.42	1.19	30.2	7.3	55.9	0.5

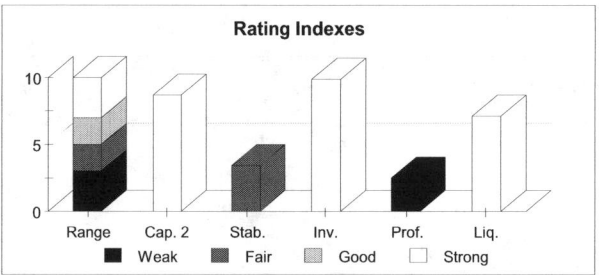

CDPHP UNIVERSAL BENEFITS INC   E   Very Weak

Major Rating Factors: Weak profitability index (0.9 on a scale of 0 to 10). Weak liquidity (0.5) as a spike in claims may stretch capacity. Fair capitalization (3.3) based on weak current risk-adjusted capital (moderate loss scenario).
Other Rating Factors: High quality investment portfolio (9.1).
Principal Business: Comp med (83%), Medicare (9%), FEHB (7%)
Mem Phys: 13: 16,516   **12:** 15,092   **13 MLR** 94.2%   **/ 13 Admin Exp** N/A
Enroll(000): Q2 14: 165   **13:** 171   **12:** 136   **Med Exp PMPM:** $340
Principal Investments: Long-term bonds (88%), cash and equiv (12%)
Provider Compensation ($000): Contr fee ($593,823), capitation ($15,093), other ($29,287)
Total Member Encounters: Phys (1,096,891), non-phys (382,657)
Group Affiliation: CDPHP Universal Benefits Inc
Licensed in: NY
Address: 500 Patroon Creek Blvd, Albany, NY 12206-1057
Phone: (518) 641-3000   **Dom State:** NY   **Commenced Bus:** January 1998

Data Date	Rating	RACR #1	RACR #2	Total Assets ($mil)	Capital ($mil)	Net Premium ($mil)	Net Income ($mil)
6-14	E	0.67	0.56	136.5	35.4	374.9	-44.2
6-13	E	0.72	0.60	92.2	26.9	332.1	-19.8
2013	E	1.52	1.26	160.6	79.3	687.6	-67.0
2012	D	0.22	0.18	84.5	15.4	537.7	-26.1
2011	B	0.74	0.62	84.6	40.9	412.7	11.1
2010	B	0.65	0.54	71.8	30.1	334.1	2.3
2009	C+	0.80	0.67	56.5	28.3	245.8	-7.9

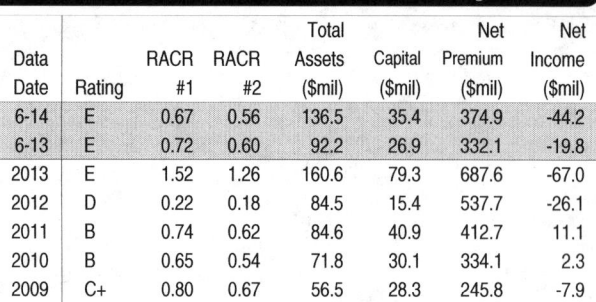

Rating Indexes

Range, Cap. 2, Stab., Inv., Prof., Liq.
■ Weak   ▨ Fair   ▧ Good   □ Strong

CELTIC INSURANCE COMPANY   C   Fair

Major Rating Factors: Fair overall results on stability tests (4.2 on a scale of 0 to 10) including fair financial strength of affiliated Centene Corp and negative cash flow from operations for 2013. Good current capitalization (6.7) based on good risk adjusted capital (severe loss scenario), although results have slipped from the excellent range during the last year. Good liquidity (6.4).
Other Rating Factors: Weak profitability (2.0). High quality investment portfolio (8.2).
Principal Business: Individual health insurance (57%) and group health insurance (42%).
Principal Investments: NonCMO investment grade bonds (79%), cash (12%), CMOs and structured securities (8%), and noninv. grade bonds (2%).
Investments in Affiliates: None
Group Affiliation: Centene Corp
Licensed in: All states except NY, PR
Commenced Business: January 1950
Address: 233 S Wacker Dr Suite 700, Chicago, IL 60606-6393
Phone: (312) 332-5401   **Domicile State:** IL   **NAIC Code:** 80799

Data Date	Rating	RACR #1	RACR #2	Total Assets ($mil)	Capital ($mil)	Net Premium ($mil)	Net Income ($mil)
6-14	C	1.22	0.96	96.7	28.5	55.4	4.6
6-13	C	1.45	1.17	88.0	44.3	68.0	0.7
2013	C	1.82	1.45	83.5	43.8	125.1	0.3
2012	C	1.39	1.13	100.0	43.7	154.7	-19.0
2011	C+	1.25	1.01	68.8	25.5	98.2	-5.3
2010	B	1.19	0.96	57.0	20.7	81.4	0.7
2009	B	1.19	0.95	58.2	19.8	79.4	2.3

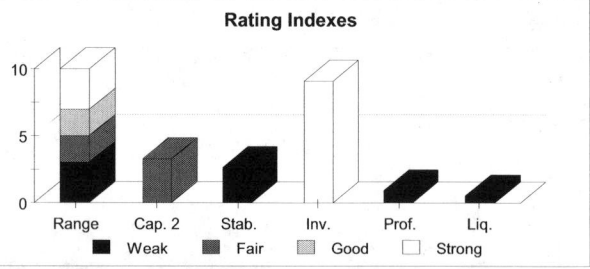

Centene Corp Composite Group Rating: C Largest Group Members	Assets ($mil)	Rating
BANKERS RESERVE LIFE INS CO OF WI	435	C-
SUPERIOR HEALTHPLAN INC	349	C
KENTUCKY SPIRIT HEALTH PLAN INC	218	C-
SUNFLOWER STATE HEALTH PLAN INC	215	D+
BUCKEYE COMMUNITY HEALTH PLAN INC	199	C+

CELTICARE HEALTH PLAN OF MA INC   C+   Fair

Major Rating Factors: Fair profitability index (3.4 on a scale of 0 to 10). Good liquidity (6.7) with sufficient resources (cash flows and marketable investments) to handle a spike in claims. Strong capitalization (10.0) based on excellent current risk-adjusted capital (severe loss scenario).
Other Rating Factors: High quality investment portfolio (9.3).
Principal Business: Comp med (100%)
Mem Phys: 13: 12,005   **12:** 11,369   **13 MLR** 95.9%   **/ 13 Admin Exp** N/A
Enroll(000): Q2 14: 35   **13:** 12   **12:** 20   **Med Exp PMPM:** $313
Principal Investments: Long-term bonds (77%), cash and equiv (23%)
Provider Compensation ($000): Contr fee ($53,949), salary ($2,334), capitation ($781), bonus arrang ($448)
Total Member Encounters: Phys (82,448), non-phys (69,150)
Group Affiliation: Centene Corp
Licensed in: MA
Address: 1380 Soldiers Field Rd, Brighton, MA 02135
Phone: (314) 725-4706   **Dom State:** MA   **Commenced Bus:** May 2009

Data Date	Rating	RACR #1	RACR #2	Total Assets ($mil)	Capital ($mil)	Net Premium ($mil)	Net Income ($mil)
6-14	C+	4.45	3.71	49.4	18.1	102.6	3.4
6-13	B-	1.74	1.45	21.0	13.0	34.8	0.3
2013	C	3.00	2.50	18.2	11.6	54.4	-1.5
2012	B-	1.69	1.41	32.2	13.2	119.8	0.1
2011	B-	1.55	1.29	34.8	11.1	106.5	-0.1
2010	C-	1.65	1.38	29.8	8.1	78.1	-0.1
2009	U	3.40	2.83	14.5	5.5	11.6	-0.8

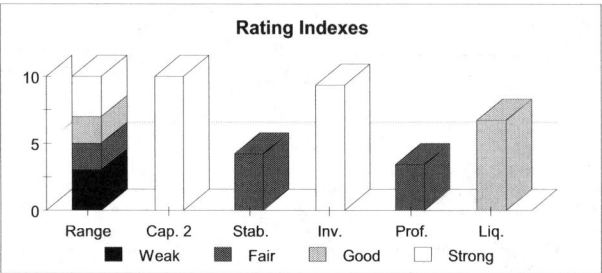

Rating Indexes

Range, Cap. 2, Stab., Inv., Prof., Liq.
■ Weak   ▨ Fair   ▧ Good   □ Strong

CENTRAL HEALTH PLAN OF CALIFORNIA   E+   Very Weak

Major Rating Factors: Poor capitalization index (0.0 on a scale of 0 to 10) based on weak current risk-adjusted capital (severe loss scenario). Weak liquidity (0.0) as a spike in claims may stretch capacity. Fair overall results on stability tests (3.8) based on poor risk diversification due to the company's size.
Other Rating Factors: Excellent overall profitability index (6.9).
Principal Business: Medicare (100%)
Mem Phys: 13: N/A   **12:** N/A   **13 MLR** 86.3%   / **13 Admin Exp** N/A
Enroll(000): Q2 14: 17   **13:** 13   **12:** 13   **Med Exp PMPM:** $733
Principal Investments ($000): Cash and equiv ($18,284)
Provider Compensation ($000): None
Total Member Encounters: N/A
Group Affiliation: AHMC Central Health LLC
Licensed in: CA
Address: 1051 Pakrview Dr Suite 120, Covina, CA 91724
Phone: (626) 388-2390   **Dom State:** CA   **Commenced Bus:** October 2004

Data Date	Rating	RACR #1	RACR #2	Total Assets ($mil)	Capital ($mil)	Net Premium ($mil)	Net Income ($mil)
6-14	E+	0.11	0.07	19.7	7.9	76.1	-0.9
6-13	E+	0.17	0.11	23.9	7.9	59.0	0.4
2013	E+	0.18	0.11	25.0	8.8	128.6	1.2
2012	E+	0.14	0.09	27.5	7.6	127.2	4.4
2011	E+	N/A	N/A	21.8	4.2	105.1	4.0
2010	E+	0.22	0.13	13.5	3.7	59.2	2.2
2009	E+	0.22	0.13	10.4	1.7	41.7	-0.1

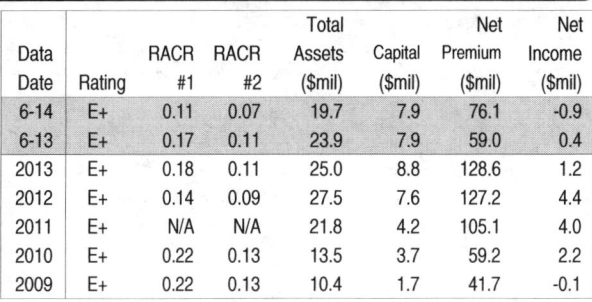

Rating Indexes

Range   Cap. 2   Stab.   Inv.   Prof.   Liq.
■ Weak   ▨ Fair   ▧ Good   □ Strong

CENTRAL STATES HEALTH & LIFE COMPANY OF OMAHA *   A-   Excellent

Major Rating Factors: Good quality investment portfolio (5.8 on a scale of 0 to 10) despite mixed results such as: minimal exposure to mortgages and substantial holdings of BBB bonds but minimal holdings in junk bonds. Good overall results on stability tests (6.9). Strengths that enhance stability include excellent operational trends and excellent risk diversification. Strong capitalization (9.7) based on excellent risk adjusted capital (severe loss scenario).
Other Rating Factors: Excellent profitability (7.9). Excellent liquidity (8.0).
Principal Business: Credit life insurance (51%), credit health insurance (33%), individual health insurance (12%), group health insurance (2%), and individual life insurance (2%).
Principal Investments: NonCMO investment grade bonds (44%), CMOs and structured securities (26%), common & preferred stock (12%), mortgages in good standing (4%), and misc. investments (15%).
Investments in Affiliates: 6%
Group Affiliation: Central States Group
Licensed in: All states except NY
Commenced Business: June 1932
Address: 1212 N 96th St, Omaha, NE 68114
Phone: (402) 397-1111   **Domicile State:** NE   **NAIC Code:** 61751

Data Date	Rating	RACR #1	RACR #2	Total Assets ($mil)	Capital ($mil)	Net Premium ($mil)	Net Income ($mil)
6-14	A-	3.97	2.83	405.9	121.2	38.3	2.4
6-13	A-	4.06	2.89	382.0	112.5	36.8	1.7
2013	A-	3.98	2.85	395.5	119.6	77.1	0.2
2012	A-	4.26	3.06	372.0	111.0	72.2	3.8
2011	A-	4.12	2.95	343.8	104.5	61.8	8.6
2010	B	4.12	2.91	331.4	102.3	65.9	5.7
2009	B	4.33	3.08	329.7	98.1	57.8	4.2

Adverse Trends in Operations

Decrease in premium volume from 2010 to 2011 (6%)

CENTRAL STATES INDEMNITY CO OF OMAHA *   B+   Good

Major Rating Factors: Good overall results on stability tests (5.3 on a scale of 0 to 10) despite potential drain of affiliation with Berkshire-Hathaway. Strong long-term capitalization index (9.7) based on excellent current risk adjusted capital (severe and moderate loss scenarios). Moreover, capital levels have been consistent in recent years.
Other Rating Factors: Ample reserve history (7.7) that can protect against increases in claims costs. Excellent profitability (8.1) with operating gains in each of the last five years. Superior liquidity (9.1) with ample operational cash flow and liquid investments.
Principal Business: Other accident & health (41%), inland marine (32%), aggregate write-ins for other lines of business (15%), credit accident & health (6%), aircraft (5%), and group accident & health (1%).
Principal Investments: Misc. investments (63%), investment grade bonds (36%), and cash (1%).
Investments in Affiliates: 4%
Group Affiliation: Berkshire-Hathaway
Licensed in: All states, the District of Columbia and Puerto Rico
Commenced Business: June 1977
Address: 1212 N 96th St, Omaha, NE 68114
Phone: (402) 997-8000   **Domicile State:** NE   **NAIC Code:** 34274

Data Date	Rating	RACR #1	RACR #2	Loss Ratio %	Total Assets ($mil)	Capital ($mil)	Net Premium ($mil)	Net Income ($mil)
6-14	B+	4.28	2.75	N/A	424.9	355.6	24.4	2.5
6-13	B+	4.15	2.57	N/A	368.2	311.4	20.2	5.5
2013	B+	4.34	2.79	36.2	412.3	346.0	43.0	17.7
2012	B+	4.34	2.69	18.3	335.1	285.5	32.2	13.1
2011	B+	4.37	2.58	10.3	287.0	249.6	29.8	12.8
2010	B+	4.38	2.57	20.2	272.9	235.2	33.6	9.7
2009	B+	4.14	2.45	29.9	252.4	216.5	40.7	8.4

Berkshire-Hathaway Composite Group Rating: B- Largest Group Members	Assets ($mil)	Rating
NATIONAL INDEMNITY CO	151912	B-
GOVERNMENT EMPLOYEES INS CO	25779	B+
COLUMBIA INS CO	19013	B-
GENERAL REINSURANCE CORP	16220	B-
BERKSHIRE HATHAWAY LIFE INS CO OF NE	13768	C+

CENTRAL UNITED LIFE INSURANCE COMPANY   C   Fair

Major Rating Factors: Fair capitalization for the current period (3.5 on a scale of 0 to 10) based on fair risk adjusted capital (severe loss scenario) reflecting some improvement over results in 2009. Fair overall results on stability tests (3.5) including weak risk adjusted capital in prior years, negative cash flow from operations for 2013. Good quality investment portfolio (5.2).
Other Rating Factors: Good overall profitability (6.7). Good liquidity (6.6).
Principal Business: Individual health insurance (79%), reinsurance (12%), group health insurance (5%), and individual life insurance (4%).
Principal Investments: Common & preferred stock (41%), nonCMO investment grade bonds (41%), real estate (8%), cash (5%), and misc. investments (4%).
Investments in Affiliates: 41%
Group Affiliation: Harris Insurance Holdings Inc
Licensed in: All states except AK, CT, DC, DE, HI, MI, NJ, NY, RI, VT, PR
Commenced Business: September 1963
Address: 2727 Allen Parkway,6th Floor, Houston, TX 77019-2115
Phone: (713) 529-0045 **Domicile State:** AR **NAIC Code:** 61883

Data Date	Rating	RACR #1	RACR #2	Total Assets ($mil)	Capital ($mil)	Net Premium ($mil)	Net Income ($mil)
6-14	C	0.61	0.56	303.5	79.1	43.0	2.8
6-13	C	0.81	0.66	308.7	74.0	44.5	3.1
2013	C	0.59	0.54	307.2	76.6	88.8	3.8
2012	C	0.77	0.67	302.0	59.7	92.0	8.8
2011	D+	0.70	0.61	312.5	56.6	97.6	3.9
2010	D+	0.67	0.59	321.8	53.9	102.6	12.1
2009	D+	0.53	0.47	332.6	44.6	98.2	4.2

Risk-Adjusted Capital Ratio #2
(Severe Loss Scenario)

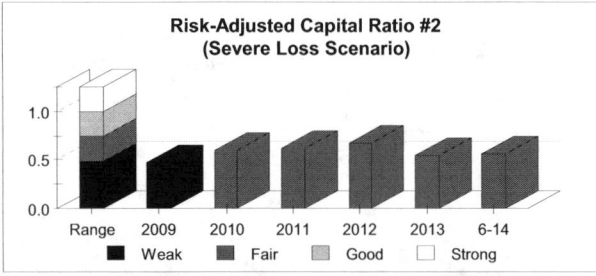

Range 2009 2010 2011 2012 2013 6-14
■ Weak ■ Fair ▨ Good ☐ Strong

CENTRE LIFE INSURANCE COMPANY   B-   Good

Major Rating Factors: Good quality investment portfolio (6.8 on a scale of 0 to 10) with no exposure to mortgages and minimal holdings in junk bonds. Fair overall results on stability tests (4.9) including fair financial strength of affiliated Zurich Financial Services Group and negative cash flow from operations for 2013. Strong capitalization (9.5) based on excellent risk adjusted capital (severe loss scenario).
Other Rating Factors: Excellent profitability (8.3) despite modest operating losses during 2009. Excellent liquidity (8.7).
Principal Business: Reinsurance (61%) and individual health insurance (39%).
Principal Investments: NonCMO investment grade bonds (84%) and CMOs and structured securities (16%).
Investments in Affiliates: None
Group Affiliation: Zurich Financial Services Group
Licensed in: All states except PR
Commenced Business: October 1927
Address: 1600 McConnor Parkway, Schaumburg, IL 60196-6801
Phone: (847) 874-7400 **Domicile State:** MA **NAIC Code:** 80896

Data Date	Rating	RACR #1	RACR #2	Total Assets ($mil)	Capital ($mil)	Net Premium ($mil)	Net Income ($mil)
6-14	B-	4.11	2.67	1,928.5	100.2	0.0	-0.7
6-13	B-	4.21	2.76	1,807.8	99.2	0.0	-0.4
2013	B-	4.13	2.67	1,927.7	101.2	0.0	1.9
2012	C+	4.15	2.72	1,815.1	98.8	0.0	0.3
2011	C+	4.18	2.78	1,811.6	100.5	-1.5	0.3
2010	C+	3.64	2.01	1,841.2	89.2	3.1	16.2
2009	C+	2.98	1.35	1,969.0	77.1	10.2	-4.8

Zurich Financial Services Group
Composite Group Rating: C
Largest Group Members

Largest Group Members	Assets ($mil)	Rating
ZURICH AMERICAN INS CO	30184	C+
ZURICH AMERICAN LIFE INS CO	12969	C
FARMERS NEW WORLD LIFE INS CO	7141	B-
CENTRE LIFE INS CO	1928	B-
FARMERS REINS CO	1400	B-

CENTURION LIFE INSURANCE COMPANY   D   Weak

Major Rating Factors: Weak profitability (1.5 on a scale of 0 to 10). Excellent expense controls. Weak overall results on stability tests (1.5) including weak results on operational trends. Good quality investment portfolio (6.5) despite mixed results such as: no exposure to mortgages and large holdings of BBB rated bonds but no exposure to junk bonds.
Other Rating Factors: Good liquidity (6.5). Strong capitalization (9.9) based on excellent risk adjusted capital (severe loss scenario).
Principal Business: Reinsurance (99%).
Principal Investments: CMOs and structured securities (55%), nonCMO investment grade bonds (33%), noninv. grade bonds (8%), common & preferred stock (3%), and cash (1%).
Investments in Affiliates: None
Group Affiliation: Wells Fargo Group
Licensed in: All states except ME, NY, VT, PR
Commenced Business: July 1956
Address: 206 Eighth Street, Des Moines, IA 50309
Phone: (515) 243-2131 **Domicile State:** IA **NAIC Code:** 62383

Data Date	Rating	RACR #1	RACR #2	Total Assets ($mil)	Capital ($mil)	Net Premium ($mil)	Net Income ($mil)
3-14	D	4.98	2.92	1,211.1	406.3	64.5	8.5
3-13	D	11.68	5.95	1,183.3	372.6	33.0	-259.3
2013	D	4.92	2.88	1,209.0	397.3	204.6	-227.0
2012	C+	20.93	10.33	1,475.0	599.9	13.7	39.4
2011	C+	16.61	8.13	1,472.9	545.1	23.8	47.0
2010	B	30.68	15.76	1,965.1	1,066.4	81.1	41.6
2009	B-	29.31	15.09	1,887.8	1,023.4	202.2	37.5

Adverse Trends in Operations

Decrease in capital during 2013 (34%)
Decrease in premium volume from 2011 to 2012 (43%)
Decrease in premium volume from 2010 to 2011 (71%)
Decrease in capital during 2011 (49%)
Decrease in premium volume from 2009 to 2010 (60%)

CHA HMO INC   C   Fair

Major Rating Factors: Weak profitability index (1.1 on a scale of 0 to 10). Good overall results on stability tests (5.6). Rating is significantly influenced by the fair financial results of Humana Inc. Good liquidity (6.9) with sufficient resources (cash flows and marketable investments) to handle a spike in claims.
Other Rating Factors: Strong capitalization index (10.0) based on excellent current risk-adjusted capital (severe loss scenario). High quality investment portfolio (8.9).
Principal Business: Medicare (99%)
Mem Phys: 13: 26,294 **12:** N/A **13 MLR** 92.5% **/ 13 Admin Exp** N/A
Enroll(000): Q2 14: 5 **13:** 4 **12:** N/A **Med Exp PMPM:** $471
Principal Investments: Long-term bonds (92%), cash and equiv (8%)
Provider Compensation ($000): Contr fee ($20,007), capitation ($1,090), FFS ($29)
Total Member Encounters: Phys (52,652), non-phys (28,182)
Group Affiliation: Humana Inc
Licensed in: IN, KY
Address: 500 W Main St, Louisville, KY 40202-2946
Phone: (502) 580-1000 **Dom State:** KY **Commenced Bus:** July 1995

Data Date	Rating	RACR #1	RACR #2	Total Assets ($mil)	Capital ($mil)	Net Premium ($mil)	Net Income ($mil)
6-14	C	9.56	7.96	34.0	29.0	16.7	-0.3
6-13	N/A	N/A	N/A	34.3	31.5	12.7	-0.1
2013	C	9.65	8.04	33.3	29.2	25.8	-2.6
2012	N/A	N/A	N/A	31.6	31.5	N/A	0.9
2011	N/A	N/A	N/A	30.9	30.8	N/A	0.7
2010	N/A	N/A	N/A	28.2	27.9	N/A	0.8
2009	C	N/A	N/A	26.8	26.8	0.4	0.5

Rating Indexes

CHILDRENS COMMUNITY HEALTH PLAN INC   C-   Fair

Major Rating Factors: Weak profitability index (1.9 on a scale of 0 to 10). Good capitalization (6.6) based on good current risk-adjusted capital (severe loss scenario). Good liquidity (6.9) with sufficient resources (cash flows and marketable investments) to handle a spike in claims.
Other Rating Factors: High quality investment portfolio (9.9).
Principal Business: Medicaid (100%)
Mem Phys: 13: 10,832 **12:** 10,250 **13 MLR** 94.9% **/ 13 Admin Exp** N/A
Enroll(000): Q2 14: 131 **13:** 136 **12:** 70 **Med Exp PMPM:** $180
Principal Investments: Cash and equiv (77%), long-term bonds (23%)
Provider Compensation ($000): Contr fee ($154,821), capitation ($9,926), bonus arrang ($14), other ($74,396)
Total Member Encounters: Phys (378,018), non-phys (69,502)
Group Affiliation: Childrens Hospital and Health System
Licensed in: WI
Address: 9000 W Wisconsin Ave, Milwaukee, WI 53226
Phone: (800) 482-8010 **Dom State:** WI **Commenced Bus:** January 2010

Data Date	Rating	RACR #1	RACR #2	Total Assets ($mil)	Capital ($mil)	Net Premium ($mil)	Net Income ($mil)
6-14	C-	1.17	0.97	58.9	25.2	148.9	5.2
6-13	C-	0.82	0.68	38.1	7.5	109.9	-4.7
2013	C-	0.93	0.77	67.0	20.0	274.9	-2.0
2012	C-	0.99	0.83	27.8	9.0	103.6	-3.3
2011	C	0.95	0.79	20.2	7.6	96.9	-7.6
2010	C-	0.94	0.78	33.1	5.5	84.8	0.1
2009	N/A	N/A	N/A	N/A	N/A	N/A	N/A

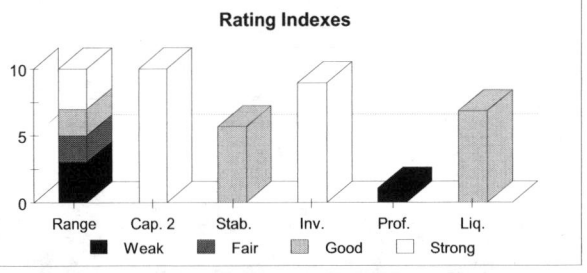

Rating Indexes

CHINESE COMMUNITY HEALTH PLAN   B-   Good

Major Rating Factors: Good overall profitability index (6.5 on a scale of 0 to 10). Good overall results on stability tests (6.0) despite fair risk diversification due to the company's size but steady enrollment growth, averaging 3% over the past five years. Strong capitalization index (7.8) based on excellent current risk-adjusted capital (severe loss scenario).
Other Rating Factors: Excellent liquidity (7.3) with ample operational cash flow and liquid investments.
Principal Business: Medicare (79%)
Mem Phys: 13: N/A **12:** N/A **13 MLR** 83.9% **/ 13 Admin Exp** N/A
Enroll(000): Q2 14: 28 **13:** 16 **12:** 15 **Med Exp PMPM:** $588
Principal Investments ($000): Cash and equiv ($16,720)
Provider Compensation ($000): None
Total Member Encounters: N/A
Group Affiliation: Chinese Hospital Association
Licensed in: CA
Address: 445 Grant Avenue Suite 700, San Francisco, CA 94108
Phone: (415) 955-8800 **Dom State:** CA **Commenced Bus:** August 1987

Data Date	Rating	RACR #1	RACR #2	Total Assets ($mil)	Capital ($mil)	Net Premium ($mil)	Net Income ($mil)
6-14	B-	2.58	1.69	61.0	32.9	84.8	5.5
6-13	B-	2.06	1.35	36.1	24.8	59.6	2.0
2013	B-	2.15	1.41	37.2	27.4	128.1	4.6
2012	B-	1.85	1.22	33.5	22.8	115.8	4.1
2011	B-	1.65	1.07	28.0	18.7	111.1	2.8
2010	B-	1.52	0.98	26.6	15.9	108.1	-0.9
2009	B-	1.65	1.05	36.0	16.8	99.8	1.4

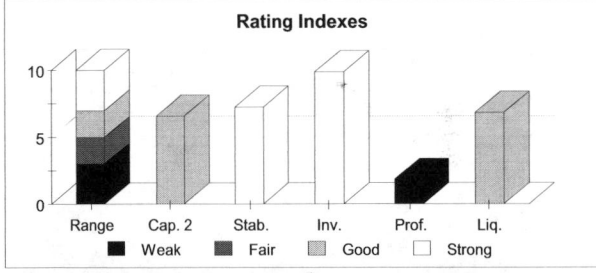

Rating Indexes

CHOICE PHYSICIANS NETWORK — D+ — Weak

Major Rating Factors: Fair capitalization index (3.9 on a scale of 0 to 10) based on weak current risk-adjusted capital (moderate loss scenario). Fair overall results on stability tests (3.4) in spite of healthy premium and capital growth during 2013. Good liquidity (6.9) with sufficient resources (cash flows and marketable investments) to handle a spike in claims.

Other Rating Factors: Excellent profitability (8.9).

Principal Business: Managed care (100%)

Mem Phys: 13: N/A **12:** N/A **13 MLR** 92.3% **/ 13 Admin Exp** N/A

Enroll(000): Q2 14: 7 **13:** 6 **12:** 6 **Med Exp PMPM:** $734

Principal Investments ($000): Cash and equiv ($5,108)

Provider Compensation ($000): None

Total Member Encounters: N/A

Group Affiliation: None

Licensed in: CA

Address: 18564 Highway Suite 108, Apple Valley, CA 92307

Phone: (626) 229-9828 **Dom State:** CA **Commenced Bus:** September 2009

Data Date	Rating	RACR #1	RACR #2	Total Assets ($mil)	Capital ($mil)	Net Premium ($mil)	Net Income ($mil)
6-14	D+	0.64	0.39	8.4	3.3	28.2	0.2
6-13	D	0.71	0.43	7.4	3.2	22.7	0.6
2013	D+	0.59	0.36	8.4	3.1	50.0	2.4
2012	D-	0.58	0.35	6.4	2.6	43.4	0.2
2011	N/A	N/A	N/A	7.2	2.4	41.2	0.5
2010	E+	0.53	0.33	7.0	2.0	32.0	1.0
2009	D+	N/A	N/A	1.0	1.0	N/A	N/A

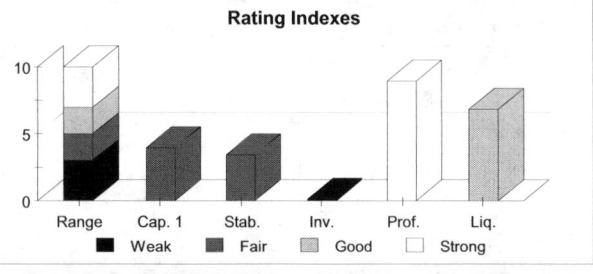

Rating Indexes — Range, Cap. 1, Stab., Inv., Prof., Liq. — Weak, Fair, Good, Strong

CHRISTIAN FIDELITY LIFE INSURANCE COMPANY — B- — Good

Major Rating Factors: Good overall results on stability tests (5.3 on a scale of 0 to 10) despite fair financial strength of affiliated Amerco Corp. Other stability subfactors include good operational trends and good risk diversification. Strong overall capitalization (8.4) based on excellent risk adjusted capital (severe loss scenario). Nevertheless, capital levels have fluctuated during prior years. High quality investment portfolio (7.8).

Other Rating Factors: Excellent profitability (7.1) with operating gains in each of the last five years. Excellent liquidity (7.1).

Principal Business: Individual health insurance (88%), group health insurance (9%), and individual life insurance (3%).

Principal Investments: NonCMO investment grade bonds (87%), mortgages in good standing (5%), CMOs and structured securities (5%), noninv. grade bonds (1%), and misc. investments (2%).

Investments in Affiliates: None

Group Affiliation: Amerco Corp

Licensed in: AL, AZ, AR, CO, FL, GA, ID, IL, IN, KS, KY, LA, MS, MO, MT, NE, NV, NM, ND, OH, OK, OR, SC, SD, TN, TX, UT, VA, WA, WV, WY

Commenced Business: December 1935

Address: 2721 N Central Ave, Phoenix, AZ 85004-1172

Phone: (972) 937-4420 **Domicile State:** TX **NAIC Code:** 61859

Data Date	Rating	RACR #1	RACR #2	Total Assets ($mil)	Capital ($mil)	Net Premium ($mil)	Net Income ($mil)
6-14	B-	2.60	1.92	78.6	32.8	22.4	4.0
6-13	B-	2.33	1.74	81.7	31.7	25.0	3.9
2013	B-	2.20	1.63	75.4	28.8	48.9	9.6
2012	B-	2.00	1.49	77.9	28.0	54.3	8.7
2011	B	1.64	1.34	85.3	36.2	49.1	8.5
2010	B-	1.49	1.22	83.2	32.8	52.0	4.3
2009	B-	1.87	1.52	88.1	39.8	53.9	6.4

Amerco Corp
Composite Group Rating: C
Largest Group Members

Largest Group Members	Assets ($mil)	Rating
OXFORD LIFE INS CO	1098	B-
REPWEST INS CO	285	D-
CHRISTIAN FIDELITY LIFE INS CO	75	B-
NORTH AMERICAN INS CO	22	C
ARCOA RRG INC	10	E

CHRISTUS HEALTH PLAN — B- — Good

Major Rating Factors: Good overall profitability index (6.4 on a scale of 0 to 10). Strong capitalization (9.1) based on excellent current risk-adjusted capital (severe loss scenario). High quality investment portfolio (9.9).

Other Rating Factors: Excellent liquidity (8.0) with ample operational cash flow and liquid investments.

Principal Business: Medicaid (100%)

Mem Phys: 13: 1,091 **12:** 816 **13 MLR** 77.4% **/ 13 Admin Exp** N/A

Enroll(000): Q2 14: 23 **13:** 8 **12:** 10 **Med Exp PMPM:** $189

Principal Investments: Cash and equiv (100%)

Provider Compensation ($000): FFS ($22,303), capitation ($719)

Total Member Encounters: Phys (214,779), non-phys (23,787)

Group Affiliation: CHRISTUS Health Group

Licensed in: TX

Address: 100 NE Loop 410 Suite 800, San Antonio, TX 78216

Phone: (469) 282-2000 **Dom State:** TX **Commenced Bus:** March 2012

Data Date	Rating	RACR #1	RACR #2	Total Assets ($mil)	Capital ($mil)	Net Premium ($mil)	Net Income ($mil)
6-14	B-	3.07	2.56	18.9	15.0	10.5	-0.7
6-13	B-	4.77	3.98	24.1	15.2	15.0	2.1
2013	B-	3.91	3.26	18.5	14.9	29.7	1.7
2012	C-	4.12	3.43	21.9	13.1	17.9	0.6
2011	N/A	N/A	N/A	12.5	12.5	N/A	N/A
2010	N/A	N/A	N/A	N/A	N/A	N/A	N/A
2009	N/A	N/A	N/A	N/A	N/A	N/A	N/A

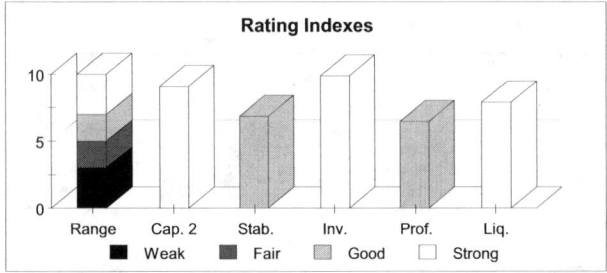

Rating Indexes — Range, Cap. 2, Stab., Inv., Prof., Liq. — Weak, Fair, Good, Strong

CIGNA HEALTH & LIFE INSURANCE COMPANY

B   **Good**

Major Rating Factors: Good overall results on stability tests (5.6 on a scale of 0 to 10) despite excessive premium growth. Other stability subfactors include good operational trends and excellent risk diversification. Good liquidity (6.5) with sufficient resources to handle a spike in claims. Fair quality investment portfolio (3.7).

Other Rating Factors: Strong capitalization (7.1) based on excellent risk adjusted capital (severe loss scenario). Excellent profitability (9.6) with operating gains in each of the last five years.

Principal Business: Group health insurance (99%) and reinsurance (1%).

Principal Investments: NonCMO investment grade bonds (60%), mortgages in good standing (14%), noninv. grade bonds (9%), common & preferred stock (8%), and misc. investments (9%).

Investments in Affiliates: 15%
Group Affiliation: CIGNA Corp
Licensed in: All states except PR
Commenced Business: February 1964
Address: 900 Cottage Grove Rd, Hartford, CT 06152
Phone: (303) 729-7462 **Domicile State:** CT **NAIC Code:** 67369

Data Date	Rating	RACR #1	RACR #2	Total Assets ($mil)	Capital ($mil)	Net Premium ($mil)	Net Income ($mil)
6-14	B	1.84	1.44	5,195.8	2,103.0	4,772.6	456.1
6-13	B	1.84	1.47	3,214.2	1,242.5	3,017.9	231.1
2013	B	1.68	1.37	4,139.3	1,713.2	6,456.2	489.1
2012	B	1.92	1.66	1,681.4	1,017.9	1,883.9	300.7
2011	B	10.20	6.05	713.4	543.4	296.6	122.8
2010	B	9.56	8.61	65.2	51.0	23.6	12.1
2009	B	9.19	8.27	50.0	42.0	26.9	17.9

Adverse Trends in Operations

Change in asset mix during 2013 (5%)
Change in asset mix during 2011 (10.1%)
Decrease in premium volume from 2009 to 2010 (12%)
Change in asset mix during 2010 (6.8%)

CIGNA HEALTHCARE OF ARIZONA INC

C   **Fair**

Major Rating Factors: Fair overall results on stability tests (3.7 on a scale of 0 to 10) based on a steep decline in capital during 2013. Rating is significantly influenced by the good financial results of CIGNA Corp. Fair liquidity (4.4) as cash resources may not be adequate to cover a spike in claims. Weak profitability index (0.8).

Other Rating Factors: Good quality investment portfolio (5.8). Strong capitalization index (7.5) based on excellent current risk-adjusted capital (severe loss scenario).

Principal Business: Medicare (86%), comp med (18%)
Mem Phys: 13: 14,999 **12:** 14,155 **13 MLR** 95.8% **/ 13 Admin Exp** N/A
Enroll(000): Q2 14: 55 **13:** 57 **12:** 54 **Med Exp PMPM:** $709
Principal Investments: Long-term bonds (60%), real estate (47%)
Provider Compensation ($000): Contr fee ($306,212), salary ($65,452), FFS ($49,491), capitation ($25,183), other ($36,921)
Total Member Encounters: Phys (540,308), non-phys (129,150)
Group Affiliation: CIGNA Corp
Licensed in: AZ
Address: 11001 N Black Canyon Hwy, Phoenix, AZ 85029
Phone: (623) 277-2171 **Dom State:** AZ **Commenced Bus:** March 1979

Data Date	Rating	RACR #1	RACR #2	Total Assets ($mil)	Capital ($mil)	Net Premium ($mil)	Net Income ($mil)
6-14	C	1.79	1.49	114.3	45.0	237.0	-10.5
6-13	B	2.75	2.29	121.3	68.7	267.6	10.2
2013	C+	1.82	1.51	104.6	45.8	505.4	1.1
2012	C	2.34	1.95	120.7	58.3	488.6	8.9
2011	C	1.90	1.58	115.6	51.2	508.7	-2.9
2010	C	1.92	1.60	124.7	51.5	529.0	-14.0
2009	B	2.62	2.18	146.8	72.4	546.4	18.8

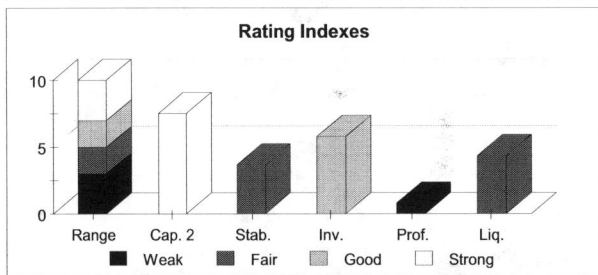

Rating Indexes

(Range, Cap. 2, Stab., Inv., Prof., Liq.)
Weak ■ Fair ■ Good ▨ Strong □

CIGNA HEALTHCARE OF CALIFORNIA INC

B   **Good**

Major Rating Factors: Good capitalization index (5.4 on a scale of 0 to 10) based on good current risk-adjusted capital (severe loss scenario). Good overall results on stability tests (5.1). Rating is significantly influenced by the good financial results of CIGNA Corp. Fair profitability index (3.1).

Other Rating Factors: Excellent liquidity (7.0) with sufficient resources (cash flows and marketable investments) to handle a spike in claims.

Principal Business: Managed care (101%)
Mem Phys: 13: N/A **12:** N/A **13 MLR** 94.9% **/ 13 Admin Exp** N/A
Enroll(000): Q2 14: 186 **13:** 200 **12:** 217 **Med Exp PMPM:** $1,498
Principal Investments ($000): Cash and equiv ($85,369)
Provider Compensation ($000): None
Total Member Encounters: N/A
Group Affiliation: CIGNA Corp
Licensed in: CA
Address: 400 N Brand Blvd, Glendale, CA 91203
Phone: (818) 500-6284 **Dom State:** CA **Commenced Bus:** November 1978

Data Date	Rating	RACR #1	RACR #2	Total Assets ($mil)	Capital ($mil)	Net Premium ($mil)	Net Income ($mil)
6-14	B	1.36	0.83	180.3	47.2	478.6	-3.1
6-13	B	1.95	1.20	174.1	66.7	470.4	12.6
2013	B	1.43	0.87	156.0	49.9	944.4	5.9
2012	C+	1.67	1.02	160.3	54.9	950.7	6.1
2011	C	1.34	0.81	139.8	41.8	934.2	-0.4
2010	C	1.35	0.82	140.6	41.3	896.3	-1.4
2009	C	1.24	0.75	155.4	42.1	788.6	-12.0

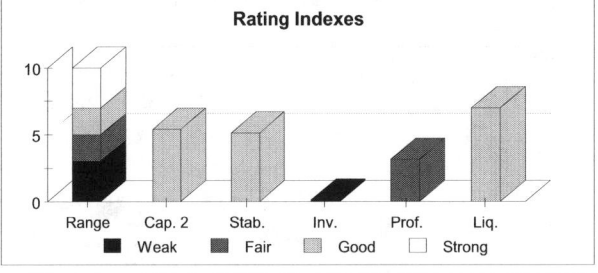

Rating Indexes

(Range, Cap. 2, Stab., Inv., Prof., Liq.)
Weak ■ Fair ■ Good ▨ Strong □

CIGNA HEALTHCARE OF COLORADO INC

C **Fair**

Major Rating Factors: Weak overall results on stability tests (2.3 on a scale of 0 to 10) based on a significant 19% decrease in enrollment during the period. Rating is significantly influenced by the good financial results of CIGNA Corp. Good overall profitability index (5.2). Strong capitalization index (10.0) based on excellent current risk-adjusted capital (severe loss scenario).

Other Rating Factors: High quality investment portfolio (9.9). Excellent liquidity (7.1) with ample operational cash flow and liquid investments.

Principal Business: Comp med (100%)

Mem Phys: 13: 12,209 **12:** 11,446 **13 MLR** 72.2% **/ 13 Admin Exp** N/A

Enroll(000): Q2 14: 2 **13:** 2 **12:** 2 **Med Exp PMPM:** $302

Principal Investments: Long-term bonds (76%), cash and equiv (24%)

Provider Compensation ($000): Contr fee ($5,694), FFS ($1,613), capitation ($284)

Total Member Encounters: Phys (8,725), non-phys (2,043)

Group Affiliation: CIGNA Corp

Licensed in: CO

Address: 3900 E Mexico Ave Suite 1100, Denver, CO 80210

Phone: (303) 782-1500 **Dom State:** CO **Commenced Bus:** May 1986

Data Date	Rating	RACR #1	RACR #2	Total Assets ($mil)	Capital ($mil)	Net Premium ($mil)	Net Income ($mil)
6-14	C	7.10	5.92	5.8	4.4	4.0	0.0
6-13	C	4.59	3.82	5.5	3.9	5.1	0.6
2013	C	7.07	5.90	5.5	4.4	9.8	1.1
2012	C	5.82	4.85	7.0	5.3	11.4	0.0
2011	C	4.11	3.43	9.9	7.4	22.5	0.8
2010	C	4.56	3.80	14.5	10.7	25.2	2.1
2009	C	2.65	2.21	13.0	6.2	29.4	-0.5

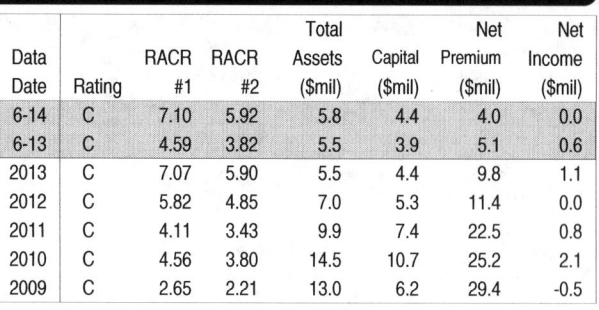

Rating Indexes

CIGNA HEALTHCARE OF CONNECTICUT INC

C- **Fair**

Major Rating Factors: Fair profitability index (4.6 on a scale of 0 to 10). Good overall results on stability tests (5.0). Rating is significantly influenced by the good financial results of CIGNA Corp. Strong capitalization index (10.0) based on excellent current risk-adjusted capital (severe loss scenario).

Other Rating Factors: High quality investment portfolio (9.9). Excellent liquidity (8.9) with ample operational cash flow and liquid investments.

Principal Business: Dental (91%), comp med (9%)

Mem Phys: 13: 10,123 **12:** 9,527 **13 MLR** 66.9% **/ 13 Admin Exp** N/A

Enroll(000): Q2 14: 35 **13:** 35 **12:** 37 **Med Exp PMPM:** $17

Principal Investments: Long-term bonds (67%), cash and equiv (33%)

Provider Compensation ($000): FFS ($4,032), capitation ($2,642), contr fee ($840)

Total Member Encounters: Phys (900), non-phys (210)

Group Affiliation: CIGNA Corp

Licensed in: CT

Address: 900 Cottage Grove Rd., B228, Hartford, CT 06152-1118

Phone: (860) 226-4014 **Dom State:** CT **Commenced Bus:** May 1986

Data Date	Rating	RACR #1	RACR #2	Total Assets ($mil)	Capital ($mil)	Net Premium ($mil)	Net Income ($mil)
6-14	C-	34.73	28.94	32.9	32.0	5.2	1.4
6-13	C-	31.42	26.19	30.7	29.4	5.6	1.2
2013	C-	33.30	27.75	31.6	30.6	11.0	2.5
2012	C-	30.29	25.24	31.1	28.3	11.9	2.9
2011	C-	5.53	4.61	39.8	25.0	63.7	2.0
2010	C-	4.50	3.75	52.0	22.0	110.1	-5.5
2009	C	2.40	2.00	21.9	10.7	67.8	-1.8

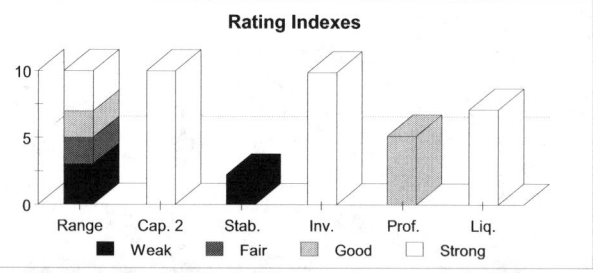

Rating Indexes

CIGNA HEALTHCARE OF FLORIDA INC

C **Fair**

Major Rating Factors: Fair profitability index (4.1 on a scale of 0 to 10). Weak overall results on stability tests (2.2) based on a significant 79% decrease in enrollment during the period. Rating is significantly influenced by the good financial results of CIGNA Corp. Strong capitalization index (10.0) based on excellent current risk-adjusted capital (severe loss scenario).

Other Rating Factors: High quality investment portfolio (9.9). Excellent liquidity (9.2) with ample operational cash flow and liquid investments.

Principal Business: Comp med (100%)

Mem Phys: 13: 78,564 **12:** 38,992 **13 MLR** 73.5% **/ 13 Admin Exp** N/A

Enroll(000): Q2 14: 0 **13:** 0 **12:** 1 **Med Exp PMPM:** $355

Principal Investments: Cash and equiv (55%), long-term bonds (45%)

Provider Compensation ($000): Contr fee ($902), FFS ($323), capitation ($53)

Total Member Encounters: Phys (1,248), non-phys (181)

Group Affiliation: CIGNA Corp

Licensed in: FL

Address: 2701 N Rocky Point Dr Ste 800, Tampa, FL 33607

Phone: (215) 761-1000 **Dom State:** FL **Commenced Bus:** February 1981

Data Date	Rating	RACR #1	RACR #2	Total Assets ($mil)	Capital ($mil)	Net Premium ($mil)	Net Income ($mil)
6-14	C	9.02	7.51	4.5	4.1	0.7	0.0
6-13	C	9.67	8.06	4.7	4.0	0.6	0.2
2013	C	9.04	7.53	4.6	4.1	1.2	0.2
2012	C	9.58	7.98	5.1	3.9	5.6	-0.2
2011	C	8.51	7.09	5.6	4.1	8.5	0.5
2010	B-	10.03	8.36	11.0	9.0	12.3	3.3
2009	C	6.94	5.79	17.5	10.0	25.0	3.0

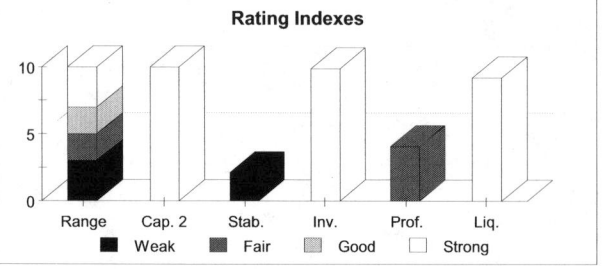

Rating Indexes

CIGNA HEALTHCARE OF GEORGIA INC   B-   Good

Major Rating Factors: Fair overall results on stability tests (3.7 on a scale of 0 to 10) based on a significant 43% decrease in enrollment during the period, a steep decline in premium revenue in 2013. Rating is significantly influenced by the good financial results of CIGNA Corp. Strong capitalization index (10.0) based on excellent current risk-adjusted capital (severe loss scenario). High quality investment portfolio (9.9).
Other Rating Factors: Excellent liquidity (7.9) with ample operational cash flow and liquid investments. Weak profitability index (2.5).
Principal Business: Comp med (100%)
Mem Phys: 13: 13,905 **12:** 13,330 **13 MLR** 86.2% **/ 13 Admin Exp** N/A
Enroll(000): Q2 14: 2 **13:** 1 **12:** 1 **Med Exp PMPM:** $553
Principal Investments: Long-term bonds (67%), cash and equiv (33%)
Provider Compensation ($000): Contr fee ($2,396), FFS ($928), capitation ($114)
Total Member Encounters: Phys (3,534), non-phys (529)
Group Affiliation: CIGNA Corp
Licensed in: GA
Address: 3500 Piedmont Rd Suite 200, Atlanta, GA 30305
Phone: (404) 443-8800 **Dom State:** GA **Commenced Bus:** December 1985

Data Date	Rating	RACR #1	RACR #2	Total Assets ($mil)	Capital ($mil)	Net Premium ($mil)	Net Income ($mil)
6-14	B-	9.78	8.15	7.7	5.2	6.0	-0.9
6-13	C	11.03	9.19	6.4	5.9	2.0	0.1
2013	C	11.43	9.52	6.7	6.1	3.9	0.3
2012	C	10.98	9.15	6.8	5.9	6.1	0.5
2011	C	7.90	6.58	6.6	5.3	7.2	0.7
2010	C	10.44	8.70	7.3	6.6	7.3	1.2
2009	C	8.71	7.26	9.2	6.6	9.6	1.0

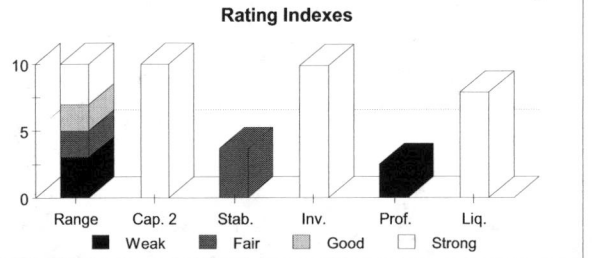

Rating Indexes

CIGNA HEALTHCARE OF ILLINOIS INC   C   Fair

Major Rating Factors: Fair profitability index (3.8 on a scale of 0 to 10). Fair overall results on stability tests (4.3). Rating is significantly influenced by the good financial results of CIGNA Corp. Strong capitalization index (10.0) based on excellent current risk-adjusted capital (severe loss scenario).
Other Rating Factors: High quality investment portfolio (9.9). Excellent liquidity (9.0) with ample operational cash flow and liquid investments.
Principal Business: Comp med (100%)
Mem Phys: 13: 17,144 **12:** 16,705 **13 MLR** 76.8% **/ 13 Admin Exp** N/A
Enroll(000): Q2 14: 0 **13:** 0 **12:** 0 **Med Exp PMPM:** $412
Principal Investments: Cash and equiv (73%), long-term bonds (27%)
Provider Compensation ($000): Contr fee ($500), FFS ($262), capitation ($46)
Total Member Encounters: Phys (724), non-phys (225)
Group Affiliation: CIGNA Corp
Licensed in: IL, IN
Address: 525 West Monroe Ste 1800, Chicago, IL 60661
Phone: (312) 648-2460 **Dom State:** IL **Commenced Bus:** July 1986

Data Date	Rating	RACR #1	RACR #2	Total Assets ($mil)	Capital ($mil)	Net Premium ($mil)	Net Income ($mil)
6-14	C	4.70	3.91	2.7	2.6	0.5	0.1
6-13	C-	4.63	3.86	2.6	2.5	0.5	0.0
2013	C	4.39	3.66	2.6	2.4	1.0	0.0
2012	C-	4.60	3.83	2.6	2.4	1.2	0.2
2011	C-	4.32	3.60	2.4	2.2	1.6	-0.2
2010	C	5.16	4.30	2.6	2.4	1.8	0.5
2009	C	6.22	5.18	4.2	2.9	2.7	0.3

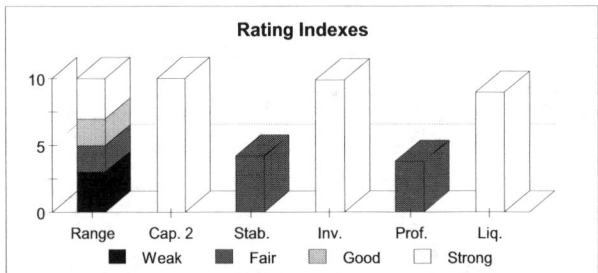

Rating Indexes

CIGNA HEALTHCARE OF INDIANA INC   C+   Fair

Major Rating Factors: Fair profitability index (3.6 on a scale of 0 to 10). Fair overall results on stability tests (4.2). Rating is significantly influenced by the good financial results of CIGNA Corp. Strong capitalization index (8.6) based on excellent current risk-adjusted capital (severe loss scenario).
Other Rating Factors: High quality investment portfolio (9.9). Excellent liquidity (7.8) with ample operational cash flow and liquid investments.
Principal Business: Comp med (100%)
Mem Phys: 13: 9,128 **12:** 8,752 **13 MLR** 86.8% **/ 13 Admin Exp** N/A
Enroll(000): Q2 14: 0 **13:** 0 **12:** 0 **Med Exp PMPM:** $508
Principal Investments: Long-term bonds (58%), cash and equiv (42%)
Provider Compensation ($000): Contr fee ($561), FFS ($168), capitation ($45)
Total Member Encounters: Phys (512), non-phys (32)
Group Affiliation: CIGNA Corp
Licensed in: IN
Address: 11595 N Meridian St, Carmel, IN 46032
Phone: (215) 761-1000 **Dom State:** IN **Commenced Bus:** September 1986

Data Date	Rating	RACR #1	RACR #2	Total Assets ($mil)	Capital ($mil)	Net Premium ($mil)	Net Income ($mil)
6-14	C+	2.61	2.18	1.7	1.4	0.5	-0.1
6-13	C	2.72	2.27	1.5	1.3	0.4	-0.2
2013	C+	2.74	2.28	1.5	1.5	0.8	0.0
2012	C	3.08	2.56	2.0	1.5	0.9	0.2
2011	C	4.00	3.33	2.0	1.8	0.9	0.3
2010	C	5.48	4.57	2.9	2.8	0.7	0.5
2009	C	6.90	5.75	4.3	3.3	5.0	0.4

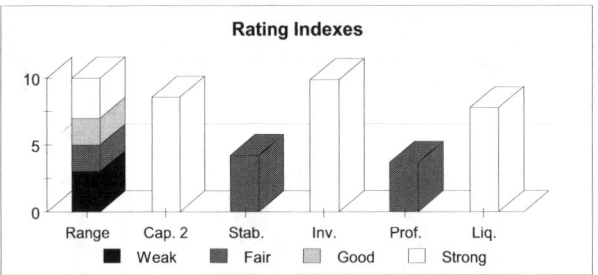

Rating Indexes

CIGNA HEALTHCARE OF NEW JERSEY INC   C   Fair

Major Rating Factors: Weak profitability index (0.9 on a scale of 0 to 10). Weak overall results on stability tests (2.2). Rating is significantly influenced by the good financial results of CIGNA Corp. Strong capitalization index (10.0) based on excellent current risk-adjusted capital (severe loss scenario).
Other Rating Factors: High quality investment portfolio (9.9). Excellent liquidity (7.3) with ample operational cash flow and liquid investments.
Principal Business: Comp med (100%)
Mem Phys: 13: 23,441   **12:** 22,321   **13 MLR** 72.9%   **/ 13 Admin Exp** N/A
Enroll(000): Q2 14: 0   **13:** 0   **12:** 0   **Med Exp PMPM:** $484
Principal Investments: Long-term bonds (86%), cash and equiv (14%)
Provider Compensation ($000): Contr fee ($1,870), FFS ($449), capitation ($98)
Total Member Encounters: Phys (2,889), non-phys (21,439)
Group Affiliation: CIGNA Corp
Licensed in: NJ
Address: 499 Washington Blvd 5th Floor, Jersey City, NJ 07310-1608
Phone: (201) 533-5001   **Dom State:** NJ   **Commenced Bus:** February 1988

Data Date	Rating	RACR #1	RACR #2	Total Assets ($mil)	Capital ($mil)	Net Premium ($mil)	Net Income ($mil)
6-14	C	4.86	4.05	5.4	2.6	0.8	-1.4
6-13	C	7.22	6.01	4.8	3.9	1.9	0.3
2013	C	7.28	6.07	4.7	4.0	3.2	0.4
2012	C	6.66	5.55	4.8	3.6	1.7	-0.1
2011	C	7.00	5.83	5.5	3.8	6.4	0.8
2010	C	15.16	12.63	8.3	7.2	7.6	2.4
2009	C	14.13	11.78	20.5	16.6	12.0	-1.6

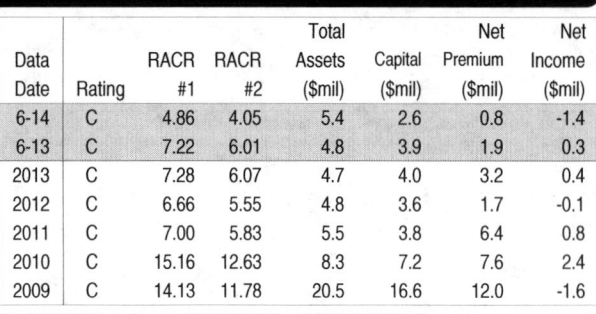

Rating Indexes

Range, Cap. 2, Stab., Inv., Prof., Liq.
■ Weak   ■ Fair   ▨ Good   □ Strong

CIGNA HEALTHCARE OF NORTH CAROLINA   C   Fair

Major Rating Factors: Fair profitability index (4.5 on a scale of 0 to 10). Fair overall results on stability tests (3.8) based on a significant 64% decrease in enrollment during the period, a steep decline in premium revenue in 2013. Rating is significantly influenced by the good financial results of CIGNA Corp. Strong capitalization index (10.0) based on excellent current risk-adjusted capital (severe loss scenario).
Other Rating Factors: High quality investment portfolio (9.9). Excellent liquidity (7.2) with ample operational cash flow and liquid investments.
Principal Business: Comp med (100%)
Mem Phys: 13: 21,318   **12:** 20,439   **13 MLR** 77.4%   **/ 13 Admin Exp** N/A
Enroll(000): Q2 14: 3   **13:** 2   **12:** 6   **Med Exp PMPM:** $327
Principal Investments: Long-term bonds (73%), cash and equiv (27%)
Provider Compensation ($000): Contr fee ($10,137), FFS ($2,422), capitation ($286)
Total Member Encounters: Phys (16,830), non-phys (3,029)
Group Affiliation: CIGNA Corp
Licensed in: NC
Address: 701 Corporate Center Dr, Raleigh, NC 27607
Phone: (919) 854-7469   **Dom State:** NC   **Commenced Bus:** April 1986

Data Date	Rating	RACR #1	RACR #2	Total Assets ($mil)	Capital ($mil)	Net Premium ($mil)	Net Income ($mil)
6-14	C	7.91	6.59	13.5	10.3	11.1	0.7
6-13	C	3.88	3.24	11.7	9.0	9.8	0.4
2013	C	7.45	6.20	11.3	9.7	15.3	1.1
2012	C	3.77	3.15	11.4	8.7	28.6	1.5
2011	C	5.12	4.27	16.6	12.2	31.2	1.7
2010	C	3.94	3.29	16.0	10.7	32.5	-0.7
2009	C	2.89	2.41	19.1	11.5	68.6	2.9

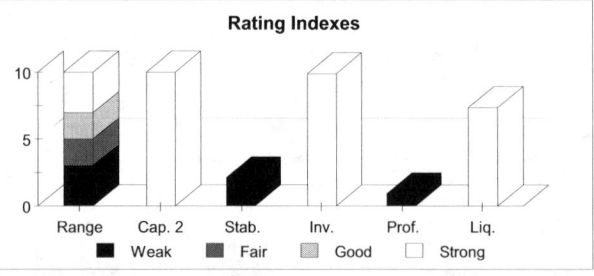

Rating Indexes

Range, Cap. 2, Stab., Inv., Prof., Liq.
■ Weak   ■ Fair   ▨ Good   □ Strong

CIGNA HEALTHCARE OF SOUTH CAROLINA   D+   Weak

Major Rating Factors: Weak profitability index (0.9 on a scale of 0 to 10). Weak overall results on stability tests (1.9). Rating is significantly influenced by the good financial results of CIGNA Corp. Strong capitalization index (7.6) based on excellent current risk-adjusted capital (severe loss scenario).
Other Rating Factors: High quality investment portfolio (9.9). Excellent liquidity (9.3) with ample operational cash flow and liquid investments.
Principal Business: Comp med (100%)
Mem Phys: 13: 12,611   **12:** 12,037   **13 MLR** 43.1%   **/ 13 Admin Exp** N/A
Enroll(000): Q2 14: 6   **13:** 0   **12:** 0   **Med Exp PMPM:** $276
Principal Investments: Cash and equiv (76%), long-term bonds (24%)
Provider Compensation ($000): Contr fee ($406), FFS ($206), capitation ($60)
Total Member Encounters: Phys (1,014), non-phys (153)
Group Affiliation: CIGNA Corp
Licensed in: SC
Address: 146 Fairchild St, Charleston, SC 29492
Phone: (800) 566-7412   **Dom State:** SC   **Commenced Bus:** January 1987

Data Date	Rating	RACR #1	RACR #2	Total Assets ($mil)	Capital ($mil)	Net Premium ($mil)	Net Income ($mil)
6-14	D+	1.82	1.52	8.8	0.7	27.4	-1.5
6-13	C	4.80	4.00	2.5	1.9	0.7	0.2
2013	C	4.41	3.68	2.7	2.2	1.5	0.5
2012	C	3.98	3.32	2.3	1.7	1.5	0.1
2011	C	6.16	5.13	3.3	2.4	3.3	0.7
2010	C	7.69	6.41	6.8	5.2	9.2	0.5
2009	C	3.96	3.30	11.6	7.8	26.4	0.5

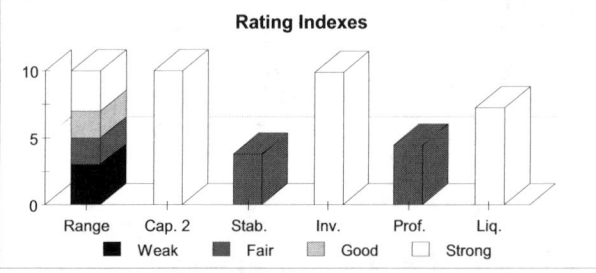

Rating Indexes

Range, Cap. 2, Stab., Inv., Prof., Liq.
■ Weak   ■ Fair   ▨ Good   □ Strong

CIGNA HEALTHCARE OF ST LOUIS

D+   Weak

Major Rating Factors: Weak profitability index (1.2 on a scale of 0 to 10). Weak overall results on stability tests (1.8) based on a steep decline in capital during 2013. Rating is significantly influenced by the good financial results of CIGNA Corp. Strong capitalization index (7.0) based on excellent current risk-adjusted capital (severe loss scenario).

Other Rating Factors: High quality investment portfolio (9.9). Excellent liquidity (7.7) with ample operational cash flow and liquid investments.

Principal Business: Comp med (100%)

Mem Phys: 13: 15,540   **12:** 14,242   **13 MLR** 87.6%   / **13 Admin Exp** N/A

Enroll(000): Q2 14: 1   **13:** 1   **12:** 1   **Med Exp PMPM:** $381

Principal Investments: Cash and equiv (64%), long-term bonds (36%)

Provider Compensation ($000): Contr fee ($3,535), FFS ($970), capitation ($271)

Total Member Encounters: Phys (5,264), non-phys (921)

Group Affiliation: CIGNA Corp

Licensed in: IL, MO

Address: 231 S BEMISTON, St Louis, MO 63105

Phone: (314) 290-7300   **Dom State:** MO   **Commenced Bus:** February 1986

Data Date	Rating	RACR #1	RACR #2	Total Assets ($mil)	Capital ($mil)	Net Premium ($mil)	Net Income ($mil)
6-14	D+	1.33	1.10	5.5	0.6	2.7	-1.9
6-13	C	4.16	3.47	4.6	2.3	2.8	-0.1
2013	C	4.28	3.57	5.1	2.3	5.5	0.2
2012	C	6.95	5.79	6.3	3.8	5.1	-0.2
2011	C+	10.70	8.91	7.8	6.0	5.1	-0.3
2010	C	3.46	2.88	8.0	6.4	6.0	0.2
2009	C	3.61	3.01	2.1	1.5	2.0	0.1

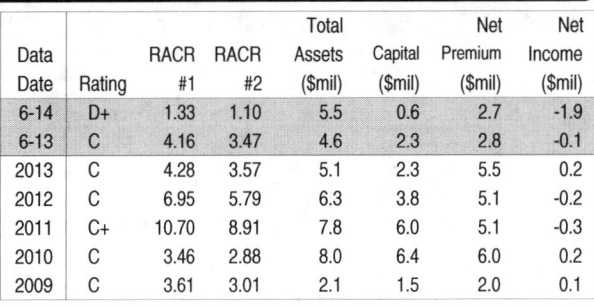

Rating Indexes

CIGNA HEALTHCARE OF TENNESSEE INC

C   Fair

Major Rating Factors: Fair profitability index (4.3 on a scale of 0 to 10). Weak overall results on stability tests (2.2) based on a significant 27% decrease in enrollment during the period. Rating is significantly influenced by the good financial results of CIGNA Corp. Strong capitalization index (9.8) based on excellent current risk-adjusted capital (severe loss scenario).

Other Rating Factors: High quality investment portfolio (8.9). Excellent liquidity (7.0) with sufficient resources (cash flows and marketable investments) to handle a spike in claims.

Principal Business: Comp med (100%)

Mem Phys: 13: 34,567   **12:** 16,017   **13 MLR** 73.4%   / **13 Admin Exp** N/A

Enroll(000): Q2 14: 4   **13:** 8   **12:** 10   **Med Exp PMPM:** $279

Principal Investments: Long-term bonds (81%), cash and equiv (7%), other (12%)

Provider Compensation ($000): Contr fee ($17,608), FFS ($7,543), capitation ($2,533)

Total Member Encounters: Phys (34,837), non-phys (6,152)

Group Affiliation: CIGNA Corp

Licensed in: MS, TN

Address: 1000 Corporate Centre Dr, Franklin, TN 37067

Phone: (860) 226-4014   **Dom State:** TN   **Commenced Bus:** November 1985

Data Date	Rating	RACR #1	RACR #2	Total Assets ($mil)	Capital ($mil)	Net Premium ($mil)	Net Income ($mil)
6-14	C	3.56	2.97	12.1	7.7	8.8	-0.3
6-13	C	2.69	2.24	13.9	8.2	18.0	1.7
2013	C	3.74	3.12	12.8	8.2	35.4	2.3
2012	C	2.31	1.92	12.7	6.6	48.1	-1.2
2011	C	4.02	3.35	17.9	11.0	49.2	3.4
2010	U	3.24	2.70	19.8	12.9	73.8	2.0
2009	C	3.76	3.13	30.0	19.5	95.0	4.6

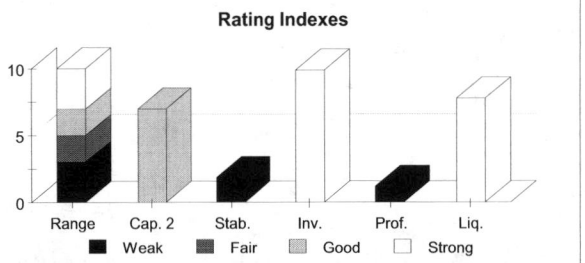

Rating Indexes

CIGNA HEALTHCARE OF TEXAS INC

B-   Good

Major Rating Factors: Fair profitability index (3.3 on a scale of 0 to 10). Fair overall results on stability tests (4.3). Rating is significantly influenced by the good financial results of CIGNA Corp. Strong capitalization index (8.3) based on excellent current risk-adjusted capital (severe loss scenario).

Other Rating Factors: High quality investment portfolio (9.9). Excellent liquidity (7.0) with ample operational cash flow and liquid investments.

Principal Business: Comp med (100%)

Mem Phys: 13: 77,910   **12:** 51,461   **13 MLR** 85.8%   / **13 Admin Exp** N/A

Enroll(000): Q2 14: 13   **13:** 17   **12:** 17   **Med Exp PMPM:** $422

Principal Investments: Long-term bonds (55%), cash and equiv (45%)

Provider Compensation ($000): Contr fee ($53,803), FFS ($17,506), capitation ($15,312)

Total Member Encounters: Phys (49,329), non-phys (10,003)

Group Affiliation: CIGNA Corp

Licensed in: TX

Address: Two Riverway, Houston, TX 77056

Phone: (972) 863-5410   **Dom State:** TX   **Commenced Bus:** January 1996

Data Date	Rating	RACR #1	RACR #2	Total Assets ($mil)	Capital ($mil)	Net Premium ($mil)	Net Income ($mil)
6-14	B-	2.38	1.98	26.6	13.2	45.7	-1.7
6-13	C	2.61	2.18	24.0	13.5	50.4	1.4
2013	B-	2.58	2.15	31.9	14.5	100.8	2.0
2012	C	2.62	2.18	21.9	12.8	95.2	1.1
2011	C	2.74	2.28	24.9	14.6	85.4	1.7
2010	C	2.75	2.29	32.6	20.6	128.4	2.9
2009	B	4.50	3.75	52.9	33.6	134.6	2.6

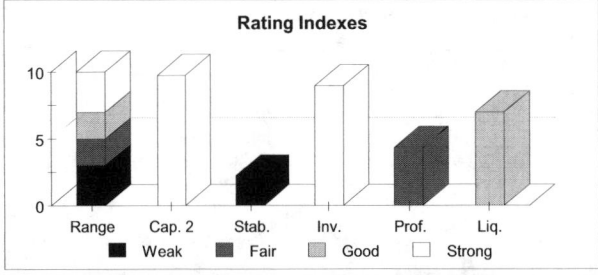

Rating Indexes

CIGNA LIFE INSURANCE COMPANY OF NEW YORK *   A-   Excellent

Major Rating Factors: Good quality investment portfolio (6.6 on a scale of 0 to 10) despite mixed results such as: no exposure to mortgages and large holdings of BBB rated bonds but small junk bond holdings. Good overall profitability (6.3). Return on equity has been excellent over the last five years averaging 18.7%. Excellent overall results on stability tests (7.0) excellent operational trends and excellent risk diversification.

Other Rating Factors: Strong capitalization (9.0) based on excellent risk adjusted capital (severe loss scenario). Excellent liquidity (7.3).

Principal Business: Group health insurance (66%) and group life insurance (33%).

Principal Investments: NonCMO investment grade bonds (86%), CMOs and structured securities (7%), and noninv. grade bonds (7%).

Investments in Affiliates: None

Group Affiliation: CIGNA Corp

Licensed in: AL, DC, MO, NY, PA, TN

Commenced Business: December 1965

Address: 499 Washington Blvd, Jersey City, NJ 07310-1995

Phone: (212) 618-5757 **Domicile State:** NY **NAIC Code:** 64548

Data Date	Rating	RACR #1	RACR #2	Total Assets ($mil)	Capital ($mil)	Net Premium ($mil)	Net Income ($mil)
6-14	A-	3.68	2.31	376.2	106.5	62.0	13.8
6-13	B+	3.67	2.32	381.5	101.2	59.5	7.9
2013	B+	3.21	2.03	375.9	93.5	119.9	16.9
2012	B+	3.54	2.38	376.0	93.8	115.6	15.8
2011	B	4.12	2.77	387.8	102.4	124.7	16.6
2010	B	3.94	2.71	395.5	103.4	131.6	26.7
2009	B-	3.91	2.73	388.0	97.2	124.1	15.5

Adverse Trends in Operations

Decrease in premium volume from 2011 to 2012 (7%)
Decrease in asset base during 2012 (3%)
Decrease in capital during 2012 (8%)
Decrease in asset base during 2011 (2%)
Decrease in premium volume from 2010 to 2011 (5%)

COLONIAL LIFE & ACCIDENT INSURANCE COMPANY   C+   Fair

Major Rating Factors: Fair overall results on stability tests (4.5 on a scale of 0 to 10). Good quality investment portfolio (6.2) despite mixed results such as: large holdings of BBB rated bonds but moderate junk bond exposure. Good liquidity (6.8) with sufficient resources to handle a spike in claims as well as a significant increase in policy surrenders.

Other Rating Factors: Strong capitalization (8.1) based on excellent risk adjusted capital (severe loss scenario). Excellent profitability (8.6) with operating gains in each of the last five years.

Principal Business: Individual health insurance (75%), individual life insurance (20%), group health insurance (4%), and group life insurance (1%).

Principal Investments: NonCMO investment grade bonds (72%), mortgages in good standing (10%), noninv. grade bonds (8%), CMOs and structured securities (4%), and misc. investments (6%).

Investments in Affiliates: None

Group Affiliation: Unum Group

Licensed in: All states except NY

Commenced Business: September 1939

Address: 6335 S. East Street, Suite A, Indianapolis, IN 46227

Phone: (803) 798-7000 **Domicile State:** SC **NAIC Code:** 62049

Data Date	Rating	RACR #1	RACR #2	Total Assets ($mil)	Capital ($mil)	Net Premium ($mil)	Net Income ($mil)
6-14	C+	2.85	1.76	2,869.7	574.1	641.7	77.2
6-13	C+	2.83	1.72	2,712.3	559.0	624.8	66.9
2013	C+	2.71	1.66	2,752.7	538.2	1,238.8	134.4
2012	C+	2.75	1.68	2,651.4	534.9	1,208.2	139.7
2011	C+	2.84	1.74	2,521.2	532.3	1,152.4	136.0
2010	C+	2.81	1.75	2,300.1	491.7	1,103.9	142.3
2009	C+	2.80	1.76	2,141.8	459.7	1,043.0	124.4

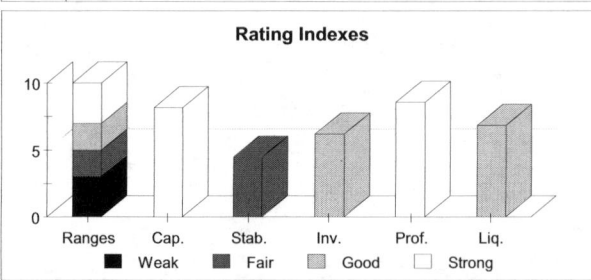

Rating Indexes

COLONIAL PENN LIFE INSURANCE COMPANY   D+   Weak

Major Rating Factors: Weak profitability (2.4 on a scale of 0 to 10) with operating losses during the first six months of 2014. Weak liquidity (0.2) as a spike in claims or a run on policy withdrawals may stretch capacity. Weak overall results on stability tests (2.2) including weak risk adjusted capital in prior years, negative cash flow from operations for 2013.

Other Rating Factors: Fair quality investment portfolio (4.5). Good capitalization (5.6) based on good risk adjusted capital (moderate loss scenario).

Principal Business: Individual health insurance (56%), individual life insurance (24%), group life insurance (20%), and reinsurance (1%).

Principal Investments: NonCMO investment grade bonds (74%), CMOs and structured securities (13%), mortgages in good standing (4%), policy loans (3%), and misc. investments (5%).

Investments in Affiliates: None

Group Affiliation: CNO Financial Group Inc

Licensed in: All states except NY

Commenced Business: September 1959

Address: 399 Market St, Philadelphia, PA 19181

Phone: (215) 928-8000 **Domicile State:** PA **NAIC Code:** 62065

Data Date	Rating	RACR #1	RACR #2	Total Assets ($mil)	Capital ($mil)	Net Premium ($mil)	Net Income ($mil)
6-14	D+	1.41	0.81	750.9	92.5	159.9	-2.0
6-13	D+	1.31	0.75	755.5	82.5	146.6	1.2
2013	D+	1.05	0.60	740.3	62.0	277.8	-19.1
2012	D+	1.20	0.68	736.6	70.6	253.5	-3.9
2011	D+	1.41	0.78	743.9	76.7	222.8	9.2
2010	D+	1.48	0.78	733.8	73.3	194.0	0.3
2009	D+	0.88	0.46	683.6	32.7	182.3	-3.8

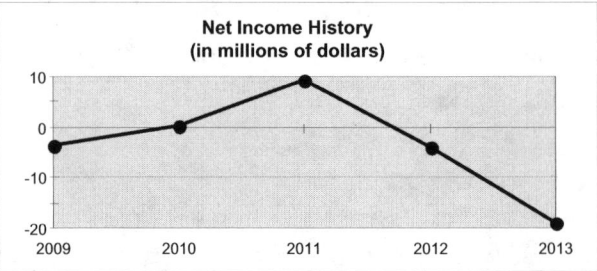

Net Income History
(in millions of dollars)

COLORADO CHOICE HEALTH PLANS   C   Fair

Major Rating Factors: Fair profitability index (2.9 on a scale of 0 to 10). Weak overall results on stability tests (2.6). Good capitalization index (5.3) based on good current risk-adjusted capital (severe loss scenario).
Other Rating Factors: High quality investment portfolio (9.9). Excellent liquidity (7.0) with sufficient resources (cash flows and marketable investments) to handle a spike in claims.
Principal Business: Comp med (81%), Medicaid (12%), Medicare (7%)
Mem Phys: 13: 4,256   **12:** 3,893   **13 MLR** 86.1%   **/ 13 Admin Exp** N/A
Enroll(000): Q2 14: 13   **13:** 6   **12:** 6   **Med Exp PMPM:** $274
Principal Investments: Cash and equiv (90%), long-term bonds (10%)
Provider Compensation ($000): Contr fee ($20,911), FFS ($186)
Total Member Encounters: N/A
Group Affiliation: None
Licensed in: CO
Address: 700 Main Street, Suite 100, Alamosa, CO 81101
Phone: (719) 589-3696   **Dom State:** CO   **Commenced Bus:** May 1975

Data Date	Rating	RACR #1	RACR #2	Total Assets ($mil)	Capital ($mil)	Net Premium ($mil)	Net Income ($mil)
6-14	C	0.97	0.81	16.3	4.6	22.6	0.9
6-13	B	1.51	1.26	10.2	5.3	12.3	-0.8
2013	C+	0.93	0.77	9.3	4.4	24.6	-1.4
2012	B	2.03	1.69	11.2	6.5	20.8	1.1
2011	B	1.82	1.51	9.6	5.8	18.9	1.1
2010	C	1.42	1.18	7.6	4.7	18.0	0.1
2009	C-	1.45	1.21	6.8	4.8	18.0	0.1

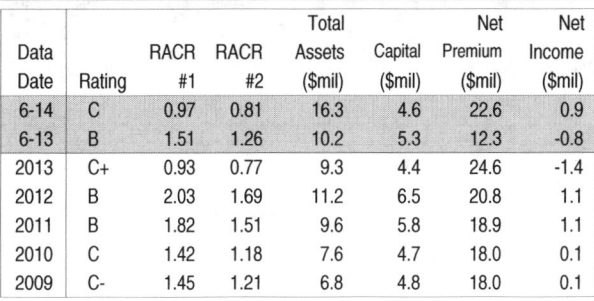

COLUMBIA UNITED PROVIDERS INC   B   Good

Major Rating Factors: Good liquidity (6.9 on a scale of 0 to 10) with sufficient resources (cash flows and marketable investments) to handle a spike in claims. Fair profitability index (3.8). Strong capitalization (7.6) based on excellent current risk-adjusted capital (severe loss scenario).
Other Rating Factors: High quality investment portfolio (9.9).
Principal Business: Medicaid (94%), comp med (5%)
Mem Phys: 13: N/A   **12:** 1,288   **13 MLR** 93.1%   **/ 13 Admin Exp** N/A
Enroll(000): Q2 14: 52   **13:** 42   **12:** 43   **Med Exp PMPM:** $173
Principal Investments: Long-term bonds (58%), cash and equiv (41%), nonaffiliate common stock (2%)
Provider Compensation ($000): FFS ($45,112), contr fee ($28,719), capitation ($16,860)
Total Member Encounters: Phys (241,621), non-phys (89,770)
Group Affiliation: Southwest Washington Health Systems
Licensed in: WA
Address: 19120 SE 34th Street #201, Vancouver, WA 98683
Phone: (360) 449-8861   **Dom State:** WA   **Commenced Bus:** January 1994

Data Date	Rating	RACR #1	RACR #2	Total Assets ($mil)	Capital ($mil)	Net Premium ($mil)	Net Income ($mil)
6-14	B	1.87	1.56	37.4	20.8	64.1	-1.7
6-13	B	1.94	1.62	32.7	21.7	47.4	-0.7
2013	B	2.13	1.78	35.4	23.8	95.5	-1.0
2012	B	2.19	1.83	36.1	24.6	108.7	2.3
2011	B	1.87	1.56	34.2	22.8	136.8	4.1
2010	N/A	N/A	N/A	27.0	18.9	103.3	4.2
2009	B	1.52	1.26	22.5	14.5	97.1	3.3

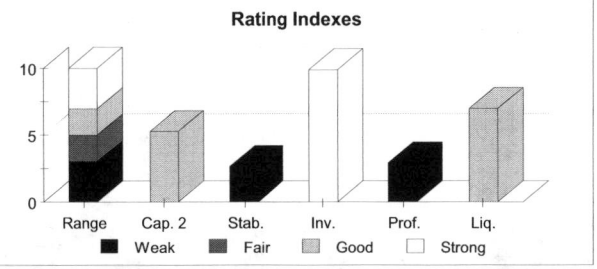

COMBINED INSURANCE COMPANY OF AMERICA   C+   Fair

Major Rating Factors: Fair overall results on stability tests (3.4 on a scale of 0 to 10). Good quality investment portfolio (6.8) despite mixed results such as: no exposure to mortgages and substantial holdings of BBB bonds but small junk bond holdings. Good overall profitability (5.8). Return on equity has been excellent over the last five years averaging 33.8%.
Other Rating Factors: Strong capitalization (8.1) based on excellent risk adjusted capital (severe loss scenario). Excellent liquidity (7.2).
Principal Business: Individual health insurance (70%), group health insurance (20%), individual life insurance (8%), reinsurance (1%), and group life insurance (1%).
Principal Investments: NonCMO investment grade bonds (63%), CMOs and structured securities (22%), common & preferred stock (6%), noninv. grade bonds (5%), and misc. investments (4%).
Investments in Affiliates: 6%
Group Affiliation: ACE Ltd
Licensed in: All states except NY
Commenced Business: January 1922
Address: 1000 North Milwakee Ave, Glenview, IL 60025
Phone: (312) 701-3000   **Domicile State:** IL   **NAIC Code:** 62146

Data Date	Rating	RACR #1	RACR #2	Total Assets ($mil)	Capital ($mil)	Net Premium ($mil)	Net Income ($mil)
6-14	C+	2.24	1.71	1,642.8	373.5	215.6	44.5
6-13	C+	1.96	1.54	1,560.4	345.5	215.2	46.1
2013	C+	1.99	1.54	1,588.9	324.6	428.1	71.8
2012	C+	2.06	1.61	1,543.6	320.7	151.5	195.8
2011	B-	1.96	1.68	1,995.5	496.6	597.2	121.4
2010	B-	3.26	2.69	2,543.8	741.7	478.9	221.9
2009	B-	2.46	2.00	2,508.2	642.7	869.2	178.9

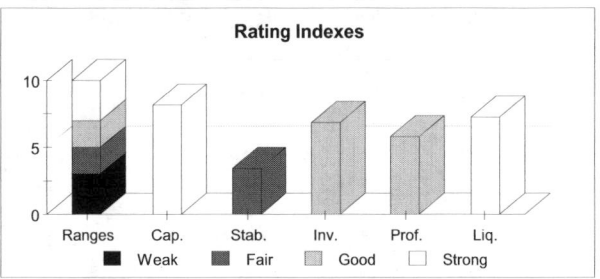

COMBINED LIFE INSURANCE COMPANY OF NEW YORK — B — Good

Major Rating Factors: Good overall results on stability tests (5.7 on a scale of 0 to 10) despite fair financial strength of affiliated ACE Ltd. Other stability subfactors include excellent operational trends and excellent risk diversification. Good overall profitability (5.2) although investment income, in comparison to reserve requirements, is below regulatory standards. Strong capitalization (7.6) based on excellent risk adjusted capital (severe loss scenario).

Other Rating Factors: High quality investment portfolio (7.6). Excellent liquidity (7.5).

Principal Business: Individual health insurance (74%), individual life insurance (14%), group health insurance (11%), and group life insurance (1%).

Principal Investments: NonCMO investment grade bonds (51%), CMOs and structured securities (47%), policy loans (2%), and noninv. grade bonds (1%).

Investments in Affiliates: None

Group Affiliation: ACE Ltd

Licensed in: FL, IL, NY

Commenced Business: June 1971

Address: 11 British Anerican Blvd, Latham, NY 12110

Phone: (518) 220-9333 **Domicile State:** NY **NAIC Code:** 78697

Data Date	Rating	RACR #1	RACR #2	Total Assets ($mil)	Capital ($mil)	Net Premium ($mil)	Net Income ($mil)
6-14	B	2.05	1.43	416.4	62.4	63.7	5.3
6-13	B	1.83	1.28	396.0	55.9	63.4	2.7
2013	B	1.85	1.29	402.9	56.4	126.0	3.7
2012	B	2.23	1.55	398.9	67.7	126.0	7.2
2011	B	1.95	1.38	382.7	60.3	132.4	15.6
2010	B	1.97	1.41	381.6	60.7	135.2	18.6
2009	B	1.92	1.36	391.1	61.6	138.0	20.5

ACE Ltd
Composite Group Rating: C+

Largest Group Members	Assets ($mil)	Rating
ACE AMERICAN INS CO	11697	B-
ACE PROPERTY CASUALTY INS CO	7214	C
PACIFIC EMPLOYERS INS CO	3309	B-
WESTCHESTER FIRE INS CO	2056	C
COMBINED INS CO OF AMERICA	1589	C+

COMMUNITY CARE BEHAVIORAL HEALTH — C — Fair

Major Rating Factors: Excellent profitability (8.4 on a scale of 0 to 10). Strong capitalization (9.3) based on excellent current risk-adjusted capital (severe loss scenario). High quality investment portfolio (9.9).

Other Rating Factors: Excellent liquidity (7.0) with ample operational cash flow and liquid investments.

Principal Business: Medicaid (99%)

Mem Phys: 13: 3,233 **12:** 2,585 **13 MLR** 89.3% **/ 13 Admin Exp** N/A

Enroll(000): Q2 14: 975 **13:** 957 **12:** 866 **Med Exp PMPM:** $59

Principal Investments: Long-term bonds (60%), cash and equiv (38%), other (2%)

Provider Compensation ($000): Contr fee ($640,919), capitation ($9,905)

Total Member Encounters: Phys (26,613,339)

Group Affiliation: UPMC Health System

Licensed in: PA

Address: 112 Washington Pl Ste 700, Pittsburgh, PA 15219

Phone: (412) 454-2120 **Dom State:** PA **Commenced Bus:** August 1997

Data Date	Rating	RACR #1	RACR #2	Total Assets ($mil)	Capital ($mil)	Net Premium ($mil)	Net Income ($mil)
6-14	C	3.21	2.68	250.7	165.9	393.1	10.7
6-13	C	2.99	2.49	227.8	149.7	353.3	9.6
2013	C	3.20	2.66	234.9	155.4	735.7	15.6
2012	C	2.79	2.32	213.5	140.2	737.1	16.5
2011	N/A	N/A	N/A	215.1	129.9	713.9	22.6
2010	N/A	N/A	N/A	209.5	123.1	680.3	22.9
2009	C	N/A	N/A	186.1	101.8	649.5	15.9

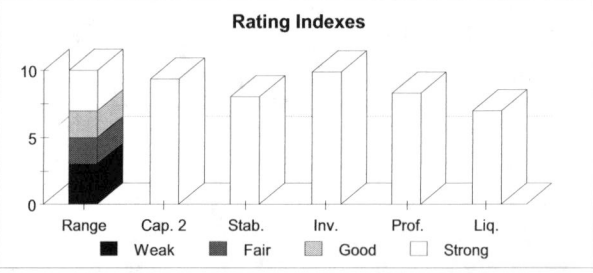

Rating Indexes

Range · Cap. 2 · Stab. · Inv. · Prof. · Liq.
■ Weak ■ Fair ▨ Good ☐ Strong

COMMUNITY CARE HEALTH PLAN INC — B- — Good

Major Rating Factors: Good capitalization (6.9 on a scale of 0 to 10) based on excellent current risk-adjusted capital (severe loss scenario). High quality investment portfolio (9.9). Excellent liquidity (7.0) with sufficient resources (cash flows and marketable investments) to handle a spike in claims.

Other Rating Factors: Weak profitability index (1.5).

Principal Business: Medicaid (60%), Medicare (40%)

Mem Phys: 13: 10,587 **12:** 7,650 **13 MLR** 89.2% **/ 13 Admin Exp** N/A

Enroll(000): Q2 14: 3 **13:** 3 **12:** 3 **Med Exp PMPM:** $2,678

Principal Investments: Cash and equiv (65%), long-term bonds (35%)

Provider Compensation ($000): Contr fee ($53,219), salary ($24,495), FFS ($320)

Total Member Encounters: Phys (35,845), non-phys (102,290)

Group Affiliation: Community Care Inc

Licensed in: WI

Address: 1555 S Layton Blvd, Milwaukee, WI 53215-1924

Phone: (414) 385-6600 **Dom State:** WI **Commenced Bus:** July 2005

Data Date	Rating	RACR #1	RACR #2	Total Assets ($mil)	Capital ($mil)	Net Premium ($mil)	Net Income ($mil)
6-14	B-	1.27	1.06	17.3	11.4	45.1	-2.6
6-13	B	1.93	1.61	24.3	16.4	45.8	0.6
2013	B	1.80	1.50	24.4	16.1	94.8	0.6
2012	B	1.84	1.54	23.7	15.7	89.0	0.0
2011	B	1.83	1.52	23.0	15.6	88.1	2.1
2010	N/A	N/A	N/A	33.6	11.5	75.7	-0.6
2009	C+	1.81	1.51	20.6	12.8	73.9	1.0

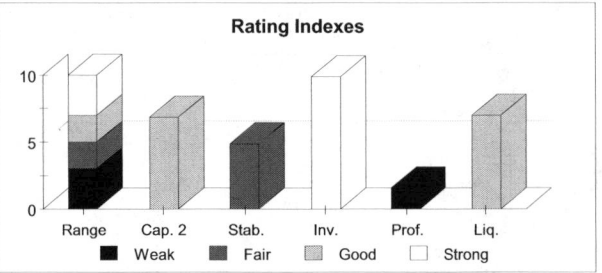

Rating Indexes

Range · Cap. 2 · Stab. · Inv. · Prof. · Liq.
■ Weak ■ Fair ▨ Good ☐ Strong

COMMUNITY FIRST HEALTH PLANS INC *   B+   Good

Major Rating Factors: Good overall profitability index (5.3 on a scale of 0 to 10). Strong capitalization index (7.7) based on excellent current risk-adjusted capital (severe loss scenario). High quality investment portfolio (9.7).
Other Rating Factors: Excellent overall results on stability tests (7.6). Excellent liquidity (7.0) with ample operational cash flow and liquid investments
Principal Business: Medicaid (77%), comp med (23%)
Mem Phys: 13: 4,552 **12:** 4,400   **13 MLR** 88.8% **/ 13 Admin Exp** N/A
Enroll(000): Q1 14: 117 **13:** 119 **12:** 115   **Med Exp PMPM:** $166
Principal Investments: Cash and equiv (64%), long-term bonds (36%)
Provider Compensation ($000): Contr fee ($233,712), capitation ($2,171)
Total Member Encounters: Phys (487,275), non-phys (618,661)
Group Affiliation: Community First Group
Licensed in: TX
Address: 4801 NW Loop 410 Ste 1000, San Antonio, TX 78229
Phone: (210) 227-2347   **Dom State:** TX   **Commenced Bus:** October 1995

Data Date	Rating	RACR #1	RACR #2	Total Assets ($mil)	Capital ($mil)	Net Premium ($mil)	Net Income ($mil)
3-14	B+	1.88	1.57	85.9	46.9	73.2	1.6
3-13	B	1.32	1.10	56.2	34.0	63.7	-4.9
2013	B+	1.75	1.46	78.1	43.8	265.0	4.6
2012	B	1.51	1.26	67.9	39.1	259.5	0.3
2011	B	1.66	1.38	77.2	39.7	256.0	12.2
2010	C	0.88	0.74	66.7	27.8	265.9	7.1
2009	C	0.61	0.51	56.5	17.2	250.6	-5.7

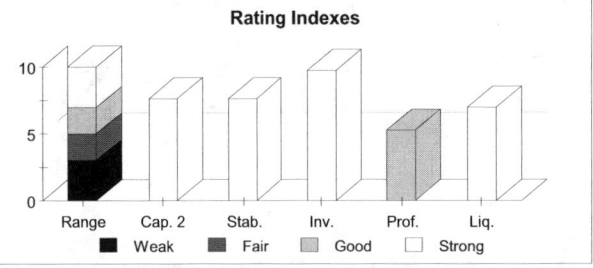

Rating Indexes

COMMUNITY HEALTH CHOICE INC   B-   Good

Major Rating Factors: Fair profitability index (3.5 on a scale of 0 to 10). Good overall results on stability tests (5.2). Strong capitalization index (7.5) based on excellent current risk-adjusted capital (severe loss scenario).
Other Rating Factors: High quality investment portfolio (9.9). Excellent liquidity (7.0) with sufficient resources (cash flows and marketable investments) to handle a spike in claims.
Principal Business: Medicaid (87%), comp med (13%)
Mem Phys: 13: 9,586 **12:** 9,804   **13 MLR** 92.7% **/ 13 Admin Exp** N/A
Enroll(000): Q2 14: 244 **13:** 237 **12:** 234   **Med Exp PMPM:** $213
Principal Investments: Cash and equiv (80%), long-term bonds (20%)
Provider Compensation ($000): Contr fee ($603,725), capitation ($20,531), bonus arrang ($659)
Total Member Encounters: Phys (1,912,987), non-phys (5,390,991)
Group Affiliation: Harris County Hospital District
Licensed in: TX
Address: 2636 South Loop West Ste 700, Houston, TX 77054
Phone: (713) 295-2200   **Dom State:** TX   **Commenced Bus:** July 1997

Data Date	Rating	RACR #1	RACR #2	Total Assets ($mil)	Capital ($mil)	Net Premium ($mil)	Net Income ($mil)
6-14	B-	1.73	1.44	174.6	96.8	346.2	9.6
6-13	B-	1.60	1.33	170.6	90.1	333.0	-0.5
2013	B-	1.47	1.22	166.6	84.3	663.4	-6.3
2012	B	1.62	1.35	172.8	91.2	636.2	-15.5
2011	A-	2.76	2.30	179.5	111.5	511.7	39.5
2010	B	1.69	1.41	123.7	73.8	473.0	1.2
2009	B+	2.01	1.68	148.9	72.8	424.0	11.7

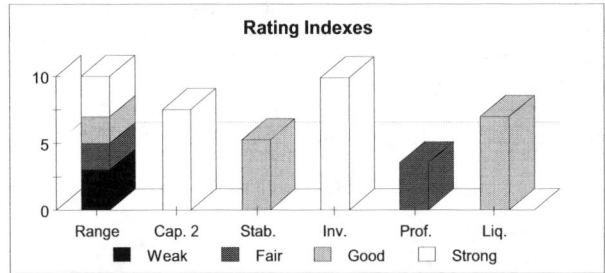

Rating Indexes

COMMUNITY HEALTH GROUP   C   Fair

Major Rating Factors: Fair profitability index (3.7 on a scale of 0 to 10). Fair overall results on stability tests (3.4) in spite of steady enrollment growth, averaging 7% over the past five years. Good capitalization index (6.9) based on good current risk-adjusted capital (moderate loss scenario).
Other Rating Factors: Excellent liquidity (6.9) with sufficient resources (cash flows and marketable investments) to handle a spike in claims.
Principal Business: Medicaid (95%), Medicare (5%)
Mem Phys: 13: N/A **12:** N/A   **13 MLR** 99.2% **/ 13 Admin Exp** N/A
Enroll(000): Q2 14: 187 **13:** 151 **12:** 149   **Med Exp PMPM:** $186
Principal Investments ($000): Cash and equiv ($31,803)
Provider Compensation ($000): None
Total Member Encounters: N/A
Group Affiliation: None
Licensed in: CA
Address: 740 Bay Blvd., Chula Vista, CA 91910
Phone: (619) 422-0422   **Dom State:** CA   **Commenced Bus:** N/A

Data Date	Rating	RACR #1	RACR #2	Total Assets ($mil)	Capital ($mil)	Net Premium ($mil)	Net Income ($mil)
6-14	C	1.03	0.65	138.7	38.9	258.6	0.5
6-13	C	1.11	0.70	90.4	37.5	166.3	-12.7
2013	C	1.02	0.64	94.5	38.3	340.7	-11.9
2012	B	1.53	0.96	98.1	50.2	312.1	-2.6
2011	B-	2.27	1.41	88.9	52.9	237.3	6.4
2010	B-	2.44	1.50	72.5	46.4	210.2	27.2
2009	C	1.10	0.67	45.1	19.2	165.1	3.5

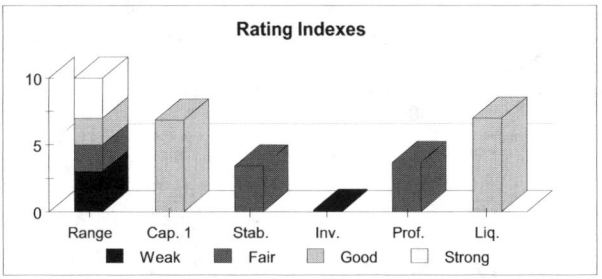

Rating Indexes

COMMUNITY HEALTH PLAN OF WASHINGTON *

A- Excellent

Major Rating Factors: Strong capitalization (7.7 on a scale of 0 to 10) based on excellent current risk-adjusted capital (severe loss scenario). High quality investment portfolio (9.9). Excellent liquidity (6.9) with sufficient resources (cash flows and marketable investments) to handle a spike in claims.
Other Rating Factors: Good overall profitability index (5.4).
Principal Business: Medicaid (74%), Medicare (19%), comp med (7%)
Mem Phys: 13: 24,507 **12:** 23,724 **13 MLR** 87.3% **/ 13 Admin Exp** N/A
Enroll(000): Q2 14: 331 **13:** 286 **12:** 295 **Med Exp PMPM:** $217
Principal Investments: Cash and equiv (47%), long-term bonds (41%), nonaffiliate common stock (12%)
Provider Compensation ($000): FFS ($516,737), capitation ($253,341), other ($16,075)
Total Member Encounters: Phys (1,080,814), non-phys (484,266)
Group Affiliation: Community Health Network Washington
Licensed in: WA
Address: 720 Olive Way Ste 300, Seattle, WA 98101
Phone: (206) 521-8833 **Dom State:** WA **Commenced Bus:** July 1996

Data Date	Rating	RACR #1	RACR #2	Total Assets ($mil)	Capital ($mil)	Net Premium ($mil)	Net Income ($mil)
6-14	A-	1.94	1.62	363.5	131.3	602.5	-8.4
6-13	B+	1.91	1.59	279.8	121.6	477.8	4.7
2013	A-	2.04	1.70	376.9	137.8	901.9	18.4
2012	B+	1.89	1.57	314.0	126.1	876.2	8.8
2011	B	2.33	1.94	210.7	105.0	706.4	11.4
2010	B	2.26	1.88	183.3	92.6	610.2	21.4
2009	C+	1.61	1.34	150.9	69.5	558.6	4.1

COMMUNITY INS CO *

B+ Good

Major Rating Factors: Good liquidity (6.2 on a scale of 0 to 10) with sufficient resources (cash flows and marketable investments) to handle a spike in claims. Excellent profitability (8.7). Strong capitalization (8.6) based on excellent current risk-adjusted capital (severe loss scenario).
Other Rating Factors: Fair quality investment portfolio (3.7).
Principal Business: Comp med (54%), Medicare (22%), FEHB (18%), med supp (2%), other (3%)
Mem Phys: 13: 61,371 **12:** 58,644 **13 MLR** 83.4% **/ 13 Admin Exp** N/A
Enroll(000): Q2 14: 2,021 **13:** 1,899 **12:** 1,876 **Med Exp PMPM:** $187
Principal Investments: Long-term bonds (86%), nonaffiliate common stock (23%), real estate (2%), other (11%)
Provider Compensation ($000): Contr fee ($2,418,700), FFS ($1,723,845), bonus arrang ($10,104), capitation ($2,103), other ($114,697)
Total Member Encounters: Phys (6,394,446), non-phys (3,997,432)
Group Affiliation: WellPoint Inc
Licensed in: IN, OH
Address: 4361 Irwin Simpson Rd, Mason, OH 45040-9498
Phone: (513) 872-8100 **Dom State:** OH **Commenced Bus:** October 1995

Data Date	Rating	RACR #1	RACR #2	Total Assets ($mil)	Capital ($mil)	Net Premium ($mil)	Net Income ($mil)
6-14	B+	2.62	2.18	2,036.0	747.1	2,664.4	139.1
6-13	B+	2.81	2.34	1,961.9	833.5	2,544.2	237.5
2013	B+	2.72	2.27	1,887.4	778.4	5,102.2	392.5
2012	B+	2.55	2.13	1,988.7	754.8	5,229.5	380.1
2011	B+	2.45	2.04	1,882.3	692.1	4,517.1	367.3
2010	B+	2.88	2.40	1,994.8	723.3	4,141.7	375.7
2009	A-	2.42	2.02	2,919.4	626.5	4,068.6	2,516.3

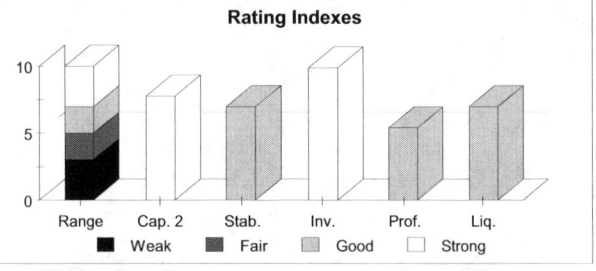

COMMUNITYCARE HMO INC *

A Excellent

Major Rating Factors: Excellent profitability (7.7 on a scale of 0 to 10). Strong capitalization index (8.8) based on excellent current risk-adjusted capital (severe loss scenario). High quality investment portfolio (9.9).
Other Rating Factors: Excellent overall results on stability tests (7.7). Excellent liquidity (7.0) with ample operational cash flow and liquid investments
Principal Business: Comp med (55%), Medicare (45%)
Mem Phys: 13: 8,179 **12:** 8,002 **13 MLR** 89.1% **/ 13 Admin Exp** N/A
Enroll(000): Q2 14: 112 **13:** 114 **12:** 108 **Med Exp PMPM:** $433
Principal Investments: Cash and equiv (71%), long-term bonds (28%), other (1%)
Provider Compensation ($000): Capitation ($288,560), contr fee ($278,526), FFS ($14)
Total Member Encounters: Phys (693,132), non-phys (751,711)
Group Affiliation: CommunityCare of Oklahoma
Licensed in: OK
Address: 218 W. 6th Street, Tulsa, OK 74119
Phone: (918) 594-5200 **Dom State:** OK **Commenced Bus:** June 1994

Data Date	Rating	RACR #1	RACR #2	Total Assets ($mil)	Capital ($mil)	Net Premium ($mil)	Net Income ($mil)
6-14	A	2.82	2.35	207.2	112.0	331.6	-1.9
6-13	A	2.91	2.43	161.7	107.9	325.0	4.1
2013	A	2.84	2.36	185.7	112.5	661.6	9.8
2012	A	2.78	2.32	153.9	102.9	606.6	8.9
2011	A	2.63	2.19	140.7	94.1	568.9	13.7
2010	A	2.37	1.98	147.5	81.8	556.0	14.6
2009	A-	1.85	1.54	126.2	70.0	562.2	4.3

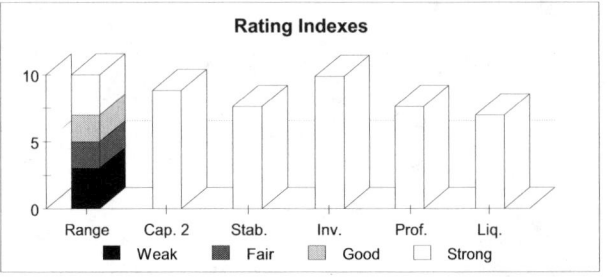

COMMUNITYCARE LIFE AND HEALTH INS CO   B-   Good

Major Rating Factors: Strong capitalization (7.7 on a scale of 0 to 10) based on excellent current risk-adjusted capital (severe loss scenario). High quality investment portfolio (9.9). Excellent liquidity (7.1) with ample operational cash flow and liquid investments.
Other Rating Factors: Weak profitability index (2.4).
Principal Business: Comp med (99%), med supp (1%)
Mem Phys: 13: 17,988 **12:** 17,982 **13 MLR** 84.0% **/ 13 Admin Exp** N/A
Enroll(000): Q2 14: 16 **13:** 17 **12:** 16 **Med Exp PMPM:** $297
Principal Investments: Cash and equiv (77%), long-term bonds (23%)
Provider Compensation ($000): Contr fee ($60,112), FFS ($2,573)
Total Member Encounters: Phys (93,681), non-phys (66,783)
Group Affiliation: CommunityCare of Oklahoma
Licensed in: OK
Address: 218 W 6th St, Tulsa, OK 74119
Phone: (918) 594-5200 **Dom State:** OK **Commenced Bus:** June 2000

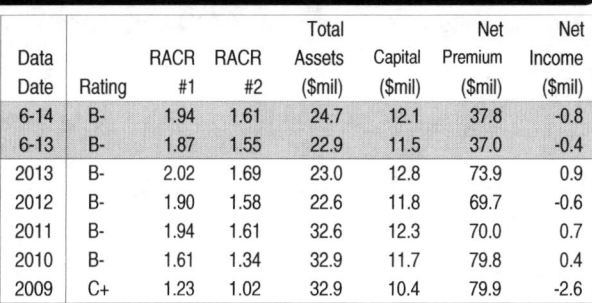

Data Date	Rating	RACR #1	RACR #2	Total Assets ($mil)	Capital ($mil)	Net Premium ($mil)	Net Income ($mil)
6-14	B-	1.94	1.61	24.7	12.1	37.8	-0.8
6-13	B-	1.87	1.55	22.9	11.5	37.0	-0.4
2013	B-	2.02	1.69	23.0	12.8	73.9	0.9
2012	B-	1.90	1.58	22.6	11.8	69.7	-0.6
2011	B-	1.94	1.61	32.6	12.3	70.0	0.7
2010	B-	1.61	1.34	32.9	11.7	79.8	0.4
2009	C+	1.23	1.02	32.9	10.4	79.9	-2.6

Rating Indexes

Range Cap. 2 Stab. Inv. Prof. Liq.
■ Weak ■ Fair ▨ Good □ Strong

COMPANION LIFE INSURANCE COMPANY *   A-   Excellent

Major Rating Factors: Good quality investment portfolio (5.7 on a scale of 0 to 10) despite mixed results such as: no exposure to mortgages and substantial holdings of BBB bonds but minimal holdings in junk bonds. Excellent overall results on stability tests (7.2). Strengths that enhance stability include excellent operational trends and excellent risk diversification. Strong capitalization (8.7) based on excellent risk adjusted capital (severe loss scenario).
Other Rating Factors: Excellent profitability (8.6) with operating gains in each of the last five years. Excellent liquidity (7.4).
Principal Business: Group health insurance (91%), group life insurance (5%), reinsurance (3%), and individual health insurance (1%).
Principal Investments: NonCMO investment grade bonds (37%), common & preferred stock (23%), cash (22%), CMOs and structured securities (17%), and noninv. grade bonds (1%).
Investments in Affiliates: 8%
Group Affiliation: Blue Cross Blue Shield of S Carolina
Licensed in: All states except CA, HI, NJ, NY, PR
Commenced Business: July 1970
Address: 2501 Faraway Dr, Columbia, SC 29219
Phone: (800) 753-0404 **Domicile State:** SC **NAIC Code:** 77828

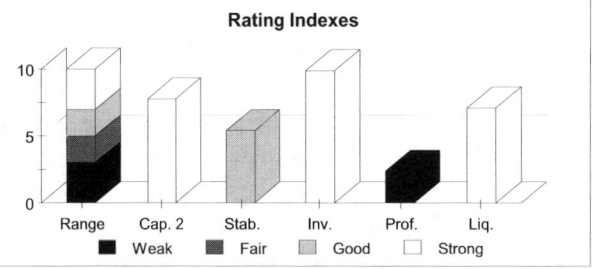

Data Date	Rating	RACR #1	RACR #2	Total Assets ($mil)	Capital ($mil)	Net Premium ($mil)	Net Income ($mil)
6-14	A-	2.76	2.16	278.1	134.8	110.9	8.4
6-13	A-	2.84	2.26	218.9	126.6	100.0	6.6
2013	A-	2.92	2.31	251.7	138.0	202.8	14.5
2012	A-	2.75	2.19	203.8	120.7	181.8	12.5
2011	A-	2.53	2.02	186.8	110.0	177.8	8.7
2010	A-	2.86	2.20	160.1	91.8	161.5	8.4
2009	A-	3.01	2.38	140.2	84.8	152.1	7.0

Rating Indexes

Ranges Cap. Stab. Inv. Prof. Liq.
■ Weak ■ Fair ▨ Good □ Strong

COMPBENEFITS INSURANCE COMPANY   B   Good

Major Rating Factors: Good overall profitability (6.1 on a scale of 0 to 10) despite operating losses during the first six months of 2014. Return on equity has been fair, averaging 9.6%. Good liquidity (6.3) with sufficient resources to handle a spike in claims. Fair overall results on stability tests (4.2) including fair financial strength of affiliated Humana Inc.
Other Rating Factors: Strong capitalization (7.9) based on excellent risk adjusted capital (severe loss scenario). High quality investment portfolio (8.8).
Principal Business: Group health insurance (97%) and individual health insurance (3%).
Principal Investments: NonCMO investment grade bonds (61%), CMOs and structured securities (38%), and cash (1%).
Investments in Affiliates: None
Group Affiliation: Humana Inc
Licensed in: AL, AZ, AR, CO, DC, FL, GA, ID, IL, IN, IA, KS, KY, LA, MD, MI, MS, MO, NE, NV, NM, NY, NC, ND, OH, OK, OR, SC, TN, TX, UT, VA, WA, WV
Commenced Business: November 1959
Address: 2929 Briar Park Suite 314, Houston, TX 77042
Phone: (770) 998-8936 **Domicile State:** TX **NAIC Code:** 60984

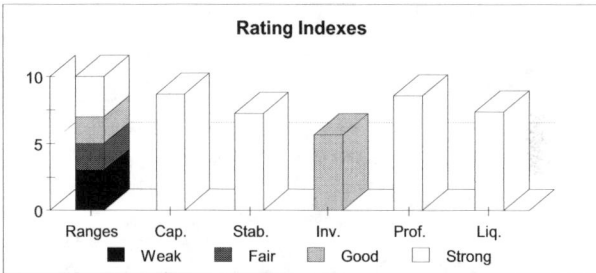

Data Date	Rating	RACR #1	RACR #2	Total Assets ($mil)	Capital ($mil)	Net Premium ($mil)	Net Income ($mil)
6-14	B	1.96	1.59	50.1	40.2	49.8	-0.5
6-13	B	1.76	1.45	51.8	40.4	60.2	1.2
2013	B	1.83	1.49	51.5	40.9	118.9	1.7
2012	B	1.83	1.50	54.2	42.8	125.4	4.1
2011	B	0.99	0.82	33.2	23.1	126.7	2.5
2010	B+	1.52	1.26	49.9	35.7	128.7	7.0
2009	B+	1.40	1.17	47.0	32.2	127.4	3.3

Humana Inc Composite Group Rating: C+ Largest Group Members	Assets ($mil)	Rating
KANAWHA INS CO	1623	C
HUMANA MEDICAL PLAN INC	1595	B
HUMANA HEALTH PLAN INC	812	C
HUMANA HEALTH BENEFIT PLAN LA	388	B
HUMANA HEALTH PLAN OF TEXAS INC	335	B

COMPCARE HEALTH SERVICES INS CORP *   A-   Excellent

Major Rating Factors: Excellent profitability (9.2 on a scale of 0 to 10). Strong capitalization index (10.0) based on excellent current risk-adjusted capital (severe loss scenario). High quality investment portfolio (7.1).

Other Rating Factors: Good overall results on stability tests (6.7) despite inconsistent enrollment growth in the past five years due to declines in 2010 and 2011, a decline in the number of member physicians during 2014 but healthy premium and capital growth during 2013. Rating is significantly influenced by the good financial results of WellPoint Inc. Good liquidity (6.6) with sufficient resources (cash flows and marketable investments) to handle a spike in claims.

Principal Business: Comp med (71%), Medicaid (25%), dental (2%), Medicare (1%)

Mem Phys: 13: 13,147 **12:** 20,365 **13 MLR** 82.6% **/ 13 Admin Exp** N/A

Enroll(000): Q2 14: 209 **13:** 201 **12:** 170 **Med Exp PMPM:** $210

Principal Investments: Long-term bonds (110%)

Provider Compensation ($000): FFS ($251,954), contr fee ($225,502), capitation ($7,367), bonus arrang ($340)

Total Member Encounters: Phys (875,543), non-phys (430,701)

Group Affiliation: WellPoint Inc

Licensed in: WI

Address: 6775 W Washington St, Milwaukee, WI 53214-5644

Phone: (414) 459-5000 **Dom State:** WI **Commenced Bus:** February 1976

Data Date	Rating	RACR #1	RACR #2	Total Assets ($mil)	Capital ($mil)	Net Premium ($mil)	Net Income ($mil)
6-14	A-	3.64	3.03	233.6	121.0	334.9	16.0
6-13	B+	3.96	3.30	192.0	105.1	282.1	22.0
2013	A-	3.15	2.63	190.2	103.9	599.3	40.6
2012	B+	3.28	2.73	163.7	86.0	471.3	32.9
2011	B+	3.51	2.92	164.4	90.9	465.6	34.5
2010	B	3.05	2.54	177.8	95.1	507.8	12.3
2009	B	2.22	1.85	128.4	63.7	473.1	13.1

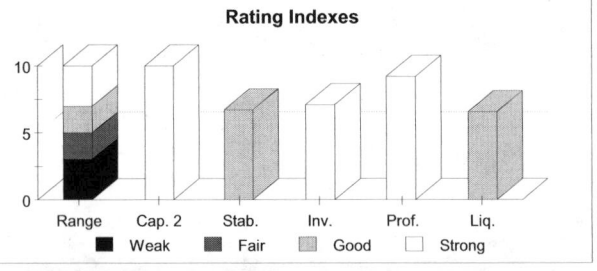

CONNECTICARE INC   B   Good

Major Rating Factors: Good overall results on stability tests (4.9 on a scale of 0 to 10) based on a significant 25% decrease in enrollment during the period. Good financial strength from affiliates. Good liquidity (6.3) with sufficient resources (cash flows and marketable investments) to handle a spike in claims. Fair profitability index (4.2).

Other Rating Factors: Strong capitalization index (8.9) based on excellent current risk-adjusted capital (severe loss scenario). High quality investment portfolio (8.5).

Principal Business: Medicare (50%), comp med (50%)

Mem Phys: 13: 19,663 **12:** 17,965 **13 MLR** 85.0% **/ 13 Admin Exp** N/A

Enroll(000): Q2 14: 99 **13:** 107 **12:** 143 **Med Exp PMPM:** $508

Principal Investments: Long-term bonds (106%)

Provider Compensation ($000): Contr fee ($619,690), FFS ($89,648), capitation ($13,865), bonus arrang ($810)

Total Member Encounters: Phys (826,111), non-phys (505,654)

Group Affiliation: EmblemHealth Inc

Licensed in: CT

Address: 175 Scott Swamp Rd, Farmington, CT 06032

Phone: (860) 674-5700 **Dom State:** CT **Commenced Bus:** July 1999

Data Date	Rating	RACR #1	RACR #2	Total Assets ($mil)	Capital ($mil)	Net Premium ($mil)	Net Income ($mil)
6-14	B	2.85	2.37	265.5	127.4	394.1	-8.5
6-13	B+	3.05	2.54	279.0	160.8	427.4	10.9
2013	B+	3.08	2.57	246.6	138.7	834.3	16.8
2012	B+	2.92	2.43	278.7	153.3	971.9	31.4
2011	B+	2.75	2.30	284.7	139.6	962.0	34.5
2010	B	3.25	2.70	273.2	129.9	768.0	27.3
2009	B	2.02	1.68	226.4	103.2	860.6	-6.1

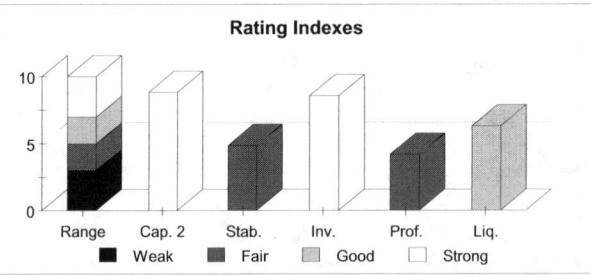

CONNECTICARE INS CO INC   C   Fair

Major Rating Factors: Good overall profitability index (6.8 on a scale of 0 to 10). Good liquidity (6.9) with sufficient resources (cash flows and marketable investments) to handle a spike in claims. Strong capitalization (7.9) based on excellent current risk-adjusted capital (severe loss scenario).

Other Rating Factors: High quality investment portfolio (9.9).

Principal Business: Comp med (99%)

Mem Phys: 13: 19,663 **12:** 17,965 **13 MLR** 79.7% **/ 13 Admin Exp** N/A

Enroll(000): Q2 14: 115 **13:** 92 **12:** 64 **Med Exp PMPM:** $310

Principal Investments: Long-term bonds (60%), cash and equiv (39%), affiliate common stock (1%)

Provider Compensation ($000): Contr fee ($257,091), FFS ($46,786), capitation ($8,792)

Total Member Encounters: Phys (343,234), non-phys (222,189)

Group Affiliation: EmblemHealth Inc

Licensed in: CT

Address: 175 Scott Swamp Rd, Farmington, CT 06032

Phone: (860) 674-5700 **Dom State:** CT **Commenced Bus:** October 2002

Data Date	Rating	RACR #1	RACR #2	Total Assets ($mil)	Capital ($mil)	Net Premium ($mil)	Net Income ($mil)
6-14	C	2.09	1.74	116.3	44.4	254.9	-2.3
6-13	C-	2.64	2.20	80.9	33.4	189.0	9.5
2013	C	1.80	1.50	90.5	37.9	404.9	14.1
2012	D+	1.92	1.60	61.7	23.7	224.5	4.1
2011	D+	2.88	2.40	48.8	21.2	139.7	8.5
2010	D	3.11	2.59	29.1	14.7	80.6	4.7
2009	D	1.24	1.03	31.5	9.1	144.8	-6.5

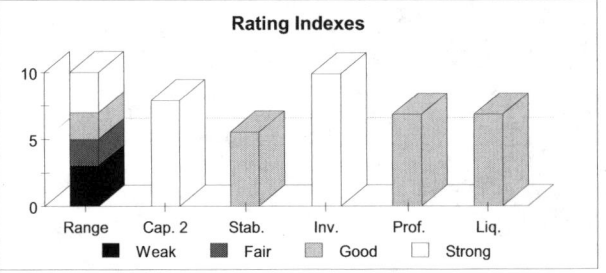

CONNECTICARE OF MASSACHUSETTS INC   C   Fair

Major Rating Factors: Weak overall results on stability tests (2.1 on a scale of 0 to 10) based on a steep decline in capital during 2013. Rating is significantly influenced by the good financial results of EmblemHealth Inc. Excellent overall profitability index (6.9). Strong capitalization index (8.7) based on excellent current risk-adjusted capital (severe loss scenario).
Other Rating Factors: High quality investment portfolio (9.9). Excellent liquidity (6.9) with sufficient resources (cash flows and marketable investments) to handle a spike in claims.
Principal Business: Comp med (100%)
Mem Phys: 13: 19,663 **12:** 17,965 **13 MLR** 81.4% **/ 13 Admin Exp** N/A
Enroll(000): Q2 14: 2 **13:** 3 **12:** 4 **Med Exp PMPM:** $307
Principal Investments: Long-term bonds (67%), cash and equiv (33%)
Provider Compensation ($000): Contr fee ($9,560), FFS ($2,037), capitation ($442)
Total Member Encounters: Phys (15,202), non-phys (6,704)
Group Affiliation: EmblemHealth Inc
Licensed in: MA
Address: 260 Franklin St, Boston, MA 02110-3173
Phone: (860) 674-5700 **Dom State:** MA **Commenced Bus:** July 2000

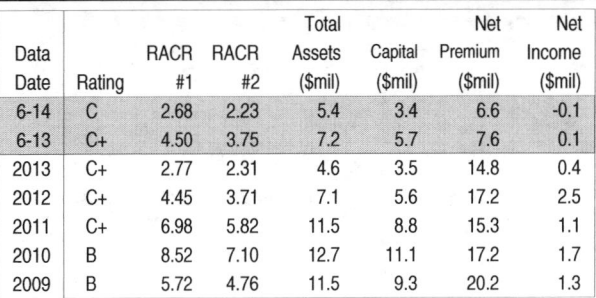

Data Date	Rating	RACR #1	RACR #2	Total Assets ($mil)	Capital ($mil)	Net Premium ($mil)	Net Income ($mil)
6-14	C	2.68	2.23	5.4	3.4	6.6	-0.1
6-13	C+	4.50	3.75	7.2	5.7	7.6	0.1
2013	C+	2.77	2.31	4.6	3.5	14.8	0.4
2012	C+	4.45	3.71	7.1	5.6	17.2	2.5
2011	C+	6.98	5.82	11.5	8.8	15.3	1.1
2010	B	8.52	7.10	12.7	11.1	17.2	1.7
2009	B	5.72	4.76	11.5	9.3	20.2	1.3

Rating Indexes

Range Cap. 2 Stab. Inv. Prof. Liq.
■ Weak ■ Fair ▨ Good □ Strong

CONNECTICUT GENERAL LIFE INSURANCE COMPANY   B-   Good

Major Rating Factors: Good liquidity (6.1 on a scale of 0 to 10) with sufficient resources to handle a spike in claims as well as a significant increase in policy surrenders. Fair quality investment portfolio (4.4) with substantial holdings of BBB bonds in addition to moderate junk bond exposure. Fair overall results on stability tests (3.8) including negative cash flow from operations for 2013.
Other Rating Factors: Strong capitalization (7.5) based on excellent risk adjusted capital (severe loss scenario). Excellent profitability (8.9) with operating gains in each of the last five years.
Principal Business: Group health insurance (47%), individual health insurance (36%), individual life insurance (8%), group life insurance (6%), and reinsurance (2%).
Principal Investments: NonCMO investment grade bonds (31%), common & preferred stock (20%), policy loans (16%), noninv. grade bonds (11%), and misc. investments (22%).
Investments in Affiliates: 24%
Group Affiliation: CIGNA Corp
Licensed in: All states, the District of Columbia and Puerto Rico
Commenced Business: October 1865
Address: 900 Cottage Grove Rd, S-330, Bloomfield, CT 06002
Phone: (860) 726-7234 **Domicile State:** CT **NAIC Code:** 62308

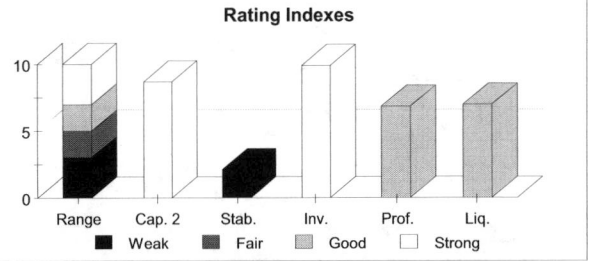

Data Date	Rating	RACR #1	RACR #2	Total Assets ($mil)	Capital ($mil)	Net Premium ($mil)	Net Income ($mil)
6-14	B-	1.61	1.31	18,669.3	3,248.7	628.7	131.1
6-13	B-	1.85	1.40	20,205.5	3,054.3	2,048.8	318.7
2013	B-	1.63	1.33	18,573.6	3,283.0	3,440.5	601.8
2012	B-	1.78	1.35	20,921.6	3,040.9	7,272.6	588.9
2011	B-	2.04	1.48	20,751.9	2,918.2	6,803.9	590.3
2010	C+	2.64	1.77	20,055.5	3,014.5	8,750.9	676.4
2009	C+	2.89	1.93	19,037.0	2,919.2	6,821.0	647.1

Rating Indexes

Ranges Cap. Stab. Inv. Prof. Liq.
■ Weak ■ Fair ▨ Good □ Strong

CONSTITUTION LIFE INSURANCE COMPANY   C+   Fair

Major Rating Factors: Fair overall results on stability tests (4.5 on a scale of 0 to 10) including fair financial strength of affiliated Universal American Corp and excessive premium growth. Good quality investment portfolio (6.9) despite mixed results such as: no exposure to mortgages and large holdings of BBB rated bonds but minimal holdings in junk bonds. Weak profitability (2.9) with investment income below regulatory standards in relation to interest assumptions of reserves.
Other Rating Factors: Strong capitalization (7.3) based on excellent risk adjusted capital (severe loss scenario). Excellent liquidity (7.3).
Principal Business: Reinsurance (50%), individual health insurance (41%), and individual life insurance (8%).
Principal Investments: NonCMO investment grade bonds (59%), CMOs and structured securities (41%), and noninv. grade bonds (1%).
Investments in Affiliates: None
Group Affiliation: Universal American Corp
Licensed in: All states except NJ, NY, PR
Commenced Business: June 1929
Address: 4211 Norbourne Blvd, Louisville, KY 40207-4048
Phone: (214) 954-7111 **Domicile State:** TX **NAIC Code:** 62359

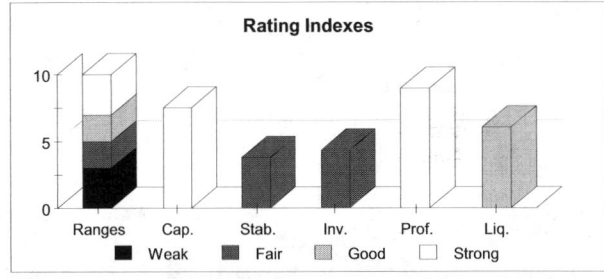

Data Date	Rating	RACR #1	RACR #2	Total Assets ($mil)	Capital ($mil)	Net Premium ($mil)	Net Income ($mil)
6-14	C+	1.76	1.17	319.1	36.7	49.6	3.9
6-13	B	1.24	0.94	53.2	22.1	31.5	2.2
2013	C+	1.56	1.05	317.3	33.5	109.5	9.2
2012	B-	1.52	1.16	57.4	28.4	69.2	4.5
2011	C	1.66	1.26	56.7	27.1	56.0	4.9
2010	C+	2.32	1.76	62.9	37.2	54.7	11.7
2009	C+	2.08	1.59	54.7	27.5	-3.8	3.7

Universal American Corp Composite Group Rating: C Largest Group Members	Assets ($mil)	Rating
CONSTITUTION LIFE INS CO	317	C+
AMERICAN PROGRESSIVE LH I C OF NY	236	B
PYRAMID LIFE INS CO	212	C
SELECTCARE OF TEXAS LLC	133	C
AMERICAN PIONEER LIFE INS CO	77	D+

CONTINENTAL AMERICAN INSURANCE COMPANY   B   Good

Major Rating Factors: Good overall results on stability tests (5.7 on a scale of 0 to 10). Strengths include good financial support from affiliation with AFLAC Inc, excellent operational trends and excellent risk diversification. Weak profitability (1.9). Return on equity has been low, averaging -13.6%. Strong capitalization (9.2) based on excellent risk adjusted capital (severe loss scenario).

Other Rating Factors: High quality investment portfolio (8.5). Excellent liquidity (7.4).

Principal Business: Group health insurance (92%), group life insurance (4%), and reinsurance (3%).

Principal Investments: NonCMO investment grade bonds (81%), cash (17%), policy loans (1%), and real estate (1%).

Investments in Affiliates: None

Group Affiliation: AFLAC Inc

Licensed in: All states except NY, PR

Commenced Business: January 1969

Address: 2801 Devine St, Columbia, SC 29205

Phone: (803) 256-6265   **Domicile State:** SC   **NAIC Code:** 71730

Data Date	Rating	RACR #1	RACR #2	Total Assets ($mil)	Capital ($mil)	Net Premium ($mil)	Net Income ($mil)
6-14	B	3.41	2.45	404.2	139.8	124.1	7.6
6-13	B	3.76	2.70	365.1	134.9	119.5	6.7
2013	B	3.47	2.49	382.4	138.0	233.4	18.8
2012	B	4.36	3.13	344.0	137.4	183.7	-21.2
2011	B	1.68	1.32	167.4	36.0	162.6	-32.4
2010	A-	2.30	1.78	116.8	31.5	104.0	-2.1
2009	A-	3.08	2.36	118.0	38.5	87.3	5.8

AFLAC Inc Composite Group Rating: B+ Largest Group Members	Assets ($mil)	Rating
AMERICAN FAMILY LIFE ASR CO OF COLUM	107913	B+
AMERICAN FAMILY LIFE ASR CO OF NY	645	A-
CONTINENTAL AMERICAN INS CO	382	B

CONTINENTAL LIFE INSURANCE COMPANY OF BRENTWOOD   B   Good

Major Rating Factors: Good current capitalization (6.4 on a scale of 0 to 10) based on good risk adjusted capital (severe loss scenario), although results have slipped from the excellent range during the last year. Good quality investment portfolio (6.7) with no exposure to mortgages and no exposure to junk bonds. Good overall results on stability tests (5.5) despite excessive premium growth and fair risk adjusted capital in prior years good operational trends and excellent risk diversification.

Other Rating Factors: Weak profitability (2.9) with operating losses during the first six months of 2014. Excellent liquidity (7.0).

Principal Business: Individual health insurance (96%), group health insurance (3%), and individual life insurance (2%).

Principal Investments: NonCMO investment grade bonds (30%), cash (29%), common & preferred stock (27%), CMOs and structured securities (14%), and policy loans (1%).

Investments in Affiliates: 27%

Group Affiliation: Aetna Inc

Licensed in: AL, AZ, AR, CO, DE, FL, GA, ID, IL, IN, IA, KS, KY, LA, MD, MI, MN, MS, MO, MT, NE, NV, NM, NC, ND, OH, OK, PA, RI, SC, SD, TN, TX, UT, VA, WV, WI, WY

Commenced Business: December 1983

Address: 800 Crescent Centre Dr, Franklin, TN 37067

Phone: (800) 264-4000   **Domicile State:** TN   **NAIC Code:** 68500

Data Date	Rating	RACR #1	RACR #2	Total Assets ($mil)	Capital ($mil)	Net Premium ($mil)	Net Income ($mil)
6-14	B	1.05	0.93	211.8	96.6	161.1	-3.5
6-13	B	0.76	0.69	170.4	67.3	120.8	-1.3
2013	B	1.12	1.01	205.6	97.0	256.6	3.2
2012	B	0.97	0.89	175.6	80.2	166.4	9.7
2011	C	0.71	0.65	144.3	54.2	139.0	5.7
2010	B	0.93	0.83	143.9	59.0	142.5	11.6
2009	B+	1.53	1.29	146.0	61.4	152.2	11.1

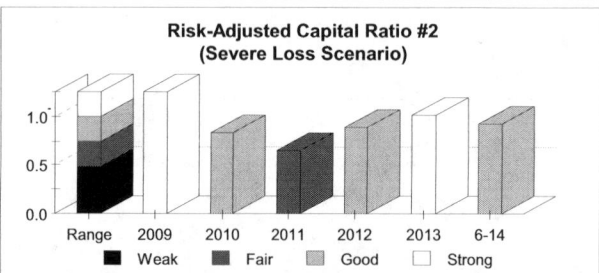

Risk-Adjusted Capital Ratio #2 (Severe Loss Scenario)

Range — 2009 — 2010 — 2011 — 2012 — 2013 — 6-14
■ Weak ■ Fair ▨ Good □ Strong

CONTRA COSTA HEALTH PLAN   D   Weak

Major Rating Factors: Poor capitalization index (1.6 on a scale of 0 to 10) based on weak current risk-adjusted capital (moderate loss scenario). Good overall results on stability tests (6.4) based on steady enrollment growth, averaging 10% over the past five years, healthy premium and capital growth during 2013. Excellent profitability (7.6).

Other Rating Factors: Excellent liquidity (6.9) with sufficient resources (cash flows and marketable investments) to handle a spike in claims.

Principal Business: Medicaid (82%).

Mem Phys: 13: N/A **12:** N/A **13 MLR** 106.9% **/ 13 Admin Exp** N/A

Enroll(000): Q2 14: 120 **13:** 118 **12:** 109 **Med Exp PMPM:** $285

Principal Investments ($000): None

Provider Compensation ($000): None

Total Member Encounters: N/A

Group Affiliation: None

Licensed in: CA

Address: 50 Doutlas Suite 310, Martinez, CA 94553

Phone: (925) 313-6000   **Dom State:** CA   **Commenced Bus:** November 1973

Data Date	Rating	RACR #1	RACR #2	Total Assets ($mil)	Capital ($mil)	Net Premium ($mil)	Net Income ($mil)
6-14	D	0.57	0.38	59.1	14.8	177.7	0.9
6-13	D	0.60	0.39	78.1	12.6	128.4	0.5
2013	D	0.53	0.35	139.4	13.9	356.1	1.8
2012	D	0.58	0.37	97.1	12.1	255.9	4.0
2011	D-	0.49	0.31	88.5	8.1	214.7	0.7
2010	D-	0.45	0.29	67.9	7.3	184.4	2.7
2009	E+	0.33	0.21	48.4	4.6	163.1	0.2

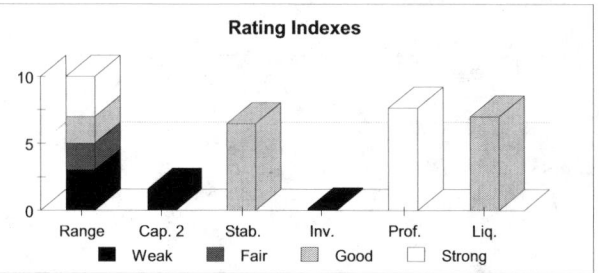

Rating Indexes

Range — Cap. 2 — Stab. — Inv. — Prof. — Liq.
■ Weak ■ Fair ▨ Good □ Strong

COOK CHILDRENS HEALTH PLAN   E+   Very Weak

Major Rating Factors: Good overall profitability index (5.4 on a scale of 0 to 10). Good capitalization index (5.9) based on good current risk-adjusted capital (severe loss scenario). Good overall results on stability tests (6.3).
Other Rating Factors: High quality investment portfolio (9.9). Excellent liquidity (7.1) with ample operational cash flow and liquid investments.
Principal Business: Medicaid (77%), comp med (23%)
Mem Phys: 13: 2,624 **12:** 2,588 **13 MLR** 91.2% **/ 13 Admin Exp** N/A
Enroll(000): Q2 14: 114 **13:** 109 **12:** 108 **Med Exp PMPM:** $181
Principal Investments: Cash and equiv (100%)
Provider Compensation ($000): Contr fee ($231,374), capitation ($2,077), bonus arrang ($166)
Total Member Encounters: Phys (2,032,465), non-phys (271,911)
Group Affiliation: Cook Childrens Health Care System
Licensed in: TX
Address: 801 Seventh Ave, Fort Worth, TX 76104
Phone: (817) 334-2247 **Dom State:** TX **Commenced Bus:** April 1999

Data Date	Rating	RACR #1	RACR #2	Total Assets ($mil)	Capital ($mil)	Net Premium ($mil)	Net Income ($mil)
6-14	E+	1.07	0.89	71.2	33.5	136.8	-2.5
6-13	E+	1.13	0.94	58.2	27.9	127.6	-3.1
2013	E+	1.16	0.97	68.6	36.1	265.2	4.1
2012	E+	1.27	1.05	57.3	31.2	237.4	8.4
2011	E+	1.18	0.99	51.5	24.3	195.5	8.8
2010	E+	0.87	0.73	34.9	16.0	169.1	4.8
2009	E	0.02	0.02	28.6	9.8	131.5	-4.1

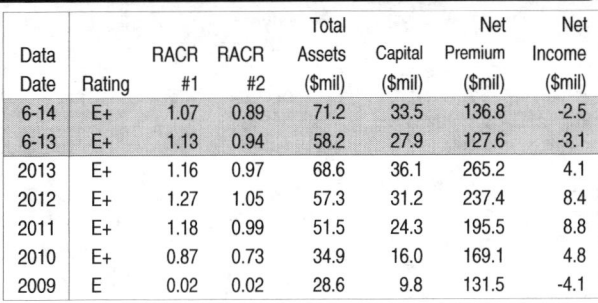

Rating Indexes

COORDINATED CARE CORP   C+   Fair

Major Rating Factors: Fair profitability index (4.7 on a scale of 0 to 10). Good overall results on stability tests (6.6). Fair financial strength from affiliates. Good liquidity (6.9) with sufficient resources (cash flows and marketable investments) to handle a spike in claims.
Other Rating Factors: Strong capitalization index (8.3) based on excellent current risk-adjusted capital (severe loss scenario). High quality investment portfolio (9.9).
Principal Business: Medicaid (99%)
Mem Phys: 13: 23,988 **12:** 21,344 **13 MLR** 85.7% **/ 13 Admin Exp** N/A
Enroll(000): Q2 14: 394 **13:** 277 **12:** 259 **Med Exp PMPM:** $152
Principal Investments: Cash and equiv (51%), long-term bonds (42%), affiliate common stock (6%), other (1%)
Provider Compensation ($000): Contr fee ($357,647), bonus arrang ($50,078), capitation ($48,944), salary ($9,637)
Total Member Encounters: Phys (1,432,861), non-phys (1,037,783)
Group Affiliation: Centene Corp
Licensed in: IN, WA
Address: 1099 N Meridian St Ste 400, Indianapolis, IN 46204-1041
Phone: (314) 725-4706 **Dom State:** IN **Commenced Bus:** August 1996

Data Date	Rating	RACR #1	RACR #2	Total Assets ($mil)	Capital ($mil)	Net Premium ($mil)	Net Income ($mil)
6-14	C+	2.41	2.01	319.9	69.0	462.7	-6.5
6-13	B-	2.89	2.41	143.9	56.3	283.2	9.0
2013	C+	2.03	1.70	188.3	57.1	570.0	4.9
2012	B-	2.54	2.12	154.1	51.0	387.5	1.2
2011	B-	2.69	2.25	82.7	46.8	297.1	11.9
2010	B-	2.44	2.03	79.8	45.8	314.1	11.3
2009	B	1.45	1.21	78.0	37.0	382.3	1.9

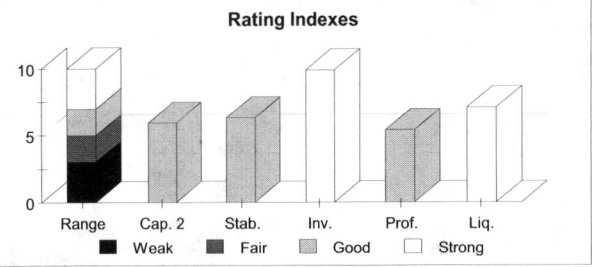

Rating Indexes

COUNTY OF LOS ANGELES DEPT HEALTH   D   Weak

Major Rating Factors: Weak overall results on stability tests (0.2 on a scale of 0 to 10). Good overall profitability index (5.6). Strong capitalization index (10.0) based on excellent current risk-adjusted capital (severe loss scenario).
Other Rating Factors: Excellent liquidity (10.0) with ample operational cash flow and liquid investments.
Principal Business: Medicaid (100%)
Mem Phys: 13: N/A **12:** N/A **13 MLR** 125.7% **/ 13 Admin Exp** N/A
Enroll(000): Q1 14: N/A **13:** N/A **12:** 12 **Med Exp PMPM:** N/A
Principal Investments ($000): Cash and equiv ($26,952)
Provider Compensation ($000): None
Total Member Encounters: N/A
Group Affiliation: None
Licensed in: CA
Address: 1000 S Fremont Ave Bldg A9, Alhambra, CA 91803
Phone: (626) 299-5300 **Dom State:** CA **Commenced Bus:** December 1985

Data Date	Rating	RACR #1	RACR #2	Total Assets ($mil)	Capital ($mil)	Net Premium ($mil)	Net Income ($mil)
3-14	D	32.41	21.55	14.3	12.8	N/A	0.6
3-13	C-	3.72	2.29	35.6	46.1	2.6	1.6
2013	C-	N/A	N/A	27.7	13.2	2.1	0.8
2012	C-	3.56	2.19	35.6	44.5	184.1	24.4
2011	D	0.81	0.50	69.3	18.5	306.5	18.3
2010	D	0.62	0.39	69.3	13.6	284.7	16.6
2009	D+	0.90	0.57	68.3	17.3	262.9	23.6

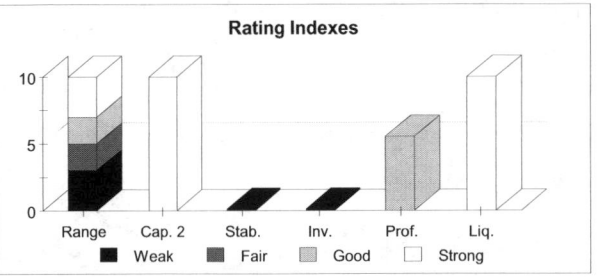

Rating Indexes

COVENTRY HEALTH & LIFE INS CO *

B+　　**Good**

Major Rating Factors: Good quality investment portfolio (6.6 on a scale of 0 to 10). Good liquidity (6.8) with sufficient resources (cash flows and marketable investments) to handle a spike in claims. Excellent profitability (7.2).
Other Rating Factors: Strong capitalization (9.6) based on excellent current risk-adjusted capital (severe loss scenario).
Principal Business: Comp med (44%), Medicaid (32%), Medicare (20%), other (3%)
Mem Phys: 13: N/A　**12:** N/A　**13 MLR** 81.5%　**/ 13 Admin Exp** N/A
Enroll(000): Q2 14: 1,016　**13:** 830　**12:** 767　**Med Exp PMPM:** $289
Principal Investments: Long-term bonds (77%), cash and equiv (23%)
Provider Compensation ($000): Contr fee ($2,458,303), FFS ($175,254), capitation ($103,666), bonus arrang ($208), other ($1,968)
Total Member Encounters: Phys (7,345,518), non-phys (1,736,746)
Group Affiliation: Aetna Inc
Licensed in: AL, AZ, AR, CO, DC, DE, FL, GA, IL, IN, IA, KS, KY, LA, ME, MD, MA, MI, MS, MO, NE, NV, NC, ND, OH, OK, PA, SC, SD, TN, TX, UT, VA, WA, WV, WI, WY
Address: 550 Maryville Center Dr #300, St Louis, MO 63141
Phone: (800) 843-7421　**Dom State:** MO　**Commenced Bus:** May 1968

Data Date	Rating	RACR #1	RACR #2	Total Assets ($mil)	Capital ($mil)	Net Premium ($mil)	Net Income ($mil)
6-14	B+	3.41	2.84	1,547.4	654.0	2,272.5	61.6
6-13	B+	2.81	2.35	1,058.7	542.2	1,654.0	61.1
2013	B+	3.08	2.57	1,162.5	585.9	3,441.1	117.9
2012	B+	2.50	2.09	936.0	478.1	3,303.6	39.8
2011	B+	2.71	2.26	813.4	339.9	2,393.7	70.4
2010	B+	4.18	3.48	792.8	425.9	2,496.3	139.8
2009	B+	2.22	1.85	950.7	418.6	3,593.2	1.6

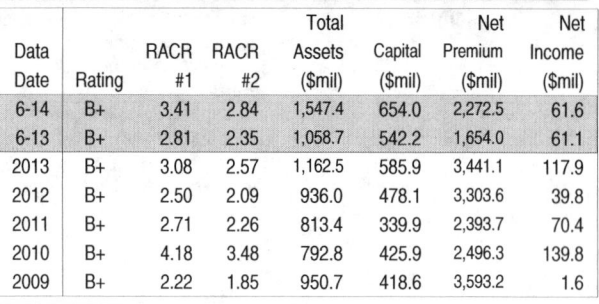

Rating Indexes

COVENTRY HEALTH CARE CAROLINAS INC

B　　**Good**

Major Rating Factors: Good quality investment portfolio (6.6 on a scale of 0 to 10). Good overall results on stability tests (6.3). Rating is significantly influenced by the good financial results of Aetna Inc. Good liquidity (6.7) with sufficient resources (cash flows and marketable investments) to handle a spike in claims.
Other Rating Factors: Excellent profitability (8.6). Strong capitalization index (8.7) based on excellent current risk-adjusted capital (severe loss scenario).
Principal Business: Comp med (100%)
Mem Phys: 13: 27,419　**12:** 25,576　**13 MLR** 81.7%　**/ 13 Admin Exp** N/A
Enroll(000): Q2 14: 178　**13:** 103　**12:** 87　**Med Exp PMPM:** $231
Principal Investments: Long-term bonds (74%), cash and equiv (26%)
Provider Compensation ($000): Contr fee ($218,849), FFS ($27,233), capitation ($272)
Total Member Encounters: Phys (79,916), non-phys (373,837)
Group Affiliation: Aetna Inc
Licensed in: NC, SC
Address: 2801 Slater Rd Suite 200, Morrisville, NC 27560
Phone: (804) 747-3700　**Dom State:** NC　**Commenced Bus:** January 1996

Data Date	Rating	RACR #1	RACR #2	Total Assets ($mil)	Capital ($mil)	Net Premium ($mil)	Net Income ($mil)
6-14	B	2.68	2.24	144.8	44.7	277.7	7.0
6-13	B	2.68	2.23	86.9	42.6	148.8	3.5
2013	B	2.30	1.91	89.8	37.8	307.7	3.6
2012	B	2.48	2.07	82.1	39.3	303.4	10.8
2011	B	3.37	2.81	93.2	42.6	247.7	9.2
2010	B	3.25	2.71	71.7	43.0	220.1	10.1
2009	B	2.03	1.69	54.3	29.5	228.0	5.2

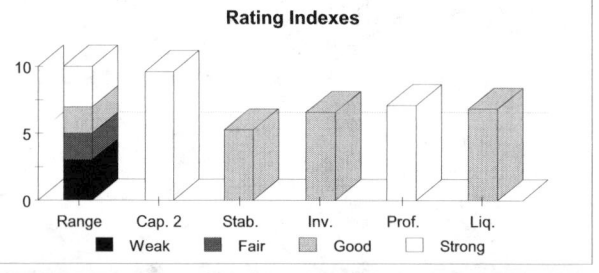

Rating Indexes

COVENTRY HEALTH CARE OF DELAWARE INC

B　　**Good**

Major Rating Factors: Good overall profitability index (6.6 on a scale of 0 to 10). Good quality investment portfolio (5.6). Good liquidity (6.8) with sufficient resources (cash flows and marketable investments) to handle a spike in claims.
Other Rating Factors: Fair overall results on stability tests (4.3) based on a significant 36% decrease in enrollment during the period. Rating is significantly influenced by the good financial results of Aetna Inc. Strong capitalization index (10.0) based on excellent current risk-adjusted capital (severe loss scenario).
Principal Business: Comp med (74%), Medicaid (23%), FEHB (4%)
Mem Phys: 13: 16,243　**12:** 15,251　**13 MLR** 81.4%　**/ 13 Admin Exp** N/A
Enroll(000): Q2 14: 29　**13:** 32　**12:** 50　**Med Exp PMPM:** $281
Principal Investments: Long-term bonds (91%), cash and equiv (9%)
Provider Compensation ($000): Contr fee ($144,650), FFS ($6,972), capitation ($6,402)
Total Member Encounters: Phys (237,813), non-phys (45,663)
Group Affiliation: Aetna Inc
Licensed in: DE, MD
Address: 750 Prides Crossing Suite 300, Newark, DE 19713
Phone: (800) 727-9951　**Dom State:** DE　**Commenced Bus:** November 1986

Data Date	Rating	RACR #1	RACR #2	Total Assets ($mil)	Capital ($mil)	Net Premium ($mil)	Net Income ($mil)
6-14	B	4.56	3.80	67.0	40.7	64.6	2.1
6-13	B	3.30	2.75	74.2	32.8	104.8	2.8
2013	B	4.30	3.58	65.0	37.9	189.1	7.7
2012	B-	4.09	3.41	83.7	43.5	222.6	11.2
2011	B-	2.41	2.00	77.6	28.6	262.1	7.8
2010	B+	3.18	2.65	87.2	43.5	299.3	9.9
2009	B	2.17	1.81	72.7	32.6	320.9	1.6

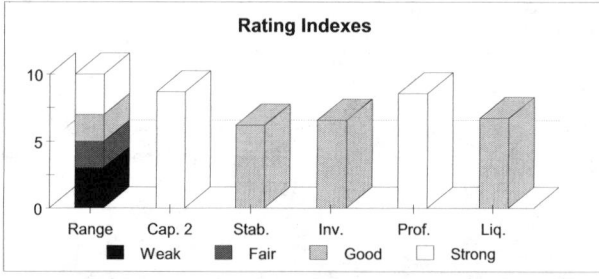

Rating Indexes

COVENTRY HEALTH CARE OF FLORIDA INC · B · Good

Major Rating Factors: Good liquidity (6.7 on a scale of 0 to 10) with sufficient resources (cash flows and marketable investments) to handle a spike in claims. Fair overall results on stability tests (3.5) based on a significant 19% decrease in enrollment during the period. Rating is significantly influenced by the good financial results of Aetna Inc. Strong capitalization index (7.8) based on excellent current risk-adjusted capital (severe loss scenario).

Other Rating Factors: High quality investment portfolio (9.2). Weak profitability index (1.9).

Principal Business: Comp med (65%), Medicaid (24%), Medicare (11%)

Mem Phys: 13: 27,466 **12:** 23,033 **13 MLR** 85.6% **/ 13 Admin Exp** N/A

Enroll(000): Q2 14: 354 **13:** 131 **12:** 160 **Med Exp PMPM:** $286

Principal Investments: Long-term bonds (74%), cash and equiv (24%), real estate (2%)

Provider Compensation ($000): Contr fee ($351,537), capitation ($55,796), FFS ($39,059)

Total Member Encounters: Phys (796,800), non-phys (102,897)

Group Affiliation: Aetna Inc

Licensed in: FL

Address: 1340 Concord Terrace, Sunrise, FL 33323

Phone: (954) 858-3000 **Dom State:** FL **Commenced Bus:** January 1985

Data Date	Rating	RACR #1	RACR #2	Total Assets ($mil)	Capital ($mil)	Net Premium ($mil)	Net Income ($mil)
6-14	B	2.02	1.68	311.3	54.2	535.6	-26.9
6-13	B	2.72	2.26	165.2	96.5	241.8	4.2
2013	B	3.48	2.90	178.6	103.4	523.1	14.5
2012	B	2.61	2.18	167.4	92.4	692.6	32.3
2011	C+	1.38	1.15	158.2	58.6	819.1	8.9
2010	C+	1.20	1.00	152.8	39.7	790.5	0.7
2009	D+	0.85	0.71	151.2	33.9	771.4	-3.4

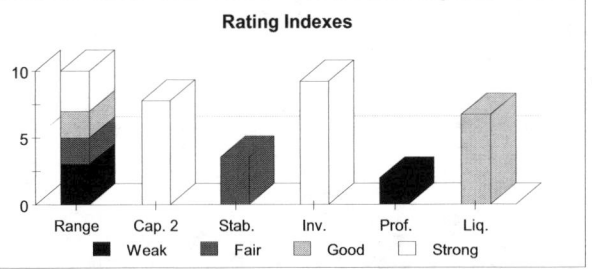

Rating Indexes

COVENTRY HEALTH CARE OF GEORGIA · B · Good

Major Rating Factors: Good liquidity (6.2 on a scale of 0 to 10) with sufficient resources (cash flows and marketable investments) to handle a spike in claims. Fair overall results on stability tests (4.5). Rating is significantly influenced by the good financial results of Aetna Inc. Excellent profitability (8.2).

Other Rating Factors: Strong capitalization index (8.5) based on excellent current risk-adjusted capital (severe loss scenario). High quality investment portfolio (9.1).

Principal Business: Comp med (95%), Medicare (5%)

Mem Phys: 13: 15,782 **12:** 14,819 **13 MLR** 84.4% **/ 13 Admin Exp** N/A

Enroll(000): Q2 14: 140 **13:** 162 **12:** 158 **Med Exp PMPM:** $233

Principal Investments: Long-term bonds (99%), cash and equiv (1%)

Provider Compensation ($000): Contr fee ($410,074), FFS ($22,695), capitation ($19,010)

Total Member Encounters: Phys (827,530), non-phys (27,889)

Group Affiliation: Aetna Inc

Licensed in: GA

Address: 1100 Circle 75 Pkwy Ste 1400, Atlanta, GA 30339

Phone: (678) 202-2100 **Dom State:** GA **Commenced Bus:** January 1994

Data Date	Rating	RACR #1	RACR #2	Total Assets ($mil)	Capital ($mil)	Net Premium ($mil)	Net Income ($mil)
6-14	B	2.59	2.16	167.6	73.7	249.9	4.4
6-13	B+	2.62	2.18	130.6	69.9	261.7	8.5
2013	B	2.44	2.03	130.3	69.1	534.1	7.1
2012	B+	2.97	2.48	138.4	79.8	512.7	19.0
2011	B+	2.71	2.26	118.2	60.6	423.8	10.0
2010	B+	3.35	2.79	93.0	55.6	341.1	18.0
2009	B+	3.16	2.63	75.6	43.5	279.3	14.2

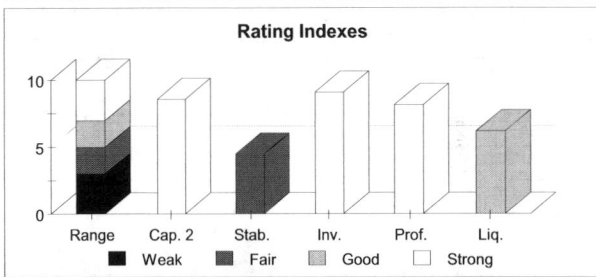

Rating Indexes

COVENTRY HEALTH CARE OF ILLINOIS INC * · B+ · Good

Major Rating Factors: Good overall profitability index (6.8 on a scale of 0 to 10). Good liquidity (6.9) with sufficient resources (cash flows and marketable investments) to handle a spike in claims. Strong capitalization (9.8) based on excellent current risk-adjusted capital (severe loss scenario).

Other Rating Factors: High quality investment portfolio (9.2).

Principal Business: Comp med (56%), Medicare (44%)

Mem Phys: 13: 29,896 **12:** 26,871 **13 MLR** 85.5% **/ 13 Admin Exp** N/A

Enroll(000): Q2 14: 52 **13:** 43 **12:** 51 **Med Exp PMPM:** $415

Principal Investments: Long-term bonds (77%), cash and equiv (20%), other (3%)

Provider Compensation ($000): Contr fee ($179,859), capitation ($33,841), FFS ($18,005)

Total Member Encounters: Phys (839,656), non-phys (145,951)

Group Affiliation: Aetna Inc

Licensed in: IL

Address: 2110 Fox Dr, Champaign, IL 61820

Phone: (217) 366-1226 **Dom State:** IL **Commenced Bus:** December 1988

Data Date	Rating	RACR #1	RACR #2	Total Assets ($mil)	Capital ($mil)	Net Premium ($mil)	Net Income ($mil)
6-14	B+	3.58	2.98	104.8	44.6	159.3	-0.6
6-13	B+	3.20	2.67	87.1	41.8	131.3	6.1
2013	B+	3.54	2.95	88.3	44.0	263.5	7.7
2012	B+	3.33	2.77	99.2	43.8	272.1	9.2
2011	B+	3.12	2.60	110.8	55.2	364.4	12.6
2010	A-	4.16	3.46	121.3	73.1	329.4	17.1
2009	B+	3.83	3.19	90.0	55.9	295.2	19.2

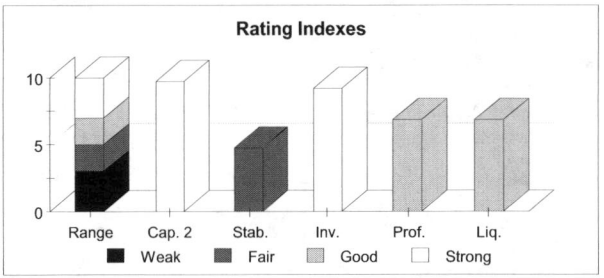

Rating Indexes

COVENTRY HEALTH CARE OF IOWA INC
B   Good

Major Rating Factors: Fair overall results on stability tests (4.5 on a scale of 0 to 10). Rating is significantly influenced by the good financial results of Aetna Inc. Excellent profitability (8.7). Strong capitalization index (9.6) based on excellent current risk-adjusted capital (severe loss scenario).

Other Rating Factors: High quality investment portfolio (9.2). Excellent liquidity (7.0) with sufficient resources (cash flows and marketable investments) to handle a spike in claims.

Principal Business: Comp med (59%), Medicare (28%), FEHB (13%)

Mem Phys: 13: 20,152   **12:** 14,232   **13 MLR** 79.8%   **/ 13 Admin Exp** N/A

Enroll(000): Q2 14: 57   **13:** 36   **12:** 32   **Med Exp PMPM:** $234

Principal Investments: Long-term bonds (73%), cash and equiv (27%)

Provider Compensation ($000): Contr fee ($90,740), capitation ($1,709), FFS ($548)

Total Member Encounters: Phys (155,865), non-phys (68,290)

Group Affiliation: Aetna Inc

Licensed in: IA

Address: 3333 Farnam St Suite 300, Omaha, NE 68131-3406

Phone: (800) 471-0240   **Dom State:** IA   **Commenced Bus:** January 1986

Data Date	Rating	RACR #1	RACR #2	Total Assets ($mil)	Capital ($mil)	Net Premium ($mil)	Net Income ($mil)
6-14	B	3.40	2.84	59.2	24.0	93.8	2.7
6-13	B	3.41	2.84	39.7	21.0	58.6	6.1
2013	B	3.01	2.51	46.5	21.1	118.6	6.3
2012	B	3.88	3.24	43.1	24.3	110.6	9.4
2011	B	2.86	2.38	48.9	26.2	141.1	7.2
2010	N/A	N/A	N/A	51.3	24.7	145.2	5.2
2009	B	2.06	1.72	46.2	19.3	167.3	5.5

Rating Indexes

COVENTRY HEALTH CARE OF KANSAS INC
B   Good

Major Rating Factors: Good quality investment portfolio (6.7 on a scale of 0 to 10). Good overall results on stability tests (5.7). Rating is significantly influenced by the good financial results of Aetna Inc. Excellent profitability (7.1).

Other Rating Factors: Strong capitalization index (9.8) based on excellent current risk-adjusted capital (severe loss scenario). Excellent liquidity (7.3) with ample operational cash flow and liquid investments.

Principal Business: Comp med (48%), Medicare (47%), FEHB (5%)

Mem Phys: 13: 17,773   **12:** 15,168   **13 MLR** 62.6%   **/ 13 Admin Exp** N/A

Enroll(000): Q2 14: 87   **13:** 90   **12:** 271   **Med Exp PMPM:** $340

Principal Investments: Long-term bonds (73%), cash and equiv (27%)

Provider Compensation ($): Contr fee ($564,714), capitation ($30,223), FFS ($27,929), bonus arrang ($2,117)

Total Member Encounters: Phys (484,075), non-phys (301,554)

Group Affiliation: Aetna Inc

Licensed in: KS, MO

Address: 8301 E 21st St N Ste 300, Wichita, KS 67206

Phone: (913) 202-5400   **Dom State:** KS   **Commenced Bus:** October 1981

Data Date	Rating	RACR #1	RACR #2	Total Assets ($mil)	Capital ($mil)	Net Premium ($mil)	Net Income ($mil)
6-14	B	3.60	3.00	270.2	128.3	321.0	10.7
6-13	B	1.85	1.54	210.7	103.2	380.4	24.6
2013	B	3.26	2.72	204.4	115.5	699.7	33.9
2012	B	2.03	1.69	248.1	113.7	1,040.2	-29.7
2011	B	3.69	3.08	209.2	114.5	595.9	31.6
2010	B-	3.24	2.70	168.7	85.1	532.2	19.7
2009	B-	5.32	4.43	176.1	99.6	572.1	18.5

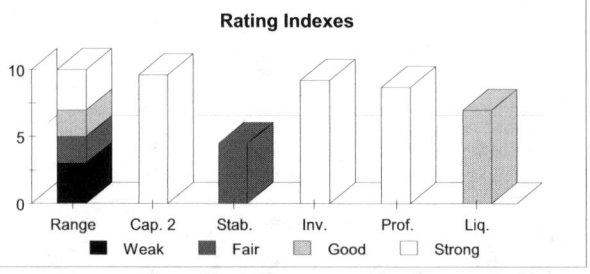

Rating Indexes

COVENTRY HEALTH CARE OF LOUISIANA
B   Good

Major Rating Factors: Good liquidity (6.8 on a scale of 0 to 10) with sufficient resources (cash flows and marketable investments) to handle a spike in claims. Fair overall results on stability tests (4.9). Rating is significantly influenced by the good financial results of Aetna Inc. Excellent profitability (7.7).

Other Rating Factors: Strong capitalization index (8.8) based on excellent current risk-adjusted capital (severe loss scenario). High quality investment portfolio (9.3).

Principal Business: Comp med (94%), FEHB (6%)

Mem Phys: 13: 9,688   **12:** 8,060   **13 MLR** 82.3%   **/ 13 Admin Exp** N/A

Enroll(000): Q2 14: 43   **13:** 44   **12:** 41   **Med Exp PMPM:** $269

Principal Investments: Long-term bonds (82%), cash and equiv (18%)

Provider Compensation ($000): Contr fee ($128,124), FFS ($9,581), capitation ($1,921)

Total Member Encounters: Phys (555,655), non-phys (27,685)

Group Affiliation: Aetna Inc

Licensed in: LA

Address: 3838 N.Causeway Blvd.,Ste 3350, Metairie, LA 70002

Phone: (504) 834-0840   **Dom State:** LA   **Commenced Bus:** July 1985

Data Date	Rating	RACR #1	RACR #2	Total Assets ($mil)	Capital ($mil)	Net Premium ($mil)	Net Income ($mil)
6-14	B	2.77	2.31	50.3	24.1	96.1	5.1
6-13	B	3.17	2.64	47.5	25.0	86.0	6.3
2013	B	2.75	2.30	47.0	24.0	171.1	5.2
2012	B	3.36	2.80	47.1	26.6	156.2	8.0
2011	B	2.87	2.39	45.1	24.6	165.3	6.2
2010	B	3.90	3.25	44.4	23.9	138.9	4.7
2009	B-	5.37	4.47	44.0	23.6	109.0	4.9

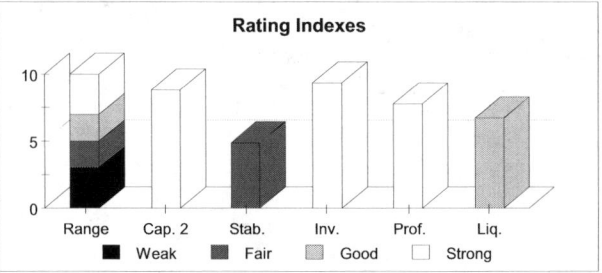

Rating Indexes

COVENTRY HEALTH CARE OF MISSOURI INC

B   **Good**

Major Rating Factors: Good quality investment portfolio (6.6 on a scale of 0 to 10). Fair overall results on stability tests (4.0). Rating is significantly influenced by the good financial results of Aetna Inc. Excellent profitability (7.9).

Other Rating Factors: Strong capitalization index (10.0) based on excellent current risk-adjusted capital (severe loss scenario). Weak liquidity (2.6) as a spike in claims may stretch capacity.

Principal Business: Medicare (90%), comp med (10%)

Mem Phys: 13: 15,877   **12:** 15,492   **13 MLR** 114.4%   / **13 Admin Exp** N/A

Enroll(000): Q2 14: 76   **13:** 63   **12:** 62   **Med Exp PMPM:** $697

Principal Investments: Long-term bonds (81%), cash and equiv (19%)

Provider Compensation ($000): Contr fee ($269,912), capitation ($181,064), bonus arrang ($58,969), FFS ($8,032)

Total Member Encounters: Phys (603,586), non-phys (171,000)

Group Affiliation: Aetna Inc

Licensed in: IL, MO

Address: 550 Maryville Centre Dr #300, St Louis, MO 63141-5818

Phone: (314) 506-1700   **Dom State:** MO   **Commenced Bus:** November 1985

Data Date	Rating	RACR #1	RACR #2	Total Assets ($mil)	Capital ($mil)	Net Premium ($mil)	Net Income ($mil)
6-14	B	4.51	3.76	248.8	92.6	265.3	6.9
6-13	B	5.50	4.58	224.6	112.6	229.8	14.1
2013	B	3.92	3.27	201.4	79.6	456.8	18.1
2012	B-	4.81	4.01	207.7	97.6	458.9	34.6
2011	B-	4.47	3.73	229.5	101.1	469.1	30.8
2010	B-	4.38	3.65	229.7	110.2	607.3	26.9
2009	B	4.14	3.45	272.7	131.6	781.8	23.9

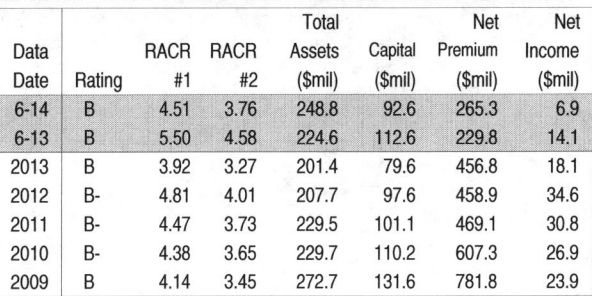

Rating Indexes

COVENTRY HEALTH CARE OF NEBRASKA INC *

B+   **Good**

Major Rating Factors: Good overall profitability index (6.6 on a scale of 0 to 10). Good liquidity (6.4) with sufficient resources (cash flows and marketable investments) to handle a spike in claims. Strong capitalization index (9.1) based on excellent current risk-adjusted capital (severe loss scenario).

Other Rating Factors: High quality investment portfolio (8.9). Excellent overall results on stability tests (7.3) based on healthy premium and capital growth during 2013. Rating is significantly influenced by the good financial results of Aetna Inc.

Principal Business: Medicaid (66%), comp med (27%), Medicare (7%)

Mem Phys: 13: 20,105   **12:** 14,894   **13 MLR** 84.9%   / **13 Admin Exp** N/A

Enroll(000): Q2 14: 132   **13:** 126   **12:** 129   **Med Exp PMPM:** $207

Principal Investments: Long-term bonds (74%), cash and equiv (26%)

Provider Compensation ($000): Contr fee ($308,683), capitation ($5,386), FFS ($1,261)

Total Member Encounters: Phys (670,381), non-phys (243,425)

Group Affiliation: Aetna Inc

Licensed in: IA, NE

Address: 15950 W Dodge Rd, Omaha, NE 68118

Phone: (800) 471-0240   **Dom State:** NE   **Commenced Bus:** October 1987

Data Date	Rating	RACR #1	RACR #2	Total Assets ($mil)	Capital ($mil)	Net Premium ($mil)	Net Income ($mil)
6-14	B+	3.00	2.50	142.3	55.4	211.1	5.5
6-13	B	3.02	2.52	131.1	51.7	183.7	9.2
2013	B+	2.72	2.27	127.9	49.6	375.4	14.0
2012	B-	2.50	2.09	112.8	42.1	316.5	8.6
2011	C+	1.77	1.47	82.0	32.5	269.4	-2.6
2010	C+	2.02	1.68	66.2	22.4	199.9	-4.0
2009	B-	2.39	1.99	46.2	20.5	155.7	0.7

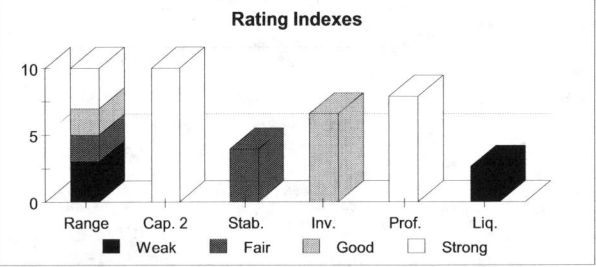

Rating Indexes

COVENTRY HEALTH CARE OF TEXAS INC

B   **Good**

Major Rating Factors: Strong capitalization (10.0 on a scale of 0 to 10) based on excellent current risk-adjusted capital (severe loss scenario). High quality investment portfolio (9.9). Excellent liquidity (10.0) with ample operational cash flow and liquid investments.

Other Rating Factors: Weak profitability index (0.9).

Principal Business: Comp med (100%)

Mem Phys: 13: 2,383   **12:** N/A   **13 MLR** 86.9%   / **13 Admin Exp** N/A

Enroll(000): Q2 14: 2   **13:** 1   **12:** N/A   **Med Exp PMPM:** $196

Principal Investments: Cash and equiv (99%), long-term bonds (1%)

Provider Compensation ($000): Contr fee ($542), FFS ($180), capitation ($17), other ($17)

Total Member Encounters: Phys (1,653), non-phys (561)

Group Affiliation: Aetna Inc

Licensed in: TX

Address: 2110 Fox Dr, Champaign, IL 61820

Phone: (217) 366-1226   **Dom State:** TX   **Commenced Bus:** April 2012

Data Date	Rating	RACR #1	RACR #2	Total Assets ($mil)	Capital ($mil)	Net Premium ($mil)	Net Income ($mil)
6-14	B	16.50	13.75	13.6	11.7	6.5	0.4
6-13	N/A	N/A	N/A	11.9	11.6	0.3	-0.3
2013	B	16.00	13.33	11.6	11.3	1.0	-0.5
2012	N/A	N/A	N/A	12.1	11.8	N/A	-1.0
2011	N/A	N/A	N/A	N/A	N/A	N/A	N/A
2010	N/A	N/A	N/A	N/A	N/A	N/A	N/A
2009	N/A	N/A	N/A	N/A	N/A	N/A	N/A

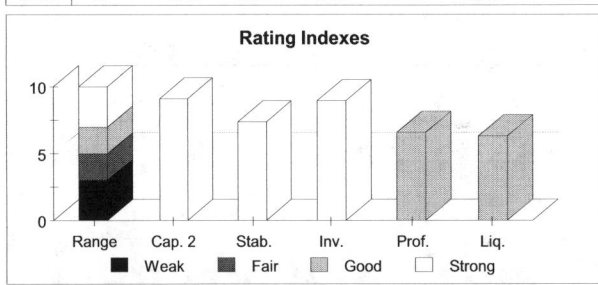

Rating Indexes

COVENTRY HEALTH CARE OF VIRGINIA INC

B **Good**

Major Rating Factors: Good overall results on stability tests (5.6 on a scale of 0 to 10). Rating is significantly influenced by the good financial results of Aetna Inc. Excellent overall profitability index (7.0). Strong capitalization index (7.8) based on excellent current risk-adjusted capital (severe loss scenario).

Other Rating Factors: High quality investment portfolio (9.0). Excellent liquidity (6.9) with sufficient resources (cash flows and marketable investments) to handle a spike in claims.

Principal Business: Comp med (54%), Medicaid (46%)

Mem Phys: 13: 17,346 **12:** 16,721 **13 MLR** 85.0% **/ 13 Admin Exp** N/A

Enroll(000): Q2 14: 106 **13:** 82 **12:** 71 **Med Exp PMPM:** $279

Principal Investments: Long-term bonds (66%), cash and equiv (31%), real estate (3%)

Provider Compensation ($000): Contr fee ($246,045), FFS ($11,423), capitation ($9,566)

Total Member Encounters: Phys (448,982), non-phys (251,187)

Group Affiliation: Aetna Inc

Licensed in: VA

Address: 9881 Mayland Dr, Richmond, VA 23233

Phone: (804) 747-3700 **Dom State:** VA **Commenced Bus:** April 1991

Data Date	Rating	RACR #1	RACR #2	Total Assets ($mil)	Capital ($mil)	Net Premium ($mil)	Net Income ($mil)
6-14	B	1.96	1.63	88.6	33.3	189.7	-2.6
6-13	B	2.19	1.83	69.0	29.3	150.9	8.1
2013	B	2.10	1.75	74.5	35.9	315.4	13.9
2012	B-	2.80	2.33	76.0	38.5	258.7	17.0
2011	C+	3.62	3.01	77.9	43.6	222.0	13.3
2010	B	4.68	3.90	95.7	60.0	242.7	14.0
2009	B	3.86	3.22	98.1	60.5	276.0	4.5

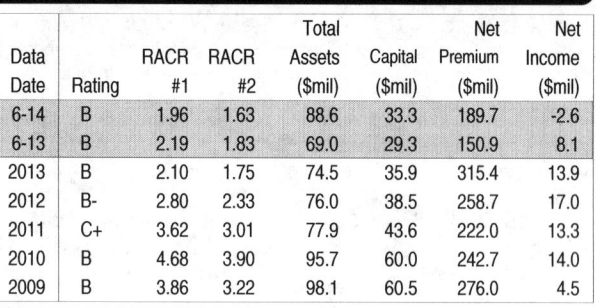

Rating Indexes

COVENTRY HEALTH CARE OF WEST VA INC *

B+ **Good**

Major Rating Factors: Good overall results on stability tests (5.5 on a scale of 0 to 10). Rating is significantly influenced by the good financial results of Aetna Inc. Excellent profitability (8.6). Strong capitalization index (9.0) based on excellent current risk-adjusted capital (severe loss scenario).

Other Rating Factors: High quality investment portfolio (8.9). Excellent liquidity (6.9) with sufficient resources (cash flows and marketable investments) to handle a spike in claims.

Principal Business: Medicaid (76%), comp med (24%)

Mem Phys: 13: 4,791 **12:** 4,606 **13 MLR** 80.0% **/ 13 Admin Exp** N/A

Enroll(000): Q2 14: 88 **13:** 81 **12:** 77 **Med Exp PMPM:** $204

Principal Investments: Long-term bonds (70%), cash and equiv (30%)

Provider Compensation ($000): Contr fee ($177,897), FFS ($7,078), capitation ($2,376), other ($1)

Total Member Encounters: Phys (408,419), non-phys (84,040)

Group Affiliation: Aetna Inc

Licensed in: OH, WV

Address: 500 Virginia St E Ste 400, Charleston, WV 25301

Phone: (800) 788-6445 **Dom State:** WV **Commenced Bus:** January 1995

Data Date	Rating	RACR #1	RACR #2	Total Assets ($mil)	Capital ($mil)	Net Premium ($mil)	Net Income ($mil)
6-14	B+	2.99	2.49	90.8	36.7	152.0	9.4
6-13	B+	N/A	N/A	69.6	31.4	109.4	4.9
2013	A-	3.57	2.97	78.3	44.4	235.1	17.3
2012	B+	3.46	2.88	69.0	37.0	189.0	8.5
2011	B+	3.82	3.19	64.4	37.7	165.3	10.1
2010	B+	3.96	3.30	58.3	33.9	160.1	9.1
2009	B+	3.63	3.02	58.8	33.7	167.8	7.6

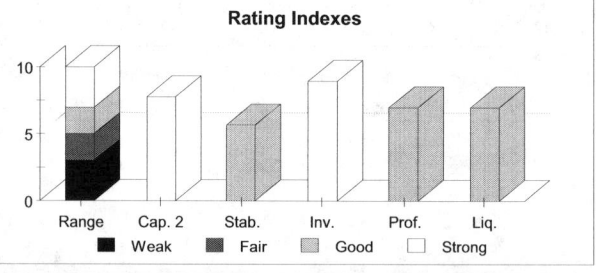

Rating Indexes

COVENTRY HEALTH PLAN OF FLORIDA INC *

A- **Excellent**

Major Rating Factors: Excellent profitability (8.6 on a scale of 0 to 10). Strong capitalization index (10.0) based on excellent current risk-adjusted capital (severe loss scenario). High quality investment portfolio (9.1).

Other Rating Factors: Good overall results on stability tests (6.2). Rating is significantly influenced by the good financial results of Aetna Inc. Good liquidity (6.8) with sufficient resources (cash flows and marketable investments) to handle a spike in claims.

Principal Business: Medicare (42%), comp med (28%), Medicaid (24%), FEHB (5%)

Mem Phys: 13: 25,691 **12:** 21,898 **13 MLR** 82.2% **/ 13 Admin Exp** N/A

Enroll(000): Q2 14: 78 **13:** 54 **12:** 56 **Med Exp PMPM:** $328

Principal Investments: Long-term bonds (80%), cash and equiv (20%)

Provider Compensation ($000): Contr fee ($176,591), capitation ($35,617), FFS ($13,423)

Total Member Encounters: Phys (354,951), non-phys (52,216)

Group Affiliation: Aetna Inc

Licensed in: FL

Address: 1340 Concord Terrace, Sunrise, FL 33021

Phone: (954) 858-3000 **Dom State:** FL **Commenced Bus:** November 1994

Data Date	Rating	RACR #1	RACR #2	Total Assets ($mil)	Capital ($mil)	Net Premium ($mil)	Net Income ($mil)
6-14	A-	6.14	5.11	215.5	97.1	369.3	-0.8
6-13	A-	3.43	2.85	88.6	49.9	134.0	7.0
2013	A-	3.32	2.77	83.1	51.3	268.0	8.5
2012	B+	3.01	2.51	81.2	43.5	293.5	19.8
2011	B	2.94	2.45	96.4	41.6	269.9	3.7
2010	B-	2.54	2.12	93.0	37.4	278.9	6.3
2009	D+	1.85	1.55	88.3	30.1	313.3	5.6

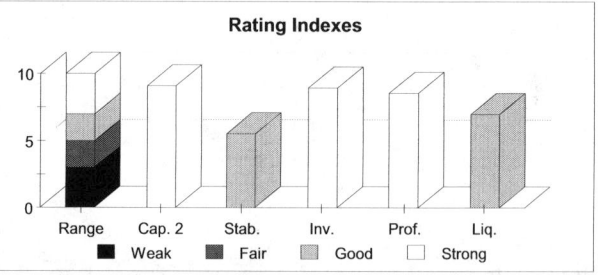

Rating Indexes

COVENTRYCARES OF MICHIGAN INC   B   Good

Major Rating Factors: Excellent profitability (7.2 on a scale of 0 to 10). Strong capitalization (9.1) based on excellent current risk-adjusted capital (severe loss scenario). High quality investment portfolio (9.3).
Other Rating Factors: Excellent liquidity (6.9) with sufficient resources (cash flows and marketable investments) to handle a spike in claims.
Principal Business: Medicaid (99%)
Mem Phys: 13: 5,408   **12:** 4,718   **13 MLR** 87.2%   **/ 13 Admin Exp** N/A
Enroll(000): Q2 14: 45   **13:** 40   **12:** 43   **Med Exp PMPM:** $295
Principal Investments: Cash and equiv (56%), long-term bonds (44%)
Provider Compensation ($000): Contr fee ($79,241), capitation ($48,919), FFS ($16,625), bonus arrang ($1,610)
Total Member Encounters: Phys (385,374), non-phys (67,108)
Group Affiliation: Aetna Inc
Licensed in: MI
Address: 1333 Gratiot Suite 400, Detroit, MI 48207
Phone: (313) 465-1519   **Dom State:** MI   **Commenced Bus:** October 2004

Data Date	Rating	RACR #1	RACR #2	Total Assets ($mil)	Capital ($mil)	Net Premium ($mil)	Net Income ($mil)
6-14	B	3.07	2.55	50.1	23.8	82.6	2.0
6-13	B	2.52	2.10	39.8	19.7	82.4	2.5
2013	B	2.84	2.36	41.9	21.8	163.7	4.4
2012	B	3.02	2.52	46.7	24.3	173.2	7.1
2011	B	3.12	2.60	49.0	25.9	185.2	4.6
2010	B	2.99	2.49	45.4	24.6	187.8	3.6
2009	B	2.77	2.30	43.9	23.0	186.4	1.6

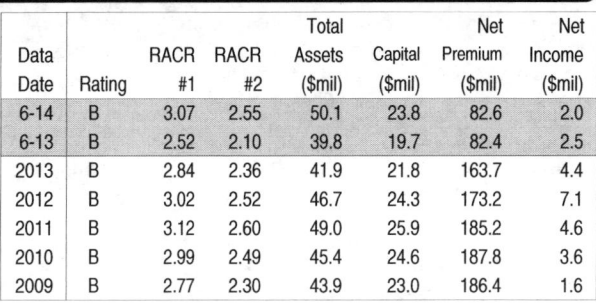

Rating Indexes

COX HEALTH SYSTEMS HMO INC   C   Fair

Major Rating Factors: Fair profitability index (4.7 on a scale of 0 to 10). Fair quality investment portfolio (3.0). Fair overall results on stability tests (4.3).
Other Rating Factors: Strong capitalization index (7.4) based on excellent current risk-adjusted capital (severe loss scenario). Excellent liquidity (8.7) with ample operational cash flow and liquid investments.
Principal Business: Comp med (100%)
Mem Phys: 13: 2,558   **12:** 2,457   **13 MLR** 90.9%   **/ 13 Admin Exp** N/A
Enroll(000): Q2 14: 0   **13:** 1   **12:** 1   **Med Exp PMPM:** $355
Principal Investments: Affiliate common stock (63%), cash and equiv (13%), other (24%)
Provider Compensation ($000): Contr fee ($4,589), FFS ($181)
Total Member Encounters: Phys (6,943), non-phys (1,329)
Group Affiliation: Cox Health Systems
Licensed in: MO
Address: 3200 S National Bldg B, Springfield, MO 65801-5750
Phone: (417) 269-6762   **Dom State:** MO   **Commenced Bus:** January 1997

Data Date	Rating	RACR #1	RACR #2	Total Assets ($mil)	Capital ($mil)	Net Premium ($mil)	Net Income ($mil)
6-14	C	1.66	1.38	25.7	23.7	1.7	-0.6
6-13	C	1.34	1.12	22.2	21.2	2.5	-0.3
2013	C	1.58	1.32	23.9	22.6	4.9	2.6
2012	C	1.25	1.04	21.1	19.7	5.4	0.0
2011	C+	1.62	1.35	24.4	22.0	9.2	-0.5
2010	B-	1.55	1.29	24.2	20.6	11.6	1.6
2009	C+	1.46	1.21	23.3	18.9	16.1	1.9

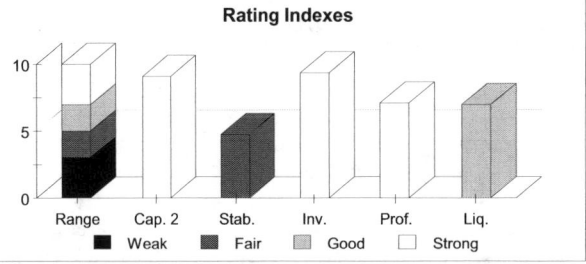

Rating Indexes

COX HEALTH SYSTEMS INS CO   B-   Good

Major Rating Factors: Fair profitability index (3.6 on a scale of 0 to 10). Good capitalization (5.9) based on good current risk-adjusted capital (severe loss scenario). Good liquidity (6.8) with sufficient resources (cash flows and marketable investments) to handle a spike in claims.
Other Rating Factors: High quality investment portfolio (9.9).
Principal Business: Comp med (100%)
Mem Phys: 13: 2,562   **12:** 2,476   **13 MLR** 86.5%   **/ 13 Admin Exp** N/A
Enroll(000): Q2 14: 34   **13:** 33   **12:** 33   **Med Exp PMPM:** $240
Principal Investments: Cash and equiv (55%), long-term bonds (45%)
Provider Compensation ($000): Contr fee ($91,394), FFS ($2,352)
Total Member Encounters: Phys (152,202), non-phys (24,835)
Group Affiliation: Cox Health Systems
Licensed in: MO
Address: 3200 S National Building B, Springfield, MO 65801-5750
Phone: (417) 269-6762   **Dom State:** MO   **Commenced Bus:** January 1995

Data Date	Rating	RACR #1	RACR #2	Total Assets ($mil)	Capital ($mil)	Net Premium ($mil)	Net Income ($mil)
6-14	B-	1.07	0.89	39.0	14.8	58.5	0.5
6-13	B-	N/A	N/A	33.2	14.1	54.7	0.7
2013	B-	1.06	0.88	36.7	14.6	109.8	1.6
2012	B-	N/A	N/A	29.9	10.5	101.8	-4.8
2011	B-	1.06	0.88	27.4	11.9	91.4	1.6
2010	C+	0.74	0.62	23.8	9.7	80.1	1.1
2009	C+	0.78	0.65	21.7	9.2	74.0	0.9

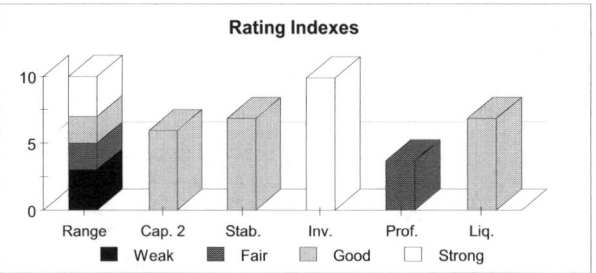

Rating Indexes

CRESTPOINT HEALTH INS CO D Weak

Major Rating Factors: Weak profitability index (0.7 on a scale of 0 to 10). Strong capitalization (10.0) based on excellent current risk-adjusted capital (severe loss scenario). High quality investment portfolio (9.9).
Other Rating Factors: Excellent liquidity (7.0) with sufficient resources (cash flows and marketable investments) to handle a spike in claims.
Principal Business: Medicare (100%)
Mem Phys: 13: 3,863 **12:** N/A **13 MLR** 103.5% **/ 13 Admin Exp** N/A
Enroll(000): Q2 14: 3 **13:** 0 **12:** N/A **Med Exp PMPM:** $737
Principal Investments: Cash and equiv (79%), long-term bonds (21%)
Provider Compensation ($000): Contr fee ($1,338)
Total Member Encounters: Phys (545), non-phys (641)
Group Affiliation: Mountain States Health Alliance
Licensed in: TN
Address: 208 Sunset Dr Suite 101, Johnson City, TN 37604
Phone: (423) 952-2111 **Dom State:** TN **Commenced Bus:** March 1930

Data Date	Rating	RACR #1	RACR #2	Total Assets ($mil)	Capital ($mil)	Net Premium ($mil)	Net Income ($mil)
6-14	D	4.84	4.03	10.7	5.2	9.3	-1.4
6-13	N/A	N/A	N/A	4.6	2.0	1.0	-3.9
2013	D	3.09	2.57	8.0	3.4	2.2	-8.6
2012	N/A	N/A	N/A	2.5	2.1	N/A	N/A
2011	N/A	N/A	N/A	2.4	2.4	N/A	N/A
2010	N/A	N/A	N/A	3.7	3.3	N/A	N/A
2009	N/A	N/A	N/A	6.6	2.4	N/A	N/A

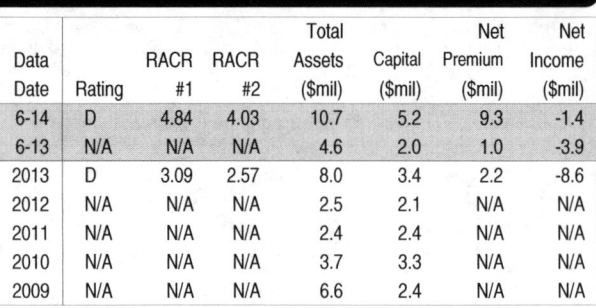

Rating Indexes

CUATRO LLC E Very Weak

Major Rating Factors: Weak profitability index (0.2 on a scale of 0 to 10). Poor capitalization (0.6) based on weak current risk-adjusted capital (moderate loss scenario). Weak liquidity (0.0) as a spike in claims may stretch capacity.
Other Rating Factors: High quality investment portfolio (9.9).
Principal Business: Medicare (100%)
Mem Phys: 13: N/A **12:** N/A **13 MLR** 89.0% **/ 13 Admin Exp** N/A
Enroll(000): Q2 14: 3 **13:** 3 **12:** 2 **Med Exp PMPM:** $1,075
Principal Investments: Cash and equiv (100%)
Provider Compensation ($000): FFS ($28,580), capitation ($2,963)
Total Member Encounters: N/A
Group Affiliation: None
Licensed in: (No states)
Address: 9320 Roosevelt Ave, Jackson Heights, NY 11372
Phone: (917) 348-9976 **Dom State:** NY **Commenced Bus:** May 2010

Data Date	Rating	RACR #1	RACR #2	Total Assets ($mil)	Capital ($mil)	Net Premium ($mil)	Net Income ($mil)
6-14	E	0.36	0.30	4.5	2.3	21.8	-0.9
6-13	E-	0.26	0.22	2.7	0.7	17.2	-1.6
2013	E-	0.21	0.18	4.8	1.3	38.4	-3.9
2012	E-	0.11	0.09	2.8	-0.1	19.7	-4.3
2011	E-	N/A	N/A	1.2	-0.7	6.0	-3.2
2010	N/A	N/A	N/A	0.8	-0.3	N/A	N/A
2009	N/A	N/A	N/A	N/A	N/A	N/A	N/A

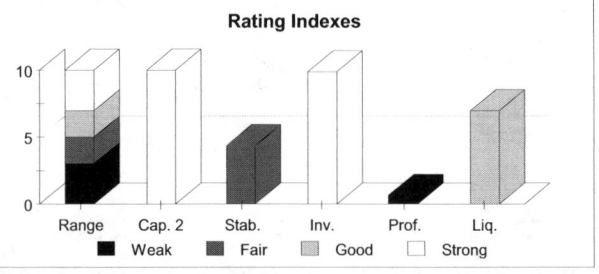

Rating Indexes

DEAN HEALTH PLAN INC B Good

Major Rating Factors: Good overall results on stability tests (5.0 on a scale of 0 to 10). Fair profitability index (2.9). Strong capitalization index (7.0) based on excellent current risk-adjusted capital (severe loss scenario).
Other Rating Factors: High quality investment portfolio (8.2). Excellent liquidity (7.0) with sufficient resources (cash flows and marketable investments) to handle a spike in claims.
Principal Business: Comp med (78%), Medicaid (8%), Medicare (7%), FEHB (4%), med supp (3%)
Mem Phys: 13: 3,214 **12:** 2,288 **13 MLR** 91.3% **/ 13 Admin Exp** N/A
Enroll(000): Q2 14: 268 **13:** 257 **12:** 257 **Med Exp PMPM:** $322
Principal Investments: Cash and equiv (41%), long-term bonds (32%), nonaffiliate common stock (21%), real estate (6%)
Provider Compensation ($000): Capitation ($976,815), contr fee ($7,820), FFS ($2,848)
Total Member Encounters: Phys (952,838), non-phys (787,238)
Group Affiliation: Dean Health Group
Licensed in: WI
Address: 1277 Deming Way, Madison, WI 53717
Phone: (608) 836-1400 **Dom State:** WI **Commenced Bus:** January 1984

Data Date	Rating	RACR #1	RACR #2	Total Assets ($mil)	Capital ($mil)	Net Premium ($mil)	Net Income ($mil)
6-14	B	1.38	1.15	263.5	79.2	581.5	-3.4
6-13	B	1.74	1.45	251.7	92.9	537.4	-3.1
2013	B	1.55	1.29	159.6	86.6	1,076.7	32.0
2012	A-	1.74	1.45	151.8	89.0	1,042.3	-1.3
2011	A-	1.69	1.41	137.4	81.5	1,020.8	-1.5
2010	A-	1.79	1.49	133.0	82.3	955.6	8.6
2009	B	1.57	1.31	121.5	70.9	943.1	8.8

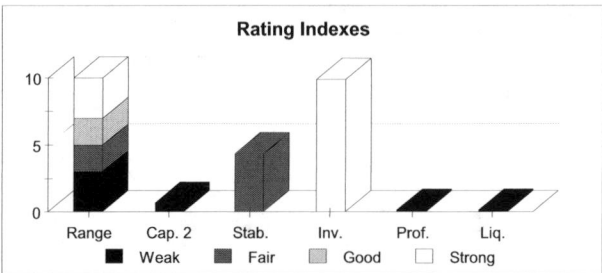

Rating Indexes

DEARBORN NATIONAL LIFE INSURANCE COMPANY * A- Excellent

Major Rating Factors: Good quality investment portfolio (6.4 on a scale of 0 to 10) despite mixed results such as: large holdings of BBB rated bonds but moderate junk bond exposure. Good overall profitability (5.1). Return on equity has been low, averaging 2.5%. Good liquidity (6.6) with sufficient resources to handle a spike in claims.

Other Rating Factors: Good overall results on stability tests (5.7) despite negative cash flow from operations for 2013 excellent risk diversification. Strong capitalization (8.0) based on excellent risk adjusted capital (severe loss scenario).

Principal Business: Group life insurance (55%), group health insurance (43%), individual life insurance (2%), and individual annuities (1%).

Principal Investments: NonCMO investment grade bonds (62%), CMOs and structured securities (29%), noninv. grade bonds (6%), and common & preferred stock (2%).

Investments in Affiliates: 2%
Group Affiliation: HCSC Group
Licensed in: All states except NY
Commenced Business: April 1969
Address: 300 East Randolph Street, Chicago, IL 60601-5099
Phone: (800) 633-3696 **Domicile State:** IL **NAIC Code:** 71129

Data Date	Rating	RACR #1	RACR #2	Total Assets ($mil)	Capital ($mil)	Net Premium ($mil)	Net Income ($mil)
6-14	A-	2.50	1.68	2,193.1	476.7	192.2	24.8
6-13	A-	1.98	1.31	2,414.6	413.6	260.7	16.5
2013	A-	2.27	1.52	2,324.1	439.7	495.5	42.3
2012	A-	1.85	1.21	2,621.0	402.8	563.1	-6.1
2011	A-	1.75	1.10	2,895.8	399.7	694.6	-10.8
2010	A-	1.77	1.09	3,077.2	451.5	747.2	-10.3
2009	A-	1.90	1.13	3,093.1	457.4	1,142.2	-39.8

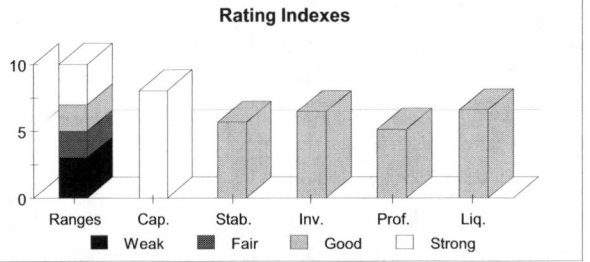

Rating Indexes

Ranges Cap. Stab. Inv. Prof. Liq.
■ Weak ▨ Fair ▧ Good ☐ Strong

DELAWARE AMERICAN LIFE INSURANCE COMPANY B Good

Major Rating Factors: Good overall results on stability tests (6.2 on a scale of 0 to 10). Stability strengths include excellent operational trends and excellent risk diversification. Strong capitalization (10.0) based on excellent risk adjusted capital (severe loss scenario). Moreover, capital has steadily grown over the last five years. High quality investment portfolio (7.7).

Other Rating Factors: Excellent profitability (8.7) with operating gains in each of the last five years. Excellent liquidity (7.6).

Principal Business: Group health insurance (53%), reinsurance (32%), group life insurance (13%), and individual life insurance (2%).

Principal Investments: NonCMO investment grade bonds (66%), CMOs and structured securities (19%), cash (9%), and noninv. grade bonds (1%).

Investments in Affiliates: 5%
Group Affiliation: MetLife Inc
Licensed in: All states except MN, MO, NH, NY, NC, PR
Commenced Business: August 1966
Address: 600 King St, Wilmington, DE 19801
Phone: (302) 594-2000 **Domicile State:** DE **NAIC Code:** 62634

Data Date	Rating	RACR #1	RACR #2	Total Assets ($mil)	Capital ($mil)	Net Premium ($mil)	Net Income ($mil)
6-14	B	5.18	3.71	145.7	82.0	50.5	6.9
6-13	B	4.00	2.96	119.3	63.0	43.1	6.5
2013	B	4.89	3.54	137.1	74.3	91.1	17.1
2012	B	3.60	2.62	128.7	54.6	76.1	7.7
2011	B	3.08	2.23	135.8	51.4	72.4	12.6
2010	B	2.09	1.59	86.1	29.4	72.7	6.5
2009	B	3.85	2.83	65.3	25.9	-5.8	2.7

Adverse Trends in Operations

Decrease in asset base during 2012 (5%)
Change in asset mix during 2011 (4.8%)
Change in premium mix from 2009 to 2010 (117.4%)

DELAWARE LIFE INSURANCE COMPANY OF NEW YORK C Fair

Major Rating Factors: Fair overall capitalization (4.0 on a scale of 0 to 10) based on mixed results -- excessive policy leverage mitigated by excellent risk adjusted capital (severe loss scenario). Moreover, capital levels have been consistently high over the last five years. Good quality investment portfolio (6.4) despite mixed results such as: minimal exposure to mortgages and large holdings of BBB rated bonds but minimal holdings in junk bonds. Good overall profitability (6.8).

Other Rating Factors: Weak overall results on stability tests (2.9) including potential financial drain due to affiliation with Delaware Life Partners LLC and weak results on operational trends. Excellent liquidity (7.5).

Principal Business: N/A

Principal Investments: NonCMO investment grade bonds (74%), CMOs and structured securities (20%), mortgages in good standing (4%), noninv. grade bonds (1%), and common & preferred stock (1%).

Investments in Affiliates: None
Group Affiliation: Delaware Life Partners LLC
Licensed in: CT, NY, RI
Commenced Business: August 1985
Address: 1115 Broadway 12th Floor, New York, NY 10010
Phone: (781) 237-6030 **Domicile State:** NY **NAIC Code:** 72664

Data Date	Rating	RACR #1	RACR #2	Total Assets ($mil)	Capital ($mil)	Net Premium ($mil)	Net Income ($mil)
6-14	C	8.36	4.10	3,113.3	405.9	15.1	25.3
6-13	C	5.07	2.80	3,433.9	363.4	77.6	3.7
2013	C	7.96	3.91	3,194.6	399.9	-8.7	16.9
2012	C	4.96	2.73	3,509.7	348.6	145.0	37.6
2011	C	4.65	2.48	3,503.0	304.9	387.8	5.3
2010	C	4.14	2.25	3,426.7	295.7	433.2	55.5
2009	C	3.27	1.78	3,071.4	232.4	728.9	17.6

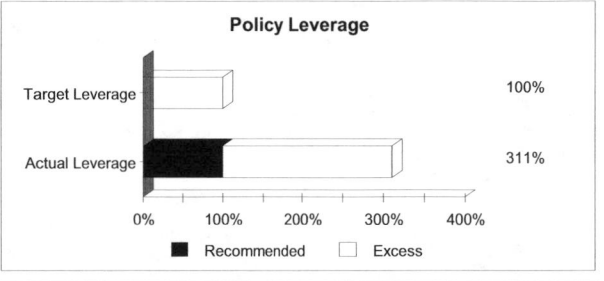

Policy Leverage

Target Leverage 100%

Actual Leverage 311%

0% 100% 200% 300% 400%
■ Recommended ☐ Excess

DELTA DENTAL PLAN OF VERMONT

C-   **Fair**

Major Rating Factors: Excellent profitability (8.2 on a scale of 0 to 10). Strong capitalization (10.0) based on excellent current risk-adjusted capital (severe loss scenario). High quality investment portfolio (7.4).
Other Rating Factors: Excellent liquidity (7.2) with ample operational cash flow and liquid investments.
Principal Business: Dental (100%)
Mem Phys: 13: 340   **12:** 344   **13 MLR** 77.1%   / **13 Admin Exp** N/A
Enroll(000): **13:** 56   **12:** 57   **Med Exp PMPM:** $28
Principal Investments: Long-term bonds (46%), cash and equiv (24%), nonaffiliate common stock (23%), affiliate common stock (6%)
Provider Compensation ($000): FFS ($20,208)
Total Member Encounters: N/A
Group Affiliation: Northeast Delta Dental
Licensed in: ME
Address: 135 College St, Burlington, VT 03302-2002
Phone: (603) 223-1000   **Dom State:** VT   **Commenced Bus:** September 1966

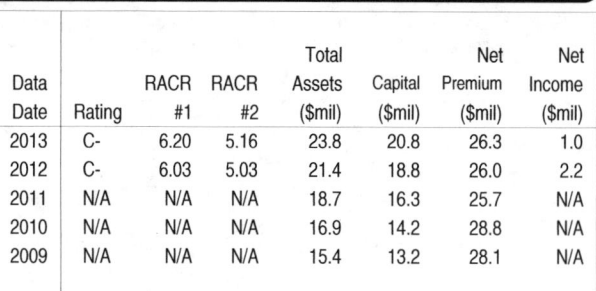

Data Date	Rating	RACR #1	RACR #2	Total Assets ($mil)	Capital ($mil)	Net Premium ($mil)	Net Income ($mil)
2013	C-	6.20	5.16	23.8	20.8	26.3	1.0
2012	C-	6.03	5.03	21.4	18.8	26.0	2.2
2011	N/A	N/A	N/A	18.7	16.3	25.7	N/A
2010	N/A	N/A	N/A	16.9	14.2	28.8	N/A
2009	N/A	N/A	N/A	15.4	13.2	28.1	N/A

Rating Indexes

Range   Cap. 2   Stab.   Inv.   Prof.   Liq.
■ Weak   ■ Fair   ▨ Good   ☐ Strong

DENVER HEALTH MEDICAL PLAN INC

B   **Good**

Major Rating Factors: Good overall results on stability tests (6.1 on a scale of 0 to 10). Good liquidity (6.8) with sufficient resources (cash flows and marketable investments) to handle a spike in claims. Excellent profitability (8.3).
Other Rating Factors: Strong capitalization index (9.1) based on excellent current risk-adjusted capital (severe loss scenario). High quality investment portfolio (9.4).
Principal Business: Comp med (58%), Medicare (42%)
Mem Phys: 13: 15,888   **12:** 15,061   **13 MLR** 82.7%   / **13 Admin Exp** N/A
Enroll(000): Q2 14: 20   **13:** 20   **12:** 20   **Med Exp PMPM:** $390
Principal Investments: Long-term bonds (97%), cash and equiv (3%)
Provider Compensation ($000): Contr fee ($38,116), FFS ($30,734), capitation ($21,484)
Total Member Encounters: Phys (141,676), non-phys (1,501)
Group Affiliation: Denver Health & Hospital Authority
Licensed in: CO
Address: 777 Bannock St, MC6000, Denver, CO 80204
Phone: (303) 602-2100   **Dom State:** CO   **Commenced Bus:** January 1997

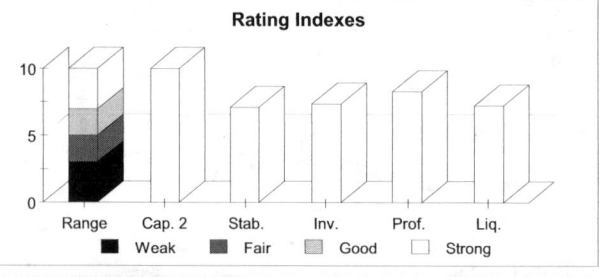

Data Date	Rating	RACR #1	RACR #2	Total Assets ($mil)	Capital ($mil)	Net Premium ($mil)	Net Income ($mil)
6-14	B	3.04	2.54	45.7	31.4	54.4	-3.1
6-13	B	4.14	3.45	50.3	38.4	52.7	4.8
2013	B	3.39	2.82	45.9	34.9	108.9	7.2
2012	B	3.74	3.12	47.8	34.8	101.5	12.8
2011	B	2.86	2.38	40.8	26.2	94.7	9.7
2010	B	2.21	1.85	30.0	19.5	88.4	8.2
2009	C+	1.56	1.30	23.7	13.3	81.9	5.4

Rating Indexes

Range   Cap. 2   Stab.   Inv.   Prof.   Liq.
■ Weak   ■ Fair   ▨ Good   ☐ Strong

DRISCOLL CHILDRENS HEALTH PLAN

D   **Weak**

Major Rating Factors: Fair capitalization index (3.4 on a scale of 0 to 10) based on weak current risk-adjusted capital (moderate loss scenario). Fair overall results on stability tests (3.6). Good overall profitability index (5.1).
Other Rating Factors: High quality investment portfolio (9.9). Excellent liquidity (6.9) with sufficient resources (cash flows and marketable investments) to handle a spike in claims.
Principal Business: Medicaid (94%), other (6%)
Mem Phys: 13: 3,542   **12:** 3,556   **13 MLR** 89.0%   / **13 Admin Exp** N/A
Enroll(000): Q2 14: 120   **13:** 110   **12:** 106   **Med Exp PMPM:** $216
Principal Investments: Cash and equiv (70%), nonaffiliate common stock (28%), long-term bonds (3%)
Provider Compensation ($000): Contr fee ($190,050), FFS ($66,480), bonus arrang ($15,658), capitation ($8,055)
Total Member Encounters: Phys (891,110), non-phys (48,664)
Group Affiliation: Driscoll Childrens Hospital
Licensed in: TX
Address: 615 N Upper Broadway St, 1621, Corpus Christi, TX 78477-0046
Phone: (361) 694-6432   **Dom State:** TX   **Commenced Bus:** April 1997

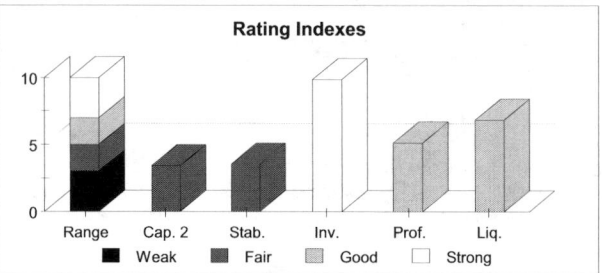

Data Date	Rating	RACR #1	RACR #2	Total Assets ($mil)	Capital ($mil)	Net Premium ($mil)	Net Income ($mil)
6-14	D	0.68	0.57	57.7	21.8	177.3	-5.8
6-13	D	0.87	0.72	50.3	22.3	154.2	2.0
2013	D	0.96	0.80	63.1	30.3	315.6	1.4
2012	D	1.17	0.98	63.0	30.2	290.0	22.0
2011	D	1.39	1.15	37.1	19.3	149.0	3.8
2010	D	1.84	1.53	44.9	25.0	150.5	10.2
2009	E+	0.95	0.80	28.9	12.7	134.1	-0.3

Rating Indexes

Range   Cap. 2   Stab.   Inv.   Prof.   Liq.
■ Weak   ■ Fair   ▨ Good   ☐ Strong

EASY CHOICE HEALTH PLAN   E+   Very Weak

Major Rating Factors: Weak profitability index (0.9 on a scale of 0 to 10). Poor capitalization index (2.4) based on weak current risk-adjusted capital (moderate loss scenario). Good overall results on stability tests (6.1) based on healthy premium and capital growth during 2013.
Other Rating Factors: Good liquidity (6.8) with sufficient resources (cash flows and marketable investments) to handle a spike in claims.
Principal Business: Medicare (100%)
Mem Phys: 13: N/A **12:** N/A **13 MLR** 93.7% **/ 13 Admin Exp** N/A
Enroll(000): Q2 14: 62 **13:** 56 **12:** 40 **Med Exp PMPM:** $809
Principal Investments ($000): Cash and equiv ($66,674)
Provider Compensation ($000): None
Total Member Encounters: N/A
Group Affiliation: None
Licensed in: CA
Address: 20411 SW Birch St Suite 200, Newport Beach, CA 92660
Phone: (866) 999-3945 **Dom State:** CA **Commenced Bus:** September 2006

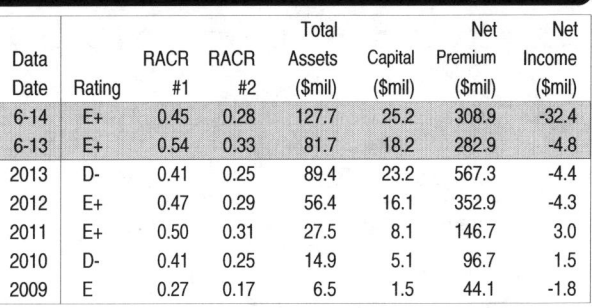

Data Date	Rating	RACR #1	RACR #2	Total Assets ($mil)	Capital ($mil)	Net Premium ($mil)	Net Income ($mil)
6-14	E+	0.45	0.28	127.7	25.2	308.9	-32.4
6-13	E+	0.54	0.33	81.7	18.2	282.9	-4.8
2013	D-	0.41	0.25	89.4	23.2	567.3	-4.4
2012	E+	0.47	0.29	56.4	16.1	352.9	-4.3
2011	E+	0.50	0.31	27.5	8.1	146.7	3.0
2010	D-	0.41	0.25	14.9	5.1	96.7	1.5
2009	E	0.27	0.17	6.5	1.5	44.1	-1.8

EL PASO FIRST HEALTH PLANS INC   B   Good

Major Rating Factors: Excellent profitability (8.8 on a scale of 0 to 10). Strong capitalization index (8.0) based on excellent current risk-adjusted capital (severe loss scenario). High quality investment portfolio (9.9).
Other Rating Factors: Excellent overall results on stability tests (7.2). Excellent liquidity (7.2) with ample operational cash flow and liquid investments
Principal Business: Medicaid (84%), comp med (15%)
Mem Phys: 13: 2,130 **12:** 1,969 **13 MLR** 83.8% **/ 13 Admin Exp** N/A
Enroll(000): Q2 14: 70 **13:** 65 **12:** 62 **Med Exp PMPM:** $139
Principal Investments: Cash and equiv (100%)
Provider Compensation ($000): Contr fee ($101,666), FFS ($3,031), capitation ($1,104), other ($656)
Total Member Encounters: Phys (437,788), non-phys (101,246)
Group Affiliation: El Paso County Hospital District
Licensed in: TX
Address: 2501 N Mesa Street, El Paso, TX 79902
Phone: (915) 298-7198 **Dom State:** TX **Commenced Bus:** October 2000

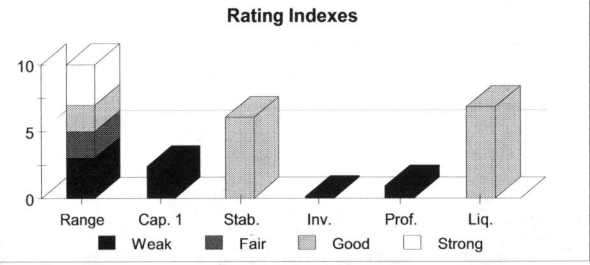

Data Date	Rating	RACR #1	RACR #2	Total Assets ($mil)	Capital ($mil)	Net Premium ($mil)	Net Income ($mil)
6-14	B	2.15	1.79	40.7	29.1	69.2	0.9
6-13	B	2.02	1.68	40.9	26.2	59.3	1.9
2013	B	2.07	1.72	38.2	28.0	126.9	3.7
2012	B	1.86	1.55	37.4	24.2	126.7	6.8
2011	B	2.24	1.87	44.9	26.3	117.8	7.2
2010	B	2.11	1.76	36.1	23.5	112.0	7.2
2009	C+	1.63	1.36	27.1	16.3	98.4	1.8

ELDERPLAN INC   C-   Fair

Major Rating Factors: Fair overall results on stability tests (4.7 on a scale of 0 to 10). Good overall profitability index (5.1). Strong capitalization index (7.8) based on excellent current risk-adjusted capital (severe loss scenario).
Other Rating Factors: High quality investment portfolio (9.9). Excellent liquidity (7.0) with sufficient resources (cash flows and marketable investments) to handle a spike in claims.
Principal Business: Medicaid (71%), Medicare (29%)
Mem Phys: 13: N/A **12:** 32,092 **13 MLR** 79.7% **/ 13 Admin Exp** N/A
Enroll(000): Q2 14: 24 **13:** 25 **12:** 22 **Med Exp PMPM:** $1,890
Principal Investments: Long-term bonds (57%), cash and equiv (35%), nonaffiliate common stock (7%), other (1%)
Provider Compensation ($000): FFS ($427,753), contr fee ($61,426), capitation ($10,830)
Total Member Encounters: Phys (261,988), non-phys (132,561)
Group Affiliation: None
Licensed in: NY
Address: 6323 7th Ave, Brooklyn, NY 11220
Phone: (718) 921-7990 **Dom State:** NY **Commenced Bus:** March 1985

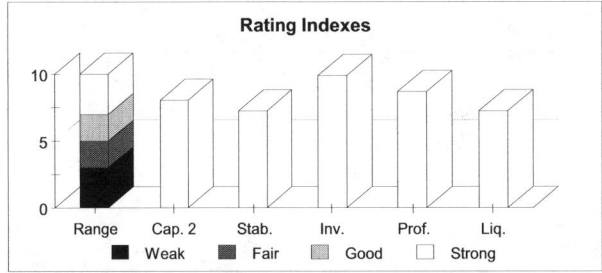

Data Date	Rating	RACR #1	RACR #2	Total Assets ($mil)	Capital ($mil)	Net Premium ($mil)	Net Income ($mil)
6-14	C-	2.02	1.69	240.3	110.0	379.2	11.8
6-13	D	1.62	1.35	155.8	76.5	282.2	2.5
2013	D+	1.90	1.58	200.2	103.0	645.9	28.9
2012	D	1.52	1.27	151.0	72.5	514.7	12.0
2011	D	1.58	1.31	143.1	58.9	388.9	-21.3
2010	C-	1.90	1.59	142.6	84.7	362.2	-0.1
2009	C+	2.14	1.78	103.4	45.3	234.0	-7.6

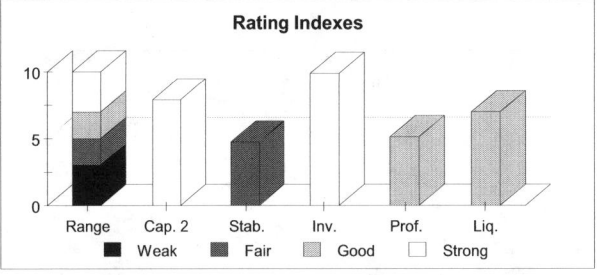

EMI HEALTH   B-   Good

Major Rating Factors: Good overall profitability index (5.9 on a scale of 0 to 10). Strong capitalization (10.0) based on excellent current risk-adjusted capital (severe loss scenario). High quality investment portfolio (8.4).
Other Rating Factors: Excellent liquidity (8.0) with ample operational cash flow and liquid investments.
Principal Business: Dental (17%), med supp (13%), other (68%)
Mem Phys: 13: 11,423 **12:** N/A **13 MLR** 91.7% **/ 13 Admin Exp** N/A
Enroll(000): Q2 14: 76 **13:** 76 **12:** 84 **Med Exp PMPM:** $33
Principal Investments: Long-term bonds (53%), cash and equiv (33%), affiliate common stock (10%), real estate (2%), pref stock (2%)
Provider Compensation ($000): FFS ($19,112), contr fee ($13,834)
Total Member Encounters: Phys (131,877), non-phys (114,456)
Group Affiliation: Educators Mutual Group
Licensed in: ID, UT
Address: 852 E Arrowhead Ln, Murray, UT 84107
Phone: (801) 262-7476 **Dom State:** UT **Commenced Bus:** June 1935

Data Date	Rating	RACR #1	RACR #2	Total Assets ($mil)	Capital ($mil)	Net Premium ($mil)	Net Income ($mil)
6-14	B-	4.35	3.63	86.2	54.4	16.3	2.9
6-13	N/A	N/A	N/A	72.6	50.2	17.9	1.3
2013	C-	4.21	3.51	75.9	52.8	35.1	4.1
2012	N/A	N/A	N/A	72.1	46.4	35.4	N/A
2011	N/A	N/A	N/A	68.9	41.0	45.7	N/A
2010	N/A	N/A	N/A	74.0	47.3	58.7	N/A
2009	N/A	N/A	N/A	72.6	36.2	58.8	N/A

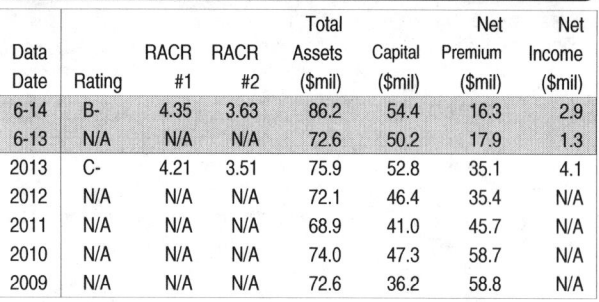
Rating Indexes

EMPIRE HEALTHCHOICE ASSURANCE INC   B-   Good

Major Rating Factors: Good overall profitability index (6.3 on a scale of 0 to 10). Good quality investment portfolio (5.4). Good liquidity (6.5) with sufficient resources (cash flows and marketable investments) to handle a spike in claims.
Other Rating Factors: Strong capitalization (10.0) based on excellent current risk-adjusted capital (severe loss scenario).
Principal Business: Comp med (73%), FEHB (13%), Medicare (11%), med supp (2%)
Mem Phys: 13: 72,308 **12:** 71,377 **13 MLR** 88.6% **/ 13 Admin Exp** N/A
Enroll(000): Q2 14: 876 **13:** 1,792 **12:** 1,864 **Med Exp PMPM:** $190
Principal Investments: Long-term bonds (85%), affiliate common stock (19%), pref stock (1%), other (8%)
Provider Compensation ($000): Contr fee ($3,895,770), FFS ($196,723), bonus arrang ($6,740), capitation ($5,266), other ($17,932)
Total Member Encounters: Phys (6,324,415), non-phys (1,593,264)
Group Affiliation: WellPoint Inc
Licensed in: NY
Address: 1 Liberty Plaza 165 Broadway, New York, NY 10006
Phone: (212) 476-1000 **Dom State:** NY **Commenced Bus:** June 1974

Data Date	Rating	RACR #1	RACR #2	Total Assets ($mil)	Capital ($mil)	Net Premium ($mil)	Net Income ($mil)
6-14	B-	4.14	3.45	3,006.6	1,367.8	1,265.2	101.5
6-13	B+	4.45	3.71	3,527.2	1,655.6	2,281.5	195.4
2013	B	5.14	4.28	3,533.3	1,711.9	4,591.4	263.0
2012	B+	4.58	3.82	3,655.5	1,712.2	5,130.5	291.0
2011	B+	3.61	3.01	3,557.0	1,446.1	5,547.3	329.8
2010	B+	5.37	4.47	3,099.0	1,531.1	4,926.4	324.4
2009	A-	3.13	2.61	3,042.4	1,363.2	5,884.6	199.5

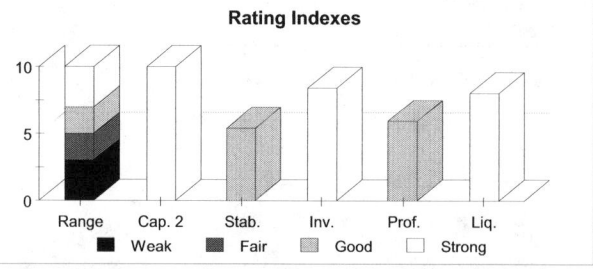
Rating Indexes

EMPIRE HEALTHCHOICE HMO INC   B   Good

Major Rating Factors: Good overall profitability index (5.2 on a scale of 0 to 10). Good liquidity (6.6) with sufficient resources (cash flows and marketable investments) to handle a spike in claims. Strong capitalization index (10.0) based on excellent current risk-adjusted capital (severe loss scenario).
Other Rating Factors: High quality investment portfolio (7.5). Weak overall results on stability tests (2.4) based on a significant 25% decrease in enrollment during the period. Rating is significantly influenced by the good financial results of WellPoint Inc.
Principal Business: Medicare (56%), comp med (44%)
Mem Phys: 13: 70,315 **12:** 68,824 **13 MLR** 88.5% **/ 13 Admin Exp** N/A
Enroll(000): Q2 14: 191 **13:** 164 **12:** 219 **Med Exp PMPM:** $603
Principal Investments: Long-term bonds (98%), other (5%)
Provider Compensation ($000): Contr fee ($1,248,147), FFS ($107,873), capitation ($14,309), bonus arrang ($3,119)
Total Member Encounters: Phys (2,541,837), non-phys (450,881)
Group Affiliation: WellPoint Inc
Licensed in: NY
Address: 1 Liberty Plaza 165 Broadway, New York, NY 10006
Phone: (212) 476-1000 **Dom State:** NY **Commenced Bus:** March 1996

Data Date	Rating	RACR #1	RACR #2	Total Assets ($mil)	Capital ($mil)	Net Premium ($mil)	Net Income ($mil)
6-14	B	3.78	3.15	873.6	311.5	725.9	-31.9
6-13	B+	5.07	4.23	770.7	475.7	812.3	15.7
2013	B+	5.53	4.61	750.6	477.3	1,539.6	22.3
2012	A-	5.79	4.83	850.1	548.8	1,699.5	83.8
2011	A-	4.87	4.06	969.0	495.7	1,863.3	104.6
2010	A-	5.84	4.86	878.6	559.4	1,959.3	178.8
2009	A-	4.03	3.36	813.9	482.3	2,293.8	138.9

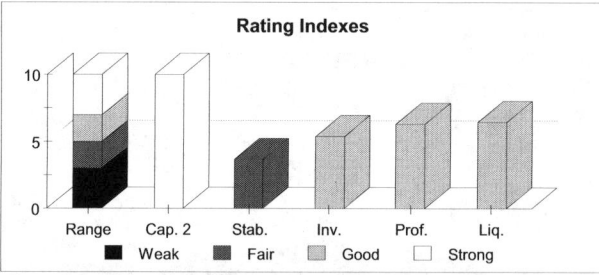
Rating Indexes

EMPLOYER CHOICE INS CO

E   **Very Weak**

Major Rating Factors: Weak profitability index (0.0 on a scale of 0 to 10). Strong capitalization (9.1) based on excellent current risk-adjusted capital (severe loss scenario). High quality investment portfolio (9.9).
Other Rating Factors: Excellent liquidity (8.1) with ample operational cash flow and liquid investments.
Principal Business: Comp med (100%)
Mem Phys: 13: 2,296   **12:** 2,542   **13 MLR** 84.6%   **/ 13 Admin Exp** N/A
Enroll(000): Q2 14: 0   **13:** 1   **12:** 1   **Med Exp PMPM:** $143
Principal Investments: Cash and equiv (100%)
Provider Compensation ($000): Contr fee ($1,897)
Total Member Encounters: N/A
Group Affiliation: North American Health Services Inc
Licensed in: FL
Address: 602 Courtland St Suite 310, Orlando, FL 32804
Phone: (407) 691-5414   **Dom State:** FL   **Commenced Bus:** July 2009

Data Date	Rating	RACR #1	RACR #2	Total Assets ($mil)	Capital ($mil)	Net Premium ($mil)	Net Income ($mil)
6-14	E	3.07	2.56	2.9	2.4	0.6	-0.1
6-13	D	4.72	3.93	3.9	3.6	1.1	-0.1
2013	E	3.39	2.83	3.3	2.6	2.2	-1.1
2012	D	5.02	4.19	4.2	3.7	1.7	-0.6
2011	D	3.30	2.75	4.6	4.5	0.7	-0.4
2010	N/A	N/A	N/A	4.8	4.8	N/A	-0.2
2009	E	N/A	N/A	5.0	5.0	N/A	N/A

ENVISION INS CO

C   **Fair**

Major Rating Factors: Weak liquidity (2.2 on a scale of 0 to 10) as a spike in claims may stretch capacity. Good capitalization (6.9) based on excellent current risk-adjusted capital (severe loss scenario). Excellent profitability (7.1).
Other Rating Factors: High quality investment portfolio (9.9).
Principal Business: Other (100%)
Mem Phys: 13: 68,394   **12:** N/A   **13 MLR** 373.2%   **/ 13 Admin Exp** N/A
Enroll(000): Q2 14: 372   **13:** 484   **12:** 376   **Med Exp PMPM:** $89
Principal Investments: Cash and equiv (68%), long-term bonds (31%), real estate (1%)
Provider Compensation ($000): Other ($499,164)
Total Member Encounters: N/A
Group Affiliation: Envision Pharmaceutical Holdings Inc
Licensed in: (No states)
Address: 2181 East Aurora Rd, Twinsburg, OH 44087-1974
Phone: (330) 405-8089   **Dom State:** OH   **Commenced Bus:** January 2007

Data Date	Rating	RACR #1	RACR #2	Total Assets ($mil)	Capital ($mil)	Net Premium ($mil)	Net Income ($mil)
6-14	C	1.27	1.06	465.7	25.2	60.8	-0.1
6-13	N/A	N/A	N/A	313.7	23.8	69.1	0.6
2013	U	1.28	1.06	309.6	25.5	134.7	1.8
2012	N/A	N/A	N/A	237.8	22.0	107.4	N/A
2011	N/A	N/A	N/A	93.2	20.8	121.1	N/A
2010	N/A	N/A	N/A	97.0	19.3	58.0	N/A
2009	C	N/A	N/A	37.6	21.6	34.0	2.4

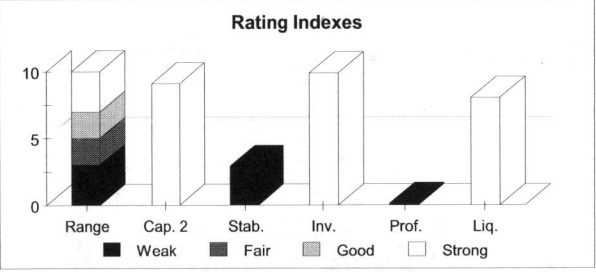

EPIC HEALTH PLAN

D+   **Weak**

Major Rating Factors: Weak liquidity (0.0 on a scale of 0 to 10) as a spike in claims may stretch capacity. Good capitalization index (5.0) based on fair current risk-adjusted capital (moderate loss scenario). Good overall results on stability tests (5.2) based on healthy premium and capital growth during 2013.
Other Rating Factors: Excellent profitability (7.2).
Principal Business: Managed care (100%)
Mem Phys: 13: N/A   **12:** N/A   **13 MLR** 97.1%   **/ 13 Admin Exp** N/A
Enroll(000): Q2 14: 62   **13:** 34   **12:** 2   **Med Exp PMPM:** $450
Principal Investments ($000): Cash and equiv ($9,572)
Provider Compensation ($000): None
Total Member Encounters: N/A
Group Affiliation: None
Licensed in: CA
Address: 10393 Enterprise Dr, Redlands, CA 92373
Phone: (909) 478-5110   **Dom State:** CA   **Commenced Bus:** October 2010

Data Date	Rating	RACR #1	RACR #2	Total Assets ($mil)	Capital ($mil)	Net Premium ($mil)	Net Income ($mil)
6-14	D+	0.78	0.47	17.3	5.6	138.6	N/A
6-13	C-	1.42	0.85	9.0	3.4	19.2	0.5
2013	D+	0.55	0.33	11.6	4.1	65.4	0.7
2012	C-	1.20	0.73	6.3	2.9	21.0	N/A
2011	N/A	N/A	N/A	5.1	2.9	11.4	N/A
2010	N/A	N/A	N/A	3.0	2.9	N/A	-0.1
2009	N/A	N/A	N/A	N/A	N/A	N/A	N/A

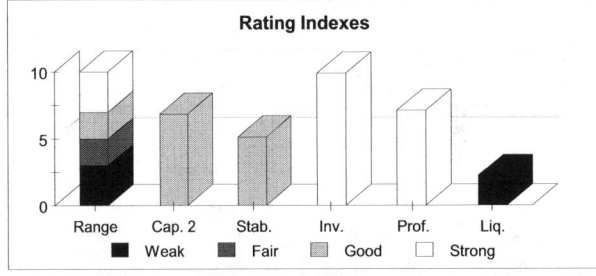

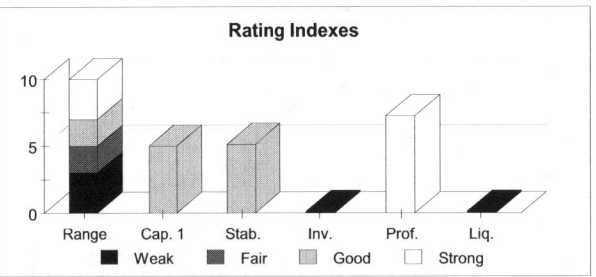

EPIC LIFE INSURANCE COMPANY   B   Good

Major Rating Factors: Good overall results on stability tests (5.9 on a scale of 0 to 10) despite fair financial strength of affiliated Wisconsin Physicians Ins Group. Other stability subfactors include excellent operational trends and good risk diversification. Good quality investment portfolio (5.3) with no exposure to mortgages and no exposure to junk bonds. Strong capitalization (9.1) based on excellent risk adjusted capital (severe loss scenario).

Other Rating Factors: Excellent profitability (7.9) despite operating losses during the first six months of 2014. Excellent liquidity (7.1).

Principal Business: Group health insurance (66%), group life insurance (27%), reinsurance (5%), and individual health insurance (2%).

Principal Investments: NonCMO investment grade bonds (67%), common & preferred stock (20%), CMOs and structured securities (9%), and cash (3%).

Investments in Affiliates: None

Group Affiliation: Wisconsin Physicians Ins Group

Licensed in: AZ, AR, CO, FL, IL, IN, IA, KS, KY, MD, MI, MN, MO, NE, NV, ND, OH, OK, OR, PA, SC, SD, TN, TX, VA, WV, WI

Commenced Business: August 1984

Address: 1717 W Broadway, Madison, WI 53713

Phone: (608) 221-6882 **Domicile State:** WI **NAIC Code:** 64149

Data Date	Rating	RACR #1	RACR #2	Total Assets ($mil)	Capital ($mil)	Net Premium ($mil)	Net Income ($mil)
6-14	B	3.56	2.40	61.0	31.5	13.1	-0.4
6-13	B	3.37	2.28	59.0	30.0	12.7	0.6
2013	B	2.95	1.99	61.8	31.6	25.5	1.4
2012	B+	2.55	1.73	56.9	28.2	24.5	2.4
2011	B+	2.55	1.74	54.5	26.6	21.7	2.2
2010	B+	2.82	1.89	51.5	25.9	18.2	1.1
2009	B+	2.78	1.88	47.8	23.9	18.3	1.2

Wisconsin Physicians Ins Group Composite Group Rating: C+ Largest Group Members	Assets ($mil)	Rating
WISCONSIN PHYSICIANS SERVICE INS	345	C+
EPIC LIFE INSURANCE CO	62	B
WPS HEALTH PLAN INC	23	C

EQUITABLE LIFE & CASUALTY INSURANCE COMPANY   C+   Fair

Major Rating Factors: Fair profitability (4.8 on a scale of 0 to 10). Excellent expense controls. Return on equity has been low, averaging 0.3%. Fair overall results on stability tests (4.4). Strong capitalization (8.1) based on excellent risk adjusted capital (severe loss scenario). Capital levels have been relatively consistent over the last five years.

Other Rating Factors: High quality investment portfolio (7.7). Excellent liquidity (7.2).

Principal Business: Individual health insurance (88%), individual life insurance (9%), and reinsurance (3%).

Principal Investments: NonCMO investment grade bonds (68%), CMOs and structured securities (22%), mortgages in good standing (5%), and cash (4%).

Investments in Affiliates: None

Group Affiliation: Insurance Investment Co

Licensed in: All states except CA, FL, MN, NJ, NY, PR

Commenced Business: June 1935

Address: 3 Triad Center Suite 200, Salt Lake City, UT 84180

Phone: (801) 579-3400 **Domicile State:** UT **NAIC Code:** 62952

Data Date	Rating	RACR #1	RACR #2	Total Assets ($mil)	Capital ($mil)	Net Premium ($mil)	Net Income ($mil)
6-14	C+	2.49	1.71	284.9	41.6	34.5	3.9
6-13	D+	1.41	1.00	250.1	26.9	49.5	-3.4
2013	D+	2.15	1.51	275.8	39.1	91.1	-0.3
2012	C-	1.51	1.08	243.0	30.3	111.1	1.8
2011	C-	1.61	1.15	230.6	30.9	110.1	1.4
2010	C	1.55	1.08	215.8	29.5	77.4	-5.4
2009	B-	1.43	1.04	233.1	30.0	109.1	-1.5

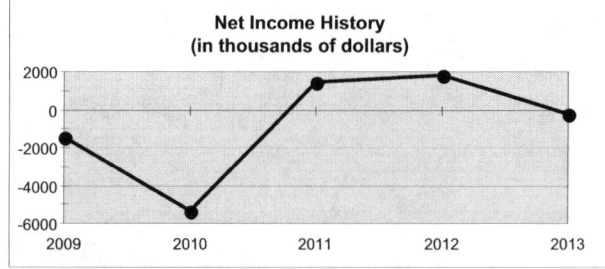

Net Income History (in thousands of dollars)

ESSENCE HEALTHCARE INC   B   Good

Major Rating Factors: Good overall profitability index (6.4 on a scale of 0 to 10). Strong capitalization (7.1) based on excellent current risk-adjusted capital (severe loss scenario). High quality investment portfolio (8.9).

Other Rating Factors: Excellent liquidity (6.9) with sufficient resources (cash flows and marketable investments) to handle a spike in claims.

Principal Business: Medicare (100%)

Mem Phys: 13: 3,604 **12:** 8,758 **13 MLR** 82.9% **/ 13 Admin Exp** N/A

Enroll(000): Q2 14: 41 **13:** 38 **12:** 39 **Med Exp PMPM:** $764

Principal Investments: Long-term bonds (72%), cash and equiv (25%), affiliate common stock (3%)

Provider Compensation ($000): Contr fee ($263,430), capitation ($95,695)

Total Member Encounters: Phys (277,342), non-phys (56,001)

Group Affiliation: Essence Group Holdings Corp

Licensed in: IL, IN, KY, MO, WA

Address: 12655 Olive Blvd 4th Floor, St Louis, MO 63141

Phone: (314) 209-2780 **Dom State:** MO **Commenced Bus:** July 2004

Data Date	Rating	RACR #1	RACR #2	Total Assets ($mil)	Capital ($mil)	Net Premium ($mil)	Net Income ($mil)
6-14	B	1.44	1.20	109.3	50.9	221.6	6.6
6-13	B	1.28	1.07	116.0	47.5	208.1	11.5
2013	B	1.23	1.02	111.3	44.3	411.8	20.3
2012	B	1.40	1.17	135.2	51.1	432.7	20.8
2011	B	1.15	0.96	137.8	53.2	409.5	19.8
2010	C	0.56	0.46	113.1	38.0	461.5	-11.9
2009	C+	0.72	0.60	105.0	24.5	317.5	1.1

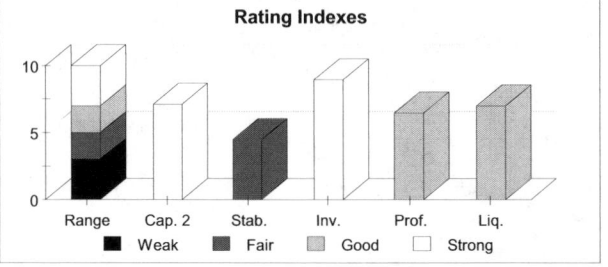

Rating Indexes

Range   Cap. 2   Stab.   Inv.   Prof.   Liq.

■ Weak   ▨ Fair   ▥ Good   □ Strong

EXCELLUS HEALTH PLAN INC *

A **Excellent**

Major Rating Factors: Strong capitalization (9.5 on a scale of 0 to 10) based on excellent current risk-adjusted capital (severe loss scenario). Good quality investment portfolio (5.1). Good liquidity (6.8) with sufficient resources (cash flows and marketable investments) to handle a spike in claims.
Other Rating Factors: Fair profitability index (4.3).
Principal Business: Comp med (64%), Medicare (17%), Medicaid (15%), FEHB (2%), other (1%)
Mem Phys: 13: 26,677 **12:** 26,400 **13 MLR** 90.5% **/ 13 Admin Exp** N/A
Enroll(000): Q2 14: 1,351 **13:** 1,615 **12:** 1,624 **Med Exp PMPM:** $293
Principal Investments: Long-term bonds (61%), nonaffiliate common stock (18%), affiliate common stock (10%), real estate (2%), cash and equiv (1%), other (7%)
Provider Compensation ($000): Contr fee ($5,426,168), capitation ($282,034), bonus arrang ($12,117)
Total Member Encounters: Phys (11,239,018), non-phys (2,796,311)
Group Affiliation: Lifetime Healthcare Inc
Licensed in: NY
Address: 165 Court St, Rochester, NY 14647
Phone: (585) 454-1700 **Dom State:** NY **Commenced Bus:** January 1936

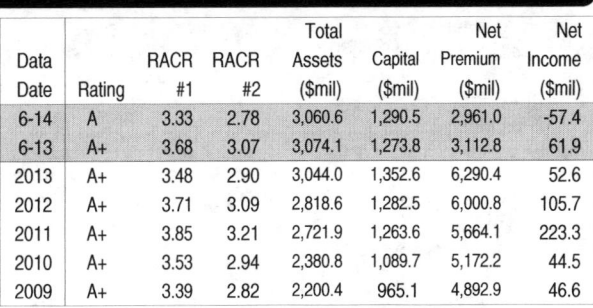

Data Date	Rating	RACR #1	RACR #2	Total Assets ($mil)	Capital ($mil)	Net Premium ($mil)	Net Income ($mil)
6-14	A	3.33	2.78	3,060.6	1,290.5	2,961.0	-57.4
6-13	A+	3.68	3.07	3,074.1	1,273.8	3,112.8	61.9
2013	A+	3.48	2.90	3,044.0	1,352.6	6,290.4	52.6
2012	A+	3.71	3.09	2,818.6	1,282.5	6,000.8	105.7
2011	A+	3.85	3.21	2,721.9	1,263.6	5,664.1	223.3
2010	A+	3.53	2.94	2,380.8	1,089.7	5,172.2	44.5
2009	A+	3.39	2.82	2,200.4	965.1	4,892.9	46.6

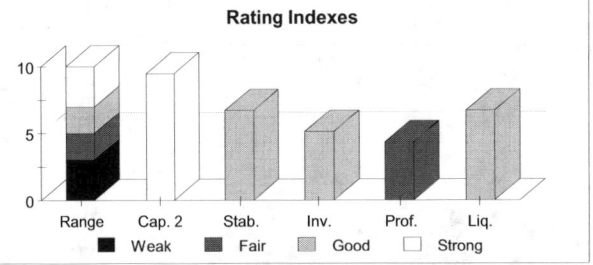

Rating Indexes

Range / Cap. 2 / Stab. / Inv. / Prof. / Liq.
■ Weak ■ Fair ▩ Good ☐ Strong

EXPRESS SCRIPTS INS CO

B **Good**

Major Rating Factors: Excellent profitability (7.4 on a scale of 0 to 10). Strong capitalization (8.1) based on excellent current risk-adjusted capital (severe loss scenario). High quality investment portfolio (9.9).
Other Rating Factors: Excellent liquidity (8.9) with ample operational cash flow and liquid investments.
Principal Business: Other (100%)
Mem Phys: 13: N/A **12:** N/A **13 MLR** 81.1% **/ 13 Admin Exp** N/A
Enroll(000): Q2 14: 345 **13:** 243 **12:** 154 **Med Exp PMPM:** $141
Principal Investments: Cash and equiv (100%)
Provider Compensation ($000): None
Total Member Encounters: N/A
Group Affiliation: New York Life Group
Licensed in: All states, the District of Columbia and Puerto Rico
Address: 7909 S Hardy Dr, Tempe, AZ 85284
Phone: (800) 332-5455 **Dom State:** AZ **Commenced Bus:** February 1994

Data Date	Rating	RACR #1	RACR #2	Total Assets ($mil)	Capital ($mil)	Net Premium ($mil)	Net Income ($mil)
6-14	B	2.22	1.85	108.0	49.5	62.9	-2.1
6-13	A-	1.80	1.50	63.2	29.3	72.8	0.3
2013	A-	2.71	2.26	240.3	60.4	172.3	31.3
2012	B+	1.11	0.92	80.6	18.0	84.1	-0.2
2011	B	2.28	1.90	31.8	18.2	44.8	4.9
2010	B	2.41	2.01	39.1	13.3	30.5	1.9
2009	B	N/A	N/A	19.1	11.5	20.6	2.5

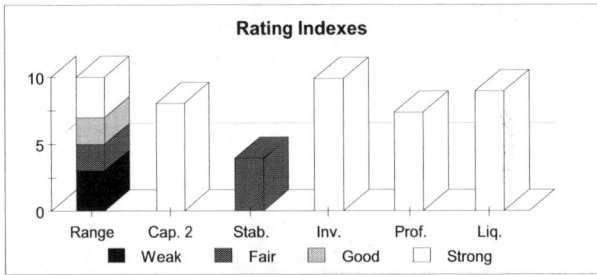

Rating Indexes

Range / Cap. 2 / Stab. / Inv. / Prof. / Liq.
■ Weak ■ Fair ▩ Good ☐ Strong

FALLON COMMUNITY HEALTH PLAN

B- **Good**

Major Rating Factors: Good profitability index (4.9 on a scale of 0 to 10). Good quality investment portfolio (5.2). Good liquidity (5.5) with sufficient resources (cash flows and marketable investments) to handle a spike in claims.
Other Rating Factors: Strong capitalization index (7.6) based on excellent current risk-adjusted capital (severe loss scenario). Excellent overall results on stability tests (7.0).
Principal Business: Comp med (61%), Medicare (32%), Medicaid (6%), FEHB (1%)
Mem Phys: 13: 40,702 **12:** 42,494 **13 MLR** 88.7% **/ 13 Admin Exp** N/A
Enroll(000): Q2 14: 151 **13:** 155 **12:** 155 **Med Exp PMPM:** $566
Principal Investments: Long-term bonds (49%), nonaffiliate common stock (45%), cash and equiv (4%), affiliate common stock (2%), other (1%)
Provider Compensation ($000): Contr fee ($810,983), capitation ($232,203), salary ($12,309), bonus arrang ($1,281)
Total Member Encounters: Phys (653,313), non-phys (303,393)
Group Affiliation: Fallon Health
Licensed in: MA
Address: 10 Chestnut St, Worcester, MA 01608-2810
Phone: (508) 799-2100 **Dom State:** MA **Commenced Bus:** February 1977

Data Date	Rating	RACR #1	RACR #2	Total Assets ($mil)	Capital ($mil)	Net Premium ($mil)	Net Income ($mil)
6-14	B-	1.86	1.55	407.4	173.8	547.7	8.9
6-13	B-	1.74	1.45	366.8	154.9	591.2	14.2
2013	B-	1.78	1.49	396.4	167.0	1,195.4	28.9
2012	B-	1.73	1.44	367.7	154.5	1,107.5	23.7
2011	B-	1.50	1.25	342.9	127.9	1,096.3	46.3
2010	C	1.03	0.86	296.4	93.6	1,093.5	4.1
2009	B+	1.12	0.93	272.3	101.0	1,075.8	-19.0

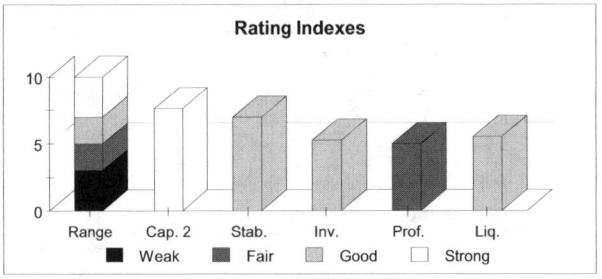

Rating Indexes

Range / Cap. 2 / Stab. / Inv. / Prof. / Liq.
■ Weak ■ Fair ▩ Good ☐ Strong

FALLON HEALTH & LIFE ASR CO   E   Very Weak

Major Rating Factors: Weak profitability index (1.1 on a scale of 0 to 10). Good capitalization (5.8) based on good current risk-adjusted capital (severe loss scenario). High quality investment portfolio (9.9).
Other Rating Factors: Excellent liquidity (7.1) with ample operational cash flow and liquid investments.
Principal Business: Comp med (94%), med supp (6%)
Mem Phys: 13: 40,702 **12:** 42,494 **13 MLR** 114.0% **/ 13 Admin Exp** N/A
Enroll(000): Q2 14: 8 **13:** 8 **12:** 6 **Med Exp PMPM:** $477
Principal Investments: Cash and equiv (100%), affiliate common stock (3%)
Provider Compensation ($000): Contr fee ($39,632), bonus arrang ($91), capitation ($81)
Total Member Encounters: Phys (27,342), non-phys (10,126)
Group Affiliation: Fallon Health
Licensed in: MA
Address: 10 Chestnut St, Worcester, MA 01608
Phone: (508) 799-2100 **Dom State:** MA **Commenced Bus:** January 1993

Data Date	Rating	RACR #1	RACR #2	Total Assets ($mil)	Capital ($mil)	Net Premium ($mil)	Net Income ($mil)
6-14	E	1.05	0.87	29.7	5.4	19.1	-5.8
6-13	E	1.02	0.85	27.6	4.9	17.1	-4.4
2013	E	1.08	0.90	30.8	5.6	35.2	-9.3
2012	C	1.31	1.09	25.8	6.4	28.2	-8.9
2011	C	1.10	0.91	23.6	4.7	25.2	-8.0
2010	D+	0.82	0.68	16.3	4.4	25.2	-13.0
2009	C+	0.79	0.66	13.5	3.9	21.3	-10.4

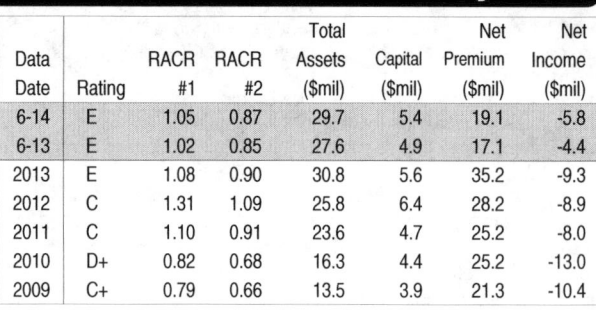

FAMILY HEALTH HAWAII MBS   D+   Weak

Major Rating Factors: Weak profitability index (0.6 on a scale of 0 to 10). Fair capitalization (2.9) based on good current risk-adjusted capital (moderate loss scenario). High quality investment portfolio (9.9).
Other Rating Factors: Excellent liquidity (9.4) with ample operational cash flow and liquid investments.
Principal Business: Comp med (100%)
Mem Phys: 13: 3,923 **12:** N/A **13 MLR** 93.4% **/ 13 Admin Exp** N/A
Enroll(000): Q2 14: 3 **13:** 0 **12:** N/A **Med Exp PMPM:** $268
Principal Investments: Cash and equiv (100%)
Provider Compensation ($000): Contr fee ($33), capitation ($12)
Total Member Encounters: Phys (119), non-phys (92)
Group Affiliation: None
Licensed in: HI
Address: 1440 Kapiolani Blvd Suite 1020, Honolulu, HI 96814
Phone: (808) 951-4645 **Dom State:** HI **Commenced Bus:** February 2013

Data Date	Rating	RACR #1	RACR #2	Total Assets ($mil)	Capital ($mil)	Net Premium ($mil)	Net Income ($mil)
6-14	D+	2.33	1.94	3.2	2.0	4.7	0.0
6-13	N/A	N/A	N/A	2.2	2.2	N/A	-0.1
2013	D+	2.33	1.94	2.2	2.0	0.2	-0.3
2012	N/A	N/A	N/A	N/A	N/A	N/A	N/A
2011	N/A	N/A	N/A	N/A	N/A	N/A	N/A
2010	N/A	N/A	N/A	N/A	N/A	N/A	N/A
2009	N/A	N/A	N/A	N/A	N/A	N/A	N/A

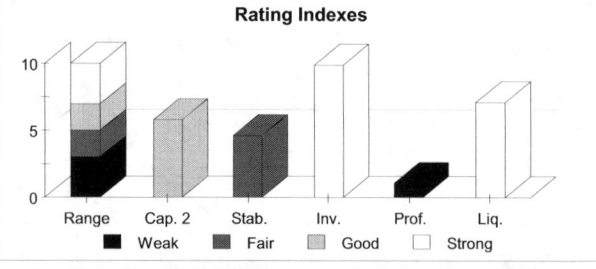

FAMILY HERITAGE LIFE INSURANCE COMPANY OF AMERICA *   A-   Excellent

Major Rating Factors: Excellent overall results on stability tests (7.3 on a scale of 0 to 10). Strengths that enhance stability include excellent operational trends and excellent risk diversification. Strong capitalization (7.5) based on excellent risk adjusted capital (severe loss scenario). Furthermore, this high level of risk adjusted capital has been consistently maintained over the last five years. High quality investment portfolio (7.5).
Other Rating Factors: Excellent profitability (9.6) with operating gains in each of the last five years. Excellent liquidity (8.2).
Principal Business: Individual health insurance (97%), group health insurance (3%), and individual life insurance (1%).
Principal Investments: NonCMO investment grade bonds (99%).
Investments in Affiliates: None
Group Affiliation: Torchmark Corp
Licensed in: All states except NY
Commenced Business: November 1989
Address: 6001 E Royalton Rd Suite 200, Cleveland, OH 44147-3529
Phone: (440) 922-5200 **Domicile State:** OH **NAIC Code:** 77968

Data Date	Rating	RACR #1	RACR #2	Total Assets ($mil)	Capital ($mil)	Net Premium ($mil)	Net Income ($mil)
6-14	A-	1.84	1.30	706.7	67.1	123.1	8.2
6-13	A-	2.48	1.77	609.4	76.0	94.6	8.8
2013	A-	2.09	1.48	641.5	66.9	192.7	17.0
2012	B+	2.15	1.57	571.1	62.1	177.0	16.5
2011	B+	2.22	1.71	488.5	55.3	161.0	15.6
2010	B+	2.19	1.72	431.9	48.3	145.9	14.0
2009	B+	2.06	1.63	365.4	41.7	132.0	13.3

Adverse Trends in Operations

Increase in policy surrenders from 2012 to 2013 (77%)
Increase in policy surrenders from 2010 to 2011 (33%)
Increase in policy surrenders from 2009 to 2010 (119%)

FAMILY LIFE INSURANCE COMPANY

C **Fair**

Major Rating Factors: Fair overall results on stability tests (4.2 on a scale of 0 to 10). Good liquidity (6.6) with sufficient resources to handle a spike in claims as well as a significant increase in policy surrenders. Weak profitability (2.9) with investment income below regulatory standards in relation to interest assumptions of reserves.

Other Rating Factors: Strong capitalization (9.6) based on excellent risk adjusted capital (severe loss scenario). High quality investment portfolio (8.7).

Principal Business: Individual health insurance (71%) and individual life insurance (29%).

Principal Investments: NonCMO investment grade bonds (67%), cash (14%), policy loans (11%), CMOs and structured securities (6%), and mortgages in good standing (2%).

Investments in Affiliates: None

Group Affiliation: Harris Insurance Holdings Inc

Licensed in: All states except NY, PR

Commenced Business: June 1949

Address: 1200 6th Ave Park Place Bldg, Seattle, WA 98101

Phone: (512) 404-5284 **Domicile State:** TX **NAIC Code:** 63053

Data Date	Rating	RACR #1	RACR #2	Total Assets ($mil)	Capital ($mil)	Net Premium ($mil)	Net Income ($mil)
6-14	C	3.51	2.71	146.9	32.9	12.8	3.0
6-13	C+	3.34	2.61	151.5	31.3	12.7	1.9
2013	C	3.41	2.69	147.6	31.9	26.0	3.5
2012	C	3.39	2.63	147.4	31.7	27.9	5.8
2011	C	3.23	2.77	126.4	29.5	23.2	3.7
2010	C+	3.20	2.58	130.3	29.3	27.4	5.1
2009	C+	2.84	2.55	122.3	26.0	16.2	4.4

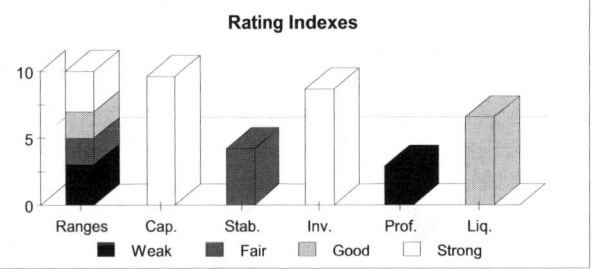

Rating Indexes

Ranges / Cap. / Stab. / Inv. / Prof. / Liq.
■ Weak ▨ Fair ▨ Good ☐ Strong

FAMILYCARE HEALTH PLANS INC

C- **Fair**

Major Rating Factors: Weak profitability index (0.9 on a scale of 0 to 10). Good liquidity (5.2) with sufficient resources (cash flows and marketable investments) to handle a spike in claims. Strong capitalization (7.2) based on excellent current risk-adjusted capital (severe loss scenario).

Other Rating Factors: High quality investment portfolio (7.9).

Principal Business: Medicare (100%)

Mem Phys: 13: 1,828 **12:** 2,453 **13 MLR** 84.3% **/ 13 Admin Exp** N/A

Enroll(000): Q2 14: 3 **13:** 3 **12:** 3 **Med Exp PMPM:** $819

Principal Investments: Long-term bonds (72%), nonaffiliate common stock (36%)

Provider Compensation ($000): Contr fee ($23,572), FFS ($2,520), capitation ($144), bonus arrang ($14)

Total Member Encounters: Phys (44,880), non-phys (21,258)

Group Affiliation: FamilyCare Inc

Licensed in: OR

Address: 2121 SW Broadway Suite 300, Portland, OR 97201

Phone: (503) 222-3205 **Dom State:** OR **Commenced Bus:** June 1997

Data Date	Rating	RACR #1	RACR #2	Total Assets ($mil)	Capital ($mil)	Net Premium ($mil)	Net Income ($mil)
6-14	C-	1.49	1.24	14.4	7.1	16.0	-2.8
6-13	C-	0.70	0.58	9.6	3.2	14.1	-0.4
2013	C-	0.99	0.82	10.7	4.7	31.1	-0.2
2012	C-	0.85	0.71	10.3	3.9	28.6	-0.4
2011	D+	0.86	0.72	11.8	4.5	31.8	0.2
2010	D	0.61	0.51	10.0	3.4	30.9	-2.4
2009	B	1.28	1.06	12.4	6.3	26.9	1.0

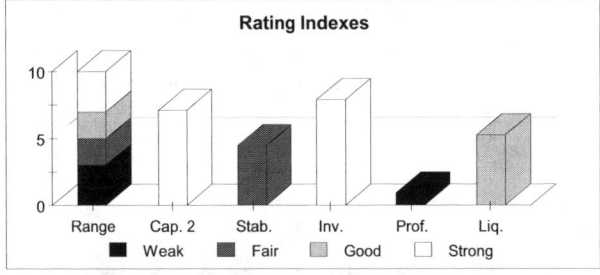

Rating Indexes

Range / Cap. 2 / Stab. / Inv. / Prof. / Liq.
■ Weak ▨ Fair ▨ Good ☐ Strong

FEDERATED MUTUAL INS CO *

A- **Excellent**

Major Rating Factors: Strong long-term capitalization index (10.0 on a scale of 0 to 10) based on excellent current risk adjusted capital (severe and moderate loss scenarios). Moreover, capital levels have been consistent in recent years. Ample reserve history (8.9) that helps to protect the company against sharp claims increases.

Other Rating Factors: Good overall results on stability tests (5.5) despite potential drain of affiliation with Federated Mutual Ins Group. Good overall profitability index (6.8). Fair expense controls. Good liquidity (6.9) with sufficient resources (cash flows and marketable investments) to handle a spike in claims.

Principal Business: Group accident & health (33%), workers compensation (17%), other liability (13%), auto liability (12%), commercial multiple peril (6%), auto physical damage (4%), and other lines (14%).

Principal Investments: Investment grade bonds (75%), misc. investments (24%), and real estate (1%).

Investments in Affiliates: 14%

Group Affiliation: Federated Mutual Ins Group

Licensed in: All states except AK, HI, PR

Commenced Business: August 1904

Address: 121 E Park Square, Owatonna, MN 55060

Phone: (507) 455-5200 **Domicile State:** MN **NAIC Code:** 13935

Data Date	Rating	RACR #1	RACR #2	Loss Ratio %	Total Assets ($mil)	Capital ($mil)	Net Premium ($mil)	Net Income ($mil)
6-14	A-	3.70	2.99	N/A	4,667.2	2,616.8	562.3	79.8
6-13	A-	3.85	3.13	N/A	4,383.3	2,424.1	490.5	69.1
2013	A-	3.67	3.00	69.6	4,523.5	2,518.3	1,083.5	127.9
2012	A-	3.86	3.19	74.6	4,233.8	2,365.4	942.3	106.1
2011	A-	3.71	3.03	79.6	4,075.1	2,237.2	875.9	52.5
2010	A-	3.83	3.12	65.8	4,019.4	2,190.9	784.6	152.3
2009	A-	3.61	2.90	64.8	3,944.9	2,017.8	809.2	137.1

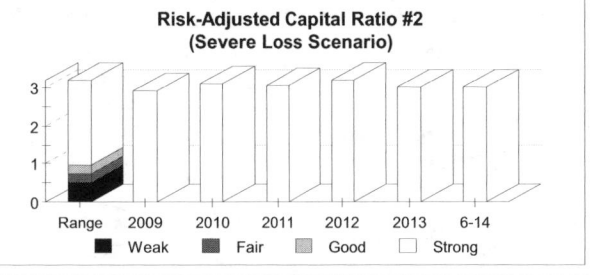

Risk-Adjusted Capital Ratio #2
(Severe Loss Scenario)

Range / 2009 / 2010 / 2011 / 2012 / 2013 / 6-14
■ Weak ▨ Fair ▨ Good ☐ Strong

FIDELIS SECURECARE OF MICHIGAN INC   C   Fair

Major Rating Factors: Good profitability index (5.0 on a scale of 0 to 10). Strong capitalization (7.2) based on excellent current risk-adjusted capital (severe loss scenario). High quality investment portfolio (9.9).
Other Rating Factors: Excellent liquidity (7.1) with ample operational cash flow and liquid investments.
Principal Business: Medicare (100%)
Mem Phys: 13: 106 **12:** 86 **13 MLR** 87.5% **/ 13 Admin Exp** N/A
Enroll(000): Q2 14: 2 **13:** 1 **12:** 1 **Med Exp PMPM:** $1,572
Principal Investments: Cash and equiv (91%), long-term bonds (9%)
Provider Compensation ($000): Contr fee ($6,925), FFS ($6,267), capitation ($4,931), bonus arrang ($278)
Total Member Encounters: N/A
Group Affiliation: Fidelis SeniorCare Inc
Licensed in: MI
Address: 38777 W Six Mile Rd Suite 207, Livonia, MI 48152
Phone: (847) 605-0501 **Dom State:** MI **Commenced Bus:** July 2005

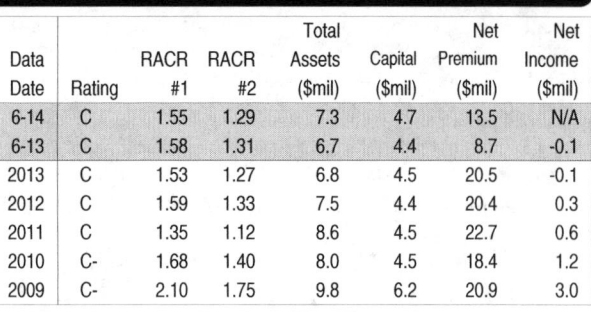

Data Date	Rating	RACR #1	RACR #2	Total Assets ($mil)	Capital ($mil)	Net Premium ($mil)	Net Income ($mil)
6-14	C	1.55	1.29	7.3	4.7	13.5	N/A
6-13	C	1.58	1.31	6.7	4.4	8.7	-0.1
2013	C	1.53	1.27	6.8	4.5	20.5	-0.1
2012	C	1.59	1.33	7.5	4.4	20.4	0.3
2011	C	1.35	1.12	8.6	4.5	22.7	0.6
2010	C-	1.68	1.40	8.0	4.5	18.4	1.2
2009	C-	2.10	1.75	9.8	6.2	20.9	3.0

Rating Indexes

Range | Cap. 2 | Stab. | Inv. | Prof. | Liq.
■ Weak ■ Fair ▨ Good ☐ Strong

FIDELIS SECURECARE OF NORTH CAROLINA   D+   Weak

Major Rating Factors: Weak profitability index (1.6 on a scale of 0 to 10). Strong capitalization (10.0) based on excellent current risk-adjusted capital (severe loss scenario). High quality investment portfolio (9.9).
Other Rating Factors: Excellent liquidity (7.4) with ample operational cash flow and liquid investments.
Principal Business: Medicare (100%)
Mem Phys: 13: 10 **12:** 13 **13 MLR** 99.1% **/ 13 Admin Exp** N/A
Enroll(000): **13:** 0 **12:** 0 **Med Exp PMPM:** $2,193
Principal Investments: Cash and equiv (100%)
Provider Compensation ($000): FFS ($1,186), contr fee ($1,186), bonus arrang ($271), capitation ($172)
Total Member Encounters: N/A
Group Affiliation: Fidelis SeniorCare Inc
Licensed in: NC
Address: 9300 Harris Corners Pkwy #100, Charlotte, NC 28269
Phone: (847) 605-0501 **Dom State:** NC **Commenced Bus:** July 2005

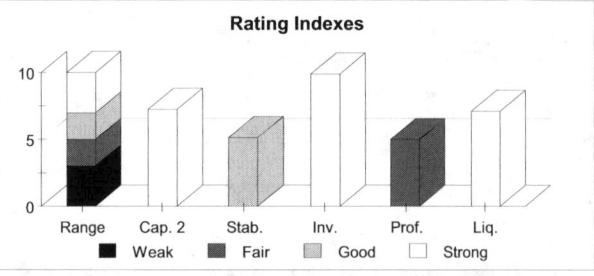

Data Date	Rating	RACR #1	RACR #2	Total Assets ($mil)	Capital ($mil)	Net Premium ($mil)	Net Income ($mil)
2013	D+	3.92	3.26	2.3	2.0	2.6	-0.8
2012	C	4.51	3.76	4.5	3.9	5.8	-0.2
2011	C-	2.89	2.41	5.3	4.1	10.1	0.8
2010	D	2.38	1.98	5.0	3.5	10.6	0.8
2009	D	1.03	0.86	5.1	2.6	12.5	0.7

Rating Indexes

Range | Cap. 2 | Stab. | Inv. | Prof. | Liq.
■ Weak ■ Fair ▨ Good ☐ Strong

FIDELITY SECURITY LIFE INSURANCE COMPANY   B-   Good

Major Rating Factors: Good quality investment portfolio (6.4 on a scale of 0 to 10) despite mixed results such as: minimal exposure to mortgages and large holdings of BBB rated bonds but small junk bond holdings. Good overall profitability (6.6). Return on equity has been good over the last five years, averaging 10.1%. Good liquidity (6.2).
Other Rating Factors: Fair overall results on stability tests (3.5) including weak results on operational trends. Strong capitalization (8.5) based on excellent risk adjusted capital (severe loss scenario).
Principal Business: Group health insurance (88%), reinsurance (5%), individual annuities (2%), individual health insurance (2%), and other lines (3%).
Principal Investments: NonCMO investment grade bonds (49%), CMOs and structured securities (40%), noninv. grade bonds (4%), common & preferred stock (2%), and misc. investments (5%).
Investments in Affiliates: 1%
Group Affiliation: Fidelity Security Group
Licensed in: All states except PR
Commenced Business: July 1969
Address: 3130 Broadway, Kansas City, MO 64111
Phone: (816) 750-1060 **Domicile State:** MO **NAIC Code:** 71870

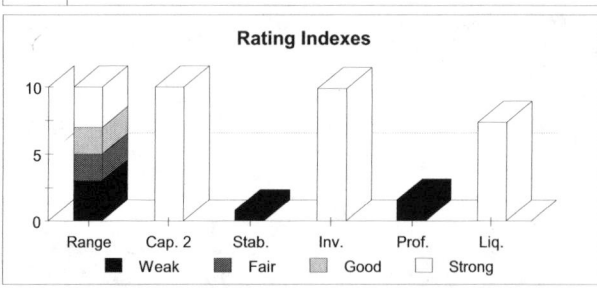

Data Date	Rating	RACR #1	RACR #2	Total Assets ($mil)	Capital ($mil)	Net Premium ($mil)	Net Income ($mil)
6-14	B-	3.21	1.98	824.9	141.6	48.7	7.4
6-13	B	3.15	1.93	802.8	128.7	57.9	6.3
2013	B-	2.99	1.83	819.5	135.3	109.2	13.9
2012	B	2.79	1.67	789.7	123.2	202.7	2.3
2011	B+	3.01	1.85	702.7	122.8	117.3	14.9
2010	B+	2.87	1.82	664.4	109.4	207.9	16.0
2009	B+	1.74	1.24	608.5	93.9	361.9	10.4

Rating Indexes

Ranges | Cap. | Stab. | Inv. | Prof. | Liq.
■ Weak ■ Fair ▨ Good ☐ Strong

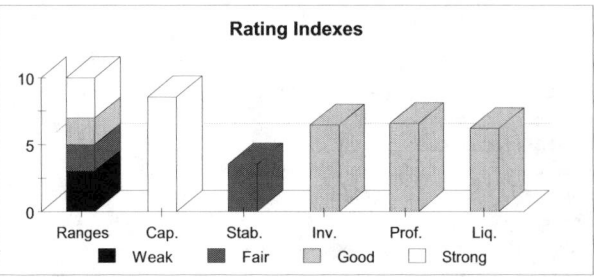

FIRST ASSURANCE LIFE OF AMERICA   B   Good

Major Rating Factors: Good overall results on stability tests (5.7 on a scale of 0 to 10). Stability strengths include good operational trends and good risk diversification. Strong capitalization (10.0) based on excellent risk adjusted capital (severe loss scenario). Moreover, capital levels have been consistently high over the last five years. High quality investment portfolio (8.8).
Other Rating Factors: Excellent profitability (8.3) with operating gains in each of the last five years. Excellent liquidity (9.1).
Principal Business: Credit life insurance (74%) and credit health insurance (26%).
Principal Investments: NonCMO investment grade bonds (69%), common & preferred stock (26%), and cash (5%).
Investments in Affiliates: 26%
Group Affiliation: LDS Group
Licensed in: AL, LA, MS, TN
Commenced Business: September 1981
Address: 9016 Bluebonnet Blvd, Baton Rouge, LA 70884-2810
Phone: (504) 769-9923 **Domicile State:** LA **NAIC Code:** 94579

Data Date	Rating	RACR #1	RACR #2	Total Assets ($mil)	Capital ($mil)	Net Premium ($mil)	Net Income ($mil)
6-14	B	3.17	3.01	37.4	32.0	1.6	0.3
6-13	B	3.13	2.98	36.4	31.4	1.8	0.3
2013	B	3.14	2.98	36.8	31.7	3.0	0.7
2012	B	3.10	2.95	35.8	31.1	3.2	0.9
2011	B	4.02	3.78	31.3	27.0	2.7	1.0
2010	B	4.15	3.93	30.9	25.6	-2.2	1.0
2009	B	3.70	3.44	30.7	24.3	4.3	0.9

Adverse Trends in Operations

Decrease in premium volume from 2012 to 2013 (4%)
Change in premium mix from 2010 to 2011 (38.2%)
Decrease in premium volume from 2009 to 2010 (150%)

FIRST COMMUNITY HEALTH PLAN INC   B   Good

Major Rating Factors: Good overall profitability index (5.0 on a scale of 0 to 10). Strong capitalization (10.0) based on excellent current risk-adjusted capital (severe loss scenario). High quality investment portfolio (9.9).
Other Rating Factors: Excellent liquidity (7.8) with ample operational cash flow and liquid investments.
Principal Business: Med supp (100%)
Mem Phys: 13: N/A **12:** N/A **13 MLR** 62.4% **/ 13 Admin Exp** N/A
Enroll(000): Q2 14: 4 **13:** 4 **12:** 4 **Med Exp PMPM:** $95
Principal Investments: Long-term bonds (52%), cash and equiv (48%)
Provider Compensation ($000): FFS ($4,272)
Total Member Encounters: Phys (210,196), non-phys (16,624)
Group Affiliation: First Community Health Plans Group
Licensed in: AL
Address: 699 Gallatin St Ste A2, Huntsville, AL 35801-4912
Phone: (256) 532-2780 **Dom State:** AL **Commenced Bus:** January 1996

Data Date	Rating	RACR #1	RACR #2	Total Assets ($mil)	Capital ($mil)	Net Premium ($mil)	Net Income ($mil)
6-14	B	8.29	6.91	6.4	5.3	3.6	-0.1
6-13	B	7.67	6.40	6.5	5.4	3.4	0.4
2013	B	8.35	6.96	6.5	5.3	6.8	0.8
2012	B-	6.92	5.76	6.3	5.0	6.3	0.3
2011	C	8.00	6.66	6.1	4.6	6.3	0.4
2010	C-	6.23	5.19	5.6	4.3	6.3	0.4
2009	C-	5.11	4.26	4.6	3.4	5.6	-1.8

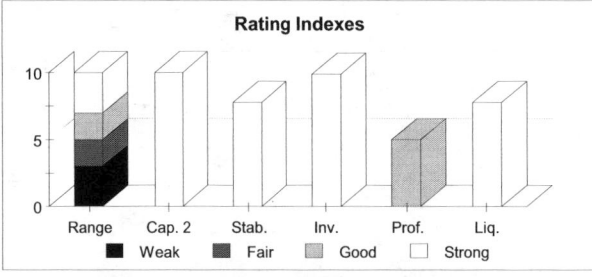

Rating Indexes

Range | Cap. 2 | Stab. | Inv. | Prof. | Liq.

■ Weak ▦ Fair ▨ Good □ Strong

FIRST HEALTH LIFE & HEALTH INSURANCE COMPANY   B   Good

Major Rating Factors: Good current capitalization (5.4 on a scale of 0 to 10) based on mixed results -- excessive policy leverage mitigated by good risk adjusted capital (severe loss scenario), although results have slipped from the excellent range over the last two years. Fair overall results on stability tests (4.1) including negative cash flow from operations for 2013, weak risk adjusted capital in prior years. Weak profitability (1.8) with operating losses during the first six months of 2014.
Other Rating Factors: Weak liquidity (0.2). High quality investment portfolio (9.1).
Principal Business: Individual health insurance (99%) and group health insurance (1%).
Principal Investments: NonCMO investment grade bonds (50%), cash (43%), and CMOs and structured securities (7%).
Investments in Affiliates: None
Group Affiliation: Aetna Inc
Licensed in: All states except NY, PR
Commenced Business: June 1979
Address: 300 W 11th St, Kansas City, MO 64199-3487
Phone: (816) 391-2231 **Domicile State:** TX **NAIC Code:** 90328

Data Date	Rating	RACR #1	RACR #2	Total Assets ($mil)	Capital ($mil)	Net Premium ($mil)	Net Income ($mil)
6-14	B	1.04	0.87	501.4	216.1	472.1	-17.3
6-13	B-	1.21	1.01	501.1	328.0	733.6	-82.9
2013	B	1.02	0.85	525.6	253.3	1,420.5	-175.3
2012	C+	1.46	1.22	600.2	412.2	1,494.9	48.3
2011	C+	1.19	0.99	577.0	363.5	1,156.5	28.4
2010	C+	1.61	1.33	592.4	329.3	1,125.2	64.8
2009	C+	0.59	0.49	811.1	269.5	2,729.2	-49.4

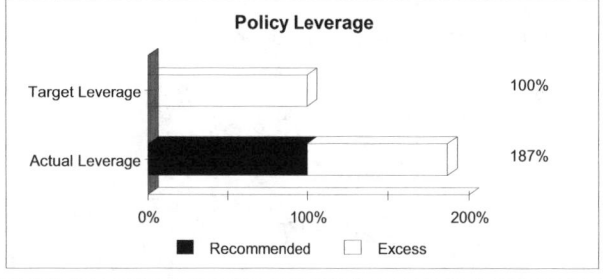

Policy Leverage

Target Leverage — 100%
Actual Leverage — 187%

0%   100%   200%

■ Recommended □ Excess

FIRST MEDICAL HEALTH PLAN INC   E   Very Weak

Major Rating Factors: Poor capitalization index (0.0 on a scale of 0 to 10) based on weak current risk-adjusted capital (severe loss scenario). Fair profitability index (3.2). Fair overall results on stability tests (4.4).
Other Rating Factors: Good liquidity (6.9) with sufficient resources (cash flows and marketable investments) to handle a spike in claims. High quality investment portfolio (9.1).
Principal Business: Comp med (72%), Medicare (28%)
Mem Phys: 13: N/A **12:** 8,124 **13 MLR** 87.7% **/ 13 Admin Exp** N/A
Enroll(000): Q2 14: 324 **13:** 332 **12:** 344 **Med Exp PMPM:** $140
Principal Investments: Cash and equiv (68%), long-term bonds (31%)
Provider Compensation ($000): Contr fee ($555,448), capitation ($8,508), other ($505)
Total Member Encounters: Phys (1,595,472), non-phys (597)
Group Affiliation: None
Licensed in: PR
Address: Ext Villa Caparra Mar Buch 530, Guaynabo, PR 00968
Phone: (787) 474-3999 **Dom State:** PR **Commenced Bus:** March 1977

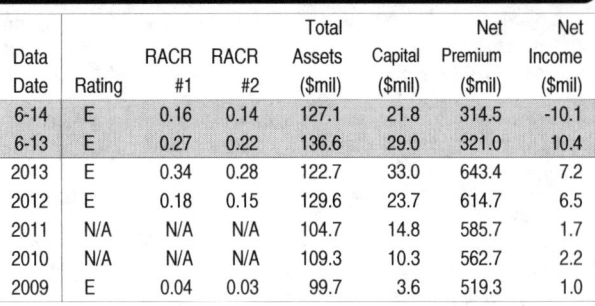

Data Date	Rating	RACR #1	RACR #2	Total Assets ($mil)	Capital ($mil)	Net Premium ($mil)	Net Income ($mil)
6-14	E	0.16	0.14	127.1	21.8	314.5	-10.1
6-13	E	0.27	0.22	136.6	29.0	321.0	10.4
2013	E	0.34	0.28	122.7	33.0	643.4	7.2
2012	E	0.18	0.15	129.6	23.7	614.7	6.5
2011	N/A	N/A	N/A	104.7	14.8	585.7	1.7
2010	N/A	N/A	N/A	109.3	10.3	562.7	2.2
2009	E	0.04	0.03	99.7	3.6	519.3	1.0

Rating Indexes

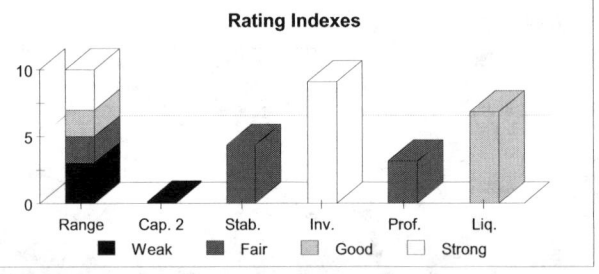

Range Cap. 2 Stab. Inv. Prof. Liq.
■ Weak   ▨ Fair   ▦ Good   □ Strong

FIRST PRIORITY LIFE INS CO   C   Fair

Major Rating Factors: Weak profitability index (1.7 on a scale of 0 to 10). Good quality investment portfolio (6.4). Good liquidity (6.7) with sufficient resources (cash flows and marketable investments) to handle a spike in claims.
Other Rating Factors: Strong capitalization (9.6) based on excellent current risk-adjusted capital (severe loss scenario).
Principal Business: Comp med (100%)
Mem Phys: 13: 6,726 **12:** 6,669 **13 MLR** 82.2% **/ 13 Admin Exp** N/A
Enroll(000): Q2 14: 121 **13:** 104 **12:** 86 **Med Exp PMPM:** $308
Principal Investments: Long-term bonds (60%), nonaffiliate common stock (25%), cash and equiv (11%), other (4%)
Provider Compensation ($000): FFS ($230,647), contr fee ($105,207), bonus arrang ($455)
Total Member Encounters: Phys (447,910), non-phys (5,336)
Group Affiliation: Hospital Svc Assoc of NE PA
Licensed in: PA
Address: 19 N Main St, Wilkes-Barre, PA 18711
Phone: (888) 338-2211 **Dom State:** PA **Commenced Bus:** August 1998

Data Date	Rating	RACR #1	RACR #2	Total Assets ($mil)	Capital ($mil)	Net Premium ($mil)	Net Income ($mil)
6-14	C	3.44	2.87	253.7	125.9	253.9	-14.2
6-13	B-	4.48	3.74	237.6	145.0	201.2	-0.8
2013	B-	3.86	3.22	246.3	142.3	416.5	-12.9
2012	C+	4.46	3.72	224.0	145.1	390.1	7.3
2011	C-	4.32	3.60	207.9	132.8	380.4	2.0
2010	N/A	N/A	N/A	189.7	130.0	408.9	5.2
2009	C	N/A	N/A	179.2	122.5	402.1	4.7

Rating Indexes

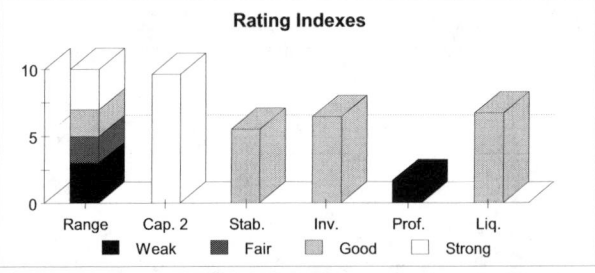

Range Cap. 2 Stab. Inv. Prof. Liq.
■ Weak   ▨ Fair   ▦ Good   □ Strong

FIRST RELIANCE STANDARD LIFE INSURANCE COMPANY *   A   Excellent

Major Rating Factors: Good overall results on stability tests (6.2 on a scale of 0 to 10). Strengths that enhance stability include excellent operational trends and excellent risk diversification. Good quality investment portfolio (6.8) despite mixed results such as: no exposure to mortgages and substantial holdings of BBB bonds but small junk bond holdings. Strong capitalization (10.0) based on excellent risk adjusted capital (severe loss scenario).
Other Rating Factors: Excellent profitability (7.6) with operating gains in each of the last five years. Excellent liquidity (7.0).
Principal Business: Group health insurance (58%) and group life insurance (42%).
Principal Investments: NonCMO investment grade bonds (66%), CMOs and structured securities (24%), and noninv. grade bonds (5%).
Investments in Affiliates: None
Group Affiliation: Tokio Marine Holdings Inc
Licensed in: DC, DE, NY
Commenced Business: October 1984
Address: 590 Madison Ave 29th Floor, New York, NY 10022
Phone: (215) 787-4000 **Domicile State:** NY **NAIC Code:** 71005

Data Date	Rating	RACR #1	RACR #2	Total Assets ($mil)	Capital ($mil)	Net Premium ($mil)	Net Income ($mil)
6-14	A	6.02	3.89	188.3	67.7	27.1	3.1
6-13	A	6.03	4.00	191.2	63.6	28.8	0.1
2013	A	5.71	3.72	182.7	64.2	56.8	5.9
2012	A	6.69	4.70	176.2	63.6	53.5	6.7
2011	B	6.47	4.93	166.3	60.5	48.3	4.1
2010	B	6.51	4.94	160.5	60.6	52.1	4.3
2009	B	4.54	3.33	147.7	56.8	58.1	6.1

Adverse Trends in Operations

Decrease in premium volume from 2010 to 2011 (7%)
Decrease in premium volume from 2009 to 2010 (10%)
Increase in policy surrenders from 2009 to 2010 (568%)

FIRST UNITED AMERICAN LIFE INSURANCE COMPANY *   B+   Good

Major Rating Factors: Good overall results on stability tests (6.7 on a scale of 0 to 10). Stability strengths include excellent operational trends and excellent risk diversification. Good quality investment portfolio (5.0) despite mixed results such as: large holdings of BBB rated bonds but moderate junk bond exposure. Good overall profitability (6.8). Excellent expense controls.

Other Rating Factors: Good liquidity (5.2). Strong capitalization (7.7) based on excellent risk adjusted capital (severe loss scenario).

Principal Business: Individual health insurance (58%), individual life insurance (30%), individual annuities (9%), and group health insurance (3%).

Principal Investments: NonCMO investment grade bonds (79%), CMOs and structured securities (6%), noninv. grade bonds (6%), policy loans (4%), and cash (3%).

Investments in Affiliates: None
Group Affiliation: Torchmark Corp
Licensed in: NY
Commenced Business: December 1984
Address: 1020 7th North St, Liverpool, NY 13088
Phone: (315) 451-2544 **Domicile State:** NY **NAIC Code:** 74101

Data Date	Rating	RACR #1	RACR #2	Total Assets ($mil)	Capital ($mil)	Net Premium ($mil)	Net Income ($mil)
6-14	B+	2.25	1.46	187.3	35.6	39.2	4.7
6-13	B+	2.53	1.66	174.5	36.4	41.6	5.2
2013	B+	2.18	1.42	178.0	34.2	78.7	3.1
2012	B+	2.31	1.49	165.4	34.3	88.7	9.9
2011	B+	2.46	1.60	140.4	33.5	66.2	4.4
2010	A-	2.78	1.85	132.7	38.0	65.5	9.3
2009	A-	3.02	2.03	126.8	38.4	64.5	4.9

Adverse Trends in Operations

Decrease in premium volume from 2012 to 2013 (11%)
Change in premium mix from 2011 to 2012 (5%)
Decrease in capital during 2011 (12%)

FIRST UNUM LIFE INSURANCE COMPANY   C+   Fair

Major Rating Factors: Fair overall results on stability tests (4.8 on a scale of 0 to 10) including fair financial strength of affiliated Unum Group. Fair quality investment portfolio (4.5) with large holdings of BBB rated bonds in addition to junk bond exposure equal to 87% of capital. Strong capitalization (7.5) based on excellent risk adjusted capital (severe loss scenario).

Other Rating Factors: Excellent profitability (7.5) despite operating losses during the first six months of 2014. Excellent liquidity (7.3).

Principal Business: Group health insurance (54%), individual health insurance (26%), group life insurance (18%), and individual life insurance (2%).

Principal Investments: NonCMO investment grade bonds (75%), CMOs and structured securities (9%), noninv. grade bonds (9%), and mortgages in good standing (6%).

Investments in Affiliates: None
Group Affiliation: Unum Group
Licensed in: NY
Commenced Business: January 1960
Address: Christiana Bldg Suite 100, Tarrytown, NY 10591
Phone: (914) 524-4056 **Domicile State:** NY **NAIC Code:** 64297

Data Date	Rating	RACR #1	RACR #2	Total Assets ($mil)	Capital ($mil)	Net Premium ($mil)	Net Income ($mil)
6-14	C+	2.67	1.36	2,768.6	265.2	179.3	-0.4
6-13	C+	2.48	1.29	2,638.8	239.9	175.5	17.9
2013	C+	2.75	1.42	2,704.1	266.3	348.7	20.4
2012	C+	2.65	1.41	2,682.6	251.8	360.2	11.3
2011	C+	3.16	1.82	2,398.7	269.3	381.1	30.7
2010	C+	2.69	1.63	2,123.3	239.4	392.8	27.2
2009	C+	2.41	1.45	2,012.2	218.3	401.7	7.5

Unum Group
Composite Group Rating: C+
Largest Group Members

	Assets ($mil)	Rating
UNUM LIFE INS CO OF AMERICA	19079	C+
PROVIDENT LIFE ACCIDENT INS CO	8348	C+
PAUL REVERE LIFE INS CO	4302	C+
COLONIAL LIFE ACCIDENT INS CO	2753	C+
FIRST UNUM LIFE INS CO	2704	C+

FIRSTCAROLINACARE INS CO INC   B   Good

Major Rating Factors: Good liquidity (6.6 on a scale of 0 to 10) with sufficient resources (cash flows and marketable investments) to handle a spike in claims. Strong capitalization (7.0) based on excellent current risk-adjusted capital (severe loss scenario). High quality investment portfolio (9.2).

Other Rating Factors: Weak profitability index (0.9).

Principal Business: Comp med (84%), Medicare (16%)

Mem Phys: 13: 2,800 **12:** 2,795 **13 MLR** 87.6% **/ 13 Admin Exp** N/A

Enroll(000): Q2 14: 14 **13:** 13 **12:** 11 **Med Exp PMPM:** $371

Principal Investments: Long-term bonds (46%), cash and equiv (35%), nonaffiliate common stock (19%)

Provider Compensation ($000): Contr fee ($52,925), FFS ($3,258)

Total Member Encounters: Phys (116,029), non-phys (16,466)

Group Affiliation: FirstHealth of the Carolinas
Licensed in: NC, SC
Address: 42 Memorial Dr, Pinehurst, NC 28374
Phone: (910) 715-8100 **Dom State:** NC **Commenced Bus:** April 2007

Data Date	Rating	RACR #1	RACR #2	Total Assets ($mil)	Capital ($mil)	Net Premium ($mil)	Net Income ($mil)
6-14	B	1.38	1.15	21.2	11.4	38.0	-3.0
6-13	B	1.98	1.65	21.2	12.5	31.7	-0.7
2013	B	1.74	1.45	24.0	14.4	65.2	-4.0
2012	B+	2.15	1.79	21.1	13.6	49.4	-0.1
2011	B+	2.32	1.93	20.3	13.3	43.1	0.5
2010	B+	2.63	2.19	18.6	12.8	34.3	0.3
2009	B+	2.80	2.34	16.2	12.3	28.6	-0.6

Rating Indexes

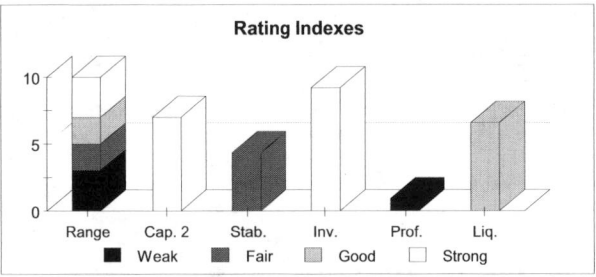

FLORIDA HEALTH CARE PLAN INC *   A-   Excellent

Major Rating Factors: Excellent profitability (9.1 on a scale of 0 to 10). Strong capitalization (10.0) based on excellent current risk-adjusted capital (severe loss scenario). High quality investment portfolio (8.3).

Other Rating Factors: Excellent liquidity (6.9) with sufficient resources (cash flows and marketable investments) to handle a spike in claims.

Principal Business: Comp med (53%), Medicare (47%)

Mem Phys: 13: 657   **12:** 596   **13 MLR** 84.9%   **/ 13 Admin Exp** N/A

Enroll(000): Q2 14: 54   **13:** 49   **12:** 48   **Med Exp PMPM:** $454

Principal Investments: Long-term bonds (63%), cash and equiv (30%), real estate (7%)

Provider Compensation ($000): Contr fee ($157,766), salary ($38,509), FFS ($20,407), capitation ($14,427), other ($32,821)

Total Member Encounters: Phys (181,845), non-phys (40,889)

Group Affiliation: Blue Cross Blue Shield Of Florida

Licensed in: FL

Address: 1340 Ridgewood Ave, Holly Hill, FL 32117-2320

Phone: (386) 676-7100   **Dom State:** FL   **Commenced Bus:** January 2009

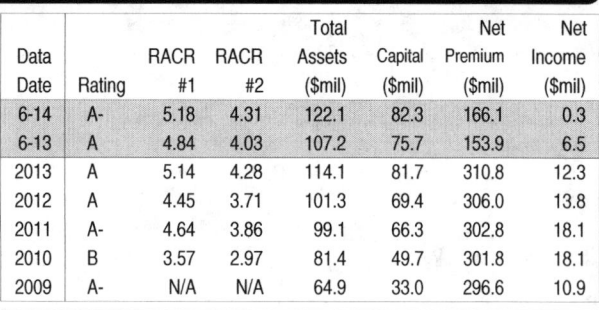

Data Date	Rating	RACR #1	RACR #2	Total Assets ($mil)	Capital ($mil)	Net Premium ($mil)	Net Income ($mil)
6-14	A-	5.18	4.31	122.1	82.3	166.1	0.3
6-13	A	4.84	4.03	107.2	75.7	153.9	6.5
2013	A	5.14	4.28	114.1	81.7	310.8	12.3
2012	A	4.45	3.71	101.3	69.4	306.0	13.8
2011	A-	4.64	3.86	99.1	66.3	302.8	18.1
2010	B	3.57	2.97	81.4	49.7	301.8	18.1
2009	A-	N/A	N/A	64.9	33.0	296.6	10.9

Rating Indexes

Range   Cap. 2   Stab.   Inv.   Prof.   Liq.

■ Weak   ▨ Fair   ▧ Good   ☐ Strong

FLORIDA TRUE HEALTH INC   E   Very Weak

Major Rating Factors: Weak profitability index (0.0 on a scale of 0 to 10). Good liquidity (5.8) with sufficient resources (cash flows and marketable investments) to handle a spike in claims. Strong capitalization (10.0) based on excellent current risk-adjusted capital (severe loss scenario).

Other Rating Factors: High quality investment portfolio (9.9).

Principal Business: Medicaid (100%)

Mem Phys: 13: 7,145   **12:** N/A   **13 MLR** 85.0%   **/ 13 Admin Exp** N/A

Enroll(000): Q2 14: 5   **13:** 7   **12:** N/A   **Med Exp PMPM:** $200

Principal Investments: Cash and equiv (97%), other (3%)

Provider Compensation ($000): Contr fee ($5,544), capitation ($19)

Total Member Encounters: Phys (18,398), non-phys (7,158)

Group Affiliation: Independence Blue Cross Inc

Licensed in: FL

Address: 11601 Kew Gardens Ave Ste 200, Palm Beach Gardens, FL 33410

Phone: (215) 937-8000   **Dom State:** FL   **Commenced Bus:** July 2012

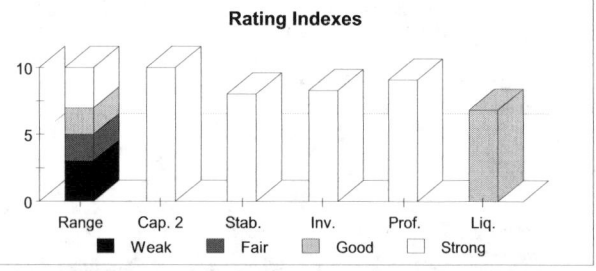

Data Date	Rating	RACR #1	RACR #2	Total Assets ($mil)	Capital ($mil)	Net Premium ($mil)	Net Income ($mil)
6-14	E	6.75	5.62	21.8	11.2	9.0	-8.3
6-13	N/A	N/A	N/A	9.6	7.3	2.4	-6.1
2013	E	2.01	1.67	12.1	3.3	10.4	-13.8
2012	N/A	N/A	N/A	19.2	10.3	N/A	-9.5
2011	N/A	N/A	N/A	N/A	N/A	N/A	N/A
2010	N/A	N/A	N/A	N/A	N/A	N/A	N/A
2009	N/A	N/A	N/A	N/A	N/A	N/A	N/A

Rating Indexes

Range   Cap. 2   Stab.   Inv.   Prof.   Liq.

■ Weak   ▨ Fair   ▧ Good   ☐ Strong

FREELANCERS INS CO   B   Good

Major Rating Factors: Good overall profitability index (6.1 on a scale of 0 to 10). Good liquidity (6.7) with sufficient resources (cash flows and marketable investments) to handle a spike in claims. Strong capitalization (8.1) based on excellent current risk-adjusted capital (severe loss scenario).

Other Rating Factors: High quality investment portfolio (9.9).

Principal Business: Comp med (100%)

Mem Phys: 13: 75,000   **12:** 73,271   **13 MLR** 77.9%   **/ 13 Admin Exp** N/A

Enroll(000): Q2 14: 23   **13:** 27   **12:** 24   **Med Exp PMPM:** $284

Principal Investments: Long-term bonds (84%), nonaffiliate common stock (9%), cash and equiv (8%)

Provider Compensation ($000): Contr fee ($76,339), capitation ($2,293), other ($6,381)

Total Member Encounters: Phys (179,443), non-phys (67,284)

Group Affiliation: Freelancers Union Inc

Licensed in: NY

Address: N/A

Phone: (718) 532-1515   **Dom State:** NY   **Commenced Bus:** January 2009

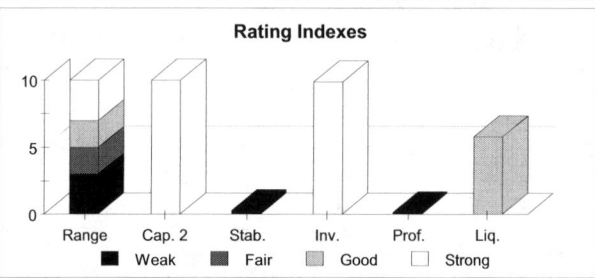

Data Date	Rating	RACR #1	RACR #2	Total Assets ($mil)	Capital ($mil)	Net Premium ($mil)	Net Income ($mil)
6-14	B	2.22	1.85	53.8	24.5	53.7	-2.4
6-13	C+	2.84	2.37	59.5	26.7	55.5	3.6
2013	B-	2.70	2.25	58.4	29.5	112.2	7.2
2012	C	2.43	2.03	54.3	23.0	105.9	6.5
2011	D+	1.70	1.42	40.7	17.4	96.1	6.1
2010	D	0.84	0.70	31.6	10.8	83.1	2.0
2009	E	0.91	0.76	28.9	9.5	67.4	-5.0

Rating Indexes

Range   Cap. 2   Stab.   Inv.   Prof.   Liq.

■ Weak   ▨ Fair   ▧ Good   ☐ Strong

FRESNO-KINGS-MADERA REGIONAL HEALTH
E   Very Weak

Major Rating Factors: Poor capitalization index (0.0 on a scale of 0 to 10) based on weak current risk-adjusted capital (severe loss scenario). Good overall results on stability tests (6.3) based on healthy premium and capital growth during 2013. Excellent profitability (8.9).
Other Rating Factors: Excellent liquidity (6.9) with sufficient resources (cash flows and marketable investments) to handle a spike in claims.
Principal Business: Medicaid (100%)
Mem Phys: 13: N/A **12:** N/A **13 MLR** 89.8% **/ 13 Admin Exp** N/A
Enroll(000): Q2 14: 213 **13:** 210 **12:** 186 **Med Exp PMPM:** N/A
Principal Investments ($000): Cash and equiv ($21,581)
Provider Compensation ($000): None
Total Member Encounters: N/A
Group Affiliation: None
Licensed in: CA
Address: 1315 Van Ness Ave Suite 103, Fresno, CA 93721
Phone: (888) 893-1569 **Dom State:** CA **Commenced Bus:** March 2011

Data Date	Rating	RACR #1	RACR #2	Total Assets ($mil)	Capital ($mil)	Net Premium ($mil)	Net Income ($mil)
6-14	E	0.37	0.23	70.6	11.3	232.9	1.3
6-13	E	0.31	0.19	55.3	7.9	196.5	2.6
2013	E	0.33	0.20	70.4	9.9	454.5	4.6
2012	E	0.20	0.12	48.0	5.3	361.0	4.9
2011	N/A	N/A	N/A	44.9	0.4	97.1	0.5
2010	N/A	N/A	N/A	N/A	N/A	N/A	N/A
2009	N/A	N/A	N/A	N/A	N/A	N/A	N/A

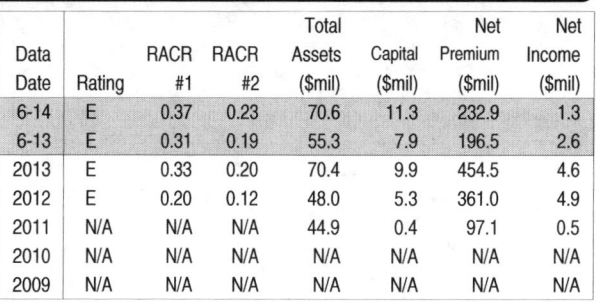

Rating Indexes

GATEWAY HEALTH PLAN INC
B   Good

Major Rating Factors: Good overall results on stability tests (6.3 on a scale of 0 to 10). Rating is significantly influenced by the good financial results of Highmark Inc. Good liquidity (6.8) with sufficient resources (cash flows and marketable investments) to handle a spike in claims. Fair profitability index (4.3).
Other Rating Factors: Strong capitalization index (8.3) based on excellent current risk-adjusted capital (severe loss scenario). High quality investment portfolio (8.8).
Principal Business: Medicaid (74%), Medicare (26%)
Mem Phys: 13: 18,127 **12:** 17,737 **13 MLR** 84.5% **/ 13 Admin Exp** N/A
Enroll(000): Q2 14: 307 **13:** 303 **12:** 306 **Med Exp PMPM:** $420
Principal Investments: Long-term bonds (43%), nonaffiliate common stock (33%), cash and equiv (24%)
Provider Compensation ($000): Contr fee ($1,420,715), capitation ($116,176)
Total Member Encounters: Phys (1,630,372), non-phys (587,285)
Group Affiliation: Highmark Inc
Licensed in: PA
Address: 600 Grant St US Steel Tower 41, Pittsburgh, PA 15219-2713
Phone: (412) 255-4640 **Dom State:** PA **Commenced Bus:** August 1986

Data Date	Rating	RACR #1	RACR #2	Total Assets ($mil)	Capital ($mil)	Net Premium ($mil)	Net Income ($mil)
6-14	B	2.37	1.97	540.6	220.8	934.0	-16.0
6-13	B	2.63	2.19	507.6	215.8	882.9	14.7
2013	B	2.52	2.10	470.7	236.7	1,809.5	20.2
2012	B	2.42	2.02	440.0	197.6	1,616.6	28.9
2011	B	2.28	1.90	386.5	171.7	1,543.2	3.7
2010	B	2.26	1.88	387.1	170.9	1,460.8	11.5
2009	B	2.16	1.80	344.0	145.9	1,354.2	-12.8

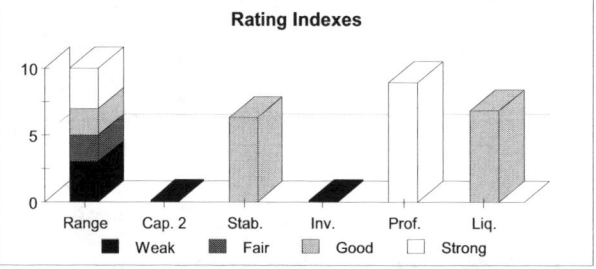

Rating Indexes

GEISINGER HEALTH PLAN
B   Good

Major Rating Factors: Good overall results on stability tests (6.3 on a scale of 0 to 10) based on healthy premium and capital growth during 2013. Good liquidity (6.9) with sufficient resources (cash flows and marketable investments) to handle a spike in claims. Excellent profitability (8.5).
Other Rating Factors: Strong capitalization index (7.2) based on excellent current risk-adjusted capital (severe loss scenario). High quality investment portfolio (7.8).
Principal Business: Medicare (40%), comp med (30%), Medicaid (29%)
Mem Phys: 13: 29,920 **12:** 27,611 **13 MLR** 85.8% **/ 13 Admin Exp** N/A
Enroll(000): Q2 14: 271 **13:** 280 **12:** 145 **Med Exp PMPM:** $417
Principal Investments: Long-term bonds (53%), nonaffiliate common stock (32%), cash and equiv (10%), real estate (5%)
Provider Compensation ($000): Contr fee ($820,945), FFS ($289,005), capitation ($75,781), bonus arrang ($23,730)
Total Member Encounters: Phys (1,791,421), non-phys (325,025)
Group Affiliation: Geisinger Health System Foundation
Licensed in: PA
Address: 100 N Academy Ave, Danville, PA 17822-3051
Phone: (570) 271-8777 **Dom State:** PA **Commenced Bus:** March 1985

Data Date	Rating	RACR #1	RACR #2	Total Assets ($mil)	Capital ($mil)	Net Premium ($mil)	Net Income ($mil)
6-14	B	1.52	1.27	406.2	174.5	788.5	10.5
6-13	B	2.13	1.77	328.9	152.2	651.4	22.0
2013	B	1.46	1.21	338.1	166.9	1,466.3	44.0
2012	B	1.75	1.46	239.3	125.6	935.6	46.5
2011	B	1.40	1.17	211.5	96.9	903.1	46.2
2010	B	1.71	1.42	219.6	113.0	851.9	36.1
2009	B	1.77	1.47	200.9	104.1	785.6	39.8

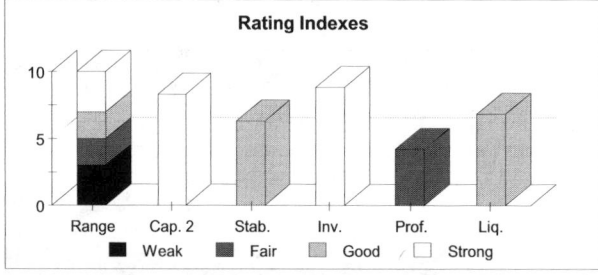

Rating Indexes

GEISINGER INDEMNITY INS CO

C　　**Fair**

Major Rating Factors: Weak profitability index (1.8 on a scale of 0 to 10). Good liquidity (6.6) with sufficient resources (cash flows and marketable investments) to handle a spike in claims. Strong capitalization (7.4) based on excellent current risk-adjusted capital (severe loss scenario).
Other Rating Factors: High quality investment portfolio (9.9).
Principal Business: Medicare (97%), med supp (2%), other (1%)
Mem Phys: 13: 36,640　**12:** 27,611　**13 MLR** 87.9%　**/ 13 Admin Exp** N/A
Enroll(000): Q2 14: 29　**13:** 23　**12:** 16　**Med Exp PMPM:** $527
Principal Investments: Long-term bonds (63%), cash and equiv (37%)
Provider Compensation ($000): Contr fee ($115,646), FFS ($11,378), capitation ($5,222), bonus arrang ($2,070)
Total Member Encounters: Phys (238,878), non-phys (55,286)
Group Affiliation: Geisinger Health System Foundation
Licensed in: PA, WV
Address: 100 N Academy Ave, Danville, PA 17822
Phone: (570) 271-8777　**Dom State:** PA　**Commenced Bus:** February 1996

Data Date	Rating	RACR #1	RACR #2	Total Assets ($mil)	Capital ($mil)	Net Premium ($mil)	Net Income ($mil)
6-14	C	1.65	1.38	62.0	24.0	99.2	3.8
6-13	C	1.23	1.03	44.0	13.2	75.2	-4.2
2013	C	1.43	1.19	53.7	20.8	158.1	-7.8
2012	C	1.64	1.37	40.7	17.8	122.0	-8.7
2011	B	1.59	1.32	29.8	13.0	92.0	1.6
2010	B	1.89	1.57	16.8	8.6	47.6	3.5
2009	B	1.65	1.38	13.0	5.4	27.1	-0.9

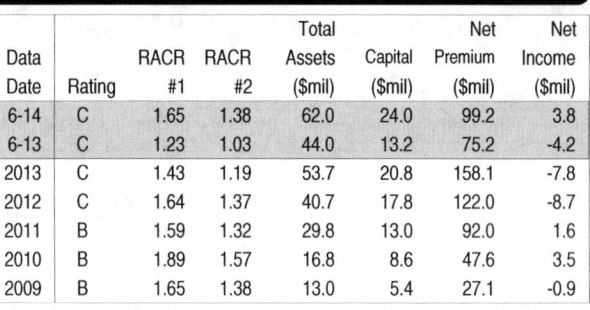

Rating Indexes

GEISINGER QUALITY OPTIONS INC

C　　**Fair**

Major Rating Factors: Fair profitability index (3.9 on a scale of 0 to 10). Good liquidity (6.3) with sufficient resources (cash flows and marketable investments) to handle a spike in claims. Strong capitalization (7.1) based on excellent current risk-adjusted capital (severe loss scenario).
Other Rating Factors: High quality investment portfolio (9.6).
Principal Business: Comp med (99%)
Mem Phys: 13: 29,973　**12:** 27,611　**13 MLR** 85.0%　**/ 13 Admin Exp** N/A
Enroll(000): Q2 14: 70　**13:** 83　**12:** 94　**Med Exp PMPM:** $276
Principal Investments: Long-term bonds (92%), cash and equiv (8%)
Provider Compensation ($000): Contr fee ($166,516), FFS ($101,855), capitation ($19,749), bonus arrang ($4,198)
Total Member Encounters: Phys (402,528), non-phys (53,747)
Group Affiliation: Geisinger Health System Foundation
Licensed in: PA
Address: 100 N Academy Ave MC 30-51, Danville, PA 17822
Phone: (570) 271-8777　**Dom State:** PA　**Commenced Bus:** March 2007

Data Date	Rating	RACR #1	RACR #2	Total Assets ($mil)	Capital ($mil)	Net Premium ($mil)	Net Income ($mil)
6-14	C	1.46	1.22	94.2	40.2	148.9	-4.8
6-13	C	1.68	1.40	95.8	47.8	174.9	5.0
2013	C	1.65	1.38	99.1	45.9	341.5	2.4
2012	C	1.52	1.27	92.4	43.5	354.8	1.7
2011	N/A	N/A	N/A	91.5	42.6	349.5	7.5
2010	N/A	N/A	N/A	78.9	35.4	284.4	5.4
2009	C	N/A	N/A	59.4	28.9	217.1	1.2

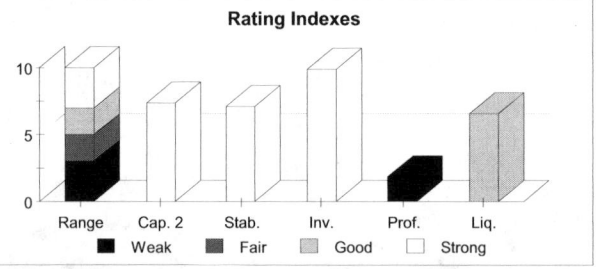

Rating Indexes

GEMCARE HEALTH PLAN INC

E　　**Very Weak**

Major Rating Factors: Poor capitalization index (0.0 on a scale of 0 to 10) based on weak current risk-adjusted capital (severe loss scenario). Weak liquidity (0.0) as a spike in claims may stretch capacity. Fair profitability index (4.2).
Other Rating Factors: Fair overall results on stability tests (4.1) based on poor risk diversification due to the company's size.
Principal Business: Medicare (61%)
Mem Phys: 13: N/A　**12:** N/A　**13 MLR** 89.7%　**/ 13 Admin Exp** N/A
Enroll(000): Q2 14: 21　**13:** 21　**12:** 20　**Med Exp PMPM:** $504
Principal Investments ($000): Cash and equiv ($13,921)
Provider Compensation ($000): None
Total Member Encounters: N/A
Group Affiliation: GEMCare Invest/Managed Care Systems
Licensed in: CA
Address: 4550 California Ave Suite 100, Bakersfield, CA 93309
Phone: (661) 716-8800　**Dom State:** CA　**Commenced Bus:** November 2005

Data Date	Rating	RACR #1	RACR #2	Total Assets ($mil)	Capital ($mil)	Net Premium ($mil)	Net Income ($mil)
6-14	E	0.08	0.05	16.7	6.3	72.6	-0.4
6-13	E	0.27	0.17	18.1	6.9	69.8	1.0
2013	E	0.10	0.06	16.1	6.6	140.0	0.7
2012	E	0.20	0.12	15.8	5.9	131.9	0.7
2011	N/A	N/A	N/A	15.2	5.3	107.5	0.9
2010	N/A	N/A	N/A	13.5	4.4	71.3	1.0
2009	E	N/A	N/A	9.6	3.4	69.3	-0.7

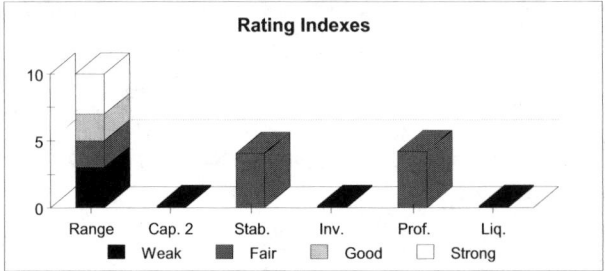

Rating Indexes

GENWORTH LIFE INSURANCE COMPANY   B-   Good

Major Rating Factors: Good overall results on stability tests (5.1 on a scale of 0 to 10) despite fair financial strength of affiliated Genworth Financial and excessive premium growth. Other stability subfactors include good operational trends and excellent risk diversification. Good capitalization (6.0) based on good risk adjusted capital (severe loss scenario). Capital levels have been relatively consistent over the last five years. Good quality investment portfolio (6.7).

Other Rating Factors: Excellent profitability (7.2) despite modest operating losses during 2009 and 2010. Excellent liquidity (7.4).

Principal Business: Individual health insurance (56%), individual annuities (15%), individual life insurance (11%), reinsurance (10%), and group health insurance (7%).

Principal Investments: NonCMO investment grade bonds (59%), CMOs and structured securities (15%), mortgages in good standing (10%), common & preferred stock (8%), and misc. investments (7%).

Investments in Affiliates: 8%

Group Affiliation: Genworth Financial

Licensed in: All states except NY

Commenced Business: October 1956

Address: 6604 West Broad St, Richmond, VA 23230

Phone: (800) 255-7836 **Domicile State:** DE **NAIC Code:** 70025

Data Date	Rating	RACR #1	RACR #2	Total Assets ($mil)	Capital ($mil)	Net Premium ($mil)	Net Income ($mil)
6-14	B-	1.10	0.87	36,940.5	3,610.0	809.3	94.5
6-13	C+	0.98	0.78	36,078.6	3,247.6	611.4	66.8
2013	C+	1.06	0.85	36,445.4	3,487.2	2,578.1	329.8
2012	C+	1.01	0.80	36,783.8	3,410.5	1,659.0	201.0
2011	C+	1.04	0.80	35,784.2	3,097.3	1,607.6	22.9
2010	C+	0.98	0.76	33,585.1	2,983.6	1,273.4	-137.4
2009	C+	0.99	0.76	32,974.6	3,164.8	1,252.2	-199.4

Genworth Financial Composite Group Rating: C+ Largest Group Members	Assets ($mil)	Rating
GENWORTH LIFE INS CO	36445	B-
GENWORTH LIFE ANNUITY INS CO	24162	B-
GENWORTH LIFE INS CO OF NEW YORK	8139	B
GENWORTH MORTGAGE INS CORP	2373	C-
RIVER LAKE INS CO	1338	C-

GENWORTH LIFE INSURANCE COMPANY OF NEW YORK   B   Good

Major Rating Factors: Good overall results on stability tests (5.6 on a scale of 0 to 10) despite fair financial strength of affiliated Genworth Financial and excessive premium growth. Other stability subfactors include excellent operational trends, good risk adjusted capital for prior years and excellent risk diversification. Good quality investment portfolio (5.2) despite large holdings of BBB rated bonds in addition to junk bond exposure equal to 55% of capital. Exposure to mortgages is significant, but the mortgage default rate has been low. Good overall profitability (6.4).

Other Rating Factors: Good liquidity (6.6). Strong capitalization (7.3) based on excellent risk adjusted capital (severe loss scenario).

Principal Business: Individual annuities (52%), individual health insurance (25%), individual life insurance (12%), reinsurance (9%), and group health insurance (2%).

Principal Investments: NonCMO investment grade bonds (57%), CMOs and structured securities (24%), mortgages in good standing (12%), noninv. grade bonds (5%), and common & preferred stock (1%).

Investments in Affiliates: None

Group Affiliation: Genworth Financial

Licensed in: CT, DC, DE, FL, IL, NJ, NY, RI, VA

Commenced Business: October 1988

Address: 125 Park Ave 6th Floor, New York, NY 10017-5529

Phone: (800) 357-1066 **Domicile State:** NY **NAIC Code:** 72990

Data Date	Rating	RACR #1	RACR #2	Total Assets ($mil)	Capital ($mil)	Net Premium ($mil)	Net Income ($mil)
6-14	B	2.39	1.20	8,216.0	550.7	282.6	33.3
6-13	B	2.48	1.24	7,803.0	546.9	152.7	37.5
2013	B	2.29	1.15	8,139.0	527.3	610.9	13.1
2012	B	2.36	1.18	7,815.8	540.1	542.6	19.1
2011	B-	2.45	1.23	7,691.7	559.5	576.6	6.5
2010	B-	2.39	1.18	7,432.0	549.1	329.8	130.0
2009	C	1.85	0.92	7,218.4	429.5	340.0	40.9

Genworth Financial Composite Group Rating: C+ Largest Group Members	Assets ($mil)	Rating
GENWORTH LIFE INS CO	36445	B-
GENWORTH LIFE ANNUITY INS CO	24162	B-
GENWORTH LIFE INS CO OF NEW YORK	8139	B
GENWORTH MORTGAGE INS CORP	2373	C-
RIVER LAKE INS CO	1338	C-

GERBER LIFE INSURANCE COMPANY *   A-   Excellent

Major Rating Factors: Good quality investment portfolio (6.4 on a scale of 0 to 10) despite mixed results such as: no exposure to mortgages and large holdings of BBB rated bonds but small junk bond holdings. Good liquidity (5.5) with sufficient resources to handle a spike in claims as well as a significant increase in policy surrenders. Strong capitalization (7.3) based on excellent risk adjusted capital (severe loss scenario).

Other Rating Factors: Excellent profitability (7.7) with operating gains in each of the last five years. Excellent overall results on stability tests (7.2) excellent operational trends and excellent risk diversification.

Principal Business: Individual life insurance (40%), group health insurance (35%), individual health insurance (18%), and reinsurance (7%).

Principal Investments: NonCMO investment grade bonds (73%), CMOs and structured securities (17%), policy loans (5%), common & preferred stock (3%), and noninv. grade bonds (3%).

Investments in Affiliates: None

Group Affiliation: Nestle SA

Licensed in: All states, the District of Columbia and Puerto Rico

Commenced Business: September 1968

Address: 1311 Mamaroneck Ave, White Plains, NY 10605

Phone: (877) 778-0839 **Domicile State:** NY **NAIC Code:** 70939

Data Date	Rating	RACR #1	RACR #2	Total Assets ($mil)	Capital ($mil)	Net Premium ($mil)	Net Income ($mil)
6-14	A-	1.97	1.19	2,680.4	269.0	288.6	6.3
6-13	A-	1.98	1.19	2,429.6	245.3	265.1	10.2
2013	A-	2.00	1.21	2,548.1	263.5	506.8	22.7
2012	A-	1.96	1.17	2,306.7	237.9	464.1	20.2
2011	A-	1.91	1.15	2,110.0	215.5	432.2	4.9
2010	A-	2.01	1.21	1,901.1	213.0	393.7	14.9
2009	A-	2.07	1.29	1,712.6	194.3	379.0	17.6

Rating Indexes

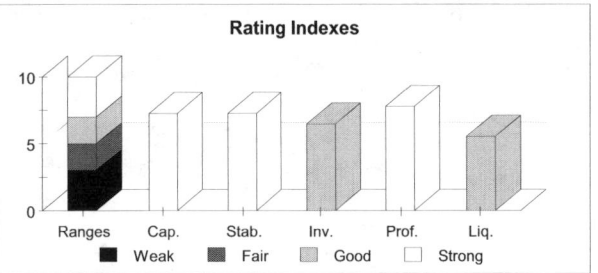

GHS MANAGED HEALTH CARE PLANS INC   B-   Good

Major Rating Factors: Strong capitalization (7.6 on a scale of 0 to 10) based on excellent current risk-adjusted capital (severe loss scenario). High quality investment portfolio (9.9). Excellent liquidity (7.0) with ample operational cash flow and liquid investments.
Other Rating Factors: Weak profitability index (0.9).
Principal Business: Medicare (100%)
Mem Phys: 13: 1,821 **12:** 898 **13 MLR** 106.2% / **13 Admin Exp** N/A
Enroll(000): Q2 14: 3 **13:** 2 **12:** 0 **Med Exp PMPM:** $767
Principal Investments: Cash and equiv (100%)
Provider Compensation ($000): Contr fee ($11,517), FFS ($1,440)
Total Member Encounters: Phys (29,347), non-phys (3,145)
Group Affiliation: Ardent Health Services LLC
Licensed in: OK
Address: 1400 S Boston Ave, Tulsa, OK 74119
Phone: (312) 653-6716 **Dom State:** OK **Commenced Bus:** February 2011

Data Date	Rating	RACR #1	RACR #2	Total Assets ($mil)	Capital ($mil)	Net Premium ($mil)	Net Income ($mil)
6-14	B-	1.82	1.52	14.7	2.8	12.4	0.2
6-13	D	2.16	1.80	6.6	1.9	6.3	-1.3
2013	D	1.22	1.02	8.6	2.6	12.9	-7.9
2012	C+	2.54	2.12	3.5	2.2	3.2	-1.6
2011	N/A	N/A	N/A	1.7	1.5	N/A	-0.2
2010	N/A	N/A	N/A	N/A	N/A	N/A	N/A
2009	N/A	N/A	N/A	N/A	N/A	N/A	N/A

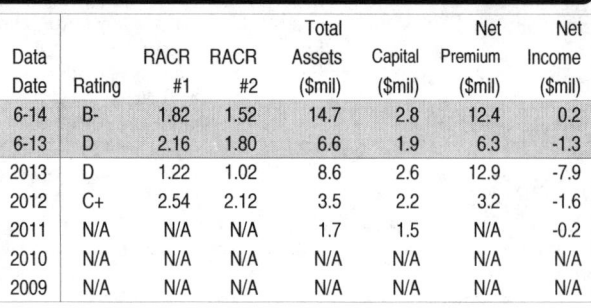

GLOBALHEALTH INC   C+   Fair

Major Rating Factors: Good capitalization (5.2 on a scale of 0 to 10) based on good current risk-adjusted capital (severe loss scenario). Weak profitability index (2.0). High quality investment portfolio (9.9).
Other Rating Factors: Excellent liquidity (7.0) with sufficient resources (cash flows and marketable investments) to handle a spike in claims.
Principal Business: Comp med (96%), FEHB (4%)
Mem Phys: 13: 2,717 **12:** 2,506 **13 MLR** 86.6% / **13 Admin Exp** N/A
Enroll(000): Q2 14: 42 **13:** 39 **12:** 33 **Med Exp PMPM:** $292
Principal Investments: Cash and equiv (58%), long-term bonds (42%)
Provider Compensation ($000): Capitation ($133,941), contr fee ($665), FFS ($629)
Total Member Encounters: N/A
Group Affiliation: Oklahoma City Clinic
Licensed in: OK
Address: 4888 Loop Central Dr Suite 700, Houston, TX 77081
Phone: (405) 280-5656 **Dom State:** OK **Commenced Bus:** July 2009

Data Date	Rating	RACR #1	RACR #2	Total Assets ($mil)	Capital ($mil)	Net Premium ($mil)	Net Income ($mil)
6-14	C+	0.96	0.80	20.4	9.0	90.4	-1.5
6-13	B-	1.28	1.07	15.2	9.6	77.7	0.3
2013	B	1.16	0.97	14.6	10.7	156.0	0.8
2012	C-	0.97	0.81	12.4	7.5	121.8	0.9
2011	N/A	N/A	N/A	10.2	7.9	32.7	-0.1
2010	N/A	N/A	N/A	1.6	1.6	-0.1	N/A
2009	C+	N/A	N/A	1.6	1.6	N/A	N/A

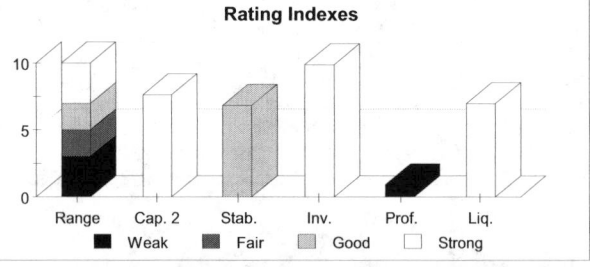

GOLDEN RULE INSURANCE COMPANY   B   Good

Major Rating Factors: Good overall results on stability tests (5.4 on a scale of 0 to 10) despite fair financial strength of affiliated UnitedHealth Group Inc. Other stability subfactors include excellent operational trends and excellent risk diversification. Good overall capitalization (5.0) based on mixed results -- excessive policy leverage mitigated by good risk adjusted capital (severe loss scenario). Capital levels have been relatively consistent over the last five years. Good liquidity (6.2).
Other Rating Factors: High quality investment portfolio (8.1). Excellent profitability (8.7) with operating gains in each of the last five years.
Principal Business: Group health insurance (82%), individual health insurance (15%), and individual life insurance (2%).
Principal Investments: NonCMO investment grade bonds (79%), CMOs and structured securities (18%), real estate (1%), and , and misc. investments (2%).
Investments in Affiliates: None
Group Affiliation: UnitedHealth Group Inc
Licensed in: All states except NY, PR
Commenced Business: June 1961
Address: 712 Eleventh St, Lawrenceville, IL 62439-2395
Phone: (317) 290-8100 **Domicile State:** IN **NAIC Code:** 62286

Data Date	Rating	RACR #1	RACR #2	Total Assets ($mil)	Capital ($mil)	Net Premium ($mil)	Net Income ($mil)
6-14	B	1.24	0.98	772.3	297.5	955.0	43.1
6-13	B	1.47	1.16	826.0	333.8	980.2	100.7
2013	B	1.12	0.89	759.8	293.5	2,020.6	129.4
2012	B	1.19	0.94	782.5	292.3	1,879.5	127.6
2011	B	1.43	1.13	814.9	312.1	1,673.4	104.6
2010	B	1.49	1.18	694.0	304.8	1,566.3	202.0
2009	B	1.03	0.81	524.4	175.8	1,324.3	156.3

UnitedHealth Group Inc Composite Group Rating: C+ Largest Group Members	Assets ($mil)	Rating
UNITED HEALTHCARE INS CO	14513	C
OXFORD HEALTH INS INC	2078	C+
UNITED HEALTHCARE INS CO OF NY	1983	B-
OXFORD HEALTH PLANS (NY) INC	1820	A+
UNITEDHEALTHCARE PLAN RIVER VALLEY	1094	B+

GOLDEN SECURITY LIFE INS CO   B   Good

Major Rating Factors: Good liquidity (6.8 on a scale of 0 to 10) with sufficient resources (cash flows and marketable investments) to handle a spike in claims. Excellent profitability (9.1). Strong capitalization (7.8) based on excellent current risk-adjusted capital (severe loss scenario).
Other Rating Factors: High quality investment portfolio (9.3).
Principal Business: Other (100%)
Mem Phys: 13: N/A **12:** N/A **13 MLR** 94.9% **/ 13 Admin Exp** N/A
Enroll(000): Q2 14: 192 **13:** 161 **12:** 166 **Med Exp PMPM:** $12
Principal Investments: Long-term bonds (61%), cash and equiv (39%)
Provider Compensation ($000): Other ($21,308)
Total Member Encounters: N/A
Group Affiliation: BlueCross BlueShield of Tennessee
Licensed in: AL, AR, MS, TN, TX
Address: 254 Court Avenue, Memphis, TN 38103
Phone: (423) 535-5600 **Dom State:** TN **Commenced Bus:** January 1984

Data Date	Rating	RACR #1	RACR #2	Total Assets ($mil)	Capital ($mil)	Net Premium ($mil)	Net Income ($mil)
6-14	B	1.99	1.66	22.1	9.1	16.9	1.3
6-13	N/A	N/A	N/A	18.6	5.8	11.5	0.6
2013	B	1.75	1.46	18.6	7.9	24.0	2.7
2012	N/A	N/A	N/A	15.3	5.2	16.4	1.8
2011	N/A	N/A	N/A	3.4	3.4	N/A	N/A
2010	N/A	N/A	N/A	3.3	3.3	N/A	N/A
2009	N/A	N/A	N/A	3.2	3.2	N/A	N/A

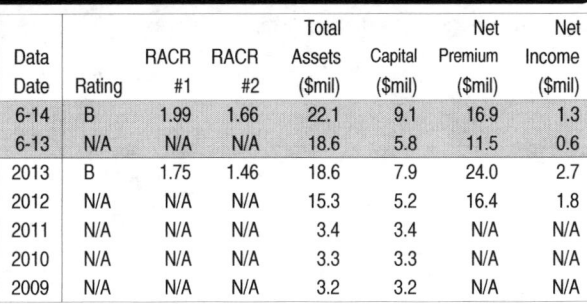

Rating Indexes

GOLDEN STATE MEDICARE HEALTH PLAN   C-   Fair

Major Rating Factors: Fair overall results on stability tests (3.0 on a scale of 0 to 10) based on an excessive 324% enrollment growth during the period. Weak profitability index (2.5). Strong capitalization index (10.0) based on excellent current risk-adjusted capital (severe loss scenario).
Other Rating Factors: Excellent liquidity (8.9) with ample operational cash flow and liquid investments.
Principal Business: Medicare (100%)
Mem Phys: 13: N/A **12:** N/A **13 MLR** 93.7% **/ 13 Admin Exp** N/A
Enroll(000): Q2 14: 2 **13:** 3 **12:** 1 **Med Exp PMPM:** $804
Principal Investments ($000): Cash and equiv ($5,023)
Provider Compensation ($000): None
Total Member Encounters: N/A
Group Affiliation: None
Licensed in: (No states)
Address: 3010 Old Ranch Pkwy Suite 260, Seal Beach, CA 90740
Phone: (877) 541-4111 **Dom State:** CA **Commenced Bus:** May 2009

Data Date	Rating	RACR #1	RACR #2	Total Assets ($mil)	Capital ($mil)	Net Premium ($mil)	Net Income ($mil)
6-14	C-	12.66	8.08	14.2	12.2	10.0	-0.5
6-13	C-	0.97	0.61	1.4	1.2	4.2	-0.2
2013	C-	4.99	3.19	5.8	5.3	8.7	-0.8
2012	C-	1.12	0.70	1.5	1.3	10.7	0.7
2011	C-	1.78	1.13	1.6	1.4	6.6	0.1
2010	N/A	N/A	N/A	1.4	1.3	2.7	-0.3
2009	C-	N/A	N/A	1.3	1.3	N/A	-0.2

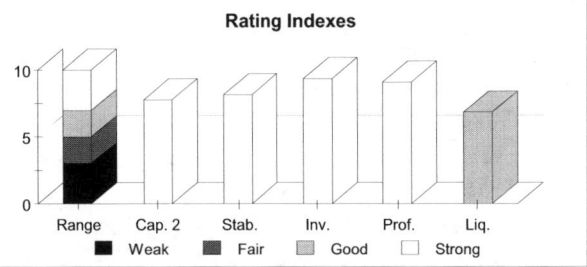

Rating Indexes

GOOD HEALTH HMO INC   C   Fair

Major Rating Factors: Fair overall results on stability tests (4.2 on a scale of 0 to 10) based on a significant 38% decrease in enrollment during the period. Weak profitability index (1.6). Good liquidity (6.6) with sufficient resources (cash flows and marketable investments) to handle a spike in claims
Other Rating Factors: Strong capitalization index (10.0) based on excellent current risk-adjusted capital (severe loss scenario). High quality investment portfolio (9.1).
Principal Business: Comp med (100%)
Mem Phys: 13: 4,986 **12:** 4,747 **13 MLR** 91.6% **/ 13 Admin Exp** N/A
Enroll(000): Q2 14: 31 **13:** 46 **12:** 74 **Med Exp PMPM:** $359
Principal Investments: Long-term bonds (97%), cash and equiv (3%)
Provider Compensation ($000): Contr fee ($219,277), FFS ($21,686), capitation ($806)
Total Member Encounters: Phys (271,500), non-phys (122,565)
Group Affiliation: RightCHOICE Managed Care Inc
Licensed in: KS, MO
Address: 2301 Main St, Kansas City, MO 64108-2428
Phone: (816) 395-2222 **Dom State:** MO **Commenced Bus:** January 1989

Data Date	Rating	RACR #1	RACR #2	Total Assets ($mil)	Capital ($mil)	Net Premium ($mil)	Net Income ($mil)
6-14	C	3.82	3.18	88.3	64.4	79.7	-3.1
6-13	A	N/A	N/A	103.3	68.4	136.6	-5.9
2013	B	3.76	3.14	89.1	63.4	252.0	-6.5
2012	A	N/A	N/A	118.8	74.5	389.4	-5.1
2011	A+	2.92	2.43	119.7	79.6	401.9	0.6
2010	A+	2.46	2.05	113.8	70.9	422.3	7.5
2009	A	2.44	2.04	113.8	71.0	434.1	15.6

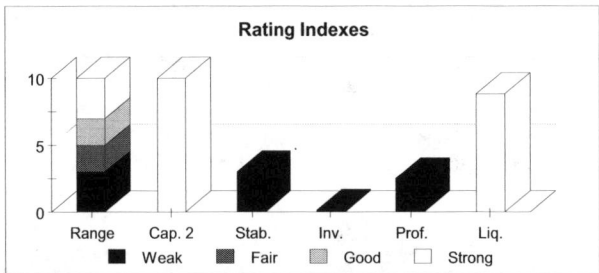

Rating Indexes

GOVERNMENT PERSONNEL MUTUAL LIFE INSURANCE CO * B+ Good

Major Rating Factors: Good liquidity (5.2 on a scale of 0 to 10) with sufficient resources to cover a large increase in policy surrenders. Good overall results on stability tests (6.4). Stability strengths include excellent operational trends and excellent risk diversification. Strong capitalization (8.0) based on excellent risk adjusted capital (severe loss scenario).

Other Rating Factors: High quality investment portfolio (7.0). Excellent profitability (7.4) with operating gains in each of the last five years.

Principal Business: Individual life insurance (63%), individual health insurance (37%), group life insurance (1%), individual annuities (1%), and reinsurance (1%).

Principal Investments: NonCMO investment grade bonds (68%), mortgages in good standing (15%), policy loans (9%), common & preferred stock (3%), and misc. investments (5%).

Investments in Affiliates: 2%

Group Affiliation: GPM Life Group

Licensed in: All states except NJ, NY, PR

Commenced Business: October 1934

Address: 2211 NW Loop 410, San Antonio, TX 78217

Phone: (800) 938-9765 **Domicile State:** TX **NAIC Code:** 63967

Data Date	Rating	RACR #1	RACR #2	Total Assets ($mil)	Capital ($mil)	Net Premium ($mil)	Net Income ($mil)
6-14	B+	2.65	1.69	833.6	108.4	23.5	0.9
6-13	B+	2.66	1.71	833.6	105.4	24.3	1.5
2013	B+	2.69	1.72	830.9	109.2	46.9	4.1
2012	B+	2.64	1.69	833.7	104.8	51.1	4.9
2011	B+	3.51	1.92	834.1	97.0	54.6	6.8
2010	B+	2.98	1.71	821.2	92.0	56.5	7.2
2009	B+	2.54	1.47	801.9	87.8	55.0	0.6

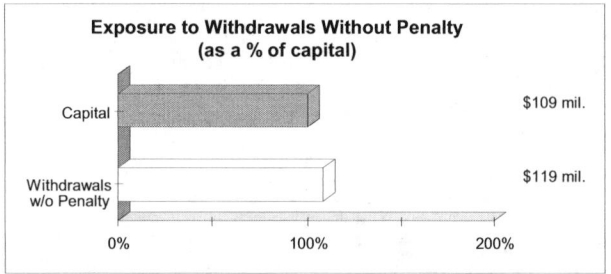

Exposure to Withdrawals Without Penalty (as a % of capital)

Capital — $109 mil.
Withdrawals w/o Penalty — $119 mil.

GRAND VALLEY HEALTH PLAN INC D+ Weak

Major Rating Factors: Weak profitability index (1.0 on a scale of 0 to 10). Fair capitalization index (4.6) based on fair current risk-adjusted capital (moderate loss scenario). Fair overall results on stability tests (3.5) based on a significant 24% decrease in enrollment during the period, an inordinate decline in premium revenue in 2013 and a steep decline in capital during 2013.

Other Rating Factors: Good liquidity (6.9) with sufficient resources (cash flows and marketable investments) to handle a spike in claims. High quality investment portfolio (9.9).

Principal Business: Comp med (76%), FEHB (24%)

Mem Phys: 13: 3,971 **12:** 3,490 **13 MLR** 91.6% **/ 13 Admin Exp** N/A

Enroll(000): Q2 14: 6 **13:** 5 **12:** 6 **Med Exp PMPM:** $337

Principal Investments: Cash and equiv (81%), real estate (19%)

Provider Compensation ($000): Contr fee ($10,067), salary ($9,748), FFS ($299), capitation ($188)

Total Member Encounters: Phys (18,984), non-phys (5,865)

Group Affiliation: Grand Valley Health Corp

Licensed in: MI

Address: 829 Forest Hill Ave SE, Grand Rapids, MI 49546

Phone: (616) 949-2410 **Dom State:** MI **Commenced Bus:** February 1982

Data Date	Rating	RACR #1	RACR #2	Total Assets ($mil)	Capital ($mil)	Net Premium ($mil)	Net Income ($mil)
6-14	D+	0.88	0.73	5.3	2.2	10.3	0.0
6-13	D+	0.78	0.65	5.9	2.5	11.0	-0.1
2013	D+	0.81	0.68	5.0	2.0	22.0	-0.4
2012	D	0.81	0.67	5.8	2.6	25.9	0.3
2011	D	0.79	0.66	6.6	2.6	30.6	-0.8
2010	D	1.10	0.92	6.0	3.3	29.3	0.7
2009	D	0.84	0.70	6.7	2.6	28.3	-1.2

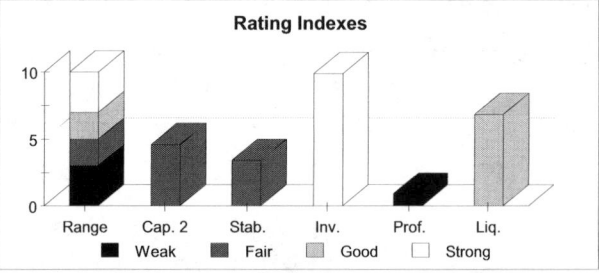

Rating Indexes

Range, Cap. 2, Stab., Inv., Prof., Liq.
■ Weak ▨ Fair ▥ Good ☐ Strong

GREAT CORNERSTONE LIFE & HEALTH INS C- Fair

Major Rating Factors: Weak profitability index (2.1 on a scale of 0 to 10). Strong capitalization (10.0) based on excellent current risk-adjusted capital (severe loss scenario). High quality investment portfolio (9.7).

Other Rating Factors: Excellent liquidity (7.0) with ample operational cash flow and liquid investments.

Principal Business: Dental (56%), other (44%)

Mem Phys: 12: N/A **11:** N/A **12 MLR** 50.3% **/ 12 Admin Exp** N/A

Enroll(000): Q2 13: 2 **12:** 4 **11:** 5 **Med Exp PMPM:** $16

Principal Investments: Long-term bonds (85%), cash and equiv (8%), nonaffiliate common stock (7%), mortgs (1%)

Provider Compensation ($000): FFS ($931)

Total Member Encounters: N/A

Group Affiliation: Great Cornerstone Corp

Licensed in: OK, TX

Address: 1601 S State St Suite 100, Edmond, OK 73013

Phone: (405) 285-0838 **Dom State:** OK **Commenced Bus:** May 2002

Data Date	Rating	RACR #1	RACR #2	Total Assets ($mil)	Capital ($mil)	Net Premium ($mil)	Net Income ($mil)
6-13	C-	6.85	5.71	2.4	2.2	0.5	-0.1
6-12	N/A	N/A	N/A	2.7	2.4	0.9	N/A
2012	C-	7.18	5.98	2.7	2.3	1.8	0.0
2011	N/A	N/A	N/A	2.6	2.3	1.9	0.1
2010	N/A	N/A	N/A	2.5	2.2	2.0	N/A
2009	N/A	N/A	N/A	2.4	2.2	2.1	N/A
2008	N/A	N/A	N/A	2.3	2.1	1.8	N/A

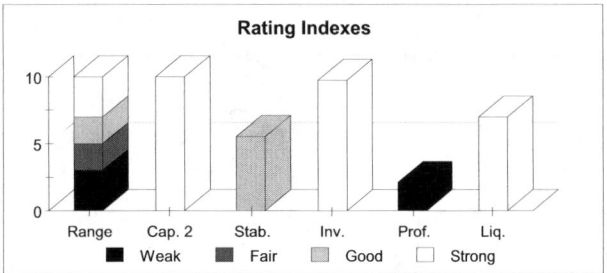

Rating Indexes

Range, Cap. 2, Stab., Inv., Prof., Liq.
■ Weak ▨ Fair ▥ Good ☐ Strong

GROUP HEALTH COOP OF EAU CLAIRE   E+   Very Weak

Major Rating Factors: Fair profitability index (3.8 on a scale of 0 to 10). Fair overall results on stability tests (4.7). Good capitalization index (6.3) based on good current risk-adjusted capital (severe loss scenario).
Other Rating Factors: Good liquidity (6.8) with sufficient resources (cash flows and marketable investments) to handle a spike in claims. High quality investment portfolio (9.9).
Principal Business: Medicaid (65%), comp med (33%)
Mem Phys: 13: 8,978   **12:** 7,521   **13 MLR** 86.1%   **/ 13 Admin Exp** N/A
Enroll(000): Q2 14: 38   **13:** 41   **12:** 46   **Med Exp PMPM:** $282
Principal Investments: Long-term bonds (62%), cash and equiv (38%)
Provider Compensation ($000): Contr fee ($68,950), FFS ($63,174), capitation ($1,167), bonus arrang ($46), other ($15,348)
Total Member Encounters: Phys (245,695), non-phys (142,919)
Group Affiliation: None
Licensed in: WI
Address: 2503 N Hillcrest Parkway, Altoona, WI 54720
Phone: (715) 552-4300   **Dom State:** WI   **Commenced Bus:** November 1976

Data Date	Rating	RACR #1	RACR #2	Total Assets ($mil)	Capital ($mil)	Net Premium ($mil)	Net Income ($mil)
6-14	E+	1.13	0.94	43.9	22.1	73.3	4.0
6-13	E+	0.60	0.50	40.4	15.1	88.9	1.4
2013	E+	0.91	0.76	42.2	18.2	170.9	4.4
2012	E+	0.54	0.45	40.6	13.9	198.3	2.2
2011	E	0.30	0.25	51.0	11.7	273.0	-8.7
2010	D+	0.57	0.47	91.8	20.4	286.5	-8.5
2009	C+	0.88	0.73	58.5	22.9	247.1	3.1

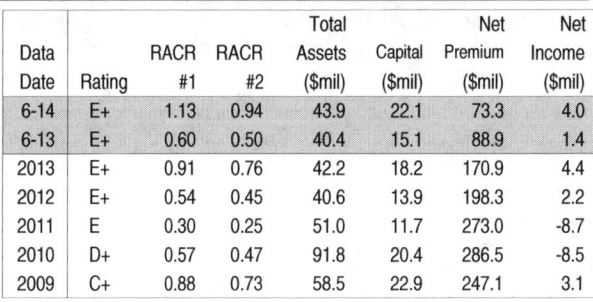

Rating Indexes

GROUP HEALTH COOP OF S CENTRAL WI   D+   Weak

Major Rating Factors: Weak profitability index (0.8 on a scale of 0 to 10). Low quality investment portfolio (1.7). Fair overall results on stability tests (3.5) based on a steep decline in capital during 2013 but steady enrollment growth, averaging 4% over the past five years.
Other Rating Factors: Good liquidity (5.1) with sufficient resources (cash flows and marketable investments) to handle a spike in claims. Strong capitalization index (7.3) based on excellent current risk-adjusted capital (severe loss scenario).
Principal Business: Comp med (90%), FEHB (7%), Medicaid (2%)
Mem Phys: 13: N/A   **12:** N/A   **13 MLR** 95.6%   **/ 13 Admin Exp** N/A
Enroll(000): Q2 14: 80   **13:** 73   **12:** 70   **Med Exp PMPM:** $351
Principal Investments: Nonaffiliate common stock (71%), real estate (17%), cash and equiv (8%), long-term bonds (4%)
Provider Compensation ($000): Capitation ($103,197), FFS ($102,901), contr fee ($47,249), salary ($46,681), other ($8,812)
Total Member Encounters: Phys (251,450), non-phys (272,523)
Group Affiliation: None
Licensed in: WI
Address: 1265 John Q Hammons Dr, Madison, WI 53717
Phone: (608) 251-4156   **Dom State:** WI   **Commenced Bus:** March 1976

Data Date	Rating	RACR #1	RACR #2	Total Assets ($mil)	Capital ($mil)	Net Premium ($mil)	Net Income ($mil)
6-14	D+	1.58	1.32	90.0	50.0	183.0	-7.6
6-13	C-	1.56	1.30	100.9	70.7	157.4	-4.1
2013	D+	1.92	1.60	101.9	59.2	317.4	-13.5
2012	C	1.71	1.43	116.4	76.5	296.7	-5.5
2011	B-	2.50	2.08	124.2	80.8	279.9	7.1
2010	B-	2.92	2.43	117.9	75.6	257.1	4.3
2009	B+	2.73	2.27	101.6	68.8	241.2	2.1

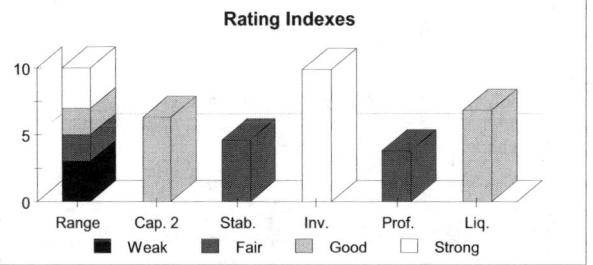

Rating Indexes

GROUP HEALTH COOPERATIVE *   A-   Excellent

Major Rating Factors: Strong capitalization index (10.0 on a scale of 0 to 10) based on excellent current risk-adjusted capital (severe loss scenario). Excellent liquidity (7.0) with sufficient resources (cash flows and marketable investments) to handle a spike in claims. Good quality investment portfolio (6.4).
Other Rating Factors: Good overall results on stability tests (5.5). Fair profitability index (4.1).
Principal Business: Comp med (47%), Medicare (43%), FEHB (11%)
Mem Phys: 13: 16,848   **12:** 15,793   **13 MLR** 87.8%   **/ 13 Admin Exp** N/A
Enroll(000): Q2 14: 359   **13:** 348   **12:** 339   **Med Exp PMPM:** $481
Principal Investments: Long-term bonds (36%), real estate (22%), cash and equiv (15%), nonaffiliate common stock (15%), affiliate common stock (8%), other (4%)
Provider Compensation ($000): Contr fee ($784,524), FFS ($360,283), capitation ($359,199), bonus arrang ($23,732), other ($429,631)
Total Member Encounters: Phys (1,471,136), non-phys (173,363)
Group Affiliation: Group Health Cooperative
Licensed in: WA
Address: 320 Westlake Ave N Suite 100, Seattle, WA 98109-5233
Phone: (206) 448-5600   **Dom State:** WA   **Commenced Bus:** December 1945

Data Date	Rating	RACR #1	RACR #2	Total Assets ($mil)	Capital ($mil)	Net Premium ($mil)	Net Income ($mil)
6-14	A-	5.34	4.45	1,617.8	912.8	1,193.0	97.4
6-13	A-	3.25	2.71	1,445.6	638.2	1,138.6	98.2
2013	A-	4.57	3.81	1,531.0	803.5	2,245.8	107.8
2012	A-	2.03	1.69	1,255.4	431.3	2,122.0	4.4
2011	A-	2.55	2.12	1,494.1	482.5	1,973.2	-13.6
2010	A+	3.74	3.12	1,379.8	605.8	1,874.0	-32.9
2009	A+	3.85	3.20	1,358.0	593.2	1,925.8	16.2

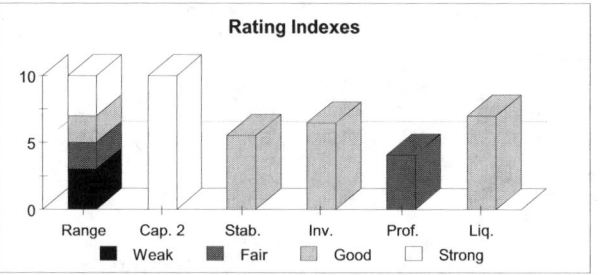

Rating Indexes

GROUP HEALTH INCORPORATED | D | Weak

Major Rating Factors: Weak profitability index (0.9 on a scale of 0 to 10). Fair quality investment portfolio (4.5). Good capitalization (6.1) based on good current risk-adjusted capital (severe loss scenario).
Other Rating Factors: Good liquidity (4.9) as cash resources may not be adequate to cover a spike in claims.
Principal Business: Comp med (76%), Medicare (9%), FEHB (7%), dental (3%), other (4%)
Mem Phys: 13: 82,123 **12:** 85,587 **13 MLR** 88.5% **/ 13 Admin Exp** N/A
Enroll(000): Q2 14: 1,488 **13:** 1,568 **12:** 1,594 **Med Exp PMPM:** $167
Principal Investments: Long-term bonds (73%), real estate (32%), nonaffiliate common stock (6%)
Provider Compensation ($000): Contr fee ($3,091,163), capitation ($1,073), other ($109,534)
Total Member Encounters: N/A
Group Affiliation: EmblemHealth Inc
Licensed in: NY
Address: 441 Ninth Ave, New York, NY 10001
Phone: (212) 615-0000 **Dom State:** NY **Commenced Bus:** December 1940

Data Date	Rating	RACR #1	RACR #2	Total Assets ($mil)	Capital ($mil)	Net Premium ($mil)	Net Income ($mil)
6-14	D	1.10	0.91	1,100.4	284.1	1,536.5	3.8
6-13	D	0.53	0.44	1,032.6	157.7	1,802.4	8.0
2013	D	1.06	0.89	991.9	276.3	3,614.6	-66.2
2012	D	0.37	0.30	967.1	120.2	3,571.3	-51.9
2011	C-	0.61	0.51	877.0	144.9	3,496.1	-33.0
2010	C+	0.95	0.79	1,032.3	213.1	3,594.1	-32.7
2009	C-	0.71	0.59	824.5	146.4	3,156.3	-8.9

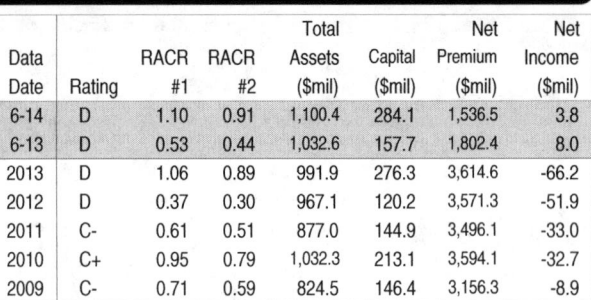

Rating Indexes

GROUP HEALTH OPTIONS INC | B- | Good

Major Rating Factors: Good liquidity (5.8 on a scale of 0 to 10) with sufficient resources (cash flows and marketable investments) to handle a spike in claims. Strong capitalization (8.5) based on excellent current risk-adjusted capital (severe loss scenario). High quality investment portfolio (8.7).
Other Rating Factors: Weak profitability index (2.2).
Principal Business: Comp med (97%), Medicare (3%)
Mem Phys: 13: 39,368 **12:** 37,214 **13 MLR** 85.6% **/ 13 Admin Exp** N/A
Enroll(000): Q2 14: 141 **13:** 174 **12:** 201 **Med Exp PMPM:** $354
Principal Investments: Long-term bonds (100%), real estate (3%)
Provider Compensation ($000): FFS ($574,458), capitation ($207,165)
Total Member Encounters: Phys (611,554), non-phys (49,772)
Group Affiliation: Group Health Cooperative
Licensed in: ID, WA
Address: 320 Westlake Ave N Suite 100, Seattle, WA 98109-5233
Phone: (206) 448-5600 **Dom State:** WA **Commenced Bus:** October 1990

Data Date	Rating	RACR #1	RACR #2	Total Assets ($mil)	Capital ($mil)	Net Premium ($mil)	Net Income ($mil)
6-14	B-	2.55	2.12	224.9	103.6	380.8	-6.7
6-13	C+	1.77	1.48	215.3	115.5	459.1	6.5
2013	B-	2.65	2.21	219.4	111.5	893.6	2.0
2012	C+	1.54	1.29	219.2	109.9	1,010.9	-8.2
2011	B	2.57	2.14	200.0	117.5	1,015.9	7.9
2010	B	3.12	2.60	183.6	109.8	862.3	7.4
2009	B	2.44	2.03	123.8	69.6	651.6	-4.6

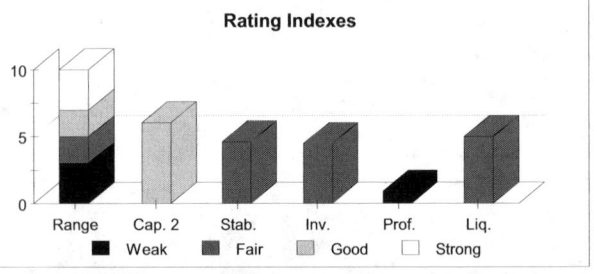

Rating Indexes

GROUP HEALTH PLAN INC * | A+ | Excellent

Major Rating Factors: Excellent profitability (8.9 on a scale of 0 to 10). Strong capitalization index (10.0) based on excellent current risk-adjusted capital (severe loss scenario). High quality investment portfolio (9.7).
Other Rating Factors: Excellent overall results on stability tests (7.9) despite a decline in the number of member physicians during 2014. Excellent liquidity (7.4) with ample operational cash flow and liquid investments.
Principal Business: Comp med (54%), Medicare (38%), FEHB (4%), dental (4%)
Mem Phys: 13: 49,353 **12:** 67,042 **13 MLR** 89.9% **/ 13 Admin Exp** N/A
Enroll(000): Q2 14: 60 **13:** 55 **12:** 53 **Med Exp PMPM:** $1,438
Principal Investments: Long-term bonds (48%), cash and equiv (22%), real estate (16%), nonaffiliate common stock (13%), other (1%)
Provider Compensation ($000): Bonus arrang ($239,275), contr fee ($58,389)
Total Member Encounters: Phys (1,088,243), non-phys (104,044)
Group Affiliation: HealthPartners Inc
Licensed in: MN
Address: 8100 34th Ave S, Minneapolis, MN 55440-1309
Phone: (952) 883-6000 **Dom State:** MN **Commenced Bus:** August 1957

Data Date	Rating	RACR #1	RACR #2	Total Assets ($mil)	Capital ($mil)	Net Premium ($mil)	Net Income ($mil)
6-14	A+	4.68	3.90	693.0	170.1	525.6	3.4
6-13	B-	3.86	3.22	645.4	121.6	500.2	12.8
2013	A-	4.37	3.65	764.3	158.8	1,040.2	43.0
2012	C-	3.10	2.58	606.1	98.8	968.4	20.3
2011	N/A	N/A	N/A	647.2	98.7	931.1	N/A
2010	N/A	N/A	N/A	552.2	85.5	825.0	N/A
2009	N/A	N/A	N/A	492.8	79.4	841.1	N/A

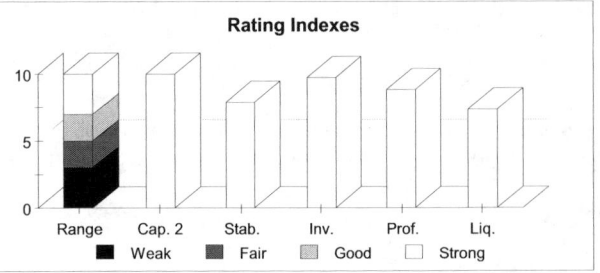

Rating Indexes

GROUP HOSP & MEDICAL SERVICES INC   B-   Good

Major Rating Factors: Good quality investment portfolio (5.7 on a scale of 0 to 10). Good liquidity (6.7) with sufficient resources (cash flows and marketable investments) to handle a spike in claims. Strong capitalization (10.0) based on excellent current risk-adjusted capital (severe loss scenario).
Other Rating Factors: Weak profitability index (2.5).
Principal Business: FEHB (57%), comp med (40%), dental (1%), med supp (1%)
Mem Phys: 13: 46,263   **12:** 46,896   **13 MLR** 92.4%   / **13 Admin Exp** N/A
Enroll(000): Q2 14: 781   **13:** 728   **12:** 803   **Med Exp PMPM:** $325
Principal Investments: Long-term bonds (48%), nonaffiliate common stock (11%), other (41%)
Provider Compensation ($000): Contr fee ($2,830,656), FFS ($107,628), capitation ($5,439)
Total Member Encounters: Phys (9,239,208), non-phys (3,560,465)
Group Affiliation: CareFirst Inc
Licensed in: DC, MD, VA
Address: 840 First Street NE, Washington, DC 20065
Phone: (410) 581-3000   **Dom State:** DC   **Commenced Bus:** March 1934

Data Date	Rating	RACR #1	RACR #2	Total Assets ($mil)	Capital ($mil)	Net Premium ($mil)	Net Income ($mil)
6-14	B-	5.13	4.28	2,279.9	894.3	1,636.4	-47.6
6-13	B	5.34	4.45	2,237.5	941.2	1,561.9	8.3
2013	B	5.36	4.47	2,216.0	934.8	3,161.9	9.0
2012	A-	5.34	4.45	2,251.3	941.1	3,165.9	-7.5
2011	A+	5.84	4.87	2,293.3	963.6	3,059.4	53.6
2010	A+	6.49	5.41	2,173.6	969.5	2,917.4	86.7
2009	A+	5.40	4.50	1,887.6	761.5	2,890.9	44.8

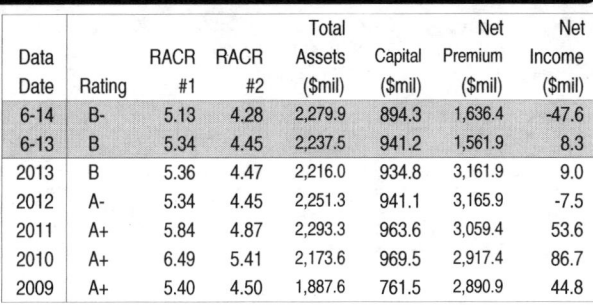

Rating Indexes

GUARANTEE TRUST LIFE INSURANCE COMPANY   B   Good

Major Rating Factors: Good quality investment portfolio (6.4 on a scale of 0 to 10) despite mixed results such as: minimal exposure to mortgages and substantial holdings of BBB bonds but small junk bond holdings. Good overall results on stability tests (5.9). Stability strengths include excellent operational trends, good risk adjusted capital for prior years and excellent risk diversification. Strong capitalization (7.1) based on excellent risk adjusted capital (severe loss scenario).
Other Rating Factors: Excellent profitability (7.7) with operating gains in each of the last five years. Excellent liquidity (7.4).
Principal Business: Individual health insurance (66%), group health insurance (19%), individual life insurance (9%), reinsurance (3%), and other lines (3%).
Principal Investments: NonCMO investment grade bonds (51%), CMOs and structured securities (34%), mortgages in good standing (8%), noninv. grade bonds (3%), and misc. investments (4%).
Investments in Affiliates: 2%
Group Affiliation: Guarantee Trust
Licensed in: All states except NY
Commenced Business: June 1936
Address: 1275 Milwaukee Ave, Glenview, IL 60025
Phone: (847) 699-0600   **Domicile State:** IL   **NAIC Code:** 64211

Data Date	Rating	RACR #1	RACR #2	Total Assets ($mil)	Capital ($mil)	Net Premium ($mil)	Net Income ($mil)
6-14	B	1.52	1.04	382.3	55.8	97.1	3.2
6-13	B	1.36	0.95	335.4	46.1	91.0	2.6
2013	B	1.49	1.03	366.1	54.3	196.4	7.1
2012	B	1.36	0.97	325.0	44.2	182.9	3.3
2011	B	1.38	0.98	283.7	42.1	165.2	4.9
2010	B-	1.26	0.88	258.0	40.1	164.0	3.2
2009	C+	1.29	0.91	232.5	40.4	164.6	1.6

Adverse Trends in Operations

Increase in policy surrenders from 2012 to 2013 (127%)
Increase in policy surrenders from 2011 to 2012 (33%)

GUARDIAN LIFE INSURANCE COMPANY OF AMERICA *   A   Excellent

Major Rating Factors: Good quality investment portfolio (6.4 on a scale of 0 to 10) despite mixed results such as: large holdings of BBB rated bonds but moderate junk bond exposure. Good liquidity (5.9) with sufficient resources to handle a spike in claims as well as a significant increase in policy surrenders. Strong capitalization (8.2) based on excellent risk adjusted capital (severe loss scenario).
Other Rating Factors: Excellent profitability (7.5) with operating gains in each of the last five years. Excellent overall results on stability tests (7.5) excellent operational trends and excellent risk diversification.
Principal Business: Individual life insurance (51%), group health insurance (33%), reinsurance (6%), group life insurance (6%), and individual health insurance (3%).
Principal Investments: NonCMO investment grade bonds (62%), mortgages in good standing (8%), policy loans (8%), CMOs and structured securities (7%), and misc. investments (14%).
Investments in Affiliates: 4%
Group Affiliation: Guardian Group
Licensed in: All states except PR
Commenced Business: July 1860
Address: 7 Hanover Square, New York, NY 10004-4025
Phone: (212) 598-8000   **Domicile State:** NY   **NAIC Code:** 64246

Data Date	Rating	RACR #1	RACR #2	Total Assets ($mil)	Capital ($mil)	Net Premium ($mil)	Net Income ($mil)
6-14	A	2.75	1.79	44,344.6	5,693.7	3,478.7	172.0
6-13	A	2.59	1.68	40,918.5	4,851.0	3,321.2	126.2
2013	A	2.64	1.73	42,066.0	5,011.9	6,705.6	285.5
2012	A	2.59	1.70	37,530.7	4,752.0	6,011.2	253.3
2011	A	2.63	1.70	35,130.0	4,572.6	5,874.6	195.9
2010	A	2.63	1.72	33,178.0	4,431.0	5,943.5	205.3
2009	A	2.58	1.72	30,895.2	4,188.0	5,925.4	27.7

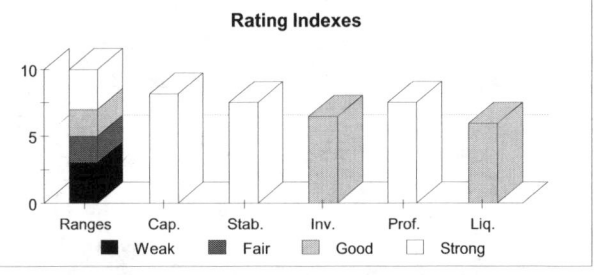

Rating Indexes

GUNDERSEN HEALTH PLAN INC   B   Good

Major Rating Factors: Good overall profitability index (6.6 on a scale of 0 to 10). Good capitalization index (6.3) based on good current risk-adjusted capital (severe loss scenario). Good overall results on stability tests (6.2).
Other Rating Factors: High quality investment portfolio (9.9). Excellent liquidity (7.0) with sufficient resources (cash flows and marketable investments) to handle a spike in claims.
Principal Business: Comp med (46%), Medicare (43%), Medicaid (12%)
Mem Phys: 13: 2,666 **12:** 2,633   **13 MLR** 93.5% **/ 13 Admin Exp** N/A
Enroll(000): Q2 14: 59 **13:** 56 **12:** 56   **Med Exp PMPM:** $394
Principal Investments: Cash and equiv (66%), long-term bonds (29%), other (5%)
Provider Compensation ($000): Capitation ($258,966), FFS ($6,906)
Total Member Encounters: Phys (270,005), non-phys (161,256)
Group Affiliation: Gundersen Lutheran Health System Inc
Licensed in: IA, WI
Address: 1836 South Ave, La Crosse, WI 54601
Phone: (608) 782-7300   **Dom State:** WI   **Commenced Bus:** September 1995

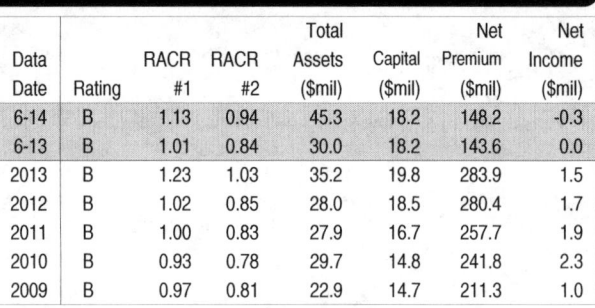

Data Date	Rating	RACR #1	RACR #2	Total Assets ($mil)	Capital ($mil)	Net Premium ($mil)	Net Income ($mil)
6-14	B	1.13	0.94	45.3	18.2	148.2	-0.3
6-13	B	1.01	0.84	30.0	18.2	143.6	0.0
2013	B	1.23	1.03	35.2	19.8	283.9	1.5
2012	B	1.02	0.85	28.0	18.5	280.4	1.7
2011	B	1.00	0.83	27.9	16.7	257.7	1.9
2010	B	0.93	0.78	29.7	14.8	241.8	2.3
2009	B	0.97	0.81	22.9	14.7	211.3	1.0

Rating Indexes

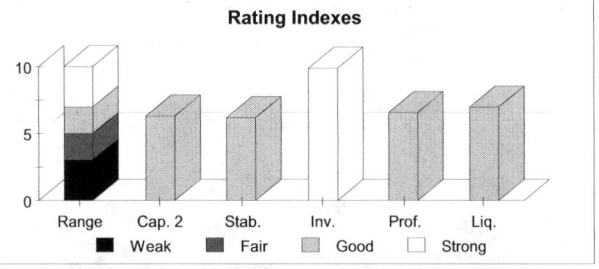

GUNDERSEN HEALTH PLAN MN   B-   Good

Major Rating Factors: Fair capitalization (3.6 on a scale of 0 to 10) based on weak current risk-adjusted capital (moderate loss scenario). High quality investment portfolio (9.9). Excellent liquidity (7.7) with ample operational cash flow and liquid investments.
Other Rating Factors: Weak profitability index (1.0).
Principal Business: Medicare (93%), comp med (7%)
Mem Phys: 13: 696 **12:** 2,633   **13 MLR** 92.9% **/ 13 Admin Exp** N/A
Enroll(000): Q2 14: 1 **13:** 0 **12:** 0   **Med Exp PMPM:** $448
Principal Investments: Cash and equiv (66%), long-term bonds (34%)
Provider Compensation ($000): Capitation ($1,874), FFS ($142)
Total Member Encounters: Phys (2,512), non-phys (1,432)
Group Affiliation: Gundersen Lutheran Health System Inc
Licensed in: WI
Address: 1900 South Ave, La Crosse, WI 54601-5467
Phone: (608) 782-7300   **Dom State:** MN   **Commenced Bus:** February 2012

Data Date	Rating	RACR #1	RACR #2	Total Assets ($mil)	Capital ($mil)	Net Premium ($mil)	Net Income ($mil)
6-14	B-	0.72	0.60	1.7	1.4	1.8	-0.1
6-13	U	0.74	0.62	1.6	1.5	1.0	0.0
2013	B-	0.76	0.63	1.6	1.5	2.2	0.0
2012	U	0.74	0.62	1.6	1.5	0.0	0.0
2011	N/A	N/A	N/A	N/A	1.6	N/A	N/A
2010	N/A	N/A	N/A	N/A	N/A	N/A	N/A
2009	N/A	N/A	N/A	N/A	N/A	N/A	N/A

Rating Indexes

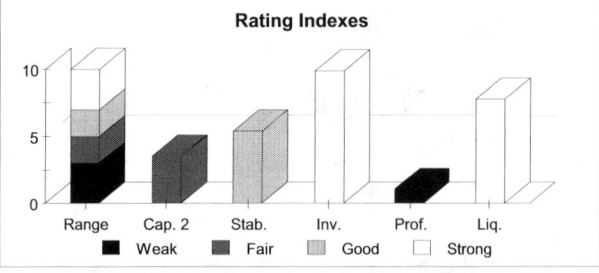

HAP MIDWEST HEALTH PLAN INC   B-   Good

Major Rating Factors: Good overall results on stability tests (5.8 on a scale of 0 to 10). Excellent profitability (7.7). Strong capitalization index (7.8) based on excellent current risk-adjusted capital (severe loss scenario).
Other Rating Factors: High quality investment portfolio (9.9). Excellent liquidity (7.1) with ample operational cash flow and liquid investments.
Principal Business: Medicaid (96%), Medicare (3%)
Mem Phys: 13: 1,815 **12:** 1,309   **13 MLR** 88.1% **/ 13 Admin Exp** N/A
Enroll(000): Q2 14: 93 **13:** 79 **12:** 82   **Med Exp PMPM:** $270
Principal Investments: Cash and equiv (99%), long-term bonds (1%)
Provider Compensation ($000): Contr fee ($155,891), capitation ($86,135), FFS ($9,439), bonus arrang ($2,779)
Total Member Encounters: Phys (486,050), non-phys (323,312)
Group Affiliation: Henry Ford Health System
Licensed in: MI
Address: 4700 Schaefear Rd Suite 340, Dearborn, MI 48126
Phone: (313) 581-3700   **Dom State:** MI   **Commenced Bus:** January 1994

Data Date	Rating	RACR #1	RACR #2	Total Assets ($mil)	Capital ($mil)	Net Premium ($mil)	Net Income ($mil)
6-14	B-	1.96	1.63	103.4	38.3	169.1	7.8
6-13	B-	1.68	1.40	77.7	30.9	147.6	4.1
2013	B-	1.62	1.35	82.1	31.4	294.6	9.4
2012	B-	1.49	1.24	66.7	26.8	274.5	7.1
2011	D-	0.90	0.75	49.9	19.1	265.1	5.9
2010	A+	2.52	2.10	77.8	48.4	247.8	8.5
2009	A+	2.65	2.21	71.9	46.0	223.4	7.1

Rating Indexes

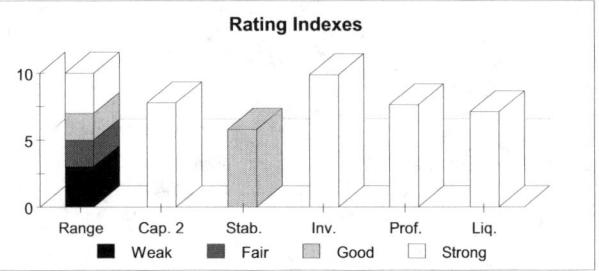

HARBOR HEALTH PLAN INC   E-   Very Weak

Major Rating Factors: Fair profitability index (3.7 on a scale of 0 to 10). Fair overall results on stability tests (4.9). Strong capitalization index (10.0) based on excellent current risk-adjusted capital (severe loss scenario).
Other Rating Factors: High quality investment portfolio (9.9). Excellent liquidity (7.7) with ample operational cash flow and liquid investments.
Principal Business: Medicaid (100%)
Mem Phys: 13: 1,487   **12:** 1,545   **13 MLR** 84.7%   **/ 13 Admin Exp** N/A
Enroll(000): Q2 14: 6   **13:** 3   **12:** 2   **Med Exp PMPM:** $261
Principal Investments: Cash and equiv (100%)
Provider Compensation ($000): Contr fee ($7,135), capitation ($85)
Total Member Encounters: Phys (402), non-phys (32,933)
Group Affiliation: Vanguard Health Systems Inc
Licensed in: MI
Address: 4707 St Antoine 5 South, Detroit, MI 48201
Phone: (800) 543-0161   **Dom State:** MI   **Commenced Bus:** December 2000

Data Date	Rating	RACR #1	RACR #2	Total Assets ($mil)	Capital ($mil)	Net Premium ($mil)	Net Income ($mil)
6-14	E-	5.33	4.44	10.5	7.5	7.9	0.5
6-13	E-	3.16	2.64	4.7	3.4	4.1	0.4
2013	E-	3.55	2.96	6.5	4.8	8.9	-0.3
2012	C+	1.75	1.46	3.4	1.7	8.0	-0.1
2011	C+	2.20	1.83	4.4	1.8	7.4	0.2
2010	C	1.54	1.29	4.6	2.2	6.5	0.0
2009	D+	3.02	2.52	3.6	2.1	4.4	0.3

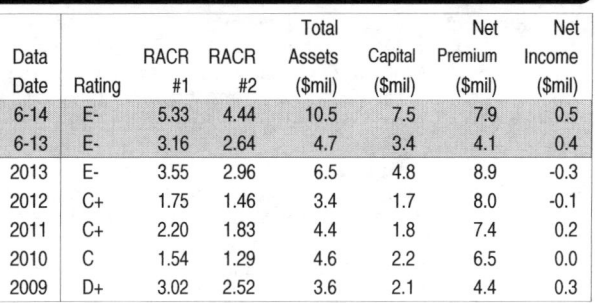

Rating Indexes (Range, Cap. 2, Stab., Inv., Prof., Liq. — Weak, Fair, Good, Strong)

HARMONY HEALTH PLAN OF ILLINOIS INC   B-   Good

Major Rating Factors: Fair quality investment portfolio (4.0 on a scale of 0 to 10). Fair overall results on stability tests (4.5). Rating is significantly influenced by the fair financial results of WellCare Health Plans Inc. Excellent profitability (8.1).
Other Rating Factors: Strong capitalization index (9.7) based on excellent current risk-adjusted capital (severe loss scenario). Excellent liquidity (7.0) with sufficient resources (cash flows and marketable investments) to handle a spike in claims.
Principal Business: Medicaid (53%), Medicare (47%)
Mem Phys: 13: 16,200   **12:** 4,600   **13 MLR** 85.4%   **/ 13 Admin Exp** N/A
Enroll(000): Q2 14: 149   **13:** 159   **12:** 156   **Med Exp PMPM:** $163
Principal Investments: Cash and equiv (95%), long-term bonds (5%)
Provider Compensation ($000): Contr fee ($196,620), capitation ($111,957)
Total Member Encounters: Phys (330,251), non-phys (84,707)
Group Affiliation: WellCare Health Plans Inc
Licensed in: IL, IN, MO
Address: 200 W Adams St 8th Floor, Chicago, IL 60606
Phone: (813) 290-6200   **Dom State:** IL   **Commenced Bus:** July 1996

Data Date	Rating	RACR #1	RACR #2	Total Assets ($mil)	Capital ($mil)	Net Premium ($mil)	Net Income ($mil)
6-14	B-	3.52	2.93	106.1	46.6	187.1	1.3
6-13	B+	4.81	4.00	106.3	55.9	183.6	6.4
2013	B	3.13	2.61	97.3	43.2	368.1	6.6
2012	B+	4.09	3.41	98.9	49.5	323.1	14.0
2011	B+	4.45	3.71	118.1	53.9	310.6	21.0
2010	B	2.81	2.34	109.9	41.1	338.3	11.7
2009	C	1.76	1.46	116.1	29.6	386.6	2.3

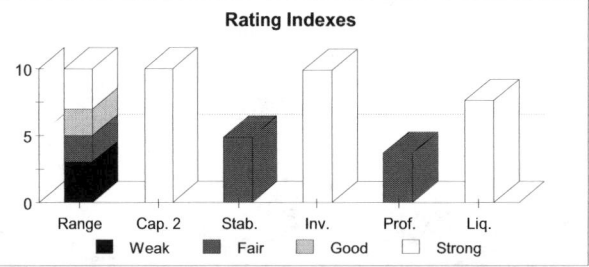

Rating Indexes (Range, Cap. 2, Stab., Inv., Prof., Liq. — Weak, Fair, Good, Strong)

HARTFORD LIFE & ACCIDENT INSURANCE COMPANY   C-   Fair

Major Rating Factors: Poor current capitalization (0.5 on a scale of 0 to 10) based on weak risk adjusted capital (severe loss scenario), although results have slipped from the excellent range during the last year. Low quality investment portfolio (0.6). Weak overall results on stability tests (1.8) including excessive premium growth and negative cash flow from operations for 2013.
Other Rating Factors: Fair profitability (3.6) with operating losses during the first six months of 2014. Good liquidity (6.9).
Principal Business: Group health insurance (53%), group life insurance (35%), reinsurance (11%), and individual life insurance (1%).
Principal Investments: NonCMO investment grade bonds (40%), common & preferred stock (39%), CMOs and structured securities (8%), mortgages in good standing (5%), and misc. investments (5%).
Investments in Affiliates: 38%
Group Affiliation: Hartford Financial Services Inc
Licensed in: All states, the District of Columbia and Puerto Rico
Commenced Business: February 1967
Address: 200 Hopmeadow St, Simsbury, CT 06070
Phone: (860) 547-5000   **Domicile State:** CT   **NAIC Code:** 70815

Data Date	Rating	RACR #1	RACR #2	Total Assets ($mil)	Capital ($mil)	Net Premium ($mil)	Net Income ($mil)
6-14	C-	0.30	0.29	9,108.6	1,478.8	1,338.8	-463.8
6-13	B-	1.12	1.05	14,719.6	6,144.3	730.5	-62.1
2013	B-	1.05	1.00	13,890.8	5,595.2	1,974.0	-174.0
2012	B-	1.07	1.01	14,404.8	5,767.3	2,878.5	-397.8
2011	B-	1.06	1.01	15,388.3	6,737.2	3,178.7	-23.0
2010	B-	1.04	1.00	14,950.7	6,577.1	3,314.6	164.8
2009	B-	1.02	0.98	14,254.5	6,005.3	3,350.8	70.4

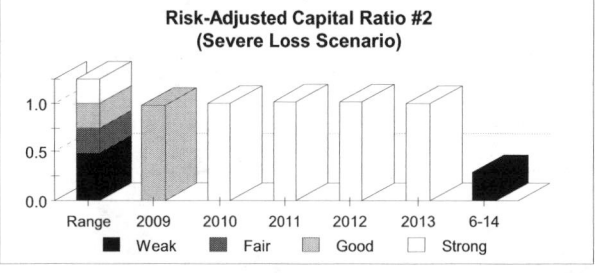

Risk-Adjusted Capital Ratio #2
(Severe Loss Scenario) (Range, 2009, 2010, 2011, 2012, 2013, 6-14 — Weak, Fair, Good, Strong)

HARVARD PILGRIM HC OF NEW ENGLAND — B — Good

Major Rating Factors: Good overall profitability index (5.1 on a scale of 0 to 10). Good overall results on stability tests (5.2). Strong capitalization index (10.0) based on excellent current risk-adjusted capital (severe loss scenario).
Other Rating Factors: High quality investment portfolio (9.9). Excellent liquidity (6.9) with sufficient resources (cash flows and marketable investments) to handle a spike in claims.
Principal Business: Comp med (100%)
Mem Phys: 13: 55,628 **12:** 47,769 **13 MLR** 79.5% **/ 13 Admin Exp** N/A
Enroll(000): Q2 14: 51 **13:** 46 **12:** 35 **Med Exp PMPM:** $363
Principal Investments: Long-term bonds (84%), cash and equiv (16%)
Provider Compensation ($000): Contr fee ($86,183), bonus arrang ($79,617), capitation ($8,193), FFS ($6,705), other ($3,990)
Total Member Encounters: Phys (191,142), non-phys (80,958)
Group Affiliation: Harvard Pilgrim Health Care
Licensed in: MA, NH
Address: 93 Worcester St, Wellesley, MA 02481
Phone: (781) 263-6000 **Dom State:** MA **Commenced Bus:** October 1980

Data Date	Rating	RACR #1	RACR #2	Total Assets ($mil)	Capital ($mil)	Net Premium ($mil)	Net Income ($mil)
6-14	B	4.21	3.51	94.5	62.1	134.0	5.2
6-13	B	4.60	3.83	80.9	59.0	112.0	9.1
2013	B	4.12	3.43	84.8	59.4	230.8	13.3
2012	B	3.97	3.31	72.9	50.1	195.0	7.3
2011	B	2.75	2.29	70.1	44.0	267.0	11.4
2010	B	1.53	1.27	64.7	31.7	301.2	-4.0
2009	C+	1.40	1.16	78.7	36.6	359.9	-12.4

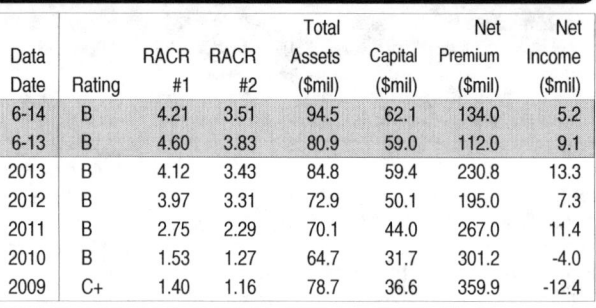

Rating Indexes

HARVARD PILGRIM HEALTH CARE INC * — B+ — Good

Major Rating Factors: Good profitability index (5.0 on a scale of 0 to 10). Good quality investment portfolio (6.4). Good overall results on stability tests (5.3).
Other Rating Factors: Good liquidity (6.6) with sufficient resources (cash flows and marketable investments) to handle a spike in claims. Strong capitalization index (8.8) based on excellent current risk-adjusted capital (severe loss scenario).
Principal Business: Comp med (100%)
Mem Phys: 13: 55,628 **12:** 47,769 **13 MLR** 87.5% **/ 13 Admin Exp** N/A
Enroll(000): Q2 14: 299 **13:** 329 **12:** 345 **Med Exp PMPM:** $389
Principal Investments: Long-term bonds (69%), nonaffiliate common stock (20%), affiliate common stock (8%), real estate (4%)
Provider Compensation ($000): Bonus arrang ($860,979), contr fee ($411,659), capitation ($237,889), FFS ($64,383), other ($20,898)
Total Member Encounters: Phys (1,726,042), non-phys (652,160)
Group Affiliation: Harvard Pilgrim Health Care
Licensed in: ME, MA
Address: 93 Worcester St, Wellesley, MA 02481
Phone: (781) 263-6000 **Dom State:** MA **Commenced Bus:** February 1969

Data Date	Rating	RACR #1	RACR #2	Total Assets ($mil)	Capital ($mil)	Net Premium ($mil)	Net Income ($mil)
6-14	B+	2.78	2.32	837.3	450.9	835.9	-8.6
6-13	B+	2.96	2.47	842.1	466.8	902.2	-2.6
2013	B+	3.08	2.56	853.5	496.6	1,786.0	11.5
2012	A	3.03	2.52	882.6	481.1	1,923.0	16.4
2011	A	3.00	2.50	826.3	479.5	2,046.4	74.2
2010	A	2.22	1.85	793.9	412.7	2,302.0	44.2
2009	B+	2.26	1.88	801.1	382.0	2,077.8	24.0

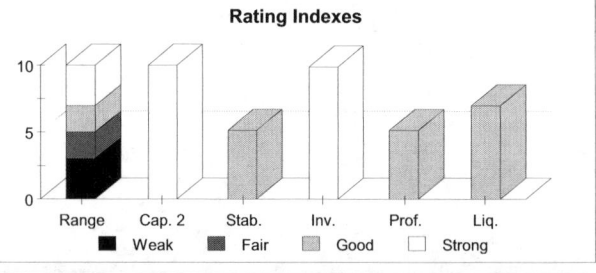

Rating Indexes

HAWAII MANAGEMENT ALLIANCE ASSOC — C — Fair

Major Rating Factors: Weak profitability index (1.9 on a scale of 0 to 10). Weak liquidity (2.2) as a spike in claims may stretch capacity. Good capitalization (6.8) based on excellent current risk-adjusted capital (severe loss scenario).
Other Rating Factors: High quality investment portfolio (9.2).
Principal Business: Comp med (86%), dental (3%), other (10%)
Mem Phys: 13: 7,173 **12:** 6,757 **13 MLR** 140.7% **/ 13 Admin Exp** N/A
Enroll(000): Q2 14: 44 **13:** 42 **12:** 39 **Med Exp PMPM:** $245
Principal Investments: Cash and equiv (67%), long-term bonds (32%), nonaffiliate common stock (1%)
Provider Compensation ($000): FFS ($112,994)
Total Member Encounters: Phys (5,912)
Group Affiliation: None
Licensed in: HI
Address: 737 Bishop St Ste 1200, Honolulu, HI 96813
Phone: (808) 791-7550 **Dom State:** HI **Commenced Bus:** October 1990

Data Date	Rating	RACR #1	RACR #2	Total Assets ($mil)	Capital ($mil)	Net Premium ($mil)	Net Income ($mil)
6-14	C	1.21	1.01	37.0	13.0	42.5	0.0
6-13	C	1.45	1.21	28.1	12.3	41.2	-0.1
2013	C	1.21	1.01	34.9	12.9	82.0	0.5
2012	C	1.45	1.21	29.1	11.4	58.8	0.0
2011	N/A	N/A	N/A	26.7	12.4	64.5	-4.2
2010	N/A	N/A	N/A	27.2	15.5	52.2	-2.8
2009	C+	3.66	3.05	28.9	19.5	38.3	0.3

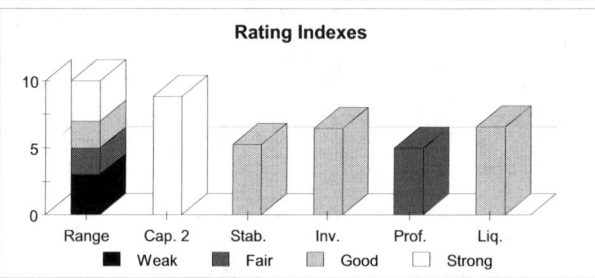

Rating Indexes

HAWAII MEDICAL SERVICE ASSOCIATION   C   Fair

Major Rating Factors: Weak profitability index (1.8 on a scale of 0 to 10). Good quality investment portfolio (6.4). Good liquidity (6.8) with sufficient resources (cash flows and marketable investments) to handle a spike in claims.
Other Rating Factors: Strong capitalization (7.6) based on excellent current risk-adjusted capital (severe loss scenario).
Principal Business: Comp med (59%), Medicaid (15%), Medicare (14%), FEHB (11%)
Mem Phys: 13: 6,702 **12:** 6,424 **13 MLR** 95.0% **/ 13 Admin Exp** N/A
Enroll(000): Q2 14: 723 **13:** 717 **12:** 701 **Med Exp PMPM:** $292
Principal Investments: Nonaffiliate common stock (50%), cash and equiv (28%), long-term bonds (10%), real estate (7%), affiliate common stock (3%), other (2%)
Provider Compensation ($000): Contr fee ($2,360,731), capitation ($67,394), bonus arrang ($42,217), salary ($7,368)
Total Member Encounters: Phys (5,079,661)
Group Affiliation: Hawaii Medical Service Assoc
Licensed in: HI
Address: 818 Keeaumoku St, Honolulu, HI 96814
Phone: (808) 948-5145 **Dom State:** HI **Commenced Bus:** June 1938

Data Date	Rating	RACR #1	RACR #2	Total Assets ($mil)	Capital ($mil)	Net Premium ($mil)	Net Income ($mil)
6-14	C	1.87	1.56	933.2	391.7	1,438.3	-8.4
6-13	C	2.26	1.88	858.4	442.1	1,310.8	-5.9
2013	C	1.87	1.56	945.2	391.5	2,640.0	-44.4
2012	C	2.32	1.93	864.4	452.2	2,481.8	36.0
2011	C	2.50	2.08	756.9	406.2	2,064.4	43.8
2010	C	3.16	2.63	740.2	389.6	1,763.5	5.3
2009	C	2.73	2.28	664.8	356.1	1,643.2	-64.4

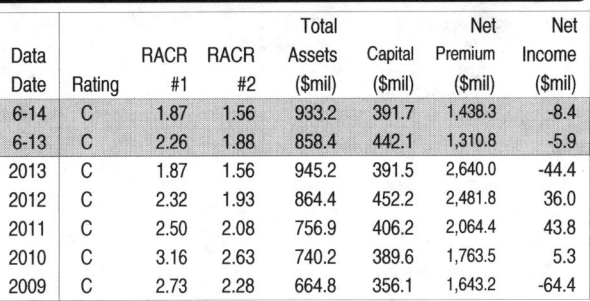

Rating Indexes

HCC LIFE INSURANCE COMPANY   B   Good

Major Rating Factors: Good overall results on stability tests (6.1 on a scale of 0 to 10). Stability strengths include excellent operational trends and excellent risk diversification. Good liquidity (6.9) with sufficient resources to handle a spike in claims. Strong capitalization (10.0) based on excellent risk adjusted capital (severe loss scenario).
Other Rating Factors: High quality investment portfolio (7.7). Excellent profitability (9.4) with operating gains in each of the last five years.
Principal Business: Group health insurance (94%), individual health insurance (4%), and reinsurance (1%).
Principal Investments: NonCMO investment grade bonds (77%), CMOs and structured securities (20%), and common & preferred stock (3%).
Investments in Affiliates: 3%
Group Affiliation: HCC Ins Holdings Inc
Licensed in: All states except PR
Commenced Business: March 1981
Address: 300 N Meridian St Ste 2700, Indianapolis, IN 46204
Phone: (713) 996-1200 **Domicile State:** IN **NAIC Code:** 92711

Data Date	Rating	RACR #1	RACR #2	Total Assets ($mil)	Capital ($mil)	Net Premium ($mil)	Net Income ($mil)
6-14	B	3.87	3.16	841.1	487.9	470.8	49.6
6-13	B	3.07	2.64	772.7	459.9	424.8	48.1
2013	B	3.61	2.96	750.2	436.9	854.6	142.1
2012	B	2.72	2.34	731.2	413.7	821.0	100.2
2011	B	2.97	2.57	655.7	400.2	686.0	89.0
2010	B	3.01	2.60	608.3	390.3	637.0	78.6
2009	B	2.81	2.43	598.0	367.7	651.8	66.0

Adverse Trends in Operations

Decrease in premium volume from 2009 to 2010 (2%)

HCSC INS SERVICES CO   B   Good

Major Rating Factors: Strong capitalization (10.0 on a scale of 0 to 10) based on excellent current risk-adjusted capital (severe loss scenario). High quality investment portfolio (9.9). Excellent liquidity (7.5) with ample operational cash flow and liquid investments.
Other Rating Factors: Weak profitability index (1.0).
Principal Business: Medicaid (29%), Medicare (1%), other (69%)
Mem Phys: 13: 21,971 **12:** 9,668 **13 MLR** 81.8% **/ 13 Admin Exp** N/A
Enroll(000): Q2 14: 443 **13:** 348 **12:** 339 **Med Exp PMPM:** $88
Principal Investments: Cash and equiv (75%), long-term bonds (25%)
Provider Compensation ($000): FFS ($61,585), contr fee ($51,528), capitation ($1,179), other ($252,594)
Total Member Encounters: Phys (158,553), non-phys (132,531)
Group Affiliation: HCSC Group
Licensed in: All states except CT, HI, ME, NH, NJ, NY, VT, PR
Address: 300 E Randolph St, Chicago, IL 60601-5099
Phone: (312) 653-6000 **Dom State:** IL **Commenced Bus:** February 1958

Data Date	Rating	RACR #1	RACR #2	Total Assets ($mil)	Capital ($mil)	Net Premium ($mil)	Net Income ($mil)
6-14	B	6.17	5.14	405.2	160.9	502.8	-35.9
6-13	A-	5.78	4.82	195.2	140.2	226.7	-2.9
2013	B+	7.86	6.55	300.3	205.9	442.8	-43.3
2012	A-	5.92	4.93	188.5	143.5	425.1	8.9
2011	B	6.09	5.07	185.0	134.6	412.9	19.5
2010	B	4.88	4.07	157.1	98.3	432.2	23.0
2009	B	3.84	3.20	166.3	71.3	428.8	5.4

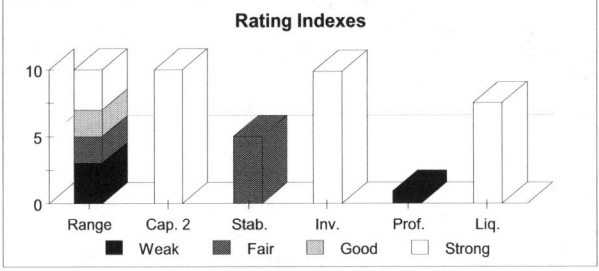

Rating Indexes

HEALTH ALLIANCE MEDICAL PLANS *   A   Excellent

Major Rating Factors: Strong capitalization (8.6 on a scale of 0 to 10) based on excellent current risk-adjusted capital (severe loss scenario). High quality investment portfolio (6.9). Excellent liquidity (7.1) with ample operational cash flow and liquid investments.

Other Rating Factors: Good overall profitability index (5.6).

Principal Business: Comp med (83%), Medicare (12%), FEHB (3%), Medicaid (1%)

Mem Phys: 13: 21,791 **12:** 15,755 **13 MLR** 89.0% **/ 13 Admin Exp** N/A

Enroll(000): Q2 14: 194 **13:** 207 **12:** 205 **Med Exp PMPM:** $411

Principal Investments: Long-term bonds (51%), nonaffiliate common stock (40%), cash and equiv (6%), affiliate common stock (4%)

Provider Compensation ($000): Contr fee ($613,194), capitation ($403,959), FFS ($13,721)

Total Member Encounters: Phys (874,029), non-phys (1,934,388)

Group Affiliation: Health Alliance Group

Licensed in: IL

Address: 301 S Vine, Urbana, IL 61801

Phone: (217) 337-8406 **Dom State:** IL **Commenced Bus:** December 1989

Data Date	Rating	RACR #1	RACR #2	Total Assets ($mil)	Capital ($mil)	Net Premium ($mil)	Net Income ($mil)
6-14	A	2.62	2.18	521.4	191.2	586.0	-10.4
6-13	A	2.55	2.12	521.8	178.4	535.1	6.7
2013	A	2.75	2.29	509.3	200.8	1,119.0	11.4
2012	B+	2.36	1.97	477.1	165.3	1,069.8	11.8
2011	B+	2.42	2.02	410.7	161.0	1,046.7	25.8
2010	B+	2.03	1.69	362.1	140.6	1,003.0	22.8
2009	B-	1.85	1.55	312.5	127.3	947.5	11.9

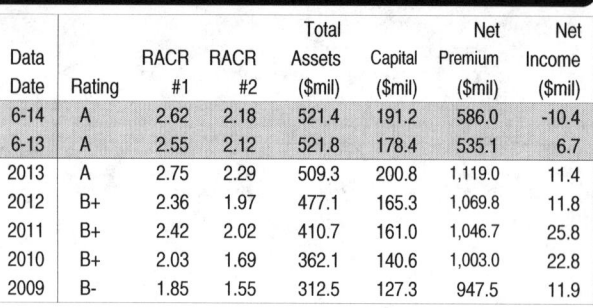

Rating Indexes

HEALTH ALLIANCE PLAN OF MICHIGAN   B   Good

Major Rating Factors: Good overall profitability index (5.3 on a scale of 0 to 10). Fair overall results on stability tests (4.8). Strong capitalization index (7.1) based on excellent current risk-adjusted capital (severe loss scenario).

Other Rating Factors: High quality investment portfolio (9.9). Excellent liquidity (6.9) with sufficient resources (cash flows and marketable investments) to handle a spike in claims.

Principal Business: Comp med (68%), Medicare (26%), FEHB (6%)

Mem Phys: 13: 8,832 **12:** 9,706 **13 MLR** 89.1% **/ 13 Admin Exp** N/A

Enroll(000): Q2 14: 313 **13:** 329 **12:** 342 **Med Exp PMPM:** $416

Principal Investments: Cash and equiv (45%), affiliate common stock (32%), long-term bonds (18%), other (6%)

Provider Compensation ($000): Contr fee ($820,723), capitation ($784,206), FFS ($52,515), bonus arrang ($16,242)

Total Member Encounters: Phys (1,373,741), non-phys (147,865)

Group Affiliation: Henry Ford Health System

Licensed in: MI

Address: 2850 W Grand Blvd, Detroit, MI 48202

Phone: (313) 872-8100 **Dom State:** MI **Commenced Bus:** February 1979

Data Date	Rating	RACR #1	RACR #2	Total Assets ($mil)	Capital ($mil)	Net Premium ($mil)	Net Income ($mil)
6-14	B	1.44	1.20	483.1	208.6	928.6	-5.0
6-13	B	1.34	1.12	490.2	196.1	941.1	11.2
2013	B	1.45	1.21	456.7	210.2	1,869.0	17.9
2012	B+	1.57	1.31	500.0	231.5	1,895.1	21.8
2011	B+	1.68	1.40	501.5	238.6	1,791.3	23.8
2010	B+	2.12	1.77	454.8	285.0	1,733.2	25.8
2009	A-	2.06	1.72	405.3	256.3	1,718.1	22.8

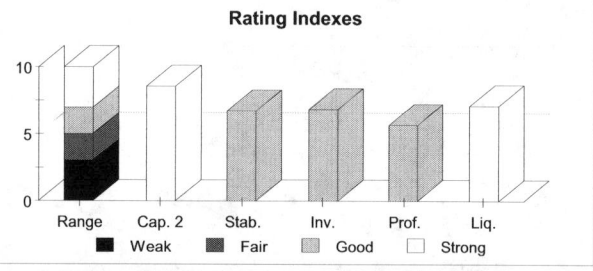

Rating Indexes

HEALTH ALLIANCE-MIDWEST INC   E   Very Weak

Major Rating Factors: Weak profitability index (0.9 on a scale of 0 to 10). Weak overall results on stability tests (2.6) based on a steep decline in capital during 2013. Rating is significantly influenced by the strong financial results of Health Alliance Group. Good liquidity (6.3) with sufficient resources (cash flows and marketable investments) to handle a spike in claims.

Other Rating Factors: Strong capitalization index (9.6) based on excellent current risk-adjusted capital (severe loss scenario). High quality investment portfolio (9.2).

Principal Business: Comp med (96%), FEHB (4%)

Mem Phys: 13: 6,072 **12:** 5,062 **13 MLR** 92.0% **/ 13 Admin Exp** N/A

Enroll(000): Q2 14: 3 **13:** 3 **12:** 3 **Med Exp PMPM:** $340

Principal Investments: Long-term bonds (87%), cash and equiv (13%)

Provider Compensation ($000): Contr fee ($8,834), capitation ($1,809)

Total Member Encounters: Phys (8,959), non-phys (18,197)

Group Affiliation: Health Alliance Group

Licensed in: IL, IA

Address: 301 S Vine, Urbana, IL 61801

Phone: (217) 337-8406 **Dom State:** IL **Commenced Bus:** May 1997

Data Date	Rating	RACR #1	RACR #2	Total Assets ($mil)	Capital ($mil)	Net Premium ($mil)	Net Income ($mil)
6-14	E	3.42	2.85	10.4	6.1	6.8	-2.0
6-13	C-	2.54	2.12	7.5	4.6	5.7	0.0
2013	D	1.78	1.49	8.6	3.1	11.8	-1.5
2012	D+	2.52	2.10	7.9	4.6	12.2	-1.1
2011	D+	2.77	2.31	9.0	5.7	17.0	0.2
2010	D+	2.64	2.20	8.2	5.5	15.3	-0.4
2009	C	1.39	1.16	5.3	2.4	10.6	0.0

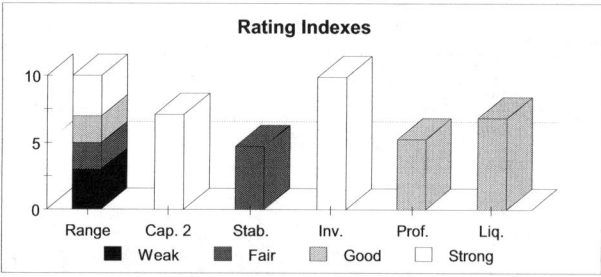

Rating Indexes

HEALTH CARE SVC CORP A MUT LEG RES *   A+   Excellent

Major Rating Factors: Excellent profitability (8.3 on a scale of 0 to 10). Strong capitalization (10.0) based on excellent current risk-adjusted capital (severe loss scenario). High quality investment portfolio (9.9).
Other Rating Factors: Excellent liquidity (7.1) with ample operational cash flow and liquid investments.
Principal Business: Comp med (73%), FEHB (18%), med supp (6%), other (2%)
Mem Phys: 13: 149,259 **12:** 141,524 **13 MLR** 85.0% **/ 13 Admin Exp** N/A
Enroll(000): Q2 14: 9,658 **13:** 8,512 **12:** 8,065 **Med Exp PMPM:** $192
Principal Investments: Long-term bonds (47%), cash and equiv (27%), real estate (9%), nonaffiliate common stock (9%), affiliate common stock (6%), other (1%)
Provider Compensation ($000): FFS ($11,090,004), contr fee ($6,673,427), capitation ($970,015), bonus arrang ($222,219), other ($433,754)
Total Member Encounters: Phys (41,614,901), non-phys (14,993,676)
Group Affiliation: HCSC Group
Licensed in: AK, AZ, AR, CO, CT, DC, DE, FL, GA, ID, IL, IN, KY, ME, MD, MA, MI, MN, MO, MT, NE, NJ, NM, OH, OK, OR, PA, SC, TX, UT, VA, WV, WI
Address: 300 East Randolph Street, Chicago, IL 60601-5099
Phone: (312) 653-6000 **Dom State:** IL **Commenced Bus:** January 1937

Data Date	Rating	RACR #1	RACR #2	Total Assets ($mil)	Capital ($mil)	Net Premium ($mil)	Net Income ($mil)
6-14	A+	7.18	5.98	18,206.4	10,353.6	13,266.7	121.8
6-13	A+	7.71	6.43	16,699.9	10,209.9	11,086.9	611.2
2013	A+	7.13	5.94	16,713.6	10,271.6	22,686.7	684.3
2012	A+	7.22	6.02	15,517.6	9,553.7	20,653.4	1,007.1
2011	A+	7.15	5.96	14,603.8	8,909.8	19,911.8	1,203.9
2010	A+	6.32	5.27	12,718.6	7,793.5	19,527.9	1,092.6
2009	A+	5.85	4.87	11,377.9	6,692.4	17,335.6	514.5

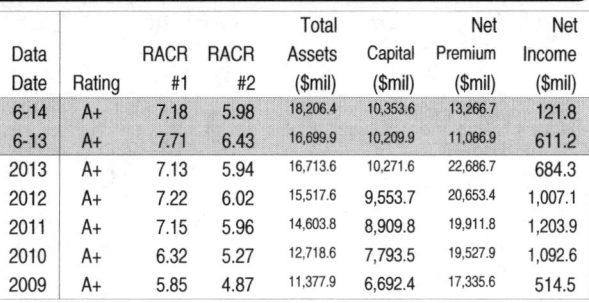

Rating Indexes

Range   Cap. 2   Stab.   Inv.   Prof.   Liq.
■ Weak   ■ Fair   ▩ Good   □ Strong

HEALTH CHOICE UTAH INC   D+   Weak

Major Rating Factors: Excellent profitability (9.8 on a scale of 0 to 10). Strong capitalization (8.0) based on excellent current risk-adjusted capital (severe loss scenario). High quality investment portfolio (9.9).
Other Rating Factors: Excellent liquidity (8.6) with ample operational cash flow and liquid investments.
Principal Business: Medicaid (100%)
Mem Phys: 13: N/A **12:** N/A **13 MLR** 78.7% **/ 13 Admin Exp** N/A
Enroll(000): Q2 14: 4 **13:** 3 **12:** 1 **Med Exp PMPM:** $225
Principal Investments: Cash and equiv (82%), long-term bonds (18%)
Provider Compensation ($000): FFS ($4,423)
Total Member Encounters: Phys (8,565), non-phys (7,519)
Group Affiliation: Iasis Healthcare LLC
Licensed in: UT
Address: 406 W South Jordan Pkwy #500, South Jordan, UT 84095-3945
Phone: (801) 984-3388 **Dom State:** UT **Commenced Bus:** April 2012

Data Date	Rating	RACR #1	RACR #2	Total Assets ($mil)	Capital ($mil)	Net Premium ($mil)	Net Income ($mil)
6-14	D+	2.17	1.81	4.4	2.8	5.6	0.2
6-13	D+	0.70	0.59	3.0	2.2	1.9	0.1
2013	D+	2.04	1.70	6.6	2.6	6.2	0.6
2012	D	0.47	0.39	2.5	1.5	0.7	0.0
2011	N/A	N/A	N/A	N/A	N/A	N/A	N/A
2010	N/A	N/A	N/A	N/A	N/A	N/A	N/A
2009	N/A	N/A	N/A	N/A	N/A	N/A	N/A

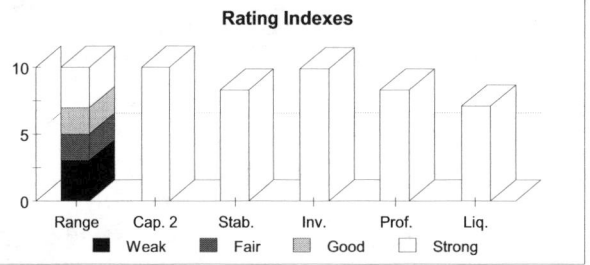

Rating Indexes

Range   Cap. 2   Stab.   Inv.   Prof.   Liq.
■ Weak   ■ Fair   ▩ Good   □ Strong

HEALTH FIRST HEALTH PLANS   C-   Fair

Major Rating Factors: Good overall results on stability tests (6.3 on a scale of 0 to 10). Excellent profitability (8.3). Strong capitalization index (7.8) based on excellent current risk-adjusted capital (severe loss scenario).
Other Rating Factors: High quality investment portfolio (9.9). Excellent liquidity (7.0) with ample operational cash flow and liquid investments.
Principal Business: Medicare (72%), comp med (27%)
Mem Phys: 13: 1,773 **12:** 1,130 **13 MLR** 82.7% **/ 13 Admin Exp** N/A
Enroll(000): Q2 14: 44 **13:** 45 **12:** 44 **Med Exp PMPM:** $556
Principal Investments: Cash and equiv (61%), long-term bonds (32%), real estate (6%)
Provider Compensation ($000): FFS ($153,094), contr fee ($137,877), capitation ($6,601)
Total Member Encounters: Phys (596,219), non-phys (251,293)
Group Affiliation: Health First Inc
Licensed in: FL
Address: 6450 U.S. Highway 1, Rockledge, FL 32955
Phone: (321) 434-5600 **Dom State:** FL **Commenced Bus:** January 1996

Data Date	Rating	RACR #1	RACR #2	Total Assets ($mil)	Capital ($mil)	Net Premium ($mil)	Net Income ($mil)
6-14	C-	1.96	1.63	112.5	61.5	182.6	4.6
6-13	C-	1.61	1.34	96.7	54.6	177.7	4.2
2013	C-	1.79	1.49	97.8	56.3	353.1	8.0
2012	C-	1.49	1.24	91.2	50.6	362.8	0.6
2011	N/A	N/A	N/A	100.4	55.0	393.0	11.5
2010	N/A	N/A	N/A	84.8	44.2	361.0	7.9
2009	C-	N/A	N/A	74.1	39.0	374.7	7.2

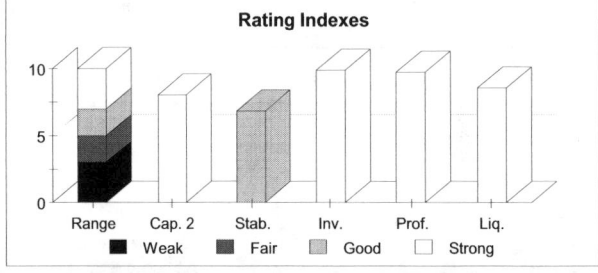

Rating Indexes

Range   Cap. 2   Stab.   Inv.   Prof.   Liq.
■ Weak   ■ Fair   ▩ Good   □ Strong

HEALTH FIRST INS INC

D+   **Weak**

Major Rating Factors: Weak profitability index (0.9 on a scale of 0 to 10). Strong capitalization (10.0) based on excellent current risk-adjusted capital (severe loss scenario). High quality investment portfolio (9.9).
Other Rating Factors: Excellent liquidity (9.0) with ample operational cash flow and liquid investments.
Principal Business: Comp med (86%), med supp (14%)
Mem Phys: 13: 1,181   **12:** 1,130   **13 MLR** 74.6%   **/ 13 Admin Exp** N/A
Enroll(000): Q2 14: 5   **13:** 1   **12:** 0   **Med Exp PMPM:** $189
Principal Investments: Cash and equiv (100%)
Provider Compensation ($000): Contr fee ($402), capitation ($13)
Total Member Encounters: Phys (2,127), non-phys (1,571)
Group Affiliation: Health First Inc
Licensed in: FL
Address: 6450 US Highway One, Rockledge, FL 32955-5747
Phone: (321) 434-5600   **Dom State:** FL   **Commenced Bus:** January 2012

Data Date	Rating	RACR #1	RACR #2	Total Assets ($mil)	Capital ($mil)	Net Premium ($mil)	Net Income ($mil)
6-14	D+	4.64	3.86	8.1	3.6	9.0	-0.6
6-13	U	15.45	12.87	2.3	1.7	0.1	-0.8
2013	D+	5.41	4.51	5.4	4.3	1.0	-1.2
2012	U	22.72	18.94	2.6	2.5	0.0	-0.5
2011	N/A	N/A	N/A	2.5	2.5	N/A	N/A
2010	N/A	N/A	N/A	N/A	N/A	N/A	N/A
2009	N/A	N/A	N/A	N/A	N/A	N/A	N/A

Rating Indexes

Range   Cap. 2   Stab.   Inv.   Prof.   Liq.
■ Weak   ▨ Fair   ▤ Good   □ Strong

HEALTH INSURANCE PLAN OF GREATER NY

B   **Good**

Major Rating Factors: Good overall profitability index (6.5 on a scale of 0 to 10). Good liquidity (6.9) with sufficient resources (cash flows and marketable investments) to handle a spike in claims. Strong capitalization (10.0) based on excellent current risk-adjusted capital (severe loss scenario).
Other Rating Factors: High quality investment portfolio (6.9).
Principal Business: Comp med (45%), Medicare (34%), Medicaid (21%)
Mem Phys: 13: 69,789   **12:** 45,059   **13 MLR** 84.7%   **/ 13 Admin Exp** N/A
Enroll(000): Q2 14: 741   **13:** 695   **12:** 718   **Med Exp PMPM:** $497
Principal Investments: Long-term bonds (64%), affiliate common stock (35%), cash and equiv (7%), real estate (5%)
Provider Compensation ($000): Contr fee ($2,007,935), capitation ($1,404,147), FFS ($795,111), salary ($63,608), other ($36,347)
Total Member Encounters: Phys (7,391,913), non-phys (3,889,608)
Group Affiliation: EmblemHealth Inc
Licensed in: NY
Address: 55 Water Street, New York, NY 10041-8190
Phone: (646) 447-5000   **Dom State:** NY   **Commenced Bus:** March 1947

Data Date	Rating	RACR #1	RACR #2	Total Assets ($mil)	Capital ($mil)	Net Premium ($mil)	Net Income ($mil)
6-14	B	3.83	3.19	2,126.2	1,334.5	2,512.5	-58.9
6-13	B	4.18	3.48	2,293.7	1,447.2	2,475.1	2.0
2013	B+	4.14	3.45	2,118.6	1,442.8	4,988.5	179.0
2012	B+	4.32	3.60	2,310.2	1,498.9	5,026.5	173.7
2011	B+	4.33	3.61	2,049.2	1,347.5	4,730.3	201.1
2010	B+	4.27	3.56	1,880.2	1,184.5	4,905.9	239.7
2009	B+	3.29	2.75	1,652.3	923.1	4,763.9	91.8

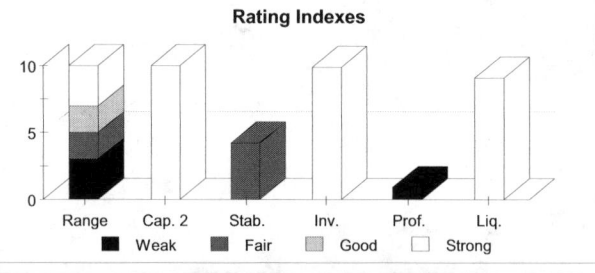

Rating Indexes

Range   Cap. 2   Stab.   Inv.   Prof.   Liq.
■ Weak   ▨ Fair   ▤ Good   □ Strong

HEALTH NET COMMUNITY SOLUTIONS INC

B-   **Good**

Major Rating Factors: Fair overall results on stability tests (4.9 on a scale of 0 to 10). Good overall profitability index (5.6). Strong capitalization index (8.0) based on excellent current risk-adjusted capital (severe loss scenario).
Other Rating Factors: Excellent liquidity (7.1) with ample operational cash flow and liquid investments.
Principal Business: Medicaid (78%)
Mem Phys: 13: N/A   **12:** N/A   **13 MLR** 86.6%   **/ 13 Admin Exp** N/A
Enroll(000): Q2 14: 1,345   **13:** 1,098   **12:** 915   **Med Exp PMPM:** $149
Principal Investments ($000): Cash and equiv ($201,004)
Provider Compensation ($000): None
Total Member Encounters: N/A
Group Affiliation: Health Net Inc
Licensed in: CA
Address: 11971 Foundation Place, Rancho Cordova, CA 95670
Phone: (818) 676-8394   **Dom State:** CA   **Commenced Bus:** June 2005

Data Date	Rating	RACR #1	RACR #2	Total Assets ($mil)	Capital ($mil)	Net Premium ($mil)	Net Income ($mil)
6-14	B-	2.90	1.80	871.0	293.2	1,885.2	59.3
6-13	N/A	N/A	N/A	442.8	200.7	1,074.6	43.1
2013	C	2.32	1.44	577.6	233.0	2,158.4	75.3
2012	N/A	N/A	N/A	358.2	158.5	1,722.8	4.5
2011	N/A	N/A	N/A	2,343.1	1,215.3	9,378.1	181.1
2010	N/A	N/A	N/A	2,537.8	1,316.9	8,953.0	146.9
2009	B-	N/A	N/A	2,354.6	1,283.6	8,721.3	172.2

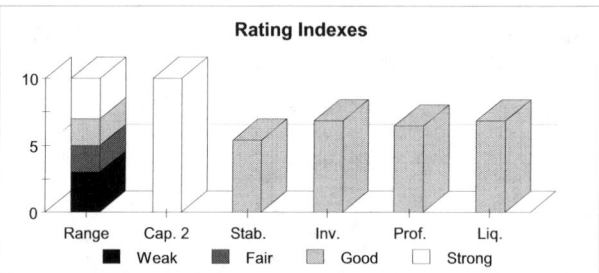

Rating Indexes

Range   Cap. 2   Stab.   Inv.   Prof.   Liq.
■ Weak   ▨ Fair   ▤ Good   □ Strong

HEALTH NET HEALTH PLAN OF OREGON INC   E   Very Weak

Major Rating Factors: Weak profitability index (1.8 on a scale of 0 to 10). Fair overall results on stability tests (3.0) based on a decline in the number of member physicians during 2014, a significant 17% decrease in enrollment during the period and a steep decline in premium revenue in 2013. Rating is significantly influenced by the fair financial results of Health Net Inc. Good liquidity (5.4) with sufficient resources (cash flows and marketable investments) to handle a spike in claims.

Other Rating Factors: Strong capitalization index (7.6) based on excellent current risk-adjusted capital (severe loss scenario). High quality investment portfolio (7.9).

Principal Business: Comp med (93%), Medicare (5%)

Mem Phys: 13: 33,361 **12:** 39,226 **13 MLR** 83.4% **/ 13 Admin Exp** N/A

Enroll(000): Q2 14: 70 **13:** 70 **12:** 84 **Med Exp PMPM:** $298

Principal Investments: Long-term bonds (112%)

Provider Compensation ($000): FFS ($251,558), capitation ($3,692)

Total Member Encounters: Phys (260,838), non-phys (222,700)

Group Affiliation: Health Net Inc

Licensed in: OR, WA

Address: 13221 SW 68th Pkwy., Ste 200, Tigard, OR 97223

Phone: (888) 802-7001 **Dom State:** OR **Commenced Bus:** September 1989

Data Date	Rating	RACR #1	RACR #2	Total Assets ($mil)	Capital ($mil)	Net Premium ($mil)	Net Income ($mil)
6-14	E	1.86	1.55	105.6	47.8	161.3	-16.3
6-13	B	1.86	1.55	114.2	56.1	147.1	5.4
2013	B-	2.11	1.76	94.6	53.3	294.1	4.6
2012	B	2.21	1.85	121.4	66.7	368.8	10.6
2011	B	2.62	2.18	113.3	70.0	354.5	21.5
2010	B	2.34	1.95	109.3	63.3	363.7	16.6
2009	B+	1.86	1.55	120.6	73.7	434.2	-3.2

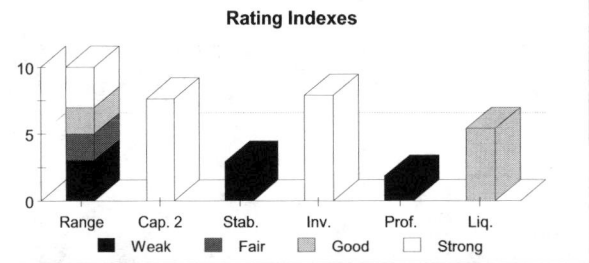

Rating Indexes

HEALTH NET LIFE INSURANCE COMPANY   B   Good

Major Rating Factors: Good liquidity (5.5 on a scale of 0 to 10) with sufficient resources to handle a spike in claims. Fair overall results on stability tests (4.9) including fair financial strength of affiliated Health Net Inc. Fair profitability (3.9) with operating losses during the first six months of 2014. Return on equity has been fair, averaging 9.0%.

Other Rating Factors: Strong capitalization (7.4) based on excellent risk adjusted capital (severe loss scenario). High quality investment portfolio (8.3).

Principal Business: Group health insurance (55%) and individual health insurance (45%).

Principal Investments: NonCMO investment grade bonds (79%), CMOs and structured securities (25%), and noninv. grade bonds (1%).

Investments in Affiliates: None

Group Affiliation: Health Net Inc

Licensed in: All states except NY, PR

Commenced Business: January 1987

Address: 225 N Main St, Pueblo, CO 81003

Phone: (719) 585-8017 **Domicile State:** CA **NAIC Code:** 66141

Data Date	Rating	RACR #1	RACR #2	Total Assets ($mil)	Capital ($mil)	Net Premium ($mil)	Net Income ($mil)
6-14	B	1.59	1.29	554.9	218.9	467.3	-36.6
6-13	B	2.58	2.08	626.5	394.3	473.0	30.7
2013	B	1.88	1.52	485.1	257.2	916.1	22.9
2012	C+	2.25	1.82	632.0	365.6	1,079.4	107.7
2011	C+	1.99	1.63	548.6	352.9	1,178.4	22.6
2010	B+	2.33	1.89	680.5	414.5	1,159.6	26.9
2009	B	2.14	1.74	643.1	383.6	1,161.6	58.2

Health Net Inc

Composite Group Rating: C+ Largest Group Members	Assets ($mil)	Rating
HEALTH NET OF CALIFORNIA INC	1948	C+
HEALTH NET COMMUNITY SOLUTIONS INC	578	C
HEALTH NET LIFE INS CO	485	B
HEALTH NET OF ARIZONA INC	350	C
HEALTH NET HEALTH PLAN OF OREGON INC	95	B-

HEALTH NET OF ARIZONA INC   D+   Weak

Major Rating Factors: Weak profitability index (1.0 on a scale of 0 to 10). Weak liquidity (0.0) as a spike in claims may stretch capacity. Fair overall results on stability tests (3.3).

Other Rating Factors: Good capitalization index (5.3) based on good current risk-adjusted capital (severe loss scenario). High quality investment portfolio (9.7).

Principal Business: Medicare (69%), comp med (21%), FEHB (11%)

Mem Phys: 13: 15,924 **12:** 13,742 **13 MLR** 90.3% **/ 13 Admin Exp** N/A

Enroll(000): Q2 14: 153 **13:** 94 **12:** 98 **Med Exp PMPM:** $572

Principal Investments: Long-term bonds (91%), cash and equiv (9%)

Provider Compensation ($000): Contr fee ($453,740), capitation ($170,076), bonus arrang ($2,020)

Total Member Encounters: Phys (726,971), non-phys (687,073)

Group Affiliation: Health Net Inc

Licensed in: AZ

Address: 1230 W.Washington St., Ste 401, Tempe, AZ 85281-1245

Phone: (602) 794-1400 **Dom State:** AZ **Commenced Bus:** November 1981

Data Date	Rating	RACR #1	RACR #2	Total Assets ($mil)	Capital ($mil)	Net Premium ($mil)	Net Income ($mil)
6-14	D+	0.97	0.81	419.2	43.9	412.9	-32.4
6-13	C	1.15	0.96	279.6	69.2	362.3	-9.2
2013	C	1.84	1.54	350.3	85.3	721.0	-4.7
2012	C+	1.34	1.11	218.1	77.5	724.9	-10.2
2011	C+	1.51	1.26	168.1	89.5	661.9	-17.2
2010	B	1.66	1.39	162.8	82.5	688.4	0.9
2009	B	1.87	1.56	196.9	108.8	802.8	19.3

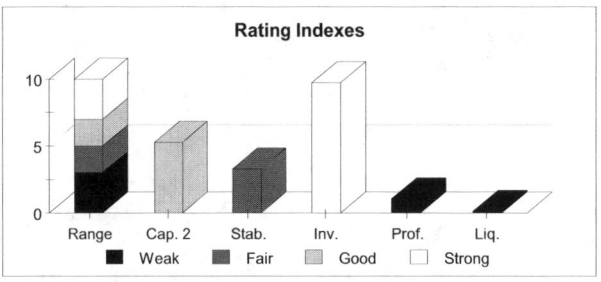

Rating Indexes

HEALTH NET OF CALIFORNIA INC   C+   Fair

Major Rating Factors: Fair overall results on stability tests (4.4 on a scale of 0 to 10) based on a significant 19% decrease in enrollment during the period. Good overall profitability index (5.4). Strong capitalization index (7.7) based on excellent current risk-adjusted capital (severe loss scenario)

Other Rating Factors: Excellent liquidity (7.1) with ample operational cash flow and liquid investments.

Principal Business: Medicare (32%), Medicaid (1%)

Mem Phys: 13: N/A **12:** N/A **13 MLR** 88.5% **/ 13 Admin Exp** N/A

Enroll(000): Q2 14: 1,284 **13:** 1,123 **12:** 1,381 **Med Exp PMPM:** $442

Principal Investments ($000): Cash and equiv ($1,349,472)

Provider Compensation ($000): None

Total Member Encounters: N/A

Group Affiliation: Health Net Inc

Licensed in: CA

Address: 21281 Burbank Blvd, Woodland Hills, CA 91367

Phone: (818) 676-6775 **Dom State:** CA **Commenced Bus:** March 1979

Data Date	Rating	RACR #1	RACR #2	Total Assets ($mil)	Capital ($mil)	Net Premium ($mil)	Net Income ($mil)
6-14	C+	2.57	1.59	2,315.3	955.5	3,645.2	7.3
6-13	B-	2.38	1.47	2,098.9	1,008.7	3,598.5	41.5
2013	C+	2.42	1.50	1,948.3	922.2	7,078.8	65.4
2012	B-	2.54	1.57	2,196.0	1,068.9	7,836.5	113.9
2011	B	2.51	1.55	2,343.1	1,215.3	9,378.1	181.1
2010	B	2.72	1.69	2,537.8	1,316.9	8,953.0	146.9
2009	B+	2.66	1.66	2,354.6	1,283.6	8,721.3	172.2

Rating Indexes

HEALTH NEW ENGLAND INC   B   Good

Major Rating Factors: Good capitalization index (5.9 on a scale of 0 to 10) based on good current risk-adjusted capital (severe loss scenario). Good liquidity (6.2) with sufficient resources (cash flows and marketable investments) to handle a spike in claims. Fair profitability index (4.7).

Other Rating Factors: High quality investment portfolio (8.6). Excellent overall results on stability tests (7.3).

Principal Business: Comp med (73%), Medicare (15%), Medicaid (12%)

Mem Phys: 13: 10,269 **12:** 9,192 **13 MLR** 89.6% **/ 13 Admin Exp** N/A

Enroll(000): Q2 14: 113 **13:** 110 **12:** 105 **Med Exp PMPM:** $376

Principal Investments: Long-term bonds (66%), nonaffiliate common stock (15%), cash and equiv (13%), affiliate common stock (4%), other (1%)

Provider Compensation ($000): Contr fee ($324,027), FFS ($99,442), bonus arrang ($59,015), capitation ($5,086)

Total Member Encounters: Phys (777,914), non-phys (94,065)

Group Affiliation: Baystate Health Inc

Licensed in: MA

Address: 1 Monarch Pl, Ste 1500, Springfield, MA 01144-1006

Phone: (413) 787-4000 **Dom State:** MA **Commenced Bus:** January 1986

Data Date	Rating	RACR #1	RACR #2	Total Assets ($mil)	Capital ($mil)	Net Premium ($mil)	Net Income ($mil)
6-14	B	1.07	0.89	144.3	55.3	285.9	-3.0
6-13	B-	0.79	0.66	124.6	37.8	267.8	-4.1
2013	B-	1.02	0.85	137.0	52.6	546.6	2.3
2012	A-	1.17	0.98	127.6	50.3	494.2	2.2
2011	A	1.27	1.06	133.6	53.7	460.6	10.1
2010	A	1.24	1.04	102.2	46.8	392.3	7.3
2009	B+	1.35	1.13	82.4	41.7	307.6	3.2

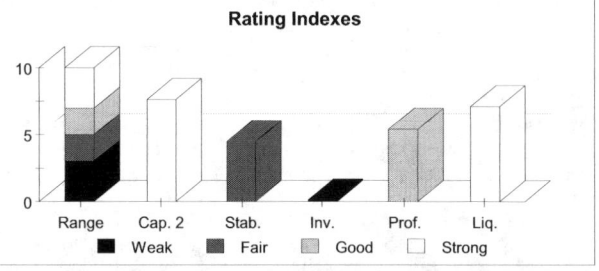

Rating Indexes

HEALTH PARTNERS PLANS INC   B   Good

Major Rating Factors: Good liquidity (6.8 on a scale of 0 to 10) with sufficient resources (cash flows and marketable investments) to handle a spike in claims. Fair profitability index (4.3). Strong capitalization index (6.9) based on excellent current risk-adjusted capital (severe loss scenario).

Other Rating Factors: High quality investment portfolio (9.9). Excellent overall results on stability tests (7.6).

Principal Business: Medicaid (99%), other (1%)

Mem Phys: 13: 5,109 **12:** 4,828 **13 MLR** 85.3% **/ 13 Admin Exp** N/A

Enroll(000): Q2 14: 188 **13:** 185 **12:** 165 **Med Exp PMPM:** $409

Principal Investments: Cash and equiv (51%), long-term bonds (49%)

Provider Compensation ($000): Contr fee ($691,077), capitation ($26,243)

Total Member Encounters: Phys (1,351,081), non-phys (227,709)

Group Affiliation: None

Licensed in: PA

Address: 901 Market St Suite 500, Philadelphia, PA 19107-3111

Phone: (215) 849-9606 **Dom State:** PA **Commenced Bus:** October 1988

Data Date	Rating	RACR #1	RACR #2	Total Assets ($mil)	Capital ($mil)	Net Premium ($mil)	Net Income ($mil)
6-14	B	1.31	1.09	332.9	90.4	535.0	-0.5
6-13	B	1.26	1.05	296.2	87.3	469.7	-0.3
2013	B	1.30	1.08	296.5	89.9	1,000.3	-0.2
2012	B	1.25	1.04	273.6	86.7	1,034.9	-1.6
2011	B	1.30	1.09	259.2	87.6	1,048.4	7.6
2010	B	1.28	1.07	265.0	80.5	963.0	9.2
2009	B	1.26	1.05	191.6	70.8	805.5	2.9

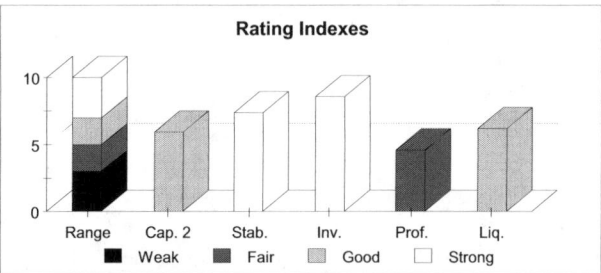

Rating Indexes

HEALTH PLAN OF CAREOREGON INC   B   Good

Major Rating Factors: Good liquidity (6.7 on a scale of 0 to 10) with sufficient resources (cash flows and marketable investments) to handle a spike in claims. Excellent profitability (7.8). Strong capitalization (9.1) based on excellent current risk-adjusted capital (severe loss scenario).

Other Rating Factors: High quality investment portfolio (9.9).

Principal Business: Medicare (100%)

Mem Phys: 13: 1,521 **12:** 1,483 **13 MLR** 86.6% **/ 13 Admin Exp** N/A

Enroll(000): Q2 14: 10 **13:** 9 **12:** 9 **Med Exp PMPM:** $919

Principal Investments: Long-term bonds (91%), cash and equiv (9%)

Provider Compensation ($000): Contr fee ($74,174), FFS ($25,112)

Total Member Encounters: Phys (66,299), non-phys (38,953)

Group Affiliation: CareOregon Inc

Licensed in: OR

Address: 315 SW Fifth Ave Suite 900, Portland, OR 97204-1753

Phone: (503) 416-4100 **Dom State:** OR **Commenced Bus:** March 2005

Data Date	Rating	RACR #1	RACR #2	Total Assets ($mil)	Capital ($mil)	Net Premium ($mil)	Net Income ($mil)
6-14	B	3.01	2.51	65.7	38.6	62.7	-0.3
6-13	B	3.36	2.80	63.3	38.9	56.4	0.0
2013	B	3.13	2.61	66.9	40.1	115.5	0.5
2012	B	3.35	2.79	57.9	38.7	105.6	3.9
2011	B	3.64	3.04	49.8	34.6	95.2	6.4
2010	N/A	N/A	N/A	41.7	28.6	79.0	2.3
2009	C+	3.86	3.22	40.7	27.0	70.6	3.7

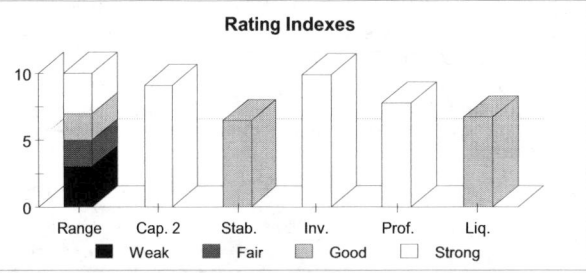

Rating Indexes

■ Weak ▩ Fair ▤ Good □ Strong

HEALTH PLAN OF NEVADA INC   B   Good

Major Rating Factors: Good overall profitability index (6.8 on a scale of 0 to 10). Good liquidity (6.9) with sufficient resources (cash flows and marketable investments) to handle a spike in claims. Fair overall results on stability tests (4.5). Rating is significantly influenced by the fair financial results of UnitedHealth Group Inc.

Other Rating Factors: Strong capitalization index (8.6) based on excellent current risk-adjusted capital (severe loss scenario). High quality investment portfolio (9.5).

Principal Business: Comp med (49%), Medicare (37%), Medicaid (12%), FEHB (1%)

Mem Phys: 13: 5,579 **12:** 5,487 **13 MLR** 82.3% **/ 13 Admin Exp** N/A

Enroll(000): Q2 14: 496 **13:** 415 **12:** 393 **Med Exp PMPM:** $264

Principal Investments: Long-term bonds (79%), cash and equiv (13%), real estate (6%), pref stock (1%)

Provider Compensation ($000): Contr fee ($654,080), capitation ($630,809), FFS ($2,324)

Total Member Encounters: Phys (2,315,987), non-phys (1,106,011)

Group Affiliation: UnitedHealth Group Inc

Licensed in: NV

Address: 2720 N Tenaya Way, Las Vegas, NV 89128

Phone: (702) 242-7732 **Dom State:** NV **Commenced Bus:** August 1982

Data Date	Rating	RACR #1	RACR #2	Total Assets ($mil)	Capital ($mil)	Net Premium ($mil)	Net Income ($mil)
6-14	B	2.66	2.21	423.1	159.5	911.3	30.2
6-13	B	3.10	2.58	326.3	173.2	781.5	46.5
2013	B	3.63	3.02	381.5	224.3	1,564.2	97.6
2012	B	3.56	2.97	342.4	201.7	1,493.7	115.1
2011	B	3.23	2.69	365.7	202.0	1,580.4	97.4
2010	B	2.31	1.93	363.1	152.4	1,525.8	36.4
2009	B	1.80	1.50	335.3	121.9	1,526.8	-3.2

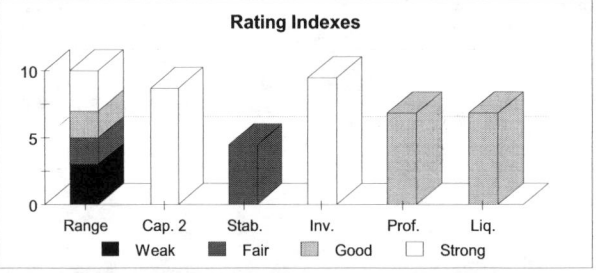

Rating Indexes

■ Weak ▩ Fair ▤ Good □ Strong

HEALTH PLAN OF SAN JOAQUIN   B   Good

Major Rating Factors: Good overall profitability index (5.4 on a scale of 0 to 10). Good overall results on stability tests (5.3). Strong capitalization index (7.3) based on excellent current risk-adjusted capital (severe loss scenario).

Other Rating Factors: Excellent liquidity (7.1) with ample operational cash flow and liquid investments.

Principal Business: Medicaid (100%)

Mem Phys: 13: N/A **12:** N/A **13 MLR** 92.7% **/ 13 Admin Exp** N/A

Enroll(000): Q2 14: 192 **13:** 189 **12:** 130 **Med Exp PMPM:** $154

Principal Investments ($000): Cash and equiv ($50,214)

Provider Compensation ($000): None

Total Member Encounters: N/A

Group Affiliation: None

Licensed in: CA

Address: 7751 S Manthey, French Camp, CA 95231-9802

Phone: (209) 939-3500 **Dom State:** CA **Commenced Bus:** February 1996

Data Date	Rating	RACR #1	RACR #2	Total Assets ($mil)	Capital ($mil)	Net Premium ($mil)	Net Income ($mil)
6-14	B	2.14	1.32	127.9	51.3	190.3	-2.1
6-13	B	2.62	1.62	79.4	46.2	115.8	-4.2
2013	B	2.23	1.38	115.1	53.4	301.5	3.0
2012	B	2.92	1.81	81.3	50.4	204.0	0.8
2011	B-	3.88	2.40	70.9	49.6	160.6	6.9
2010	B-	3.43	2.13	63.4	42.7	147.1	6.4
2009	C+	3.18	1.98	53.0	36.3	127.1	2.1

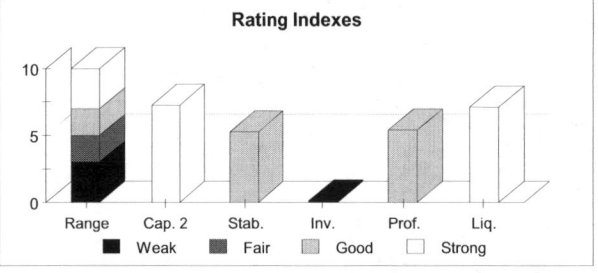

Rating Indexes

■ Weak ▩ Fair ▤ Good □ Strong

HEALTH PLAN OF THE UPPER OHIO VALLEY *   B+   Good

Major Rating Factors: Good overall profitability index (6.1 on a scale of 0 to 10). Good quality investment portfolio (6.8). Good liquidity (6.7) with sufficient resources (cash flows and marketable investments) to handle a spike in claims.
Other Rating Factors: Strong capitalization index (9.8) based on excellent current risk-adjusted capital (severe loss scenario). Excellent overall results on stability tests (7.2).
Principal Business: Comp med (39%), Medicare (38%), Medicaid (20%), FEHB (2%)
Mem Phys: 13: 15,403   **12:** 14,327   **13 MLR** 91.2%   **/ 13 Admin Exp** N/A
Enroll(000): Q2 14: 79   **13:** 78   **12:** 81   **Med Exp PMPM:** $359
Principal Investments: Nonaffiliate common stock (43%), long-term bonds (41%), affiliate common stock (7%), cash and equiv (7%), real estate (2%)
Provider Compensation ($000): Contr fee ($322,320), FFS ($8,523)
Total Member Encounters: Phys (696,112), non-phys (141,795)
Group Affiliation: Health Plan Group
Licensed in: OH, WV
Address: 52160 National Rd E, St Clairsville, OH 43950
Phone: (740) 695-3585   **Dom State:** WV   **Commenced Bus:** November 1979

Data Date	Rating	RACR #1	RACR #2	Total Assets ($mil)	Capital ($mil)	Net Premium ($mil)	Net Income ($mil)
6-14	B+	3.58	2.98	253.1	196.4	191.9	7.4
6-13	B	3.76	3.14	246.6	190.6	188.4	0.5
2013	B+	3.58	2.98	248.8	196.0	364.6	16.2
2012	B+	3.76	3.14	243.1	190.0	376.9	9.0
2011	B+	3.52	2.93	235.6	179.7	383.3	22.8
2010	B+	4.03	3.36	226.8	175.7	380.5	33.9
2009	B	3.14	2.62	198.1	148.1	399.8	14.8

HEALTH TRADITION HEALTH PLAN   B   Good

Major Rating Factors: Good overall profitability index (6.7 on a scale of 0 to 10). Good capitalization index (5.9) based on good current risk-adjusted capital (severe loss scenario). High quality investment portfolio (9.9).
Other Rating Factors: Excellent overall results on stability tests (7.9). Excellent liquidity (7.0) with sufficient resources (cash flows and marketable investments) to handle a spike in claims
Principal Business: Comp med (86%), Medicaid (12%), med supp (3%)
Mem Phys: 13: 1,439   **12:** 1,387   **13 MLR** 90.9%   **/ 13 Admin Exp** N/A
Enroll(000): Q2 14: 38   **13:** 36   **12:** 37   **Med Exp PMPM:** $317
Principal Investments: Cash and equiv (68%), long-term bonds (32%)
Provider Compensation ($000): Capitation ($91,902), FFS ($29,222), other ($16,099)
Total Member Encounters: Phys (220,774), non-phys (116,336)
Group Affiliation: Mayo Clinic
Licensed in: WI
Address: 1808 E Main St, Onalaska, WI 54650
Phone: (507) 538-5212   **Dom State:** WI   **Commenced Bus:** April 1986

Data Date	Rating	RACR #1	RACR #2	Total Assets ($mil)	Capital ($mil)	Net Premium ($mil)	Net Income ($mil)
6-14	B	1.07	0.89	25.3	12.5	84.0	0.3
6-13	B	1.07	0.89	30.2	12.6	74.3	0.3
2013	B	1.07	0.89	30.2	12.5	151.3	0.3
2012	B	1.04	0.87	27.7	12.2	144.5	0.5
2011	B	1.06	0.88	33.8	11.9	139.1	0.3
2010	B	0.96	0.80	29.7	11.6	137.1	0.4
2009	B-	0.77	0.64	16.5	8.3	131.8	0.3

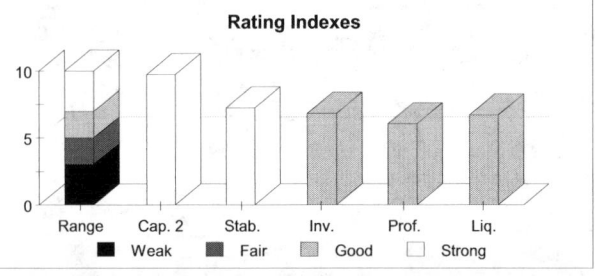

HEALTHAMERICA PENNSYLVANIA INC   B   Good

Major Rating Factors: Good quality investment portfolio (5.5 on a scale of 0 to 10). Good liquidity (6.0) with sufficient resources (cash flows and marketable investments) to handle a spike in claims. Fair overall results on stability tests (3.4) based on a steep decline in capital during 2013, an excessive 57% enrollment growth during the period. Rating is significantly influenced by the good financial results of Aetna Inc.
Other Rating Factors: Excellent profitability (7.1). Strong capitalization index (7.8) based on excellent current risk-adjusted capital (severe loss scenario).
Principal Business: Medicare (50%), Medicaid (43%), FEHB (3%), comp med (3%)
Mem Phys: 13: 50,810   **12:** 47,784   **13 MLR** 87.0%   **/ 13 Admin Exp** N/A
Enroll(000): Q2 14: 165   **13:** 142   **12:** 91   **Med Exp PMPM:** $454
Principal Investments: Long-term bonds (94%), cash and equiv (6%)
Provider Compensation ($000): Contr fee ($618,002), capitation ($32,734), FFS ($15,093), other ($1)
Total Member Encounters: Phys (1,316,705), non-phys (121,558)
Group Affiliation: Aetna Inc
Licensed in: OH, PA
Address: 600 N Second St Suite 500, Harrisburg, PA 17101
Phone: (800) 788-6445   **Dom State:** PA   **Commenced Bus:** January 1975

Data Date	Rating	RACR #1	RACR #2	Total Assets ($mil)	Capital ($mil)	Net Premium ($mil)	Net Income ($mil)
6-14	B	1.98	1.65	307.0	76.3	554.3	-10.1
6-13	B	4.29	3.58	219.8	102.0	382.0	13.5
2013	B	2.13	1.78	227.7	83.0	809.5	20.1
2012	B	4.54	3.79	199.5	108.8	563.0	60.8
2011	B-	3.87	3.23	194.9	78.0	473.3	28.9
2010	B-	4.17	3.48	197.5	87.5	478.0	36.1
2009	B+	3.52	2.94	206.9	97.8	608.3	23.5

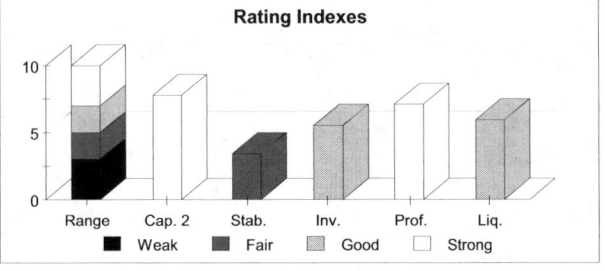

HEALTHASSURANCE PENNSYLVANIA INC   B   Good

Major Rating Factors: Good quality investment portfolio (5.1 on a scale of 0 to 10). Good liquidity (6.5) with sufficient resources (cash flows and marketable investments) to handle a spike in claims. Fair overall results on stability tests (4.7). Rating is significantly influenced by the good financial results of Aetna Inc.
Other Rating Factors: Excellent profitability (8.2). Strong capitalization index (9.4) based on excellent current risk-adjusted capital (severe loss scenario).
Principal Business: Comp med (58%), Medicare (42%)
Mem Phys: 13: 50,801   **12:** 47,765   **13 MLR** 86.0%   **/ 13 Admin Exp** N/A
Enroll(000): Q2 14: 182   **13:** 188   **12:** 203   **Med Exp PMPM:** $391
Principal Investments: Long-term bonds (95%), cash and equiv (4%)
Provider Compensation ($000): Contr fee ($856,127), capitation ($46,669), FFS ($27,369), other ($38)
Total Member Encounters: Phys (1,619,062), non-phys (293,236)
Group Affiliation: Aetna Inc
Licensed in: PA
Address: 3721 Tecport Dr. PO Box 67103, Harrisburg, PA 17106-7103
Phone: (800) 788-6445   **Dom State:** PA   **Commenced Bus:** June 2001

Data Date	Rating	RACR #1	RACR #2	Total Assets ($mil)	Capital ($mil)	Net Premium ($mil)	Net Income ($mil)
6-14	B	3.26	2.71	341.5	185.1	565.4	11.6
6-13	B+	2.85	2.37	271.9	157.7	536.3	21.2
2013	B	3.02	2.52	283.5	170.5	1,065.1	30.0
2012	B+	3.42	2.85	315.1	192.2	1,051.0	39.4
2011	B+	2.98	2.49	316.1	165.6	1,068.6	35.3
2010	B+	3.19	2.66	283.2	158.6	994.4	44.5
2009	B	2.72	2.26	213.5	114.3	827.9	26.3

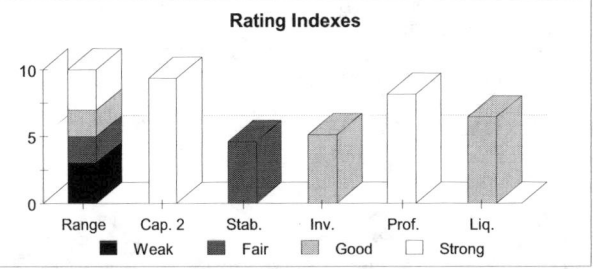

Rating Indexes

HEALTHCARE USA OF MISSOURI LLC *   A-   Excellent

Major Rating Factors: Excellent profitability (7.8 on a scale of 0 to 10). Strong capitalization index (10.0) based on excellent current risk-adjusted capital (severe loss scenario). High quality investment portfolio (8.9).
Other Rating Factors: Excellent overall results on stability tests (7.6). Rating is significantly influenced by the good financial results of Aetna Inc. Excellent liquidity (7.0) with sufficient resources (cash flows and marketable investments) to handle a spike in claims.
Principal Business: Medicaid (100%)
Mem Phys: 13: 12,772   **12:** 9,572   **13 MLR** 85.1%   **/ 13 Admin Exp** N/A
Enroll(000): Q2 14: 234   **13:** 243   **12:** 253   **Med Exp PMPM:** $190
Principal Investments: Long-term bonds (72%), cash and equiv (28%)
Provider Compensation ($000): Contr fee ($376,650), capitation ($168,862), FFS ($18,525)
Total Member Encounters: Phys (1,053,246), non-phys (182,040)
Group Affiliation: Aetna Inc
Licensed in: MO
Address: 10 S Broadway #1200, St Louis, MO 63102-1712
Phone: (314) 241-5300   **Dom State:** MO   **Commenced Bus:** July 1995

Data Date	Rating	RACR #1	RACR #2	Total Assets ($mil)	Capital ($mil)	Net Premium ($mil)	Net Income ($mil)
6-14	A-	3.61	3.01	203.4	102.7	330.3	-1.7
6-13	A-	3.27	2.72	168.1	93.3	337.7	23.8
2013	A-	3.65	3.05	164.0	104.0	669.4	32.9
2012	B+	3.33	2.77	152.1	95.2	658.5	19.7
2011	B+	3.50	2.92	144.6	89.4	499.3	3.5
2010	B+	3.22	2.68	126.2	76.5	499.9	15.1
2009	B+	2.63	2.19	128.4	70.2	557.4	10.2

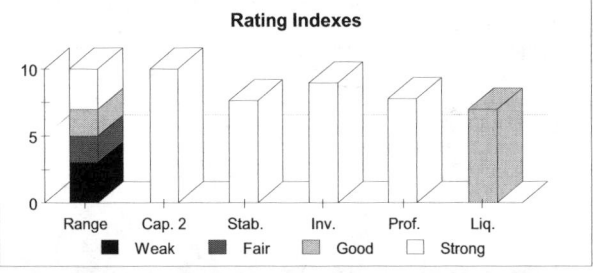

Rating Indexes

HEALTHFIRST HEALTH PLAN NEW JERSEY   E   Very Weak

Major Rating Factors: Weak profitability index (0.9 on a scale of 0 to 10). Fair capitalization (3.4) based on weak current risk-adjusted capital (moderate loss scenario). Good liquidity (6.4) with sufficient resources (cash flows and marketable investments) to handle a spike in claims.
Other Rating Factors: High quality investment portfolio (9.9).
Principal Business: Medicaid (68%), Medicare (32%)
Mem Phys: 13: 4,345   **12:** 3,565   **13 MLR** 93.4%   **/ 13 Admin Exp** N/A
Enroll(000): Q2 14: 49   **13:** 48   **12:** 51   **Med Exp PMPM:** $460
Principal Investments: Cash and equiv (100%)
Provider Compensation ($000): Contr fee ($195,914), FFS ($43,205), capitation ($2,508)
Total Member Encounters: Phys (630,166), non-phys (1,960,665)
Group Affiliation: HF Management Services LLC
Licensed in: NJ
Address: 25 Broadway, New York, NY 10004
Phone: (212) 801-6000   **Dom State:** NJ   **Commenced Bus:** January 2008

Data Date	Rating	RACR #1	RACR #2	Total Assets ($mil)	Capital ($mil)	Net Premium ($mil)	Net Income ($mil)
6-14	E	0.69	0.58	82.6	23.1	158.4	-0.2
6-13	B-	0.90	0.75	61.2	28.3	122.4	0.0
2013	E	0.37	0.31	55.2	13.2	265.3	-15.9
2012	B-	0.81	0.67	65.4	25.7	279.4	0.1
2011	C	0.68	0.57	52.7	14.7	181.1	0.0
2010	C+	0.65	0.54	26.7	8.7	98.2	0.5
2009	C	0.68	0.57	14.4	5.9	39.2	-0.2

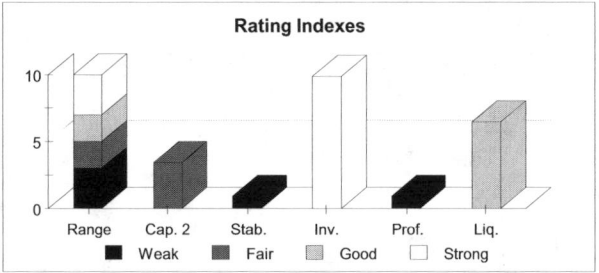

Rating Indexes

HEALTHKEEPERS INC *

A-   Excellent

Major Rating Factors: Excellent profitability (8.6 on a scale of 0 to 10). Strong capitalization index (8.9) based on excellent current risk-adjusted capital (severe loss scenario). Good quality investment portfolio (6.3).

Other Rating Factors: Good liquidity (6.8) with sufficient resources (cash flows and marketable investments) to handle a spike in claims. Fair overall results on stability tests (4.7). Rating is significantly influenced by the good financial results of WellPoint Inc.

Principal Business: Medicaid (54%), comp med (46%)

Mem Phys: 13: 18,897 **12:** 17,015 **13 MLR** 86.8% **/ 13 Admin Exp** N/A

Enroll(000): Q2 14: 495 **13:** 424 **12:** 465 **Med Exp PMPM:** $283

Principal Investments: Long-term bonds (69%), nonaffiliate common stock (25%), cash and equiv (6%)

Provider Compensation ($000): Contr fee ($1,148,415), bonus arrang ($224,108), FFS ($36,984), capitation ($23,973)

Total Member Encounters: Phys (4,808,518), non-phys (596,530)

Group Affiliation: WellPoint Inc

Licensed in: VA

Address: 2015 Staples Mills Road, Richmond, VA 23230

Phone: (804) 354-7000 **Dom State:** VA **Commenced Bus:** September 1986

Data Date	Rating	RACR #1	RACR #2	Total Assets ($mil)	Capital ($mil)	Net Premium ($mil)	Net Income ($mil)
6-14	A-	2.88	2.40	650.1	271.9	932.4	20.7
6-13	A	2.12	1.77	547.8	209.6	803.1	29.7
2013	A-	2.65	2.21	490.8	249.2	1,658.7	70.3
2012	A+	2.78	2.32	515.3	278.8	1,762.2	104.4
2011	A+	2.50	2.08	509.6	252.7	1,808.4	103.5
2010	A+	3.77	3.14	511.9	279.7	1,365.7	129.3
2009	A+	3.29	2.74	490.8	257.2	1,292.2	42.2

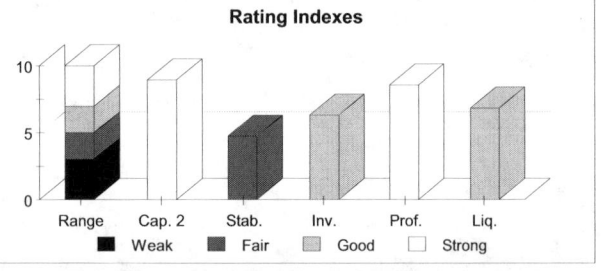

Rating Indexes

Range, Cap. 2, Stab., Inv., Prof., Liq.
■ Weak ■ Fair ▨ Good ☐ Strong

HEALTHNOW NY INC *

B+   Good

Major Rating Factors: Good liquidity (6.8 on a scale of 0 to 10) with sufficient resources (cash flows and marketable investments) to handle a spike in claims. Strong capitalization (9.2) based on excellent current risk-adjusted capital (severe loss scenario). High quality investment portfolio (8.9).

Other Rating Factors: Fair profitability index (4.0).

Principal Business: Comp med (55%), Medicare (29%), Medicaid (9%), FEHB (2%), other (4%)

Mem Phys: 13: 26,318 **12:** 24,778 **13 MLR** 89.9% **/ 13 Admin Exp** N/A

Enroll(000): Q2 14: 441 **13:** 458 **12:** 473 **Med Exp PMPM:** $399

Principal Investments: Long-term bonds (76%), nonaffiliate common stock (19%), pref stock (1%), cash and equiv (1%), affiliate common stock (1%), other (2%)

Provider Compensation ($000): Contr fee ($2,165,931), capitation ($42,105)

Total Member Encounters: Phys (7,209,228), non-phys (4,421,232)

Group Affiliation: HealthNow Systems Inc

Licensed in: NY

Address: 257 W Genesee St, Buffalo, NY 14202

Phone: (716) 887-6900 **Dom State:** NY **Commenced Bus:** March 1940

Data Date	Rating	RACR #1	RACR #2	Total Assets ($mil)	Capital ($mil)	Net Premium ($mil)	Net Income ($mil)
6-14	B+	3.15	2.62	1,063.7	573.4	1,211.8	-24.7
6-13	A	3.15	2.62	1,002.2	558.2	1,229.1	-0.5
2013	A	3.27	2.72	1,009.5	591.7	2,463.2	31.7
2012	A	3.20	2.66	1,010.3	556.8	2,455.4	31.5
2011	A	2.97	2.47	983.0	528.9	2,396.6	3.9
2010	A	3.31	2.75	945.6	567.6	2,397.1	52.7
2009	A-	3.15	2.63	896.6	546.2	2,454.1	62.0

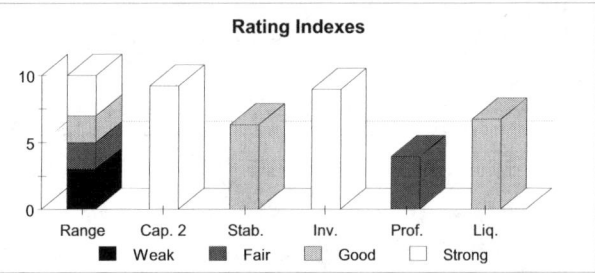

Rating Indexes

Range, Cap. 2, Stab., Inv., Prof., Liq.
■ Weak ■ Fair ▨ Good ☐ Strong

HEALTHPARTNERS *

B+   Good

Major Rating Factors: Good overall results on stability tests (6.0 on a scale of 0 to 10) despite a decline in the number of member physicians during 2014. Excellent profitability (8.7). Strong capitalization index (10.0) based on excellent current risk-adjusted capital (severe loss scenario)

Other Rating Factors: High quality investment portfolio (9.9). Excellent liquidity (7.4) with ample operational cash flow and liquid investments.

Principal Business: Comp med (51%), Medicaid (44%), dental (4%), Medicare (1%)

Mem Phys: 13: 49,353 **12:** 67,042 **13 MLR** 86.1% **/ 13 Admin Exp** N/A

Enroll(000): Q2 14: 250 **13:** 224 **12:** 235 **Med Exp PMPM:** $412

Principal Investments: Cash and equiv (45%), long-term bonds (45%), nonaffiliate common stock (9%), other (1%)

Provider Compensation ($000): Bonus arrang ($697,533), contr fee ($321,987)

Total Member Encounters: Phys (1,934,994), non-phys (253,763)

Group Affiliation: HealthPartners Inc

Licensed in: MN

Address: 8100 34th Ave S, Minneapolis, MN 55440-1309

Phone: (952) 883-6000 **Dom State:** MN **Commenced Bus:** March 1984

Data Date	Rating	RACR #1	RACR #2	Total Assets ($mil)	Capital ($mil)	Net Premium ($mil)	Net Income ($mil)
6-14	B+	3.94	3.28	1,138.9	899.0	665.2	23.7
6-13	B-	3.72	3.10	934.5	784.4	636.4	29.8
2013	B+	3.71	3.09	1,055.6	846.4	1,279.2	65.6
2012	C-	3.30	2.75	866.7	709.1	1,379.2	106.4
2011	N/A	N/A	N/A	810.4	616.9	1,352.1	N/A
2010	N/A	N/A	N/A	644.5	497.4	1,519.3	N/A
2009	N/A	N/A	N/A	544.9	386.6	1,590.7	N/A

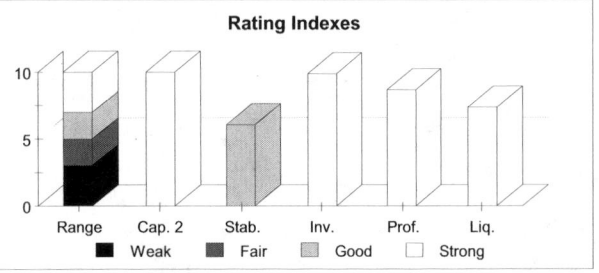

Rating Indexes

Range, Cap. 2, Stab., Inv., Prof., Liq.
■ Weak ■ Fair ▨ Good ☐ Strong

HEALTHPARTNERS INS CO *   A-   Excellent

Major Rating Factors: Excellent profitability (7.5 on a scale of 0 to 10). Strong capitalization (9.1) based on excellent current risk-adjusted capital (severe loss scenario). High quality investment portfolio (9.9).
Other Rating Factors: Good liquidity (6.7) with sufficient resources (cash flows and marketable investments) to handle a spike in claims.
Principal Business: Comp med (93%), dental (1%), other (6%)
Mem Phys: 13: 49,353 **12:** 48,557 **13 MLR** 85.9% **/ 13 Admin Exp** N/A
Enroll(000): Q2 14: 538 **13:** 493 **12:** 518 **Med Exp PMPM:** $128
Principal Investments: Long-term bonds (73%), cash and equiv (27%)
Provider Compensation ($000): Bonus arrang ($402,292), contr fee ($370,603)
Total Member Encounters: Phys (1,158,665), non-phys (143,702)
Group Affiliation: HealthPartners Inc
Licensed in: MN, WI
Address: 8170 33rd Ave S, Minneapolis, MN 55440-1309
Phone: (952) 883-6000 **Dom State:** MN **Commenced Bus:** January 1991

Data Date	Rating	RACR #1	RACR #2	Total Assets ($mil)	Capital ($mil)	Net Premium ($mil)	Net Income ($mil)
6-14	A-	3.05	2.54	325.5	166.5	465.7	17.6
6-13	A-	3.10	2.59	284.2	164.8	459.7	16.1
2013	A-	2.75	2.29	279.0	148.9	892.7	1.3
2012	A-	2.76	2.30	272.3	148.9	880.7	14.0
2011	A-	1.64	1.36	248.8	113.2	861.4	32.7
2010	A-	1.45	1.21	194.6	84.2	663.5	16.7
2009	B	1.41	1.17	128.0	64.2	447.4	11.6

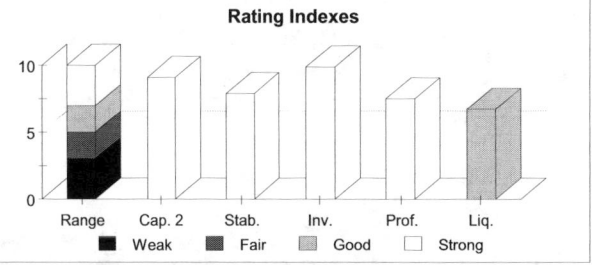

HEALTHPLUS INS CO   C   Fair

Major Rating Factors: Weak profitability index (0.9 on a scale of 0 to 10). Good capitalization (6.5) based on good current risk-adjusted capital (severe loss scenario). High quality investment portfolio (9.9).
Other Rating Factors: Excellent liquidity (7.0) with sufficient resources (cash flows and marketable investments) to handle a spike in claims.
Principal Business: Comp med (92%), Medicare (8%)
Mem Phys: 13: 6,828 **12:** 6,153 **13 MLR** 92.7% **/ 13 Admin Exp** N/A
Enroll(000): Q2 14: 55 **13:** 51 **12:** 51 **Med Exp PMPM:** $304
Principal Investments: Cash and equiv (99%), long-term bonds (1%)
Provider Compensation ($000): Contr fee ($129,637), FFS ($60,146)
Total Member Encounters: Phys (77,041), non-phys (258,945)
Group Affiliation: HealthPlus of Michigan
Licensed in: MI
Address: 2050 S Linden Rd, Flint, MI 48532
Phone: (810) 230-2000 **Dom State:** MI **Commenced Bus:** January 2007

Data Date	Rating	RACR #1	RACR #2	Total Assets ($mil)	Capital ($mil)	Net Premium ($mil)	Net Income ($mil)
6-14	C	1.15	0.96	46.8	22.2	107.7	2.2
6-13	B-	0.92	0.77	51.2	17.8	100.5	-8.9
2013	C	1.06	0.89	51.6	20.3	200.1	-6.3
2012	B	0.74	0.61	50.1	14.2	180.5	-12.0
2011	B	1.08	0.90	38.8	15.2	132.9	0.8
2010	N/A	N/A	N/A	35.1	14.4	84.7	N/A
2009	N/A	N/A	N/A	25.5	13.1	44.0	N/A

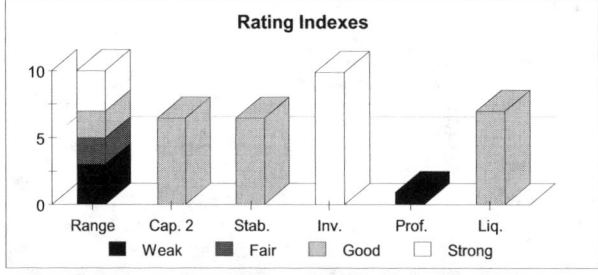

HEALTHPLUS OF MICHIGAN   B-   Good

Major Rating Factors: Fair overall results on stability tests (4.6 on a scale of 0 to 10) based on inconsistent enrollment growth in the past five years due to declines in 2010 and 2011. Good capitalization index (6.2) based on good current risk-adjusted capital (severe loss scenario). Good liquidity (6.9) with sufficient resources (cash flows and marketable investments) to handle a spike in claims.
Other Rating Factors: High quality investment portfolio (8.1). Weak profitability index (2.4).
Principal Business: Comp med (54%), Medicare (42%), FEHB (4%)
Mem Phys: 13: 7,479 **12:** 7,071 **13 MLR** 91.0% **/ 13 Admin Exp** N/A
Enroll(000): Q2 14: 77 **13:** 79 **12:** 74 **Med Exp PMPM:** $489
Principal Investments: Cash and equiv (44%), affiliate common stock (38%), nonaffiliate common stock (15%), real estate (3%)
Provider Compensation ($000): Contr fee ($284,658), capitation ($141,343), FFS ($29,350)
Total Member Encounters: Phys (228,621), non-phys (564,200)
Group Affiliation: HealthPlus of Michigan
Licensed in: MI
Address: 2050 S Linden Rd, Flint, MI 48532
Phone: (800) 332-9161 **Dom State:** MI **Commenced Bus:** October 1979

Data Date	Rating	RACR #1	RACR #2	Total Assets ($mil)	Capital ($mil)	Net Premium ($mil)	Net Income ($mil)
6-14	B-	1.12	0.93	145.2	81.1	253.0	-0.3
6-13	B+	1.29	1.08	155.0	87.6	244.0	2.6
2013	B	1.17	0.97	155.5	84.5	490.4	-7.0
2012	A	1.42	1.18	174.9	95.9	505.1	10.2
2011	A	1.56	1.30	170.3	96.1	481.3	8.7
2010	A	1.66	1.38	159.4	91.1	444.0	3.1
2009	A-	1.72	1.43	164.7	86.4	435.6	0.7

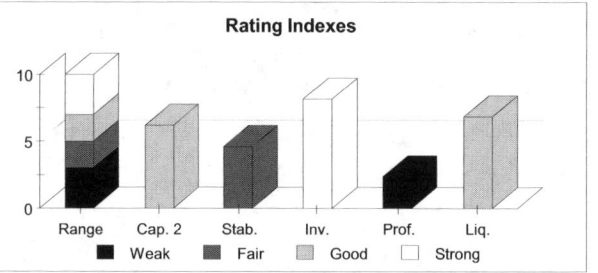

HEALTHPLUS PARTNERS INC

B   **Good**

Major Rating Factors: Good liquidity (6.9 on a scale of 0 to 10) with sufficient resources (cash flows and marketable investments) to handle a spike in claims. Fair profitability index (3.2). Strong capitalization (7.6) based on excellent current risk-adjusted capital (severe loss scenario).

Other Rating Factors: High quality investment portfolio (9.3).

Principal Business: Medicaid (100%)

Mem Phys: 13: 3,254 **12:** 2,595 **13 MLR** 91.3% / **13 Admin Exp** N/A

Enroll(000): Q2 14: 82 **13:** 66 **12:** 67 **Med Exp PMPM:** $262

Principal Investments: Cash and equiv (54%), nonaffiliate common stock (46%)

Provider Compensation ($000): Capitation ($115,049), contr fee ($76,528), FFS ($15,074)

Total Member Encounters: Phys (178,207), non-phys (359,406)

Group Affiliation: HealthPlus of Michigan

Licensed in: MI

Address: 2050 S Linden Rd, Flint, MI 48532

Phone: (810) 230-2000 **Dom State:** MI **Commenced Bus:** January 2003

Data Date	Rating	RACR #1	RACR #2	Total Assets ($mil)	Capital ($mil)	Net Premium ($mil)	Net Income ($mil)
6-14	B	1.83	1.52	60.1	28.7	124.7	-2.4
6-13	B	1.86	1.55	55.1	25.6	113.0	-3.0
2013	B	1.92	1.60	53.6	30.1	226.3	0.9
2012	B	2.01	1.68	52.1	27.7	211.6	0.4
2011	B	1.92	1.60	49.5	26.9	220.4	-3.3
2010	B	2.40	2.00	56.9	32.4	229.6	9.0
2009	C+	1.71	1.42	48.0	23.4	219.6	5.5

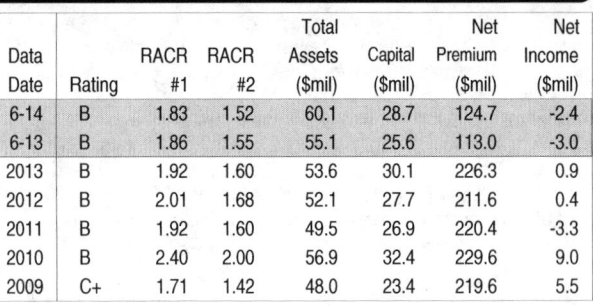

Rating Indexes

Range | Cap. 2 | Stab. | Inv. | Prof. | Liq.
■ Weak ▨ Fair ▥ Good ☐ Strong

HEALTHSPAN INTEGRATED CARE

D   **Weak**

Major Rating Factors: Weak profitability index (0.7 on a scale of 0 to 10). Fair overall results on stability tests (3.3). Strong capitalization index (9.4) based on excellent current risk-adjusted capital (severe loss scenario).

Other Rating Factors: High quality investment portfolio (9.0). Excellent liquidity (7.1) with ample operational cash flow and liquid investments.

Principal Business: Comp med (58%), Medicare (33%), FEHB (9%)

Mem Phys: 13: 2,075 **12:** 2,093 **13 MLR** 93.4% / **13 Admin Exp** N/A

Enroll(000): Q2 14: 77 **13:** 82 **12:** 86 **Med Exp PMPM:** $449

Principal Investments: Cash and equiv (68%), real estate (31%)

Provider Compensation ($000): Salary ($291,412), contr fee ($83,049), FFS ($20,573)

Total Member Encounters: Phys (497,352), non-phys (81,480)

Group Affiliation: HealthSpan Partners

Licensed in: OH

Address: 1001 Lakeside Ave Ste 1200, Cleveland, OH 44114

Phone: (216) 621-5600 **Dom State:** OH **Commenced Bus:** October 1976

Data Date	Rating	RACR #1	RACR #2	Total Assets ($mil)	Capital ($mil)	Net Premium ($mil)	Net Income ($mil)
6-14	D	3.28	2.73	194.8	80.0	209.5	-30.2
6-13	D	1.41	1.17	284.8	45.9	237.4	-19.7
2013	D	4.72	3.94	263.1	109.3	476.8	-89.4
2012	D	2.07	1.73	302.3	68.3	494.6	-59.6
2011	D	0.80	0.66	234.1	28.2	527.1	-36.7
2010	C	1.08	0.90	246.3	42.1	559.4	-44.8
2009	B	1.75	1.46	205.4	40.6	567.2	-6.4

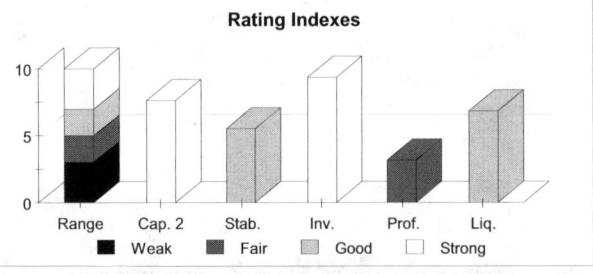

Rating Indexes

Range | Cap. 2 | Stab. | Inv. | Prof. | Liq.
■ Weak ▨ Fair ▥ Good ☐ Strong

HEALTHSPRING LIFE & HLTH INS CO INC

B-   **Good**

Major Rating Factors: Excellent profitability (7.3 on a scale of 0 to 10). Strong capitalization (9.5) based on excellent current risk-adjusted capital (severe loss scenario). High quality investment portfolio (9.4).

Other Rating Factors: Excellent liquidity (7.0) with sufficient resources (cash flows and marketable investments) to handle a spike in claims.

Principal Business: Medicare (62%), Medicaid (15%), other (24%)

Mem Phys: 13: 10,847 **12:** 14,607 **13 MLR** 81.7% / **13 Admin Exp** N/A

Enroll(000): Q2 14: 514 **13:** 592 **12:** 742 **Med Exp PMPM:** $240

Principal Investments: Long-term bonds (64%), cash and equiv (36%)

Provider Compensation ($000): Contr fee ($1,000,235), capitation ($335,410), bonus arrang ($2,800), other ($399,916)

Total Member Encounters: Phys (2,463,011), non-phys (807,385)

Group Affiliation: CIGNA Corp

Licensed in: All states except FL, NM, PR

Address: 2900 North Loop West STE 1300, Houston, TX 77092

Phone: (615) 291-7000 **Dom State:** TX **Commenced Bus:** February 2007

Data Date	Rating	RACR #1	RACR #2	Total Assets ($mil)	Capital ($mil)	Net Premium ($mil)	Net Income ($mil)
6-14	B-	3.33	2.77	627.9	301.6	1,102.5	-13.1
6-13	B	3.83	3.19	703.9	332.9	1,091.5	16.1
2013	B	4.22	3.52	671.9	384.7	2,124.3	57.4
2012	B	5.04	4.20	796.2	439.3	2,167.8	118.0
2011	C	2.21	1.84	529.7	317.5	2,066.1	74.6
2010	N/A	N/A	N/A	265.1	141.1	1,113.3	N/A
2009	N/A	N/A	N/A	220.7	51.2	774.6	N/A

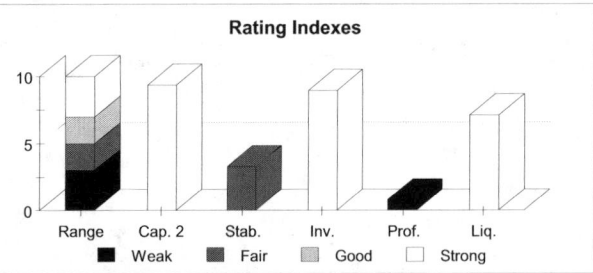

Rating Indexes

Range | Cap. 2 | Stab. | Inv. | Prof. | Liq.
■ Weak ▨ Fair ▥ Good ☐ Strong

HEALTHSPRING OF ALABAMA INC　　　　　　B　　　Good

Major Rating Factors: Good liquidity (6.7 on a scale of 0 to 10) with sufficient resources (cash flows and marketable investments) to handle a spike in claims. Fair overall results on stability tests (4.6). Rating is significantly influenced by the good financial results of CIGNA Corp. Excellent profitability (8.3).
Other Rating Factors: Strong capitalization index (8.6) based on excellent current risk-adjusted capital (severe loss scenario). High quality investment portfolio (8.2).
Principal Business: Medicare (100%)
Mem Phys: 13: 4,041　**12:** 3,535　**13 MLR** 82.3%　**/ 13 Admin Exp** N/A
Enroll(000): Q2 14: 46　**13:** 44　**12:** 39　**Med Exp PMPM:** $814
Principal Investments: Long-term bonds (93%), cash and equiv (7%)
Provider Compensation ($000): Contr fee ($284,150), capitation ($105,254), FFS ($18,808)
Total Member Encounters: Phys (372,633), non-phys (384,581)
Group Affiliation: CIGNA Corp
Licensed in: AL
Address: Two Chase Corporate Dr #300, Birmingham, AL 35244
Phone: (205) 423-1000　**Dom State:** AL　**Commenced Bus:** May 1986

Data Date	Rating	RACR #1	RACR #2	Total Assets ($mil)	Capital ($mil)	Net Premium ($mil)	Net Income ($mil)
6-14	B	2.60	2.17	148.9	63.9	263.0	3.3
6-13	B	3.44	2.87	138.0	76.8	254.4	10.8
2013	B	3.28	2.73	139.8	81.0	502.9	14.9
2012	B	4.12	3.43	141.5	92.3	473.7	26.2
2011	B	2.16	1.80	102.9	67.1	412.0	27.9
2010	C+	2.48	2.07	94.8	59.5	394.8	28.1
2009	C	1.62	1.35	78.7	41.9	376.5	12.0

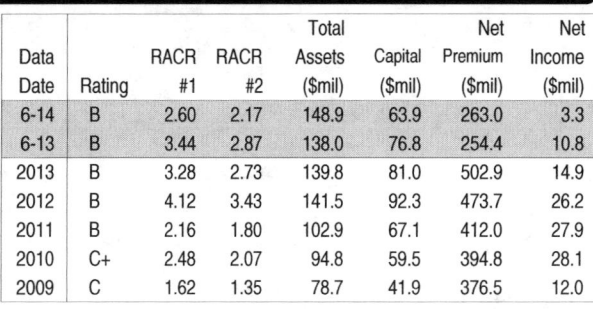

HEALTHSPRING OF FLORIDA INC　　　　　　B　　　Good

Major Rating Factors: Good liquidity (5.8 on a scale of 0 to 10) with sufficient resources (cash flows and marketable investments) to handle a spike in claims. Excellent profitability (8.3). Strong capitalization (7.2) based on excellent current risk-adjusted capital (severe loss scenario).
Other Rating Factors: High quality investment portfolio (8.3).
Principal Business: Medicare (100%)
Mem Phys: 13: 1,468　**12:** 1,304　**13 MLR** 81.4%　**/ 13 Admin Exp** N/A
Enroll(000): Q2 14: 47　**13:** 44　**12:** 42　**Med Exp PMPM:** $1,175
Principal Investments: Long-term bonds (93%), cash and equiv (7%)
Provider Compensation ($000): Capitation ($336,992), contr fee ($213,690), FFS ($62,948)
Total Member Encounters: Phys (828,685), non-phys (763,056)
Group Affiliation: CIGNA Corp
Licensed in: FL
Address: 11501 SW 40th St, Miami, FL 33165
Phone: (305) 642-5366　**Dom State:** FL　**Commenced Bus:** August 2002

Data Date	Rating	RACR #1	RACR #2	Total Assets ($mil)	Capital ($mil)	Net Premium ($mil)	Net Income ($mil)
6-14	B	1.52	1.27	127.4	47.8	384.8	2.1
6-13	B	1.31	1.09	102.5	39.5	379.5	6.4
2013	B	1.55	1.29	98.7	48.5	752.5	14.8
2012	B-	1.11	0.92	78.3	33.5	711.2	6.9
2011	C	0.52	0.44	66.3	27.1	613.6	8.2
2010	C-	0.51	0.43	59.9	26.5	541.1	9.8
2009	D+	0.62	0.52	60.6	27.4	492.9	12.6

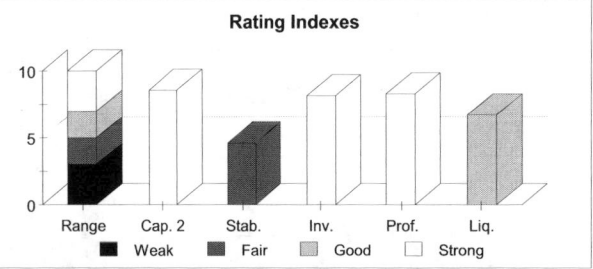

HEALTHSPRING OF TENNESSEE INC　　　　　C+　　　Fair

Major Rating Factors: Fair overall results on stability tests (3.2 on a scale of 0 to 10). Rating is significantly influenced by the good financial results of CIGNA Corp. Good overall profitability index (6.9). Good liquidity (6.2) with sufficient resources (cash flows and marketable investments) to handle a spike in claims.
Other Rating Factors: Strong capitalization index (7.3) based on excellent current risk-adjusted capital (severe loss scenario). High quality investment portfolio (9.9).
Principal Business: Medicare (100%)
Mem Phys: 13: 10,971　**12:** 7,015　**13 MLR** 84.2%　**/ 13 Admin Exp** N/A
Enroll(000): Q2 14: 119　**13:** 112　**12:** 96　**Med Exp PMPM:** $759
Principal Investments: Long-term bonds (81%), cash and equiv (19%)
Provider Compensation ($000): FFS ($717,750), capitation ($236,389), bonus arrang ($4,747)
Total Member Encounters: Phys (2,033,320), non-phys (631,638)
Group Affiliation: CIGNA Corp
Licensed in: IL, MS, TN
Address: 44 Vantage Way Suite 300, Nashville, TN 37228-1513
Phone: (615) 291-7000　**Dom State:** TN　**Commenced Bus:** July 1995

Data Date	Rating	RACR #1	RACR #2	Total Assets ($mil)	Capital ($mil)	Net Premium ($mil)	Net Income ($mil)
6-14	C+	1.62	1.35	303.9	114.8	640.6	7.3
6-13	B	2.11	1.75	262.2	120.4	589.5	13.2
2013	C+	1.64	1.37	260.0	116.0	1,170.1	9.5
2012	B	2.76	2.30	270.2	157.4	1,052.2	51.0
2011	B	2.07	1.72	207.1	106.4	981.5	39.1
2010	C	1.32	1.10	163.1	77.8	896.7	29.8
2009	C	1.52	1.27	172.3	90.3	983.1	-6.4

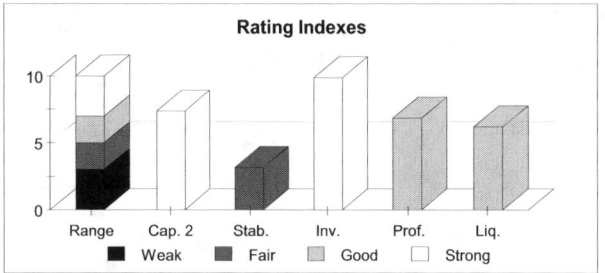

HEALTHSUN HEALTH PLANS

C   **Fair**

Major Rating Factors: Fair capitalization (3.8 on a scale of 0 to 10) based on fair current risk-adjusted capital (moderate loss scenario). Excellent profitability (8.5). High quality investment portfolio (9.9).

Other Rating Factors: Excellent liquidity (7.0) with sufficient resources (cash flows and marketable investments) to handle a spike in claims.

Principal Business: Medicare (100%)

Mem Phys: 13: 1,707   **12:** 1,463   **13 MLR** 88.1%   / **13 Admin Exp** N/A

Enroll(000): Q2 14: 24   **13:** 21   **12:** 16   **Med Exp PMPM:** $1,615

Principal Investments: Cash and equiv (100%)

Provider Compensation ($000): Capitation ($151,568), FFS ($141,387), contr fee ($73,391)

Total Member Encounters: Phys (616,408), non-phys (293,753)

Group Affiliation: None

Licensed in: FL

Address: 1205 SW 37th Ave, Miami, FL 33135

Phone: (305) 448-8100   **Dom State:** FL   **Commenced Bus:** August 2005

Data Date	Rating	RACR #1	RACR #2	Total Assets ($mil)	Capital ($mil)	Net Premium ($mil)	Net Income ($mil)
6-14	C	0.76	0.63	73.4	20.4	237.0	5.8
6-13	C	0.64	0.53	51.4	11.6	185.1	6.0
2013	C-	0.48	0.40	55.7	13.2	414.0	11.3
2012	C+	0.73	0.61	56.3	13.3	309.5	12.1
2011	D+	0.51	0.42	23.9	4.6	129.3	3.0
2010	C-	0.55	0.46	12.9	4.6	69.2	2.0
2009	D	0.67	0.56	9.9	4.5	54.3	1.7

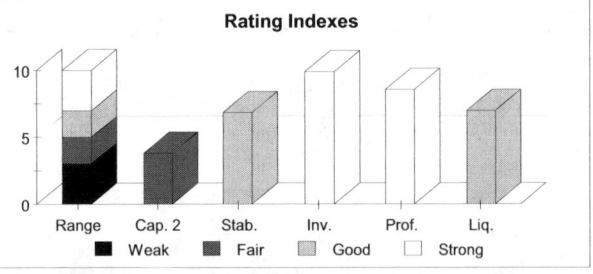

HEALTHY ALLIANCE LIFE INS CO *

A-   **Excellent**

Major Rating Factors: Excellent profitability (9.8 on a scale of 0 to 10). Strong capitalization (10.0) based on excellent current risk-adjusted capital (severe loss scenario). High quality investment portfolio (7.4).

Other Rating Factors: Good liquidity (6.9) with sufficient resources (cash flows and marketable investments) to handle a spike in claims.

Principal Business: Comp med (75%), FEHB (17%), med supp (5%), dental (1%), other (1%)

Mem Phys: 13: 16,383   **12:** 16,033   **13 MLR** 81.3%   / **13 Admin Exp** N/A

Enroll(000): Q2 14: 727   **13:** 717   **12:** 716   **Med Exp PMPM:** $180

Principal Investments: Long-term bonds (85%), cash and equiv (2%), other (13%)

Provider Compensation ($000): Contr fee ($947,712), FFS ($566,095), bonus arrang ($392), other ($11,993)

Total Member Encounters: Phys (2,454,371), non-phys (1,844,365)

Group Affiliation: WellPoint Inc

Licensed in: AL, IL, IN, KS, MD, MS, MO, NV, OH, UT, WV

Address: 1831 Chestnut St, St Louis, MO 63103-2275

Phone: (314) 923-4444   **Dom State:** MO   **Commenced Bus:** June 1971

Data Date	Rating	RACR #1	RACR #2	Total Assets ($mil)	Capital ($mil)	Net Premium ($mil)	Net Income ($mil)
6-14	A-	4.60	3.83	954.2	428.2	943.6	56.2
6-13	A-	4.57	3.81	849.2	414.5	948.0	84.1
2013	A-	3.89	3.24	840.1	358.9	1,883.4	133.4
2012	A-	3.70	3.08	763.0	331.5	1,845.0	107.9
2011	A-	4.03	3.36	775.2	332.0	1,748.1	133.9
2010	B+	3.76	3.13	661.2	283.1	1,707.3	144.5
2009	N/A	N/A	N/A	624.3	252.1	1,591.3	N/A

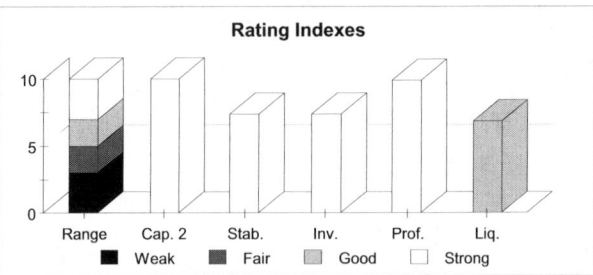

HEALTHY PALM BEACHES INC

D   **Weak**

Major Rating Factors: Weak profitability index (1.3 on a scale of 0 to 10). Fair overall results on stability tests (4.3). Strong capitalization index (7.7) based on excellent current risk-adjusted capital (severe loss scenario).

Other Rating Factors: High quality investment portfolio (9.9). Excellent liquidity (7.4) with ample operational cash flow and liquid investments.

Principal Business: Medicaid (54%), other (46%)

Mem Phys: 13: 1,695   **12:** 1,375   **13 MLR** 94.2%   / **13 Admin Exp** N/A

Enroll(000): Q2 14: 25   **13:** 27   **12:** 23   **Med Exp PMPM:** $157

Principal Investments: Cash and equiv (100%)

Provider Compensation ($000): Contr fee ($24,873), capitation ($22,976)

Total Member Encounters: Phys (298,915), non-phys (321,916)

Group Affiliation: None

Licensed in: FL

Address: 324 Datura St Suite 401, West Palm Beach, FL 33401

Phone: (561) 659-1270   **Dom State:** FL   **Commenced Bus:** January 1998

Data Date	Rating	RACR #1	RACR #2	Total Assets ($mil)	Capital ($mil)	Net Premium ($mil)	Net Income ($mil)
6-14	D	1.93	1.61	19.5	11.2	23.7	-3.1
6-13	D	3.63	3.03	23.2	16.7	23.2	0.5
2013	D	2.47	2.06	23.1	14.3	51.2	-1.9
2012	D	3.52	2.94	23.7	16.2	42.0	-0.4
2011	D	4.38	3.65	23.9	16.6	37.3	-1.2
2010	B	5.41	4.50	25.3	17.8	39.1	10.2
2009	B	2.20	1.84	15.0	7.6	24.1	1.9

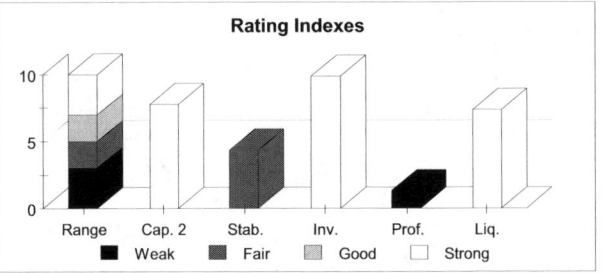

HERITAGE PROVIDER NETWORK INC   D   Weak

Major Rating Factors: Fair capitalization index (4.4 on a scale of 0 to 10) based on weak current risk-adjusted capital (moderate loss scenario). Good overall profitability index (6.4). Good liquidity (6.9) with sufficient resources (cash flows and marketable investments) to handle a spike in claims.
Other Rating Factors: Excellent overall results on stability tests (7.3).
Principal Business: Managed care (98%), indemnity (2%)
Mem Phys: 13: N/A **12:** N/A **13 MLR** 93.6% **/ 13 Admin Exp** N/A
Enroll(000): Q2 14: 492 **13:** 427 **12:** 431 **Med Exp PMPM:** $338
Principal Investments ($000): Cash and equiv ($237,779)
Provider Compensation ($000): None
Total Member Encounters: N/A
Group Affiliation: Heritage California Medical Groups
Licensed in: CA
Address: 8510 Balboa Blvd., Ste 285, Northridge, CA 91325
Phone: (818) 654-3461 **Dom State:** CA **Commenced Bus:** May 1996

Data Date	Rating	RACR #1	RACR #2	Total Assets ($mil)	Capital ($mil)	Net Premium ($mil)	Net Income ($mil)
6-14	D	0.70	0.43	378.3	109.2	994.5	1.3
6-13	D-	0.61	0.37	369.5	100.0	929.5	1.3
2013	D	0.64	0.39	333.8	105.9	1,857.4	2.4
2012	D-	0.57	0.35	363.0	97.6	1,751.0	2.8
2011	D-	0.47	0.29	322.6	91.0	1,598.0	2.2
2010	D	0.46	0.28	288.1	90.5	1,499.4	1.5
2009	D	0.72	0.44	242.0	70.8	1,143.1	0.2

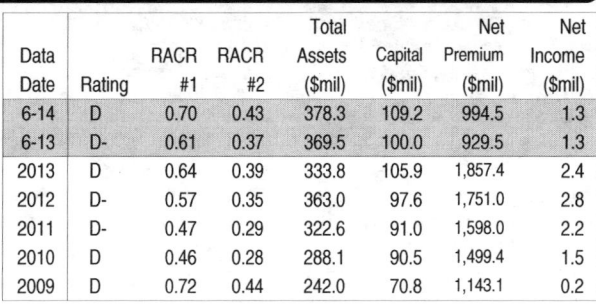

Rating Indexes

HIGHMARK BCBSD INC   B   Good

Major Rating Factors: Good quality investment portfolio (6.5 on a scale of 0 to 10). Good liquidity (6.8) with sufficient resources (cash flows and marketable investments) to handle a spike in claims. Strong capitalization (10.0) based on excellent current risk-adjusted capital (severe loss scenario).
Other Rating Factors: Weak profitability index (2.3).
Principal Business: Comp med (78%), FEHB (20%), med supp (2%)
Mem Phys: 13: 5,671 **12:** 3,235 **13 MLR** 83.5% **/ 13 Admin Exp** N/A
Enroll(000): Q2 14: 117 **13:** 107 **12:** 110 **Med Exp PMPM:** $337
Principal Investments: Long-term bonds (59%), nonaffiliate common stock (30%), cash and equiv (9%), other (2%)
Provider Compensation ($000): Contr fee ($421,226), capitation ($195)
Total Member Encounters: Phys (1,404,644), non-phys (264,714)
Group Affiliation: Highmark Inc
Licensed in: DE
Address: 800 Delaware Ave, Wilmington, DE 19801-1368
Phone: (800) 292-9525 **Dom State:** DE **Commenced Bus:** September 1935

Data Date	Rating	RACR #1	RACR #2	Total Assets ($mil)	Capital ($mil)	Net Premium ($mil)	Net Income ($mil)
6-14	B	5.68	4.73	376.5	164.6	286.5	-4.7
6-13	B+	5.05	4.20	340.9	139.2	250.4	1.3
2013	B	5.45	4.54	334.2	157.7	512.1	-8.4
2012	A	6.08	5.07	312.5	168.7	532.2	-11.1
2011	A+	5.64	4.70	305.8	158.6	516.5	4.1
2010	A+	6.33	5.28	306.7	171.1	498.8	14.8
2009	A+	5.13	4.28	262.0	139.7	482.1	0.8

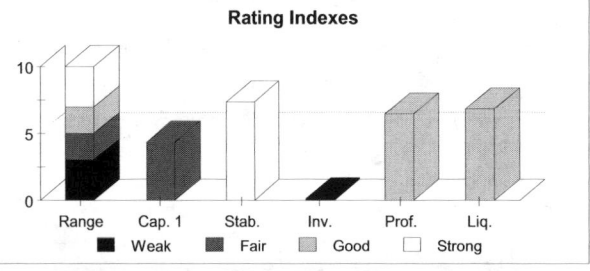

Rating Indexes

HIGHMARK CASUALTY INS CO   C   Fair

Major Rating Factors: Fair overall results on stability tests (4.0 on a scale of 0 to 10) including fair financial strength of affiliated Highmark Inc and weak results on operational trends. The largest net exposure for one risk is conservative at 1.5% of capital. Good long-term capitalization (6.8) based on good current risk adjusted capital (moderate loss scenario) reflecting improvement over results in 2013.
Other Rating Factors: Good liquidity (5.6) with sufficient resources (cash flows and marketable investments) to handle a spike in claims. Ample reserve history (9.4) that helps to protect the company against sharp claims increases. Excellent profitability (8.7) with operating gains in each of the last five years. Return on equity has been good over the last five years, averaging 11.6%.
Principal Business: Group accident & health (67%) and workers compensation (33%).
Principal Investments: Investment grade bonds (78%), misc. investments (11%), non investment grade bonds (10%), and cash (1%).
Investments in Affiliates: None
Group Affiliation: Highmark Inc
Licensed in: AL, FL, GA, ID, IL, IN, KS, KY, MD, MI, MS, MO, NV, NJ, NM, NC, OR, PA, SC, TX, UT, VA, WA, WV
Commenced Business: February 1978
Address: Fifth Avenue Pl 120 Fifth Ave, Pittsburgh, PA 15222-3099
Phone: (800) 328-5433 **Domicile State:** PA **NAIC Code:** 35599

Data Date	Rating	RACR #1	RACR #2	Loss Ratio %	Total Assets ($mil)	Capital ($mil)	Net Premium ($mil)	Net Income ($mil)
6-14	C	1.59	1.10	N/A	413.1	162.7	149.6	1.0
6-13	C	1.85	1.25	N/A	371.5	156.1	136.6	8.2
2013	C	1.23	0.84	75.7	398.5	160.9	290.7	12.6
2012	C	1.37	0.93	72.1	344.9	148.5	253.0	20.0
2011	C	1.66	1.10	70.3	324.2	131.3	204.3	21.0
2010	C	3.95	2.84	69.1	226.4	111.6	88.5	13.4
2009	C	1.55	0.94	66.2	217.1	112.9	75.0	15.8

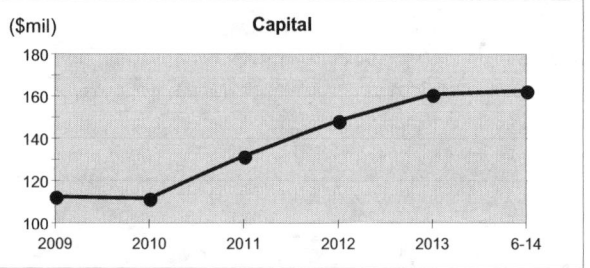

($mil)   **Capital**

HIGHMARK INC
B-   **Good**

Major Rating Factors: Good overall profitability index (6.7 on a scale of 0 to 10). Good quality investment portfolio (4.9). Strong capitalization (10.0) based on excellent current risk-adjusted capital (severe loss scenario).

Other Rating Factors: Excellent liquidity (7.1) with ample operational cash flow and liquid investments.

Principal Business: Comp med (46%), Medicare (36%), FEHB (12%), med supp (5%)

Mem Phys: 13: 71,224 **12:** 68,346 **13 MLR** 90.6% **/ 13 Admin Exp** N/A

Enroll(000): Q2 14: 1,339 **13:** 1,294 **12:** 1,346 **Med Exp PMPM:** $356

Principal Investments: Affiliate common stock (33%), long-term bonds (30%), nonaffiliate common stock (13%), cash and equiv (8%), real estate (1%), other (15%)

Provider Compensation ($000): Contr fee ($5,062,237), FFS ($526,655), bonus arrang ($28,441), capitation ($14,091)

Total Member Encounters: Phys (16,293,529), non-phys (4,416,479)

Group Affiliation: Highmark Inc

Licensed in: PA

Address: 1800 Center St, Camp Hill, PA 17089

Phone: (412) 544-7000 **Dom State:** PA **Commenced Bus:** December 1996

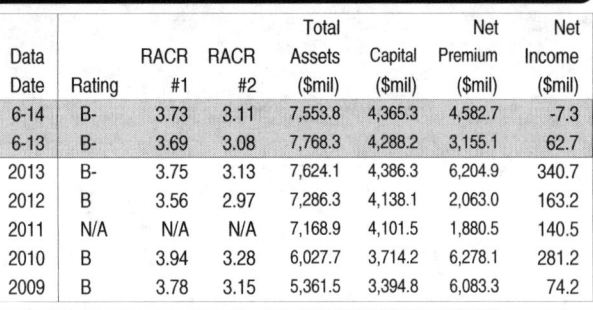

Data Date	Rating	RACR #1	RACR #2	Total Assets ($mil)	Capital ($mil)	Net Premium ($mil)	Net Income ($mil)
6-14	B-	3.73	3.11	7,553.8	4,365.3	4,582.7	-7.3
6-13	B-	3.69	3.08	7,768.3	4,288.2	3,155.1	62.7
2013	B-	3.75	3.13	7,624.1	4,386.3	6,204.9	340.7
2012	B	3.56	2.97	7,286.3	4,138.1	2,063.0	163.2
2011	N/A	N/A	N/A	7,168.9	4,101.5	1,880.5	140.5
2010	B	3.94	3.28	6,027.7	3,714.2	6,278.1	281.2
2009	B	3.78	3.15	5,361.5	3,394.8	6,083.3	74.2

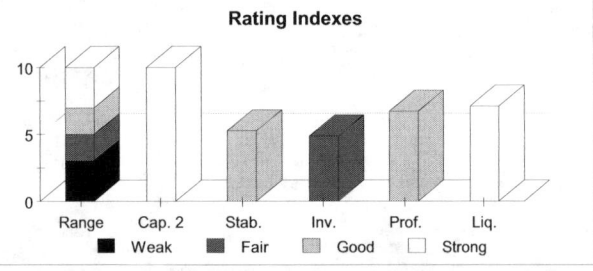

Rating Indexes

HIGHMARK WEST VIRGINIA INC *
B+   **Good**

Major Rating Factors: Good overall profitability index (6.2 on a scale of 0 to 10). Good quality investment portfolio (6.6). Good liquidity (6.9) with sufficient resources (cash flows and marketable investments) to handle a spike in claims.

Other Rating Factors: Strong capitalization (10.0) based on excellent current risk-adjusted capital (severe loss scenario).

Principal Business: Comp med (62%), FEHB (33%), med supp (2%), other (3%)

Mem Phys: 13: 12,158 **12:** 11,536 **13 MLR** 90.9% **/ 13 Admin Exp** N/A

Enroll(000): Q2 14: 204 **13:** 192 **12:** 184 **Med Exp PMPM:** $359

Principal Investments: Long-term bonds (73%), cash and equiv (9%), nonaffiliate common stock (7%), real estate (5%), other (5%)

Provider Compensation ($000): Contr fee ($781,927), FFS ($16,410), bonus arrang ($4,337)

Total Member Encounters: Phys (1,438,544), non-phys (346,247)

Group Affiliation: Highmark Inc

Licensed in: WV

Address: 614 Market St, Parkersburg, WV 26102

Phone: (304) 424-7700 **Dom State:** WV **Commenced Bus:** January 1983

Data Date	Rating	RACR #1	RACR #2	Total Assets ($mil)	Capital ($mil)	Net Premium ($mil)	Net Income ($mil)
6-14	B+	6.22	5.19	623.7	311.3	485.8	10.0
6-13	B+	7.28	6.06	560.7	316.3	441.5	6.7
2013	B+	6.16	5.13	574.6	308.1	894.3	1.4
2012	A-	7.42	6.18	545.0	322.6	824.0	32.2
2011	A-	7.36	6.13	500.9	288.1	770.0	51.7
2010	A-	5.90	4.91	439.1	241.7	788.9	30.6
2009	A-	5.15	4.29	365.8	212.8	763.0	5.3

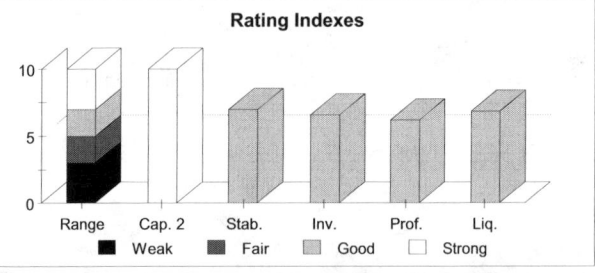

Rating Indexes

HIP INS CO OF NEW YORK
D-   **Weak**

Major Rating Factors: Weak profitability index (0.9 on a scale of 0 to 10). Good liquidity (6.1) with sufficient resources (cash flows and marketable investments) to handle a spike in claims. Strong capitalization (10.0) based on excellent current risk-adjusted capital (severe loss scenario).

Other Rating Factors: High quality investment portfolio (8.8).

Principal Business: Comp med (99%)

Mem Phys: 13: 46,354 **12:** 42,784 **13 MLR** 87.9% **/ 13 Admin Exp** N/A

Enroll(000): Q2 14: 17 **13:** 28 **12:** 37 **Med Exp PMPM:** $350

Principal Investments: Long-term bonds (93%), cash and equiv (7%)

Provider Compensation ($000): Contr fee ($68,042), FFS ($66,151)

Total Member Encounters: Phys (158,433), non-phys (97,001)

Group Affiliation: EmblemHealth Inc

Licensed in: NY

Address: 55 Water St, New York, NY 10041-8190

Phone: (646) 447-5000 **Dom State:** NY **Commenced Bus:** September 1994

Data Date	Rating	RACR #1	RACR #2	Total Assets ($mil)	Capital ($mil)	Net Premium ($mil)	Net Income ($mil)
6-14	D-	4.36	3.64	64.6	42.2	37.7	-0.9
6-13	E+	3.63	3.03	72.2	45.2	74.3	4.7
2013	D-	4.47	3.72	67.3	43.3	146.8	4.3
2012	E+	3.23	2.69	75.1	40.0	169.6	-13.6
2011	D+	1.10	0.91	80.1	12.3	155.6	-7.0
2010	D+	1.21	1.01	83.1	17.3	199.5	-7.0
2009	B-	2.03	1.69	62.9	27.5	187.9	-11.2

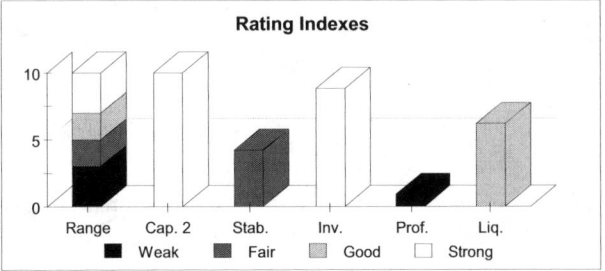

Rating Indexes

HM HEALTH INS CO   C-   Fair

Major Rating Factors: Fair profitability index (3.2 on a scale of 0 to 10). Fair quality investment portfolio (3.7). Poor capitalization (1.0) based on weak current risk-adjusted capital (moderate loss scenario).
Other Rating Factors: Good liquidity (5.9) with sufficient resources (cash flows and marketable investments) to handle a spike in claims.
Principal Business: Comp med (80%), Medicare (11%), other (9%)
Mem Phys: 13: 7,065 **12:** 6,972 **13 MLR** 89.8% **/ 13 Admin Exp** N/A
Enroll(000): Q2 14: 315 **13:** 307 **12:** 404 **Med Exp PMPM:** $271
Principal Investments: Long-term bonds (73%), cash and equiv (24%), other (3%)
Provider Compensation ($000): Contr fee ($1,033,952), bonus arrang ($7,702), capitation ($923)
Total Member Encounters: Phys (1,489,455), non-phys (631,481)
Group Affiliation: Highmark Inc
Licensed in: All states except FL, ME, NH, NY, PR
Address: 120 Fifth Ave, Pittsburgh, PA 15222-3099
Phone: (412) 544-7000 **Dom State:** PA **Commenced Bus:** January 1955

Data Date	Rating	RACR #1	RACR #2	Total Assets ($mil)	Capital ($mil)	Net Premium ($mil)	Net Income ($mil)
6-14	C-	0.40	0.33	291.9	31.1	N/A	2.4
6-13	C+	0.66	0.55	341.5	182.0	583.1	4.7
2013	C+	2.27	1.89	348.0	177.7	1,143.8	-9.6
2012	B	2.33	1.94	1,335.8	641.3	5,064.6	41.5
2011	B	2.24	1.87	1,279.9	597.3	5,094.5	129.5
2010	B	2.56	2.13	179.8	66.6	434.2	12.2
2009	C+	1.39	1.16	28.5	11.4	91.7	-1.2

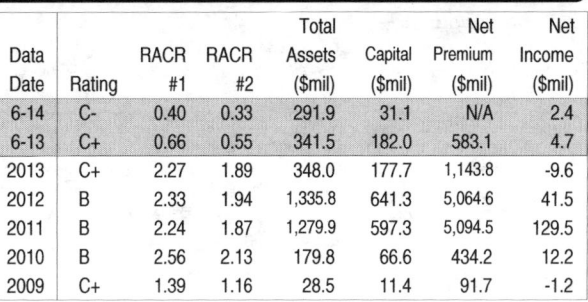

Rating Indexes

HM LIFE INSURANCE COMPANY   B   Good

Major Rating Factors: Good overall results on stability tests (6.1 on a scale of 0 to 10). Stability strengths include excellent operational trends and excellent risk diversification. Good quality investment portfolio (5.1) with no exposure to mortgages and small junk bond holdings. Good liquidity (6.8) with sufficient resources to handle a spike in claims.
Other Rating Factors: Strong capitalization (9.0) based on excellent risk adjusted capital (severe loss scenario). Excellent profitability (8.7) with operating gains in each of the last five years.
Principal Business: Group health insurance (87%) and reinsurance (13%).
Principal Investments: NonCMO investment grade bonds (60%), CMOs and structured securities (14%), noninv. grade bonds (11%), cash (7%), and common & preferred stock (1%).
Investments in Affiliates: 1%
Group Affiliation: Highmark Inc
Licensed in: All states except NY, PR
Commenced Business: May 1981
Address: 120 Fifth Avenue, Pittsburgh, PA 15222
Phone: (800) 328-5433 **Domicile State:** PA **NAIC Code:** 93440

Data Date	Rating	RACR #1	RACR #2	Total Assets ($mil)	Capital ($mil)	Net Premium ($mil)	Net Income ($mil)
6-14	B	3.10	2.36	570.6	291.7	327.6	6.3
6-13	B	2.95	2.26	529.8	264.6	312.1	17.7
2013	B	3.07	2.35	557.9	284.6	634.0	35.5
2012	B	2.87	2.20	491.3	250.0	588.8	25.4
2011	B-	2.64	2.03	471.6	219.5	568.8	27.7
2010	B-	2.69	2.04	415.2	189.2	491.9	25.8
2009	B-	2.86	2.15	346.2	157.8	394.1	12.7

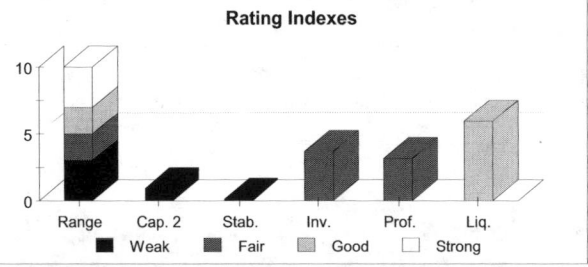

Rating Indexes

HM LIFE INSURANCE COMPANY OF NEW YORK *   B+   Good

Major Rating Factors: Good overall results on stability tests (5.8 on a scale of 0 to 10). Stability strengths include good operational trends and good risk diversification. Good overall profitability (6.3). Return on equity has been fair, averaging 5.8%. Strong capitalization (8.5) based on excellent risk adjusted capital (severe loss scenario).
Other Rating Factors: High quality investment portfolio (8.7). Excellent liquidity (7.1).
Principal Business: N/A
Principal Investments: NonCMO investment grade bonds (44%), cash (32%), and CMOs and structured securities (24%).
Investments in Affiliates: None
Group Affiliation: Highmark Inc
Licensed in: DC, NY, RI
Commenced Business: March 1997
Address: 420 Fifth Ave 3rd Floor, New York, NY 10018
Phone: (800) 328-5433 **Domicile State:** NY **NAIC Code:** 60213

Data Date	Rating	RACR #1	RACR #2	Total Assets ($mil)	Capital ($mil)	Net Premium ($mil)	Net Income ($mil)
6-14	B+	2.55	2.01	72.5	32.3	36.5	0.2
6-13	B+	1.97	1.56	69.2	31.0	43.0	-0.8
2013	B+	2.28	1.81	76.1	31.9	85.4	-0.4
2012	B+	2.00	1.59	66.5	31.8	88.4	9.0
2011	B-	1.90	1.50	44.9	22.9	63.1	2.5
2010	B-	1.51	1.21	44.3	20.1	71.0	-0.3
2009	B	1.91	1.52	41.1	20.6	61.2	-1.1

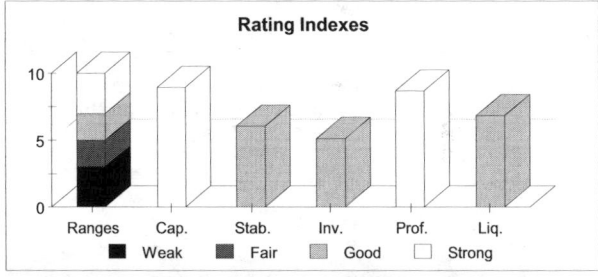

Adverse Trends in Operations

Decrease in premium volume from 2012 to 2013 (3%)
Decrease in premium volume from 2010 to 2011 (11%)
Decrease in capital during 2010 (2%)

HMO COLORADO
B-　**Good**

Major Rating Factors: Fair quality investment portfolio (3.8 on a scale of 0 to 10). Fair overall results on stability tests (4.4). Rating is significantly influenced by the good financial results of WellPoint Inc. Excellent profitability (7.2).
Other Rating Factors: Strong capitalization index (10.0) based on excellent current risk-adjusted capital (severe loss scenario). Excellent liquidity (7.1) with ample operational cash flow and liquid investments.
Principal Business: Comp med (98%), Medicare (2%)
Mem Phys: 13: 27,355　**12:** 21,848　**13 MLR** 85.2%　**/ 13 Admin Exp** N/A
Enroll(000): Q2 14: 49　**13:** 30　**12:** 31　**Med Exp PMPM:** $353
Principal Investments: Long-term bonds (139%), affiliate common stock (5%)
Provider Compensation ($000): Contr fee ($120,574), capitation ($657), bonus arrang ($349), other ($1,232)
Total Member Encounters: Phys (2,736,183), non-phys (370,758)
Group Affiliation: WellPoint Inc
Licensed in: CO, NV
Address: 700 Broadway, Denver, CO 80273
Phone: (303) 831-2131　**Dom State:** CO　**Commenced Bus:** January 1980

Data Date	Rating	RACR #1	RACR #2	Total Assets ($mil)	Capital ($mil)	Net Premium ($mil)	Net Income ($mil)
6-14	B-	4.77	3.97	87.9	45.8	99.2	-1.1
6-13	B-	6.43	5.36	79.9	59.2	70.8	3.7
2013	B-	4.90	4.08	65.7	47.2	145.1	8.5
2012	B-	6.01	5.01	75.0	55.0	155.5	15.6
2011	B-	4.09	3.41	68.3	43.5	163.8	3.4
2010	B	4.78	3.99	80.7	58.2	206.2	8.5
2009	B	3.57	2.98	82.5	55.9	281.2	10.2

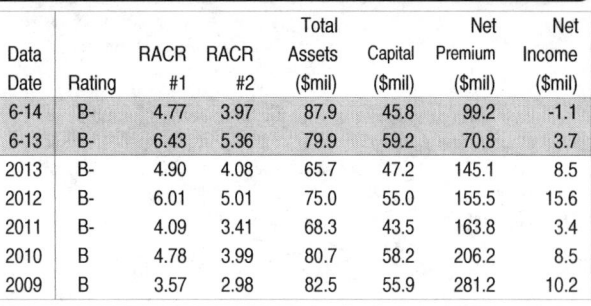

Rating Indexes

HMO LOUISIANA INC *
A+　**Excellent**

Major Rating Factors: Excellent profitability (9.5 on a scale of 0 to 10). Strong capitalization index (10.0) based on excellent current risk-adjusted capital (severe loss scenario). High quality investment portfolio (9.0).
Other Rating Factors: Excellent overall results on stability tests (7.2) despite a decline in enrollment during 2013. Excellent liquidity (7.4) with ample operational cash flow and liquid investments.
Principal Business: Comp med (100%)
Mem Phys: 13: 13,253　**12:** 11,064　**13 MLR** 77.3%　**/ 13 Admin Exp** N/A
Enroll(000): Q2 14: 111　**13:** 95　**12:** 108　**Med Exp PMPM:** $309
Principal Investments: Long-term bonds (58%), nonaffiliate common stock (22%), cash and equiv (15%), other (5%)
Provider Compensation ($000): Contr fee ($375,013)
Total Member Encounters: Phys (874,721), non-phys (510,784)
Group Affiliation: Louisiana Health Services
Licensed in: LA
Address: 5525 Reitz Ave, Baton Rouge, LA 70809
Phone: (225) 295-3307　**Dom State:** LA　**Commenced Bus:** July 1986

Data Date	Rating	RACR #1	RACR #2	Total Assets ($mil)	Capital ($mil)	Net Premium ($mil)	Net Income ($mil)
6-14	A+	12.40	10.34	497.8	361.6	255.9	11.9
6-13	A+	10.37	8.64	405.6	317.9	240.6	20.1
2013	A+	11.94	9.95	434.9	347.9	472.4	47.9
2012	A+	9.67	8.06	395.7	296.2	499.6	32.9
2011	A+	8.97	7.47	361.8	263.4	483.7	32.1
2010	A+	8.09	6.74	341.6	238.9	468.6	19.8
2009	A+	7.56	6.30	301.2	208.2	423.9	17.2

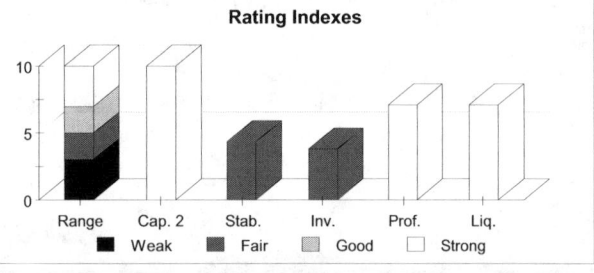

Rating Indexes

HMO MINNESOTA *
A-　**Excellent**

Major Rating Factors: Strong capitalization index (10.0 on a scale of 0 to 10) based on excellent current risk-adjusted capital (severe loss scenario). Good overall profitability index (6.9). Good quality investment portfolio (6.6).
Other Rating Factors: Good overall results on stability tests (6.6). Good liquidity (6.7) with sufficient resources (cash flows and marketable investments) to handle a spike in claims.
Principal Business: Medicaid (60%), Medicare (39%), comp med (2%)
Mem Phys: 13: 17,377　**12:** 16,098　**13 MLR** 90.9%　**/ 13 Admin Exp** N/A
Enroll(000): Q2 14: 107　**13:** 143　**12:** 138　**Med Exp PMPM:** $528
Principal Investments: Long-term bonds (71%), nonaffiliate common stock (23%), cash and equiv (6%)
Provider Compensation ($000): Contr fee ($557,516), bonus arrang ($290,685), FFS ($93,000)
Total Member Encounters: Phys (955,823), non-phys (649,838)
Group Affiliation: Aware Integrated Inc
Licensed in: MN
Address: 3535 Blue Cross Rd, 43179, St Paul, MN 55164
Phone: (651) 662-8000　**Dom State:** MN　**Commenced Bus:** November 1974

Data Date	Rating	RACR #1	RACR #2	Total Assets ($mil)	Capital ($mil)	Net Premium ($mil)	Net Income ($mil)
6-14	A-	7.75	6.46	715.0	510.4	417.6	59.6
6-13	A-	5.84	4.87	747.8	378.8	517.2	15.9
2013	A-	6.84	5.70	629.8	448.9	1,016.7	73.2
2012	A-	5.56	4.63	572.8	359.6	956.9	-4.4
2011	A-	5.46	4.55	563.7	357.2	1,090.3	50.6
2010	A-	5.18	4.31	501.2	317.6	1,034.5	70.9
2009	B+	3.96	3.30	423.9	250.9	967.4	28.7

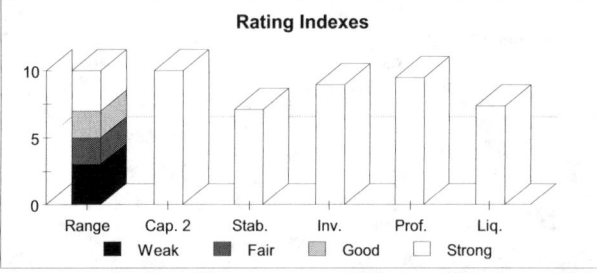

Rating Indexes

HMO MISSOURI INC

B- **Good**

Major Rating Factors: Excellent profitability (7.8 on a scale of 0 to 10). Strong capitalization index (10.0) based on excellent current risk-adjusted capital (severe loss scenario). High quality investment portfolio (9.8).

Other Rating Factors: Excellent liquidity (7.0) with ample operational cash flow and liquid investments. Weak overall results on stability tests (1.8) based on a significant 21% decrease in enrollment during the period, a steep decline in capital during 2013. Rating is significantly influenced by the good financial results of WellPoint Inc.

Principal Business: Comp med (61%), FEHB (39%)

Mem Phys: 13: 13,698 **12:** 12,935 **13 MLR** 83.3% **/ 13 Admin Exp** N/A

Enroll(000): Q2 14: 28 **13:** 33 **12:** 42 **Med Exp PMPM:** $330

Principal Investments: Long-term bonds (72%), cash and equiv (28%)

Provider Compensation ($000): Contr fee ($77,063), FFS ($63,089), bonus arrang ($67)

Total Member Encounters: Phys (186,536), non-phys (118,244)

Group Affiliation: WellPoint Inc

Licensed in: IL, MO

Address: 1831 Chestnut, St Louis, MO 63103-2275

Phone: (314) 923-4444 **Dom State:** MO **Commenced Bus:** December 1987

Data Date	Rating	RACR #1	RACR #2	Total Assets ($mil)	Capital ($mil)	Net Premium ($mil)	Net Income ($mil)
6-14	B-	6.00	5.00	72.9	44.7	72.0	5.2
6-13	B-	9.27	7.72	112.5	71.5	86.9	5.7
2013	B-	5.31	4.42	71.2	39.3	169.1	9.1
2012	B-	8.52	7.10	115.9	65.5	184.3	13.6
2011	B-	5.45	4.54	101.3	50.2	242.8	18.3
2010	B	7.00	5.83	126.7	78.7	273.4	18.3
2009	B	5.15	4.29	135.2	75.7	329.5	20.0

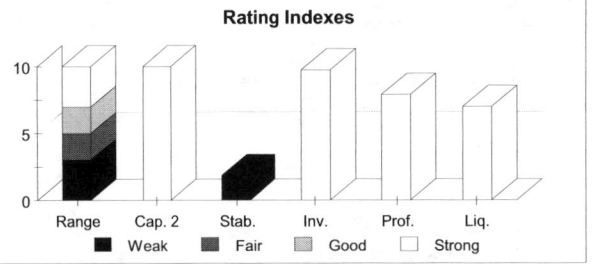

Rating Indexes

HMO OF NORTHEASTERN PENNSYLVANIA INC

C **Fair**

Major Rating Factors: Fair profitability index (4.5 on a scale of 0 to 10). Fair quality investment portfolio (4.4). Fair overall results on stability tests (3.9) based on an inordinate decline in premium revenue in 2013.

Other Rating Factors: Strong capitalization index (10.0) based on excellent current risk-adjusted capital (severe loss scenario). Excellent liquidity (7.0) with ample operational cash flow and liquid investments.

Principal Business: Comp med (100%)

Mem Phys: 13: 6,813 **12:** 6,459 **13 MLR** 81.7% **/ 13 Admin Exp** N/A

Enroll(000): Q2 14: 19 **13:** 21 **12:** 25 **Med Exp PMPM:** $246

Principal Investments: Long-term bonds (58%), nonaffiliate common stock (23%), cash and equiv (14%), other (5%)

Provider Compensation ($000): FFS ($32,648), contr fee ($30,610), capitation ($2,783), bonus arrang ($83)

Total Member Encounters: Phys (120,286), non-phys (3,441)

Group Affiliation: Hospital Svc Assoc of NE PA

Licensed in: PA

Address: 19 N Main St, Wilkes Barre, PA 18711

Phone: (800) 822-8753 **Dom State:** PA **Commenced Bus:** January 1987

Data Date	Rating	RACR #1	RACR #2	Total Assets ($mil)	Capital ($mil)	Net Premium ($mil)	Net Income ($mil)
6-14	C	7.59	6.33	85.0	72.9	34.8	1.4
6-13	C	7.13	5.94	80.8	65.5	40.5	1.3
2013	C	7.42	6.18	83.2	70.9	79.9	6.4
2012	C	6.95	5.79	78.7	64.0	93.9	9.9
2011	C	6.95	5.79	103.7	82.9	116.6	-3.3
2010	C+	5.21	4.34	107.7	85.2	166.1	3.9
2009	B	4.48	3.74	140.0	111.2	228.7	2.7

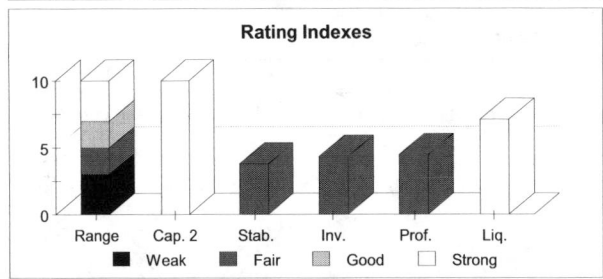

Rating Indexes

HMO PARTNERS INC *

A+ **Excellent**

Major Rating Factors: Excellent profitability (7.9 on a scale of 0 to 10). Strong capitalization index (10.0) based on excellent current risk-adjusted capital (severe loss scenario). High quality investment portfolio (9.9).

Other Rating Factors: Excellent overall results on stability tests (8.0). Good liquidity (6.8) with sufficient resources (cash flows and marketable investments) to handle a spike in claims.

Principal Business: Comp med (100%)

Mem Phys: 13: 13,092 **12:** 12,315 **13 MLR** 128.8% **/ 13 Admin Exp** N/A

Enroll(000): Q2 14: 70 **13:** 72 **12:** 67 **Med Exp PMPM:** $352

Principal Investments: Long-term bonds (51%), cash and equiv (31%), nonaffiliate common stock (17%)

Provider Compensation ($000): Bonus arrang ($201,336), FFS ($2,737)

Total Member Encounters: Phys (63,431), non-phys (74,644)

Group Affiliation: Arkansas Bl Cross Bl Shield Group

Licensed in: AR

Address: 320 West Capitol, Little Rock, AR 72203-8069

Phone: (501) 221-1800 **Dom State:** AR **Commenced Bus:** January 1994

Data Date	Rating	RACR #1	RACR #2	Total Assets ($mil)	Capital ($mil)	Net Premium ($mil)	Net Income ($mil)
6-14	A+	11.37	9.47	171.0	119.0	85.7	3.4
6-13	A+	11.56	9.64	148.4	111.9	75.0	6.1
2013	A+	11.17	9.31	157.2	116.9	153.8	7.5
2012	A+	11.32	9.43	148.0	109.3	143.2	8.4
2011	A+	10.19	8.49	146.0	102.0	143.8	8.7
2010	A+	9.61	8.01	142.8	95.6	136.2	9.7
2009	A	8.68	7.23	128.4	84.1	122.8	5.4

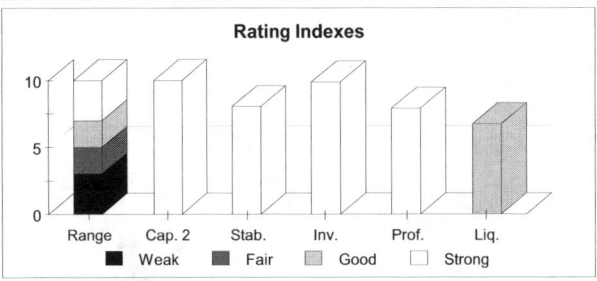

Rating Indexes

HOME STATE HEALTH PLAN INC   C-   Fair

Major Rating Factors: Weak profitability index (0.9 on a scale of 0 to 10). Good liquidity (5.3) with sufficient resources (cash flows and marketable investments) to handle a spike in claims. Strong capitalization (8.5) based on excellent current risk-adjusted capital (severe loss scenario).
Other Rating Factors: High quality investment portfolio (9.9).
Principal Business: Medicaid (100%)
Mem Phys: 13: 12,008   **12:** 10,344   **13 MLR** 96.0%   **/ 13 Admin Exp** N/A
Enroll(000): Q2 14: 57   **13:** 58   **12:** 60   **Med Exp PMPM:** $253
Principal Investments: Long-term bonds (75%), affiliate common stock (14%), cash and equiv (11%)
Provider Compensation ($000): Contr fee ($148,196), capitation ($20,177), salary ($2,379), bonus arrang ($1,690)
Total Member Encounters: Phys (286,069), non-phys (258,729)
Group Affiliation: Centene Corp
Licensed in: MO
Address: 16090 Swingley Ridge Rd #500, St Louis, MO 63105
Phone: (314) 725-4477   **Dom State:** MO   **Commenced Bus:** July 2012

Data Date	Rating	RACR #1	RACR #2	Total Assets ($mil)	Capital ($mil)	Net Premium ($mil)	Net Income ($mil)
6-14	C-	2.55	2.12	45.7	18.5	89.9	-0.7
6-13	C-	3.59	2.99	54.6	25.4	94.2	4.8
2013	C-	2.44	2.03	47.4	17.2	185.2	-2.8
2012	C-	2.77	2.31	52.8	20.3	77.8	-15.6
2011	N/A	N/A	N/A	N/A	N/A	N/A	N/A
2010	N/A	N/A	N/A	N/A	N/A	N/A	N/A
2009	N/A	N/A	N/A	N/A	N/A	N/A	N/A

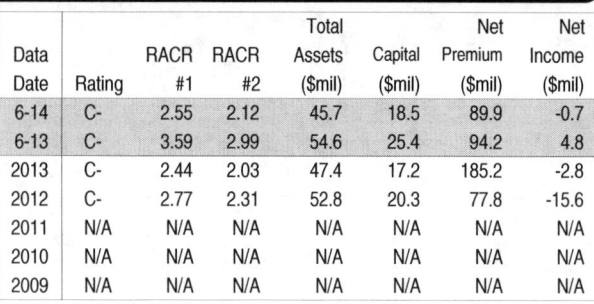

Rating Indexes

Range · Cap. 2 · Stab. · Inv. · Prof. · Liq.
■ Weak   ▨ Fair   ▨ Good   □ Strong

HOMETOWN HEALTH PLAN INC   C   Fair

Major Rating Factors: Fair overall results on stability tests (4.7 on a scale of 0 to 10). Weak profitability index (1.4). Good capitalization index (5.4) based on good current risk-adjusted capital (severe loss scenario).
Other Rating Factors: High quality investment portfolio (9.8). Excellent liquidity (7.0) with sufficient resources (cash flows and marketable investments) to handle a spike in claims.
Principal Business: Medicare (53%), comp med (47%)
Mem Phys: 13: 2,601   **12:** 2,224   **13 MLR** 90.2%   **/ 13 Admin Exp** N/A
Enroll(000): Q2 14: 33   **13:** 33   **12:** 30   **Med Exp PMPM:** $550
Principal Investments: Cash and equiv (65%), long-term bonds (27%), real estate (7%), nonaffiliate common stock (1%)
Provider Compensation ($000): FFS ($198,534), capitation ($2,186)
Total Member Encounters: Phys (278,309), non-phys (564,801)
Group Affiliation: Renown Health
Licensed in: NV
Address: 830 Harvard Way, Reno, NV 89502
Phone: (775) 982-3100   **Dom State:** NV   **Commenced Bus:** February 1988

Data Date	Rating	RACR #1	RACR #2	Total Assets ($mil)	Capital ($mil)	Net Premium ($mil)	Net Income ($mil)
6-14	C	1.00	0.83	75.3	25.2	126.1	-11.2
6-13	C	1.36	1.13	114.8	37.5	146.7	6.2
2013	C	1.39	1.16	88.1	35.5	237.4	4.8
2012	C	1.11	0.93	84.9	32.5	245.2	8.2
2011	C	1.35	1.13	49.7	20.6	210.4	-1.5
2010	N/A	N/A	N/A	45.1	23.3	196.0	10.1
2009	D+	0.95	0.79	35.5	13.6	177.3	-5.7

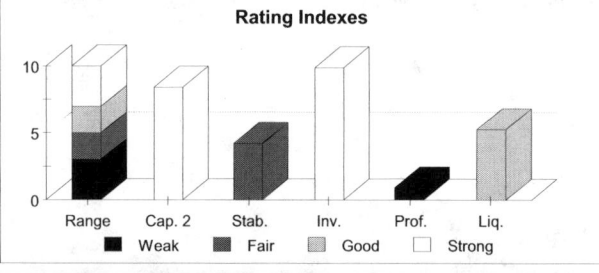

Rating Indexes

Range · Cap. 2 · Stab. · Inv. · Prof. · Liq.
■ Weak   ▨ Fair   ▨ Good   □ Strong

HOMETOWN HEALTH PROVIDERS INS CO   B   Good

Major Rating Factors: Good overall profitability index (5.1 on a scale of 0 to 10). Strong capitalization (10.0) based on excellent current risk-adjusted capital (severe loss scenario). High quality investment portfolio (9.3).
Other Rating Factors: Excellent liquidity (7.3) with ample operational cash flow and liquid investments.
Principal Business: Comp med (96%), Medicare (4%)
Mem Phys: 13: 2,601   **12:** 2,224   **13 MLR** 82.1%   **/ 13 Admin Exp** N/A
Enroll(000): Q2 14: 22   **13:** 19   **12:** 18   **Med Exp PMPM:** $188
Principal Investments: Cash and equiv (55%), long-term bonds (30%), real estate (14%), nonaffiliate common stock (1%)
Provider Compensation ($000): FFS ($40,711)
Total Member Encounters: Phys (39,636), non-phys (70,498)
Group Affiliation: Renown Health
Licensed in: NV
Address: 830 Harvard Way, Reno, NV 89502
Phone: (775) 982-3100   **Dom State:** NV   **Commenced Bus:** March 1982

Data Date	Rating	RACR #1	RACR #2	Total Assets ($mil)	Capital ($mil)	Net Premium ($mil)	Net Income ($mil)
6-14	B	4.18	3.49	40.8	29.9	28.8	1.5
6-13	N/A	N/A	N/A	43.7	30.4	29.1	1.3
2013	B	4.18	3.48	46.1	29.1	53.6	0.3
2012	N/A	N/A	N/A	40.8	29.3	59.6	1.6
2011	N/A	N/A	N/A	36.3	27.3	5.8	3.9
2010	N/A	N/A	N/A	30.9	23.1	53.9	2.7
2009	B	2.68	2.23	28.3	20.4	59.4	0.3

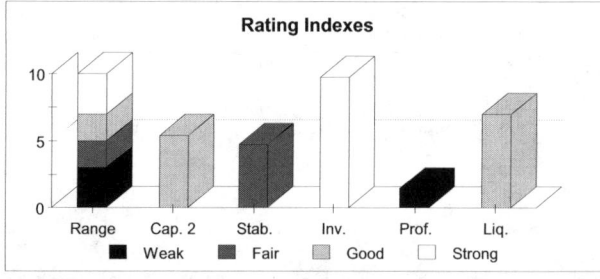

Rating Indexes

Range · Cap. 2 · Stab. · Inv. · Prof. · Liq.
■ Weak   ▨ Fair   ▨ Good   □ Strong

HONORED CITIZENS CHOICE HEALTH PLAN   E   Very Weak

Major Rating Factors: Weak profitability index (0.9 on a scale of 0 to 10). Weak overall results on stability tests (0.1). Weak liquidity (0.0) as a spike in claims may stretch capacity.

Other Rating Factors: Fair capitalization index (3.7) based on weak current risk-adjusted capital (moderate loss scenario).

Principal Business: Medicare (100%)

Mem Phys: 13: N/A **12:** N/A **13 MLR** 91.2% **/ 13 Admin Exp** N/A

Enroll(000): Q2 14: 13 **13:** 15 **12:** 12 **Med Exp PMPM:** $836

Principal Investments ($000): Cash and equiv ($5,509)

Provider Compensation ($000): None

Total Member Encounters: N/A

Group Affiliation: None

Licensed in: CA

Address: 5400 E Olympi Suite 130, Los Angeles, CA 90703

Phone: (323) 728-7232 **Dom State:** CA **Commenced Bus:** May 2004

Data Date	Rating	RACR #1	RACR #2	Total Assets ($mil)	Capital ($mil)	Net Premium ($mil)	Net Income ($mil)
6-14	E	0.61	0.38	43.7	15.4	61.7	-13.2
6-13	D-	0.15	0.09	35.4	6.4	82.3	0.5
2013	E	N/A	N/A	28.6	1.7	161.2	-3.8
2012	D-	0.12	0.07	29.3	6.0	145.7	1.9
2011	D-	0.13	0.08	28.4	5.8	159.3	4.8
2010	D-	0.06	0.03	24.3	4.3	124.3	1.7
2009	D-	0.21	0.13	15.9	3.3	87.8	0.4

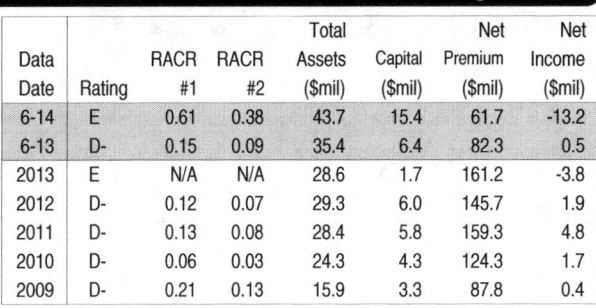

Rating Indexes

HORIZON HEALTHCARE OF NEW JERSEY INC *   A-   Excellent

Major Rating Factors: Strong capitalization index (8.3 on a scale of 0 to 10) based on excellent current risk-adjusted capital (severe loss scenario). High quality investment portfolio (9.9). Good overall profitability index (5.4).

Other Rating Factors: Good overall results on stability tests (6.8) despite a decline in enrollment during 2013. Good liquidity (6.1) with sufficient resources (cash flows and marketable investments) to handle a spike in claims.

Principal Business: Medicaid (55%), Medicare (23%), comp med (22%)

Mem Phys: 13: 74,179 **12:** 63,698 **13 MLR** 89.3% **/ 13 Admin Exp** N/A

Enroll(000): Q2 14: 740 **13:** 755 **12:** 896 **Med Exp PMPM:** $359

Principal Investments: Long-term bonds (87%), nonaffiliate common stock (14%)

Provider Compensation ($000): Contr fee ($3,302,738), FFS ($222,040), capitation ($199,791)

Total Member Encounters: Phys (9,554,264), non-phys (4,933,155)

Group Affiliation: Horizon Healthcare Services Inc

Licensed in: NJ

Address: 3 Penn Plaza East- PP-15D, Newark, NJ 07105-2248

Phone: (973) 466-5607 **Dom State:** NJ **Commenced Bus:** June 1986

Data Date	Rating	RACR #1	RACR #2	Total Assets ($mil)	Capital ($mil)	Net Premium ($mil)	Net Income ($mil)
6-14	A-	2.36	1.97	1,300.1	558.0	1,788.1	-16.3
6-13	A	2.46	2.05	1,278.9	558.6	2,121.0	28.8
2013	A	2.44	2.04	1,318.4	577.6	4,115.5	36.1
2012	A	2.39	1.99	1,235.9	542.6	4,099.9	50.4
2011	A	2.73	2.28	1,100.7	486.7	3,460.9	65.6
2010	A+	3.29	2.74	1,007.9	499.8	2,932.5	93.9
2009	A+	2.81	2.34	954.2	406.1	2,769.4	90.8

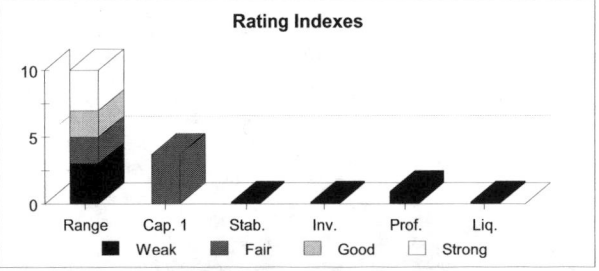

Rating Indexes

HORIZON HEALTHCARE SERVICES INC *   B+   Good

Major Rating Factors: Good overall profitability index (6.2 on a scale of 0 to 10). Good quality investment portfolio (6.4). Good liquidity (6.9) with sufficient resources (cash flows and marketable investments) to handle a spike in claims.

Other Rating Factors: Strong capitalization (10.0) based on excellent current risk-adjusted capital (severe loss scenario).

Principal Business: Comp med (82%), FEHB (12%), dental (3%), med supp (2%)

Mem Phys: 13: 76,483 **12:** 65,516 **13 MLR** 84.9% **/ 13 Admin Exp** N/A

Enroll(000): **13:** 1,466 **12:** 1,903 **Med Exp PMPM:** $269

Principal Investments: Long-term bonds (62%), affiliate common stock (24%), nonaffiliate common stock (10%), other (10%)

Provider Compensation ($000): Contr fee ($4,097,039), capitation ($233,332), FFS ($100,962), other ($37,722)

Total Member Encounters: Phys (14,419,313), non-phys (11,725,831)

Group Affiliation: Horizon Healthcare Services Inc

Licensed in: NJ

Address: 3 Penn Plaza East, PP-15D, Newark, NJ 07105-2248

Phone: (973) 466-5607 **Dom State:** NJ **Commenced Bus:** December 1932

Data Date	Rating	RACR #1	RACR #2	Total Assets ($mil)	Capital ($mil)	Net Premium ($mil)	Net Income ($mil)
2013	B+	4.11	3.42	3,679.0	2,212.0	5,243.6	519.9
2012	B	3.87	3.23	3,624.1	2,106.9	4,940.8	152.6
2011	B	4.17	3.48	3,464.7	1,973.2	4,836.1	124.8
2010	B	3.95	3.29	3,370.0	1,771.1	5,005.3	65.5
2009	B	3.51	2.92	3,100.4	1,560.0	5,058.8	-4.3

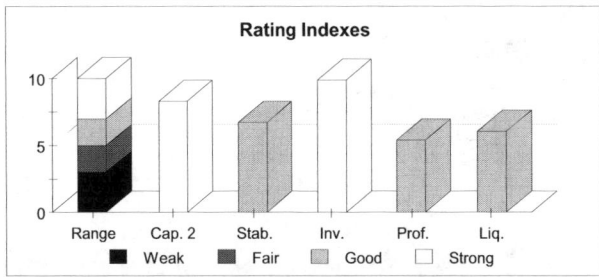

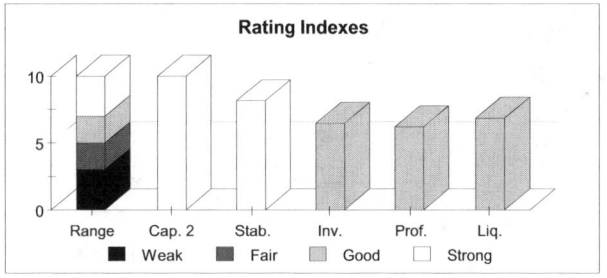

Rating Indexes

HORIZON INS CO

B   **Good**

Major Rating Factors: Good liquidity (6.1 on a scale of 0 to 10) with sufficient resources (cash flows and marketable investments) to handle a spike in claims. Excellent profitability (9.0). Strong capitalization (7.0) based on excellent current risk-adjusted capital (severe loss scenario).
Other Rating Factors: High quality investment portfolio (9.9).
Principal Business: Med supp (100%)
Mem Phys: 13: 76,483   **12:** N/A   **13 MLR** 78.8%   **/ 13 Admin Exp** N/A
Enroll(000):   **13:** 92   **12:** N/A   **Med Exp PMPM:** $181
Principal Investments: Long-term bonds (80%), cash and equiv (20%)
Provider Compensation ($000): Bonus arrang ($67,292), contr fee ($5,863)
Total Member Encounters: Phys (1,312,282), non-phys (606,567)
Group Affiliation: Horizon Healthcare Services Inc
Licensed in: NJ
Address: 3 Penn Plaza East PP-15D, Newark, NJ 07105-2248
Phone: (973) 466-5607   **Dom State:** NJ   **Commenced Bus:** December 2012

Data Date	Rating	RACR #1	RACR #2	Total Assets ($mil)	Capital ($mil)	Net Premium ($mil)	Net Income ($mil)
2013	B	1.40	1.16	68.0	9.9	122.6	1.5
2012	N/A	N/A	N/A	4.2	4.2	N/A	N/A
2011	N/A	N/A	N/A	N/A	N/A	N/A	N/A
2010	N/A	N/A	N/A	N/A	N/A	N/A	N/A
2009	N/A	N/A	N/A	N/A	N/A	N/A	N/A

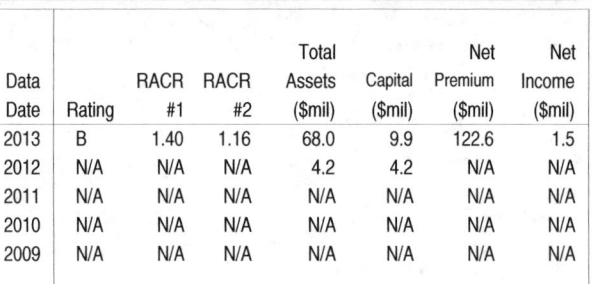

Rating Indexes

Range, Cap. 2, Stab., Inv., Prof., Liq.
■ Weak ▨ Fair ▨ Good □ Strong

HOSPITAL SERV ASSN OF NORTH EAST PA

C   **Fair**

Major Rating Factors: Fair profitability index (3.4 on a scale of 0 to 10). Good quality investment portfolio (5.0). Strong capitalization (10.0) based on excellent current risk-adjusted capital (severe loss scenario).
Other Rating Factors: Excellent liquidity (7.3) with ample operational cash flow and liquid investments.
Principal Business: Medicaid (46%), FEHB (28%), med supp (17%), comp med (7%), other (2%)
Mem Phys: 13: 778   **12:** 766   **13 MLR** 48.5%   **/ 13 Admin Exp** N/A
Enroll(000): Q2 14: 102   **13:** 102   **12:** 75   **Med Exp PMPM:** $93
Principal Investments: Long-term bonds (44%), affiliate common stock (30%), nonaffiliate common stock (17%), real estate (3%), cash and equiv (2%), other (3%)
Provider Compensation ($000): FFS ($78,117), contr fee ($26,316)
Total Member Encounters: N/A
Group Affiliation: Hospital Svc Assoc of NE PA
Licensed in: PA
Address: 19 N Main St, Wilkes-Barre, PA 18711
Phone: (800) 829-8599   **Dom State:** PA   **Commenced Bus:** December 1938

Data Date	Rating	RACR #1	RACR #2	Total Assets ($mil)	Capital ($mil)	Net Premium ($mil)	Net Income ($mil)
6-14	C	4.94	4.12	493.0	348.3	89.9	6.4
6-13	C	4.21	3.51	513.1	275.6	96.2	8.9
2013	C	4.86	4.05	497.7	341.4	215.6	50.6
2012	C-	3.93	3.27	496.6	258.2	113.0	32.4
2011	C-	3.41	2.84	485.8	209.5	141.9	-25.8
2010	C-	3.36	2.80	520.4	261.5	128.7	-7.1
2009	C	2.67	2.22	542.2	250.7	122.6	-59.5

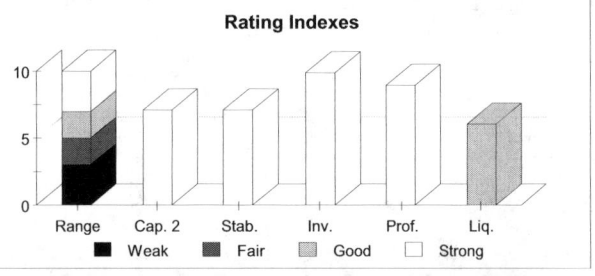

Rating Indexes

Range, Cap. 2, Stab., Inv., Prof., Liq.
■ Weak ▨ Fair ▨ Good □ Strong

HPHC INS CO INC

B-   **Good**

Major Rating Factors: Fair capitalization (4.9 on a scale of 0 to 10) based on good current risk-adjusted capital (severe loss scenario). Fair liquidity (4.0) as cash resources may not be adequate to cover a spike in claims. High quality investment portfolio (9.3).
Other Rating Factors: Weak profitability index (1.9).
Principal Business: Comp med (78%), med supp (6%), other (16%)
Mem Phys: 13: 55,628   **12:** 47,769   **13 MLR** 88.4%   **/ 13 Admin Exp** N/A
Enroll(000): Q2 14: 173   **13:** 172   **12:** 149   **Med Exp PMPM:** $270
Principal Investments: Long-term bonds (99%), cash and equiv (1%)
Provider Compensation ($000): Contr fee ($393,300), FFS ($68,498), bonus arrang ($27,435), capitation ($18,213), other ($36,791)
Total Member Encounters: Phys (884,123), non-phys (402,856)
Group Affiliation: Harvard Community Health Plan Inc
Licensed in: CT, ME, MA, NH
Address: 93 Worcester St, Wellesley, MA 02481
Phone: (781) 263-6000   **Dom State:** MA   **Commenced Bus:** January 1992

Data Date	Rating	RACR #1	RACR #2	Total Assets ($mil)	Capital ($mil)	Net Premium ($mil)	Net Income ($mil)
6-14	B-	0.91	0.76	164.3	38.0	301.8	-5.8
6-13	B	1.20	1.00	161.2	39.5	305.3	2.9
2013	B	1.02	0.85	158.0	42.0	616.1	-3.8
2012	B	1.24	1.03	150.3	40.7	542.5	-2.0
2011	B	1.44	1.20	132.5	42.6	455.9	5.4
2010	B+	1.41	1.17	113.4	36.7	361.3	7.4
2009	B	1.38	1.15	81.8	29.0	263.7	7.9

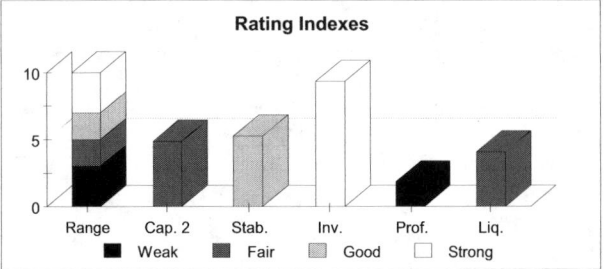

Rating Indexes

Range, Cap. 2, Stab., Inv., Prof., Liq.
■ Weak ▨ Fair ▨ Good □ Strong

HUMANA BENEFIT PLAN OF ILLINOIS   B   Good

Major Rating Factors: Good liquidity (6.8 on a scale of 0 to 10) with sufficient resources (cash flows and marketable investments) to handle a spike in claims. Excellent profitability (7.4). Strong capitalization (10.0) based on excellent current risk-adjusted capital (severe loss scenario).
Other Rating Factors: High quality investment portfolio (8.6).
Principal Business: Medicare (96%), FEHB (4%)
Mem Phys: 13: 136,449 **12:** N/A **13 MLR** 84.2% **/ 13 Admin Exp** N/A
Enroll(000): Q2 14: 30 **13:** 18 **12:** 18 **Med Exp PMPM:** $653
Principal Investments: Long-term bonds (100%)
Provider Compensation ($000): Contr fee ($117,657), capitation ($23,565), FFS ($3,463)
Total Member Encounters: Phys (340,439), non-phys (181,231)
Group Affiliation: Humana Inc
Licensed in: IL, PA
Address: 7915 N Hale Ave Suite D, Peoria, IL 61615
Phone: (502) 580-1000 **Dom State:** IL **Commenced Bus:** February 1995

Data Date	Rating	RACR #1	RACR #2	Total Assets ($mil)	Capital ($mil)	Net Premium ($mil)	Net Income ($mil)
6-14	B	5.60	4.67	98.9	51.8	142.5	7.7
6-13	C+	4.50	3.75	67.8	45.7	88.6	4.9
2013	B	4.99	4.16	66.4	45.9	172.3	4.7
2012	C+	4.40	3.66	64.3	44.6	164.5	3.8
2011	C	4.21	3.51	61.4	39.7	172.4	9.0
2010	C+	4.56	3.80	80.0	55.0	201.3	12.4
2009	C	2.42	2.01	82.1	39.7	269.6	1.1

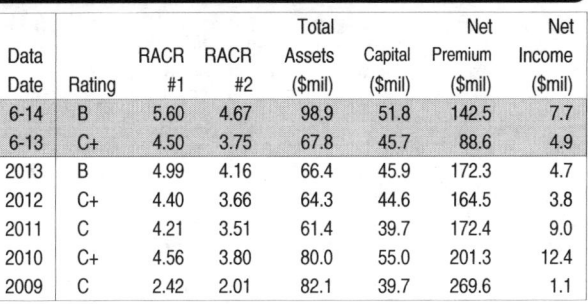

Rating Indexes

HUMANA EMPLOYERS HEALTH PLAN OF GA   D   Weak

Major Rating Factors: Weak profitability index (0.9 on a scale of 0 to 10). Fair overall results on stability tests (4.9) based on an excessive 38% enrollment growth during the period. Rating is significantly influenced by the fair financial results of Humana Inc. Good liquidity (6.8) with sufficient resources (cash flows and marketable investments) to handle a spike in claims.
Other Rating Factors: Strong capitalization index (9.6) based on excellent current risk-adjusted capital (severe loss scenario). High quality investment portfolio (9.9).
Principal Business: Comp med (69%), Medicare (28%), FEHB (3%)
Mem Phys: 13: 76,389 **12:** 4,496 **13 MLR** 80.1% **/ 13 Admin Exp** N/A
Enroll(000): Q2 14: 462 **13:** 209 **12:** 151 **Med Exp PMPM:** $225
Principal Investments: Long-term bonds (75%), cash and equiv (25%)
Provider Compensation ($000): Contr fee ($376,193), FFS ($83,563), capitation ($24,111)
Total Member Encounters: Phys (1,117,937), non-phys (337,986)
Group Affiliation: Humana Inc
Licensed in: GA
Address: 900 Ashwood Pkwy., Suite 400, Atlanta, GA 30338
Phone: (770) 393-9226 **Dom State:** GA **Commenced Bus:** February 1997

Data Date	Rating	RACR #1	RACR #2	Total Assets ($mil)	Capital ($mil)	Net Premium ($mil)	Net Income ($mil)
6-14	D	3.45	2.87	416.5	115.9	750.7	5.0
6-13	D	3.27	2.73	167.4	66.0	295.1	-3.0
2013	D	2.21	1.84	194.7	73.9	628.6	-31.9
2012	D	1.72	1.43	105.4	34.0	393.2	-7.5
2011	B	2.99	2.49	104.4	43.1	286.2	-7.3
2010	C+	7.42	6.18	81.9	44.0	112.4	0.1
2009	C+	7.52	6.27	67.7	30.6	75.8	6.0

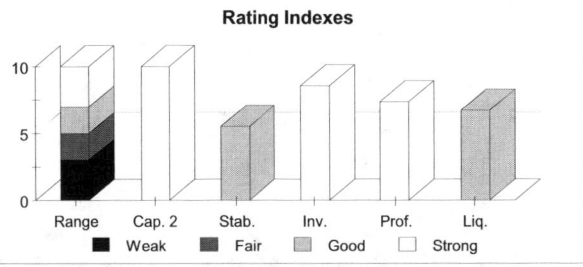

Rating Indexes

HUMANA HEALTH BENEFIT PLAN LA   B   Good

Major Rating Factors: Good overall results on stability tests (5.5 on a scale of 0 to 10). Fair financial strength from affiliates. Good liquidity (6.9) with sufficient resources (cash flows and marketable investments) to handle a spike in claims. Excellent profitability (8.6).
Other Rating Factors: Strong capitalization index (9.3) based on excellent current risk-adjusted capital (severe loss scenario). High quality investment portfolio (9.9).
Principal Business: Medicare (82%), comp med (17%)
Mem Phys: 13: 76,284 **12:** 9,774 **13 MLR** 78.3% **/ 13 Admin Exp** N/A
Enroll(000): Q2 14: 237 **13:** 213 **12:** 192 **Med Exp PMPM:** $467
Principal Investments: Long-term bonds (83%), cash and equiv (17%)
Provider Compensation ($000): Contr fee ($763,303), capitation ($308,122), FFS ($80,578)
Total Member Encounters: Phys (2,628,316), non-phys (1,551,094)
Group Affiliation: Humana Inc
Licensed in: LA
Address: 1 Galleria Blvd Suite 850, Metairie, LA 70001
Phone: (504) 219-6600 **Dom State:** LA **Commenced Bus:** November 1994

Data Date	Rating	RACR #1	RACR #2	Total Assets ($mil)	Capital ($mil)	Net Premium ($mil)	Net Income ($mil)
6-14	B	3.21	2.68	414.2	200.6	822.1	39.1
6-13	B	3.38	2.82	392.0	201.0	738.3	52.0
2013	B	3.74	3.11	388.0	236.6	1,464.8	88.3
2012	B	3.44	2.86	357.8	204.7	1,371.7	79.7
2011	B	3.67	3.06	362.2	208.4	1,318.2	83.9
2010	B	3.31	2.76	347.1	188.9	1,263.1	51.1
2009	B	3.24	2.70	340.5	176.8	1,190.1	49.9

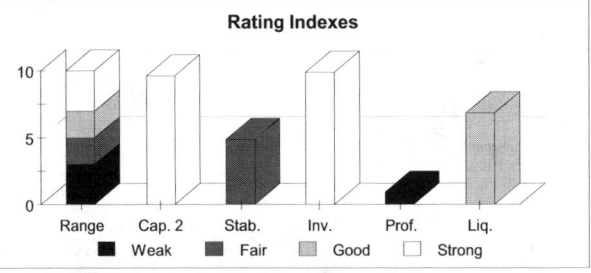

Rating Indexes

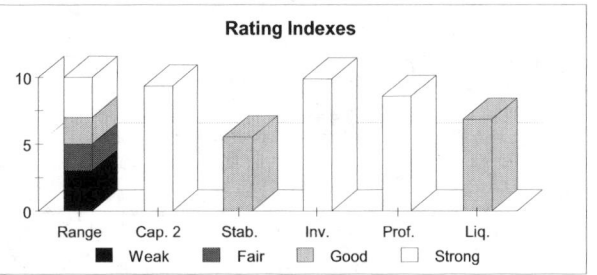

HUMANA HEALTH CO OF NEW YORK INC   E   Very Weak

Major Rating Factors: Weak profitability index (0.9 on a scale of 0 to 10). Strong capitalization (10.0) based on excellent current risk-adjusted capital (severe loss scenario). High quality investment portfolio (9.9).

Other Rating Factors: Excellent liquidity (10.0) with ample operational cash flow and liquid investments.

Principal Business: Medicare (100%)

Mem Phys: 13: 21,555   **12:** N/A   **13 MLR** 87.8%   **/ 13 Admin Exp** N/A

Enroll(000): Q2 14: 2   **13:** 1   **12:** 1   **Med Exp PMPM:** $588

Principal Investments: Cash and equiv (100%)

Provider Compensation ($000): Contr fee ($3,863), FFS ($370), capitation ($28)

Total Member Encounters: Phys (10,543), non-phys (4,865)

Group Affiliation: Humana Inc

Licensed in: NY

Address: 100 Elwood Davis Rd, North Syracuse, NY 13212

Phone: (510) 832-0311   **Dom State:** NY   **Commenced Bus:** January 2009

Data Date	Rating	RACR #1	RACR #2	Total Assets ($mil)	Capital ($mil)	Net Premium ($mil)	Net Income ($mil)
6-14	E	19.40	16.17	29.4	26.9	6.6	0.1
6-13	E	18.32	15.27	28.1	25.3	2.3	0.2
2013	E	19.34	16.12	27.5	26.8	4.5	1.4
2012	E	2.92	2.43	8.3	5.0	6.7	-3.2
2011	E-	0.60	0.50	3.7	2.1	12.0	0.2
2010	E-	0.45	0.38	2.8	1.4	11.0	-0.8
2009	E+	0.50	0.42	1.5	0.8	1.5	-1.0

HUMANA HEALTH INS CO OF FL INC   C   Fair

Major Rating Factors: Good quality investment portfolio (6.8 on a scale of 0 to 10). Good liquidity (6.7) with sufficient resources (cash flows and marketable investments) to handle a spike in claims. Excellent profitability (7.5).

Other Rating Factors: Strong capitalization (9.3) based on excellent current risk-adjusted capital (severe loss scenario).

Principal Business: Comp med (50%), Medicare (47%), med supp (2%), other (1%)

Mem Phys: 13: 194,793   **12:** 22,401   **13 MLR** 80.8%   **/ 13 Admin Exp** N/A

Enroll(000): Q2 14: 121   **13:** 133   **12:** 125   **Med Exp PMPM:** $162

Principal Investments: Long-term bonds (92%), cash and equiv (6%), other (2%)

Provider Compensation ($000): Contr fee ($209,668), FFS ($54,399), capitation ($36)

Total Member Encounters: Phys (673,626), non-phys (343,733)

Group Affiliation: Humana Inc

Licensed in: FL

Address: 3501 SW 160th Avenue, Miramar, FL 33027

Phone: (305) 626-5616   **Dom State:** FL   **Commenced Bus:** May 1984

Data Date	Rating	RACR #1	RACR #2	Total Assets ($mil)	Capital ($mil)	Net Premium ($mil)	Net Income ($mil)
6-14	C	3.22	2.68	131.9	57.3	147.1	6.2
6-13	B-	3.50	2.92	128.4	57.9	170.6	12.2
2013	C	3.28	2.73	127.8	58.5	323.7	10.2
2012	B	5.50	4.59	167.9	95.1	326.9	25.9
2011	C+	6.13	5.11	160.0	73.0	248.9	10.1
2010	B	4.54	3.78	168.8	97.8	489.7	36.9
2009	B	3.02	2.52	169.8	80.4	558.6	13.7

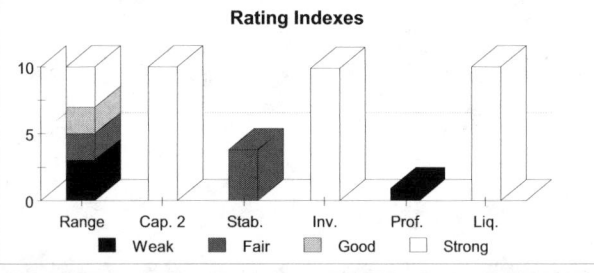

HUMANA HEALTH PLAN INC   C   Fair

Major Rating Factors: Weak profitability index (0.9 on a scale of 0 to 10). Good overall results on stability tests (5.9). Good liquidity (5.2) with sufficient resources (cash flows and marketable investments) to handle a spike in claims.

Other Rating Factors: Strong capitalization index (8.0) based on excellent current risk-adjusted capital (severe loss scenario). High quality investment portfolio (8.4).

Principal Business: Medicare (76%), comp med (21%), FEHB (3%)

Mem Phys: 13: 712,559   **12:** 50,830   **13 MLR** 88.2%   **/ 13 Admin Exp** N/A

Enroll(000): Q2 14: 742   **13:** 586   **12:** 477   **Med Exp PMPM:** $476

Principal Investments: Long-term bonds (85%), cash and equiv (7%), affiliate common stock (4%), mortgs (4%)

Provider Compensation ($000): Contr fee ($1,803,694), capitation ($1,185,544), FFS ($189,887), salary ($8,120)

Total Member Encounters: Phys (6,648,574), non-phys (3,028,637)

Group Affiliation: Humana Inc

Licensed in: AL, AZ, AR, CO, ID, IL, IN, KS, KY, MO, NE, NV, NM, SC, TN, VA, WA, WV

Address: 321 W Main St 12th Floor, Louisville, KY 40202

Phone: (502) 580-1000   **Dom State:** KY   **Commenced Bus:** September 1983

Data Date	Rating	RACR #1	RACR #2	Total Assets ($mil)	Capital ($mil)	Net Premium ($mil)	Net Income ($mil)
6-14	C	2.14	1.78	1,031.3	352.6	2,386.1	-45.8
6-13	C+	2.26	1.89	786.3	318.9	1,848.9	-5.7
2013	C	2.29	1.91	811.6	379.2	3,694.2	-38.5
2012	B-	2.19	1.82	645.2	307.9	2,992.3	-28.9
2011	B	2.49	2.08	528.8	265.5	2,341.6	5.5
2010	B	3.23	2.69	509.9	280.9	1,966.5	30.4
2009	C	2.07	1.73	405.4	175.6	1,767.2	-8.9

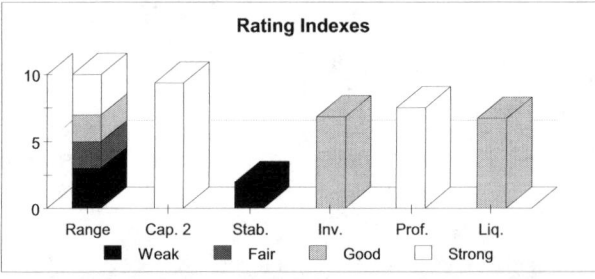

HUMANA HEALTH PLAN OF CALIFORNIA INC   C-   Fair

Major Rating Factors: Weak profitability index (0.9 on a scale of 0 to 10). Weak overall results on stability tests (1.3) based on an excessive 53% enrollment growth during the period. Rating is significantly influenced by the fair financial results of Humana Inc. Weak liquidity (0.0) as a spike in claims may stretch capacity.
Other Rating Factors: Good capitalization index (5.8) based on good current risk-adjusted capital (severe loss scenario).
Principal Business: Medicare (100%)
Mem Phys: 13: N/A **12:** N/A **13 MLR** 92.4% **/ 13 Admin Exp** N/A
Enroll(000): Q2 14: 40 **13:** 25 **12:** 16 **Med Exp PMPM:** $648
Principal Investments ($000): Cash and equiv ($866)
Provider Compensation ($000): None
Total Member Encounters: N/A
Group Affiliation: Humana Inc
Licensed in: CA
Address: 5421 Avenida Encinas Suite N, Carlsbad, CA 92008
Phone: (502) 580-3806 **Dom State:** CA **Commenced Bus:** May 2009

Data Date	Rating	RACR #1	RACR #2	Total Assets ($mil)	Capital ($mil)	Net Premium ($mil)	Net Income ($mil)
6-14	C-	1.28	0.87	81.9	27.8	168.3	-11.2
6-13	C-	3.98	2.68	73.7	47.5	103.0	1.9
2013	C-	2.22	1.51	64.0	38.0	205.0	-7.3
2012	C-	1.81	1.15	34.7	16.5	125.2	-11.5
2011	C	0.87	0.55	6.0	2.5	45.9	-1.8
2010	C	14.56	9.14	5.3	4.3	5.6	0.3
2009	C-	N/A	N/A	4.0	4.0	N/A	N/A

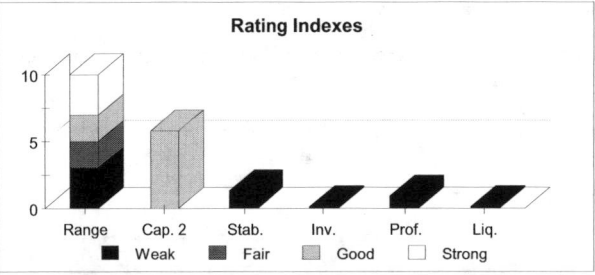

HUMANA HEALTH PLAN OF OHIO INC   C   Fair

Major Rating Factors: Weak profitability index (1.5 on a scale of 0 to 10). Good overall results on stability tests (6.3). Rating is significantly influenced by the fair financial results of Humana Inc. Good liquidity (6.0) with sufficient resources (cash flows and marketable investments) to handle a spike in claims.
Other Rating Factors: Strong capitalization index (8.1) based on excellent current risk-adjusted capital (severe loss scenario). High quality investment portfolio (8.7).
Principal Business: Comp med (51%), Medicare (49%)
Mem Phys: 13: 119,882 **12:** 3,493 **13 MLR** 82.5% **/ 13 Admin Exp** N/A
Enroll(000): Q2 14: 94 **13:** 75 **12:** 63 **Med Exp PMPM:** $348
Principal Investments: Long-term bonds (95%), cash and equiv (4%), other (1%)
Provider Compensation ($000): Contr fee ($238,120), FFS ($37,534), capitation ($21,755)
Total Member Encounters: Phys (630,238), non-phys (296,285)
Group Affiliation: Humana Inc
Licensed in: IN, KY, OH
Address: 640 Eden Park Dr, Cincinnati, OH 45202-6056
Phone: (513) 784-5320 **Dom State:** OH **Commenced Bus:** March 1979

Data Date	Rating	RACR #1	RACR #2	Total Assets ($mil)	Capital ($mil)	Net Premium ($mil)	Net Income ($mil)
6-14	C	2.27	1.89	116.3	45.5	246.4	-4.1
6-13	C	2.90	2.41	92.8	48.2	179.5	6.2
2013	C	2.41	2.01	90.7	48.6	367.0	5.6
2012	C	2.49	2.08	77.4	41.2	284.7	5.4
2011	C	2.94	2.45	78.7	39.5	224.2	-1.4
2010	C	5.46	4.55	87.7	41.6	98.3	-19.5
2009	C	5.37	4.47	43.5	16.2	44.7	-4.7

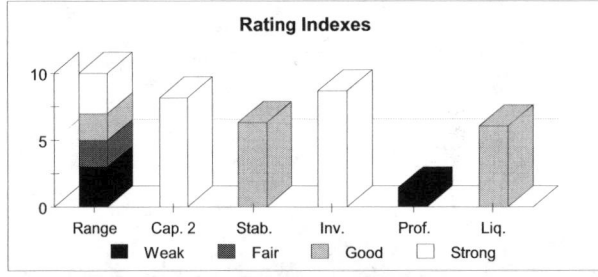

HUMANA HEALTH PLAN OF TEXAS INC   B   Good

Major Rating Factors: Good liquidity (6.4 on a scale of 0 to 10) with sufficient resources (cash flows and marketable investments) to handle a spike in claims. Fair profitability index (4.7). Strong capitalization index (10.0) based on excellent current risk-adjusted capital (severe loss scenario).
Other Rating Factors: High quality investment portfolio (9.9). Excellent overall results on stability tests (7.1) based on healthy premium and capital growth during 2013. Rating is significantly influenced by the fair financial results of Humana Inc.
Principal Business: Comp med (49%), Medicare (46%), FEHB (5%)
Mem Phys: 13: 223,854 **12:** 13,879 **13 MLR** 83.1% **/ 13 Admin Exp** N/A
Enroll(000): Q2 14: 386 **13:** 284 **12:** 259 **Med Exp PMPM:** $335
Principal Investments: Long-term bonds (91%), cash and equiv (7%), real estate (1%), other (1%)
Provider Compensation ($000): Contr fee ($558,280), salary ($380,992), FFS ($140,487), capitation ($44,506)
Total Member Encounters: Phys (2,214,210), non-phys (845,663)
Group Affiliation: Humana Inc
Licensed in: TX
Address: 1221 S Mopac Suite 200, Austin, TX 78746
Phone: (502) 580-1000 **Dom State:** TX **Commenced Bus:** July 1984

Data Date	Rating	RACR #1	RACR #2	Total Assets ($mil)	Capital ($mil)	Net Premium ($mil)	Net Income ($mil)
6-14	B	4.16	3.46	494.7	229.1	900.9	4.6
6-13	B	2.75	2.30	322.9	154.8	687.4	14.8
2013	B	3.20	2.66	335.2	174.7	1,362.4	9.6
2012	B	1.87	1.55	243.9	102.6	1,171.2	6.4
2011	B	2.12	1.77	255.8	107.8	1,017.4	34.4
2010	B-	2.36	1.97	217.1	75.8	636.1	-4.1
2009	B-	1.60	1.33	182.3	35.6	482.3	-4.3

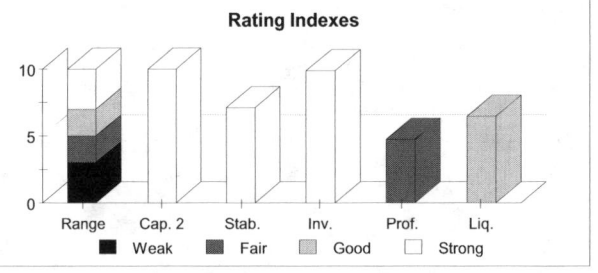

HUMANA HEALTH PLANS OF PUERTO RICO   B   Good

Major Rating Factors: Good liquidity (6.0 on a scale of 0 to 10) with sufficient resources (cash flows and marketable investments) to handle a spike in claims. Fair profitability index (3.1). Fair overall results on stability tests (4.3) based on a significant 92% decrease in enrollment during the period. Rating is significantly influenced by the fair financial results of Humana Inc.

Other Rating Factors: Strong capitalization index (7.4) based on excellent current risk-adjusted capital (severe loss scenario). High quality investment portfolio (9.4).

Principal Business: Medicaid (69%), Medicare (28%), FEHB (2%), comp med (1%)

Mem Phys: 13: 12,531   **12:** 12,119   **13 MLR** 93.0%   / **13 Admin Exp** N/A

Enroll(000): Q2 14: 57   **13:** 47   **12:** 568   **Med Exp PMPM:** $159

Principal Investments: Long-term bonds (96%), cash and equiv (4%)

Provider Compensation ($000): FFS ($768,054), capitation ($133,483)

Total Member Encounters: Phys (3,169,234), non-phys (317,193)

Group Affiliation: Humana Inc

Licensed in: PR

Address: 383 FD Roosevelt Ave 3rd Fl, San Juan, PR 00918-2131

Phone: (787) 282-7900   **Dom State:** PR   **Commenced Bus:** May 1986

Data Date	Rating	RACR #1	RACR #2	Total Assets ($mil)	Capital ($mil)	Net Premium ($mil)	Net Income ($mil)
6-14	B	1.68	1.40	189.1	82.9	192.2	-3.9
6-13	B	1.63	1.36	266.0	87.6	548.9	-16.4
2013	B	1.75	1.46	189.5	87.0	907.2	-15.0
2012	B	1.82	1.52	260.8	102.5	1,025.2	19.3
2011	B	1.74	1.45	226.3	82.4	917.7	15.7
2010	B	1.82	1.52	228.3	67.9	689.4	9.4
2009	B	1.84	1.54	192.7	61.0	592.1	6.4

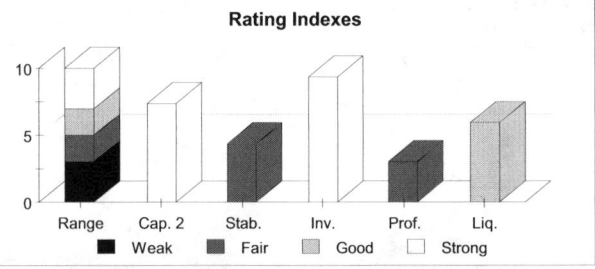

Rating Indexes

HUMANA INS CO OF NEW YORK   B   Good

Major Rating Factors: Fair profitability index (3.1 on a scale of 0 to 10). Strong capitalization (10.0) based on excellent current risk-adjusted capital (severe loss scenario). High quality investment portfolio (9.9).

Other Rating Factors: Excellent liquidity (7.0) with ample operational cash flow and liquid investments.

Principal Business: Medicare (43%), med supp (2%), other (55%)

Mem Phys: 13: 120,399   **12:** N/A   **13 MLR** 84.1%   / **13 Admin Exp** N/A

Enroll(000): Q2 14: 131   **13:** 99   **12:** 80   **Med Exp PMPM:** $140

Principal Investments: Long-term bonds (72%), cash and equiv (28%)

Provider Compensation ($000): Contr fee ($150,897), FFS ($1,838)

Total Member Encounters: Phys (201,810), non-phys (105,900)

Group Affiliation: Humana Inc

Licensed in: NY

Address: 125 Wolf Rd, Albany, NY 12205

Phone: (518) 435-0459   **Dom State:** NY   **Commenced Bus:** August 2006

Data Date	Rating	RACR #1	RACR #2	Total Assets ($mil)	Capital ($mil)	Net Premium ($mil)	Net Income ($mil)
6-14	B	6.15	5.13	96.7	58.3	119.7	-4.9
6-13	B	9.73	8.11	95.6	68.2	97.4	1.9
2013	B	6.73	5.61	82.8	64.0	185.5	-1.8
2012	B	9.18	7.65	78.3	64.2	146.7	3.1
2011	B	7.10	5.92	112.1	71.9	133.0	15.7
2010	N/A	N/A	N/A	111.5	73.6	137.9	5.1
2009	B	13.19	10.99	110.0	75.4	120.7	8.5

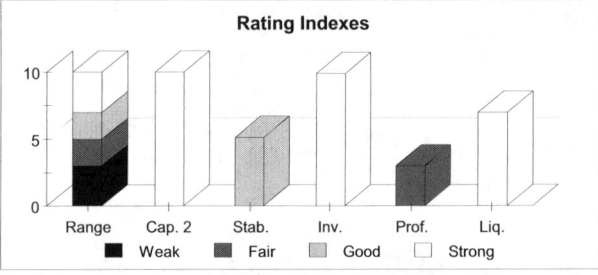

Rating Indexes

HUMANA INSURANCE COMPANY OF KENTUCKY   B-   Good

Major Rating Factors: Good overall results on stability tests (5.1 on a scale of 0 to 10) despite fair financial strength of affiliated Humana Inc. Other stability subfactors include good operational trends and good risk diversification. Good liquidity (6.7) with sufficient resources to handle a spike in claims. Weak profitability (2.9) with investment income below regulatory standards in relation to interest assumptions of reserves.

Other Rating Factors: Strong capitalization (8.0) based on excellent risk adjusted capital (severe loss scenario). High quality investment portfolio (8.1).

Principal Business: Reinsurance (60%), individual health insurance (20%), group life insurance (17%), and group health insurance (3%).

Principal Investments: NonCMO investment grade bonds (61%), CMOs and structured securities (36%), and cash (3%).

Investments in Affiliates: None

Group Affiliation: Humana Inc

Licensed in: KY

Commenced Business: January 2001

Address: 500 W Main St, Louisville, KY 40202

Phone: (502) 580-1000   **Domicile State:** KY   **NAIC Code:** 60219

Data Date	Rating	RACR #1	RACR #2	Total Assets ($mil)	Capital ($mil)	Net Premium ($mil)	Net Income ($mil)
6-14	B-	2.18	1.67	115.2	66.7	58.6	5.6
6-13	B-	2.08	1.62	48.8	30.5	22.1	5.6
2013	B-	2.03	1.57	108.6	61.1	111.5	15.7
2012	B-	1.73	1.35	42.3	24.8	40.8	6.4
2011	B-	1.40	1.10	35.9	18.5	36.6	-1.9
2010	B-	1.54	1.21	37.4	19.9	37.9	-0.1
2009	B-	1.74	1.37	34.2	19.6	33.7	0.1

Humana Inc Composite Group Rating: C+ Largest Group Members	Assets ($mil)	Rating
KANAWHA INS CO	1623	C
HUMANA MEDICAL PLAN INC	1595	B
HUMANA HEALTH PLAN INC	812	C
HUMANA HEALTH BENEFIT PLAN LA	388	B
HUMANA HEALTH PLAN OF TEXAS INC	335	B

HUMANA INSURANCE COMPANY OF PUERTO RICO INCORPORA   B-   Good

Major Rating Factors: Good overall results on stability tests (5.2 on a scale of 0 to 10) despite fair financial strength of affiliated Humana Inc. Other stability subfactors include good operational trends and good risk diversification. Good liquidity (6.6) with sufficient resources to handle a spike in claims. Strong capitalization (9.2) based on excellent risk adjusted capital (severe loss scenario).

Other Rating Factors: High quality investment portfolio (8.4). Excellent profitability (7.6) despite operating losses during the first six months of 2014.

Principal Business: Group health insurance (78%) and individual health insurance (22%).

Principal Investments: CMOs and structured securities (59%), nonCMO investment grade bonds (42%), and noninv. grade bonds (2%).

Investments in Affiliates: None

Group Affiliation: Humana Inc

Licensed in: PR

Commenced Business: September 1971

Address: 383 F D Roosevelt Ave, San Juan, PR 00918-2131

Phone: (787) 282-7900 **Domicile State:** PR **NAIC Code:** 84603

Data Date	Rating	RACR #1	RACR #2	Total Assets ($mil)	Capital ($mil)	Net Premium ($mil)	Net Income ($mil)
6-14	B-	3.12	2.46	73.6	55.0	47.1	-1.4
6-13	C+	3.27	2.60	73.9	58.7	46.5	5.7
2013	B-	3.20	2.52	73.3	57.0	93.2	4.7
2012	C+	2.86	2.27	70.2	52.1	98.6	4.6
2011	C	3.28	2.60	73.6	48.8	88.1	7.9
2010	C	N/A	N/A	57.5	40.9	89.2	8.1
2009	C	2.25	1.84	49.8	32.8	80.6	1.3

Humana Inc Composite Group Rating: C+ Largest Group Members	Assets ($mil)	Rating
KANAWHA INS CO	1623	C
HUMANA MEDICAL PLAN INC	1595	B
HUMANA HEALTH PLAN INC	812	C
HUMANA HEALTH BENEFIT PLAN LA	388	B
HUMANA HEALTH PLAN OF TEXAS INC	335	B

HUMANA MEDICAL PLAN INC   B   Good

Major Rating Factors: Good liquidity (5.2 on a scale of 0 to 10) with sufficient resources (cash flows and marketable investments) to handle a spike in claims. Fair overall results on stability tests (4.2). Fair financial strength from affiliates. Excellent profitability (8.0).

Other Rating Factors: Strong capitalization index (9.0) based on excellent current risk-adjusted capital (severe loss scenario). High quality investment portfolio (9.5).

Principal Business: Medicare (84%), comp med (12%), Medicaid (4%)

Mem Phys: 13: 210,805 **12:** 23,150 **13 MLR** 80.0% **/ 13 Admin Exp** N/A

Enroll(000): Q2 14: 825 **13:** 533 **12:** 485 **Med Exp PMPM:** $705

Principal Investments: Long-term bonds (90%), cash and equiv (9%), affiliate common stock (2%)

Provider Compensation ($000): Capitation ($2,344,324), contr fee ($906,834), salary ($807,210), FFS ($226,848)

Total Member Encounters: Phys (6,997,913), non-phys (3,256,858)

Group Affiliation: Humana Inc

Licensed in: FL, MS, NC, OR

Address: 3501 SW 160th Ave, Miramar, FL 33027

Phone: (305) 626-5616 **Dom State:** FL **Commenced Bus:** June 1987

Data Date	Rating	RACR #1	RACR #2	Total Assets ($mil)	Capital ($mil)	Net Premium ($mil)	Net Income ($mil)
6-14	B	2.92	2.43	1,670.8	380.0	3,234.4	124.4
6-13	B	2.96	2.46	1,506.0	335.5	2,675.1	162.8
2013	B	3.77	3.14	1,595.0	530.7	5,391.4	348.6
2012	B	4.80	4.00	1,618.6	631.5	5,242.2	461.2
2011	B	4.82	4.01	1,661.0	599.1	4,931.3	432.9
2010	B	3.86	3.22	1,587.0	447.5	4,664.0	276.0
2009	B	4.20	3.50	1,387.6	467.7	4,352.6	291.9

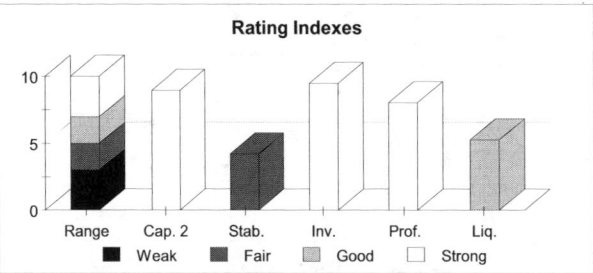

Rating Indexes

HUMANA MEDICAL PLAN OF MICHIGAN INC   B   Good

Major Rating Factors: Excellent profitability (8.8 on a scale of 0 to 10). Strong capitalization (10.0) based on excellent current risk-adjusted capital (severe loss scenario). High quality investment portfolio (9.9).

Other Rating Factors: Excellent liquidity (9.5) with ample operational cash flow and liquid investments.

Principal Business: Medicare (99%)

Mem Phys: 13: 28,292 **12:** N/A **13 MLR** 70.2% **/ 13 Admin Exp** N/A

Enroll(000): Q2 14: 32 **13:** 0 **12:** N/A **Med Exp PMPM:** $482

Principal Investments: Cash and equiv (98%), long-term bonds (2%)

Provider Compensation ($000): Contr fee ($917), capitation ($197), FFS ($34)

Total Member Encounters: Phys (2,754), non-phys (1,277)

Group Affiliation: Humana Inc

Licensed in: MI

Address: 5555 Glenwood Hills Pkwy 150, Grand Rapids, MI 49512

Phone: (502) 580-1000 **Dom State:** MI **Commenced Bus:** February 2012

Data Date	Rating	RACR #1	RACR #2	Total Assets ($mil)	Capital ($mil)	Net Premium ($mil)	Net Income ($mil)
6-14	B	12.07	10.06	35.9	17.8	29.8	3.1
6-13	N/A	N/A	N/A	5.3	5.0	0.8	N/A
2013	C	3.49	2.91	5.6	5.2	1.8	0.2
2012	N/A	N/A	N/A	5.0	5.0	N/A	N/A
2011	N/A	N/A	N/A	5.0	5.0	N/A	N/A
2010	N/A	N/A	N/A	N/A	N/A	N/A	N/A
2009	N/A	N/A	N/A	N/A	N/A	N/A	N/A

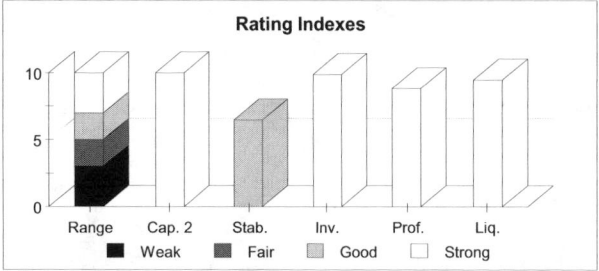

Rating Indexes

HUMANA MEDICAL PLAN OF UTAH INC

D   **Weak**

Major Rating Factors: Weak profitability index (0.9 on a scale of 0 to 10). Good liquidity (6.7) with sufficient resources (cash flows and marketable investments) to handle a spike in claims. Strong capitalization (10.0) based on excellent current risk-adjusted capital (severe loss scenario).
Other Rating Factors: High quality investment portfolio (9.9).
Principal Business: Medicare (99%), dental (1%)
Mem Phys: 13: 11,768   **12:** N/A   **13 MLR** 86.7%   **/ 13 Admin Exp** N/A
Enroll(000): Q2 14: 22   **13:** 7   **12:** 15   **Med Exp PMPM:** $383
Principal Investments: Long-term bonds (83%), cash and equiv (17%)
Provider Compensation ($000): Contr fee ($27,108), capitation ($9,798), FFS ($822)
Total Member Encounters: Phys (72,349), non-phys (55,800)
Group Affiliation: Humana Inc
Licensed in: UT
Address: 9815 S Monroe St Suite 300, Sandy, UT 84070
Phone: (801) 256-6200   **Dom State:** UT   **Commenced Bus:** March 2007

Data Date	Rating	RACR #1	RACR #2	Total Assets ($mil)	Capital ($mil)	Net Premium ($mil)	Net Income ($mil)
6-14	D	10.09	8.41	38.7	27.8	35.7	2.2
6-13	D	3.10	2.58	33.6	21.8	18.9	-0.2
2013	D	9.42	7.85	32.0	25.9	37.3	4.4
2012	D	3.08	2.57	39.3	21.7	93.1	-13.5
2011	D	1.44	1.20	7.7	4.0	31.1	-0.5
2010	B	3.26	2.72	6.4	4.3	10.7	0.0
2009	C	3.13	2.61	4.9	4.3	3.2	-0.2

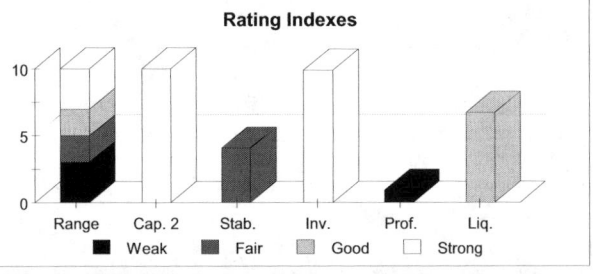

Rating Indexes

HUMANA WISCONSIN HEALTH ORGANIZATION

B   **Good**

Major Rating Factors: Good overall profitability index (6.5 on a scale of 0 to 10). Good overall results on stability tests (5.6). Rating is significantly influenced by the fair financial results of Humana Inc. Good liquidity (6.5) with sufficient resources (cash flows and marketable investments) to handle a spike in claims.
Other Rating Factors: Strong capitalization index (8.8) based on excellent current risk-adjusted capital (severe loss scenario). High quality investment portfolio (9.7).
Principal Business: Comp med (78%), Medicare (22%)
Mem Phys: 13: 45,141   **12:** 15,633   **13 MLR** 88.5%   **/ 13 Admin Exp** N/A
Enroll(000): Q2 14: 51   **13:** 49   **12:** 58   **Med Exp PMPM:** $382
Principal Investments: Long-term bonds (81%), cash and equiv (19%)
Provider Compensation ($000): Contr fee ($158,228), FFS ($42,806), capitation ($14,988)
Total Member Encounters: Phys (370,074), non-phys (171,875)
Group Affiliation: Humana Inc
Licensed in: WI
Address: N19-W24133 Riverwood Dr., #300, Waukesha, WI 53188
Phone: (262) 408-4300   **Dom State:** WI   **Commenced Bus:** September 1985

Data Date	Rating	RACR #1	RACR #2	Total Assets ($mil)	Capital ($mil)	Net Premium ($mil)	Net Income ($mil)
6-14	B	2.79	2.33	81.8	41.7	144.1	0.7
6-13	B	2.54	2.11	75.6	40.1	116.0	-0.1
2013	B	2.63	2.19	76.2	39.2	241.8	2.3
2012	B	2.38	1.98	73.3	37.4	286.3	0.6
2011	B	2.60	2.17	59.9	34.3	226.5	1.4
2010	C	3.16	2.63	59.8	33.7	176.8	6.1
2009	C	3.28	2.73	57.9	31.6	151.6	0.2

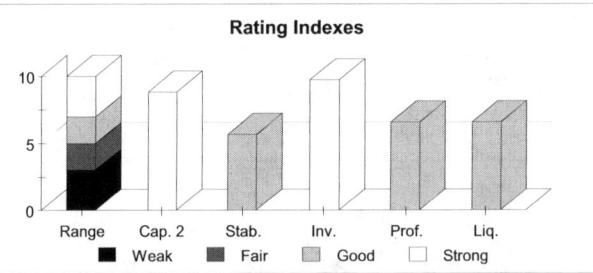

Rating Indexes

ILLINICARE HEALTH PLAN INC

C+   **Fair**

Major Rating Factors: Good overall profitability index (5.9 on a scale of 0 to 10). Good liquidity (6.8) with sufficient resources (cash flows and marketable investments) to handle a spike in claims. Strong capitalization (8.0) based on excellent current risk-adjusted capital (severe loss scenario).
Other Rating Factors: High quality investment portfolio (9.2).
Principal Business: Medicaid (100%)
Mem Phys: 13: 9,384   **12:** 7,902   **13 MLR** 89.1%   **/ 13 Admin Exp** N/A
Enroll(000): Q2 14: 27   **13:** 22   **12:** 17   **Med Exp PMPM:** $1,152
Principal Investments: Long-term bonds (64%), cash and equiv (32%), affiliate common stock (5%)
Provider Compensation ($000): Contr fee ($206,622), capitation ($23,023), salary ($11,401)
Total Member Encounters: Phys (199,888), non-phys (250,507)
Group Affiliation: Centene Corp
Licensed in: (No states)
Address: 999 Oakmont Plaza Dr, Westmont, IL 60559
Phone: (314) 725-4477   **Dom State:** IL   **Commenced Bus:** May 2011

Data Date	Rating	RACR #1	RACR #2	Total Assets ($mil)	Capital ($mil)	Net Premium ($mil)	Net Income ($mil)
6-14	C+	2.15	1.79	124.8	32.5	200.7	2.3
6-13	B-	1.46	1.22	69.6	21.5	141.5	2.1
2013	C+	1.93	1.61	114.7	28.6	309.4	1.8
2012	B-	1.22	1.01	46.8	19.0	226.2	5.9
2011	C-	1.51	1.26	38.1	10.9	81.6	-2.7
2010	N/A	N/A	N/A	N/A	N/A	N/A	N/A
2009	N/A	N/A	N/A	N/A	N/A	N/A	N/A

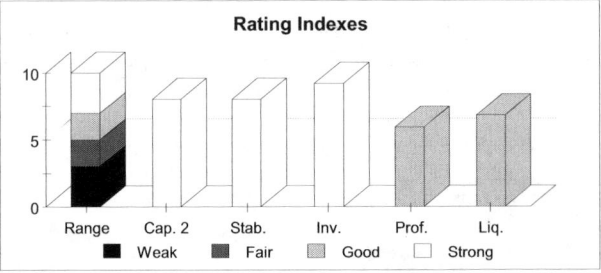

Rating Indexes

ILLINOIS MUTUAL LIFE INSURANCE COMPANY *   A-   Excellent

Major Rating Factors: Good quality investment portfolio (6.5 on a scale of 0 to 10) despite mixed results such as: minimal exposure to mortgages and large holdings of BBB rated bonds but minimal holdings in junk bonds. Good liquidity (6.6) with sufficient resources to handle a spike in claims as well as a significant increase in policy surrenders. Good overall results on stability tests (6.9) excellent operational trends, good risk adjusted capital for prior years and excellent risk diversification.

Other Rating Factors: Strong capitalization (8.2) based on excellent risk adjusted capital (severe loss scenario). Excellent profitability (7.0).

Principal Business: Individual health insurance (51%), individual life insurance (46%), individual annuities (2%), and group health insurance (1%).

Principal Investments: NonCMO investment grade bonds (72%), CMOs and structured securities (21%), common & preferred stock (2%), policy loans (1%), and misc. investments (4%).

Investments in Affiliates: None

Group Affiliation: None

Licensed in: All states except AK, DC, HI, NY, PR

Commenced Business: July 1912

Address: 300 SW Adams, Peoria, IL 61634

Phone: (309) 674-8255 **Domicile State:** IL **NAIC Code:** 64580

Data Date	Rating	RACR #1	RACR #2	Total Assets ($mil)	Capital ($mil)	Net Premium ($mil)	Net Income ($mil)
6-14	A-	3.20	1.81	1,354.0	181.8	50.4	8.0
6-13	A-	3.28	1.91	1,309.1	152.7	53.2	8.6
2013	A-	3.57	2.05	1,329.4	173.7	104.2	26.7
2012	B	3.07	1.76	1,289.1	144.2	102.0	27.0
2011	B	2.58	1.46	1,227.9	115.6	104.3	22.3
2010	B	1.85	1.05	1,211.6	104.1	104.5	-63.5
2009	B+	1.67	0.89	1,248.0	136.4	138.4	1.0

Adverse Trends in Operations

Decrease in premium volume from 2011 to 2012 (2%)
Decrease in asset base during 2010 (3%)
Change in premium mix from 2009 to 2010 (5.4%)
Decrease in capital during 2010 (24%)
Decrease in premium volume from 2009 to 2010 (25%)

INDEPENDENCE AMERICAN INS CO   C   Fair

Major Rating Factors: Fair overall results on stability tests (4.2 on a scale of 0 to 10) including fair financial strength of affiliated Geneve Holdings Inc. The largest net exposure for one risk is conservative at 1.7% of capital. Vulnerable liquidity (2.1) as a spike in claims may stretch capacity.

Other Rating Factors: History of adequate reserve strength (6.4) as reserves have been consistently at an acceptable level. Strong long-term capitalization index (7.7) based on excellent current risk adjusted capital (severe and moderate loss scenarios). Moreover, capital levels have been consistent in recent years. Excellent profitability (8.6) with operating gains in each of the last five years.

Principal Business: Group accident & health (65%), aggregate write-ins for other lines of business (21%), and inland marine (13%).

Principal Investments: Investment grade bonds (85%), misc. investments (12%), and cash (3%).

Investments in Affiliates: None

Group Affiliation: Geneve Holdings Inc

Licensed in: All states except NH, PR

Commenced Business: March 1973

Address: 1013 Centre Rd, New Castle, DE 19805-1297

Phone: (212) 355-4141   **Domicile State:** DE   **NAIC Code:** 26581

Data Date	Rating	RACR #1	RACR #2	Loss Ratio %	Total Assets ($mil)	Capital ($mil)	Net Premium ($mil)	Net Income ($mil)
6-14	C	2.54	1.49	N/A	103.4	58.9	66.1	1.6
6-13	C	3.00	1.72	N/A	97.6	56.2	61.6	1.7
2013	C	2.39	1.41	68.7	102.1	57.9	128.8	3.2
2012	C	3.72	2.14	67.9	84.7	54.4	85.8	3.3
2011	C	4.06	2.32	66.0	73.4	51.4	72.7	3.4
2010	C	3.67	2.10	68.5	72.5	47.4	73.8	2.7
2009	C	2.50	1.45	69.8	72.5	44.2	85.5	2.8

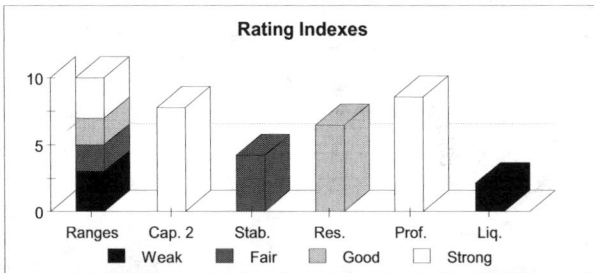

Rating Indexes
Ranges / Cap. 2 / Stab. / Res. / Prof. / Liq.
■ Weak ■ Fair ▥ Good □ Strong

INDEPENDENCE BLUE CROSS   C   Fair

Major Rating Factors: Fair profitability index (3.4 on a scale of 0 to 10). Low quality investment portfolio (2.2). Strong capitalization (10.0) based on excellent current risk-adjusted capital (severe loss scenario).

Other Rating Factors: Excellent liquidity (7.0) with ample operational cash flow and liquid investments.

Principal Business: FEHB (66%), med supp (18%), comp med (15%).

Mem Phys: 13: 793 **12:** 795 **13 MLR** 90.4% **/ 13 Admin Exp** N/A

Enroll(000): Q2 14: 135 **13:** 141 **12:** 67 **Med Exp PMPM:** $192

Principal Investments: Affiliate common stock (83%), long-term bonds (5%), cash and equiv (3%), nonaffiliate common stock (1%), other (8%)

Provider Compensation ($000): Contr fee ($272,937), FFS ($67,760)

Total Member Encounters: Non-phys (316,625)

Group Affiliation: Independence Blue Cross Inc

Licensed in: PA

Address: 1901 Market St, Philadelphia, PA 19103-1480

Phone: (215) 241-2400 **Dom State:** PA **Commenced Bus:** November 1938

Data Date	Rating	RACR #1	RACR #2	Total Assets ($mil)	Capital ($mil)	Net Premium ($mil)	Net Income ($mil)
6-14	C	3.80	3.16	2,773.2	2,125.0	185.8	23.8
6-13	C	3.87	3.23	2,657.9	2,024.0	174.1	-27.2
2013	C	4.02	3.35	2,866.2	2,250.1	363.5	-74.4
2012	C	3.86	3.21	2,693.0	2,014.9	402.7	126.2
2011	C+	3.80	3.17	2,505.4	1,913.0	413.5	117.0
2010	C+	3.38	2.82	2,186.9	1,678.7	405.7	-15.4
2009	C+	2.29	1.91	1,703.9	1,285.6	384.3	-43.1

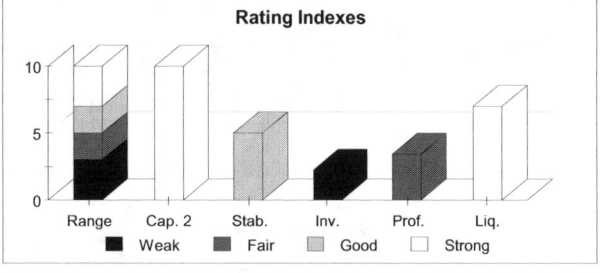

Rating Indexes
Range / Cap. 2 / Stab. / Inv. / Prof. / Liq.
■ Weak ■ Fair ▥ Good □ Strong

INDEPENDENT CARE HEALTH PLAN

B   **Good**

Major Rating Factors: Good liquidity (5.9 on a scale of 0 to 10) with sufficient resources (cash flows and marketable investments) to handle a spike in claims. Fair profitability index (4.1). Strong capitalization (8.4) based on excellent current risk-adjusted capital (severe loss scenario).
Other Rating Factors: High quality investment portfolio (9.9).
Principal Business: Medicaid (54%), Medicare (46%)
Mem Phys: 13: 4,137 **12:** 5,773 **13 MLR** 85.6% **/ 13 Admin Exp** N/A
Enroll(000): Q2 14: 15 **13:** 15 **12:** 15 **Med Exp PMPM:** $817
Principal Investments: Long-term bonds (65%), cash and equiv (35%)
Provider Compensation ($000): Contr fee ($134,566), capitation ($3,251), other ($10,736)
Total Member Encounters: Phys (242,448), non-phys (150,865)
Group Affiliation: Humana Inc
Licensed in: WI
Address: 1555 N RiverCenter Dr 202A, Milwaukee, WI 53212
Phone: (414) 223-4847 **Dom State:** WI **Commenced Bus:** June 2003

Data Date	Rating	RACR #1	RACR #2	Total Assets ($mil)	Capital ($mil)	Net Premium ($mil)	Net Income ($mil)
6-14	B	2.44	2.03	51.8	18.5	88.4	-2.3
6-13	B	2.70	2.25	53.0	18.7	84.8	-1.9
2013	B	2.66	2.22	56.1	20.8	174.3	0.6
2012	B	2.87	2.39	54.5	20.3	162.8	1.6
2011	B	2.88	2.40	51.5	17.9	145.5	3.6
2010	B	2.92	2.43	68.8	18.2	141.7	2.4
2009	B	2.53	2.11	46.0	15.5	139.8	4.3

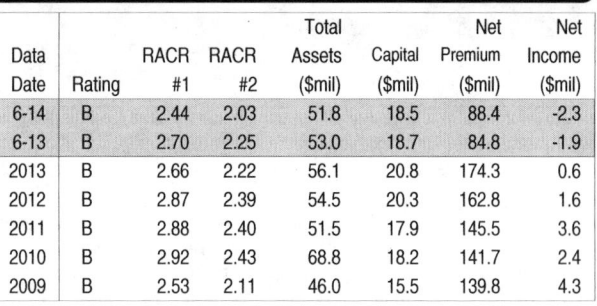

Rating Indexes

INDEPENDENT HEALTH ASSOC INC

B   **Good**

Major Rating Factors: Good overall results on stability tests (6.1 on a scale of 0 to 10). Good liquidity (6.9) with sufficient resources (cash flows and marketable investments) to handle a spike in claims. Strong capitalization index (10.0) based on excellent current risk-adjusted capital (severe loss scenario).
Other Rating Factors: High quality investment portfolio (8.3). Weak profitability index (2.7).
Principal Business: Medicare (56%), comp med (18%), Medicaid (18%), FEHB (7%)
Mem Phys: 13: 3,771 **12:** 3,521 **13 MLR** 89.5% **/ 13 Admin Exp** N/A
Enroll(000): Q2 14: 176 **13:** 181 **12:** 180 **Med Exp PMPM:** $566
Principal Investments: Long-term bonds (58%), nonaffiliate common stock (9%), cash and equiv (8%), real estate (4%), affiliate common stock (2%), other (19%)
Provider Compensation ($000): Capitation ($960,498), FFS ($218,548), other ($14,689)
Total Member Encounters: Phys (717,046), non-phys (1,571,283)
Group Affiliation: Independent Health Assoc Inc
Licensed in: NY
Address: 511 Farber Lakes Dr, Buffalo, NY 14221
Phone: (716) 635-3800 **Dom State:** NY **Commenced Bus:** January 1980

Data Date	Rating	RACR #1	RACR #2	Total Assets ($mil)	Capital ($mil)	Net Premium ($mil)	Net Income ($mil)
6-14	B	4.72	3.93	646.2	436.4	657.8	-27.6
6-13	B+	5.06	4.21	646.4	443.0	663.2	10.3
2013	B+	5.03	4.19	658.7	461.6	1,356.1	26.7
2012	B+	4.63	3.86	606.3	411.8	1,354.9	-49.4
2011	A+	6.83	5.69	603.4	452.7	1,213.1	28.8
2010	A+	6.62	5.51	596.1	451.3	1,087.1	70.2
2009	A+	5.79	4.82	521.6	374.3	1,060.4	29.9

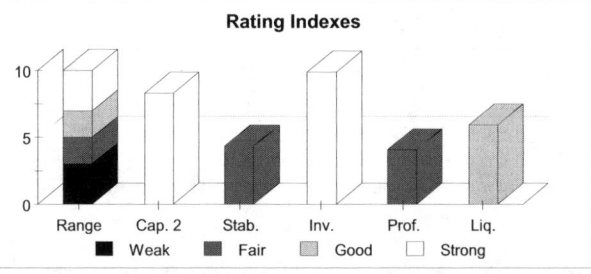

Rating Indexes

INDEPENDENT HEALTH BENEFITS CORP

C+   **Fair**

Major Rating Factors: Fair profitability index (3.1 on a scale of 0 to 10). Strong capitalization (8.7) based on excellent current risk-adjusted capital (severe loss scenario). High quality investment portfolio (9.4).
Other Rating Factors: Excellent liquidity (7.1) with ample operational cash flow and liquid investments.
Principal Business: Comp med (90%), Medicare (9%)
Mem Phys: 13: 3,762 **12:** 3,512 **13 MLR** 85.3% **/ 13 Admin Exp** N/A
Enroll(000): Q2 14: 108 **13:** 108 **12:** 115 **Med Exp PMPM:** $322
Principal Investments: Cash and equiv (58%), long-term bonds (42%)
Provider Compensation ($000): FFS ($400,039), capitation ($1,085)
Total Member Encounters: Phys (1,304,373), non-phys (2,148,803)
Group Affiliation: Independent Health Assoc Inc
Licensed in: NY
Address: 511 Farber Lakes Dr, Buffalo, NY 14221
Phone: (716) 635-3800 **Dom State:** NY **Commenced Bus:** December 1995

Data Date	Rating	RACR #1	RACR #2	Total Assets ($mil)	Capital ($mil)	Net Premium ($mil)	Net Income ($mil)
6-14	C+	2.69	2.24	173.6	103.6	252.3	7.5
6-13	B	2.64	2.20	165.0	109.6	239.8	5.8
2013	C+	2.60	2.16	174.5	98.9	485.9	-7.0
2012	B	2.39	1.99	164.4	100.2	508.2	-0.7
2011	B	2.64	2.20	161.1	101.2	469.3	-0.6
2010	B	2.49	2.08	149.8	99.7	477.9	3.0
2009	B	2.27	1.89	153.8	92.9	470.0	8.3

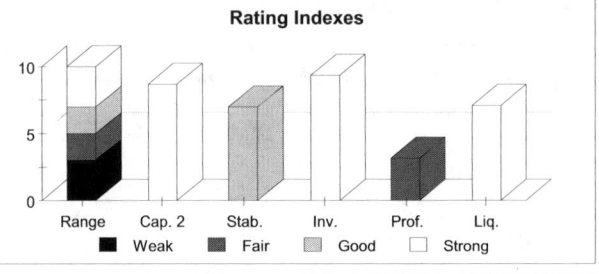

Rating Indexes

INDIANA UNIVERSITY HEALTH PLANS INC   D-   Weak

Major Rating Factors: Weak profitability index (1.9 on a scale of 0 to 10). Good capitalization (6.9) based on excellent current risk-adjusted capital (severe loss scenario). High quality investment portfolio (9.9).
Other Rating Factors: Excellent liquidity (7.0) with sufficient resources (cash flows and marketable investments) to handle a spike in claims.
Principal Business: Medicare (100%)
Mem Phys: 13: 6,557 **12:** N/A **13 MLR** 89.4% **/ 13 Admin Exp** N/A
Enroll(000): Q2 14: 10 **13:** 9 **12:** 12 **Med Exp PMPM:** $837
Principal Investments: Cash and equiv (100%)
Provider Compensation ($000): Capitation ($87,285), other ($604)
Total Member Encounters: N/A
Group Affiliation: Indiana University Health
Licensed in: IN
Address: 340 W 10th St Suite 6100, Indianapolis, IN 46206
Phone: (317) 963-9780 **Dom State:** IN **Commenced Bus:** May 2008

Data Date	Rating	RACR #1	RACR #2	Total Assets ($mil)	Capital ($mil)	Net Premium ($mil)	Net Income ($mil)
6-14	D-	1.27	1.05	10.0	7.7	57.1	0.7
6-13	D-	1.02	0.85	9.6	7.3	47.7	0.1
2013	D-	1.21	1.01	9.0	7.3	98.3	0.6
2012	D-	1.04	0.86	10.1	7.4	118.3	-1.1
2011	D-	0.85	0.71	7.3	5.6	107.6	-2.0
2010	E+	1.23	1.02	8.3	6.7	88.1	-3.9
2009	E	0.92	0.77	9.0	2.8	34.9	-8.6

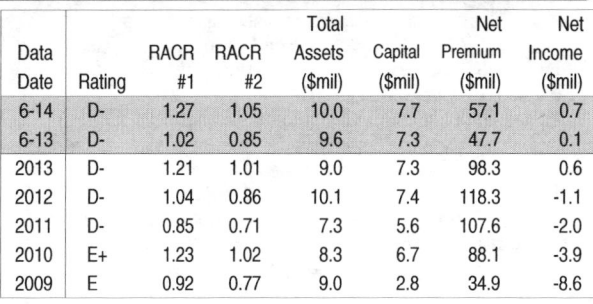

Rating Indexes

INLAND EMPIRE HEALTH PLAN   B   Good

Major Rating Factors: Good overall profitability index (5.3 on a scale of 0 to 10). Fair overall results on stability tests (4.1). Strong capitalization index (6.9) based on good current risk-adjusted capital (moderate loss scenario).
Other Rating Factors: Excellent liquidity (6.9) with sufficient resources (cash flows and marketable investments) to handle a spike in claims.
Principal Business: Medicaid (90%), Medicare (10%)
Mem Phys: 13: N/A **12:** N/A **13 MLR** 93.8% **/ 13 Admin Exp** N/A
Enroll(000): Q2 14: 640 **13:** 625 **12:** 569 **Med Exp PMPM:** $627
Principal Investments ($000): Cash and equiv ($116,049)
Provider Compensation ($000): None
Total Member Encounters: N/A
Group Affiliation: None
Licensed in: CA
Address: 303 E Vanderbilt Way Ste 400, San Bernardino, CA 92408
Phone: (909) 890-2000 **Dom State:** CA **Commenced Bus:** September 1996

Data Date	Rating	RACR #1	RACR #2	Total Assets ($mil)	Capital ($mil)	Net Premium ($mil)	Net Income ($mil)
6-14	B	1.08	0.68	347.0	99.3	663.2	-19.2
6-13	B	1.51	0.92	218.4	93.6	561.3	-14.1
2013	B	1.39	0.87	280.5	118.5	1,240.9	10.8
2012	B	1.78	1.09	237.7	107.7	990.3	37.1
2011	C+	1.38	0.85	164.8	70.6	868.0	27.0
2010	C+	0.89	0.55	138.7	43.6	675.8	9.3
2009	C	0.84	0.52	88.9	34.3	514.5	4.7

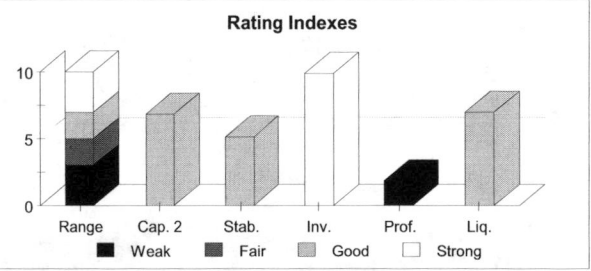

Rating Indexes

INNOVATION HEALTH INS CO   B   Good

Major Rating Factors: Strong capitalization (10.0 on a scale of 0 to 10) based on excellent current risk-adjusted capital (severe loss scenario). High quality investment portfolio (7.9). Excellent liquidity (7.8) with ample operational cash flow and liquid investments.
Other Rating Factors: Weak profitability index (0.9).
Principal Business: Comp med (100%)
Mem Phys: 13: 45,711 **12:** N/A **13 MLR** 19.1% **/ 13 Admin Exp** N/A
Enroll(000): Q2 14: 36 **13:** 3 **12:** N/A **Med Exp PMPM:** $284
Principal Investments: Cash and equiv (55%), affiliate common stock (42%), long-term bonds (4%)
Provider Compensation ($000): FFS ($226)
Total Member Encounters: Phys (77), non-phys (80)
Group Affiliation: Aetna Inc
Licensed in: VA
Address: 3130 Farview Park Dr Suite 300, Falls Church, VA 22042-4517
Phone: (860) 273-0123 **Dom State:** VA **Commenced Bus:** April 2013

Data Date	Rating	RACR #1	RACR #2	Total Assets ($mil)	Capital ($mil)	Net Premium ($mil)	Net Income ($mil)
6-14	B	4.63	3.86	42.0	14.6	51.3	-0.4
6-13	N/A	N/A	N/A	16.7	13.8	N/A	-3.1
2013	B	3.99	3.33	15.8	12.6	4.3	-6.2
2012	N/A	N/A	N/A	N/A	-0.2	N/A	N/A
2011	N/A	N/A	N/A	N/A	N/A	N/A	N/A
2010	N/A	N/A	N/A	N/A	N/A	N/A	N/A
2009	N/A	N/A	N/A	N/A	N/A	N/A	N/A

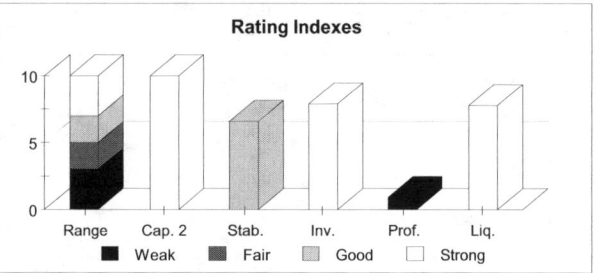

Rating Indexes

INNOVATION HEALTH PLAN INC   B   Good

Major Rating Factors: Strong capitalization (10.0 on a scale of 0 to 10) based on excellent current risk-adjusted capital (severe loss scenario). High quality investment portfolio (9.9). Excellent liquidity (7.5) with ample operational cash flow and liquid investments.

Other Rating Factors: Weak profitability index (0.9).

Principal Business: Comp med (100%)

Mem Phys: 13: 45,711   **12:** N/A   **13 MLR** 8.2%   **/ 13 Admin Exp** N/A

Enroll(000): Q2 14: 9   **13:** 4   **12:** N/A   **Med Exp PMPM:** $167

Principal Investments: Cash and equiv (55%), long-term bonds (45%)

Provider Compensation ($000): FFS ($83), contr fee ($74), capitation ($1)

Total Member Encounters: Phys (147), non-phys (121)

Group Affiliation: Aetna Inc

Licensed in: VA

Address: 3130 Farview Park Dr Suite 300, Falls Church, VA 22042-4517

Phone: (860) 273-0123   **Dom State:** VA   **Commenced Bus:** April 2013

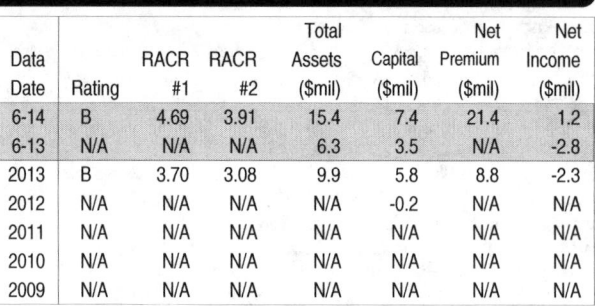

Data Date	Rating	RACR #1	RACR #2	Total Assets ($mil)	Capital ($mil)	Net Premium ($mil)	Net Income ($mil)
6-14	B	4.69	3.91	15.4	7.4	21.4	1.2
6-13	N/A	N/A	N/A	6.3	3.5	N/A	-2.8
2013	B	3.70	3.08	9.9	5.8	8.8	-2.3
2012	N/A	N/A	N/A	N/A	-0.2	N/A	N/A
2011	N/A	N/A	N/A	N/A	N/A	N/A	N/A
2010	N/A	N/A	N/A	N/A	N/A	N/A	N/A
2009	N/A	N/A	N/A	N/A	N/A	N/A	N/A

Rating Indexes

Range, Cap. 2, Stab., Inv., Prof., Liq.

■ Weak ■ Fair ■ Good □ Strong

INS CO OF NORTH AMERICA   C   Fair

Major Rating Factors: Fair profitability index (3.4 on a scale of 0 to 10) with operating losses during the first six months of 2014. Return on equity has been fair, averaging 7.8% over the past five years. Fair overall results on stability tests (4.3) including fair financial strength of affiliated ACE Ltd.

Other Rating Factors: Good liquidity (6.5) with sufficient resources (cash flows and marketable investments) to handle a spike in claims. Strong long-term capitalization index (7.3) based on excellent current risk adjusted capital (severe and moderate loss scenarios), despite some fluctuation in capital levels. Ample reserve history (8.3) that helps to protect the company against sharp claims increases.

Principal Business: International (19%), other accident & health (17%), group accident & health (17%), other liability (16%), fire (12%), ocean marine (8%), and other lines (11%).

Principal Investments: Investment grade bonds (91%), cash (6%), and real estate (5%).

Investments in Affiliates: None

Group Affiliation: ACE Ltd

Licensed in: All states, the District of Columbia and Puerto Rico

Commenced Business: January 1792

Address: 1601 Chestnut St, Philadelphia, PA 19192

Phone: (215) 640-1000   **Domicile State:** PA   **NAIC Code:** 22713

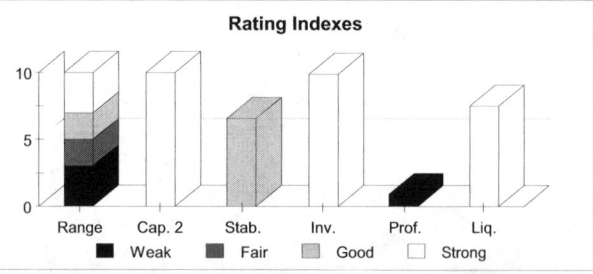

Data Date	Rating	RACR #1	RACR #2	Loss Ratio %	Total Assets ($mil)	Capital ($mil)	Net Premium ($mil)	Net Income ($mil)
6-14	C	1.66	1.11	N/A	758.6	167.4	98.2	-15.5
6-13	C	2.29	1.49	N/A	798.6	208.1	90.1	11.2
2013	C	1.88	1.26	72.2	787.1	182.8	217.7	15.3
2012	C	2.22	1.46	89.9	831.8	195.6	224.1	3.2
2011	C	2.13	1.37	80.7	755.6	180.5	212.8	29.2
2010	C	1.97	1.35	67.1	811.4	303.7	174.6	22.6
2009	C	2.07	1.37	66.8	780.0	281.1	151.6	52.4

Income Trends ($mil)

▲ Underwriting Income   ■ Net Income

INS CO OF SCOTT AND WHITE   D+   Weak

Major Rating Factors: Weak profitability index (0.9 on a scale of 0 to 10). Strong capitalization (7.0) based on excellent current risk-adjusted capital (severe loss scenario). High quality investment portfolio (9.9).

Other Rating Factors: Excellent liquidity (7.5) with ample operational cash flow and liquid investments.

Principal Business: Comp med (100%)

Mem Phys: 13: 3,208   **12:** N/A   **13 MLR** 77.0%   **/ 13 Admin Exp** N/A

Enroll(000): Q2 14: 8   **13:** 7   **12:** 7   **Med Exp PMPM:** $133

Principal Investments: Cash and equiv (86%), nonaffiliate common stock (8%), long-term bonds (6%)

Provider Compensation ($000): Contr fee ($9,022), FFS ($1,100), bonus arrang ($897)

Total Member Encounters: Phys (15,607), non-phys (11,677)

Group Affiliation: Scott & White Group

Licensed in: TX

Address: 1206 W Campus Dr, Temple, TX 76502

Phone: (254) 298-3000   **Dom State:** TX   **Commenced Bus:** May 2003

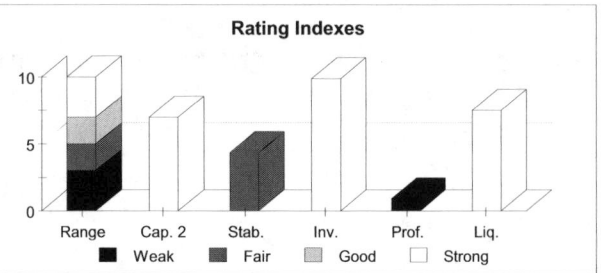

Data Date	Rating	RACR #1	RACR #2	Total Assets ($mil)	Capital ($mil)	Net Premium ($mil)	Net Income ($mil)
6-14	D+	1.35	1.13	9.6	2.4	12.2	-1.4
6-13	N/A	N/A	N/A	8.6	4.0	7.3	-0.3
2013	C+	1.98	1.65	8.3	3.8	14.2	-0.5
2012	N/A	N/A	N/A	6.6	4.2	8.3	N/A
2011	N/A	N/A	N/A	3.0	2.9	1.0	N/A
2010	N/A	N/A	N/A	3.0	2.8	0.7	N/A
2009	N/A	N/A	N/A	2.9	2.7	0.7	N/A

Rating Indexes

Range, Cap. 2, Stab., Inv., Prof., Liq.

■ Weak ■ Fair ■ Good □ Strong

INSTIL HEALTH INS CO   B   Good

Major Rating Factors: Good overall profitability index (5.6 on a scale of 0 to 10). Strong capitalization (10.0) based on excellent current risk-adjusted capital (severe loss scenario). High quality investment portfolio (8.8).
Other Rating Factors: Excellent liquidity (6.9) with sufficient resources (cash flows and marketable investments) to handle a spike in claims.
Principal Business: FEHB (100%)
Mem Phys: 12: N/A   **11:** N/A   **12 MLR** 97.0%   **/ 12 Admin Exp** N/A
Enroll(000): Q2 13: 132   **12:** 133   **11:** 107   **Med Exp PMPM:** $150
Principal Investments: Long-term bonds (67%), nonaffiliate common stock (18%), cash and equiv (14%)
Provider Compensation ($000): Contr fee ($200,743), FFS ($24,743), salary ($511)
Total Member Encounters: N/A
Group Affiliation: Blue Cross Blue Shield of S Carolina
Licensed in: AL, AZ, AR, GA, IL, KY, LA, NV, NM, OR, SC, TX, UT
Address: 17 Technology Cir, Columbia, SC 29202
Phone: (877) 446-7845   **Dom State:** SC   **Commenced Bus:** September 2004

Data Date	Rating	RACR #1	RACR #2	Total Assets ($mil)	Capital ($mil)	Net Premium ($mil)	Net Income ($mil)
6-13	B	14.24	11.87	108.7	74.0	124.8	2.1
6-12	B-	18.93	15.77	102.3	67.3	113.9	3.3
2012	B	13.78	11.48	104.6	71.3	235.9	7.4
2011	B-	17.98	14.99	94.8	63.5	199.0	8.7
2010	B-	13.31	11.09	84.8	54.3	190.9	10.3
2009	B-	4.13	3.44	104.0	44.1	295.7	3.7
2008	B-	4.23	3.53	114.2	38.9	279.1	-9.7

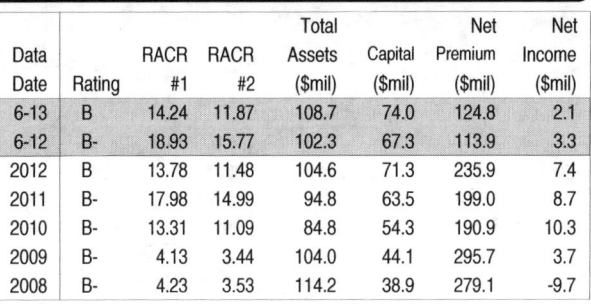

Rating Indexes
Range, Cap. 2, Stab., Inv., Prof., Liq.
■ Weak ▨ Fair ▧ Good □ Strong

INTERVALLEY HEALTH PLAN   D   Weak

Major Rating Factors: Good overall profitability index (5.8 on a scale of 0 to 10). Good overall results on stability tests (5.3). Strong capitalization index (7.0) based on good current risk-adjusted capital (moderate loss scenario).
Other Rating Factors: Excellent liquidity (6.9) with sufficient resources (cash flows and marketable investments) to handle a spike in claims.
Principal Business: Medicare (100%)
Mem Phys: 13: N/A   **12:** N/A   **13 MLR** 90.3%   **/ 13 Admin Exp** N/A
Enroll(000): Q2 14: 20   **13:** 20   **12:** 18   **Med Exp PMPM:** $895
Principal Investments ($000): Cash and equiv ($14,393)
Provider Compensation ($000): None
Total Member Encounters: N/A
Group Affiliation: None
Licensed in: CA
Address: 300 S Park Ave Suite 300, Pomona, CA 91766
Phone: (909) 623-6333   **Dom State:** CA   **Commenced Bus:** July 1979

Data Date	Rating	RACR #1	RACR #2	Total Assets ($mil)	Capital ($mil)	Net Premium ($mil)	Net Income ($mil)
6-14	D	1.10	0.70	27.9	22.1	123.6	-0.9
6-13	D	1.24	0.79	29.7	22.6	113.6	1.3
2013	D	1.15	0.73	30.4	23.0	225.2	1.7
2012	D	1.16	0.74	48.6	21.3	201.8	2.5
2011	D	1.24	0.78	25.8	18.7	169.9	0.6
2010	D	1.52	0.95	24.6	18.1	143.3	2.2
2009	D	1.56	0.97	21.5	16.0	130.2	4.6

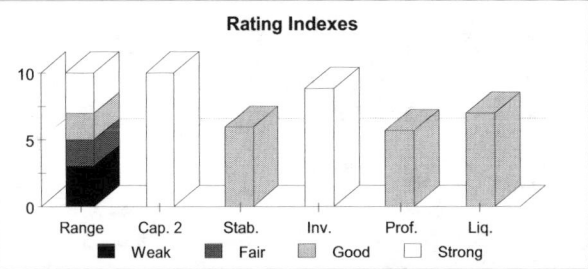

Rating Indexes
Range, Cap. 1, Stab., Inv., Prof., Liq.
■ Weak ▨ Fair ▧ Good □ Strong

INTOTAL HEALTH LLC *   B+   Good

Major Rating Factors: Good overall profitability index (5.5 on a scale of 0 to 10). Strong capitalization (9.6) based on excellent current risk-adjusted capital (severe loss scenario). High quality investment portfolio (9.9).
Other Rating Factors: Excellent liquidity (7.0) with sufficient resources (cash flows and marketable investments) to handle a spike in claims.
Principal Business: Medicaid (100%)
Mem Phys: 13: 13,805   **12:** 11,237   **13 MLR** 85.1%   **/ 13 Admin Exp** N/A
Enroll(000): Q2 14: 56   **13:** 55   **12:** 57   **Med Exp PMPM:** $223
Principal Investments: Cash and equiv (67%), long-term bonds (33%)
Provider Compensation ($000): Capitation ($3,558)
Total Member Encounters: Phys (433,039), non-phys (148,451)
Group Affiliation: INOVA Health System Foundation
Licensed in: VA
Address: 8110 Gatehouse Rd Suite 400W, Falls Church, VA 22042
Phone: (703) 289-2455   **Dom State:** VA   **Commenced Bus:** September 2005

Data Date	Rating	RACR #1	RACR #2	Total Assets ($mil)	Capital ($mil)	Net Premium ($mil)	Net Income ($mil)
6-14	B+	3.39	2.83	55.3	29.1	87.9	-4.4
6-13	B	1.89	1.57	51.2	25.9	87.2	-1.7
2013	B+	3.75	3.12	54.4	32.1	178.2	0.4
2012	B	1.43	1.19	39.9	24.0	147.4	5.4
2011	B	3.03	2.53	28.0	18.2	106.4	5.2
2010	B	3.38	2.82	31.7	18.1	95.0	5.4
2009	B	2.90	2.42	21.4	12.7	75.6	3.9

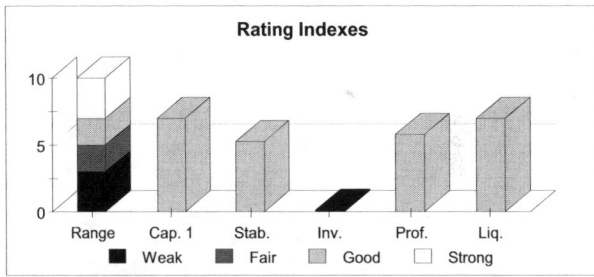

Rating Indexes
Range, Cap. 2, Stab., Inv., Prof., Liq.
■ Weak ▨ Fair ▧ Good □ Strong

JOHN ALDEN LIFE INSURANCE COMPANY   B   Good

Major Rating Factors: Good quality investment portfolio (6.5 on a scale of 0 to 10) despite mixed results such as: large holdings of BBB rated bonds but moderate junk bond exposure. Good overall profitability (6.3). Return on equity has been excellent over the last five years averaging 19.7%. Good liquidity (6.1) with sufficient resources to handle a spike in claims.

Other Rating Factors: Fair overall results on stability tests (4.4) including negative cash flow from operations for 2013. Strong capitalization (7.9) based on excellent risk adjusted capital (severe loss scenario).

Principal Business: Group health insurance (84%), individual health insurance (13%), individual life insurance (2%), and group life insurance (1%).

Principal Investments: NonCMO investment grade bonds (70%), CMOs and structured securities (12%), policy loans (6%), noninv. grade bonds (6%), and mortgages in good standing (5%).

Investments in Affiliates: None

Group Affiliation: Assurant Inc

Licensed in: All states except NY, PR

Commenced Business: January 1974

Address: 7300 Corporate Center Dr, Miami, FL 33102-0270

Phone: (305) 715-3772   **Domicile State:** WI   **NAIC Code:** 65080

Data Date	Rating	RACR #1	RACR #2	Total Assets ($mil)	Capital ($mil)	Net Premium ($mil)	Net Income ($mil)
6-14	B	2.28	1.63	349.9	64.7	94.2	6.2
6-13	B	1.94	1.40	397.8	82.7	167.9	6.9
2013	B	1.93	1.40	362.8	68.4	314.5	18.1
2012	B	1.76	1.28	410.7	82.6	410.7	30.8
2011	B	1.91	1.40	486.8	107.5	474.1	14.7
2010	B-	1.73	1.26	472.4	100.7	494.1	19.9
2009	B-	1.53	1.13	462.7	85.2	486.8	1.8

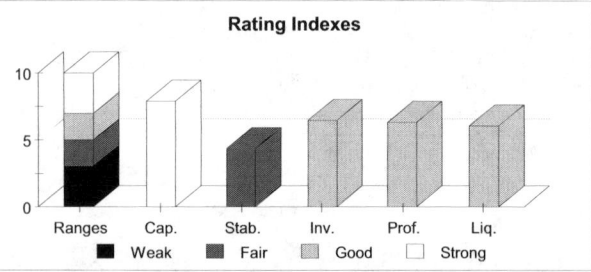

Rating Indexes

JOHN HANCOCK LIFE & HEALTH INSURANCE COMPANY   B   Good

Major Rating Factors: Good quality investment portfolio (5.2 on a scale of 0 to 10) despite mixed results such as: minimal exposure to mortgages and substantial holdings of BBB bonds but minimal holdings in junk bonds. Fair overall results on stability tests (4.0) including weak results on operational trends. Weak profitability (2.8) with operating losses during the first six months of 2014.

Other Rating Factors: Strong capitalization (8.2) based on excellent risk adjusted capital (severe loss scenario). Excellent liquidity (8.1).

Principal Business: Group health insurance (67%), individual health insurance (24%), reinsurance (8%), and group retirement contracts (1%).

Principal Investments: NonCMO investment grade bonds (66%), mortgages in good standing (9%), real estate (5%), CMOs and structured securities (5%), and misc. investments (9%).

Investments in Affiliates: 1%

Group Affiliation: Manulife Financial Group

Licensed in: All states, the District of Columbia and Puerto Rico

Commenced Business: October 1981

Address: 2711 Centerville Rd Ste 400, Wilmington, DE 19808

Phone: (617) 572-6000   **Domicile State:** MA   **NAIC Code:** 93610

Data Date	Rating	RACR #1	RACR #2	Total Assets ($mil)	Capital ($mil)	Net Premium ($mil)	Net Income ($mil)
6-14	B	3.00	1.80	10,136.3	690.5	286.6	-19.6
6-13	B	3.48	1.95	10,157.9	678.9	275.1	3.7
2013	B	3.05	1.81	9,737.6	682.7	565.5	82.4
2012	B	3.50	1.94	10,039.5	664.9	562.3	12.0
2011	B	3.09	1.78	8,947.4	597.9	491.2	93.1
2010	B	2.22	1.29	7,615.6	461.8	528.4	-218.5
2009	B	1.22	0.79	6,443.0	350.9	1,149.2	-1.4

Adverse Trends in Operations

Decrease in asset base during 2013 (3%)
Decrease in premium volume from 2010 to 2011 (7%)
Change in premium mix from 2009 to 2010 (5.8%)
Change in asset mix during 2010 (5.0%)
Decrease in premium volume from 2009 to 2010 (54%)

K S PLAN ADMINISTRATORS LLC   B   Good

Major Rating Factors: Excellent profitability (9.2 on a scale of 0 to 10). Strong capitalization (7.4) based on excellent current risk-adjusted capital (severe loss scenario). High quality investment portfolio (8.2).

Other Rating Factors: Excellent liquidity (7.1) with ample operational cash flow and liquid investments.

Principal Business: Medicare (100%)

Mem Phys: 13: 758   **12:** 781   **13 MLR** 85.8%   **/ 13 Admin Exp** N/A

Enroll(000): Q2 14: 27   **13:** 25   **12:** 24   **Med Exp PMPM:** $795

Principal Investments: Cash and equiv (70%), nonaffiliate common stock (30%)

Provider Compensation ($000): FFS ($115,938), capitation ($111,558), bonus arrang ($2,947)

Total Member Encounters: Phys (425,867), non-phys (7,803)

Group Affiliation: St Lukes Episcopal Health System

Licensed in: TX

Address: 2727 W Holcombe Blvd, Houston, TX 77025

Phone: (713) 442-0757   **Dom State:** TX   **Commenced Bus:** December 2006

Data Date	Rating	RACR #1	RACR #2	Total Assets ($mil)	Capital ($mil)	Net Premium ($mil)	Net Income ($mil)
6-14	B	1.68	1.40	67.4	38.1	144.3	1.2
6-13	C-	1.30	1.09	53.8	29.5	132.9	5.2
2013	C	1.58	1.31	57.7	35.8	266.9	11.5
2012	C-	1.10	0.91	50.8	24.8	259.1	9.1
2011	D+	0.78	0.65	35.5	15.3	214.1	4.5
2010	D+	0.78	0.65	25.2	11.0	149.2	1.7
2009	D	0.68	0.57	17.1	7.8	104.9	2.6

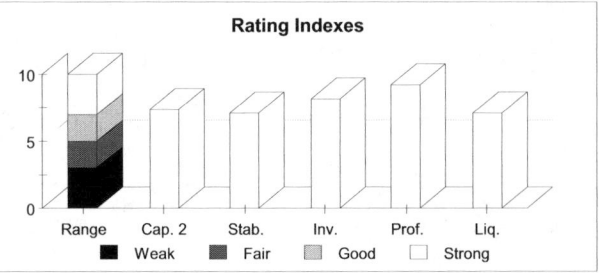

Rating Indexes

KAISER FOUNDATION HEALTH PLAN INC *   A   Excellent

Major Rating Factors: Strong capitalization index (9.5 on a scale of 0 to 10) based on excellent current risk-adjusted capital (severe loss scenario). Excellent overall results on stability tests (7.7) based on steady enrollment growth, averaging 2% over the past five years. Excellent liquidity (7.2) with ample operational cash flow and liquid investments.

Other Rating Factors: Good overall profitability index (6.8).

Principal Business: Medicare (26%), Medicaid (1%)

Mem Phys: 13: N/A   **12:** N/A   **13 MLR** 98.6%   **/ 13 Admin Exp** N/A

Enroll(000): Q2 14: 7,427   **13:** 7,124   **12:** 7,042   **Med Exp PMPM:** $575

Principal Investments ($000): Cash and equiv ($6,285,407)

Provider Compensation ($000): None

Total Member Encounters: N/A

Group Affiliation: Kaiser Foundation

Licensed in: CA, HI

Address: One Kaiser Plaza, Oakland, CA 94612

Phone: (510) 271-5910   **Dom State:** CA   **Commenced Bus:** N/A

Data Date	Rating	RACR #1	RACR #2	Total Assets ($mil)	Capital ($mil)	Net Premium ($mil)	Net Income ($mil)
6-14	A	3.91	2.80	60,291.5	25,427.0	26,239.3	2,143.9
6-13	A-	2.74	1.94	54,750.5	15,747.3	25,044.3	1,521.3
2013	A	3.71	2.64	56,878.4	23,048.8	49,772.6	2,684.8
2012	A-	2.56	1.81	52,812.8	14,283.6	47,488.3	2,595.6
2011	A-	2.56	1.80	46,698.6	12,495.0	44,763.1	2,013.2
2010	A-	2.91	2.04	42,848.9	12,887.7	41,565.7	1,991.3
2009	A-	3.03	2.10	37,798.0	11,837.6	39,673.5	2,108.6

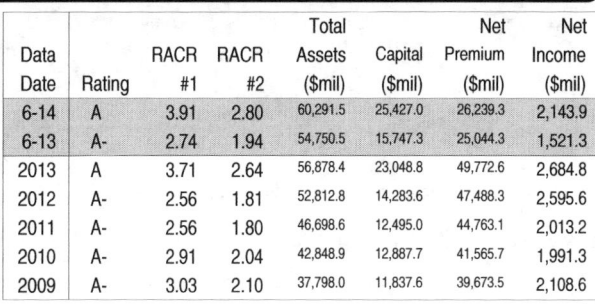

Rating Indexes

KAISER FOUNDATION HP INC HI   B   Good

Major Rating Factors: Good overall results on stability tests (5.2 on a scale of 0 to 10) despite inconsistent enrollment growth in the past five years due to declines in 2011 and 2012. Rating is significantly influenced by the strong financial results of Kaiser Foundation. Fair quality investment portfolio (3.2). Strong capitalization index (9.8) based on excellent current risk-adjusted capital (severe loss scenario).

Other Rating Factors: Excellent liquidity (7.1) with ample operational cash flow and liquid investments. Weak profitability index (1.9).

Principal Business: Comp med (59%), Medicare (30%), FEHB (6%), Medicaid (5%)

Mem Phys: 13: 426   **12:** 427   **13 MLR** 95.3%   **/ 13 Admin Exp** N/A

Enroll(000): Q2 14: 230   **13:** 227   **12:** 225   **Med Exp PMPM:** $410

Principal Investments: Real estate (98%), cash and equiv (2%)

Provider Compensation ($000): Salary ($654,406), contr fee ($103,773), FFS ($12,832), other ($338,248)

Total Member Encounters: Phys (782,556), non-phys (342,219)

Group Affiliation: Kaiser Foundation

Licensed in: HI

Address: 711 Kapiolani Blvd, Honolulu, HI 96813

Phone: (808) 432-5955   **Dom State:** HI   **Commenced Bus:** February 1958

Data Date	Rating	RACR #1	RACR #2	Total Assets ($mil)	Capital ($mil)	Net Premium ($mil)	Net Income ($mil)
6-14	B	3.57	2.98	362.8	120.3	591.3	-4.8
6-13	B	3.29	2.74	340.0	103.2	571.9	-1.5
2013	B	3.89	3.24	356.3	130.7	1,159.0	-1.0
2012	B	3.41	2.84	334.5	107.0	1,126.1	1.7
2011	B-	4.01	3.34	325.6	121.0	1,064.1	4.3
2010	B-	4.84	4.03	297.5	132.0	957.0	-5.1
2009	B-	4.58	3.82	296.2	130.7	902.5	-8.7

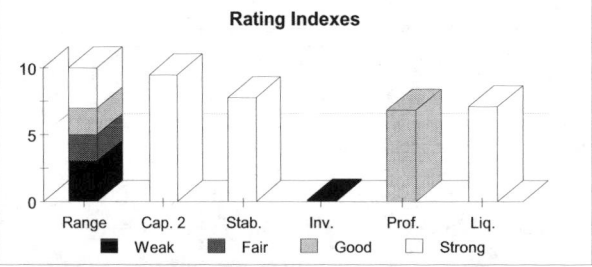

Rating Indexes

KAISER FOUNDATION HP MID-ATL STATES   B   Good

Major Rating Factors: Good quality investment portfolio (5.9 on a scale of 0 to 10). Good overall results on stability tests (5.5). Rating is significantly influenced by the strong financial results of Kaiser Foundation. Good liquidity (6.8) with sufficient resources (cash flows and marketable investments) to handle a spike in claims.

Other Rating Factors: Strong capitalization index (7.1) based on excellent current risk-adjusted capital (severe loss scenario). Weak profitability index (1.9).

Principal Business: Comp med (56%), FEHB (27%), Medicare (17%)

Mem Phys: 13: 19,358   **12:** 18,697   **13 MLR** 91.3%   **/ 13 Admin Exp** N/A

Enroll(000): Q2 14: 512   **13:** 480   **12:** 478   **Med Exp PMPM:** $382

Principal Investments: Real estate (71%), long-term bonds (28%), cash and equiv (1%)

Provider Compensation ($000): Salary ($670,703), contr fee ($320,929), FFS ($207,979), capitation ($8,971), other ($905,770)

Total Member Encounters: Phys (1,719,352), non-phys (736,596)

Group Affiliation: Kaiser Foundation

Licensed in: DC, MD, VA

Address: 2101 E Jefferson St, Rockville, MD 20852

Phone: (301) 816-2424   **Dom State:** MD   **Commenced Bus:** October 1972

Data Date	Rating	RACR #1	RACR #2	Total Assets ($mil)	Capital ($mil)	Net Premium ($mil)	Net Income ($mil)
6-14	B	1.43	1.19	1,128.9	202.1	1,289.7	10.8
6-13	B	1.63	1.36	1,124.1	201.6	1,199.5	15.5
2013	B	1.32	1.10	1,120.9	176.0	2,409.1	-19.4
2012	B	1.41	1.18	1,121.8	182.3	2,302.0	-21.3
2011	B	1.68	1.40	912.7	150.0	2,182.9	-59.5
2010	B	2.74	2.28	695.6	187.2	2,084.6	-33.8
2009	A	3.60	3.00	695.3	218.5	1,987.6	-7.1

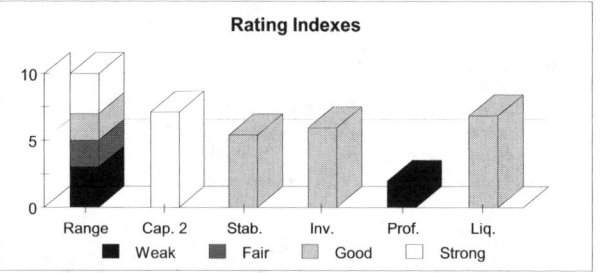

Rating Indexes

KAISER FOUNDATION HP NORTHWEST   B   Good

Major Rating Factors: Good overall results on stability tests (6.2 on a scale of 0 to 10) despite inconsistent enrollment growth in the past five years due to declines in 2010 and 2012. Rating is significantly influenced by the strong financial results of Kaiser Foundation. Good liquidity (6.9) with sufficient resources (cash flows and marketable investments) to handle a spike in claims. Strong capitalization index (10.0) based on excellent current risk-adjusted capital (severe loss scenario).

Other Rating Factors: High quality investment portfolio (9.1). Weak profitability index (2.7).

Principal Business: Comp med (62%), Medicare (28%), FEHB (5%), dental (4%), other (2%)

Mem Phys: 13: 1,238   **12:** 1,176   **13 MLR** 93.7%   **/ 13 Admin Exp** N/A

Enroll(000): Q2 14: 468   **13:** 473   **12:** 465   **Med Exp PMPM:** $501

Principal Investments: Long-term bonds (76%), real estate (19%), cash and equiv (5%)

Provider Compensation ($000): Salary ($1,194,287), contr fee ($409,227), FFS ($103,864), other ($1,115,957)

Total Member Encounters: Phys (1,845,373), non-phys (975,493)

Group Affiliation: Kaiser Foundation

Licensed in: OR, WA

Address: 500 NE Multnomah St, Suite 100, Portland, OR 97232-2099

Phone: (503) 813-2800   **Dom State:** OR   **Commenced Bus:** May 1942

Data Date	Rating	RACR #1	RACR #2	Total Assets ($mil)	Capital ($mil)	Net Premium ($mil)	Net Income ($mil)
6-14	B	5.07	4.23	1,257.7	454.4	1,556.7	-10.1
6-13	A-	5.65	4.71	1,191.2	452.4	1,491.1	-4.1
2013	B	5.36	4.46	1,216.5	480.1	3,008.0	-14.9
2012	A-	5.89	4.91	1,152.7	471.7	2,862.6	22.0
2011	A	6.48	5.40	1,097.9	490.6	2,698.8	33.0
2010	A	6.82	5.68	966.2	500.0	2,528.8	39.5
2009	A	6.97	5.80	941.7	494.9	2,431.0	36.3

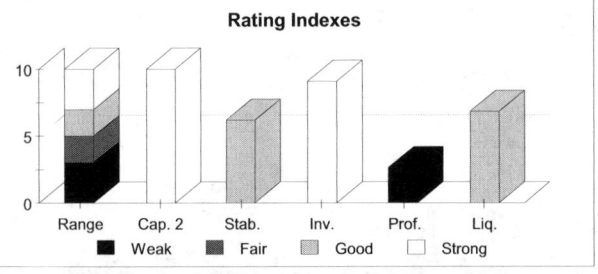

Rating Indexes

KAISER FOUNDATION HP OF CO *   B+   Good

Major Rating Factors: Good overall profitability index (6.0 on a scale of 0 to 10). Good overall results on stability tests (5.6). Rating is significantly influenced by the strong financial results of Kaiser Foundation. Good liquidity (6.9) with sufficient resources (cash flows and marketable investments) to handle a spike in claims.

Other Rating Factors: Strong capitalization index (9.5) based on excellent current risk-adjusted capital (severe loss scenario). High quality investment portfolio (7.3).

Principal Business: Comp med (59%), Medicare (33%), FEHB (6%), other (1%)

Mem Phys: 13: 642   **12:** 601   **13 MLR** 92.1%   **/ 13 Admin Exp** N/A

Enroll(000): Q2 14: 566   **13:** 502   **12:** 503   **Med Exp PMPM:** $452

Principal Investments: Long-term bonds (56%), real estate (29%), nonaffiliate common stock (15%)

Provider Compensation ($000): Contr fee ($1,038,055), salary ($511,010), FFS ($78,007), capitation ($857), other ($1,115,995)

Total Member Encounters: Phys (3,910,775), non-phys (1,414,357)

Group Affiliation: Kaiser Foundation

Licensed in: CO

Address: 10350 E Dakota Ave, Denver, CO 80231

Phone: (800) 632-9700   **Dom State:** CO   **Commenced Bus:** July 1969

Data Date	Rating	RACR #1	RACR #2	Total Assets ($mil)	Capital ($mil)	Net Premium ($mil)	Net Income ($mil)
6-14	B+	3.38	2.82	1,274.6	468.0	1,592.5	34.9
6-13	B+	3.91	3.26	1,199.4	493.1	1,467.6	23.3
2013	B+	3.04	2.53	1,182.0	419.8	2,958.0	83.9
2012	B+	3.58	2.99	1,128.7	451.5	2,830.7	64.0
2011	B+	3.48	2.90	1,089.0	411.7	2,692.9	58.4
2010	B+	7.51	6.26	1,067.2	666.0	2,437.8	66.2
2009	B+	7.69	6.41	987.8	626.2	2,228.0	44.4

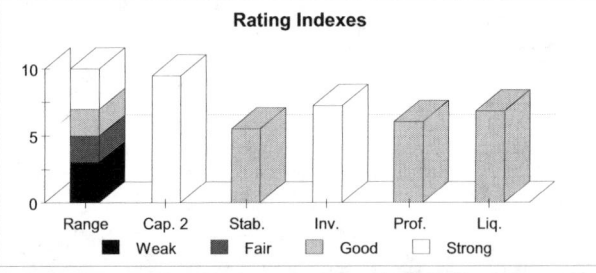

Rating Indexes

KAISER FOUNDATION HP OF GA   D   Weak

Major Rating Factors: Weak profitability index (0.9 on a scale of 0 to 10). Fair capitalization index (2.9) based on good current risk-adjusted capital (moderate loss scenario). Good overall results on stability tests (5.2). Rating is significantly influenced by the strong financial results of Kaiser Foundation.

Other Rating Factors: Good liquidity (6.1) with sufficient resources (cash flows and marketable investments) to handle a spike in claims. High quality investment portfolio (7.6).

Principal Business: Comp med (66%), Medicare (18%), FEHB (13%), other (2%)

Mem Phys: 13: 490   **12:** 487   **13 MLR** 98.3%   **/ 13 Admin Exp** N/A

Enroll(000): Q2 14: 249   **13:** 229   **12:** 224   **Med Exp PMPM:** $394

Principal Investments: Long-term bonds (51%), real estate (43%), cash and equiv (6%)

Provider Compensation ($000): Contr fee ($394,284), FFS ($24,852), capitation ($372), other ($663,660)

Total Member Encounters: Phys (964,275), non-phys (171,338)

Group Affiliation: Kaiser Foundation

Licensed in: GA

Address: 3495 Piedmont Road NE, Atlanta, GA 30305-1736

Phone: (404) 364-7000   **Dom State:** GA   **Commenced Bus:** October 1985

Data Date	Rating	RACR #1	RACR #2	Total Assets ($mil)	Capital ($mil)	Net Premium ($mil)	Net Income ($mil)
6-14	D	1.38	1.15	505.3	119.4	595.2	-40.5
6-13	D	0.88	0.73	461.2	76.1	547.8	-29.0
2013	D	1.02	0.85	479.8	88.4	1,099.4	-80.6
2012	C-	1.04	0.87	455.7	89.7	1,084.5	-71.6
2011	C-	0.88	0.73	327.7	70.4	1,026.5	-36.2
2010	B	1.45	1.21	328.8	111.7	897.2	-125.6
2009	B	2.01	1.67	247.0	99.7	999.8	-12.0

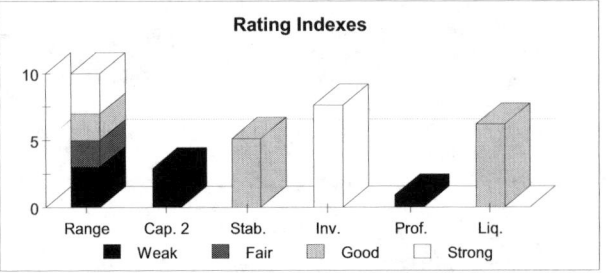

Rating Indexes

KAISER PERMANENTE INS CO *   B+   Good

Major Rating Factors: Good overall profitability index (6.9 on a scale of 0 to 10). Strong capitalization (10.0) based on excellent current risk-adjusted capital (severe loss scenario). High quality investment portfolio (9.9).
Other Rating Factors: Excellent liquidity (7.1) with ample operational cash flow and liquid investments.
Principal Business: Comp med (80%), dental (19%), other (1%)
Mem Phys: 13: 732,783 **12:** 700,892 **13 MLR** 80.3% **/ 13 Admin Exp** N/A
Enroll(000): Q2 14: 167 **13:** 308 **12:** 237 **Med Exp PMPM:** $51
Principal Investments: Long-term bonds (63%), cash and equiv (37%)
Provider Compensation ($000): Contr fee ($100,221), bonus arrang ($77,546), FFS ($22,839), other ($2,226)
Total Member Encounters: Phys (66,452), non-phys (356,020)
Group Affiliation: Kaiser Foundation
Licensed in: CA, CO, DC, GA, HI, KS, MD, MO, OH, OR, SC, VA, WA
Address: 300 Lakeside Dr 26th Floor, Oakland, CA 94612
Phone: (877) 847-7572 **Dom State:** CA **Commenced Bus:** January 1995

Data Date	Rating	RACR #1	RACR #2	Total Assets ($mil)	Capital ($mil)	Net Premium ($mil)	Net Income ($mil)
6-14	B+	5.75	4.79	179.4	84.8	72.8	-3.0
6-13	A	5.57	4.64	174.7	92.2	125.9	8.9
2013	A	5.99	4.99	180.0	88.5	245.8	5.1
2012	A	5.03	4.19	160.8	83.1	291.9	10.3
2011	A	4.53	3.78	163.0	70.8	272.2	3.2
2010	A	4.49	3.74	126.5	65.9	250.2	3.8
2009	A	4.98	4.15	118.6	60.1	213.8	1.6

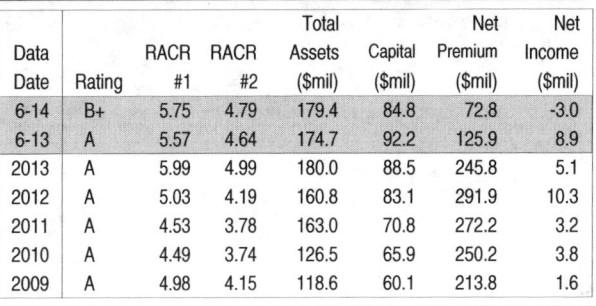

Rating Indexes

Range   Cap. 2   Stab.   Inv.   Prof.   Liq.
■ Weak   ▨ Fair   ▦ Good   ☐ Strong

KANAWHA INSURANCE COMPANY   C   Fair

Major Rating Factors: Fair overall results on stability tests (3.5 on a scale of 0 to 10). Good quality investment portfolio (6.6) despite mixed results such as: minimal exposure to mortgages and large holdings of BBB rated bonds but small junk bond holdings. Weak profitability (1.5) with operating losses during the first six months of 2014. Return on equity has been low, averaging -71.0%.
Other Rating Factors: Strong capitalization (7.5) based on excellent risk adjusted capital (severe loss scenario). Excellent liquidity (7.8).
Principal Business: Individual health insurance (40%), group health insurance (30%), group life insurance (17%), individual life insurance (12%), and reinsurance (2%).
Principal Investments: NonCMO investment grade bonds (81%), CMOs and structured securities (11%), cash (5%), noninv. grade bonds (1%), and policy loans (1%).
Investments in Affiliates: None
Group Affiliation: Humana Inc
Licensed in: All states except AK, ME, NY, PR
Commenced Business: December 1958
Address: 210 S White St, Lancaster, SC 29721
Phone: (803) 283-5300 **Domicile State:** SC **NAIC Code:** 65110

Data Date	Rating	RACR #1	RACR #2	Total Assets ($mil)	Capital ($mil)	Net Premium ($mil)	Net Income ($mil)
6-14	C	2.20	1.35	1,638.6	133.2	109.2	-23.8
6-13	C	4.43	2.80	1,465.3	276.5	122.2	20.9
2013	C	2.68	1.67	1,623.0	155.1	228.1	-174.9
2012	C	4.02	2.54	1,456.8	255.5	252.2	-112.4
2011	C	3.22	2.03	1,288.9	190.5	206.5	-77.4
2010	C	1.45	0.91	1,109.0	80.8	178.4	-87.0
2009	C	1.88	1.22	926.4	92.7	156.6	-77.1

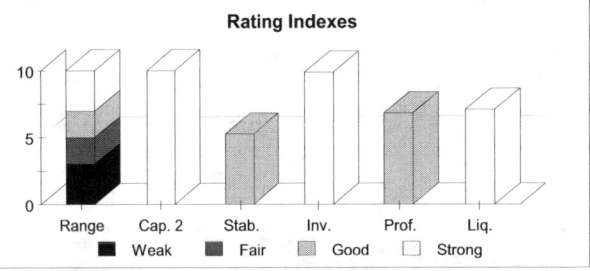

Rating Indexes

Ranges   Cap.   Stab.   Inv.   Prof.   Liq.
■ Weak   ▨ Fair   ▦ Good   ☐ Strong

KENTUCKY SPIRIT HEALTH PLAN INC   C-   Fair

Major Rating Factors: Fair liquidity (3.5 on a scale of 0 to 10) as cash resources may not be adequate to cover a spike in claims. Weak profitability index (0.9). Strong capitalization (7.6) based on excellent current risk-adjusted capital (severe loss scenario).
Other Rating Factors: High quality investment portfolio (9.9).
Principal Business: Medicaid (100%)
Mem Phys: 12: 7,180 **11:** 7,255 **12 MLR** 116.1% **/ 12 Admin Exp** N/A
Enroll(000): Q2 13: 131 **12:** 137 **11:** 180 **Med Exp PMPM:** $361
Principal Investments: Cash and equiv (62%), long-term bonds (38%)
Provider Compensation ($000): Contr fee ($489,885), capitation ($87,432), salary ($41,311)
Total Member Encounters: Phys (916,992), non-phys (1,135,534)
Group Affiliation: Centene Corp
Licensed in: (No states)
Address: 201 E Main St Suite 501, Lexington, KY 40507
Phone: (314) 725-4477 **Dom State:** KY **Commenced Bus:** November 2011

Data Date	Rating	RACR #1	RACR #2	Total Assets ($mil)	Capital ($mil)	Net Premium ($mil)	Net Income ($mil)
6-13	C-	1.82	1.51	176.2	79.0	235.0	18.6
6-12	C-	5.20	4.34	202.8	58.7	291.8	-81.1
2012	C-	1.22	1.01	218.0	57.3	555.5	-139.4
2011	C-	1.64	1.37	106.9	19.3	128.7	-22.7
2010	N/A	N/A	N/A	N/A	N/A	N/A	N/A
2009	N/A	N/A	N/A	N/A	N/A	N/A	N/A
2008	N/A	N/A	N/A	N/A	N/A	N/A	N/A

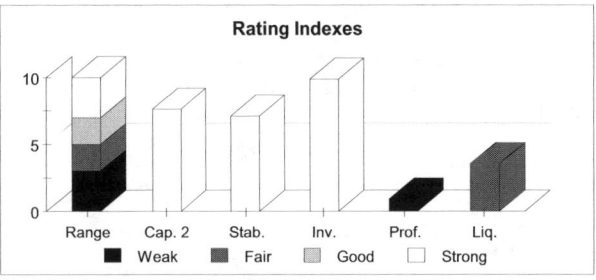

Rating Indexes

Range   Cap. 2   Stab.   Inv.   Prof.   Liq.
■ Weak   ▨ Fair   ▦ Good   ☐ Strong

KERN HEALTH SYSTEMS

C   **Fair**

Major Rating Factors: Fair overall results on stability tests (4.0 on a scale of 0 to 10) in spite of steady enrollment growth, averaging 6% over the past five years. Weak profitability index (1.6). Strong capitalization index (8.9) based on excellent current risk-adjusted capital (severe loss scenario).

Other Rating Factors: Excellent liquidity (7.3) with ample operational cash flow and liquid investments.

Principal Business: Medicaid (100%)

Mem Phys: 13: N/A   **12:** N/A   **13 MLR** 99.3%   **/ 13 Admin Exp** N/A

Enroll(000): Q2 14: 161   **13:** 126   **12:** 116   **Med Exp PMPM:** $151

Principal Investments ($000): Cash and equiv ($56,830)

Provider Compensation ($000): None

Total Member Encounters: N/A

Group Affiliation: None

Licensed in: CA

Address: 9700 Stockdale Hwy, Bakersfield, CA 93311-3617

Phone: (661) 664-5000   **Dom State:** CA   **Commenced Bus:** June 1996

Data Date	Rating	RACR #1	RACR #2	Total Assets ($mil)	Capital ($mil)	Net Premium ($mil)	Net Income ($mil)
6-14	C	3.87	2.37	131.9	75.7	155.8	-2.2
6-13	C	4.24	2.65	117.2	80.9	110.6	13.8
2013	C	3.70	2.26	134.6	72.6	232.1	5.5
2012	C	3.39	2.12	105.1	67.1	198.4	-31.3
2011	B+	7.05	4.33	125.2	98.4	173.1	10.7
2010	B+	7.01	4.31	117.8	87.8	156.1	16.6
2009	B+	5.56	3.42	106.9	71.2	141.8	2.0

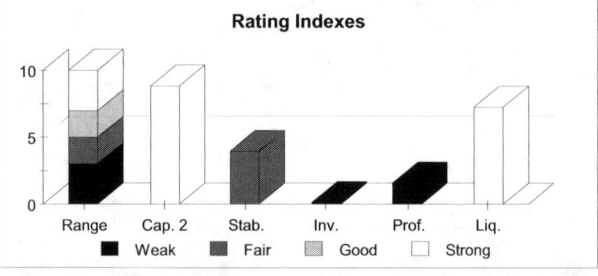

Rating Indexes

KEYSTONE HEALTH PLAN CENTRAL INC

B   **Good**

Major Rating Factors: Fair overall results on stability tests (4.9 on a scale of 0 to 10). Excellent profitability (7.0). Strong capitalization index (10.0) based on excellent current risk-adjusted capital (severe loss scenario).

Other Rating Factors: High quality investment portfolio (8.2). Excellent liquidity (6.9) with sufficient resources (cash flows and marketable investments) to handle a spike in claims.

Principal Business: Medicare (62%), comp med (38%)

Mem Phys: 13: 3,529   **12:** 3,392   **13 MLR** 81.8%   **/ 13 Admin Exp** N/A

Enroll(000): Q2 14: 39   **13:** 45   **12:** 50   **Med Exp PMPM:** $387

Principal Investments: Long-term bonds (90%), cash and equiv (10%)

Provider Compensation ($000): Contr fee ($200,457), capitation ($12,745)

Total Member Encounters: Phys (768,426), non-phys (135,400)

Group Affiliation: Capital Blue Cross Group

Licensed in: PA

Address: 2500 Elmerton Avenue, Harrisburg, PA 17177

Phone: (717) 541-7000   **Dom State:** PA   **Commenced Bus:** November 1988

Data Date	Rating	RACR #1	RACR #2	Total Assets ($mil)	Capital ($mil)	Net Premium ($mil)	Net Income ($mil)
6-14	B	6.02	5.01	135.2	88.0	120.1	0.4
6-13	B	6.13	5.11	131.5	98.0	131.6	5.4
2013	B	6.03	5.02	126.8	88.1	258.1	10.1
2012	B	5.79	4.83	129.3	92.5	283.3	13.2
2011	B	5.28	4.40	135.5	94.9	326.3	16.6
2010	B	4.39	3.66	142.1	88.6	379.7	10.1
2009	B	4.07	3.39	141.0	92.1	420.3	15.2

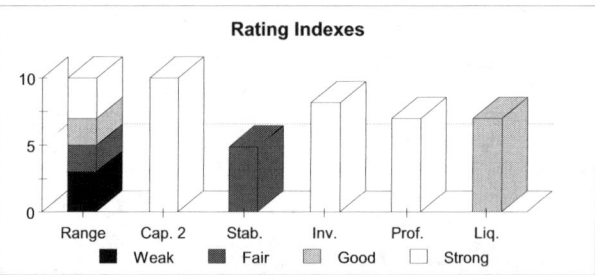

Rating Indexes

KEYSTONE HEALTH PLAN EAST INC *

B+   **Good**

Major Rating Factors: Good overall profitability index (6.4 on a scale of 0 to 10). Good quality investment portfolio (6.6). Good overall results on stability tests (5.4) despite a decline in enrollment during 2013.

Other Rating Factors: Strong capitalization index (10.0) based on excellent current risk-adjusted capital (severe loss scenario). Excellent liquidity (6.9) with sufficient resources (cash flows and marketable investments) to handle a spike in claims.

Principal Business: Comp med (63%), Medicare (37%)

Mem Phys: 13: 30,368   **12:** 29,079   **13 MLR** 81.0%   **/ 13 Admin Exp** N/A

Enroll(000): Q2 14: 516   **13:** 423   **12:** 446   **Med Exp PMPM:** $420

Principal Investments: Long-term bonds (63%), nonaffiliate common stock (16%), cash and equiv (8%), pref stock (2%), other (11%)

Provider Compensation ($000): Contr fee ($1,996,699), capitation ($168,498), FFS ($42,655)

Total Member Encounters: Phys (5,363,492), non-phys (1,181,031)

Group Affiliation: Independence Blue Cross Inc

Licensed in: PA

Address: 1901 Market St, Philadelphia, PA 19101

Phone: (215) 241-2400   **Dom State:** PA   **Commenced Bus:** January 1987

Data Date	Rating	RACR #1	RACR #2	Total Assets ($mil)	Capital ($mil)	Net Premium ($mil)	Net Income ($mil)
6-14	B+	5.83	4.85	1,543.2	924.3	1,458.1	34.8
6-13	B+	5.20	4.34	1,279.7	827.3	1,380.0	75.0
2013	B+	5.78	4.82	1,325.1	916.5	2,685.7	145.5
2012	B+	4.82	4.02	1,257.4	763.2	2,844.6	168.9
2011	B+	4.77	3.97	1,260.1	780.1	3,062.9	207.6
2010	B+	3.57	2.97	1,093.7	622.4	3,449.7	112.8
2009	B+	2.65	2.21	1,072.8	557.9	4,105.4	-18.2

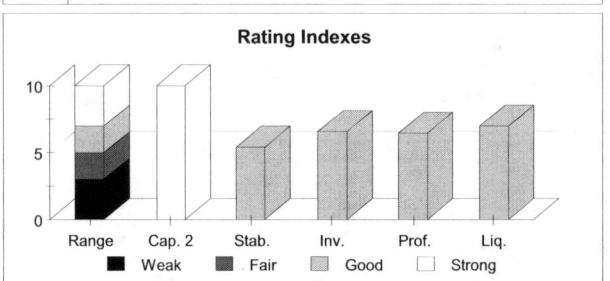

Rating Indexes

KEYSTONE HEALTH PLAN WEST INC   D+   Weak

Major Rating Factors: Poor capitalization index (0.0 on a scale of 0 to 10) based on weak current risk-adjusted capital (severe loss scenario). Weak overall results on stability tests (2.5) based on a steep decline in capital during 2013. Rating is significantly influenced by the good financial results of Highmark Inc. Good overall profitability index (6.7).

Other Rating Factors: High quality investment portfolio (9.9). Excellent liquidity (7.0) with sufficient resources (cash flows and marketable investments) to handle a spike in claims.

Principal Business: Medicare (92%), comp med (8%)

Mem Phys: 13: 23,105 **12:** 21,711 **13 MLR** 87.2% **/ 13 Admin Exp** N/A

Enroll(000): Q2 14: 143 **13:** 157 **12:** 172 **Med Exp PMPM:** $798

Principal Investments: Cash and equiv (50%), long-term bonds (47%), nonaffiliate common stock (2%)

Provider Compensation ($000): Contr fee ($1,573,964), capitation ($8,970), bonus arrang ($4,073)

Total Member Encounters: Phys (2,358,673), non-phys (1,011,885)

Group Affiliation: Highmark Inc

Licensed in: PA

Address: 120 Fifth Ave, Pittsburgh, PA 15222-3099

Phone: (412) 544-7000 **Dom State:** PA **Commenced Bus:** September 1986

Data Date	Rating	RACR #1	RACR #2	Total Assets ($mil)	Capital ($mil)	Net Premium ($mil)	Net Income ($mil)
6-14	D+	0.27	0.23	321.7	34.9	N/A	-1.8
6-13	B	3.09	2.58	688.3	370.1	928.8	59.0
2013	B-	1.46	1.22	482.4	287.0	1,791.3	104.7
2012	A-	3.42	2.85	658.3	407.2	1,892.7	95.3
2011	A-	3.28	2.73	690.4	431.5	2,044.1	73.2
2010	A-	3.45	2.87	782.3	482.2	2,302.8	131.8
2009	A-	3.11	2.59	758.4	479.9	2,446.0	143.2

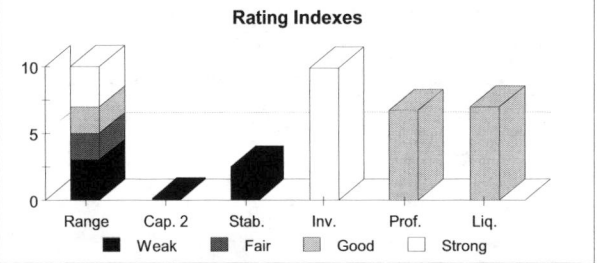

Rating Indexes

KPS HEALTH PLANS   C   Fair

Major Rating Factors: Fair profitability index (4.4 on a scale of 0 to 10). Good liquidity (6.8) with sufficient resources (cash flows and marketable investments) to handle a spike in claims. Strong capitalization (10.0) based on excellent current risk-adjusted capital (severe loss scenario).

Other Rating Factors: High quality investment portfolio (8.7).

Principal Business: FEHB (72%), comp med (25%), med supp (3%)

Mem Phys: 13: 11,696 **12:** 7,987 **13 MLR** 88.7% **/ 13 Admin Exp** N/A

Enroll(000): Q2 14: 22 **13:** 23 **12:** 23 **Med Exp PMPM:** $396

Principal Investments: Long-term bonds (77%), cash and equiv (23%)

Provider Compensation ($000): Contr fee ($103,450), FFS ($6,163)

Total Member Encounters: Phys (195,645), non-phys (154,173)

Group Affiliation: Group Health Cooperative

Licensed in: WA

Address: 400 Warren Ave, Bremerton, WA 98310

Phone: (360) 377-5576 **Dom State:** WA **Commenced Bus:** June 1948

Data Date	Rating	RACR #1	RACR #2	Total Assets ($mil)	Capital ($mil)	Net Premium ($mil)	Net Income ($mil)
6-14	C	5.16	4.30	47.6	18.8	56.6	-0.7
6-13	C	3.65	3.05	45.0	16.0	56.0	1.2
2013	C	5.08	4.24	40.8	19.2	115.0	1.9
2012	C	3.09	2.57	53.8	14.6	123.2	3.4
2011	C+	2.01	1.68	45.5	11.0	126.6	2.4
2010	B-	1.84	1.53	44.5	12.5	149.2	-0.6
2009	B	1.90	1.58	48.5	13.7	146.1	-1.9

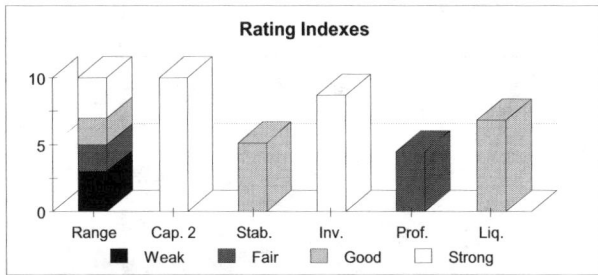

Rating Indexes

LA HEALTH SERVICE & INDEMNITY CO *   A+   Excellent

Major Rating Factors: Strong capitalization (10.0 on a scale of 0 to 10) based on excellent current risk-adjusted capital (severe loss scenario). Excellent liquidity (6.9) with sufficient resources (cash flows and marketable investments) to handle a spike in claims. Good overall profitability index (6.8).

Other Rating Factors: Good quality investment portfolio (6.8).

Principal Business: Comp med (77%), FEHB (17%), med supp (5%), other (1%)

Mem Phys: 13: 23,388 **12:** 21,872 **13 MLR** 83.6% **/ 13 Admin Exp** N/A

Enroll(000): Q2 14: 683 **13:** 648 **12:** 634 **Med Exp PMPM:** $238

Principal Investments: Long-term bonds (39%), affiliate common stock (26%), nonaffiliate common stock (16%), cash and equiv (10%), real estate (5%), other (4%)

Provider Compensation ($000): FFS ($955,161), contr fee ($884,144)

Total Member Encounters: Phys (5,376,899), non-phys (2,447,519)

Group Affiliation: Louisiana Health Services

Licensed in: LA

Address: 5525 Reitz Ave, Baton Rouge, LA 70809-

Phone: (225) 295-3307 **Dom State:** LA **Commenced Bus:** January 1975

Data Date	Rating	RACR #1	RACR #2	Total Assets ($mil)	Capital ($mil)	Net Premium ($mil)	Net Income ($mil)
6-14	A+	7.40	6.17	1,813.5	1,169.3	1,191.7	52.1
6-13	A+	6.82	5.68	1,619.8	1,041.5	1,073.5	69.2
2013	A+	6.98	5.82	1,644.0	1,102.4	2,181.0	68.7
2012	A+	6.50	5.42	1,505.4	992.5	2,094.6	58.1
2011	A+	5.95	4.96	1,411.3	873.8	2,024.7	50.4
2010	A+	5.97	4.97	1,326.4	816.9	1,834.9	63.7
2009	A+	5.14	4.28	1,115.3	697.5	1,798.3	52.7

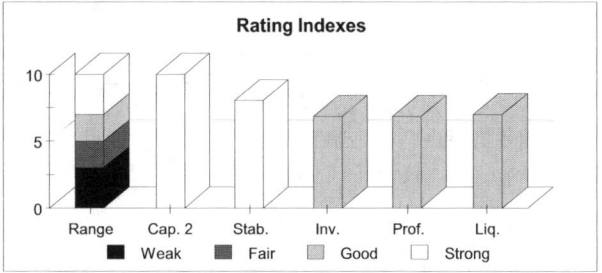

Rating Indexes

LIBERTY LIFE ASSURANCE COMPANY OF BOSTON   B   Good

Major Rating Factors: Good overall results on stability tests (6.2 on a scale of 0 to 10). Stability strengths include excellent operational trends, good risk adjusted capital for prior years and excellent risk diversification. Good quality investment portfolio (6.4) despite mixed results such as: large holdings of BBB rated bonds but moderate junk bond exposure. Good overall profitability (6.6).

Other Rating Factors: Good liquidity (6.9). Strong capitalization (7.4) based on excellent risk adjusted capital (severe loss scenario).

Principal Business: N/A

Principal Investments: NonCMO investment grade bonds (78%), CMOs and structured securities (12%), mortgages in good standing (3%), noninv. grade bonds (2%), and policy loans (1%).

Investments in Affiliates: None

Group Affiliation: Liberty Mutual Group

Licensed in: All states except PR

Commenced Business: January 1964

Address: 175 Berkeley St, Boston, MA 02117

Phone: (617) 357-9500 **Domicile State:** NH **NAIC Code:** 65315

Data Date	Rating	RACR #1	RACR #2	Total Assets ($mil)	Capital ($mil)	Net Premium ($mil)	Net Income ($mil)
6-14	B	2.21	1.29	14,171.0	896.1	1,164.2	21.2
6-13	B	1.71	1.08	12,575.7	728.1	1,044.5	135.0
2013	B	1.83	1.07	13,115.1	716.9	2,095.9	39.2
2012	B	1.63	1.03	12,403.2	688.6	1,807.1	31.3
2011	B	1.65	1.04	15,165.1	660.6	1,641.5	53.4
2010	B	1.69	1.07	14,160.7	637.7	1,390.3	40.3
2009	B-	1.58	0.96	12,983.2	597.5	1,208.7	-23.5

Adverse Trends in Operations

Increase in policy surrenders from 2012 to 2013 (38%)
Decrease in asset base during 2012 (18%)
Increase in policy surrenders from 2009 to 2010 (44%)

LIBERTY UNION LIFE ASR CO   C-   Fair

Major Rating Factors: Fair profitability index (3.0 on a scale of 0 to 10). Good liquidity (5.0) as cash resources may not be adequate to cover a spike in claims. Strong capitalization (7.7) based on excellent current risk-adjusted capital (severe loss scenario).

Other Rating Factors: High quality investment portfolio (9.6).

Principal Business: Comp med (71%), dental (10%), other (17%)

Mem Phys: 13: N/A **12:** N/A **13 MLR** 74.3% **/ 13 Admin Exp** N/A

Enroll(000): Q2 14: 15 **13:** 19 **12:** 18 **Med Exp PMPM:** $71

Principal Investments: Long-term bonds (83%), cash and equiv (15%), other (2%)

Provider Compensation ($000): Contr fee ($14,861), FFS ($893)

Total Member Encounters: Phys (30,364), non-phys (15,544)

Group Affiliation: Mid-America Associates Inc

Licensed in: MI, WV

Address: 30775 Barrington Ave, Madison Heights, MI 48071

Phone: (248) 583-7123 **Dom State:** MI **Commenced Bus:** June 1964

Data Date	Rating	RACR #1	RACR #2	Total Assets ($mil)	Capital ($mil)	Net Premium ($mil)	Net Income ($mil)
6-14	C-	1.94	1.61	11.8	4.1	9.6	-0.3
6-13	C-	2.77	2.30	11.0	4.6	10.7	0.0
2013	C-	2.12	1.76	11.6	4.7	21.7	0.5
2012	C-	2.73	2.28	11.2	4.5	21.2	0.9
2011	N/A	N/A	N/A	11.5	4.5	21.8	N/A
2010	N/A	N/A	N/A	N/A	N/A	N/A	N/A
2009	N/A	N/A	N/A	N/A	N/A	N/A	N/A

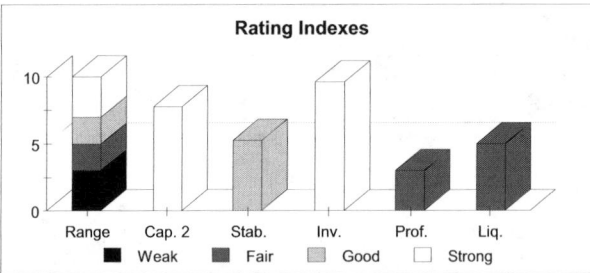

Rating Indexes — Range, Cap. 2, Stab., Inv., Prof., Liq. — Weak, Fair, Good, Strong

LIFE INSURANCE COMPANY OF ALABAMA *   A-   Excellent

Major Rating Factors: Good quality investment portfolio (6.2 on a scale of 0 to 10) despite mixed results such as: no exposure to mortgages and large holdings of BBB rated bonds but minimal holdings in junk bonds. Good liquidity (6.7) with sufficient resources to handle a spike in claims. Good overall results on stability tests (6.3) excellent operational trends and good risk diversification.

Other Rating Factors: Strong capitalization (8.4) based on excellent risk adjusted capital (severe loss scenario). Excellent profitability (9.0) with operating gains in each of the last five years.

Principal Business: Individual health insurance (77%), individual life insurance (17%), and group health insurance (6%).

Principal Investments: NonCMO investment grade bonds (84%), common & preferred stock (7%), policy loans (3%), noninv. grade bonds (3%), and misc. investments (4%).

Investments in Affiliates: None

Group Affiliation: None

Licensed in: AL, AR, FL, GA, KY, LA, MS, NC, OK, SC, TN

Commenced Business: August 1952

Address: 302 Broad St, Gadsden, AL 35901

Phone: (205) 543-2022 **Domicile State:** AL **NAIC Code:** 65412

Data Date	Rating	RACR #1	RACR #2	Total Assets ($mil)	Capital ($mil)	Net Premium ($mil)	Net Income ($mil)
6-14	A-	2.96	1.96	112.7	35.8	18.7	1.8
6-13	A-	2.59	1.79	103.8	30.6	18.8	1.0
2013	A-	2.88	1.95	108.0	33.0	37.2	2.7
2012	A-	2.52	1.74	102.6	29.4	38.0	3.0
2011	A-	2.03	1.43	94.9	25.0	39.2	3.1
2010	B+	1.91	1.39	96.6	22.8	40.9	3.5
2009	B+	1.56	1.13	88.8	18.9	40.7	3.3

Adverse Trends in Operations

Decrease in premium volume from 2012 to 2013 (2%)
Decrease in premium volume from 2011 to 2012 (3%)
Decrease in asset base during 2011 (2%)
Decrease in premium volume from 2010 to 2011 (4%)

LIFE INSURANCE COMPANY OF NORTH AMERICA   B   Good

Major Rating Factors: Good overall results on stability tests (5.8 on a scale of 0 to 10). Stability strengths include excellent operational trends and excellent risk diversification. Good quality investment portfolio (5.4) despite large holdings of BBB rated bonds in addition to junk bond exposure equal to 50% of capital. Exposure to mortgages is significant, but the mortgage default rate has been low. Strong capitalization (7.8) based on excellent risk adjusted capital (severe loss scenario).

Other Rating Factors: Excellent profitability (7.9) with operating gains in each of the last five years. Excellent liquidity (7.0).

Principal Business: Group health insurance (52%), group life insurance (40%), and reinsurance (7%).

Principal Investments: NonCMO investment grade bonds (61%), mortgages in good standing (18%), noninv. grade bonds (10%), CMOs and structured securities (5%), and misc. investments (6%).

Investments in Affiliates: 5%

Group Affiliation: CIGNA Corp

Licensed in: All states, the District of Columbia and Puerto Rico

Commenced Business: September 1957

Address: 1601 Chestnut ST,2 Liberty Pl, Philadelphia, PA 19192-2235

Phone: (860) 726-7234 **Domicile State:** PA **NAIC Code:** 65498

Data Date	Rating	RACR #1	RACR #2	Total Assets ($mil)	Capital ($mil)	Net Premium ($mil)	Net Income ($mil)
6-14	B	2.46	1.55	6,882.4	1,238.8	1,586.6	149.1
6-13	B	2.08	1.32	5,980.8	886.1	1,496.1	46.6
2013	B	2.20	1.39	6,711.9	1,103.5	3,232.7	173.3
2012	B	2.10	1.34	6,089.4	884.4	2,705.9	198.7
2011	B-	2.28	1.47	5,628.9	872.4	2,474.3	202.0
2010	B-	2.31	1.50	5,815.7	841.7	2,350.8	721.7
2009	B-	1.87	1.27	5,732.7	769.4	2,304.5	215.6

Adverse Trends in Operations

Increase in policy surrenders from 2011 to 2012 (72%)
Decrease in asset base during 2011 (3%)
Change in asset mix during 2010 (8.3%)

LIFEMAP ASSURANCE COMPANY   B   Good

Major Rating Factors: Good liquidity (6.7 on a scale of 0 to 10) with sufficient resources to handle a spike in claims. Good overall results on stability tests (5.9). Strengths include good financial support from affiliation with Regence Group, excellent operational trends and excellent risk diversification. Fair quality investment portfolio (4.6).

Other Rating Factors: Weak profitability (2.7) with operating losses during the first six months of 2014. Strong capitalization (7.5) based on excellent risk adjusted capital (severe loss scenario).

Principal Business: Group health insurance (58%), group life insurance (30%), individual health insurance (11%), and reinsurance (1%).

Principal Investments: NonCMO investment grade bonds (53%), common & preferred stock (26%), and CMOs and structured securities (21%).

Investments in Affiliates: 2%

Group Affiliation: Regence Group

Licensed in: AK, ID, MT, OR, UT, WA, WY

Commenced Business: July 1966

Address: 100 SW Market St, Portland, OR 97201

Phone: (503) 225-6048 **Domicile State:** OR **NAIC Code:** 97985

Data Date	Rating	RACR #1	RACR #2	Total Assets ($mil)	Capital ($mil)	Net Premium ($mil)	Net Income ($mil)
6-14	B	1.83	1.32	91.5	43.3	34.1	-0.1
6-13	B+	2.06	1.48	89.1	44.9	31.0	-0.1
2013	B	1.96	1.41	89.6	45.3	64.1	-0.5
2012	B+	2.17	1.56	86.1	44.9	55.0	-1.8
2011	B+	2.38	1.71	89.5	46.8	49.5	-0.1
2010	B+	2.39	1.70	87.1	46.1	44.0	3.0
2009	B+	2.27	1.63	89.2	42.7	44.9	2.8

Regence Group
Composite Group Rating: B+
Largest Group Members

	Assets ($mil)	Rating
REGENCE BLUESHIELD	1692	B+
REGENCE BL CROSS BL SHIELD OREGON	1008	B+
REGENCE BLUE CROSS BLUE SHIELD OF UT	535	B
REGENCE BLUESHIELD OF IDAHO INC	274	B
ASURIS NORTHWEST HEALTH	100	B

LIFESECURE INSURANCE COMPANY   D-   Weak

Major Rating Factors: Weak profitability (1.8 on a scale of 0 to 10) with operating losses during the first six months of 2014. Weak overall results on stability tests (1.4). Strong current capitalization (8.1) based on excellent risk adjusted capital (severe loss scenario) reflecting improvement over results in 2009.

Other Rating Factors: High quality investment portfolio (7.5). Excellent liquidity (8.4).

Principal Business: Reinsurance (54%), individual health insurance (25%), individual life insurance (17%), and individual annuities (4%).

Principal Investments: NonCMO investment grade bonds (100%).

Investments in Affiliates: None

Group Affiliation: Blue Cross Blue Shield of Michigan

Licensed in: All states except CT, ME, MA, NH, NJ, NY, VT, PR

Commenced Business: July 1954

Address: 1005 Congress Ave, Ste 825, Austin, TX 78701

Phone: (847) 402-5000 **Domicile State:** MI **NAIC Code:** 77720

Data Date	Rating	RACR #1	RACR #2	Total Assets ($mil)	Capital ($mil)	Net Premium ($mil)	Net Income ($mil)
6-14	D-	2.63	1.70	209.5	27.7	20.3	-4.1
6-13	E+	2.11	1.42	184.0	19.9	16.1	-5.1
2013	D-	2.10	1.34	189.7	20.2	33.4	-3.9
2012	E+	2.50	1.79	174.9	23.8	28.2	-6.2
2011	E+	2.78	2.11	148.3	26.0	25.2	-3.1
2010	E+	1.49	1.20	119.2	13.5	23.3	-7.6
2009	E	1.11	0.95	96.1	9.7	12.6	-12.0

Net Income History
(in millions of dollars)

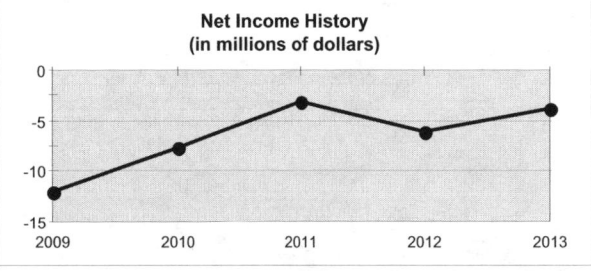

LIFEWISE ASSURANCE COMPANY *

A   **Excellent**

Major Rating Factors: Excellent overall results on stability tests (7.0 on a scale of 0 to 10). Strengths that enhance stability include excellent operational trends and good risk diversification. Strong capitalization (10.0) based on excellent risk adjusted capital (severe loss scenario). Furthermore, this high level of risk adjusted capital has been consistently maintained over the last five years. High quality investment portfolio (8.5).

Other Rating Factors: Excellent profitability (9.2) with operating gains in each of the last five years. Excellent liquidity (7.0).

Principal Business: Group health insurance (93%) and group life insurance (6%).

Principal Investments: NonCMO investment grade bonds (53%), CMOs and structured securities (40%), cash (5%), and noninv. grade bonds (2%).

Investments in Affiliates: None

Group Affiliation: PREMERA

Licensed in: AK, AZ, CA, ID, MT, NM, ND, OR, UT, WA, WY

Commenced Business: November 1981

Address: 7007 220th SW, Mountlake Terrace, WA 98043

Phone: (206) 670-4584   **Domicile State:** WA   **NAIC Code:** 94188

Data Date	Rating	RACR #1	RACR #2	Total Assets ($mil)	Capital ($mil)	Net Premium ($mil)	Net Income ($mil)
6-14	A	6.52	4.94	129.7	83.9	46.6	2.9
6-13	A	6.56	4.91	118.9	78.1	43.1	6.4
2013	A	6.19	4.70	119.4	81.1	85.4	9.5
2012	A	5.90	4.42	118.4	71.6	84.3	12.8
2011	A	2.94	2.22	94.5	57.8	89.7	4.3
2010	A	3.21	2.40	94.8	52.3	66.5	7.2
2009	A	2.82	2.02	76.4	45.4	51.6	4.4

Adverse Trends in Operations

Decrease in premium volume from 2011 to 2012 (6%)

LIFEWISE HEALTH PLAN OF OREGON

B   **Good**

Major Rating Factors: Good liquidity (6.7 on a scale of 0 to 10) with sufficient resources (cash flows and marketable investments) to handle a spike in claims. Strong capitalization (10.0) based on excellent current risk-adjusted capital (severe loss scenario). High quality investment portfolio (8.9).

Other Rating Factors: Weak profitability index (2.4).

Principal Business: Comp med (95%), med supp (3%), dental (2%)

Mem Phys: 13: 9,753   **12:** 12,365   **13 MLR** 77.4%   **/ 13 Admin Exp** N/A

Enroll(000): Q2 14: 47   **13:** 51   **12:** 53   **Med Exp PMPM:** $189

Principal Investments: Long-term bonds (94%), cash and equiv (6%)

Provider Compensation ($000): Contr fee ($109,475), FFS ($10,919)

Total Member Encounters: Phys (254,315), non-phys (113,199)

Group Affiliation: PREMERA

Licensed in: ID, OR

Address: 2020 SW 4th St Suite 1000, Portland, OR 97201

Phone: (503) 295-6707   **Dom State:** OR   **Commenced Bus:** January 1987

Data Date	Rating	RACR #1	RACR #2	Total Assets ($mil)	Capital ($mil)	Net Premium ($mil)	Net Income ($mil)
6-14	B	7.12	5.93	106.7	62.4	77.8	-3.3
6-13	B	6.79	5.66	97.3	64.0	76.6	-0.5
2013	B	7.47	6.22	97.9	65.6	151.3	1.0
2012	B	6.87	5.72	99.7	64.7	160.1	-0.2
2011	B	6.54	5.45	91.6	62.5	171.2	4.3
2010	B	5.39	4.49	97.0	54.8	190.3	-4.2
2009	B	4.92	4.10	97.4	58.5	217.9	0.8

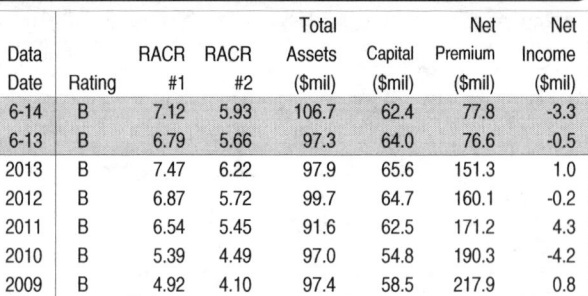

Rating Indexes

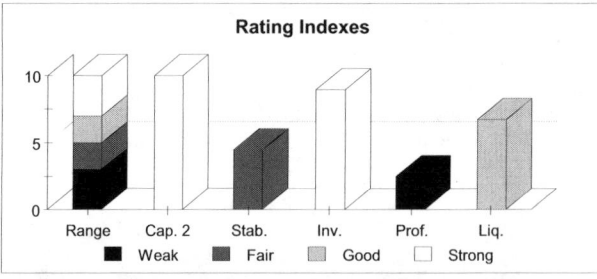

Range   Cap. 2   Stab.   Inv.   Prof.   Liq.

■ Weak   ▨ Fair   ▥ Good   □ Strong

LIFEWISE HEALTH PLAN OF WASHINGTON *

B+   **Good**

Major Rating Factors: Good liquidity (6.6 on a scale of 0 to 10) with sufficient resources (cash flows and marketable investments) to handle a spike in claims. Strong capitalization (9.7) based on excellent current risk-adjusted capital (severe loss scenario). High quality investment portfolio (9.6).

Other Rating Factors: Fair profitability index (4.9).

Principal Business: Comp med (100%)

Mem Phys: 13: 33,542   **12:** 31,792   **13 MLR** 72.2%   **/ 13 Admin Exp** N/A

Enroll(000): Q2 14: 83   **13:** 94   **12:** 114   **Med Exp PMPM:** $202

Principal Investments: Long-term bonds (89%), cash and equiv (9%), other (2%)

Provider Compensation ($000): Contr fee ($249,751), FFS ($3,212), bonus arrang ($50)

Total Member Encounters: Phys (713,675), non-phys (293,532)

Group Affiliation: PREMERA

Licensed in: WA

Address: 7001 220th St SW, Mountlake Terrace, WA 98043

Phone: (425) 918-4000   **Dom State:** WA   **Commenced Bus:** April 2001

Data Date	Rating	RACR #1	RACR #2	Total Assets ($mil)	Capital ($mil)	Net Premium ($mil)	Net Income ($mil)
6-14	B+	3.50	2.92	150.0	59.1	149.9	-3.6
6-13	B+	2.78	2.32	127.4	50.8	179.7	4.9
2013	B+	3.66	3.05	117.8	61.8	345.0	15.7
2012	B+	2.54	2.12	110.5	46.2	326.0	-1.4
2011	B+	2.92	2.43	113.8	46.3	287.0	-4.6
2010	A-	4.61	3.84	108.1	51.5	220.4	6.9
2009	A-	4.27	3.56	97.3	46.9	210.2	7.1

Rating Indexes

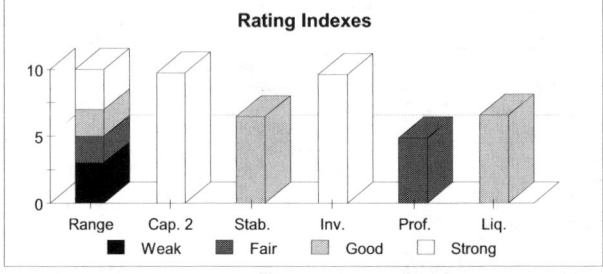

Range   Cap. 2   Stab.   Inv.   Prof.   Liq.

■ Weak   ▨ Fair   ▥ Good   □ Strong

LOCAL INITIATIVE HEALTH AUTH LA   C   Fair

Major Rating Factors: Weak liquidity (0.0 on a scale of 0 to 10) as a spike in claims may stretch capacity. Good overall profitability index (5.5). Good capitalization index (6.8) based on good current risk-adjusted capital (moderate loss scenario).

Other Rating Factors: Good overall results on stability tests (6.4) based on healthy premium and capital growth during 2013.

Principal Business: Medicaid (92%), Medicare (2%)

Mem Phys: 13: N/A **12:** N/A **13 MLR** 94.3% / **13 Admin Exp** N/A

Enroll(000): Q2 14: 1,394 **13:** 1,197 **12:** 1,060 **Med Exp PMPM:** $185

Principal Investments ($000): Cash and equiv ($849,378)

Provider Compensation ($000): None

Total Member Encounters: N/A

Group Affiliation: None

Licensed in: CA

Address: 555 W Fifth St 29th Floor, Los Angeles, CA 90013-3036

Phone: (213) 694-1250 **Dom State:** CA **Commenced Bus:** April 1997

Data Date	Rating	RACR #1	RACR #2	Total Assets ($mil)	Capital ($mil)	Net Premium ($mil)	Net Income ($mil)
6-14	C	1.00	0.61	1,194.7	190.2	1,690.2	14.2
6-13	C	0.96	0.59	481.7	122.5	1,136.0	-16.7
2013	C	0.91	0.55	1,233.9	175.9	2,687.4	36.7
2012	C	1.13	0.68	509.3	139.3	1,933.6	-11.5
2011	C	1.95	1.19	368.0	150.7	1,334.8	5.2
2010	C	2.34	1.42	351.7	145.5	1,127.6	20.3
2009	C-	2.16	1.31	378.3	125.2	1,127.4	7.9

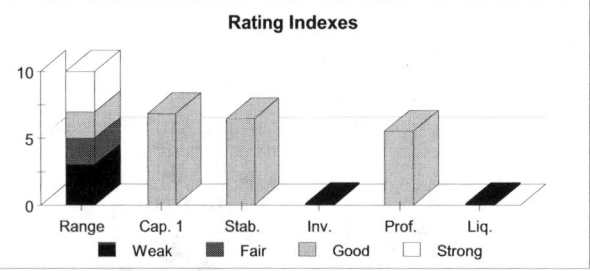

Rating Indexes

LONDON LIFE REINSURANCE COMPANY   C+   Fair

Major Rating Factors: Fair overall capitalization (4.0 on a scale of 0 to 10) based on mixed results -- excessive policy leverage mitigated by excellent risk adjusted capital (severe loss scenario). Nevertheless, capital levels have fluctuated during prior years. Fair overall results on stability tests (3.0) including weak results on operational trends. Weak profitability (2.9) with investment income below regulatory standards in relation to interest assumptions of reserves.

Other Rating Factors: High quality investment portfolio (7.9). Excellent liquidity (9.1).

Principal Business: Reinsurance (100%).

Principal Investments: NonCMO investment grade bonds (82%), CMOs and structured securities (13%), cash (3%), noninv. grade bonds (2%), and common & preferred stock (1%).

Investments in Affiliates: None

Group Affiliation: Great West Life Asr

Licensed in: All states, the District of Columbia and Puerto Rico

Commenced Business: December 1969

Address: 1787 Sentry Parkway, Ste 420, Blue Bell, PA 1942-22

Phone: (215) 542-7200 **Domicile State:** PA **NAIC Code:** 76694

Data Date	Rating	RACR #1	RACR #2	Total Assets ($mil)	Capital ($mil)	Net Premium ($mil)	Net Income ($mil)
6-14	C+	4.46	2.26	330.2	54.4	1.2	1.4
6-13	C+	4.89	2.48	358.5	67.8	-9.3	0.6
2013	C+	4.74	2.39	344.1	52.9	-8.1	2.3
2012	C+	4.67	2.38	424.6	67.2	29.9	1.6
2011	B-	3.85	2.06	464.4	69.9	39.2	2.0
2010	B	3.68	2.02	515.6	71.6	34.3	2.0
2009	B	3.26	1.80	704.5	74.0	51.1	6.8

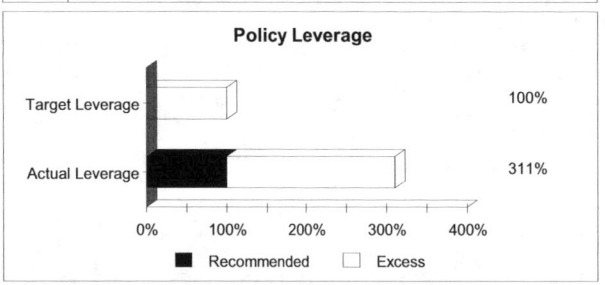

Policy Leverage

LOUISIANA HEALTHCARE CONNECTIONS INC   C-   Fair

Major Rating Factors: Weak profitability index (1.1 on a scale of 0 to 10). Good liquidity (6.9) with sufficient resources (cash flows and marketable investments) to handle a spike in claims. Strong capitalization (7.7) based on excellent current risk-adjusted capital (severe loss scenario).

Other Rating Factors: High quality investment portfolio (9.9).

Principal Business: Medicaid (100%).

Mem Phys: 13: 9,632 **12:** 7,881 **13 MLR** 85.6% / **13 Admin Exp** N/A

Enroll(000): Q2 14: 148 **13:** 152 **12:** 166 **Med Exp PMPM:** $208

Principal Investments: Cash and equiv (52%), long-term bonds (48%)

Provider Compensation ($000): Contr fee ($383,301), capitation ($12,303), salary ($6,568), bonus arrang ($419)

Total Member Encounters: Phys (743,061), non-phys (682,892)

Group Affiliation: Centene Corp

Licensed in: LA

Address: 7700 Forsyth Blvd, St Louis, MO 63105

Phone: (314) 725-4477 **Dom State:** LA **Commenced Bus:** July 2011

Data Date	Rating	RACR #1	RACR #2	Total Assets ($mil)	Capital ($mil)	Net Premium ($mil)	Net Income ($mil)
6-14	C-	1.90	1.58	91.3	47.1	215.8	0.0
6-13	C-	1.73	1.44	83.3	34.9	231.0	1.9
2013	C-	1.92	1.60	88.4	47.6	456.7	4.1
2012	C-	1.68	1.40	89.3	35.2	271.1	-16.4
2011	N/A	N/A	N/A	N/A	N/A	N/A	N/A
2010	N/A	N/A	N/A	N/A	N/A	N/A	N/A
2009	N/A	N/A	N/A	N/A	N/A	N/A	N/A

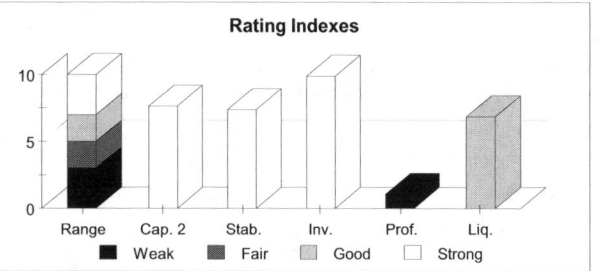

Rating Indexes

LOVELACE HEALTH SYSTEMS INC

C+   Fair

Major Rating Factors: Fair quality investment portfolio (4.0 on a scale of 0 to 10). Fair overall results on stability tests (3.4) based on a significant 63% decrease in enrollment during the period, a steep decline in premium revenue in 2013. Good overall profitability index (5.5).
Other Rating Factors: Good liquidity (6.8) with sufficient resources (cash flows and marketable investments) to handle a spike in claims. Strong capitalization index (9.4) based on excellent current risk-adjusted capital (severe loss scenario).
Principal Business: Medicare (41%), Medicaid (25%), comp med (11%), FEHB (10%), other (13%)
Mem Phys: 13: 16,757 **12:** 17,900 **13 MLR** 79.3% **/ 13 Admin Exp** N/A
Enroll(000): Q1 14: 54 **13:** 56 **12:** 152 **Med Exp PMPM:** $434
Principal Investments: Real estate (83%), cash and equiv (12%), affiliate common stock (1%), other (5%)
Provider Compensation ($000): Contr fee ($548,472), FFS ($41,474), capitation ($2,358)
Total Member Encounters: Phys (1,180,098), non-phys (284,202)
Group Affiliation: Ardent Health Services LLC
Licensed in: NM
Address: 4101 Indian School Rd NE 110 S, Albuquerque, NM 87110
Phone: (505) 727-5683 **Dom State:** NM **Commenced Bus:** March 1985

Data Date	Rating	RACR #1	RACR #2	Total Assets ($mil)	Capital ($mil)	Net Premium ($mil)	Net Income ($mil)
3-14	C+	3.27	2.73	325.1	183.8	127.0	-6.9
3-13	B	3.79	3.16	401.0	250.1	216.7	6.0
2013	B-	3.63	3.03	320.9	202.8	704.3	15.2
2012	B	3.77	3.14	406.2	248.7	918.1	70.0
2011	B	3.11	2.59	373.0	213.6	970.5	50.4
2010	B	2.68	2.23	333.7	181.2	973.0	75.1
2009	B-	2.29	1.91	304.6	164.1	973.7	70.7

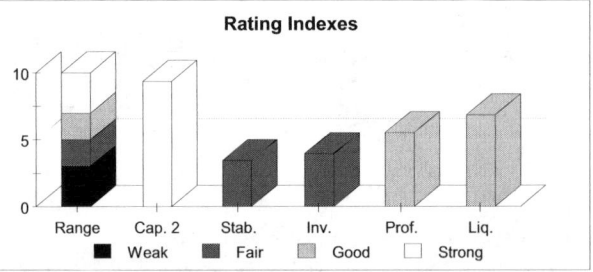

Rating Indexes

LOVELACE INS CO INC

D   Weak

Major Rating Factors: Weak profitability index (0.9 on a scale of 0 to 10). Poor capitalization (2.0) based on weak current risk-adjusted capital (moderate loss scenario). Weak liquidity (2.6) as a spike in claims may stretch capacity.
Other Rating Factors: High quality investment portfolio (9.9).
Principal Business: Comp med (99%)
Mem Phys: 13: 15,570 **12:** 15,883 **13 MLR** 92.8% **/ 13 Admin Exp** N/A
Enroll(000): Q1 14: 20 **13:** 25 **12:** 27 **Med Exp PMPM:** $297
Principal Investments: Cash and equiv (99%), long-term bonds (1%)
Provider Compensation ($000): Contr fee ($84,220), FFS ($7,924), capitation ($275)
Total Member Encounters: Phys (324,925), non-phys (99,211)
Group Affiliation: Ardent Health Services LLC
Licensed in: NM
Address: 4101 Indian School Rd NE #110S, Albuquerque, NM 87110
Phone: (505) 727-5683 **Dom State:** NM **Commenced Bus:** January 2005

Data Date	Rating	RACR #1	RACR #2	Total Assets ($mil)	Capital ($mil)	Net Premium ($mil)	Net Income ($mil)
3-14	D	0.50	0.42	29.2	10.9	21.8	-5.2
3-13	C+	0.74	0.62	31.0	13.0	26.0	-2.5
2013	D	0.51	0.42	30.5	10.9	101.1	-15.4
2012	C+	0.75	0.62	27.9	13.1	91.7	-10.9
2011	N/A	N/A	N/A	23.5	10.2	68.7	-9.3
2010	N/A	N/A	N/A	19.7	7.0	38.1	-4.4
2009	D	N/A	N/A	9.8	2.9	24.8	-5.2

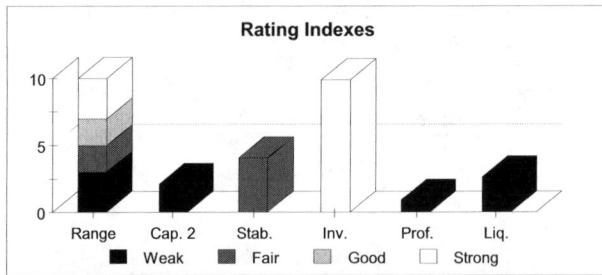

Rating Indexes

LOYAL AMERICAN LIFE INSURANCE COMPANY

C   Fair

Major Rating Factors: Fair profitability (4.5 on a scale of 0 to 10) with investment income below regulatory standards in relation to interest assumptions of reserves. Fair overall results on stability tests (3.7) including fair risk adjusted capital in prior years. Good quality investment portfolio (6.4).
Other Rating Factors: Good liquidity (6.9). Strong capitalization (7.0) based on excellent risk adjusted capital (severe loss scenario).
Principal Business: Reinsurance (54%), individual health insurance (41%), individual life insurance (2%), and group health insurance (2%).
Principal Investments: NonCMO investment grade bonds (97%), common & preferred stock (4%), and CMOs and structured securities (1%).
Investments in Affiliates: 4%
Group Affiliation: CIGNA Corp
Licensed in: All states except NY, PR
Commenced Business: July 1955
Address: 525 Vine Street, 20th Floor, Cincinnati, OH 45202
Phone: (800) 633-6752 **Domicile State:** OH **NAIC Code:** 65722

Data Date	Rating	RACR #1	RACR #2	Total Assets ($mil)	Capital ($mil)	Net Premium ($mil)	Net Income ($mil)
6-14	C	1.35	1.01	242.4	68.0	123.7	7.7
6-13	C	7.65	5.34	249.9	78.8	131.6	7.5
2013	C	1.53	1.18	244.0	71.5	260.0	14.3
2012	C	1.71	1.32	282.3	78.2	-80.2	-22.2
2011	C	0.97	0.67	438.9	40.8	103.3	2.8
2010	C+	0.94	0.64	452.9	37.9	87.4	10.6
2009	C+	0.90	0.60	465.8	33.3	52.9	2.3

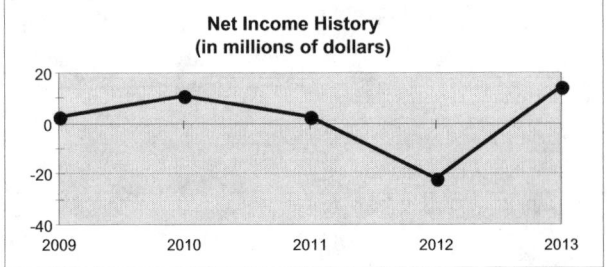

Net Income History
(in millions of dollars)

MADISON NATIONAL LIFE INSURANCE COMPANY INCORPORAT   C+   Fair

Major Rating Factors: Fair profitability (4.5 on a scale of 0 to 10) with investment income below regulatory standards in relation to interest assumptions of reserves. Fair overall results on stability tests (3.1) including negative cash flow from operations for 2013. Weak liquidity (0.7) as a spike in claims or a run on policy withdrawals may stretch capacity.

Other Rating Factors: Strong capitalization (7.0) based on excellent risk adjusted capital (severe loss scenario). High quality investment portfolio (7.9).

Principal Business: Group health insurance (65%), reinsurance (11%), group life insurance (10%), individual life insurance (9%), and individual annuities (5%).

Principal Investments: NonCMO investment grade bonds (78%), common & preferred stock (12%), policy loans (2%), CMOs and structured securities (2%), and cash (2%).

Investments in Affiliates: 13%

Group Affiliation: Geneve Holdings Inc

Licensed in: All states except PR

Commenced Business: March 1962

Address: 6120 University Ave, Middleton, WI 53562

Phone: (608) 238-2691 **Domicile State:** WI **NAIC Code:** 65781

Data Date	Rating	RACR #1	RACR #2	Total Assets ($mil)	Capital ($mil)	Net Premium ($mil)	Net Income ($mil)
6-14	C+	1.23	1.02	496.5	77.6	78.5	3.1
6-13	B	1.35	1.10	497.7	83.9	83.8	15.5
2013	C+	1.20	1.00	488.6	78.0	168.8	11.7
2012	B	1.12	0.89	689.7	72.3	136.4	11.9
2011	B	1.09	0.84	686.7	70.3	140.2	15.1
2010	B	0.97	0.88	801.7	174.2	141.1	12.8
2009	C+	0.95	0.86	784.4	169.3	121.2	21.4

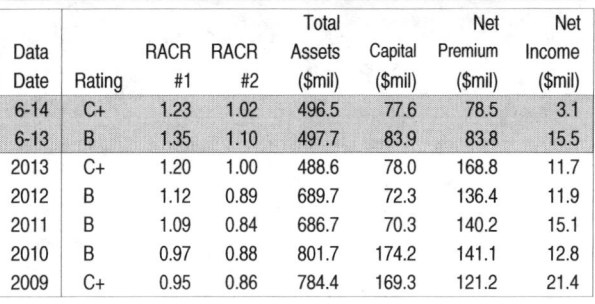

Net Income History
(in millions of dollars)

MAGELLAN BEHAVIORAL HEALTH OF NE   D+   Weak

Major Rating Factors: Weak profitability index (0.9 on a scale of 0 to 10). Strong capitalization (7.0) based on excellent current risk-adjusted capital (severe loss scenario). High quality investment portfolio (9.9).

Other Rating Factors: Excellent liquidity (6.9) with sufficient resources (cash flows and marketable investments) to handle a spike in claims.

Principal Business: Medicaid (100%)

Mem Phys: 13: 1,618 **12:** N/A **13 MLR** 95.5% **/ 13 Admin Exp** N/A

Enroll(000): Q2 14: 229 **13:** 235 **12:** N/A **Med Exp PMPM:** $34

Principal Investments: Cash and equiv (100%)

Provider Compensation ($000): FFS ($20,022)

Total Member Encounters: Phys (21,067), non-phys (310,845)

Group Affiliation: Magellan Health Inc

Licensed in: NE

Address: 1221 N Street Suite 700, Lincoln, NE 68508

Phone: (402) 437-4214 **Dom State:** NE **Commenced Bus:** July 2012

Data Date	Rating	RACR #1	RACR #2	Total Assets ($mil)	Capital ($mil)	Net Premium ($mil)	Net Income ($mil)
6-14	D+	1.37	1.14	22.7	3.1	56.3	-1.3
6-13	N/A	N/A	N/A	0.1	0.1	N/A	N/A
2013	D+	1.98	1.65	17.1	4.4	33.2	-0.6
2012	N/A	N/A	N/A	0.1	0.1	N/A	N/A
2011	N/A	N/A	N/A	N/A	N/A	N/A	N/A
2010	N/A	N/A	N/A	N/A	N/A	N/A	N/A
2009	N/A	N/A	N/A	N/A	N/A	N/A	N/A

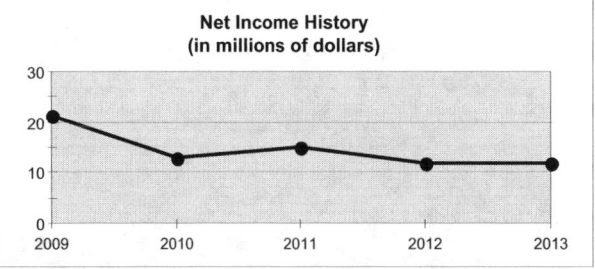

Rating Indexes

Range Cap. 2 Stab. Inv. Prof. Liq.

■ Weak   ■ Fair   ▨ Good   □ Strong

MAGELLAN BEHAVIORAL HEALTH OF PA INC   D+   Weak

Major Rating Factors: Good overall profitability index (5.6 on a scale of 0 to 10). Strong capitalization (10.0) based on excellent current risk-adjusted capital (severe loss scenario). High quality investment portfolio (9.9).

Other Rating Factors: Excellent liquidity (7.1) with ample operational cash flow and liquid investments.

Principal Business: Medicaid (100%)

Mem Phys: 13: 290 **12:** 260 **13 MLR** 90.2% **/ 13 Admin Exp** N/A

Enroll(000): Q2 14: 284 **13:** 273 **12:** 266 **Med Exp PMPM:** $99

Principal Investments: Cash and equiv (97%), long-term bonds (3%)

Provider Compensation ($000): Contr fee ($318,685)

Total Member Encounters: Phys (1,396,870), non-phys (4,529,337)

Group Affiliation: Magellan Health Inc

Licensed in: PA

Address: 105 Terry Dr Ste 103, Newtown, PA 18940

Phone: (215) 504-3907 **Dom State:** PA **Commenced Bus:** February 1997

Data Date	Rating	RACR #1	RACR #2	Total Assets ($mil)	Capital ($mil)	Net Premium ($mil)	Net Income ($mil)
6-14	D+	18.17	15.14	93.8	42.3	178.7	-2.9
6-13	N/A	N/A	N/A	86.1	47.4	177.7	2.5
2013	E+	19.86	16.55	89.7	45.3	358.5	4.8
2012	N/A	N/A	N/A	84.0	44.9	355.1	4.6
2011	N/A	N/A	N/A	84.5	43.2	349.7	4.9
2010	C-	1.22	1.02	79.0	39.9	334.6	5.0
2009	D+	N/A	N/A	70.4	34.9	315.0	4.0

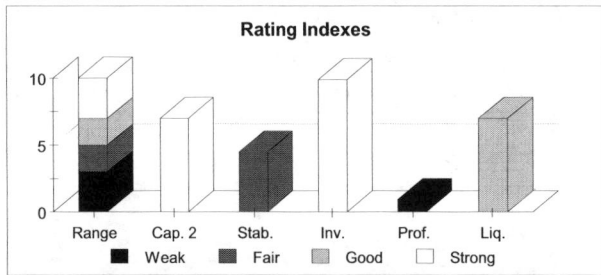

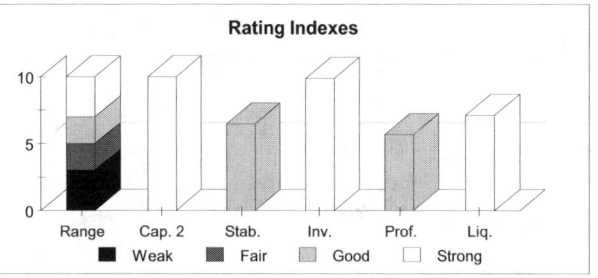

Rating Indexes

Range Cap. 2 Stab. Inv. Prof. Liq.

■ Weak   ■ Fair   ▨ Good   □ Strong

MAGNOLIA HEALTH PLAN INC | D | Weak

Major Rating Factors: Weak profitability index (0.9 on a scale of 0 to 10). Good liquidity (6.8) with sufficient resources (cash flows and marketable investments) to handle a spike in claims. Strong capitalization (7.2) based on excellent current risk-adjusted capital (severe loss scenario).
Other Rating Factors: High quality investment portfolio (9.5).
Principal Business: Medicaid (100%)
Mem Phys: 13: 14,981 **12:** 5,960 **13 MLR** 90.7% **/ 13 Admin Exp** N/A
Enroll(000): Q2 14: 97 **13:** 78 **12:** 77 **Med Exp PMPM:** $398
Principal Investments: Cash and equiv (52%), long-term bonds (48%)
Provider Compensation ($000): Contr fee ($270,677), capitation ($48,276), bonus arrang ($39,407), salary ($6,910)
Total Member Encounters: Phys (473,389), non-phys (425,431)
Group Affiliation: Centene Corp
Licensed in: MS
Address: 111 E Capitol St Suite 500, Jackson, MS 39201
Phone: (314) 725-4477 **Dom State:** MS **Commenced Bus:** January 2011

Data Date	Rating	RACR #1	RACR #2	Total Assets ($mil)	Capital ($mil)	Net Premium ($mil)	Net Income ($mil)
6-14	D	1.54	1.28	98.0	31.2	262.7	-13.0
6-13	C-	2.62	2.18	49.2	22.2	205.3	-9.3
2013	C-	1.75	1.46	57.1	36.3	406.6	-10.1
2012	C	2.26	1.89	40.3	19.3	195.6	10.1
2011	C-	0.96	0.80	56.1	15.1	187.0	-6.6
2010	N/A	N/A	N/A	1.5	1.5	N/A	N/A
2009	N/A	N/A	N/A	1.5	1.5	N/A	N/A

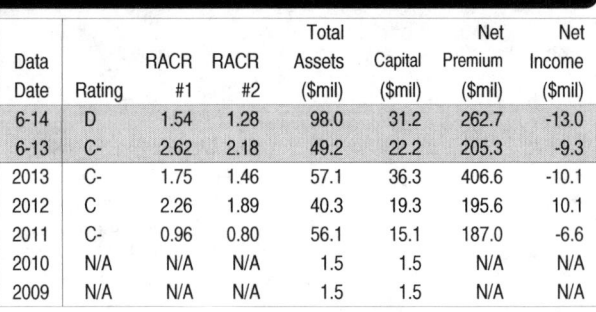

Rating Indexes

MAINE DENTAL SERVICE CORP | C- | Fair

Major Rating Factors: Good quality investment portfolio (5.5 on a scale of 0 to 10). Excellent profitability (7.8). Strong capitalization (10.0) based on excellent current risk-adjusted capital (severe loss scenario).
Other Rating Factors: Excellent liquidity (7.1) with ample operational cash flow and liquid investments.
Principal Business: Dental (100%)
Mem Phys: 13: 533 **12:** 515 **13 MLR** 80.3% **/ 13 Admin Exp** N/A
Enroll(000): 13: 138 **12:** 137 **Med Exp PMPM:** $25
Principal Investments: Long-term bonds (53%), nonaffiliate common stock (28%), cash and equiv (16%), affiliate common stock (3%)
Provider Compensation ($000): FFS ($43,265)
Total Member Encounters: N/A
Group Affiliation: Northeast Delta Dental
Licensed in: ME
Address: 84 Marginal Way Suite 600, Portlanad, ME 04101-2480
Phone: (603) 223-1000 **Dom State:** ME **Commenced Bus:** September 1966

Data Date	Rating	RACR #1	RACR #2	Total Assets ($mil)	Capital ($mil)	Net Premium ($mil)	Net Income ($mil)
2013	C-	5.35	4.46	44.4	39.9	53.9	1.4
2012	C-	5.62	4.68	41.2	36.8	52.4	2.7
2011	N/A	N/A	N/A	38.7	32.9	52.9	N/A
2010	N/A	N/A	N/A	37.4	30.7	55.3	N/A
2009	N/A	N/A	N/A	34.6	27.6	53.2	N/A

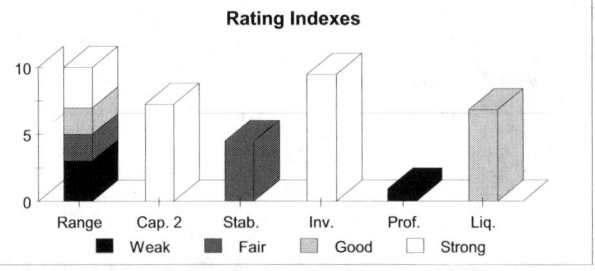

Rating Indexes

MAMSI LIFE & HEALTH INS CO | B- | Good

Major Rating Factors: Excellent profitability (8.0 on a scale of 0 to 10). Strong capitalization (10.0) based on excellent current risk-adjusted capital (severe loss scenario). High quality investment portfolio (9.9).
Other Rating Factors: Excellent liquidity (7.3) with ample operational cash flow and liquid investments.
Principal Business: Comp med (100%)
Mem Phys: 13: 36,157 **12:** 35,400 **13 MLR** 76.7% **/ 13 Admin Exp** N/A
Enroll(000): Q2 14: 13 **13:** 16 **12:** 12 **Med Exp PMPM:** $318
Principal Investments: Cash and equiv (90%), long-term bonds (10%)
Provider Compensation ($000): Contr fee ($55,435), bonus arrang ($20)
Total Member Encounters: Phys (138,294), non-phys (5,946)
Group Affiliation: UnitedHealth Group Inc
Licensed in: CA, DC, DE, GA, IN, KS, LA, MD, MO, NM, ND, TX, VA, WV
Address: 800 King Farm Blvd, Rockville, MD 20850
Phone: (301) 762-8205 **Dom State:** MD **Commenced Bus:** November 1955

Data Date	Rating	RACR #1	RACR #2	Total Assets ($mil)	Capital ($mil)	Net Premium ($mil)	Net Income ($mil)
6-14	B-	4.04	3.37	25.0	15.9	36.5	1.1
6-13	C+	4.05	3.38	20.2	11.7	34.2	2.5
2013	B-	4.00	3.34	24.4	15.7	73.3	6.6
2012	C+	3.39	2.83	15.7	9.2	54.4	4.7
2011	C+	6.95	5.79	21.7	15.9	44.9	5.9
2010	C+	7.41	6.17	25.6	20.2	56.3	11.9
2009	C+	6.23	5.19	51.2	38.0	127.8	21.3

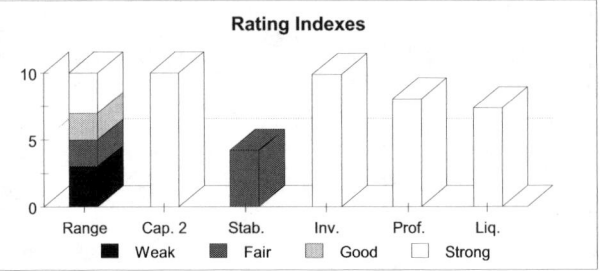

Rating Indexes

MANAGED HEALTH INC — B- — Good

Major Rating Factors: Good overall results on stability tests (6.1 on a scale of 0 to 10) based on steady enrollment growth, averaging 7% over the past five years. Good liquidity (5.7) with sufficient resources (cash flows and marketable investments) to handle a spike in claims. Strong capitalization index (7.1) based on excellent current risk-adjusted capital (severe loss scenario).

Other Rating Factors: High quality investment portfolio (9.9). Weak profitability index (1.8).

Principal Business: Medicare (100%)

Mem Phys: 13: 25,095 **12:** 24,138 **13 MLR** 87.1% **/ 13 Admin Exp** N/A

Enroll(000): Q2 14: 120 **13:** 116 **12:** 106 **Med Exp PMPM:** $1,050

Principal Investments: Long-term bonds (80%), cash and equiv (19%), nonaffiliate common stock (1%)

Provider Compensation ($000): Contr fee ($1,301,714), FFS ($90,696), capitation ($17,339)

Total Member Encounters: Phys (3,106,137), non-phys (2,009,299)

Group Affiliation: HealthFirst Inc

Licensed in: NY

Address: 100 Church St, New York, NY 10007

Phone: (212) 801-6000 **Dom State:** NY **Commenced Bus:** October 1990

Data Date	Rating	RACR #1	RACR #2	Total Assets ($mil)	Capital ($mil)	Net Premium ($mil)	Net Income ($mil)
6-14	B-	1.45	1.21	485.4	177.7	871.8	-32.8
6-13	B+	1.90	1.58	512.4	207.9	791.8	-1.9
2013	B+	1.59	1.32	476.3	195.1	1,613.4	-10.2
2012	B+	1.89	1.58	502.9	207.4	1,472.4	16.7
2011	B+	1.88	1.57	451.3	184.9	1,391.5	22.9
2010	B+	2.06	1.72	367.3	160.1	1,295.1	16.5
2009	B	1.34	1.12	373.7	132.7	1,215.6	7.3

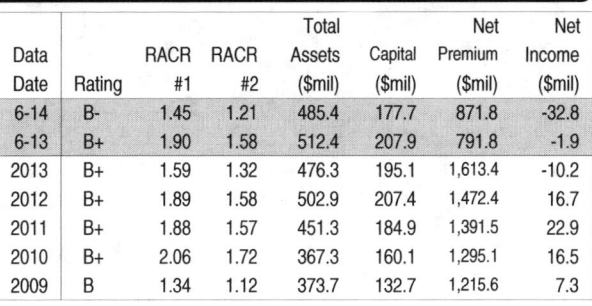

Rating Indexes

MANAGED HEALTH SERVICES INS CORP — C+ — Fair

Major Rating Factors: Fair overall results on stability tests (4.4 on a scale of 0 to 10). Rating is significantly influenced by the fair financial results of Centene Corp. Good overall profitability index (6.6). Strong capitalization index (9.2) based on excellent current risk-adjusted capital (severe loss scenario).

Other Rating Factors: High quality investment portfolio (9.4). Excellent liquidity (6.9) with sufficient resources (cash flows and marketable investments) to handle a spike in claims.

Principal Business: Medicaid (94%), Medicare (6%)

Mem Phys: 13: 13,440 **12:** 12,013 **13 MLR** 86.2% **/ 13 Admin Exp** N/A

Enroll(000): Q2 14: 36 **13:** 38 **12:** 39 **Med Exp PMPM:** $372

Principal Investments: Long-term bonds (53%), cash and equiv (43%), affiliate common stock (2%), other (1%)

Provider Compensation ($000): Contr fee ($107,383), capitation ($13,548), salary ($4,124), bonus arrang ($405), other ($45,248)

Total Member Encounters: Phys (229,817), non-phys (230,654)

Group Affiliation: Centene Corp

Licensed in: WI

Address: 10700 W Research Dr Suite 300, Milwaukee, WI 53226

Phone: (314) 505-6972 **Dom State:** WI **Commenced Bus:** December 1990

Data Date	Rating	RACR #1	RACR #2	Total Assets ($mil)	Capital ($mil)	Net Premium ($mil)	Net Income ($mil)
6-14	C+	3.12	2.60	56.7	26.8	102.4	0.4
6-13	C	2.38	1.98	48.8	21.3	97.0	3.0
2013	C+	3.09	2.57	56.9	26.5	203.7	8.2
2012	C	2.01	1.67	53.1	18.2	201.9	7.1
2011	B-	2.99	2.49	51.6	27.1	201.0	6.9
2010	B-	2.08	1.74	105.2	31.2	299.6	-1.6
2009	B+	2.73	2.28	78.0	51.9	378.7	9.7

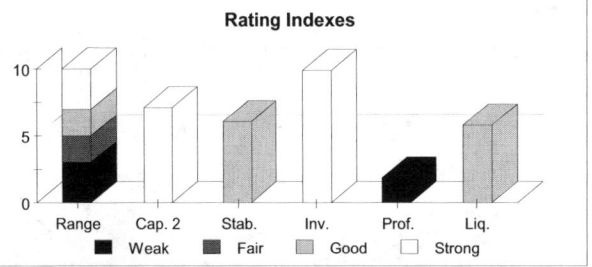

Rating Indexes

MAPFRE LIFE INSURANCE COMPANY OF PUERTO RICO — C+ — Fair

Major Rating Factors: Fair overall results on stability tests (3.6 on a scale of 0 to 10) including weak risk adjusted capital in prior years, negative cash flow from operations for 2013. Good liquidity (6.9) with sufficient resources to handle a spike in claims. Weak profitability (1.9). Return on equity has been low, averaging -2.6%.

Other Rating Factors: Strong capitalization (7.6) based on excellent risk adjusted capital (severe loss scenario). High quality investment portfolio (8.4).

Principal Business: Group health insurance (85%), individual health insurance (9%), credit life insurance (3%), group life insurance (2%), and reinsurance (1%).

Principal Investments: NonCMO investment grade bonds (68%), cash (32%), and common & preferred stock (2%).

Investments in Affiliates: None

Group Affiliation: MAPFRE Ins Group

Licensed in: PR

Commenced Business: February 1984

Address: 297 Ave Carlos Chardon, San Juan, PR 00918-1410

Phone: (787) 250-6500 **Domicile State:** PR **NAIC Code:** 77054

Data Date	Rating	RACR #1	RACR #2	Total Assets ($mil)	Capital ($mil)	Net Premium ($mil)	Net Income ($mil)
6-14	C+	1.72	1.37	69.5	31.8	51.8	2.9
6-13	D	0.29	0.24	46.9	7.7	46.0	1.9
2013	C+	1.61	1.29	64.0	27.9	88.4	5.5
2012	D	0.25	0.21	62.6	8.8	158.4	-11.4
2011	B-	0.57	0.47	73.8	19.5	166.3	0.8
2010	B-	0.76	0.62	74.7	22.5	149.4	3.3
2009	C	0.83	0.67	82.0	24.5	151.8	16.0

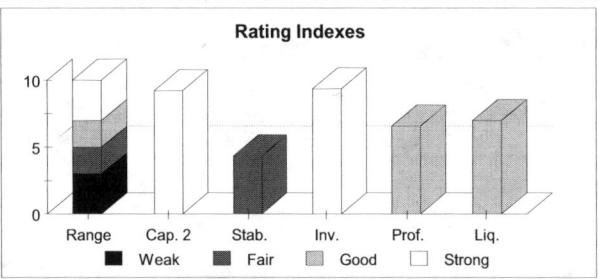

Rating Indexes

MARTINS POINT GENERATIONS LLC

D   **Weak**

Major Rating Factors: Weak profitability index (0.9 on a scale of 0 to 10). Fair capitalization (3.9) based on fair current risk-adjusted capital (moderate loss scenario). Good liquidity (6.9) with sufficient resources (cash flows and marketable investments) to handle a spike in claims.
Other Rating Factors: High quality investment portfolio (9.9).
Principal Business: Medicare (100%)
Mem Phys: 13: 9,072   **12:** 7,312   **13 MLR** 94.6%   **/ 13 Admin Exp** N/A
Enroll(000): Q2 14: 30   **13:** 25   **12:** 18   **Med Exp PMPM:** $578
Principal Investments: Cash and equiv (100%)
Provider Compensation ($000): FFS ($155,114), capitation ($2,277)
Total Member Encounters: Phys (387,688), non-phys (47,175)
Group Affiliation: Martins Point Health Care
Licensed in: ME
Address: 891 Washington Ave, Portland, ME 04103
Phone: (207) 774-5801   **Dom State:** ME   **Commenced Bus:** January 2007

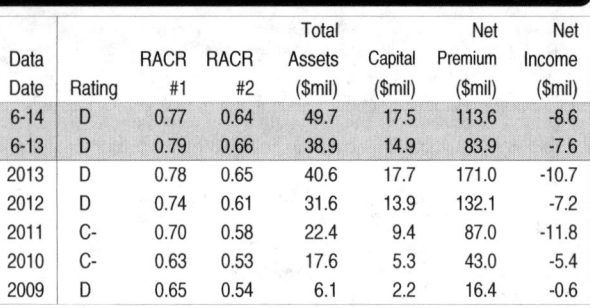

Data Date	Rating	RACR #1	RACR #2	Total Assets ($mil)	Capital ($mil)	Net Premium ($mil)	Net Income ($mil)
6-14	D	0.77	0.64	49.7	17.5	113.6	-8.6
6-13	D	0.79	0.66	38.9	14.9	83.9	-7.6
2013	D	0.78	0.65	40.6	17.7	171.0	-10.7
2012	D	0.74	0.61	31.6	13.9	132.1	-7.2
2011	C-	0.70	0.58	22.4	9.4	87.0	-11.8
2010	C-	0.63	0.53	17.6	5.3	43.0	-5.4
2009	D	0.65	0.54	6.1	2.2	16.4	-0.6

Rating Indexes

Range   Cap. 2   Stab.   Inv.   Prof.   Liq.
■ Weak   ■ Fair   ▨ Good   □ Strong

MATTHEW THORNTON HEALTH PLAN *

A-   **Excellent**

Major Rating Factors: Excellent profitability (8.7 on a scale of 0 to 10). Strong capitalization index (9.6) based on excellent current risk-adjusted capital (severe loss scenario). High quality investment portfolio (8.2).
Other Rating Factors: Excellent overall results on stability tests (7.3). Rating is significantly influenced by the good financial results of WellPoint Inc. Excellent liquidity (6.9) with sufficient resources (cash flows and marketable investments) to handle a spike in claims.
Principal Business: Comp med (100%)
Mem Phys: 13: 13,039   **12:** 12,586   **13 MLR** 81.3%   **/ 13 Admin Exp** N/A
Enroll(000): Q2 14: 124   **13:** 94   **12:** 103   **Med Exp PMPM:** $350
Principal Investments: Long-term bonds (105%)
Provider Compensation ($000): FFS ($277,928), contr fee ($116,856), other ($1,090)
Total Member Encounters: Phys (554,604), non-phys (365,779)
Group Affiliation: WellPoint Inc
Licensed in: NH
Address: 3000 Goffs Falls Rd, Manchester, NH 03111-0001
Phone: (603) 695-7000   **Dom State:** NH   **Commenced Bus:** November 1971

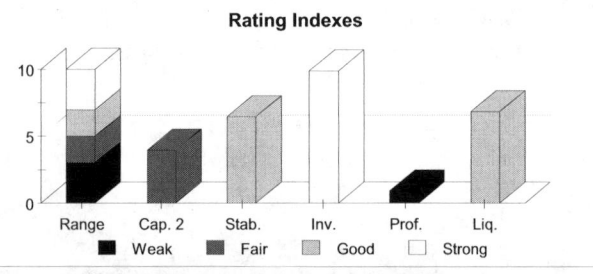

Data Date	Rating	RACR #1	RACR #2	Total Assets ($mil)	Capital ($mil)	Net Premium ($mil)	Net Income ($mil)
6-14	A-	3.44	2.87	220.6	105.4	290.2	13.2
6-13	B	3.15	2.62	161.1	99.3	247.2	13.7
2013	A-	3.03	2.52	187.5	92.2	492.1	25.3
2012	B	2.84	2.37	155.2	89.3	511.6	28.0
2011	B	2.71	2.26	169.0	75.1	457.7	26.6
2010	B	3.13	2.61	153.3	74.2	401.0	17.9
2009	B	3.31	2.76	158.3	82.2	400.0	10.5

Rating Indexes

Range   Cap. 2   Stab.   Inv.   Prof.   Liq.
■ Weak   ■ Fair   ▨ Good   □ Strong

MCLAREN HEALTH PLAN INC

B-   **Good**

Major Rating Factors: Fair overall results on stability tests (4.7 on a scale of 0 to 10). Good overall profitability index (6.3). Good capitalization index (5.2) based on good current risk-adjusted capital (severe loss scenario).
Other Rating Factors: Good liquidity (6.8) with sufficient resources (cash flows and marketable investments) to handle a spike in claims. High quality investment portfolio (8.9).
Principal Business: Medicaid (82%), comp med (17%), Medicare (1%)
Mem Phys: 13: 13,452   **12:** 13,815   **13 MLR** 94.9%   **/ 13 Admin Exp** N/A
Enroll(000): Q2 14: 192   **13:** 159   **12:** 144   **Med Exp PMPM:** $279
Principal Investments: Cash and equiv (70%), nonaffiliate common stock (17%), affiliate common stock (11%), real estate (2%)
Provider Compensation ($000): Contr fee ($514,975), capitation ($116,672), FFS ($6,584)
Total Member Encounters: Phys (1,157,801), non-phys (235,441)
Group Affiliation: McLaren Health Care
Licensed in: MI
Address: 2369 WOODLAKE DR, SUITE 200, Okemos, MI 48864
Phone: (810) 733-9723   **Dom State:** MI   **Commenced Bus:** August 1996

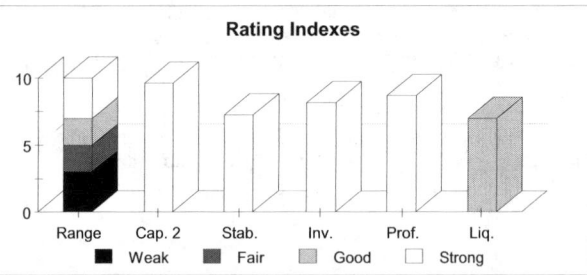

Data Date	Rating	RACR #1	RACR #2	Total Assets ($mil)	Capital ($mil)	Net Premium ($mil)	Net Income ($mil)
6-14	B-	0.96	0.80	143.4	46.5	310.8	4.9
6-13	C	1.36	1.14	123.1	50.1	256.9	7.8
2013	C	0.92	0.77	130.3	44.2	532.6	-0.2
2012	C	1.32	1.10	116.7	42.4	453.2	14.8
2011	B-	2.54	2.11	164.1	102.2	429.4	2.0
2010	B	2.71	2.25	124.3	78.1	301.4	10.3
2009	C+	2.31	1.92	110.3	69.8	266.8	20.3

Rating Indexes

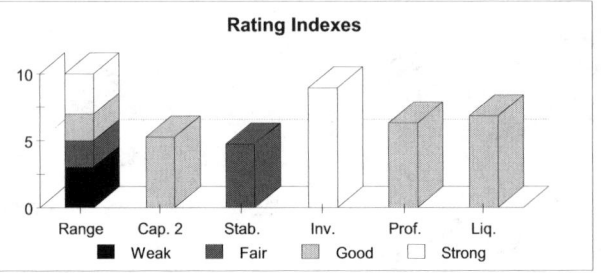

Range   Cap. 2   Stab.   Inv.   Prof.   Liq.
■ Weak   ■ Fair   ▨ Good   □ Strong

MCS ADVANTAGE INC

E   **Very Weak**

Major Rating Factors: Weak profitability index (0.9 on a scale of 0 to 10). Poor capitalization (0.2) based on weak current risk-adjusted capital (moderate loss scenario). Good liquidity (5.7) with sufficient resources (cash flows and marketable investments) to handle a spike in claims.
Other Rating Factors: High quality investment portfolio (9.9).
Principal Business: Medicare (100%)
Mem Phys: 13: 10,311   **12:** 12,571   **13 MLR** 84.2%   **/ 13 Admin Exp** N/A
Enroll(000): Q2 14: 172   **13:** 130   **12:** 113   **Med Exp PMPM:** $663
Principal Investments: Long-term bonds (84%), cash and equiv (16%)
Provider Compensation ($000): Contr fee ($861,639), capitation ($111,775)
Total Member Encounters: Phys (1,325,293), non-phys (201,104)
Group Affiliation: MCS Inc
Licensed in: PR
Address: 255 Ponce de Leon Ave Ste 203, San Juan, PR 00917
Phone: (787) 758-2500   **Dom State:** PR   **Commenced Bus:** February 2007

Data Date	Rating	RACR #1	RACR #2	Total Assets ($mil)	Capital ($mil)	Net Premium ($mil)	Net Income ($mil)
6-14	E	0.32	0.27	234.8	25.8	721.8	-33.5
6-13	D	0.47	0.39	187.8	43.4	560.4	-16.5
2013	C-	0.75	0.63	189.0	63.1	1,173.8	3.7
2012	C-	0.84	0.70	200.1	62.8	1,146.4	27.3
2011	N/A	N/A	N/A	207.6	48.6	1,183.6	-11.8
2010	N/A	N/A	N/A	249.3	78.0	1,165.1	N/A
2009	E	N/A	N/A	180.2	36.4	818.4	28.1

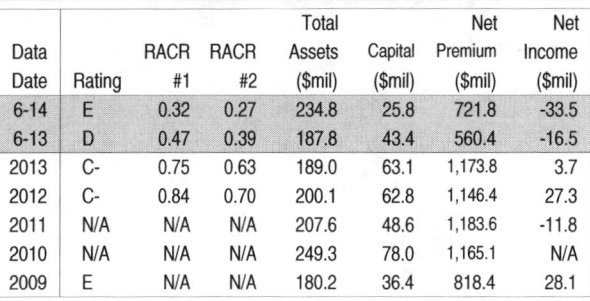

Rating Indexes

Range, Cap. 2, Stab., Inv., Prof., Liq.
Weak, Fair, Good, Strong

MD CARE INC

C   **Fair**

Major Rating Factors: Fair overall results on stability tests (3.4 on a scale of 0 to 10) based on a steep decline in premium revenue in 2013, a significant 100% decrease in enrollment during the period. Rating is significantly influenced by the fair financial results of Humana Inc. Weak profitability index (0.9). Strong capitalization index (10.0) based on excellent current risk-adjusted capital (severe loss scenario).
Other Rating Factors: Excellent liquidity (9.8) with ample operational cash flow and liquid investments.
Principal Business: Medicare (100%)
Mem Phys: 13: N/A   **12:** N/A   **13 MLR** -700.0%   **/ 13 Admin Exp** N/A
Enroll(000): Q2 14: 0   **13:** 0   **12:** 10   **Med Exp PMPM:** N/A
Principal Investments ($000): Cash and equiv ($9,528)
Provider Compensation ($000): None
Total Member Encounters: N/A
Group Affiliation: Humana Inc
Licensed in: CA
Address: 10941 Bloomfield St Suite F, Los Alamitos, CA 90720
Phone: (562) 344-3400   **Dom State:** CA   **Commenced Bus:** January 2008

Data Date	Rating	RACR #1	RACR #2	Total Assets ($mil)	Capital ($mil)	Net Premium ($mil)	Net Income ($mil)
6-14	C	9.16	7.24	50.8	44.9	0.0	-1.7
6-13	E	2.26	1.56	50.8	44.1	0.6	3.2
2013	C	12.47	9.84	45.8	40.1	0.5	3.2
2012	E	1.83	1.27	52.0	38.2	129.4	-41.4
2011	E+	0.61	0.38	92.2	61.5	176.9	-23.8
2010	E+	0.01	0.01	19.4	0.2	147.9	0.2
2009	C	N/A	N/A	11.3	-1.5	78.8	-5.1

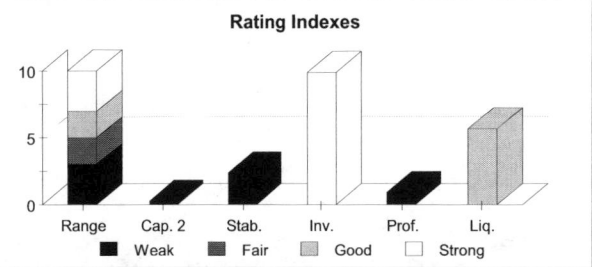

Rating Indexes

Range, Cap. 2, Stab., Inv., Prof., Liq.
Weak, Fair, Good, Strong

MD INDIVIDUAL PRACTICE ASSOC INC

B-   **Good**

Major Rating Factors: Fair overall results on stability tests (4.5 on a scale of 0 to 10) based on a significant 17% decrease in enrollment during the period. Rating is significantly influenced by the fair financial results of UnitedHealth Group Inc. Excellent profitability (8.6). Strong capitalization index (10.0) based on excellent current risk-adjusted capital (severe loss scenario).
Other Rating Factors: High quality investment portfolio (9.9). Excellent liquidity (7.2) with ample operational cash flow and liquid investments.
Principal Business: FEHB (99%)
Mem Phys: 13: 30,581   **12:** 29,935   **13 MLR** 82.3%   **/ 13 Admin Exp** N/A
Enroll(000): Q2 14: 73   **13:** 83   **12:** 100   **Med Exp PMPM:** $343
Principal Investments: Cash and equiv (99%), long-term bonds (1%)
Provider Compensation ($000): Contr fee ($342,024), capitation ($11,236), bonus arrang ($459)
Total Member Encounters: Phys (670,256), non-phys (44,657)
Group Affiliation: UnitedHealth Group Inc
Licensed in: DC, MD, VA
Address: 800 King Farm Blvd, Rockville, MD 20850-5979
Phone: (240) 683-5250   **Dom State:** MD   **Commenced Bus:** December 1980

Data Date	Rating	RACR #1	RACR #2	Total Assets ($mil)	Capital ($mil)	Net Premium ($mil)	Net Income ($mil)
6-14	B-	10.49	8.74	115.6	67.4	202.2	17.3
6-13	C+	5.52	4.60	88.5	33.4	213.1	17.6
2013	B-	8.17	6.81	93.4	50.7	417.3	34.8
2012	C+	5.24	4.37	76.4	31.2	485.7	42.4
2011	C	3.66	3.05	92.2	29.6	560.8	41.5
2010	C+	6.31	5.25	113.9	56.0	526.2	48.5
2009	C	3.97	3.30	123.5	42.2	590.3	38.4

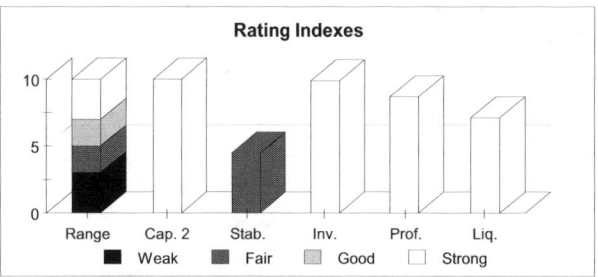

Rating Indexes

Range, Cap. 2, Stab., Inv., Prof., Liq.
Weak, Fair, Good, Strong

MDWISE INC

C+　　**Fair**

Major Rating Factors: Fair profitability index (3.4 on a scale of 0 to 10). Fair overall results on stability tests (4.1). Good capitalization index (6.5) based on good current risk-adjusted capital (severe loss scenario).
Other Rating Factors: High quality investment portfolio (9.9). Excellent liquidity (6.9) with sufficient resources (cash flows and marketable investments) to handle a spike in claims.
Principal Business: Medicaid (100%)
Mem Phys: 13: 1,701 **12:** 1,609 **13 MLR** 80.8% **/ 13 Admin Exp** N/A
Enroll(000): Q2 14: 315 **13:** 282 **12:** 285 **Med Exp PMPM:** $106
Principal Investments: Cash and equiv (54%), long-term bonds (46%), nonaffiliate common stock (1%)
Provider Compensation ($000): Capitation ($363,526)
Total Member Encounters: Phys (1,626,577)
Group Affiliation: Clarian Health Partners Inc
Licensed in: IN
Address: 1200 Madison Ave Suite 400, Indianapolis, IN 46225-1616
Phone: (317) 822-7300 **Dom State:** IN **Commenced Bus:** May 1989

Data Date	Rating	RACR #1	RACR #2	Total Assets ($mil)	Capital ($mil)	Net Premium ($mil)	Net Income ($mil)
6-14	C+	1.15	0.96	76.8	28.7	281.0	0.0
6-13	B-	1.68	1.40	55.1	40.0	225.9	2.3
2013	C+	1.25	1.04	47.9	31.0	449.9	-2.7
2012	B-	1.56	1.30	45.6	37.4	445.4	2.5
2011	B	1.44	1.20	44.0	35.3	435.9	2.3
2010	B-	1.32	1.10	46.7	37.9	478.4	2.1
2009	C	1.05	0.88	52.5	40.2	622.7	7.0

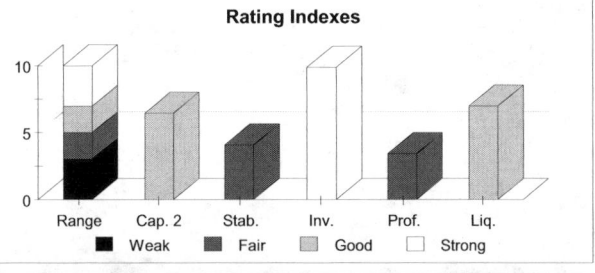

Rating Indexes

MEDAMERICA INSURANCE COMPANY

B　　**Good**

Major Rating Factors: Good current capitalization (5.9 on a scale of 0 to 10) based on good risk adjusted capital (severe loss scenario), although results have slipped from the excellent range during the last year. Good overall results on stability tests (5.9). Strengths include potential support from affiliation with Lifetime Healthcare Inc, excellent operational trends and excellent risk diversification. Low quality investment portfolio (2.0).
Other Rating Factors: Weak profitability (2.0) with operating losses during the first six months of 2014. Excellent liquidity (9.0).
Principal Business: Individual health insurance (60%), reinsurance (30%), and group health insurance (10%).
Principal Investments: NonCMO investment grade bonds (76%), CMOs and structured securities (6%), noninv. grade bonds (5%), and cash (2%).
Investments in Affiliates: None
Group Affiliation: Lifetime Healthcare Inc
Licensed in: All states except FL, NY, PR
Commenced Business: August 1966
Address: Foster Plaza VIII 730 Holiday, Pittsburgh, PA 15220
Phone: (410) 684-3200 **Domicile State:** PA **NAIC Code:** 69515

Data Date	Rating	RACR #1	RACR #2	Total Assets ($mil)	Capital ($mil)	Net Premium ($mil)	Net Income ($mil)
6-14	B	1.60	0.86	860.2	39.4	30.7	-3.1
6-13	B	0.98	0.53	782.5	19.3	26.8	-6.1
2013	B	1.85	1.00	866.2	43.6	54.6	1.7
2012	B	1.44	0.78	733.7	28.7	49.0	-7.7
2011	B	1.71	0.99	678.0	33.8	50.0	-8.1
2010	B	2.00	1.19	552.6	37.3	43.4	0.5
2009	B-	1.91	1.21	497.1	33.1	42.8	4.5

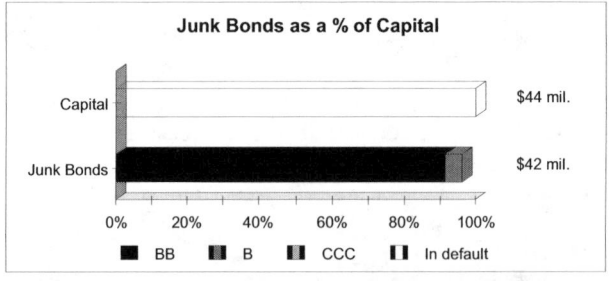

Junk Bonds as a % of Capital

MEDCO CONTAINMENT INS CO OF NY *

B+　　**Good**

Major Rating Factors: Strong capitalization (10.0 on a scale of 0 to 10) based on excellent current risk-adjusted capital (severe loss scenario). High quality investment portfolio (9.9). Excellent liquidity (8.3) with ample operational cash flow and liquid investments.
Other Rating Factors: Fair profitability index (4.2).
Principal Business: Other (100%)
Mem Phys: 13: N/A **12:** N/A **13 MLR** 78.9% **/ 13 Admin Exp** N/A
Enroll(000): Q2 14: 74 **13:** 59 **12:** 68 **Med Exp PMPM:** $82
Principal Investments: Cash and equiv (99%), long-term bonds (1%)
Provider Compensation ($000): FFS ($64,812)
Total Member Encounters: N/A
Group Affiliation: Medco Health Solutions
Licensed in: NY
Address: 500 Executive Blvd, Elmsford, NY 10523
Phone: (800) 426-0152 **Dom State:** NY **Commenced Bus:** July 1989

Data Date	Rating	RACR #1	RACR #2	Total Assets ($mil)	Capital ($mil)	Net Premium ($mil)	Net Income ($mil)
6-14	B+	16.24	13.53	69.9	48.6	56.1	-3.6
6-13	B+	14.22	11.85	56.7	46.7	43.8	-1.4
2013	A-	17.98	14.98	62.0	53.8	77.2	6.2
2012	B+	14.63	12.19	54.9	48.3	83.3	5.5
2011	B	12.18	10.15	48.3	42.7	78.2	2.3
2010	B	12.89	10.74	54.6	40.4	59.9	-2.1
2009	C	4.43	3.70	23.3	12.7	48.8	0.9

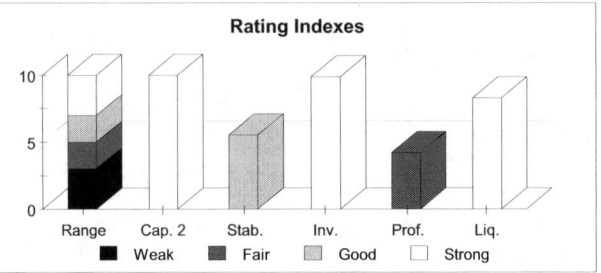

Rating Indexes

MEDCO CONTAINMENT LIFE INS CO *   B+   Good

Major Rating Factors: Excellent profitability (9.0 on a scale of 0 to 10). Strong capitalization (10.0) based on excellent current risk-adjusted capital (severe loss scenario). High quality investment portfolio (9.9).
Other Rating Factors: Excellent liquidity (9.0) with ample operational cash flow and liquid investments.
Principal Business: Other (100%)
Mem Phys: 13: N/A   **12:** N/A   **13 MLR** 81.7%   **/ 13 Admin Exp** N/A
Enroll(000): Q2 14: 369   **13:** 369   **12:** 472   **Med Exp PMPM:** $92
Principal Investments: Cash and equiv (99%), long-term bonds (1%)
Provider Compensation ($000): FFS ($416,505)
Total Member Encounters: N/A
Group Affiliation: Medco Health Solutions
Licensed in: All states except NY
Address: 5010 Ritter Rd Suite 115, Mechanicsburg, PA 17055
Phone: (201) 269-3400   **Dom State:** PA   **Commenced Bus:** July 1955

Data Date	Rating	RACR #1	RACR #2	Total Assets ($mil)	Capital ($mil)	Net Premium ($mil)	Net Income ($mil)
6-14	B+	9.17	7.64	507.6	279.1	335.8	5.4
6-13	B+	7.13	5.94	418.0	230.9	276.5	6.0
2013	B+	9.38	7.82	807.0	284.4	513.3	70.9
2012	B+	7.00	5.83	396.9	226.3	598.0	42.6
2011	B	3.91	3.26	244.0	183.5	627.8	9.2
2010	B	2.96	2.47	260.1	138.5	641.2	12.4
2009	C-	3.07	2.56	208.7	107.4	494.6	9.2

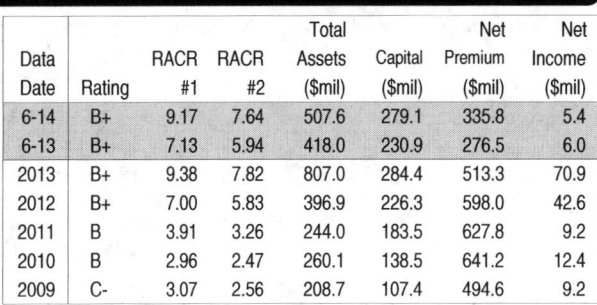

Rating Indexes

MEDICA HEALTH PLANS *   B+   Good

Major Rating Factors: Good overall results on stability tests (5.4 on a scale of 0 to 10). Strong capitalization index (9.4) based on excellent current risk-adjusted capital (severe loss scenario). High quality investment portfolio (7.7).
Other Rating Factors: Excellent liquidity (7.2) with ample operational cash flow and liquid investments. Fair profitability index (4.4).
Principal Business: Medicaid (69%), comp med (30%)
Mem Phys: 13: 60,865   **12:** 57,735   **13 MLR** 68.2%   **/ 13 Admin Exp** N/A
Enroll(000): Q2 14: 168   **13:** 141   **12:** 139   **Med Exp PMPM:** $709
Principal Investments: Long-term bonds (60%), real estate (19%), nonaffiliate common stock (8%), cash and equiv (7%), other (7%)
Provider Compensation ($000): Contr fee ($763,460), bonus arrang ($389,483), capitation ($4,860), other ($19,722)
Total Member Encounters: Phys (1,965,566), non-phys (1,541,238)
Group Affiliation: Medica Holding Co
Licensed in: MN, ND, SD
Address: 401 Carlson Parkway, Minnetonka, MN 55305
Phone: (952) 992-2900   **Dom State:** MN   **Commenced Bus:** December 1974

Data Date	Rating	RACR #1	RACR #2	Total Assets ($mil)	Capital ($mil)	Net Premium ($mil)	Net Income ($mil)
6-14	B+	3.30	2.75	760.3	414.5	937.8	14.7
6-13	A	3.99	3.32	723.1	433.9	854.5	1.1
2013	A-	3.20	2.66	686.5	404.5	1,778.6	-4.3
2012	A	4.09	3.41	681.8	442.1	1,594.5	44.5
2011	A	3.95	3.29	718.9	416.3	1,586.8	14.6
2010	A-	3.39	2.83	675.3	399.3	1,706.2	29.1
2009	A-	3.41	2.84	586.3	361.3	1,367.5	49.7

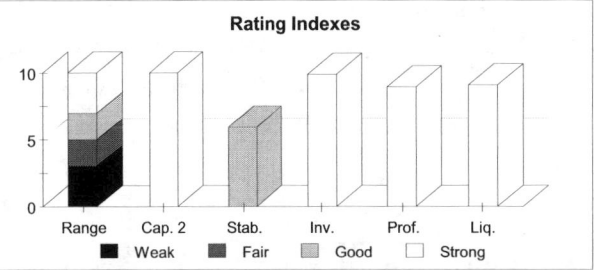

Rating Indexes

MEDICA HEALTH PLANS OF FLORIDA INC   E   Very Weak

Major Rating Factors: Weak profitability index (0.9 on a scale of 0 to 10). Fair liquidity (4.9) as cash resources may not be adequate to cover a spike in claims. Strong capitalization (7.1) based on excellent current risk-adjusted capital (severe loss scenario).
Other Rating Factors: High quality investment portfolio (9.9).
Principal Business: Medicaid (86%), comp med (14%)
Mem Phys: 13: 6,113   **12:** 1,207   **13 MLR** 103.5%   **/ 13 Admin Exp** N/A
Enroll(000): Q2 14: 7   **13:** 8   **12:** 9   **Med Exp PMPM:** $346
Principal Investments: Cash and equiv (100%)
Provider Compensation ($000): Contr fee ($29,603), FFS ($5,722), capitation ($1,564)
Total Member Encounters: Phys (56,464), non-phys (27,426)
Group Affiliation: UnitedHealth Group Inc
Licensed in: FL
Address: 4000 Ponce de Leon Blvd # 650, Coral Gables, FL 33146
Phone: (305) 460-0600   **Dom State:** FL   **Commenced Bus:** February 2007

Data Date	Rating	RACR #1	RACR #2	Total Assets ($mil)	Capital ($mil)	Net Premium ($mil)	Net Income ($mil)
6-14	E	1.46	1.21	11.4	6.1	17.7	0.5
6-13	E	1.92	1.60	12.9	7.0	17.7	-1.0
2013	E	1.33	1.11	12.4	5.6	35.9	-2.4
2012	C	0.83	0.69	9.2	3.0	34.4	-1.2
2011	N/A	N/A	N/A	7.1	1.7	29.2	-0.7
2010	N/A	N/A	N/A	7.2	2.0	18.3	-1.9
2009	E	N/A	N/A	4.8	2.4	5.0	-2.2

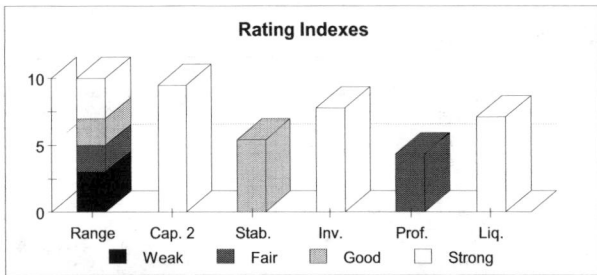

Rating Indexes

MEDICA HEALTHCARE PLANS INC

E-   **Very Weak**

Major Rating Factors: Weak profitability index (0.8 on a scale of 0 to 10). Good capitalization (5.6) based on good current risk-adjusted capital (severe loss scenario). Good liquidity (6.9) with sufficient resources (cash flows and marketable investments) to handle a spike in claims.
Other Rating Factors: High quality investment portfolio (9.8).
Principal Business: Medicare (100%)
Mem Phys: 13: 6,113   **12:** 8,546   **13 MLR** 96.1%   **/ 13 Admin Exp** N/A
Enroll(000): Q2 14: 33   **13:** 33   **12:** 36   **Med Exp PMPM:** $1,257
Principal Investments: Cash and equiv (94%), real estate (6%)
Provider Compensation ($000): Contr fee ($423,937), capitation ($65,593), bonus arrang ($847), other ($4,368)
Total Member Encounters: Phys (557,222), non-phys (381,917)
Group Affiliation: UnitedHealth Group Inc
Licensed in: FL
Address: 4000 Ponce de Leon Blvd # 650, Coral Gables, FL 33146
Phone: (305) 460-0600   **Dom State:** FL   **Commenced Bus:** June 2005

Data Date	Rating	RACR #1	RACR #2	Total Assets ($mil)	Capital ($mil)	Net Premium ($mil)	Net Income ($mil)
6-14	E-	1.02	0.85	113.4	31.2	238.7	3.1
6-13	E-	0.41	0.34	75.6	19.1	261.1	-2.0
2013	E-	0.66	0.55	100.3	20.0	513.4	-21.6
2012	E-	0.47	0.39	84.9	21.3	554.3	-8.4
2011	E-	N/A	N/A	60.3	-5.3	538.9	-11.7
2010	E+	0.19	0.16	51.0	6.7	395.2	2.1
2009	E+	0.33	0.28	41.5	11.8	258.4	10.1

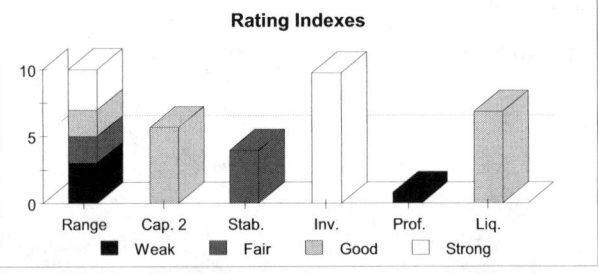

Rating Indexes

MEDICA INS CO

C+   **Fair**

Major Rating Factors: Good overall profitability index (6.6 on a scale of 0 to 10). Weak liquidity (2.2) as a spike in claims may stretch capacity. Strong capitalization (8.9) based on excellent current risk-adjusted capital (severe loss scenario).
Other Rating Factors: High quality investment portfolio (9.3).
Principal Business: Medicare (53%), comp med (44%), other (3%)
Mem Phys: 13: 60,865   **12:** 57,735   **13 MLR** 115.3%   **/ 13 Admin Exp** N/A
Enroll(000): Q2 14: 388   **13:** 432   **12:** 426   **Med Exp PMPM:** $323
Provider Compensation ($000): Contr fee ($952,511), bonus arrang ($682,413), other ($45,344)
Total Member Encounters: Phys (3,371,929), non-phys (839,021)
Group Affiliation: Medica Holding Co
Licensed in: MN, ND, SD, WI
Address: 401 Carlson Parkway, Minnetonka, MN 55305
Phone: (952) 992-2900   **Dom State:** MN   **Commenced Bus:** June 1984

Data Date	Rating	RACR #1	RACR #2	Total Assets ($mil)	Capital ($mil)	Net Premium ($mil)	Net Income ($mil)
6-14	C+	2.89	2.41	626.0	275.6	704.1	7.6
6-13	A-	2.67	2.22	608.8	247.4	748.3	11.3
2013	B	2.79	2.32	544.3	267.5	1,463.9	32.9
2012	A-	2.76	2.30	582.8	255.3	1,381.0	-2.6
2011	A-	3.16	2.63	496.4	248.6	1,230.3	50.9
2010	B+	2.58	2.15	430.7	190.7	1,117.0	44.1
2009	B	2.45	2.05	447.9	196.9	1,064.8	17.4

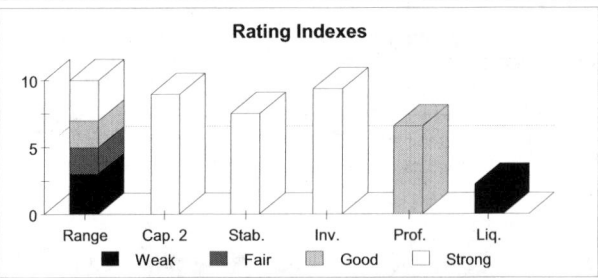

Rating Indexes

MEDICAL ASSOC CLINIC HEALTH PLAN

B-   **Good**

Major Rating Factors: Good capitalization index (6.9 on a scale of 0 to 10) based on excellent current risk-adjusted capital (severe loss scenario). Excellent profitability (7.2). High quality investment portfolio (8.3).
Other Rating Factors: Excellent overall results on stability tests (7.4). Excellent liquidity (6.9) with sufficient resources (cash flows and marketable investments) to handle a spike in claims
Principal Business: Comp med (56%), Medicare (44%)
Mem Phys: 13: 343   **12:** 337   **13 MLR** 91.9%   **/ 13 Admin Exp** N/A
Enroll(000): Q2 14: 7   **13:** 7   **12:** 7   **Med Exp PMPM:** $359
Principal Investments: Cash and equiv (43%), nonaffiliate common stock (35%), long-term bonds (22%)
Provider Compensation ($000): Capitation ($28,423)
Total Member Encounters: Phys (109,934)
Group Affiliation: Medical Associates Clinic PC
Licensed in: WI
Address: 1605 Associates Dr., Suite 101, Dubuque, IA 52002-2270
Phone: (563) 556-8070   **Dom State:** WI   **Commenced Bus:** January 1985

Data Date	Rating	RACR #1	RACR #2	Total Assets ($mil)	Capital ($mil)	Net Premium ($mil)	Net Income ($mil)
6-14	B-	1.26	1.05	3.8	3.3	11.0	0.2
6-13	B-	1.21	1.01	4.0	3.1	15.5	0.1
2013	B-	1.17	0.97	3.9	3.0	30.9	0.1
2012	B-	1.17	0.97	3.4	3.0	30.0	0.2
2011	B-	1.01	0.84	2.9	2.6	31.3	0.2
2010	B-	1.04	0.86	3.4	2.6	29.1	0.3
2009	C+	0.97	0.81	3.3	2.3	27.0	0.3

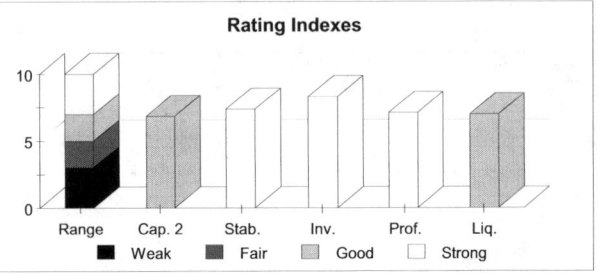

Rating Indexes

MEDICAL ASSOCIATES HEALTH PLAN INC   B   Good

Major Rating Factors: Good quality investment portfolio (6.0 on a scale of 0 to 10). Good liquidity (6.9) with sufficient resources (cash flows and marketable investments) to handle a spike in claims. Excellent profitability (7.6).

Other Rating Factors: Strong capitalization index (7.7) based on excellent current risk-adjusted capital (severe loss scenario). Excellent overall results on stability tests (7.3).

Principal Business: Comp med (59%), Medicare (41%)

Mem Phys: 13: 343   **12:** 337   **13 MLR** 87.2%   / **13 Admin Exp** N/A

Enroll(000): Q2 14: 25   **13:** 25   **12:** 25   **Med Exp PMPM:** $334

Principal Investments: Nonaffiliate common stock (51%), cash and equiv (25%), long-term bonds (24%)

Provider Compensation ($000): Contr fee ($57,491), capitation ($43,012)

Total Member Encounters: Phys (378,165)

Group Affiliation: Medical Associates Clinic PC

Licensed in: IL, IA

Address: 1605 Associates Dr., Suite 101, Dubuque, IA 52002-2270

Phone: (563) 556-8070   **Dom State:** IA   **Commenced Bus:** August 1987

Data Date	Rating	RACR #1	RACR #2	Total Assets ($mil)	Capital ($mil)	Net Premium ($mil)	Net Income ($mil)
6-14	B	1.94	1.62	31.3	20.6	42.8	-0.5
6-13	B	2.00	1.66	32.5	20.9	57.6	2.3
2013	B	1.96	1.63	30.8	20.9	115.3	3.6
2012	B	1.81	1.51	32.0	19.0	109.7	1.7
2011	B	1.66	1.38	29.4	16.8	104.8	1.2
2010	B	1.66	1.38	26.7	15.4	102.3	1.3
2009	B	1.62	1.35	24.0	14.2	97.6	0.9

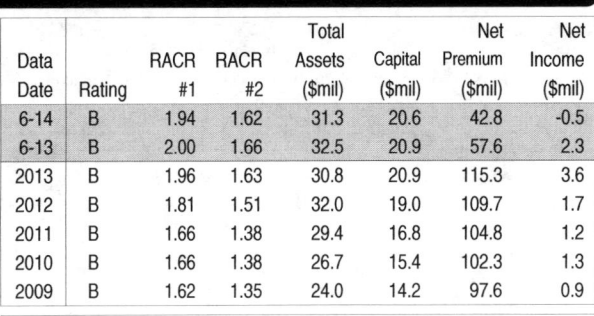

Rating Indexes

MEDICAL HEALTH INS CORP OF OHIO *   B+   Good

Major Rating Factors: Strong capitalization index (10.0 on a scale of 0 to 10) based on excellent current risk-adjusted capital (severe loss scenario). High quality investment portfolio (9.9). Excellent liquidity (8.8) with ample operational cash flow and liquid investments.

Other Rating Factors: Fair overall results on stability tests (3.2) based on a steep decline in premium revenue in 2013, a significant 30% decrease in enrollment during the period. Rating is significantly influenced by the strong financial results of Medical Mutual of Ohio Group. Weak profitability index (1.8).

Principal Business: Comp med (96%), FEHB (4%)

Mem Phys: 13: 44,798   **12:** 42,976   **13 MLR** 91.7%   / **13 Admin Exp** N/A

Enroll(000): Q2 14: 38   **13:** 3   **12:** 4   **Med Exp PMPM:** $354

Principal Investments: Long-term bonds (86%), cash and equiv (14%)

Provider Compensation ($000): Contr fee ($11,588), FFS ($64), bonus arrang ($12), capitation ($6)

Total Member Encounters: Phys (23,996), non-phys (15,509)

Group Affiliation: Medical Mutual of Ohio Group

Licensed in: OH

Address: 2060 E Ninth St, Cleveland, OH 44115-1355

Phone: (216) 687-7000   **Dom State:** OH   **Commenced Bus:** January 1985

Data Date	Rating	RACR #1	RACR #2	Total Assets ($mil)	Capital ($mil)	Net Premium ($mil)	Net Income ($mil)
6-14	B+	56.24	46.87	114.5	77.0	56.7	-11.8
6-13	B+	53.18	44.32	91.2	88.1	6.2	1.4
2013	B+	64.64	53.86	92.4	88.6	12.3	2.0
2012	B+	52.34	43.62	90.3	86.7	24.0	3.8
2011	B+	43.70	36.41	88.3	83.8	32.3	3.1
2010	B+	35.12	29.27	85.1	79.8	36.6	5.0
2009	B+	31.08	25.90	83.3	74.9	41.0	5.0

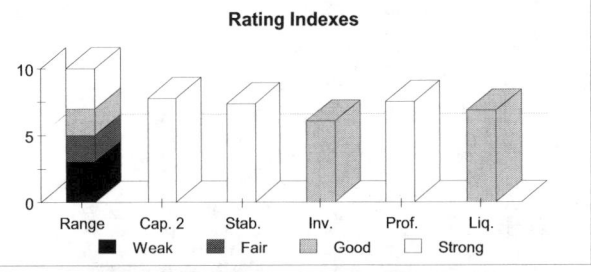

Rating Indexes

MEDICAL MUTUAL OF OHIO *   A-   Excellent

Major Rating Factors: Strong capitalization (10.0 on a scale of 0 to 10) based on excellent current risk-adjusted capital (severe loss scenario). High quality investment portfolio (8.0). Good overall profitability index (5.5).

Other Rating Factors: Good liquidity (6.9) with sufficient resources (cash flows and marketable investments) to handle a spike in claims.

Principal Business: Comp med (94%), med supp (1%), other (4%)

Mem Phys: 13: 94,582   **12:** 90,545   **13 MLR** 80.4%   / **13 Admin Exp** N/A

Enroll(000): Q2 14: 1,060   **13:** 1,112   **12:** 1,160   **Med Exp PMPM:** $148

Principal Investments: Long-term bonds (52%), affiliate common stock (9%), cash and equiv (8%), nonaffiliate common stock (8%), other (23%)

Provider Compensation ($000): Contr fee ($1,918,556), FFS ($36,572), capitation ($3,298), bonus arrang ($3,042), other ($70,900)

Total Member Encounters: Phys (3,921,530), non-phys (3,949,602)

Group Affiliation: Medical Mutual of Ohio Group

Licensed in: GA, IN, MI, NC, OH, PA, WV, WI

Address: 2060 E Ninth St, Cleveland, OH 44115

Phone: (216) 687-7000   **Dom State:** OH   **Commenced Bus:** January 1934

Data Date	Rating	RACR #1	RACR #2	Total Assets ($mil)	Capital ($mil)	Net Premium ($mil)	Net Income ($mil)
6-14	A-	6.08	5.07	1,798.4	1,271.5	1,130.9	68.3
6-13	A-	5.44	4.53	1,648.6	1,168.3	1,239.8	63.4
2013	A-	5.85	4.87	1,684.6	1,221.8	2,473.5	97.7
2012	A	5.28	4.40	1,634.4	1,133.6	2,371.9	43.4
2011	A+	5.89	4.91	1,558.7	1,120.9	2,122.8	66.2
2010	A+	5.61	4.68	1,495.7	1,065.3	2,078.7	-25.4
2009	A	5.26	4.38	1,454.9	975.0	1,979.3	43.5

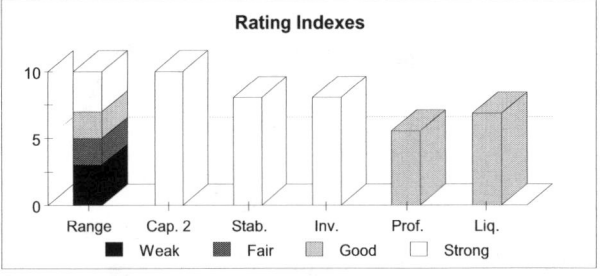

Rating Indexes

MEDICO INSURANCE COMPANY   B   Good

Major Rating Factors: Good liquidity (6.8 on a scale of 0 to 10) with sufficient resources to handle a spike in claims. Fair overall results on stability tests (4.7) including negative cash flow from operations for 2013. Weak profitability (1.9). Return on equity has been low, averaging -20.4%.

Other Rating Factors: Strong capitalization (10.0) based on excellent risk adjusted capital (severe loss scenario). High quality investment portfolio (7.4).

Principal Business: Individual health insurance (68%), group health insurance (28%), individual life insurance (2%), and reinsurance (1%).

Principal Investments: NonCMO investment grade bonds (56%), CMOs and structured securities (26%), cash (8%), common & preferred stock (2%), and misc. investments (8%).

Investments in Affiliates: None

Group Affiliation: American Enterprise Mutual Holding

Licensed in: All states except CT, NJ, NY, PR

Commenced Business: April 1930

Address: 1515 S 75th St, Omaha, NE 68124

Phone: (402) 391-6900 **Domicile State:** NE **NAIC Code:** 31119

Data Date	Rating	RACR #1	RACR #2	Total Assets ($mil)	Capital ($mil)	Net Premium ($mil)	Net Income ($mil)
6-14	B	4.26	3.83	69.5	31.2	0.5	0.2
6-13	B	4.51	3.97	68.0	30.9	0.5	1.2
2013	B	4.06	3.66	65.7	29.7	0.9	0.8
2012	B	4.07	2.82	55.1	31.5	25.4	-12.4
2011	D+	2.06	1.28	91.0	21.0	39.9	-13.7
2010	C	4.26	2.74	102.6	36.9	26.7	-5.3
2009	C+	5.03	4.27	113.1	44.7	18.6	-4.0

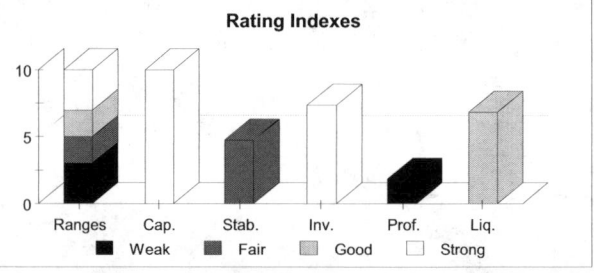

Rating Indexes

MEDISUN INC   B   Good

Major Rating Factors: Good capitalization index (5.2 on a scale of 0 to 10) based on good current risk-adjusted capital (severe loss scenario). Excellent profitability (8.9). High quality investment portfolio (9.9).

Other Rating Factors: Excellent overall results on stability tests (8.0) based on steady enrollment growth, averaging 5% over the past five years. Excellent liquidity (7.1) with ample operational cash flow and liquid investments.

Principal Business: Medicare (100%)

Mem Phys: 13: 2,170 **12:** 2,170 **13 MLR** 89.9% **/ 13 Admin Exp** N/A

Enroll(000): Q2 14: 23 **13:** 23 **12:** 23 **Med Exp PMPM:** $766

Principal Investments: Cash and equiv (100%)

Provider Compensation ($000): Capitation ($214,222), FFS ($1,760)

Total Member Encounters: Phys (486,015), non-phys (114,209)

Group Affiliation: Banner Health

Licensed in: AZ

Address: 13950 W Meeker Blvd, Sun City West, AZ 85375-9939

Phone: (480) 684-7744 **Dom State:** AZ **Commenced Bus:** May 1985

Data Date	Rating	RACR #1	RACR #2	Total Assets ($mil)	Capital ($mil)	Net Premium ($mil)	Net Income ($mil)
6-14	B	0.96	0.80	51.2	25.0	115.2	0.2
6-13	B	1.05	0.87	36.3	21.5	122.2	2.9
2013	B	0.95	0.79	37.2	24.7	238.1	4.9
2012	B	0.91	0.76	33.0	18.8	239.0	2.8
2011	B	0.99	0.83	32.2	16.7	228.2	3.0
2010	B	1.16	0.97	22.6	15.4	206.4	1.0
2009	B	1.00	0.83	22.2	10.7	203.5	2.9

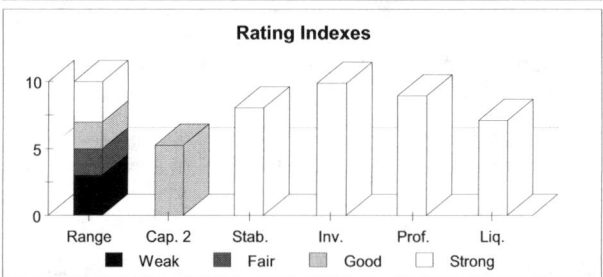

Rating Indexes

MEDSTAR FAMILY CHOICE INC   C-   Fair

Major Rating Factors: Good overall profitability index (5.4 on a scale of 0 to 10). Good capitalization (5.5) based on good current risk-adjusted capital (severe loss scenario). High quality investment portfolio (9.8).

Other Rating Factors: Excellent liquidity (7.0) with sufficient resources (cash flows and marketable investments) to handle a spike in claims.

Principal Business: Medicaid (100%)

Mem Phys: 13: 1,286 **12:** 1,060 **13 MLR** 90.4% **/ 13 Admin Exp** N/A

Enroll(000): Q2 14: 107 **13:** 75 **12:** 32 **Med Exp PMPM:** $303

Principal Investments: Cash and equiv (100%)

Provider Compensation ($000): FFS ($111,805), contr fee ($62,061), capitation ($7,569)

Total Member Encounters: N/A

Group Affiliation: MedStar Health Inc

Licensed in: MD

Address: 8094 Sandpiper Circle Suite O, Baltimore, MD 21236

Phone: (410) 933-3035 **Dom State:** MD **Commenced Bus:** July 1997

Data Date	Rating	RACR #1	RACR #2	Total Assets ($mil)	Capital ($mil)	Net Premium ($mil)	Net Income ($mil)
6-14	C-	1.01	0.84	124.1	27.8	208.0	6.7
6-13	C-	1.47	1.23	57.2	24.5	77.1	0.7
2013	C-	0.79	0.66	63.7	21.5	224.8	-1.4
2012	C-	1.43	1.20	40.8	23.8	115.4	0.1
2011	N/A	N/A	N/A	40.2	21.0	122.2	N/A
2010	N/A	N/A	N/A	36.1	20.5	113.6	N/A
2009	N/A	N/A	N/A	33.4	14.9	98.3	N/A

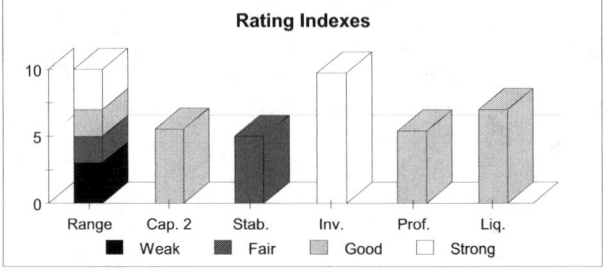

Rating Indexes

MEGA LIFE & HEALTH INSURANCE COMPANY

B-   **Good**

Major Rating Factors: Good quality investment portfolio (6.8 on a scale of 0 to 10) with no exposure to mortgages and no exposure to junk bonds. Fair overall results on stability tests (4.1). Strong current capitalization (8.3) based on excellent risk adjusted capital (severe loss scenario) reflecting improvement over results in 2011.

Other Rating Factors: Excellent profitability (7.0) with operating gains in each of the last five years. Excellent liquidity (7.2).

Principal Business: Group health insurance (71%), individual health insurance (25%), and individual life insurance (3%).

Principal Investments: NonCMO investment grade bonds (77%), common & preferred stock (8%), real estate (6%), CMOs and structured securities (4%), and cash (1%).

Investments in Affiliates: 10%

Group Affiliation: HealthMarkets

Licensed in: All states except NY, PR

Commenced Business: June 1982

Address: 9151 Grapevine Highway, North Richland Hills, TX 76180

Phone: (817) 255-3100 **Domicile State:** OK **NAIC Code:** 97055

Data Date	Rating	RACR #1	RACR #2	Total Assets ($mil)	Capital ($mil)	Net Premium ($mil)	Net Income ($mil)
6-14	B-	2.34	1.87	268.9	113.0	79.3	8.1
6-13	B-	1.48	1.22	287.4	95.3	116.9	12.8
2013	B-	1.95	1.57	281.0	109.2	229.2	26.8
2012	B-	1.26	1.04	289.5	90.9	289.1	27.6
2011	B-	1.15	0.96	346.0	110.5	362.7	47.1
2010	B-	2.34	1.93	590.8	291.8	489.8	119.5
2009	B-	1.62	1.32	643.8	235.1	688.5	67.6

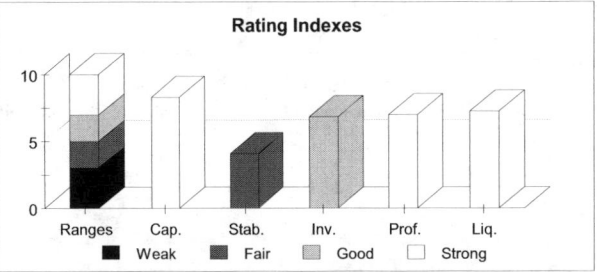

Rating Indexes

MEMBERS HEALTH INS CO

C   **Fair**

Major Rating Factors: Weak profitability index (2.4 on a scale of 0 to 10). Strong capitalization (10.0) based on excellent current risk-adjusted capital (severe loss scenario). High quality investment portfolio (9.2).

Other Rating Factors: Excellent liquidity (8.9) with ample operational cash flow and liquid investments.

Principal Business: Med supp (100%)

Mem Phys: 13: N/A **12:** N/A **13 MLR** 79.0% **/ 13 Admin Exp** N/A

Enroll(000): Q2 14: 1 **13:** 1 **12:** 0 **Med Exp PMPM:** $105

Principal Investments: Long-term bonds (81%), nonaffiliate common stock (13%), cash and equiv (5%).

Provider Compensation ($000): FFS ($426)

Total Member Encounters: Phys (6,467), non-phys (1,579)

Group Affiliation: Tennessee Rural Health Improvement

Licensed in: AL, AZ, AR, CO, FL, GA, ID, IL, IN, MD, MN, MS, MO, MT, NE, NM, ND, OR, PA, SC, SD, TN, TX, UT, WA, WV

Address: 5025 N Central Ave Suite 546, Phoenix, AZ 85012

Phone: (931) 388-7872 **Dom State:** AZ **Commenced Bus:** May 1982

Data Date	Rating	RACR #1	RACR #2	Total Assets ($mil)	Capital ($mil)	Net Premium ($mil)	Net Income ($mil)
6-14	C	17.45	14.54	33.0	31.3	0.6	0.0
6-13	N/A	N/A	N/A	32.0	31.9	0.3	0.3
2013	C	17.27	14.39	32.7	31.1	0.7	-0.9
2012	N/A	N/A	N/A	32.0	31.8	N/A	0.4
2011	N/A	N/A	N/A	29.7	29.5	N/A	0.4
2010	N/A	N/A	N/A	28.9	28.9	N/A	0.5
2009	C	N/A	N/A	10.9	10.9	N/A	-0.2

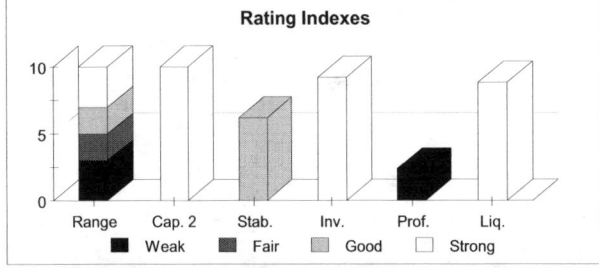

Rating Indexes

MEMORIAL HERMANN HEALTH INS CO

C-   **Fair**

Major Rating Factors: Weak profitability index (0.9 on a scale of 0 to 10). Strong capitalization (8.2) based on excellent current risk-adjusted capital (severe loss scenario). High quality investment portfolio (9.9).

Other Rating Factors: Excellent liquidity (7.3) with ample operational cash flow and liquid investments.

Principal Business: Comp med (100%)

Mem Phys: 13: 7,089 **12:** 5,956 **13 MLR** 111.4% **/ 13 Admin Exp** N/A

Enroll(000): Q2 14: 10 **13:** 8 **12:** 3 **Med Exp PMPM:** $305

Principal Investments: Cash and equiv (100%)

Provider Compensation ($000): FFS ($20,986)

Total Member Encounters: Phys (21,128), non-phys (20,965)

Group Affiliation: MHealth Inc

Licensed in: TX

Address: 929 Gessner Suite 1500, Houston, TX 77024

Phone: (713) 338-6480 **Dom State:** TX **Commenced Bus:** January 2001

Data Date	Rating	RACR #1	RACR #2	Total Assets ($mil)	Capital ($mil)	Net Premium ($mil)	Net Income ($mil)
6-14	C-	2.33	1.94	22.4	11.8	20.7	-1.0
6-13	C-	4.04	3.36	13.6	6.2	8.0	-1.2
2013	C-	1.68	1.40	18.7	8.7	20.9	-3.4
2012	C-	2.48	2.06	9.4	3.9	5.2	-0.7
2011	N/A	N/A	N/A	5.4	2.4	6.6	1.8
2010	C+	3.89	3.24	7.8	3.0	13.0	-2.3
2009	C+	1.76	1.47	7.4	3.7	13.8	-1.8

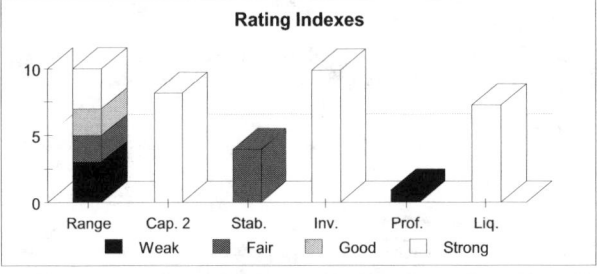

Rating Indexes

MERCYCARE HMO
C   Fair

Major Rating Factors: Fair quality investment portfolio (3.8 on a scale of 0 to 10). Good profitability index (4.9). Good liquidity (6.1) with sufficient resources (cash flows and marketable investments) to handle a spike in claims.
Other Rating Factors: Strong capitalization (7.4) based on excellent current risk-adjusted capital (severe loss scenario).
Principal Business: Comp med (69%), Medicaid (27%), Medicare (3%)
Mem Phys: 13: 275 **12:** 265 **13 MLR** 93.8% **/ 13 Admin Exp** N/A
Enroll(000): Q2 14: 30 **13:** 33 **12:** 32 **Med Exp PMPM:** $260
Principal Investments: Nonaffiliate common stock (60%), long-term bonds (27%), cash and equiv (13%)
Provider Compensation ($000): Contr fee ($70,035), capitation ($23,727), other ($7,693)
Total Member Encounters: Phys (214,080), non-phys (51,070)
Group Affiliation: Mercy Alliance Inc
Licensed in: WI
Address: 3430 Palmer Dr, Janesville, WI 53546
Phone: (608) 752-3431 **Dom State:** WI **Commenced Bus:** September 2004

Data Date	Rating	RACR #1	RACR #2	Total Assets ($mil)	Capital ($mil)	Net Premium ($mil)	Net Income ($mil)
6-14	C	1.71	1.42	34.6	19.0	52.9	0.1
6-13	C	1.42	1.18	30.3	16.2	54.0	0.3
2013	C	1.59	1.32	30.6	17.7	109.0	0.2
2012	C	1.24	1.03	26.2	14.2	114.3	0.4
2011	C	1.15	0.96	23.9	12.2	112.4	0.1
2010	C-	1.22	1.02	31.0	12.7	110.2	0.0
2009	D+	1.12	0.93	25.9	11.4	110.3	0.0

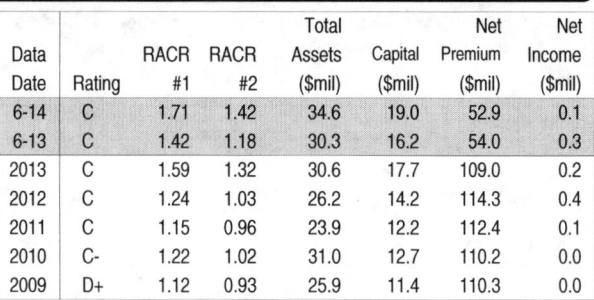

Rating Indexes

MERCYCARE INS CO
C-   Fair

Major Rating Factors: Fair profitability index (3.3 on a scale of 0 to 10). Low quality investment portfolio (2.6). Good liquidity (6.8) with sufficient resources (cash flows and marketable investments) to handle a spike in claims.
Other Rating Factors: Strong capitalization (7.4) based on excellent current risk-adjusted capital (severe loss scenario).
Principal Business: Comp med (100%)
Mem Phys: 13: N/A **12:** 265 **13 MLR** 88.8% **/ 13 Admin Exp** N/A
Enroll(000): Q2 14: 3 **13:** 4 **12:** 4 **Med Exp PMPM:** $15
Principal Investments: Affiliate common stock (90%), long-term bonds (11%)
Provider Compensation ($000): FFS ($512), contr fee ($80), capitation ($12), other ($5)
Total Member Encounters: Phys (1,562), non-phys (249)
Group Affiliation: Mercy Alliance Inc
Licensed in: IL, WI
Address: 3430 Palmer Dr, Janesville, WI 53546
Phone: (608) 752-3431 **Dom State:** WI **Commenced Bus:** January 1994

Data Date	Rating	RACR #1	RACR #2	Total Assets ($mil)	Capital ($mil)	Net Premium ($mil)	Net Income ($mil)
6-14	C-	1.69	1.41	21.2	21.0	0.4	0.1
6-13	C-	1.42	1.19	18.2	18.1	0.4	0.0
2013	C-	1.57	1.31	19.8	19.6	0.7	0.0
2012	C-	1.26	1.05	16.4	16.0	0.7	0.0
2011	C-	1.17	0.98	14.4	14.1	0.7	0.0
2010	C-	1.23	1.02	15.3	14.6	1.0	0.0
2009	C-	0.99	0.82	13.5	13.3	1.0	-1.4

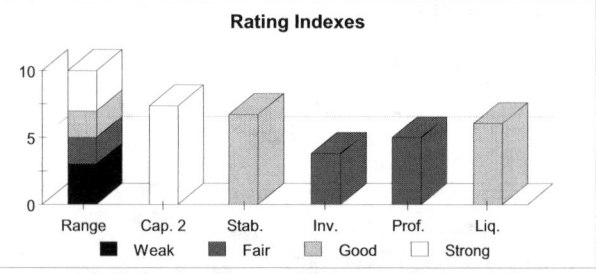

Rating Indexes

MERIDIAN HEALTH PLAN OF ILLINOIS INC
B   Good

Major Rating Factors: Good overall profitability index (5.3 on a scale of 0 to 10). Good capitalization (6.7) based on good current risk-adjusted capital (severe loss scenario). High quality investment portfolio (9.9).
Other Rating Factors: Excellent liquidity (7.1) with ample operational cash flow and liquid investments.
Principal Business: Medicaid (100%)
Mem Phys: 13: 10,231 **12:** 4,342 **13 MLR** 90.0% **/ 13 Admin Exp** N/A
Enroll(000): Q2 14: 45 **13:** 32 **12:** 9 **Med Exp PMPM:** $183
Principal Investments: Cash and equiv (96%), long-term bonds (4%)
Provider Compensation ($000): Contr fee ($17,245), FFS ($7,121), bonus arrang ($410), capitation ($207)
Total Member Encounters: Phys (119,000), non-phys (50,825)
Group Affiliation: Caidan Enterprises Inc
Licensed in: IL
Address: 222 N LaSalle Suite 930, Chicago, IL 60601
Phone: (312) 705-2900 **Dom State:** IL **Commenced Bus:** December 2008

Data Date	Rating	RACR #1	RACR #2	Total Assets ($mil)	Capital ($mil)	Net Premium ($mil)	Net Income ($mil)
6-14	B	1.19	0.99	43.0	6.2	81.3	1.3
6-13	B-	1.66	1.38	8.9	2.5	8.7	0.2
2013	B-	0.94	0.78	24.2	4.9	40.9	0.4
2012	B-	1.52	1.26	6.7	2.3	11.4	0.1
2011	B-	1.78	1.48	4.4	1.7	6.6	-0.2
2010	U	5.10	4.25	2.7	2.0	1.9	0.0
2009	B	N/A	N/A	2.4	2.0	0.7	N/A

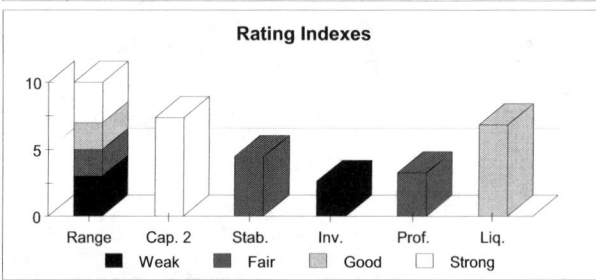

Rating Indexes

MERIDIAN HEALTH PLAN OF IOWA INC
E — Very Weak

Major Rating Factors: Weak profitability index (0.7 on a scale of 0 to 10). Poor capitalization (2.5) based on weak current risk-adjusted capital (moderate loss scenario). Good liquidity (6.8) with sufficient resources (cash flows and marketable investments) to handle a spike in claims.
Other Rating Factors: High quality investment portfolio (9.9).
Principal Business: Medicaid (100%)
Mem Phys: 13: 7,212 **12:** 2,452 **13 MLR** 99.7% **/ 13 Admin Exp** N/A
Enroll(000): Q2 14: 56 **13:** 40 **12:** 12 **Med Exp PMPM:** $186
Principal Investments: Cash and equiv (100%)
Provider Compensation ($000): Contr fee ($35,673), FFS ($12,926), bonus arrang ($462)
Total Member Encounters: Phys (181,143), non-phys (69,971)
Group Affiliation: Caidan Enterprises Inc
Licensed in: IA
Address: 666 Grand Ave 14th Floor, Des Moines, IA 50309
Phone: (313) 324-3700 **Dom State:** IA **Commenced Bus:** March 2012

Data Date	Rating	RACR #1	RACR #2	Total Assets ($mil)	Capital ($mil)	Net Premium ($mil)	Net Income ($mil)
6-14	E	0.56	0.46	23.1	4.8	61.1	-5.5
6-13	E	0.78	0.65	4.5	1.0	17.5	-1.2
2013	E	1.31	1.09	20.1	10.3	57.0	-4.6
2012	B-	1.11	0.92	3.8	1.4	8.5	0.2
2011	N/A	N/A	N/A	1.0	1.0	N/A	N/A
2010	N/A	N/A	N/A	N/A	N/A	N/A	N/A
2009	N/A	N/A	N/A	N/A	N/A	N/A	N/A

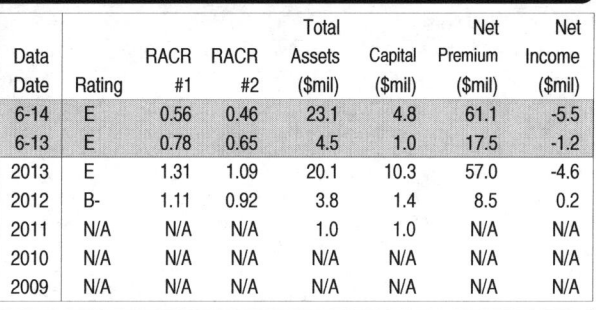

Rating Indexes

Range, Cap. 2, Stab., Inv., Prof., Liq.
Weak ■ Fair ▨ Good ▨ Strong □

MERIDIAN HEALTH PLAN OF MICHIGAN INC *
B+ — Good

Major Rating Factors: Good capitalization index (6.8 on a scale of 0 to 10) based on excellent current risk-adjusted capital (severe loss scenario). Good liquidity (6.8) with sufficient resources (cash flows and marketable investments) to handle a spike in claims. Excellent profitability (7.9).
Other Rating Factors: High quality investment portfolio (9.8). Excellent overall results on stability tests (8.5) based on steady enrollment growth, averaging 6% over the past five years.
Principal Business: Medicaid (99%)
Mem Phys: 13: 32,380 **12:** 25,981 **13 MLR** 88.5% **/ 13 Admin Exp** N/A
Enroll(000): Q2 14: 373 **13:** 297 **12:** 295 **Med Exp PMPM:** $264
Principal Investments: Cash and equiv (68%), long-term bonds (26%), nonaffiliate common stock (6%)
Provider Compensation ($000): Contr fee ($550,024), capitation ($276,132), FFS ($82,907), bonus arrang ($15,977)
Total Member Encounters: Phys (3,245,697), non-phys (3,588,244)
Group Affiliation: Caidan Enterprises Inc
Licensed in: MI
Address: 777 Woodward Ave Suite 600, Detroit, MI 48226
Phone: (313) 324-3700 **Dom State:** MI **Commenced Bus:** December 1995

Data Date	Rating	RACR #1	RACR #2	Total Assets ($mil)	Capital ($mil)	Net Premium ($mil)	Net Income ($mil)
6-14	B+	1.20	1.00	263.1	91.5	624.7	3.0
6-13	B	1.15	0.96	201.5	82.5	509.8	0.1
2013	B	1.16	0.97	210.5	88.6	1,058.6	5.7
2012	B	1.14	0.95	191.6	82.0	957.4	5.2
2011	B	1.09	0.91	182.8	77.6	960.6	12.9
2010	B+	0.97	0.81	156.6	65.1	873.2	11.6
2009	A-	1.20	1.00	117.1	60.0	651.9	14.3

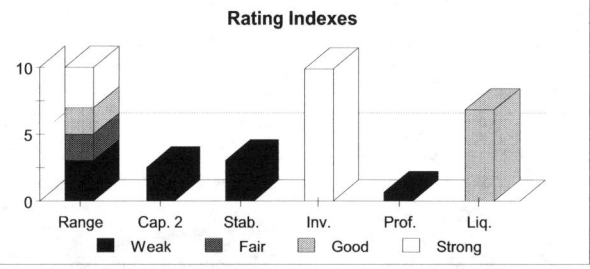

Rating Indexes

Range, Cap. 2, Stab., Inv., Prof., Liq.
Weak ■ Fair ▨ Good ▨ Strong □

MERIT HEALTH INS CO
C — Fair

Major Rating Factors: Good overall profitability index (6.0 on a scale of 0 to 10). Strong capitalization (10.0) based on excellent current risk-adjusted capital (severe loss scenario). High quality investment portfolio (9.9).
Other Rating Factors: Excellent liquidity (7.3) with ample operational cash flow and liquid investments.
Principal Business: Medicaid (100%)
Mem Phys: 13: 3,493 **12:** 1,403 **13 MLR** 81.1% **/ 13 Admin Exp** N/A
Enroll(000): Q2 14: 282 **13:** 289 **12:** 293 **Med Exp PMPM:** $31
Principal Investments: Cash and equiv (76%), long-term bonds (19%), affiliate common stock (5%)
Provider Compensation ($000): FFS ($109,871)
Total Member Encounters: Phys (160,994), non-phys (1,120)
Group Affiliation: Magellan Health Inc
Licensed in: IL, LA, NM
Address: 125 S Wacker Dr Suite 1450, Chicago, IL 60606
Phone: (224) 935-9809 **Dom State:** IL **Commenced Bus:** January 1993

Data Date	Rating	RACR #1	RACR #2	Total Assets ($mil)	Capital ($mil)	Net Premium ($mil)	Net Income ($mil)
6-14	C	5.50	4.58	71.8	32.7	62.8	-5.7
6-13	N/A	N/A	N/A	93.1	41.6	64.0	6.5
2013	D+	6.45	5.38	78.4	37.8	128.6	12.6
2012	N/A	N/A	N/A	76.4	34.9	106.7	11.7
2011	N/A	N/A	N/A	25.7	25.6	N/A	1.2
2010	N/A	N/A	N/A	7.4	7.4	N/A	-0.1
2009	C	N/A	N/A	6.9	6.9	N/A	0.5

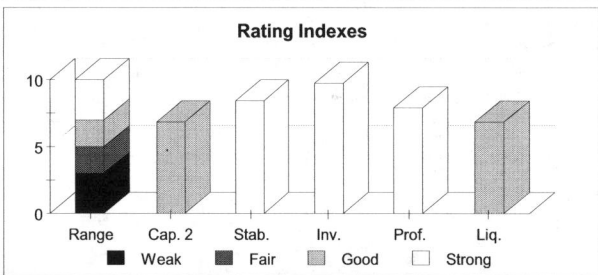

Rating Indexes

Range, Cap. 2, Stab., Inv., Prof., Liq.
Weak ■ Fair ▨ Good ▨ Strong □

MERIT LIFE INSURANCE COMPANY * | B+ Good

Major Rating Factors: Good quality investment portfolio (6.1 on a scale of 0 to 10) despite significant exposure to mortgages . Mortgage default rate has been low. large holdings of BBB rated bonds in addition to minimal holdings in junk bonds. Good overall profitability (5.7). Excellent expense controls. Return on equity has been fair, averaging 5.3%. Good overall results on stability tests (6.2) good operational trends and excellent risk diversification.

Other Rating Factors: Strong capitalization (10.0) based on excellent risk adjusted capital (severe loss scenario). Excellent liquidity (9.1).

Principal Business: Credit health insurance (37%), credit life insurance (29%), individual life insurance (18%), individual health insurance (13%), and group life insurance (2%).

Principal Investments: NonCMO investment grade bonds (60%), mortgages in good standing (20%), CMOs and structured securities (16%), noninv. grade bonds (4%), and cash (1%).

Investments in Affiliates: None

Group Affiliation: American General Finance Inc

Licensed in: All states except AK, MA, VT

Commenced Business: October 1957

Address: 601 NW Second St, Evansville, IN 47708-1013

Phone: (812) 424-8031 **Domicile State:** IN **NAIC Code:** 65951

Data Date	Rating	RACR #1	RACR #2	Total Assets ($mil)	Capital ($mil)	Net Premium ($mil)	Net Income ($mil)
6-14	B+	6.31	4.06	560.2	190.2	68.9	2.9
6-13	B+	10.16	5.86	578.8	254.2	59.9	1.7
2013	B+	6.34	4.09	532.0	184.5	128.1	3.3
2012	B+	10.53	5.92	549.0	245.4	85.9	10.1
2011	B+	13.33	7.16	630.4	334.8	79.3	8.5
2010	B	13.42	6.72	646.3	341.2	62.9	17.7
2009	B	11.74	5.72	659.6	316.1	56.9	28.0

Adverse Trends in Operations

Decrease in asset base during 2013 (3%)
Decrease in capital during 2013 (25%)
Decrease in asset base during 2012 (13%)
Decrease in capital during 2012 (27%)
Decrease in asset base during 2011 (2%)

METROPOLITAN HEALTH PLAN | C- Fair

Major Rating Factors: Good overall results on stability tests (5.5 on a scale of 0 to 10). Excellent profitability (9.1). Strong capitalization index (7.8) based on excellent current risk-adjusted capital (severe loss scenario).

Other Rating Factors: High quality investment portfolio (8.5). Excellent liquidity (7.3) with ample operational cash flow and liquid investments.

Principal Business: Medicaid (53%), Medicare (47%)

Mem Phys: 13: 13,808 **12:** 7,045 **13 MLR** 85.0% **/ 13 Admin Exp** N/A

Enroll(000): Q2 14: 12 **13:** 10 **12:** 10 **Med Exp PMPM:** $1,065

Principal Investments: Cash and equiv (100%)

Provider Compensation ($000): Contr fee ($95,127), bonus arrang ($40,570)

Total Member Encounters: Phys (140,963), non-phys (47,222)

Group Affiliation: None

Licensed in: MN

Address: 400 S 4th St Suite 201, Minneapolis, MN 55415

Phone: (612) 543-3397 **Dom State:** MN **Commenced Bus:** June 1984

Data Date	Rating	RACR #1	RACR #2	Total Assets ($mil)	Capital ($mil)	Net Premium ($mil)	Net Income ($mil)
6-14	C-	2.01	1.68	69.8	29.3	81.3	0.5
6-13	C-	1.97	1.64	62.5	24.7	74.9	0.6
2013	C-	1.95	1.63	64.6	28.3	154.5	4.0
2012	C-	1.98	1.65	57.1	24.7	132.4	5.5
2011	N/A	N/A	N/A	52.7	19.0	163.8	N/A
2010	N/A	N/A	N/A	36.8	10.6	141.6	N/A
2009	N/A	N/A	N/A	27.4	8.1	140.0	N/A

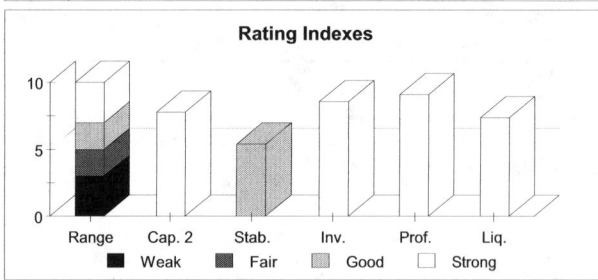

Rating Indexes

Range / Cap. 2 / Stab. / Inv. / Prof. / Liq.
■ Weak ▨ Fair ▧ Good ☐ Strong

MHNET LIFE & HEALTH INS CO | B- Good

Major Rating Factors: Good overall profitability index (6.4 on a scale of 0 to 10). Strong capitalization (10.0) based on excellent current risk-adjusted capital (severe loss scenario). High quality investment portfolio (9.9).

Other Rating Factors: Excellent liquidity (10.0) with ample operational cash flow and liquid investments.

Principal Business: Other (100%)

Mem Phys: 13: 35,883 **12:** 37,621 **13 MLR** 26.2% **/ 13 Admin Exp** N/A

Enroll(000): Q2 14: 5 **13:** 6 **12:** 9 **Med Exp PMPM:** $2

Principal Investments: Cash and equiv (100%)

Provider Compensation ($000): Contr fee ($95), FFS ($84)

Total Member Encounters: Phys (875), non-phys (752)

Group Affiliation: Aetna Inc

Licensed in: TX

Address: 9606 N Mopac Expwy Suite 600, Austin, TX 78759

Phone: (301) 581-0600 **Dom State:** TX **Commenced Bus:** January 2006

Data Date	Rating	RACR #1	RACR #2	Total Assets ($mil)	Capital ($mil)	Net Premium ($mil)	Net Income ($mil)
6-14	B-	87.79	73.16	4.3	4.0	0.5	0.1
6-13	B-	81.70	68.08	4.0	3.9	0.3	0.1
2013	B-	85.36	71.13	4.0	3.9	0.7	0.1
2012	C+	80.44	67.03	3.9	3.8	0.6	0.0
2011	N/A	N/A	N/A	3.9	3.8	0.6	N/A
2010	N/A	N/A	N/A	4.0	3.7	0.7	0.2
2009	B-	N/A	N/A	3.9	3.5	1.9	0.2

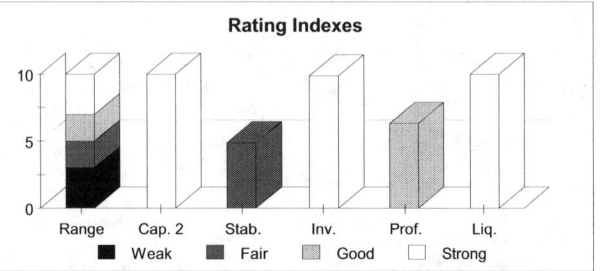

Rating Indexes

Range / Cap. 2 / Stab. / Inv. / Prof. / Liq.
■ Weak ▨ Fair ▧ Good ☐ Strong

MID ROGUE HEALTH PLAN

E   Very Weak

Major Rating Factors: Weak profitability index (0.9 on a scale of 0 to 10). Fair capitalization (3.1) based on weak current risk-adjusted capital (moderate loss scenario). Fair quality investment portfolio (3.1).
Other Rating Factors: Good liquidity (6.7) with sufficient resources (cash flows and marketable investments) to handle a spike in claims.
Principal Business: Medicare (100%)
Mem Phys: 13: 1,066 **12:** 926 **13 MLR** 96.9% **/ 13 Admin Exp** N/A
Enroll(000): Q2 14: 4 **13:** 4 **12:** 4 **Med Exp PMPM:** $820
Principal Investments: Cash and equiv (75%), long-term bonds (25%)
Provider Compensation ($000): Contr fee ($40,326), FFS ($3,436), bonus arrang ($311)
Total Member Encounters: Phys (91,112), non-phys (29,068)
Group Affiliation: Mid Rogue Holding Co
Licensed in: OR
Address: 740 NE 7th St, Grants Pass, OR 97526-1635
Phone: (541) 471-4106 **Dom State:** OR **Commenced Bus:** January 2005

Data Date	Rating	RACR #1	RACR #2	Total Assets ($mil)	Capital ($mil)	Net Premium ($mil)	Net Income ($mil)
6-14	E	0.65	0.54	12.2	6.0	21.1	-1.6
6-13	E	0.71	0.59	11.9	5.4	22.8	-2.8
2013	E	0.85	0.71	13.1	7.4	43.5	-1.7
2012	D-	1.21	1.01	14.6	8.4	41.3	0.1
2011	D-	1.04	0.87	15.1	8.2	51.2	2.5
2010	D-	0.67	0.56	13.6	5.6	44.4	-0.6
2009	D	0.54	0.45	14.1	5.7	56.6	-0.5

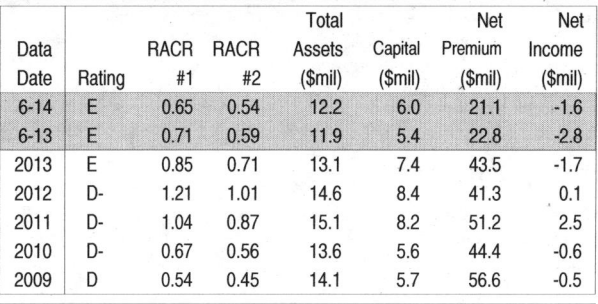

Rating Indexes

Range, Cap. 2, Stab., Inv., Prof., Liq.
■ Weak ▨ Fair ▒ Good ☐ Strong

MID-WEST NATIONAL LIFE INSURANCE COMPANY OF TENNES:

B-   Good

Major Rating Factors: Good overall profitability (6.2 on a scale of 0 to 10). Return on equity has been excellent over the last five years averaging 25.4%. Fair overall results on stability tests (4.1) including fair financial strength of affiliated HealthMarkets. Strong capitalization (10.0) based on excellent risk adjusted capital (severe loss scenario).
Other Rating Factors: High quality investment portfolio (9.0). Excellent liquidity (8.2).
Principal Business: Group health insurance (82%), individual health insurance (12%), and individual life insurance (5%).
Principal Investments: NonCMO investment grade bonds (95%), CMOs and structured securities (3%), and cash (1%).
Investments in Affiliates: 1%
Group Affiliation: HealthMarkets
Licensed in: All states except ME, NH, NY, VT
Commenced Business: May 1965
Address: 9151 Grapevine Highway, North Richland Hills, TX 76180
Phone: (817) 255-3100 **Domicile State:** TX **NAIC Code:** 66087

Data Date	Rating	RACR #1	RACR #2	Total Assets ($mil)	Capital ($mil)	Net Premium ($mil)	Net Income ($mil)
6-14	B-	5.72	4.47	92.7	52.3	27.5	0.3
6-13	B-	4.69	3.66	105.8	60.9	42.5	3.3
2013	B-	4.24	3.34	92.0	51.7	80.4	6.4
2012	B-	3.78	2.95	103.9	56.6	108.9	13.3
2011	B-	3.78	2.92	137.8	73.7	141.5	12.8
2010	B	3.39	2.62	177.2	96.0	206.3	48.7
2009	B	2.29	1.74	197.3	77.8	247.5	31.9

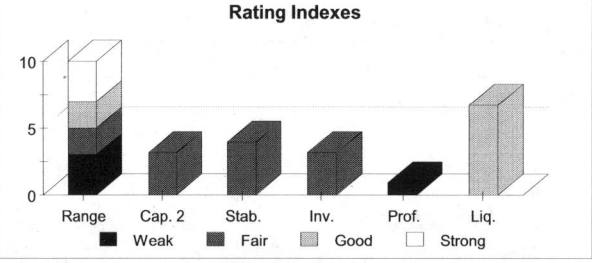

HealthMarkets Composite Group Rating: C+ Largest Group Members	Assets ($mil)	Rating
MEGA LIFE HEALTH INS CO	281	B-
MID-WEST NATIONAL LIFE INS CO OF TN	92	B-
CHESAPEAKE LIFE INS CO	42	C+
HEALTHMARKETS INS CO	16	B-

MII LIFE INC

B   Good

Major Rating Factors: Good quality investment portfolio (5.0 on a scale of 0 to 10). Fair profitability index (3.8). Strong capitalization (8.2) based on excellent current risk-adjusted capital (severe loss scenario).
Other Rating Factors: Excellent liquidity (9.0) with ample operational cash flow and liquid investments.
Principal Business: Other (3%)
Mem Phys: 13: N/A **12:** N/A **13 MLR** 121.5% **/ 13 Admin Exp** N/A
Enroll(000): Q2 14: 20 **13:** 20 **12:** 27 **Med Exp PMPM:** $73
Principal Investments: Long-term bonds (68%), cash and equiv (16%), nonaffiliate common stock (11%), other (5%)
Provider Compensation ($000): Other ($18,236)
Total Member Encounters: N/A
Group Affiliation: Aware Integrated Inc
Licensed in: MI, MN, ND, SD, WI
Address: 3535 Blue Cross Rd, St Paul, MN 55122
Phone: (651) 662-8000 **Dom State:** MN **Commenced Bus:** September 1959

Data Date	Rating	RACR #1	RACR #2	Total Assets ($mil)	Capital ($mil)	Net Premium ($mil)	Net Income ($mil)
6-14	B	2.33	1.94	490.7	28.2	0.2	1.4
6-13	N/A	N/A	N/A	419.6	14.6	0.2	2.2
2013	B	1.29	1.08	438.0	15.7	15.1	3.5
2012	N/A	N/A	N/A	405.2	14.4	11.9	2.8
2011	N/A	N/A	N/A	252.1	10.2	10.2	1.2
2010	N/A	N/A	N/A	201.4	9.8	7.0	-1.7
2009	N/A	N/A	N/A	164.4	6.5	6.7	N/A

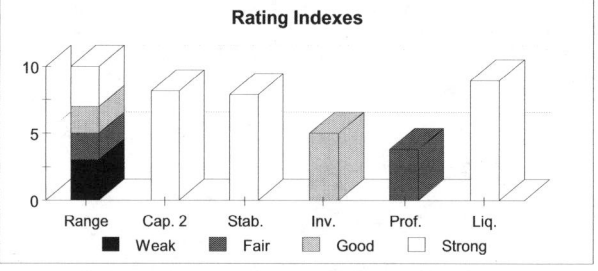

Rating Indexes

Range, Cap. 2, Stab., Inv., Prof., Liq.
■ Weak ▨ Fair ▒ Good ☐ Strong

MISSOURI CARE INC

E **Very Weak**

Major Rating Factors: Good overall profitability index (5.2 on a scale of 0 to 10). Strong capitalization (8.5) based on excellent current risk-adjusted capital (severe loss scenario). High quality investment portfolio (9.9).
Other Rating Factors: Excellent liquidity (7.1) with ample operational cash flow and liquid investments.
Principal Business: Medicaid (95%), comp med (5%)
Mem Phys: 13: 20,200 **12:** 11,311 **13 MLR** 89.5% **/ 13 Admin Exp** N/A
Enroll(000): Q2 14: 97 **13:** 104 **12:** 108 **Med Exp PMPM:** $214
Principal Investments: Cash and equiv (98%), long-term bonds (2%)
Provider Compensation ($000): Contr fee ($259,023), capitation ($10,398)
Total Member Encounters: Phys (382,484), non-phys (117,851)
Group Affiliation: WellCare Health Plans Inc
Licensed in: MO
Address: 2404 Forum Blvd, Columbia, MO 65203
Phone: (813) 206-6200 **Dom State:** MO **Commenced Bus:** July 2006

Data Date	Rating	RACR #1	RACR #2	Total Assets ($mil)	Capital ($mil)	Net Premium ($mil)	Net Income ($mil)
6-14	E	2.52	2.10	96.2	44.6	142.4	2.8
6-13	E	2.22	1.85	86.2	32.4	154.5	1.4
2013	E	2.28	1.90	86.1	42.7	305.2	11.4
2012	C	0.92	0.76	57.1	17.6	228.4	-2.7
2011	N/A	N/A	N/A	38.9	20.4	138.0	-3.6
2010	N/A	N/A	N/A	32.5	15.8	125.2	-2.9
2009	E	N/A	N/A	27.0	11.1	123.9	-4.1

Rating Indexes

MMM HEALTHCARE INC

C **Fair**

Major Rating Factors: Fair capitalization (4.1 on a scale of 0 to 10) based on fair current risk-adjusted capital (moderate loss scenario). Good liquidity (5.6) with sufficient resources (cash flows and marketable investments) to handle a spike in claims. Excellent profitability (8.5).
Other Rating Factors: High quality investment portfolio (9.4).
Principal Business: Medicare (100%)
Mem Phys: 13: N/A **12:** N/A **13 MLR** 83.9% **/ 13 Admin Exp** N/A
Enroll(000): Q2 14: 156 **13:** 190 **12:** 181 **Med Exp PMPM:** $636
Principal Investments: Long-term bonds (97%), cash and equiv (2%)
Provider Compensation ($000): FFS ($905,109), capitation ($162,463), bonus arrang ($61,658), other ($388,137)
Total Member Encounters: N/A
Group Affiliation: InnovaCare Inc
Licensed in: PR
Address: 350 Chardon Ave Suite 500, San Juan, PR 00918
Phone: (787) 622-3000 **Dom State:** PR **Commenced Bus:** January 2001

Data Date	Rating	RACR #1	RACR #2	Total Assets ($mil)	Capital ($mil)	Net Premium ($mil)	Net Income ($mil)
6-14	C	0.80	0.66	305.4	113.8	722.9	0.0
6-13	C	0.84	0.70	353.8	118.2	884.6	33.7
2013	C+	0.87	0.72	314.2	123.7	1,733.0	46.8
2012	C	0.63	0.53	306.5	89.8	1,698.3	77.4
2011	C	0.56	0.46	333.3	69.5	1,531.8	104.3
2010	C	0.60	0.50	292.1	59.5	1,328.3	79.8
2009	D	0.43	0.36	301.2	53.4	1,319.1	99.5

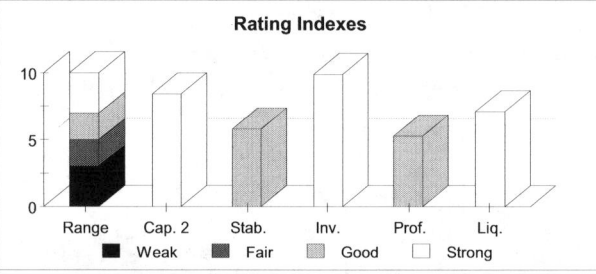

Rating Indexes

MODA HEALTH PLAN INC

B- **Good**

Major Rating Factors: Fair profitability index (3.1 on a scale of 0 to 10). Fair quality investment portfolio (4.4). Good liquidity (5.4) with sufficient resources (cash flows and marketable investments) to handle a spike in claims.
Other Rating Factors: Strong capitalization (8.0) based on excellent current risk-adjusted capital (severe loss scenario).
Principal Business: Comp med (93%), Medicare (5%), other (2%)
Mem Phys: 13: 25,141 **12:** 21,671 **13 MLR** 90.0% **/ 13 Admin Exp** N/A
Enroll(000): Q2 14: 199 **13:** 86 **12:** 75 **Med Exp PMPM:** $267
Principal Investments: Long-term bonds (69%), nonaffiliate common stock (25%), affiliate common stock (12%), other (7%)
Provider Compensation ($000): Contr fee ($240,134), FFS ($19,666)
Total Member Encounters: Phys (188,696), non-phys (126,765)
Group Affiliation: Oregon Dental Association
Licensed in: AK, ID, OR, WA
Address: 601 SW Second Ave, Portland, OR 97204
Phone: (503) 228-6554 **Dom State:** OR **Commenced Bus:** December 1988

Data Date	Rating	RACR #1	RACR #2	Total Assets ($mil)	Capital ($mil)	Net Premium ($mil)	Net Income ($mil)
6-14	B-	2.13	1.78	273.2	73.9	334.6	-3.6
6-13	B-	2.65	2.21	227.9	80.9	142.0	3.8
2013	B-	2.17	1.81	208.8	74.9	293.0	7.5
2012	B-	2.45	2.04	284.1	75.9	249.4	5.3
2011	B	2.60	2.16	257.7	80.8	217.4	5.9
2010	C+	2.47	2.05	244.1	76.6	216.4	3.6
2009	B	2.47	2.06	231.7	71.4	216.9	-10.0

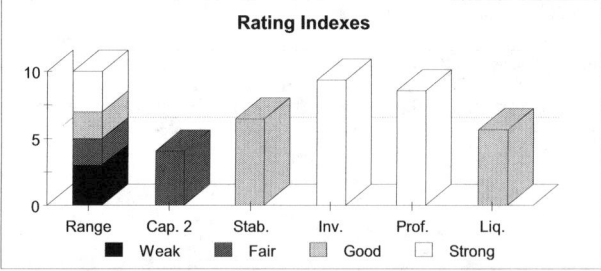

Rating Indexes

MOLINA HEALTHCARE OF CALIFORNIA   C-   Fair

Major Rating Factors: Good overall profitability index (6.2 on a scale of 0 to 10). Good capitalization index (5.8) based on good current risk-adjusted capital (severe loss scenario). Good overall results on stability tests (6.0).
Other Rating Factors: Good liquidity (6.2) with sufficient resources (cash flows and marketable investments) to handle a spike in claims.
Principal Business: Medicaid (66%), Medicare (13%)
Mem Phys: 13: N/A   **12:** N/A   **13 MLR** 88.6%   **/ 13 Admin Exp** N/A
Enroll(000): Q2 14: 456   **13:** 368   **12:** 336   **Med Exp PMPM:** $161
Principal Investments ($000): Cash and equiv ($74,360)
Provider Compensation ($000): None
Total Member Encounters: N/A
Group Affiliation: Molina Healthcare Inc
Licensed in: CA, UT, WA
Address: One Golden Shore Dr, Long Beach, CA 90802
Phone: (562) 499-6191   **Dom State:** CA   **Commenced Bus:** April 1989

Data Date	Rating	RACR #1	RACR #2	Total Assets ($mil)	Capital ($mil)	Net Premium ($mil)	Net Income ($mil)
6-14	C-	1.36	0.88	323.8	83.8	685.6	26.9
6-13	C-	0.84	0.52	132.8	50.3	378.9	-2.2
2013	C-	0.81	0.52	246.8	56.9	770.4	-1.3
2012	C-	0.76	0.47	119.0	47.5	671.3	-4.0
2011	C-	0.82	0.51	111.0	49.8	575.2	8.8
2010	C-	1.02	0.65	104.7	56.8	506.9	14.9
2009	C-	0.81	0.51	107.3	49.9	481.7	-19.4

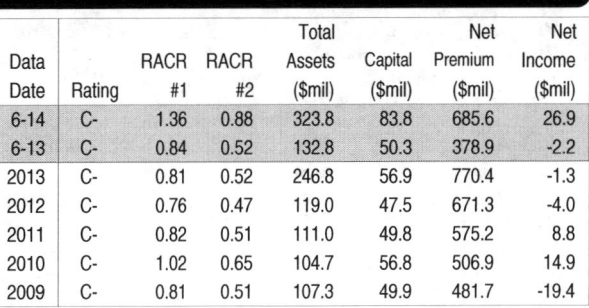

Rating Indexes

Range · Cap. 2 · Stab. · Inv. · Prof. · Liq.
■ Weak   ■ Fair   ▨ Good   □ Strong

MOLINA HEALTHCARE OF FLORIDA INC   D   Weak

Major Rating Factors: Weak profitability index (0.9 on a scale of 0 to 10). Fair capitalization (4.3) based on fair current risk-adjusted capital (moderate loss scenario). Good liquidity (6.8) with sufficient resources (cash flows and marketable investments) to handle a spike in claims.
Other Rating Factors: High quality investment portfolio (9.9).
Principal Business: Medicaid (92%), Medicare (3%), other (4%)
Mem Phys: 13: 8,494   **12:** 5,819   **13 MLR** 84.7%   **/ 13 Admin Exp** N/A
Enroll(000): Q2 14: 59   **13:** 89   **12:** 73   **Med Exp PMPM:** $230
Principal Investments: Cash and equiv (85%), long-term bonds (15%)
Provider Compensation ($000): FFS ($179,365), capitation ($27,991)
Total Member Encounters: Phys (493,619), non-phys (365,681)
Group Affiliation: Molina Healthcare Inc
Licensed in: FL
Address: 8300 NW 33rd St Suite 400, Doral, FL 33122
Phone: (866) 422-2541   **Dom State:** FL   **Commenced Bus:** March 2008

Data Date	Rating	RACR #1	RACR #2	Total Assets ($mil)	Capital ($mil)	Net Premium ($mil)	Net Income ($mil)
6-14	D	0.83	0.69	62.0	18.0	212.5	-0.1
6-13	D	1.28	1.06	41.3	21.0	119.9	-1.5
2013	D	0.79	0.66	53.1	17.3	264.9	-5.6
2012	D	1.15	0.95	42.7	19.1	228.6	0.0
2011	D	0.92	0.76	34.5	14.8	203.5	-9.9
2010	D-	0.82	0.68	47.6	9.7	170.2	-9.0
2009	D	1.85	1.54	50.3	17.3	102.1	-4.4

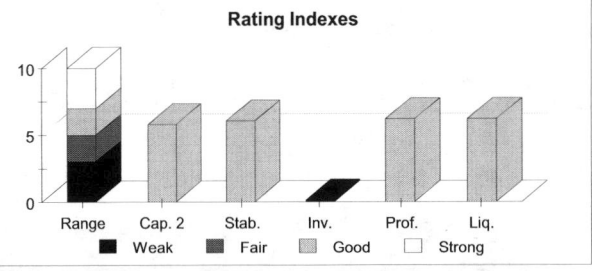

Rating Indexes

Range · Cap. 2 · Stab. · Inv. · Prof. · Liq.
■ Weak   ■ Fair   ▨ Good   □ Strong

MOLINA HEALTHCARE OF ILLINOIS INC   E   Very Weak

Major Rating Factors: Weak profitability index (0.6 on a scale of 0 to 10). Fair liquidity (4.8) as cash resources may not be adequate to cover a spike in claims. Strong capitalization (7.0) based on excellent current risk-adjusted capital (severe loss scenario).
Other Rating Factors: High quality investment portfolio (9.9).
Principal Business: Medicaid (100%)
Mem Phys: 13: 2,861   **12:** N/A   **13 MLR** 102.1%   **/ 13 Admin Exp** N/A
Enroll(000): Q2 14: 6   **13:** 4   **12:** N/A   **Med Exp PMPM:** $1,220
Principal Investments: Cash and equiv (96%), long-term bonds (4%)
Provider Compensation ($000): Contr fee ($2,155), FFS ($722), capitation ($23)
Total Member Encounters: Phys (2,919), non-phys (3,843)
Group Affiliation: Molina Healthcare Inc
Licensed in: IL
Address: 200 Oceangate Suite 100, Long Beach, CA 90802
Phone: (562) 435-3666   **Dom State:** IL   **Commenced Bus:** June 2011

Data Date	Rating	RACR #1	RACR #2	Total Assets ($mil)	Capital ($mil)	Net Premium ($mil)	Net Income ($mil)
6-14	E	1.39	1.16	22.1	3.7	34.6	-4.2
6-13	N/A	N/A	N/A	4.8	3.0	N/A	-1.8
2013	C+	2.01	1.67	13.8	5.0	8.3	-5.8
2012	N/A	N/A	N/A	2.3	2.2	N/A	N/A
2011	N/A	N/A	N/A	2.0	2.0	N/A	N/A
2010	N/A	N/A	N/A	N/A	N/A	N/A	N/A
2009	N/A	N/A	N/A	N/A	N/A	N/A	N/A

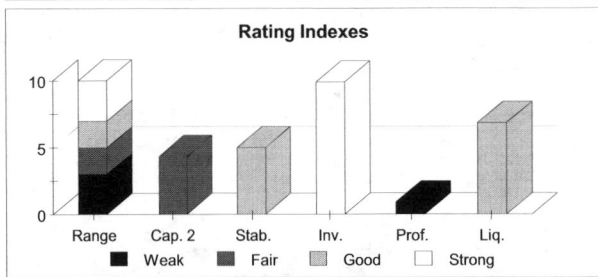

Rating Indexes

Range · Cap. 2 · Stab. · Inv. · Prof. · Liq.
■ Weak   ■ Fair   ▨ Good   □ Strong

MOLINA HEALTHCARE OF MICHIGAN INC

B **Good**

Major Rating Factors: Excellent profitability (8.1 on a scale of 0 to 10). Strong capitalization index (7.9) based on excellent current risk-adjusted capital (severe loss scenario). High quality investment portfolio (9.6).
Other Rating Factors: Excellent overall results on stability tests (7.1). Good financial strength from affiliates. Excellent liquidity (7.0) with sufficient resources (cash flows and marketable investments) to handle a spike in claims.
Principal Business: Medicaid (82%), Medicare (17%)
Mem Phys: 13: 16,155 **12:** 13,185 **13 MLR** 85.4% **/ 13 Admin Exp** N/A
Enroll(000): Q2 14: 244 **13:** 213 **12:** 220 **Med Exp PMPM:** $292
Principal Investments: Cash and equiv (82%), long-term bonds (18%)
Provider Compensation ($000): Contr fee ($453,279), capitation ($213,639), FFS ($80,618)
Total Member Encounters: Phys (1,144,269), non-phys (1,648,853)
Group Affiliation: Molina Healthcare Inc
Licensed in: MI
Address: 100 W Big Beaver Ste 600, Troy, MI 48084-5209
Phone: (248) 925-1700 **Dom State:** MI **Commenced Bus:** January 1998

Data Date	Rating	RACR #1	RACR #2	Total Assets ($mil)	Capital ($mil)	Net Premium ($mil)	Net Income ($mil)
6-14	B	2.09	1.74	229.7	107.0	496.0	3.8
6-13	B	1.76	1.47	187.7	89.0	436.8	5.8
2013	B	1.98	1.65	193.7	102.7	883.4	18.6
2012	B	1.57	1.31	174.4	80.5	841.2	9.4
2011	B	1.62	1.35	164.6	77.8	844.3	15.1
2010	B	1.38	1.15	151.9	63.5	806.4	3.7
2009	B	1.71	1.43	145.6	69.3	718.7	10.0

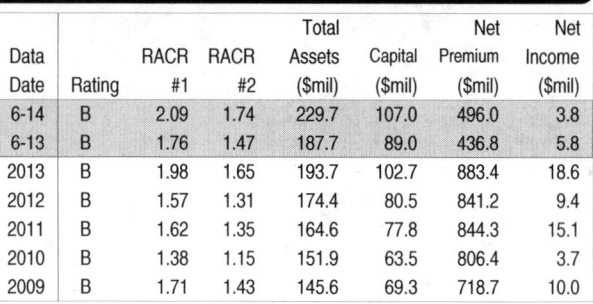

Rating Indexes

MOLINA HEALTHCARE OF NEW MEXICO

B **Good**

Major Rating Factors: Good liquidity (6.8 on a scale of 0 to 10) with sufficient resources (cash flows and marketable investments) to handle a spike in claims. Fair profitability index (4.0). Fair overall results on stability tests (4.4) based on an excessive 86% enrollment growth during the period.
Other Rating Factors: Strong capitalization index (7.0) based on excellent current risk-adjusted capital (severe loss scenario). High quality investment portfolio (9.9).
Principal Business: Medicaid (96%), Medicare (2%), other (2%)
Mem Phys: 13: 12,816 **12:** 11,404 **13 MLR** 81.1% **/ 13 Admin Exp** N/A
Enroll(000): Q2 14: 195 **13:** 168 **12:** 90 **Med Exp PMPM:** $271
Principal Investments: Cash and equiv (64%), long-term bonds (36%)
Provider Compensation ($000): Contr fee ($307,946), capitation ($66,266), FFS ($15,289)
Total Member Encounters: Phys (511,160), non-phys (846,638)
Group Affiliation: Molina Healthcare Inc
Licensed in: NM
Address: 8801 Horizon Blvd., NE, Albuquerque, NM 87113
Phone: (505) 348-0410 **Dom State:** NM **Commenced Bus:** December 1993

Data Date	Rating	RACR #1	RACR #2	Total Assets ($mil)	Capital ($mil)	Net Premium ($mil)	Net Income ($mil)
6-14	B	1.38	1.15	203.0	36.0	511.3	-7.2
6-13	B	2.56	2.13	75.4	47.6	188.3	4.6
2013	B	1.53	1.27	95.3	40.9	499.7	1.0
2012	B	2.50	2.09	74.1	47.5	337.5	6.0
2011	B	2.56	2.13	81.3	46.8	344.0	12.6
2010	B	2.00	1.67	83.3	39.1	366.3	14.3
2009	B	1.81	1.51	83.8	44.0	403.7	5.4

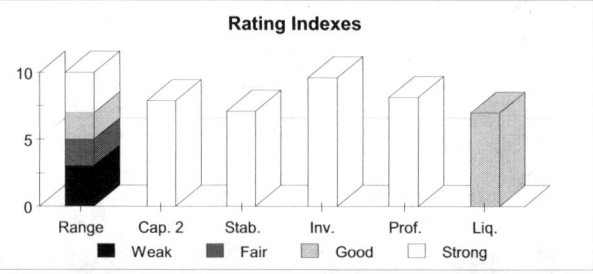

Rating Indexes

MOLINA HEALTHCARE OF OHIO INC

B **Good**

Major Rating Factors: Excellent profitability (8.0 on a scale of 0 to 10). Strong capitalization (8.1) based on excellent current risk-adjusted capital (severe loss scenario). High quality investment portfolio (9.9).
Other Rating Factors: Excellent liquidity (6.9) with sufficient resources (cash flows and marketable investments) to handle a spike in claims.
Principal Business: Medicaid (100%)
Mem Phys: 13: 21,623 **12:** 14,731 **13 MLR** 76.9% **/ 13 Admin Exp** N/A
Enroll(000): Q2 14: 302 **13:** 255 **12:** 244 **Med Exp PMPM:** $319
Principal Investments: Cash and equiv (71%), long-term bonds (29%)
Provider Compensation ($000): Contr fee ($657,519), capitation ($232,715), FFS ($48,200)
Total Member Encounters: Phys (1,210,006), non-phys (2,172,577)
Group Affiliation: Molina Healthcare Inc
Licensed in: OH
Address: 8101 N High St Suite 210, Columbus, OH 43235
Phone: (888) 562-5442 **Dom State:** OH **Commenced Bus:** October 2005

Data Date	Rating	RACR #1	RACR #2	Total Assets ($mil)	Capital ($mil)	Net Premium ($mil)	Net Income ($mil)
6-14	B	2.26	1.88	351.1	151.7	719.0	23.4
6-13	B-	1.74	1.45	207.7	122.2	595.3	26.2
2013	B	1.90	1.58	267.3	128.9	1,248.2	34.0
2012	B-	1.35	1.12	199.9	96.4	1,216.3	18.8
2011	C+	2.09	1.74	214.6	115.8	1,000.5	45.3
2010	C+	1.92	1.60	192.3	98.9	857.9	37.9
2009	C-	1.37	1.14	225.8	73.6	801.9	-2.0

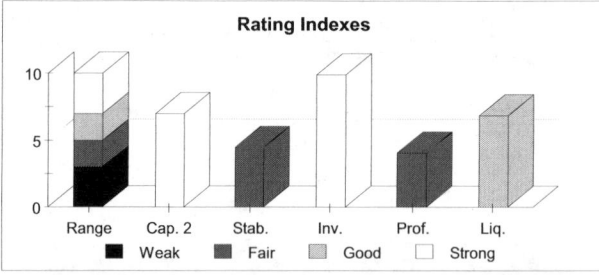

Rating Indexes

MOLINA HEALTHCARE OF TEXAS INC   C   Fair

Major Rating Factors: Weak profitability index (1.9 on a scale of 0 to 10). Good capitalization (5.8) based on good current risk-adjusted capital (severe loss scenario). High quality investment portfolio (9.9).
Other Rating Factors: Excellent liquidity (6.9) with sufficient resources (cash flows and marketable investments) to handle a spike in claims.
Principal Business: Medicaid (89%), comp med (8%), Medicare (3%)
Mem Phys: 13: 35,995 **12:** 28,113 **13 MLR** 81.8% **/ 13 Admin Exp** N/A
Enroll(000): Q2 14: 200 **13:** 252 **12:** 282 **Med Exp PMPM:** $338
Principal Investments: Cash and equiv (68%), long-term bonds (30%), affiliate common stock (2%)
Provider Compensation ($000): Contr fee ($974,683), FFS ($98,073), capitation ($1,427)
Total Member Encounters: Phys (1,391,160), non-phys (2,037,545)
Group Affiliation: Molina Healthcare Inc
Licensed in: TX
Address: 84 Northeast Loop 410 Ste 200, San Antonio, TX 78216-8419
Phone: (877) 665-4622 **Dom State:** TX **Commenced Bus:** June 2005

Data Date	Rating	RACR #1	RACR #2	Total Assets ($mil)	Capital ($mil)	Net Premium ($mil)	Net Income ($mil)
6-14	C	1.06	0.88	257.2	89.2	669.5	-16.9
6-13	C	1.24	1.03	205.1	111.6	660.5	22.8
2013	C	1.28	1.07	227.3	110.0	1,312.4	16.7
2012	C	0.97	0.81	232.4	88.3	1,257.3	-21.5
2011	C	1.26	1.05	86.9	39.8	408.8	-17.3
2010	N/A	N/A	N/A	42.8	18.2	188.3	-1.4
2009	B-	1.47	1.23	38.8	17.3	134.4	3.0

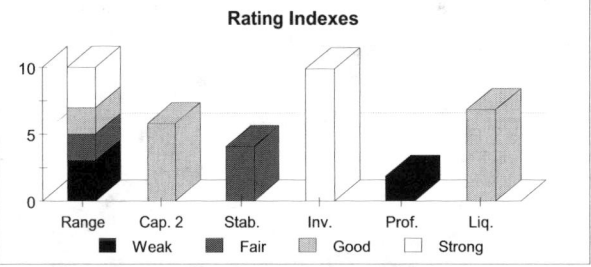

Rating Indexes

Range, Cap. 2, Stab., Inv., Prof., Liq.
■ Weak ▨ Fair ▤ Good ☐ Strong

MOLINA HEALTHCARE OF UTAH INC   B   Good

Major Rating Factors: Good overall profitability index (6.6 on a scale of 0 to 10). Good overall results on stability tests (5.4) despite a decline in the number of member physicians during 2014. Strong capitalization index (8.2) based on excellent current risk-adjusted capital (severe loss scenario).
Other Rating Factors: High quality investment portfolio (9.2). Excellent liquidity (6.9) with sufficient resources (cash flows and marketable investments) to handle a spike in claims.
Principal Business: Medicaid (59%), Medicare (35%), comp med (6%)
Mem Phys: 13: 4,498 **12:** 9,200 **13 MLR** 83.3% **/ 13 Admin Exp** N/A
Enroll(000): Q2 14: 83 **13:** 86 **12:** 87 **Med Exp PMPM:** $278
Principal Investments: Long-term bonds (59%), cash and equiv (41%)
Provider Compensation ($000): Contr fee ($262,325), FFS ($16,477), capitation ($3,120)
Total Member Encounters: Phys (523,231), non-phys (446,046)
Group Affiliation: Molina Healthcare Inc
Licensed in: UT
Address: 7050 Union Park Ctr Ste 200, Midvale, UT 84047
Phone: (801) 858-0400 **Dom State:** UT **Commenced Bus:** May 1996

Data Date	Rating	RACR #1	RACR #2	Total Assets ($mil)	Capital ($mil)	Net Premium ($mil)	Net Income ($mil)
6-14	B	2.34	1.95	90.3	53.0	173.9	-2.5
6-13	B	2.85	2.37	88.1	57.5	161.9	6.4
2013	B	2.50	2.09	107.5	57.6	347.3	10.8
2012	B	2.48	2.07	82.6	50.8	310.8	18.0
2011	C	2.19	1.82	84.8	39.5	292.4	22.3
2010	C-	1.17	0.98	74.3	24.8	256.7	-2.2
2009	C-	1.19	0.99	54.6	14.1	114.0	-1.0

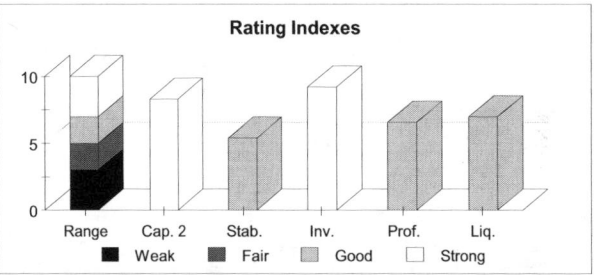

Rating Indexes

Range, Cap. 2, Stab., Inv., Prof., Liq.
■ Weak ▨ Fair ▤ Good ☐ Strong

MOLINA HEALTHCARE OF WASHINGTON INC *   B+   Good

Major Rating Factors: Excellent profitability (8.9 on a scale of 0 to 10). Strong capitalization index (7.6) based on excellent current risk-adjusted capital (severe loss scenario). High quality investment portfolio (9.9).
Other Rating Factors: Excellent overall results on stability tests (8.4). Good financial strength from affiliates. Excellent liquidity (7.0) with sufficient resources (cash flows and marketable investments) to handle a spike in claims.
Principal Business: Medicaid (88%), Medicare (8%), comp med (4%)
Mem Phys: 13: 21,768 **12:** 17,965 **13 MLR** 85.1% **/ 13 Admin Exp** N/A
Enroll(000): Q2 14: 461 **13:** 403 **12:** 418 **Med Exp PMPM:** $207
Principal Investments: Cash and equiv (67%), long-term bonds (33%)
Provider Compensation ($000): Contr fee ($725,141), FFS ($230,667), capitation ($41,380)
Total Member Encounters: Phys (2,039,281), non-phys (1,845,336)
Group Affiliation: Molina Healthcare Inc
Licensed in: WA
Address: 21540 30th Dr SE Ste 400, Bothell, WA 98021
Phone: (425) 424-1100 **Dom State:** WA **Commenced Bus:** December 1986

Data Date	Rating	RACR #1	RACR #2	Total Assets ($mil)	Capital ($mil)	Net Premium ($mil)	Net Income ($mil)
6-14	B+	1.88	1.56	386.8	149.4	834.3	3.2
6-13	A-	1.82	1.51	222.2	121.8	608.9	12.3
2013	A-	1.50	1.25	331.7	120.0	1,201.2	5.0
2012	A-	1.67	1.39	294.0	113.8	1,050.1	19.3
2011	A-	1.87	1.56	157.1	99.5	834.8	25.9
2010	A-	1.98	1.65	141.1	92.2	757.6	26.6
2009	A-	1.76	1.47	124.1	81.0	725.0	22.4

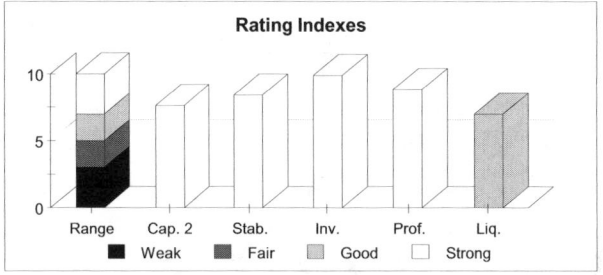

Rating Indexes

Range, Cap. 2, Stab., Inv., Prof., Liq.
■ Weak ▨ Fair ▤ Good ☐ Strong

MOLINA HEALTHCARE OF WISCONSIN INC   D   Weak

Major Rating Factors: Fair profitability index (4.6 on a scale of 0 to 10). Strong capitalization (7.6) based on excellent current risk-adjusted capital (severe loss scenario). High quality investment portfolio (9.9).
Other Rating Factors: Excellent liquidity (7.0) with sufficient resources (cash flows and marketable investments) to handle a spike in claims.
Principal Business: Medicaid (100%)
Mem Phys: 13: 8,526 **12:** 12,193 **13 MLR** 82.5% **/ 13 Admin Exp** N/A
Enroll(000): Q2 14: 85 **13:** 93 **12:** 46 **Med Exp PMPM:** $152
Principal Investments: Cash and equiv (78%), long-term bonds (22%)
Provider Compensation ($000): Contr fee ($133,292), FFS ($13,392), capitation ($6,102)
Total Member Encounters: Phys (384,693), non-phys (406,926)
Group Affiliation: Molina Healthcare Inc
Licensed in: WI
Address: 2400 S 102nd St, West Allis, WI 53227
Phone: (414) 847-1777 **Dom State:** WI **Commenced Bus:** May 2004

Data Date	Rating	RACR #1	RACR #2	Total Assets ($mil)	Capital ($mil)	Net Premium ($mil)	Net Income ($mil)
6-14	D	1.84	1.54	46.3	25.2	127.8	1.7
6-13	D	1.92	1.60	38.3	16.5	101.3	0.9
2013	D	1.60	1.33	47.0	22.1	195.1	6.1
2012	D	1.66	1.38	32.1	14.6	96.5	-5.9
2011	D	1.53	1.28	25.7	12.7	96.3	3.3
2010	D	1.40	1.17	43.8	4.8	64.3	-3.3
2009	D	1.03	0.86	14.6	7.0	58.1	1.3

Rating Indexes

Range, Cap. 2, Stab., Inv., Prof., Liq.
■ Weak ▨ Fair ▦ Good ☐ Strong

MONARCH HEALTH PLAN   E-   Very Weak

Major Rating Factors: Weak profitability index (0.9 on a scale of 0 to 10). Poor capitalization index (0.0) based on weak current risk-adjusted capital (severe loss scenario). Weak overall results on stability tests (0.7).
Other Rating Factors: Weak liquidity (0.0) as a spike in claims may stretch capacity.
Principal Business: Managed care (100%)
Mem Phys: 13: N/A **12:** N/A **13 MLR** 99.3% **/ 13 Admin Exp** N/A
Enroll(000): Q2 14: 20 **13:** 15 **12:** 13 **Med Exp PMPM:** $8,671
Principal Investments ($000): Cash and equiv ($22,506)
Provider Compensation ($000): None
Total Member Encounters: N/A
Group Affiliation: None
Licensed in: CA
Address: 7 Technology Dr, Irvine, CA 92618
Phone: (949) 923-3200 **Dom State:** CA **Commenced Bus:** January 2008

Data Date	Rating	RACR #1	RACR #2	Total Assets ($mil)	Capital ($mil)	Net Premium ($mil)	Net Income ($mil)
6-14	E-	N/A	N/A	34.5	1.4	85.5	0.2
6-13	E-	N/A	N/A	26.1	1.6	64.5	-1.8
2013	E-	N/A	N/A	24.1	1.2	133.1	-1.4
2012	E-	N/A	N/A	23.7	2.6	117.7	0.8
2011	E-	N/A	N/A	21.2	1.9	105.9	3.3
2010	E-	N/A	N/A	19.7	-1.6	91.1	-3.6
2009	E	N/A	N/A	11.4	2.0	68.9	0.4

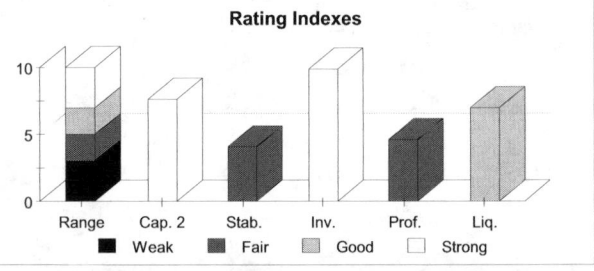

Rating Indexes

Range, Cap. 2, Stab., Inv., Prof., Liq.
■ Weak ▨ Fair ▦ Good ☐ Strong

MOUNT CARMEL HEALTH INS CO   D   Weak

Major Rating Factors: Weak profitability index (2.7 on a scale of 0 to 10). Strong capitalization (10.0) based on excellent current risk-adjusted capital (severe loss scenario). High quality investment portfolio (9.9).
Other Rating Factors: Excellent liquidity (7.7) with ample operational cash flow and liquid investments.
Principal Business: Medicare (100%)
Mem Phys: 13: 5,881 **12:** 4,873 **13 MLR** 88.6% **/ 13 Admin Exp** N/A
Enroll(000): Q2 14: 1 **13:** 1 **12:** 1 **Med Exp PMPM:** $803
Principal Investments: Cash and equiv (66%), long-term bonds (34%)
Provider Compensation ($000): Contr fee ($7,003), FFS ($1,009)
Total Member Encounters: N/A
Group Affiliation: Mount Carmel Health System
Licensed in: OH
Address: 6150 E Broad St, Columbus, OH 43213
Phone: (614) 546-3211 **Dom State:** OH **Commenced Bus:** January 2009

Data Date	Rating	RACR #1	RACR #2	Total Assets ($mil)	Capital ($mil)	Net Premium ($mil)	Net Income ($mil)
6-14	D	3.99	3.33	8.1	6.8	6.7	-0.1
6-13	D	3.85	3.21	7.4	6.5	4.3	-0.3
2013	D	4.04	3.37	7.9	6.9	9.3	0.1
2012	D	4.00	3.33	7.5	6.8	7.3	1.0
2011	D	3.40	2.83	6.8	5.9	8.7	-0.2
2010	D	3.13	2.61	7.0	6.1	9.6	-1.2
2009	D	2.86	2.38	6.9	5.9	5.6	-1.1

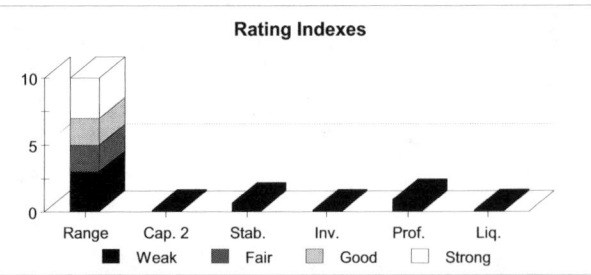

Rating Indexes

Range, Cap. 2, Stab., Inv., Prof., Liq.
■ Weak ▨ Fair ▦ Good ☐ Strong

MOUNT CARMEL HEALTH PLAN INC *

A   **Excellent**

Major Rating Factors: Excellent profitability (9.2 on a scale of 0 to 10). Strong capitalization index (10.0) based on excellent current risk-adjusted capital (severe loss scenario). High quality investment portfolio (9.6).
Other Rating Factors: Excellent overall results on stability tests (8.0). Excellent liquidity (7.5) with ample operational cash flow and liquid investments
Principal Business: Medicare (100%)
Mem Phys: 13: 5,881   **12:** 4,873   **13 MLR** 84.4%   **/ 13 Admin Exp** N/A
Enroll(000): Q2 14: 46   **13:** 38   **12:** 30   **Med Exp PMPM:** $804
Principal Investments: Long-term bonds (43%), cash and equiv (35%), nonaffiliate common stock (22%).
Provider Compensation ($000): Contr fee ($334,133), FFS ($20,083)
Total Member Encounters: N/A
Group Affiliation: Mount Carmel Health System
Licensed in: OH
Address: 6150 E Broad St EE320, Columbus, OH 43213
Phone: (614) 546-3211   **Dom State:** OH   **Commenced Bus:** April 1997

Data Date	Rating	RACR #1	RACR #2	Total Assets ($mil)	Capital ($mil)	Net Premium ($mil)	Net Income ($mil)
6-14	A	7.37	6.15	336.9	305.8	246.6	21.0
6-13	A	8.07	6.72	314.4	272.8	203.0	16.3
2013	A	6.99	5.83	327.1	291.4	424.8	43.4
2012	A	7.81	6.51	294.6	264.7	359.3	49.6
2011	A	7.00	5.83	259.3	229.1	340.9	36.7
2010	A	5.77	4.81	218.3	195.6	310.2	34.7
2009	B-	5.70	4.75	190.3	166.5	312.6	30.6

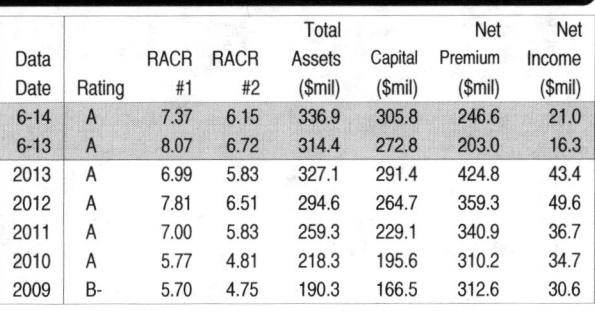

Rating Indexes — Range, Cap. 2, Stab., Inv., Prof., Liq.
■ Weak   ▨ Fair   ▦ Good   ☐ Strong

MUTUAL OF OMAHA INSURANCE COMPANY *

B+   **Good**

Major Rating Factors: Good overall results on stability tests (6.5 on a scale of 0 to 10). Stability strengths include excellent operational trends, good risk adjusted capital for prior years and excellent risk diversification. Good quality investment portfolio (6.1) despite mixed results such as: minimal exposure to mortgages and substantial holdings of BBB bonds but minimal holdings in junk bonds. Strong capitalization (7.1) based on excellent risk adjusted capital (severe loss scenario).
Other Rating Factors: Excellent profitability (8.6) with operating gains in each of the last five years. Excellent liquidity (7.2).
Principal Business: Reinsurance (53%), individual health insurance (35%), and group health insurance (12%).
Principal Investments: Common & preferred stock (38%), nonCMO investment grade bonds (29%), CMOs and structured securities (17%), mortgages in good standing (5%), and misc. investments (9%).
Investments in Affiliates: 42%
Group Affiliation: Mutual Of Omaha Group
Licensed in: All states, the District of Columbia and Puerto Rico
Commenced Business: January 1910
Address: Mutual Of Omaha Plaza, Omaha, NE 68175
Phone: (402) 342-7600   **Domicile State:** NE   **NAIC Code:** 71412

Data Date	Rating	RACR #1	RACR #2	Total Assets ($mil)	Capital ($mil)	Net Premium ($mil)	Net Income ($mil)
6-14	B+	1.16	1.07	6,375.2	2,850.2	1,066.7	55.1
6-13	B+	1.10	1.02	5,710.8	2,450.5	1,011.3	69.0
2013	B+	1.11	1.04	5,795.4	2,674.5	2,071.2	105.8
2012	B+	1.09	1.02	5,549.8	2,406.0	1,946.8	56.8
2011	B+	1.05	0.97	5,247.4	2,314.9	1,909.5	33.0
2010	B+	1.12	1.05	5,239.9	2,580.8	1,752.5	40.5
2009	B+	1.03	0.97	4,730.2	2,237.9	1,620.4	26.0

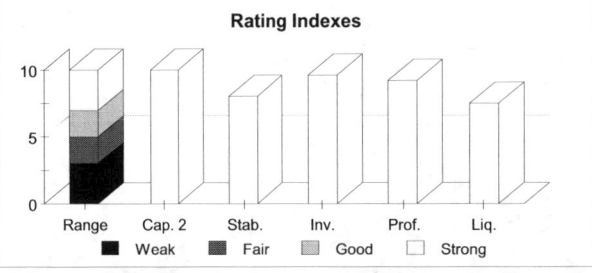

Adverse Trends in Operations

Decrease in capital during 2011 (10%)

MVP HEALTH INS CO

E   **Very Weak**

Major Rating Factors: Weak profitability index (0.6 on a scale of 0 to 10). Good capitalization (5.8) based on good current risk-adjusted capital (severe loss scenario). Good liquidity (5.5) with sufficient resources (cash flows and marketable investments) to handle a spike in claims.
Other Rating Factors: High quality investment portfolio (9.7).
Principal Business: Comp med (100%)
Mem Phys: 13: 46,208   **12:** 44,909   **13 MLR** 86.0%   **/ 13 Admin Exp** N/A
Enroll(000): Q2 14: 79   **13:** 116   **12:** 158   **Med Exp PMPM:** $308
Principal Investments: Long-term bonds (81%), nonaffiliate common stock (11%), cash and equiv (7%), other (1%)
Provider Compensation ($000): Contr fee ($419,664), capitation ($9,557), bonus arrang ($4,375), FFS ($2,848), other ($23,302)
Total Member Encounters: Phys (1,022,999), non-phys (461,349)
Group Affiliation: MVP Health Care Inc
Licensed in: NY, VT
Address: 625 State St, Schenectady, NY 12305
Phone: (518) 370-4793   **Dom State:** NY   **Commenced Bus:** July 2001

Data Date	Rating	RACR #1	RACR #2	Total Assets ($mil)	Capital ($mil)	Net Premium ($mil)	Net Income ($mil)
6-14	E	1.05	0.87	133.1	58.2	192.8	-12.8
6-13	E	1.44	1.20	163.0	91.5	271.2	-8.6
2013	E	1.45	1.21	155.5	72.6	527.1	-29.6
2012	E	1.67	1.39	182.0	102.9	695.6	-22.7
2011	E-	1.61	1.34	213.7	123.1	732.6	-46.7
2010	E-	1.02	0.85	192.9	78.6	696.3	-72.7
2009	E-	0.89	0.74	143.8	56.1	429.0	-65.6

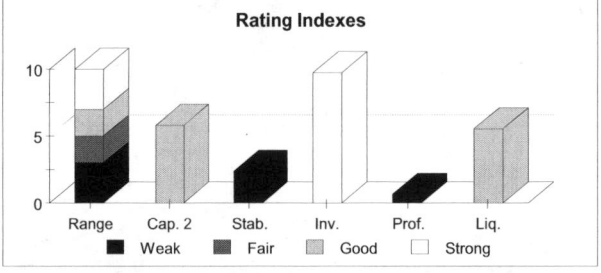

Rating Indexes — Range, Cap. 2, Stab., Inv., Prof., Liq.
■ Weak   ▨ Fair   ▦ Good   ☐ Strong

MVP HEALTH INS CO OF NEW HAMPSHIRE | D | Weak

Major Rating Factors: Weak profitability index (0.9 on a scale of 0 to 10). Good liquidity (6.1) with sufficient resources (cash flows and marketable investments) to handle a spike in claims. Strong capitalization (7.3) based on excellent current risk-adjusted capital (severe loss scenario).
Other Rating Factors: High quality investment portfolio (9.5).
Principal Business: Comp med (100%)
Mem Phys: 13: 5,877 **12:** 5,723 **13 MLR** 88.0% **/ 13 Admin Exp** N/A
Enroll(000): Q2 14: 2 **13:** 6 **12:** 11 **Med Exp PMPM:** $398
Principal Investments: Long-term bonds (89%), cash and equiv (11%)
Provider Compensation ($000): Contr fee ($35,941), capitation ($516), FFS ($86), other ($1,089)
Total Member Encounters: Phys (56,882), non-phys (44,193)
Group Affiliation: MVP Health Care Inc
Licensed in: NH
Address: 33 S Commercial St, Manchester, NH 03101
Phone: (518) 370-4793 **Dom State:** NH **Commenced Bus:** January 2008

Data Date	Rating	RACR #1	RACR #2	Total Assets ($mil)	Capital ($mil)	Net Premium ($mil)	Net Income ($mil)
6-14	D	1.58	1.32	7.9	5.0	8.5	-2.5
6-13	D	2.02	1.68	13.7	8.9	23.0	0.2
2013	D	2.32	1.93	12.0	7.9	41.0	-1.3
2012	D	2.01	1.68	15.2	8.8	56.1	-3.9
2011	E+	2.08	1.73	20.1	12.9	86.4	-1.0
2010	E	1.32	1.10	33.3	12.0	108.5	-20.7
2009	E	0.73	0.61	27.9	7.2	100.1	-24.3

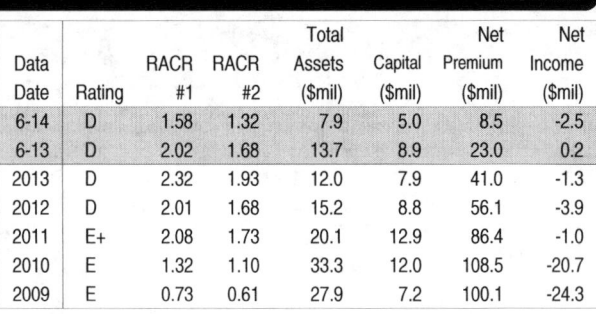

MVP HEALTH PLAN INC | B- | Good

Major Rating Factors: Fair overall results on stability tests (3.7 on a scale of 0 to 10) based on an inordinate decline in premium revenue in 2013. Good profitability index (4.9). Strong capitalization index (9.0) based on excellent current risk-adjusted capital (severe loss scenario).
Other Rating Factors: High quality investment portfolio (6.9). Excellent liquidity (7.0) with ample operational cash flow and liquid investments.
Principal Business: Medicare (54%), comp med (26%), Medicaid (9%), FEHB (8%), other (3%)
Mem Phys: 13: 45,890 **12:** 44,829 **13 MLR** 90.4% **/ 13 Admin Exp** N/A
Enroll(000): Q2 14: 230 **13:** 223 **12:** 255 **Med Exp PMPM:** $561
Principal Investments: Long-term bonds (55%), nonaffiliate common stock (12%), other (35%)
Provider Compensation ($000): Contr fee ($1,015,287), capitation ($493,235), bonus arrang ($10,908), FFS ($6,905), other ($18,570)
Total Member Encounters: Phys (3,609,447), non-phys (2,083,567)
Group Affiliation: MVP Health Care Inc
Licensed in: NY, VT
Address: 625 State St, Schenectady, NY 12305
Phone: (518) 370-4793 **Dom State:** NY **Commenced Bus:** July 1983

Data Date	Rating	RACR #1	RACR #2	Total Assets ($mil)	Capital ($mil)	Net Premium ($mil)	Net Income ($mil)
6-14	B-	2.93	2.44	491.0	289.1	821.8	-36.5
6-13	B-	3.05	2.55	486.2	352.2	837.0	6.8
2013	B	3.97	3.31	538.2	380.9	1,678.6	27.5
2012	B	3.02	2.51	535.7	345.1	1,959.8	61.4
2011	B-	2.69	2.24	489.6	298.4	1,972.5	75.5
2010	B+	3.05	2.54	528.8	329.8	2,084.4	124.4
2009	A-	2.17	1.81	570.0	327.2	2,352.1	122.5

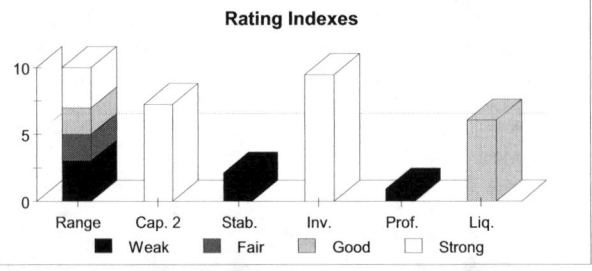

NATIONAL GUARDIAN LIFE INSURANCE COMPANY | B | Good

Major Rating Factors: Good quality investment portfolio (5.7 on a scale of 0 to 10) despite mixed results such as: minimal exposure to mortgages and large holdings of BBB rated bonds but small junk bond holdings. Good overall profitability (6.8). Good liquidity (6.0) with sufficient resources to handle a spike in claims as well as a significant increase in policy surrenders.
Other Rating Factors: Good overall results on stability tests (6.0) excellent operational trends, good risk adjusted capital for prior years and excellent risk diversification. Strong capitalization (7.0) based on excellent risk adjusted capital (severe loss scenario).
Principal Business: Group health insurance (36%), group life insurance (32%), individual life insurance (21%), reinsurance (6%), and other lines (4%).
Principal Investments: NonCMO investment grade bonds (77%), common & preferred stock (6%), CMOs and structured securities (6%), mortgages in good standing (4%), and misc. investments (6%).
Investments in Affiliates: 3%
Group Affiliation: NGL Ins Group
Licensed in: All states except NY, PR
Commenced Business: October 1910
Address: 2 E Gilman St, Madison, WI 53703
Phone: (608) 257-5611 **Domicile State:** WI **NAIC Code:** 66583

Data Date	Rating	RACR #1	RACR #2	Total Assets ($mil)	Capital ($mil)	Net Premium ($mil)	Net Income ($mil)
6-14	B	1.56	1.02	2,823.3	255.2	216.4	10.5
6-13	B	1.46	0.94	2,610.4	216.5	200.5	13.6
2013	B	1.51	0.99	2,730.8	241.3	416.1	28.8
2012	B	1.43	0.93	2,532.8	196.4	395.8	18.9
2011	B	1.29	0.84	2,331.4	182.4	494.2	8.7
2010	B+	1.45	0.97	2,043.2	196.4	385.5	3.3
2009	B+	1.48	0.99	1,776.3	187.4	238.9	8.2

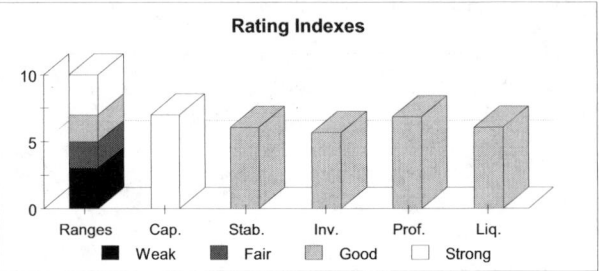

NATIONAL TEACHERS ASSOCIATES LIFE INSURANCE COMPAN   B   Good

Major Rating Factors: Good overall results on stability tests (6.0 on a scale of 0 to 10). Stability strengths include excellent operational trends and good risk diversification. Fair profitability (4.6) with investment income below regulatory standards in relation to interest assumptions of reserves. Strong capitalization (8.3) based on excellent risk adjusted capital (severe loss scenario).
Other Rating Factors: High quality investment portfolio (7.6). Excellent liquidity (8.4).
Principal Business: Individual health insurance (98%) and individual life insurance (2%).
Principal Investments: NonCMO investment grade bonds (47%), CMOs and structured securities (44%), noninv. grade bonds (3%), common & preferred stock (2%), and misc. investments (3%).
Investments in Affiliates: 2%
Group Affiliation: Ellard Enterprises Inc
Licensed in: All states except MA, NH, NY, RI, VT, PR
Commenced Business: July 1938
Address: 4949 Keller Springs Rd, Addison, TX 75001-5910
Phone: (972) 532-2100 **Domicile State:** TX **NAIC Code:** 87963

Data Date	Rating	RACR #1	RACR #2	Total Assets ($mil)	Capital ($mil)	Net Premium ($mil)	Net Income ($mil)
6-14	B	2.62	1.88	401.6	77.1	57.9	3.7
6-13	B+	3.55	2.43	366.9	73.2	53.2	5.1
2013	B	2.55	1.84	381.8	73.1	108.1	7.0
2012	B+	3.40	2.34	347.2	67.1	99.0	9.2
2011	B+	2.95	2.01	325.6	56.3	92.8	12.0
2010	B	2.43	1.65	309.4	44.5	88.1	8.8
2009	B	2.02	1.38	272.9	35.3	83.4	4.7

Adverse Trends in Operations

Increase in policy surrenders from 2012 to 2013 (29%)
Increase in policy surrenders from 2009 to 2010 (57%)

NEIGHBORHOOD HEALTH PARTNERSHIP INC   B-   Good

Major Rating Factors: Fair overall results on stability tests (3.9 on a scale of 0 to 10). Rating is significantly influenced by the fair financial results of UnitedHealth Group Inc. Good liquidity (6.3) with sufficient resources (cash flows and marketable investments) to handle a spike in claims. Excellent profitability (8.0).
Other Rating Factors: Strong capitalization index (7.6) based on excellent current risk-adjusted capital (severe loss scenario). High quality investment portfolio (8.7).
Principal Business: Comp med (100%)
Mem Phys: 13: 11,699 **12:** 11,320 **13 MLR** 79.3% **/ 13 Admin Exp** N/A
Enroll(000): Q2 14: 101 **13:** 107 **12:** 105 **Med Exp PMPM:** $295
Principal Investments: Long-term bonds (102%)
Provider Compensation ($000): Contr fee ($342,836), FFS ($27,597), capitation ($13,153)
Total Member Encounters: Phys (522,793), non-phys (9,306)
Group Affiliation: UnitedHealth Group Inc
Licensed in: FL
Address: 7600 Corporate Center Dr, Miami, FL 33126
Phone: (800) 825-8792 **Dom State:** FL **Commenced Bus:** November 2000

Data Date	Rating	RACR #1	RACR #2	Total Assets ($mil)	Capital ($mil)	Net Premium ($mil)	Net Income ($mil)
6-14	B-	1.81	1.50	109.3	39.4	242.3	4.2
6-13	B	2.93	2.44	124.4	57.5	232.0	15.2
2013	B-	1.63	1.36	94.4	35.0	477.4	30.6
2012	B	2.27	1.89	106.1	43.3	448.2	42.1
2011	B	2.67	2.22	127.2	48.4	409.9	16.9
2010	B	2.70	2.25	123.8	54.1	390.1	18.8
2009	B	2.11	1.76	117.9	48.1	431.6	14.9

Rating Indexes

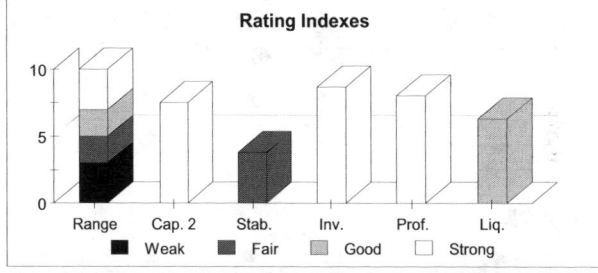

Range   Cap. 2   Stab.   Inv.   Prof.   Liq.
■ Weak   ■ Fair   ▨ Good   □ Strong

NEIGHBORHOOD HEALTH PLAN   C+   Fair

Major Rating Factors: Fair profitability index (3.6 on a scale of 0 to 10). Good liquidity (6.2) with sufficient resources (cash flows and marketable investments) to handle a spike in claims. Low quality investment portfolio (2.8).
Other Rating Factors: Strong capitalization index (7.2) based on excellent current risk-adjusted capital (severe loss scenario). Excellent overall results on stability tests (7.0) based on steady enrollment growth, averaging 8% over the past five years.
Principal Business: Medicaid (64%), comp med (36%)
Mem Phys: 13: 23,001 **12:** 20,760 **13 MLR** 91.6% **/ 13 Admin Exp** N/A
Enroll(000): Q2 14: 328 **13:** 274 **12:** 252 **Med Exp PMPM:** $400
Principal Investments: Nonaffiliate common stock (72%), cash and equiv (19%), long-term bonds (9%)
Provider Compensation ($000): Contr fee ($952,623), capitation ($258,089), FFS ($21,953), other ($24,758)
Total Member Encounters: Phys (1,898,905), non-phys (1,767,410)
Group Affiliation: None
Licensed in: MA
Address: 253 Summer St, Boston, MA 02210-1120
Phone: (617) 772-5500 **Dom State:** MA **Commenced Bus:** January 1988

Data Date	Rating	RACR #1	RACR #2	Total Assets ($mil)	Capital ($mil)	Net Premium ($mil)	Net Income ($mil)
6-14	C+	1.48	1.23	412.0	170.7	821.4	-13.8
6-13	C+	1.62	1.35	319.0	177.5	660.5	19.9
2013	C+	1.54	1.28	340.4	178.4	1,363.0	19.4
2012	C+	1.41	1.18	321.9	154.0	1,268.8	10.7
2011	B-	1.53	1.28	282.9	141.0	1,212.5	3.8
2010	B-	1.73	1.44	296.5	136.1	1,038.8	10.7
2009	B	1.60	1.33	261.3	122.0	923.9	-31.0

Rating Indexes

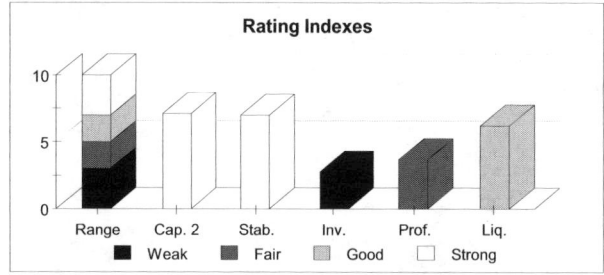

Range   Cap. 2   Stab.   Inv.   Prof.   Liq.
■ Weak   ■ Fair   ▨ Good   □ Strong

NEIGHBORHOOD HEALTH PLAN OF RI INC

B- **Good**

Major Rating Factors: Fair profitability index (4.5 on a scale of 0 to 10). Fair capitalization index (4.7) based on fair current risk-adjusted capital (moderate loss scenario). Fair overall results on stability tests (4.3).
Other Rating Factors: High quality investment portfolio (9.9). Excellent liquidity (6.9) with sufficient resources (cash flows and marketable investments) to handle a spike in claims.
Principal Business: Medicaid (100%)
Mem Phys: 13: 3,403 **12:** 3,307 **13 MLR** 89.7% **/ 13 Admin Exp** N/A
Enroll(000): Q2 14: 145 **13:** 99 **12:** 91 **Med Exp PMPM:** $345
Principal Investments: Cash and equiv (62%), long-term bonds (38%)
Provider Compensation ($000): Contr fee ($363,167), capitation ($10,167), bonus arrang ($7,387)
Total Member Encounters: Phys (1,556,240), non-phys (334,630)
Group Affiliation: None
Licensed in: RI
Address: 299 Promenade St, Providence, RI 02908
Phone: (401) 459-6000 **Dom State:** RI **Commenced Bus:** December 1994

Data Date	Rating	RACR #1	RACR #2	Total Assets ($mil)	Capital ($mil)	Net Premium ($mil)	Net Income ($mil)
6-14	B-	0.88	0.74	170.6	38.0	408.6	11.2
6-13	B-	0.83	0.69	84.3	35.7	204.8	-1.5
2013	B-	0.83	0.69	134.5	35.7	428.2	-3.8
2012	B-	0.99	0.83	149.5	42.1	427.6	-0.7
2011	B-	1.05	0.87	155.0	43.4	431.5	11.2
2010	D+	0.83	0.69	113.5	32.7	386.1	13.4
2009	D-	0.51	0.43	108.3	18.8	338.5	-19.7

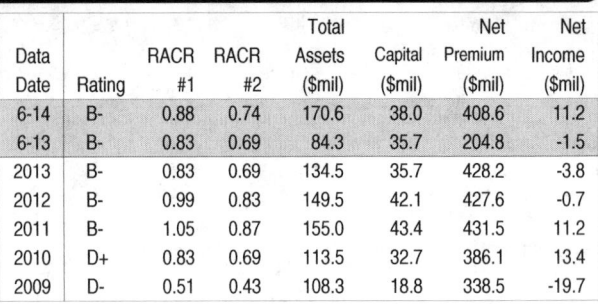

Rating Indexes

NETWORK HEALTH INS CORP

C- **Fair**

Major Rating Factors: Weak profitability index (1.6 on a scale of 0 to 10). Good liquidity (6.2) with sufficient resources (cash flows and marketable investments) to handle a spike in claims. Strong capitalization (7.1) based on excellent current risk-adjusted capital (severe loss scenario).
Other Rating Factors: High quality investment portfolio (9.9).
Principal Business: Medicare (98%), comp med (1%)
Mem Phys: 13: 6,679 **12:** N/A **13 MLR** 89.4% **/ 13 Admin Exp** N/A
Enroll(000): Q2 14: 67 **13:** 62 **12:** 60 **Med Exp PMPM:** $572
Principal Investments: Long-term bonds (83%), cash and equiv (17%)
Provider Compensation ($000): Contr fee ($412,829), FFS ($7,705)
Total Member Encounters: Phys (481,194), non-phys (149,085)
Group Affiliation: Ministry Health Care Inc
Licensed in: WI
Address: 1570 Midway Place, Menasha, WI 54952-1165
Phone: (920) 720-1452 **Dom State:** WI **Commenced Bus:** April 2013

Data Date	Rating	RACR #1	RACR #2	Total Assets ($mil)	Capital ($mil)	Net Premium ($mil)	Net Income ($mil)
6-14	C-	1.45	1.21	117.8	58.4	248.7	-6.0
6-13	N/A	N/A	N/A	126.7	64.2	234.7	0.7
2013	C-	1.59	1.33	122.1	64.4	474.2	4.2
2012	N/A	N/A	N/A	110.8	55.5	446.3	N/A
2011	N/A	N/A	N/A	93.5	49.9	408.1	N/A
2010	N/A	N/A	N/A	77.5	39.9	314.5	N/A
2009	N/A	N/A	N/A	51.6	27.0	204.6	N/A

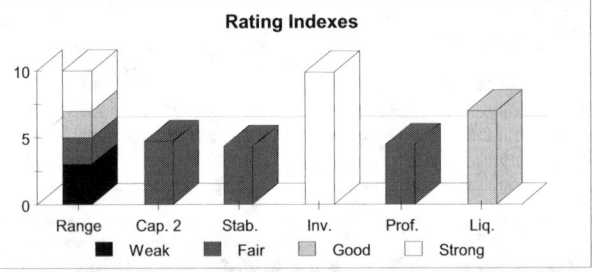

Rating Indexes

NETWORK HEALTH LLC

C+ **Fair**

Major Rating Factors: Good quality investment portfolio (4.9 on a scale of 0 to 10). Good liquidity (6.2) with sufficient resources (cash flows and marketable investments) to handle a spike in claims. Weak profitability index (0.9).
Other Rating Factors: Strong capitalization (7.8) based on excellent current risk-adjusted capital (severe loss scenario).
Principal Business: Medicaid (68%), comp med (32%)
Mem Phys: 13: 25,722 **12:** 24,404 **13 MLR** 97.8% **/ 13 Admin Exp** N/A
Enroll(000): Q2 14: 243 **13:** 221 **12:** 217 **Med Exp PMPM:** $396
Principal Investments: Nonaffiliate common stock (74%), cash and equiv (25%)
Provider Compensation ($000): Contr fee ($700,817), bonus arrang ($234,769), FFS ($98,911)
Total Member Encounters: Phys (2,883,085), non-phys (930,264)
Group Affiliation: Tufts Associated Health Plans Inc
Licensed in: MA
Address: 101 Station Landing 4th Floor, Medford, MA 02155-5134
Phone: (781) 393-3504 **Dom State:** MA **Commenced Bus:** November 2011

Data Date	Rating	RACR #1	RACR #2	Total Assets ($mil)	Capital ($mil)	Net Premium ($mil)	Net Income ($mil)
6-14	C+	2.00	1.67	312.6	148.3	611.0	-0.7
6-13	C+	1.96	1.63	234.5	124.5	527.8	-9.9
2013	C+	1.86	1.55	268.0	136.8	1,072.8	-66.1
2012	C+	1.78	1.48	217.6	113.7	999.1	-5.1
2011	C	1.57	1.31	211.3	108.8	137.5	-5.8
2010	N/A	N/A	N/A	N/A	N/A	N/A	N/A
2009	N/A	N/A	N/A	N/A	N/A	N/A	N/A

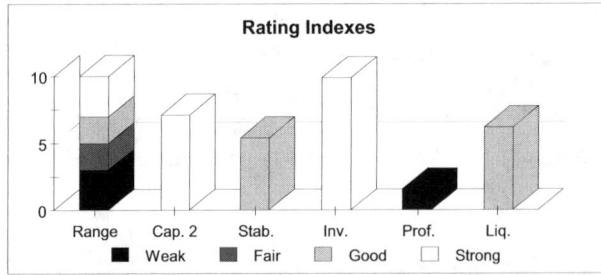

Rating Indexes

NETWORK HEALTH PLAN — D — Weak

Major Rating Factors: Weak overall results on stability tests (0.6 on a scale of 0 to 10). Good liquidity (6.9) with sufficient resources (cash flows and marketable investments) to handle a spike in claims. Excellent profitability (7.2). **Other Rating Factors:** Strong capitalization index (7.2) based on excellent current risk-adjusted capital (severe loss scenario). High quality investment portfolio (8.1).
Principal Business: Comp med (81%), Medicaid (19%)
Mem Phys: 13: 7,310 **12:** 7,046 **13 MLR** 87.1% **/ 13 Admin Exp** N/A
Enroll(000): Q2 14: 102 **13:** 105 **12:** 113 **Med Exp PMPM:** $282
Principal Investments: Long-term bonds (59%), cash and equiv (38%), real estate (3%)
Provider Compensation ($000): Contr fee ($267,945), capitation ($77,123), FFS ($26,180)
Total Member Encounters: Phys (556,543), non-phys (179,335)
Group Affiliation: Ministry Health Care Inc
Licensed in: WI
Address: 1570 Midway Pl, Menasha, WI 54952
Phone: (920) 720-1200 **Dom State:** WI **Commenced Bus:** April 1983

Data Date	Rating	RACR #1	RACR #2	Total Assets ($mil)	Capital ($mil)	Net Premium ($mil)	Net Income ($mil)
6-14	D	1.49	1.25	95.8	46.8	207.6	6.3
6-13	C	0.49	0.41	83.4	38.6	210.6	10.9
2013	D+	1.30	1.09	94.3	40.6	418.0	13.1
2012	B	1.24	1.03	144.9	91.2	435.4	5.1
2011	B+	1.35	1.13	133.8	91.9	415.1	12.1
2010	B	1.30	1.08	104.6	75.4	396.1	19.5
2009	B-	1.37	1.14	103.1	69.8	424.4	10.5

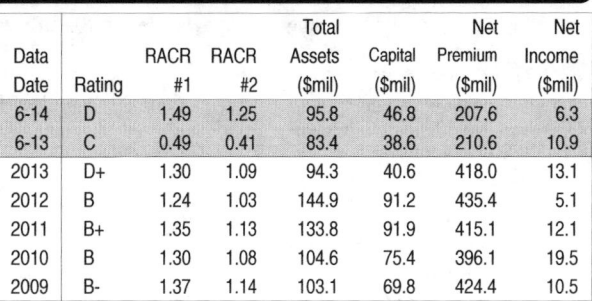

Rating Indexes

NEW ERA LIFE INSURANCE COMPANY — C — Fair

Major Rating Factors: Fair capitalization (4.6 on a scale of 0 to 10) based on fair risk adjusted capital (moderate loss scenario). Fair overall results on stability tests (3.5) including excessive premium growth and fair risk adjusted capital in prior years. Good quality investment portfolio (5.3) despite large holdings of BBB rated bonds in addition to moderate junk bond exposure. Exposure to mortgages is significant, but the mortgage default rate has been low.
Other Rating Factors: Good overall profitability (6.0). Good liquidity (6.5).
Principal Business: Individual health insurance (62%), individual annuities (36%), and individual life insurance (1%).
Principal Investments: NonCMO investment grade bonds (44%), CMOs and structured securities (18%), common & preferred stock (13%), mortgages in good standing (12%), and misc. investments (13%).
Investments in Affiliates: 11%
Group Affiliation: New Era Life Group
Licensed in: AL, AZ, CA, CO, DE, FL, GA, IN, LA, MS, NM, NC, OH, OK, PA, SC, SD, TN, TX, UT, WV
Commenced Business: June 1924
Address: 200 Westlake Park Blvd, Houston, TX 77079
Phone: (713) 368-7200 **Domicile State:** TX **NAIC Code:** 78743

Data Date	Rating	RACR #1	RACR #2	Total Assets ($mil)	Capital ($mil)	Net Premium ($mil)	Net Income ($mil)
6-14	C	0.92	0.70	390.8	61.1	54.1	1.8
6-13	C	0.88	0.66	360.7	53.4	38.4	1.3
2013	C	0.90	0.69	371.3	58.0	77.3	4.6
2012	C	0.86	0.65	352.2	52.0	68.3	2.1
2011	C	0.81	0.62	353.6	47.1	67.0	-4.2
2010	C	0.86	0.64	344.3	48.2	78.6	0.8
2009	C	0.81	0.57	320.1	45.2	71.4	-3.7

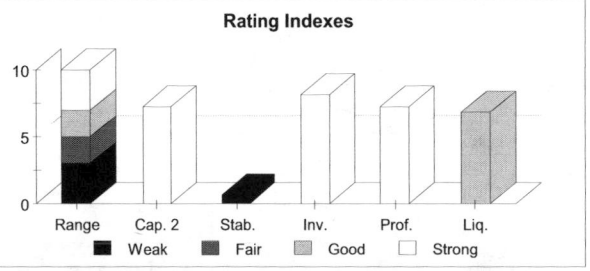

Risk-Adjusted Capital Ratio #1 (Moderate Loss Scenario)

NEW WEST HEALTH SERVICES — E+ — Very Weak

Major Rating Factors: Weak profitability index (0.7 on a scale of 0 to 10). Poor capitalization index (0.0) based on weak current risk-adjusted capital (severe loss scenario). Low quality investment portfolio (0.0).
Other Rating Factors: Weak liquidity (0.0) as a spike in claims may stretch capacity. Fair overall results on stability tests (4.9) based on an excessive 69% enrollment growth during the period.
Principal Business: Medicare (100%)
Mem Phys: 13: 5,550 **12:** 5,532 **13 MLR** 98.1% **/ 13 Admin Exp** N/A
Enroll(000): Q2 14: 23 **13:** 20 **12:** 12 **Med Exp PMPM:** $660
Principal Investments: Nonaffiliate common stock (425%)
Provider Compensation ($000): Contr fee ($132,938), FFS ($15,546)
Total Member Encounters: Phys (174,989), non-phys (111,477)
Group Affiliation: None
Licensed in: MT
Address: 130 Neill Ave, Helena, MT 59601
Phone: (406) 457-2200 **Dom State:** MT **Commenced Bus:** March 1998

Data Date	Rating	RACR #1	RACR #2	Total Assets ($mil)	Capital ($mil)	Net Premium ($mil)	Net Income ($mil)
6-14	E+	0.26	0.21	45.4	9.9	90.3	-8.5
6-13	E+	0.18	0.15	20.1	4.5	75.7	-5.9
2013	E+	0.26	0.21	27.6	9.9	155.2	-15.7
2012	D-	0.40	0.33	23.6	9.9	92.6	-14.3
2011	D	0.59	0.49	38.6	19.7	158.1	1.4
2010	D	0.68	0.56	33.7	18.3	119.4	-2.9
2009	E+	0.98	0.81	35.9	20.5	98.2	0.7

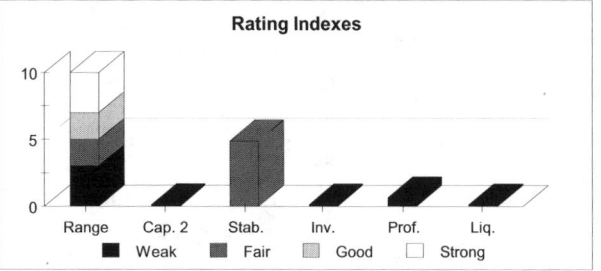

Rating Indexes

NIPPON LIFE INSURANCE COMPANY OF AMERICA *   A-   Excellent

Major Rating Factors: Good liquidity (6.4 on a scale of 0 to 10) with sufficient resources to handle a spike in claims. Strong capitalization (9.2) based on excellent risk adjusted capital (severe loss scenario). Furthermore, this high level of risk adjusted capital has been consistently maintained over the last five years. High quality investment portfolio (8.1).

Other Rating Factors: Excellent profitability (9.0) with operating gains in each of the last five years. Excellent overall results on stability tests (7.0) excellent operational trends and excellent risk diversification.

Principal Business: Group health insurance (99%) and group life insurance (1%).

Principal Investments: NonCMO investment grade bonds (78%), CMOs and structured securities (13%), cash (5%), common & preferred stock (1%), and noninv. grade bonds (1%).

Investments in Affiliates: None

Group Affiliation: Nippon Life Ins Co Japan

Licensed in: All states except ME, NH, WY, PR

Commenced Business: July 1973

Address: 650 8th St, Des Moines, IA 50309

Phone: (212) 682-3992 **Domicile State:** IA **NAIC Code:** 81264

Data Date	Rating	RACR #1	RACR #2	Total Assets ($mil)	Capital ($mil)	Net Premium ($mil)	Net Income ($mil)
6-14	A-	3.10	2.48	222.1	133.6	165.2	0.5
6-13	A-	3.32	2.62	219.7	133.2	167.9	2.7
2013	A-	2.96	2.35	225.1	136.7	351.2	6.7
2012	A-	3.44	2.71	213.7	134.6	295.4	8.4
2011	A-	3.83	2.99	196.5	129.8	251.6	7.6
2010	A-	3.77	2.84	167.9	121.3	229.2	7.0
2009	A-	3.91	3.00	157.9	114.7	211.5	0.7

Rating Indexes

Ranges · Cap. · Stab. · Inv. · Prof. · Liq.
■ Weak ▦ Fair ▒ Good ☐ Strong

NORIDIAN MUTUAL INS CO   C+   Fair

Major Rating Factors: Good liquidity (6.5 on a scale of 0 to 10) with sufficient resources (cash flows and marketable investments) to handle a spike in claims. Weak profitability index (1.7). Strong capitalization (7.3) based on excellent current risk-adjusted capital (severe loss scenario).

Other Rating Factors: High quality investment portfolio (9.2).

Principal Business: Comp med (76%), FEHB (8%), med supp (6%), other (9%)

Mem Phys: 13: 2,486 **12:** 2,166 **13 MLR** 91.7% **/ 13 Admin Exp** N/A

Enroll(000): 13: 386 **12:** 300 **Med Exp PMPM:** $275

Principal Investments: Long-term bonds (49%), cash and equiv (23%), nonaffiliate common stock (20%), real estate (7%), affiliate common stock (1%)

Provider Compensation ($000): FFS ($553,694), contr fee ($536,255)

Total Member Encounters: Phys (3,528,050), non-phys (2,728,171)

Group Affiliation: Noridian Mutual Ins Co

Licensed in: MN, ND

Address: 4510 13th Ave S, Fargo, ND 58121

Phone: (701) 282-1100 **Dom State:** ND **Commenced Bus:** April 1940

Data Date	Rating	RACR #1	RACR #2	Total Assets ($mil)	Capital ($mil)	Net Premium ($mil)	Net Income ($mil)
2013	C+	1.58	1.31	458.2	199.1	1,195.6	-80.8
2012	B+	2.29	1.91	506.8	272.0	1,106.3	22.1
2011	A-	2.51	2.09	508.5	270.3	1,027.9	22.9
2010	A-	2.42	2.02	454.8	258.0	961.4	18.9
2009	A-	2.24	1.87	392.6	216.1	909.4	10.0

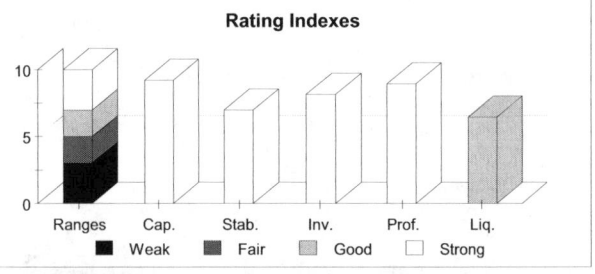

Rating Indexes

Range · Cap. 2 · Stab. · Inv. · Prof. · Liq.
■ Weak ▦ Fair ▒ Good ☐ Strong

NORTHWESTERN LONG TERM CARE INSURANCE COMPANY   B   Good

Major Rating Factors: Good overall results on stability tests (6.3 on a scale of 0 to 10). Strengths include potential support from affiliation with Northwestern Mutual Group, excellent operational trends, good risk adjusted capital for prior years and excellent risk diversification. Fair quality investment portfolio (4.4) with large holdings of BBB rated bonds in addition to junk bond exposure equal to 84% of capital. Exposure to mortgages is significant, but the mortgage default rate has been low. Weak profitability (1.7).

Other Rating Factors: Strong capitalization (7.1) based on excellent risk adjusted capital (severe loss scenario). Excellent liquidity (9.4).

Principal Business: Individual health insurance (100%).

Principal Investments: NonCMO investment grade bonds (68%), mortgages in good standing (12%), noninv. grade bonds (10%), and common & preferred stock (8%).

Investments in Affiliates: None

Group Affiliation: Northwestern Mutual Group

Licensed in: All states except PR

Commenced Business: October 1953

Address: 720 E Wisconsin Ave, Milwaukee, WI 53202

Phone: (414) 299-3136 **Domicile State:** WI **NAIC Code:** 69000

Data Date	Rating	RACR #1	RACR #2	Total Assets ($mil)	Capital ($mil)	Net Premium ($mil)	Net Income ($mil)
6-14	B	1.91	1.06	2,475.9	261.5	237.7	5.0
6-13	B	2.66	1.49	2,038.8	319.9	220.7	19.2
2013	B	1.76	0.99	2,220.1	213.8	457.3	-84.2
2012	B	2.45	1.40	1,861.6	274.7	387.1	-192.9
2011	B	2.14	1.29	1,193.9	210.1	300.6	10.5
2010	B-	1.91	1.27	926.2	149.6	338.6	-49.5
2009	B-	1.66	1.10	528.2	71.4	186.5	-17.1

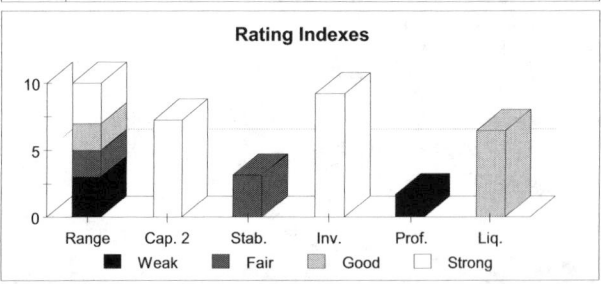

Northwestern Mutual Group Composite Group Rating: A- Largest Group Members	Assets ($mil)	Rating
NORTHWESTERN MUTUAL LIFE INS CO	215165	A-
NORTHWESTERN LONG TERM CARE INS CO	2220	B

OLD REPUBLIC LIFE INSURANCE COMPANY   B-   Good

Major Rating Factors: Good quality investment portfolio (6.1 on a scale of 0 to 10) despite mixed results such as: no exposure to mortgages and large holdings of BBB rated bonds but no exposure to junk bonds. Good overall results on stability tests (5.3) despite negative cash flow from operations for 2013. Strengths include good financial support from affiliation with Old Republic Group, excellent operational trends and excellent risk diversification. Weak profitability (2.9) with operating losses during the first six months of 2014.
Other Rating Factors: Strong capitalization (8.6) based on excellent risk adjusted capital (severe loss scenario). Excellent liquidity (7.0).
Principal Business: Individual life insurance (40%), group health insurance (40%), reinsurance (19%), and individual annuities (1%).
Principal Investments: NonCMO investment grade bonds (94%), common & preferred stock (4%), policy loans (1%), and cash (1%).
Investments in Affiliates: None
Group Affiliation: Old Republic Group
Licensed in: All states except NY
Commenced Business: April 1923
Address: 307 N Michigan Ave, Chicago, IL 60601
Phone: (312) 346-8100 **Domicile State:** IL **NAIC Code:** 67261

Data Date	Rating	RACR #1	RACR #2	Total Assets ($mil)	Capital ($mil)	Net Premium ($mil)	Net Income ($mil)
6-14	B-	3.28	2.06	132.3	33.4	10.0	-2.0
6-13	B	4.50	2.87	137.4	39.9	10.5	1.3
2013	B-	4.30	2.81	131.7	36.4	21.2	2.2
2012	B	4.68	3.13	138.4	40.6	21.0	1.6
2011	B+	4.69	3.12	142.3	41.0	22.4	4.8
2010	B+	4.41	2.85	149.1	40.6	26.4	4.0
2009	B+	4.45	2.90	151.9	41.0	25.5	5.1

Old Republic Group
Composite Group Rating: B

Largest Group Members	Assets ($mil)	Rating
OLD REPUBLIC INS CO	2473	A-
REPUBLIC MORTGAGE INS CO	1933	F
GREAT WEST CASUALTY CO	1737	A-
OLD REPUBLIC GENERAL INS CORP	1731	A-
BITUMINOUS CASUALTY CORP	788	A-

OLD UNITED LIFE INSURANCE COMPANY   B   Good

Major Rating Factors: Good overall results on stability tests (6.2 on a scale of 0 to 10). Stability strengths include excellent operational trends and good risk diversification. Good quality investment portfolio (5.1) despite mixed results such as: no exposure to mortgages and large holdings of BBB rated bonds but small junk bond holdings. Strong capitalization (10.0) based on excellent risk adjusted capital (severe loss scenario).
Other Rating Factors: Excellent profitability (7.1) with operating gains in each of the last five years. Excellent liquidity (9.4).
Principal Business: Credit life insurance (51%) and credit health insurance (49%).
Principal Investments: NonCMO investment grade bonds (59%), common & preferred stock (18%), CMOs and structured securities (16%), and noninv. grade bonds (7%).
Investments in Affiliates: None
Group Affiliation: Van Enterprises Group
Licensed in: All states except ME, NH, NY, PR
Commenced Business: January 1964
Address: 8500 W Shawnee Mission Pky 200, Merriam, KS 66202
Phone: (913) 432-6400 **Domicile State:** AZ **NAIC Code:** 76007

Data Date	Rating	RACR #1	RACR #2	Total Assets ($mil)	Capital ($mil)	Net Premium ($mil)	Net Income ($mil)
6-14	B	5.92	3.44	89.7	45.7	4.2	0.3
6-13	B	6.17	3.61	84.8	44.6	4.2	0.4
2013	B	6.08	3.55	87.4	44.9	8.5	0.4
2012	B	5.95	3.86	82.3	43.9	9.8	1.0
2011	B	6.03	5.15	76.2	43.6	4.9	2.2
2010	B	5.79	5.21	75.9	41.8	5.2	1.5
2009	B-	5.57	5.02	73.5	40.2	3.4	4.2

Adverse Trends in Operations

Decrease in premium volume from 2012 to 2013 (13%)
Decrease in premium volume from 2010 to 2011 (6%)
Increase in policy surrenders from 2010 to 2011 (96%)
Change in premium mix from 2009 to 2010 (4.3%)

ON LOK SENIOR HEALTH SERVICES   B   Good

Major Rating Factors: Good overall profitability index (5.3 on a scale of 0 to 10). Good overall results on stability tests (6.3) based on steady enrollment growth, averaging 5% over the past five years. Strong capitalization index (9.4) based on excellent current risk-adjusted capital (severe loss scenario).
Other Rating Factors: Excellent liquidity (7.1) with ample operational cash flow and liquid investments.
Principal Business: Medicaid (61%), Medicare (36%)
Mem Phys: 13: N/A **12:** N/A **13 MLR** 93.9% **/ 13 Admin Exp** N/A
Enroll(000): Q2 14: 1 **13:** 1 **12:** 1 **Med Exp PMPM:** $24,682
Principal Investments ($000): Cash and equiv ($2,690)
Provider Compensation ($000): None
Total Member Encounters: N/A
Group Affiliation: None
Licensed in: CA
Address: 1333 Bush St, San Francisco, CA 94109-5611
Phone: (415) 292-8888 **Dom State:** CA **Commenced Bus:** September 1971

Data Date	Rating	RACR #1	RACR #2	Total Assets ($mil)	Capital ($mil)	Net Premium ($mil)	Net Income ($mil)
6-14	B	3.72	2.72	126.1	94.0	50.8	4.7
6-13	B	3.65	2.68	117.1	88.6	49.1	4.9
2013	B	3.55	2.59	118.8	89.4	97.0	5.7
2012	B	3.70	2.69	115.4	83.7	95.7	1.6
2011	B	3.68	2.69	107.3	82.1	88.9	11.5
2010	B	3.83	2.76	96.6	70.7	84.7	6.6
2009	B	3.70	2.64	89.7	64.0	83.1	-4.2

Rating Indexes

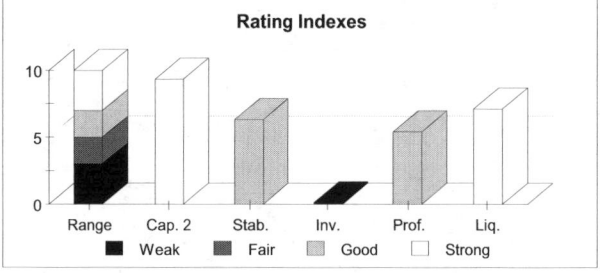

OPTIMA HEALTH INS CO

C **Fair**

Major Rating Factors: Weak profitability index (0.9 on a scale of 0 to 10). Good liquidity (5.3) with sufficient resources (cash flows and marketable investments) to handle a spike in claims. Strong capitalization (8.0) based on excellent current risk-adjusted capital (severe loss scenario).
Other Rating Factors: High quality investment portfolio (9.9).
Principal Business: Comp med (95%), Medicare (5%)
Mem Phys: 13: 8,243 **12:** 14,235 **13 MLR** 92.4% **/ 13 Admin Exp** N/A
Enroll(000): Q2 14: 28 **13:** 31 **12:** 27 **Med Exp PMPM:** $298
Principal Investments: Long-term bonds (84%), nonaffiliate common stock (9%), cash and equiv (6%)
Provider Compensation ($000): Contr fee ($98,548), capitation ($2,598), bonus arrang ($3)
Total Member Encounters: Phys (4,463), non-phys (39,870)
Group Affiliation: Sentara Healthcare
Licensed in: NC, VA
Address: 4417 Corporation Lane, Virginia Beach, VA 23462
Phone: (757) 552-7401 **Dom State:** VA **Commenced Bus:** October 1992

Data Date	Rating	RACR #1	RACR #2	Total Assets ($mil)	Capital ($mil)	Net Premium ($mil)	Net Income ($mil)
6-14	C	2.12	1.77	38.9	22.5	56.0	-7.0
6-13	B-	2.41	2.01	41.0	21.4	51.8	-3.7
2013	B	1.74	1.45	36.0	18.2	113.6	-6.0
2012	B-	2.81	2.34	41.3	25.3	93.2	-4.5
2011	B	1.31	1.09	65.4	27.1	215.7	-14.9
2010	B	1.46	1.22	59.1	25.7	185.6	-12.4
2009	B	1.79	1.49	46.2	23.0	155.1	1.4

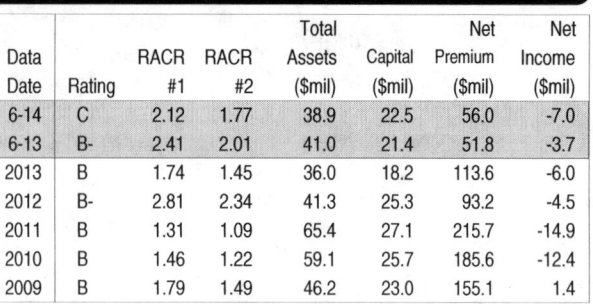

Rating Indexes

OPTIMA HEALTH PLAN *

B+ **Good**

Major Rating Factors: Good overall results on stability tests (5.2 on a scale of 0 to 10). Excellent profitability (7.5). Strong capitalization index (7.5) based on excellent current risk-adjusted capital (severe loss scenario).
Other Rating Factors: High quality investment portfolio (9.9). Excellent liquidity (7.0) with sufficient resources (cash flows and marketable investments) to handle a spike in claims.
Principal Business: Medicaid (49%), comp med (41%), FEHB (10%)
Mem Phys: 13: 14,380 **12:** 12,278 **13 MLR** 89.6% **/ 13 Admin Exp** N/A
Enroll(000): Q2 14: 315 **13:** 320 **12:** 321 **Med Exp PMPM:** $305
Principal Investments: Long-term bonds (48%), cash and equiv (45%), nonaffiliate common stock (8%)
Provider Compensation ($000): Contr fee ($1,103,525), capitation ($45,164), bonus arrang ($91)
Total Member Encounters: Phys (1,730,492), non-phys (3,937,106)
Group Affiliation: Sentara Healthcare
Licensed in: VA
Address: 4417 Corporation Lane, Virginia Beach, VA 23462
Phone: (757) 552-7401 **Dom State:** VA **Commenced Bus:** December 1984

Data Date	Rating	RACR #1	RACR #2	Total Assets ($mil)	Capital ($mil)	Net Premium ($mil)	Net Income ($mil)
6-14	B+	1.74	1.45	320.8	165.7	666.8	15.6
6-13	A-	2.15	1.79	370.5	196.7	633.7	22.3
2013	A-	2.07	1.72	349.5	196.6	1,302.4	48.9
2012	A-	1.85	1.54	316.0	170.2	1,238.4	29.6
2011	A+	2.54	2.11	336.9	199.6	1,136.7	84.5
2010	A+	2.32	1.94	310.8	183.6	1,091.5	70.0
2009	A+	1.70	1.42	247.4	130.8	985.1	18.3

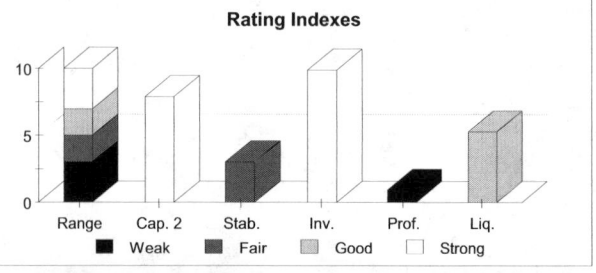

Rating Indexes

OPTIMUM CHOICE INC

C+ **Fair**

Major Rating Factors: Fair overall results on stability tests (4.0 on a scale of 0 to 10). Rating is significantly influenced by the fair financial results of UnitedHealth Group Inc. Excellent profitability (8.0). Strong capitalization index (10.0) based on excellent current risk-adjusted capital (severe loss scenario).
Other Rating Factors: High quality investment portfolio (9.9). Excellent liquidity (7.0) with ample operational cash flow and liquid investments.
Principal Business: Comp med (100%)
Mem Phys: 13: 36,157 **12:** 35,400 **13 MLR** 74.9% **/ 13 Admin Exp** N/A
Enroll(000): Q2 14: 46 **13:** 51 **12:** 53 **Med Exp PMPM:** $306
Principal Investments: Long-term bonds (75%), cash and equiv (25%)
Provider Compensation ($000): Contr fee ($168,798), capitation ($8,340), bonus arrang ($157)
Total Member Encounters: Phys (299,751), non-phys (18,337)
Group Affiliation: UnitedHealth Group Inc
Licensed in: DC, DE, MD, VA, WV
Address: 800 King Farm Blvd, Rockville, MD 20850
Phone: (240) 632-8109 **Dom State:** MD **Commenced Bus:** September 1988

Data Date	Rating	RACR #1	RACR #2	Total Assets ($mil)	Capital ($mil)	Net Premium ($mil)	Net Income ($mil)
6-14	C+	5.65	4.71	88.4	53.6	114.3	12.8
6-13	C+	3.13	2.61	69.0	30.0	115.6	13.5
2013	C+	4.41	3.67	70.1	41.0	233.5	24.5
2012	C+	2.81	2.35	56.3	26.5	242.9	22.1
2011	C+	4.60	3.83	73.8	41.6	252.9	30.0
2010	C+	6.06	5.05	124.5	91.3	324.9	47.4
2009	C+	4.44	3.70	162.3	102.7	459.9	45.5

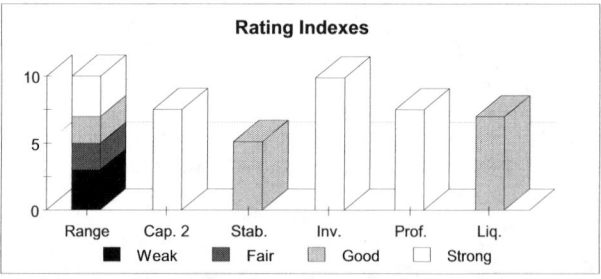

Rating Indexes

ORANGE PREVENTION & TREATMENT INTEGR | B | Good

Major Rating Factors: Good overall profitability index (6.7 on a scale of 0 to 10). Strong capitalization index (6.9) based on excellent current risk-adjusted capital (severe loss scenario). Excellent overall results on stability tests (7.7) based on healthy premium and capital growth during 2013.
Other Rating Factors: Excellent liquidity (6.9) with sufficient resources (cash flows and marketable investments) to handle a spike in claims.
Principal Business: Medicaid (88%), Medicare (12%)
Mem Phys: 13: N/A **12:** N/A **13 MLR** 92.1% **/ 13 Admin Exp** N/A
Enroll(000): Q2 14: 492 **13:** 471 **12:** 424 **Med Exp PMPM:** $303
Principal Investments ($000): Cash and equiv ($159,355)
Provider Compensation ($000): None
Total Member Encounters: N/A
Group Affiliation: None
Licensed in: CA
Address: 1120 West La Veta Ave, Orange, CA 92868
Phone: (714) 246-8400 **Dom State:** CA **Commenced Bus:** June 2000

Data Date	Rating	RACR #1	RACR #2	Total Assets ($mil)	Capital ($mil)	Net Premium ($mil)	Net Income ($mil)
6-14	B	1.66	1.07	610.1	224.7	773.7	12.8
6-13	B-	1.26	0.80	445.8	162.5	689.2	5.6
2013	B	1.58	1.01	690.4	211.9	1,743.2	55.1
2012	B-	1.17	0.75	464.9	156.9	1,493.1	3.5
2011	B-	1.22	0.78	389.9	153.3	1,464.5	4.3
2010	C+	1.32	0.85	370.5	149.0	1,225.1	17.7
2009	C	1.29	0.83	327.4	131.4	1,078.2	-17.5

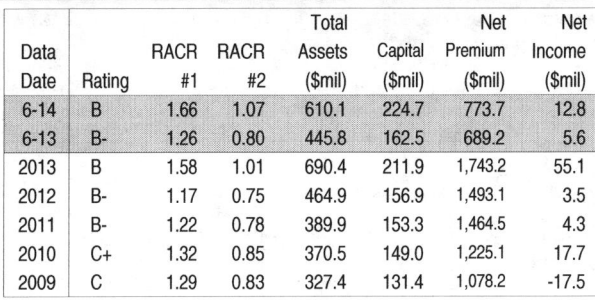

OXFORD HEALTH INS INC | C+ | Fair

Major Rating Factors: Weak liquidity (2.1 on a scale of 0 to 10) as a spike in claims may stretch capacity. Excellent profitability (9.8). Strong capitalization (10.0) based on excellent current risk-adjusted capital (severe loss scenario).
Other Rating Factors: High quality investment portfolio (9.6).
Principal Business: Comp med (100%)
Mem Phys: 13: 112,000 **12:** 104,000 **13 MLR** 162.7% **/ 13 Admin Exp** N/A
Enroll(000): Q2 14: 858 **13:** 984 **12:** 1,039 **Med Exp PMPM:** $399
Principal Investments: Long-term bonds (84%), cash and equiv (15%), other (1%)
Provider Compensation ($000): Contr fee ($3,943,413), FFS ($609,726), capitation ($128,925), bonus arrang ($11,533)
Total Member Encounters: Phys (4,653,235), non-phys (4,582,627)
Group Affiliation: UnitedHealth Group Inc
Licensed in: CT, NJ, NY, PA
Address: Two Penn Plaza, New York, NY 10121
Phone: (203) 459-6000 **Dom State:** NY **Commenced Bus:** July 1987

Data Date	Rating	RACR #1	RACR #2	Total Assets ($mil)	Capital ($mil)	Net Premium ($mil)	Net Income ($mil)
6-14	C+	5.90	4.92	1,963.7	895.4	2,097.0	43.8
6-13	C+	5.32	4.43	2,002.8	791.6	1,417.1	86.1
2013	C+	5.65	4.70	2,078.4	855.2	2,862.9	141.4
2012	C+	4.83	4.03	2,004.7	721.8	2,832.7	160.7
2011	C+	4.01	3.34	1,880.7	573.7	2,755.4	161.7
2010	C+	3.31	2.76	1,450.2	432.6	2,416.9	129.9
2009	C+	2.54	2.12	1,018.9	315.1	2,177.5	75.1

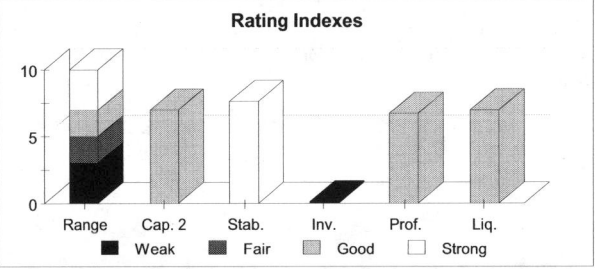

OXFORD HEALTH PLANS (CT) INC | B | Good

Major Rating Factors: Good overall profitability index (5.1 on a scale of 0 to 10). Good liquidity (6.8) with sufficient resources (cash flows and marketable investments) to handle a spike in claims. Fair overall results on stability tests (4.5). Rating is significantly influenced by the fair financial results of UnitedHealth Group Inc.
Other Rating Factors: Strong capitalization index (9.2) based on excellent current risk-adjusted capital (severe loss scenario). High quality investment portfolio (9.9).
Principal Business: Medicare (81%), comp med (19%)
Mem Phys: 13: 111,635 **12:** 104,243 **13 MLR** 86.8% **/ 13 Admin Exp** N/A
Enroll(000): Q2 14: 55 **13:** 68 **12:** 69 **Med Exp PMPM:** $670
Principal Investments: Long-term bonds (69%), cash and equiv (31%)
Provider Compensation ($000): Contr fee ($503,571), FFS ($47,842), capitation ($15,002), bonus arrang ($468)
Total Member Encounters: Phys (1,187,876), non-phys (609,453)
Group Affiliation: UnitedHealth Group Inc
Licensed in: CT
Address: 48 Monroe Turnpike, Trumbull, CT 06611
Phone: (203) 459-6000 **Dom State:** CT **Commenced Bus:** October 1993

Data Date	Rating	RACR #1	RACR #2	Total Assets ($mil)	Capital ($mil)	Net Premium ($mil)	Net Income ($mil)
6-14	B	3.14	2.61	232.1	110.8	271.6	5.8
6-13	B-	2.93	2.44	234.6	102.4	330.8	6.9
2013	B	3.28	2.73	240.7	116.2	653.1	7.0
2012	B-	2.79	2.33	231.7	104.2	652.6	27.5
2011	B-	2.32	1.93	253.1	122.2	686.7	19.5
2010	C+	2.44	2.04	246.0	112.6	1,062.0	-2.8
2009	C+	2.78	2.32	313.9	145.1	1,183.3	0.2

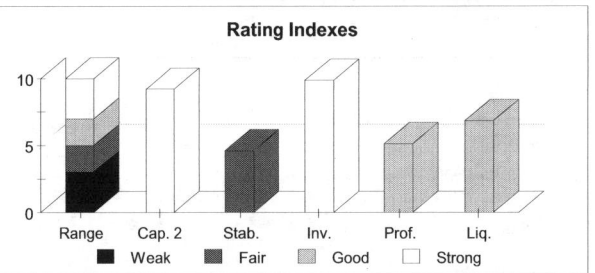

OXFORD HEALTH PLANS (NJ) INC

B   **Good**

Major Rating Factors: Good liquidity (6.3 on a scale of 0 to 10) with sufficient resources (cash flows and marketable investments) to handle a spike in claims. Fair overall results on stability tests (4.8). Rating is significantly influenced by the fair financial results of UnitedHealth Group Inc. Excellent profitability (7.3).
Other Rating Factors: Strong capitalization index (8.1) based on excellent current risk-adjusted capital (severe loss scenario). High quality investment portfolio (9.9).
Principal Business: Medicare (51%), comp med (49%)
Mem Phys: 13: 111,000   **12:** 104,000   **13 MLR** 85.7%   **/ 13 Admin Exp** N/A
Enroll(000): Q2 14: 131   **13:** 168   **12:** 173   **Med Exp PMPM:** $473
Principal Investments: Long-term bonds (96%), cash and equiv (4%)
Provider Compensation ($000): Contr fee ($684,667), FFS ($266,882), capitation ($14,532), bonus arrang ($894)
Total Member Encounters: Phys (1,747,421), non-phys (866,224)
Group Affiliation: UnitedHealth Group Inc
Licensed in: NJ
Address: 170 Wood Ave Floor 3, Iselin, NJ 08830
Phone: (203) 459-6000   **Dom State:** NJ   **Commenced Bus:** September 1985

Data Date	Rating	RACR #1	RACR #2	Total Assets ($mil)	Capital ($mil)	Net Premium ($mil)	Net Income ($mil)
6-14	B	2.23	1.85	342.5	134.0	554.0	6.1
6-13	B+	2.21	1.84	353.5	127.0	563.4	16.7
2013	B+	2.33	1.94	337.3	140.8	1,143.7	34.0
2012	B+	2.05	1.71	317.3	124.1	1,118.0	62.8
2011	B+	2.30	1.92	340.7	156.9	1,059.1	46.2
2010	B+	3.41	2.84	355.0	186.0	1,089.1	62.8
2009	B+	4.23	3.52	363.7	198.3	1,109.8	28.1

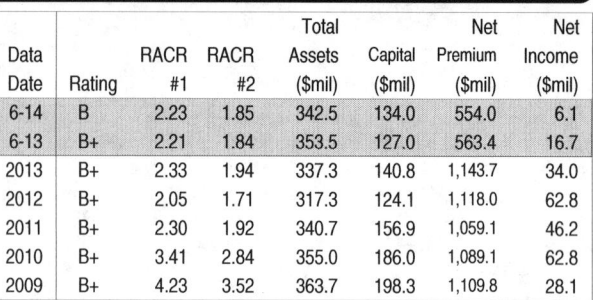

Rating Indexes

OXFORD HEALTH PLANS (NY) INC *

A+   **Excellent**

Major Rating Factors: Strong capitalization index (7.1 on a scale of 0 to 10) based on excellent current risk-adjusted capital (severe loss scenario). High quality investment portfolio (7.1). Good overall profitability index (5.9).
Other Rating Factors: Good liquidity (6.9) with sufficient resources (cash flows and marketable investments) to handle a spike in claims. Fair overall results on stability tests (3.8).
Principal Business: Comp med (69%), Medicare (31%)
Mem Phys: 13: 111,635   **12:** 104,243   **13 MLR** 87.0%   **/ 13 Admin Exp** N/A
Enroll(000): Q2 14: 273   **13:** 351   **12:** 378   **Med Exp PMPM:** $513
Principal Investments: Affiliate common stock (53%), long-term bonds (31%), cash and equiv (15%)
Provider Compensation ($000): Contr fee ($1,616,408), FFS ($521,577), capitation ($53,847), bonus arrang ($15,232)
Total Member Encounters: Phys (3,018,507), non-phys (1,896,926)
Group Affiliation: UnitedHealth Group Inc
Licensed in: NY
Address: One Penn Plaza Floor 8, New York, NY 10119
Phone: (203) 459-6000   **Dom State:** NY   **Commenced Bus:** June 1986

Data Date	Rating	RACR #1	RACR #2	Total Assets ($mil)	Capital ($mil)	Net Premium ($mil)	Net Income ($mil)
6-14	A+	1.40	1.17	817.8	407.2	1,084.4	-26.4
6-13	A+	4.43	3.69	1,751.2	1,288.3	1,278.5	57.9
2013	A+	4.58	3.82	1,820.5	1,386.7	2,524.6	77.7
2012	A+	3.95	3.29	1,626.5	1,175.8	2,524.0	108.3
2011	A+	4.06	3.38	1,518.6	1,148.6	2,338.7	148.0
2010	A+	3.71	3.09	1,417.8	967.9	2,305.4	125.9
2009	A+	2.90	2.42	1,115.1	747.7	2,436.7	498.9

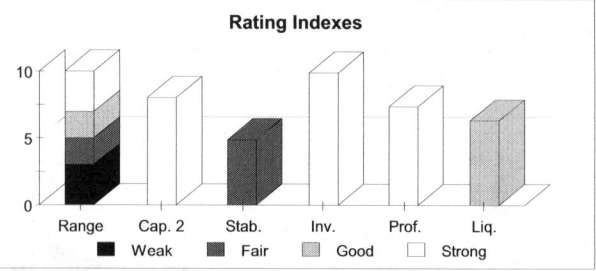

Rating Indexes

PACIFIC GUARDIAN LIFE INSURANCE COMPANY LIMITED *

A-   **Excellent**

Major Rating Factors: Good quality investment portfolio (6.6 on a scale of 0 to 10) despite large exposure to mortgages . Mortgage default rate has been low. substantial holdings of BBB bonds in addition to no exposure to junk bonds. Good liquidity (6.2) with sufficient resources to handle a spike in claims as well as a significant increase in policy surrenders. Strong capitalization (9.6) based on excellent risk adjusted capital (severe loss scenario).
Other Rating Factors: Excellent profitability (7.7) with operating gains in each of the last five years. Excellent overall results on stability tests (7.0) excellent operational trends and excellent risk diversification.
Principal Business: Individual life insurance (42%), group health insurance (42%), and group life insurance (16%).
Principal Investments: NonCMO investment grade bonds (41%), mortgages in good standing (35%), CMOs and structured securities (18%), and policy loans (6%).
Investments in Affiliates: None
Group Affiliation: Meiji Yasuda Life Ins Co
Licensed in: AK, AZ, CA, CO, HI, ID, IA, LA, MO, MT, NE, NV, NM, OK, OR, SD, TX, UT, WA, WY
Commenced Business: June 1962
Address: 1440 Kapiolani Blvd Ste 1700, Honolulu, HI 96814
Phone: (808) 955-2236   **Domicile State:** HI   **NAIC Code:** 64343

Data Date	Rating	RACR #1	RACR #2	Total Assets ($mil)	Capital ($mil)	Net Premium ($mil)	Net Income ($mil)
6-14	A-	4.81	2.75	518.1	105.2	38.2	4.1
6-13	A-	4.70	2.72	507.9	97.1	37.8	3.4
2013	A-	5.09	2.93	504.7	108.0	69.8	6.9
2012	A-	4.98	2.91	486.8	99.8	70.5	6.2
2011	A-	4.90	2.87	464.2	99.6	66.3	7.0
2010	A-	4.84	2.85	448.4	96.4	63.4	9.9
2009	A-	3.73	2.23	433.3	87.5	66.3	6.6

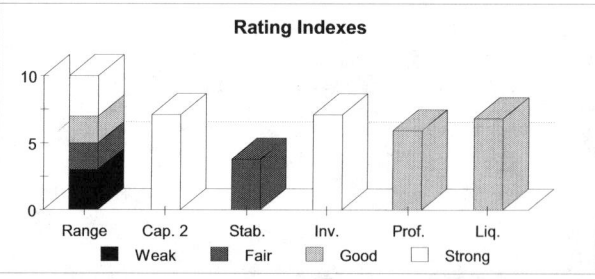

Rating Indexes

PACIFICARE LIFE & HEALTH INSURANCE COMPANY   C+   Fair

Major Rating Factors: Fair overall results on stability tests (3.5 on a scale of 0 to 10) including fair financial strength of affiliated UnitedHealth Group Inc. Good overall profitability (6.4). Excellent expense controls. Return on equity has been fair, averaging 9.9%. Strong capitalization (10.0) based on excellent risk adjusted capital (severe loss scenario).

Other Rating Factors: High quality investment portfolio (8.4). Excellent liquidity (9.3).

Principal Business: Group health insurance (58%) and individual health insurance (42%).

Principal Investments: NonCMO investment grade bonds (86%) and CMOs and structured securities (15%).

Investments in Affiliates: None

Group Affiliation: UnitedHealth Group Inc

Licensed in: All states except NY, PR

Commenced Business: September 1967

Address: 23046 Avenida Dela Carlota 700, Laguna Hills, CA 92653-1519

Phone: (714) 226-3321 **Domicile State:** IN **NAIC Code:** 70785

Data Date	Rating	RACR #1	RACR #2	Total Assets ($mil)	Capital ($mil)	Net Premium ($mil)	Net Income ($mil)
6-14	C+	34.61	22.36	554.9	538.2	23.8	4.2
6-13	C+	25.21	16.78	619.5	591.5	56.6	11.6
2013	C+	29.46	19.62	616.2	592.6	104.7	13.2
2012	C+	23.08	15.56	622.2	582.0	139.3	18.7
2011	C+	19.76	14.03	695.3	650.6	205.8	87.4
2010	B-	20.19	14.98	848.3	677.6	225.6	117.6
2009	B-	15.23	11.50	745.7	680.5	322.1	120.7

UnitedHealth Group Inc Composite Group Rating: C+ Largest Group Members	Assets ($mil)	Rating
UNITED HEALTHCARE INS CO	14513	C
OXFORD HEALTH INS INC	2078	C+
UNITED HEALTHCARE INS CO OF NY	1983	B-
OXFORD HEALTH PLANS (NY) INC	1820	A+
UNITEDHEALTHCARE PLAN RIVER VALLEY	1094	B+

PACIFICARE OF ARIZONA INC   B   Good

Major Rating Factors: Good overall results on stability tests (5.2 on a scale of 0 to 10). Rating is significantly influenced by the fair financial results of UnitedHealth Group Inc. Good liquidity (6.8) with sufficient resources (cash flows and marketable investments) to handle a spike in claims. Excellent profitability (7.9).

Other Rating Factors: Strong capitalization index (8.7) based on excellent current risk-adjusted capital (severe loss scenario). High quality investment portfolio (9.6).

Principal Business: Medicare (100%)

Mem Phys: 13: 12,620 **12:** 11,953 **13 MLR** 85.2% **/ 13 Admin Exp** N/A

Enroll(000): Q2 14: 93 **13:** 96 **12:** 93 **Med Exp PMPM:** $730

Principal Investments: Long-term bonds (96%), cash and equiv (4%)

Provider Compensation ($000): Capitation ($442,132), contr fee ($361,567), bonus arrang ($3,395)

Total Member Encounters: Phys (345,764), non-phys (31,329)

Group Affiliation: UnitedHealth Group Inc

Licensed in: AZ

Address: 2390 E Camelback Rd #300, Phoenix, AZ 85016

Phone: (800) 985-2356 **Dom State:** AZ **Commenced Bus:** July 1997

Data Date	Rating	RACR #1	RACR #2	Total Assets ($mil)	Capital ($mil)	Net Premium ($mil)	Net Income ($mil)
6-14	B	2.68	2.23	255.6	98.0	501.7	6.5
6-13	C+	2.90	2.42	194.9	92.0	491.7	10.5
2013	B	2.51	2.09	190.3	91.3	986.4	38.8
2012	C+	2.62	2.18	162.5	82.3	970.4	46.4
2011	B	2.56	2.14	175.4	99.8	977.5	5.8
2010	B	2.09	1.74	193.0	100.5	1,040.6	9.7
2009	B	1.90	1.59	190.7	106.2	1,158.1	13.3

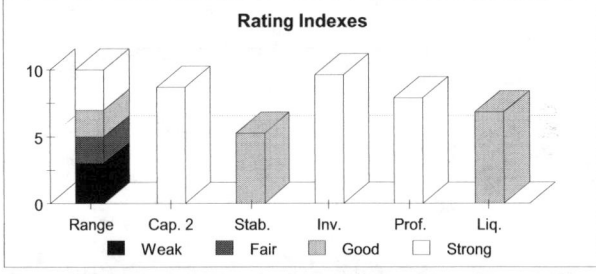

Rating Indexes — Range, Cap. 2, Stab., Inv., Prof., Liq. — Weak, Fair, Good, Strong

PACIFICARE OF COLORADO INC   B-   Good

Major Rating Factors: Fair overall results on stability tests (4.0 on a scale of 0 to 10). Rating is significantly influenced by the fair financial results of UnitedHealth Group Inc. Good liquidity (6.9) with sufficient resources (cash flows and marketable investments) to handle a spike in claims. Excellent profitability (8.2).

Other Rating Factors: Strong capitalization index (8.8) based on excellent current risk-adjusted capital (severe loss scenario). High quality investment portfolio (9.9).

Principal Business: Medicare (100%)

Mem Phys: 13: 579 **12:** 561 **13 MLR** 80.9% **/ 13 Admin Exp** N/A

Enroll(000): Q2 14: 96 **13:** 89 **12:** 79 **Med Exp PMPM:** $651

Principal Investments: Long-term bonds (76%), cash and equiv (24%)

Provider Compensation ($000): Contr fee ($391,767), capitation ($273,028), bonus arrang ($9,592)

Total Member Encounters: Phys (441,547), non-phys (51,831)

Group Affiliation: UnitedHealth Group Inc

Licensed in: CO

Address: 6465 Greenwood Plaza Blvd #300, Centennial, CO 80111

Phone: (303) 267-3570 **Dom State:** CO **Commenced Bus:** November 1987

Data Date	Rating	RACR #1	RACR #2	Total Assets ($mil)	Capital ($mil)	Net Premium ($mil)	Net Income ($mil)
6-14	B-	2.80	2.33	249.8	102.4	478.0	17.9
6-13	B-	2.99	2.49	195.4	105.9	426.7	22.5
2013	B	3.65	3.04	211.3	134.2	849.8	50.9
2012	B-	2.39	1.99	164.0	83.7	813.0	62.5
2011	B-	2.38	1.98	142.4	81.9	756.6	58.0
2010	B-	2.98	2.49	160.3	103.9	729.0	69.8
2009	B-	2.93	2.44	195.7	124.9	848.6	46.4

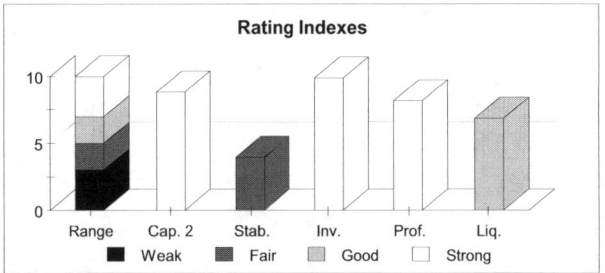

Rating Indexes — Range, Cap. 2, Stab., Inv., Prof., Liq. — Weak, Fair, Good, Strong

PACIFICARE OF NEVADA INC   E   Very Weak

Major Rating Factors: Weak profitability index (0.9 on a scale of 0 to 10). Weak overall results on stability tests (2.8) based on an excessive 265% enrollment growth during the period. Rating is significantly influenced by the fair financial results of UnitedHealth Group Inc. Fair liquidity (3.5) as cash resources may not be adequate to cover a spike in claims.

Other Rating Factors: Strong capitalization index (8.9) based on excellent current risk-adjusted capital (severe loss scenario). High quality investment portfolio (9.9).

Principal Business: Medicare (100%)

Mem Phys: 13: 4,126   **12:** 4,453   **13 MLR** 102.2%   / **13 Admin Exp** N/A

Enroll(000): Q2 14: 11   **13:** 10   **12:** 3   **Med Exp PMPM:** $813

Principal Investments: Cash and equiv (88%), long-term bonds (12%)

Provider Compensation ($000): Contr fee ($49,720), capitation ($31,843), FFS ($126)

Total Member Encounters: Phys (830), non-phys (1,997)

Group Affiliation: UnitedHealth Group Inc

Licensed in: NV

Address: 2720 N Tenaya Way, Las Vegas, NV 89128

Phone: (702) 242-7000   **Dom State:** NV   **Commenced Bus:** September 1997

Data Date	Rating	RACR #1	RACR #2	Total Assets ($mil)	Capital ($mil)	Net Premium ($mil)	Net Income ($mil)
6-14	E	2.88	2.40	27.5	13.9	54.3	0.3
6-13	E	3.59	2.99	12.7	3.2	40.7	-3.2
2013	E	1.86	1.55	26.0	8.3	86.6	-11.3
2012	C	4.84	4.03	10.5	5.9	28.5	-0.2
2011	C	15.78	13.15	17.4	15.9	20.0	3.5
2010	C	15.61	13.01	41.4	37.2	43.5	0.7
2009	C+	16.72	13.94	76.3	65.8	74.2	0.5

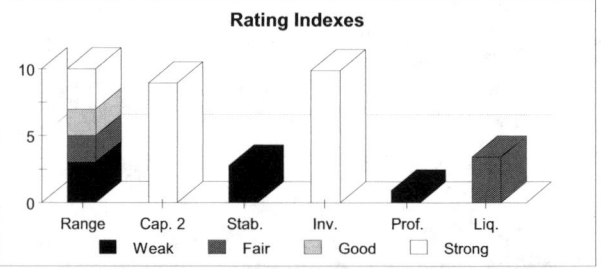

Rating Indexes

PACIFICARE OF OKLAHOMA INC   B   Good

Major Rating Factors: Good overall results on stability tests (5.6 on a scale of 0 to 10) despite a decline in enrollment during 2013. Rating is significantly influenced by the fair financial results of UnitedHealth Group Inc. Good liquidity (6.8) with sufficient resources (cash flows and marketable investments) to handle a spike in claims. Excellent profitability (9.1).

Other Rating Factors: Strong capitalization index (9.5) based on excellent current risk-adjusted capital (severe loss scenario). High quality investment portfolio (9.9).

Principal Business: Medicare (86%), comp med (14%)

Mem Phys: 13: 13,140   **12:** 7,298   **13 MLR** 81.5%   / **13 Admin Exp** N/A

Enroll(000): Q2 14: 41   **13:** 41   **12:** 52   **Med Exp PMPM:** $599

Principal Investments: Long-term bonds (87%), cash and equiv (13%)

Provider Compensation ($000): Contr fee ($270,280), FFS ($13,389), capitation ($5,297), bonus arrang ($4,258)

Total Member Encounters: Phys (310,963), non-phys (41,625)

Group Affiliation: UnitedHealth Group Inc

Licensed in: OK

Address: 7666 E 61st St, Tulsa, OK 74133

Phone: (512) 347-2600   **Dom State:** OK   **Commenced Bus:** September 1985

Data Date	Rating	RACR #1	RACR #2	Total Assets ($mil)	Capital ($mil)	Net Premium ($mil)	Net Income ($mil)
6-14	B	3.32	2.77	119.0	65.8	189.8	7.5
6-13	B	2.83	2.36	107.6	62.1	182.6	12.7
2013	B	2.95	2.46	105.0	58.2	362.3	21.4
2012	B	2.26	1.88	97.3	48.8	418.7	25.8
2011	B	2.08	1.73	83.8	41.4	400.9	32.5
2010	B	2.07	1.73	77.7	38.9	357.5	18.4
2009	B	2.54	2.11	72.0	42.8	331.9	22.8

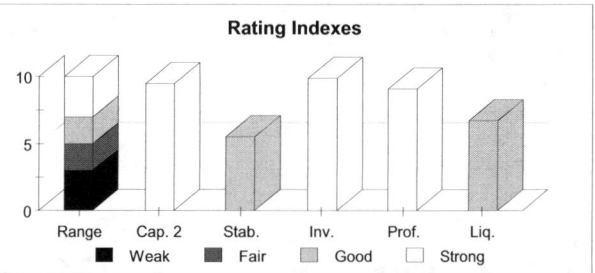

Rating Indexes

PACIFICSOURCE COMMUNITY HEALTH PLANS   C   Fair

Major Rating Factors: Weak profitability index (0.9 on a scale of 0 to 10). Good quality investment portfolio (4.9). Good liquidity (5.3) with sufficient resources (cash flows and marketable investments) to handle a spike in claims.

Other Rating Factors: Strong capitalization (7.2) based on excellent current risk-adjusted capital (severe loss scenario).

Principal Business: Medicare (100%)

Mem Phys: 13: 16,314   **12:** 13,088   **13 MLR** 94.0%   / **13 Admin Exp** N/A

Enroll(000): Q2 14: 38   **13:** 37   **12:** 18   **Med Exp PMPM:** $673

Principal Investments: Affiliate common stock (53%), long-term bonds (26%), cash and equiv (17%), other (4%)

Provider Compensation ($000): Contr fee ($246,010), FFS ($19,068), bonus arrang ($2,648), capitation ($929)

Total Member Encounters: Phys (283,223), non-phys (67,986)

Group Affiliation: PacificSource Health Plan

Licensed in: MT, OR

Address: 2965 NE Conners Ave, Bend, OR 97701

Phone: (541) 385-5315   **Dom State:** OR   **Commenced Bus:** March 2007

Data Date	Rating	RACR #1	RACR #2	Total Assets ($mil)	Capital ($mil)	Net Premium ($mil)	Net Income ($mil)
6-14	C	1.48	1.24	92.4	46.2	162.4	-7.0
6-13	C	2.23	1.86	76.9	45.4	149.6	2.2
2013	C	1.33	1.11	78.8	41.5	300.4	-6.6
2012	C	2.15	1.79	70.4	44.0	165.5	-4.1
2011	C	2.73	2.27	69.6	45.3	121.8	-1.5
2010	C	2.36	1.97	82.4	46.3	134.3	-1.3
2009	C	N/A	N/A	82.7	44.4	146.9	-7.5

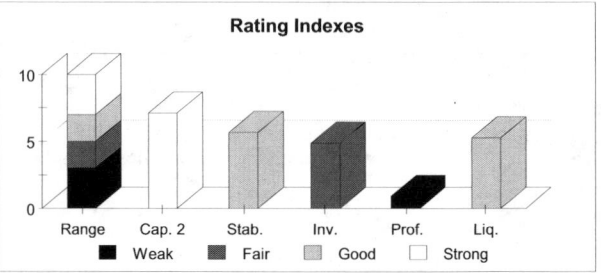

Rating Indexes

PACIFICSOURCE HEALTH PLANS   B-   Good

Major Rating Factors: Good quality investment portfolio (6.4 on a scale of 0 to 10). Good liquidity (6.5) with sufficient resources (cash flows and marketable investments) to handle a spike in claims. Strong capitalization (7.3) based on excellent current risk-adjusted capital (severe loss scenario).
Other Rating Factors: Weak profitability index (2.7).
Principal Business: Comp med (98%)
Mem Phys: 13: 47,359   **12:** 44,328   **13 MLR** 88.3%   **/ 13 Admin Exp** N/A
Enroll(000): Q2 14: 178   **13:** 207   **12:** 224   **Med Exp PMPM:** $247
Principal Investments: Long-term bonds (48%), affiliate common stock (26%), cash and equiv (19%), nonaffiliate common stock (6%), other (1%)
Provider Compensation ($000): Contr fee ($371,164), FFS ($264,163), bonus arrang ($9,268), capitation ($94)
Total Member Encounters: Phys (554,168), non-phys (289,387)
Group Affiliation: PacificSource Health Plan
Licensed in: ID, OR, WA
Address: 110 International Way, Springfield, OR 97477
Phone: (541) 686-1242   **Dom State:** OR   **Commenced Bus:** July 1939

Data Date	Rating	RACR #1	RACR #2	Total Assets ($mil)	Capital ($mil)	Net Premium ($mil)	Net Income ($mil)
6-14	B-	1.58	1.32	237.9	152.0	317.4	-4.9
6-13	B-	1.42	1.18	213.6	126.1	367.0	12.8
2013	B-	1.57	1.31	230.1	151.3	724.1	14.7
2012	B-	1.23	1.02	209.2	109.8	722.2	-25.9
2011	B	1.73	1.44	203.5	125.7	644.2	10.9
2010	B+	1.51	1.26	196.4	114.1	583.0	8.1
2009	B	2.17	1.80	173.6	107.1	520.6	4.3

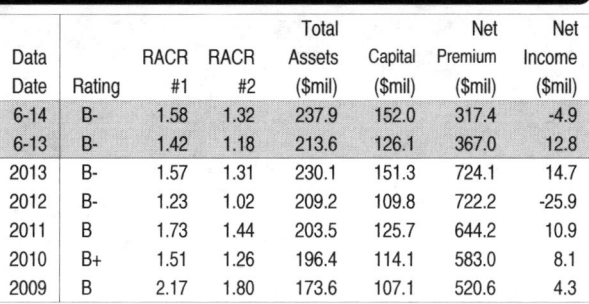

PAN-AMERICAN LIFE INSURANCE COMPANY   B   Good

Major Rating Factors: Good quality investment portfolio (5.4 on a scale of 0 to 10) despite mixed results such as: large holdings of BBB rated bonds but moderate junk bond exposure. Good overall profitability (6.4). Return on equity has been fair, averaging 7.1%. Good liquidity (6.2) with sufficient resources to handle a spike in claims as well as a significant increase in policy surrenders.
Other Rating Factors: Good overall results on stability tests (6.0) despite negative cash flow from operations for 2013 excellent operational trends and excellent risk diversification. Strong capitalization (7.7) based on excellent risk adjusted capital (severe loss scenario).
Principal Business: Group health insurance (65%), individual life insurance (15%), reinsurance (11%), individual health insurance (5%), and group life insurance (3%).
Principal Investments: NonCMO investment grade bonds (67%), noninv. grade bonds (9%), CMOs and structured securities (7%), policy loans (6%), and misc. investments (10%).
Investments in Affiliates: 2%
Group Affiliation: Pan-American Life
Licensed in: All states except ME, NY, VT
Commenced Business: March 1912
Address: Pan American Life Center, New Orleans, LA 70130
Phone: (504) 566-1300   **Domicile State:** LA   **NAIC Code:** 67539

Data Date	Rating	RACR #1	RACR #2	Total Assets ($mil)	Capital ($mil)	Net Premium ($mil)	Net Income ($mil)
6-14	B	2.34	1.45	1,420.2	253.7	136.0	12.1
6-13	B	2.13	1.31	1,463.6	235.9	139.8	20.7
2013	B	2.29	1.43	1,425.5	244.6	270.3	27.3
2012	B	2.12	1.31	1,444.4	226.6	255.0	15.3
2011	B	2.36	1.45	1,478.2	248.4	239.3	23.0
2010	B	2.41	1.45	1,487.7	256.7	218.3	24.8
2009	B	2.48	1.47	1,515.4	259.4	190.3	9.0

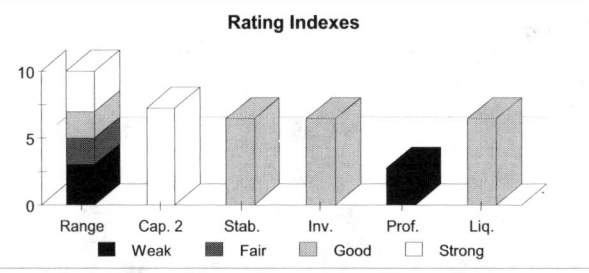

PARAMOUNT ADVANTAGE *   A-   Excellent

Major Rating Factors: Excellent profitability (8.9 on a scale of 0 to 10). Strong capitalization (8.0) based on excellent current risk-adjusted capital (severe loss scenario). High quality investment portfolio (9.9).
Other Rating Factors: Excellent liquidity (6.9) with sufficient resources (cash flows and marketable investments) to handle a spike in claims.
Principal Business: Medicaid (100%)
Mem Phys: 13: 16,930   **12:** 1,654   **13 MLR** 81.2%   **/ 13 Admin Exp** N/A
Enroll(000): Q2 14: 182   **13:** 141   **12:** 95   **Med Exp PMPM:** $224
Principal Investments: Long-term bonds (56%), cash and equiv (44%)
Provider Compensation ($000): Contr fee ($143,200), FFS ($128,918), capitation ($24,842)
Total Member Encounters: Phys (31,068), non-phys (55,730)
Group Affiliation: ProMedica Health System Inc
Licensed in: OH
Address: 1901 Indian Wood Cir, Maumee, OH 43537
Phone: (419) 887-2500   **Dom State:** OH   **Commenced Bus:** December 2005

Data Date	Rating	RACR #1	RACR #2	Total Assets ($mil)	Capital ($mil)	Net Premium ($mil)	Net Income ($mil)
6-14	A-	2.12	1.77	172.9	65.1	285.6	1.9
6-13	B+	2.36	1.96	91.6	57.7	147.6	-0.3
2013	B+	2.08	1.73	130.2	63.7	390.0	5.5
2012	B+	2.37	1.97	95.1	58.0	294.8	9.6
2011	B+	2.16	1.80	84.1	48.4	240.8	6.4
2010	B+	2.13	1.78	67.4	42.1	213.5	10.1
2009	C	1.46	1.22	74.2	31.9	210.9	2.6

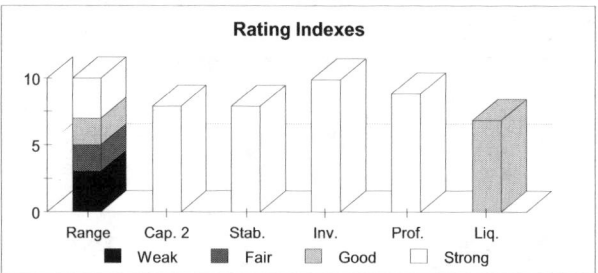

PARAMOUNT CARE OF MI INC

B-   **Good**

Major Rating Factors: Fair overall results on stability tests (4.1 on a scale of 0 to 10) based on a steep decline in premium revenue in 2013, a significant 60% decrease in enrollment during the period. Rating is significantly influenced by the good financial results of ProMedica Health System Inc. Strong capitalization index (7.7) based on excellent current risk-adjusted capital (severe loss scenario). High quality investment portfolio (9.9).

Other Rating Factors: Excellent liquidity (7.4) with ample operational cash flow and liquid investments. Weak profitability index (1.4).

Principal Business: Medicare (70%), comp med (30%)

Mem Phys: 13: 1,487 **12:** 1,332 **13 MLR** 95.9% **/ 13 Admin Exp** N/A

Enroll(000): Q2 14: 2 **13:** 2 **12:** 5 **Med Exp PMPM:** $583

Principal Investments: Cash and equiv (100%)

Provider Compensation ($000): FFS ($12,041), contr fee ($11,569)

Total Member Encounters: Phys (1,617), non-phys (3,850)

Group Affiliation: ProMedica Health System Inc

Licensed in: MI

Address: 106 Park Pl, Dundee, MI 48131

Phone: (734) 529-7800 **Dom State:** MI **Commenced Bus:** June 1996

Data Date	Rating	RACR #1	RACR #2	Total Assets ($mil)	Capital ($mil)	Net Premium ($mil)	Net Income ($mil)
6-14	B-	1.88	1.57	10.3	6.8	8.4	-0.7
6-13	C	1.70	1.42	13.2	7.7	13.4	-0.4
2013	C+	2.06	1.72	10.8	7.5	23.1	0.0
2012	C+	1.78	1.48	13.3	8.0	30.4	-1.9
2011	B	1.93	1.61	13.7	9.5	31.7	0.7
2010	B	1.73	1.44	12.9	8.3	32.8	0.1
2009	B	2.08	1.73	14.5	10.5	33.9	0.5

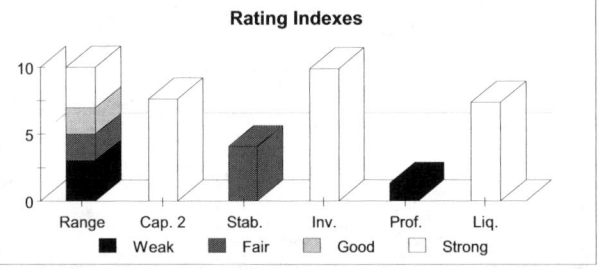

Rating Indexes

PARAMOUNT HEALTH CARE

C   **Fair**

Major Rating Factors: Fair profitability index (3.2 on a scale of 0 to 10). Fair overall results on stability tests (4.4) based on a significant 72% decrease in enrollment during the period. Good liquidity (6.9) with sufficient resources (cash flows and marketable investments) to handle a spike in claims.

Other Rating Factors: Strong capitalization index (9.3) based on excellent current risk-adjusted capital (severe loss scenario). High quality investment portfolio (8.3).

Principal Business: Medicare (67%), comp med (33%)

Mem Phys: 13: 2,093 **12:** 1,861 **13 MLR** 91.4% **/ 13 Admin Exp** N/A

Enroll(000): Q2 14: 12 **13:** 12 **12:** 44 **Med Exp PMPM:** $558

Principal Investments: Long-term bonds (60%), nonaffiliate common stock (25%), cash and equiv (15%)

Provider Compensation ($000): Contr fee ($108,583), FFS ($100,689)

Total Member Encounters: Phys (12,250), non-phys (28,727)

Group Affiliation: ProMedica Health System Inc

Licensed in: OH

Address: 1901 Indian Wood Cir, Maumee, OH 43537-4068

Phone: (419) 887-2500 **Dom State:** OH **Commenced Bus:** January 1988

Data Date	Rating	RACR #1	RACR #2	Total Assets ($mil)	Capital ($mil)	Net Premium ($mil)	Net Income ($mil)
6-14	C	3.17	2.64	97.9	65.1	71.7	0.9
6-13	C-	2.11	1.76	108.6	59.5	131.3	1.2
2013	C	3.13	2.61	98.8	64.4	212.8	7.2
2012	C-	2.06	1.72	111.6	58.2	270.3	-8.6
2011	D+	1.58	1.31	120.8	65.1	277.9	4.4
2010	D+	1.59	1.33	160.7	43.1	280.9	-14.2
2009	B	1.74	1.45	146.1	56.1	331.1	10.9

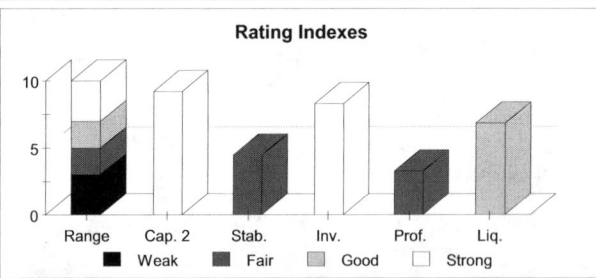

Rating Indexes

PARAMOUNT INS CO

B-   **Good**

Major Rating Factors: Fair profitability index (3.6 on a scale of 0 to 10). Strong capitalization (7.9) based on excellent current risk-adjusted capital (severe loss scenario). High quality investment portfolio (9.9).

Other Rating Factors: Excellent liquidity (7.2) with ample operational cash flow and liquid investments.

Principal Business: Comp med (96%), med supp (4%)

Mem Phys: 13: 2,093 **12:** 1,861 **13 MLR** 82.4% **/ 13 Admin Exp** N/A

Enroll(000): Q2 14: 40 **13:** 40 **12:** 9 **Med Exp PMPM:** $237

Principal Investments: Cash and equiv (83%), long-term bonds (17%)

Provider Compensation ($000): FFS ($36,682), contr fee ($20,299)

Total Member Encounters: Phys (8,571), non-phys (18,970)

Group Affiliation: ProMedica Health System Inc

Licensed in: MI, OH

Address: 1901 Indian Wood Cir, Maumee, OH 43537

Phone: (419) 887-2500 **Dom State:** OH **Commenced Bus:** September 2002

Data Date	Rating	RACR #1	RACR #2	Total Assets ($mil)	Capital ($mil)	Net Premium ($mil)	Net Income ($mil)
6-14	B-	2.12	1.76	53.7	16.7	74.5	2.5
6-13	C	3.19	2.66	18.9	12.2	15.1	-0.5
2013	C+	1.87	1.56	35.0	14.6	79.2	1.9
2012	C	3.32	2.77	18.6	12.8	26.9	-0.9
2011	C	4.03	3.36	19.6	13.7	23.0	1.5
2010	C	1.99	1.66	19.6	12.0	37.3	-1.0
2009	C	1.43	1.20	18.2	6.1	34.3	-7.0

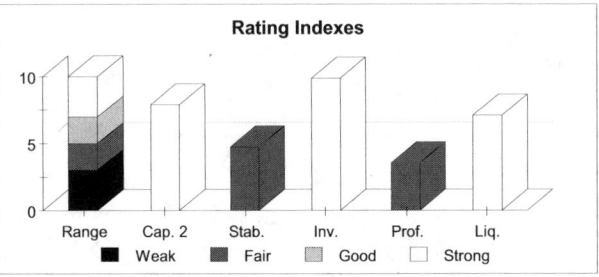

Rating Indexes

PARKLAND COMMUNITY HEALTH PLAN INC　　　　　　B　　　　Good

Major Rating Factors: Good overall results on stability tests (5.5 on a scale of 0 to 10). Excellent profitability (7.0). Strong capitalization index (9.2) based on excellent current risk-adjusted capital (severe loss scenario).
Other Rating Factors: High quality investment portfolio (9.9). Excellent liquidity (7.0) with ample operational cash flow and liquid investments.
Principal Business: Medicaid (86%), comp med (14%)
Mem Phys: 13: 5,863　**12:** 5,678　**13 MLR** 83.6%　**/ 13 Admin Exp** N/A
Enroll(000): Q2 14: 200　**13:** 198　**12:** 204　**Med Exp PMPM:** $177
Principal Investments: Long-term bonds (52%), cash and equiv (48%)
Provider Compensation ($000): Contr fee ($431,705), capitation ($3,539)
Total Member Encounters: Phys (1,587,699), non-phys (460,285)
Group Affiliation: Dallas County Hospital District
Licensed in: TX
Address: 2777 N Stemmons Fwy Suite 1750, Dallas, TX 75207
Phone: (214) 266-2100　**Dom State:** TX　**Commenced Bus:** January 1998

Data Date	Rating	RACR #1	RACR #2	Total Assets ($mil)	Capital ($mil)	Net Premium ($mil)	Net Income ($mil)
6-14	B	3.09	2.58	188.4	125.6	250.4	19.0
6-13	B	1.87	1.55	123.6	78.8	257.6	-0.6
2013	B	2.63	2.19	157.6	106.7	518.6	27.3
2012	B	1.88	1.57	130.3	79.4	514.1	24.2
2011	B-	2.80	2.34	150.7	95.1	469.0	44.3
2010	C	1.31	1.09	131.0	55.6	454.9	0.6
2009	C	2.22	1.85	135.6	80.3	399.2	5.9

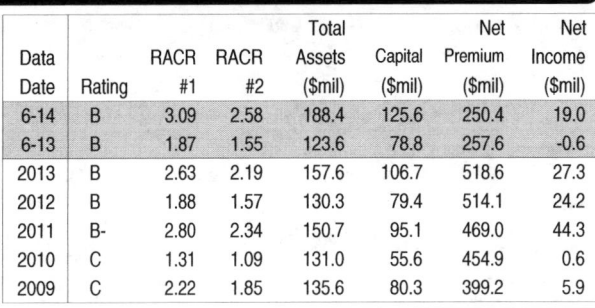

PARTNERRE AMERICA INS CO　　　　　　　　　　　C　　　　Fair

Major Rating Factors: Fair overall results on stability tests (4.0 on a scale of 0 to 10) including potential drain of affiliation with PartnerRe Ltd, excessive premium growth, weak results on operational trends and negative cash flow from operations for 2013. Good overall profitability index (6.1). Weak expense controls. Return on equity has been good over the last five years, averaging 10.5%.
Other Rating Factors: Strong long-term capitalization index (10.0) based on excellent current risk adjusted capital (severe and moderate loss scenarios), despite some fluctuation in capital levels. Ample reserve history (7.0) that can protect against increases in claims costs. Excellent liquidity (7.0) with ample operational cash flow and liquid investments.
Principal Business: Other liability (34%), other accident & health (32%), aircraft (24%), auto liability (8%), and auto physical damage (3%).
Principal Investments: Investment grade bonds (61%) and cash (40%).
Investments in Affiliates: None
Group Affiliation: PartnerRe Ltd
Licensed in: All states except ME, NH, VT
Commenced Business: August 1919
Address: 1209 Orange St, Wilmington, DE 19801
Phone: (305) 377-1292　**Domicile State:** DE　**NAIC Code:** 11835

Data Date	Rating	RACR #1	RACR #2	Loss Ratio %	Total Assets ($mil)	Capital ($mil)	Net Premium ($mil)	Net Income ($mil)
6-14	C	14.93	13.43	N/A	270.4	132.3	11.1	3.9
6-13	C	33.96	30.56	N/A	146.1	122.6	1.5	0.8
2013	C	23.52	21.17	64.9	169.4	128.5	-0.2	0.8
2012	C	13.77	9.39	N/A	185.7	121.8	2.1	34.1
2011	C	2.12	1.53	73.4	206.6	83.9	9.3	17.5
2010	C	2.01	1.46	73.0	327.3	149.4	80.4	0.2
2009	C	5.11	3.67	60.3	283.5	158.3	29.8	8.3

PartnerRe Ltd Composite Group Rating: C- Largest Group Members	Assets ($mil)	Rating
PARTNER REINSURANCE CO OF THE US	4887	C-
PARTNERRE AMERICA INS CO	169	C
PARTNERRE INS CO OF NEW YORK	136	C

PARTNERSHIP HEALTHPLAN OF CALIFORNIA *　　　A-　　　Excellent

Major Rating Factors: Excellent profitability (9.4 on a scale of 0 to 10). Strong capitalization index (10.0) based on excellent current risk-adjusted capital (severe loss scenario). Excellent overall results on stability tests (7.0).
Other Rating Factors: Excellent liquidity (7.3) with ample operational cash flow and liquid investments.
Principal Business: Medicaid (87%), Medicare (13%)
Mem Phys: 13: N/A　**12:** N/A　**13 MLR** 86.4%　**/ 13 Admin Exp** N/A
Enroll(000): Q2 14: 351　**13:** 221　**12:** 204　**Med Exp PMPM:** $323
Principal Investments ($000): Cash and equiv ($209,647)
Provider Compensation ($000): None
Total Member Encounters: N/A
Group Affiliation: None
Licensed in: CA
Address: 360 Campus Lane Suite 100, Fairfield, CA 94534-4036
Phone: (707) 863-4100　**Dom State:** CA　**Commenced Bus:** November 2005

Data Date	Rating	RACR #1	RACR #2	Total Assets ($mil)	Capital ($mil)	Net Premium ($mil)	Net Income ($mil)
6-14	A-	7.26	4.45	502.0	286.3	665.2	50.2
6-13	A-	4.63	2.83	311.3	190.5	428.9	16.5
2013	A-	6.00	3.68	378.0	236.0	928.9	62.0
2012	B+	4.23	2.58	351.9	174.1	906.2	51.4
2011	B	3.79	2.32	248.4	122.6	696.6	50.2
2010	B	2.32	1.42	180.6	72.4	605.5	31.5
2009	C+	2.03	1.24	111.3	40.9	429.8	17.1

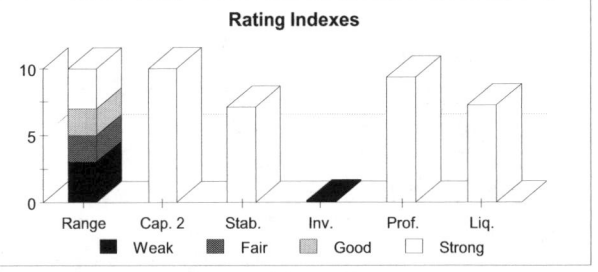

PAUL REVERE LIFE INSURANCE COMPANY

C+   **Fair**

Major Rating Factors: Fair overall results on stability tests (4.8 on a scale of 0 to 10) including fair financial strength of affiliated Unum Group and negative cash flow from operations for 2013. Fair quality investment portfolio (4.6) with large holdings of BBB rated bonds in addition to junk bond exposure equal to 81% of capital. Good overall profitability (5.9).

Other Rating Factors: Strong capitalization (7.3) based on excellent risk adjusted capital (severe loss scenario). Excellent liquidity (7.6).

Principal Business: Individual health insurance (66%), reinsurance (28%), group health insurance (4%), and individual life insurance (3%).

Principal Investments: NonCMO investment grade bonds (78%), noninv. grade bonds (7%), CMOs and structured securities (6%), common & preferred stock (5%), and mortgages in good standing (3%).

Investments in Affiliates: 3%

Group Affiliation: Unum Group

Licensed in: All states except PR

Commenced Business: July 1930

Address: 18 Chestnut St, Worcester, MA 01608

Phone: (508) 792-6377 **Domicile State:** MA **NAIC Code:** 67598

Data Date	Rating	RACR #1	RACR #2	Total Assets ($mil)	Capital ($mil)	Net Premium ($mil)	Net Income ($mil)
6-14	C+	1.89	1.20	4,273.4	360.8	46.7	38.9
6-13	C+	2.02	1.26	4,398.1	376.2	46.6	36.7
2013	C+	1.78	1.13	4,301.8	336.1	90.4	66.5
2012	C+	1.99	1.23	4,458.2	368.3	91.9	81.7
2011	C+	2.21	1.36	4,602.4	408.0	93.4	89.8
2010	C+	2.25	1.39	4,678.4	419.5	90.4	64.9
2009	C+	2.54	1.54	4,744.8	450.5	92.0	131.4

Unum Group Composite Group Rating: C+ Largest Group Members	Assets ($mil)	Rating
UNUM LIFE INS CO OF AMERICA	19079	C+
PROVIDENT LIFE ACCIDENT INS CO	8348	C+
PAUL REVERE LIFE INS CO	4302	C+
COLONIAL LIFE ACCIDENT INS CO	2753	C+
FIRST UNUM LIFE INS CO	2704	C+

PEACH STATE HEALTH PLAN INC

C   **Fair**

Major Rating Factors: Weak profitability index (2.7 on a scale of 0 to 10). Strong capitalization (8.2) based on excellent current risk-adjusted capital (severe loss scenario). High quality investment portfolio (9.9).

Other Rating Factors: Excellent liquidity (6.9) with sufficient resources (cash flows and marketable investments) to handle a spike in claims.

Principal Business: Medicaid (100%)

Mem Phys: 13: 15,244 **12:** 14,271 **13 MLR** 86.2% **/ 13 Admin Exp** N/A

Enroll(000): Q2 14: 373 **13:** 319 **12:** 314 **Med Exp PMPM:** $187

Principal Investments: Cash and equiv (71%), long-term bonds (19%), affiliate common stock (10%)

Provider Compensation ($000): Contr fee ($559,420), capitation ($103,273), salary ($8,920), bonus arrang ($2,959)

Total Member Encounters: Phys (1,452,751), non-phys (1,022,989)

Group Affiliation: Centene Corp

Licensed in: GA

Address: 3200 Highlands Pkwy SE Ste 300, Smyrna, GA 30082

Phone: (314) 725-4477 **Dom State:** GA **Commenced Bus:** June 2006

Data Date	Rating	RACR #1	RACR #2	Total Assets ($mil)	Capital ($mil)	Net Premium ($mil)	Net Income ($mil)
6-14	C	2.33	1.94	213.4	93.8	502.4	1.7
6-13	C	2.12	1.77	152.9	83.6	387.5	-2.0
2013	C	2.23	1.86	170.5	89.5	799.0	-3.9
2012	C	2.07	1.72	155.2	85.0	764.1	-18.0
2011	C	2.16	1.80	160.3	100.1	777.6	16.5
2010	C	1.83	1.52	172.8	88.2	751.1	23.7
2009	C	1.26	1.05	158.5	63.0	752.0	-36.3

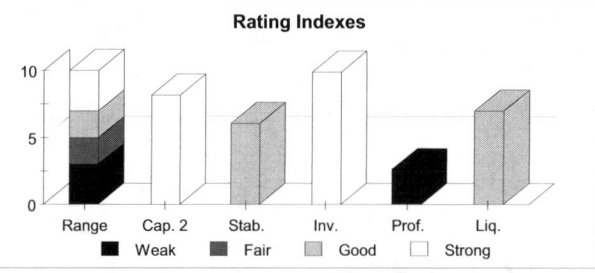

Rating Indexes

PEKIN LIFE INSURANCE COMPANY

B   **Good**

Major Rating Factors: Good overall profitability (6.4 on a scale of 0 to 10). Return on equity has been low, averaging 1.0%. Good liquidity (5.9) with sufficient resources to cover a large increase in policy surrenders. Good overall results on stability tests (6.2). Stability strengths include excellent operational trends and excellent risk diversification.

Other Rating Factors: Strong capitalization (7.6) based on excellent risk adjusted capital (severe loss scenario). High quality investment portfolio (7.0).

Principal Business: Individual life insurance (29%), group health insurance (22%), group life insurance (18%), individual health insurance (12%), and other lines (19%).

Principal Investments: NonCMO investment grade bonds (66%), CMOs and structured securities (25%), policy loans (1%), and common & preferred stock (1%).

Investments in Affiliates: None

Group Affiliation: Farmers Automobile Ins Assn

Licensed in: AL, AZ, AR, IL, IN, IA, KS, KY, LA, MI, MN, MS, MO, NE, OH, PA, WI

Commenced Business: September 1965

Address: 2505 Court St, Pekin, IL 61558

Phone: (309) 346-1161 **Domicile State:** IL **NAIC Code:** 67628

Data Date	Rating	RACR #1	RACR #2	Total Assets ($mil)	Capital ($mil)	Net Premium ($mil)	Net Income ($mil)
6-14	B	2.30	1.40	1,304.1	125.4	103.4	3.7
6-13	B	2.20	1.36	1,249.9	119.6	118.4	2.8
2013	B	2.24	1.37	1,301.6	122.7	227.0	2.4
2012	B	2.24	1.39	1,209.2	119.2	221.1	7.6
2011	B+	2.31	1.44	1,124.2	117.9	224.4	3.1
2010	B+	2.08	1.32	1,095.9	112.9	245.8	4.2
2009	B+	2.26	1.44	926.0	111.8	245.4	-2.7

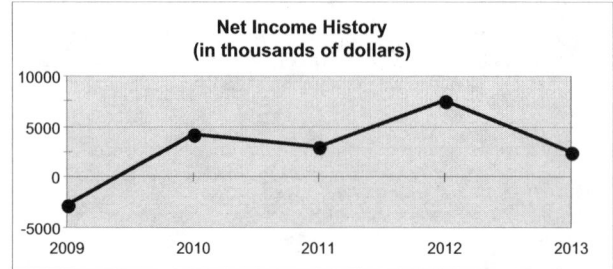

Net Income History
(in thousands of dollars)

PENNSYLVANIA LIFE INS CO　　　　　　　　　　　　C　　　　Fair

Major Rating Factors: Good overall profitability index (6.3 on a scale of 0 to 10). Strong capitalization (10.0) based on excellent current risk-adjusted capital (severe loss scenario). High quality investment portfolio (9.9).
Other Rating Factors: Excellent liquidity (9.1) with ample operational cash flow and liquid investments.
Principal Business: Med supp (12%), dental (1%), other (75%)
Mem Phys: 13: 68,000　**12:** 67,000　**13 MLR** -44.7%　**/ 13 Admin Exp** N/A
Enroll(000): Q2 14: 76　**13:** 81　**12:** 2,278　**Med Exp PMPM:** $-10
Principal Investments: Cash and equiv (81%), long-term bonds (19%)
Provider Compensation ($000): None
Total Member Encounters: N/A
Group Affiliation: CVS Caremark Corp
Licensed in: All states except NY
Address: 27 N Front St, Harrisburg, PA 17101
Phone: (401) 770-7699　**Dom State:** PA　**Commenced Bus:** January 1948

Data Date	Rating	RACR #1	RACR #2	Total Assets ($mil)	Capital ($mil)	Net Premium ($mil)	Net Income ($mil)
6-14	C	204.37	170.31	613.1	420.5	6.3	0.4
6-13	C	3.68	3.07	679.9	386.5	12.5	18.4
2013	C	211.50	176.30	633.9	420.8	23.7	40.9
2012	C-	4.05	3.38	1,002.0	389.6	2,496.5	-17.9
2011	N/A	N/A	N/A	917.0	398.6	1,877.0	N/A
2010	N/A	N/A	N/A	789.3	268.9	2,105.4	N/A
2009	N/A	N/A	N/A	901.4	261.0	1,928.4	N/A

Rating Indexes

PEOPLES HEALTH INC　　　　　　　　　　　　　　　D　　　　Weak

Major Rating Factors: Low quality investment portfolio (0.2 on a scale of 0 to 10). Fair capitalization (3.5) based on weak current risk-adjusted capital (moderate loss scenario). Good overall profitability index (6.8).
Other Rating Factors: Excellent liquidity (7.0) with sufficient resources (cash flows and marketable investments) to handle a spike in claims.
Principal Business: Medicare (100%)
Mem Phys: 13: 2,916　**12:** 2,728　**13 MLR** 84.7%　**/ 13 Admin Exp** N/A
Enroll(000): Q2 14: 57　**13:** 56　**12:** 53　**Med Exp PMPM:** $902
Principal Investments: Cash and equiv (100%)
Provider Compensation ($000): Capitation ($593,135)
Total Member Encounters: Phys (903,132), non-phys (724,835)
Group Affiliation: New Orleans Regional Physician Hosp
Licensed in: LA
Address: 3838 N Causeway Blvd, Metairie, LA 70002-8306
Phone: (504) 849-4500　**Dom State:** LA　**Commenced Bus:** March 2009

Data Date	Rating	RACR #1	RACR #2	Total Assets ($mil)	Capital ($mil)	Net Premium ($mil)	Net Income ($mil)
6-14	D	0.71	0.59	62.1	31.7	356.4	0.6
6-13	D+	0.71	0.59	76.1	30.5	353.9	0.6
2013	D+	0.69	0.58	50.9	31.1	699.7	1.2
2012	D+	0.69	0.58	55.3	29.9	678.0	1.1
2011	D+	0.69	0.57	49.8	28.8	643.4	2.0
2010	D+	0.68	0.57	41.3	26.5	585.7	0.4
2009	D	0.95	0.79	41.2	26.2	393.9	3.9

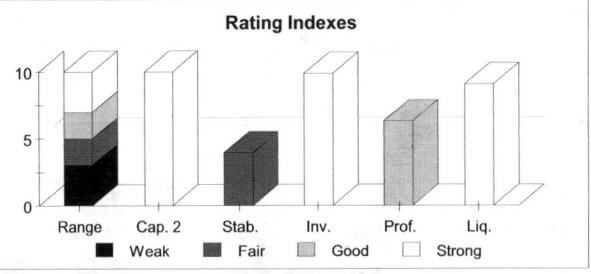

Rating Indexes

PHARMACY INS CORP OF AMERICA INC　　　　　　C-　　　　Fair

Major Rating Factors: Fair profitability index (2.9 on a scale of 0 to 10). Strong capitalization (10.0) based on excellent current risk-adjusted capital (severe loss scenario). High quality investment portfolio (9.9).
Other Rating Factors: Excellent liquidity (7.0) with ample operational cash flow and liquid investments.
Principal Business: Other (100%)
Mem Phys: 13: N/A　**12:** 19,500　**13 MLR** 96.2%　**/ 13 Admin Exp** N/A
Enroll(000): **13:** 7　**12:** 9　**Med Exp PMPM:** $102
Principal Investments: Long-term bonds (52%), cash and equiv (26%), nonaffiliate common stock (14%), other (9%)
Provider Compensation ($000): Contr fee ($10,214)
Total Member Encounters: N/A
Group Affiliation: None
Licensed in: PR
Address: 650 Munoz Rivera Suite 702, San Juan, PR 00918
Phone: (787) 625-4343　**Dom State:** PR　**Commenced Bus:** January 2006

Data Date	Rating	RACR #1	RACR #2	Total Assets ($mil)	Capital ($mil)	Net Premium ($mil)	Net Income ($mil)
2013	C-	4.30	3.58	8.2	5.2	9.5	-0.5
2012	N/A	N/A	N/A	8.3	4.7	13.1	0.5
2011	N/A	N/A	N/A	8.2	4.8	14.5	N/A
2010	N/A	N/A	N/A	6.8	3.1	15.0	N/A
2009	C-	N/A	N/A	8.4	4.5	18.9	0.2

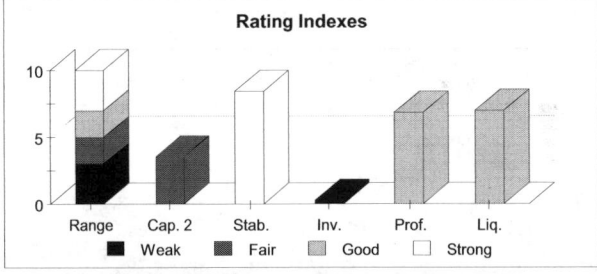

Rating Indexes

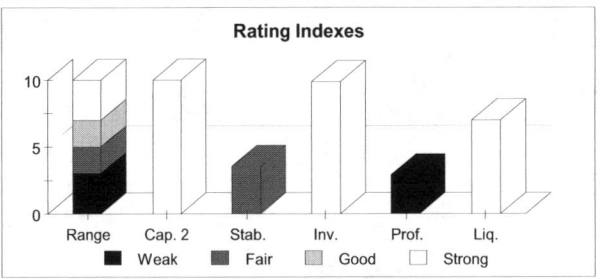

PHILADELPHIA AMERICAN LIFE INSURANCE COMPANY   B-   Good

Major Rating Factors: Good overall results on stability tests (5.0 on a scale of 0 to 10) despite fair financial strength of affiliated New Era Life Group and excessive premium growth. Other stability subfactors include excellent operational trends and good risk diversification. Good capitalization (5.9) based on good risk adjusted capital (severe loss scenario). Moreover, capital levels have been consistent over the last five years. Good quality investment portfolio (5.0).

Other Rating Factors: Good liquidity (6.1). Excellent profitability (9.0) with operating gains in each of the last five years.

Principal Business: Individual health insurance (85%), individual annuities (11%), group health insurance (3%), and individual life insurance (1%).

Principal Investments: NonCMO investment grade bonds (60%), CMOs and structured securities (25%), noninv. grade bonds (8%), cash (3%), and mortgages in good standing (3%).

Investments in Affiliates: None

Group Affiliation: New Era Life Group

Licensed in: All states except NY, RI, PR

Commenced Business: March 1978

Address: 3121 Buffalo Speedway, Houston, TX 77098

Phone: (281) 368-7247 **Domicile State:** TX **NAIC Code:** 67784

Data Date	Rating	RACR #1	RACR #2	Total Assets ($mil)	Capital ($mil)	Net Premium ($mil)	Net Income ($mil)
6-14	B-	1.33	0.86	210.8	30.2	72.6	1.8
6-13	B-	1.44	0.89	203.1	26.4	56.6	0.6
2013	B-	1.38	0.88	205.7	29.0	120.4	3.1
2012	B-	1.68	0.99	197.6	26.1	69.5	4.3
2011	C+	1.70	0.95	194.8	24.5	62.9	3.4
2010	C	1.73	1.00	190.8	22.1	62.4	1.2
2009	C	1.71	0.96	175.2	20.9	51.3	0.2

New Era Life Group
Composite Group Rating: C

Largest Group Members	Assets ($mil)	Rating
NEW ERA LIFE INS CO	371	C
PHILADELPHIA AMERICAN LIFE INS CO	206	B-
NEW ERA LIFE INS CO OF THE MIDWEST	74	C
LIFE OF AMERICA INS CO	12	C

PHOENIX HEALTH PLANS INC   D+   Weak

Major Rating Factors: Weak profitability index (0.7 on a scale of 0 to 10). Fair capitalization (3.4) based on weak current risk-adjusted capital (moderate loss scenario). High quality investment portfolio (9.9).

Other Rating Factors: Excellent liquidity (7.2) with ample operational cash flow and liquid investments.

Principal Business: Medicare (100%)

Mem Phys: 13: 2,419 **12:** 2,419 **13 MLR** 100.3% **/ 13 Admin Exp** N/A

Enroll(000): Q2 14: 9 **13:** 7 **12:** 4 **Med Exp PMPM:** $938

Principal Investments: Cash and equiv (93%), long-term bonds (4%), other (2%)

Provider Compensation ($000): Contr fee ($64,179)

Total Member Encounters: N/A

Group Affiliation: Vanguard Health Systems Inc

Licensed in: AZ

Address: 7878 N 16th St Suite 105, Phoenix, AZ 85020

Phone: (602) 824-3700 **Dom State:** AZ **Commenced Bus:** July 2005

Data Date	Rating	RACR #1	RACR #2	Total Assets ($mil)	Capital ($mil)	Net Premium ($mil)	Net Income ($mil)
6-14	D+	0.70	0.58	30.7	7.5	41.2	-6.8
6-13	B	3.30	2.75	44.0	20.6	31.8	0.7
2013	C-	1.26	1.05	36.9	13.1	68.7	-6.5
2012	B	3.18	2.65	38.5	19.7	41.0	0.0
2011	B-	3.48	2.90	35.4	20.1	31.6	0.5
2010	D	4.09	3.41	38.0	19.5	33.3	1.2
2009	D-	4.25	3.54	34.1	18.1	36.9	2.8

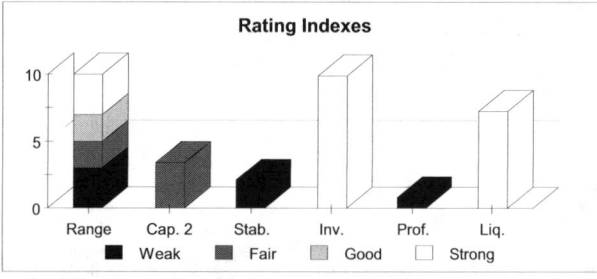

Rating Indexes

Range · Cap. 2 · Stab. · Inv. · Prof. · Liq.
■ Weak ▨ Fair ▥ Good □ Strong

PHP FAMILYCARE   C+   Fair

Major Rating Factors: Fair profitability index (3.4 on a scale of 0 to 10). Strong capitalization (6.9) based on excellent current risk-adjusted capital (severe loss scenario). High quality investment portfolio (9.9).

Other Rating Factors: Excellent liquidity (7.0) with sufficient resources (cash flows and marketable investments) to handle a spike in claims.

Principal Business: Medicaid (100%)

Mem Phys: 13: N/A **12:** 1,362 **13 MLR** 91.9% **/ 13 Admin Exp** N/A

Enroll(000): Q2 14: 20 **13:** 18 **12:** 18 **Med Exp PMPM:** $239

Principal Investments: Cash and equiv (64%), nonaffiliate common stock (35%), other (1%)

Provider Compensation ($000): Contr fee ($45,362), bonus arrang ($2,015), FFS ($306)

Total Member Encounters: Phys (105,230), non-phys (60,846)

Group Affiliation: Sparrow Health System

Licensed in: MI

Address: 1400 E Michigan Ave, Lansing, MI 48912

Phone: (517) 364-8400 **Dom State:** MI **Commenced Bus:** January 2003

Data Date	Rating	RACR #1	RACR #2	Total Assets ($mil)	Capital ($mil)	Net Premium ($mil)	Net Income ($mil)
6-14	C+	1.30	1.08	19.7	8.2	30.4	0.2
6-13	C+	1.10	0.92	12.9	6.7	27.2	0.3
2013	C+	1.23	1.02	16.8	7.7	54.3	0.8
2012	C+	1.03	0.85	13.5	6.3	53.0	-0.5
2011	C+	1.22	1.02	14.0	6.6	54.7	-0.5
2010	C+	1.25	1.04	12.9	6.6	54.8	-0.3
2009	C+	1.05	0.88	14.3	6.6	53.6	0.1

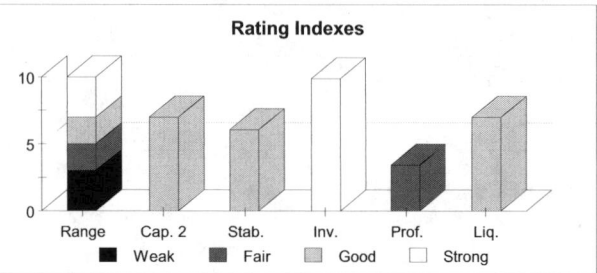

Rating Indexes

Range · Cap. 2 · Stab. · Inv. · Prof. · Liq.
■ Weak ▨ Fair ▥ Good □ Strong

PHP INS CO

C **Fair**

Major Rating Factors: Weak profitability index (0.9 on a scale of 0 to 10). Strong capitalization (7.1) based on excellent current risk-adjusted capital (severe loss scenario). High quality investment portfolio (9.9).
Other Rating Factors: Excellent liquidity (7.1) with ample operational cash flow and liquid investments.
Principal Business: Comp med (100%)
Mem Phys: 13: N/A **12:** 1,295 **13 MLR** 91.1% **/ 13 Admin Exp** N/A
Enroll(000): Q2 14: 11 **13:** 11 **12:** 9 **Med Exp PMPM:** $309
Principal Investments: Cash and equiv (100%)
Provider Compensation ($000): Contr fee ($23,560), FFS ($11,739)
Total Member Encounters: Phys (100,269), non-phys (61,960)
Group Affiliation: Sparrow Health System
Licensed in: MI
Address: 1400 E Michigan Ave, Lansing, MI 48912-2107
Phone: (517) 364-8400 **Dom State:** MI **Commenced Bus:** December 2006

Data Date	Rating	RACR #1	RACR #2	Total Assets ($mil)	Capital ($mil)	Net Premium ($mil)	Net Income ($mil)
6-14	C	1.42	1.19	16.5	7.6	23.0	-1.3
6-13	B	2.42	2.02	13.0	9.0	19.8	-0.2
2013	C+	1.55	1.29	14.9	8.4	41.2	-1.0
2012	B	2.46	2.05	13.7	9.2	27.9	0.6
2011	C	3.08	2.57	11.5	8.7	18.8	-0.1
2010	N/A	N/A	N/A	10.8	8.8	8.9	N/A
2009	N/A	N/A	N/A	10.0	9.1	6.5	N/A

Rating Indexes

Range Cap. 2 Stab. Inv. Prof. Liq.
■ Weak ■ Fair ▨ Good □ Strong

PHP INS CO OF INDIANA INC

C+ **Fair**

Major Rating Factors: Fair profitability index (3.5 on a scale of 0 to 10). Strong capitalization (10.0) based on excellent current risk-adjusted capital (severe loss scenario). High quality investment portfolio (9.9).
Other Rating Factors: Excellent liquidity (8.1) with ample operational cash flow and liquid investments.
Principal Business: Dental (100%)
Mem Phys: 13: N/A **12:** N/A **13 MLR** 81.2% **/ 13 Admin Exp** N/A
Enroll(000): **13:** 2 **12:** 2 **Med Exp PMPM:** $23
Principal Investments: Long-term bonds (59%), cash and equiv (21%), nonaffiliate common stock (20%)
Provider Compensation ($000): FFS ($672)
Total Member Encounters: Phys (3,377)
Group Affiliation: Physicians HP Northern Indiana
Licensed in: IN
Address: 8101 W Jefferson Blvd, Ft Wayne, IN 46804
Phone: (260) 432-6690 **Dom State:** IN **Commenced Bus:** May 2006

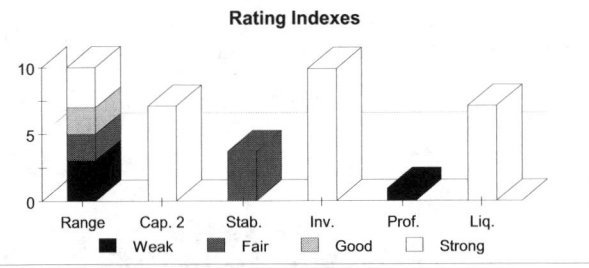

Data Date	Rating	RACR #1	RACR #2	Total Assets ($mil)	Capital ($mil)	Net Premium ($mil)	Net Income ($mil)
2013	C+	14.18	11.82	2.5	2.4	0.8	0.1
2012	C+	15.40	12.84	2.4	2.3	0.7	0.0
2011	C	16.08	13.40	2.3	2.2	0.7	0.1
2010	C	16.35	13.63	2.3	2.2	0.6	0.0
2009	C	22.07	18.39	2.2	2.1	0.3	-0.1

Rating Indexes

Range Cap. 2 Stab. Inv. Prof. Liq.
■ Weak ■ Fair ▨ Good □ Strong

PHYSICIANS HEALTH CHOICE OF TEXAS

B- **Good**

Major Rating Factors: Good overall profitability index (5.4 on a scale of 0 to 10). Strong capitalization (8.8) based on excellent current risk-adjusted capital (severe loss scenario). High quality investment portfolio (9.9).
Other Rating Factors: Excellent liquidity (7.0) with sufficient resources (cash flows and marketable investments) to handle a spike in claims.
Principal Business: Medicare (100%)
Mem Phys: 13: 360 **12:** 308 **13 MLR** 89.5% **/ 13 Admin Exp** N/A
Enroll(000): Q2 14: 28 **13:** 32 **12:** 32 **Med Exp PMPM:** $918
Principal Investments: Long-term bonds (63%), cash and equiv (37%)
Provider Compensation ($000): Capitation ($309,115), contr fee ($91,691)
Total Member Encounters: Phys (632,759), non-phys (374,615)
Group Affiliation: UnitedHealth Group Inc
Licensed in: TX
Address: 8637 Fredericksburg Ste 400, San Antonio, TX 78240
Phone: (856) 550-4736 **Dom State:** TX **Commenced Bus:** August 2002

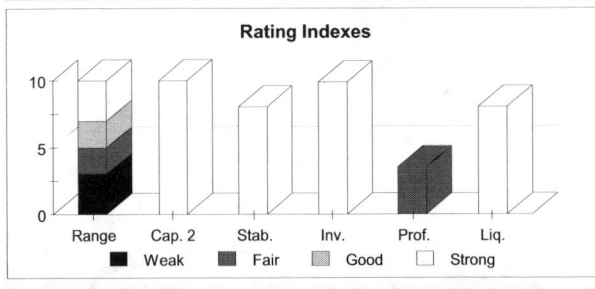

Data Date	Rating	RACR #1	RACR #2	Total Assets ($mil)	Capital ($mil)	Net Premium ($mil)	Net Income ($mil)
6-14	B-	2.78	2.31	88.3	52.1	167.7	-2.1
6-13	N/A	N/A	N/A	92.1	49.7	209.5	4.0
2013	B-	3.00	2.50	73.5	56.4	404.1	9.6
2012	N/A	N/A	N/A	123.5	38.8	410.8	6.9
2011	N/A	N/A	N/A	41.0	38.4	350.6	8.8
2010	D	0.92	0.77	20.1	13.0	316.6	-2.0
2009	C-	1.10	0.92	18.4	12.8	215.0	-1.6

Rating Indexes

Range Cap. 2 Stab. Inv. Prof. Liq.
■ Weak ■ Fair ▨ Good □ Strong

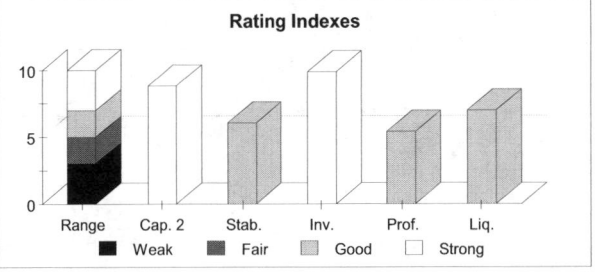

265

* Denotes a Weiss Ratings Recommended Company

PHYSICIANS HEALTH PLAN OF NO IN — B — Good

Major Rating Factors: Good liquidity (6.6 on a scale of 0 to 10) with sufficient resources (cash flows and marketable investments) to handle a spike in claims. Fair profitability index (4.8). Strong capitalization index (8.5) based on excellent current risk-adjusted capital (severe loss scenario).
Other Rating Factors: High quality investment portfolio (8.2). Excellent overall results on stability tests (8.0).
Principal Business: Comp med (98%), FEHB (1%)
Mem Phys: 13: 6,032 **12:** 5,803 **13 MLR** 88.1% **/ 13 Admin Exp** N/A
Enroll(000): Q2 14: 53 **13:** 45 **12:** 41 **Med Exp PMPM:** $290
Principal Investments: Long-term bonds (61%), nonaffiliate common stock (21%), cash and equiv (12%), affiliate common stock (3%), real estate (3%)
Provider Compensation ($000): FFS ($126,511), contr fee ($12,219), bonus arrang ($7,606)
Total Member Encounters: Phys (187,562), non-phys (140,819)
Group Affiliation: Physicians HP Northern Indiana
Licensed in: IN
Address: 8101 W Jefferson Blvd, Ft Wayne, IN 46804
Phone: (260) 432-6690 **Dom State:** IN **Commenced Bus:** December 1983

Data Date	Rating	RACR #1	RACR #2	Total Assets ($mil)	Capital ($mil)	Net Premium ($mil)	Net Income ($mil)
6-14	B	2.52	2.10	90.1	50.5	102.7	6.2
6-13	B-	2.58	2.15	71.2	46.2	81.0	3.4
2013	B	2.22	1.85	74.6	44.9	167.1	0.4
2012	B-	2.34	1.95	70.0	42.4	151.8	2.9
2011	B-	2.15	1.79	64.5	38.7	152.5	5.0
2010	B-	1.86	1.55	64.6	34.9	152.5	2.6
2009	B	1.74	1.45	61.6	31.9	143.8	-7.2

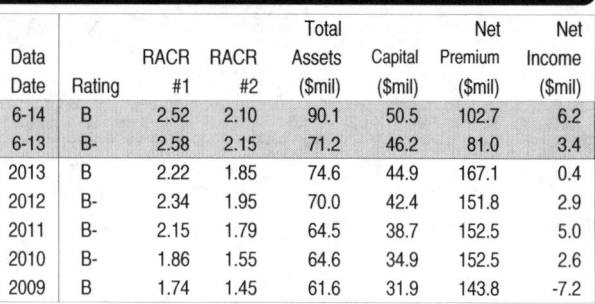

Rating Indexes

PHYSICIANS HP OF MID-MICHIGAN — B — Good

Major Rating Factors: Good profitability index (5.0 on a scale of 0 to 10). Good overall results on stability tests (6.1) despite a decline in enrollment during 2013. Strong capitalization index (7.7) based on excellent current risk-adjusted capital (severe loss scenario).
Other Rating Factors: High quality investment portfolio (8.1). Excellent liquidity (7.0) with sufficient resources (cash flows and marketable investments) to handle a spike in claims.
Principal Business: Comp med (81%), other (18%)
Mem Phys: 13: 2,857 **12:** 1,713 **13 MLR** 92.0% **/ 13 Admin Exp** N/A
Enroll(000): Q2 14: 31 **13:** 32 **12:** 37 **Med Exp PMPM:** $443
Principal Investments: Nonaffiliate common stock (44%), cash and equiv (32%), affiliate common stock (11%), real estate (2%), other (11%)
Provider Compensation ($000): Contr fee ($105,937), FFS ($42,288), bonus arrang ($35,451), capitation ($879)
Total Member Encounters: Phys (238,609), non-phys (117,994)
Group Affiliation: Sparrow Health System
Licensed in: MI
Address: 1400 E Michigan Ave, Lansing, MI 48912
Phone: (517) 364-8400 **Dom State:** MI **Commenced Bus:** October 1981

Data Date	Rating	RACR #1	RACR #2	Total Assets ($mil)	Capital ($mil)	Net Premium ($mil)	Net Income ($mil)
6-14	B	1.92	1.60	85.7	58.4	80.0	-1.1
6-13	B	1.81	1.51	79.7	54.6	118.0	0.7
2013	B	1.91	1.60	83.2	58.2	195.3	3.0
2012	B	1.74	1.45	79.9	52.7	214.6	0.0
2011	B-	1.36	1.13	70.3	46.8	171.9	4.0
2010	B	1.86	1.55	73.9	51.5	164.3	1.4
2009	B	1.77	1.48	80.0	51.1	178.3	6.0

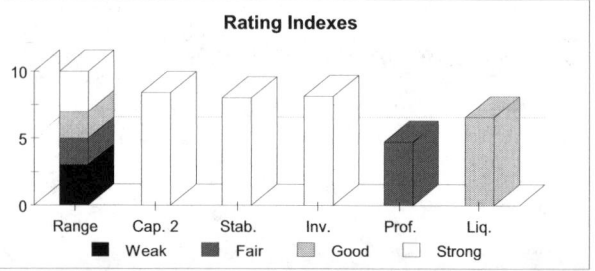

Rating Indexes

PHYSICIANS LIFE INSURANCE COMPANY * — A- — Excellent

Major Rating Factors: Good quality investment portfolio (5.7 on a scale of 0 to 10) despite mixed results such as: large holdings of BBB rated bonds but junk bond exposure equal to 87% of capital. Good overall profitability (6.2). Return on equity has been fair, averaging 5.9%. Good liquidity (5.8).
Other Rating Factors: Good overall results on stability tests (6.9) excellent operational trends and excellent risk diversification. Strong capitalization (7.6) based on excellent risk adjusted capital (severe loss scenario).
Principal Business: Individual life insurance (47%), individual health insurance (25%), individual annuities (16%), group life insurance (11%), and reinsurance (1%).
Principal Investments: NonCMO investment grade bonds (66%), CMOs and structured securities (22%), noninv. grade bonds (8%), policy loans (2%), and common & preferred stock (1%).
Investments in Affiliates: None
Group Affiliation: Physicians Mutual Group
Licensed in: All states except NY, PR
Commenced Business: January 1970
Address: 2600 Dodge St, Omaha, NE 68131-2671
Phone: (402) 633-1000 **Domicile State:** NE **NAIC Code:** 72125

Data Date	Rating	RACR #1	RACR #2	Total Assets ($mil)	Capital ($mil)	Net Premium ($mil)	Net Income ($mil)
6-14	A-	2.89	1.41	1,406.1	123.4	126.7	3.4
6-13	A-	3.09	1.54	1,302.3	116.8	118.1	3.2
2013	A-	2.94	1.45	1,378.7	122.7	248.6	8.3
2012	A-	3.02	1.50	1,285.0	115.8	211.2	8.7
2011	A-	2.78	1.40	1,268.9	108.7	200.9	4.4
2010	A-	2.79	1.40	1,257.5	106.1	197.5	5.0
2009	A-	2.55	1.26	1,252.7	101.5	193.8	6.3

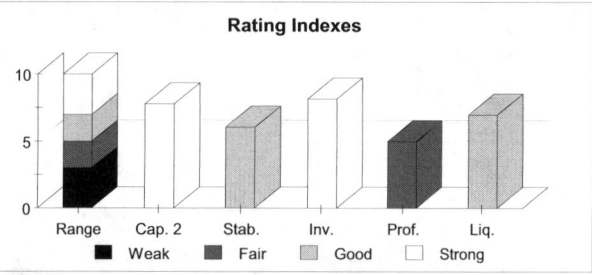

Rating Indexes

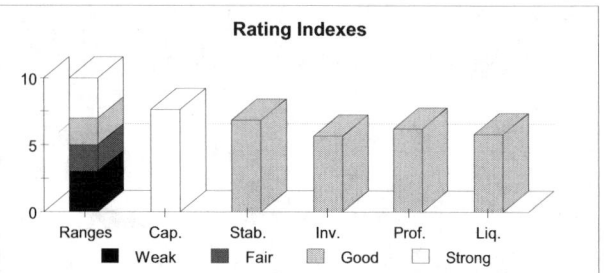

PHYSICIANS MUTUAL INSURANCE COMPANY *   A+   Excellent

Major Rating Factors: Good quality investment portfolio (6.5 on a scale of 0 to 10) despite mixed results such as: no exposure to mortgages and large holdings of BBB rated bonds but small junk bond holdings. Strong capitalization (10.0) based on excellent risk adjusted capital (severe loss scenario). Furthermore, this high level of risk adjusted capital has been consistently maintained over the last five years. Excellent profitability (8.9) with operating gains in each of the last five years.

Other Rating Factors: Excellent liquidity (7.4). Excellent overall results on stability tests (7.9) excellent operational trends and excellent risk diversification.

Principal Business: Individual health insurance (61%), reinsurance (36%), and group health insurance (4%).

Principal Investments: NonCMO investment grade bonds (72%), common & preferred stock (12%), noninv. grade bonds (8%), CMOs and structured securities (8%), and real estate (1%).

Investments in Affiliates: 7%

Group Affiliation: Physicians Mutual Group

Licensed in: All states except PR

Commenced Business: February 1902

Address: 2600 Dodge St, Omaha, NE 68131-2671

Phone: (402) 633-1000 **Domicile State:** NE **NAIC Code:** 80578

Data Date	Rating	RACR #1	RACR #2	Total Assets ($mil)	Capital ($mil)	Net Premium ($mil)	Net Income ($mil)
6-14	A+	4.26	3.22	1,968.0	953.3	210.1	23.6
6-13	A+	4.13	3.13	1,877.2	881.3	232.2	14.5
2013	A+	4.23	3.22	1,920.5	931.1	453.9	33.6
2012	A+	4.02	3.04	1,829.7	866.1	447.6	30.2
2011	A+	4.19	3.19	1,732.5	843.4	434.3	35.8
2010	A+	4.28	3.25	1,641.1	824.6	380.5	35.4
2009	A+	4.39	3.36	1,539.4	799.1	386.0	25.0

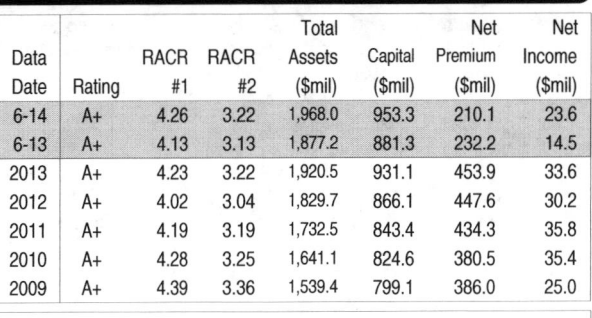

PHYSICIANS PLUS INS CORP   D   Weak

Major Rating Factors: Weak profitability index (0.8 on a scale of 0 to 10). Poor capitalization index (2.2) based on weak current risk-adjusted capital (moderate loss scenario). Fair overall results on stability tests (4.3) based on a significant 29% decrease in enrollment during the period, an inordinate decline in premium revenue in 2013.

Other Rating Factors: Good liquidity (6.1) with sufficient resources (cash flows and marketable investments) to handle a spike in claims. High quality investment portfolio (8.8).

Principal Business: Comp med (93%), Medicaid (5%)

Mem Phys: 13: 2,603 **12:** 2,350 **13 MLR** 95.1% **/ 13 Admin Exp** N/A

Enroll(000): Q2 14: 62 **13:** 74 **12:** 104 **Med Exp PMPM:** $337

Principal Investments: Long-term bonds (52%), cash and equiv (34%), nonaffiliate common stock (14%)

Provider Compensation ($000): Contr fee ($183,012), capitation ($115,817), FFS ($37,106)

Total Member Encounters: Phys (706,930), non-phys (82,697)

Group Affiliation: UnityPoint Health

Licensed in: WI

Address: 2650 Novation Parkway, Madison, WI 53713

Phone: (608) 282-8900 **Dom State:** WI **Commenced Bus:** October 1986

Data Date	Rating	RACR #1	RACR #2	Total Assets ($mil)	Capital ($mil)	Net Premium ($mil)	Net Income ($mil)
6-14	D	0.51	0.43	81.7	32.1	120.4	-6.2
6-13	D	0.38	0.32	84.7	28.4	181.3	-15.0
2013	D	0.55	0.46	89.9	33.5	352.4	-16.5
2012	D	0.52	0.43	80.5	25.9	438.3	-30.3
2011	B-	0.83	0.69	79.3	34.8	468.1	-10.5
2010	A	1.24	1.03	89.5	47.6	431.8	0.4
2009	A	1.40	1.17	81.0	46.4	394.3	3.2

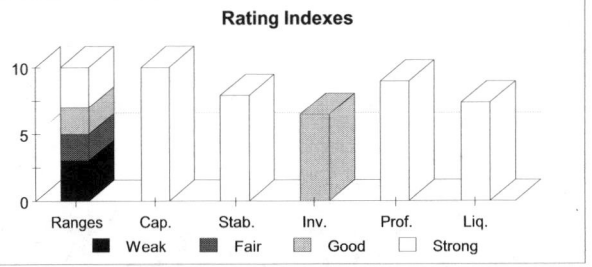

PIEDMONT COMMUNITY HEALTHCARE   B   Good

Major Rating Factors: Good overall profitability index (5.7 on a scale of 0 to 10). Good capitalization index (5.2) based on good current risk-adjusted capital (severe loss scenario). High quality investment portfolio (9.9).

Other Rating Factors: Excellent overall results on stability tests (7.4) based on healthy premium and capital growth during 2013. Excellent liquidity (7.0) with sufficient resources (cash flows and marketable investments) to handle a spike in claims.

Principal Business: Comp med (64%), Medicare (34%), FEHB (1%)

Mem Phys: 13: 990 **12:** 974 **13 MLR** 90.3% **/ 13 Admin Exp** N/A

Enroll(000): Q2 14: 12 **13:** 11 **12:** 10 **Med Exp PMPM:** $374

Principal Investments: Cash and equiv (100%)

Provider Compensation ($000): Contr fee ($31,421), bonus arrang ($18,816), FFS ($1,685), capitation ($47)

Total Member Encounters: Phys (101,516), non-phys (52,793)

Group Affiliation: Centra Health/Integrated Healthcare

Licensed in: VA

Address: 2512 Langhorne Rd, Lynchburg, VA 24501

Phone: (434) 947-4463 **Dom State:** VA **Commenced Bus:** January 1999

Data Date	Rating	RACR #1	RACR #2	Total Assets ($mil)	Capital ($mil)	Net Premium ($mil)	Net Income ($mil)
6-14	B	0.96	0.80	14.3	7.7	33.1	0.2
6-13	B	0.96	0.80	20.1	6.5	29.4	0.1
2013	B	0.93	0.77	16.6	7.5	57.8	0.2
2012	B	0.94	0.79	15.4	6.4	47.9	0.1
2011	B	1.00	0.84	14.1	6.3	44.8	0.0
2010	B	0.96	0.80	13.9	6.2	46.3	0.0
2009	B-	1.00	0.84	17.2	6.0	46.6	0.0

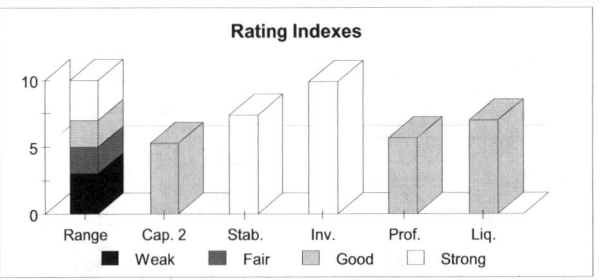

PMC MEDICARE CHOICE INC

B-   Good

Major Rating Factors: Good capitalization (5.0 on a scale of 0 to 10) based on good current risk-adjusted capital (severe loss scenario). Good liquidity (6.3) with sufficient resources (cash flows and marketable investments) to handle a spike in claims. Excellent profitability (8.3).

Other Rating Factors: High quality investment portfolio (9.2).

Principal Business: Medicare (100%)

Mem Phys: 13: N/A   **12:** N/A   **13 MLR** 85.2%   **/ 13 Admin Exp** N/A

Enroll(000): Q2 14: 34   **13:** 41   **12:** 39   **Med Exp PMPM:** $684

Principal Investments: Long-term bonds (83%), cash and equiv (16%), other (1%)

Provider Compensation ($000): FFS ($218,244), capitation ($35,817), bonus arrang ($14,599), other ($87,318)

Total Member Encounters: N/A

Group Affiliation: InnovaCare Inc

Licensed in: PR

Address: 350 Chardon Ave, San Juan, PR 00917

Phone: (787) 622-3000   **Dom State:** PR   **Commenced Bus:** August 2004

Data Date	Rating	RACR #1	RACR #2	Total Assets ($mil)	Capital ($mil)	Net Premium ($mil)	Net Income ($mil)
6-14	B-	0.93	0.78	84.9	31.9	175.6	1.7
6-13	C	0.92	0.77	94.6	32.8	208.1	3.1
2013	B-	0.99	0.82	83.1	33.7	402.7	6.2
2012	C	0.83	0.69	87.5	29.6	415.5	16.9
2011	C-	0.62	0.51	118.8	24.9	462.7	20.3
2010	D	0.56	0.47	113.9	26.7	510.4	24.5
2009	D	0.48	0.40	113.7	26.0	538.1	41.5

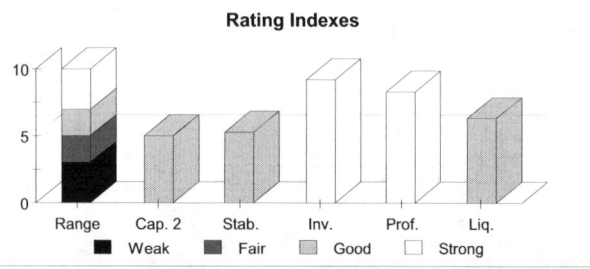

PREFERRED CARE PARTNERS INC

E-   Very Weak

Major Rating Factors: Weak liquidity (0.0 on a scale of 0 to 10) as a spike in claims may stretch capacity. Fair capitalization (3.8) based on fair current risk-adjusted capital (moderate loss scenario). Good overall profitability index (5.0).

Other Rating Factors: High quality investment portfolio (9.6).

Principal Business: Medicare (96%), Medicaid (4%)

Mem Phys: 13: 6,689   **12:** 5,387   **13 MLR** 90.1%   **/ 13 Admin Exp** N/A

Enroll(000): Q2 14: 46   **13:** 51   **12:** 57   **Med Exp PMPM:** $836

Principal Investments: Long-term bonds (65%), cash and equiv (35%)

Provider Compensation ($000): Contr fee ($358,550), capitation ($87,336), FFS ($64,048), bonus arrang ($11,418)

Total Member Encounters: Phys (144,292), non-phys (107,568)

Group Affiliation: UnitedHealth Group Inc

Licensed in: FL

Address: 9100 S Dadeland Blvd Ste 1250, Miami, FL 33156

Phone: (305) 670-8438   **Dom State:** FL   **Commenced Bus:** August 2002

Data Date	Rating	RACR #1	RACR #2	Total Assets ($mil)	Capital ($mil)	Net Premium ($mil)	Net Income ($mil)
6-14	E-	0.76	0.63	108.8	26.5	292.6	8.7
6-13	E-	0.46	0.39	129.5	26.0	285.3	7.0
2013	E-	0.68	0.57	110.5	23.9	566.5	14.1
2012	E-	N/A	N/A	110.2	-8.9	671.1	N/A
2011	D	0.03	0.02	78.9	12.0	574.0	8.9
2010	C-	0.82	0.68	74.9	31.2	431.8	11.6
2009	C-	0.82	0.68	72.8	41.4	329.9	9.5

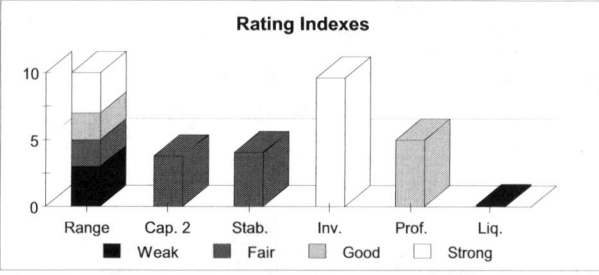

PREFERRED MEDICAL PLAN INC

D+   Weak

Major Rating Factors: Weak overall results on stability tests (0.1 on a scale of 0 to 10). Excellent profitability (7.3). Strong capitalization index (8.1) based on excellent current risk-adjusted capital (severe loss scenario).

Other Rating Factors: High quality investment portfolio (9.9). Excellent liquidity (6.9) with sufficient resources (cash flows and marketable investments) to handle a spike in claims.

Principal Business: Comp med (50%), Medicaid (45%), Medicare (3%), other (1%)

Mem Phys: 13: 5,633   **12:** 5,464   **13 MLR** 79.9%   **/ 13 Admin Exp** N/A

Enroll(000): Q2 14: 116   **13:** 38   **12:** 39   **Med Exp PMPM:** $190

Principal Investments: Cash and equiv (90%), long-term bonds (5%), real estate (5%)

Provider Compensation ($000): Contr fee ($64,672), capitation ($16,006), FFS ($7,238)

Total Member Encounters: Phys (79,923)

Group Affiliation: None

Licensed in: FL

Address: 4950 SW 8th Street, Coral Gables, FL 33134

Phone: (305) 648-4000   **Dom State:** FL   **Commenced Bus:** April 1975

Data Date	Rating	RACR #1	RACR #2	Total Assets ($mil)	Capital ($mil)	Net Premium ($mil)	Net Income ($mil)
6-14	D+	2.19	1.83	136.4	19.5	140.1	9.8
6-13	C+	1.46	1.21	38.3	11.7	54.8	2.0
2013	D+	0.54	0.45	33.0	2.7	108.5	0.6
2012	C+	1.25	1.04	39.6	9.6	109.0	7.1
2011	C	0.76	0.63	30.0	5.7	108.5	4.2
2010	C+	1.82	1.51	37.1	12.3	113.7	10.9
2009	B-	1.10	0.91	37.6	10.1	123.3	8.8

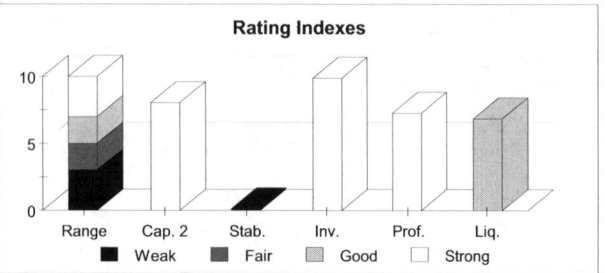

PREFERREDONE COMMUNITY HEALTH PLAN   D   Weak

Major Rating Factors: Weak profitability index (1.0 on a scale of 0 to 10). Fair overall results on stability tests (3.4) based on a steep decline in capital during 2013. Good capitalization index (5.9) based on good current risk-adjusted capital (severe loss scenario).
Other Rating Factors: Good liquidity (6.3) with sufficient resources (cash flows and marketable investments) to handle a spike in claims. High quality investment portfolio (9.2).
Principal Business: Comp med (100%)
Mem Phys: 13: 45,585 **12:** 45,340 **13 MLR** 90.1% / **13 Admin Exp** N/A
Enroll(000): Q2 14: 15 **13:** 17 **12:** 16 **Med Exp PMPM:** $279
Principal Investments: Long-term bonds (60%), cash and equiv (22%), nonaffiliate common stock (18%)
Provider Compensation ($000): Contr fee ($40,728), FFS ($9,950), bonus arrang ($5,345)
Total Member Encounters: N/A
Group Affiliation: PreferredOne Group
Licensed in: MN
Address: 6105 Golden Hills Dr, Golden Valley, MN 55416
Phone: (763) 847-4000 **Dom State:** MN **Commenced Bus:** January 1996

Data Date	Rating	RACR #1	RACR #2	Total Assets ($mil)	Capital ($mil)	Net Premium ($mil)	Net Income ($mil)
6-14	D	1.07	0.89	16.6	8.1	29.4	0.3
6-13	D+	1.35	1.12	18.8	10.7	29.4	0.2
2013	D	1.01	0.84	14.1	7.7	59.6	-2.7
2012	D+	1.28	1.07	18.4	10.2	62.9	-0.8
2011	D+	0.89	0.74	22.4	10.6	103.8	1.2
2010	D	0.80	0.67	30.4	11.9	138.1	0.4
2009	D	0.72	0.60	27.9	11.4	136.1	-2.1

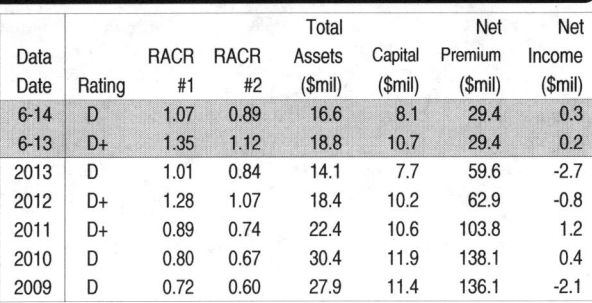

Rating Indexes

PREFERREDONE INS CO   B   Good

Major Rating Factors: Good liquidity (6.4 on a scale of 0 to 10) with sufficient resources (cash flows and marketable investments) to handle a spike in claims. Strong capitalization (7.4) based on excellent current risk-adjusted capital (severe loss scenario). High quality investment portfolio (8.9).
Other Rating Factors: Weak profitability index (2.4).
Principal Business: Comp med (91%), other (9%)
Mem Phys: 13: 45,585 **12:** 45,340 **13 MLR** 87.5% / **13 Admin Exp** N/A
Enroll(000): Q2 14: 205 **13:** 112 **12:** 87 **Med Exp PMPM:** $114
Principal Investments: Long-term bonds (67%), nonaffiliate common stock (19%), cash and equiv (14%)
Provider Compensation ($000): Contr fee ($95,215), FFS ($23,530), bonus arrang ($12,283), other ($11,729)
Total Member Encounters: N/A
Group Affiliation: PreferredOne Group
Licensed in: MN
Address: 6105 Golden Hills Dr, Golden Valley, MN 55416-1023
Phone: (763) 847-4000 **Dom State:** MN **Commenced Bus:** October 2003

Data Date	Rating	RACR #1	RACR #2	Total Assets ($mil)	Capital ($mil)	Net Premium ($mil)	Net Income ($mil)
6-14	B	1.66	1.38	107.0	36.6	189.0	-3.5
6-13	B+	1.80	1.50	58.7	32.9	84.7	1.9
2013	B+	1.33	1.11	58.1	29.8	165.7	-1.6
2012	B+	1.66	1.38	51.5	30.5	144.8	3.1
2011	B	1.63	1.36	45.6	26.3	119.2	1.9
2010	B	1.52	1.27	38.2	21.7	103.8	1.6
2009	B	1.68	1.40	32.0	19.6	79.7	2.0

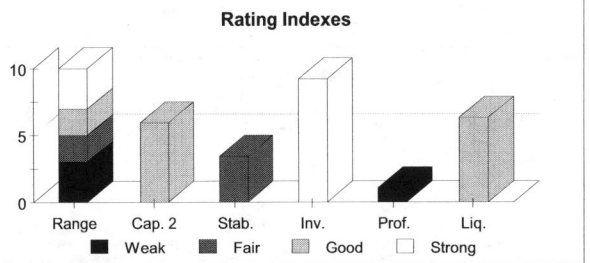

Rating Indexes

PREMERA BLUE CROSS *   A-   Excellent

Major Rating Factors: Excellent profitability (8.3 on a scale of 0 to 10). Strong capitalization (10.0) based on excellent current risk-adjusted capital (severe loss scenario). Good liquidity (6.9) with sufficient resources (cash flows and marketable investments) to handle a spike in claims.
Other Rating Factors: Fair quality investment portfolio (4.7).
Principal Business: Comp med (74%), FEHB (20%), med supp (3%), dental (2%)
Mem Phys: 13: 41,201 **12:** 39,051 **13 MLR** 86.3% / **13 Admin Exp** N/A
Enroll(000): Q2 14: 742 **13:** 654 **12:** 670 **Med Exp PMPM:** $280
Principal Investments: Long-term bonds (39%), nonaffiliate common stock (27%), affiliate common stock (14%), cash and equiv (3%), real estate (2%), other (14%)
Provider Compensation ($000): Contr fee ($2,136,123), FFS ($161,464), bonus arrang ($148)
Total Member Encounters: Phys (3,752,235), non-phys (1,683,367)
Group Affiliation: PREMERA
Licensed in: AK, WA
Address: 7001 220th St SW, Mountlake Terrace, WA 98043
Phone: (425) 918-4000 **Dom State:** WA **Commenced Bus:** May 1945

Data Date	Rating	RACR #1	RACR #2	Total Assets ($mil)	Capital ($mil)	Net Premium ($mil)	Net Income ($mil)
6-14	A-	6.49	5.41	2,178.3	1,367.6	1,486.9	6.7
6-13	A-	6.44	5.36	1,879.6	1,241.6	1,264.4	45.9
2013	A-	6.45	5.38	2,009.4	1,359.9	2,556.1	86.3
2012	A-	6.02	5.02	1,781.7	1,160.4	2,574.5	93.1
2011	A-	5.70	4.75	1,564.5	972.7	2,501.0	119.2
2010	A-	5.73	4.78	1,482.1	879.4	2,375.4	119.0
2009	A-	4.68	3.90	1,287.5	790.0	2,439.7	21.0

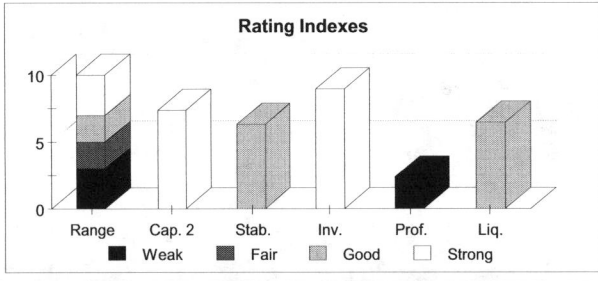
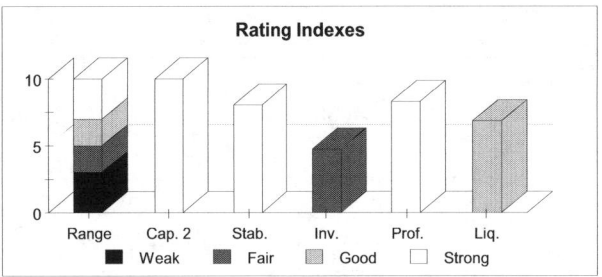

Rating Indexes

PREMIER HEALTH PLAN SERVICES INC

C-   **Fair**

Major Rating Factors: Fair overall results on stability tests (3.4 on a scale of 0 to 10) based on poor risk diversification due to the company's size. Excellent profitability (8.2). Strong capitalization index (10.0) based on excellent current risk-adjusted capital (severe loss scenario).
Other Rating Factors: Excellent liquidity (7.4) with ample operational cash flow and liquid investments.
Principal Business: Managed care (100%)
Mem Phys: 13: N/A **12:** N/A **13 MLR** 90.5% **/ 13 Admin Exp** N/A
Enroll(000): Q2 14: 44 **13:** 2 **12:** 2 **Med Exp PMPM:** $667
Principal Investments ($000): Cash and equiv ($3,860)
Provider Compensation ($000): None
Total Member Encounters: N/A
Group Affiliation: Lakewood IPA
Licensed in: (No states)
Address: 4909 Lakewood Blvd Suite 200, Lakewood, CA 90712
Phone: (Phone number   **Dom State:** CA **Commenced Bus:** June 2009

Data Date	Rating	RACR #1	RACR #2	Total Assets ($mil)	Capital ($mil)	Net Premium ($mil)	Net Income ($mil)
6-14	C-	6.89	4.58	17.4	5.2	35.4	2.5
6-13	C-	11.02	10.59	4.5	2.3	9.3	0.2
2013	C-	2.81	1.85	4.6	2.1	17.9	0.0
2012	C-	9.88	9.49	5.1	2.1	17.3	0.6
2011	C-	26.16	23.25	3.0	1.5	4.1	0.0
2010	N/A	N/A	N/A	1.5	1.5	N/A	-0.1
2009	N/A	N/A	N/A	N/A	N/A	N/A	N/A

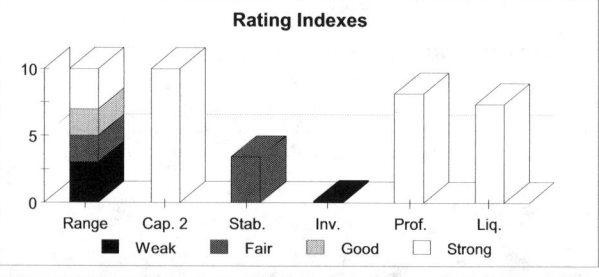

Rating Indexes

PRESBYTERIAN HEALTH PLAN INC *

B+   **Good**

Major Rating Factors: Good overall results on stability tests (5.0 on a scale of 0 to 10) based on a decline in the number of member physicians during 2014. Good liquidity (6.8) with sufficient resources (cash flows and marketable investments) to handle a spike in claims. Excellent profitability (8.0)
Other Rating Factors: Strong capitalization index (8.9) based on excellent current risk-adjusted capital (severe loss scenario). High quality investment portfolio (9.2).
Principal Business: Medicaid (52%), Medicare (23%), comp med (20%), FEHB (6%)
Mem Phys: 13: 7,646 **12:** 10,145 **13 MLR** 88.7% **/ 13 Admin Exp** N/A
Enroll(000): Q2 14: 282 **13:** 271 **12:** 268 **Med Exp PMPM:** $309
Principal Investments: Long-term bonds (52%), cash and equiv (25%), nonaffiliate common stock (21%), other (1%)
Provider Compensation ($000): Contr fee ($505,551), capitation ($430,222), FFS ($70,423), bonus arrang ($467)
Total Member Encounters: Phys (1,882,643), non-phys (873,423)
Group Affiliation: Presbyterian HealthCare Services
Licensed in: NM
Address: 2501 Buena Vista SE, Albuquerque, NM 87106-4270
Phone: (505) 923-5700 **Dom State:** NM **Commenced Bus:** July 1987

Data Date	Rating	RACR #1	RACR #2	Total Assets ($mil)	Capital ($mil)	Net Premium ($mil)	Net Income ($mil)
6-14	B+	2.88	2.40	415.3	198.1	714.3	28.4
6-13	B+	2.41	2.01	304.4	164.0	571.6	9.1
2013	B+	2.45	2.05	305.7	169.1	1,142.5	16.6
2012	A-	2.25	1.87	319.2	153.4	1,069.4	37.6
2011	A-	2.49	2.07	299.3	164.5	1,076.6	36.2
2010	A	2.92	2.44	331.4	196.4	1,117.6	55.9
2009	B+	1.98	1.65	291.6	138.6	1,125.6	38.0

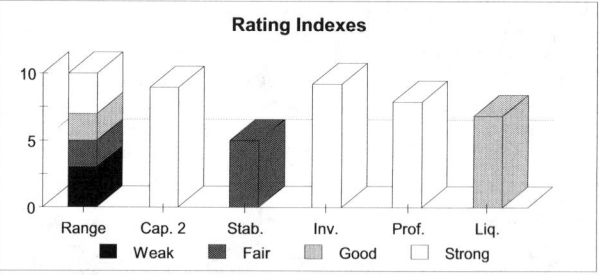

Rating Indexes

PRESBYTERIAN INS CO INC

B   **Good**

Major Rating Factors: Excellent profitability (8.2 on a scale of 0 to 10). Strong capitalization (8.4) based on excellent current risk-adjusted capital (severe loss scenario). High quality investment portfolio (9.9).
Other Rating Factors: Excellent liquidity (6.9) with sufficient resources (cash flows and marketable investments) to handle a spike in claims.
Principal Business: Medicare (62%), comp med (38%)
Mem Phys: 13: 6,539 **12:** 8,609 **13 MLR** 85.5% **/ 13 Admin Exp** N/A
Enroll(000): Q2 14: 31 **13:** 25 **12:** 45 **Med Exp PMPM:** $439
Principal Investments: Long-term bonds (40%), cash and equiv (39%), nonaffiliate common stock (21%)
Provider Compensation ($000): Contr fee ($107,760), FFS ($21,419), capitation ($99)
Total Member Encounters: Phys (232,397), non-phys (117,502)
Group Affiliation: Presbyterian Health Services
Licensed in: NM
Address: 2301 Buena Vista Dr SE, Albuquerque, NM 87106
Phone: (505) 923-5700 **Dom State:** NM **Commenced Bus:** July 2002

Data Date	Rating	RACR #1	RACR #2	Total Assets ($mil)	Capital ($mil)	Net Premium ($mil)	Net Income ($mil)
6-14	B	2.47	2.06	63.8	32.7	100.2	3.6
6-13	B	1.53	1.28	43.6	23.9	76.9	1.8
2013	B	2.07	1.72	48.5	27.6	150.8	5.4
2012	B	1.40	1.17	54.4	22.0	181.8	4.1
2011	B+	1.85	1.54	54.6	26.0	160.8	6.0
2010	B	2.48	2.07	39.9	22.1	107.8	4.6
2009	B	1.97	1.64	31.8	17.8	102.1	2.2

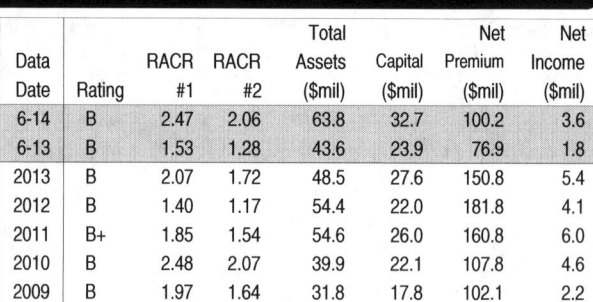

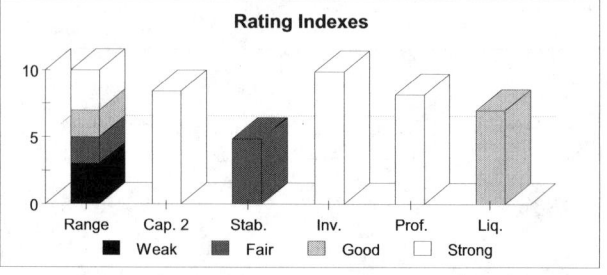

Rating Indexes

PRIMECARE MEDICAL NETWORK INC — C — Fair

Major Rating Factors: Good capitalization index (6.2 on a scale of 0 to 10) based on good current risk-adjusted capital (severe loss scenario). Good overall results on stability tests (5.7). Excellent profitability (7.9).
Other Rating Factors: Excellent liquidity (7.1) with ample operational cash flow and liquid investments.
Principal Business: Managed care (100%)
Mem Phys: 13: N/A **12:** N/A **13 MLR** 82.4% **/ 13 Admin Exp** N/A
Enroll(000): Q2 14: 214 **13:** 198 **12:** 205 **Med Exp PMPM:** $213
Principal Investments ($000): Cash and equiv ($150,436)
Provider Compensation ($000): None
Total Member Encounters: N/A
Group Affiliation: InnovaCare Inc
Licensed in: CA
Address: 3281 E Guasti Rd 7th Fl, Ontario, CA 91761-7643
Phone: (909) 605-8000 **Dom State:** CA **Commenced Bus:** October 1998

Data Date	Rating	RACR #1	RACR #2	Total Assets ($mil)	Capital ($mil)	Net Premium ($mil)	Net Income ($mil)
6-14	C	1.49	0.93	167.1	53.7	328.9	10.6
6-13	C	0.94	0.58	146.1	32.0	305.3	10.7
2013	C	1.15	0.72	154.5	42.7	620.8	21.7
2012	C	0.62	0.38	127.3	21.6	559.2	25.5
2011	C	0.62	0.39	108.5	19.7	510.9	24.9
2010	C-	0.88	0.55	98.7	23.8	431.0	16.3
2009	C	N/A	N/A	88.7	19.4	411.1	15.7

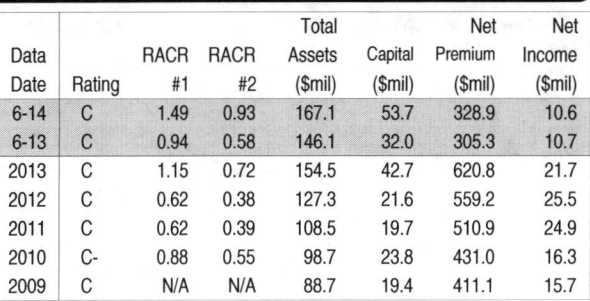

Rating Indexes

PRIORITY HEALTH — B — Good

Major Rating Factors: Good overall profitability index (5.8 on a scale of 0 to 10). Good overall results on stability tests (6.6) despite a decline in enrollment during 2013. Strong capitalization index (8.4) based on excellent current risk-adjusted capital (severe loss scenario).
Other Rating Factors: High quality investment portfolio (9.8). Excellent liquidity (7.0) with sufficient resources (cash flows and marketable investments) to handle a spike in claims.
Principal Business: Comp med (63%), Medicare (37%)
Mem Phys: 13: 15,568 **12:** 13,620 **13 MLR** 88.3% **/ 13 Admin Exp** N/A
Enroll(000): Q2 14: 365 **13:** 362 **12:** 398 **Med Exp PMPM:** $381
Principal Investments: Cash and equiv (39%), long-term bonds (34%), nonaffiliate common stock (14%), affiliate common stock (13%)
Provider Compensation ($000): Contr fee ($1,007,830), bonus arrang ($542,806), FFS ($91,269), capitation ($16,416)
Total Member Encounters: Phys (4,155,530), non-phys (550,179)
Group Affiliation: Spectrum Health System & Munson HC
Licensed in: MI
Address: 1231 E Beltline Ave NE, Grand Rapids, MI 49525
Phone: (616) 942-0954 **Dom State:** MI **Commenced Bus:** October 1986

Data Date	Rating	RACR #1	RACR #2	Total Assets ($mil)	Capital ($mil)	Net Premium ($mil)	Net Income ($mil)
6-14	B	2.47	2.06	670.3	431.9	993.5	46.9
6-13	B	1.81	1.51	558.6	340.3	941.2	27.2
2013	B	2.22	1.85	624.0	394.9	1,878.2	58.6
2012	B	1.60	1.34	542.5	307.2	1,936.8	60.7
2011	B	1.14	0.95	472.9	227.8	1,857.7	33.2
2010	B	1.09	0.91	425.2	204.1	1,654.2	-7.2
2009	A-	1.66	1.39	426.5	234.9	1,324.4	17.8

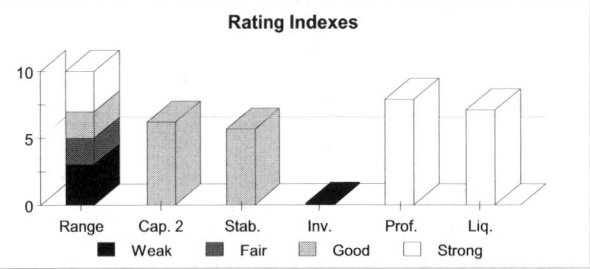

Rating Indexes

PRIORITY HEALTH CHOICE INC * — B+ — Good

Major Rating Factors: Good overall profitability index (5.3 on a scale of 0 to 10). Good liquidity (6.9) with sufficient resources (cash flows and marketable investments) to handle a spike in claims. Strong capitalization (7.7) based on excellent current risk-adjusted capital (severe loss scenario).
Other Rating Factors: High quality investment portfolio (9.1).
Principal Business: Medicaid (98%), comp med (2%)
Mem Phys: 13: 6,731 **12:** 5,061 **13 MLR** 93.4% **/ 13 Admin Exp** N/A
Enroll(000): Q2 14: 97 **13:** 75 **12:** 70 **Med Exp PMPM:** $251
Principal Investments: Cash and equiv (63%), nonaffiliate common stock (36%), long-term bonds (2%)
Provider Compensation ($000): Capitation ($110,336), bonus arrang ($65,360), contr fee ($27,113), FFS ($6,811)
Total Member Encounters: Phys (739,849), non-phys (77,412)
Group Affiliation: Spectrum Health System & Munson HC
Licensed in: MI
Address: 1231 E Beltline Ave NE, Grand Rapids, MI 49525
Phone: (616) 942-0954 **Dom State:** MI **Commenced Bus:** October 2002

Data Date	Rating	RACR #1	RACR #2	Total Assets ($mil)	Capital ($mil)	Net Premium ($mil)	Net Income ($mil)
6-14	B+	1.90	1.58	76.2	28.0	131.8	-2.0
6-13	B	2.19	1.82	54.8	26.3	110.1	-3.2
2013	B+	1.97	1.64	62.0	29.5	231.5	-0.1
2012	B	2.44	2.04	52.0	29.7	192.6	4.0
2011	C+	2.25	1.88	46.5	25.7	188.2	5.6
2010	C+	1.86	1.55	39.4	20.1	180.6	8.4
2009	C+	1.66	1.38	34.2	16.7	172.1	10.3

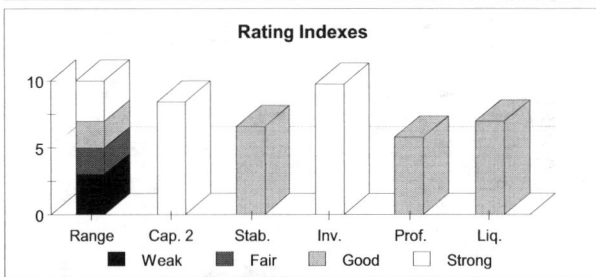

Rating Indexes

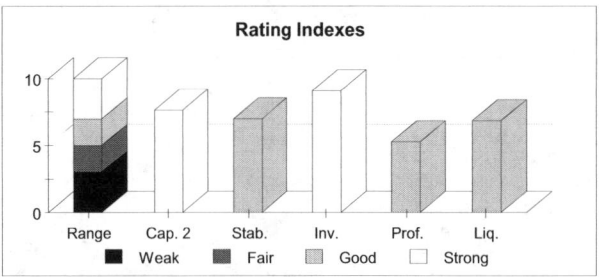

PRIORITY HEALTH INS CO C   Fair

Major Rating Factors: Fair profitability index (4.3 on a scale of 0 to 10). Strong capitalization (8.9) based on excellent current risk-adjusted capital (severe loss scenario). High quality investment portfolio (9.4).
Other Rating Factors: Excellent liquidity (7.2) with ample operational cash flow and liquid investments.
Principal Business: Comp med (95%), other (5%)
Mem Phys: 13: 16,943 **12:** 13,620 **13 MLR** 75.2% / **13 Admin Exp** N/A
Enroll(000): Q2 14: 54 **13:** 57 **12:** 58 **Med Exp PMPM:** $242
Principal Investments: Cash and equiv (58%), nonaffiliate common stock (41%), long-term bonds (1%)
Provider Compensation ($000): Contr fee ($78,549), bonus arrang ($43,769), FFS ($32,583)
Total Member Encounters: Phys (400,802), non-phys (28,429)
Group Affiliation: Spectrum Health Corp & Munson Health
Licensed in: MI
Address: 1231 E Beltline NE, Grand Rapids, MI 49525-4501
Phone: (616) 942-0954 **Dom State:** MI **Commenced Bus:** September 2004

Data Date	Rating	RACR #1	RACR #2	Total Assets ($mil)	Capital ($mil)	Net Premium ($mil)	Net Income ($mil)
6-14	C	2.88	2.40	107.2	44.9	109.8	-1.5
6-13	C	1.91	1.59	80.6	35.3	97.0	4.7
2013	C	2.88	2.40	88.3	45.5	197.3	14.5
2012	C	1.65	1.38	74.8	30.9	224.4	1.1
2011	C	1.29	1.08	76.5	29.7	251.3	-6.6
2010	N/A	N/A	N/A	65.9	26.3	217.0	N/A
2009	N/A	N/A	N/A	41.9	16.2	130.4	N/A

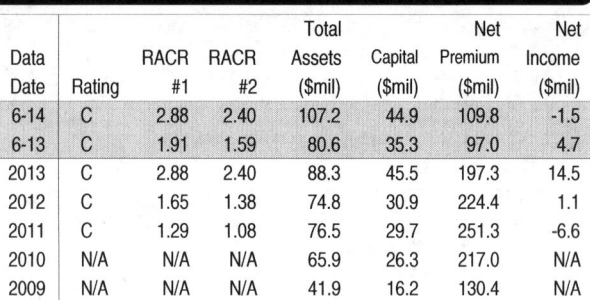

PROFESSIONAL INSURANCE COMPANY C-   Fair

Major Rating Factors: Fair overall results on stability tests (3.2 on a scale of 0 to 10) including potential financial drain due to affiliation with Sun Life Assurance Group and negative cash flow from operations for 2013. Weak profitability (2.6). Excellent expense controls. Return on equity has been low, averaging -6.5%. Good liquidity (6.7).
Other Rating Factors: Strong capitalization (9.3) based on excellent risk adjusted capital (severe loss scenario). High quality investment portfolio (7.0).
Principal Business: Individual health insurance (95%) and individual life insurance (5%).
Principal Investments: NonCMO investment grade bonds (85%), CMOs and structured securities (8%), policy loans (4%), noninv. grade bonds (1%), and misc. investments (1%).
Investments in Affiliates: None
Group Affiliation: Sun Life Assurance Group
Licensed in: All states except AK, DE, ME, NH, NJ, NY, RI, VT, PR
Commenced Business: September 1937
Address: 4850 Street Road, Trevose, PA 19049
Phone: (800) 730-6484 **Domicile State:** TX **NAIC Code:** 68047

Data Date	Rating	RACR #1	RACR #2	Total Assets ($mil)	Capital ($mil)	Net Premium ($mil)	Net Income ($mil)
6-14	C-	3.68	2.55	106.1	33.0	16.3	1.3
6-13	D	2.84	2.00	106.1	29.4	19.2	1.9
2013	C-	3.16	2.21	105.1	29.5	37.1	3.4
2012	D	2.61	1.84	108.6	28.6	44.6	1.1
2011	D	1.52	1.09	104.5	20.8	53.8	-9.2
2010	C	1.82	1.30	105.5	29.4	70.1	-6.8
2009	C	2.07	1.43	111.2	33.6	71.5	0.0

Sun Life Assurance Group Composite Group Rating: D+ Largest Group Members	Assets ($mil)	Rating
SUN LIFE ASR CO OF CANADA	15369	D
INDEPENDENCE LIFE ANNUITY CO	2284	C
SUN LIFE HEALTH INS CO	354	C-
PROFESSIONAL INS CO	105	C-

PROMINENCE HEALTHFIRST D+   Weak

Major Rating Factors: Weak profitability index (0.9 on a scale of 0 to 10). Fair capitalization index (3.0) based on weak current risk-adjusted capital (moderate loss scenario). Fair quality investment portfolio (3.8).
Other Rating Factors: Fair overall results on stability tests (4.5). Good liquidity (6.4) with sufficient resources (cash flows and marketable investments) to handle a spike in claims.
Principal Business: Comp med (100%)
Mem Phys: 13: 4,008 **12:** 3,513 **13 MLR** 88.5% / **13 Admin Exp** N/A
Enroll(000): Q2 14: 25 **13:** 21 **12:** 19 **Med Exp PMPM:** $315
Principal Investments: Nonaffiliate common stock (32%), cash and equiv (31%), affiliate common stock (31%), real estate (6%)
Provider Compensation ($000): Contr fee ($69,229), capitation ($1,595)
Total Member Encounters: Phys (23,888), non-phys (1,809)
Group Affiliation: Universal Health Services Inc
Licensed in: NV
Address: 1510 Meadow Wood Lane, Reno, NV 89502
Phone: (775) 770-6000 **Dom State:** NV **Commenced Bus:** June 1993

Data Date	Rating	RACR #1	RACR #2	Total Assets ($mil)	Capital ($mil)	Net Premium ($mil)	Net Income ($mil)
6-14	D+	0.62	0.52	37.6	11.3	51.3	-6.4
6-13	D+	0.69	0.57	30.7	12.6	42.2	-1.3
2013	D+	1.00	0.83	43.5	18.6	83.7	-3.7
2012	D+	0.82	0.69	31.2	15.3	84.7	0.0
2011	N/A	N/A	N/A	33.7	10.7	86.6	-2.7
2010	N/A	N/A	N/A	40.6	11.0	82.8	-2.9
2009	C-	1.03	0.86	33.5	12.4	87.9	-7.2

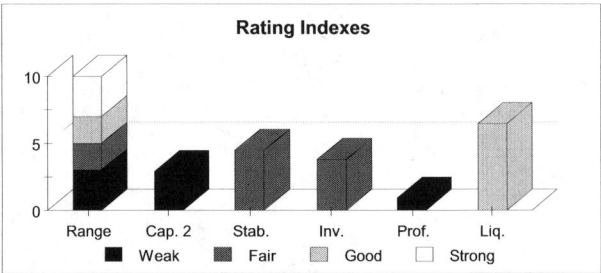

PROMINENCE PREFERRED HEALTH INS CO — D — Weak

Major Rating Factors: Weak profitability index (0.7 on a scale of 0 to 10). Fair capitalization (3.8) based on weak current risk-adjusted capital (moderate loss scenario). High quality investment portfolio (9.7).
Other Rating Factors: Excellent liquidity (6.9) with sufficient resources (cash flows and marketable investments) to handle a spike in claims.
Principal Business: Comp med (99%)
Mem Phys: 13: 8,399 **12:** 7,722 **13 MLR** 88.0% **/ 13 Admin Exp** N/A
Enroll(000): Q2 14: 14 **13:** 15 **12:** 15 **Med Exp PMPM:** $351
Principal Investments: Cash and equiv (92%), real estate (8%)
Provider Compensation ($000): Contr fee ($55,437), capitation ($1,312)
Total Member Encounters: Phys (17,525), non-phys (1,522)
Group Affiliation: Universal Health Services Inc
Licensed in: NV
Address: 1510 Meadow Wood Lane, Reno, NV 89502
Phone: (775) 770-6679 **Dom State:** NV **Commenced Bus:** April 2000

Data Date	Rating	RACR #1	RACR #2	Total Assets ($mil)	Capital ($mil)	Net Premium ($mil)	Net Income ($mil)
6-14	D	0.74	0.62	27.8	6.1	35.9	-6.2
6-13	D	0.56	0.47	15.0	5.3	34.3	-1.4
2013	D	1.22	1.02	26.6	10.2	69.2	-7.8
2012	D	0.72	0.60	17.0	6.7	80.9	-3.4
2011	D	0.73	0.61	24.0	8.2	100.5	-5.3
2010	D+	0.72	0.60	27.7	7.2	86.6	-2.0
2009	D+	0.61	0.51	24.7	5.9	65.7	-3.0

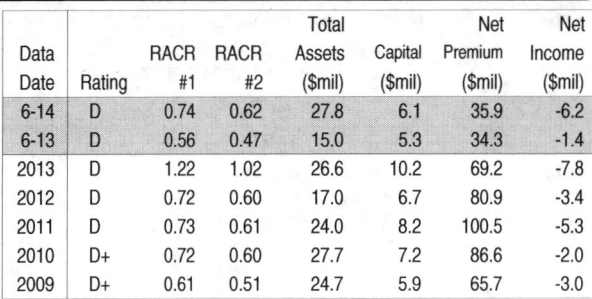

Rating Indexes

Range Cap. 2 Stab. Inv. Prof. Liq.
■ Weak ■ Fair ▨ Good ☐ Strong

PROVIDENCE HEALTH PLAN * — A+ — Excellent

Major Rating Factors: Excellent profitability (7.5 on a scale of 0 to 10). Strong capitalization index (10.0) based on excellent current risk-adjusted capital (severe loss scenario). High quality investment portfolio (9.5).
Other Rating Factors: Excellent overall results on stability tests (8.0). Good liquidity (6.8) with sufficient resources (cash flows and marketable investments) to handle a spike in claims.
Principal Business: Comp med (58%), Medicare (42%)
Mem Phys: 13: 27,992 **12:** 23,642 **13 MLR** 88.9% **/ 13 Admin Exp** N/A
Enroll(000): Q2 14: 187 **13:** 184 **12:** 186 **Med Exp PMPM:** $427
Principal Investments: Long-term bonds (81%), real estate (10%), cash and equiv (7%), affiliate common stock (1%)
Provider Compensation ($000): Contr fee ($500,647), bonus arrang ($223,436), FFS ($199,067), capitation ($28,395)
Total Member Encounters: Phys (958,371), non-phys (845,772)
Group Affiliation: Sisters of Providence
Licensed in: OR, WA
Address: 4400 NE Halsey Bldg 2 Ste 690, Portland, OR 97213-1545
Phone: (503) 574-7500 **Dom State:** OR **Commenced Bus:** January 1985

Data Date	Rating	RACR #1	RACR #2	Total Assets ($mil)	Capital ($mil)	Net Premium ($mil)	Net Income ($mil)
6-14	A+	6.06	5.05	738.7	522.3	548.2	15.2
6-13	A+	4.65	3.87	678.5	489.8	542.0	25.2
2013	A+	5.85	4.88	692.9	506.8	1,076.2	47.2
2012	A+	4.43	3.69	654.4	470.3	1,057.6	49.8
2011	A+	5.42	4.52	582.9	431.5	1,035.6	69.0
2010	A+	5.46	4.55	545.7	418.2	980.5	54.7
2009	A-	4.88	4.06	505.5	373.5	967.5	28.8

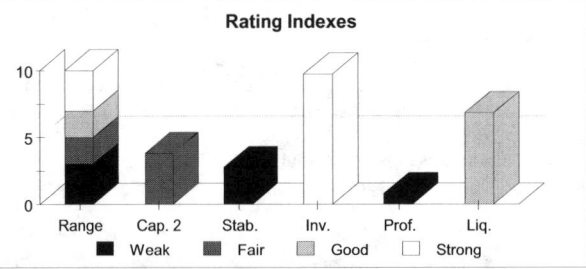

Rating Indexes

Range Cap. 2 Stab. Inv. Prof. Liq.
■ Weak ■ Fair ▨ Good ☐ Strong

PROVIDENT LIFE & ACCIDENT INSURANCE COMPANY — C+ — Fair

Major Rating Factors: Fair overall results on stability tests (4.8 on a scale of 0 to 10) including fair financial strength of affiliated Unum Group. Fair quality investment portfolio (4.4) with large holdings of BBB rated bonds in addition to junk bond exposure equal to 100% of capital. Good overall profitability (6.8). Excellent expense controls. Return on equity has been excellent over the last five years averaging 21.7%.
Other Rating Factors: Strong capitalization (7.5) based on excellent risk adjusted capital (severe loss scenario). Excellent liquidity (7.3).
Principal Business: Individual health insurance (69%), individual life insurance (28%), group health insurance (1%), reinsurance (1%), and group life insurance (1%).
Principal Investments: NonCMO investment grade bonds (72%), noninv. grade bonds (9%), CMOs and structured securities (8%), mortgages in good standing (5%), and misc. investments (6%).
Investments in Affiliates: None
Group Affiliation: Unum Group
Licensed in: All states except NY
Commenced Business: May 1887
Address: 1 Fountain Square, Chattanooga, TN 37402
Phone: (423) 755-1373 **Domicile State:** TN **NAIC Code:** 68195

Data Date	Rating	RACR #1	RACR #2	Total Assets ($mil)	Capital ($mil)	Net Premium ($mil)	Net Income ($mil)
6-14	C+	2.60	1.31	8,355.4	700.5	473.6	89.5
6-13	C+	2.43	1.22	8,333.0	668.0	466.3	102.6
2013	C+	2.55	1.28	8,347.6	699.7	898.5	166.4
2012	C+	2.30	1.16	8,452.0	642.8	960.1	168.9
2011	C+	2.35	1.19	8,417.2	653.0	924.9	170.4
2010	C+	2.47	1.25	8,271.6	654.6	887.4	130.3
2009	C+	2.26	1.16	8,004.3	567.1	862.5	113.3

Unum Group
Composite Group Rating: C+

Largest Group Members	Assets ($mil)	Rating
UNUM LIFE INS CO OF AMERICA	19079	C+
PROVIDENT LIFE ACCIDENT INS CO	8348	C+
PAUL REVERE LIFE INS CO	4302	C+
COLONIAL LIFE ACCIDENT INS CO	2753	C+
FIRST UNUM LIFE INS CO	2704	C+

PROVIDENT LIFE & CASUALTY INSURANCE COMPANY   B-   Good

Major Rating Factors: Good overall results on stability tests (5.3 on a scale of 0 to 10) despite fair financial strength of affiliated Unum Group. Other stability subfactors include excellent operational trends and excellent risk diversification. Fair quality investment portfolio (4.6) with large holdings of BBB rated bonds in addition to junk bond exposure equal to 55% of capital. Strong capitalization (9.3) based on excellent risk adjusted capital (severe loss scenario).

Other Rating Factors: Excellent profitability (8.4) with operating gains in each of the last five years. Excellent liquidity (7.2).

Principal Business: Individual health insurance (90%), reinsurance (6%), and individual life insurance (3%).

Principal Investments: NonCMO investment grade bonds (74%), noninv. grade bonds (11%), CMOs and structured securities (9%), and mortgages in good standing (4%).

Investments in Affiliates: None

Group Affiliation: Unum Group

Licensed in: AK, AR, CO, CT, DC, DE, GA, HI, ID, IL, IA, KY, LA, MA, MS, MO, NE, NH, NJ, NM, NY, NC, ND, OH, OK, PA, RI, SC, SD, TN, VA, WA

Commenced Business: January 1952

Address: 1 Fountain Square, Chattanooga, TN 37402

Phone: (423) 755-1373 **Domicile State:** TN **NAIC Code:** 68209

Data Date	Rating	RACR #1	RACR #2	Total Assets ($mil)	Capital ($mil)	Net Premium ($mil)	Net Income ($mil)
6-14	B-	4.69	2.50	765.1	154.5	42.9	8.3
6-13	B-	4.46	2.33	771.3	153.3	44.4	9.6
2013	B-	4.65	2.46	764.1	150.9	86.2	18.3
2012	B-	4.43	2.33	777.6	145.9	87.8	17.8
2011	B-	4.45	2.37	768.3	142.0	85.3	14.5
2010	B-	4.55	2.44	747.2	142.6	84.0	13.3
2009	B-	4.20	2.29	722.0	130.2	86.6	6.1

Unum Group
Composite Group Rating: C+

Largest Group Members	Assets ($mil)	Rating
UNUM LIFE INS CO OF AMERICA	19079	C+
PROVIDENT LIFE ACCIDENT INS CO	8348	C+
PAUL REVERE LIFE INS CO	4302	C+
COLONIAL LIFE ACCIDENT INS CO	2753	C+
FIRST UNUM LIFE INS CO	2704	C+

PUPIL BENEFITS PLAN INC   C-   Fair

Major Rating Factors: Fair profitability index (4.8 on a scale of 0 to 10). Strong capitalization (7.5) based on excellent current risk-adjusted capital (severe loss scenario). High quality investment portfolio (9.9).

Other Rating Factors: Excellent liquidity (7.1) with ample operational cash flow and liquid investments.

Principal Business: Other (100%)

Mem Phys: 13: N/A **12:** N/A **13 MLR** 79.0% **/ 13 Admin Exp** N/A

Enroll(000): Q2 14: 745 **13:** 745 **12:** 742 **Med Exp PMPM:** $0

Principal Investments: Cash and equiv (59%), long-term bonds (31%), nonaffiliate common stock (7%), real estate (2%).

Provider Compensation ($000): FFS ($6,160)

Total Member Encounters: N/A

Group Affiliation: None

Licensed in: NY

Address: 101 Dutch Meadows Lane, Glenville, NY 12302

Phone: (518) 377-5144 **Dom State:** NY **Commenced Bus:** July 1941

Data Date	Rating	RACR #1	RACR #2	Total Assets ($mil)	Capital ($mil)	Net Premium ($mil)	Net Income ($mil)
6-14	C-	1.71	1.43	7.0	2.6	4.3	0.7
6-13	C-	1.93	1.61	7.0	2.5	4.0	0.7
2013	C-	1.25	1.04	11.5	1.9	8.3	0.0
2012	C-	1.34	1.11	10.6	1.7	7.3	0.1
2011	N/A	N/A	N/A	9.1	1.6	6.3	N/A
2010	N/A	N/A	N/A	8.8	1.7	5.8	0.8
2009	C-	N/A	N/A	8.2	0.8	5.4	-1.0

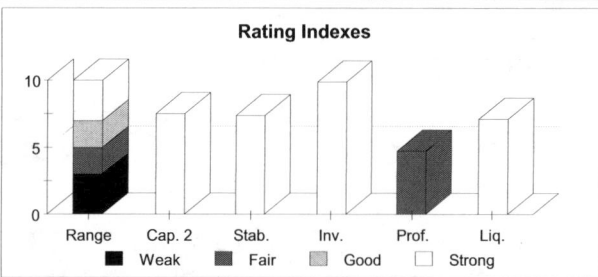

Rating Indexes

Range, Cap. 2, Stab., Inv., Prof., Liq.
■ Weak ■ Fair ▥ Good □ Strong

PYRAMID LIFE INSURANCE COMPANY   C   Fair

Major Rating Factors: Good current capitalization (6.0 on a scale of 0 to 10) based on excellent risk adjusted capital (severe loss scenario) reflecting significant improvement over results in 2010. Good overall profitability (5.9). Excellent expense controls. Return on equity has been good over the last five years, averaging 12.9%. Good liquidity (5.8).

Other Rating Factors: Weak overall results on stability tests (2.9) including weak results on operational trends. High quality investment portfolio (7.5).

Principal Business: Individual health insurance (99%) and individual life insurance (1%).

Principal Investments: NonCMO investment grade bonds (72%), CMOs and structured securities (23%), and common & preferred stock (4%).

Investments in Affiliates: None

Group Affiliation: Universal American Corp

Licensed in: AL, AZ, AR, CA, CO, DE, FL, GA, ID, IL, IN, IA, KS, KY, LA, MD, MA, MI, MN, MS, MO, MT, NE, NV, NM, NC, ND, OH, OK, OR, PA, SC, SD, TN, TX, UT, VA, WA, WI, WY

Commenced Business: August 1914

Address: 6201 Johnson Dr, Shawnee Mission, KS 66202

Phone: (913) 722-1110 **Domicile State:** KS **NAIC Code:** 68284

Data Date	Rating	RACR #1	RACR #2	Total Assets ($mil)	Capital ($mil)	Net Premium ($mil)	Net Income ($mil)
6-14	C	1.73	1.37	196.1	105.6	108.0	1.7
6-13	C	1.00	0.81	203.1	89.2	217.9	8.7
2013	C	1.29	1.03	211.8	104.2	425.6	23.5
2012	C	1.86	1.49	307.4	187.0	532.9	12.6
2011	C	1.59	1.28	385.2	253.5	748.1	14.4
2010	C-	0.65	0.53	477.2	239.0	1,754.8	38.1
2009	C-	0.73	0.60	369.3	179.5	1,063.5	24.4

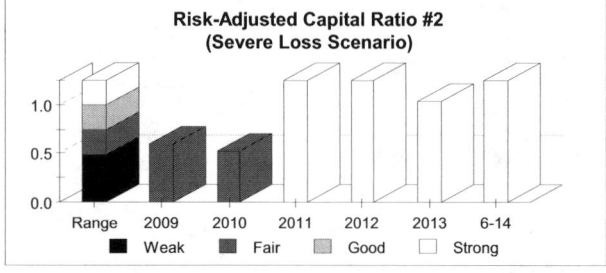

Risk-Adjusted Capital Ratio #2
(Severe Loss Scenario)

Range, 2009, 2010, 2011, 2012, 2013, 6-14
■ Weak ■ Fair ▥ Good □ Strong

QCA HEALTH PLAN INC
C- Fair

Major Rating Factors: Weak profitability index (0.9 on a scale of 0 to 10). Good capitalization index (6.8) based on excellent current risk-adjusted capital (severe loss scenario). Good overall results on stability tests (5.1).
Other Rating Factors: Good liquidity (5.2) with sufficient resources (cash flows and marketable investments) to handle a spike in claims. High quality investment portfolio (8.5).
Principal Business: Comp med (99%), FEHB (1%)
Mem Phys: 13: 13,168 **12:** 11,049 **13 MLR** 89.4% **/ 13 Admin Exp** N/A
Enroll(000): Q2 14: 39 **13:** 41 **12:** 45 **Med Exp PMPM:** $255
Principal Investments: Long-term bonds (38%), cash and equiv (32%), nonaffiliate common stock (24%), other (5%)
Provider Compensation ($000): Contr fee ($106,952), FFS ($21,075)
Total Member Encounters: Phys (345,510), non-phys (101,303)
Group Affiliation: Catholic Health Initiatives
Licensed in: AR
Address: 12615 Chenal Parkway Suite 300, Little Rock, AR 72211-3323
Phone: (501) 228-7111 **Dom State:** AR **Commenced Bus:** July 1996

Data Date	Rating	RACR #1	RACR #2	Total Assets ($mil)	Capital ($mil)	Net Premium ($mil)	Net Income ($mil)
6-14	C-	1.21	1.01	47.9	19.7	71.9	-1.1
6-13	C-	0.72	0.60	33.8	11.7	71.1	-1.7
2013	C-	0.78	0.65	31.0	12.8	141.3	-3.6
2012	C-	0.80	0.66	39.1	12.9	147.2	-6.2
2011	B-	1.18	0.99	42.9	18.8	146.1	-4.6
2010	B	1.50	1.25	44.8	23.2	146.8	2.0
2009	B	1.66	1.39	39.9	21.7	124.2	2.4

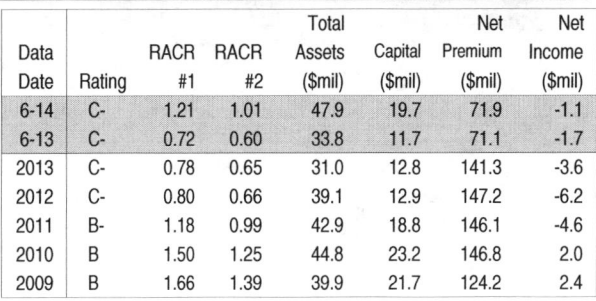

Rating Indexes

Range, Cap. 2, Stab., Inv., Prof., Liq.
Weak, Fair, Good, Strong

QCC INS CO
B Good

Major Rating Factors: Good quality investment portfolio (6.7 on a scale of 0 to 10). Good liquidity (6.9) with sufficient resources (cash flows and marketable investments) to handle a spike in claims. Fair profitability index (4.6).
Other Rating Factors: Strong capitalization (10.0) based on excellent current risk-adjusted capital (severe loss scenario).
Principal Business: Comp med (91%), Medicare (4%), dental (2%), other (2%)
Mem Phys: 13: 54,545 **12:** 51,931 **13 MLR** 83.8% **/ 13 Admin Exp** N/A
Enroll(000): Q2 14: 418 **13:** 353 **12:** 372 **Med Exp PMPM:** $386
Principal Investments: Long-term bonds (47%), nonaffiliate common stock (35%), cash and equiv (7%), other (11%)
Provider Compensation ($000): Contr fee ($1,625,830), FFS ($40,540), capitation ($10,263)
Total Member Encounters: Phys (7,344,310), non-phys (1,429,317)
Group Affiliation: Independence Blue Cross Inc
Licensed in: AZ, CO, DC, DE, FL, GA, IN, KS, KY, LA, MD, MA, MS, MT, NE, NV, NJ, NM, ND, OH, OK, PA, SC, SD, TN, TX, UT, VT, WA, WV
Address: 1901 Market St 39th Floor, Philadelphia, PA 19103
Phone: (215) 241-2400 **Dom State:** PA **Commenced Bus:** December 1981

Data Date	Rating	RACR #1	RACR #2	Total Assets ($mil)	Capital ($mil)	Net Premium ($mil)	Net Income ($mil)
6-14	B	4.68	3.90	1,334.2	690.4	1,156.7	-3.8
6-13	B	5.16	4.30	1,220.9	701.3	1,025.9	21.5
2013	B	4.93	4.11	1,211.6	730.7	2,002.2	36.1
2012	B	5.23	4.36	1,335.2	711.5	2,146.4	58.3
2011	B	5.78	4.81	1,373.8	743.0	2,144.7	112.6
2010	B	5.62	4.68	1,323.6	772.4	2,457.9	238.9
2009	B-	3.26	2.72	1,046.2	503.8	2,851.9	-6.5

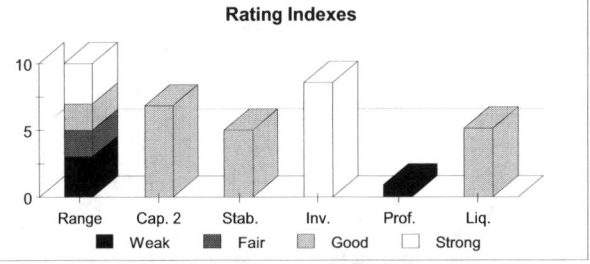

Rating Indexes

Range, Cap. 2, Stab., Inv., Prof., Liq.
Weak, Fair, Good, Strong

QUALCHOICE LIFE & HEALTH INS CO
C Fair

Major Rating Factors: Weak profitability index (2.4 on a scale of 0 to 10). Good capitalization (6.4) based on good current risk-adjusted capital (severe loss scenario). High quality investment portfolio (9.9).
Other Rating Factors: Excellent liquidity (7.3) with ample operational cash flow and liquid investments.
Principal Business: Comp med (95%), med supp (3%)
Mem Phys: 13: 13,168 **12:** 11,049 **13 MLR** 83.8% **/ 13 Admin Exp** N/A
Enroll(000): Q2 14: 2 **13:** 2 **12:** 2 **Med Exp PMPM:** $224
Principal Investments: Cash and equiv (96%), long-term bonds (4%)
Provider Compensation ($000): Contr fee ($4,247), FFS ($834)
Total Member Encounters: Phys (14,514), non-phys (5,553)
Group Affiliation: Catholic Health Initiatives
Licensed in: AR
Address: 12615 Chenal Pkwy Suite 300, Little Rock, AR 72211
Phone: (501) 228-7111 **Dom State:** AR **Commenced Bus:** April 1965

Data Date	Rating	RACR #1	RACR #2	Total Assets ($mil)	Capital ($mil)	Net Premium ($mil)	Net Income ($mil)
6-14	C	1.15	0.95	3.1	2.2	3.0	0.0
6-13	C	1.10	0.92	2.4	1.8	2.9	0.0
2013	C	0.90	0.75	2.4	1.7	6.1	0.0
2012	C-	1.00	0.84	2.5	1.7	5.9	-0.1
2011	C	0.84	0.70	2.7	1.8	4.7	0.2
2010	N/A	N/A	N/A	1.7	1.7	N/A	N/A
2009	N/A	N/A	N/A	N/A	N/A	N/A	N/A

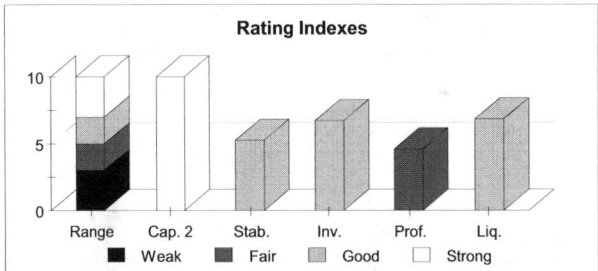

Rating Indexes

Range, Cap. 2, Stab., Inv., Prof., Liq.
Weak, Fair, Good, Strong

QUALITY HEALTH PLANS OF NEW YORK INC   E   Very Weak

Major Rating Factors: Weak profitability index (0.0 on a scale of 0 to 10). Fair capitalization (2.9) based on good current risk-adjusted capital (moderate loss scenario). Fair liquidity (4.1) as cash resources may not be adequate to cover a spike in claims.
Other Rating Factors: High quality investment portfolio (9.9).
Principal Business: Medicare (100%)
Mem Phys: 13: 2,356 **12:** 1,076 **13 MLR** 88.6% **/ 13 Admin Exp** N/A
Enroll(000): Q2 14: 0 **13:** 0 **12:** 0 **Med Exp PMPM:** $689
Principal Investments: Cash and equiv (100%)
Provider Compensation ($000): FFS ($815), capitation ($20)
Total Member Encounters: Phys (2,668), non-phys (290)
Group Affiliation: QHP Group Inc
Licensed in: NY
Address: 620 Belle Terre Rd Suite 4, Port Jefferson, NY 11777
Phone: (813) 463-0099 **Dom State:** NY **Commenced Bus:** January 2010

Data Date	Rating	RACR #1	RACR #2	Total Assets ($mil)	Capital ($mil)	Net Premium ($mil)	Net Income ($mil)
6-14	E	1.10	0.92	1.7	0.7	1.1	0.2
6-13	E	1.38	1.15	1.5	0.8	0.5	-0.4
2013	E	0.41	0.34	2.5	0.2	1.2	-2.9
2012	E-	2.42	2.02	2.4	1.5	0.2	-2.6
2011	E	4.92	4.10	1.7	1.5	0.1	0.0
2010	U	10.48	8.73	10.3	9.7	0.2	-0.3
2009	N/A	N/A	N/A	10.1	10.0	N/A	N/A

Rating Indexes

REGENCE BL CROSS BL SHIELD OREGON *   B+   Good

Major Rating Factors: Good overall profitability index (5.6 on a scale of 0 to 10). Good quality investment portfolio (6.3). Good liquidity (6.8) with sufficient resources (cash flows and marketable investments) to handle a spike in claims.
Other Rating Factors: Strong capitalization (10.0) based on excellent current risk-adjusted capital (severe loss scenario).
Principal Business: Comp med (46%), Medicare (33%), FEHB (17%), med supp (1%), other (1%)
Mem Phys: 13: 18,996 **12:** 18,173 **13 MLR** 85.9% **/ 13 Admin Exp** N/A
Enroll(000): Q2 14: 470 **13:** 498 **12:** 473 **Med Exp PMPM:** $273
Principal Investments: Long-term bonds (63%), nonaffiliate common stock (25%), cash and equiv (8%), real estate (1%), affiliate common stock (1%), other (3%)
Provider Compensation ($000): Contr fee ($1,179,569), FFS ($428,429), bonus arrang ($1,329), capitation ($45), other ($9,515)
Total Member Encounters: Phys (4,810,649), non-phys (6,169,004)
Group Affiliation: Regence Group
Licensed in: OR, WA
Address: 100 SW Market St, Portland, OR 97201
Phone: (503) 225-5221 **Dom State:** OR **Commenced Bus:** June 1942

Data Date	Rating	RACR #1	RACR #2	Total Assets ($mil)	Capital ($mil)	Net Premium ($mil)	Net Income ($mil)
6-14	B+	5.95	4.96	1,047.9	636.5	933.9	-0.8
6-13	B+	6.32	5.27	986.3	604.6	936.9	23.2
2013	B+	5.87	4.89	1,008.2	627.3	1,891.2	18.0
2012	B+	5.92	4.94	938.4	565.0	1,852.5	43.2
2011	B+	5.36	4.47	934.7	522.0	1,865.9	6.9
2010	B+	5.78	4.82	933.5	544.2	1,892.9	75.2
2009	B	4.28	3.56	1,000.3	565.2	2,440.4	21.9

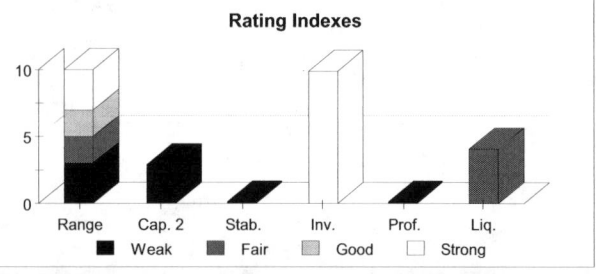

Rating Indexes

REGENCE BLUE CROSS BLUE SHIELD OF UT   B   Good

Major Rating Factors: Good quality investment portfolio (6.4 on a scale of 0 to 10). Good liquidity (6.8) with sufficient resources (cash flows and marketable investments) to handle a spike in claims. Fair profitability index (3.9).
Other Rating Factors: Strong capitalization (10.0) based on excellent current risk-adjusted capital (severe loss scenario).
Principal Business: Comp med (40%), FEHB (37%), Medicare (18%), med supp (3%), other (2%)
Mem Phys: 13: 12,397 **12:** 11,927 **13 MLR** 87.2% **/ 13 Admin Exp** N/A
Enroll(000): Q2 14: 251 **13:** 259 **12:** 251 **Med Exp PMPM:** $305
Principal Investments: Long-term bonds (69%), nonaffiliate common stock (15%), cash and equiv (8%), affiliate common stock (8%), real estate (1%)
Provider Compensation ($000): Contr fee ($605,267), FFS ($322,684), capitation ($244), bonus arrang ($57), other ($3,464)
Total Member Encounters: Phys (3,212,845), non-phys (3,225,605)
Group Affiliation: Regence Group
Licensed in: UT
Address: 2980 E Cottonwood Pkwy, Salt Lake City, UT 84109
Phone: (801) 333-2000 **Dom State:** UT **Commenced Bus:** January 1945

Data Date	Rating	RACR #1	RACR #2	Total Assets ($mil)	Capital ($mil)	Net Premium ($mil)	Net Income ($mil)
6-14	B	5.18	4.32	550.8	273.5	562.0	-1.2
6-13	B	6.02	5.02	521.5	281.8	528.4	11.0
2013	B	5.44	4.53	534.8	287.5	1,086.4	8.6
2012	B	5.98	4.99	511.8	279.9	1,000.0	112.7
2011	B-	4.60	3.83	503.9	236.9	1,011.6	-10.8
2010	B	4.78	3.98	473.9	243.7	1,040.4	16.2
2009	B-	3.42	2.85	486.5	215.5	1,079.1	-25.0

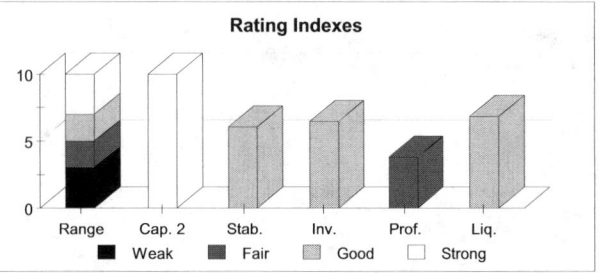

Rating Indexes

REGENCE BLUESHIELD   B   Good

Major Rating Factors: Good quality investment portfolio (6.3 on a scale of 0 to 10). Good liquidity (6.8) with sufficient resources (cash flows and marketable investments) to handle a spike in claims. Fair profitability index (3.7).
Other Rating Factors: Strong capitalization (10.0) based on excellent current risk-adjusted capital (severe loss scenario).
Principal Business: Comp med (73%), Medicare (14%), FEHB (10%), med supp (2%), dental (1%)
Mem Phys: 13: 33,050   **12:** 32,142   **13 MLR** 83.1%   **/ 13 Admin Exp** N/A
Enroll(000): Q2 14: 474   **13:** 542   **12:** 547   **Med Exp PMPM:** $276
Principal Investments: Long-term bonds (60%), nonaffiliate common stock (25%), affiliate common stock (8%), cash and equiv (2%), real estate (1%), other (4%)
Provider Compensation ($000): Contr fee ($1,325,469), FFS ($495,713), bonus arrang ($5,501), capitation ($161)
Total Member Encounters: Phys (6,204,410), non-phys (7,396,151)
Group Affiliation: Regence Group
Licensed in: WA
Address: 1800 9th Ave, Seattle, WA 98101
Phone: (206) 464-3600   **Dom State:** WA   **Commenced Bus:** April 1933

Data Date	Rating	RACR #1	RACR #2	Total Assets ($mil)	Capital ($mil)	Net Premium ($mil)	Net Income ($mil)
6-14	B	6.78	5.65	1,684.2	1,106.2	931.0	-27.6
6-13	B+	7.62	6.35	1,753.7	1,151.8	1,103.5	37.7
2013	B+	7.22	6.02	1,692.1	1,178.5	2,190.6	48.3
2012	B+	7.15	5.96	1,583.5	1,079.7	2,157.8	30.0
2011	B+	6.33	5.28	1,551.3	994.1	2,209.8	-10.2
2010	A-	6.00	5.00	1,471.8	956.5	2,320.2	51.3
2009	B+	5.45	4.54	1,427.9	892.8	2,394.4	10.5

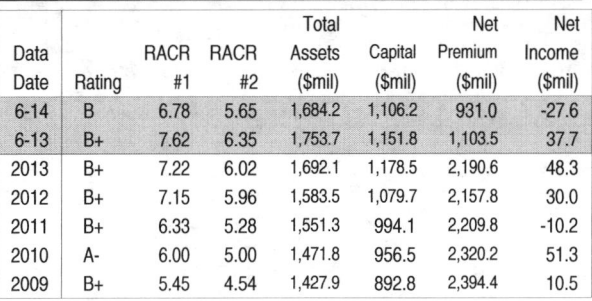

Rating Indexes

REGENCE BLUESHIELD OF IDAHO INC   B   Good

Major Rating Factors: Good quality investment portfolio (6.4 on a scale of 0 to 10). Good liquidity (6.8) with sufficient resources (cash flows and marketable investments) to handle a spike in claims. Fair profitability index (3.8).
Other Rating Factors: Strong capitalization (10.0) based on excellent current risk-adjusted capital (severe loss scenario).
Principal Business: Comp med (78%), Medicare (13%), FEHB (3%), med supp (3%), dental (1%), other (2%)
Mem Phys: 13: 8,422   **12:** 8,053   **13 MLR** 81.0%   **/ 13 Admin Exp** N/A
Enroll(000): Q2 14: 125   **13:** 139   **12:** 146   **Med Exp PMPM:** $223
Principal Investments: Long-term bonds (65%), cash and equiv (16%), nonaffiliate common stock (15%), real estate (3%), affiliate common stock (1%)
Provider Compensation ($000): Contr fee ($224,973), FFS ($139,683), bonus arrang ($14,912), capitation ($459), other ($3,624)
Total Member Encounters: Phys (1,262,283), non-phys (1,478,541)
Group Affiliation: Regence Group
Licensed in: ID, WA
Address: 1602 21st Ave, Lewiston, ID 83501
Phone: (208) 746-2671   **Dom State:** ID   **Commenced Bus:** April 1946

Data Date	Rating	RACR #1	RACR #2	Total Assets ($mil)	Capital ($mil)	Net Premium ($mil)	Net Income ($mil)
6-14	B	6.00	5.00	275.4	149.9	222.7	-8.8
6-13	B	6.65	5.54	287.8	156.4	242.1	8.3
2013	B	6.33	5.28	273.8	158.5	479.6	14.0
2012	B	6.23	5.19	258.9	146.1	460.6	15.1
2011	B	5.05	4.21	242.6	128.1	465.7	-1.1
2010	B	4.83	4.02	233.3	122.5	487.1	3.1
2009	B-	4.31	3.59	237.5	116.7	512.4	-5.1

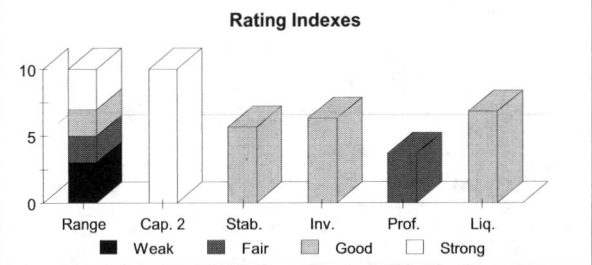

Rating Indexes

RELIANCE STANDARD LIFE INSURANCE COMPANY   B   Good

Major Rating Factors: Good overall results on stability tests (5.9 on a scale of 0 to 10) despite excessive premium growth. Other stability subfactors include excellent operational trends, excellent risk adjusted capital for prior years and excellent risk diversification. Good current capitalization (6.7) based on good risk adjusted capital (severe loss scenario), although results have slipped from the excellent range during the last year. Good overall profitability (6.5).
Other Rating Factors: Good liquidity (6.7). Fair quality investment portfolio (4.8).
Principal Business: Group health insurance (37%), individual annuities (29%), group life insurance (22%), group retirement contracts (8%), and reinsurance (3%).
Principal Investments: CMOs and structured securities (49%), nonCMO investment grade bonds (35%), noninv. grade bonds (7%), common & preferred stock (3%), and mortgages in good standing (1%).
Investments in Affiliates: 2%
Group Affiliation: Tokio Marine Holdings Inc
Licensed in: All states, the District of Columbia and Puerto Rico
Commenced Business: April 1907
Address: 111 S Wacker Dr Suite 4400, Chicago, IL 60606-4410
Phone: (215) 787-4000   **Domicile State:** IL   **NAIC Code:** 68381

Data Date	Rating	RACR #1	RACR #2	Total Assets ($mil)	Capital ($mil)	Net Premium ($mil)	Net Income ($mil)
6-14	B	1.69	0.96	7,240.6	671.9	989.4	74.7
6-13	B	1.76	1.05	5,542.2	594.2	702.4	67.9
2013	B	1.78	1.06	5,980.4	598.4	1,642.5	134.6
2012	B	1.74	1.02	5,186.9	561.5	1,386.6	88.4
2011	B-	1.72	1.04	4,618.0	522.3	1,320.9	76.9
2010	B-	1.97	1.19	4,193.8	530.6	1,148.0	64.3
2009	B-	1.78	1.12	3,821.3	541.0	1,212.9	-29.1

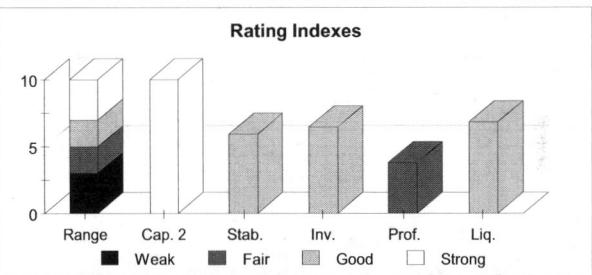

Adverse Trends in Operations

Increase in policy surrenders from 2012 to 2013 (50%)
Decrease in capital during 2011 (2%)
Decrease in capital during 2010 (2%)
Decrease in premium volume from 2009 to 2010 (5%)

RESERVE NATIONAL INSURANCE COMPANY *   A   Excellent

Major Rating Factors: Good liquidity (6.6 on a scale of 0 to 10) with sufficient resources to handle a spike in claims. Excellent overall results on stability tests (7.6). Strengths that enhance stability include excellent operational trends and excellent risk diversification. Strong capitalization (8.2) based on excellent risk adjusted capital (severe loss scenario). Furthermore, this high level of risk adjusted capital has been consistently maintained over the last five years.

Other Rating Factors: High quality investment portfolio (8.0). Excellent profitability (7.1) with operating gains in each of the last five years.

Principal Business: Individual health insurance (90%), individual life insurance (8%), and group health insurance (2%).

Principal Investments: NonCMO investment grade bonds (92%), CMOs and structured securities (5%), and , and , and misc. investments (3%).

Investments in Affiliates: None

Group Affiliation: Kemper Corporation

Licensed in: AL, AZ, AR, CO, FL, GA, ID, IL, IN, IA, KS, KY, LA, MI, MS, MO, MT, NE, NV, NM, NC, OH, OK, OR, PA, SC, SD, TN, TX, UT, VA, WA, WV, WI, WY

Commenced Business: September 1956

Address: 601 E Britton Rd, Oklahoma City, OK 73114

Phone: (405) 848-7931 **Domicile State:** OK **NAIC Code:** 68462

Data Date	Rating	RACR #1	RACR #2	Total Assets ($mil)	Capital ($mil)	Net Premium ($mil)	Net Income ($mil)
6-14	A	2.38	1.83	112.3	51.6	68.7	0.3
6-13	A	2.67	2.04	114.6	58.0	71.7	0.5
2013	A	2.27	1.76	111.2	52.4	143.6	4.9
2012	A	2.66	2.04	116.0	58.4	135.2	8.8
2011	B	2.63	1.95	118.6	60.6	135.2	9.9
2010	B	2.21	1.62	109.3	50.2	131.7	7.4
2009	B	2.09	1.52	107.9	47.3	128.0	2.7

Adverse Trends in Operations

Decrease in asset base during 2013 (4%)
Decrease in capital during 2013 (10%)
Decrease in asset base during 2012 (2%)
Decrease in capital during 2012 (4%)

RGA REINSURANCE COMPANY   B   Good

Major Rating Factors: Good capitalization (6.0 on a scale of 0 to 10) based on good risk adjusted capital (severe loss scenario). Good quality investment portfolio (5.1) despite large holdings of BBB rated bonds in addition to junk bond exposure equal to 84% of capital. Exposure to mortgages is significant, but the mortgage default rate has been low. Good overall profitability (6.8). Excellent expense controls.

Other Rating Factors: Good liquidity (5.5). Fair overall results on stability tests (4.4).

Principal Business: Reinsurance (100%).

Principal Investments: NonCMO investment grade bonds (50%), mortgages in good standing (15%), CMOs and structured securities (14%), policy loans (8%), and misc. investments (13%).

Investments in Affiliates: 3%

Group Affiliation: RGA Inc

Licensed in: All states except PR

Commenced Business: October 1982

Address: 660 Mason Ridge Center Dr, St Louis, MO 63141

Phone: (314) 453-7368 **Domicile State:** MO **NAIC Code:** 93572

Data Date	Rating	RACR #1	RACR #2	Total Assets ($mil)	Capital ($mil)	Net Premium ($mil)	Net Income ($mil)
6-14	B	1.67	0.88	23,561.5	1,506.8	1,025.9	93.8
6-13	B	1.68	0.90	23,251.4	1,515.0	1,188.5	-76.2
2013	B	1.70	0.90	23,259.8	1,550.1	2,305.6	115.8
2012	B	1.75	0.95	22,835.1	1,644.6	5,213.8	3.5
2011	B	1.97	1.13	16,913.0	1,515.9	3,176.5	129.7
2010	B	2.03	1.17	15,327.9	1,528.9	2,225.9	68.0
2009	B	1.90	1.11	14,893.4	1,416.5	2,239.6	63.2

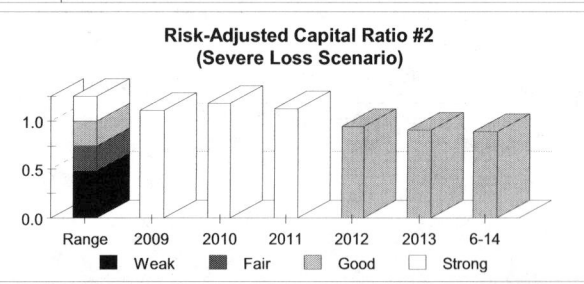

Risk-Adjusted Capital Ratio #2 (Severe Loss Scenario)

Range, 2009, 2010, 2011, 2012, 2013, 6-14 — Weak, Fair, Good, Strong

ROCKY MOUNTAIN HEALTH MAINT ORG *   A-   Excellent

Major Rating Factors: Strong capitalization index (10.0 on a scale of 0 to 10) based on excellent current risk-adjusted capital (severe loss scenario). High quality investment portfolio (9.3). Good liquidity (6.7) with sufficient resources (cash flows and marketable investments) to handle a spike in claims.

Other Rating Factors: Fair profitability index (4.3). Fair overall results on stability tests (4.3).

Principal Business: Comp med (73%), Medicare (30%).

Mem Phys: 13: 20,368 **12:** 18,298 **13 MLR** 82.6% **/ 13 Admin Exp** N/A

Enroll(000): Q2 14: 194 **13:** 129 **12:** 101 **Med Exp PMPM:** $94

Principal Investments: Long-term bonds (71%), cash and equiv (13%), nonaffiliate common stock (9%), real estate (6%)

Provider Compensation ($000): Bonus arrang ($73,553), contr fee ($52,749), FFS ($2,243), capitation ($525)

Total Member Encounters: Phys (694,192)

Group Affiliation: Rocky Mountain Health Co

Licensed in: CO, WY

Address: 2775 Crossroads Blvd, Grand Junction, CO 81506

Phone: (970) 244-7760 **Dom State:** CO **Commenced Bus:** June 1974

Data Date	Rating	RACR #1	RACR #2	Total Assets ($mil)	Capital ($mil)	Net Premium ($mil)	Net Income ($mil)
6-14	A-	5.05	4.20	147.0	80.8	143.7	-4.9
6-13	A+	7.19	5.99	170.9	111.0	79.6	5.7
2013	A-	5.79	4.83	142.6	91.0	160.4	4.1
2012	A+	6.88	5.73	168.1	106.5	171.8	14.2
2011	A+	6.19	5.16	148.2	101.2	171.3	8.0
2010	A+	6.62	5.51	150.9	110.1	179.6	16.0
2009	A+	6.37	5.31	139.9	98.9	215.5	16.2

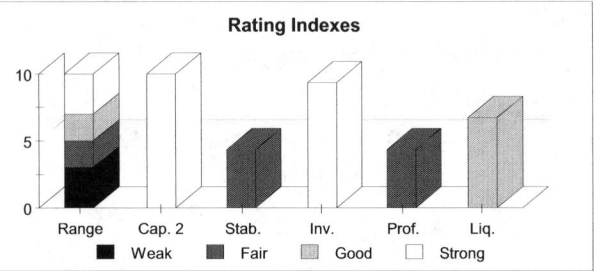

Rating Indexes

Range, Cap. 2, Stab., Inv., Prof., Liq. — Weak, Fair, Good, Strong

ROCKY MOUNTAIN HEALTHCARE OPTIONS   E   Very Weak

Major Rating Factors: Weak profitability index (0.9 on a scale of 0 to 10). Poor capitalization (2.3) based on weak current risk-adjusted capital (moderate loss scenario). Weak liquidity (2.4) as a spike in claims may stretch capacity.
Other Rating Factors: High quality investment portfolio (9.7).
Principal Business: Comp med (99%)
Mem Phys: 13: 17,323 **12:** 18,183   **13 MLR** 89.1% / **13 Admin Exp** N/A
Enroll(000): Q2 14: 20 **13:** 38 **12:** 51   **Med Exp PMPM:** $283
Principal Investments: Long-term bonds (85%), cash and equiv (8%), affiliate common stock (7%)
Provider Compensation ($000): Contr fee ($114,010), FFS ($18,099), bonus arrang ($16,392), capitation ($1,602), other ($818)
Total Member Encounters: Phys (317,181)
Group Affiliation: Rocky Mountain Health Co
Licensed in: CO
Address: 2775 Crossroads Blvd, Grand Junction, CO 81506
Phone: (970) 244-7760   **Dom State:** CO   **Commenced Bus:** May 1993

Data Date	Rating	RACR #1	RACR #2	Total Assets ($mil)	Capital ($mil)	Net Premium ($mil)	Net Income ($mil)
6-14	E	0.53	0.44	42.2	16.6	55.4	-1.6
6-13	E	0.43	0.36	43.9	11.1	86.5	-2.6
2013	E	0.50	0.41	40.8	13.6	170.4	-4.2
2012	E	0.59	0.49	44.7	13.8	168.5	-14.2
2011	D+	1.10	0.92	42.3	18.1	159.3	-6.6
2010	D+	0.75	0.63	29.2	9.7	129.8	-3.2
2009	B-	0.96	0.80	27.5	11.2	103.9	-0.4

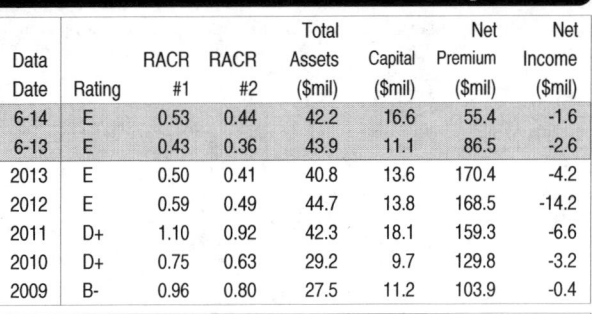

Rating Indexes

ROCKY MOUNTAIN HOSPITAL & MEDICAL *   B+   Good

Major Rating Factors: Good liquidity (6.6 on a scale of 0 to 10) with sufficient resources (cash flows and marketable investments) to handle a spike in claims. Excellent profitability (9.1). Strong capitalization (10.0) based on excellent current risk-adjusted capital (severe loss scenario).
Other Rating Factors: Fair quality investment portfolio (3.7).
Principal Business: Comp med (57%), FEHB (35%), med supp (4%), dental (2%), other (1%)
Mem Phys: 13: 23,023 **12:** 25,167   **13 MLR** 84.5% / **13 Admin Exp** N/A
Enroll(000): Q2 14: 687 **13:** 634 **12:** 601   **Med Exp PMPM:** $217
Principal Investments: Long-term bonds (82%), affiliate common stock (30%), real estate (2%)
Provider Compensation ($000): Contr fee ($1,450,047), FFS ($137,933), bonus arrang ($2,745), capitation ($97), other ($20,133)
Total Member Encounters: Phys (26,219,461), non-phys (3,729,382)
Group Affiliation: WellPoint Inc
Licensed in: CO, NV
Address: 700 Broadway, Denver, CO 80273
Phone: (303) 831-2131   **Dom State:** CO   **Commenced Bus:** October 1938

Data Date	Rating	RACR #1	RACR #2	Total Assets ($mil)	Capital ($mil)	Net Premium ($mil)	Net Income ($mil)
6-14	B+	3.83	3.19	889.3	449.7	982.3	74.5
6-13	A-	3.63	3.03	850.9	450.4	933.7	71.2
2013	B+	3.46	2.89	815.5	405.7	1,921.6	110.9
2012	A-	3.01	2.51	826.9	370.2	1,992.2	95.9
2011	B+	2.55	2.12	846.8	343.5	2,019.4	94.7
2010	B+	2.80	2.34	696.3	316.7	1,684.3	96.9
2009	B+	2.71	2.26	662.9	315.0	1,626.6	102.1

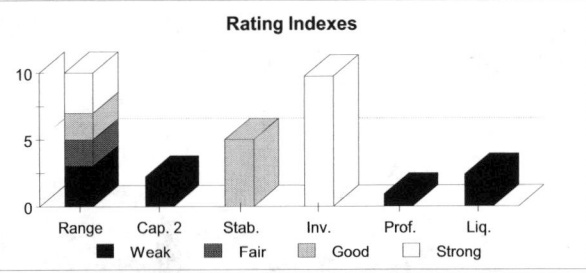

Rating Indexes

ROYAL STATE NATIONAL INSURANCE COMPANY LIMITED   B-   Good

Major Rating Factors: Good quality investment portfolio (6.1 on a scale of 0 to 10) despite mixed results such as: no exposure to mortgages and substantial holdings of BBB bonds but no exposure to junk bonds. Good overall profitability (5.4). Return on equity has been low, averaging 1.8%. Good liquidity (6.9) with sufficient resources to handle a spike in claims.
Other Rating Factors: Good overall results on stability tests (5.1) good operational trends and good risk diversification. Strong capitalization (8.8) based on excellent risk adjusted capital (severe loss scenario).
Principal Business: Group life insurance (65%), group health insurance (26%), individual life insurance (6%), and reinsurance (3%).
Principal Investments: NonCMO investment grade bonds (70%), common & preferred stock (16%), CMOs and structured securities (9%), cash (5%), and policy loans (1%).
Investments in Affiliates: 3%
Group Affiliation: Royal State Group
Licensed in: HI
Commenced Business: August 1961
Address: 819 S Beretania St, Honolulu, HI 96813
Phone: (808) 539-1600   **Domicile State:** HI   **NAIC Code:** 68551

Data Date	Rating	RACR #1	RACR #2	Total Assets ($mil)	Capital ($mil)	Net Premium ($mil)	Net Income ($mil)
6-14	B-	3.12	2.20	46.2	29.3	5.4	0.5
6-13	B-	3.24	2.32	45.7	29.1	5.4	0.3
2013	B-	3.29	2.33	45.6	28.9	10.6	0.4
2012	B-	3.29	2.38	44.6	28.9	10.5	-0.1
2011	B-	4.44	3.08	43.3	28.6	5.8	0.8
2010	B-	4.63	3.42	48.7	28.2	5.9	1.1
2009	B-	4.54	3.78	48.1	27.8	6.0	0.6

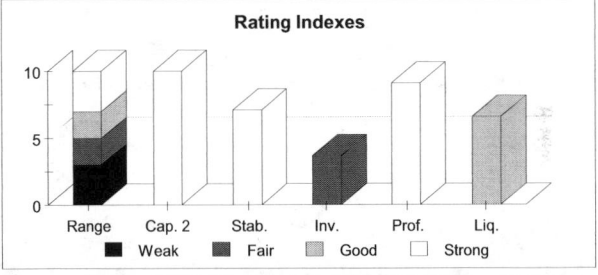

Rating Indexes

RYDER HEALTH PLAN INC

D   Weak

Major Rating Factors: Weak profitability index (2.3 on a scale of 0 to 10). Poor capitalization index (1.8) based on weak current risk-adjusted capital (moderate loss scenario). Fair overall results on stability tests (4.6).
Other Rating Factors: High quality investment portfolio (9.8). Excellent liquidity (7.6) with ample operational cash flow and liquid investments.
Principal Business: Comp med (96%), med supp (3%)
Mem Phys: 13: N/A **12:** N/A **13 MLR** 86.9% **/ 13 Admin Exp** N/A
Enroll(000): Q2 14: 4 **13:** 4 **12:** 4 **Med Exp PMPM:** $49
Principal Investments: Cash and equiv (83%), long-term bonds (17%)
Provider Compensation ($000): Capitation ($2,057), other ($304)
Total Member Encounters: N/A
Group Affiliation: None
Licensed in: PR
Address: 353 Font Martelo Ave Suite 1, Humacao, PR 00791
Phone: (787) 852-0846 **Dom State:** PR **Commenced Bus:** October 1984

Data Date	Rating	RACR #1	RACR #2	Total Assets ($mil)	Capital ($mil)	Net Premium ($mil)	Net Income ($mil)
6-14	D	0.48	0.40	1.4	0.6	1.3	0.0
6-13	E+	0.21	0.17	1.6	0.6	1.3	0.1
2013	D	0.60	0.50	1.5	0.7	2.6	0.0
2012	D	0.23	0.19	1.5	0.7	2.8	0.0
2011	C-	0.90	0.75	1.5	0.7	2.6	0.0
2010	U	1.03	0.86	1.6	0.8	2.8	0.0
2009	N/A	N/A	N/A	1.5	0.7	2.9	N/A

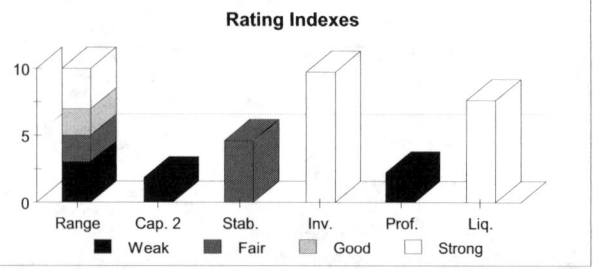

SAMARITAN HEALTH PLANS INC

B-   Good

Major Rating Factors: Fair capitalization (4.8 on a scale of 0 to 10) based on good current risk-adjusted capital (severe loss scenario). Good liquidity (6.1) with sufficient resources (cash flows and marketable investments) to handle a spike in claims. High quality investment portfolio (9.7).
Other Rating Factors: Weak profitability index (2.4).
Principal Business: Medicare (98%), other (2%)
Mem Phys: 13: 4,316 **12:** 4,236 **13 MLR** 91.4% **/ 13 Admin Exp** N/A
Enroll(000): Q2 14: 5 **13:** 5 **12:** 6 **Med Exp PMPM:** $769
Principal Investments: Long-term bonds (61%), cash and equiv (29%), nonaffiliate common stock (10%)
Provider Compensation ($000): Contr fee ($50,562)
Total Member Encounters: Phys (25,220), non-phys (18,159)
Group Affiliation: Samaritan Health Services
Licensed in: OR
Address: 3600 NW Samaritan Dr, Corvallis, OR 97330
Phone: (541) 768-5328 **Dom State:** OR **Commenced Bus:** January 2005

Data Date	Rating	RACR #1	RACR #2	Total Assets ($mil)	Capital ($mil)	Net Premium ($mil)	Net Income ($mil)
6-14	B-	0.90	0.75	17.5	7.5	27.7	-0.2
6-13	C+	0.95	0.79	15.2	7.8	28.2	0.1
2013	B-	0.97	0.81	16.6	8.0	55.4	-0.5
2012	C+	0.95	0.79	15.7	7.7	55.6	1.3
2011	C	0.73	0.61	13.4	6.6	57.1	-0.4
2010	C+	0.74	0.62	15.2	7.0	56.3	-0.8
2009	C-	0.68	0.57	15.0	7.4	55.4	0.3

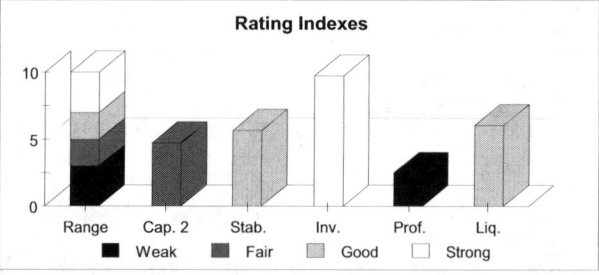

SAN FRANCISCO HEALTH AUTHORITY

C+   Fair

Major Rating Factors: Fair profitability index (4.6 on a scale of 0 to 10). Good overall results on stability tests (5.2) based on healthy premium and capital growth during 2013, steady enrollment growth, averaging 10% over the past five years. Strong capitalization index (6.9) based on excellent current risk-adjusted capital (severe loss scenario).
Other Rating Factors: Excellent liquidity (7.6) with ample operational cash flow and liquid investments.
Principal Business: Medicare (100%)
Mem Phys: 13: N/A **12:** N/A **13 MLR** 89.3% **/ 13 Admin Exp** N/A
Enroll(000): Q2 14: 82 **13:** 81 **12:** 77 **Med Exp PMPM:** $234
Principal Investments ($000): Cash and equiv ($93,105)
Provider Compensation ($000): None
Total Member Encounters: N/A
Group Affiliation: None
Licensed in: CA
Address: 201 Third St 7th Floor, San Francisco, CA 94103
Phone: (415) 547-7818 **Dom State:** CA **Commenced Bus:** March 1996

Data Date	Rating	RACR #1	RACR #2	Total Assets ($mil)	Capital ($mil)	Net Premium ($mil)	Net Income ($mil)
6-14	C+	1.66	1.08	174.9	40.4	127.4	4.1
6-13	C	1.26	0.82	133.8	26.7	114.4	1.0
2013	C+	1.49	0.97	159.5	36.2	250.1	10.5
2012	C	1.21	0.79	121.7	25.7	201.1	-4.5
2011	C+	1.94	1.30	106.5	30.1	132.1	-0.4
2010	B-	2.62	1.69	96.7	30.6	129.4	-0.4
2009	B	2.76	1.77	77.8	31.0	109.8	-3.1

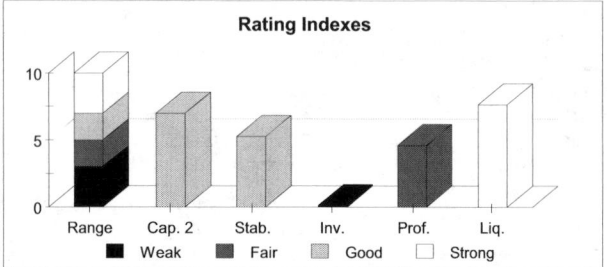

SAN MATEO HEALTH COMMISSION *   B+   Good

Major Rating Factors: Excellent profitability (8.8 on a scale of 0 to 10). Strong capitalization index (10.0) based on excellent current risk-adjusted capital (severe loss scenario). Excellent overall results on stability tests (7.7).
Other Rating Factors: Excellent liquidity (7.7) with ample operational cash flow and liquid investments.
Principal Business: Medicaid (73%), Medicare (27%)
Mem Phys: 13: N/A   **12:** N/A   **13 MLR** 82.5%   **/ 13 Admin Exp** N/A
Enroll(000): Q2 14: 115   **13:** 90   **12:** 81   **Med Exp PMPM:** $413
Principal Investments ($000): Cash and equiv ($181,150)
Provider Compensation ($000): None
Total Member Encounters: N/A
Group Affiliation: None
Licensed in: CA
Address: 701 Gateway Blvd Ste 400, S San Francisco, CA 94080
Phone: (650) 616-0050   **Dom State:** CA   **Commenced Bus:** December 1987

Data Date	Rating	RACR #1	RACR #2	Total Assets ($mil)	Capital ($mil)	Net Premium ($mil)	Net Income ($mil)
6-14	B+	5.56	3.40	298.4	158.7	299.6	13.5
6-13	B+	3.02	1.84	205.8	93.9	221.6	6.2
2013	B+	5.12	3.13	256.2	145.2	503.9	57.4
2012	B	2.78	1.70	209.9	87.8	478.7	11.9
2011	C+	2.48	1.52	191.9	75.8	452.8	4.0
2010	B	2.49	1.53	183.1	71.8	430.6	14.3
2009	B	2.70	1.65	110.2	57.5	302.7	15.0

SANFORD HEALTH PLAN   B   Good

Major Rating Factors: Good profitability index (4.9 on a scale of 0 to 10). Good liquidity (6.5) with sufficient resources (cash flows and marketable investments) to handle a spike in claims. Strong capitalization index (7.5) based on excellent current risk-adjusted capital (severe loss scenario).
Other Rating Factors: High quality investment portfolio (9.9). Excellent overall results on stability tests (7.6).
Principal Business: Comp med (97%), med supp (3%)
Mem Phys: 13: 28,485   **12:** 25,504   **13 MLR** 91.0%   **/ 13 Admin Exp** N/A
Enroll(000): Q2 14: 50   **13:** 37   **12:** 35   **Med Exp PMPM:** $306
Principal Investments: Long-term bonds (78%), cash and equiv (17%), pref stock (2%), other (3%)
Provider Compensation ($000): Contr fee ($126,010)
Total Member Encounters: Phys (112,698), non-phys (92,299)
Group Affiliation: Sanford Health
Licensed in: IA, ND, SD
Address: 300 Cherapa Pl Suite 201, Sioux Falls, SD 57103
Phone: (605) 328-6868   **Dom State:** SD   **Commenced Bus:** January 1998

Data Date	Rating	RACR #1	RACR #2	Total Assets ($mil)	Capital ($mil)	Net Premium ($mil)	Net Income ($mil)
6-14	B	1.73	1.45	62.7	28.7	112.3	2.5
6-13	B	1.78	1.48	44.8	28.1	70.8	2.7
2013	B	1.56	1.30	51.3	26.0	143.3	1.8
2012	B	1.69	1.41	47.8	26.8	138.2	2.8
2011	B	1.69	1.41	42.2	25.1	128.0	0.6
2010	B	1.69	1.41	40.9	24.1	122.0	0.2
2009	C+	0.77	0.65	24.4	9.5	105.9	-0.5

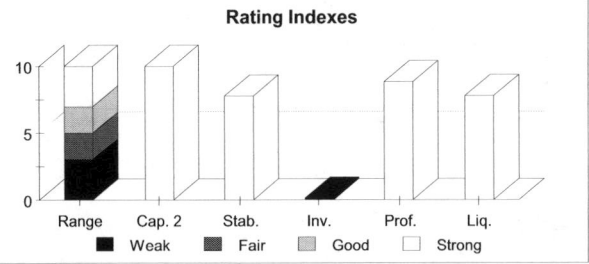

SANFORD HEALTH PLAN OF MINNESOTA   E   Very Weak

Major Rating Factors: Weak profitability index (0.6 on a scale of 0 to 10). Fair overall results on stability tests (4.4). Rating is significantly influenced by the good financial results of Sanford Health. Good capitalization index (6.8) based on excellent current risk-adjusted capital (severe loss scenario).
Other Rating Factors: High quality investment portfolio (9.9). Excellent liquidity (7.3) with ample operational cash flow and liquid investments.
Principal Business: Comp med (84%), med supp (16%)
Mem Phys: 13: 28,485   **12:** 25,504   **13 MLR** 102.5%   **/ 13 Admin Exp** N/A
Enroll(000): Q2 14: 0   **13:** 1   **12:** 1   **Med Exp PMPM:** $359
Principal Investments: Cash and equiv (100%)
Provider Compensation ($000): Contr fee ($3,285)
Total Member Encounters: Phys (2,632), non-phys (2,244)
Group Affiliation: Sanford Health
Licensed in: MN
Address: 300 Cherapa Pl Suite 201, Sioux Falls, SD 57103
Phone: (605) 328-7226   **Dom State:** MN   **Commenced Bus:** January 1998

Data Date	Rating	RACR #1	RACR #2	Total Assets ($mil)	Capital ($mil)	Net Premium ($mil)	Net Income ($mil)
6-14	E	1.22	1.02	1.8	1.1	1.2	-0.1
6-13	E	0.70	0.58	2.0	1.1	1.6	-0.5
2013	E	1.35	1.13	2.0	1.3	3.0	-0.4
2012	E	0.42	0.35	1.8	0.7	3.1	-1.2
2011	D+	1.33	1.11	1.9	1.3	3.2	0.0
2010	D+	1.39	1.16	2.0	1.3	2.7	-0.4
2009	C	2.16	1.80	2.3	1.7	3.0	-0.3

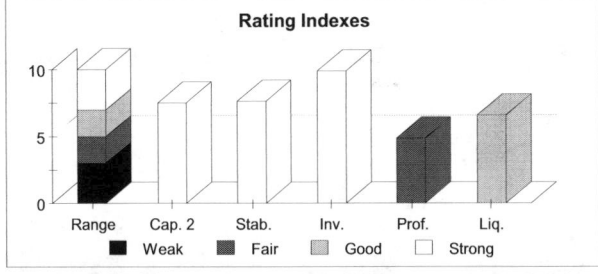

SANFORD HEART OF AMERICA HEALTH PLAN   D+   Weak

Major Rating Factors: Weak profitability index (0.9 on a scale of 0 to 10). Fair capitalization index (3.8) based on fair current risk-adjusted capital (moderate loss scenario). Fair overall results on stability tests (4.5).

Other Rating Factors: Good liquidity (6.9) with sufficient resources (cash flows and marketable investments) to handle a spike in claims. High quality investment portfolio (9.4).

Principal Business: Comp med (63%), FEHB (9%), other (28%)

Mem Phys: 13: 51 **12:** 47 **13 MLR** 97.4% **/ 13 Admin Exp** N/A

Enroll(000): Q2 14: 1 **13:** 1 **12:** 1 **Med Exp PMPM:** $306

Principal Investments: Cash and equiv (56%), long-term bonds (44%)

Provider Compensation ($000): FFS ($3,341), capitation ($377), contr fee ($116)

Total Member Encounters: Phys (3,290), non-phys (782)

Group Affiliation: None

Licensed in: ND

Address: 810 S Main Ave, Rugby, ND 58368

Phone: (701) 776-5848 **Dom State:** ND **Commenced Bus:** August 1982

Data Date	Rating	RACR #1	RACR #2	Total Assets ($mil)	Capital ($mil)	Net Premium ($mil)	Net Income ($mil)
6-14	D+	0.75	0.63	2.1	1.1	1.9	-0.2
6-13	C-	0.93	0.77	1.4	0.8	1.9	0.0
2013	D+	0.87	0.72	2.0	1.2	3.8	-0.4
2012	C-	0.96	0.80	1.5	0.9	4.1	-0.3
2011	C+	1.39	1.16	1.8	1.2	4.5	-0.1
2010	B	1.61	1.34	2.1	1.3	4.4	-0.2
2009	B	2.00	1.66	2.1	1.5	4.4	0.0

Rating Indexes

Range, Cap. 2, Stab., Inv., Prof., Liq.

■ Weak ■ Fair ▨ Good ☐ Strong

SANTA BARBARA SAN LUIS OBISPO REGION   E+   Very Weak

Major Rating Factors: Poor capitalization index (0.0 on a scale of 0 to 10) based on weak current risk-adjusted capital (severe loss scenario). Weak liquidity (0.0) as a spike in claims may stretch capacity. Fair overall results on stability tests (4.1).

Other Rating Factors: Good overall profitability index (6.4).

Principal Business: Medicaid (96%)

Mem Phys: 13: N/A **12:** N/A **13 MLR** 89.5% **/ 13 Admin Exp** N/A

Enroll(000): Q2 14: 112 **13:** 108 **12:** 106 **Med Exp PMPM:** $245

Principal Investments ($000): Cash and equiv ($22,022)

Provider Compensation ($000): None

Total Member Encounters: N/A

Group Affiliation: None

Licensed in: CA

Address: 110 Castilian Dr, Goleta, CA 93117-3028

Phone: (805) 685-9525 **Dom State:** CA **Commenced Bus:** September 1983

Data Date	Rating	RACR #1	RACR #2	Total Assets ($mil)	Capital ($mil)	Net Premium ($mil)	Net Income ($mil)
6-14	E+	0.29	0.18	109.7	39.7	178.9	4.7
6-13	E+	N/A	N/A	72.5	21.1	158.4	-0.5
2013	E+	0.08	0.05	121.5	35.0	343.9	13.4
2012	E+	N/A	N/A	81.5	21.6	328.7	0.7
2011	E+	N/A	N/A	75.8	20.9	370.5	6.7
2010	E+	N/A	N/A	58.0	14.2	291.8	-6.3
2009	E+	N/A	N/A	71.1	20.6	250.5	5.0

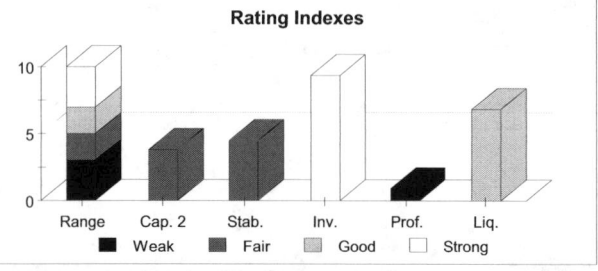

Rating Indexes

Range, Cap. 2, Stab., Inv., Prof., Liq.

■ Weak ■ Fair ▨ Good ☐ Strong

SANTA CLARA COUNTY HEALTH AUTHORITY   C-   Fair

Major Rating Factors: Fair overall results on stability tests (4.8 on a scale of 0 to 10) in spite of steady enrollment growth, averaging 7% over the past five years. Good overall profitability index (5.6). Good capitalization index (5.7) based on good current risk-adjusted capital (severe loss scenario).

Other Rating Factors: Excellent liquidity (7.2) with ample operational cash flow and liquid investments.

Principal Business: Medicaid (100%)

Mem Phys: 13: N/A **12:** N/A **13 MLR** 69.7% **/ 13 Admin Exp** N/A

Enroll(000): Q2 14: 153 **13:** 155 **12:** 140 **Med Exp PMPM:** $578

Principal Investments ($000): Cash and equiv ($61,584)

Provider Compensation ($000): None

Total Member Encounters: N/A

Group Affiliation: None

Licensed in: CA

Address: 210 E Hacienda Ave, Campbell, CA 95008

Phone: (408) 376-2000 **Dom State:** CA **Commenced Bus:** February 1997

Data Date	Rating	RACR #1	RACR #2	Total Assets ($mil)	Capital ($mil)	Net Premium ($mil)	Net Income ($mil)
6-14	C-	1.41	0.86	69.7	32.9	162.5	0.3
6-13	D+	1.10	0.69	63.7	23.8	151.0	-0.4
2013	C-	1.39	0.85	95.4	32.6	384.2	8.3
2012	D+	1.12	0.71	60.0	24.2	246.4	0.1
2011	D+	2.01	1.30	60.2	36.1	212.0	11.0
2010	D+	1.45	0.90	54.3	25.1	224.5	14.3
2009	D+	0.49	0.31	39.1	10.8	218.2	-2.8

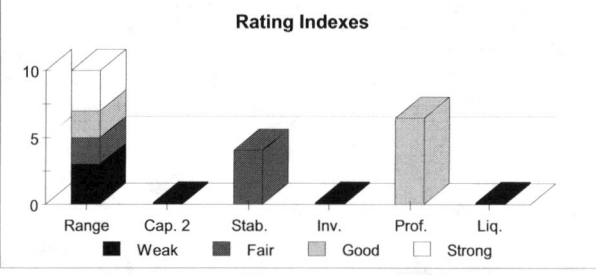

Rating Indexes

Range, Cap. 2, Stab., Inv., Prof., Liq.

■ Weak ■ Fair ▨ Good ☐ Strong

SANTA CLARA VALLEY   C   Fair

Major Rating Factors: Fair overall results on stability tests (2.9 on a scale of 0 to 10) in spite of steady enrollment growth, averaging 8% over the past five years. Good overall profitability index (6.8). Good capitalization index (5.8) based on good current risk-adjusted capital (severe loss scenario).
Other Rating Factors: Excellent liquidity (7.1) with ample operational cash flow and liquid investments.
Principal Business: Managed care (100%)
Mem Phys: 13: N/A **12:** N/A **13 MLR** 91.0% **/ 13 Admin Exp** N/A
Enroll(000): Q2 14: 93 **13:** 92 **12:** 85 **Med Exp PMPM:** $180
Principal Investments ($000): Cash and equiv ($29,325)
Provider Compensation ($000): None
Total Member Encounters: N/A
Group Affiliation: None
Licensed in: CA
Address: 2325 Enborg Lane Suite 290, San Jose, CA 95128
Phone: (408) 885-4080 **Dom State:** CA **Commenced Bus:** September 1985

Data Date	Rating	RACR #1	RACR #2	Total Assets ($mil)	Capital ($mil)	Net Premium ($mil)	Net Income ($mil)
6-14	C	1.44	0.88	42.8	20.8	114.6	5.5
6-13	C	2.06	1.26	42.2	25.7	103.7	4.1
2013	C	1.05	0.64	29.6	15.3	212.1	7.3
2012	C	1.72	1.05	35.0	21.5	182.7	7.1
2011	C-	1.32	0.81	26.5	14.8	158.9	6.4
2010	D	0.79	0.49	19.7	8.4	142.7	5.0
2009	D-	0.30	0.19	17.5	3.4	130.1	0.3

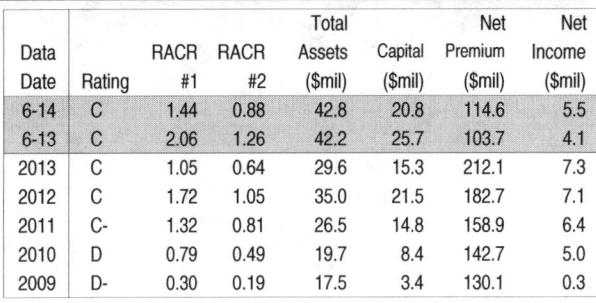

Rating Indexes
Range, Cap. 2, Stab., Inv., Prof., Liq.
■ Weak ■ Fair ▨ Good □ Strong

SANTA CRUZ-MONTEREY-MERCED MGD MED   B-   Good

Major Rating Factors: Excellent profitability (9.6 on a scale of 0 to 10). Strong capitalization index (10.0) based on excellent current risk-adjusted capital (severe loss scenario). Excellent overall results on stability tests (7.8) based on healthy premium and capital growth during 2013.
Other Rating Factors: Excellent liquidity (7.9) with ample operational cash flow and liquid investments.
Principal Business: Medicaid (100%)
Mem Phys: 13: N/A **12:** N/A **13 MLR** 76.4% **/ 13 Admin Exp** N/A
Enroll(000): Q2 14: 268 **13:** 220 **12:** 206 **Med Exp PMPM:** $203
Principal Investments ($000): Cash and equiv ($115,000)
Provider Compensation ($000): None
Total Member Encounters: N/A
Group Affiliation: None
Licensed in: CA
Address: 1600 Green Hills Rd, Ste 101, Scott Valley, CA 95066
Phone: (800) 700-3874 **Dom State:** CA **Commenced Bus:** N/A

Data Date	Rating	RACR #1	RACR #2	Total Assets ($mil)	Capital ($mil)	Net Premium ($mil)	Net Income ($mil)
6-14	B-	11.16	6.88	492.8	346.6	360.5	33.4
6-13	B-	6.03	3.70	366.4	193.0	288.5	7.4
2013	B-	10.15	6.25	418.3	313.2	684.4	127.6
2012	B-	5.73	3.51	325.9	185.6	588.3	26.0
2011	B-	5.05	3.09	260.0	159.6	578.2	31.3
2010	B-	4.12	2.52	227.9	128.3	549.1	38.8
2009	C+	3.75	2.30	182.9	89.5	385.5	4.9

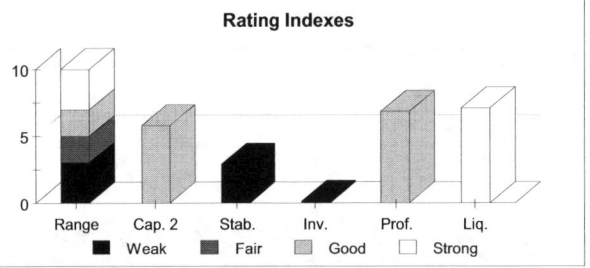

Rating Indexes
Range, Cap. 2, Stab., Inv., Prof., Liq.
■ Weak ■ Fair ▨ Good □ Strong

SCAN HEALTH PLAN   C   Fair

Major Rating Factors: Weak profitability index (1.8 on a scale of 0 to 10). Good overall results on stability tests (5.3). Strong capitalization index (10.0) based on excellent current risk-adjusted capital (severe loss scenario).
Other Rating Factors: Excellent liquidity (7.3) with ample operational cash flow and liquid investments.
Principal Business: Medicare (98%), Medicaid (2%)
Mem Phys: 13: N/A **12:** N/A **13 MLR** 90.8% **/ 13 Admin Exp** N/A
Enroll(000): Q2 14: 153 **13:** 139 **12:** 116 **Med Exp PMPM:** $1,045
Principal Investments ($000): Cash and equiv ($532,733)
Provider Compensation ($000): None
Total Member Encounters: N/A
Group Affiliation: SCAN Group
Licensed in: CA
Address: 3800 Kilroy Airport Way, Long Beach, CA 90806-2460
Phone: (562) 989-5100 **Dom State:** CA **Commenced Bus:** March 1985

Data Date	Rating	RACR #1	RACR #2	Total Assets ($mil)	Capital ($mil)	Net Premium ($mil)	Net Income ($mil)
6-14	C	5.01	3.11	668.0	461.0	1,002.8	-0.5
6-13	C	6.41	3.96	728.7	518.3	940.9	19.8
2013	C	5.00	3.10	647.6	461.5	1,862.2	38.0
2012	C	6.11	3.78	721.7	498.5	1,682.1	59.8
2011	C+	5.18	3.28	1,005.8	468.7	1,635.0	-178.1
2010	B+	7.68	4.77	984.1	646.8	1,629.9	-65.3
2009	A-	9.80	5.95	934.9	712.1	1,588.9	130.9

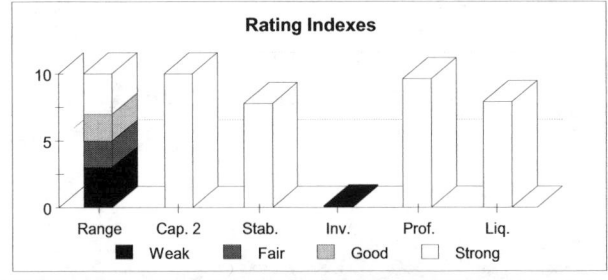

Rating Indexes
Range, Cap. 2, Stab., Inv., Prof., Liq.
■ Weak ■ Fair ▨ Good □ Strong

SCAN HEALTH PLAN ARIZONA   E   Very Weak

Major Rating Factors: Weak profitability index (0.7 on a scale of 0 to 10). Fair capitalization (2.9) based on good current risk-adjusted capital (moderate loss scenario). High quality investment portfolio (9.9).
Other Rating Factors: Excellent liquidity (7.1) with ample operational cash flow and liquid investments.
Principal Business: Medicare (100%)
Mem Phys: 13: N/A **12:** 4,415 **13 MLR** 94.5% **/ 13 Admin Exp** N/A
Enroll(000): Q2 14: 18 **13:** 13 **12:** 12   **Med Exp PMPM:** $707
Principal Investments: Cash and equiv (95%), long-term bonds (5%)
Provider Compensation ($000): Capitation ($107,175), contr fee ($21,900), FFS ($957)
Total Member Encounters: N/A
Group Affiliation: SCAN Group
Licensed in: AZ
Address: 1313 E Osborn Rd Suite 150, Phoenix, AZ 85014
Phone: (562) 989-5100   **Dom State:** AZ   **Commenced Bus:** July 2005

Data Date	Rating	RACR #1	RACR #2	Total Assets ($mil)	Capital ($mil)	Net Premium ($mil)	Net Income ($mil)
6-14	E	1.43	1.19	31.5	20.8	79.5	-5.6
6-13	E	0.49	0.41	45.0	12.9	60.6	-8.0
2013	E	1.83	1.53	34.0	27.6	116.8	6.5
2012	C-	0.73	0.61	62.7	20.5	129.4	-32.8
2011	N/A	N/A	N/A	64.8	23.7	145.7	2.7
2010	N/A	N/A	N/A	81.5	22.1	56.9	-56.5
2009	E	N/A	N/A	20.6	7.6	29.4	-6.7

Rating Indexes
Range, Cap. 2, Stab., Inv., Prof., Liq.
■ Weak ■ Fair ▨ Good □ Strong

SCOTT & WHITE HEALTH PLAN   B   Good

Major Rating Factors: Good overall profitability index (6.2 on a scale of 0 to 10). Good overall results on stability tests (5.5). Strong capitalization index (7.5) based on excellent current risk-adjusted capital (severe loss scenario).
Other Rating Factors: High quality investment portfolio (8.3). Excellent liquidity (6.9) with sufficient resources (cash flows and marketable investments) to handle a spike in claims.
Principal Business: Comp med (57%), Medicare (25%), Medicaid (18%)
Mem Phys: 13: 3,750 **12:** N/A **13 MLR** 84.8% **/ 13 Admin Exp** N/A
Enroll(000): Q2 14: 151 **13:** 146 **12:** 134 **Med Exp PMPM:** $304
Principal Investments: Cash and equiv (35%), long-term bonds (29%), real estate (19%), nonaffiliate common stock (12%), affiliate common stock (4%)
Provider Compensation ($000): Capitation ($259,091), contr fee ($207,130), FFS ($26,852), bonus arrang ($10,881)
Total Member Encounters: Phys (501,564), non-phys (439,166)
Group Affiliation: Scott & White Group
Licensed in: TX
Address: 2401 S 31st St, Temple, TX 76508
Phone: (254) 298-3000   **Dom State:** TX   **Commenced Bus:** January 1982

Data Date	Rating	RACR #1	RACR #2	Total Assets ($mil)	Capital ($mil)	Net Premium ($mil)	Net Income ($mil)
6-14	B	1.79	1.49	174.6	72.7	328.8	10.4
6-13	B	1.46	1.21	144.1	61.4	281.2	3.2
2013	B	1.53	1.28	149.9	63.1	589.6	2.9
2012	B-	1.37	1.14	140.6	57.4	579.4	6.1
2011	C+	1.25	1.04	126.5	51.3	563.5	-9.7
2010	A-	1.58	1.31	145.2	63.8	562.0	-3.1
2009	B	1.45	1.21	150.2	67.4	626.9	9.3

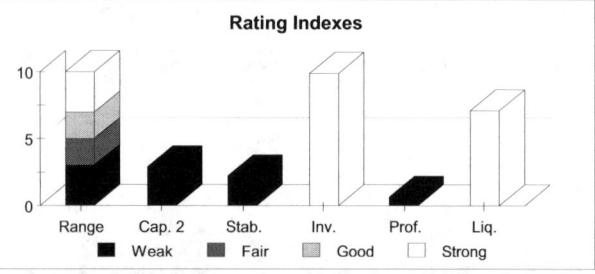

Rating Indexes
Range, Cap. 2, Stab., Inv., Prof., Liq.
■ Weak ■ Fair ▨ Good □ Strong

SCRIPPS CLINIC HEALTH PLAN SERVICES   D   Weak

Major Rating Factors: Fair capitalization index (4.9 on a scale of 0 to 10) based on fair current risk-adjusted capital (moderate loss scenario). Good overall profitability index (6.4). Good overall results on stability tests (6.3) despite fair risk diversification due to the company's size.
Other Rating Factors: Good liquidity (6.9) with sufficient resources (cash flows and marketable investments) to handle a spike in claims.
Principal Business: Managed care (100%)
Mem Phys: 13: N/A **12:** N/A **13 MLR** 99.9% **/ 13 Admin Exp** N/A
Enroll(000): Q2 14: 68 **13:** 40 **12:** 27 **Med Exp PMPM:** $580
Principal Investments ($000): Cash and equiv ($55,031)
Provider Compensation ($000): None
Total Member Encounters: N/A
Group Affiliation: Scripps Health
Licensed in: CA
Address: 10170 Sorrento Valley Rd, San Diego, CA 92121
Phone: (858) 784-5961   **Dom State:** CA   **Commenced Bus:** October 1997

Data Date	Rating	RACR #1	RACR #2	Total Assets ($mil)	Capital ($mil)	Net Premium ($mil)	Net Income ($mil)
6-14	D	0.76	0.46	77.5	14.9	139.6	0.1
6-13	E	0.43	0.26	40.4	8.2	119.3	0.2
2013	E+	0.46	0.28	56.8	9.3	249.8	0.2
2012	E	0.42	0.26	36.3	8.1	229.3	0.3
2011	N/A	N/A	N/A	39.4	8.8	226.6	0.5
2010	N/A	N/A	N/A	36.4	8.3	226.3	0.6
2009	D	N/A	N/A	34.1	8.3	232.8	0.2

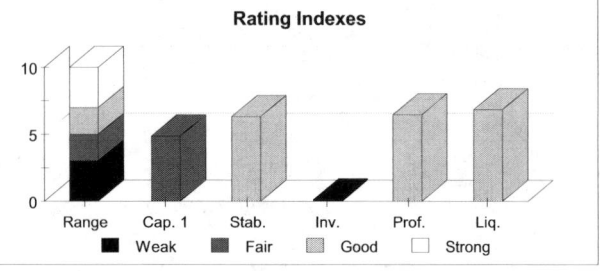

Rating Indexes
Range, Cap. 1, Stab., Inv., Prof., Liq.
■ Weak ■ Fair ▨ Good □ Strong

SD STATE MEDICAL HOLDING CO   B   Good

Major Rating Factors: Good quality investment portfolio (5.1 on a scale of 0 to 10). Good overall results on stability tests (5.0) based on inconsistent enrollment growth in the past five years due to declines in 2011 and 2012. Excellent profitability (7.1)

Other Rating Factors: Strong capitalization index (7.0) based on excellent current risk-adjusted capital (severe loss scenario). Excellent liquidity (7.0) with sufficient resources (cash flows and marketable investments) to handle a spike in claims.

Principal Business: Comp med (100%)

Mem Phys: 13: 2,425 **12:** 2,160 **13 MLR** 83.8% **/ 13 Admin Exp** N/A

Enroll(000): Q2 14: 26 **13:** 28 **12:** 27 **Med Exp PMPM:** $296

Principal Investments: Cash and equiv (52%), long-term bonds (30%), affiliate common stock (11%), mortgs (5%), nonaffiliate common stock (1%), other (1%)

Provider Compensation ($000): Contr fee ($74,057), FFS ($18,086), bonus arrang ($2,338)

Total Member Encounters: Phys (176,934), non-phys (20,255)

Group Affiliation: South Dakota State Medical Holding

Licensed in: SD

Address: 2600 W 49th St, Sioux Falls, SD 57105

Phone: (605) 334-4000 **Dom State:** SD **Commenced Bus:** April 1985

Data Date	Rating	RACR #1	RACR #2	Total Assets ($mil)	Capital ($mil)	Net Premium ($mil)	Net Income ($mil)
6-14	B	1.37	1.14	39.9	19.1	56.1	0.3
6-13	B	1.44	1.20	39.7	19.8	56.9	1.8
2013	B	1.66	1.38	42.4	23.3	113.9	3.2
2012	B	1.73	1.44	41.5	23.7	110.3	4.4
2011	B	1.69	1.41	42.4	23.0	108.5	2.2
2010	B	1.63	1.36	39.5	20.9	100.9	3.7
2009	B-	1.32	1.10	33.8	17.6	92.4	0.6

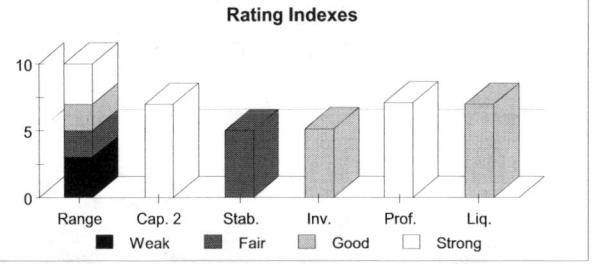

Rating Indexes

SECURIAN LIFE INSURANCE COMPANY   B   Good

Major Rating Factors: Good liquidity (6.9 on a scale of 0 to 10) with sufficient resources to handle a spike in claims. Good overall results on stability tests (6.3). Stability strengths include excellent operational trends and excellent risk diversification. Fair profitability (4.7). Excellent expense controls. Return on equity has been low, averaging 1.7%.

Other Rating Factors: Strong capitalization (10.0) based on excellent risk adjusted capital (severe loss scenario). High quality investment portfolio (8.2).

Principal Business: Group life insurance (37%), group health insurance (31%), reinsurance (12%), individual life insurance (11%), and other lines (9%).

Principal Investments: NonCMO investment grade bonds (90%), CMOs and structured securities (7%), cash (2%), and noninv. grade bonds (1%).

Investments in Affiliates: None

Group Affiliation: Securian Financial Group

Licensed in: All states except PR

Commenced Business: December 1981

Address: 400 Robert St N, St Paul, MN 55101

Phone: (651) 665-3500 **Domicile State:** MN **NAIC Code:** 93742

Data Date	Rating	RACR #1	RACR #2	Total Assets ($mil)	Capital ($mil)	Net Premium ($mil)	Net Income ($mil)
6-14	B	6.50	4.56	225.6	133.6	44.1	2.6
6-13	A-	7.97	5.60	207.3	133.8	40.9	-1.2
2013	B	6.47	4.56	207.8	131.5	83.2	-3.0
2012	A-	8.20	5.79	190.1	134.9	72.0	0.3
2011	B+	8.60	6.17	167.6	134.2	65.5	4.7
2010	B+	10.79	7.66	155.2	129.7	50.5	3.3
2009	B+	11.07	7.70	149.7	126.5	44.6	3.9

Adverse Trends in Operations

Decrease in capital during 2013 (2%)
Change in premium mix from 2012 to 2013 (4.2%)
Increase in policy surrenders from 2012 to 2013 (291%)
Increase in policy surrenders from 2010 to 2011 (132%)

SECURITY HEALTH PLAN OF WI INC *   A-   Excellent

Major Rating Factors: Strong capitalization index (7.6 on a scale of 0 to 10) based on excellent current risk-adjusted capital (severe loss scenario). Good liquidity (6.2) with sufficient resources (cash flows and marketable investments) to handle a spike in claims. Fair profitability index (3.7).

Other Rating Factors: Fair quality investment portfolio (3.9). Fair overall results on stability tests (4.5).

Principal Business: Comp med (45%), Medicare (41%), Medicaid (13%)

Mem Phys: 13: 3,794 **12:** 3,227 **13 MLR** 94.3% **/ 13 Admin Exp** N/A

Enroll(000): Q2 14: 196 **13:** 181 **12:** 176 **Med Exp PMPM:** $435

Principal Investments: Nonaffiliate common stock (48%), long-term bonds (30%), cash and equiv (7%), real estate (1%), other (14%)

Provider Compensation ($000): Contr fee ($636,283), capitation ($181,543), FFS ($134,474)

Total Member Encounters: N/A

Group Affiliation: Marshfield Clinic

Licensed in: WI

Address: 1515 Saint Joseph Ave, Marshfield, WI 54449

Phone: (715) 221-9555 **Dom State:** WI **Commenced Bus:** September 1986

Data Date	Rating	RACR #1	RACR #2	Total Assets ($mil)	Capital ($mil)	Net Premium ($mil)	Net Income ($mil)
6-14	A-	1.85	1.54	322.0	163.9	552.6	8.7
6-13	A+	2.25	1.87	290.2	185.5	499.8	12.6
2013	A-	1.72	1.43	280.1	152.5	1,001.8	-19.3
2012	A+	2.13	1.78	308.6	176.3	978.0	8.5
2011	A+	2.10	1.75	297.1	167.7	942.2	34.4
2010	A+	1.74	1.45	254.4	123.5	910.0	31.7
2009	A-	1.96	1.64	214.0	124.9	804.1	37.0

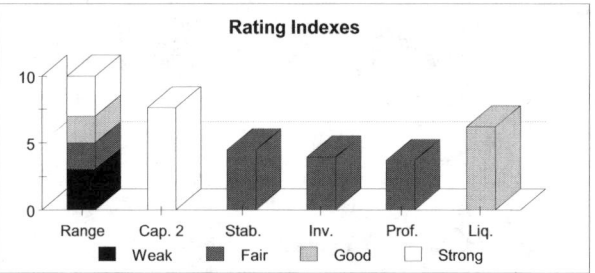

Rating Indexes

SEECHANGE HEALTH INS CO INC

D   **Weak**

Major Rating Factors: Weak profitability index (0.2 on a scale of 0 to 10). Poor capitalization (2.4) based on weak current risk-adjusted capital (moderate loss scenario). Weak liquidity (0.1) as a spike in claims may stretch capacity.
Other Rating Factors: High quality investment portfolio (9.9).
Principal Business: Comp med (100%)
Mem Phys: 13: 600,000   **12:** N/A   **13 MLR** 111.4%   / **13 Admin Exp** N/A
Enroll(000): Q2 14: 31   **13:** 38   **12:** 22   **Med Exp PMPM:** $283
Principal Investments: Cash and equiv (53%), long-term bonds (47%)
Provider Compensation ($000): Contr fee ($111,959), FFS ($5,864)
Total Member Encounters: Phys (160,040), non-phys (117,795)
Group Affiliation: SeeChange Health LLC
Licensed in: AZ, AR, CA, CO, FL, ID, IL, IN, IA, KS, KY, MD, MI, MS, MO, NE, NV, ND, OH, OK, SD, TN, VA, WV, WI
Address: 12711 Ventura Blvd Suite 180, Studio City, CA 91604
Phone: (763) 746-8475   **Dom State:** CA   **Commenced Bus:** November 1956

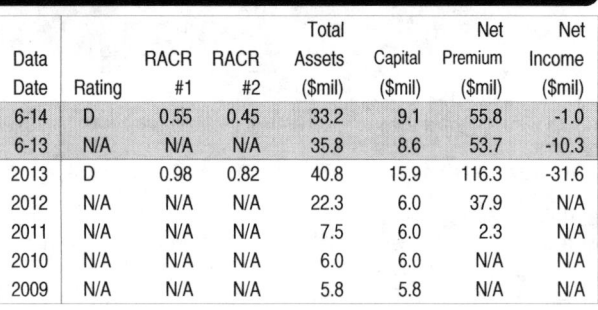

Data Date	Rating	RACR #1	RACR #2	Total Assets ($mil)	Capital ($mil)	Net Premium ($mil)	Net Income ($mil)
6-14	D	0.55	0.45	33.2	9.1	55.8	-1.0
6-13	N/A	N/A	N/A	35.8	8.6	53.7	-10.3
2013	D	0.98	0.82	40.8	15.9	116.3	-31.6
2012	N/A	N/A	N/A	22.3	6.0	37.9	N/A
2011	N/A	N/A	N/A	7.5	6.0	2.3	N/A
2010	N/A	N/A	N/A	6.0	6.0	N/A	N/A
2009	N/A	N/A	N/A	5.8	5.8	N/A	N/A

Rating Indexes

Range   Cap. 2   Stab.   Inv.   Prof.   Liq.
■ Weak   ■ Fair   ▨ Good   □ Strong

SELECT HEALTH OF SOUTH CAROLINA INC

B   **Good**

Major Rating Factors: Good liquidity (6.7 on a scale of 0 to 10) with sufficient resources (cash flows and marketable investments) to handle a spike in claims. Excellent profitability (8.9). Strong capitalization index (7.5) based on excellent current risk-adjusted capital (severe loss scenario).
Other Rating Factors: High quality investment portfolio (9.9). Excellent overall results on stability tests (8.2). Rating is significantly influenced by the good financial results of Independence Blue Cross Inc.
Principal Business: Medicaid (100%)
Mem Phys: 13: 9,764   **12:** 7,776   **13 MLR** 91.6%   / **13 Admin Exp** N/A
Enroll(000): Q2 14: 331   **13:** 282   **12:** 248   **Med Exp PMPM:** $245
Principal Investments: Long-term bonds (47%), cash and equiv (33%), nonaffiliate common stock (20%)
Provider Compensation ($000): Contr fee ($601,299), FFS ($144,584), capitation ($5,273)
Total Member Encounters: Phys (2,093,022), non-phys (282,395)
Group Affiliation: Independence Blue Cross Inc
Licensed in: KY, MS, SC
Address: 4390 Belle Oaks Dr Suite 400, Charleston, SC 29405
Phone: (843) 569-1759   **Dom State:** SC   **Commenced Bus:** December 1996

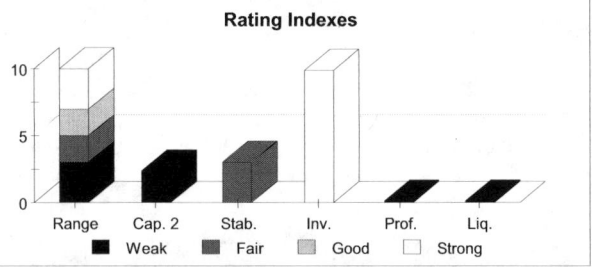

Data Date	Rating	RACR #1	RACR #2	Total Assets ($mil)	Capital ($mil)	Net Premium ($mil)	Net Income ($mil)
6-14	B	1.72	1.44	236.2	88.8	530.8	5.4
6-13	B	1.66	1.38	178.8	63.1	396.4	-5.6
2013	B	1.61	1.34	198.2	82.5	848.7	9.7
2012	B	2.01	1.68	166.2	78.5	678.4	14.7
2011	B	1.94	1.61	144.7	65.1	608.2	29.4
2010	B	1.06	0.88	163.6	38.0	608.5	8.1
2009	C+	0.73	0.61	142.0	22.4	516.7	0.2

Rating Indexes

Range   Cap. 2   Stab.   Inv.   Prof.   Liq.
■ Weak   ■ Fair   ▨ Good   □ Strong

SELECTCARE HEALTH PLANS INC

C   **Fair**

Major Rating Factors: Fair profitability index (4.6 on a scale of 0 to 10). Good liquidity (6.6) with sufficient resources (cash flows and marketable investments) to handle a spike in claims. Strong capitalization (8.7) based on excellent current risk-adjusted capital (severe loss scenario).
Other Rating Factors: High quality investment portfolio (9.2).
Principal Business: Medicare (100%)
Mem Phys: 13: N/A   **12:** 2,799   **13 MLR** 83.2%   / **13 Admin Exp** N/A
Enroll(000): Q2 14: 5   **13:** 5   **12:** 4   **Med Exp PMPM:** $828
Principal Investments: Long-term bonds (98%), cash and equiv (2%)
Provider Compensation ($000): Contr fee ($44,852), capitation ($1,388)
Total Member Encounters: Phys (53,013), non-phys (16,559)
Group Affiliation: Universal American Corp
Licensed in: IN, TX
Address: 4888 Loop Central Dr Suite 700, Houston, TX 77018
Phone: (713) 965-9444   **Dom State:** TX   **Commenced Bus:** July 2005

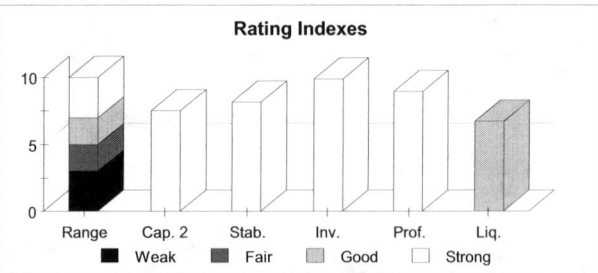

Data Date	Rating	RACR #1	RACR #2	Total Assets ($mil)	Capital ($mil)	Net Premium ($mil)	Net Income ($mil)
6-14	C	2.75	2.29	22.2	14.8	26.9	0.0
6-13	C	3.39	2.82	22.1	15.1	28.9	2.0
2013	C	2.73	2.28	20.3	14.7	56.0	1.6
2012	C	4.03	3.36	23.5	17.6	54.2	4.9
2011	N/A	N/A	N/A	23.6	12.6	71.6	1.3
2010	N/A	N/A	N/A	22.4	11.1	84.4	-2.6
2009	C	N/A	N/A	15.4	7.4	62.5	-1.1

Rating Indexes

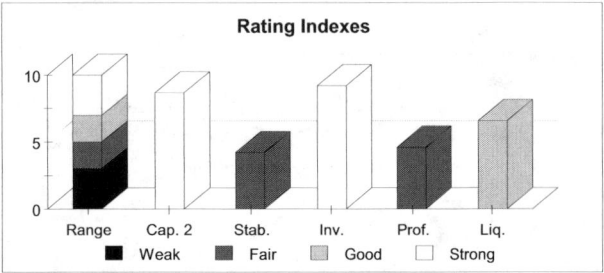

Range   Cap. 2   Stab.   Inv.   Prof.   Liq.
■ Weak   ■ Fair   ▨ Good   □ Strong

SELECTCARE OF OKLAHOMA INC   B-   Good

Major Rating Factors: Fair profitability index (3.8 on a scale of 0 to 10). Strong capitalization (8.7) based on excellent current risk-adjusted capital (severe loss scenario). High quality investment portfolio (9.9).
Other Rating Factors: Excellent liquidity (7.5) with ample operational cash flow and liquid investments.
Principal Business: Medicare (100%)
Mem Phys: 13: 189 **12:** 189 **13 MLR** 77.9% **/ 13 Admin Exp** N/A
Enroll(000): Q2 14: 0 **13:** 0 **12:** 0 **Med Exp PMPM:** $1,590
Principal Investments: Cash and equiv (76%), long-term bonds (24%)
Provider Compensation ($000): Contr fee ($1,740), capitation ($530), bonus arrang ($6)
Total Member Encounters: N/A
Group Affiliation: Universal American Corp
Licensed in: OK
Address: 201 Robert S Kerr Ave Ste 600, Oklahoma City, OK 73012
Phone: (713) 965-9444 **Dom State:** OK **Commenced Bus:** December 2004

Data Date	Rating	RACR #1	RACR #2	Total Assets ($mil)	Capital ($mil)	Net Premium ($mil)	Net Income ($mil)
6-14	B-	2.68	2.23	2.9	1.9	1.6	0.1
6-13	C	2.88	2.40	2.2	1.8	1.6	0.0
2013	C	2.55	2.12	2.4	1.8	3.2	0.0
2012	C	2.95	2.46	2.2	1.8	3.3	0.1
2011	C-	2.22	1.85	1.8	1.4	3.0	-0.2
2010	C-	3.12	2.60	2.2	1.7	3.6	0.1
2009	C-	3.95	3.29	2.5	1.5	3.5	-0.2

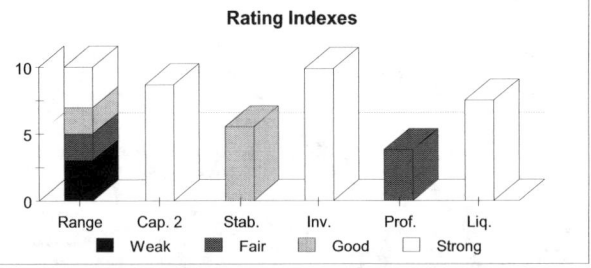

Rating Indexes

SELECTCARE OF TEXAS LLC   C-   Fair

Major Rating Factors: Weak overall results on stability tests (2.0 on a scale of 0 to 10) based on a decline in the number of member physicians during 2014. Good overall profitability index (6.8). Good quality investment portfolio (5.7)
Other Rating Factors: Good liquidity (6.8) with sufficient resources (cash flows and marketable investments) to handle a spike in claims. Strong capitalization index (7.6) based on excellent current risk-adjusted capital (severe loss scenario).
Principal Business: Medicare (100%)
Mem Phys: 13: 2,541 **12:** 3,059 **13 MLR** 85.3% **/ 13 Admin Exp** N/A
Enroll(000): Q2 14: 56 **13:** 50 **12:** 46 **Med Exp PMPM:** $931
Principal Investments: Long-term bonds (98%), pref stock (2%)
Provider Compensation ($000): Capitation ($327,032), contr fee ($227,061)
Total Member Encounters: Phys (667,616), non-phys (95,933)
Group Affiliation: Universal American Corp
Licensed in: TX
Address: 4888 Loop Central Dr Ste 700, Houston, TX 77081
Phone: (713) 965-9444 **Dom State:** TX **Commenced Bus:** May 2001

Data Date	Rating	RACR #1	RACR #2	Total Assets ($mil)	Capital ($mil)	Net Premium ($mil)	Net Income ($mil)
6-14	C-	1.82	1.52	153.2	64.7	365.7	-0.3
6-13	B	1.95	1.62	192.1	60.6	330.3	8.6
2013	C	1.81	1.51	133.1	64.2	652.0	11.7
2012	B	3.35	2.79	180.5	103.7	614.3	15.6
2011	B-	3.87	3.23	183.8	112.0	594.1	23.6
2010	C+	4.31	3.59	207.1	111.0	607.9	24.9
2009	B-	3.53	2.94	159.4	84.2	542.2	9.6

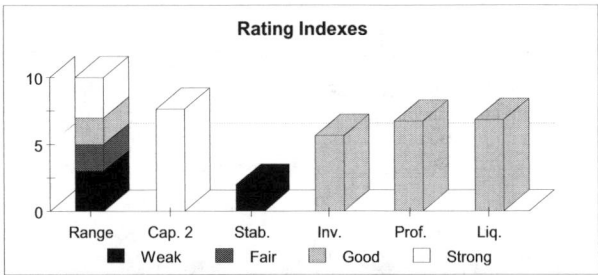

Rating Indexes

SELECTHEALTH BENEFIT ASR CO INC   B   Good

Major Rating Factors: Good overall profitability index (5.9 on a scale of 0 to 10). Strong capitalization (10.0) based on excellent current risk-adjusted capital (severe loss scenario). High quality investment portfolio (9.6).
Other Rating Factors: Excellent liquidity (8.4) with ample operational cash flow and liquid investments.
Principal Business: Other (100%)
Mem Phys: 13: N/A **12:** N/A **13 MLR** 40.1% **/ 13 Admin Exp** N/A
Enroll(000): Q2 14: 2 **13:** 2 **12:** 1 **Med Exp PMPM:** $159
Principal Investments: Long-term bonds (74%), cash and equiv (24%), other (1%)
Provider Compensation ($000): FFS ($3,318)
Total Member Encounters: Phys (1,101), non-phys (489)
Group Affiliation: Intermountain Health Care Inc
Licensed in: UT
Address: 5381 Green St, Murray, UT 84123
Phone: (801) 442-5000 **Dom State:** UT **Commenced Bus:** July 1992

Data Date	Rating	RACR #1	RACR #2	Total Assets ($mil)	Capital ($mil)	Net Premium ($mil)	Net Income ($mil)
6-14	B	6.45	5.38	21.3	12.4	7.9	-0.2
6-13	B	6.24	5.20	17.5	11.8	4.3	1.3
2013	B	6.74	5.61	18.0	13.1	7.3	2.6
2012	B	5.45	4.54	15.8	10.4	7.4	1.0
2011	B	3.54	2.95	13.7	9.6	7.9	-0.6
2010	B	4.61	3.84	14.5	10.0	6.5	1.1
2009	B	5.56	4.63	20.8	14.0	16.3	0.8

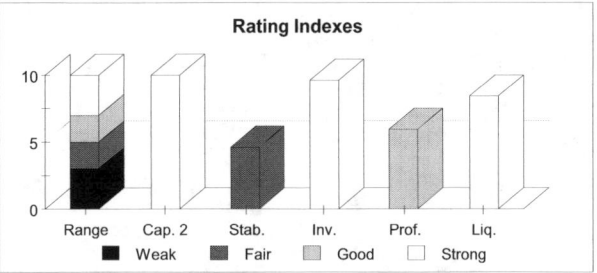

Rating Indexes

SELECTHEALTH INC *   A   Excellent

Major Rating Factors: Excellent profitability (8.3 on a scale of 0 to 10). Strong capitalization index (10.0) based on excellent current risk-adjusted capital (severe loss scenario). Excellent overall results on stability tests (8.2) based on healthy premium and capital growth during 2013.
Other Rating Factors: Good quality investment portfolio (6.1). Good liquidity (6.7) with sufficient resources (cash flows and marketable investments) to handle a spike in claims.
Principal Business: Comp med (79%), Medicaid (17%), Medicare (2%).
Mem Phys: 13: 9,432 **12:** 4,000 **13 MLR** 87.1% **/ 13 Admin Exp** N/A
Enroll(000): Q2 14: 575 **13:** 492 **12:** 415 **Med Exp PMPM:** $217
Principal Investments: Long-term bonds (47%), nonaffiliate common stock (42%), cash and equiv (8%), affiliate common stock (2%), other (2%).
Provider Compensation ($000): Contr fee ($825,822), FFS ($222,715), bonus arrang ($167,655), capitation ($1,980)
Total Member Encounters: Phys (2,173,721), non-phys (1,101,798)
Group Affiliation: Intermountain Health Care Inc
Licensed in: ID, UT
Address: 5381 Green St, Murray, UT 84123
Phone: (801) 442-5000 **Dom State:** UT **Commenced Bus:** February 1984

Data Date	Rating	RACR #1	RACR #2	Total Assets ($mil)	Capital ($mil)	Net Premium ($mil)	Net Income ($mil)
6-14	A	4.06	3.38	849.6	493.7	899.9	13.1
6-13	A	4.54	3.78	774.7	432.0	718.6	51.3
2013	A	3.78	3.15	767.6	464.8	1,461.4	50.8
2012	A	3.88	3.23	573.3	376.0	1,160.2	33.4
2011	A-	3.47	2.90	487.7	327.0	1,178.5	51.3
2010	A-	3.21	2.68	430.4	279.8	1,076.9	33.7
2009	A-	3.09	2.57	371.5	247.9	994.2	52.9

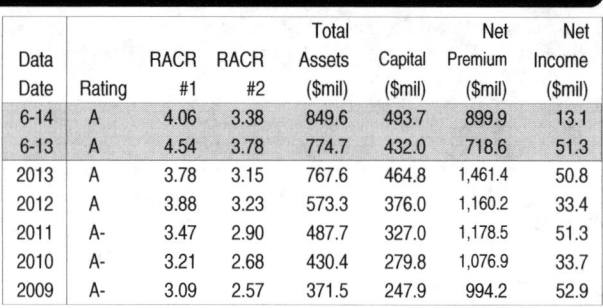

Rating Indexes

SENIOR HEALTH INSURANCE COMPANY OF PENNSYLVANIA   D+   Weak

Major Rating Factors: Low quality investment portfolio (2.0 on a scale of 0 to 10) containing large holdings of BBB rated bonds in addition to significant exposure to junk bonds. Weak profitability (1.8) with operating losses during the first six months of 2014. Return on equity has been low, averaging -4.8%. Weak overall results on stability tests (2.8) including negative cash flow from operations for 2013.
Other Rating Factors: Good capitalization (5.3) based on good risk adjusted capital (moderate loss scenario). Good liquidity (6.8).
Principal Business: Individual health insurance (92%), reinsurance (7%), and group health insurance (1%).
Principal Investments: NonCMO investment grade bonds (72%), CMOs and structured securities (15%), noninv. grade bonds (6%), common & preferred stock (3%), and mortgages in good standing (3%).
Investments in Affiliates: None
Group Affiliation: Senior Health Care Oversight Trust
Licensed in: All states except CT, NY, RI, VT, PR
Commenced Business: February 1965
Address: 11815 N Pennsylvania St, Carmel, IN 46032
Phone: (317) 817-3700 **Domicile State:** PA **NAIC Code:** 76325

Data Date	Rating	RACR #1	RACR #2	Total Assets ($mil)	Capital ($mil)	Net Premium ($mil)	Net Income ($mil)
6-14	D+	1.21	0.60	2,932.4	88.6	81.2	-1.9
6-13	D+	1.48	0.73	3,046.0	121.5	90.3	19.3
2013	D+	1.25	0.62	2,985.9	98.2	173.7	-3.4
2012	D+	1.22	0.60	3,080.7	105.5	194.0	-4.0
2011	D+	1.22	0.60	3,161.1	114.4	213.8	-57.2
2010	D+	1.74	0.83	3,317.0	177.3	234.2	-15.0
2009	D+	1.94	0.92	3,252.0	193.4	249.9	-17.5

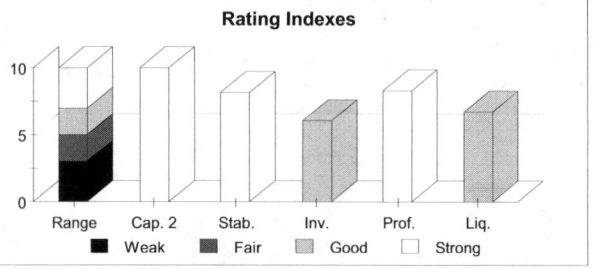

Junk Bonds as a % of Capital

Capital — $98 mil.
Junk Bonds — $169 mil.

0% 20% 40% 60% 80% 100% 120% 140% 160% 180%
■ BB ▨ B ▥ CCC ▤ In default

SENIOR WHOLE HEALTH OF NEW YORK INC   E   Very Weak

Major Rating Factors: Weak profitability index (0.6 on a scale of 0 to 10). Strong capitalization (7.0) based on excellent current risk-adjusted capital (severe loss scenario). High quality investment portfolio (9.9).
Other Rating Factors: Excellent liquidity (7.0) with sufficient resources (cash flows and marketable investments) to handle a spike in claims.
Principal Business: Medicaid (100%).
Mem Phys: 13: 5,604 **12:** 10,035 **13 MLR** 91.5% **/ 13 Admin Exp** N/A
Enroll(000): Q2 14: 1 **13:** 1 **12:** 1 **Med Exp PMPM:** $3,593
Principal Investments: Cash and equiv (100%).
Provider Compensation ($000): None
Total Member Encounters: Phys (1,208), non-phys (8,012)
Group Affiliation: Senior Health Holdings LLC
Licensed in: NY
Address: 200 S Pearl St, Albany, NY 12202
Phone: (617) 494-5353 **Dom State:** NY **Commenced Bus:** January 2007

Data Date	Rating	RACR #1	RACR #2	Total Assets ($mil)	Capital ($mil)	Net Premium ($mil)	Net Income ($mil)
6-14	E	1.33	1.11	19.5	5.6	18.6	-2.6
6-13	E	0.32	0.27	11.6	2.3	6.3	-1.4
2013	D-	1.23	1.02	11.3	5.2	17.8	-0.7
2012	E	0.01	0.01	8.7	0.1	27.6	-8.7
2011	N/A	N/A	N/A	5.2	0.8	24.9	-3.8
2010	N/A	N/A	N/A	6.9	3.0	21.1	-4.0
2009	E	N/A	N/A	8.3	4.8	18.1	-3.5

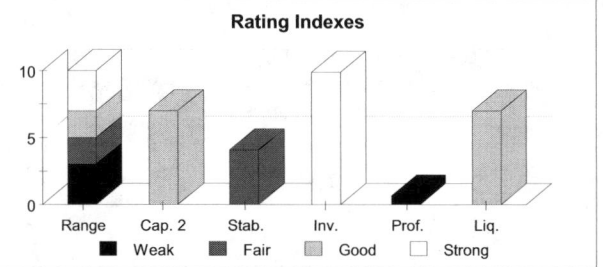

Rating Indexes

SETON HEALTH PLAN INC   B-   Good

Major Rating Factors: Fair quality investment portfolio (4.4 on a scale of 0 to 10). Good overall profitability index (6.6). Good overall results on stability tests (6.5).

Other Rating Factors: Strong capitalization index (8.2) based on excellent current risk-adjusted capital (severe loss scenario). Excellent liquidity (7.2) with ample operational cash flow and liquid investments.

Principal Business: Medicaid (61%), comp med (39%)

Mem Phys: 13: 4,352   **12:** 4,307   **13 MLR** 81.3%   **/ 13 Admin Exp** N/A

Enroll(000): Q2 14: 24   **13:** 24   **12:** 26   **Med Exp PMPM:** $138

Principal Investments: Nonaffiliate common stock (58%), cash and equiv (42%)

Provider Compensation ($000): Contr fee ($33,248), FFS ($1,321), capitation ($1,070), other ($7,410)

Total Member Encounters: Phys (166,469), non-phys (36,542)

Group Affiliation: Ascension Health System

Licensed in: TX

Address: 1201 W 28th St, Austin, TX 75705

Phone: (512) 324-3350   **Dom State:** TX   **Commenced Bus:** July 1995

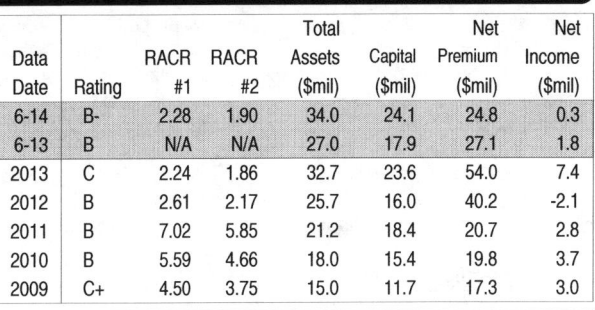

Data Date	Rating	RACR #1	RACR #2	Total Assets ($mil)	Capital ($mil)	Net Premium ($mil)	Net Income ($mil)
6-14	B-	2.28	1.90	34.0	24.1	24.8	0.3
6-13	B	N/A	N/A	27.0	17.9	27.1	1.8
2013	C	2.24	1.86	32.7	23.6	54.0	7.4
2012	B	2.61	2.17	25.7	16.0	40.2	-2.1
2011	B	7.02	5.85	21.2	18.4	20.7	2.8
2010	B	5.59	4.66	18.0	15.4	19.8	3.7
2009	C+	4.50	3.75	15.0	11.7	17.3	3.0

Rating Indexes

Range, Cap. 2, Stab., Inv., Prof., Liq.

■ Weak   ▨ Fair   ▤ Good   ☐ Strong

SHA LLC   E   Very Weak

Major Rating Factors: Weak profitability index (0.9 on a scale of 0 to 10). Poor capitalization index (2.8) based on weak current risk-adjusted capital (moderate loss scenario). Fair overall results on stability tests (4.0).

Other Rating Factors: Good quality investment portfolio (6.8). Good liquidity (5.7) with sufficient resources (cash flows and marketable investments) to handle a spike in claims.

Principal Business: Medicaid (60%), comp med (29%), Medicare (11%)

Mem Phys: 13: N/A   **12:** 8,597   **13 MLR** 90.6%   **/ 13 Admin Exp** N/A

Enroll(000): Q2 14: 143   **13:** 138   **12:** 138   **Med Exp PMPM:** $318

Principal Investments: Nonaffiliate common stock (46%), cash and equiv (43%), affiliate common stock (8%), real estate (2%), long-term bonds (1%)

Provider Compensation ($000): Contr fee ($401,991), FFS ($30,498), capitation ($2,170)

Total Member Encounters: Phys (180,859), non-phys (112,175)

Group Affiliation: FirstCare Group

Licensed in: TX

Address: 12940 N Hwy 183, Austin, TX 78750-3203

Phone: (512) 257-6001   **Dom State:** TX   **Commenced Bus:** August 1994

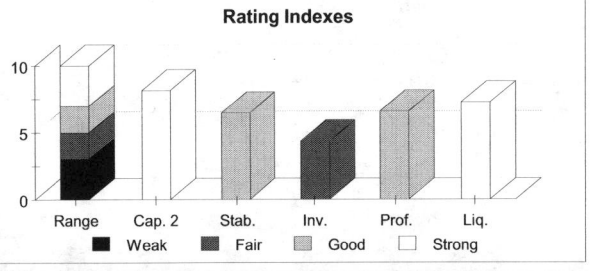

Data Date	Rating	RACR #1	RACR #2	Total Assets ($mil)	Capital ($mil)	Net Premium ($mil)	Net Income ($mil)
6-14	E	0.58	0.48	105.3	31.4	252.7	-21.7
6-13	E	0.75	0.62	93.6	34.9	232.1	-18.2
2013	E	1.09	0.90	115.3	55.4	478.0	-9.1
2012	C+	1.12	0.94	116.5	49.1	414.1	2.9
2011	C	1.37	1.14	79.1	41.8	253.5	0.0
2010	C	1.38	1.15	73.2	39.9	244.4	-1.8
2009	C	0.96	0.80	68.3	35.8	322.2	-9.0

Rating Indexes

Range, Cap. 2, Stab., Inv., Prof., Liq.

■ Weak   ▨ Fair   ▤ Good   ☐ Strong

SHARP HEALTH PLAN   B   Good

Major Rating Factors: Good capitalization index (6.7 on a scale of 0 to 10) based on good current risk-adjusted capital (severe loss scenario). Excellent profitability (8.4). Excellent overall results on stability tests (7.2) based on healthy premium and capital growth during 2013.

Other Rating Factors: Excellent liquidity (7.0) with sufficient resources (cash flows and marketable investments) to handle a spike in claims.

Principal Business: Managed care (100%)

Mem Phys: 13: N/A   **12:** N/A   **13 MLR** 90.9%   **/ 13 Admin Exp** N/A

Enroll(000): Q2 14: 81   **13:** 71   **12:** 66   **Med Exp PMPM:** $351

Principal Investments ($000): Cash and equiv ($24,241)

Provider Compensation ($000): None

Total Member Encounters: N/A

Group Affiliation: San Diego Hospital Assoc

Licensed in: CA

Address: 4305 University Ave Suite 200, San Diego, CA 92105

Phone: (619) 228-2377   **Dom State:** CA   **Commenced Bus:** November 1992

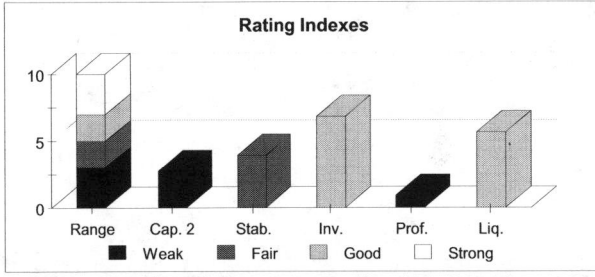

Data Date	Rating	RACR #1	RACR #2	Total Assets ($mil)	Capital ($mil)	Net Premium ($mil)	Net Income ($mil)
6-14	B	1.52	0.99	77.6	51.1	180.5	3.9
6-13	B	1.41	0.92	65.6	43.1	156.2	3.2
2013	B	1.41	0.92	65.8	47.2	320.4	7.1
2012	B-	1.32	0.86	60.1	40.0	277.3	5.8
2011	B-	1.46	0.95	49.1	34.2	227.2	3.8
2010	B-	1.39	0.92	44.7	30.4	193.7	4.4
2009	B-	1.58	1.00	38.4	26.0	171.3	3.4

Rating Indexes

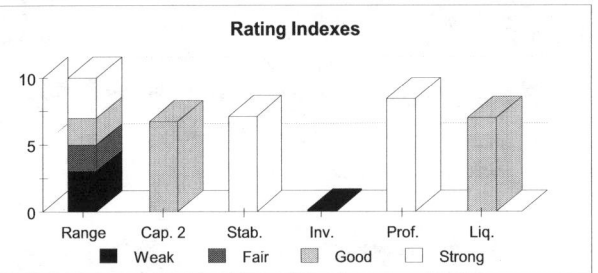

Range, Cap. 2, Stab., Inv., Prof., Liq.

■ Weak   ▨ Fair   ▤ Good   ☐ Strong

SHELTERPOINT LIFE INSURANCE COMPANY *

A   **Excellent**

Major Rating Factors: Good quality investment portfolio (6.4 on a scale of 0 to 10) despite mixed results such as: no exposure to mortgages and substantial holdings of BBB bonds but minimal holdings in junk bonds. Good overall results on stability tests (6.6). Strengths that enhance stability include excellent operational trends and good risk diversification. Strong capitalization (8.8) based on excellent risk adjusted capital (severe loss scenario).

Other Rating Factors: Excellent profitability (7.9) despite operating losses during the first six months of 2014. Excellent liquidity (7.2).

Principal Business: Group health insurance (98%) and group life insurance (2%).

Principal Investments: NonCMO investment grade bonds (78%), CMOs and structured securities (14%), noninv. grade bonds (5%), and cash (3%).

Investments in Affiliates: None

Group Affiliation: Rehab Services Corp

Licensed in: CO, CT, DC, DE, IL, MD, MA, MI, MN, NJ, NY, NC, PA, RI, SC, TN

Commenced Business: November 1972

Address: 600 Northern Blvd, Great Neck, NY 11021-5202

Phone: (516) 829-8100 **Domicile State:** NY **NAIC Code:** 81434

Data Date	Rating	RACR #1	RACR #2	Total Assets ($mil)	Capital ($mil)	Net Premium ($mil)	Net Income ($mil)
6-14	A	3.00	2.18	103.8	50.1	48.5	-0.1
6-13	A	3.92	2.99	99.0	50.2	44.4	2.2
2013	A	3.82	2.91	100.4	48.2	82.4	5.7
2012	A-	4.13	3.18	93.5	47.3	71.9	4.5
2011	B	3.87	3.01	87.2	43.4	69.2	4.5
2010	B-	2.87	2.26	94.3	42.4	95.2	3.5
2009	C	2.85	2.22	93.5	42.0	95.3	2.4

Adverse Trends in Operations

Decrease in asset base during 2011 (7%)
Decrease in premium volume from 2010 to 2011 (27%)

SIERRA HEALTH AND LIFE INS CO INC

C+   **Fair**

Major Rating Factors: Excellent profitability (7.8 on a scale of 0 to 10). Strong capitalization (10.0) based on excellent current risk-adjusted capital (severe loss scenario). High quality investment portfolio (9.9).

Other Rating Factors: Excellent liquidity (6.9) with sufficient resources (cash flows and marketable investments) to handle a spike in claims.

Principal Business: Comp med (82%), Medicare (10%), med supp (7%)

Mem Phys: 13: 5,477 **12:** N/A **13 MLR** 79.3% **/ 13 Admin Exp** N/A

Enroll(000): Q2 14: 122 **13:** 105 **12:** 117 **Med Exp PMPM:** $163

Principal Investments: Long-term bonds (67%), cash and equiv (30%), real estate (3%)

Provider Compensation ($000): Contr fee ($214,505), FFS ($2,603), capitation ($597)

Total Member Encounters: Phys (547,766), non-phys (254,656)

Group Affiliation: UnitedHealth Group Inc

Licensed in: All states except FL, MI, MN, NH, NY, VT, WI, PR

Address: 2720 N Tenaya Way, Las Vegas, NV 89128

Phone: (702) 242-7732 **Dom State:** NV **Commenced Bus:** August 1906

Data Date	Rating	RACR #1	RACR #2	Total Assets ($mil)	Capital ($mil)	Net Premium ($mil)	Net Income ($mil)
6-14	C+	6.16	5.13	155.4	77.8	201.2	7.3
6-13	N/A	N/A	N/A	132.2	70.3	129.3	5.4
2013	C	5.65	4.71	127.0	70.8	257.1	11.6
2012	N/A	N/A	N/A	133.6	65.5	317.3	N/A
2011	N/A	N/A	N/A	128.7	72.7	261.8	N/A
2010	N/A	N/A	N/A	128.4	81.3	238.4	N/A
2009	N/A	N/A	N/A	121.4	70.4	215.5	N/A

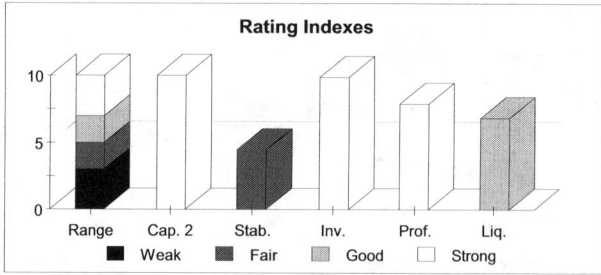

Rating Indexes

SILVERSCRIPT INS CO

D   **Weak**

Major Rating Factors: Weak liquidity (2.0 on a scale of 0 to 10) as a spike in claims may stretch capacity. Good overall profitability index (6.2). Strong capitalization (7.9) based on excellent current risk-adjusted capital (severe loss scenario).

Other Rating Factors: High quality investment portfolio (9.9).

Principal Business: Other (100%)

Mem Phys: 13: 68,000 **12:** 67,000 **13 MLR** 105.1% **/ 13 Admin Exp** N/A

Enroll(000): Q2 14: 3,047 **13:** 3,355 **12:** 1,527 **Med Exp PMPM:** $75

Principal Investments: Cash and equiv (94%), long-term bonds (6%), other (1%)

Provider Compensation ($000): Other ($2,926,978)

Total Member Encounters: N/A

Group Affiliation: CVS Caremark Corp

Licensed in: All states except PR

Address: 445 Great Circle Rd, Nashville, TN 37228

Phone: (615) 743-6600 **Dom State:** TN **Commenced Bus:** January 2006

Data Date	Rating	RACR #1	RACR #2	Total Assets ($mil)	Capital ($mil)	Net Premium ($mil)	Net Income ($mil)
6-14	D	2.04	1.70	2,788.6	270.3	1,403.3	-27.6
6-13	D	2.15	1.79	806.8	154.9	1,679.9	-76.4
2013	D	2.71	2.25	2,481.6	349.9	2,994.3	100.1
2012	B-	4.26	3.55	775.9	286.0	1,389.7	111.4
2011	C	2.95	2.45	487.6	181.7	870.3	45.8
2010	C	1.79	1.49	362.0	139.6	925.4	-14.5
2009	B-	2.20	1.83	439.0	144.9	1,157.5	12.1

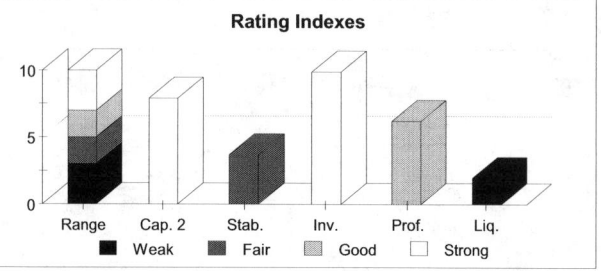

Rating Indexes

SIRIUS AMERICA INS CO   C+   Fair

Major Rating Factors: Fair overall results on stability tests (4.5 on a scale of 0 to 10) including potential drain of affiliation with White Mountains Group and negative cash flow from operations for 2013. The largest net exposure for one risk is high at 3.9% of capital. Fair profitability index (3.7). Fair expense controls. Return on equity has been fair, averaging 9.8% over the past five years.

Other Rating Factors: History of adequate reserve strength (5.0) as reserves have been consistently at an acceptable level. Strong long-term capitalization index (7.0) based on excellent current risk adjusted capital (severe and moderate loss scenarios), despite some fluctuation in capital levels. Excellent liquidity (7.0) with ample operational cash flow and liquid investments.

Principal Business: Group accident & health (71%), aggregate write-ins for other lines of business (23%), and inland marine (5%).

Principal Investments: Investment grade bonds (77%), misc. investments (21%), cash (1%), and non investment grade bonds (1%).

Investments in Affiliates: None

Group Affiliation: White Mountains Group

Licensed in: All states, the District of Columbia and Puerto Rico

Commenced Business: January 1980

Address: One Liberty Plaza, 19th Floor, New York, NY 10006

Phone: (212) 312-2500   **Domicile State:** NY   **NAIC Code:** 38776

Data Date	Rating	RACR #1	RACR #2	Loss Ratio %	Total Assets ($mil)	Capital ($mil)	Net Premium ($mil)	Net Income ($mil)
6-14	C+	2.37	1.35	N/A	1,556.0	597.4	128.5	27.6
6-13	C	1.91	1.20	N/A	1,633.7	575.2	119.4	28.2
2013	C+	2.14	1.21	48.9	1,559.4	548.4	252.8	55.9
2012	C	1.64	1.03	76.8	1,669.7	528.3	271.2	26.2
2011	C	1.50	0.95	71.7	1,807.7	533.7	485.3	101.4
2010	C	2.01	1.32	79.7	2,400.5	742.6	527.2	70.2
2009	C	2.23	1.51	68.6	2,438.1	832.0	489.1	46.9

White Mountains Group Composite Group Rating: B+ Largest Group Members	Assets ($mil)	Rating
SYMETRA LIFE INS CO	27220	B+
ATLANTIC SPECIALTY INS CO	2259	C
SIRIUS AMERICA INS CO	1559	C+
ONEBEACON INS CO	1086	C
FIRST SYMETRA NATL LIFE INS CO OF NY	813	A-

SISTEMAS MEDICOS NACIONALES SA DE CV   C+   Fair

Major Rating Factors: Good overall results on stability tests (5.7 on a scale of 0 to 10). Excellent profitability (7.1). Strong capitalization index (7.5) based on excellent current risk-adjusted capital (severe loss scenario).

Other Rating Factors: Excellent liquidity (7.3) with ample operational cash flow and liquid investments.

Principal Business: Managed care (91%), indemnity (9%)

Mem Phys: 13: N/A   **12:** N/A   **13 MLR** 57.1%   **/ 13 Admin Exp** N/A

Enroll(000): Q2 14: 37   **13:** 35   **12:** 32   **Med Exp PMPM:** $74

Principal Investments ($000): Cash and equiv ($7,962)

Provider Compensation ($000): None

Total Member Encounters: N/A

Group Affiliation: None

Licensed in: CA

Address: 303 H Street Suite 390, Chula Vista, CA 91910

Phone: (619) 407-4082   **Dom State:** CA   **Commenced Bus:** January 2000

Data Date	Rating	RACR #1	RACR #2	Total Assets ($mil)	Capital ($mil)	Net Premium ($mil)	Net Income ($mil)
6-14	C+	2.17	1.44	21.7	11.2	32.8	5.1
6-13	C+	3.10	2.06	20.4	14.0	26.7	5.0
2013	C+	1.76	1.17	15.1	9.2	52.8	4.7
2012	C+	1.94	1.29	14.1	9.0	44.5	3.2
2011	C	1.25	0.82	8.1	5.8	36.6	1.1
2010	C	1.24	0.85	7.0	4.7	27.3	-0.8
2009	C	2.00	1.37	7.9	5.4	24.5	2.5

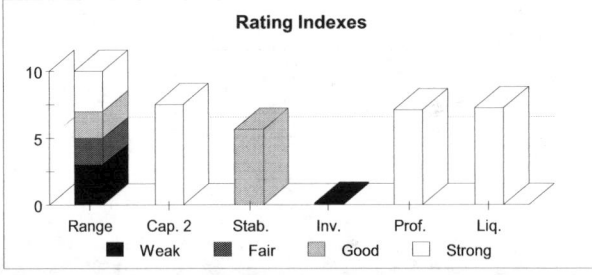

Rating Indexes

Range | Cap. 2 | Stab. | Inv. | Prof. | Liq.
■ Weak   ▨ Fair   ▩ Good   □ Strong

SOLSTICE BENEFITS INC   D   Weak

Major Rating Factors: Weak profitability index (1.1 on a scale of 0 to 10). Fair capitalization (3.1) based on weak current risk-adjusted capital (moderate loss scenario). Good liquidity (6.9) with sufficient resources (cash flows and marketable investments) to handle a spike in claims.

Other Rating Factors: High quality investment portfolio (9.6).

Principal Business: Dental (79%), vision (1%), other (19%)

Mem Phys: 13: 19,576   **12:** 14,012   **13 MLR** 50.1%   **/ 13 Admin Exp** N/A

Enroll(000): Q1 14: 349   **13:** 634   **12:** 521   **Med Exp PMPM:** $1

Principal Investments: Cash and equiv (90%), affiliate common stock (10%)

Provider Compensation ($000): FFS ($12,143)

Total Member Encounters: N/A

Group Affiliation: None

Licensed in: FL

Address: 7901 Southwest 6th Court #400, Plantation, FL 33324

Phone: (954) 370-1700   **Dom State:** FL   **Commenced Bus:** April 2005

Data Date	Rating	RACR #1	RACR #2	Total Assets ($mil)	Capital ($mil)	Net Premium ($mil)	Net Income ($mil)
3-14	D	0.65	0.54	5.3	2.2	4.3	-0.7
3-13	C-	1.72	1.43	5.8	4.1	4.9	0.3
2013	D	0.74	0.61	5.4	2.5	25.7	-1.4
2012	C-	1.74	1.45	5.8	4.1	21.0	0.8
2011	N/A	N/A	N/A	1.7	0.7	15.1	N/A
2010	N/A	N/A	N/A	1.6	0.6	12.3	N/A
2009	N/A	N/A	N/A	1.2	0.2	8.6	N/A

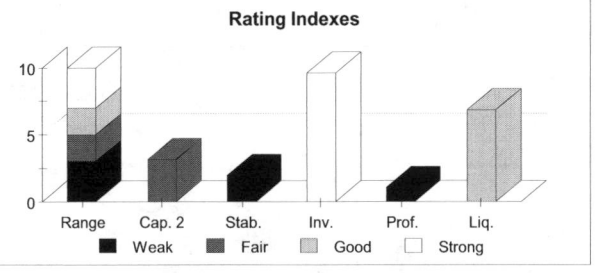

Rating Indexes

Range | Cap. 2 | Stab. | Inv. | Prof. | Liq.
■ Weak   ▨ Fair   ▩ Good   □ Strong

SOUNDPATH HEALTH   C   Fair

Major Rating Factors: Weak profitability index (1.4 on a scale of 0 to 10). Strong capitalization (7.0) based on excellent current risk-adjusted capital (severe loss scenario). High quality investment portfolio (9.9).
Other Rating Factors: Excellent liquidity (6.9) with sufficient resources (cash flows and marketable investments) to handle a spike in claims.
Principal Business: Medicare (100%)
Mem Phys: 13: 7,334 **12:** 7,391 **13 MLR** 87.7% **/ 13 Admin Exp** N/A
Enroll(000): Q2 14: 17 **13:** 17 **12:** 17 **Med Exp PMPM:** $658
Principal Investments: Cash and equiv (75%), long-term bonds (25%)
Provider Compensation ($000): Capitation ($77,969), contr fee ($44,217), FFS ($835), other ($8,030)
Total Member Encounters: Phys (133,691), non-phys (60,801)
Group Affiliation: None
Licensed in: WA
Address: 32129 Weyerhaeuser Way S #201, Federal Way, WA 98001-9346
Phone: (253) 517-4301 **Dom State:** WA **Commenced Bus:** January 2008

Data Date	Rating	RACR #1	RACR #2	Total Assets ($mil)	Capital ($mil)	Net Premium ($mil)	Net Income ($mil)
6-14	C	1.39	1.15	33.7	16.3	68.7	-2.8
6-13	C-	1.56	1.30	28.7	16.1	75.1	0.8
2013	C	1.61	1.34	31.4	18.9	150.0	2.4
2012	D-	0.36	0.30	19.7	2.4	128.0	-0.4
2011	D	0.73	0.61	20.9	4.1	50.1	-1.3
2010	C	1.03	0.86	18.8	5.8	51.7	0.0
2009	C-	1.15	0.96	7.9	5.6	53.4	0.6

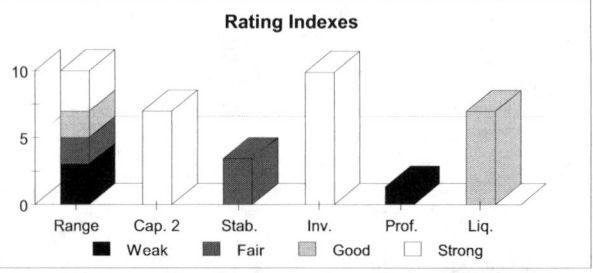

Rating Indexes

SOUTHEASTERN INDIANA HEALTH ORG INC   B   Good

Major Rating Factors: Good overall profitability index (6.9 on a scale of 0 to 10). Strong capitalization index (7.3) based on excellent current risk-adjusted capital (severe loss scenario). High quality investment portfolio (9.5).
Other Rating Factors: Excellent overall results on stability tests (7.0) despite a decline in enrollment during 2013. Excellent liquidity (7.1) with ample operational cash flow and liquid investments.
Principal Business: Comp med (99%)
Mem Phys: 13: 25,571 **12:** 25,402 **13 MLR** 80.2% **/ 13 Admin Exp** N/A
Enroll(000): Q2 14: 9 **13:** 10 **12:** 11 **Med Exp PMPM:** $321
Principal Investments: Cash and equiv (80%), real estate (16%), long-term bonds (4%)
Provider Compensation ($000): Contr fee ($33,818), bonus arrang ($5,039), capitation ($406), FFS ($184)
Total Member Encounters: Phys (45,510), non-phys (17,610)
Group Affiliation: None
Licensed in: IN
Address: 417 Washington St, Columbus, IN 47201
Phone: (812) 378-7000 **Dom State:** IN **Commenced Bus:** December 1986

Data Date	Rating	RACR #1	RACR #2	Total Assets ($mil)	Capital ($mil)	Net Premium ($mil)	Net Income ($mil)
6-14	B	1.63	1.35	17.6	9.6	24.0	0.6
6-13	B	1.40	1.17	16.7	8.4	25.0	0.9
2013	B	1.56	1.30	16.6	9.3	50.4	1.9
2012	B	1.29	1.07	15.3	7.9	47.4	2.0
2011	C	0.88	0.74	11.8	5.7	45.6	1.0
2010	D+	0.63	0.53	9.8	4.5	50.3	0.3
2009	D+	0.54	0.45	10.5	3.9	48.3	-1.1

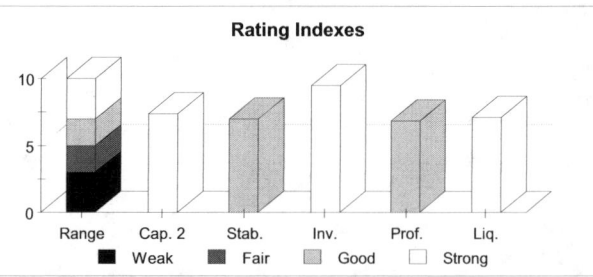

Rating Indexes

SOUTHWEST LIFE & HEALTH INS CO   C   Fair

Major Rating Factors: Weak profitability index (0.9 on a scale of 0 to 10). Strong capitalization (7.6) based on excellent current risk-adjusted capital (severe loss scenario). High quality investment portfolio (9.9).
Other Rating Factors: Excellent liquidity (7.3) with ample operational cash flow and liquid investments.
Principal Business: Comp med (99%)
Mem Phys: 13: 8,148 **12:** 8,927 **13 MLR** 84.6% **/ 13 Admin Exp** N/A
Enroll(000): Q2 14: 6 **13:** 6 **12:** 7 **Med Exp PMPM:** $241
Principal Investments: Cash and equiv (76%), long-term bonds (24%)
Provider Compensation ($000): Contr fee ($9,871), FFS ($9,350), capitation ($43)
Total Member Encounters: Phys (21,125), non-phys (11,664)
Group Affiliation: FirstCare Group
Licensed in: LA, NM, TX
Address: 12940 N Hwy 183, Austin, TX 78750-3203
Phone: (512) 257-6001 **Dom State:** TX **Commenced Bus:** March 1962

Data Date	Rating	RACR #1	RACR #2	Total Assets ($mil)	Capital ($mil)	Net Premium ($mil)	Net Income ($mil)
6-14	C	1.80	1.50	9.9	6.3	10.2	-1.1
6-13	C	1.58	1.32	11.0	7.5	11.2	-0.3
2013	C	2.26	1.88	10.8	7.6	21.7	-0.2
2012	C	1.72	1.43	11.9	7.8	26.5	-1.4
2011	C	1.86	1.55	15.8	9.3	34.8	0.0
2010	C	1.80	1.50	15.5	9.4	43.0	0.6
2009	C-	1.44	1.20	15.8	8.8	53.7	1.8

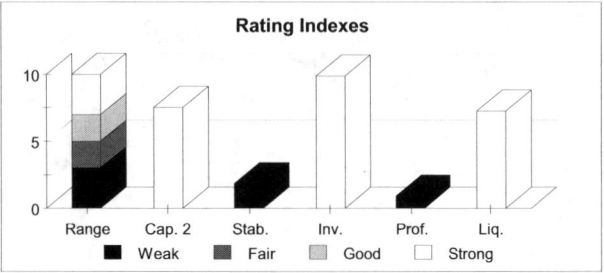

Rating Indexes

STANDARD INSURANCE COMPANY *   B+   Good

Major Rating Factors: Good quality investment portfolio (5.8 on a scale of 0 to 10) despite substantial holdings of BBB bonds in addition to moderate junk bond exposure. Exposure to mortgages is large, but the mortgage default rate has been low. Good liquidity (6.7) with sufficient resources to cover a large increase in policy surrenders. Good overall results on stability tests (6.5) despite excessive premium growth good operational trends and excellent risk diversification.

Other Rating Factors: Strong capitalization (7.4) based on excellent risk adjusted capital (severe loss scenario). Excellent profitability (7.8) with operating gains in each of the last five years.

Principal Business: Group retirement contracts (36%), group health insurance (28%), group life insurance (19%), individual annuities (8%), and other lines (9%).

Principal Investments: NonCMO investment grade bonds (49%), mortgages in good standing (43%), noninv. grade bonds (3%), CMOs and structured securities (2%), and cash (1%).

Investments in Affiliates: None

Group Affiliation: Stancorp Financial Group

Licensed in: All states except NY, PR

Commenced Business: April 1906

Address: 1100 SW Sixth Ave, Portland, OR 97204

Phone: (503) 321-7000 **Domicile State:** OR **NAIC Code:** 69019

Data Date	Rating	RACR #1	RACR #2	Total Assets ($mil)	Capital ($mil)	Net Premium ($mil)	Net Income ($mil)
6-14	B+	2.23	1.24	19,996.4	1,287.9	2,249.0	86.9
6-13	B+	2.33	1.30	17,996.4	1,200.0	1,644.4	66.7
2013	B+	2.37	1.32	19,118.7	1,287.3	3,489.3	195.8
2012	B+	2.36	1.33	17,250.3	1,190.3	3,506.4	125.4
2011	B+	2.44	1.42	16,014.1	1,139.2	3,547.4	127.2
2010	B+	2.51	1.49	15,616.8	1,171.5	3,263.5	190.1
2009	B+	2.66	1.58	14,524.9	1,193.7	3,359.4	217.8

Adverse Trends in Operations

Decrease in capital during 2011 (3%)
Increase in policy surrenders from 2010 to 2011 (33%)
Decrease in capital during 2010 (2%)
Increase in policy surrenders from 2009 to 2010 (38%)
Decrease in premium volume from 2009 to 2010 (3%)

STANDARD LIFE & ACCIDENT INSURANCE COMPANY *   A-   Excellent

Major Rating Factors: Good overall results on stability tests (6.9 on a scale of 0 to 10). Strengths that enhance stability include excellent operational trends and excellent risk diversification. Good liquidity (6.9) with sufficient resources to handle a spike in claims as well as a significant increase in policy surrenders. Fair quality investment portfolio (4.9).

Other Rating Factors: Strong capitalization (10.0) based on excellent risk adjusted capital (severe loss scenario). Excellent profitability (8.7) with operating gains in each of the last five years.

Principal Business: Individual health insurance (38%), reinsurance (35%), group health insurance (21%), individual life insurance (6%), and individual annuities (1%).

Principal Investments: NonCMO investment grade bonds (70%), common & preferred stock (18%), mortgages in good standing (7%), noninv. grade bonds (3%), and misc. investments (3%).

Investments in Affiliates: None

Group Affiliation: American National Group Inc

Licensed in: All states except ME, NH, NJ, NY, PR

Commenced Business: June 1976

Address: One Moody Plaza, Galveston, TX 77550

Phone: (409) 763-4661 **Domicile State:** TX **NAIC Code:** 86355

Data Date	Rating	RACR #1	RACR #2	Total Assets ($mil)	Capital ($mil)	Net Premium ($mil)	Net Income ($mil)
6-14	A-	5.02	3.08	525.1	250.0	60.3	10.0
6-13	A-	5.41	3.32	521.9	243.2	53.8	8.3
2013	A-	5.22	3.20	527.6	252.2	108.7	18.0
2012	A-	5.88	3.59	527.8	255.8	106.2	22.4
2011	A-	5.71	3.50	515.1	235.5	105.2	26.5
2010	A-	5.19	3.19	512.9	222.5	111.4	21.5
2009	A-	5.29	3.24	505.9	217.7	121.0	3.2

Adverse Trends in Operations

Decrease in capital during 2013 (1%)
Decrease in premium volume from 2010 to 2011 (6%)
Decrease in premium volume from 2009 to 2010 (8%)

STANDARD LIFE INSURANCE COMPANY OF NEW YORK *   A-   Excellent

Major Rating Factors: Good overall profitability (6.7 on a scale of 0 to 10) despite operating losses during the first six months of 2014. Return on equity has been fair, averaging 6.3%. Good liquidity (6.8) with sufficient resources to handle a spike in claims. Excellent overall results on stability tests (7.2) excellent operational trends and excellent risk diversification.

Other Rating Factors: Strong capitalization (8.8) based on excellent risk adjusted capital (severe loss scenario). High quality investment portfolio (7.4).

Principal Business: Group health insurance (56%) and group life insurance (43%).

Principal Investments: Mortgages in good standing (48%), nonCMO investment grade bonds (48%), noninv. grade bonds (2%), and cash (2%).

Investments in Affiliates: None

Group Affiliation: Stancorp Financial Group

Licensed in: NY

Commenced Business: January 2001

Address: 360 Hamilton Ave Suite 210, White Plains, NY 10601-1871

Phone: (503) 321-7859 **Domicile State:** NY **NAIC Code:** 89009

Data Date	Rating	RACR #1	RACR #2	Total Assets ($mil)	Capital ($mil)	Net Premium ($mil)	Net Income ($mil)
6-14	A-	3.27	2.17	269.3	71.0	47.6	-0.2
6-13	A-	3.05	2.05	260.9	68.7	48.4	-1.0
2013	A-	3.28	2.19	265.6	71.6	98.0	2.7
2012	A-	3.07	2.10	251.1	69.3	100.1	6.1
2011	A-	3.34	2.21	231.3	53.8	65.9	-1.3
2010	B+	3.50	2.34	212.1	55.3	65.0	5.4
2009	B+	3.46	2.31	196.2	49.5	61.2	6.7

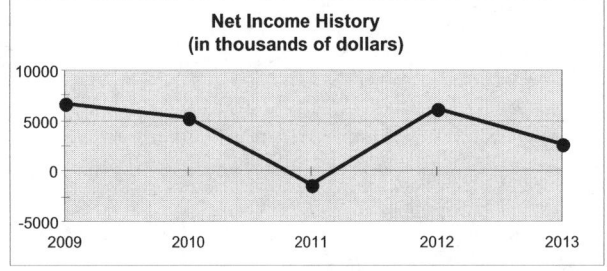

Net Income History
(in thousands of dollars)

STANDARD SECURITY LIFE INSURANCE CO OF NEW YORK — B — Good

Major Rating Factors: Good overall results on stability tests (5.9 on a scale of 0 to 10) despite fair financial strength of affiliated Geneve Holdings Inc. Other stability subfactors include excellent operational trends and excellent risk diversification. Good liquidity (6.8) with sufficient resources to handle a spike in claims. Strong capitalization (9.4) based on excellent risk adjusted capital (severe loss scenario).

Other Rating Factors: High quality investment portfolio (7.1). Excellent profitability (7.2) with operating gains in each of the last five years.

Principal Business: Group health insurance (79%) and reinsurance (20%).

Principal Investments: NonCMO investment grade bonds (68%), common & preferred stock (19%), CMOs and structured securities (2%), and cash (1%).

Investments in Affiliates: 16%

Group Affiliation: Geneve Holdings Inc

Licensed in: All states, the District of Columbia and Puerto Rico

Commenced Business: December 1958

Address: 485 Madison Ave, New York, NY 10022-5872

Phone: (212) 355-4141 **Domicile State:** NY **NAIC Code:** 69078

Data Date	Rating	RACR #1	RACR #2	Total Assets ($mil)	Capital ($mil)	Net Premium ($mil)	Net Income ($mil)
6-14	B	3.25	2.62	249.3	112.7	106.8	4.3
6-13	B	3.82	3.08	258.1	120.0	104.6	4.0
2013	B	3.29	2.67	249.5	114.0	214.4	9.2
2012	B	4.05	3.25	239.5	116.3	148.4	15.8
2011	A-	3.38	2.63	371.6	106.5	151.6	7.7
2010	B+	3.28	2.61	363.5	109.3	141.3	3.3
2009	B+	3.03	2.45	370.8	115.1	180.2	8.8

Geneve Holdings Inc
Composite Group Rating: C+

Largest Group Members	Assets ($mil)	Rating
MADISON NATIONAL LIFE INS CO INC	489	C+
STANDARD SECURITY LIFE INS CO OF NY	250	B
INDEPENDENCE AMERICAN INS CO	102	C

STATE MUTUAL INSURANCE COMPANY — C — Fair

Major Rating Factors: Fair profitability (3.8 on a scale of 0 to 10) with investment income below regulatory standards in relation to interest assumptions of reserves. Fair overall results on stability tests (3.5) including negative cash flow from operations for 2013, fair risk adjusted capital in prior years. Good quality investment portfolio (5.4).

Other Rating Factors: Good liquidity (6.1). Strong capitalization (7.0) based on excellent risk adjusted capital (severe loss scenario).

Principal Business: Reinsurance (47%), individual life insurance (34%), and individual health insurance (19%).

Principal Investments: NonCMO investment grade bonds (41%), CMOs and structured securities (20%), mortgages in good standing (15%), policy loans (9%), and misc. investments (16%).

Investments in Affiliates: 7%

Group Affiliation: None

Licensed in: All states except AK, CA, CT, ME, MA, MI, NH, NJ, NY, PR

Commenced Business: October 1890

Address: 210 E Second Ave Suite 301, Rome, GA 30161-1714

Phone: (706) 291-1054 **Domicile State:** GA **NAIC Code:** 69132

Data Date	Rating	RACR #1	RACR #2	Total Assets ($mil)	Capital ($mil)	Net Premium ($mil)	Net Income ($mil)
6-14	C	1.66	1.00	296.3	29.3	9.3	1.0
6-13	C	1.87	1.09	296.3	27.0	11.6	0.8
2013	C	1.73	1.04	296.8	30.0	21.5	0.8
2012	C	1.93	1.11	298.0	29.4	16.3	1.4
2011	C-	2.04	1.18	304.6	32.7	-134.3	-0.5
2010	C-	1.06	0.69	383.5	25.8	28.9	-1.3
2009	C	1.21	0.81	392.8	29.9	30.1	1.3

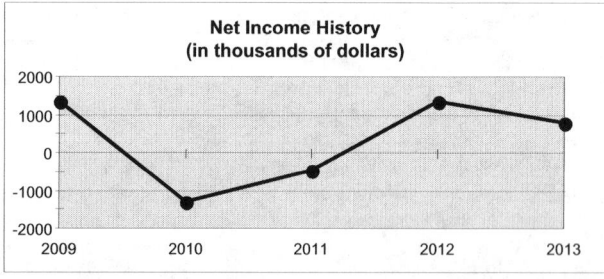

Net Income History
(in thousands of dollars)

STERLING LIFE INS CO — D — Weak

Major Rating Factors: Fair profitability index (4.1 on a scale of 0 to 10). Strong capitalization (10.0) based on excellent current risk-adjusted capital (severe loss scenario). High quality investment portfolio (9.9).

Other Rating Factors: Excellent liquidity (7.0) with sufficient resources (cash flows and marketable investments) to handle a spike in claims.

Principal Business: Med supp (49%), Medicare (9%), other (40%)

Mem Phys: 13: 63,648 **12:** 59,966 **13 MLR** 97.3% **/ 13 Admin Exp** N/A

Enroll(000): Q2 14: 108 **13:** 141 **12:** 144 **Med Exp PMPM:** $124

Principal Investments: Long-term bonds (87%), cash and equiv (13%)

Provider Compensation ($000): Contr fee ($159,549), other ($79,196)

Total Member Encounters: N/A

Group Affiliation: WellCare Health Plans Inc

Licensed in: All states except PR

Address: 30 S Wacker Dr, Chicago, IL 60025-2423

Phone: (360) 647-9080 **Dom State:** IL **Commenced Bus:** January 1958

Data Date	Rating	RACR #1	RACR #2	Total Assets ($mil)	Capital ($mil)	Net Premium ($mil)	Net Income ($mil)
6-14	D	5.42	4.52	99.4	40.7	86.8	6.2
6-13	D	4.48	3.74	182.4	106.6	106.2	17.9
2013	D	5.89	4.91	113.0	44.4	205.4	28.1
2012	D	3.80	3.16	224.8	88.7	442.6	-17.6
2011	D	3.81	3.17	212.2	108.6	468.5	-34.1
2010	C	3.47	2.89	272.0	148.0	793.9	33.2
2009	C+	3.83	3.19	331.7	209.0	947.6	12.3

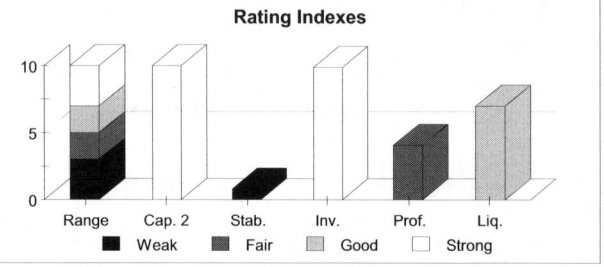

Rating Indexes

STONEBRIDGE LIFE INSURANCE COMPANY　　　　B-　　　Good

Major Rating Factors: Good overall results on stability tests (5.3 on a scale of 0 to 10). Stability strengths include good operational trends, good risk adjusted capital for prior years and excellent risk diversification. Good overall profitability (5.4). Return on equity has been excellent over the last five years averaging 106.7%. Fair quality investment portfolio (4.6).

Other Rating Factors: Strong capitalization (7.2) based on excellent risk adjusted capital (severe loss scenario). Excellent liquidity (7.3).

Principal Business: Group health insurance (46%), group life insurance (21%), individual life insurance (15%), individual health insurance (9%), and reinsurance (8%).

Principal Investments: NonCMO investment grade bonds (64%), CMOs and structured securities (14%), mortgages in good standing (6%), noninv. grade bonds (4%), and misc. investments (8%).

Investments in Affiliates: None

Group Affiliation: AEGON USA Group

Licensed in: All states except NY, PR

Commenced Business: May 1906

Address: 187 West St, Rutland, VT 05701

Phone: (319) 355-8511　**Domicile State:** VT　**NAIC Code:** 65021

Data Date	Rating	RACR #1	RACR #2	Total Assets ($mil)	Capital ($mil)	Net Premium ($mil)	Net Income ($mil)
6-14	B-	2.03	1.11	1,753.9	159.8	198.4	54.0
6-13	C+	1.66	0.89	1,753.3	124.8	180.0	38.3
2013	C+	1.44	0.78	1,739.9	108.5	360.5	83.6
2012	C+	1.55	0.83	1,676.9	113.7	362.5	383.1
2011	C+	2.09	1.14	1,749.6	161.1	372.8	163.4
2010	B+	4.34	2.33	2,157.6	368.5	-297.2	136.8
2009	B+	1.87	1.05	2,024.8	182.1	509.9	135.0

Adverse Trends in Operations

Decrease in capital during 2013 (5%)
Decrease in capital during 2012 (29%)
Decrease in asset base during 2011 (19%)
Decrease in capital during 2011 (56%)
Decrease in premium volume from 2009 to 2010 (158%)

SUMMA INS CO　　　　　　　　　　　　　　D　　　Weak

Major Rating Factors: Weak profitability index (0.7 on a scale of 0 to 10). Poor capitalization (2.9) based on weak current risk-adjusted capital (moderate loss scenario). Good liquidity (6.9) with sufficient resources (cash flows and marketable investments) to handle a spike in claims.

Other Rating Factors: High quality investment portfolio (9.9).

Principal Business: Comp med (99%)

Mem Phys: 13: 7,000　**12:** 6,000　**13 MLR** 94.7%　**/ 13 Admin Exp** N/A

Enroll(000): Q2 14: 57　**13:** 59　**12:** 56　**Med Exp PMPM:** $305

Principal Investments: Long-term bonds (61%), cash and equiv (39%)

Provider Compensation ($000): Contr fee ($205,437), capitation ($524), bonus arrang ($72)

Total Member Encounters: Phys (93,095), non-phys (124,396)

Group Affiliation: Summa Health Systems

Licensed in: OH

Address: 10 N Main St, Akron, OH 44308

Phone: (330) 996-8410　**Dom State:** OH　**Commenced Bus:** February 1996

Data Date	Rating	RACR #1	RACR #2	Total Assets ($mil)	Capital ($mil)	Net Premium ($mil)	Net Income ($mil)
6-14	D	0.61	0.51	64.3	26.2	117.7	-2.4
6-13	C	2.06	1.72	91.4	60.0	105.7	-3.0
2013	D+	0.69	0.57	61.9	29.8	219.6	-10.6
2012	C	1.99	1.66	95.3	58.0	205.2	-1.6
2011	C	1.96	1.63	85.8	53.9	175.7	-0.2
2010	C-	1.82	1.52	75.1	48.2	154.0	-0.8
2009	C-	1.70	1.42	69.4	40.8	145.8	-7.4

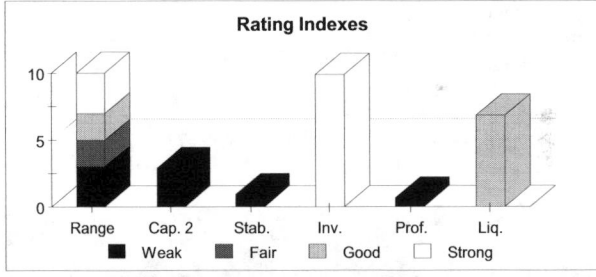

Rating Indexes (Range, Cap. 2, Stab., Inv., Prof., Liq.)
■ Weak　■ Fair　▨ Good　□ Strong

SUMMACARE INC　　　　　　　　　　　　　C-　　　Fair

Major Rating Factors: Weak overall results on stability tests (1.7 on a scale of 0 to 10). Good liquidity (6.9) with sufficient resources (cash flows and marketable investments) to handle a spike in claims. Excellent profitability (7.1).

Other Rating Factors: Strong capitalization index (7.1) based on excellent current risk-adjusted capital (severe loss scenario). High quality investment portfolio (9.9).

Principal Business: Medicare (100%)

Mem Phys: 13: 7,000　**12:** 6,000　**13 MLR** 85.1%　**/ 13 Admin Exp** N/A

Enroll(000): Q2 14: 33　**13:** 28　**12:** 25　**Med Exp PMPM:** $701

Principal Investments: Long-term bonds (66%), cash and equiv (29%), other (4%)

Provider Compensation ($000): Contr fee ($228,768), capitation ($2,888), bonus arrang ($28)

Total Member Encounters: Phys (122,114), non-phys (187,889)

Group Affiliation: Summa Health Systems

Licensed in: OH

Address: 10 N Main St, Akron, OH 44309

Phone: (330) 996-8410　**Dom State:** OH　**Commenced Bus:** March 1993

Data Date	Rating	RACR #1	RACR #2	Total Assets ($mil)	Capital ($mil)	Net Premium ($mil)	Net Income ($mil)
6-14	C-	1.46	1.22	81.9	34.8	154.2	3.5
6-13	B	2.65	2.20	96.1	56.9	137.5	4.6
2013	C	1.30	1.09	105.3	30.6	277.6	9.1
2012	B	2.43	2.02	88.3	52.2	283.3	3.9
2011	B-	2.24	1.87	93.1	48.5	277.3	3.6
2010	B-	1.86	1.55	87.0	44.4	294.2	5.1
2009	B-	1.73	1.44	44.7	27.8	265.4	2.9

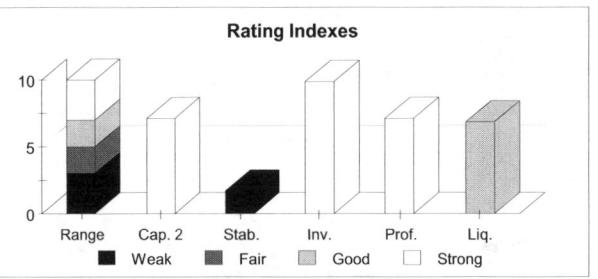

Rating Indexes (Range, Cap. 2, Stab., Inv., Prof., Liq.)
■ Weak　■ Fair　▨ Good　□ Strong

SUN LIFE & HEALTH INSURANCE COMPANY

C-   Fair

Major Rating Factors: Fair overall results on stability tests (3.3 on a scale of 0 to 10) including potential financial drain due to affiliation with Sun Life Assurance Group and negative cash flow from operations for 2013. Weak profitability (2.4) with investment income below regulatory standards in relation to interest assumptions of reserves. Good liquidity (6.9).

Other Rating Factors: Strong capitalization (10.0) based on excellent risk adjusted capital (severe loss scenario). High quality investment portfolio (7.2).

Principal Business: Reinsurance (50%), group health insurance (30%), and group life insurance (20%).

Principal Investments: CMOs and structured securities (46%), nonCMO investment grade bonds (42%), and mortgages in good standing (11%).

Investments in Affiliates: None

Group Affiliation: Sun Life Assurance Group

Licensed in: All states, the District of Columbia and Puerto Rico

Commenced Business: January 1975

Address: 100 Bright Meadow Blvd, Enfield, CT 06083-1900

Phone: (860) 403-1179   **Domicile State:** CT   **NAIC Code:** 80926

Data Date	Rating	RACR #1	RACR #2	Total Assets ($mil)	Capital ($mil)	Net Premium ($mil)	Net Income ($mil)
6-14	C-	5.25	3.48	366.3	187.4	86.7	7.1
6-13	C-	5.89	2.89	67.0	48.7	0.0	0.1
2013	C-	5.38	3.67	353.7	182.0	166.8	-35.8
2012	C-	6.10	2.98	64.6	48.1	0.0	1.8
2011	C	5.80	2.84	65.1	44.3	0.0	1.6
2010	C	5.41	2.54	65.7	42.3	0.0	2.6
2009	C	5.30	3.12	72.7	40.8	0.0	-1.1

Sun Life Assurance Group Composite Group Rating: D+ Largest Group Members	Assets ($mil)	Rating
SUN LIFE ASR CO OF CANADA	15369	D
INDEPENDENCE LIFE ANNUITY CO	2284	C
SUN LIFE HEALTH INS CO	354	C-
PROFESSIONAL INS CO	105	C-

SUN LIFE ASSURANCE COMPANY OF CANADA

D   Weak

Major Rating Factors: Low quality investment portfolio (2.1 on a scale of 0 to 10) containing large holdings of BBB rated bonds in addition to moderate junk bond exposure. Exposure to mortgages is significant, but the mortgage default rate has been low. Weak profitability (2.5) with operating losses during the first six months of 2014. Weak liquidity (1.8).

Other Rating Factors: Weak overall results on stability tests (2.3) including weak risk adjusted capital in prior years, negative cash flow from operations for 2013. Fair overall capitalization (4.0) based on mixed results -- excessive policy leverage mitigated by fair risk adjusted capital (moderate loss scenario).

Principal Business: N/A

Principal Investments: NonCMO investment grade bonds (51%), mortgages in good standing (20%), real estate (8%), CMOs and structured securities (7%), and misc. investments (12%).

Investments in Affiliates: 2%

Group Affiliation: Sun Life Assurance Group

Licensed in: All states, the District of Columbia and Puerto Rico

Commenced Business: May 1871

Address: One Sun Life Executive Park, Wellesley Hills, MA 02481

Phone: (781) 237-6030   **Domicile State:** MI   **NAIC Code:** 80802

Data Date	Rating	RACR #1	RACR #2	Total Assets ($mil)	Capital ($mil)	Net Premium ($mil)	Net Income ($mil)
6-14	D	0.90	0.47	15,974.7	892.4	1,126.3	-56.5
6-13	C-	1.00	0.56	15,576.7	1,185.5	-189.1	320.2
2013	D	0.53	0.30	15,368.9	766.7	-919.7	234.8
2012	C-	0.79	0.45	17,403.4	1,037.6	2,283.3	119.1
2011	C-	0.77	0.44	17,348.7	1,017.6	2,397.5	-253.2
2010	C	0.80	0.45	16,039.3	890.8	2,513.6	159.1
2009	C	0.54	0.30	15,278.5	662.0	2,600.1	156.5

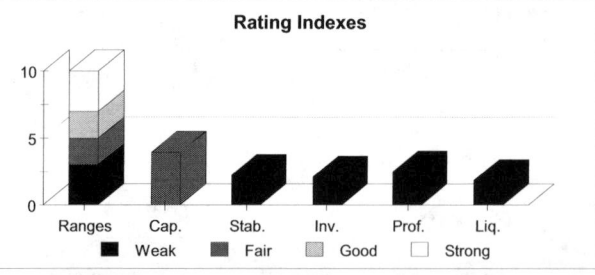

Rating Indexes

Ranges | Cap. | Stab. | Inv. | Prof. | Liq.
■ Weak   ■ Fair   ▨ Good   □ Strong

SUNFLOWER STATE HEALTH PLAN INC

D+   Weak

Major Rating Factors: Weak profitability index (0.9 on a scale of 0 to 10). Good liquidity (6.8) with sufficient resources (cash flows and marketable investments) to handle a spike in claims. Strong capitalization (7.1) based on excellent current risk-adjusted capital (severe loss scenario).

Other Rating Factors: High quality investment portfolio (9.9).

Principal Business: Medicaid (100%)

Mem Phys: 13: 7,550   **12:** N/A   **13 MLR** 100.0% / **13 Admin Exp** N/A

Enroll(000): Q2 14: 146   **13:** 140   **12:** N/A   **Med Exp PMPM:** $484

Principal Investments: Cash and equiv (81%), long-term bonds (19%)

Provider Compensation ($000): Contr fee ($575,346), capitation ($128,003), salary ($11,014)

Total Member Encounters: Phys (726,080), non-phys (1,755,311)

Group Affiliation: Centene Corp

Licensed in: KS

Address: 8325 Lenexa Dr, Lenexa, KS 66214

Phone: (314) 725-4477   **Dom State:** KS   **Commenced Bus:** January 2013

Data Date	Rating	RACR #1	RACR #2	Total Assets ($mil)	Capital ($mil)	Net Premium ($mil)	Net Income ($mil)
6-14	D+	1.46	1.21	201.6	81.6	483.2	-10.8
6-13	N/A	N/A	N/A	157.7	79.2	353.9	-26.5
2013	D+	1.45	1.21	215.1	81.5	801.7	-91.0
2012	N/A	N/A	N/A	3.2	3.0	N/A	N/A
2011	N/A	N/A	N/A	N/A	N/A	N/A	N/A
2010	N/A	N/A	N/A	N/A	N/A	N/A	N/A
2009	N/A	N/A	N/A	N/A	N/A	N/A	N/A

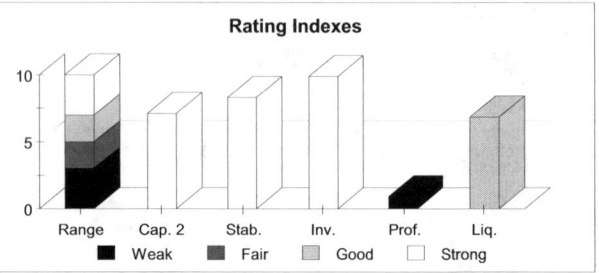

Rating Indexes

Range | Cap. 2 | Stab. | Inv. | Prof. | Liq.
■ Weak   ■ Fair   ▨ Good   □ Strong

SUNSHINE HEALTH   E   Very Weak

Major Rating Factors: Weak profitability index (0.9 on a scale of 0 to 10). Good liquidity (6.5) with sufficient resources (cash flows and marketable investments) to handle a spike in claims. Strong capitalization (6.9) based on excellent current risk-adjusted capital (severe loss scenario).

Other Rating Factors: High quality investment portfolio (9.9).

Principal Business: Medicaid (73%), comp med (27%)

Mem Phys: 13: 16,502 **12:** 11,578 **13 MLR** 89.5% **/ 13 Admin Exp** N/A

Enroll(000): Q2 14: 324 **13:** 221 **12:** 214 **Med Exp PMPM:** $266

Principal Investments: Cash and equiv (63%), long-term bonds (37%)

Provider Compensation ($000): Contr fee ($458,465), capitation ($79,021), bonus arrang ($50,015), salary ($18,863)

Total Member Encounters: Phys (1,232,505), non-phys (815,052)

Group Affiliation: Centene Corp

Licensed in: FL

Address: 400 Sawgrass Corporate Pkwy, Sunrise, FL 33325

Phone: (314) 725-4477 **Dom State:** FL **Commenced Bus:** February 2009

Data Date	Rating	RACR #1	RACR #2	Total Assets ($mil)	Capital ($mil)	Net Premium ($mil)	Net Income ($mil)
6-14	E	1.28	1.07	264.1	54.3	902.7	-29.1
6-13	E	1.65	1.37	103.1	51.6	297.2	2.3
2013	E	1.31	1.10	195.9	55.8	771.3	5.9
2012	E	1.25	1.04	86.9	40.8	559.1	0.4
2011	E	1.01	0.84	94.8	36.4	488.0	1.1
2010	E	0.96	0.80	116.8	23.4	283.0	-38.1
2009	E	1.29	1.07	64.8	13.6	106.8	-10.8

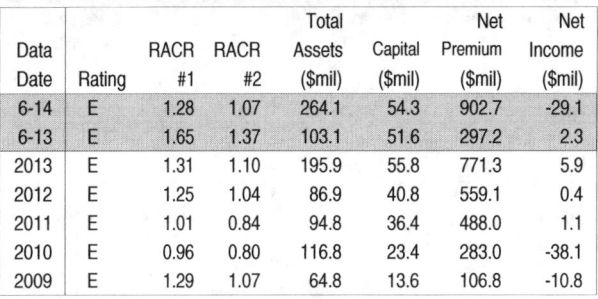

Rating Indexes

SUPERIOR HEALTHPLAN INC   C   Fair

Major Rating Factors: Weak profitability index (2.2 on a scale of 0 to 10). Good liquidity (6.9) with sufficient resources (cash flows and marketable investments) to handle a spike in claims. Strong capitalization index (7.8) based on excellent current risk-adjusted capital (severe loss scenario).

Other Rating Factors: High quality investment portfolio (9.9). Excellent overall results on stability tests (7.8).

Principal Business: Medicaid (93%), comp med (4%), Medicare (2%)

Mem Phys: 13: 40,176 **12:** 36,531 **13 MLR** 87.4% **/ 13 Admin Exp** N/A

Enroll(000): Q2 14: 391 **13:** 395 **12:** 411 **Med Exp PMPM:** $305

Principal Investments: Long-term bonds (49%), cash and equiv (47%), affiliate common stock (3%), other (1%)

Provider Compensation ($000): Contr fee ($1,408,028), capitation ($67,498), bonus arrang ($26,754), salary ($16,221)

Total Member Encounters: Phys (2,305,418), non-phys (2,674,188)

Group Affiliation: Centene Corp

Licensed in: TX

Address: 2100 South IH 35 Suite 202, Austin, TX 78704

Phone: (314) 725-4477 **Dom State:** TX **Commenced Bus:** February 1997

Data Date	Rating	RACR #1	RACR #2	Total Assets ($mil)	Capital ($mil)	Net Premium ($mil)	Net Income ($mil)
6-14	C	1.97	1.64	371.7	189.4	833.6	-1.5
6-13	C	1.84	1.53	299.2	167.7	846.7	2.0
2013	C	1.95	1.63	349.1	188.0	1,703.5	16.8
2012	C	1.72	1.43	332.2	162.9	1,559.3	-40.6
2011	B-	1.32	1.10	213.7	93.3	1,085.8	-4.6
2010	B-	1.26	1.05	157.9	74.2	877.3	-1.9
2009	B	1.45	1.21	182.4	76.8	809.3	32.0

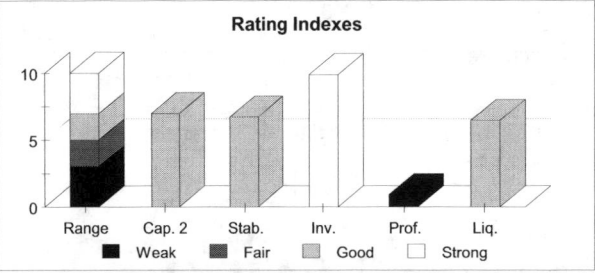

Rating Indexes

SWISS RE LIFE & HEALTH AMERICA INCORPORATED   C+   Fair

Major Rating Factors: Fair overall results on stability tests (4.7 on a scale of 0 to 10). Good overall profitability (6.5). Excellent expense controls. Return on equity has been fair, averaging 6.3%. Good liquidity (6.8) with sufficient resources to handle a spike in claims as well as a significant increase in policy surrenders.

Other Rating Factors: Strong capitalization (7.5) based on excellent risk adjusted capital (severe loss scenario). High quality investment portfolio (7.1).

Principal Business: Reinsurance (100%).

Principal Investments: NonCMO investment grade bonds (72%), CMOs and structured securities (15%), common & preferred stock (4%), mortgages in good standing (4%), and misc. investments (5%).

Investments in Affiliates: 10%

Group Affiliation: Swiss Reinsurance Group

Licensed in: All states, the District of Columbia and Puerto Rico

Commenced Business: September 1967

Address: 969 High Ridge Rd, Stamford, CT 06904-2060

Phone: (203) 321-3141 **Domicile State:** CT **NAIC Code:** 82627

Data Date	Rating	RACR #1	RACR #2	Total Assets ($mil)	Capital ($mil)	Net Premium ($mil)	Net Income ($mil)
6-14	C+	1.90	1.32	10,140.4	1,658.0	806.4	58.0
6-13	C-	1.53	1.09	9,848.2	1,333.5	929.4	-20.8
2013	C	1.86	1.31	9,994.7	1,644.0	1,644.4	95.4
2012	D+	1.35	0.97	9,138.9	1,185.3	1,557.8	95.4
2011	D	4.69	2.13	9,006.5	1,050.2	315.6	-889.9
2010	B-	1.32	1.04	10,408.9	1,621.3	1,152.6	114.4
2009	B-	2.21	1.67	12,176.2	3,039.5	311.5	367.3

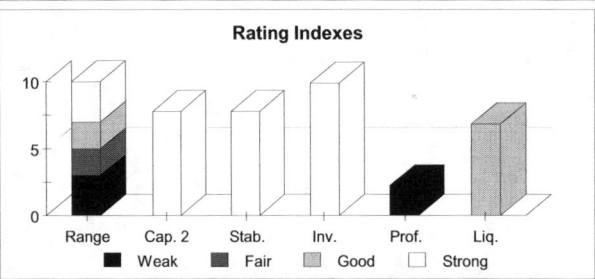

Rating Indexes

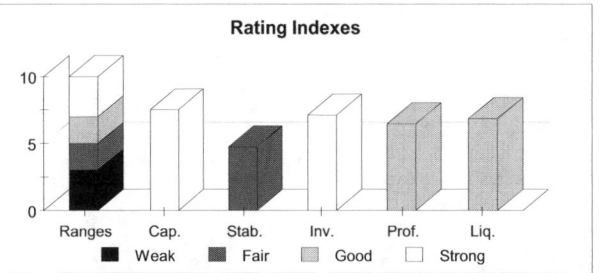

TEXAS CHILDRENS HEALTH PLAN INC

B-   **Good**

Major Rating Factors: Fair overall results on stability tests (4.2 on a scale of 0 to 10). Good overall profitability index (5.3). Good capitalization index (5.9) based on good current risk-adjusted capital (severe loss scenario).
Other Rating Factors: Good liquidity (6.9) with sufficient resources (cash flows and marketable investments) to handle a spike in claims. High quality investment portfolio (9.9).
Principal Business: Medicaid (78%), comp med (22%)
Mem Phys: 13: 6,001   **12:** 4,219   **13 MLR** 91.1%   **/ 13 Admin Exp** N/A
Enroll(000): Q2 14: 360   **13:** 350   **12:** 355   **Med Exp PMPM:** $168
Principal Investments: Cash and equiv (55%), long-term bonds (40%), affiliate common stock (5%)
Provider Compensation ($000): FFS ($530,848), contr fee ($186,136), capitation ($9,864), bonus arrang ($5,754)
Total Member Encounters: Phys (1,733,496), non-phys (1,063,350)
Group Affiliation: Texas Childrens Hospital System Inc
Licensed in: TX
Address: 2450 Holcombe Suite 34L, Houston, TX 77021
Phone: (832) 828-1020   **Dom State:** TX   **Commenced Bus:** February 1996

Data Date	Rating	RACR #1	RACR #2	Total Assets ($mil)	Capital ($mil)	Net Premium ($mil)	Net Income ($mil)
6-14	B-	1.07	0.89	136.2	80.6	414.6	-7.4
6-13	B-	1.49	1.24	157.4	96.8	388.9	-13.8
2013	B-	1.23	1.02	150.5	90.6	792.8	2.8
2012	B	1.67	1.39	175.4	108.2	734.6	18.7
2011	C+	2.83	2.36	195.5	134.6	552.3	47.4
2010	N/A	N/A	N/A	140.2	87.3	493.1	34.4
2009	C+	1.22	1.02	100.4	50.3	416.5	7.8

Rating Indexes

THP INS CO

D   **Weak**

Major Rating Factors: Weak profitability index (0.5 on a scale of 0 to 10). Weak liquidity (0.2) as a spike in claims may stretch capacity. Fair capitalization (4.6) based on fair current risk-adjusted capital (moderate loss scenario).
Other Rating Factors: High quality investment portfolio (9.0).
Principal Business: Comp med (77%), Medicare (21%), other (2%)
Mem Phys: 13: 15,403   **12:** 14,327   **13 MLR** 106.8%   **/ 13 Admin Exp** N/A
Enroll(000): Q2 14: 16   **13:** 19   **12:** 10   **Med Exp PMPM:** $319
Principal Investments: Cash and equiv (67%), nonaffiliate common stock (21%), long-term bonds (12%)
Provider Compensation ($000): Contr fee ($46,140), FFS ($5,906)
Total Member Encounters: Phys (68,629), non-phys (18,511)
Group Affiliation: Health Plan Group
Licensed in: OH, PA, WV
Address: 52160 Natonal Road East E, St Clairsville, OH 43950-9306
Phone: (740) 695-3585   **Dom State:** WV   **Commenced Bus:** March 1999

Data Date	Rating	RACR #1	RACR #2	Total Assets ($mil)	Capital ($mil)	Net Premium ($mil)	Net Income ($mil)
6-14	D	0.86	0.72	25.1	7.4	35.9	-9.3
6-13	D	2.80	2.33	24.4	16.2	21.6	-3.0
2013	D	1.78	1.48	30.4	15.2	53.2	-12.3
2012	D	3.28	2.73	28.2	19.0	46.5	-7.4
2011	D	3.39	2.82	30.9	21.1	41.1	-10.4
2010	C	2.83	2.36	25.8	16.9	45.0	-3.9
2009	C	1.92	1.60	19.7	10.5	41.2	-5.6

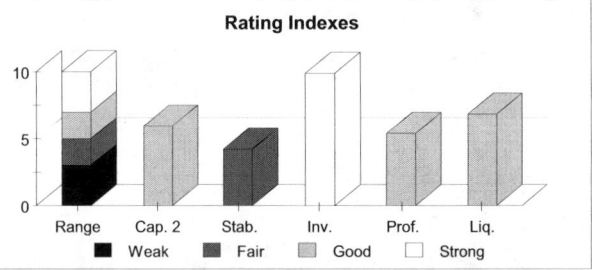

Rating Indexes

TIMBER PRODUCTS MANUFACTURERS TRUST

C+   **Fair**

Major Rating Factors: Good overall profitability index (5.4 on a scale of 0 to 10). Good capitalization (6.9) based on excellent current risk-adjusted capital (severe loss scenario). Good liquidity (6.6) with sufficient resources (cash flows and marketable investments) to handle a spike in claims.
Other Rating Factors: High quality investment portfolio (9.4).
Principal Business: Comp med (97%), dental (2%)
Mem Phys: 13: N/A   **12:** N/A   **13 MLR** 92.5%   **/ 13 Admin Exp** N/A
Enroll(000): Q2 14: 19   **13:** 17   **12:** 12   **Med Exp PMPM:** $175
Principal Investments: Long-term bonds (42%), cash and equiv (41%), nonaffiliate common stock (16%), other (1%)
Provider Compensation ($000): Contr fee ($31,900)
Total Member Encounters: Phys (50,200), non-phys (9,273)
Group Affiliation: None
Licensed in: ID, MT, OR, WA
Address: 951 E Third Ave, Spokane, WA 99202
Phone: (509) 535-4646   **Dom State:** WA   **Commenced Bus:** August 1960

Data Date	Rating	RACR #1	RACR #2	Total Assets ($mil)	Capital ($mil)	Net Premium ($mil)	Net Income ($mil)
6-14	C+	1.28	1.06	13.0	7.4	21.5	0.3
6-13	C+	1.65	1.38	12.2	8.1	16.6	1.7
2013	C+	1.22	1.01	12.4	7.1	35.3	0.7
2012	C	1.27	1.06	11.2	6.4	29.8	1.4
2011	D+	1.10	0.91	8.6	5.0	25.2	2.2
2010	E+	0.49	0.41	6.9	2.8	26.4	-0.1
2009	E	0.43	0.36	8.2	2.8	28.8	-2.7

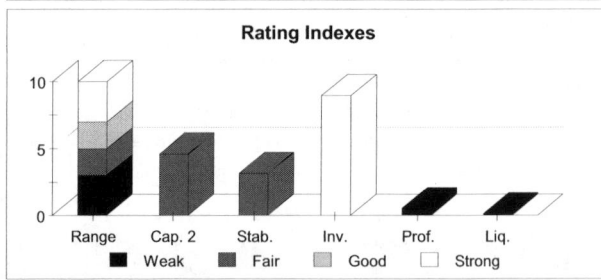

Rating Indexes

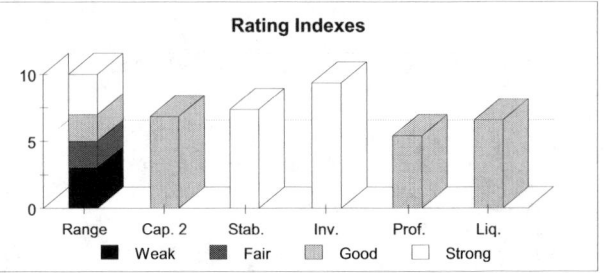

TIME INSURANCE COMPANY   B-   Good

Major Rating Factors: Good overall capitalization (5.3 on a scale of 0 to 10) based on mixed results -- excessive policy leverage mitigated by good risk adjusted capital (severe loss scenario). Nevertheless, capital levels have fluctuated during prior years. Good quality investment portfolio (6.2) despite significant exposure to mortgages . Mortgage default rate has been low. large holdings of BBB rated bonds in addition to small junk bond holdings. Good liquidity (5.2).

Other Rating Factors: Fair profitability (4.1) with operating losses during the first six months of 2014. Fair overall results on stability tests (4.9) including excessive premium growth.

Principal Business: Group health insurance (57%), individual health insurance (40%), and individual life insurance (3%).

Principal Investments: NonCMO investment grade bonds (65%), mortgages in good standing (13%), CMOs and structured securities (9%), common & preferred stock (8%), and misc. investments (6%).

Investments in Affiliates: None
Group Affiliation: Assurant Inc
Licensed in: All states except NY, PR
Commenced Business: March 1910
Address: 501 W Michigan, Milwaukee, WI 53201
Phone: (612) 738-4449 **Domicile State:** WI **NAIC Code:** 69477

Data Date	Rating	RACR #1	RACR #2	Total Assets ($mil)	Capital ($mil)	Net Premium ($mil)	Net Income ($mil)
6-14	B-	1.26	0.98	740.1	255.5	836.9	-12.7
6-13	B-	1.27	0.97	653.8	215.4	608.6	13.7
2013	B-	1.14	0.88	691.5	212.0	1,269.5	5.6
2012	B-	1.20	0.92	645.4	205.8	1,164.5	48.7
2011	B-	1.51	1.16	748.7	273.0	1,215.0	34.5
2010	B-	1.40	1.07	748.3	274.5	1,321.0	44.2
2009	B-	1.20	0.92	795.8	239.5	1,310.8	-43.5

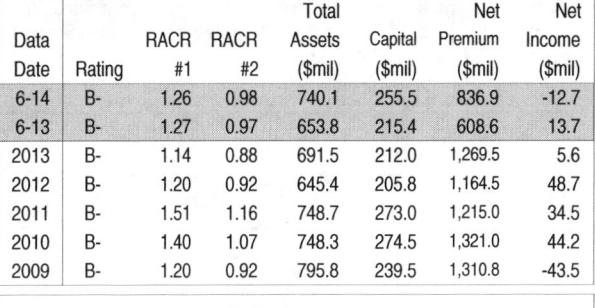

Policy Leverage

Target Leverage — 100%
Actual Leverage — 196%

■ Recommended □ Excess

TODAYS OPTIONS OF OKLAHOMA INC   C   Fair

Major Rating Factors: Weak profitability index (2.6 on a scale of 0 to 10). Good liquidity (6.7) with sufficient resources (cash flows and marketable investments) to handle a spike in claims. Strong capitalization (7.7) based on excellent current risk-adjusted capital (severe loss scenario).

Other Rating Factors: High quality investment portfolio (9.9).
Principal Business: Medicare (100%)
Mem Phys: 13: 1,230 **12:** 2,171 **13 MLR** 87.1% **/ 13 Admin Exp** N/A
Enroll(000): Q2 14: 6 **13:** 6 **12:** 6 **Med Exp PMPM:** $785
Principal Investments: Long-term bonds (84%), cash and equiv (16%)
Provider Compensation ($000): Contr fee ($45,179), capitation ($8,408), bonus arrang ($607)
Total Member Encounters: N/A
Group Affiliation: Universal American Corp
Licensed in: OK
Address: 4888 Loop Central Dr Suite 700, Oklahoma City, OK 73102
Phone: (713) 965-9444 **Dom State:** OK **Commenced Bus:** June 2003

Data Date	Rating	RACR #1	RACR #2	Total Assets ($mil)	Capital ($mil)	Net Premium ($mil)	Net Income ($mil)
6-14	C	1.90	1.58	18.5	11.1	32.0	0.5
6-13	C	2.23	1.86	17.7	11.1	32.0	1.3
2013	C	1.82	1.52	16.1	10.7	63.3	0.9
2012	C	1.96	1.63	14.9	9.6	61.1	2.0
2011	C	0.85	0.71	18.2	7.6	134.3	-6.3
2010	N/A	N/A	N/A	27.0	11.1	151.1	-0.5
2009	B-	1.33	1.11	24.0	9.1	127.1	0.0

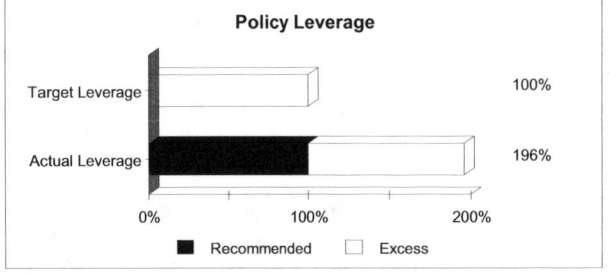

Rating Indexes

Range Cap. 2 Stab. Inv. Prof. Liq.

■ Weak ▨ Fair ▤ Good □ Strong

TOKIO MARINE PACIFIC INS LTD   B-   Good

Major Rating Factors: Fair liquidity (3.0 on a scale of 0 to 10) as cash resources may not be adequate to cover a spike in claims. Fair overall results on stability tests (4.1) including weak results on operational trends. The largest net exposure for one risk is conservative at 1.5% of capital.

Other Rating Factors: Strong long-term capitalization index (8.3) based on excellent current risk adjusted capital (severe and moderate loss scenarios), despite some fluctuation in capital levels. Ample reserve history (9.3) that helps to protect the company against sharp claims increases. Excellent profitability (8.5) with operating gains in each of the last five years. Return on equity has been excellent over the last five years averaging 19.6%.

Principal Business: Group accident & health (89%), auto physical damage (3%), commercial multiple peril (2%), auto liability (2%), workers compensation (1%), homeowners multiple peril (1%), and other lines (2%).

Principal Investments: Cash (40%), investment grade bonds (31%), and misc. investments (29%).

Investments in Affiliates: None
Group Affiliation: Tokio Marine Holdings Inc
Licensed in: (No states)
Commenced Business: February 2002
Address: 250 Route 4 Suite 202, Hagatna, GU 96910
Phone: (671) 475-8671 **Domicile State:** GU **NAIC Code:** 11216

Data Date	Rating	RACR #1	RACR #2	Loss Ratio %	Total Assets ($mil)	Capital ($mil)	Net Premium ($mil)	Net Income ($mil)
6-14	B-	3.75	2.11	N/A	107.1	65.0	57.5	3.8
6-13	B	4.73	2.56	N/A	109.3	63.2	57.6	2.2
2013	B-	3.79	2.11	80.3	105.9	60.5	122.5	5.2
2012	B	4.52	2.46	75.8	105.7	61.7	125.2	16.7
2011	N/A	N/A	N/A	73.7	97.2	44.8	129.9	7.6
2010	N/A	N/A	N/A	77.9	69.0	39.5	104.9	8.4
2009	N/A	N/A	N/A	74.4	54.0	30.1	85.8	8.4

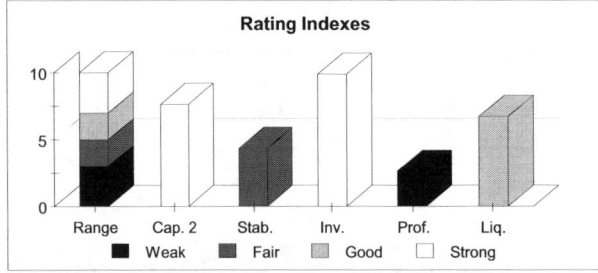

Liquidity Index

Range 2010 2011 2012 2013

■ Weak ▨ Fair ▤ Good □ Strong

TOTAL HEALTH CARE INC

D+   **Weak**

Major Rating Factors: Weak profitability index (1.1 on a scale of 0 to 10). Fair capitalization index (3.7) based on weak current risk-adjusted capital (moderate loss scenario). Fair overall results on stability tests (3.7).

Other Rating Factors: Good liquidity (6.4) with sufficient resources (cash flows and marketable investments) to handle a spike in claims. High quality investment portfolio (8.1).

Principal Business: Medicaid (99%)

Mem Phys: 13: 4,570 **12:** 4,278 **13 MLR** 92.5% **/ 13 Admin Exp** N/A

Enroll(000): Q2 14: 67 **13:** 58 **12:** 60 **Med Exp PMPM:** $298

Principal Investments: Cash and equiv (62%), affiliate common stock (37%), long-term bonds (2%)

Provider Compensation ($000): Contr fee ($135,433), capitation ($70,267), FFS ($379), bonus arrang ($153)

Total Member Encounters: Phys (364,751), non-phys (150,183)

Group Affiliation: Total Health Care Inc

Licensed in: MI

Address: 3011 W Grand Blvd Suite 1600, Detroit, MI 48202

Phone: (313) 871-2000 **Dom State:** MI **Commenced Bus:** May 1976

Data Date	Rating	RACR #1	RACR #2	Total Assets ($mil)	Capital ($mil)	Net Premium ($mil)	Net Income ($mil)
6-14	D+	0.73	0.61	50.7	23.3	119.3	0.6
6-13	D+	0.92	0.76	46.3	23.3	112.4	-6.0
2013	D+	0.72	0.60	44.6	23.2	224.0	-6.4
2012	D+	1.16	0.96	50.5	29.6	200.3	0.1
2011	D+	1.26	1.05	48.3	29.2	187.2	1.9
2010	D+	1.31	1.10	45.5	27.1	180.4	-2.4
2009	D	1.05	0.87	39.8	21.6	180.0	-5.3

Rating Indexes

TOTAL HEALTH CARE USA INC

C+   **Fair**

Major Rating Factors: Good overall profitability index (6.6 on a scale of 0 to 10). Strong capitalization (7.0) based on excellent current risk-adjusted capital (severe loss scenario). High quality investment portfolio (9.9).

Other Rating Factors: Excellent liquidity (7.1) with ample operational cash flow and liquid investments.

Principal Business: Comp med (100%)

Mem Phys: 13: 4,822 **12:** 4,278 **13 MLR** 84.0% **/ 13 Admin Exp** N/A

Enroll(000): Q2 14: 50 **13:** 36 **12:** 29 **Med Exp PMPM:** $247

Principal Investments: Cash and equiv (97%), long-term bonds (3%)

Provider Compensation ($000): Contr fee ($87,843), capitation ($5,906), FFS ($1,535)

Total Member Encounters: Phys (203,724), non-phys (70,138)

Group Affiliation: Total Health Care Inc

Licensed in: MI

Address: 3011 W Grand Blvd Suite 1600, Detroit, MI 48202

Phone: (313) 871-2000 **Dom State:** MI **Commenced Bus:** February 1994

Data Date	Rating	RACR #1	RACR #2	Total Assets ($mil)	Capital ($mil)	Net Premium ($mil)	Net Income ($mil)
6-14	C+	1.36	1.13	40.3	15.2	80.4	0.1
6-13	C+	1.60	1.34	28.9	15.4	54.6	0.0
2013	C+	1.38	1.15	30.1	15.5	114.8	0.1
2012	B-	1.64	1.36	26.8	15.5	96.9	0.2
2011	B-	1.67	1.39	29.1	15.3	90.9	0.1
2010	B-	2.28	1.90	25.7	15.4	71.5	7.1
2009	B-	1.36	1.13	17.9	8.3	54.8	2.1

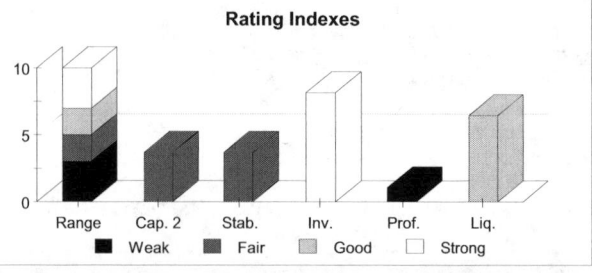

Rating Indexes

TOUCHSTONE HEALTH HMO INC

E   **Very Weak**

Major Rating Factors: Weak profitability index (0.9 on a scale of 0 to 10). Poor capitalization (0.2) based on weak current risk-adjusted capital (moderate loss scenario). High quality investment portfolio (9.8).

Other Rating Factors: Excellent liquidity (6.9) with sufficient resources (cash flows and marketable investments) to handle a spike in claims.

Principal Business: Medicare (100%)

Mem Phys: 13: 3,421 **12:** 7,100 **13 MLR** 86.8% **/ 13 Admin Exp** N/A

Enroll(000): Q2 14: 14 **13:** 39 **12:** 11 **Med Exp PMPM:** $872

Principal Investments: Cash and equiv (100%)

Provider Compensation ($000): Capitation ($100,820), contr fee ($1,931), other ($29,786)

Total Member Encounters: N/A

Group Affiliation: Touchstone Health Partnership Inc

Licensed in: NY

Address: 14 Wall St 9th Floor, New York, NY 10005-2101

Phone: (914) 288-1000 **Dom State:** NY **Commenced Bus:** September 2007

Data Date	Rating	RACR #1	RACR #2	Total Assets ($mil)	Capital ($mil)	Net Premium ($mil)	Net Income ($mil)
6-14	E	0.32	0.27	21.9	9.2	80.9	-0.1
6-13	E	N/A	N/A	19.4	0.6	78.6	N/A
2013	E	N/A	N/A	12.9	-0.5	152.9	-1.3
2012	E	N/A	N/A	14.8	0.9	157.1	-1.5
2011	E	0.03	0.02	21.8	2.5	219.2	5.7
2010	N/A	N/A	N/A	34.7	-2.1	222.4	-4.7
2009	E-	N/A	N/A	15.8	-24.2	175.1	-27.4

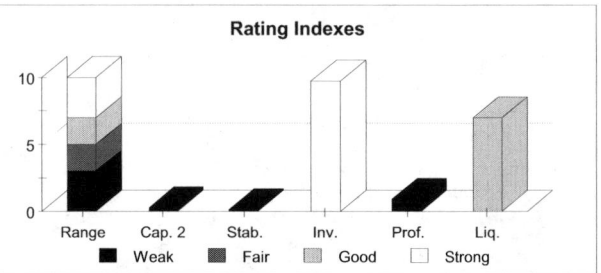

Rating Indexes

TRANS OCEANIC LIFE INSURANCE COMPANY *   A   Excellent

Major Rating Factors: Good overall results on stability tests (6.4 on a scale of 0 to 10). Strengths that enhance stability include excellent operational trends, good risk adjusted capital for prior years and good risk diversification. Strong current capitalization (8.2) based on excellent risk adjusted capital (severe loss scenario) reflecting improvement over results in 2009. High quality investment portfolio (7.2).

Other Rating Factors: Excellent profitability (9.0) with operating gains in each of the last five years. Excellent liquidity (8.7).

Principal Business: Individual health insurance (91%) and individual life insurance (8%).

Principal Investments: Cash (32%), nonCMO investment grade bonds (32%), CMOs and structured securities (27%), real estate (8%), and common & preferred stock (1%).

Investments in Affiliates: None

Group Affiliation: Trans-Oceanic Group Inc

Licensed in: FL, PR

Commenced Business: December 1959

Address: 3 Munet Court, Guaynabo, PR 00936-3467

Phone: (787) 782-2680 **Domicile State:** PR **NAIC Code:** 69523

Data Date	Rating	RACR #1	RACR #2	Total Assets ($mil)	Capital ($mil)	Net Premium ($mil)	Net Income ($mil)
6-14	A	2.71	1.81	61.6	30.7	14.9	1.8
6-13	B+	2.22	1.54	53.1	24.1	14.9	1.8
2013	B+	2.67	1.83	58.9	29.5	29.8	6.0
2012	B+	2.11	1.46	49.6	22.5	28.5	3.7
2011	B+	1.80	1.26	42.9	17.3	26.1	3.3
2010	B	1.53	1.08	38.1	13.7	24.8	2.0
2009	C-	1.06	0.78	32.1	9.0	24.9	2.4

Adverse Trends in Operations

Increase in policy surrenders from 2012 to 2013 (257%)
Increase in policy surrenders from 2009 to 2010 (594%)

TRANSAMERICA PREMIER LIFE INSURANCE COMPANY   C+   Fair

Major Rating Factors: Fair quality investment portfolio (4.2 on a scale of 0 to 10) with large holdings of BBB rated bonds in addition to significant exposure to junk bonds. Exposure to mortgages is significant, but the mortgage default rate has been low. Fair overall results on stability tests (4.7) including fair risk adjusted capital in prior years. Good capitalization (5.8) based on good risk adjusted capital (moderate loss scenario).

Other Rating Factors: Good overall profitability (5.6). Good liquidity (6.4).

Principal Business: Individual life insurance (31%), individual annuities (27%), group health insurance (20%), reinsurance (7%), and other lines (14%).

Principal Investments: NonCMO investment grade bonds (57%), CMOs and structured securities (15%), mortgages in good standing (10%), noninv. grade bonds (6%), and misc. investments (9%).

Investments in Affiliates: 3%

Group Affiliation: AEGON USA Group

Licensed in: All states except NY

Commenced Business: May 1860

Address: 4333 Edgewood Rd NE, Cedar Rapids, IA 52499

Phone: (319) 355-8511 **Domicile State:** IA **NAIC Code:** 66281

Data Date	Rating	RACR #1	RACR #2	Total Assets ($mil)	Capital ($mil)	Net Premium ($mil)	Net Income ($mil)
6-14	C+	1.54	0.77	32,077.6	921.4	839.0	86.3
6-13	C+	1.28	0.63	30,975.8	840.4	795.8	46.5
2013	C+	1.58	0.78	31,879.6	971.2	1,586.3	166.9
2012	C+	1.20	0.59	31,057.2	811.3	1,497.6	143.5
2011	C+	1.31	0.64	31,107.3	980.9	1,391.7	481.7
2010	C+	1.43	0.68	32,851.2	1,174.4	1,347.6	-0.5
2009	C+	1.62	0.77	34,728.0	1,436.6	1,846.9	191.7

Junk Bonds as a % of Capital

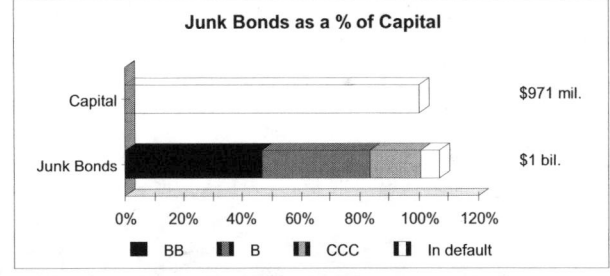

Capital — $971 mil.
Junk Bonds — $1 bil.

0% 20% 40% 60% 80% 100% 120%

■ BB   ■ B   ■ CCC   ■ In default

TRH HEALTH INS CO   C+   Fair

Major Rating Factors: Good liquidity (6.5 on a scale of 0 to 10) with sufficient resources (cash flows and marketable investments) to handle a spike in claims. Weak profitability index (2.9). Strong capitalization (9.0) based on excellent current risk-adjusted capital (severe loss scenario).

Other Rating Factors: High quality investment portfolio (9.4).

Principal Business: Comp med (100%)

Mem Phys: 13: 29,744 **12:** 26,466 **13 MLR** 87.6% **/ 13 Admin Exp** N/A

Enroll(000): Q2 14: 67 **13:** 71 **12:** 77 **Med Exp PMPM:** $175

Principal Investments: Long-term bonds (84%), cash and equiv (10%), nonaffiliate common stock (6%)

Provider Compensation ($000): FFS ($154,356)

Total Member Encounters: Phys (1,142,868), non-phys (59,309)

Group Affiliation: Tennessee Rural Health Improvement

Licensed in: TN

Address: 147 Bear Creek Pike, Columbia, TN 38401-2266

Phone: (931) 388-7872 **Dom State:** TN **Commenced Bus:** February 1999

Data Date	Rating	RACR #1	RACR #2	Total Assets ($mil)	Capital ($mil)	Net Premium ($mil)	Net Income ($mil)
6-14	C+	2.96	2.46	86.0	56.7	81.6	3.5
6-13	B	3.12	2.60	83.2	62.8	89.8	6.9
2013	B-	2.86	2.39	87.3	55.1	175.9	-6.3
2012	B-	2.89	2.41	82.6	58.6	182.2	13.5
2011	C-	1.74	1.45	80.4	43.5	186.5	-11.9
2010	C-	1.79	1.49	72.5	40.6	146.8	-1.8
2009	N/A	N/A	N/A	16.1	14.9	N/A	N/A

Rating Indexes

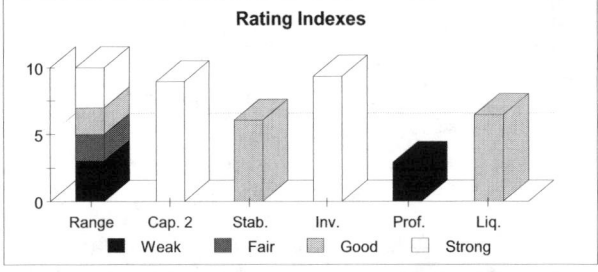

Range   Cap. 2   Stab.   Inv.   Prof.   Liq.

■ Weak   ■ Fair   ▨ Good   □ Strong

TRILLIUM COMMUNITY HEALTH PLAN INC

C+   Fair

Major Rating Factors: Good overall profitability index (6.6 on a scale of 0 to 10). Good capitalization (5.2) based on good current risk-adjusted capital (severe loss scenario). Good liquidity (6.9) with sufficient resources (cash flows and marketable investments) to handle a spike in claims.
Other Rating Factors: High quality investment portfolio (9.9).
Principal Business: Medicaid (81%), Medicare (19%)
Mem Phys: 13: 6,847 **12:** 790 **13 MLR** 88.9% **/ 13 Admin Exp** N/A
Enroll(000): Q2 14: 90 **13:** 58 **12:** 54 **Med Exp PMPM:** $309
Principal Investments: Cash and equiv (80%), long-term bonds (15%), nonaffiliate common stock (4%)
Provider Compensation ($000): Contr fee ($117,602), FFS ($87,383), bonus arrang ($5,800), capitation ($645)
Total Member Encounters: Phys (598,616), non-phys (239,833)
Group Affiliation: Agate Resources Inc
Licensed in: OR
Address: 1800 Millrace Dr, Eugene, OR 97403
Phone: (541) 338-2938 **Dom State:** OR **Commenced Bus:** February 2006

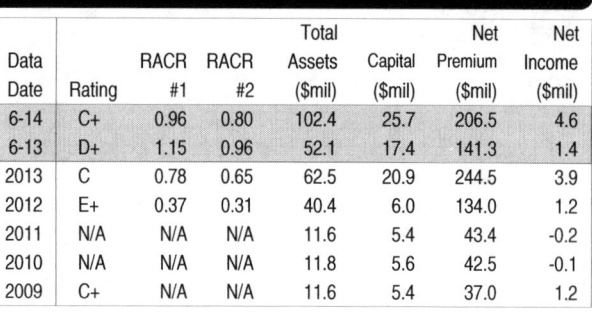

Data Date	Rating	RACR #1	RACR #2	Total Assets ($mil)	Capital ($mil)	Net Premium ($mil)	Net Income ($mil)
6-14	C+	0.96	0.80	102.4	25.7	206.5	4.6
6-13	D+	1.15	0.96	52.1	17.4	141.3	1.4
2013	C	0.78	0.65	62.5	20.9	244.5	3.9
2012	E+	0.37	0.31	40.4	6.0	134.0	1.2
2011	N/A	N/A	N/A	11.6	5.4	43.4	-0.2
2010	N/A	N/A	N/A	11.8	5.6	42.5	-0.1
2009	C+	N/A	N/A	11.6	5.4	37.0	1.2

Rating Indexes

Range Cap. 2 Stab. Inv. Prof. Liq.
■ Weak ▨ Fair ▦ Good ☐ Strong

TRIPLE S VIDA INCORPORATED

B-   Good

Major Rating Factors: Good capitalization (5.1 on a scale of 0 to 10) based on good risk adjusted capital (moderate loss scenario). Good overall results on stability tests (5.1) despite fair risk adjusted capital in prior years. Strengths include good financial support from affiliation with Triple-S Management Corp, excellent operational trends and good risk diversification. Fair quality investment portfolio (4.8).
Other Rating Factors: Fair liquidity (4.1). Excellent profitability (7.6) despite modest operating losses during 2009.
Principal Business: Individual life insurance (53%), individual health insurance (31%), individual annuities (6%), group health insurance (6%), and group life insurance (5%).
Principal Investments: NonCMO investment grade bonds (73%), common & preferred stock (14%), CMOs and structured securities (10%), policy loans (1%), and cash (1%).
Investments in Affiliates: 2%
Group Affiliation: Triple-S Management Corp
Licensed in: PR
Commenced Business: September 1964
Address: 1052 Munoz Rivera Ave, Rio Piedras, PR 00927
Phone: (787) 758-4888 **Domicile State:** PR **NAIC Code:** 73814

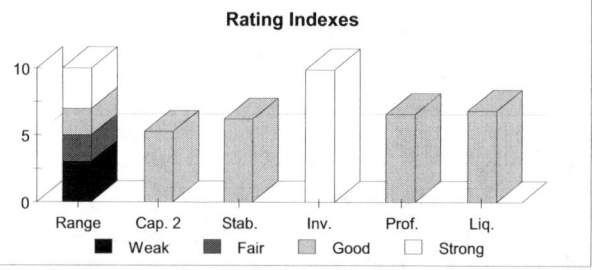

Data Date	Rating	RACR #1	RACR #2	Total Assets ($mil)	Capital ($mil)	Net Premium ($mil)	Net Income ($mil)
6-14	B-	1.04	0.71	529.2	62.2	76.4	7.1
6-13	B-	1.19	0.77	502.4	63.8	74.6	5.5
2013	B-	1.00	0.69	513.0	61.7	147.3	6.0
2012	B-	1.16	0.75	480.8	57.4	172.6	4.5
2011	B-	1.21	0.78	424.9	57.6	151.5	5.5
2010	C+	1.48	0.98	380.6	54.1	122.4	5.2
2009	C+	1.26	0.82	352.5	49.3	112.1	-1.1

Risk-Adjusted Capital Ratio #1
(Moderate Loss Scenario)

Range 2009 2010 2011 2012 2013 6-14
■ Weak ▨ Fair ☐ Good

TRIPLE-S SALUD INC *

B+   Good

Major Rating Factors: Good liquidity (6.4 on a scale of 0 to 10) with sufficient resources (cash flows and marketable investments) to handle a spike in claims. Excellent profitability (7.3). Strong capitalization (9.2) based on excellent current risk-adjusted capital (severe loss scenario).
Other Rating Factors: High quality investment portfolio (8.5).
Principal Business: Comp med (52%), Medicare (35%), FEHB (11%), med supp (2%)
Mem Phys: 13: N/A **12:** N/A **13 MLR** 88.7% **/ 13 Admin Exp** N/A
Enroll(000): Q2 14: 2,112 **13:** 2,159 **12:** 1,670 **Med Exp PMPM:** $60
Principal Investments: Long-term bonds (60%), nonaffiliate common stock (21%), affiliate common stock (11%), cash and equiv (8%)
Provider Compensation ($000): FFS ($39,463), capitation ($30,489), other ($1,230,311)
Total Member Encounters: Phys (5,902,520), non-phys (59,801)
Group Affiliation: Triple-S Management Corp
Licensed in: PR
Address: F D Roosevelt Ave 1441, San Juan, PR 00920
Phone: (787) 749-4949 **Dom State:** PR **Commenced Bus:** March 1960

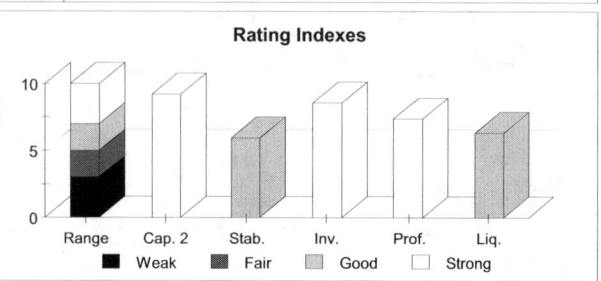

Data Date	Rating	RACR #1	RACR #2	Total Assets ($mil)	Capital ($mil)	Net Premium ($mil)	Net Income ($mil)
6-14	B+	3.11	2.59	713.6	398.9	700.5	16.0
6-13	A-	2.74	2.28	755.0	369.4	730.7	19.1
2013	A-	2.94	2.45	719.4	387.0	1,455.1	17.8
2012	A-	2.47	2.06	702.5	334.3	1,497.2	43.0
2011	A-	3.49	2.90	626.1	290.7	1,416.8	49.4
2010	B+	3.12	2.60	694.1	299.7	1,700.3	46.1
2009	B+	2.40	2.00	661.8	257.3	1,678.1	33.7

Rating Indexes

Range Cap. 2 Stab. Inv. Prof. Liq.
■ Weak ▨ Fair ▦ Good ☐ Strong

TRITON INS CO   C+   Fair

Major Rating Factors: Fair overall results on stability tests (4.4 on a scale of 0 to 10). History of adequate reserve strength (6.4) as reserves have been consistently at an acceptable level.

Other Rating Factors: Weak profitability index (2.8). Good expense controls. Return on equity has been fair, averaging 25.3% over the past five years. Strong long-term capitalization index (10.0) based on excellent current risk adjusted capital (severe and moderate loss scenarios), despite some fluctuation in capital levels. Excellent liquidity (7.3) with ample operational cash flow and liquid investments.

Principal Business: Aggregate write-ins for other lines of business (69%), credit accident & health (29%), and inland marine (2%).

Principal Investments: Investment grade bonds (86%), misc. investments (10%), cash (3%), and non investment grade bonds (1%).

Investments in Affiliates: None

Group Affiliation: Citigroup Inc

Licensed in: All states except PR

Commenced Business: July 1982

Address: 3001 Meacham Blvd Ste 200, Fort Worth, TX 76137-4615

Phone: (800) 316-5607   **Domicile State:** TX   **NAIC Code:** 41211

Data Date	Rating	RACR #1	RACR #2	Loss Ratio %	Total Assets ($mil)	Capital ($mil)	Net Premium ($mil)	Net Income ($mil)
6-14	C+	11.16	6.11	N/A	548.8	238.2	65.8	30.7
6-13	C+	11.81	6.51	N/A	571.0	249.5	70.5	32.5
2013	C+	10.15	5.58	32.3	527.8	205.9	138.6	64.0
2012	C+	10.46	5.85	30.9	554.4	219.4	147.3	74.9
2011	B	13.05	7.36	34.1	633.2	292.0	142.7	79.6
2010	B	12.95	7.41	36.2	677.7	311.4	117.5	94.0
2009	B	11.66	6.79	77.0	819.9	385.5	135.4	14.1

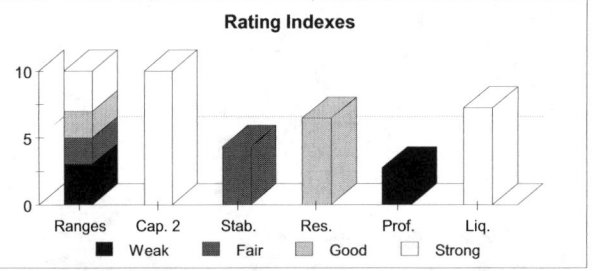

Rating Indexes

Ranges   Cap. 2   Stab.   Res.   Prof.   Liq.
■ Weak   ■ Fair   ▨ Good   □ Strong

TRUSTED HEALTH PLAN INC   C-   Fair

Major Rating Factors: Fair profitability index (3.9 on a scale of 0 to 10). Fair capitalization (4.6) based on fair current risk-adjusted capital (moderate loss scenario). High quality investment portfolio (9.9).

Other Rating Factors: Excellent liquidity (6.9) with sufficient resources (cash flows and marketable investments) to handle a spike in claims.

Principal Business: Medicaid (95%), comp med (5%)

Mem Phys: 13: 2,248 **12:** N/A **13 MLR** 89.3% **/ 13 Admin Exp** N/A

Enroll(000): Q2 14: 30 **13:** 27 **12:** N/A **Med Exp PMPM:** $278

Principal Investments: Cash and equiv (100%)

Provider Compensation ($000): Contr fee ($35,610), capitation ($1,833)

Total Member Encounters: Phys (29,492), non-phys (7,947)

Group Affiliation: None

Licensed in: DC

Address: 1100 New Jersey Ave SE # 840, Washington, DC 20003

Phone: (202) 821-1100 **Dom State:** DC **Commenced Bus:** March 2012

Data Date	Rating	RACR #1	RACR #2	Total Assets ($mil)	Capital ($mil)	Net Premium ($mil)	Net Income ($mil)
6-14	C-	0.88	0.73	17.4	6.6	54.4	1.3
6-13	N/A	N/A	N/A	5.2	5.2	N/A	-0.6
2013	D-	0.43	0.36	12.7	3.5	50.5	-0.2
2012	N/A	N/A	N/A	1.5	1.5	N/A	-0.2
2011	N/A	N/A	N/A	1.7	1.7	N/A	N/A
2010	N/A	N/A	N/A	N/A	N/A	N/A	N/A
2009	N/A	N/A	N/A	N/A	N/A	N/A	N/A

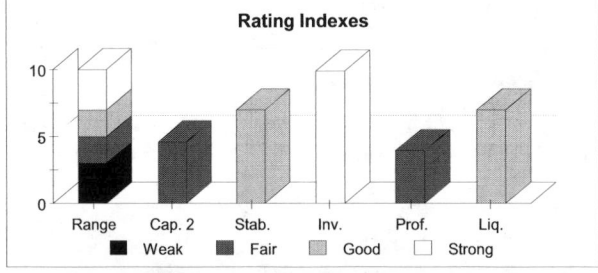

Rating Indexes

Range   Cap. 2   Stab.   Inv.   Prof.   Liq.
■ Weak   ■ Fair   ▨ Good   □ Strong

TRUSTMARK INSURANCE COMPANY *   B+   Good

Major Rating Factors: Good quality investment portfolio (5.0 on a scale of 0 to 10) despite mixed results such as: substantial holdings of BBB bonds but moderate junk bond exposure. Good overall results on stability tests (6.8). Stability strengths include excellent operational trends and excellent risk diversification. Strong capitalization (8.1) based on excellent risk adjusted capital (severe loss scenario).

Other Rating Factors: Excellent profitability (7.4) with operating gains in each of the last five years. Excellent liquidity (7.4).

Principal Business: Group life insurance (43%), group health insurance (25%), individual health insurance (23%), individual life insurance (7%), and reinsurance (1%).

Principal Investments: NonCMO investment grade bonds (46%), CMOs and structured securities (27%), common & preferred stock (12%), noninv. grade bonds (6%), and misc. investments (9%).

Investments in Affiliates: 1%

Group Affiliation: Trustmark Group Inc

Licensed in: All states, the District of Columbia and Puerto Rico

Commenced Business: January 1913

Address: 400 Field Dr, Lake Forest, IL 60045-2581

Phone: (847) 615-1500 **Domicile State:** IL **NAIC Code:** 61425

Data Date	Rating	RACR #1	RACR #2	Total Assets ($mil)	Capital ($mil)	Net Premium ($mil)	Net Income ($mil)
6-14	B+	2.94	1.71	1,404.7	310.3	152.3	11.0
6-13	B+	2.79	1.64	1,349.3	283.2	145.4	15.4
2013	B+	3.24	1.89	1,369.8	297.8	294.0	30.0
2012	B+	3.00	1.78	1,320.0	266.5	307.6	22.3
2011	B	3.19	1.85	1,264.8	256.4	283.3	22.7
2010	B	3.16	1.84	1,234.3	237.8	270.6	27.1
2009	B	3.45	1.99	1,172.0	240.3	261.3	26.2

Adverse Trends in Operations

Decrease in premium volume from 2012 to 2013 (4%)
Decrease in capital during 2010 (1%)

TRUSTMARK LIFE INSURANCE COMPANY *

B+   Good

Major Rating Factors: Good quality investment portfolio (6.5 on a scale of 0 to 10) with no exposure to mortgages and small junk bond holdings. Good overall profitability (6.3). Return on equity has been fair, averaging 5.6%. Good liquidity (6.7) with sufficient resources to handle a spike in claims.

Other Rating Factors: Good overall results on stability tests (6.6) good operational trends and excellent risk diversification. Strong capitalization (9.9) based on excellent risk adjusted capital (severe loss scenario).

Principal Business: Group health insurance (96%) and group life insurance (4%).

Principal Investments: NonCMO investment grade bonds (64%), common & preferred stock (16%), CMOs and structured securities (10%), noninv. grade bonds (8%), and misc. investments (2%).

Investments in Affiliates: 2%

Group Affiliation: Trustmark Group Inc

Licensed in: All states except PR

Commenced Business: February 1925

Address: 400 Field Dr, Lake Forest, IL 60045-2581

Phone: (847) 615-1500 **Domicile State:** IL **NAIC Code:** 62863

Data Date	Rating	RACR #1	RACR #2	Total Assets ($mil)	Capital ($mil)	Net Premium ($mil)	Net Income ($mil)
6-14	B+	4.31	2.96	380.8	167.4	109.6	6.7
6-13	B+	3.75	2.64	376.2	174.2	140.2	10.0
2013	B+	3.61	2.53	365.5	160.6	264.5	13.9
2012	B+	3.28	2.34	367.8	165.8	320.1	15.1
2011	B+	2.99	2.25	370.2	168.2	383.3	13.2
2010	B	3.14	2.38	360.0	177.0	392.0	7.8
2009	B	4.57	3.40	362.2	184.6	380.6	2.1

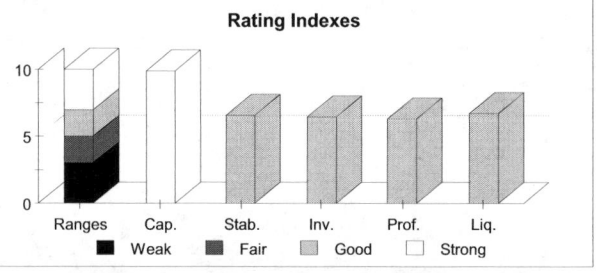

Rating Indexes

TUFTS ASSOCIATED HEALTH MAINT ORG

B   Good

Major Rating Factors: Good liquidity (6.5 on a scale of 0 to 10) with sufficient resources (cash flows and marketable investments) to handle a spike in claims. Fair quality investment portfolio (3.4). Excellent profitability (7.5).

Other Rating Factors: Strong capitalization index (9.2) based on excellent current risk-adjusted capital (severe loss scenario). Excellent overall results on stability tests (7.1) despite a decline in enrollment during 2013.

Principal Business: Comp med (52%), Medicare (47%), other (1%)

Mem Phys: 13: 38,500 **12:** 36,907 **13 MLR** 86.6% **/ 13 Admin Exp** N/A

Enroll(000): Q2 14: 334 **13:** 331 **12:** 350 **Med Exp PMPM:** $536

Principal Investments: Affiliate common stock (27%), long-term bonds (23%), nonaffiliate common stock (22%), real estate (9%), cash and equiv (4%), other (15%)

Provider Compensation ($000): Contr fee ($900,995), capitation ($750,510), bonus arrang ($300,327), FFS ($280,866)

Total Member Encounters: Phys (2,252,503), non-phys (490,829)

Group Affiliation: Tufts Associated Health Plans Inc

Licensed in: MA, RI

Address: 705 Mount Auburn St, Watertown, MA 02472-1508

Phone: (617) 972-9400 **Dom State:** MA **Commenced Bus:** October 1981

Data Date	Rating	RACR #1	RACR #2	Total Assets ($mil)	Capital ($mil)	Net Premium ($mil)	Net Income ($mil)
6-14	B	3.13	2.61	1,054.7	712.3	1,291.1	-5.0
6-13	B	3.29	2.75	1,048.4	689.1	1,245.6	45.1
2013	B	3.14	2.62	1,030.3	715.4	2,509.4	62.4
2012	B	3.11	2.59	1,062.2	661.6	2,528.0	65.0
2011	B	2.32	1.93	927.8	532.8	2,536.0	106.6
2010	B	3.41	2.84	869.3	551.7	2,338.6	38.4
2009	B	3.02	2.52	801.3	516.8	2,273.0	13.8

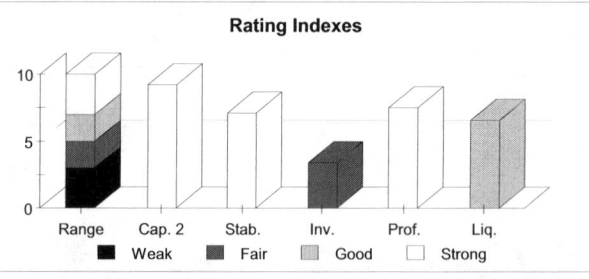

Rating Indexes

TUFTS INS CO

D+   Weak

Major Rating Factors: Weak profitability index (0.9 on a scale of 0 to 10). Strong capitalization (8.3) based on excellent current risk-adjusted capital (severe loss scenario). High quality investment portfolio (9.2).

Other Rating Factors: Excellent liquidity (6.9) with sufficient resources (cash flows and marketable investments) to handle a spike in claims.

Principal Business: Comp med (81%), med supp (12%), other (7%)

Mem Phys: 13: 38,500 **12:** 36,907 **13 MLR** 86.8% **/ 13 Admin Exp** N/A

Enroll(000): Q2 14: 74 **13:** 66 **12:** 69 **Med Exp PMPM:** $261

Principal Investments: Nonaffiliate common stock (60%), cash and equiv (40%)

Provider Compensation ($000): Contr fee ($155,246), FFS ($37,696), other ($12,993)

Total Member Encounters: Phys (266,503), non-phys (81,829)

Group Affiliation: Tufts Associated Health Plans Inc

Licensed in: CT, MA, RI, VT

Address: 705 Mount Auburn St, Watertown, MA 02472-1508

Phone: (617) 972-9400 **Dom State:** MA **Commenced Bus:** August 1996

Data Date	Rating	RACR #1	RACR #2	Total Assets ($mil)	Capital ($mil)	Net Premium ($mil)	Net Income ($mil)
6-14	D+	2.43	2.02	87.9	38.5	122.6	-10.2
6-13	D+	3.25	2.71	87.8	49.9	115.6	2.1
2013	D+	3.03	2.53	87.6	48.6	233.9	1.2
2012	D+	3.10	2.58	92.1	48.4	207.0	2.0
2011	D+	2.25	1.87	86.1	47.4	163.9	-5.0
2010	D+	2.50	2.09	64.4	33.1	139.2	-10.5
2009	C	1.93	1.60	48.9	23.7	100.9	-10.4

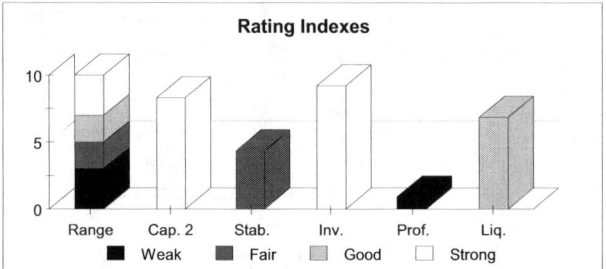

Rating Indexes

U S HEALTH & LIFE INS CO INC   C-   Fair

Major Rating Factors: Fair liquidity (4.9 on a scale of 0 to 10) as cash resources may not be adequate to cover a spike in claims. Weak profitability index (0.9). Strong capitalization (7.1) based on excellent current risk-adjusted capital (severe loss scenario).
Other Rating Factors: High quality investment portfolio (9.9).
Principal Business: Comp med (90%), dental (1%), other (9%)
Mem Phys: 13: N/A **12:** N/A **13 MLR** 91.1% **/ 13 Admin Exp** N/A
Enroll(000): Q2 14: 19 **13:** 23 **12:** 17 **Med Exp PMPM:** $220
Principal Investments: Long-term bonds (84%), cash and equiv (13%), other (3%)
Provider Compensation ($000): Contr fee ($59,251)
Total Member Encounters: Phys (77,661), non-phys (30,274)
Group Affiliation: U.S. Health Holdings Ltd
Licensed in: AK, AZ, DC, DE, ID, IL, IN, LA, MI, NE, NM, ND, OH, OR, SC, SD, TN, TX, UT, VA
Address: 8220 Irving Rd, Sterling Heights, MI 48312-4621
Phone: (586) 693-4300 **Dom State:** MI **Commenced Bus:** January 1984

Data Date	Rating	RACR #1	RACR #2	Total Assets ($mil)	Capital ($mil)	Net Premium ($mil)	Net Income ($mil)
6-14	C-	1.45	1.21	28.0	7.8	29.3	-1.8
6-13	N/A	N/A	N/A	32.2	9.0	34.3	0.3
2013	C-	1.48	1.23	26.2	8.0	67.8	-1.4
2012	N/A	N/A	N/A	26.3	8.8	52.1	-0.2
2011	N/A	N/A	N/A	27.1	9.5	27.5	0.7
2010	N/A	N/A	N/A	30.8	9.4	25.6	N/A
2009	N/A	N/A	N/A	30.3	9.4	31.6	N/A

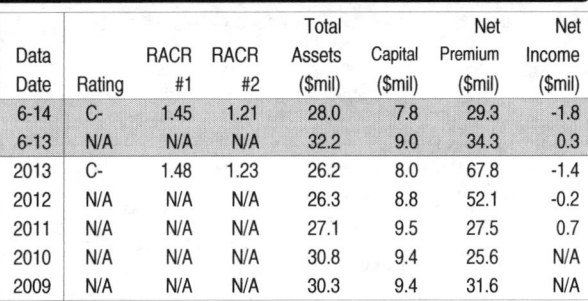

Rating Indexes

UCARE HEALTH INC   D   Weak

Major Rating Factors: Weak profitability index (0.9 on a scale of 0 to 10). Fair capitalization (2.9) based on weak current risk-adjusted capital (moderate loss scenario). High quality investment portfolio (9.9).
Other Rating Factors: Excellent liquidity (7.0) with sufficient resources (cash flows and marketable investments) to handle a spike in claims.
Principal Business: Medicare (100%)
Mem Phys: 13: 44,564 **12:** 41,322 **13 MLR** 101.3% **/ 13 Admin Exp** N/A
Enroll(000): Q2 14: 10 **13:** 7 **12:** 7 **Med Exp PMPM:** $712
Principal Investments: Cash and equiv (100%)
Provider Compensation ($000): Contr fee ($58,705), FFS ($3,054), capitation ($232)
Total Member Encounters: Phys (28,000), non-phys (34,728)
Group Affiliation: UCare Group
Licensed in: WI
Address: 500 Stinson Blvd NE, Minneapolis, MN 55413
Phone: (612) 676-6500 **Dom State:** WI **Commenced Bus:** January 2008

Data Date	Rating	RACR #1	RACR #2	Total Assets ($mil)	Capital ($mil)	Net Premium ($mil)	Net Income ($mil)
6-14	D	0.66	0.55	19.9	7.5	37.0	-1.9
6-13	D	1.24	1.03	22.6	13.8	30.4	-1.0
2013	D	0.80	0.67	19.9	9.5	59.0	-5.3
2012	D	1.36	1.13	26.7	14.7	66.4	-0.5
2011	D	0.72	0.60	16.2	5.4	58.9	-5.8
2010	B-	1.57	1.31	15.8	8.8	42.1	-3.4
2009	C	0.51	0.42	8.6	3.1	24.5	-1.8

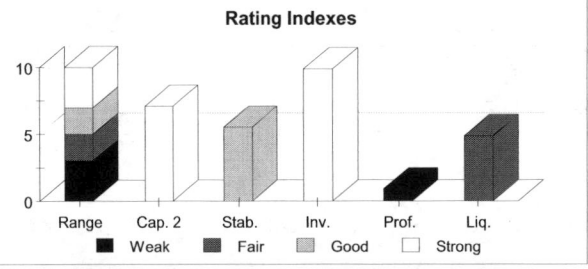

Rating Indexes

UCARE MINNESOTA *   A-   Excellent

Major Rating Factors: Excellent profitability (8.5 on a scale of 0 to 10). Strong capitalization index (8.7) based on excellent current risk-adjusted capital (severe loss scenario). High quality investment portfolio (9.5).
Other Rating Factors: Excellent overall results on stability tests (7.3). Good liquidity (6.9) with sufficient resources (cash flows and marketable investments) to handle a spike in claims.
Principal Business: Medicaid (64%), Medicare (36%)
Mem Phys: 13: 47,479 **12:** 43,957 **13 MLR** 90.9% **/ 13 Admin Exp** N/A
Enroll(000): Q2 14: 417 **13:** 311 **12:** 293 **Med Exp PMPM:** $600
Principal Investments: Long-term bonds (63%), cash and equiv (29%), nonaffiliate common stock (8%)
Provider Compensation ($000): Contr fee ($2,061,414), FFS ($107,230), capitation ($40,697)
Total Member Encounters: Phys (1,406,570), non-phys (904,228)
Group Affiliation: UCare Group
Licensed in: MN
Address: 500 Stinson Blvd NE, Minneapolis, MN 55413
Phone: (612) 676-6500 **Dom State:** MN **Commenced Bus:** April 1988

Data Date	Rating	RACR #1	RACR #2	Total Assets ($mil)	Capital ($mil)	Net Premium ($mil)	Net Income ($mil)
6-14	A-	2.68	2.23	969.6	480.9	1,491.4	40.0
6-13	A-	2.51	2.09	836.3	421.1	1,198.8	29.2
2013	A-	2.45	2.04	856.4	443.2	2,413.2	47.2
2012	A-	2.30	1.91	781.3	387.7	2,229.5	70.7
2011	A-	2.48	2.06	626.1	321.9	1,742.5	33.9
2010	B+	2.53	2.11	574.4	308.4	1,604.3	61.0
2009	B	2.12	1.76	503.1	246.1	1,461.3	37.5

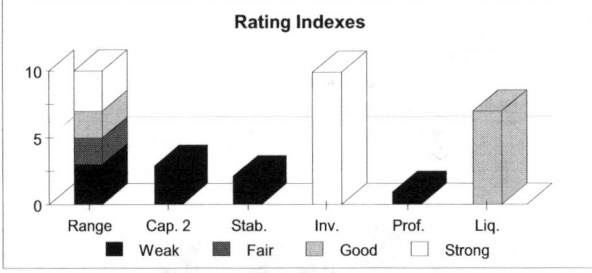

Rating Indexes

UHC OF CALIFORNIA INC

C+   Fair

Major Rating Factors: Fair overall results on stability tests (3.0 on a scale of 0 to 10). Rating is significantly influenced by the good financial results of UnitedHealth Group Inc. Good overall profitability index (6.1). Good capitalization index (5.3) based on good current risk-adjusted capital (severe loss scenario).

Other Rating Factors: Excellent liquidity (6.9) with sufficient resources (cash flows and marketable investments) to handle a spike in claims.

Principal Business: Medicare (63%)

Mem Phys: 13: N/A   **12:** N/A   **13 MLR** 86.7%   **/ 13 Admin Exp** N/A

Enroll(000): Q2 14: 780   **13:** 823   **12:** 825   **Med Exp PMPM:** $565

Principal Investments ($000): Cash and equiv ($430,880)

Provider Compensation ($000): None

Total Member Encounters: N/A

Group Affiliation: UnitedHealth Group Inc

Licensed in: CA

Address: 5995 Plaza Drive, Cypress, CA 90630

Phone: (714) 952-1121   **Dom State:** CA   **Commenced Bus:** March 1975

Data Date	Rating	RACR #1	RACR #2	Total Assets ($mil)	Capital ($mil)	Net Premium ($mil)	Net Income ($mil)
6-14	C+	1.31	0.81	971.2	322.5	3,133.4	83.2
6-13	C+	1.39	0.86	914.7	314.2	3,293.6	126.3
2013	B-	1.57	0.97	903.9	386.7	6,487.2	277.2
2012	C+	1.54	0.95	1,018.6	351.1	6,404.9	327.4
2011	C+	2.73	1.68	1,188.5	631.1	6,343.0	269.4
2010	B	3.65	2.25	1,473.1	847.0	6,242.0	310.2
2009	B	3.29	2.03	1,668.2	891.1	6,967.8	320.0

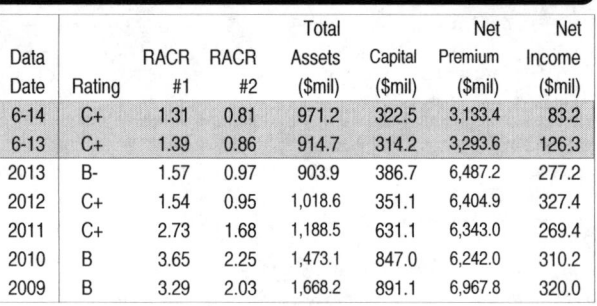

Rating Indexes

ULTIMATE HEALTH PLAN INC

E   Very Weak

Major Rating Factors: Weak profitability index (0.0 on a scale of 0 to 10). Weak liquidity (1.2) as a spike in claims may stretch capacity. Good capitalization (6.4) based on good current risk-adjusted capital (severe loss scenario).

Other Rating Factors: High quality investment portfolio (9.7).

Principal Business: Medicare (100%)

Mem Phys: 13: 282   **12:** N/A   **13 MLR** 97.1%   **/ 13 Admin Exp** N/A

Enroll(000): Q2 14: 3   **13:** 1   **12:** N/A   **Med Exp PMPM:** $833

Principal Investments: Cash and equiv (91%), other (9%)

Provider Compensation ($000): FFS ($3,129), contr fee ($281), capitation ($158), bonus arrang ($17)

Total Member Encounters: Phys (16,925), non-phys (964)

Group Affiliation: None

Licensed in: FL

Address: 12900 Cortez Blvd Suite 204, Brooksville, FL 34613

Phone: (352) 835-7151   **Dom State:** FL   **Commenced Bus:** October 2011

Data Date	Rating	RACR #1	RACR #2	Total Assets ($mil)	Capital ($mil)	Net Premium ($mil)	Net Income ($mil)
6-14	E	1.14	0.95	5.6	2.0	12.4	0.0
6-13	N/A	N/A	N/A	6.6	5.9	2.0	-1.6
2013	E	1.24	1.03	5.6	2.2	4.5	-7.6
2012	N/A	N/A	N/A	4.8	4.7	N/A	-1.8
2011	N/A	N/A	N/A	2.3	2.3	N/A	N/A
2010	N/A	N/A	N/A	N/A	N/A	N/A	N/A
2009	N/A	N/A	N/A	N/A	N/A	N/A	N/A

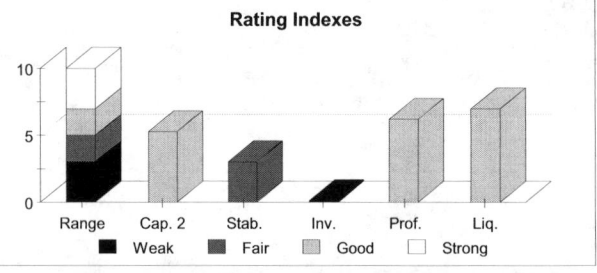

Rating Indexes

UNICARE HEALTH PLAN OF WEST VIRGINIA *

B+   Good

Major Rating Factors: Excellent profitability (9.1 on a scale of 0 to 10). Strong capitalization (10.0) based on excellent current risk-adjusted capital (severe loss scenario). High quality investment portfolio (9.6).

Other Rating Factors: Excellent liquidity (6.9) with sufficient resources (cash flows and marketable investments) to handle a spike in claims.

Principal Business: Medicaid (100%)

Mem Phys: 13: 1,273   **12:** 1,410   **13 MLR** 83.9%   **/ 13 Admin Exp** N/A

Enroll(000): Q2 14: 93   **13:** 87   **12:** 82   **Med Exp PMPM:** $182

Principal Investments: Long-term bonds (58%), cash and equiv (42%)

Provider Compensation ($000): Contr fee ($170,516), capitation ($5,986)

Total Member Encounters: Phys (575,901), non-phys (110,090)

Group Affiliation: WellPoint Inc

Licensed in: WV

Address: 707 Virginia St E, Charleston, WV 25301

Phone: (877) 864-2273   **Dom State:** WV   **Commenced Bus:** November 2003

Data Date	Rating	RACR #1	RACR #2	Total Assets ($mil)	Capital ($mil)	Net Premium ($mil)	Net Income ($mil)
6-14	B+	4.23	3.53	82.1	52.7	139.8	13.4
6-13	A-	3.47	2.89	60.4	35.4	98.7	3.5
2013	A-	3.29	2.74	70.1	40.5	215.5	11.7
2012	A-	3.13	2.61	55.1	31.8	167.1	5.8
2011	A-	2.90	2.42	52.6	28.4	160.1	2.4
2010	A-	3.31	2.76	47.9	28.0	151.3	4.9
2009	A-	5.15	4.29	59.2	43.5	155.1	13.3

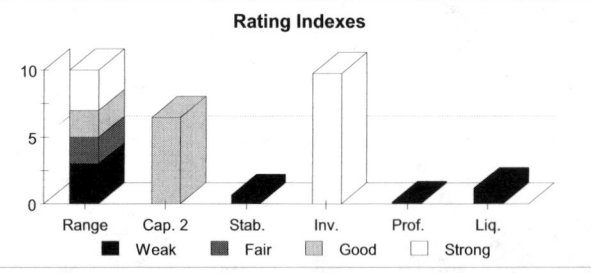

Rating Indexes

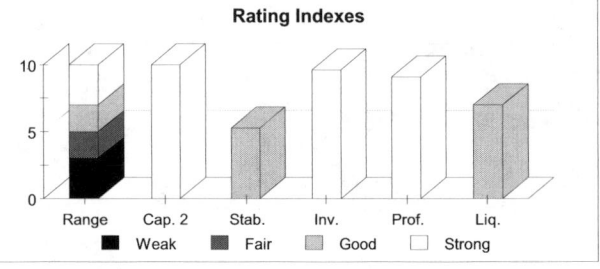

UNICARE LIFE & HEALTH INSURANCE COMPANY   B   Good

Major Rating Factors: Good overall profitability (6.6 on a scale of 0 to 10). Excellent expense controls. Return on equity has been excellent over the last five years averaging 40.8%. Good liquidity (6.5) with sufficient resources to handle a spike in claims. Fair quality investment portfolio (3.8).

Other Rating Factors: Fair overall results on stability tests (4.1). Strong capitalization (7.6) based on excellent risk adjusted capital (severe loss scenario).

Principal Business: Group life insurance (33%), reinsurance (29%), individual health insurance (21%), and group health insurance (17%).

Principal Investments: NonCMO investment grade bonds (75%), noninv. grade bonds (13%), cash (9%), and CMOs and structured securities (2%).

Investments in Affiliates: None

Group Affiliation: WellPoint Inc

Licensed in: All states, the District of Columbia and Puerto Rico

Commenced Business: December 1980

Address: 1209 Orange St, Wilmington, DE 19801

Phone: (877) 864-2273   **Domicile State:** IN   **NAIC Code:** 80314

Data Date	Rating	RACR #1	RACR #2	Total Assets ($mil)	Capital ($mil)	Net Premium ($mil)	Net Income ($mil)
6-14	B	1.85	1.37	402.8	76.5	159.0	12.4
6-13	B	1.94	1.39	426.1	93.6	159.9	20.9
2013	B	3.13	2.32	469.1	126.3	321.7	43.7
2012	B	2.83	2.05	554.2	158.8	439.4	74.4
2011	B	2.27	1.66	642.9	149.3	632.5	51.2
2010	B	1.43	1.04	971.9	168.9	987.0	68.2
2009	B	1.27	0.96	1,482.4	381.3	2,429.2	156.5

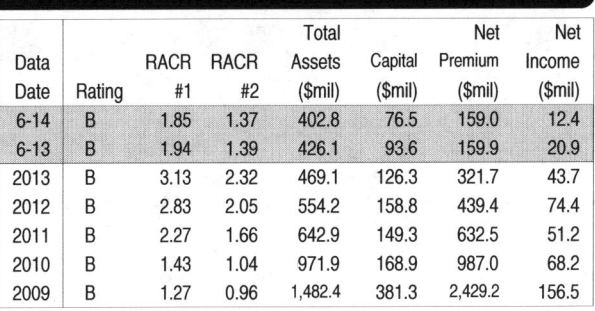

Net Income History
(in millions of dollars)

UNIMERICA INSURANCE COMPANY   B   Good

Major Rating Factors: Good overall results on stability tests (5.8 on a scale of 0 to 10) despite fair financial strength of affiliated UnitedHealth Group Inc and excessive premium growth. Other stability subfactors include excellent operational trends and excellent risk diversification. Strong capitalization (9.3) based on excellent risk adjusted capital (severe loss scenario). Capital levels have been relatively consistent over the last five years. High quality investment portfolio (8.5).

Other Rating Factors: Excellent profitability (9.0) with operating gains in each of the last five years. Excellent liquidity (7.0).

Principal Business: Group health insurance (54%), reinsurance (43%), and group life insurance (2%).

Principal Investments: NonCMO investment grade bonds (87%) and CMOs and structured securities (14%).

Investments in Affiliates: None

Group Affiliation: UnitedHealth Group Inc

Licensed in: All states except NY, PR

Commenced Business: December 1980

Address: 711 High St, Des Moines, IA 50392

Phone: (877) 832-7734   **Domicile State:** WI   **NAIC Code:** 91529

Data Date	Rating	RACR #1	RACR #2	Total Assets ($mil)	Capital ($mil)	Net Premium ($mil)	Net Income ($mil)
6-14	B	3.20	2.54	444.3	213.6	292.1	34.8
6-13	B	3.33	2.61	368.2	170.9	198.5	17.6
2013	B	2.82	2.24	410.1	181.1	489.2	43.3
2012	B	3.17	2.48	326.6	153.2	319.8	32.2
2011	B	3.07	2.37	289.0	129.9	228.4	9.5
2010	B	3.34	2.57	264.2	133.1	199.3	20.5
2009	B	2.36	1.82	262.1	113.0	235.7	5.2

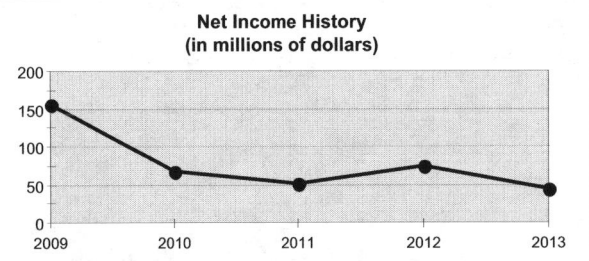

UnitedHealth Group Inc Composite Group Rating: C+ Largest Group Members	Assets ($mil)	Rating
UNITED HEALTHCARE INS CO	14513	C
OXFORD HEALTH INS INC	2078	C+
UNITED HEALTHCARE INS CO OF NY	1983	B-
OXFORD HEALTH PLANS (NY) INC	1820	A+
UNITEDHEALTHCARE PLAN RIVER VALLEY	1094	B+

UNION FIDELITY LIFE INSURANCE COMPANY   D+   Weak

Major Rating Factors: Weak profitability (1.6 on a scale of 0 to 10) with operating losses during the first six months of 2014. Return on equity has been low, averaging -41.9%. Weak overall results on stability tests (2.7) including weak risk adjusted capital in prior years, negative cash flow from operations for 2013. Fair quality investment portfolio (3.1).

Other Rating Factors: Good capitalization (5.1) based on good risk adjusted capital (moderate loss scenario). Excellent liquidity (8.6).

Principal Business: Reinsurance (86%), group health insurance (6%), group life insurance (4%), individual life insurance (2%), and individual health insurance (1%).

Principal Investments: NonCMO investment grade bonds (76%), CMOs and structured securities (12%), mortgages in good standing (5%), and noninv. grade bonds (4%).

Investments in Affiliates: 2%

Group Affiliation: General Electric Corp Group

Licensed in: All states except NY, PR

Commenced Business: February 1926

Address: 7101 College Blvd Suite 1400, Overland Park, KS 66210

Phone: (913) 982-3700   **Domicile State:** KS   **NAIC Code:** 62596

Data Date	Rating	RACR #1	RACR #2	Total Assets ($mil)	Capital ($mil)	Net Premium ($mil)	Net Income ($mil)
6-14	D+	1.05	0.54	19,518.2	536.2	139.9	-12.7
6-13	D+	0.98	0.50	19,581.7	533.8	149.8	-31.2
2013	D+	1.07	0.55	19,510.6	569.3	305.7	6.3
2012	D	1.01	0.52	19,585.3	560.1	316.1	-430.4
2011	D+	0.80	0.42	19,089.5	445.2	320.2	-598.5
2010	C-	0.74	0.40	18,522.5	438.9	335.4	-294.3
2009	C-	0.98	0.53	18,377.8	611.7	344.7	32.7

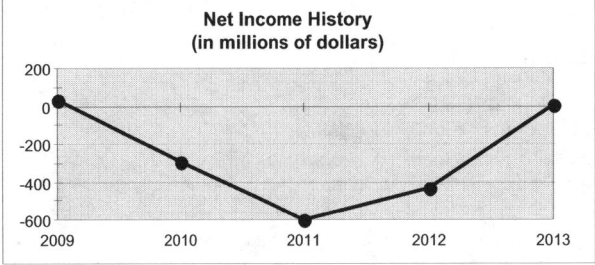

Net Income History
(in millions of dollars)

UNION HEALTH SERVICE INC

B **Good**

Major Rating Factors: Excellent profitability (8.3 on a scale of 0 to 10). Strong capitalization index (6.9) based on excellent current risk-adjusted capital (severe loss scenario). High quality investment portfolio (9.0).
Other Rating Factors: Excellent overall results on stability tests (8.2). Excellent liquidity (7.0) with ample operational cash flow and liquid investments
Principal Business: FEHB (8%), Medicare (4%), other (88%)
Mem Phys: 13: 275 **12:** 270 **13 MLR** 92.1% **/ 13 Admin Exp** N/A
Enroll(000): Q2 14: 46 **13:** 46 **12:** 47 **Med Exp PMPM:** $108
Principal Investments: Cash and equiv (39%), long-term bonds (36%), nonaffiliate common stock (20%), other (5%)
Provider Compensation ($000): FFS ($18,876), contr fee ($522), other ($40,099)
Total Member Encounters: Phys (207,880), non-phys (135,575)
Group Affiliation: None
Licensed in: IL
Address: 1634 W Polk St, Chicago, IL 60612
Phone: (312) 423-4200 **Dom State:** IL **Commenced Bus:** April 1955

Data Date	Rating	RACR #1	RACR #2	Total Assets ($mil)	Capital ($mil)	Net Premium ($mil)	Net Income ($mil)
6-14	B	1.30	1.08	23.6	14.9	33.3	0.3
6-13	B	1.28	1.06	25.0	13.0	31.6	0.4
2013	B	1.26	1.05	26.0	14.4	63.9	1.4
2012	B	1.17	0.98	23.0	11.9	62.8	2.1
2011	B	1.09	0.91	20.9	10.0	57.8	2.2
2010	B	0.95	0.79	16.6	9.4	56.8	3.4
2009	B-	0.85	0.70	14.4	7.9	54.1	2.2

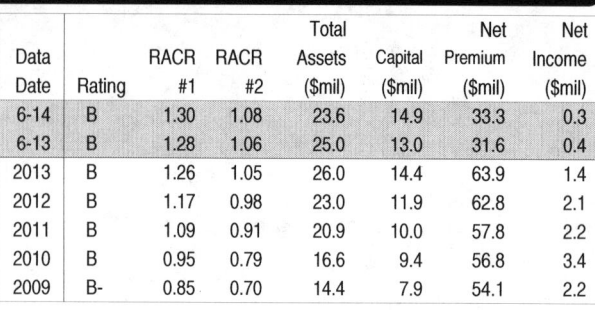

Rating Indexes

Range | Cap. 2 | Stab. | Inv. | Prof. | Liq.
■ Weak ■ Fair ▨ Good □ Strong

UNION LABOR LIFE INSURANCE COMPANY

B- **Good**

Major Rating Factors: Good liquidity (6.9 on a scale of 0 to 10) with sufficient resources to handle a spike in claims. Good overall results on stability tests (5.0) despite negative cash flow from operations for 2013. Other stability subfactors include excellent operational trends and excellent risk diversification. Weak profitability (2.9) with investment income below regulatory standards in relation to interest assumptions of reserves.
Other Rating Factors: Strong capitalization (7.1) based on excellent risk adjusted capital (severe loss scenario). High quality investment portfolio (7.7).
Principal Business: Group health insurance (45%), group life insurance (31%), reinsurance (19%), group retirement contracts (4%), and individual health insurance (1%).
Principal Investments: NonCMO investment grade bonds (55%), CMOs and structured securities (29%), common & preferred stock (7%), mortgages in good standing (7%), and misc. investments (2%).
Investments in Affiliates: 7%
Group Affiliation: Union Labor Group
Licensed in: All states except PR
Commenced Business: May 1927
Address: 111 Massachusetts Ave NW, Washington, DC 20001-1625
Phone: (202) 682-6690 **Domicile State:** MD **NAIC Code:** 69744

Data Date	Rating	RACR #1	RACR #2	Total Assets ($mil)	Capital ($mil)	Net Premium ($mil)	Net Income ($mil)
6-14	B-	1.48	1.05	3,117.1	78.2	70.2	2.4
6-13	B	1.95	1.31	2,827.5	85.7	73.1	-2.0
2013	B-	1.66	1.20	2,813.7	87.7	139.5	-11.1
2012	B-	2.22	1.50	2,905.9	96.9	148.8	7.9
2011	C+	1.82	1.15	3,495.0	91.0	156.3	2.7
2010	C+	1.89	1.25	3,928.8	93.4	147.2	7.5
2009	C+	1.72	1.10	3,882.3	92.1	155.2	8.7

Adverse Trends in Operations

Decrease in asset base during 2013 (3%)
Decrease in asset base during 2012 (17%)
Decrease in asset base during 2011 (11%)
Decrease in capital during 2011 (3%)
Decrease in premium volume from 2009 to 2010 (5%)

UNION SECURITY INSURANCE COMPANY

B **Good**

Major Rating Factors: Good overall results on stability tests (5.6 on a scale of 0 to 10) despite negative cash flow from operations for 2013. Other stability subfactors include excellent operational trends and excellent risk diversification. Good quality investment portfolio (5.4) despite large holdings of BBB rated bonds in addition to moderate junk bond exposure. Exposure to mortgages is significant, but the mortgage default rate has been low. Good overall profitability (6.4).
Other Rating Factors: Good liquidity (5.0). Strong capitalization (7.3) based on excellent risk adjusted capital (severe loss scenario).
Principal Business: Group health insurance (56%), group life insurance (16%), reinsurance (13%), individual health insurance (8%), and other lines (7%).
Principal Investments: NonCMO investment grade bonds (64%), mortgages in good standing (18%), noninv. grade bonds (4%), CMOs and structured securities (4%), and misc. investments (7%).
Investments in Affiliates: 1%
Group Affiliation: Assurant Inc
Licensed in: All states except NY, PR
Commenced Business: September 1910
Address: 500 Bielenberg Dr, Woodbury, MN 55125
Phone: (612) 738-5063 **Domicile State:** KS **NAIC Code:** 70408

Data Date	Rating	RACR #1	RACR #2	Total Assets ($mil)	Capital ($mil)	Net Premium ($mil)	Net Income ($mil)
6-14	B	1.83	1.19	5,018.5	419.4	506.8	36.6
6-13	B	2.07	1.27	4,976.0	434.4	490.2	35.8
2013	B	1.88	1.21	5,085.8	434.7	986.2	85.4
2012	B	2.10	1.28	5,015.5	438.8	986.8	95.3
2011	B	2.02	1.24	5,139.5	455.8	1,050.4	69.1
2010	B	1.89	1.15	5,529.4	449.6	1,109.5	81.0
2009	C+	1.68	1.01	5,653.2	418.4	1,103.3	59.9

Adverse Trends in Operations

Decrease in premium volume from 2011 to 2012 (6%)
Decrease in asset base during 2012 (2%)
Decrease in capital during 2012 (4%)
Decrease in premium volume from 2010 to 2011 (5%)
Decrease in asset base during 2010 (2%)

UNION SECURITY LIFE INSURANCE COMPANY OF NEW YORK *   B+   Good

Major Rating Factors: Good overall results on stability tests (5.0 on a scale of 0 to 10) despite negative cash flow from operations for 2013. Other stability subfactors include good operational trends and excellent risk diversification. Good overall profitability (5.9). Return on equity has been good over the last five years, averaging 12.1%. Good liquidity (6.8).

Other Rating Factors: Strong capitalization (10.0) based on excellent risk adjusted capital (severe loss scenario). High quality investment portfolio (7.0).

Principal Business: Group health insurance (40%), individual health insurance (25%), reinsurance (16%), group life insurance (10%), and other lines (8%).

Principal Investments: NonCMO investment grade bonds (66%), mortgages in good standing (20%), CMOs and structured securities (7%), common & preferred stock (4%), and misc. investments (2%).

Investments in Affiliates: None

Group Affiliation: Assurant Inc

Licensed in: NY

Commenced Business: April 1974

Address: 220 Salina Meadows Pkwy #255, Syracuse, NY 13212

Phone: (315) 451-0066 **Domicile State:** NY **NAIC Code:** 81477

Data Date	Rating	RACR #1	RACR #2	Total Assets ($mil)	Capital ($mil)	Net Premium ($mil)	Net Income ($mil)
6-14	B+	4.41	3.97	142.5	40.6	12.2	3.8
6-13	B+	4.74	4.04	155.7	44.2	13.9	2.0
2013	B+	4.44	4.00	147.7	40.9	27.4	5.4
2012	B	5.02	4.21	160.6	46.9	30.1	5.5
2011	B	4.32	3.39	168.1	40.7	35.2	-0.1
2010	B	4.81	3.59	174.2	45.8	37.6	7.8
2009	B	5.32	3.60	164.5	50.5	43.5	9.6

Adverse Trends in Operations

Decrease in capital during 2013 (13%)
Increase in policy surrenders from 2012 to 2013 (769%)
Decrease in premium volume from 2011 to 2012 (14%)
Decrease in capital during 2011 (11%)
Decrease in premium volume from 2009 to 2010 (14%)

UNITED AMERICAN INSURANCE COMPANY   B   Good

Major Rating Factors: Good overall results on stability tests (5.9 on a scale of 0 to 10). Stability strengths include excellent operational trends and excellent risk diversification. Good current capitalization (5.9) based on good risk adjusted capital (severe loss scenario), although results have slipped from the excellent range over the last two years. Good quality investment portfolio (5.8).

Other Rating Factors: Good overall profitability (6.8). Good liquidity (6.5).

Principal Business: Individual health insurance (75%), group health insurance (15%), individual annuities (5%), individual life insurance (3%), and reinsurance (2%).

Principal Investments: NonCMO investment grade bonds (84%), common & preferred stock (4%), noninv. grade bonds (4%), CMOs and structured securities (4%), and misc. investments (4%).

Investments in Affiliates: 4%

Group Affiliation: Torchmark Corp

Licensed in: All states except NY, PR

Commenced Business: August 1981

Address: 10306 Regency Parkway Dr, Omaha, NE 68114

Phone: (972) 529-5085 **Domicile State:** NE **NAIC Code:** 92916

Data Date	Rating	RACR #1	RACR #2	Total Assets ($mil)	Capital ($mil)	Net Premium ($mil)	Net Income ($mil)
6-14	B	1.19	0.86	1,731.7	207.9	447.0	7.0
6-13	B	1.42	1.02	1,685.1	243.0	386.7	26.6
2013	B	1.27	0.91	1,683.4	211.6	745.1	58.1
2012	B	1.47	1.05	1,722.8	256.1	779.2	78.8
2011	B	1.54	1.07	1,703.5	243.9	692.2	75.0
2010	B	1.57	1.12	1,698.1	266.2	749.5	93.6
2009	B	1.55	1.10	1,649.6	257.0	787.2	79.4

Adverse Trends in Operations

Decrease in asset base during 2013 (2%)
Decrease in capital during 2013 (17%)
Decrease in premium volume from 2012 to 2013 (4%)
Decrease in capital during 2011 (8%)
Decrease in premium volume from 2009 to 2010 (5%)

UNITED HEALTHCARE INS CO OF IL   B   Good

Major Rating Factors: Good liquidity (6.3 on a scale of 0 to 10) with sufficient resources (cash flows and marketable investments) to handle a spike in claims. Excellent profitability (8.4). Strong capitalization (7.6) based on excellent current risk-adjusted capital (severe loss scenario).

Other Rating Factors: High quality investment portfolio (9.2).

Principal Business: Comp med (100%)

Mem Phys: 13: 31,664 **12:** 29,816 **13 MLR** 83.7% **/ 13 Admin Exp** N/A

Enroll(000): Q2 14: 194 **13:** 201 **12:** 158 **Med Exp PMPM:** $321

Principal Investments: Long-term bonds (85%), cash and equiv (9%), other (6%)

Provider Compensation ($000): Contr fee ($709,494), capitation ($14,257), bonus arrang ($1,232)

Total Member Encounters: Phys (893,906), non-phys (270,253)

Group Affiliation: UnitedHealth Group Inc

Licensed in: IL

Address: 233 N Michigan Ave, Chicago, IL 60601

Phone: (312) 424-4460 **Dom State:** IL **Commenced Bus:** December 1991

Data Date	Rating	RACR #1	RACR #2	Total Assets ($mil)	Capital ($mil)	Net Premium ($mil)	Net Income ($mil)
6-14	B	1.87	1.55	228.6	89.4	465.0	10.2
6-13	B	3.24	2.70	206.3	101.6	430.7	23.0
2013	B	1.70	1.41	193.5	80.8	890.6	33.2
2012	B	2.56	2.13	159.5	79.0	626.0	40.0
2011	B	3.54	2.95	141.0	75.5	496.0	36.7
2010	B	4.27	3.56	130.0	81.2	397.8	43.7
2009	N/A	N/A	N/A	114.9	71.8	320.3	N/A

Rating Indexes

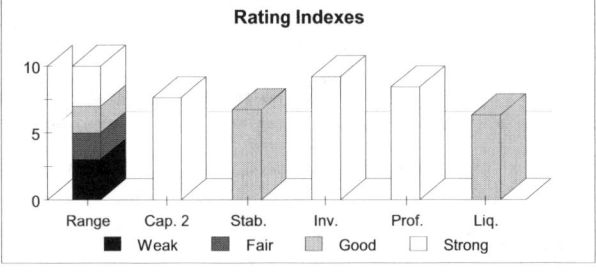

UNITED HEALTHCARE INS CO OF NY
B- **Good**

Major Rating Factors: Excellent profitability (7.9 on a scale of 0 to 10). Strong capitalization (10.0) based on excellent current risk-adjusted capital (severe loss scenario). High quality investment portfolio (9.9).
Other Rating Factors: Weak liquidity (2.1) as a spike in claims may stretch capacity.
Principal Business: Comp med (41%), med supp (22%), Medicare (18%), dental (1%), other (18%)
Mem Phys: 13: 111,635 **12:** 104,243 **13 MLR** 224.2% **/ 13 Admin Exp** N/A
Enroll(000): Q2 14: 1,336 **13:** 2,411 **12:** 2,180 **Med Exp PMPM:** $119
Principal Investments: Long-term bonds (88%), cash and equiv (12%)
Provider Compensation ($000): Contr fee ($2,938,964), FFS ($533,923), capitation ($49)
Total Member Encounters: Phys (8,066,035), non-phys (1,087,653)
Group Affiliation: UnitedHealth Group Inc
Licensed in: DC, NY
Address: 2950 Expressway Dr S Suite 240, Islandia, NY 11749-1412
Phone: (877) 832-7734 **Dom State:** NY **Commenced Bus:** December 1995

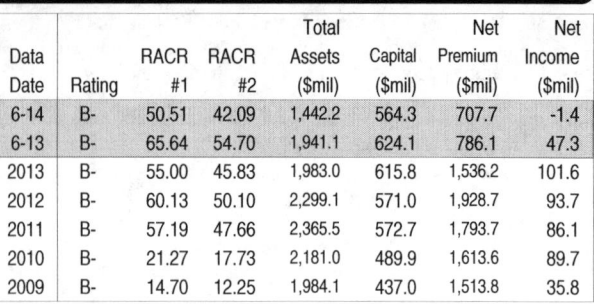

Data Date	Rating	RACR #1	RACR #2	Total Assets ($mil)	Capital ($mil)	Net Premium ($mil)	Net Income ($mil)
6-14	B-	50.51	42.09	1,442.2	564.3	707.7	-1.4
6-13	B-	65.64	54.70	1,941.1	624.1	786.5	47.3
2013	B-	55.00	45.83	1,983.0	615.8	1,536.2	101.6
2012	B-	60.13	50.10	2,299.1	571.0	1,928.7	93.7
2011	B-	57.19	47.66	2,365.5	572.7	1,793.7	86.1
2010	B-	21.27	17.73	2,181.0	489.9	1,613.6	89.7
2009	B-	14.70	12.25	1,984.1	437.0	1,513.8	35.8

Rating Indexes

Range — Cap. 2 — Stab. — Inv. — Prof. — Liq.
■ Weak ■ Fair ▨ Good ☐ Strong

UNITED HEALTHCARE INSURANCE COMPANY
C **Fair**

Major Rating Factors: Fair overall capitalization (4.0 on a scale of 0 to 10) based on mixed results -- excessive policy leverage mitigated by fair risk adjusted capital (severe loss scenario). Fair overall results on stability tests (3.5) including fair risk adjusted capital in prior years. Good quality investment portfolio (6.8).
Other Rating Factors: Weak liquidity (1.5). Excellent profitability (8.9) with operating gains in each of the last five years.
Principal Business: Group health insurance (58%), individual health insurance (31%), and reinsurance (11%).
Principal Investments: NonCMO investment grade bonds (58%), CMOs and structured securities (18%), common & preferred stock (17%), and noninv. grade bonds (5%).
Investments in Affiliates: 15%
Group Affiliation: UnitedHealth Group Inc
Licensed in: All states except NY
Commenced Business: April 1972
Address: 185 Asylum St, Hartford, CT 06103-3408
Phone: (877) 832-7734 **Domicile State:** CT **NAIC Code:** 79413

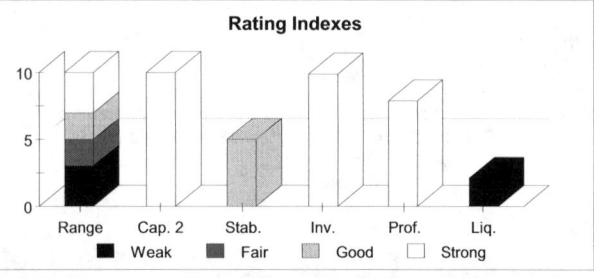

Data Date	Rating	RACR #1	RACR #2	Total Assets ($mil)	Capital ($mil)	Net Premium ($mil)	Net Income ($mil)
6-14	C	0.74	0.62	13,754.9	4,085.6	22,376.5	1,141.8
6-13	C	0.74	0.62	13,307.5	3,766.2	22,403.2	949.6
2013	C	0.76	0.64	14,512.6	5,039.5	44,680.4	2,384.0
2012	C	0.76	0.64	14,118.3	4,711.9	42,602.9	2,531.0
2011	C	0.73	0.62	15,022.1	4,421.6	41,956.3	2,430.1
2010	C+	0.70	0.59	13,677.4	4,022.0	39,966.2	2,259.1
2009	C+	0.66	0.56	11,899.7	3,425.8	35,846.0	1,993.9

Policy Leverage

Target Leverage — 100%
Actual Leverage — 293%

0% — 100% — 200% — 300%
■ Recommended ☐ Excess

UNITED HEALTHCARE OF ALABAMA INC
B **Good**

Major Rating Factors: Good liquidity (6.8 on a scale of 0 to 10) with sufficient resources (cash flows and marketable investments) to handle a spike in claims. Fair overall results on stability tests (4.6). Rating is significantly influenced by the fair financial results of UnitedHealth Group Inc. Excellent profitability (8.9).
Other Rating Factors: Strong capitalization index (10.0) based on excellent current risk-adjusted capital (severe loss scenario). High quality investment portfolio (9.4).
Principal Business: Medicare (99%)
Mem Phys: 13: 9,521 **12:** 9,258 **13 MLR** 80.9% **/ 13 Admin Exp** N/A
Enroll(000): Q2 14: 40 **13:** 40 **12:** 38 **Med Exp PMPM:** $697
Principal Investments: Long-term bonds (95%), cash and equiv (5%)
Provider Compensation ($000): Contr fee ($270,214), FFS ($53,564), capitation ($7,481)
Total Member Encounters: Phys (972,865), non-phys (446,615)
Group Affiliation: UnitedHealth Group Inc
Licensed in: AL
Address: 33 Inverness Center Parkway, Birmingham, AL 35242
Phone: (205) 437-8500 **Dom State:** AL **Commenced Bus:** March 1986

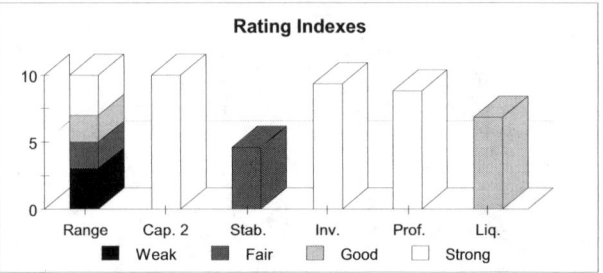

Data Date	Rating	RACR #1	RACR #2	Total Assets ($mil)	Capital ($mil)	Net Premium ($mil)	Net Income ($mil)
6-14	B	3.67	3.06	168.8	76.2	223.2	13.6
6-13	B	3.85	3.21	141.2	73.2	208.1	14.2
2013	B	3.07	2.56	132.7	62.4	406.2	26.7
2012	B	3.76	3.14	134.0	71.3	411.1	39.3
2011	B	3.73	3.11	125.6	62.8	405.3	44.3
2010	B-	2.49	2.07	100.6	44.8	374.8	28.1
2009	B	2.95	2.46	108.9	57.7	387.2	29.1

Rating Indexes

Range — Cap. 2 — Stab. — Inv. — Prof. — Liq.
■ Weak ■ Fair ▨ Good ☐ Strong

UNITED HEALTHCARE OF ARIZONA INC   B   Good

Major Rating Factors: Good overall profitability index (6.5 on a scale of 0 to 10). Good overall results on stability tests (5.0). Rating is significantly influenced by the fair financial results of UnitedHealth Group Inc. Good liquidity (6.6) with sufficient resources (cash flows and marketable investments) to handle a spike in claims.

Other Rating Factors: Strong capitalization index (8.4) based on excellent current risk-adjusted capital (severe loss scenario). High quality investment portfolio (9.3).

Principal Business: Medicare (65%), comp med (35%)

Mem Phys: 13: 14,618 **12:** 13,855 **13 MLR** 83.3% **/ 13 Admin Exp** N/A

Enroll(000): Q2 14: 40 **13:** 45 **12:** 44 **Med Exp PMPM:** $520

Principal Investments: Long-term bonds (101%)

Provider Compensation ($000): Contr fee ($244,951), FFS ($40,251), capitation ($4,830)

Total Member Encounters: Phys (715,332), non-phys (203,851)

Group Affiliation: UnitedHealth Group Inc

Licensed in: AZ

Address: 2390 E Camelback Rd #300, Phoenix, AZ 85016

Phone: (800) 985-2356 **Dom State:** AZ **Commenced Bus:** July 1985

Data Date	Rating	RACR #1	RACR #2	Total Assets ($mil)	Capital ($mil)	Net Premium ($mil)	Net Income ($mil)
6-14	B	2.48	2.06	89.1	45.0	167.0	8.4
6-13	C	1.69	1.41	80.5	30.6	171.6	8.9
2013	B-	2.07	1.73	74.4	36.9	338.9	13.9
2012	C	1.35	1.13	71.4	23.8	320.5	12.3
2011	B	4.16	3.47	154.4	117.5	293.1	15.5
2010	B	4.33	3.61	108.8	85.5	142.1	24.9
2009	B	4.26	3.55	120.9	102.0	127.3	11.8

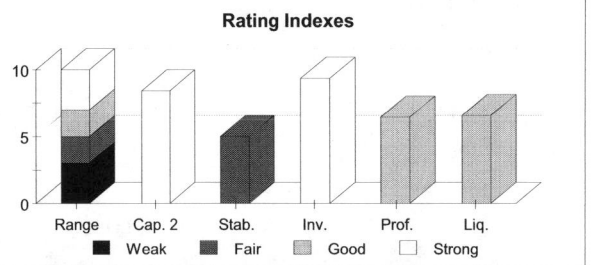

Rating Indexes

UNITED HEALTHCARE OF ARKANSAS INC   B   Good

Major Rating Factors: Excellent profitability (9.8 on a scale of 0 to 10). Strong capitalization index (9.5) based on excellent current risk-adjusted capital (severe loss scenario). High quality investment portfolio (9.9).

Other Rating Factors: Excellent overall results on stability tests (7.9). Rating is significantly influenced by the fair financial results of UnitedHealth Group Inc. Excellent liquidity (7.2) with ample operational cash flow and liquid investments.

Principal Business: Medicare (81%), comp med (19%)

Mem Phys: 13: 5,968 **12:** 5,658 **13 MLR** 82.8% **/ 13 Admin Exp** N/A

Enroll(000): Q2 14: 2 **13:** 6 **12:** 6 **Med Exp PMPM:** $512

Principal Investments: Cash and equiv (97%), long-term bonds (3%)

Provider Compensation ($000): Contr fee ($29,845), FFS ($7,029), capitation ($678), bonus arrang ($18)

Total Member Encounters: Phys (98,675), non-phys (34,967)

Group Affiliation: UnitedHealth Group Inc

Licensed in: AR

Address: 1401 Capitol Ave 3rd Fl #375, Little Rock, AR 72205

Phone: (501) 664-7700 **Dom State:** AR **Commenced Bus:** April 1992

Data Date	Rating	RACR #1	RACR #2	Total Assets ($mil)	Capital ($mil)	Net Premium ($mil)	Net Income ($mil)
6-14	B	3.32	2.77	12.1	9.6	4.5	0.5
6-13	B	3.67	3.06	17.4	10.1	23.0	1.2
2013	B	3.17	2.64	15.1	9.1	44.9	1.9
2012	B	3.28	2.73	15.6	8.9	43.7	3.3
2011	B	2.64	2.20	13.5	7.1	36.6	1.8
2010	B	3.51	2.92	10.6	6.5	23.1	1.4
2009	B	3.95	3.29	9.1	5.3	18.1	0.5

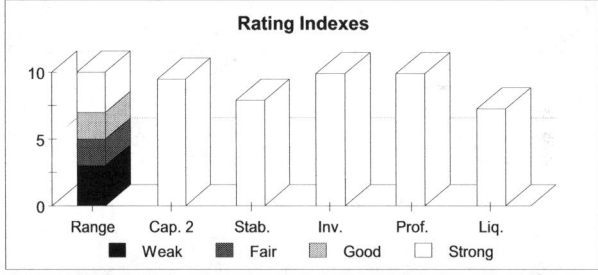

Rating Indexes

UNITED HEALTHCARE OF COLORADO INC   B   Good

Major Rating Factors: Good profitability index (5.0 on a scale of 0 to 10). Good overall results on stability tests (5.3) based on healthy premium and capital growth during 2013. Rating is significantly influenced by the fair financial results of UnitedHealth Group Inc. Strong capitalization index (10.0) based on excellent current risk-adjusted capital (severe loss scenario).

Other Rating Factors: High quality investment portfolio (9.9). Excellent liquidity (7.8) with ample operational cash flow and liquid investments.

Principal Business: Comp med (100%)

Mem Phys: 13: 13,505 **12:** 13,031 **13 MLR** 74.3% **/ 13 Admin Exp** N/A

Enroll(000): Q2 14: 8 **13:** 6 **12:** 4 **Med Exp PMPM:** $261

Principal Investments: Cash and equiv (89%), long-term bonds (11%)

Provider Compensation ($000): Contr fee ($12,481), FFS ($1,067), capitation ($852)

Total Member Encounters: Phys (25,608), non-phys (1,379)

Group Affiliation: UnitedHealth Group Inc

Licensed in: CO

Address: 6465 S Greenwood Pl Blvd 300, Centennial, CO 80111

Phone: (303) 267-3300 **Dom State:** CO **Commenced Bus:** March 1986

Data Date	Rating	RACR #1	RACR #2	Total Assets ($mil)	Capital ($mil)	Net Premium ($mil)	Net Income ($mil)
6-14	B	6.35	5.29	14.0	9.3	15.1	0.8
6-13	C	5.67	4.73	10.3	7.2	8.9	2.4
2013	B-	5.86	4.88	11.5	8.6	19.5	3.7
2012	C	3.87	3.22	9.4	4.8	12.1	-1.7
2011	C	3.89	3.24	6.3	4.7	5.3	-0.8
2010	C	4.68	3.90	6.3	5.4	2.9	-0.5
2009	C	5.26	4.38	6.4	5.9	2.6	0.2

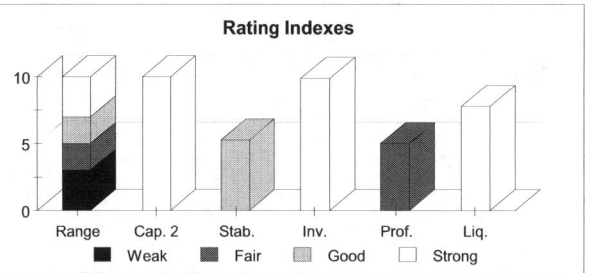

Rating Indexes

UNITED HEALTHCARE OF FLORIDA INC
C Fair

Major Rating Factors: Fair capitalization index (3.8 on a scale of 0 to 10) based on weak current risk-adjusted capital (moderate loss scenario). Fair overall results on stability tests (4.1). Rating is significantly influenced by the fair financial results of UnitedHealth Group Inc. Fair liquidity (3.2) as cash resources may not be adequate to cover a spike in claims.

Other Rating Factors: Weak profitability index (2.1). High quality investment portfolio (9.9).

Principal Business: Medicare (35%), comp med (34%), Medicaid (31%)

Mem Phys: 13: 38,172 **12:** 36,433 **13 MLR** 88.8% **/ 13 Admin Exp** N/A

Enroll(000): Q2 14: 362 **13:** 366 **12:** 332 **Med Exp PMPM:** $348

Principal Investments: Long-term bonds (72%), cash and equiv (28%)

Provider Compensation ($000): Contr fee ($1,190,761), FFS ($136,674), capitation ($86,218), bonus arrang ($3,404)

Total Member Encounters: Phys (4,122,579), non-phys (1,467,317)

Group Affiliation: UnitedHealth Group Inc

Licensed in: FL

Address: 495 N. Keller Road, Ste 200, Maitland, FL 32751

Phone: (407) 659-7041 **Dom State:** FL **Commenced Bus:** March 1973

Data Date	Rating	RACR #1	RACR #2	Total Assets ($mil)	Capital ($mil)	Net Premium ($mil)	Net Income ($mil)
6-14	C	0.74	0.62	429.1	54.1	1,037.4	-5.4
6-13	C	1.57	1.31	287.7	89.6	758.9	19.3
2013	C	0.82	0.68	339.4	62.2	1,668.5	-40.0
2012	C	1.37	1.14	256.8	75.4	1,305.2	47.9
2011	C	2.25	1.88	280.3	132.1	1,286.4	73.8
2010	U	3.04	2.54	335.3	153.3	1,074.9	53.5
2009	B-	1.74	1.45	316.5	101.2	1,299.6	6.6

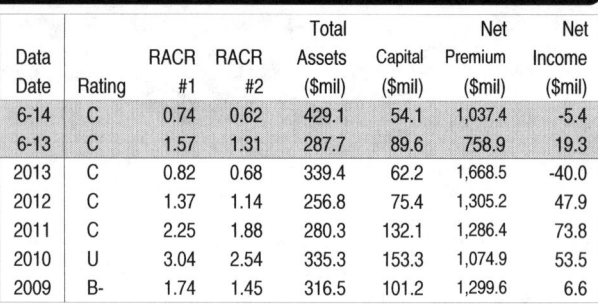

Rating Indexes

Range · Cap. 2 · Stab. · Inv. · Prof. · Liq.
■ Weak ▨ Fair ▤ Good □ Strong

UNITED HEALTHCARE OF GEORGIA INC
B- Good

Major Rating Factors: Fair overall results on stability tests (4.7 on a scale of 0 to 10) based on a significant 23% decrease in enrollment during the period. Rating is significantly influenced by the fair financial results of UnitedHealth Group Inc. Good liquidity (6.9) with sufficient resources (cash flows and marketable investments) to handle a spike in claims. Excellent profitability (7.9).

Other Rating Factors: Strong capitalization index (9.6) based on excellent current risk-adjusted capital (severe loss scenario). High quality investment portfolio (9.9).

Principal Business: Medicare (56%), comp med (44%)

Mem Phys: 13: 19,478 **12:** 18,584 **13 MLR** 82.1% **/ 13 Admin Exp** N/A

Enroll(000): Q2 14: 15 **13:** 17 **12:** 22 **Med Exp PMPM:** $470

Principal Investments: Long-term bonds (74%), cash and equiv (26%)

Provider Compensation ($000): Contr fee ($95,350), FFS ($17,222), capitation ($1,864), bonus arrang ($18)

Total Member Encounters: Phys (271,165), non-phys (73,719)

Group Affiliation: UnitedHealth Group Inc

Licensed in: GA

Address: 3720 DaVinci Ct, Ste 300, Norcross, GA 30092

Phone: (770) 300-3501 **Dom State:** GA **Commenced Bus:** April 1986

Data Date	Rating	RACR #1	RACR #2	Total Assets ($mil)	Capital ($mil)	Net Premium ($mil)	Net Income ($mil)
6-14	B-	3.43	2.86	43.6	26.3	65.4	4.9
6-13	C	2.85	2.37	41.8	22.5	73.3	5.3
2013	B-	3.18	2.65	41.1	24.1	138.1	6.6
2012	C	2.04	1.70	35.0	16.0	146.8	6.6
2011	B-	3.68	3.07	49.8	30.5	157.7	12.0
2010	B-	4.33	3.61	52.1	33.9	144.5	7.6
2009	C	2.96	2.47	48.2	25.9	157.3	8.7

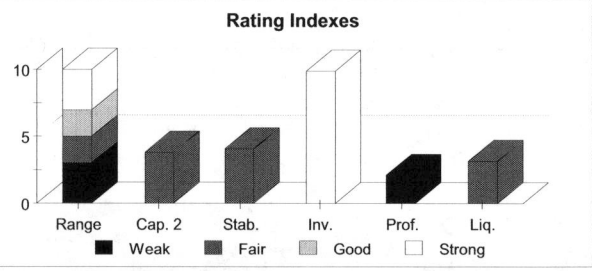

Rating Indexes

Range · Cap. 2 · Stab. · Inv. · Prof. · Liq.
■ Weak ▨ Fair ▤ Good □ Strong

UNITED HEALTHCARE OF ILLINOIS INC
C Fair

Major Rating Factors: Weak overall results on stability tests (2.7 on a scale of 0 to 10) based on an excessive 162% enrollment growth during the period. Rating is significantly influenced by the fair financial results of UnitedHealth Group Inc. Good overall profitability index (5.3). Strong capitalization index (10.0) based on excellent current risk-adjusted capital (severe loss scenario).

Other Rating Factors: High quality investment portfolio (9.9). Excellent liquidity (7.1) with ample operational cash flow and liquid investments.

Principal Business: Comp med (100%)

Mem Phys: 13: 36,328 **12:** 34,004 **13 MLR** 75.6% **/ 13 Admin Exp** N/A

Enroll(000): Q2 14: 22 **13:** 21 **12:** 8 **Med Exp PMPM:** $300

Principal Investments: Long-term bonds (59%), cash and equiv (41%)

Provider Compensation ($000): Contr fee ($48,027), FFS ($3,723), capitation ($1,302), bonus arrang ($120)

Total Member Encounters: Phys (140,602), non-phys (6,282)

Group Affiliation: UnitedHealth Group Inc

Licensed in: IL, IN

Address: 233 N Michigan Ave, Chicago, IL 60601

Phone: (312) 803-5900 **Dom State:** IL **Commenced Bus:** January 1984

Data Date	Rating	RACR #1	RACR #2	Total Assets ($mil)	Capital ($mil)	Net Premium ($mil)	Net Income ($mil)
6-14	C	3.68	3.07	31.6	15.6	51.2	0.4
6-13	C	6.72	5.60	26.9	18.5	31.6	3.3
2013	B-	5.02	4.19	32.7	21.2	76.5	6.6
2012	C	5.65	4.71	19.8	15.3	44.4	4.5
2011	B-	7.99	6.66	33.0	26.6	54.5	5.0
2010	B-	4.61	3.84	33.1	21.5	74.1	2.2
2009	B-	3.53	2.94	34.6	17.8	80.8	-6.0

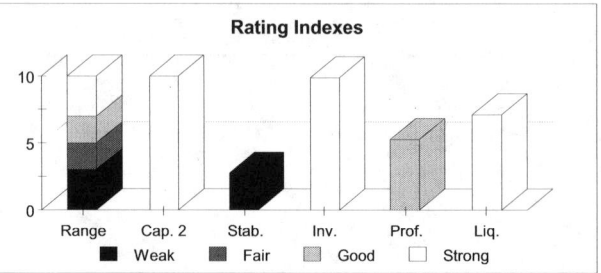

Rating Indexes

Range · Cap. 2 · Stab. · Inv. · Prof. · Liq.
■ Weak ▨ Fair ▤ Good □ Strong

UNITED HEALTHCARE OF KENTUCKY LTD   B   Good

Major Rating Factors: Good overall profitability index (6.4 on a scale of 0 to 10). Good overall results on stability tests (5.2). Rating is significantly influenced by the fair financial results of UnitedHealth Group Inc. Strong capitalization index (8.0) based on excellent current risk-adjusted capital (severe loss scenario).

Other Rating Factors: High quality investment portfolio (9.9). Excellent liquidity (7.2) with ample operational cash flow and liquid investments.

Principal Business: Comp med (100%)

Mem Phys: 13: 12,808 **12:** 12,146 **13 MLR** 80.3% **/ 13 Admin Exp** N/A

Enroll(000): Q2 14: 20 **13:** 22 **12:** 21 **Med Exp PMPM:** $295

Principal Investments: Cash and equiv (97%), long-term bonds (3%)

Provider Compensation ($000): Contr fee ($71,961), FFS ($3,397), capitation ($1,514), bonus arrang ($19)

Total Member Encounters: Phys (180,685), non-phys (7,636)

Group Affiliation: UnitedHealth Group Inc

Licensed in: IN, KY

Address: 2424 Harrodsburg Road #300, Lexington, KY 40503

Phone: (859) 825-6132 **Dom State:** KY **Commenced Bus:** May 1986

Data Date	Rating	RACR #1	RACR #2	Total Assets ($mil)	Capital ($mil)	Net Premium ($mil)	Net Income ($mil)
6-14	B	2.13	1.78	22.8	11.4	45.9	0.0
6-13	B-	2.32	1.93	21.5	11.6	46.9	3.8
2013	B	2.36	1.97	24.1	12.8	95.8	4.9
2012	B-	1.69	1.41	18.7	8.1	86.9	4.1
2011	B-	2.28	1.90	18.5	10.0	81.1	5.9
2010	B	3.18	2.65	22.1	13.4	71.6	3.1
2009	C+	3.00	2.50	18.8	10.1	48.9	-1.3

Rating Indexes

UNITED HEALTHCARE OF LOUISIANA INC   D   Weak

Major Rating Factors: Weak profitability index (2.3 on a scale of 0 to 10). Fair overall results on stability tests (4.7) based on an excessive 42% enrollment growth during the period. Rating is significantly influenced by the fair financial results of UnitedHealth Group Inc. Strong capitalization index (10.0) based on excellent current risk-adjusted capital (severe loss scenario).

Other Rating Factors: High quality investment portfolio (9.9). Excellent liquidity (10.0) with ample operational cash flow and liquid investments.

Principal Business: Comp med (100%)

Mem Phys: 13: 10,638 **12:** 9,981 **13 MLR** 58.0% **/ 13 Admin Exp** N/A

Enroll(000): Q2 14: 1 **13:** 1 **12:** 1 **Med Exp PMPM:** $289

Principal Investments: Cash and equiv (89%), long-term bonds (11%)

Provider Compensation ($000): Contr fee ($2,816), FFS ($211), capitation ($17)

Total Member Encounters: Phys (7,804), non-phys (521)

Group Affiliation: UnitedHealth Group Inc

Licensed in: LA

Address: 3838 N Causeway Blvd Ste 2600, Metairie, LA 70002

Phone: (504) 849-1603 **Dom State:** LA **Commenced Bus:** November 1986

Data Date	Rating	RACR #1	RACR #2	Total Assets ($mil)	Capital ($mil)	Net Premium ($mil)	Net Income ($mil)
6-14	D	11.11	9.26	15.1	13.4	3.8	1.0
6-13	D	5.30	4.42	7.5	6.6	2.4	-0.8
2013	D	10.28	8.57	15.4	12.4	5.1	3.0
2012	D	4.19	3.49	10.3	5.1	4.7	-4.7
2011	C	6.26	5.21	8.3	7.8	5.4	1.7
2010	C	2.07	1.73	10.3	6.1	28.0	-0.9
2009	C	2.84	2.37	15.3	7.5	29.2	-4.3

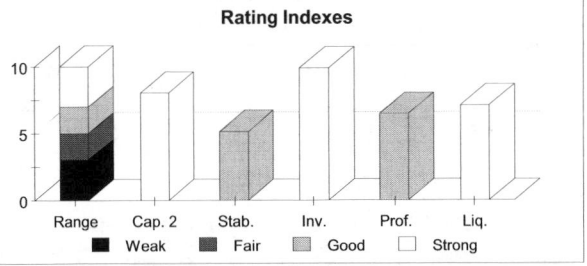

Rating Indexes

UNITED HEALTHCARE OF MID-ATLANTIC   B   Good

Major Rating Factors: Good overall results on stability tests (5.5 on a scale of 0 to 10). Rating is significantly influenced by the fair financial results of UnitedHealth Group Inc. Good liquidity (6.6) with sufficient resources (cash flows and marketable investments) to handle a spike in claims. Fair profitability index (4.8).

Other Rating Factors: Strong capitalization index (8.8) based on excellent current risk-adjusted capital (severe loss scenario). High quality investment portfolio (9.9).

Principal Business: Medicaid (89%), comp med (11%)

Mem Phys: 13: 45,153 **12:** 43,826 **13 MLR** 88.6% **/ 13 Admin Exp** N/A

Enroll(000): Q2 14: 251 **13:** 209 **12:** 189 **Med Exp PMPM:** $271

Principal Investments: Long-term bonds (81%), cash and equiv (19%)

Provider Compensation ($000): Contr fee ($596,278), FFS ($39,749), capitation ($27,784), bonus arrang ($281)

Total Member Encounters: Phys (1,750,722), non-phys (501,644)

Group Affiliation: UnitedHealth Group Inc

Licensed in: DC, MD, VA

Address: 800 King Farm Blvd, Rockville, MD 20850

Phone: (866) 297-9264 **Dom State:** MD **Commenced Bus:** December 1978

Data Date	Rating	RACR #1	RACR #2	Total Assets ($mil)	Capital ($mil)	Net Premium ($mil)	Net Income ($mil)
6-14	B	2.83	2.36	347.9	110.4	555.1	-10.2
6-13	B	3.05	2.54	267.4	110.3	360.6	-9.6
2013	B	2.92	2.44	226.7	114.4	737.0	-0.1
2012	B	3.40	2.83	210.8	124.6	701.6	22.5
2011	B	3.62	3.02	213.4	126.0	731.7	57.6
2010	B-	3.18	2.65	196.4	109.9	710.4	53.8
2009	C	1.57	1.31	196.1	56.1	678.3	-26.0

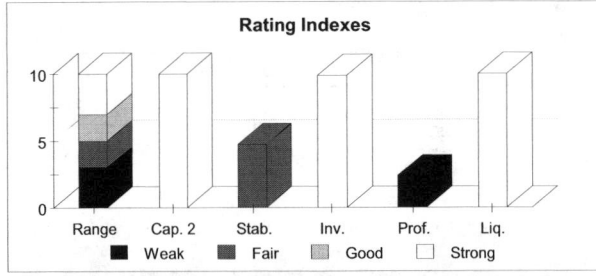

Rating Indexes

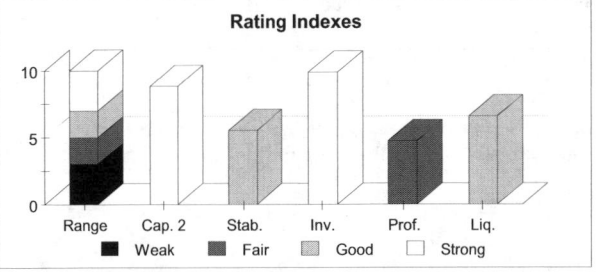

UNITED HEALTHCARE OF MISSISSIPPI INC

C **Fair**

Major Rating Factors: Fair overall results on stability tests (4.3 on a scale of 0 to 10) in spite of healthy premium and capital growth during 2013. Rating is significantly influenced by the fair financial results of UnitedHealth Group Inc. Weak profitability index (0.9). Strong capitalization index (7.8) based on excellent current risk-adjusted capital (severe loss scenario).

Other Rating Factors: High quality investment portfolio (9.9). Excellent liquidity (6.9) with sufficient resources (cash flows and marketable investments) to handle a spike in claims.

Principal Business: Medicaid (93%), comp med (7%).

Mem Phys: 13: 7,407 **12:** 6,861 **13 MLR** 88.9% **/ 13 Admin Exp** N/A

Enroll(000): Q2 14: 77 **13:** 75 **12:** 67 **Med Exp PMPM:** $381

Principal Investments: Cash and equiv (69%), long-term bonds (31%)

Provider Compensation ($000): Contr fee ($269,650), FFS ($22,371), capitation ($8,661)

Total Member Encounters: Phys (1,225,475), non-phys (374,405)

Group Affiliation: UnitedHealth Group Inc

Licensed in: MS

Address: 795 Woodlands Pkwy Ste 301, Ridgeland, MS 39157

Phone: (504) 849-1603 **Dom State:** MS **Commenced Bus:** January 1993

Data Date	Rating	RACR #1	RACR #2	Total Assets ($mil)	Capital ($mil)	Net Premium ($mil)	Net Income ($mil)
6-14	C	2.01	1.67	116.4	44.3	187.5	1.5
6-13	C	3.26	2.72	71.5	26.4	172.9	8.2
2013	C	1.67	1.40	108.5	36.7	362.2	-11.8
2012	C	2.34	1.95	73.3	18.8	126.1	3.1
2011	C	4.11	3.43	59.3	30.7	125.9	25.6
2010	U	17.26	14.38	20.7	5.3	2.9	-14.1
2009	U	2.88	2.40	4.2	4.2	0.0	0.1

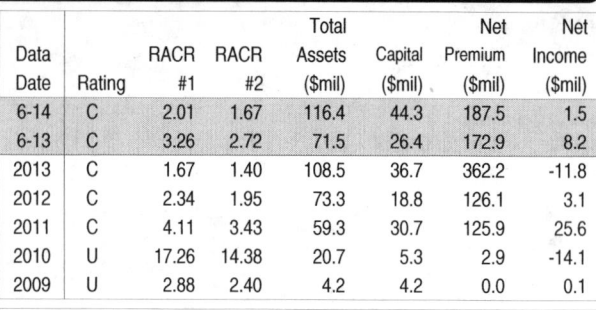

Rating Indexes

UNITED HEALTHCARE OF NC INC

B **Good**

Major Rating Factors: Good overall results on stability tests (5.9 on a scale of 0 to 10). Rating is significantly influenced by the fair financial results of UnitedHealth Group Inc. Good liquidity (6.8) with sufficient resources (cash flows and marketable investments) to handle a spike in claims. Excellent profitability (8.6).

Other Rating Factors: Strong capitalization index (8.9) based on excellent current risk-adjusted capital (severe loss scenario). High quality investment portfolio (9.7).

Principal Business: Medicare (89%), comp med (11%)

Mem Phys: 13: 22,225 **12:** 20,620 **13 MLR** 83.1% **/ 13 Admin Exp** N/A

Enroll(000): Q2 14: 103 **13:** 108 **12:** 111 **Med Exp PMPM:** $630

Principal Investments: Long-term bonds (80%), cash and equiv (20%)

Provider Compensation ($000): Contr fee ($711,419), FFS ($90,204), capitation ($12,444), bonus arrang ($756)

Total Member Encounters: Phys (1,814,855), non-phys (793,315)

Group Affiliation: UnitedHealth Group Inc

Licensed in: NC

Address: 3803 N Elm St, Greensboro, NC 27455

Phone: (336) 282-0900 **Dom State:** NC **Commenced Bus:** May 1985

Data Date	Rating	RACR #1	RACR #2	Total Assets ($mil)	Capital ($mil)	Net Premium ($mil)	Net Income ($mil)
6-14	B	2.90	2.42	287.3	146.5	516.7	16.4
6-13	B-	2.45	2.04	243.0	109.6	491.6	19.4
2013	B	2.60	2.17	249.7	130.5	969.0	40.0
2012	B-	1.97	1.64	228.2	86.0	986.5	59.5
2011	B-	2.27	1.89	224.9	102.4	933.2	57.7
2010	C+	2.32	1.93	189.4	84.2	771.3	41.6
2009	C+	3.09	2.58	233.1	122.1	774.4	42.9

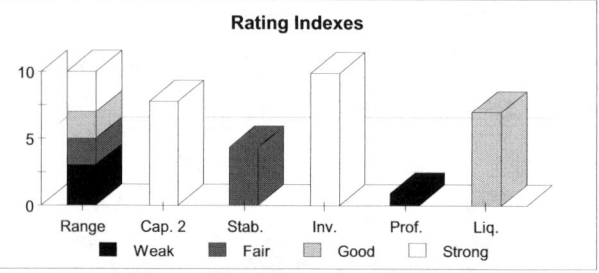

Rating Indexes

UNITED HEALTHCARE OF NEW ENGLAND INC

B **Good**

Major Rating Factors: Good liquidity (6.1 on a scale of 0 to 10) with sufficient resources (cash flows and marketable investments) to handle a spike in claims. Fair profitability index (3.9). Fair overall results on stability tests (4.7). Rating is significantly influenced by the fair financial results of UnitedHealth Group Inc.

Other Rating Factors: Strong capitalization index (10.0) based on excellent current risk-adjusted capital (severe loss scenario). High quality investment portfolio (9.4).

Principal Business: Medicare (56%), Medicaid (44%)

Mem Phys: 13: 31,226 **12:** 29,391 **13 MLR** 92.6% **/ 13 Admin Exp** N/A

Enroll(000): Q2 14: 99 **13:** 82 **12:** 80 **Med Exp PMPM:** $550

Principal Investments: Long-term bonds (93%), nonaffiliate common stock (5%), cash and equiv (3%)

Provider Compensation ($000): Contr fee ($457,450), capitation ($46,072), FFS ($39,632)

Total Member Encounters: Phys (1,218,101), non-phys (635,161)

Group Affiliation: UnitedHealth Group Inc

Licensed in: MA, RI

Address: 475 Kilvert St Suite 310, Warwick, RI 02886-1392

Phone: (203) 459-6000 **Dom State:** RI **Commenced Bus:** December 1984

Data Date	Rating	RACR #1	RACR #2	Total Assets ($mil)	Capital ($mil)	Net Premium ($mil)	Net Income ($mil)
6-14	B	3.96	3.30	258.8	135.0	332.1	13.8
6-13	B	4.41	3.68	230.7	141.1	294.5	2.4
2013	B	3.67	3.05	230.9	124.5	587.5	-2.8
2012	B	4.38	3.65	245.7	140.1	568.8	16.7
2011	B	5.33	4.44	223.8	137.2	459.8	33.1
2010	B	4.67	3.89	209.8	109.2	412.9	-14.9
2009	B	5.17	4.30	190.6	117.7	401.6	5.0

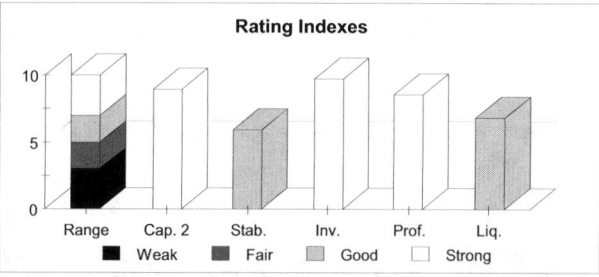

Rating Indexes

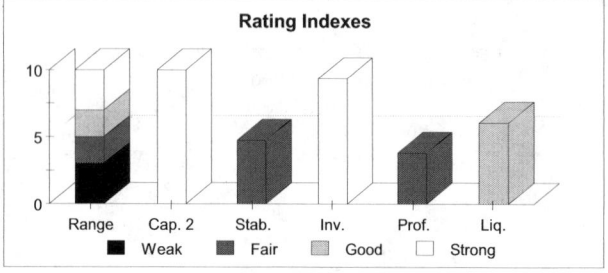

UNITED HEALTHCARE OF NY INC * — B+ — Good

Major Rating Factors: Excellent profitability (8.6 on a scale of 0 to 10). Strong capitalization index (9.0) based on excellent current risk-adjusted capital (severe loss scenario). High quality investment portfolio (9.9).
Other Rating Factors: Excellent liquidity (6.9) with sufficient resources (cash flows and marketable investments) to handle a spike in claims. Fair overall results on stability tests (4.8). Rating is significantly influenced by the fair financial results of UnitedHealth Group Inc.
Principal Business: Medicaid (76%), Medicare (21%), comp med (3%)
Mem Phys: 13: 72,908 **12:** 68,094 **13 MLR** 82.2% **/ 13 Admin Exp** N/A
Enroll(000): Q2 14: 481 **13:** 397 **12:** 350 **Med Exp PMPM:** $339
Principal Investments: Long-term bonds (66%), cash and equiv (34%)
Provider Compensation ($000): Contr fee ($1,134,942), capitation ($253,112), FFS ($142,499), bonus arrang ($2,604)
Total Member Encounters: Phys (999,756), non-phys (412,667)
Group Affiliation: UnitedHealth Group Inc
Licensed in: NY
Address: 77 Water St 14th/15th Floor, New York, NY 10005
Phone: (203) 459-6000 **Dom State:** NY **Commenced Bus:** January 1987

Data Date	Rating	RACR #1	RACR #2	Total Assets ($mil)	Capital ($mil)	Net Premium ($mil)	Net Income ($mil)
6-14	B+	2.91	2.43	564.2	271.6	1,160.5	21.1
6-13	B+	3.80	3.17	546.5	305.7	912.8	42.1
2013	B+	3.65	3.04	606.2	345.2	1,879.0	79.9
2012	B+	4.02	3.35	564.5	323.9	1,607.3	111.7
2011	B+	3.81	3.17	416.1	226.3	1,201.6	80.9
2010	B+	5.30	4.42	435.3	248.2	975.3	69.4
2009	B+	3.73	3.11	306.9	167.2	823.3	44.4

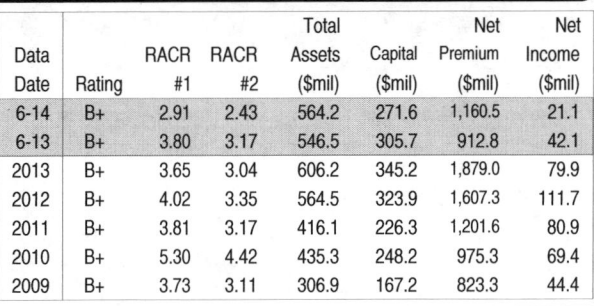

Rating Indexes

UNITED HEALTHCARE OF OHIO INC — B — Good

Major Rating Factors: Good overall profitability index (6.5 on a scale of 0 to 10). Good overall results on stability tests (6.3) based on steady enrollment growth, averaging 9% over the past five years. Rating is significantly influenced by the fair financial results of UnitedHealth Group Inc. Good liquidity (5.7) with sufficient resources (cash flows and marketable investments) to handle a spike in claims.
Other Rating Factors: Strong capitalization index (7.9) based on excellent current risk-adjusted capital (severe loss scenario). High quality investment portfolio (9.2).
Principal Business: Medicare (97%), comp med (3%)
Mem Phys: 13: 33,890 **12:** 31,626 **13 MLR** 89.6% **/ 13 Admin Exp** N/A
Enroll(000): Q2 14: 82 **13:** 109 **12:** 96 **Med Exp PMPM:** $719
Principal Investments: Long-term bonds (92%), cash and equiv (8%)
Provider Compensation ($000): Contr fee ($815,898), FFS ($74,047), capitation ($35,672), bonus arrang ($722)
Total Member Encounters: Phys (2,107,136), non-phys (1,081,327)
Group Affiliation: UnitedHealth Group Inc
Licensed in: KY, OH
Address: 9200 Worthington Rd, Westerville, OH 43082-8823
Phone: (614) 410-7000 **Dom State:** OH **Commenced Bus:** August 1985

Data Date	Rating	RACR #1	RACR #2	Total Assets ($mil)	Capital ($mil)	Net Premium ($mil)	Net Income ($mil)
6-14	B	2.06	1.72	289.1	117.0	455.8	4.6
6-13	B	2.74	2.28	294.4	127.9	527.2	4.9
2013	B	2.22	1.85	286.3	126.6	1,041.1	3.9
2012	B	2.64	2.20	256.4	122.7	926.1	34.3
2011	B	2.22	1.85	225.9	99.9	866.8	6.0
2010	B	2.35	1.96	220.7	100.1	824.4	20.9
2009	C+	2.21	1.84	191.9	78.8	749.3	8.8

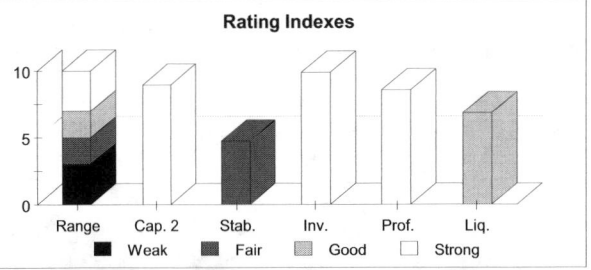

Rating Indexes

UNITED HEALTHCARE OF THE MIDLANDS * — B+ — Good

Major Rating Factors: Good liquidity (6.8 on a scale of 0 to 10) with sufficient resources (cash flows and marketable investments) to handle a spike in claims. Excellent profitability (9.1). Strong capitalization index (9.2) based on excellent current risk-adjusted capital (severe loss scenario).
Other Rating Factors: High quality investment portfolio (9.9). Excellent overall results on stability tests (7.2). Rating is significantly influenced by the fair financial results of UnitedHealth Group Inc.
Principal Business: Medicaid (73%), Medicare (27%)
Mem Phys: 13: 19,235 **12:** 18,112 **13 MLR** 81.0% **/ 13 Admin Exp** N/A
Enroll(000): Q2 14: 67 **13:** 60 **12:** 61 **Med Exp PMPM:** $226
Principal Investments: Long-term bonds (70%), cash and equiv (30%)
Provider Compensation ($000): Contr fee ($148,880), capitation ($7,757), FFS ($7,187), bonus arrang ($4,303)
Total Member Encounters: Phys (532,326), non-phys (215,461)
Group Affiliation: UnitedHealth Group Inc
Licensed in: IA, NE
Address: 2717 N. 118th Circle Ste 300, Omaha, NE 68164-9672
Phone: (402) 445-5600 **Dom State:** NE **Commenced Bus:** October 1984

Data Date	Rating	RACR #1	RACR #2	Total Assets ($mil)	Capital ($mil)	Net Premium ($mil)	Net Income ($mil)
6-14	B+	3.12	2.60	75.7	32.4	130.2	2.0
6-13	B+	2.48	2.07	61.7	22.0	101.3	1.5
2013	B+	2.92	2.43	65.8	30.0	207.0	9.8
2012	B+	2.33	1.94	53.8	20.3	186.9	8.7
2011	B+	2.52	2.10	48.6	21.6	173.8	6.9
2010	B+	2.86	2.38	46.1	22.0	151.1	4.5
2009	B+	3.27	2.72	45.1	24.0	143.4	5.6

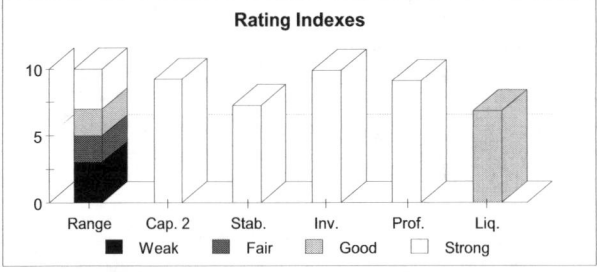

Rating Indexes

UNITED HEALTHCARE OF THE MIDWEST INC   C+   Fair

Major Rating Factors: Weak liquidity (2.1 on a scale of 0 to 10) as a spike in claims may stretch capacity. Excellent profitability (9.3). Strong capitalization index (8.7) based on excellent current risk-adjusted capital (severe loss scenario).

Other Rating Factors: High quality investment portfolio (9.9). Excellent overall results on stability tests (6.9). Rating is significantly influenced by the fair financial results of UnitedHealth Group Inc.

Principal Business: Medicare (64%), Medicaid (30%), FEHB (4%), comp med (2%)

Mem Phys: 13: 43,188   **12:** 15,706   **13 MLR** 134.0%   **/ 13 Admin Exp** N/A

Enroll(000): Q2 14: 183   **13:** 183   **12:** 58   **Med Exp PMPM:** $504

Principal Investments: Long-term bonds (79%), cash and equiv (21%)

Provider Compensation ($000): Contr fee ($915,350), FFS ($61,043), capitation ($48,931), bonus arrang ($35,642)

Total Member Encounters: Phys (2,146,653), non-phys (622,155)

Group Affiliation: UnitedHealth Group Inc

Licensed in: IL, KS, MO

Address: 13655 Riverport Dr -POB 2560, Maryland Heights, MO 63043-8560

Phone: (314) 592-7000   **Dom State:** MO   **Commenced Bus:** August 1985

Data Date	Rating	RACR #1	RACR #2	Total Assets ($mil)	Capital ($mil)	Net Premium ($mil)	Net Income ($mil)
6-14	C+	2.74	2.29	336.6	113.7	444.6	5.7
6-13	B	3.76	3.13	348.3	88.4	413.3	4.0
2013	B-	2.31	1.92	306.9	93.7	827.7	38.0
2012	B	3.77	3.14	198.3	88.8	536.6	38.9
2011	B	3.88	3.24	181.4	90.5	523.3	45.8
2010	B	3.56	2.96	173.7	80.3	516.2	41.9
2009	B-	3.05	2.54	163.2	68.8	523.1	37.0

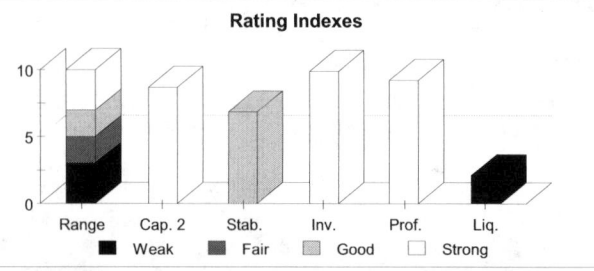

UNITED HEALTHCARE OF TX INC   C   Fair

Major Rating Factors: Weak profitability index (2.7 on a scale of 0 to 10). Weak overall results on stability tests (2.1) based on a significant 76% decrease in enrollment during the period. Rating is significantly influenced by the fair financial results of UnitedHealth Group Inc. Strong capitalization index (10.0) based on excellent current risk-adjusted capital (severe loss scenario).

Other Rating Factors: High quality investment portfolio (9.9). Excellent liquidity (10.0) with ample operational cash flow and liquid investments.

Principal Business: Comp med (100%)

Mem Phys: 13: 51,764   **12:** 49,287   **13 MLR** 50.3%   **/ 13 Admin Exp** N/A

Enroll(000): Q2 14: 0   **13:** 0   **12:** 0   **Med Exp PMPM:** $395

Principal Investments: Cash and equiv (98%), long-term bonds (2%)

Provider Compensation ($000): Contr fee ($434), FFS ($42), capitation ($2)

Total Member Encounters: Phys (1,212), non-phys (41)

Group Affiliation: UnitedHealth Group Inc

Licensed in: TX

Address: 5800 Granite Pky Stev900, Plano, TX 75024

Phone: (469) 633-8512   **Dom State:** TX   **Commenced Bus:** August 1985

Data Date	Rating	RACR #1	RACR #2	Total Assets ($mil)	Capital ($mil)	Net Premium ($mil)	Net Income ($mil)
6-14	C	5.05	4.21	6.2	6.0	0.2	-0.1
6-13	C	5.20	4.33	6.0	5.8	0.6	0.0
2013	C	5.09	4.24	6.1	6.0	0.8	0.2
2012	C	5.18	4.32	6.1	5.8	2.0	0.6
2011	C	10.91	9.10	13.4	13.2	3.3	-4.9
2010	C+	2.77	2.31	12.8	9.1	20.3	2.2
2009	C+	1.60	1.33	14.9	7.4	32.4	1.9

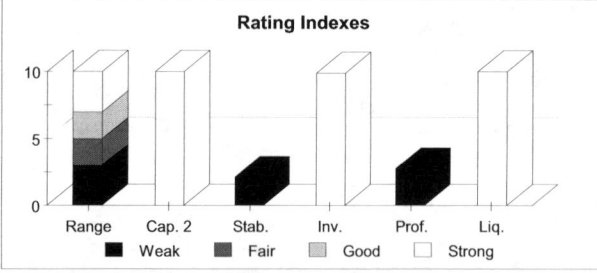

UNITED HEALTHCARE OF UTAH   B   Good

Major Rating Factors: Good overall results on stability tests (5.7 on a scale of 0 to 10) based on healthy premium and capital growth during 2013. Rating is significantly influenced by the fair financial results of UnitedHealth Group Inc. Good liquidity (6.2) with sufficient resources (cash flows and marketable investments) to handle a spike in claims. Fair profitability index (4.1).

Other Rating Factors: Strong capitalization index (8.4) based on excellent current risk-adjusted capital (severe loss scenario). High quality investment portfolio (9.9).

Principal Business: Medicare (100%)

Mem Phys: 13: 6,835   **12:** 6,326   **13 MLR** 82.7%   **/ 13 Admin Exp** N/A

Enroll(000): Q2 14: 39   **13:** 46   **12:** 40   **Med Exp PMPM:** $543

Principal Investments: Long-term bonds (91%), cash and equiv (9%)

Provider Compensation ($000): Contr fee ($268,549), FFS ($31,071), capitation ($4,000)

Total Member Encounters: Phys (722,767), non-phys (339,861)

Group Affiliation: UnitedHealth Group Inc

Licensed in: UT

Address: 2525 Lake Park Blvd, Salt Lake City, UT 84120

Phone: (801) 982-4500   **Dom State:** UT   **Commenced Bus:** March 1984

Data Date	Rating	RACR #1	RACR #2	Total Assets ($mil)	Capital ($mil)	Net Premium ($mil)	Net Income ($mil)
6-14	B	2.44	2.04	124.1	46.3	178.3	-0.8
6-13	C+	2.57	2.14	113.0	43.5	181.9	8.6
2013	B-	2.56	2.14	107.4	48.8	360.5	11.3
2012	C+	2.08	1.74	96.4	35.7	294.0	-2.3
2011	C+	1.84	1.53	70.0	19.1	261.8	1.1
2010	C+	1.48	1.23	51.1	16.0	187.6	-4.2
2009	C+	2.68	2.23	39.5	18.3	119.8	8.9

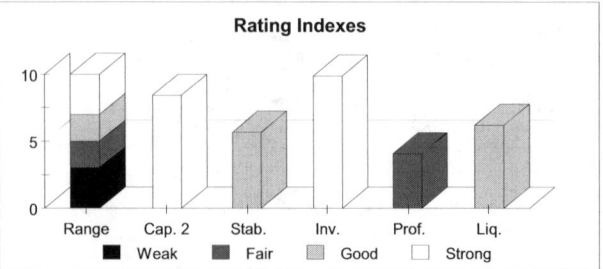

UNITED HEALTHCARE OF WISCONSIN INC   B   Good

Major Rating Factors: Good overall results on stability tests (6.0 on a scale of 0 to 10). Rating is significantly influenced by the fair financial results of UnitedHealth Group Inc. Good liquidity (6.6) with sufficient resources (cash flows and marketable investments) to handle a spike in claims. Excellent profitability (8.4).

Other Rating Factors: Strong capitalization index (8.3) based on excellent current risk-adjusted capital (severe loss scenario). High quality investment portfolio (9.9).

Principal Business: Medicare (62%), Medicaid (24%), comp med (14%)

Mem Phys: 13: 19,910   **12:** 18,733   **13 MLR** 86.1%   **/ 13 Admin Exp** N/A

Enroll(000): Q2 14: 248   **13:** 255   **12:** 221   **Med Exp PMPM:** $380

Principal Investments: Long-term bonds (79%), cash and equiv (21%)

Provider Compensation ($000): Contr fee ($953,838), capitation ($71,115), FFS ($52,255), bonus arrang ($452), other ($68,975)

Total Member Encounters: Phys (3,309,767), non-phys (1,025,416)

Group Affiliation: UnitedHealth Group Inc

Licensed in: WI

Address: 10701 West Research Dr, Wauwatosa, WI 53226

Phone: (414) 443-4000   **Dom State:** WI   **Commenced Bus:** June 1986

Data Date	Rating	RACR #1	RACR #2	Total Assets ($mil)	Capital ($mil)	Net Premium ($mil)	Net Income ($mil)
6-14	B	2.38	1.98	370.1	147.3	693.1	6.6
6-13	B	2.41	2.01	339.7	153.5	651.1	13.8
2013	B	2.52	2.10	346.3	157.0	1,328.8	20.4
2012	B	2.22	1.85	323.3	139.7	1,430.7	27.1
2011	B	2.10	1.75	313.0	132.5	1,403.0	31.5
2010	B	2.07	1.73	389.2	107.1	1,215.8	39.8
2009	C+	1.78	1.49	228.5	93.7	1,038.1	45.6

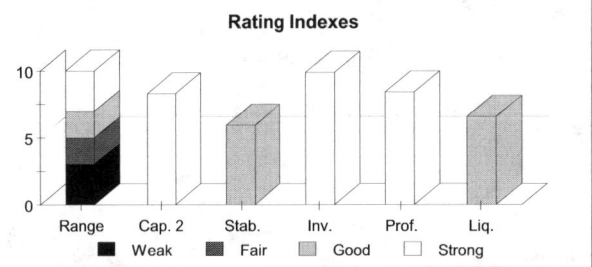

Rating Indexes

UNITED OF OMAHA LIFE INSURANCE COMPANY   B   Good

Major Rating Factors: Good quality investment portfolio (5.1 on a scale of 0 to 10) despite large holdings of BBB rated bonds in addition to moderate junk bond exposure. Exposure to mortgages is significant, but the mortgage default rate has been low. Good overall profitability (5.2). Excellent expense controls. Return on equity has been low, averaging -1.6%. Good liquidity (5.9).

Other Rating Factors: Good overall results on stability tests (5.4) good operational trends, good risk adjusted capital for prior years and excellent risk diversification. Strong capitalization (7.2) based on excellent risk adjusted capital (severe loss scenario).

Principal Business: Individual health insurance (34%), individual life insurance (31%), group health insurance (11%), group-life insurance (9%), and other lines (15%).

Principal Investments: NonCMO investment grade bonds (49%), CMOs and structured securities (26%), mortgages in good standing (13%), noninv. grade bonds (3%), and misc. investments (6%).

Investments in Affiliates: 3%

Group Affiliation: Mutual Of Omaha Group

Licensed in: All states except NY.

Commenced Business: November 1926

Address: Mutual Of Omaha Plaza, Omaha, NE 68175

Phone: (402) 342-7600   **Domicile State:** NE   **NAIC Code:** 69868

Data Date	Rating	RACR #1	RACR #2	Total Assets ($mil)	Capital ($mil)	Net Premium ($mil)	Net Income ($mil)
6-14	B	1.95	1.13	18,410.0	1,378.2	914.9	122.3
6-13	B	1.49	0.88	17,326.5	1,084.8	1,766.4	38.3
2013	B	1.71	1.00	18,122.5	1,226.9	3,428.2	69.9
2012	B	1.42	0.83	16,698.1	1,027.2	3,464.0	-31.5
2011	B	1.46	0.86	15,737.8	1,036.1	3,162.9	-207.0
2010	B	1.83	1.08	15,119.8	1,210.2	2,441.2	-110.5
2009	B+	1.95	1.13	14,037.3	1,245.1	2,416.3	-5.2

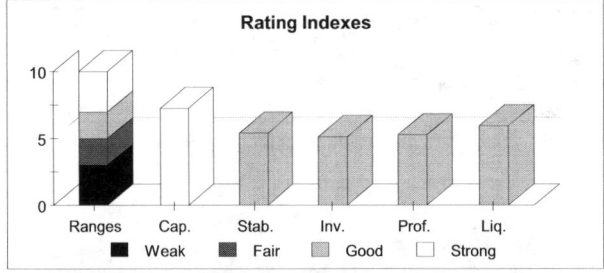

Rating Indexes

UNITED STATES FIRE INS CO   C   Fair

Major Rating Factors: Fair overall results on stability tests (3.7 on a scale of 0 to 10). Weak profitability index (2.4) with operating losses during 2010, 2011, 2012 and 2013. Average return on equity over the last five years has been poor at -2.5%.

Other Rating Factors: Good overall long-term capitalization (6.3) based on good current risk adjusted capital (moderate loss scenario). However, capital levels have fluctuated during prior years. History of adequate reserve strength (5.7) as reserves have been consistently at an acceptable level. Excellent liquidity (7.2) with ample operational cash flow and liquid investments.

Principal Business: Group accident & health (30%), inland marine (19%), workers compensation (15%), other liability (11%), ocean marine (8%), auto liability (6%), and other lines (11%).

Principal Investments: Investment grade bonds (60%), misc. investments (37%), cash (2%), and non investment grade bonds (1%).

Investments in Affiliates: 15%

Group Affiliation: Fairfax Financial

Licensed in: All states, the District of Columbia and Puerto Rico

Commenced Business: April 1824

Address: 305 Madison Avenue, Morristown, NJ 07960

Phone: (973) 490-6600   **Domicile State:** DE   **NAIC Code:** 21113

Data Date	Rating	RACR #1	RACR #2	Loss Ratio %	Total Assets ($mil)	Capital ($mil)	Net Premium ($mil)	Net Income ($mil)
6-14	C	1.26	0.95	N/A	3,271.1	955.1	484.6	50.3
6-13	C	1.47	1.09	N/A	3,214.0	967.7	437.8	-28.3
2013	C	1.14	0.87	71.4	3,154.5	812.1	971.7	-75.7
2012	C	1.42	1.07	81.2	2,924.1	881.7	810.0	-50.1
2011	C	1.39	1.06	81.0	2,722.9	894.8	697.3	-43.8
2010	C	1.34	1.03	79.5	2,511.8	901.2	462.7	-24.7
2009	C	1.44	1.03	73.7	2,743.4	1,055.5	456.0	41.3

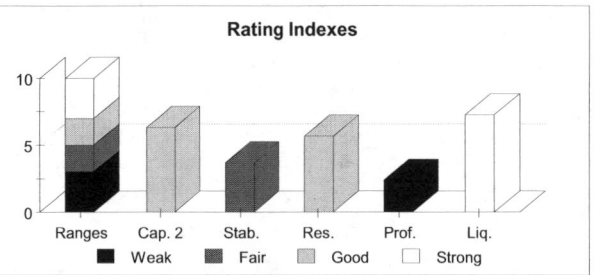

Rating Indexes

UNITED TEACHER ASSOCIATES INSURANCE COMPANY   C   Fair

Major Rating Factors: Fair overall results on stability tests (4.2 on a scale of 0 to 10). Good quality investment portfolio (5.4) despite mixed results such as: substantial holdings of BBB bonds but junk bond exposure equal to 53% of capital. Weak profitability (2.5). Return on equity has been low, averaging -2.4%.
Other Rating Factors: Strong capitalization (7.3) based on excellent risk adjusted capital (severe loss scenario). Excellent liquidity (7.2).
Principal Business: Individual health insurance (79%), group health insurance (13%), individual life insurance (3%), reinsurance (3%), and group retirement contracts (2%).
Principal Investments: NonCMO investment grade bonds (60%), CMOs and structured securities (28%), noninv. grade bonds (5%), common & preferred stock (4%), and policy loans (2%).
Investments in Affiliates: None
Group Affiliation: American Financial Group Inc
Licensed in: All states except NH, NY, RI, VT
Commenced Business: January 1959
Address: 5508 Parkcrest Dr, Austin, TX 78731
Phone: (512) 451-2224   **Domicile State:** TX   **NAIC Code:** 63479

Data Date	Rating	RACR #1	RACR #2	Total Assets ($mil)	Capital ($mil)	Net Premium ($mil)	Net Income ($mil)
6-14	C	2.14	1.18	977.5	85.4	38.0	2.4
6-13	C	1.82	0.93	897.5	60.4	39.2	-1.5
2013	C	2.13	1.16	940.0	84.4	77.7	3.5
2012	C	1.69	0.84	839.3	47.9	52.8	-14.7
2011	B-	1.51	0.92	847.1	66.9	205.7	7.2
2010	B-	1.48	0.92	772.0	69.1	224.0	8.3
2009	B-	1.38	0.86	736.9	66.2	235.8	-7.4

Rating Indexes

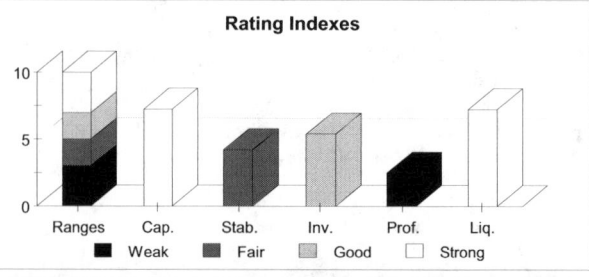

Ranges | Cap. | Stab. | Inv. | Prof. | Liq.
■ Weak   ■ Fair   □ Good   □ Strong

UNITED WORLD LIFE INSURANCE COMPANY *   B+   Good

Major Rating Factors: Good overall results on stability tests (5.3 on a scale of 0 to 10) despite negative cash flow from operations for 2013. Other stability subfactors include good operational trends and excellent risk diversification. Good overall profitability (6.7). Return on equity has been low, averaging 3.2%. Strong capitalization (8.0) based on excellent risk adjusted capital (severe loss scenario).
Other Rating Factors: High quality investment portfolio (7.6). Excellent liquidity (7.0).
Principal Business: Individual health insurance (100%).
Principal Investments: NonCMO investment grade bonds (65%), CMOs and structured securities (28%), policy loans (1%), noninv. grade bonds (1%), and cash (1%).
Investments in Affiliates: None
Group Affiliation: Mutual Of Omaha Group
Licensed in: All states except CT, NY, PR
Commenced Business: April 1970
Address: Mutual Of Omaha Plaza, Omaha, NE 68175
Phone: (402) 342-7600   **Domicile State:** NE   **NAIC Code:** 72850

Data Date	Rating	RACR #1	RACR #2	Total Assets ($mil)	Capital ($mil)	Net Premium ($mil)	Net Income ($mil)
6-14	B+	3.99	1.67	107.9	48.1	0.6	0.2
6-13	B+	3.79	1.58	99.9	47.9	0.7	0.5
2013	B+	4.19	1.76	114.9	48.6	1.6	1.2
2012	B+	3.89	1.63	103.1	47.3	1.7	0.1
2011	B+	3.67	1.53	106.1	47.3	1.9	1.9
2010	B+	3.44	1.44	101.0	45.4	2.0	2.3
2009	B+	3.22	1.35	92.8	43.2	2.2	2.3

Adverse Trends in Operations

Decrease in premium volume from 2012 to 2013 (7%)
Change in asset mix during 2013 (4%)
Decrease in asset base during 2012 (3%)
Increase in policy surrenders from 2010 to 2011 (36%)
Decrease in premium volume from 2009 to 2010 (9%)

UNITEDHEALTHCARE BENEFITS OF TEXAS *   B+   Good

Major Rating Factors: Good overall results on stability tests (6.5 on a scale of 0 to 10) based on steady enrollment growth, averaging 6% over the past five years. Rating is significantly influenced by the fair financial results of UnitedHealth Group Inc. Excellent profitability (9.3). Strong capitalization index (9.0) based on excellent current risk-adjusted capital (severe loss scenario).
Other Rating Factors: High quality investment portfolio (9.9). Excellent liquidity (7.0) with sufficient resources (cash flows and marketable investments) to handle a spike in claims.
Principal Business: Medicare (96%), comp med (3%)
Mem Phys: 13: 52,045   **12:** 51,538   **13 MLR** 83.5%   **/ 13 Admin Exp** N/A
Enroll(000): Q2 14: 189   **13:** 193   **12:** 181   **Med Exp PMPM:** $885
Principal Investments: Long-term bonds (65%), cash and equiv (35%)
Provider Compensation ($000): Contr fee ($1,050,179), capitation ($799,108), FFS ($120,088), bonus arrang ($35,941)
Total Member Encounters: Phys (1,063,980), non-phys (117,895)
Group Affiliation: UnitedHealth Group Inc
Licensed in: TX
Address: 5800 Granite Pkwy Suite 900, Plano, TX 75024-6619
Phone: (469) 633-8512   **Dom State:** TX   **Commenced Bus:** July 1986

Data Date	Rating	RACR #1	RACR #2	Total Assets ($mil)	Capital ($mil)	Net Premium ($mil)	Net Income ($mil)
6-14	B+	2.93	2.44	703.3	297.2	1,249.1	56.7
6-13	B+	3.15	2.63	655.5	274.9	1,212.1	68.8
2013	B+	3.11	2.59	599.2	315.8	2,412.0	151.4
2012	B+	2.80	2.34	585.8	242.3	2,274.1	189.2
2011	B+	2.62	2.18	432.2	226.2	2,192.2	178.8
2010	B+	2.47	2.06	386.7	213.4	2,013.6	114.6
2009	B+	2.19	1.83	351.8	187.4	1,896.3	96.8

Rating Indexes

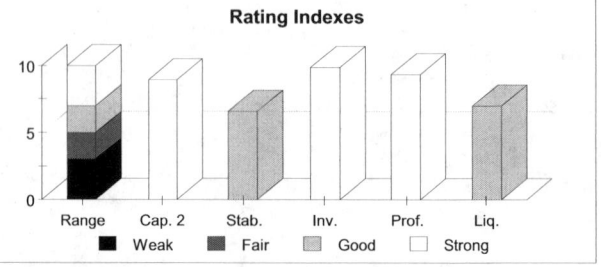

Range | Cap. 2 | Stab. | Inv. | Prof. | Liq.
■ Weak   ■ Fair   □ Good   □ Strong

UNITEDHEALTHCARE COMMUNITY PLAN INC   B   Good

Major Rating Factors: Good liquidity (6.8 on a scale of 0 to 10) with sufficient resources (cash flows and marketable investments) to handle a spike in claims. Fair profitability index (4.9). Strong capitalization index (7.6) based on excellent current risk-adjusted capital (severe loss scenario).
Other Rating Factors: High quality investment portfolio (9.9). Excellent overall results on stability tests (8.0). Rating is significantly influenced by the fair financial results of UnitedHealth Group Inc.
Principal Business: Medicaid (93%), Medicare (7%)
Mem Phys: 13: 7,844   **12:** 6,777   **13 MLR** 91.9%   **/ 13 Admin Exp** N/A
Enroll(000): Q2 14: 273   **13:** 238   **12:** 244   **Med Exp PMPM:** $289
Principal Investments: Cash and equiv (75%), long-term bonds (25%)
Provider Compensation ($000): Contr fee ($525,276), capitation ($251,221), FFS ($26,369), bonus arrang ($3,162)
Total Member Encounters: Phys (1,708,898), non-phys (871,094)
Group Affiliation: UnitedHealth Group Inc
Licensed in: MI
Address: 26957 Northwestern Hwy Ste 400, Southfield, MI 48033
Phone: (248) 559-5656   **Dom State:** MI   **Commenced Bus:** October 1994

Data Date	Rating	RACR #1	RACR #2	Total Assets ($mil)	Capital ($mil)	Net Premium ($mil)	Net Income ($mil)
6-14	B	1.83	1.53	242.2	81.9	505.6	6.9
6-13	B	1.73	1.44	192.8	66.9	445.0	-5.5
2013	B	1.71	1.43	213.4	76.0	897.8	-3.2
2012	B	1.82	1.52	175.6	70.7	875.4	4.2
2011	B	1.75	1.46	174.3	67.4	890.6	2.5
2010	B	1.97	1.65	159.6	67.2	800.2	3.3
2009	B-	1.44	1.20	111.3	40.1	671.3	-0.7

Rating Indexes — Range, Cap. 2, Stab., Inv., Prof., Liq.
■ Weak   ▨ Fair   ▩ Good   □ Strong

UNITEDHEALTHCARE COMMUNITY PLAN TX *   B+   Good

Major Rating Factors: Good liquidity (6.6 on a scale of 0 to 10) with sufficient resources (cash flows and marketable investments) to handle a spike in claims. Excellent profitability (9.2). Strong capitalization index (8.2) based on excellent current risk-adjusted capital (severe loss scenario).
Other Rating Factors: High quality investment portfolio (9.7). Excellent overall results on stability tests (7.6) based on healthy premium and capital growth during 2013. Rating is significantly influenced by the fair financial results of UnitedHealth Group Inc.
Principal Business: Medicaid (67%), Medicare (31%), comp med (2%)
Mem Phys: 13: 39,823   **12:** 37,942   **13 MLR** 85.4%   **/ 13 Admin Exp** N/A
Enroll(000): Q2 14: 219   **13:** 218   **12:** 201   **Med Exp PMPM:** $486
Principal Investments: Long-term bonds (81%), cash and equiv (19%)
Provider Compensation ($000): Contr fee ($1,090,741), FFS ($131,253), capitation ($10,207), bonus arrang ($70)
Total Member Encounters: Phys (2,913,544), non-phys (1,495,864)
Group Affiliation: UnitedHealth Group Inc
Licensed in: TX
Address: 9702 Bissonnet Ste 2200W, Houston, TX 77036
Phone: (713) 778-8664   **Dom State:** TX   **Commenced Bus:** August 2001

Data Date	Rating	RACR #1	RACR #2	Total Assets ($mil)	Capital ($mil)	Net Premium ($mil)	Net Income ($mil)
6-14	B+	2.32	1.93	394.8	166.8	747.6	6.7
6-13	B+	2.17	1.81	319.8	138.5	704.5	22.3
2013	B+	2.24	1.87	373.4	160.7	1,454.2	44.8
2012	B+	1.85	1.54	287.4	115.8	1,185.7	8.8
2011	B+	3.05	2.54	205.8	112.6	759.7	34.1
2010	B+	2.33	1.94	184.5	78.6	685.8	30.7
2009	B+	2.20	1.83	178.2	74.8	622.9	17.1

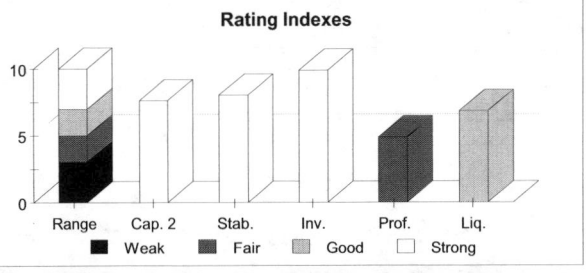

Rating Indexes — Range, Cap. 2, Stab., Inv., Prof., Liq.
■ Weak   ▨ Fair   ▩ Good   □ Strong

UNITEDHEALTHCARE COMMUNITYPLAN OHIO   B   Good

Major Rating Factors: Excellent profitability (9.9 on a scale of 0 to 10). Strong capitalization (10.0) based on excellent current risk-adjusted capital (severe loss scenario). High quality investment portfolio (9.9).
Other Rating Factors: Excellent liquidity (7.0) with sufficient resources (cash flows and marketable investments) to handle a spike in claims.
Principal Business: Medicaid (100%)
Mem Phys: 13: 33,432   **12:** 29,755   **13 MLR** 77.4%   **/ 13 Admin Exp** N/A
Enroll(000): Q2 14: 231   **13:** 168   **12:** 115   **Med Exp PMPM:** $307
Principal Investments: Long-term bonds (54%), cash and equiv (46%)
Provider Compensation ($000): Contr fee ($432,051), capitation ($51,560), bonus arrang ($747)
Total Member Encounters: Phys (1,682,813), non-phys (576,030)
Group Affiliation: UnitedHealth Group Inc
Licensed in: OH
Address: 1300 E Ninth St, Cleveland, OH 44114
Phone: (952) 979-6171   **Dom State:** OH   **Commenced Bus:** October 2005

Data Date	Rating	RACR #1	RACR #2	Total Assets ($mil)	Capital ($mil)	Net Premium ($mil)	Net Income ($mil)
6-14	B	4.62	3.85	335.0	145.8	458.7	15.4
6-13	B	4.82	4.01	170.3	118.9	261.0	12.4
2013	B	4.11	3.43	243.7	128.8	667.4	22.2
2012	B	4.37	3.65	163.4	107.1	532.7	36.2
2011	B	3.37	2.81	143.2	71.2	448.5	23.3
2010	B	3.23	2.69	119.6	60.4	413.1	32.8
2009	B	2.89	2.41	168.6	60.5	407.5	15.2

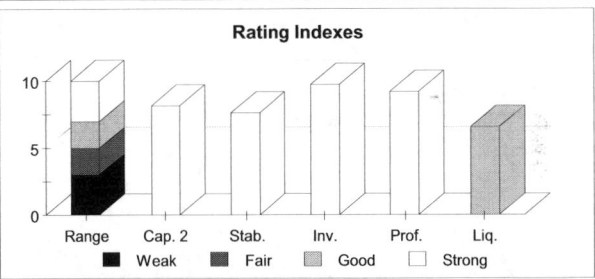

Rating Indexes — Range, Cap. 2, Stab., Inv., Prof., Liq.
■ Weak   ▨ Fair   ▩ Good   □ Strong

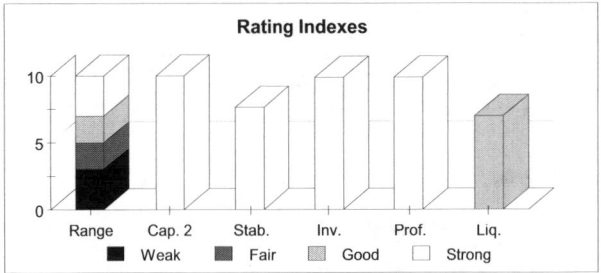

UNITEDHEALTHCARE INS CO RIVER VALLEY

B   **Good**

Major Rating Factors: Good liquidity (6.9 on a scale of 0 to 10) with sufficient resources (cash flows and marketable investments) to handle a spike in claims. Excellent profitability (9.3). Strong capitalization (8.5) based on excellent current risk-adjusted capital (severe loss scenario).
Other Rating Factors: High quality investment portfolio (9.9).
Principal Business: Comp med (99%)
Mem Phys: 13: 144,867 **12:** 113,308 **13 MLR** 81.3% **/ 13 Admin Exp** N/A
Enroll(000): Q2 14: 150 **13:** 149 **12:** 104 **Med Exp PMPM:** $240
Principal Investments: Long-term bonds (57%), cash and equiv (43%)
Provider Compensation ($000): Contr fee ($320,396), FFS ($28,256), capitation ($633), bonus arrang ($138)
Total Member Encounters: Phys (496,484), non-phys (84,633)
Group Affiliation: UnitedHealth Group Inc
Licensed in: AR, GA, IL, IA, OH, SC, TN
Address: 1300 River Dr, Moline, IL 61265
Phone: (309) 736-4600 **Dom State:** IL **Commenced Bus:** December 2004

Data Date	Rating	RACR #1	RACR #2	Total Assets ($mil)	Capital ($mil)	Net Premium ($mil)	Net Income ($mil)
6-14	B	2.58	2.15	146.6	61.7	282.5	11.8
6-13	B-	2.32	1.93	98.9	41.5	200.7	6.0
2013	B	2.15	1.79	115.5	50.8	443.3	14.6
2012	B-	2.11	1.75	89.4	37.4	327.8	8.4
2011	B-	1.30	1.08	60.4	16.3	228.3	3.9
2010	B-	1.85	1.54	29.8	11.5	107.1	4.2
2009	C+	2.19	1.82	26.0	8.3	69.3	0.3

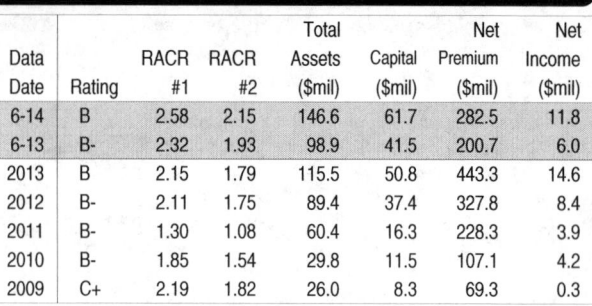

Rating Indexes

UNITEDHEALTHCARE LIFE INSURANCE COMPANY

B   **Good**

Major Rating Factors: Good overall results on stability tests (5.8 on a scale of 0 to 10) despite fair financial strength of affiliated UnitedHealth Group Inc. Other stability subfactors include good operational trends and excellent risk diversification. Strong overall capitalization (7.3) based on excellent risk adjusted capital (severe loss scenario). Nevertheless, capital levels have fluctuated during prior years. High quality investment portfolio (8.4).
Other Rating Factors: Excellent profitability (7.0) with operating gains in each of the last five years. Excellent liquidity (7.2).
Principal Business: Group health insurance (85%), individual health insurance (15%), and group life insurance (1%).
Principal Investments: NonCMO investment grade bonds (86%) and CMOs and structured securities (17%).
Investments in Affiliates: None
Group Affiliation: UnitedHealth Group Inc
Licensed in: All states except AK, CT, HI, ME, MA, NH, NJ, NY, RI, VT, PR
Commenced Business: December 1982
Address: 3100 AMS Blvd, Green Bay, WI 54313
Phone: (800) 232-5432 **Domicile State:** WI **NAIC Code:** 97179

Data Date	Rating	RACR #1	RACR #2	Total Assets ($mil)	Capital ($mil)	Net Premium ($mil)	Net Income ($mil)
6-14	B	1.50	1.20	81.0	35.6	93.3	1.5
6-13	B	1.71	1.38	51.6	27.8	43.6	4.2
2013	B	2.11	1.69	57.0	29.3	84.8	7.3
2012	B	1.50	1.21	49.0	23.8	99.9	8.9
2011	B	1.74	1.40	65.7	32.3	119.4	10.3
2010	B	1.82	1.48	70.0	41.9	142.3	24.4
2009	B	1.71	1.40	79.6	39.9	166.3	18.3

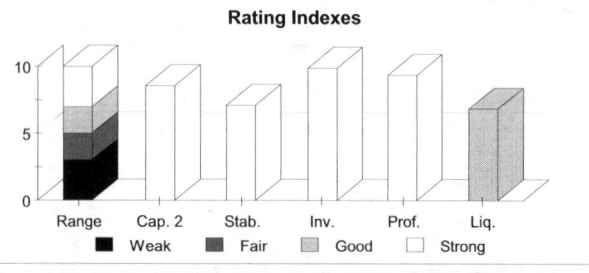

UnitedHealth Group Inc Composite Group Rating: C+ Largest Group Members	Assets ($mil)	Rating
UNITED HEALTHCARE INS CO	14513	C
OXFORD HEALTH INS INC	2078	C+
UNITED HEALTHCARE INS CO OF NY	1983	B-
OXFORD HEALTH PLANS (NY) INC	1820	A+
UNITEDHEALTHCARE PLAN RIVER VALLEY	1094	B+

UNITEDHEALTHCARE OF NEW MEXICO INC

E   **Very Weak**

Major Rating Factors: Good overall profitability index (5.0 on a scale of 0 to 10). Strong capitalization (10.0) based on excellent current risk-adjusted capital (severe loss scenario). High quality investment portfolio (9.9).
Other Rating Factors: Excellent liquidity (7.0) with sufficient resources (cash flows and marketable investments) to handle a spike in claims.
Principal Business: Medicaid (100%)
Mem Phys: 13: 5,640 **12:** 5,472 **13 MLR** 81.7% **/ 13 Admin Exp** N/A
Enroll(000): Q2 14: 62 **13:** 21 **12:** 20 **Med Exp PMPM:** $1,548
Principal Investments: Long-term bonds (56%), cash and equiv (44%)
Provider Compensation ($000): Contr fee ($295,221), FFS ($64,123), capitation ($10,671)
Total Member Encounters: Phys (317,909), non-phys (753,753)
Group Affiliation: UnitedHealth Group Inc
Licensed in: NM
Address: 8220 San Pedro NE Suite 300, Albuquerque, NM 87113
Phone: (505) 449-4131 **Dom State:** NM **Commenced Bus:** October 2008

Data Date	Rating	RACR #1	RACR #2	Total Assets ($mil)	Capital ($mil)	Net Premium ($mil)	Net Income ($mil)
6-14	E	4.49	3.74	255.5	107.3	388.0	12.1
6-13	E	5.43	4.52	178.6	114.7	225.3	7.0
2013	E	4.81	4.01	172.5	115.6	457.1	16.0
2012	E	5.14	4.29	157.0	107.9	416.5	21.9
2011	E	5.61	4.68	169.5	116.8	412.1	20.3
2010	E	4.95	4.13	183.4	106.8	411.8	33.1
2009	E	0.86	0.72	121.6	22.7	354.5	-36.9

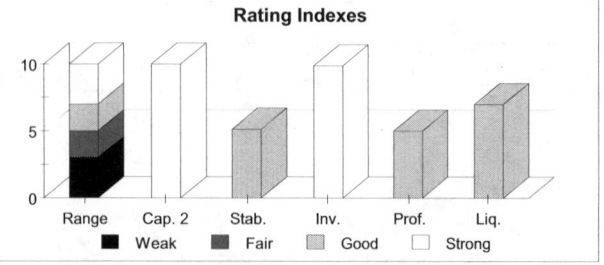

Rating Indexes

UNITEDHEALTHCARE OF OREGON   B-   Good

Major Rating Factors: Good overall results on stability tests (5.1 on a scale of 0 to 10). Rating is significantly influenced by the fair financial results of UnitedHealth Group Inc. Good liquidity (6.9) with sufficient resources (cash flows and marketable investments) to handle a spike in claims. Excellent profitability (8.6).

Other Rating Factors: Strong capitalization index (10.0) based on excellent current risk-adjusted capital (severe loss scenario). High quality investment portfolio (9.9).

Principal Business: Medicare (95%), comp med (5%)

Mem Phys: 13: 12,325   **12:** 11,775   **13 MLR** 81.4%   / **13 Admin Exp** N/A

Enroll(000): Q2 14: 21   **13:** 20   **12:** 16   **Med Exp PMPM:** $713

Principal Investments: Long-term bonds (78%), cash and equiv (22%)

Provider Compensation ($000): Contr fee ($121,541), capitation ($35,397), FFS ($3,088), bonus arrang ($718)

Total Member Encounters: Phys (111,263), non-phys (13,172)

Group Affiliation: UnitedHealth Group Inc

Licensed in: OR, WA

Address: 5 Centerpointe Dr Suite 600, Lake Oswego, OR 97035

Phone: (503) 603-7355   **Dom State:** OR   **Commenced Bus:** February 1987

Data Date	Rating	RACR #1	RACR #2	Total Assets ($mil)	Capital ($mil)	Net Premium ($mil)	Net Income ($mil)
6-14	B-	3.75	3.13	69.0	37.4	116.4	4.5
6-13	C	3.34	2.78	52.1	28.3	102.5	8.0
2013	B-	3.32	2.77	56.4	32.9	202.0	12.4
2012	C	2.45	2.05	44.4	20.3	186.3	14.0
2011	B-	3.41	2.84	53.7	32.6	207.1	15.9
2010	C	2.90	2.42	50.5	29.6	221.9	13.8
2009	C	2.31	1.92	55.0	28.4	253.4	12.7

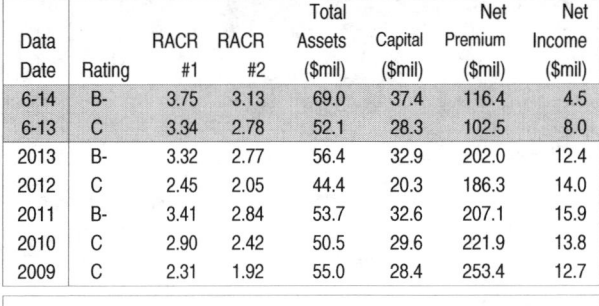

Rating Indexes

UNITEDHEALTHCARE OF PENNSYLVANIA INC   B   Good

Major Rating Factors: Good overall profitability index (5.2 on a scale of 0 to 10). Good overall results on stability tests (5.2) despite a decline in enrollment during 2013. Rating is significantly influenced by the fair financial results of UnitedHealth Group Inc. Good liquidity (6.8) with sufficient resources (cash flows and marketable investments) to handle a spike in claims.

Other Rating Factors: Strong capitalization index (8.3) based on excellent current risk-adjusted capital (severe loss scenario). High quality investment portfolio (9.9).

Principal Business: Medicaid (76%), Medicare (20%), comp med (4%)

Mem Phys: 13: 26,902   **12:** 25,293   **13 MLR** 85.2%   / **13 Admin Exp** N/A

Enroll(000): Q2 14: 202   **13:** 221   **12:** 233   **Med Exp PMPM:** $353

Principal Investments: Long-term bonds (66%), cash and equiv (34%)

Provider Compensation ($000): Contr fee ($737,225), capitation ($83,221), FFS ($74,290), bonus arrang ($34), other ($52,315)

Total Member Encounters: Phys (2,235,547), non-phys (413,329)

Group Affiliation: UnitedHealth Group Inc

Licensed in: PA

Address: 1388 Beulah Rd Bldg 801,4th fl, Pittsburgh, PA 15235

Phone: (412) 858-4000   **Dom State:** PA   **Commenced Bus:** April 1996

Data Date	Rating	RACR #1	RACR #2	Total Assets ($mil)	Capital ($mil)	Net Premium ($mil)	Net Income ($mil)
6-14	B	2.41	2.01	314.7	138.0	456.0	-10.0
6-13	B	2.39	1.99	273.5	139.3	537.9	3.4
2013	B	2.58	2.15	279.8	148.4	1,101.8	12.3
2012	B	2.32	1.93	282.4	135.3	1,160.9	16.8
2011	B	2.35	1.95	343.6	149.8	1,232.5	29.6
2010	B-	2.66	2.22	337.5	125.0	953.3	13.5
2009	B	2.76	2.30	290.1	140.9	862.8	12.9

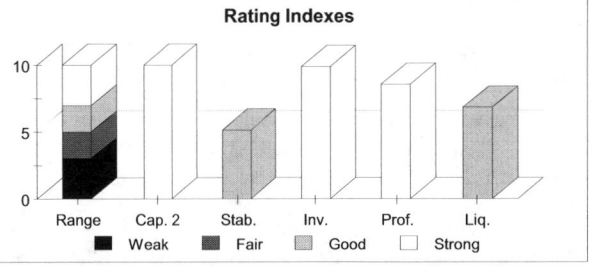

Rating Indexes

UNITEDHEALTHCARE OF WASHINGTON INC   B   Good

Major Rating Factors: Good liquidity (6.6 on a scale of 0 to 10) with sufficient resources (cash flows and marketable investments) to handle a spike in claims. Fair profitability index (4.6). Strong capitalization (10.0) based on excellent current risk-adjusted capital (severe loss scenario).

Other Rating Factors: High quality investment portfolio (9.8).

Principal Business: Medicare (73%), Medicaid (26%), comp med (1%)

Mem Phys: 13: 24,548   **12:** 22,812   **13 MLR** 89.9%   / **13 Admin Exp** N/A

Enroll(000): Q2 14: 254   **13:** 129   **12:** 97   **Med Exp PMPM:** $505

Principal Investments: Long-term bonds (74%), cash and equiv (26%)

Provider Compensation ($000): Contr fee ($604,656), capitation ($69,275), FFS ($15,162)

Total Member Encounters: Phys (914,446), non-phys (229,338)

Group Affiliation: UnitedHealth Group Inc

Licensed in: WA

Address: 7525 SE 24th, Mercer Island, WA 98040-9005

Phone: (503) 603-7106   **Dom State:** WA   **Commenced Bus:** December 1986

Data Date	Rating	RACR #1	RACR #2	Total Assets ($mil)	Capital ($mil)	Net Premium ($mil)	Net Income ($mil)
6-14	B	4.50	3.75	476.2	197.7	685.6	12.5
6-13	B	3.32	2.76	206.2	91.1	398.8	2.8
2013	B	2.73	2.28	276.1	117.5	783.7	-15.9
2012	B	3.24	2.70	195.9	88.7	567.8	17.3
2011	B	3.43	2.86	146.3	89.0	510.6	25.5
2010	B-	3.11	2.59	118.0	71.2	440.4	27.2
2009	C+	3.74	3.11	128.7	81.1	417.6	32.0

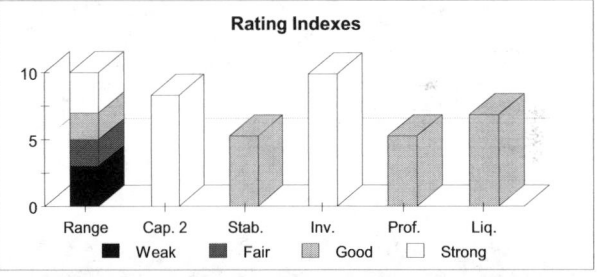

Rating Indexes

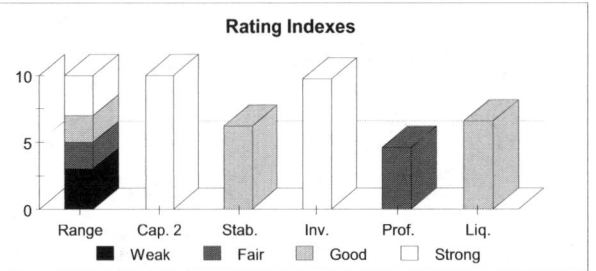

UNITEDHEALTHCARE PLAN RIVER VALLEY *   B+   Good

Major Rating Factors: Good liquidity (6.8 on a scale of 0 to 10) with sufficient resources (cash flows and marketable investments) to handle a spike in claims. Excellent profitability (8.9). Strong capitalization index (8.4) based on excellent current risk-adjusted capital (severe loss scenario).

Other Rating Factors: High quality investment portfolio (9.9). Excellent overall results on stability tests (7.4). Rating is significantly influenced by the fair financial results of UnitedHealth Group Inc.

Principal Business: Medicaid (63%), Medicare (29%), comp med (8%)

Mem Phys: 13: 124,482 **12:** 117,714 **13 MLR** 82.6% **/ 13 Admin Exp** N/A

Enroll(000): Q2 14: 788 **13:** 760 **12:** 781 **Med Exp PMPM:** $366

Principal Investments: Long-term bonds (73%), cash and equiv (25%), other (2%)

Provider Compensation ($000): Contr fee ($3,093,175), FFS ($232,194), capitation ($35,374), bonus arrang ($2,016)

Total Member Encounters: Phys (8,329,583), non-phys (4,609,374)

Group Affiliation: UnitedHealth Group Inc

Licensed in: IL, IA, TN, VA

Address: 1300 River Drive Suite 200, Moline, IL 61265

Phone: (309) 736-4600 **Dom State:** IL **Commenced Bus:** December 1985

Data Date	Rating	RACR #1	RACR #2	Total Assets ($mil)	Capital ($mil)	Net Premium ($mil)	Net Income ($mil)
6-14	B+	2.44	2.04	1,172.5	517.3	2,100.6	101.5
6-13	B+	2.26	1.89	1,047.5	466.8	2,013.3	62.9
2013	B+	2.43	2.02	1,093.7	513.4	4,071.6	152.0
2012	B+	2.15	1.79	1,017.4	441.2	4,011.4	170.0
2011	B+	2.28	1.90	1,010.0	452.8	3,923.6	211.9
2010	B+	2.17	1.81	1,126.6	359.8	3,186.8	129.4
2009	B+	2.10	1.75	814.1	268.0	2,370.7	76.3

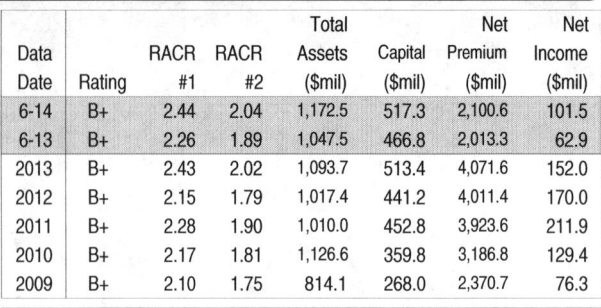

Rating Indexes

UNITY HEALTH PLANS INS CORP   B-   Good

Major Rating Factors: Fair profitability index (3.9 on a scale of 0 to 10). Fair quality investment portfolio (3.3). Good overall results on stability tests (6.2) based on healthy premium and capital growth during 2013.

Other Rating Factors: Good liquidity (6.8) with sufficient resources (cash flows and marketable investments) to handle a spike in claims. Strong capitalization index (7.2) based on excellent current risk-adjusted capital (severe loss scenario).

Principal Business: Comp med (95%), Medicaid (4%)

Mem Phys: 13: 3,857 **12:** 3,726 **13 MLR** 92.6% **/ 13 Admin Exp** N/A

Enroll(000): Q2 14: 162 **13:** 150 **12:** 120 **Med Exp PMPM:** $336

Principal Investments: Cash and equiv (44%), long-term bonds (40%), nonaffiliate common stock (15%), real estate (1%)

Provider Compensation ($000): Capitation ($563,410), other ($7,994)

Total Member Encounters: Phys (659,706), non-phys (693,928)

Group Affiliation: University Health Care Inc

Licensed in: WI

Address: 840 Carolina St, Sauk City, WI 53583

Phone: (608) 643-2491 **Dom State:** WI **Commenced Bus:** January 1984

Data Date	Rating	RACR #1	RACR #2	Total Assets ($mil)	Capital ($mil)	Net Premium ($mil)	Net Income ($mil)
6-14	B-	1.52	1.27	137.4	52.8	360.4	-1.9
6-13	B	1.18	0.99	105.9	47.3	311.1	0.5
2013	B	1.61	1.34	154.9	55.8	637.0	-0.7
2012	B	1.14	0.95	97.8	45.6	485.2	-0.1
2011	B	1.20	1.00	80.2	38.8	401.1	1.3
2010	B	1.33	1.10	87.8	41.1	376.9	6.0
2009	B-	1.45	1.21	76.6	39.8	355.0	8.1

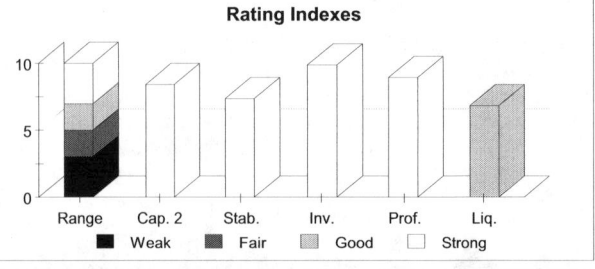

Rating Indexes

UNIVERSAL CARE   E-   Very Weak

Major Rating Factors: Weak profitability index (0.9 on a scale of 0 to 10). Poor capitalization index (0.0) based on weak current risk-adjusted capital (severe loss scenario). Weak overall results on stability tests (0.0).

Other Rating Factors: Good liquidity (6.8) with sufficient resources (cash flows and marketable investments) to handle a spike in claims.

Principal Business: Medicare (80%), Medicaid (19%)

Mem Phys: 13: N/A **12:** N/A **13 MLR** 87.7% **/ 13 Admin Exp** N/A

Enroll(000): Q2 14: 6 **13:** 21 **12:** 18 **Med Exp PMPM:** $200

Principal Investments ($000): Cash and equiv ($1,525)

Provider Compensation ($000): None

Total Member Encounters: N/A

Group Affiliation: None

Licensed in: CA

Address: 1600 E Hill St, Signal Hill, CA 90806-3682

Phone: (562) 424-6200 **Dom State:** CA **Commenced Bus:** November 1985

Data Date	Rating	RACR #1	RACR #2	Total Assets ($mil)	Capital ($mil)	Net Premium ($mil)	Net Income ($mil)
6-14	E-	N/A	N/A	24.6	-1.6	30.1	3.3
6-13	E-	N/A	N/A	17.0	-1.1	24.8	0.5
2013	E-	N/A	N/A	22.1	-4.9	50.1	-3.3
2012	E-	N/A	N/A	13.5	-1.6	40.5	-2.4
2011	E	0.12	0.08	12.0	0.5	35.5	-0.9
2010	E	0.10	0.07	8.5	0.4	32.1	-0.2
2009	E-	0.13	0.08	11.7	0.7	41.1	1.2

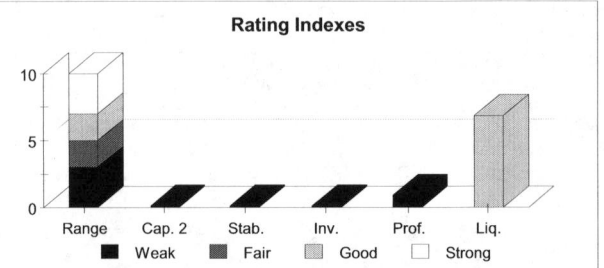

Rating Indexes

UNIVERSITY HEALTH ALLIANCE   C+   Fair

Major Rating Factors: Fair quality investment portfolio (2.9 on a scale of 0 to 10). Good liquidity (6.8) with sufficient resources (cash flows and marketable investments) to handle a spike in claims. Excellent profitability (9.1).
Other Rating Factors: Strong capitalization (7.5) based on excellent current risk-adjusted capital (severe loss scenario).
Principal Business: Comp med (80%), dental (3%), other (16%)
Mem Phys: 13: N/A **12:** N/A **13 MLR** 84.2% **/ 13 Admin Exp** N/A
Enroll(000): Q2 14: 51 **13:** 52 **12:** 49 **Med Exp PMPM:** $288
Principal Investments: Nonaffiliate common stock (67%), long-term bonds (17%), cash and equiv (16%)
Provider Compensation ($000): FFS ($136,152), contr fee ($36,282), capitation ($5,119), bonus arrang ($204), other ($2,192)
Total Member Encounters: Phys (335,219), non-phys (141,428)
Group Affiliation: None
Licensed in: HI
Address: 700 Bishop St Ste 300, Honolulu, HI 96813
Phone: (808) 532-4000 **Dom State:** HI **Commenced Bus:** March 1988

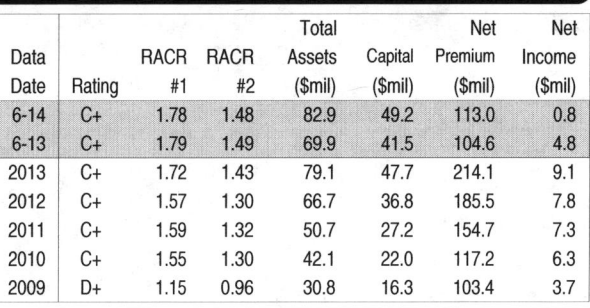

Data Date	Rating	RACR #1	RACR #2	Total Assets ($mil)	Capital ($mil)	Net Premium ($mil)	Net Income ($mil)
6-14	C+	1.78	1.48	82.9	49.2	113.0	0.8
6-13	C+	1.79	1.49	69.9	41.5	104.6	4.8
2013	C+	1.72	1.43	79.1	47.7	214.1	9.1
2012	C+	1.57	1.30	66.7	36.8	185.5	7.8
2011	C+	1.59	1.32	50.7	27.2	154.7	7.3
2010	C+	1.55	1.30	42.1	22.0	117.2	6.3
2009	D+	1.15	0.96	30.8	16.3	103.4	3.7

Rating Indexes

Range Cap. 2 Stab. Inv. Prof. Liq.
■ Weak ▨ Fair ▤ Good ☐ Strong

UNIVERSITY HEALTH CARE INC *   B+   Good

Major Rating Factors: Good overall results on stability tests (5.7 on a scale of 0 to 10). Good liquidity (6.4) with sufficient resources (cash flows and marketable investments) to handle a spike in claims. Strong capitalization index (8.1) based on excellent current risk-adjusted capital (severe loss scenario).
Other Rating Factors: High quality investment portfolio (7.1). Fair profitability index (3.4).
Principal Business: Medicaid (100%)
Mem Phys: 13: 8,681 **12:** 6,245 **13 MLR** 94.3% **/ 13 Admin Exp** N/A
Enroll(000): Q2 14: 202 **13:** 132 **12:** 178 **Med Exp PMPM:** $439
Principal Investments: Long-term bonds (43%), nonaffiliate common stock (37%), cash and equiv (20%)
Provider Compensation ($000): Contr fee ($557,703), capitation ($86,793), FFS ($13,791)
Total Member Encounters: Phys (866,270), non-phys (737,044)
Group Affiliation: Univ of Louisville Medical School
Licensed in: KY
Address: 5100 Commerce Crossings Dr, Louisville, KY 40229
Phone: (502) 585-7900 **Dom State:** KY **Commenced Bus:** October 2000

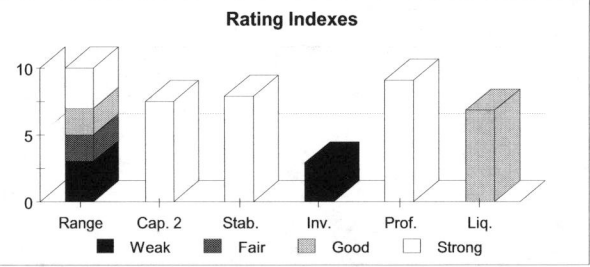

Data Date	Rating	RACR #1	RACR #2	Total Assets ($mil)	Capital ($mil)	Net Premium ($mil)	Net Income ($mil)
6-14	B+	2.21	1.84	261.3	124.7	559.1	24.9
6-13	B+	1.55	1.29	176.8	98.3	323.1	-0.8
2013	B+	1.80	1.50	177.6	100.7	685.4	-3.5
2012	B+	1.47	1.23	184.1	94.1	795.7	-1.8
2011	B+	1.27	1.06	213.0	93.2	929.9	-16.4
2010	A-	1.45	1.20	200.8	98.7	912.4	6.1
2009	B+	1.39	1.16	193.7	91.2	907.3	6.5

Rating Indexes

Range Cap. 2 Stab. Inv. Prof. Liq.
■ Weak ▨ Fair ▤ Good ☐ Strong

UNUM LIFE INSURANCE COMPANY OF AMERICA   C+   Fair

Major Rating Factors: Fair quality investment portfolio (4.0 on a scale of 0 to 10) with large holdings of BBB rated bonds in addition to significant exposure to junk bonds. Fair overall results on stability tests (4.8) including negative cash flow from operations for 2013. Good overall profitability (6.8). Return on equity has been good over the last five years, averaging 13.6%.
Other Rating Factors: Strong capitalization (7.5) based on excellent risk adjusted capital (severe loss scenario). Excellent liquidity (7.1).
Principal Business: Group health insurance (60%), group life insurance (29%), individual health insurance (9%), reinsurance (2%), and individual life insurance (1%).
Principal Investments: NonCMO investment grade bonds (76%), noninv. grade bonds (9%), CMOs and structured securities (8%), and mortgages in good standing (5%).
Investments in Affiliates: None
Group Affiliation: Unum Group
Licensed in: All states, the District of Columbia and Puerto Rico
Commenced Business: September 1966
Address: 2211 Congress St, Portland, ME 04122
Phone: (207) 770-9306 **Domicile State:** ME **NAIC Code:** 62235

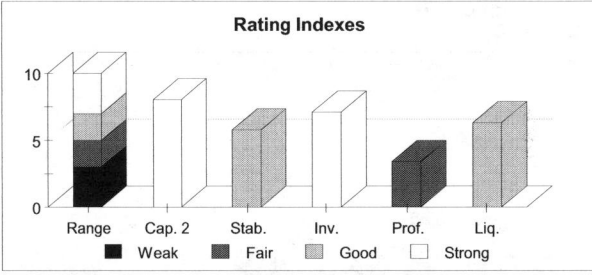

Data Date	Rating	RACR #1	RACR #2	Total Assets ($mil)	Capital ($mil)	Net Premium ($mil)	Net Income ($mil)
6-14	C+	2.41	1.30	19,334.6	1,517.4	1,437.4	88.8
6-13	C+	2.54	1.36	18,917.8	1,579.4	1,416.8	124.3
2013	C+	2.49	1.34	19,078.5	1,557.9	2,794.2	176.2
2012	C+	2.57	1.38	18,879.8	1,573.5	2,702.0	202.9
2011	C+	2.65	1.42	18,303.5	1,548.8	2,603.1	199.0
2010	C+	2.73	1.48	17,822.8	1,539.6	2,612.5	246.3
2009	C+	2.73	1.48	17,214.8	1,541.1	2,634.5	249.4

Junk Bonds as a % of Capital

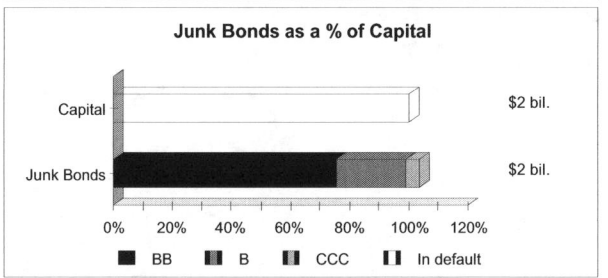

Capital $2 bil.

Junk Bonds $2 bil.

0% 20% 40% 60% 80% 100% 120%
■ BB ▨ B ▤ CCC ▥ In default

UPMC FOR YOU INC *

B+   **Good**

Major Rating Factors: Excellent profitability (8.1 on a scale of 0 to 10). Strong capitalization (7.3) based on excellent current risk-adjusted capital (severe loss scenario). High quality investment portfolio (9.4).
Other Rating Factors: Excellent liquidity (7.0) with sufficient resources (cash flows and marketable investments) to handle a spike in claims.
Principal Business: Medicaid (85%), Medicare (15%)
Mem Phys: 13: 13,454   **12:** 12,664   **13 MLR** 86.2%   **/ 13 Admin Exp** N/A
Enroll(000): Q2 14: 278   **13:** 269   **12:** 250   **Med Exp PMPM:** $425
Principal Investments: Long-term bonds (68%), cash and equiv (26%), other (5%)
Provider Compensation ($000): Contr fee ($1,317,383), capitation ($380)
Total Member Encounters: Phys (2,330,249), non-phys (2,038,176)
Group Affiliation: UPMC Health System
Licensed in: PA
Address: 600 Grant St, Pittsburgh, PA 15219
Phone: (412) 434-1200   **Dom State:** PA   **Commenced Bus:** July 2004

Data Date	Rating	RACR #1	RACR #2	Total Assets ($mil)	Capital ($mil)	Net Premium ($mil)	Net Income ($mil)
6-14	B+	1.56	1.30	421.0	175.7	820.3	4.0
6-13	B+	2.59	2.16	354.3	187.2	743.8	14.0
2013	B+	1.62	1.35	338.8	172.7	1,553.3	30.0
2012	B+	2.40	2.00	303.3	174.8	1,052.5	32.4
2011	A-	2.30	1.92	250.5	142.6	831.5	24.5
2010	A-	2.39	1.99	188.0	118.5	651.8	27.5
2009	B	1.65	1.37	185.4	91.7	793.6	2.7

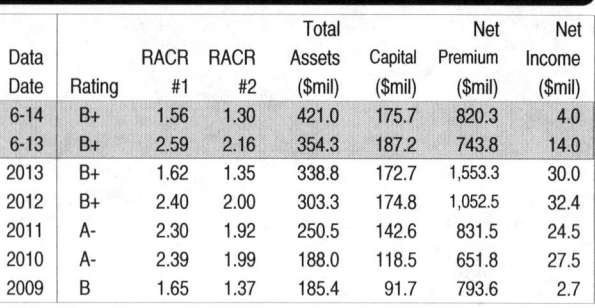

UPMC HEALTH NETWORK INC

D+   **Weak**

Major Rating Factors: Weak profitability index (0.9 on a scale of 0 to 10). Poor capitalization (0.0) based on weak current risk-adjusted capital (severe loss scenario). Good liquidity (6.8) with sufficient resources (cash flows and marketable investments) to handle a spike in claims.
Other Rating Factors: High quality investment portfolio (9.9).
Principal Business: Comp med (81%), Medicare (19%)
Mem Phys: 13: 16,053   **12:** 14,736   **13 MLR** 96.5%   **/ 13 Admin Exp** N/A
Enroll(000): Q2 14: 11   **13:** 288   **12:** 240   **Med Exp PMPM:** $352
Principal Investments: Long-term bonds (67%), cash and equiv (26%), other (6%)
Provider Compensation ($000): Contr fee ($1,148,037)
Total Member Encounters: Phys (2,296,159), non-phys (1,462,007)
Group Affiliation: UPMC Health System
Licensed in: PA
Address: 112 Washington Pl, Pittsburgh, PA 15219
Phone: (412) 434-1200   **Dom State:** PA   **Commenced Bus:** January 2005

Data Date	Rating	RACR #1	RACR #2	Total Assets ($mil)	Capital ($mil)	Net Premium ($mil)	Net Income ($mil)
6-14	D+	0.17	0.15	79.1	35.4	45.9	-7.4
6-13	C+	0.61	0.51	245.1	92.9	585.5	-17.8
2013	C+	0.76	0.64	281.4	142.1	1,208.2	-48.1
2012	B	0.84	0.70	240.8	110.9	969.5	-23.1
2011	B+	1.24	1.03	240.0	103.8	763.8	25.4
2010	A-	1.87	1.55	169.4	99.1	671.0	31.8
2009	B+	1.24	1.03	121.7	67.0	604.4	3.2

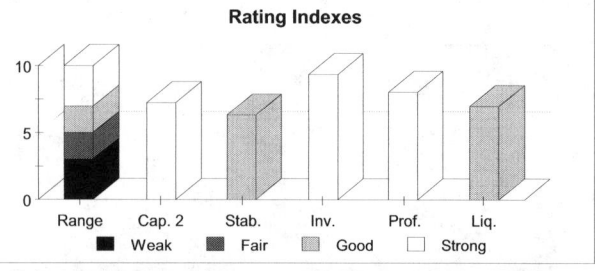

UPMC HEALTH PLAN INC

B   **Good**

Major Rating Factors: Good overall profitability index (6.1 on a scale of 0 to 10). Good overall results on stability tests (5.2). Strong capitalization index (6.9) based on excellent current risk-adjusted capital (severe loss scenario).
Other Rating Factors: High quality investment portfolio (9.9). Excellent liquidity (7.0) with ample operational cash flow and liquid investments.
Principal Business: Medicare (87%), FEHB (7%), comp med (6%)
Mem Phys: 13: 16,821   **12:** 15,669   **13 MLR** 86.8%   **/ 13 Admin Exp** N/A
Enroll(000): Q2 14: 140   **13:** 122   **12:** 119   **Med Exp PMPM:** $632
Principal Investments: Long-term bonds (63%), cash and equiv (36%), other (1%)
Provider Compensation ($000): Contr fee ($895,251), capitation ($28)
Total Member Encounters: Phys (1,507,048), non-phys (1,386,409)
Group Affiliation: UPMC Health System
Licensed in: OH, PA, WV
Address: 112 Washington Pl, Pittsburgh, PA 15219
Phone: (412) 434-1200   **Dom State:** PA   **Commenced Bus:** March 1996

Data Date	Rating	RACR #1	RACR #2	Total Assets ($mil)	Capital ($mil)	Net Premium ($mil)	Net Income ($mil)
6-14	B	1.28	1.07	322.1	121.9	598.8	12.3
6-13	B	1.24	1.03	287.5	147.5	516.7	23.3
2013	B	1.50	1.25	343.6	151.6	1,036.2	41.7
2012	C+	0.97	0.81	275.8	127.5	1,151.0	10.9
2011	B-	0.97	0.81	334.4	134.1	1,199.9	17.2
2010	B+	0.88	0.73	247.1	109.4	1,140.7	-1.8
2009	B	1.29	1.07	184.7	107.1	771.3	9.6

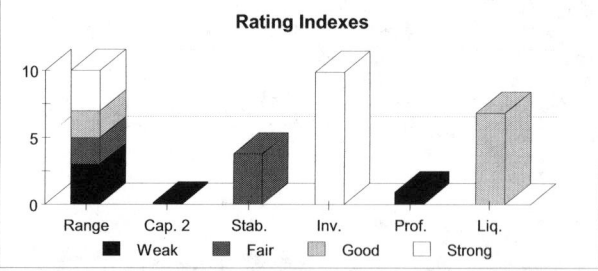

UPPER PENINSULA HEALTH PLAN INC | B- | Good

Major Rating Factors: Good overall profitability index (6.4 on a scale of 0 to 10). Good overall results on stability tests (5.6). Strong capitalization index (7.8) based on excellent current risk-adjusted capital (severe loss scenario).
Other Rating Factors: High quality investment portfolio (9.9). Excellent liquidity (7.0) with ample operational cash flow and liquid investments.
Principal Business: Medicaid (94%), Medicare (5%)
Mem Phys: 13: 1,036 **12:** 1,003 **13 MLR** 91.7% **/ 13 Admin Exp** N/A
Enroll(000): Q2 14: 41 **13:** 31 **12:** 31 **Med Exp PMPM:** $267
Principal Investments: Cash and equiv (76%), long-term bonds (24%)
Provider Compensation ($000): Contr fee ($68,897), capitation ($26,302), FFS ($3,626)
Total Member Encounters: Phys (173,961), non-phys (113,203)
Group Affiliation: Marquette General/Portage Health
Licensed in: MI
Address: 228 W Washington St, Marquette, MI 49855
Phone: (906) 225-7500 **Dom State:** MI **Commenced Bus:** August 1998

Data Date	Rating	RACR #1	RACR #2	Total Assets ($mil)	Capital ($mil)	Net Premium ($mil)	Net Income ($mil)
6-14	B-	1.95	1.63	38.0	21.3	61.2	2.2
6-13	B-	1.88	1.56	32.0	18.8	52.5	0.1
2013	B-	1.77	1.47	31.9	19.2	107.1	0.7
2012	B-	1.87	1.56	31.9	18.7	97.6	0.2
2011	C	1.94	1.62	31.2	18.4	95.5	0.1
2010	B	3.10	2.58	38.0	27.2	99.1	8.2
2009	B	2.76	2.30	35.7	23.9	93.0	5.8

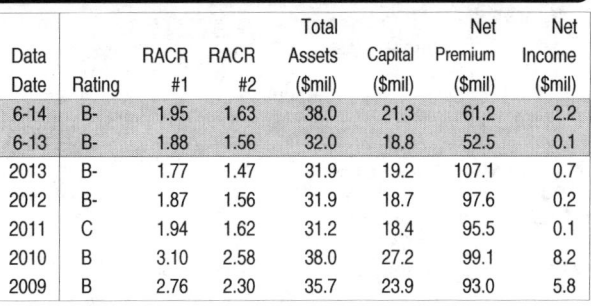

Rating Indexes
Range / Cap. 2 / Stab. / Inv. / Prof. / Liq.
■ Weak ▨ Fair ▤ Good □ Strong

USABLE LIFE * | B+ | Good

Major Rating Factors: Good quality investment portfolio (5.2 on a scale of 0 to 10) despite mixed results such as: minimal exposure to mortgages and large holdings of BBB rated bonds but minimal holdings in junk bonds. Good liquidity (5.9) with sufficient resources to handle a spike in claims. Good overall results on stability tests (6.3) good operational trends and excellent risk diversification.
Other Rating Factors: Strong capitalization (7.4) based on excellent risk adjusted capital (severe loss scenario). Excellent profitability (7.6).
Principal Business: Reinsurance (55%), group health insurance (19%), group life insurance (19%), individual health insurance (5%), and individual life insurance (1%).
Principal Investments: NonCMO investment grade bonds (68%), common & preferred stock (15%), CMOs and structured securities (7%), mortgages in good standing (4%), and misc. investments (6%).
Investments in Affiliates: 2%
Group Affiliation: Arkansas Bl Cross Bl Shield Group
Licensed in: All states except AK, NY, PR
Commenced Business: December 1980
Address: 320 W Capitol Suite 700, Little Rock, AR 72201
Phone: (501) 375-7200 **Domicile State:** AR **NAIC Code:** 94358

Data Date	Rating	RACR #1	RACR #2	Total Assets ($mil)	Capital ($mil)	Net Premium ($mil)	Net Income ($mil)
6-14	B+	1.72	1.26	426.8	182.9	294.4	12.0
6-13	B+	1.63	1.21	391.8	162.2	284.2	4.1
2013	B+	1.60	1.17	408.3	166.3	570.0	11.5
2012	B+	1.64	1.21	381.2	156.3	505.7	15.4
2011	B+	1.72	1.28	346.8	144.0	454.4	8.2
2010	B+	1.83	1.37	334.2	137.5	419.4	3.3
2009	A-	1.75	1.32	305.9	122.3	384.0	2.7

Adverse Trends in Operations

Change in asset mix during 2012 (8%)
Increase in policy surrenders from 2010 to 2011 (29%)

USABLE MUTUAL INS CO * | A+ | Excellent

Major Rating Factors: Excellent profitability (8.2 on a scale of 0 to 10). Strong capitalization (10.0) based on excellent current risk-adjusted capital (severe loss scenario). High quality investment portfolio (9.9).
Other Rating Factors: Excellent liquidity (7.4) with ample operational cash flow and liquid investments.
Principal Business: Comp med (53%), FEHB (17%), med supp (16%), Medicare (11%), other (3%)
Mem Phys: 13: 13,544 **12:** 14,099 **13 MLR** 79.8% **/ 13 Admin Exp** N/A
Enroll(000): Q2 14: 605 **13:** 448 **12:** 439 **Med Exp PMPM:** $208
Principal Investments: Cash and equiv (33%), long-term bonds (31%), affiliate common stock (15%), nonaffiliate common stock (11%), real estate (3%), other (6%)
Provider Compensation ($000): Contr fee ($1,106,021), bonus arrang ($317)
Total Member Encounters: Phys (2,440,925), non-phys (3,398,997)
Group Affiliation: Arkansas Bl Cross Bl Shield Group
Licensed in: AR
Address: 601 S Gaines, Little Rock, AR 72201
Phone: (501) 378-2000 **Dom State:** AR **Commenced Bus:** March 1949

Data Date	Rating	RACR #1	RACR #2	Total Assets ($mil)	Capital ($mil)	Net Premium ($mil)	Net Income ($mil)
6-14	A+	6.95	5.79	1,521.6	794.6	931.7	15.5
6-13	A+	6.04	5.04	1,325.9	696.7	684.5	26.5
2013	A+	6.72	5.60	1,454.5	767.2	1,393.0	37.7
2012	A+	5.90	4.92	1,283.2	678.7	1,309.6	48.0
2011	A+	4.95	4.12	1,221.7	581.7	1,262.3	46.4
2010	A+	4.85	4.04	1,139.0	572.0	1,197.9	63.3
2009	A+	4.58	3.81	951.9	482.5	1,134.4	24.1

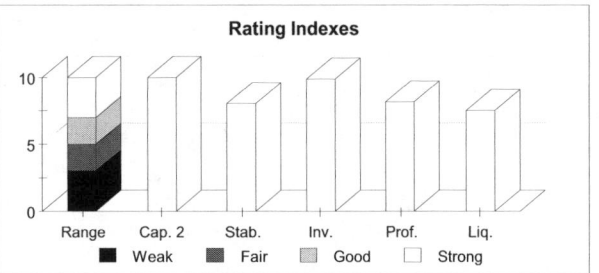

Rating Indexes
Range / Cap. 2 / Stab. / Inv. / Prof. / Liq.
■ Weak ▨ Fair ▤ Good □ Strong

UTMB HEALTH PLANS INC

B-   **Good**

Major Rating Factors: Fair profitability index (4.4 on a scale of 0 to 10). Good overall results on stability tests (5.1) despite a decline in enrollment during 2013. Strong capitalization index (10.0) based on excellent current risk-adjusted capital (severe loss scenario).
Other Rating Factors: High quality investment portfolio (8.9). Excellent liquidity (10.0) with ample operational cash flow and liquid investments.
Principal Business: Med supp (100%)
Mem Phys: 13: 30 **12:** 25 **13 MLR** 49.0% **/ 13 Admin Exp** N/A
Enroll(000): Q2 14: 0 **13:** 0 **12:** 0 **Med Exp PMPM:** $94
Principal Investments: Cash and equiv (100%)
Provider Compensation ($000): Capitation ($268), FFS ($155)
Total Member Encounters: Phys (3,607), non-phys (787)
Group Affiliation: UTMB Health Care Systems Inc
Licensed in: TX
Address: 301 University Blvd Rte 0985, Galveston, TX 77555-0116
Phone: (409) 766-4000 **Dom State:** TX **Commenced Bus:** April 1994

Data Date	Rating	RACR #1	RACR #2	Total Assets ($mil)	Capital ($mil)	Net Premium ($mil)	Net Income ($mil)
6-14	B-	46.39	38.66	7.3	6.6	1.4	1.1
6-13	C+	32.71	27.26	7.8	5.8	0.4	0.0
2013	B-	38.84	32.37	8.2	6.2	0.8	0.2
2012	C+	37.09	30.91	8.7	6.7	0.9	0.1
2011	C	43.11	35.93	9.0	7.0	1.0	0.5
2010	D+	45.33	37.78	9.9	7.6	1.0	0.1
2009	D+	44.31	36.92	11.0	8.4	0.9	-0.6

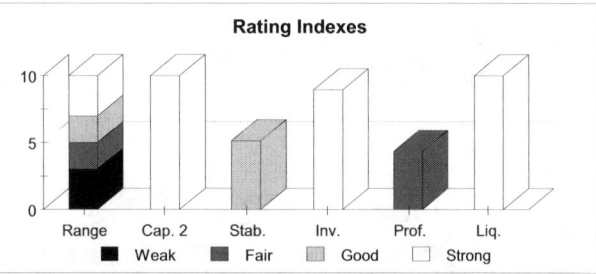

Rating Indexes

VALUE BEHAVIORAL HEALTH OF PA

E   **Very Weak**

Major Rating Factors: Good overall profitability index (6.8 on a scale of 0 to 10). Strong capitalization (7.1) based on excellent current risk-adjusted capital (severe loss scenario). High quality investment portfolio (9.9).
Other Rating Factors: Excellent liquidity (7.2) with ample operational cash flow and liquid investments.
Principal Business: Medicaid (100%)
Mem Phys: 13: 840 **12:** 750 **13 MLR** 90.3% **/ 13 Admin Exp** N/A
Enroll(000): Q2 14: 72 **13:** 71 **12:** 72 **Med Exp PMPM:** $101
Principal Investments: Cash and equiv (100%)
Provider Compensation ($000): Contr fee ($90,585)
Total Member Encounters: Phys (18,963), non-phys (745,747)
Group Affiliation: FHC Health Systems Inc
Licensed in: PA
Address: 240 Corporate Blvd, Norfolk, VA 23502
Phone: (757) 459-5200 **Dom State:** PA **Commenced Bus:** January 1999

Data Date	Rating	RACR #1	RACR #2	Total Assets ($mil)	Capital ($mil)	Net Premium ($mil)	Net Income ($mil)
6-14	E	1.40	1.17	34.1	13.3	52.3	1.3
6-13	E	1.36	1.14	32.6	12.4	49.6	-0.2
2013	E	1.50	1.25	34.0	14.3	97.8	1.6
2012	E	2.73	2.27	48.5	27.9	101.0	4.8
2011	N/A	N/A	N/A	75.6	31.1	309.0	4.7
2010	N/A	N/A	N/A	79.3	28.4	333.2	5.6
2009	E	N/A	N/A	84.5	23.1	319.2	5.2

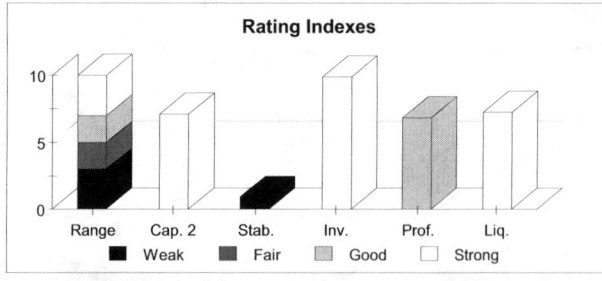

Rating Indexes

VANTAGE HEALTH PLAN INC

B-   **Good**

Major Rating Factors: Fair capitalization index (4.6 on a scale of 0 to 10) based on fair current risk-adjusted capital (moderate loss scenario). Good quality investment portfolio (5.1). Good overall results on stability tests (5.5) based on steady enrollment growth, averaging 7% over the past five years.
Other Rating Factors: Good liquidity (6.8) with sufficient resources (cash flows and marketable investments) to handle a spike in claims. Excellent profitability (8.3).
Principal Business: Medicare (67%), comp med (33%)
Mem Phys: 13: 4,701 **12:** 4,402 **13 MLR** 83.5% **/ 13 Admin Exp** N/A
Enroll(000): Q2 14: 33 **13:** 25 **12:** 24 **Med Exp PMPM:** $519
Principal Investments: Cash and equiv (31%), real estate (23%), other (46%)
Provider Compensation ($000): Contr fee ($132,547), FFS ($16,060), capitation ($264)
Total Member Encounters: Phys (305,398), non-phys (57,571)
Group Affiliation: Vantage Holdings Inc
Licensed in: LA
Address: 130 Desiard St, Ste 300, Monroe, LA 71201
Phone: (318) 361-0900 **Dom State:** LA **Commenced Bus:** January 1995

Data Date	Rating	RACR #1	RACR #2	Total Assets ($mil)	Capital ($mil)	Net Premium ($mil)	Net Income ($mil)
6-14	B-	0.87	0.73	52.9	17.2	110.6	0.7
6-13	B	0.90	0.75	43.0	16.5	91.4	-0.3
2013	B	1.01	0.85	44.7	20.2	183.7	6.0
2012	B	1.18	0.99	43.8	21.5	177.5	9.9
2011	B-	1.01	0.85	38.7	15.7	150.0	3.0
2010	B	1.03	0.86	33.8	14.5	125.9	2.6
2009	B	1.13	0.94	27.5	12.8	97.3	3.8

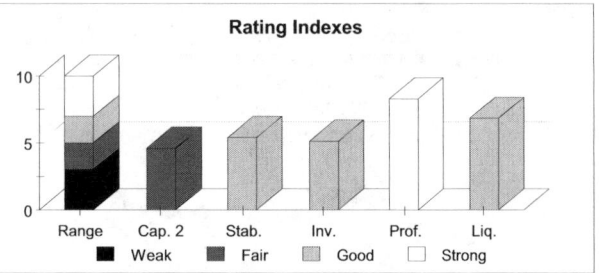

Rating Indexes

VENTURA COUNTY HEALTH CARE PLAN   B   Good

Major Rating Factors: Good overall results on stability tests (6.0 on a scale of 0 to 10). Excellent profitability (8.3). Strong capitalization index (7.0) based on excellent current risk-adjusted capital (severe loss scenario).
Other Rating Factors: Excellent liquidity (7.1) with ample operational cash flow and liquid investments.
Principal Business: Managed care (100%)
Mem Phys: 13: N/A **12:** N/A **13 MLR** 90.0% **/ 13 Admin Exp** N/A
Enroll(000): Q2 14: 15 **13:** 23 **12:** 25 **Med Exp PMPM:** $176
Principal Investments ($000): Cash and equiv ($11,566)
Provider Compensation ($000): None
Total Member Encounters: N/A
Group Affiliation: None
Licensed in: CA
Address: 233 Knoll Dr, Ventura, CA 93003
Phone: (805) 677-5157 **Dom State:** CA **Commenced Bus:** June 1996

Data Date	Rating	RACR #1	RACR #2	Total Assets ($mil)	Capital ($mil)	Net Premium ($mil)	Net Income ($mil)
6-14	B	1.85	1.16	24.8	10.4	26.4	0.2
6-13	B	1.97	1.23	23.7	10.2	28.3	0.9
2013	B	1.85	1.16	22.2	10.2	57.5	1.0
2012	B	1.79	1.12	22.1	9.2	53.7	1.7
2011	B	1.53	0.94	17.9	7.5	46.3	0.1
2010	B	1.95	1.22	15.4	7.4	36.9	1.3
2009	C	1.81	1.13	14.3	6.1	33.9	2.1

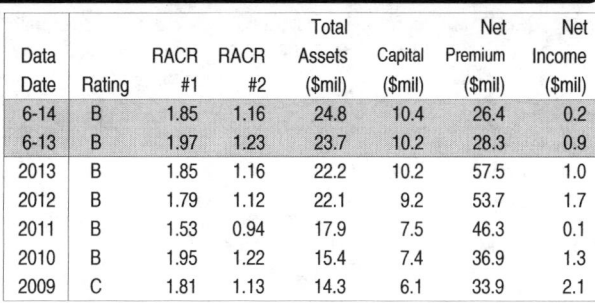

Rating Indexes

VERMONT HEALTH PLAN LLC   B   Good

Major Rating Factors: Good overall results on stability tests (5.0 on a scale of 0 to 10). Good liquidity (6.6) with sufficient resources (cash flows and marketable investments) to handle a spike in claims. Fair profitability index (4.3).
Other Rating Factors: Strong capitalization index (7.9) based on excellent current risk-adjusted capital (severe loss scenario). High quality investment portfolio (9.6).
Principal Business: Comp med (98%), med supp (2%)
Mem Phys: 13: 7,093 **12:** 6,833 **13 MLR** 93.0% **/ 13 Admin Exp** N/A
Enroll(000): Q2 14: 16 **13:** 38 **12:** 41 **Med Exp PMPM:** $343
Principal Investments: Long-term bonds (88%), cash and equiv (12%)
Provider Compensation ($000): Bonus arrang ($69,342), FFS ($58,790), contr fee ($30,398), capitation ($2,602)
Total Member Encounters: Phys (170,687), non-phys (103,433)
Group Affiliation: Blue Cross Blue Shield of Vermont
Licensed in: VT
Address: 445 Industrial Ln, Montpelier, VT 05602
Phone: (802) 223-6131 **Dom State:** VT **Commenced Bus:** January 1997

Data Date	Rating	RACR #1	RACR #2	Total Assets ($mil)	Capital ($mil)	Net Premium ($mil)	Net Income ($mil)
6-14	B	2.10	1.75	51.2	34.8	39.8	2.1
6-13	B+	2.43	2.02	67.0	40.2	87.5	3.7
2013	B	2.00	1.67	63.9	33.2	173.0	-2.8
2012	B+	2.22	1.85	68.4	36.8	183.7	7.5
2011	B	1.91	1.59	58.4	29.8	170.0	7.9
2010	B	1.69	1.41	46.9	22.9	137.0	1.9
2009	B	1.55	1.29	42.4	21.7	117.5	-2.0

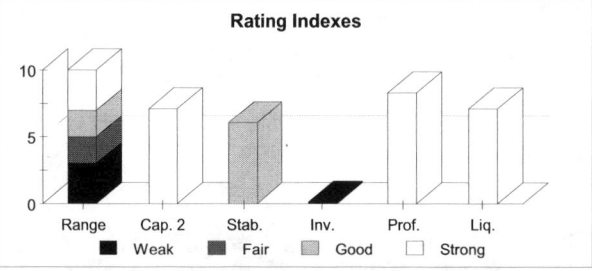

Rating Indexes

VIRGINIA PREMIER HEALTH PLAN INC *   A-   Excellent

Major Rating Factors: Strong capitalization index (7.2 on a scale of 0 to 10) based on excellent current risk-adjusted capital (severe loss scenario). High quality investment portfolio (9.9). Excellent overall results on stability tests (7.5) based on healthy premium and capital growth during 2013.
Other Rating Factors: Excellent liquidity (7.1) with ample operational cash flow and liquid investments. Good overall profitability index (5.8).
Principal Business: Medicaid (100%)
Mem Phys: 13: N/A **12:** N/A **13 MLR** 92.5% **/ 13 Admin Exp** N/A
Enroll(000): Q2 14: 176 **13:** 175 **12:** 172 **Med Exp PMPM:** $317
Principal Investments: Cash and equiv (78%), nonaffiliate common stock (18%), long-term bonds (2%), other (1%)
Provider Compensation ($000): Contr fee ($645,204), capitation ($12,426)
Total Member Encounters: N/A
Group Affiliation: University Health Services Inc
Licensed in: VA
Address: 600 E Broad St, Ste 400, Richmond, VA 23219
Phone: (804) 819-5151 **Dom State:** VA **Commenced Bus:** November 1995

Data Date	Rating	RACR #1	RACR #2	Total Assets ($mil)	Capital ($mil)	Net Premium ($mil)	Net Income ($mil)
6-14	A-	1.52	1.27	184.9	96.5	372.9	4.2
6-13	A-	1.81	1.51	165.7	93.1	343.2	20.9
2013	A-	1.56	1.30	182.2	98.7	715.4	26.8
2012	B+	1.37	1.14	167.5	73.9	586.1	10.0
2011	B	1.26	1.05	133.8	61.9	524.7	13.7
2010	B-	1.14	0.95	132.0	61.8	531.3	17.0
2009	C	0.64	0.53	90.7	37.4	471.9	-4.0

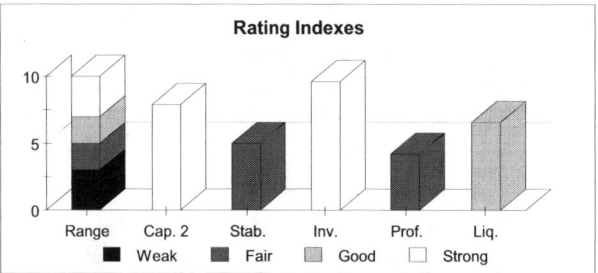

Rating Indexes

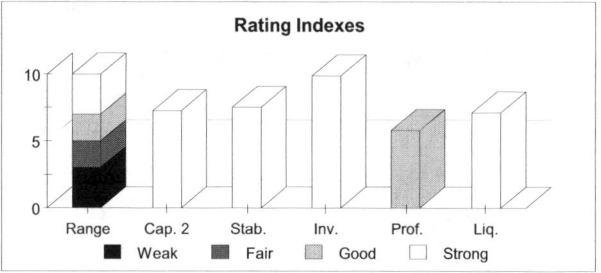

VISTA HEALTH PLAN INC　　　　　　　　　　B-　　　Good

Major Rating Factors: Strong capitalization index (7.9 on a scale of 0 to 10) based on excellent current risk-adjusted capital (severe loss scenario). High quality investment portfolio (9.9). Excellent overall results on stability tests (7.6).
Other Rating Factors: Excellent liquidity (7.0) with sufficient resources (cash flows and marketable investments) to handle a spike in claims. Weak profitability index (1.8).
Principal Business: Medicaid (100%)
Mem Phys: 13: 33,761　**12:** 28,493　**13 MLR** 97.1%　**/ 13 Admin Exp** N/A
Enroll(000): Q2 14: 479　**13:** 472　**12:** 439　**Med Exp PMPM:** $435
Principal Investments: Long-term bonds (92%), cash and equiv (8%)
Provider Compensation ($000): Capitation ($2,500,588)
Total Member Encounters: Phys (3,767,911), non-phys (965,622)
Group Affiliation: Independence Blue Cross Inc
Licensed in: PA
Address: 1901 Market St, Philadelphia, PA 19101
Phone: (215) 241-2400　**Dom State:** PA　**Commenced Bus:** November 1986

Data Date	Rating	RACR #1	RACR #2	Total Assets ($mil)	Capital ($mil)	Net Premium ($mil)	Net Income ($mil)
6-14	B-	2.08	1.73	877.1	168.2	1,449.9	-17.6
6-13	N/A	N/A	N/A	846.8	159.2	1,267.3	1.7
2013	B	1.98	1.65	447.4	160.5	2,573.7	2.9
2012	N/A	N/A	N/A	512.0	157.5	2,575.5	2.6
2011	N/A	N/A	N/A	439.2	144.6	2,413.0	2.5
2010	N/A	N/A	N/A	486.5	137.0	2,252.6	-0.8
2009	B-	2.14	1.79	475.0	137.4	2,107.2	1.7

Rating Indexes
(Range, Cap. 2, Stab., Inv., Prof., Liq. — Weak, Fair, Good, Strong)

VIVA HEALTH INC *　　　　　　　　　　B+　　　Good

Major Rating Factors: Good quality investment portfolio (6.1 on a scale of 0 to 10). Good overall results on stability tests (6.5). Excellent profitability (7.2).
Other Rating Factors: Strong capitalization index (7.8) based on excellent current risk-adjusted capital (severe loss scenario). Excellent liquidity (6.9) with sufficient resources (cash flows and marketable investments) to handle a spike in claims.
Principal Business: Medicare (83%), comp med (17%)
Mem Phys: 13: 9,786　**12:** 9,470　**13 MLR** 85.2%　**/ 13 Admin Exp** N/A
Enroll(000): Q2 14: 70　**13:** 68　**12:** 68　**Med Exp PMPM:** $586
Principal Investments: Nonaffiliate common stock (46%), cash and equiv (42%), long-term bonds (12%)
Provider Compensation ($000): Contr fee ($335,335), capitation ($128,455), FFS ($10,371)
Total Member Encounters: Phys (1,497,961), non-phys (1,831,540)
Group Affiliation: U of AL at Birmingham
Licensed in: AL
Address: 1222 14th Ave S, Birmingham, AL 35205
Phone: (205) 939-1718　**Dom State:** AL　**Commenced Bus:** February 1996

Data Date	Rating	RACR #1	RACR #2	Total Assets ($mil)	Capital ($mil)	Net Premium ($mil)	Net Income ($mil)
6-14	B+	1.99	1.66	156.2	82.3	300.7	-5.4
6-13	B+	1.84	1.54	148.1	78.1	279.5	3.0
2013	B+	2.15	1.79	147.2	87.9	554.8	13.7
2012	B+	1.85	1.54	132.5	78.2	559.8	11.0
2011	B+	1.63	1.36	131.7	66.8	571.7	33.2
2010	B-	0.92	0.76	101.2	33.6	458.0	3.1
2009	C	1.04	0.87	77.2	31.2	380.9	8.5

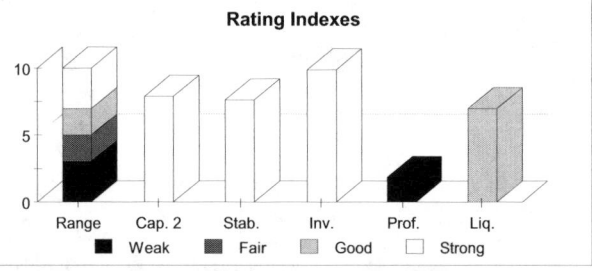

Rating Indexes
(Range, Cap. 2, Stab., Inv., Prof., Liq. — Weak, Fair, Good, Strong)

VOLUNTARY EMPLOYEES BENEFIT　　　　　D+　　　Weak

Major Rating Factors: Weak profitability index (1.0 on a scale of 0 to 10). Strong capitalization (10.0) based on excellent current risk-adjusted capital (severe loss scenario). High quality investment portfolio (7.6) containing large holdings of mortgages.
Other Rating Factors: Excellent liquidity (10.0) with ample operational cash flow and liquid investments.
Principal Business: Dental (80%), other (20%)
Mem Phys: 13: N/A　**12:** N/A　**13 MLR** 74.7%　**/ 13 Admin Exp** N/A
Enroll(000): Q2 14: 1　**13:** 1　**12:** 1　**Med Exp PMPM:** $11
Principal Investments: Long-term bonds (43%), cash and equiv (28%), affiliate common stock (15%), mortgs (10%), nonaffiliate common stock (4%)
Provider Compensation ($000): Capitation ($78)
Total Member Encounters: Non-phys (6,918)
Group Affiliation: None
Licensed in: (No states)
Address: 819 S Beretania St, Honolulu, HI 96813-2501
Phone: (808) 539-1600　**Dom State:** HI　**Commenced Bus:** January 1993

Data Date	Rating	RACR #1	RACR #2	Total Assets ($mil)	Capital ($mil)	Net Premium ($mil)	Net Income ($mil)
6-14	D+	31.57	26.31	8.4	8.3	0.1	0.0
6-13	D+	9.99	8.32	8.5	8.5	0.1	-0.1
2013	D+	31.66	26.39	8.4	8.4	0.1	-0.2
2012	D+	10.11	8.42	8.6	8.6	0.1	-0.2
2011	N/A	N/A	N/A	8.8	8.8	0.1	-0.3
2010	N/A	N/A	N/A	9.2	9.1	0.1	-0.2
2009	D+	N/A	N/A	9.6	9.2	0.1	-0.1

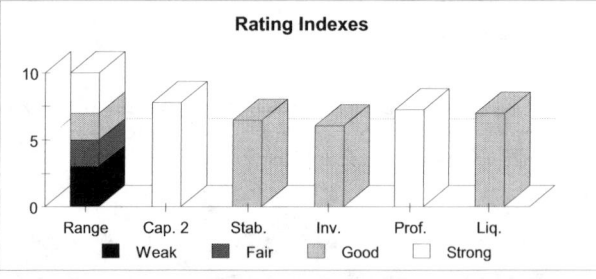
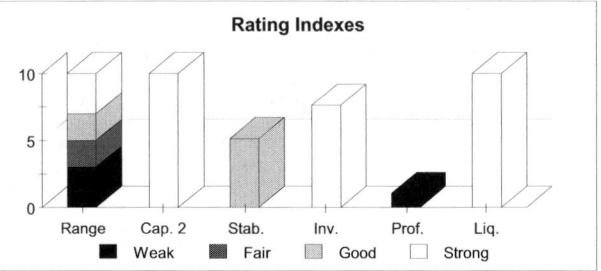

Rating Indexes
(Range, Cap. 2, Stab., Inv., Prof., Liq. — Weak, Fair, Good, Strong)

VOLUNTEER STATE HEALTH PLAN INC *   A-   Excellent

Major Rating Factors: Strong capitalization index (9.5 on a scale of 0 to 10) based on excellent current risk-adjusted capital (severe loss scenario). High quality investment portfolio (9.6). Excellent overall results on stability tests (7.5). **Other Rating Factors:** Good overall profitability index (6.6). Good liquidity (6.7) with sufficient resources (cash flows and marketable investments) to handle a spike in claims.

Principal Business: Medicaid (100%)

Mem Phys: 13: 22,572   **12:** 22,051   **13 MLR** 81.8%   **/ 13 Admin Exp** N/A

Enroll(000): Q2 14: 406   **13:** 383   **12:** 394   **Med Exp PMPM:** $294

Principal Investments: Long-term bonds (84%), cash and equiv (15%), other (1%)

Provider Compensation ($000): Contr fee ($1,334,801), capitation ($31,613), bonus arrang ($1,590)

Total Member Encounters: Phys (4,526,510), non-phys (393,610)

Group Affiliation: BlueCross BlueShield of Tennessee

Licensed in: TN

Address: 1 Cameron Hill Cir, Chattanooga, TN 37402

Phone: (423) 535-5600   **Dom State:** TN   **Commenced Bus:** November 1996

Data Date	Rating	RACR #1	RACR #2	Total Assets ($mil)	Capital ($mil)	Net Premium ($mil)	Net Income ($mil)
6-14	A-	3.33	2.78	546.3	294.6	887.2	35.7
6-13	B	2.64	2.20	461.0	233.1	839.2	16.5
2013	B+	2.93	2.44	478.2	256.9	1,673.1	42.0
2012	B	2.48	2.06	450.4	217.7	1,690.8	42.8
2011	B	2.08	1.73	393.9	175.0	1,696.0	73.5
2010	B-	1.38	1.15	490.5	104.9	1,416.3	-22.0
2009	A-	N/A	N/A	270.2	86.9	1,197.3	-64.4

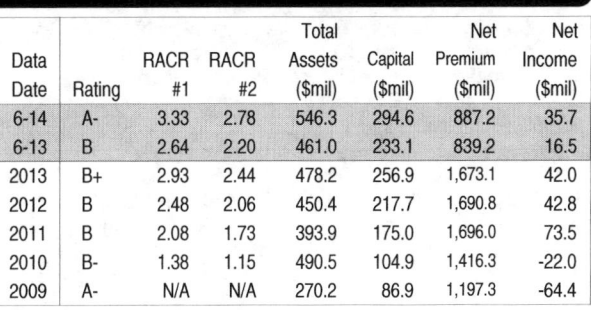

Rating Indexes

WASHINGTON NATIONAL INSURANCE COMPANY   D+   Weak

Major Rating Factors: Weak overall results on stability tests (2.7 on a scale of 0 to 10) including potential financial drain due to affiliation with CNO Financial Group Inc. Fair quality investment portfolio (4.5) with large holdings of BBB rated bonds in addition to junk bond exposure equal to 75% of capital. Good overall profitability (6.3). Excellent expense controls.

Other Rating Factors: Good liquidity (6.8). Strong capitalization (7.1) based on excellent risk adjusted capital (severe loss scenario).

Principal Business: Individual health insurance (66%), group health insurance (21%), individual life insurance (9%), individual annuities (2%), and reinsurance (2%).

Principal Investments: NonCMO investment grade bonds (56%), CMOs and structured securities (25%), mortgages in good standing (7%), noninv. grade bonds (6%), and misc. investments (7%).

Investments in Affiliates: 1%

Group Affiliation: CNO Financial Group Inc

Licensed in: All states except NY

Commenced Business: September 1923

Address: 11825 N Pennsylvania St, Carmel, I2 60069

Phone: (847) 793-3379 **Domicile State:** IN **NAIC Code:** 70319

Data Date	Rating	RACR #1	RACR #2	Total Assets ($mil)	Capital ($mil)	Net Premium ($mil)	Net Income ($mil)
6-14	D+	1.95	1.04	4,849.8	386.6	294.4	22.5
6-13	D+	2.13	1.16	5,250.2	453.3	269.5	34.4
2013	D+	2.20	1.15	5,286.1	431.9	540.7	59.6
2012	D+	2.28	1.23	5,247.6	469.4	522.4	58.6
2011	D+	2.22	1.20	5,335.9	500.9	523.9	71.3
2010	D+	2.30	1.23	4,911.7	491.8	637.4	-606.7
2009	D+	1.21	0.98	1,926.7	400.1	180.0	-43.3

CNO Financial Group Inc
Composite Group Rating: D+
Largest Group Members

Largest Group Members	Assets ($mil)	Rating
BANKERS LIFE CAS CO	15840	D+
WASHINGTON NATIONAL INS CO	5286	D+
CONSECO LIFE INS CO	3825	D+
COLONIAL PENN LIFE INS CO	740	D+
BANKERS CONSECO LIFE INS CO	383	D

WEA INSURANCE CORPORATION   C   Fair

Major Rating Factors: Fair quality investment portfolio (4.4 on a scale of 0 to 10). Fair overall results on stability tests (4.0). Good liquidity (6.7) with sufficient resources to handle a spike in claims.

Other Rating Factors: Weak profitability (2.0) with operating losses during the first six months of 2014. Return on equity has been low, averaging -5.9%. Strong capitalization (7.6) based on excellent risk adjusted capital (severe loss scenario).

Principal Business: Group health insurance (100%).

Principal Investments: NonCMO investment grade bonds (51%), CMOs and structured securities (23%), common & preferred stock (21%), and cash (5%).

Investments in Affiliates: None

Group Affiliation: WEA Inc

Licensed in: WI

Commenced Business: July 1985

Address: 45 Nob Hill Rd, Madison, WI 53713

Phone: (608) 276-4000 **Domicile State:** WI **NAIC Code:** 72273

Data Date	Rating	RACR #1	RACR #2	Total Assets ($mil)	Capital ($mil)	Net Premium ($mil)	Net Income ($mil)
6-14	C	1.99	1.40	691.0	212.5	301.0	-21.7
6-13	C	2.10	1.50	704.0	224.7	298.4	-17.3
2013	C	2.28	1.61	720.9	243.0	594.6	-15.1
2012	B-	2.19	1.59	686.8	232.1	635.9	19.1
2011	B	1.88	1.39	643.7	221.5	770.3	-0.5
2010	B+	1.84	1.37	654.4	233.2	846.5	-14.7
2009	B	1.92	1.45	596.6	240.2	863.4	2.7

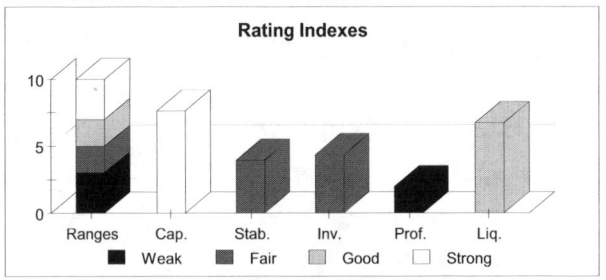

Rating Indexes

WELLCARE HEALTH INS OF ARIZONA INC

B-   **Good**

Major Rating Factors: Fair quality investment portfolio (4.8 on a scale of 0 to 10). Good overall profitability index (5.6). Strong capitalization (9.3) based on excellent current risk-adjusted capital (severe loss scenario).
Other Rating Factors: Excellent liquidity (7.1) with ample operational cash flow and liquid investments.
Principal Business: Medicaid (84%), Medicare (16%)
Mem Phys: 13: 4,600 **12:** 3,000 **13 MLR** 86.0% **/ 13 Admin Exp** N/A
Enroll(000): Q2 14: 57 **13:** 50 **12:** 37 **Med Exp PMPM:** $855
Principal Investments: Cash and equiv (98%), long-term bonds (2%)
Provider Compensation ($000): Contr fee ($423,280), capitation ($18,009)
Total Member Encounters: Phys (308,903), non-phys (355,265)
Group Affiliation: WellCare Health Plans Inc
Licensed in: AL, AZ, FL, GA, HI, ID, IN, IA, KS, KY, LA, MI, MO, NV, NM, NC, OR, SC, TX, VA, WY
Address: 2338 W Royal Plam Rd Suite J, Phoenix, AZ 85021
Phone: (813) 290-6200 **Dom State:** AZ **Commenced Bus:** January 1973

Data Date	Rating	RACR #1	RACR #2	Total Assets ($mil)	Capital ($mil)	Net Premium ($mil)	Net Income ($mil)
6-14	B-	3.22	2.68	189.0	80.9	323.0	2.5
6-13	C+	3.95	3.29	160.0	83.4	242.6	5.7
2013	B-	2.83	2.36	167.8	74.4	519.4	13.0
2012	C+	3.48	2.90	151.1	77.6	440.9	12.6
2011	N/A	N/A	N/A	141.5	90.2	391.0	29.6
2010	N/A	N/A	N/A	141.1	60.7	346.7	8.4
2009	B-	N/A	N/A	223.8	53.3	891.5	-31.4

WELLCARE HEALTH INS OF KENTUCKY INC

C+   **Fair**

Major Rating Factors: Fair profitability index (4.5 on a scale of 0 to 10). Strong capitalization (7.8) based on excellent current risk-adjusted capital (severe loss scenario). High quality investment portfolio (9.9).
Other Rating Factors: Excellent liquidity (7.0) with sufficient resources (cash flows and marketable investments) to handle a spike in claims.
Principal Business: Medicaid (87%), comp med (7%), Medicare (2%), other (4%)
Mem Phys: 13: 25,000 **12:** 3,700 **13 MLR** 88.4% **/ 13 Admin Exp** N/A
Enroll(000): Q2 14: 494 **13:** 359 **12:** 262 **Med Exp PMPM:** $320
Principal Investments: Cash and equiv (99%), long-term bonds (1%)
Provider Compensation ($000): Contr fee ($1,125,242), capitation ($75,822)
Total Member Encounters: Phys (1,796,890), non-phys (1,253,445)
Group Affiliation: WellCare Holdings LLC
Licensed in: AL, AR, CA, CO, CT, DC, DE, IL, MD, MN, MS, MT, NJ, OH, PA, RI, TN, UT, WA, WV, WI
Address: 13551 Triton Park Blvd # 1800, Louisville, KY 40223
Phone: (813) 290-6200 **Dom State:** KY **Commenced Bus:** August 1962

Data Date	Rating	RACR #1	RACR #2	Total Assets ($mil)	Capital ($mil)	Net Premium ($mil)	Net Income ($mil)
6-14	C+	1.97	1.65	434.5	151.8	1,139.9	23.1
6-13	C	2.31	1.93	261.8	110.6	619.8	25.8
2013	C	1.53	1.27	291.4	123.5	1,403.7	38.9
2012	C	1.40	1.17	184.6	68.6	743.7	-50.7
2011	N/A	N/A	N/A	112.6	42.4	155.5	-1.9
2010	N/A	N/A	N/A	56.3	41.8	52.0	10.8
2009	C+	N/A	N/A	105.4	30.6	531.5	-2.5

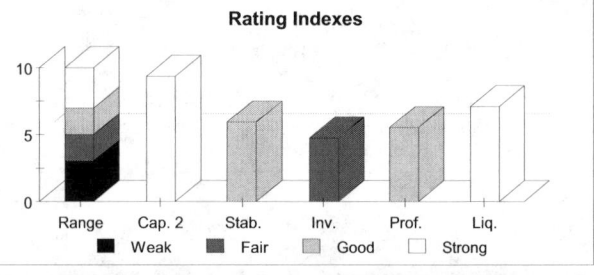

WELLCARE HEALTH PLANS OF NEW JERSEY

C   **Fair**

Major Rating Factors: Weak profitability index (0.9 on a scale of 0 to 10). Good quality investment portfolio (5.7). Strong capitalization (10.0) based on excellent current risk-adjusted capital (severe loss scenario).
Other Rating Factors: Excellent liquidity (6.9) with sufficient resources (cash flows and marketable investments) to handle a spike in claims.
Principal Business: Medicare (100%)
Mem Phys: 13: 3,200 **12:** 1,900 **13 MLR** 109.5% **/ 13 Admin Exp** N/A
Enroll(000): Q2 14: 10 **13:** 1 **12:** 2 **Med Exp PMPM:** $724
Principal Investments: Cash and equiv (60%), long-term bonds (40%)
Provider Compensation ($000): Contr fee ($13,750), capitation ($528)
Total Member Encounters: Phys (12,538), non-phys (7,087)
Group Affiliation: WellCare Health Plans Inc
Licensed in: NJ
Address: 33 Washington St 1st Floor, New York, NY 07102
Phone: (813) 290-6200 **Dom State:** NJ **Commenced Bus:** January 2008

Data Date	Rating	RACR #1	RACR #2	Total Assets ($mil)	Capital ($mil)	Net Premium ($mil)	Net Income ($mil)
6-14	C	4.18	3.48	18.4	4.4	19.8	-2.2
6-13	C+	3.88	3.23	8.0	5.9	6.6	0.0
2013	C	5.72	4.77	9.8	6.8	12.0	-1.6
2012	B-	3.63	3.02	9.9	5.9	19.4	-1.3
2011	B-	4.21	3.51	8.3	5.1	14.1	-0.7
2010	C+	2.50	2.08	6.5	2.8	16.2	-0.6
2009	C	2.56	2.13	8.0	3.4	24.0	0.5

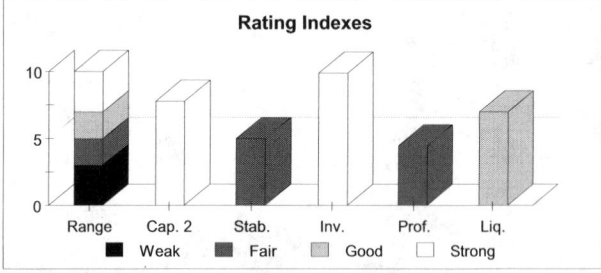

WELLCARE OF CONNECTICUT INC   C-   Fair

Major Rating Factors: Fair profitability index (3.9 on a scale of 0 to 10). Low quality investment portfolio (0.0). Good overall results on stability tests (5.4) based on healthy premium and capital growth during 2013. Rating is significantly influenced by the fair financial results of WellCare Health Plans Inc. **Other Rating Factors:** Strong capitalization index (10.0) based on excellent current risk-adjusted capital (severe loss scenario). Excellent liquidity (7.1) with ample operational cash flow and liquid investments.

Principal Business: Medicare (100%)
Mem Phys: 13: 9,800   **12:** 3,800   **13 MLR** 90.9%   **/ 13 Admin Exp** N/A
Enroll(000): Q2 14: 10   **13:** 8   **12:** 6   **Med Exp PMPM:** $861
Principal Investments: Cash and equiv (97%), long-term bonds (3%)
Provider Compensation ($000): Contr fee ($74,538), capitation ($1,752)
Total Member Encounters: Phys (87,647), non-phys (56,476)
Group Affiliation: WellCare Health Plans Inc
Licensed in: CT
Address: 127 Washington Ave 4th Floor, North Haven, CT 06473
Phone: (813) 290-6200   **Dom State:** CT   **Commenced Bus:** March 1995

Data Date	Rating	RACR #1	RACR #2	Total Assets ($mil)	Capital ($mil)	Net Premium ($mil)	Net Income ($mil)
6-14	C-	3.69	3.07	33.9	20.1	55.1	0.3
6-13	B-	4.76	3.97	31.4	19.1	39.1	2.9
2013	C	3.47	2.89	28.8	20.1	83.2	3.5
2012	B-	3.17	2.65	23.3	13.3	51.1	-1.7
2011	B-	3.72	3.10	19.9	11.6	37.1	-1.2
2010	B-	4.59	3.82	18.8	12.8	29.2	-1.1
2009	C+	4.76	3.97	19.5	14.0	36.8	0.3

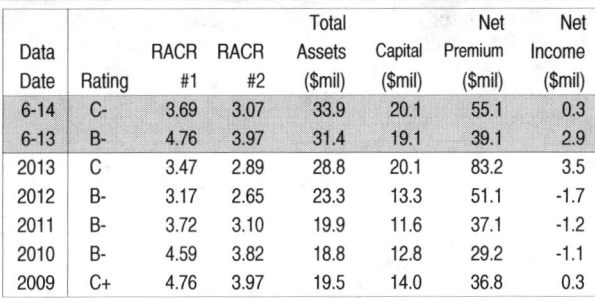

WELLCARE OF FLORIDA INC   B   Good

Major Rating Factors: Good overall profitability index (5.4 on a scale of 0 to 10). Good capitalization index (6.9) based on excellent current risk-adjusted capital (severe loss scenario). Good liquidity (6.7) with sufficient resources (cash flows and marketable investments) to handle a spike in claims. **Other Rating Factors:** Fair overall results on stability tests (4.7). High quality investment portfolio (9.9).

Principal Business: Medicaid (49%), Medicare (46%), comp med (5%)
Mem Phys: 13: 22,300   **12:** 19,400   **13 MLR** 87.8%   **/ 13 Admin Exp** N/A
Enroll(000): Q2 14: 766   **13:** 567   **12:** 522   **Med Exp PMPM:** $267
Principal Investments: Cash and equiv (68%), long-term bonds (32%)
Provider Compensation ($000): Contr fee ($1,583,332), capitation ($167,820)
Total Member Encounters: Phys (2,380,346), non-phys (1,236,060)
Group Affiliation: WellCare Health Plans Inc
Licensed in: FL
Address: 8735 Henderson Rd Ren 2, Tampa, FL 33634
Phone: (813) 290-6200   **Dom State:** FL   **Commenced Bus:** March 1986

Data Date	Rating	RACR #1	RACR #2	Total Assets ($mil)	Capital ($mil)	Net Premium ($mil)	Net Income ($mil)
6-14	B	1.23	1.03	510.7	102.9	1,200.5	-38.0
6-13	B+	2.35	1.96	414.6	179.7	976.8	20.6
2013	B+	1.56	1.30	402.1	150.7	2,021.8	42.8
2012	B+	1.93	1.61	392.9	153.3	1,696.5	80.9
2011	B+	1.38	1.15	454.7	139.7	1,553.8	37.0
2010	B	1.09	0.91	517.5	111.0	1,551.5	19.9
2009	C-	1.02	0.85	449.0	97.9	1,768.0	36.5

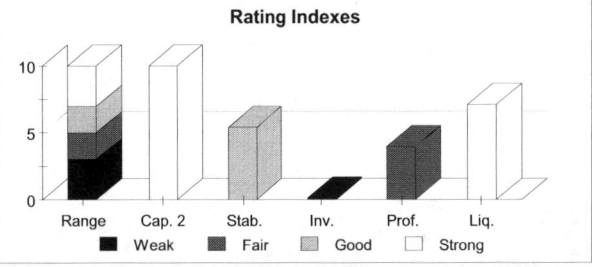

WELLCARE OF GEORGIA INC   B-   Good

Major Rating Factors: Good overall profitability index (6.5 on a scale of 0 to 10). Strong capitalization (7.5) based on excellent current risk-adjusted capital (severe loss scenario). High quality investment portfolio (9.9). **Other Rating Factors:** Excellent liquidity (6.9) with sufficient resources (cash flows and marketable investments) to handle a spike in claims.

Principal Business: Medicaid (75%), Medicare (14%), comp med (11%)
Mem Phys: 13: 32,500   **12:** 9,500   **13 MLR** 86.2%   **/ 13 Admin Exp** N/A
Enroll(000): Q2 14: 647   **13:** 568   **12:** 589   **Med Exp PMPM:** $221
Principal Investments: Cash and equiv (100%)
Provider Compensation ($000): Contr fee ($1,485,775), capitation ($36,755)
Total Member Encounters: Phys (3,106,425), non-phys (1,410,198)
Group Affiliation: WellCare Health Plans Inc
Licensed in: GA
Address: 211 Perimeter Center 8th FLoor, Atlanta, GA 30346
Phone: (813) 290-6200   **Dom State:** GA   **Commenced Bus:** July 2006

Data Date	Rating	RACR #1	RACR #2	Total Assets ($mil)	Capital ($mil)	Net Premium ($mil)	Net Income ($mil)
6-14	B-	1.72	1.43	390.6	153.2	935.5	-6.5
6-13	B	1.79	1.49	293.7	145.1	866.2	0.8
2013	B	1.55	1.29	336.8	145.4	1,805.8	10.9
2012	B+	1.55	1.29	286.1	132.5	1,657.4	0.7
2011	A-	1.98	1.65	343.9	167.7	1,579.1	53.5
2010	B	1.39	1.16	308.9	121.2	1,434.8	6.5
2009	B	1.64	1.37	272.7	127.8	1,386.6	12.3

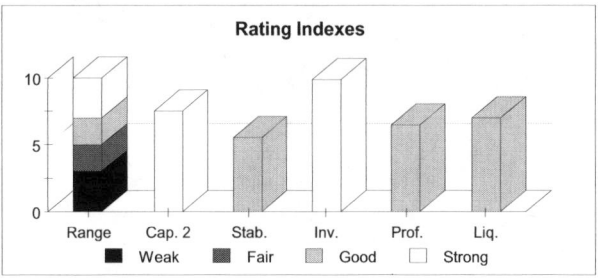

WELLCARE OF LOUISIANA INC

B-   **Good**

Major Rating Factors: Good overall profitability index (5.3 on a scale of 0 to 10). Strong capitalization (9.5) based on excellent current risk-adjusted capital (severe loss scenario). High quality investment portfolio (9.9).
Other Rating Factors: Excellent liquidity (7.1) with ample operational cash flow and liquid investments.
Principal Business: Medicare (100%)
Mem Phys: 13: 3,450   **12:** 1,600   **13 MLR** 77.6%   **/ 13 Admin Exp** N/A
Enroll(000): Q2 14: 8   **13:** 8   **12:** 7   **Med Exp PMPM:** $712
Principal Investments: Cash and equiv (100%)
Provider Compensation ($000): Contr fee ($59,676), capitation ($4,505)
Total Member Encounters: Phys (66,959), non-phys (42,955)
Group Affiliation: WellCare Health Plans Inc
Licensed in: LA
Address: 11603 Southfork Bldg C, Baton Rouge, LA 70816
Phone: (813) 290-6200   **Dom State:** LA   **Commenced Bus:** January 2004

Data Date	Rating	RACR #1	RACR #2	Total Assets ($mil)	Capital ($mil)	Net Premium ($mil)	Net Income ($mil)
6-14	B-	3.32	2.77	27.7	14.4	43.9	0.7
6-13	B-	2.89	2.41	24.3	10.4	38.4	1.2
2013	B	2.92	2.43	24.9	13.3	81.3	4.8
2012	B-	2.37	1.98	23.0	9.0	62.6	1.9
2011	B-	1.56	1.30	17.7	4.7	46.9	-0.8
2010	C+	1.42	1.19	12.8	3.9	40.1	-1.4
2009	C	1.32	1.10	13.1	4.4	49.0	-0.4

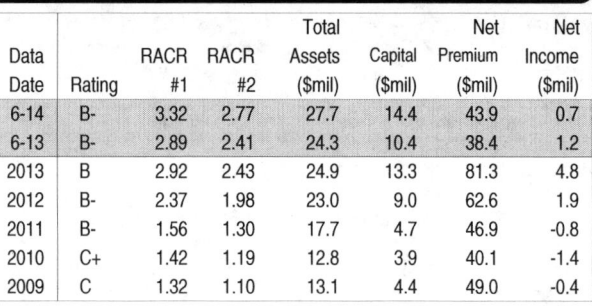

Rating Indexes

WELLCARE OF OHIO INC

C   **Fair**

Major Rating Factors: Fair profitability index (4.4 on a scale of 0 to 10). Strong capitalization (10.0) based on excellent current risk-adjusted capital (severe loss scenario). High quality investment portfolio (9.9).
Other Rating Factors: Excellent liquidity (7.2) with ample operational cash flow and liquid investments.
Principal Business: Medicaid (75%), Medicare (25%)
Mem Phys: 13: 13,000   **12:** 2,000   **13 MLR** 82.8%   **/ 13 Admin Exp** N/A
Enroll(000): Q2 14: 4   **13:** 5   **12:** 102   **Med Exp PMPM:** $265
Principal Investments: Cash and equiv (99%), long-term bonds (1%)
Provider Compensation ($000): Contr fee ($164,020), capitation ($13,235)
Total Member Encounters: Phys (266,610), non-phys (88,248)
Group Affiliation: WellCare Health Plans Inc
Licensed in: OH
Address: 6060 Rockside Woods Blvd #300, Independence, OH 44131
Phone: (813) 290-6200   **Dom State:** OH   **Commenced Bus:** January 2007

Data Date	Rating	RACR #1	RACR #2	Total Assets ($mil)	Capital ($mil)	Net Premium ($mil)	Net Income ($mil)
6-14	C	4.60	3.83	61.0	44.9	22.9	-2.1
6-13	B-	3.73	3.11	96.1	58.4	165.7	-1.1
2013	C+	4.11	3.43	63.7	42.3	199.6	7.5
2012	B-	3.26	2.72	96.0	54.2	313.9	6.8
2011	B-	4.23	3.52	104.4	60.9	260.0	8.0
2010	C+	3.56	2.97	101.0	53.5	238.7	-1.4
2009	C	3.92	3.26	115.9	57.2	252.9	11.5

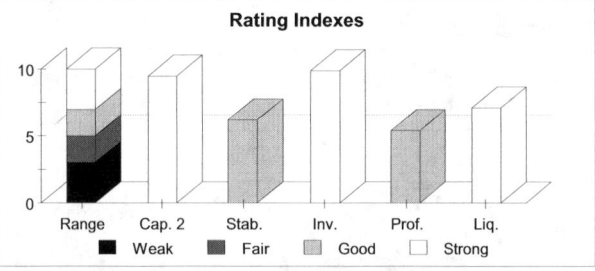

Rating Indexes

WELLCARE OF SOUTH CAROLINA INC

B-   **Good**

Major Rating Factors: Good overall profitability index (5.3 on a scale of 0 to 10). Strong capitalization (9.8) based on excellent current risk-adjusted capital (severe loss scenario). High quality investment portfolio (9.9).
Other Rating Factors: Excellent liquidity (7.2) with ample operational cash flow and liquid investments.
Principal Business: Medicaid (100%)
Mem Phys: 13: 9,200   **12:** 5,443   **13 MLR** 86.9%   **/ 13 Admin Exp** N/A
Enroll(000): Q2 14: 69   **13:** 50   **12:** 58   **Med Exp PMPM:** $228
Principal Investments: Cash and equiv (77%), long-term bonds (23%)
Provider Compensation ($000): Contr fee ($147,173), capitation ($766)
Total Member Encounters: Phys (340,790), non-phys (35,526)
Group Affiliation: WellCare Health Plan Inc
Licensed in: SC
Address: 1320 Main St Suite 300, Columbia, SC 29201
Phone: (813) 206-6200   **Dom State:** SC   **Commenced Bus:** November 2004

Data Date	Rating	RACR #1	RACR #2	Total Assets ($mil)	Capital ($mil)	Net Premium ($mil)	Net Income ($mil)
6-14	B-	3.58	2.98	71.9	33.5	108.3	0.6
6-13	C+	2.34	1.95	63.6	28.5	83.6	-1.5
2013	B-	3.54	2.95	59.2	35.4	162.9	7.7
2012	C+	2.53	2.11	59.5	29.2	218.7	9.8
2011	B	2.38	1.98	88.6	40.8	276.0	-0.2
2010	C+	2.08	1.73	111.3	33.5	269.5	-4.2
2009	B	1.18	0.98	65.7	13.6	196.8	3.0

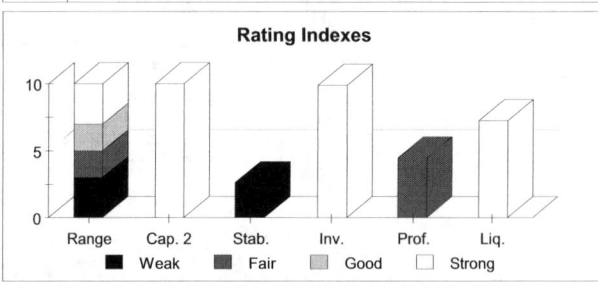

Rating Indexes

WELLCARE OF TEXAS INC   B-   Good

Major Rating Factors: Good quality investment portfolio (6.7 on a scale of 0 to 10). Strong capitalization (7.1) based on excellent current risk-adjusted capital (severe loss scenario). Excellent liquidity (6.9) with sufficient resources (cash flows and marketable investments) to handle a spike in claims.
Other Rating Factors: Weak profitability index (2.4).
Principal Business: Medicare (100%)
Mem Phys: 13: 13,900   **12:** 1,900   **13 MLR** 86.0%   / **13 Admin Exp** N/A
Enroll(000): Q2 14: 38   **13:** 33   **12:** 19   **Med Exp PMPM:** $646
Principal Investments: Cash and equiv (98%), long-term bonds (2%)
Provider Compensation ($000): Contr fee ($211,222), capitation ($8,931)
Total Member Encounters: Phys (280,737), non-phys (185,585)
Group Affiliation: WellCare Health Plans Inc
Licensed in: TX
Address: 2211 Norfolk St Suite 300, Houston, TX 77098
Phone: (813) 290-6200   **Dom State:** TX   **Commenced Bus:** January 2008

Data Date	Rating	RACR #1	RACR #2	Total Assets ($mil)	Capital ($mil)	Net Premium ($mil)	Net Income ($mil)
6-14	B-	1.47	1.22	73.8	20.2	153.3	-9.8
6-13	B	3.16	2.63	61.5	21.5	128.4	1.1
2013	B	1.63	1.35	66.1	24.2	271.9	7.0
2012	B	2.21	1.84	39.5	15.2	133.2	4.0
2011	B-	2.42	2.02	34.2	12.2	86.8	-0.9
2010	C+	3.32	2.77	25.5	13.0	68.1	1.9
2009	C	2.91	2.42	28.4	11.8	76.3	2.0

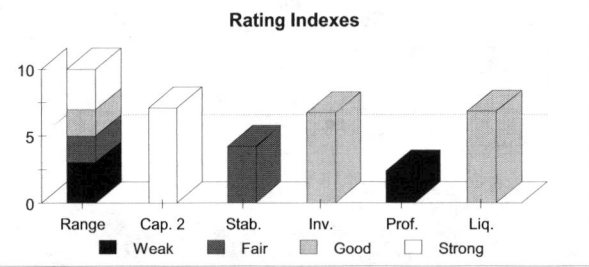

Rating Indexes

Range   Cap. 2   Stab.   Inv.   Prof.   Liq.
■ Weak   ■ Fair   ▨ Good   □ Strong

WELLCARE PRESCRIPTION INS INC   D   Weak

Major Rating Factors: Fair profitability index (4.2 on a scale of 0 to 10). Fair quality investment portfolio (3.7). Strong capitalization (10.0) based on excellent current risk-adjusted capital (severe loss scenario).
Other Rating Factors: Excellent liquidity (7.1) with ample operational cash flow and liquid investments.
Principal Business: Other (100%)
Mem Phys: 13: N/A   **12:** N/A   **13 MLR** 85.5%   / **13 Admin Exp** N/A
Enroll(000): Q2 14: 1,114   **13:** 733   **12:** 813   **Med Exp PMPM:** $71
Principal Investments: Long-term bonds (61%), cash and equiv (39%)
Provider Compensation ($000): Contr fee ($632,431)
Total Member Encounters: N/A
Group Affiliation: WellCare Health Plans Inc
Licensed in: All states except AL, AR, CO, CT, MN, MT, NH, RI, PR
Address: 8735 Henderson Rd Ren 2, Tampa, FL 33634
Phone: (813) 290-6200   **Dom State:** FL   **Commenced Bus:** October 2005

Data Date	Rating	RACR #1	RACR #2	Total Assets ($mil)	Capital ($mil)	Net Premium ($mil)	Net Income ($mil)
6-14	D	4.58	3.82	427.8	90.9	553.6	-32.2
6-13	B+	5.32	4.43	212.9	132.7	377.6	-14.6
2013	B	5.57	4.64	205.6	118.6	715.8	17.1
2012	B+	5.53	4.61	274.8	148.1	929.3	62.4
2011	B	4.01	3.34	275.8	128.3	967.7	36.7
2010	B	5.19	4.32	189.6	122.0	734.0	38.3
2009	C+	3.64	3.03	222.4	99.4	778.2	-3.1

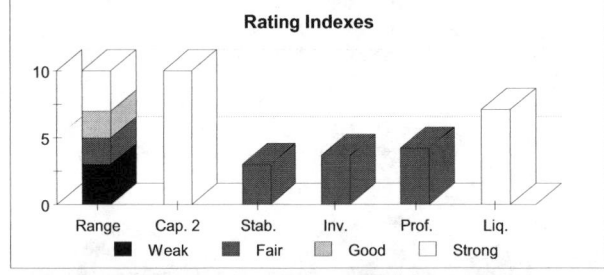

Rating Indexes

Range   Cap. 2   Stab.   Inv.   Prof.   Liq.
■ Weak   ■ Fair   ▨ Good   □ Strong

WELLINGTON LIFE INS CO   D   Weak

Major Rating Factors: Fair profitability index (3.6 on a scale of 0 to 10). Strong capitalization (10.0) based on excellent current risk-adjusted capital (severe loss scenario). High quality investment portfolio (9.9).
Other Rating Factors: Excellent liquidity (10.0) with ample operational cash flow and liquid investments.
Principal Business: Other (100%)
Mem Phys: 13: 4,378   **12:** 4,119   **13 MLR** -77.8%   / **13 Admin Exp** N/A
Enroll(000): Q2 14: 2   **13:** 3   **12:** 227   **Med Exp PMPM:** $-5
Principal Investments: Cash and equiv (100%)
Provider Compensation ($000): Contr fee ($1,518)
Total Member Encounters: Phys (51), non-phys (106)
Group Affiliation: FHC Health Systems Inc
Licensed in: AZ, AR, CA, CO, DC, DE, GA, HI, ID, IN, IA, KS, LA, MD, MS, MT, NE, NV, NM, NC, ND, OH, OK, OR, PA, SC, SD, TN, TX, UT, WA, WI
Address: 2929 N 44th St Suite 120, Phoenix, AZ 85018
Phone: (757) 459-5200   **Dom State:** AZ   **Commenced Bus:** September 1975

Data Date	Rating	RACR #1	RACR #2	Total Assets ($mil)	Capital ($mil)	Net Premium ($mil)	Net Income ($mil)
6-14	D	53.93	44.94	6.2	6.1	0.1	0.0
6-13	D	3.02	2.52	6.7	6.5	0.1	0.1
2013	D	54.05	45.04	6.2	6.1	0.2	0.2
2012	D	3.09	2.58	8.5	6.4	12.3	-0.6
2011	B	6.75	5.63	9.5	7.0	6.4	0.4
2010	B	34.16	28.47	6.7	6.6	1.0	0.0
2009	B-	35.19	29.33	7.1	6.5	1.9	0.2

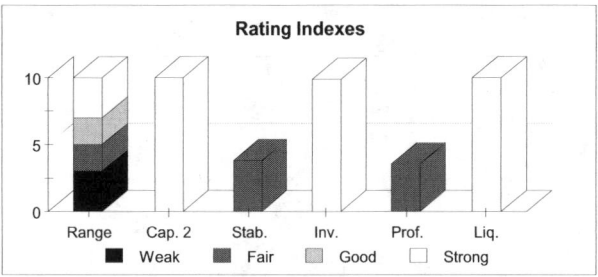

Rating Indexes

Range   Cap. 2   Stab.   Inv.   Prof.   Liq.
■ Weak   ■ Fair   ▨ Good   □ Strong

WELLMARK HEALTH PLAN OF IOWA *   B+   Good

Major Rating Factors: Good quality investment portfolio (5.1 on a scale of 0 to 10). Good overall results on stability tests (6.2). Good liquidity (6.9) with sufficient resources (cash flows and marketable investments) to handle a spike in claims.

Other Rating Factors: Excellent profitability (8.8). Strong capitalization index (10.0) based on excellent current risk-adjusted capital (severe loss scenario).

Principal Business: Comp med (100%)

Mem Phys: 13: 9,326 **12:** 8,735 **13 MLR** 83.0% **/ 13 Admin Exp** N/A

Enroll(000): Q2 14: 92 **13:** 93 **12:** 95 **Med Exp PMPM:** $252

Principal Investments: Long-term bonds (78%), nonaffiliate common stock (21%), cash and equiv (1%)

Provider Compensation ($000): Contr fee ($164,159), bonus arrang ($106,489), FFS ($10,844), capitation ($1,890)

Total Member Encounters: Phys (422,420), non-phys (230,240)

Group Affiliation: Wellmark Inc

Licensed in: IA

Address: 1331 Grand Ave, Des Moines, IA 50309-2901

Phone: (515) 376-4500 **Dom State:** IA **Commenced Bus:** January 1997

Data Date	Rating	RACR #1	RACR #2	Total Assets ($mil)	Capital ($mil)	Net Premium ($mil)	Net Income ($mil)
6-14	B+	7.30	6.08	233.7	158.6	171.7	10.3
6-13	B+	8.13	6.78	249.6	177.0	172.9	21.3
2013	B+	6.81	5.67	207.9	147.6	338.0	25.5
2012	B+	7.27	6.06	224.5	157.8	335.7	34.4
2011	B+	7.48	6.23	218.3	156.9	325.7	28.2
2010	B+	6.15	5.13	190.4	127.6	322.4	29.4
2009	B+	4.94	4.12	154.8	97.3	295.3	14.0

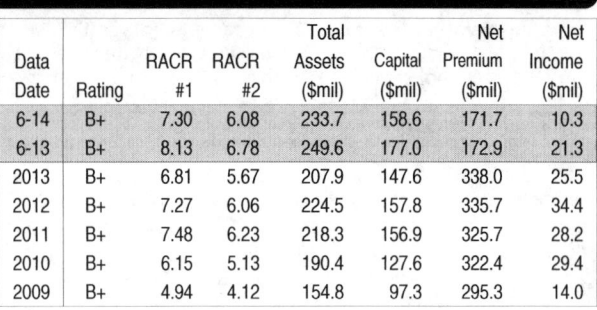

Rating Indexes

WELLMARK INC *   B+   Good

Major Rating Factors: Good overall profitability index (6.8 on a scale of 0 to 10). Good quality investment portfolio (6.8). Good liquidity (6.9) with sufficient resources (cash flows and marketable investments) to handle a spike in claims.

Other Rating Factors: Strong capitalization (10.0) based on excellent current risk-adjusted capital (severe loss scenario).

Principal Business: Comp med (67%), med supp (15%), FEHB (9%), dental (1%), other (9%)

Mem Phys: 13: 6,754 **12:** 6,337 **13 MLR** 83.8% **/ 13 Admin Exp** N/A

Enroll(000): Q2 14: 1,278 **13:** 1,280 **12:** 1,276 **Med Exp PMPM:** $127

Principal Investments: Long-term bonds (45%), affiliate common stock (22%), nonaffiliate common stock (16%), cash and equiv (10%), real estate (6%), pref stock (1%)

Provider Compensation ($000): Contr fee ($1,448,757), bonus arrang ($302,015), FFS ($93,911), other ($119,874)

Total Member Encounters: Phys (3,519,444), non-phys (1,966,061)

Group Affiliation: Wellmark Inc

Licensed in: IA, SD

Address: 636 Grand Ave, Des Moines, IA 50309

Phone: (515) 376-4500 **Dom State:** IA **Commenced Bus:** October 1939

Data Date	Rating	RACR #1	RACR #2	Total Assets ($mil)	Capital ($mil)	Net Premium ($mil)	Net Income ($mil)
6-14	B+	6.62	5.52	2,143.2	1,433.3	1,201.5	44.7
6-13	B	6.05	5.04	1,958.2	1,325.9	1,163.1	92.7
2013	B+	6.44	5.36	2,065.8	1,393.8	2,335.8	154.1
2012	B	5.61	4.68	1,873.8	1,231.2	2,316.8	85.2
2011	B-	5.03	4.19	1,703.8	1,084.3	2,269.7	70.9
2010	B-	4.41	3.68	1,595.9	1,005.4	2,200.5	73.7
2009	B-	3.94	3.29	1,452.7	880.5	2,113.9	-0.1

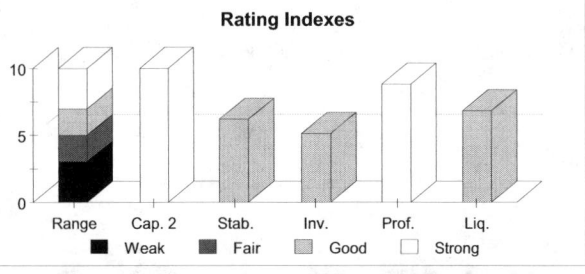

Rating Indexes

WELLMARK OF SOUTH DAKOTA INC *   B+   Good

Major Rating Factors: Good overall profitability index (5.8 on a scale of 0 to 10). Good quality investment portfolio (6.4). Strong capitalization (10.0) based on excellent current risk-adjusted capital (severe loss scenario).

Other Rating Factors: Excellent liquidity (7.0) with sufficient resources (cash flows and marketable investments) to handle a spike in claims.

Principal Business: Comp med (68%), FEHB (20%), med supp (9%), other (2%)

Mem Phys: 13: 1,904 **12:** 1,796 **13 MLR** 86.3% **/ 13 Admin Exp** N/A

Enroll(000): Q2 14: 185 **13:** 185 **12:** 187 **Med Exp PMPM:** $249

Principal Investments: Long-term bonds (61%), nonaffiliate common stock (25%), cash and equiv (13%), pref stock (1%)

Provider Compensation ($000): Contr fee ($499,265), FFS ($54,749)

Total Member Encounters: Phys (955,820), non-phys (347,356)

Group Affiliation: Wellmark Inc

Licensed in: SD

Address: 1601 W Madison St, Sioux Falls, SD 57104

Phone: (605) 373-7200 **Dom State:** SD **Commenced Bus:** August 1996

Data Date	Rating	RACR #1	RACR #2	Total Assets ($mil)	Capital ($mil)	Net Premium ($mil)	Net Income ($mil)
6-14	B+	7.19	5.99	445.3	244.8	331.3	8.8
6-13	B	6.46	5.39	370.9	219.8	316.8	19.6
2013	B+	6.93	5.77	402.5	235.8	639.9	29.9
2012	B	5.94	4.95	358.7	201.8	627.1	20.7
2011	B-	5.56	4.63	322.2	177.9	609.1	34.2
2010	C	4.53	3.77	309.0	149.0	596.3	28.4
2009	C+	3.50	2.92	277.4	119.5	570.8	-12.7

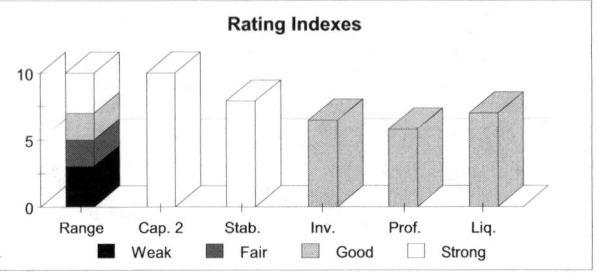

Rating Indexes

WESTERN HEALTH ADVANTAGE

D · Weak

Major Rating Factors: Weak liquidity (2.3 on a scale of 0 to 10) as a spike in claims may stretch capacity. Fair capitalization index (3.7) based on weak current risk-adjusted capital (moderate loss scenario). Good overall results on stability tests (6.5).
Other Rating Factors: Excellent profitability (7.5).
Principal Business: Managed care (100%)
Mem Phys: 13: N/A **12:** N/A **13 MLR** 92.2% **/ 13 Admin Exp** N/A
Enroll(000): Q2 14: 101 **13:** 97 **12:** 91 **Med Exp PMPM:** $362
Principal Investments ($000): Cash and equiv ($41,088)
Provider Compensation ($000): None
Total Member Encounters: N/A
Group Affiliation: None
Licensed in: CA
Address: 1331 Garden Hwy Ste 100, Sacramento, CA 95833
Phone: (916) 563-3180 **Dom State:** CA **Commenced Bus:** May 1997

Data Date	Rating	RACR #1	RACR #2	Total Assets ($mil)	Capital ($mil)	Net Premium ($mil)	Net Income ($mil)
6-14	D	0.61	0.37	55.7	20.3	242.8	0.8
6-13	D-	0.60	0.37	50.6	18.8	213.7	0.3
2013	D	0.58	0.36	49.9	19.4	444.6	0.9
2012	D-	0.59	0.36	51.0	18.5	396.9	1.5
2011	E	0.38	0.23	47.8	17.0	342.6	2.3
2010	E	0.33	0.20	30.8	14.7	294.8	1.4
2009	E+	0.30	0.19	30.2	13.3	276.3	1.7

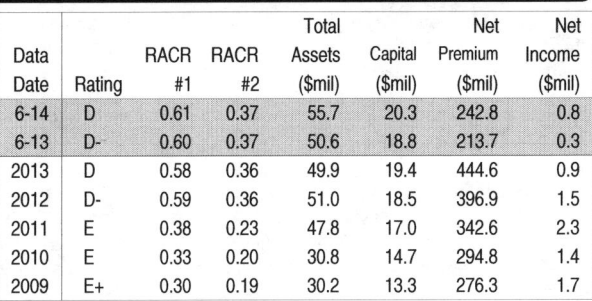

Rating Indexes

WINDSOR HEALTH PLAN OF TN INC

D+ · Weak

Major Rating Factors: Fair profitability index (4.8 on a scale of 0 to 10). Good overall results on stability tests (5.9). Strong capitalization index (9.0) based on excellent current risk-adjusted capital (severe loss scenario).
Other Rating Factors: High quality investment portfolio (9.9). Excellent liquidity (6.9) with sufficient resources (cash flows and marketable investments) to handle a spike in claims.
Principal Business: Medicare (92%), other (8%)
Mem Phys: 13: 63,648 **12:** 59,966 **13 MLR** 86.1% **/ 13 Admin Exp** N/A
Enroll(000): Q2 14: 99 **13:** 118 **12:** 107 **Med Exp PMPM:** $426
Principal Investments: Cash and equiv (93%), long-term bonds (7%)
Provider Compensation ($000): Contr fee ($563,581), other ($43,677)
Total Member Encounters: Phys (1,051,087), non-phys (376,173)
Group Affiliation: WellCare Health Plans Inc
Licensed in: AL, AR, MS, SC, TN
Address: 7100 Commerce Way Suite 285, Brentwood, TN 37027
Phone: (615) 782-7800 **Dom State:** TN **Commenced Bus:** January 1994

Data Date	Rating	RACR #1	RACR #2	Total Assets ($mil)	Capital ($mil)	Net Premium ($mil)	Net Income ($mil)
6-14	D+	2.97	2.48	217.2	123.2	250.4	5.0
6-13	D+	1.60	1.33	201.3	63.6	344.5	5.2
2013	D+	2.62	2.18	194.7	107.5	689.0	53.0
2012	D+	1.61	1.34	209.0	64.0	602.5	-65.0
2011	D+	0.80	0.67	125.5	45.4	505.9	9.5
2010	D+	1.39	1.16	143.4	29.7	231.3	13.2
2009	D-	0.38	0.32	66.4	16.2	366.6	1.0

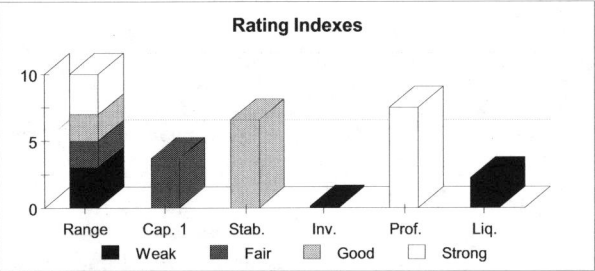

Rating Indexes

WINHEALTH PARTNERS

C- · Fair

Major Rating Factors: Fair overall results on stability tests (3.3 on a scale of 0 to 10). Weak profitability index (0.9). Good capitalization index (6.9) based on excellent current risk-adjusted capital (severe loss scenario).
Other Rating Factors: High quality investment portfolio (9.9). Excellent liquidity (7.0) with ample operational cash flow and liquid investments.
Principal Business: Comp med (100%)
Mem Phys: 13: N/A **12:** 5,523 **13 MLR** 90.7% **/ 13 Admin Exp** N/A
Enroll(000): Q2 14: 14 **13:** 6 **12:** 6 **Med Exp PMPM:** $379
Principal Investments: Cash and equiv (77%), real estate (20%), long-term bonds (3%)
Provider Compensation ($000): Contr fee ($27,535), FFS ($663)
Total Member Encounters: Phys (38,449), non-phys (26,735)
Group Affiliation: None
Licensed in: WY
Address: 1200 E 20TH ST Suite A, Cheyenne, WY 82001
Phone: (307) 773-1300 **Dom State:** WY **Commenced Bus:** May 1996

Data Date	Rating	RACR #1	RACR #2	Total Assets ($mil)	Capital ($mil)	Net Premium ($mil)	Net Income ($mil)
6-14	C-	1.27	1.06	17.8	6.1	31.4	-1.8
6-13	C-	1.80	1.50	13.6	8.7	15.5	-0.6
2013	C-	1.88	1.57	12.3	8.7	29.6	-0.7
2012	C-	1.99	1.66	13.8	9.5	32.4	1.0
2011	C-	1.58	1.31	12.8	8.6	33.8	0.0
2010	C-	1.19	0.99	13.9	8.4	44.9	-2.6
2009	B	1.79	1.49	15.4	10.9	36.8	-2.1

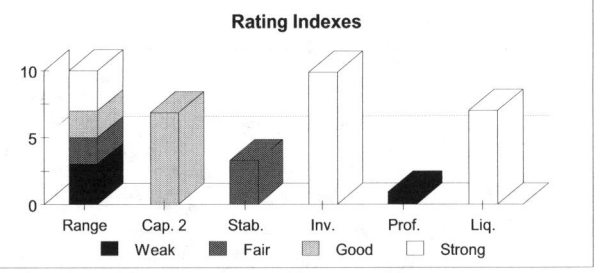

Rating Indexes

WISCONSIN PHYSICIANS SERVICE INS

C+

Fair

Major Rating Factors: Fair profitability index (3.1 on a scale of 0 to 10). Fair quality investment portfolio (4.4). Good liquidity (6.5) with sufficient resources (cash flows and marketable investments) to handle a spike in claims.
Other Rating Factors: Strong capitalization (8.3) based on excellent current risk-adjusted capital (severe loss scenario).
Principal Business: Comp med (68%), med supp (22%), dental (2%), other (8%)
Mem Phys: 13: N/A **12:** N/A **13 MLR** 80.4% **/ 13 Admin Exp** N/A
Enroll(000): Q2 14: 164 **13:** 161 **12:** 167 **Med Exp PMPM:** $209
Principal Investments: Long-term bonds (34%), nonaffiliate common stock (26%), affiliate common stock (19%), real estate (12%), cash and equiv (10%)
Provider Compensation ($000): FFS ($179,621), contr fee ($146,910), other ($66,942)
Total Member Encounters: Phys (903,776), non-phys (277,702)
Group Affiliation: Wisconsin Physicians Ins Group
Licensed in: IL, IN, MI, OH, WI
Address: 1717 West Broadway, Madison, WI 53713
Phone: (608) 221-4711 **Dom State:** WI **Commenced Bus:** April 1977

Data Date	Rating	RACR #1	RACR #2	Total Assets ($mil)	Capital ($mil)	Net Premium ($mil)	Net Income ($mil)
6-14	C+	2.42	2.02	323.1	164.6	266.6	-0.4
6-13	C+	2.12	1.77	324.4	138.3	249.5	7.4
2013	C+	2.54	2.12	345.1	172.7	499.0	10.4
2012	B-	2.19	1.83	332.5	135.5	480.9	-9.0
2011	B	2.27	1.89	327.6	141.6	490.8	7.5
2010	B+	2.87	2.40	313.3	167.2	457.8	7.9
2009	B	3.19	2.66	303.3	167.1	430.4	5.6

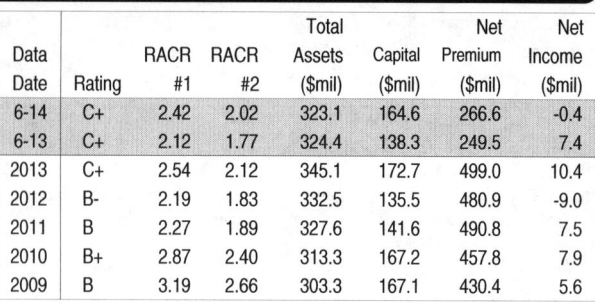

Rating Indexes

WPS HEALTH PLAN INC

C

Fair

Major Rating Factors: Fair liquidity (4.4 on a scale of 0 to 10) as cash resources may not be adequate to cover a spike in claims. Weak profitability index (0.9). Good capitalization (6.7) based on good current risk-adjusted capital (severe loss scenario).
Other Rating Factors: High quality investment portfolio (9.9).
Principal Business: Comp med (100%)
Mem Phys: 13: 4,941 **12:** 2,869 **13 MLR** 96.7% **/ 13 Admin Exp** N/A
Enroll(000): Q2 14: 31 **13:** 20 **12:** 25 **Med Exp PMPM:** $309
Principal Investments: Long-term bonds (89%), cash and equiv (11%)
Provider Compensation ($000): Contr fee ($77,656), FFS ($1,063)
Total Member Encounters: Phys (25,975), non-phys (30,442)
Group Affiliation: Wisconsin Physicians Ins Group
Licensed in: WI
Address: 2710 Executive Dr, Green Bay, WI 54304
Phone: (920) 490-6900 **Dom State:** WI **Commenced Bus:** June 2005

Data Date	Rating	RACR #1	RACR #2	Total Assets ($mil)	Capital ($mil)	Net Premium ($mil)	Net Income ($mil)
6-14	C	1.19	0.99	33.1	8.9	57.8	-3.2
6-13	C	1.01	0.84	22.3	8.5	40.0	-1.2
2013	C	1.07	0.89	23.1	7.9	78.8	-3.7
2012	C	1.23	1.02	30.3	9.9	97.3	-1.6
2011	C+	1.21	1.00	30.7	10.0	103.6	0.0
2010	B	1.33	1.11	26.2	9.8	93.6	-1.3
2009	B-	1.55	1.29	24.5	10.9	91.7	-1.2

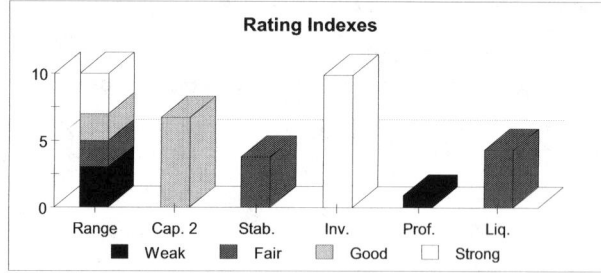

Rating Indexes

Section III

Weiss
Recommended Companies

A compilation of those

U.S. Health Insurers

receiving a Weiss Financial Strength Rating
of A+, A, A-, or B+.

Companies are listed in alphabetical order.

Section III Contents

This section provides contact addresses and phone numbers for all recommended carriers analyzed by Weiss Ratings. It contains all insurers receiving a Financial Strength Rating of A+, A, A-, or B+. If an insurer is not on this list, it should not automatically be assumed that the firm is weak. Indeed, there are many firms that have not achieved a B+ or better rating but are in relatively good condition with adequate resources to cover their risk during an average recession. Not being included in this list should not be construed as a recommendation to cancel policies.

1. Financial Strength Rating	Our rating is measured on a scale from A to F and considers a wide range of factors. Highly-rated companies are, in our opinion, less likely to experience financial difficulties than lower-rated firms. See *About Weiss Financial Strength Ratings* for more information.	
2. Insurance Company Name	The legally-registered name, which can sometimes differ from the name that the company uses for advertising. An insurer's name can be very similar to the name of other companies, so make sure you note the exact name before contacting your agent.	
3. Address	The address of the main office where you can contact the firm for additional financial data or for the location of local branches and/or registered agents.	
4. Telephone Number	The number to call for additional financial data or for the phone numbers of local branches and/or registered agents.	

Weiss Financial Strength Ratings are not deemed to be a recommendation concerning the purchase or sale of the securities of any insurance company that is publicly owned

RATING	INSURANCE COMPANY NAME	ADDRESS	CITY	STATE	ZIP	PHONE
A	4 EVER LIFE INS CO	2 MID AMERICA PLAZA SUITE 200	OAKBROOK TERRACE IL		60181	(312) 951-7700
B+	ADVANCE INS CO OF KS	1133 SW TOPEKA BLVD.	TOPEKA	KS	66629	(785) 291-7052
B+	AETNA HEALTH & LIFE INS CO	151 FARMINGTON AVENUE	HARTFORD	IL	06156	(708) 245-4001
A-	AETNA HEALTH INC (A FLORIDA CORP)	4630 WOODLAND CORPORATE BLVD	TAMPA	FL	33614	(813) 775-0000
B+	AETNA HEALTH INC (A NEW YORK CORP)	100 PARK AVE 12TH FLOOR	NEW YORK	NY	10017	(800) 872-3862
B+	AETNA LIFE INS CO	151 FARMINGTON AVE	HARTFORD	CT	06156	(860) 273-0123
B+	ALLIANCE HEALTH & LIFE INS CO	2850 W GRAND BLVD,5TH FLOOR	DETROIT	MI	48202	(313) 872-8100
A-	AMALGAMATED LIFE INS CO	333 WESTCHESTER AVE	WHITE PLAINS	NY	10604	(914) 367-5000
B+	AMERICAN FAMILY LIFE ASR CO OF COLUM	1932 WYNNTON RD	COLUMBUS	GA	31999	(706) 323-3431
A-	AMERICAN FAMILY LIFE ASR CO OF NY	22 CORPORATE WOODS BLVD #2	ALBANY	NY	12211	(706) 660-7208
B+	AMERICAN FAMILY MUT INS CO	6000 AMERICAN PKWY	MADISON	WI	53783	(608) 249-2111
B+	AMERICAN FIDELITY ASR CO	2000 N CLASSEN BLVD	OKLAHOMA CITY	OK	73106	(405) 523-2000
A-	AMERICAN REPUBLIC INS CO	601 SIXTH AVE	DES MOINES	IA	50309	(515) 245-2000
B+	AMERICAN UNITED LIFE INS CO	ONE AMERICAN SQUARE	INDIANAPOLIS	IN	46204	(317) 285-1877
A-	AMERIGROUP NEW JERSEY INC	101 WOOD AVE S 8TH FLOOR	ISELIN	NJ	08830	(757) 490-6900
B+	AMERIGROUP TEXAS INC	3800 BUFFALO SPEEDWAY STE 400	HOUSTON	TX	77098	(757) 490-6900
A-	ANTHEM HEALTH PLANS OF KENTUCKY INC	13550 TRITON PARK BLVD	LOUISVILLE	KY	40223	(888) 641-5224
B+	ANTHEM HEALTH PLANS OF NEW	3000 GOFFS FALLS RD	MANCHETER	NH	03111	(603) 695-7000
A-	ANTHEM LIFE & DISABILITY INS CO	1 LIBERTY PLAZA 165 BROADWAY	NEW YORK	NY	10006	(212) 476-1000
A-	ANTHEM LIFE INS CO	6740 N HIGH ST SUITE 200	WORTHINGTON	OH	43085	(614) 438-3959
B+	ASSURITY LIFE INS CO	2000 Q STREET	LINCOLN	NE	68503	(402) 476-6500
A	AUTO-OWNERS LIFE INS CO	6101 ANACAPRI BLVD	LANSING	MI	48917	(517) 323-1200
B+	AVMED INC	9400 S DADELAND BLVD	MIAMI	FL	33156	(352) 372-8400
A-	BALBOA LIFE INS CO	400 ROBERT STREET NORTH	ST PAUL	MN	55101	(651) 665-3500
A	BERKSHIRE LIFE INS CO OF AMERICA	700 SOUTH ST	PITTSFIELD	MA	01201	(413) 499-4321
B+	BLUE CARE NETWORK OF MICHIGAN	20500 CIVIC CENTER DRIVE	SOUTHFIELD	MI	48076	(248) 799-6400
A-	BLUE CROSS BLUE SHIELD HEALTHCARE GA	3350 PEACHTREE RD NE	ATLANTA	GA	30326	(404) 842-8000
A-	BLUE CROSS BLUE SHIELD OF ALABAMA	450 RIVERCHASE PARKWAY E	BIRMINGHAM	AL	35298	(205) 220-2100
A+	BLUE CROSS BLUE SHIELD OF ARIZONA	2444 W LAS PALMARITAS DR	PHOENIX	AZ	85021	(602) 864-4100
A	BLUE CROSS BLUE SHIELD OF MINNESOTA	3535 BLUE CROSS RD	EAGAN	MN	55122	(651) 662-8000
B+	BLUE CROSS BLUE SHIELD OF MS, MUTUAL	3545 LAKELAND DR	FLOWOOD	MS	39208	(601) 932-3704
A	BLUE CROSS BLUE SHIELD OF NC	5901 CHAPEL HILL BLVD	DURHAM	NC	27707	(919) 489-7431
A-	BLUE CROSS BLUE SHIELD OF NEBRASKA	1919 AKSARBEN DR	OMAHA	NE	68180	(402) 982-7000
A-	BLUE CROSS BLUE SHIELD OF SC INC	2501 FARAWAY DR	COLUMBIA	SC	29219	(803) 788-3860
B+	BLUE CROSS BLUE SHIELD OF VERMONT	445 INDUSTRIAL LN	MONTPELIER	VT	05602	(802) 223-6131
B+	BLUE CROSS BLUE SHIELD OF WYOMING	4000 HOUSE AVE	CHEYENNE	WY	82001	(307) 634-1393
A+	BLUE CROSS OF CALIFORNIA	1 WELLPOINT WAY	THOUSAND OAKS	CA	91362	(805) 557-6655
A-	BLUE CROSS OF IDAHO HEALTH SERVICE	3000 E PINE AVE	MERIDIAN	ID	83642	(208) 345-4550
A-	BLUE SHIELD OF CALIFORNIA L&H INS CO	50 BEALE ST	SAN FRANCISCO	CA	94105	(415) 229-5703
B+	BLUEBONNET LIFE INS CO	3475 LAKELAND DRIVE	JACKSON	MS	39208	(601) 932-8269
A	BLUECHOICE HEALTHPLAN OF SC INC	I-20 AT ALPINE RD	COLUMBIA	SC	29219	(803) 786-8466
A	BLUECROSS BLUESHIELD OF TENNESSEE	1 CAMERON HILL CIR	CHATTANOOGA	TN	37402	(423) 535-5600
B+	BLUEGRASS FAMILY HEALTH INC	651 PERIMETER PARK, STE 300	LEXINGTON	KY	40517	(859) 269-4475
B+	BOSTON MUTUAL LIFE INS CO	120 ROYALL ST	CANTON	MA	02021	(781) 828-7000
A+	CALIFORNIA PHYSICIANS SERVICE	FIFTY BEALE ST	SAN FRANCISCO	CA	94105	(415) 229-5821
A-	CAPITAL HEALTH PLAN INC	2140 CENTERVILLE PLACE	TALLAHASSEE	FL	32308	(850) 383-3333
A+	CAREFIRST BLUECHOICE INC	840 FIRST STREET NE	WASHINGTON	DC	20065	(410) 581-3000
B+	CAREMORE HEALTH PLAN	12900 PARK PLAZA DR SUITE 150	CERRITOS	CA	90703	(562) 741-4340

RATING	INSURANCE COMPANY NAME	ADDRESS	CITY	STATE	ZIP	PHONE
A	CARESOURCE	230 N MAIN ST	DAYTON	OH	45402	(937) 531-3300
A-	CENTRAL STATES H & L CO OF OMAHA	1212 N 96TH ST	OMAHA	NE	68114	(402) 397-1111
B+	CENTRAL STATES INDEMNITY CO OF OMAHA	1212 N 96TH ST	OMAHA	NE	68114	(402) 997-8000
A-	CIGNA LIFE INS CO OF NEW YORK	499 WASHINGTON BLVD	JERSEY CITY	NJ	07310	(212) 618-5757
A	CINCINNATI INS CO	6200 S GILMORE RD	FAIRFIELD	OH	45014	(513) 870-2000
B+	COLORADO BANKERS LIFE INS CO	5990 GREENWOOD PLAZA BLVD	ENGLEWOOD	CO	80111	(303) 220-8500
B+	COMMUNITY FIRST HEALTH PLANS INC	4801 NW LOOP 410 SUITE 1000	SAN ANTONIO	TX	78229	(210) 227-2347
A-	COMMUNITY HEALTH PLAN OF WASHINGTON	720 OLIVE WAY STE 300	SEATTLE	WA	98101	(206) 521-8833
B+	COMMUNITY INS CO	4361 IRWIN SIMPSON RD	MASON	OH	45040	(513) 872-8100
A	COMMUNITYCARE HMO INC	218 W 6TH STREET	TULSA	OK	74119	(918) 594-5200
A-	COMPANION LIFE INS CO	2501 FARAWAY DR	COLUMBIA	SC	29219	(803) 735-1251
A-	COMPCARE HEALTH SERVICES INS CORP	6775 W WASHINGTON ST	MILWAUKEE	WI	53214	(414) 459-5000
A-	COPIC INS CO	7800 E DORADO PL SUITE 200	ENGLEWOOD	CO	80111	(720) 858-6000
A-	COTTON STATES LIFE INS CO	13560 MORRIS RD SUITE 4000	ALPHARETTA	GA	30004	(309) 821-3000
A+	COUNTRY LIFE INS CO	1701 N TOWANDA AVE	BLOOMINGTON	IL	61701	(309) 821-3000
B+	COVENTRY HEALTH & LIFE INS CO	550 MARYVILLE CENTER DR #300	ST LOUIS	MO	63141	(800) 843-7421
B+	COVENTRY HEALTH CARE OF ILLINOIS INC	2110 FOX DR	CHAMPAIGN	IL	61820	(217) 366-1226
B+	COVENTRY HEALTH CARE OF NEBRASKA INC	15950 W DODGE RD	OMAHA	NE	68118	(800) 471-0240
B+	COVENTRY HEALTH CARE OF WEST VA INC	500 VIRGINIA ST E SUITE 400	CHARLESTON	WV	25301	(800) 788-6445
A-	COVENTRY HEALTH PLAN OF FLORIDA INC	1340 CONCORD TERRACE	SUNRISE	FL	33021	(954) 858-3000
A-	CSAA INS EXCHANGE	3055 OAK RD	WALNUT CREEK	CA	94597	(800) 207-3618
A-	DEARBORN NATIONAL LIFE INS CO	300 EAST RANDOLPH STREET	CHICAGO	IL	60601	(800) 348-4512
B+	DEARBORN NATIONAL LIFE INS CO OF NY	1250 PITTSFORD VICTOR RD # 116	PITTSFORD	NY	14534	(800) 348-4512
A-	ERIE FAMILY LIFE INS CO	100 ERIE INSURANCE PL	ERIE	PA	16530	(814) 870-2000
A	EXCELLUS HEALTH PLAN INC	165 COURT ST	ROCHESTER	NY	14647	(585) 454-1700
A-	FAMILY HERITAGE LIFE INS CO OF AMER	6001 E ROYALTON RD SUITE 200	CLEVELAND	OH	44147	(440) 922-5200
B+	FARM BUREAU LIFE INS CO	5400 UNIVERSITY AVE	WEST DES MOINES	IA	50266	(515) 225-5400
A-	FARM BUREAU LIFE INS CO OF MISSOURI	701 S COUNTRY CLUB DR	JEFFERSON CITY	MO	65109	(573) 893-1400
B+	FEDERAL INS CO	211 N PENNSYLVANIA ST #1350	INDIANAPOLIS	IN	46204	(908) 903-2000
A	FEDERATED LIFE INS CO	121 E PARK SQUARE	OWATONNA	MN	55060	(507) 455-5200
A-	FEDERATED MUTUAL INS CO	121 E PARK SQUARE	OWATONNA	MN	55060	(507) 455-5200
A	FIRST RELIANCE STANDARD LIFE INS CO	590 MADISON AVE 29TH FLOOR	NEW YORK	NY	10022	(212) 303-8400
A-	FIRST SYMETRA NATL LIFE INS CO OF NY	260 MADISON AVE 8TH FLOOR	NEW YORK	NY	10016	(425) 256-8000
B+	FIRST UNITED AMERICAN LIFE INS CO	1020 7TH NORTH ST	LIVERPOOL	NY	13088	(315) 451-2544
A-	FLORIDA HEALTH CARE PLAN INC	1340 RIDGEWOOD AVE	HOLLY HILL	FL	32117	(386) 676-7100
A-	GARDEN STATE LIFE INS CO	2450 S SHORE BLVD SUITE 301	LEAGUE CITY	TX	77573	(409) 763-4661
A-	GERBER LIFE INS CO	1311 MAMARONECK AVE	WHITE PLAINS	NY	10605	(877) 778-0839
B+	GOVERNMENT EMPLOYEES INS CO	ONE GEICO PLAZA	WASHINGTON	DC	20076	(800) 841-3000
B+	GOVERNMENT PERSONNEL MUTUAL L I C	2211 NE LOOP 410	SAN ANTONIO	TX	78217	(210) 357-2222
B+	GRANGE MUTUAL CAS CO	650 S FRONT ST	COLUMBUS	OH	43206	(614) 445-2900
B+	GREATER GEORGIA LIFE INS CO	THREE RAVINIA DR SUITE 1700	ATLANTA	GA	30346	(877) 864-2273
A-	GROUP HEALTH COOPERATIVE	320 WESTLAKE AVE N SUITE 100	SEATTLE	WA	98109	(206) 448-5600
A+	GROUP HEALTH PLAN INC	8100 34TH AVE S, PO BOX 1309	MINNEAPOLIS	MN	55440	(952) 883-6000
A	GUARDIAN LIFE INS CO OF AMERICA	7 HANOVER SQUARE	NEW YORK	NY	10004	(212) 598-1800
B+	HARVARD PILGRIM HEALTH CARE INC	93 WORCESTER ST	WELLESLEY	MA	02481	(781) 263-6000
A	HEALTH ALLIANCE MEDICAL PLANS	301 S VINE	URBANA	IL	61801	(217) 337-8406
A+	HEALTH CARE SVC CORP A MUT LEG RES	300 EAST RANDOLPH STREET	CHICAGO	IL	60601	(312) 653-6000
B+	HEALTH PLAN OF THE UPPER OHIO VALLEY	52160 NATIONAL RD E	ST CLAIRSVILLE	OH	43950	(740) 695-3585

RATING	INSURANCE COMPANY NAME	ADDRESS	CITY	STATE	ZIP	PHONE
A-	HEALTHCARE USA OF MISSOURI LLC	10 S BROADWAY #1200	ST LOUIS	MO	63102	(314) 241-5300
A-	HEALTHKEEPERS INC	2015 STAPLES MILL ROAD	RICHMOND	VA	23230	(804) 354-7000
B+	HEALTHNOW NY INC	257 W GENESEE ST	BUFFALO	NY	14202	(716) 887-6900
B+	HEALTHPARTNERS	8100 34TH AVE S, PO BOX 1309	MINNEAPOLIS	MN	55440	(952) 883-6000
A-	HEALTHPARTNERS INS CO	8170 33RD AVE S	MINNEAPOLIS	MN	55440	(952) 883-6000
A-	HEALTHY ALLIANCE LIFE INS CO	1831 CHESTNUT ST	ST LOUIS	MO	63103	(314) 923-4444
B+	HIGHMARK WEST VIRGINIA INC	614 MARKET ST	PARKERSBURG	WV	26102	(304) 424-7700
B+	HM LIFE INS CO OF NEW YORK	420 FIFTH AVE 3RD FLOOR	NEW YORK	NY	10018	(800) 235-6753
A+	HMO LOUISIANA INC	5525 REITZ AVE	BATON ROUGE	LA	70809	(225) 295-3307
A-	HMO MINNESOTA	3535 BLUE CROSS RD, 43179	ST PAUL	MN	55164	(651) 662-8000
A+	HMO PARTNERS INC	320 WEST CAPITOL	LITTLE ROCK	AR	72203	(501) 221-1800
A-	HORIZON HEALTHCARE OF NEW JERSEY INC	3 PENN PLAZA EAST- PP-15D	NEWARK	NJ	07105	(973) 466-5607
B+	HORIZON HEALTHCARE SERVICES INC	3 PENN PLAZA EAST, PP-15D	NEWARK	NJ	07105	(973) 466-5607
A-	ILLINOIS MUTUAL LIFE INS CO	300 SW ADAMS	PEORIA	IL	61634	(309) 674-8255
B+	INTOTAL HEALTH LLC	8110 GATEHOUSE RD SUITE 400W	FALLS CHURCH	VA	22042	(703) 289-2455
B+	JACKSON NATIONAL LIFE INS CO	5901 EXECUTIVE DR	LANSING	MI	48911	(517) 394-3400
A-	JOHN HANCOCK LIFE INS CO OF NY	100 SUMMIT LAKE DR 2ND FLOOR	VALHALLA	NY	10595	(914) 773-0708
A	KAISER FOUNDATION HEALTH PLAN INC	ONE KAISER PLAZA	OAKLAND	CA	94612	(510) 271-5910
B+	KAISER FOUNDATION HP OF CO	10350 E DAKOTA AVE	DENVER	CO	80231	(800) 632-9700
B+	KAISER PERMANENTE INS CO	300 LAKESIDE DR 26TH FLOOR	OAKLAND	CA	94612	(877) 847-7572
B+	KEYSTONE HEALTH PLAN EAST INC	1901 MARKET ST	PHILADELPHIA	PA	19101	(215) 241-2400
A+	LA HEALTH SERVICE & INDEMNITY CO	5525 REITZ AVE	BATON ROUGE	LA	70809	(225) 295-3307
A-	LIFE INS CO OF ALABAMA	302 BROAD ST	GADSDEN	AL	35901	(205) 543-2022
A-	LIFE INS CO OF BOSTON & NEW YORK	277 NORTH AVE SUITE 200	NEW ROCHELLE	NY	10801	(914) 712-0610
A	LIFEWISE ASR CO	7007 220TH SW	MOUNTLAKE TERRACE	WA	98043	(206) 670-4584
B+	LIFEWISE HEALTH PLAN OF WASHINGTON	7001 220TH ST SW	MOUNTLAKE TERRACE	WA	98043	(425) 918-4000
B+	LINCOLN BENEFIT LIFE CO	206 S 13TH ST, SUITE 200	LINCOLN	NE	68508	(800) 525-9287
A-	MASSACHUSETTS MUTUAL LIFE INS CO	1295 STATE ST	SPRINGFIELD	MA	01111	(413) 788-8411
A-	MATTHEW THORNTON HEALTH PLAN	3000 GOFFS FALLS RD	MANCHESTER	NH	03111	(603) 695-7000
B+	MEDCO CONTAINMENT INS CO OF NY	500 EXECUTIVE BLVD	ELMSFORD	NY	10523	(800) 426-0152
B+	MEDCO CONTAINMENT LIFE INS CO	5010 RITTER RD SUITE 115	MECHANICSBURG	PA	17055	(201) 269-3400
B+	MEDICA HEALTH PLANS	401 CARLSON PARKWAY	MINNETONKA	MN	55305	(952) 992-2900
B+	MEDICAL HEALTH INS CORP OF OHIO	2060 E NINTH ST	CLEVELAND	OH	44115	(216) 687-7000
A-	MEDICAL MUTUAL OF OHIO	2060 E NINTH ST	CLEVELAND	OH	44115	(216) 687-7000
B+	MEDICO CORP LIFE INS CO	11808 GRANT ST	OMAHA	NE	68164	(800) 822-9993
B+	MERIDIAN HEALTH PLAN OF MICHIGAN INC	777 WOODWARD AVE SUITE 600	DETROIT	MI	48226	(313) 324-3700
B+	MERIT LIFE INS CO	601 NW SECOND ST	EVANSVILLE	IN	47708	(812) 424-8031
B+	MIDLAND NATIONAL LIFE INS CO	ONE MIDLAND PLAZA	SIOUX FALLS	SD	57193	(312) 648-7600
A-	MIDWESTERN UNITED LIFE INS CO	8605 KINGS MILL PL	FORT WAYNE	IN	46804	(770) 980-5100
B+	MINNESOTA LIFE INS CO	400 N ROBERT ST	ST PAUL	MN	55101	(651) 665-3500
B+	MOLINA HEALTHCARE OF WASHINGTON INC	21540 30TH DR SE STE 400	BOTHELL	WA	98021	(425) 424-1100
A	MOUNT CARMEL HEALTH PLAN INC	6150 E BROAD ST EE320	COLUMBUS	OH	43213	(614) 546-3211
A-	MUTUAL OF AMERICA LIFE INS CO	320 PARK AVE	NEW YORK	NY	10022	(212) 224-1879
B+	MUTUAL OF OMAHA INS CO	MUTUAL OF OMAHA PLAZA	OMAHA	NE	68175	(402) 342-7600
A-	MUTUAL SAVINGS LIFE INS CO	12115 LACKLAND RD	ST LOUIS	MO	63146	(205) 552-7347
B+	NATIONAL BENEFIT LIFE INS CO	ONE COURT SQUARE	LONG ISLAND CITY	NY	11120	(718) 248-8000
B+	NATIONAL CASUALTY CO	8877 N GAINEY CENTER DR	SCOTTSDALE	AZ	85258	(480) 365-4000
B+	NATIONAL INCOME LIFE INS CO	1020 SEVENTH N ST SUITE 130	LIVERPOOL	NY	13088	(315) 451-2544

RATING	INSURANCE COMPANY NAME	ADDRESS	CITY	STATE	ZIP	PHONE
B+	NATIONAL WESTERN LIFE INS CO	1675 BROADWAY #1200	DENVER	CO	80202	(512) 836-1010
B+	NATIONWIDE MUTUAL FIRE INS CO	ONE NATIONWIDE PLAZA	COLUMBUS	OH	43216	(614) 249-7111
A-	NEW YORK LIFE INS CO	51 MADISON AVE	NEW YORK	NY	10010	(212) 576-7000
A-	NIPPON LIFE INS CO OF AMERICA	650 8TH ST	DES MOINES	IA	50309	(212) 682-3992
A-	NORTHWESTERN MUTUAL LIFE INS CO	720 E WISCONSIN AVE	MILWAUKEE	WI	53202	(414) 271-1444
B+	OHIO NATIONAL LIFE ASR CORP	ONE FINANCIAL WAY	CINCINNATI	OH	45242	(513) 794-6100
A-	OLD REPUBLIC INS CO	414 W PITTSBURGH ST	GREENSBURG	PA	15601	(724) 834-5000
B+	OPTIMA HEALTH PLAN	4417 CORPORATION LANE	VIRGINIA BEACH	VA	23462	(757) 552-7401
A+	OXFORD HEALTH PLANS (NY) INC	ONE PENN PLAZA FLOOR 8	NEW YORK	NY	10119	(203) 459-6000
A-	PACIFIC GUARDIAN LIFE INS CO LTD	1440 KAPIOLANI BLVD STE 1700	HONOLULU	HI	96814	(808) 955-2236
A-	PARAMOUNT ADVANTAGE	1901 INDIAN WOOD CIR	MAUMEE	OH	43537	(419) 887-2500
A-	PARTNERSHIP HEALTHPLAN OF CALIFORNIA	360 CAMPUS LANE SUITE 100	FAIRFIELD	CA	94534	(707) 863-4100
A-	PHYSICIANS LIFE INS CO	2600 DODGE ST	OMAHA	NE	68131	(402) 633-1000
A+	PHYSICIANS MUTUAL INS CO	2600 DODGE ST	OMAHA	NE	68131	(402) 633-1000
B+	PIONEER MUTUAL LIFE INS CO	203 N 10TH ST	FARGO	ND	58102	(701) 277-2300
A-	PREMERA BLUE CROSS	7001 220TH ST SW	MOUNTLAKE TERRACE	WA	98043	(425) 918-4000
B+	PRESBYTERIAN HEALTH PLAN INC	2501 BUENA VISTA SE	ALBUQUERQUE	NM	87106	(505) 923-5700
B+	PRINCIPAL LIFE INS CO	711 HIGH ST	DES MOINES	IA	50392	(515) 247-5111
B+	PRIORITY HEALTH CHOICE INC	1231 E BELTLINE AVE NE	GRAND RAPIDS	MI	49525	(616) 942-0954
A-	PROTECTIVE INS CO	1099 N MERIDIAN ST	INDIANAPOLIS	IN	46204	(317) 636-9800
A+	PROVIDENCE HEALTH PLAN	4400 NE HALSEY BLDG 2 STE 690	PORTLAND	OR	97213	(503) 574-7500
B+	REGENCE BL CROSS BL SHIELD OREGON	100 SW MARKET ST	PORTLAND	OR	97201	(503) 225-5221
A	RESERVE NATIONAL INS CO	601 E BRITTON RD	OKLAHOMA CITY	OK	73114	(405) 848-7931
A-	ROCKY MOUNTAIN HEALTH MAINT ORG	2775 CROSSROADS BLVD	GRAND JUNCTION	CO	81506	(970) 244-7760
B+	ROCKY MOUNTAIN HOSPITAL & MEDICAL	700 BROADWAY	DENVER	CO	80273	(303) 831-2131
B+	SAN MATEO HEALTH COMMISSION	701 GATEWAY BLVD STE 400	S SAN FRANCISCO	CA	94080	(650) 616-0050
B+	SAVINGS BANK LIFE INS CO OF MA	ONE LINSCOTT RD	WOBURN	MA	01801	(781) 938-3500
A-	SECURITY HEALTH PLAN OF WI INC	1515 SAINT JOSEPH AVE	MARSHFIELD	WI	54449	(715) 221-9555
A	SELECTHEALTH INC	5381 GREEN ST	MURRAY	UT	84123	(801) 442-5000
A	SENTRY INS A MUTUAL CO	1800 N POINT DR	STEVENS POINT	WI	54481	(715) 346-6000
A	SENTRY LIFE INS CO	1800 NORTH POINT DR	STEVENS POINT	WI	54481	(715) 346-6000
B+	SENTRY LIFE INS CO OF NEW YORK	251 SALINA MEADOWS PARKWAY	NORTH SYRACUSE	NY	13212	(715) 346-6000
B+	SENTRY SELECT INS CO	3400 80TH ST	MOLINE	IL	61265	(715) 346-6000
A-	SHELTER LIFE INS CO	1817 W BROADWAY	COLUMBIA	MO	65218	(573) 445-8441
A	SHELTERPOINT LIFE INS CO	600 NORTHERN BLVD	GREAT NECK	NY	11021	(516) 829-8100
A	SOUTHERN FARM BUREAU LIFE INS CO	1401 LIVINGSTON LANE	JACKSON	MS	39213	(601) 981-7422
B+	STANDARD INS CO	1100 SW SIXTH AVE	PORTLAND	OR	97204	(503) 321-7000
A-	STANDARD LIFE & ACCIDENT INS CO	ONE MOODY PLAZA	GALVESTON	TX	77550	(409) 763-4661
A-	STANDARD LIFE INS CO OF NY	360 HAMILTON AVE SUITE 210	WHITE PLAINS	NY	10601	(503) 321-7859
B+	STATE FARM MUTUAL AUTOMOBILE INS CO	ONE STATE FARM PLAZA	BLOOMINGTON	IL	61710	(309) 766-2311
B+	SURETY LIFE INS CO	206 S 13TH ST SUITE 300	LINCOLN	NE	68508	(800) 525-9287
B+	SYMETRA LIFE INS CO	777 108TH AVE NE SUITE 1200	BELLEVUE	WA	98004	(425) 376-8000
A+	TEACHERS INS & ANNUITY ASN OF AM	730 THIRD AVE 7TH FLOOR	NEW YORK	NY	10017	(212) 490-9000
B+	THRIVENT LIFE INS CO	625 FOURTH AVE S	MINNEAPOLIS	MN	55415	(612) 340-7214
A	TRANS OCEANIC LIFE INS CO	3 MUNET COURT	GUAYNABO	PR	00936	(787) 782-2680
B+	TRIPLE-S SALUD INC	F D ROOSEVELT AVE 1441	SAN JUAN	PR	00920	(787) 749-4949
B+	TRUSTMARK INS CO	400 FIELD DR	LAKE FOREST	IL	60045	(847) 615-1500
B+	TRUSTMARK LIFE INS CO	400 FIELD DR	LAKE FOREST	IL	60045	(847) 615-1500

RATING	INSURANCE COMPANY NAME	ADDRESS	CITY	STATE	ZIP	PHONE
A-	UCARE MINNESOTA	500 STINSON BLVD NE	MINNEAPOLIS	MN	55413	(612) 676-6500
B+	UNICARE HEALTH PLAN OF WEST VIRGINIA	707 VIRGINIA ST E	CHARLESTON	WV	25301	(877) 864-2273
B+	UNION SECURITY LIFE INS CO OF NY	220 SALINA MEADOWS PKWY #255	SYRACUSE	NY	13212	(315) 451-0066
A	UNITED FARM FAMILY LIFE INS CO	225 S EAST ST	INDIANAPOLIS	IN	46202	(317) 692-7200
B+	UNITED HEALTHCARE OF NY INC	77 WATER ST 14TH/15TH FLOOR	NEW YORK	NY	10005	(203) 459-6000
B+	UNITED HEALTHCARE OF THE MIDLANDS	2717 N. 118TH CIRCLE STE 300	OMAHA	NE	68164	(402) 445-5600
B+	UNITED WORLD LIFE INS CO	MUTUAL OF OMAHA PLAZA	OMAHA	NE	68175	(402) 342-7600
B+	UNITEDHEALTHCARE BENEFITS OF TEXAS	5800 GRANITE PKWY SUITE 900	PLANO	TX	75024	(469) 633-8512
B+	UNITEDHEALTHCARE COMMUNITY PLAN TX	9702 BISSONNET STE 2200W	HOUSTON	TX	77036	(713) 778-8664
B+	UNITEDHEALTHCARE PLAN RIVER VALLEY	1300 RIVER DRIVE SUITE 200	MOLINE	IL	61265	(309) 736-4600
B+	UNIVERSITY HEALTH CARE INC	5100 COMMERCE CROSSSINGS DR	LOUISVILLE	KY	40229	(502) 585-7900
B+	UPMC FOR YOU INC	600 GRANT ST	PITTSBURGH	PA	15219	(412) 434-1200
A	USAA LIFE INS CO	9800 FREDERICKSBURG RD	SAN ANTONIO	TX	78288	(210) 498-8000
B+	USABLE LIFE	320 W CAPITOL SUITE 700	LITTLE ROCK	AR	72201	(501) 375-7200
A+	USABLE MUTUAL INS CO	601 S GAINES	LITTLE ROCK	AR	72201	(501) 378-2000
A-	VIRGINIA PREMIER HEALTH PLAN INC	600 E BROAD ST, SUITE 400	RICHMOND	VA	23219	(804) 819-5151
B+	VIVA HEALTH INC	1222 14TH AVE S	BIRMINGHAM	AL	35205	(205) 939-1718
A-	VOLUNTEER STATE HEALTH PLAN INC	1 CAMERON HILL CIR	CHATTANOOGA	TN	37402	(423) 535-5600
B+	WELLMARK HEALTH PLAN OF IOWA	1331 GRAND AVE	DES MOINES	IA	50309	(515) 376-4500
B+	WELLMARK INC	636 GRAND AVE	DES MOINES	IA	50309	(515) 376-4500
B+	WELLMARK OF SOUTH DAKOTA INC	1601 W MADISON STREET	SIOUX FALLS	SD	57104	(605) 373-7200

Section IV

Weiss
Recommended Companies
by State

A summary analysis of those

U.S. Health Insurers

receiving a Weiss Financial Strength Rating
of A+, A, A-, or B+.

Companies are ranked by Financial Strength Rating
in each state where they are licensed to do business.

Section IV Contents

This section provides a list of the recommended carriers licensed to do business in each state. It contains all insurers receiving a Financial Strength Rating of A+, A, A-, or B+. If an insurer is not on this list, it should not automatically be assumed that the firm is weak. Indeed, there are many firms that have not achieved a B+ or better rating but are in relatively good condition with adequate resources to cover their risk during an average recession. Not being included in this list should not be construed as a recommendation to cancel policies.

Companies are ranked within each state by their Financial Strength Rating, and are listed alphabetically within each rating category. Companies with the same rating should be viewed as having the same relative strength regardless of their ranking in this table.

1. **Insurance Company Name**   The legally-registered name, which can sometimes differ from the name that the company uses for advertising. An insurer's name can be very similar to the name of other companies which may not be on our Recommended List, so make sure you note the exact name before contacting your agent.

2. **Domicile State**   The state which has primary regulatory responsibility for the company. It may differ from the location of the company's corporate headquarters. You do not have to be living in the domicile state to purchase insurance from this firm, provided it is licensed to do business in your state.

3. **Total Assets**   All assets admitted by state insurance regulators in millions of dollars as of the most recent year end. This includes investments and current business assets such as receivables from agents, reinsurers and subscribers.

Weiss Financial Strength Ratings are not deemed to be a recommendation concerning the purchase or sale of the securities of any insurance company that is publicly owned.

Alabama

INSURANCE COMPANY NAME	DOM. STATE	TOTAL ASSETS ($MIL)
Rating: A+		
COUNTRY LIFE INS CO	IL	10,519.0
PHYSICIANS MUTUAL INS CO	NE	1,968.0
TEACHERS INS & ANNUITY ASN OF AM	NY	256,932.8
Rating: A		
4 EVER LIFE INS CO	IL	202.8
AUTO-OWNERS LIFE INS CO	MI	3,557.4
BERKSHIRE LIFE INS CO OF AMERICA	MA	3,589.9
CINCINNATI INS CO	OH	10,807.9
FEDERATED LIFE INS CO	MN	1,483.1
GUARDIAN LIFE INS CO OF AMERICA	NY	44,344.6
RESERVE NATIONAL INS CO	OK	112.3
SENTRY INS A MUTUAL CO	WI	6,832.1
SENTRY LIFE INS CO	WI	5,167.7
SOUTHERN FARM BUREAU LIFE INS CO	MS	12,921.4
USAA LIFE INS CO	TX	21,633.7
Rating: A-		
AMALGAMATED LIFE INS CO	NY	107.0
AMERICAN REPUBLIC INS CO	IA	799.7
ANTHEM LIFE INS CO	IN	571.2
BALBOA LIFE INS CO	CA	58.9
BLUE CROSS BLUE SHIELD OF ALABAMA	AL	2,987.4
CENTRAL STATES H & L CO OF OMAHA	NE	405.9
CIGNA LIFE INS CO OF NEW YORK	NY	376.2
COMPANION LIFE INS CO	SC	278.1
COTTON STATES LIFE INS CO	GA	331.7
DEARBORN NATIONAL LIFE INS CO	IL	2,193.1
FAMILY HERITAGE LIFE INS CO OF AMER	OH	706.7
FEDERATED MUTUAL INS CO	MN	4,667.2
GARDEN STATE LIFE INS CO	TX	120.1
GERBER LIFE INS CO	NY	2,680.4
HEALTHY ALLIANCE LIFE INS CO	MO	954.2
ILLINOIS MUTUAL LIFE INS CO	IL	1,354.0
LIFE INS CO OF ALABAMA	AL	112.7
MASSACHUSETTS MUTUAL LIFE INS CO	MA	189,173.1
MIDWESTERN UNITED LIFE INS CO	IN	237.0
MUTUAL OF AMERICA LIFE INS CO	NY	17,180.5
MUTUAL SAVINGS LIFE INS CO	AL	473.8
NEW YORK LIFE INS CO	NY	142,089.9
NIPPON LIFE INS CO OF AMERICA	IA	222.1
NORTHWESTERN MUTUAL LIFE INS CO	WI	222,040.6
OLD REPUBLIC INS CO	PA	2,591.0
PHYSICIANS LIFE INS CO	NE	1,406.1
PROTECTIVE INS CO	IN	770.4
STANDARD LIFE & ACCIDENT INS CO	TX	525.1
Rating: B+		
AETNA HEALTH & LIFE INS CO	CT	2,193.0
AETNA LIFE INS CO	CT	22,226.6
AMERICAN FAMILY LIFE ASR CO OF COLUM	NE	111,249.2
AMERICAN FIDELITY ASR CO	OK	4,848.9
AMERICAN UNITED LIFE INS CO	IN	22,972.9
ASSURITY LIFE INS CO	NE	2,436.6
BLUEBONNET LIFE INS CO	MS	53.6
BOSTON MUTUAL LIFE INS CO	MA	1,222.3
CENTRAL STATES INDEMNITY CO OF OMAHA	NE	424.9

INSURANCE COMPANY NAME	DOM. STATE	TOTAL ASSETS ($MIL)
COLORADO BANKERS LIFE INS CO	CO	272.7
COVENTRY HEALTH & LIFE INS CO	MO	1,547.4
FEDERAL INS CO	IN	32,182.2
GOVERNMENT EMPLOYEES INS CO	MD	21,998.7
GOVERNMENT PERSONNEL MUTUAL L I C	TX	833.6
GRANGE MUTUAL CAS CO	OH	2,061.4
GREATER GEORGIA LIFE INS CO	GA	50.8
JACKSON NATIONAL LIFE INS CO	MI	176,569.5
LINCOLN BENEFIT LIFE CO	NE	13,279.3
MEDCO CONTAINMENT LIFE INS CO	PA	507.6
MEDICO CORP LIFE INS CO	NE	25.7
MERIT LIFE INS CO	IN	560.2
MIDLAND NATIONAL LIFE INS CO	IA	39,622.6
MINNESOTA LIFE INS CO	MN	34,732.2
MUTUAL OF OMAHA INS CO	NE	6,375.2
NATIONAL BENEFIT LIFE INS CO	NY	475.2
NATIONAL CASUALTY CO	WI	287.3
NATIONAL WESTERN LIFE INS CO	CO	10,001.6
NATIONWIDE MUTUAL FIRE INS CO	OH	5,596.1
OHIO NATIONAL LIFE ASR CORP	OH	3,450.3
PIONEER MUTUAL LIFE INS CO	ND	507.2
PRINCIPAL LIFE INS CO	IA	150,015.7
SAVINGS BANK LIFE INS CO OF MA	MA	2,531.7
SENTRY SELECT INS CO	WI	672.6
STANDARD INS CO	OR	19,996.4
STATE FARM MUTUAL AUTOMOBILE INS CO	IL	135,478.4
SURETY LIFE INS CO	NE	14.3
SYMETRA LIFE INS CO	WA	28,322.5
THRIVENT LIFE INS CO	MN	3,560.4
TRUSTMARK INS CO	IL	1,404.7
TRUSTMARK LIFE INS CO	IL	380.8
UNITED WORLD LIFE INS CO	NE	107.9
USABLE LIFE	AR	426.8
VIVA HEALTH INC	AL	156.2

Alaska

INSURANCE COMPANY NAME	DOM. STATE	TOTAL ASSETS ($MIL)
Rating:	**A+**	
COUNTRY LIFE INS CO	IL	10,519.0
HEALTH CARE SVC CORP A MUT LEG RES	IL	18,206.4
PHYSICIANS MUTUAL INS CO	NE	1,968.0
TEACHERS INS & ANNUITY ASN OF AM	NY	256,932.8
Rating:	**A**	
4 EVER LIFE INS CO	IL	202.8
BERKSHIRE LIFE INS CO OF AMERICA	MA	3,589.9
CINCINNATI INS CO	OH	10,807.9
GUARDIAN LIFE INS CO OF AMERICA	NY	44,344.6
LIFEWISE ASR CO	WA	129.7
RESERVE NATIONAL INS CO	OK	112.3
SENTRY INS A MUTUAL CO	WI	6,832.1
SENTRY LIFE INS CO	WI	5,167.7
USAA LIFE INS CO	TX	21,633.7
Rating:	**A-**	
AMALGAMATED LIFE INS CO	NY	107.0
AMERICAN REPUBLIC INS CO	IA	799.7
ANTHEM LIFE INS CO	IN	571.2
BALBOA LIFE INS CO	CA	58.9
CENTRAL STATES H & L CO OF OMAHA	NE	405.9
COMPANION LIFE INS CO	SC	278.1
DEARBORN NATIONAL LIFE INS CO	IL	2,193.1
FAMILY HERITAGE LIFE INS CO OF AMER	OH	706.7
FEDERATED MUTUAL INS CO	MN	4,667.2
GARDEN STATE LIFE INS CO	TX	120.1
GERBER LIFE INS CO	NY	2,680.4
MASSACHUSETTS MUTUAL LIFE INS CO	MA	189,173.1
MIDWESTERN UNITED LIFE INS CO	IN	237.0
MUTUAL OF AMERICA LIFE INS CO	NY	17,180.5
NEW YORK LIFE INS CO	NY	142,089.9
NIPPON LIFE INS CO OF AMERICA	IA	222.1
NORTHWESTERN MUTUAL LIFE INS CO	WI	222,040.6
OLD REPUBLIC INS CO	PA	2,591.0
PACIFIC GUARDIAN LIFE INS CO LTD	HI	518.1
PHYSICIANS LIFE INS CO	NE	1,406.1
PREMERA BLUE CROSS	WA	2,178.3
PROTECTIVE INS CO	IN	770.4
STANDARD LIFE & ACCIDENT INS CO	TX	525.1
Rating:	**B+**	
AETNA HEALTH & LIFE INS CO	CT	2,193.0
AETNA LIFE INS CO	CT	22,226.6
AMERICAN FAMILY LIFE ASR CO OF COLUM	NE	111,249.2
AMERICAN FIDELITY ASR CO	OK	4,848.9
AMERICAN UNITED LIFE INS CO	IN	22,972.9
ASSURITY LIFE INS CO	NE	2,436.6
BOSTON MUTUAL LIFE INS CO	MA	1,222.3
CENTRAL STATES INDEMNITY CO OF OMAHA	NE	424.9
COLORADO BANKERS LIFE INS CO	CO	272.7
FEDERAL INS CO	IN	32,182.2
GOVERNMENT EMPLOYEES INS CO	MD	21,998.7
GOVERNMENT PERSONNEL MUTUAL L I C	TX	833.6
JACKSON NATIONAL LIFE INS CO	MI	176,569.5
LINCOLN BENEFIT LIFE CO	NE	13,279.3
MEDCO CONTAINMENT LIFE INS CO	PA	507.6

INSURANCE COMPANY NAME	DOM. STATE	TOTAL ASSETS ($MIL)
MEDICO CORP LIFE INS CO	NE	25.7
MIDLAND NATIONAL LIFE INS CO	IA	39,622.6
MINNESOTA LIFE INS CO	MN	34,732.2
MUTUAL OF OMAHA INS CO	NE	6,375.2
NATIONAL BENEFIT LIFE INS CO	NY	475.2
NATIONAL CASUALTY CO	WI	287.3
NATIONAL WESTERN LIFE INS CO	CO	10,001.6
NATIONWIDE MUTUAL FIRE INS CO	OH	5,596.1
PRINCIPAL LIFE INS CO	IA	150,015.7
SAVINGS BANK LIFE INS CO OF MA	MA	2,531.7
SENTRY SELECT INS CO	WI	672.6
STANDARD INS CO	OR	19,996.4
STATE FARM MUTUAL AUTOMOBILE INS CO	IL	135,478.4
SURETY LIFE INS CO	NE	14.3
SYMETRA LIFE INS CO	WA	28,322.5
THRIVENT LIFE INS CO	MN	3,560.4
TRUSTMARK INS CO	IL	1,404.7
TRUSTMARK LIFE INS CO	IL	380.8
UNITED WORLD LIFE INS CO	NE	107.9
USABLE LIFE	AR	426.8

Arizona

INSURANCE COMPANY NAME	DOM. STATE	TOTAL ASSETS ($MIL)
Rating: A+		
BLUE CROSS BLUE SHIELD OF ARIZONA	AZ	1,642.2
COUNTRY LIFE INS CO	IL	10,519.0
HEALTH CARE SVC CORP A MUT LEG RES	IL	18,206.4
PHYSICIANS MUTUAL INS CO	NE	1,968.0
TEACHERS INS & ANNUITY ASN OF AM	NY	256,932.8
Rating: A		
4 EVER LIFE INS CO	IL	202.8
AUTO-OWNERS LIFE INS CO	MI	3,557.4
BERKSHIRE LIFE INS CO OF AMERICA	MA	3,589.9
CINCINNATI INS CO	OH	10,807.9
FEDERATED LIFE INS CO	MN	1,483.1
GUARDIAN LIFE INS CO OF AMERICA	NY	44,344.6
LIFEWISE ASR CO	WA	129.7
RESERVE NATIONAL INS CO	OK	112.3
SENTRY INS A MUTUAL CO	WI	6,832.1
SENTRY LIFE INS CO	WI	5,167.7
UNITED FARM FAMILY LIFE INS CO	IN	2,116.5
USAA LIFE INS CO	TX	21,633.7
Rating: A-		
AMALGAMATED LIFE INS CO	NY	107.0
AMERICAN REPUBLIC INS CO	IA	799.7
ANTHEM LIFE INS CO	IN	571.2
BALBOA LIFE INS CO	CA	58.9
CENTRAL STATES H & L CO OF OMAHA	NE	405.9
COMPANION LIFE INS CO	SC	278.1
COPIC INS CO	CO	523.3
DEARBORN NATIONAL LIFE INS CO	IL	2,193.1
FAMILY HERITAGE LIFE INS CO OF AMER	OH	706.7
FEDERATED MUTUAL INS CO	MN	4,667.2
GARDEN STATE LIFE INS CO	TX	120.1
GERBER LIFE INS CO	NY	2,680.4
ILLINOIS MUTUAL LIFE INS CO	IL	1,354.0
MASSACHUSETTS MUTUAL LIFE INS CO	MA	189,173.1
MIDWESTERN UNITED LIFE INS CO	IN	237.0
MUTUAL OF AMERICA LIFE INS CO	NY	17,180.5
NEW YORK LIFE INS CO	NY	142,089.9
NIPPON LIFE INS CO OF AMERICA	IA	222.1
NORTHWESTERN MUTUAL LIFE INS CO	WI	222,040.6
OLD REPUBLIC INS CO	PA	2,591.0
PACIFIC GUARDIAN LIFE INS CO LTD	HI	518.1
PHYSICIANS LIFE INS CO	NE	1,406.1
PROTECTIVE INS CO	IN	770.4
STANDARD LIFE & ACCIDENT INS CO	TX	525.1
Rating: B+		
AETNA HEALTH & LIFE INS CO	CT	2,193.0
AETNA LIFE INS CO	CT	22,226.6
AMERICAN FAMILY LIFE ASR CO OF COLUM	NE	111,249.2
AMERICAN FAMILY MUT INS CO	WI	13,709.4
AMERICAN FIDELITY ASR CO	OK	4,848.9
AMERICAN UNITED LIFE INS CO	IN	22,972.9
ASSURITY LIFE INS CO	NE	2,436.6
BOSTON MUTUAL LIFE INS CO	MA	1,222.3
CENTRAL STATES INDEMNITY CO OF OMAHA	NE	424.9
COLORADO BANKERS LIFE INS CO	CO	272.7

INSURANCE COMPANY NAME	DOM. STATE	TOTAL ASSETS ($MIL)
COVENTRY HEALTH & LIFE INS CO	MO	1,547.4
FARM BUREAU LIFE INS CO	IA	7,987.7
FEDERAL INS CO	IN	32,182.2
GOVERNMENT EMPLOYEES INS CO	MD	21,998.7
GOVERNMENT PERSONNEL MUTUAL L I C	TX	833.6
JACKSON NATIONAL LIFE INS CO	MI	176,569.5
LINCOLN BENEFIT LIFE CO	NE	13,279.3
MEDCO CONTAINMENT LIFE INS CO	PA	507.6
MEDICO CORP LIFE INS CO	NE	25.7
MERIT LIFE INS CO	IN	560.2
MIDLAND NATIONAL LIFE INS CO	IA	39,622.6
MINNESOTA LIFE INS CO	MN	34,732.2
MUTUAL OF OMAHA INS CO	NE	6,375.2
NATIONAL BENEFIT LIFE INS CO	NY	475.2
NATIONAL CASUALTY CO	WI	287.3
NATIONAL WESTERN LIFE INS CO	CO	10,001.6
NATIONWIDE MUTUAL FIRE INS CO	OH	5,596.1
OHIO NATIONAL LIFE ASR CORP	OH	3,450.3
PIONEER MUTUAL LIFE INS CO	ND	507.2
PRINCIPAL LIFE INS CO	IA	150,015.7
SAVINGS BANK LIFE INS CO OF MA	MA	2,531.7
SENTRY SELECT INS CO	WI	672.6
STANDARD INS CO	OR	19,996.4
STATE FARM MUTUAL AUTOMOBILE INS CO	IL	135,478.4
SURETY LIFE INS CO	NE	14.3
SYMETRA LIFE INS CO	WA	28,322.5
THRIVENT LIFE INS CO	MN	3,560.4
TRUSTMARK INS CO	IL	1,404.7
TRUSTMARK LIFE INS CO	IL	380.8
UNITED WORLD LIFE INS CO	NE	107.9
USABLE LIFE	AR	426.8

Arkansas

INSURANCE COMPANY NAME	DOM. STATE	TOTAL ASSETS ($MIL)
Rating:	**A+**	
COUNTRY LIFE INS CO	IL	10,519.0
HEALTH CARE SVC CORP A MUT LEG RES	IL	18,206.4
HMO PARTNERS INC	AR	171.0
PHYSICIANS MUTUAL INS CO	NE	1,968.0
TEACHERS INS & ANNUITY ASN OF AM	NY	256,932.8
USABLE MUTUAL INS CO	AR	1,521.6
Rating:	**A**	
4 EVER LIFE INS CO	IL	202.8
AUTO-OWNERS LIFE INS CO	MI	3,557.4
BERKSHIRE LIFE INS CO OF AMERICA	MA	3,589.9
CINCINNATI INS CO	OH	10,807.9
FEDERATED LIFE INS CO	MN	1,483.1
GUARDIAN LIFE INS CO OF AMERICA	NY	44,344.6
RESERVE NATIONAL INS CO	OK	112.3
SENTRY INS A MUTUAL CO	WI	6,832.1
SENTRY LIFE INS CO	WI	5,167.7
SOUTHERN FARM BUREAU LIFE INS CO	MS	12,921.4
USAA LIFE INS CO	TX	21,633.7
Rating:	**A-**	
AMALGAMATED LIFE INS CO	NY	107.0
AMERICAN REPUBLIC INS CO	IA	799.7
ANTHEM LIFE INS CO	IN	571.2
BALBOA LIFE INS CO	CA	58.9
CENTRAL STATES H & L CO OF OMAHA	NE	405.9
COMPANION LIFE INS CO	SC	278.1
DEARBORN NATIONAL LIFE INS CO	IL	2,193.1
FAMILY HERITAGE LIFE INS CO OF AMER	OH	706.7
FEDERATED MUTUAL INS CO	MN	4,667.2
GARDEN STATE LIFE INS CO	TX	120.1
GERBER LIFE INS CO	NY	2,680.4
ILLINOIS MUTUAL LIFE INS CO	IL	1,354.0
LIFE INS CO OF ALABAMA	AL	112.7
MASSACHUSETTS MUTUAL LIFE INS CO	MA	189,173.1
MIDWESTERN UNITED LIFE INS CO	IN	237.0
MUTUAL OF AMERICA LIFE INS CO	NY	17,180.5
NEW YORK LIFE INS CO	NY	142,089.9
NIPPON LIFE INS CO OF AMERICA	IA	222.1
NORTHWESTERN MUTUAL LIFE INS CO	WI	222,040.6
OLD REPUBLIC INS CO	PA	2,591.0
PHYSICIANS LIFE INS CO	NE	1,406.1
PROTECTIVE INS CO	IN	770.4
SHELTER LIFE INS CO	MO	1,097.7
STANDARD LIFE & ACCIDENT INS CO	TX	525.1
Rating:	**B+**	
AETNA HEALTH & LIFE INS CO	CT	2,193.0
AETNA LIFE INS CO	CT	22,226.6
AMERICAN FAMILY LIFE ASR CO OF COLUM	NE	111,249.2
AMERICAN FIDELITY ASR CO	OK	4,848.9
AMERICAN UNITED LIFE INS CO	IN	22,972.9
ASSURITY LIFE INS CO	NE	2,436.6
BLUEBONNET LIFE INS CO	MS	53.6
BOSTON MUTUAL LIFE INS CO	MA	1,222.3
CENTRAL STATES INDEMNITY CO OF OMAHA	NE	424.9
COLORADO BANKERS LIFE INS CO	CO	272.7

INSURANCE COMPANY NAME	DOM. STATE	TOTAL ASSETS ($MIL)
COVENTRY HEALTH & LIFE INS CO	MO	1,547.4
FEDERAL INS CO	IN	32,182.2
GOVERNMENT EMPLOYEES INS CO	MD	21,998.7
GOVERNMENT PERSONNEL MUTUAL L I C	TX	833.6
JACKSON NATIONAL LIFE INS CO	MI	176,569.5
LINCOLN BENEFIT LIFE CO	NE	13,279.3
MEDCO CONTAINMENT LIFE INS CO	PA	507.6
MEDICO CORP LIFE INS CO	NE	25.7
MERIT LIFE INS CO	IN	560.2
MIDLAND NATIONAL LIFE INS CO	IA	39,622.6
MINNESOTA LIFE INS CO	MN	34,732.2
MUTUAL OF OMAHA INS CO	NE	6,375.2
NATIONAL BENEFIT LIFE INS CO	NY	475.2
NATIONAL CASUALTY CO	WI	287.3
NATIONAL WESTERN LIFE INS CO	CO	10,001.6
NATIONWIDE MUTUAL FIRE INS CO	OH	5,596.1
OHIO NATIONAL LIFE ASR CORP	OH	3,450.3
PIONEER MUTUAL LIFE INS CO	ND	507.2
PRINCIPAL LIFE INS CO	IA	150,015.7
SAVINGS BANK LIFE INS CO OF MA	MA	2,531.7
SENTRY SELECT INS CO	WI	672.6
STANDARD INS CO	OR	19,996.4
STATE FARM MUTUAL AUTOMOBILE INS CO	IL	135,478.4
SURETY LIFE INS CO	NE	14.3
SYMETRA LIFE INS CO	WA	28,322.5
THRIVENT LIFE INS CO	MN	3,560.4
TRUSTMARK INS CO	IL	1,404.7
TRUSTMARK LIFE INS CO	IL	380.8
UNITED WORLD LIFE INS CO	NE	107.9
USABLE LIFE	AR	426.8

California

INSURANCE COMPANY NAME	DOM. STATE	TOTAL ASSETS ($MIL)
Rating: A+		
BLUE CROSS OF CALIFORNIA	CA	5,235.8
CALIFORNIA PHYSICIANS SERVICE	CA	6,941.7
PHYSICIANS MUTUAL INS CO	NE	1,968.0
TEACHERS INS & ANNUITY ASN OF AM	NY	256,932.8
Rating: A		
4 EVER LIFE INS CO	IL	202.8
BERKSHIRE LIFE INS CO OF AMERICA	MA	3,589.9
CINCINNATI INS CO	OH	10,807.9
FEDERATED LIFE INS CO	MN	1,483.1
GUARDIAN LIFE INS CO OF AMERICA	NY	44,344.6
KAISER FOUNDATION HEALTH PLAN INC	CA	60,291.5
LIFEWISE ASR CO	WA	129.7
SENTRY INS A MUTUAL CO	WI	6,832.1
SENTRY LIFE INS CO	WI	5,167.7
UNITED FARM FAMILY LIFE INS CO	IN	2,116.5
USAA LIFE INS CO	TX	21,633.7
Rating: A-		
AMALGAMATED LIFE INS CO	NY	107.0
AMERICAN REPUBLIC INS CO	IA	799.7
ANTHEM LIFE INS CO	IN	571.2
BALBOA LIFE INS CO	CA	58.9
BLUE SHIELD OF CALIFORNIA L&H INS CO	CA	838.0
CENTRAL STATES H & L CO OF OMAHA	NE	405.9
CSAA INS EXCHANGE	CA	6,888.9
DEARBORN NATIONAL LIFE INS CO	IL	2,193.1
FAMILY HERITAGE LIFE INS CO OF AMER	OH	706.7
FEDERATED MUTUAL INS CO	MN	4,667.2
GARDEN STATE LIFE INS CO	TX	120.1
GERBER LIFE INS CO	NY	2,680.4
ILLINOIS MUTUAL LIFE INS CO	IL	1,354.0
MASSACHUSETTS MUTUAL LIFE INS CO	MA	189,173.1
MIDWESTERN UNITED LIFE INS CO	IN	237.0
MUTUAL OF AMERICA LIFE INS CO	NY	17,180.5
NEW YORK LIFE INS CO	NY	142,089.9
NIPPON LIFE INS CO OF AMERICA	IA	222.1
NORTHWESTERN MUTUAL LIFE INS CO	WI	222,040.6
OLD REPUBLIC INS CO	PA	2,591.0
PACIFIC GUARDIAN LIFE INS CO LTD	HI	518.1
PARTNERSHIP HEALTHPLAN OF CALIFORNIA	CA	502.0
PHYSICIANS LIFE INS CO	NE	1,406.1
PROTECTIVE INS CO	IN	770.4
STANDARD LIFE & ACCIDENT INS CO	TX	525.1
Rating: B+		
AETNA HEALTH & LIFE INS CO	CT	2,193.0
AETNA LIFE INS CO	CT	22,226.6
AMERICAN FAMILY LIFE ASR CO OF COLUM	NE	111,249.2
AMERICAN FIDELITY ASR CO	OK	4,848.9
AMERICAN UNITED LIFE INS CO	IN	22,972.9
ASSURITY LIFE INS CO	NE	2,436.6
BOSTON MUTUAL LIFE INS CO	MA	1,222.3
CAREMORE HEALTH PLAN	CA	298.1
CENTRAL STATES INDEMNITY CO OF OMAHA	NE	424.9
COLORADO BANKERS LIFE INS CO	CO	272.7
FEDERAL INS CO	IN	32,182.2

INSURANCE COMPANY NAME	DOM. STATE	TOTAL ASSETS ($MIL)
GOVERNMENT EMPLOYEES INS CO	MD	21,998.7
GOVERNMENT PERSONNEL MUTUAL L I C	TX	833.6
JACKSON NATIONAL LIFE INS CO	MI	176,569.5
KAISER PERMANENTE INS CO	CA	179.4
LINCOLN BENEFIT LIFE CO	NE	13,279.3
MEDCO CONTAINMENT LIFE INS CO	PA	507.6
MERIT LIFE INS CO	IN	560.2
MIDLAND NATIONAL LIFE INS CO	IA	39,622.6
MINNESOTA LIFE INS CO	MN	34,732.2
MUTUAL OF OMAHA INS CO	NE	6,375.2
NATIONAL BENEFIT LIFE INS CO	NY	475.2
NATIONAL CASUALTY CO	WI	287.3
NATIONAL WESTERN LIFE INS CO	CO	10,001.6
NATIONWIDE MUTUAL FIRE INS CO	OH	5,596.1
OHIO NATIONAL LIFE ASR CORP	OH	3,450.3
PIONEER MUTUAL LIFE INS CO	ND	507.2
PRINCIPAL LIFE INS CO	IA	150,015.7
SAN MATEO HEALTH COMMISSION	CA	298.4
SAVINGS BANK LIFE INS CO OF MA	MA	2,531.7
SENTRY SELECT INS CO	WI	672.6
STANDARD INS CO	OR	19,996.4
STATE FARM MUTUAL AUTOMOBILE INS CO	IL	135,478.4
SURETY LIFE INS CO	NE	14.3
SYMETRA LIFE INS CO	WA	28,322.5
THRIVENT LIFE INS CO	MN	3,560.4
TRUSTMARK INS CO	IL	1,404.7
TRUSTMARK LIFE INS CO	IL	380.8
UNITED WORLD LIFE INS CO	NE	107.9
USABLE LIFE	AR	426.8

Colorado

INSURANCE COMPANY NAME	DOM. STATE	TOTAL ASSETS ($MIL)
Rating: A+		
COUNTRY LIFE INS CO	IL	10,519.0
HEALTH CARE SVC CORP A MUT LEG RES	IL	18,206.4
PHYSICIANS MUTUAL INS CO	NE	1,968.0
TEACHERS INS & ANNUITY ASN OF AM	NY	256,932.8
Rating: A		
4 EVER LIFE INS CO	IL	202.8
AUTO-OWNERS LIFE INS CO	MI	3,557.4
BERKSHIRE LIFE INS CO OF AMERICA	MA	3,589.9
CINCINNATI INS CO	OH	10,807.9
FEDERATED LIFE INS CO	MN	1,483.1
GUARDIAN LIFE INS CO OF AMERICA	NY	44,344.6
LIFEWISE ASR CO	WA	129.7
RESERVE NATIONAL INS CO	OK	112.3
SENTRY INS A MUTUAL CO	WI	6,832.1
SENTRY LIFE INS CO	WI	5,167.7
SHELTERPOINT LIFE INS CO	NY	103.8
SOUTHERN FARM BUREAU LIFE INS CO	MS	12,921.4
USAA LIFE INS CO	TX	21,633.7
Rating: A-		
AMALGAMATED LIFE INS CO	NY	107.0
AMERICAN REPUBLIC INS CO	IA	799.7
ANTHEM LIFE INS CO	IN	571.2
BALBOA LIFE INS CO	CA	58.9
CENTRAL STATES H & L CO OF OMAHA	NE	405.9
COMPANION LIFE INS CO	SC	278.1
COPIC INS CO	CO	523.3
DEARBORN NATIONAL LIFE INS CO	IL	2,193.1
FAMILY HERITAGE LIFE INS CO OF AMER	OH	706.7
FEDERATED MUTUAL INS CO	MN	4,667.2
GARDEN STATE LIFE INS CO	TX	120.1
GERBER LIFE INS CO	NY	2,680.4
ILLINOIS MUTUAL LIFE INS CO	IL	1,354.0
MASSACHUSETTS MUTUAL LIFE INS CO	MA	189,173.1
MIDWESTERN UNITED LIFE INS CO	IN	237.0
MUTUAL OF AMERICA LIFE INS CO	NY	17,180.5
NEW YORK LIFE INS CO	NY	142,089.9
NIPPON LIFE INS CO OF AMERICA	IA	222.1
NORTHWESTERN MUTUAL LIFE INS CO	WI	222,040.6
OLD REPUBLIC INS CO	PA	2,591.0
PACIFIC GUARDIAN LIFE INS CO LTD	HI	518.1
PHYSICIANS LIFE INS CO	NE	1,406.1
PROTECTIVE INS CO	IN	770.4
ROCKY MOUNTAIN HEALTH MAINT ORG	CO	147.0
SHELTER LIFE INS CO	MO	1,097.7
STANDARD LIFE & ACCIDENT INS CO	TX	525.1
Rating: B+		
AETNA HEALTH & LIFE INS CO	CT	2,193.0
AETNA LIFE INS CO	CT	22,226.6
AMERICAN FAMILY LIFE ASR CO OF COLUM	NE	111,249.2
AMERICAN FAMILY MUT INS CO	WI	13,709.4
AMERICAN FIDELITY ASR CO	OK	4,848.9
AMERICAN UNITED LIFE INS CO	IN	22,972.9
ASSURITY LIFE INS CO	NE	2,436.6
BOSTON MUTUAL LIFE INS CO	MA	1,222.3

INSURANCE COMPANY NAME	DOM. STATE	TOTAL ASSETS ($MIL)
CENTRAL STATES INDEMNITY CO OF OMAHA	NE	424.9
COLORADO BANKERS LIFE INS CO	CO	272.7
COVENTRY HEALTH & LIFE INS CO	MO	1,547.4
FARM BUREAU LIFE INS CO	IA	7,987.7
FEDERAL INS CO	IN	32,182.2
GOVERNMENT EMPLOYEES INS CO	MD	21,998.7
GOVERNMENT PERSONNEL MUTUAL L I C	TX	833.6
JACKSON NATIONAL LIFE INS CO	MI	176,569.5
KAISER FOUNDATION HP OF CO	CO	1,274.6
KAISER PERMANENTE INS CO	CA	179.4
LINCOLN BENEFIT LIFE CO	NE	13,279.3
MEDCO CONTAINMENT LIFE INS CO	PA	507.6
MEDICO CORP LIFE INS CO	NE	25.7
MERIT LIFE INS CO	IN	560.2
MIDLAND NATIONAL LIFE INS CO	IA	39,622.6
MINNESOTA LIFE INS CO	MN	34,732.2
MUTUAL OF OMAHA INS CO	NE	6,375.2
NATIONAL BENEFIT LIFE INS CO	NY	475.2
NATIONAL CASUALTY CO	WI	287.3
NATIONAL WESTERN LIFE INS CO	CO	10,001.6
NATIONWIDE MUTUAL FIRE INS CO	OH	5,596.1
OHIO NATIONAL LIFE ASR CORP	OH	3,450.3
PIONEER MUTUAL LIFE INS CO	ND	507.2
PRINCIPAL LIFE INS CO	IA	150,015.7
ROCKY MOUNTAIN HOSPITAL & MEDICAL	CO	889.3
SAVINGS BANK LIFE INS CO OF MA	MA	2,531.7
SENTRY SELECT INS CO	WI	672.6
STANDARD INS CO	OR	19,996.4
STATE FARM MUTUAL AUTOMOBILE INS CO	IL	135,478.4
SURETY LIFE INS CO	NE	14.3
SYMETRA LIFE INS CO	WA	28,322.5
THRIVENT LIFE INS CO	MN	3,560.4
TRUSTMARK INS CO	IL	1,404.7
TRUSTMARK LIFE INS CO	IL	380.8
UNITED WORLD LIFE INS CO	NE	107.9
USABLE LIFE	AR	426.8

Connecticut

INSURANCE COMPANY NAME	DOM. STATE	TOTAL ASSETS ($MIL)	INSURANCE COMPANY NAME	DOM. STATE	TOTAL ASSETS ($MIL)
Rating: A+			MEDCO CONTAINMENT LIFE INS CO	PA	507.6
			MERIT LIFE INS CO	IN	560.2
COUNTRY LIFE INS CO	IL	10,519.0	MIDLAND NATIONAL LIFE INS CO	IA	39,622.6
HEALTH CARE SVC CORP A MUT LEG RES	IL	18,206.4	MINNESOTA LIFE INS CO	MN	34,732.2
PHYSICIANS MUTUAL INS CO	NE	1,968.0	MUTUAL OF OMAHA INS CO	NE	6,375.2
TEACHERS INS & ANNUITY ASN OF AM	NY	256,932.8	NATIONAL BENEFIT LIFE INS CO	NY	475.2
Rating: A			NATIONAL CASUALTY CO	WI	287.3
			NATIONAL WESTERN LIFE INS CO	CO	10,001.6
4 EVER LIFE INS CO	IL	202.8	NATIONWIDE MUTUAL FIRE INS CO	OH	5,596.1
BERKSHIRE LIFE INS CO OF AMERICA	MA	3,589.9	OHIO NATIONAL LIFE ASR CORP	OH	3,450.3
CINCINNATI INS CO	OH	10,807.9	PIONEER MUTUAL LIFE INS CO	ND	507.2
FEDERATED LIFE INS CO	MN	1,483.1	PRINCIPAL LIFE INS CO	IA	150,015.7
GUARDIAN LIFE INS CO OF AMERICA	NY	44,344.6	SAVINGS BANK LIFE INS CO OF MA	MA	2,531.7
RESERVE NATIONAL INS CO	OK	112.3	SENTRY SELECT INS CO	WI	672.6
SENTRY INS A MUTUAL CO	WI	6,832.1	STANDARD INS CO	OR	19,996.4
SENTRY LIFE INS CO	WI	5,167.7	STATE FARM MUTUAL AUTOMOBILE INS CO	IL	135,478.4
SHELTERPOINT LIFE INS CO	NY	103.8	SURETY LIFE INS CO	NE	14.3
USAA LIFE INS CO	TX	21,633.7	SYMETRA LIFE INS CO	WA	28,322.5
Rating: A-			THRIVENT LIFE INS CO	MN	3,560.4
			TRUSTMARK INS CO	IL	1,404.7
AMALGAMATED LIFE INS CO	NY	107.0	TRUSTMARK LIFE INS CO	IL	380.8
AMERICAN FAMILY LIFE ASR CO OF NY	NY	706.5	USABLE LIFE	AR	426.8
AMERICAN REPUBLIC INS CO	IA	799.7			
ANTHEM LIFE INS CO	IN	571.2			
BALBOA LIFE INS CO	CA	58.9			
CENTRAL STATES H & L CO OF OMAHA	NE	405.9			
COMPANION LIFE INS CO	SC	278.1			
DEARBORN NATIONAL LIFE INS CO	IL	2,193.1			
FAMILY HERITAGE LIFE INS CO OF AMER	OH	706.7			
FEDERATED MUTUAL INS CO	MN	4,667.2			
GARDEN STATE LIFE INS CO	TX	120.1			
GERBER LIFE INS CO	NY	2,680.4			
ILLINOIS MUTUAL LIFE INS CO	IL	1,354.0			
MASSACHUSETTS MUTUAL LIFE INS CO	MA	189,173.1			
MIDWESTERN UNITED LIFE INS CO	IN	237.0			
MUTUAL OF AMERICA LIFE INS CO	NY	17,180.5			
NEW YORK LIFE INS CO	NY	142,089.9			
NIPPON LIFE INS CO OF AMERICA	IA	222.1			
NORTHWESTERN MUTUAL LIFE INS CO	WI	222,040.6			
OLD REPUBLIC INS CO	PA	2,591.0			
PHYSICIANS LIFE INS CO	NE	1,406.1			
PROTECTIVE INS CO	IN	770.4			
STANDARD LIFE & ACCIDENT INS CO	TX	525.1			
Rating: B+					
AETNA HEALTH & LIFE INS CO	CT	2,193.0			
AETNA LIFE INS CO	CT	22,226.6			
AMERICAN FAMILY LIFE ASR CO OF COLUM	NE	111,249.2			
AMERICAN FIDELITY ASR CO	OK	4,848.9			
AMERICAN UNITED LIFE INS CO	IN	22,972.9			
ASSURITY LIFE INS CO	NE	2,436.6			
BOSTON MUTUAL LIFE INS CO	MA	1,222.3			
CENTRAL STATES INDEMNITY CO OF OMAHA	NE	424.9			
COLORADO BANKERS LIFE INS CO	CO	272.7			
FEDERAL INS CO	IN	32,182.2			
GOVERNMENT EMPLOYEES INS CO	MD	21,998.7			
GOVERNMENT PERSONNEL MUTUAL L I C	TX	833.6			
JACKSON NATIONAL LIFE INS CO	MI	176,569.5			
LINCOLN BENEFIT LIFE CO	NE	13,279.3			

Delaware

INSURANCE COMPANY NAME	DOM. STATE	TOTAL ASSETS ($MIL)
Rating: A+		
COUNTRY LIFE INS CO	IL	10,519.0
HEALTH CARE SVC CORP A MUT LEG RES	IL	18,206.4
PHYSICIANS MUTUAL INS CO	NE	1,968.0
TEACHERS INS & ANNUITY ASN OF AM	NY	256,932.8
Rating: A		
4 EVER LIFE INS CO	IL	202.8
BERKSHIRE LIFE INS CO OF AMERICA	MA	3,589.9
CINCINNATI INS CO	OH	10,807.9
FEDERATED LIFE INS CO	MN	1,483.1
FIRST RELIANCE STANDARD LIFE INS CO	NY	188.3
GUARDIAN LIFE INS CO OF AMERICA	NY	44,344.6
RESERVE NATIONAL INS CO	OK	112.3
SENTRY INS A MUTUAL CO	WI	6,832.1
SENTRY LIFE INS CO	WI	5,167.7
SHELTERPOINT LIFE INS CO	NY	103.8
USAA LIFE INS CO	TX	21,633.7
Rating: A-		
AMALGAMATED LIFE INS CO	NY	107.0
AMERICAN REPUBLIC INS CO	IA	799.7
ANTHEM LIFE INS CO	IN	571.2
BALBOA LIFE INS CO	CA	58.9
CENTRAL STATES H & L CO OF OMAHA	NE	405.9
COMPANION LIFE INS CO	SC	278.1
DEARBORN NATIONAL LIFE INS CO	IL	2,193.1
FAMILY HERITAGE LIFE INS CO OF AMER	OH	706.7
FEDERATED MUTUAL INS CO	MN	4,667.2
GARDEN STATE LIFE INS CO	TX	120.1
GERBER LIFE INS CO	NY	2,680.4
ILLINOIS MUTUAL LIFE INS CO	IL	1,354.0
MASSACHUSETTS MUTUAL LIFE INS CO	MA	189,173.1
MIDWESTERN UNITED LIFE INS CO	IN	237.0
MUTUAL OF AMERICA LIFE INS CO	NY	17,180.5
NEW YORK LIFE INS CO	NY	142,089.9
NIPPON LIFE INS CO OF AMERICA	IA	222.1
NORTHWESTERN MUTUAL LIFE INS CO	WI	222,040.6
OLD REPUBLIC INS CO	PA	2,591.0
PHYSICIANS LIFE INS CO	NE	1,406.1
PROTECTIVE INS CO	IN	770.4
STANDARD LIFE & ACCIDENT INS CO	TX	525.1
Rating: B+		
AETNA HEALTH & LIFE INS CO	CT	2,193.0
AETNA LIFE INS CO	CT	22,226.6
AMERICAN FAMILY LIFE ASR CO OF COLUM	NE	111,249.2
AMERICAN FIDELITY ASR CO	OK	4,848.9
AMERICAN UNITED LIFE INS CO	IN	22,972.9
ASSURITY LIFE INS CO	NE	2,436.6
BOSTON MUTUAL LIFE INS CO	MA	1,222.3
CENTRAL STATES INDEMNITY CO OF OMAHA	NE	424.9
COLORADO BANKERS LIFE INS CO	CO	272.7
COVENTRY HEALTH & LIFE INS CO	MO	1,547.4
FEDERAL INS CO	IN	32,182.2
GOVERNMENT EMPLOYEES INS CO	MD	21,998.7
GOVERNMENT PERSONNEL MUTUAL L I C	TX	833.6
JACKSON NATIONAL LIFE INS CO	MI	176,569.5

INSURANCE COMPANY NAME	DOM. STATE	TOTAL ASSETS ($MIL)
LINCOLN BENEFIT LIFE CO	NE	13,279.3
MEDCO CONTAINMENT LIFE INS CO	PA	507.6
MEDICO CORP LIFE INS CO	NE	25.7
MERIT LIFE INS CO	IN	560.2
MIDLAND NATIONAL LIFE INS CO	IA	39,622.6
MINNESOTA LIFE INS CO	MN	34,732.2
MUTUAL OF OMAHA INS CO	NE	6,375.2
NATIONAL BENEFIT LIFE INS CO	NY	475.2
NATIONAL CASUALTY CO	WI	287.3
NATIONAL WESTERN LIFE INS CO	CO	10,001.6
NATIONWIDE MUTUAL FIRE INS CO	OH	5,596.1
OHIO NATIONAL LIFE ASR CORP	OH	3,450.3
PIONEER MUTUAL LIFE INS CO	ND	507.2
PRINCIPAL LIFE INS CO	IA	150,015.7
SAVINGS BANK LIFE INS CO OF MA	MA	2,531.7
SENTRY SELECT INS CO	WI	672.6
STANDARD INS CO	OR	19,996.4
STATE FARM MUTUAL AUTOMOBILE INS CO	IL	135,478.4
SURETY LIFE INS CO	NE	14.3
SYMETRA LIFE INS CO	WA	28,322.5
THRIVENT LIFE INS CO	MN	3,560.4
TRUSTMARK INS CO	IL	1,404.7
TRUSTMARK LIFE INS CO	IL	380.8
UNITED WORLD LIFE INS CO	NE	107.9
USABLE LIFE	AR	426.8

District of Columbia

INSURANCE COMPANY NAME	DOM. STATE	TOTAL ASSETS ($MIL)	INSURANCE COMPANY NAME	DOM. STATE	TOTAL ASSETS ($MIL)
Rating: A+			JACKSON NATIONAL LIFE INS CO	MI	176,569.5
			KAISER PERMANENTE INS CO	CA	179.4
CAREFIRST BLUECHOICE INC	DC	1,140.8	LINCOLN BENEFIT LIFE CO	NE	13,279.3
HEALTH CARE SVC CORP A MUT LEG RES	IL	18,206.4	MEDCO CONTAINMENT LIFE INS CO	PA	507.6
PHYSICIANS MUTUAL INS CO	NE	1,968.0	MEDICO CORP LIFE INS CO	NE	25.7
TEACHERS INS & ANNUITY ASN OF AM	NY	256,932.8	MERIT LIFE INS CO	IN	560.2
			MIDLAND NATIONAL LIFE INS CO	IA	39,622.6
Rating: A			MINNESOTA LIFE INS CO	MN	34,732.2
			MUTUAL OF OMAHA INS CO	NE	6,375.2
4 EVER LIFE INS CO	IL	202.8	NATIONAL BENEFIT LIFE INS CO	NY	475.2
BERKSHIRE LIFE INS CO OF AMERICA	MA	3,589.9	NATIONAL CASUALTY CO	WI	287.3
CINCINNATI INS CO	OH	10,807.9	NATIONAL WESTERN LIFE INS CO	CO	10,001.6
FIRST RELIANCE STANDARD LIFE INS CO	NY	188.3	NATIONWIDE MUTUAL FIRE INS CO	OH	5,596.1
GUARDIAN LIFE INS CO OF AMERICA	NY	44,344.6	OHIO NATIONAL LIFE ASR CORP	OH	3,450.3
RESERVE NATIONAL INS CO	OK	112.3	PIONEER MUTUAL LIFE INS CO	ND	507.2
SENTRY INS A MUTUAL CO	WI	6,832.1	PRINCIPAL LIFE INS CO	IA	150,015.7
SENTRY LIFE INS CO	WI	5,167.7	SAVINGS BANK LIFE INS CO OF MA	MA	2,531.7
SHELTERPOINT LIFE INS CO	NY	103.8	SENTRY SELECT INS CO	WI	672.6
USAA LIFE INS CO	TX	21,633.7	STANDARD INS CO	OR	19,996.4
			STATE FARM MUTUAL AUTOMOBILE INS CO	IL	135,478.4
Rating: A-			SURETY LIFE INS CO	NE	14.3
			SYMETRA LIFE INS CO	WA	28,322.5
AMALGAMATED LIFE INS CO	NY	107.0	THRIVENT LIFE INS CO	MN	3,560.4
AMERICAN REPUBLIC INS CO	IA	799.7	TRUSTMARK INS CO	IL	1,404.7
ANTHEM LIFE INS CO	IN	571.2	TRUSTMARK LIFE INS CO	IL	380.8
BALBOA LIFE INS CO	CA	58.9	UNITED WORLD LIFE INS CO	NE	107.9
CENTRAL STATES H & L CO OF OMAHA	NE	405.9	USABLE LIFE	AR	426.8
CIGNA LIFE INS CO OF NEW YORK	NY	376.2			
COMPANION LIFE INS CO	SC	278.1			
DEARBORN NATIONAL LIFE INS CO	IL	2,193.1			
ERIE FAMILY LIFE INS CO	PA	2,058.7			
FAMILY HERITAGE LIFE INS CO OF AMER	OH	706.7			
FEDERATED MUTUAL INS CO	MN	4,667.2			
GARDEN STATE LIFE INS CO	TX	120.1			
GERBER LIFE INS CO	NY	2,680.4			
MASSACHUSETTS MUTUAL LIFE INS CO	MA	189,173.1			
MIDWESTERN UNITED LIFE INS CO	IN	237.0			
MUTUAL OF AMERICA LIFE INS CO	NY	17,180.5			
NEW YORK LIFE INS CO	NY	142,089.9			
NIPPON LIFE INS CO OF AMERICA	IA	222.1			
NORTHWESTERN MUTUAL LIFE INS CO	WI	222,040.6			
OLD REPUBLIC INS CO	PA	2,591.0			
PHYSICIANS LIFE INS CO	NE	1,406.1			
PROTECTIVE INS CO	IN	770.4			
STANDARD LIFE & ACCIDENT INS CO	TX	525.1			
Rating: B+					
AETNA HEALTH & LIFE INS CO	CT	2,193.0			
AETNA LIFE INS CO	CT	22,226.6			
AMERICAN FAMILY LIFE ASR CO OF COLUM	NE	111,249.2			
AMERICAN FIDELITY ASR CO	OK	4,848.9			
AMERICAN UNITED LIFE INS CO	IN	22,972.9			
ASSURITY LIFE INS CO	NE	2,436.6			
BOSTON MUTUAL LIFE INS CO	MA	1,222.3			
CENTRAL STATES INDEMNITY CO OF OMAHA	NE	424.9			
COLORADO BANKERS LIFE INS CO	CO	272.7			
COVENTRY HEALTH & LIFE INS CO	MO	1,547.4			
FEDERAL INS CO	IN	32,182.2			
GOVERNMENT EMPLOYEES INS CO	MD	21,998.7			
GOVERNMENT PERSONNEL MUTUAL L I C	TX	833.6			
HM LIFE INS CO OF NEW YORK	NY	72.5			

Florida

INSURANCE COMPANY NAME	DOM. STATE	TOTAL ASSETS ($MIL)
Rating:	**A+**	
COUNTRY LIFE INS CO	IL	10,519.0
HEALTH CARE SVC CORP A MUT LEG RES	IL	18,206.4
PHYSICIANS MUTUAL INS CO	NE	1,968.0
TEACHERS INS & ANNUITY ASN OF AM	NY	256,932.8
Rating:	**A**	
4 EVER LIFE INS CO	IL	202.8
AUTO-OWNERS LIFE INS CO	MI	3,557.4
BERKSHIRE LIFE INS CO OF AMERICA	MA	3,589.9
CINCINNATI INS CO	OH	10,807.9
FEDERATED LIFE INS CO	MN	1,483.1
GUARDIAN LIFE INS CO OF AMERICA	NY	44,344.6
RESERVE NATIONAL INS CO	OK	112.3
SENTRY INS A MUTUAL CO	WI	6,832.1
SENTRY LIFE INS CO	WI	5,167.7
SOUTHERN FARM BUREAU LIFE INS CO	MS	12,921.4
TRANS OCEANIC LIFE INS CO	PR	61.6
USAA LIFE INS CO	TX	21,633.7
Rating:	**A-**	
AETNA HEALTH INC (A FLORIDA CORP)	FL	324.6
AMALGAMATED LIFE INS CO	NY	107.0
AMERICAN REPUBLIC INS CO	IA	799.7
ANTHEM LIFE INS CO	IN	571.2
BALBOA LIFE INS CO	CA	58.9
CAPITAL HEALTH PLAN INC	FL	468.6
CENTRAL STATES H & L CO OF OMAHA	NE	405.9
COMPANION LIFE INS CO	SC	278.1
COTTON STATES LIFE INS CO	GA	331.7
COVENTRY HEALTH PLAN OF FLORIDA INC	FL	215.5
DEARBORN NATIONAL LIFE INS CO	IL	2,193.1
FAMILY HERITAGE LIFE INS CO OF AMER	OH	706.7
FEDERATED MUTUAL INS CO	MN	4,667.2
FLORIDA HEALTH CARE PLAN INC	FL	122.1
GARDEN STATE LIFE INS CO	TX	120.1
GERBER LIFE INS CO	NY	2,680.4
ILLINOIS MUTUAL LIFE INS CO	IL	1,354.0
LIFE INS CO OF ALABAMA	AL	112.7
MASSACHUSETTS MUTUAL LIFE INS CO	MA	189,173.1
MIDWESTERN UNITED LIFE INS CO	IN	237.0
MUTUAL OF AMERICA LIFE INS CO	NY	17,180.5
MUTUAL SAVINGS LIFE INS CO	AL	473.8
NEW YORK LIFE INS CO	NY	142,089.9
NIPPON LIFE INS CO OF AMERICA	IA	222.1
NORTHWESTERN MUTUAL LIFE INS CO	WI	222,040.6
OLD REPUBLIC INS CO	PA	2,591.0
PHYSICIANS LIFE INS CO	NE	1,406.1
PROTECTIVE INS CO	IN	770.4
STANDARD LIFE & ACCIDENT INS CO	TX	525.1
Rating:	**B+**	
AETNA LIFE INS CO	CT	22,226.6
AMERICAN FAMILY LIFE ASR CO OF COLUM	NE	111,249.2
AMERICAN FIDELITY ASR CO	OK	4,848.9
AMERICAN UNITED LIFE INS CO	IN	22,972.9
ASSURITY LIFE INS CO	NE	2,436.6
AVMED INC	FL	291.3

INSURANCE COMPANY NAME	DOM. STATE	TOTAL ASSETS ($MIL)
BOSTON MUTUAL LIFE INS CO	MA	1,222.3
CENTRAL STATES INDEMNITY CO OF OMAHA	NE	424.9
COLORADO BANKERS LIFE INS CO	CO	272.7
COVENTRY HEALTH & LIFE INS CO	MO	1,547.4
FEDERAL INS CO	IN	32,182.2
GOVERNMENT EMPLOYEES INS CO	MD	21,998.7
GOVERNMENT PERSONNEL MUTUAL L I C	TX	833.6
JACKSON NATIONAL LIFE INS CO	MI	176,569.5
LINCOLN BENEFIT LIFE CO	NE	13,279.3
MEDCO CONTAINMENT LIFE INS CO	PA	507.6
MEDICO CORP LIFE INS CO	NE	25.7
MERIT LIFE INS CO	IN	560.2
MIDLAND NATIONAL LIFE INS CO	IA	39,622.6
MINNESOTA LIFE INS CO	MN	34,732.2
MUTUAL OF OMAHA INS CO	NE	6,375.2
NATIONAL BENEFIT LIFE INS CO	NY	475.2
NATIONAL CASUALTY CO	WI	287.3
NATIONAL WESTERN LIFE INS CO	CO	10,001.6
NATIONWIDE MUTUAL FIRE INS CO	OH	5,596.1
OHIO NATIONAL LIFE ASR CORP	OH	3,450.3
PIONEER MUTUAL LIFE INS CO	ND	507.2
PRINCIPAL LIFE INS CO	IA	150,015.7
SAVINGS BANK LIFE INS CO OF MA	MA	2,531.7
SENTRY SELECT INS CO	WI	672.6
STANDARD INS CO	OR	19,996.4
STATE FARM MUTUAL AUTOMOBILE INS CO	IL	135,478.4
SURETY LIFE INS CO	NE	14.3
SYMETRA LIFE INS CO	WA	28,322.5
THRIVENT LIFE INS CO	MN	3,560.4
TRUSTMARK INS CO	IL	1,404.7
TRUSTMARK LIFE INS CO	IL	380.8
UNITED WORLD LIFE INS CO	NE	107.9
USABLE LIFE	AR	426.8

Georgia

INSURANCE COMPANY NAME	DOM. STATE	TOTAL ASSETS ($MIL)
Rating: A+		
COUNTRY LIFE INS CO	IL	10,519.0
HEALTH CARE SVC CORP A MUT LEG RES	IL	18,206.4
PHYSICIANS MUTUAL INS CO	NE	1,968.0
TEACHERS INS & ANNUITY ASN OF AM	NY	256,932.8
Rating: A		
4 EVER LIFE INS CO	IL	202.8
AUTO-OWNERS LIFE INS CO	MI	3,557.4
BERKSHIRE LIFE INS CO OF AMERICA	MA	3,589.9
CINCINNATI INS CO	OH	10,807.9
FEDERATED LIFE INS CO	MN	1,483.1
GUARDIAN LIFE INS CO OF AMERICA	NY	44,344.6
RESERVE NATIONAL INS CO	OK	112.3
SENTRY INS A MUTUAL CO	WI	6,832.1
SENTRY LIFE INS CO	WI	5,167.7
SOUTHERN FARM BUREAU LIFE INS CO	MS	12,921.4
USAA LIFE INS CO	TX	21,633.7
Rating: A-		
AMALGAMATED LIFE INS CO	NY	107.0
AMERICAN REPUBLIC INS CO	IA	799.7
ANTHEM LIFE INS CO	IN	571.2
BALBOA LIFE INS CO	CA	58.9
BLUE CROSS BLUE SHIELD HEALTHCARE GA	GA	657.4
CENTRAL STATES H & L CO OF OMAHA	NE	405.9
COMPANION LIFE INS CO	SC	278.1
COTTON STATES LIFE INS CO	GA	331.7
DEARBORN NATIONAL LIFE INS CO	IL	2,193.1
FAMILY HERITAGE LIFE INS CO OF AMER	OH	706.7
FEDERATED MUTUAL INS CO	MN	4,667.2
GARDEN STATE LIFE INS CO	TX	120.1
GERBER LIFE INS CO	NY	2,680.4
ILLINOIS MUTUAL LIFE INS CO	IL	1,354.0
LIFE INS CO OF ALABAMA	AL	112.7
MASSACHUSETTS MUTUAL LIFE INS CO	MA	189,173.1
MEDICAL MUTUAL OF OHIO	OH	1,798.4
MIDWESTERN UNITED LIFE INS CO	IN	237.0
MUTUAL OF AMERICA LIFE INS CO	NY	17,180.5
MUTUAL SAVINGS LIFE INS CO	AL	473.8
NEW YORK LIFE INS CO	NY	142,089.9
NIPPON LIFE INS CO OF AMERICA	IA	222.1
NORTHWESTERN MUTUAL LIFE INS CO	WI	222,040.6
OLD REPUBLIC INS CO	PA	2,591.0
PHYSICIANS LIFE INS CO	NE	1,406.1
PROTECTIVE INS CO	IN	770.4
STANDARD LIFE & ACCIDENT INS CO	TX	525.1
Rating: B+		
AETNA HEALTH & LIFE INS CO	CT	2,193.0
AETNA LIFE INS CO	CT	22,226.6
AMERICAN FAMILY LIFE ASR CO OF COLUM	NE	111,249.2
AMERICAN FIDELITY ASR CO	OK	4,848.9
AMERICAN UNITED LIFE INS CO	IN	22,972.9
ASSURITY LIFE INS CO	NE	2,436.6
BOSTON MUTUAL LIFE INS CO	MA	1,222.3
CENTRAL STATES INDEMNITY CO OF OMAHA	NE	424.9
COLORADO BANKERS LIFE INS CO	CO	272.7

INSURANCE COMPANY NAME	DOM. STATE	TOTAL ASSETS ($MIL)
COVENTRY HEALTH & LIFE INS CO	MO	1,547.4
FEDERAL INS CO	IN	32,182.2
GOVERNMENT EMPLOYEES INS CO	MD	21,998.7
GOVERNMENT PERSONNEL MUTUAL L I C	TX	833.6
GRANGE MUTUAL CAS CO	OH	2,061.4
GREATER GEORGIA LIFE INS CO	GA	50.8
JACKSON NATIONAL LIFE INS CO	MI	176,569.5
KAISER PERMANENTE INS CO	CA	179.4
LINCOLN BENEFIT LIFE CO	NE	13,279.3
MEDCO CONTAINMENT LIFE INS CO	PA	507.6
MEDICO CORP LIFE INS CO	NE	25.7
MERIT LIFE INS CO	IN	560.2
MIDLAND NATIONAL LIFE INS CO	IA	39,622.6
MINNESOTA LIFE INS CO	MN	34,732.2
MUTUAL OF OMAHA INS CO	NE	6,375.2
NATIONAL BENEFIT LIFE INS CO	NY	475.2
NATIONAL CASUALTY CO	WI	287.3
NATIONAL WESTERN LIFE INS CO	CO	10,001.6
NATIONWIDE MUTUAL FIRE INS CO	OH	5,596.1
OHIO NATIONAL LIFE ASR CORP	OH	3,450.3
PIONEER MUTUAL LIFE INS CO	ND	507.2
PRINCIPAL LIFE INS CO	IA	150,015.7
SAVINGS BANK LIFE INS CO OF MA	MA	2,531.7
SENTRY SELECT INS CO	WI	672.6
STANDARD INS CO	OR	19,996.4
STATE FARM MUTUAL AUTOMOBILE INS CO	IL	135,478.4
SURETY LIFE INS CO	NE	14.3
SYMETRA LIFE INS CO	WA	28,322.5
TRUSTMARK INS CO	IL	1,404.7
TRUSTMARK LIFE INS CO	IL	380.8
UNITED WORLD LIFE INS CO	NE	107.9
USABLE LIFE	AR	426.8

Hawaii

INSURANCE COMPANY NAME	DOM. STATE	TOTAL ASSETS ($MIL)
Rating: A+		
PHYSICIANS MUTUAL INS CO	NE	1,968.0
TEACHERS INS & ANNUITY ASN OF AM	NY	256,932.8
Rating: A		
4 EVER LIFE INS CO	IL	202.8
BERKSHIRE LIFE INS CO OF AMERICA	MA	3,589.9
CINCINNATI INS CO	OH	10,807.9
GUARDIAN LIFE INS CO OF AMERICA	NY	44,344.6
KAISER FOUNDATION HEALTH PLAN INC	CA	60,291.5
SENTRY INS A MUTUAL CO	WI	6,832.1
SENTRY LIFE INS CO	WI	5,167.7
USAA LIFE INS CO	TX	21,633.7
Rating: A-		
AMALGAMATED LIFE INS CO	NY	107.0
AMERICAN REPUBLIC INS CO	IA	799.7
ANTHEM LIFE INS CO	IN	571.2
BALBOA LIFE INS CO	CA	58.9
CENTRAL STATES H & L CO OF OMAHA	NE	405.9
DEARBORN NATIONAL LIFE INS CO	IL	2,193.1
FAMILY HERITAGE LIFE INS CO OF AMER	OH	706.7
GARDEN STATE LIFE INS CO	TX	120.1
GERBER LIFE INS CO	NY	2,680.4
MASSACHUSETTS MUTUAL LIFE INS CO	MA	189,173.1
MIDWESTERN UNITED LIFE INS CO	IN	237.0
MUTUAL OF AMERICA LIFE INS CO	NY	17,180.5
NEW YORK LIFE INS CO	NY	142,089.9
NIPPON LIFE INS CO OF AMERICA	IA	222.1
NORTHWESTERN MUTUAL LIFE INS CO	WI	222,040.6
OLD REPUBLIC INS CO	PA	2,591.0
PACIFIC GUARDIAN LIFE INS CO LTD	HI	518.1
PHYSICIANS LIFE INS CO	NE	1,406.1
PROTECTIVE INS CO	IN	770.4
STANDARD LIFE & ACCIDENT INS CO	TX	525.1
Rating: B+		
AETNA HEALTH & LIFE INS CO	CT	2,193.0
AETNA LIFE INS CO	CT	22,226.6
AMERICAN FAMILY LIFE ASR CO OF COLUM	NE	111,249.2
AMERICAN FIDELITY ASR CO	OK	4,848.9
AMERICAN UNITED LIFE INS CO	IN	22,972.9
ASSURITY LIFE INS CO	NE	2,436.6
BOSTON MUTUAL LIFE INS CO	MA	1,222.3
CENTRAL STATES INDEMNITY CO OF OMAHA	NE	424.9
COLORADO BANKERS LIFE INS CO	CO	272.7
FEDERAL INS CO	IN	32,182.2
GOVERNMENT EMPLOYEES INS CO	MD	21,998.7
GOVERNMENT PERSONNEL MUTUAL L I C	TX	833.6
JACKSON NATIONAL LIFE INS CO	MI	176,569.5
KAISER PERMANENTE INS CO	CA	179.4
LINCOLN BENEFIT LIFE CO	NE	13,279.3
MEDCO CONTAINMENT LIFE INS CO	PA	507.6
MEDICO CORP LIFE INS CO	NE	25.7
MERIT LIFE INS CO	IN	560.2
MIDLAND NATIONAL LIFE INS CO	IA	39,622.6
MINNESOTA LIFE INS CO	MN	34,732.2
MUTUAL OF OMAHA INS CO	NE	6,375.2

INSURANCE COMPANY NAME	DOM. STATE	TOTAL ASSETS ($MIL)
NATIONAL BENEFIT LIFE INS CO	NY	475.2
NATIONAL CASUALTY CO	WI	287.3
NATIONAL WESTERN LIFE INS CO	CO	10,001.6
NATIONWIDE MUTUAL FIRE INS CO	OH	5,596.1
PIONEER MUTUAL LIFE INS CO	ND	507.2
PRINCIPAL LIFE INS CO	IA	150,015.7
SAVINGS BANK LIFE INS CO OF MA	MA	2,531.7
SENTRY SELECT INS CO	WI	672.6
STANDARD INS CO	OR	19,996.4
STATE FARM MUTUAL AUTOMOBILE INS CO	IL	135,478.4
SURETY LIFE INS CO	NE	14.3
SYMETRA LIFE INS CO	WA	28,322.5
THRIVENT LIFE INS CO	MN	3,560.4
TRUSTMARK INS CO	IL	1,404.7
TRUSTMARK LIFE INS CO	IL	380.8
UNITED WORLD LIFE INS CO	NE	107.9
USABLE LIFE	AR	426.8

Idaho

INSURANCE COMPANY NAME	DOM. STATE	TOTAL ASSETS ($MIL)
Rating: A+		
COUNTRY LIFE INS CO	IL	10,519.0
HEALTH CARE SVC CORP A MUT LEG RES	IL	18,206.4
PHYSICIANS MUTUAL INS CO	NE	1,968.0
TEACHERS INS & ANNUITY ASN OF AM	NY	256,932.8
Rating: A		
4 EVER LIFE INS CO	IL	202.8
AUTO-OWNERS LIFE INS CO	MI	3,557.4
BERKSHIRE LIFE INS CO OF AMERICA	MA	3,589.9
CINCINNATI INS CO	OH	10,807.9
FEDERATED LIFE INS CO	MN	1,483.1
GUARDIAN LIFE INS CO OF AMERICA	NY	44,344.6
LIFEWISE ASR CO	WA	129.7
RESERVE NATIONAL INS CO	OK	112.3
SELECTHEALTH INC	UT	849.6
SENTRY INS A MUTUAL CO	WI	6,832.1
SENTRY LIFE INS CO	WI	5,167.7
USAA LIFE INS CO	TX	21,633.7
Rating: A-		
AMALGAMATED LIFE INS CO	NY	107.0
AMERICAN REPUBLIC INS CO	IA	799.7
ANTHEM LIFE INS CO	IN	571.2
BALBOA LIFE INS CO	CA	58.9
BLUE CROSS OF IDAHO HEALTH SERVICE	ID	844.0
CENTRAL STATES H & L CO OF OMAHA	NE	405.9
COMPANION LIFE INS CO	SC	278.1
COPIC INS CO	CO	523.3
DEARBORN NATIONAL LIFE INS CO	IL	2,193.1
FAMILY HERITAGE LIFE INS CO OF AMER	OH	706.7
FEDERATED MUTUAL INS CO	MN	4,667.2
GARDEN STATE LIFE INS CO	TX	120.1
GERBER LIFE INS CO	NY	2,680.4
ILLINOIS MUTUAL LIFE INS CO	IL	1,354.0
MASSACHUSETTS MUTUAL LIFE INS CO	MA	189,173.1
MIDWESTERN UNITED LIFE INS CO	IN	237.0
MUTUAL OF AMERICA LIFE INS CO	NY	17,180.5
NEW YORK LIFE INS CO	NY	142,089.9
NIPPON LIFE INS CO OF AMERICA	IA	222.1
NORTHWESTERN MUTUAL LIFE INS CO	WI	222,040.6
OLD REPUBLIC INS CO	PA	2,591.0
PACIFIC GUARDIAN LIFE INS CO LTD	HI	518.1
PHYSICIANS LIFE INS CO	NE	1,406.1
PROTECTIVE INS CO	IN	770.4
STANDARD LIFE & ACCIDENT INS CO	TX	525.1
Rating: B+		
AETNA HEALTH & LIFE INS CO	CT	2,193.0
AETNA LIFE INS CO	CT	22,226.6
AMERICAN FAMILY LIFE ASR CO OF COLUM	NE	111,249.2
AMERICAN FAMILY MUT INS CO	WI	13,709.4
AMERICAN FIDELITY ASR CO	OK	4,848.9
AMERICAN UNITED LIFE INS CO	IN	22,972.9
ASSURITY LIFE INS CO	NE	2,436.6
BOSTON MUTUAL LIFE INS CO	MA	1,222.3
CENTRAL STATES INDEMNITY CO OF OMAHA	NE	424.9
COLORADO BANKERS LIFE INS CO	CO	272.7

INSURANCE COMPANY NAME	DOM. STATE	TOTAL ASSETS ($MIL)
FARM BUREAU LIFE INS CO	IA	7,987.7
FEDERAL INS CO	IN	32,182.2
GOVERNMENT EMPLOYEES INS CO	MD	21,998.7
GOVERNMENT PERSONNEL MUTUAL L I C	TX	833.6
JACKSON NATIONAL LIFE INS CO	MI	176,569.5
LINCOLN BENEFIT LIFE CO	NE	13,279.3
MEDCO CONTAINMENT LIFE INS CO	PA	507.6
MEDICO CORP LIFE INS CO	NE	25.7
MERIT LIFE INS CO	IN	560.2
MIDLAND NATIONAL LIFE INS CO	IA	39,622.6
MINNESOTA LIFE INS CO	MN	34,732.2
MUTUAL OF OMAHA INS CO	NE	6,375.2
NATIONAL BENEFIT LIFE INS CO	NY	475.2
NATIONAL CASUALTY CO	WI	287.3
NATIONAL WESTERN LIFE INS CO	CO	10,001.6
NATIONWIDE MUTUAL FIRE INS CO	OH	5,596.1
OHIO NATIONAL LIFE ASR CORP	OH	3,450.3
PIONEER MUTUAL LIFE INS CO	ND	507.2
PRINCIPAL LIFE INS CO	IA	150,015.7
SAVINGS BANK LIFE INS CO OF MA	MA	2,531.7
SENTRY SELECT INS CO	WI	672.6
STANDARD INS CO	OR	19,996.4
STATE FARM MUTUAL AUTOMOBILE INS CO	IL	135,478.4
SURETY LIFE INS CO	NE	14.3
SYMETRA LIFE INS CO	WA	28,322.5
THRIVENT LIFE INS CO	MN	3,560.4
TRUSTMARK INS CO	IL	1,404.7
TRUSTMARK LIFE INS CO	IL	380.8
UNITED WORLD LIFE INS CO	NE	107.9
USABLE LIFE	AR	426.8

Illinois

INSURANCE COMPANY NAME	DOM. STATE	TOTAL ASSETS ($MIL)
Rating:	**A+**	
COUNTRY LIFE INS CO	IL	10,519.0
HEALTH CARE SVC CORP A MUT LEG RES	IL	18,206.4
PHYSICIANS MUTUAL INS CO	NE	1,968.0
TEACHERS INS & ANNUITY ASN OF AM	NY	256,932.8
Rating:	**A**	
4 EVER LIFE INS CO	IL	202.8
AUTO-OWNERS LIFE INS CO	MI	3,557.4
BERKSHIRE LIFE INS CO OF AMERICA	MA	3,589.9
CINCINNATI INS CO	OH	10,807.9
FEDERATED LIFE INS CO	MN	1,483.1
GUARDIAN LIFE INS CO OF AMERICA	NY	44,344.6
HEALTH ALLIANCE MEDICAL PLANS	IL	521.4
RESERVE NATIONAL INS CO	OK	112.3
SENTRY INS A MUTUAL CO	WI	6,832.1
SENTRY LIFE INS CO	WI	5,167.7
SHELTERPOINT LIFE INS CO	NY	103.8
UNITED FARM FAMILY LIFE INS CO	IN	2,116.5
USAA LIFE INS CO	TX	21,633.7
Rating:	**A-**	
AMALGAMATED LIFE INS CO	NY	107.0
AMERICAN REPUBLIC INS CO	IA	799.7
ANTHEM LIFE INS CO	IN	571.2
BALBOA LIFE INS CO	CA	58.9
CENTRAL STATES H & L CO OF OMAHA	NE	405.9
COMPANION LIFE INS CO	SC	278.1
DEARBORN NATIONAL LIFE INS CO	IL	2,193.1
ERIE FAMILY LIFE INS CO	PA	2,058.7
FAMILY HERITAGE LIFE INS CO OF AMER	OH	706.7
FEDERATED MUTUAL INS CO	MN	4,667.2
GARDEN STATE LIFE INS CO	TX	120.1
GERBER LIFE INS CO	NY	2,680.4
HEALTHY ALLIANCE LIFE INS CO	MO	954.2
ILLINOIS MUTUAL LIFE INS CO	IL	1,354.0
MASSACHUSETTS MUTUAL LIFE INS CO	MA	189,173.1
MIDWESTERN UNITED LIFE INS CO	IN	237.0
MUTUAL OF AMERICA LIFE INS CO	NY	17,180.5
NEW YORK LIFE INS CO	NY	142,089.9
NIPPON LIFE INS CO OF AMERICA	IA	222.1
NORTHWESTERN MUTUAL LIFE INS CO	WI	222,040.6
OLD REPUBLIC INS CO	PA	2,591.0
PHYSICIANS LIFE INS CO	NE	1,406.1
PROTECTIVE INS CO	IN	770.4
SHELTER LIFE INS CO	MO	1,097.7
STANDARD LIFE & ACCIDENT INS CO	TX	525.1
Rating:	**B+**	
AETNA HEALTH & LIFE INS CO	CT	2,193.0
AETNA LIFE INS CO	CT	22,226.6
AMERICAN FAMILY LIFE ASR CO OF COLUM	NE	111,249.2
AMERICAN FAMILY MUT INS CO	WI	13,709.4
AMERICAN FIDELITY ASR CO	OK	4,848.9
AMERICAN UNITED LIFE INS CO	IN	22,972.9
ASSURITY LIFE INS CO	NE	2,436.6
BOSTON MUTUAL LIFE INS CO	MA	1,222.3
CENTRAL STATES INDEMNITY CO OF OMAHA	NE	424.9

INSURANCE COMPANY NAME	DOM. STATE	TOTAL ASSETS ($MIL)
COLORADO BANKERS LIFE INS CO	CO	272.7
COVENTRY HEALTH & LIFE INS CO	MO	1,547.4
COVENTRY HEALTH CARE OF ILLINOIS INC	IL	104.8
FEDERAL INS CO	IN	32,182.2
GOVERNMENT EMPLOYEES INS CO	MD	21,998.7
GOVERNMENT PERSONNEL MUTUAL L I C	TX	833.6
GRANGE MUTUAL CAS CO	OH	2,061.4
JACKSON NATIONAL LIFE INS CO	MI	176,569.5
LINCOLN BENEFIT LIFE CO	NE	13,279.3
MEDCO CONTAINMENT LIFE INS CO	PA	507.6
MEDICO CORP LIFE INS CO	NE	25.7
MERIT LIFE INS CO	IN	560.2
MIDLAND NATIONAL LIFE INS CO	IA	39,622.6
MINNESOTA LIFE INS CO	MN	34,732.2
MUTUAL OF OMAHA INS CO	NE	6,375.2
NATIONAL BENEFIT LIFE INS CO	NY	475.2
NATIONAL CASUALTY CO	WI	287.3
NATIONAL WESTERN LIFE INS CO	CO	10,001.6
NATIONWIDE MUTUAL FIRE INS CO	OH	5,596.1
OHIO NATIONAL LIFE ASR CORP	OH	3,450.3
PIONEER MUTUAL LIFE INS CO	ND	507.2
PRINCIPAL LIFE INS CO	IA	150,015.7
SAVINGS BANK LIFE INS CO OF MA	MA	2,531.7
SENTRY SELECT INS CO	WI	672.6
STANDARD INS CO	OR	19,996.4
STATE FARM MUTUAL AUTOMOBILE INS CO	IL	135,478.4
SURETY LIFE INS CO	NE	14.3
SYMETRA LIFE INS CO	WA	28,322.5
THRIVENT LIFE INS CO	MN	3,560.4
TRUSTMARK INS CO	IL	1,404.7
TRUSTMARK LIFE INS CO	IL	380.8
UNITED WORLD LIFE INS CO	NE	107.9
UNITEDHEALTHCARE PLAN RIVER VALLEY	IL	1,172.5
USABLE LIFE	AR	426.8

Indiana

INSURANCE COMPANY NAME	DOM. STATE	TOTAL ASSETS ($MIL)
Rating: A+		
COUNTRY LIFE INS CO	IL	10,519.0
HEALTH CARE SVC CORP A MUT LEG RES	IL	18,206.4
PHYSICIANS MUTUAL INS CO	NE	1,968.0
TEACHERS INS & ANNUITY ASN OF AM	NY	256,932.8
Rating: A		
4 EVER LIFE INS CO	IL	202.8
AUTO-OWNERS LIFE INS CO	MI	3,557.4
BERKSHIRE LIFE INS CO OF AMERICA	MA	3,589.9
CINCINNATI INS CO	OH	10,807.9
FEDERATED LIFE INS CO	MN	1,483.1
GUARDIAN LIFE INS CO OF AMERICA	NY	44,344.6
RESERVE NATIONAL INS CO	OK	112.3
SENTRY INS A MUTUAL CO	WI	6,832.1
SENTRY LIFE INS CO	WI	5,167.7
UNITED FARM FAMILY LIFE INS CO	IN	2,116.5
USAA LIFE INS CO	TX	21,633.7
Rating: A-		
AMALGAMATED LIFE INS CO	NY	107.0
AMERICAN REPUBLIC INS CO	IA	799.7
ANTHEM LIFE INS CO	IN	571.2
BALBOA LIFE INS CO	CA	58.9
CENTRAL STATES H & L CO OF OMAHA	NE	405.9
COMPANION LIFE INS CO	SC	278.1
CSAA INS EXCHANGE	CA	6,888.9
DEARBORN NATIONAL LIFE INS CO	IL	2,193.1
ERIE FAMILY LIFE INS CO	PA	2,058.7
FAMILY HERITAGE LIFE INS CO OF AMER	OH	706.7
FEDERATED MUTUAL INS CO	MN	4,667.2
GARDEN STATE LIFE INS CO	TX	120.1
GERBER LIFE INS CO	NY	2,680.4
HEALTHY ALLIANCE LIFE INS CO	MO	954.2
ILLINOIS MUTUAL LIFE INS CO	IL	1,354.0
MASSACHUSETTS MUTUAL LIFE INS CO	MA	189,173.1
MEDICAL MUTUAL OF OHIO	OH	1,798.4
MIDWESTERN UNITED LIFE INS CO	IN	237.0
MUTUAL OF AMERICA LIFE INS CO	NY	17,180.5
MUTUAL SAVINGS LIFE INS CO	AL	473.8
NEW YORK LIFE INS CO	NY	142,089.9
NIPPON LIFE INS CO OF AMERICA	IA	222.1
NORTHWESTERN MUTUAL LIFE INS CO	WI	222,040.6
OLD REPUBLIC INS CO	PA	2,591.0
PHYSICIANS LIFE INS CO	NE	1,406.1
PROTECTIVE INS CO	IN	770.4
SHELTER LIFE INS CO	MO	1,097.7
STANDARD LIFE & ACCIDENT INS CO	TX	525.1
Rating: B+		
AETNA HEALTH & LIFE INS CO	CT	2,193.0
AETNA LIFE INS CO	CT	22,226.6
AMERICAN FAMILY LIFE ASR CO OF COLUM	NE	111,249.2
AMERICAN FAMILY MUT INS CO	WI	13,709.4
AMERICAN FIDELITY ASR CO	OK	4,848.9
AMERICAN UNITED LIFE INS CO	IN	22,972.9
ASSURITY LIFE INS CO	NE	2,436.6
BLUEGRASS FAMILY HEALTH INC	KY	105.4

INSURANCE COMPANY NAME	DOM. STATE	TOTAL ASSETS ($MIL)
BOSTON MUTUAL LIFE INS CO	MA	1,222.3
CENTRAL STATES INDEMNITY CO OF OMAHA	NE	424.9
COLORADO BANKERS LIFE INS CO	CO	272.7
COMMUNITY INS CO	OH	2,036.0
COVENTRY HEALTH & LIFE INS CO	MO	1,547.4
FEDERAL INS CO	IN	32,182.2
GOVERNMENT EMPLOYEES INS CO	MD	21,998.7
GOVERNMENT PERSONNEL MUTUAL L I C	TX	833.6
GRANGE MUTUAL CAS CO	OH	2,061.4
JACKSON NATIONAL LIFE INS CO	MI	176,569.5
LINCOLN BENEFIT LIFE CO	NE	13,279.3
MEDCO CONTAINMENT LIFE INS CO	PA	507.6
MEDICO CORP LIFE INS CO	NE	25.7
MERIT LIFE INS CO	IN	560.2
MIDLAND NATIONAL LIFE INS CO	IA	39,622.6
MINNESOTA LIFE INS CO	MN	34,732.2
MUTUAL OF OMAHA INS CO	NE	6,375.2
NATIONAL BENEFIT LIFE INS CO	NY	475.2
NATIONAL CASUALTY CO	WI	287.3
NATIONAL WESTERN LIFE INS CO	CO	10,001.6
NATIONWIDE MUTUAL FIRE INS CO	OH	5,596.1
OHIO NATIONAL LIFE ASR CORP	OH	3,450.3
PIONEER MUTUAL LIFE INS CO	ND	507.2
PRINCIPAL LIFE INS CO	IA	150,015.7
SAVINGS BANK LIFE INS CO OF MA	MA	2,531.7
SENTRY SELECT INS CO	WI	672.6
STANDARD INS CO	OR	19,996.4
STATE FARM MUTUAL AUTOMOBILE INS CO	IL	135,478.4
SURETY LIFE INS CO	NE	14.3
SYMETRA LIFE INS CO	WA	28,322.5
THRIVENT LIFE INS CO	MN	3,560.4
TRUSTMARK INS CO	IL	1,404.7
TRUSTMARK LIFE INS CO	IL	380.8
UNITED WORLD LIFE INS CO	NE	107.9
USABLE LIFE	AR	426.8

Iowa

INSURANCE COMPANY NAME	DOM. STATE	TOTAL ASSETS ($MIL)
Rating: A+		
COUNTRY LIFE INS CO	IL	10,519.0
PHYSICIANS MUTUAL INS CO	NE	1,968.0
TEACHERS INS & ANNUITY ASN OF AM	NY	256,932.8
Rating: A		
4 EVER LIFE INS CO	IL	202.8
AUTO-OWNERS LIFE INS CO	MI	3,557.4
BERKSHIRE LIFE INS CO OF AMERICA	MA	3,589.9
CINCINNATI INS CO	OH	10,807.9
FEDERATED LIFE INS CO	MN	1,483.1
GUARDIAN LIFE INS CO OF AMERICA	NY	44,344.6
RESERVE NATIONAL INS CO	OK	112.3
SENTRY INS A MUTUAL CO	WI	6,832.1
SENTRY LIFE INS CO	WI	5,167.7
USAA LIFE INS CO	TX	21,633.7
Rating: A-		
AMALGAMATED LIFE INS CO	NY	107.0
AMERICAN REPUBLIC INS CO	IA	799.7
ANTHEM LIFE INS CO	IN	571.2
BALBOA LIFE INS CO	CA	58.9
CENTRAL STATES H & L CO OF OMAHA	NE	405.9
COMPANION LIFE INS CO	SC	278.1
COPIC INS CO	CO	523.3
DEARBORN NATIONAL LIFE INS CO	IL	2,193.1
FAMILY HERITAGE LIFE INS CO OF AMER	OH	706.7
FEDERATED MUTUAL INS CO	MN	4,667.2
GARDEN STATE LIFE INS CO	TX	120.1
GERBER LIFE INS CO	NY	2,680.4
ILLINOIS MUTUAL LIFE INS CO	IL	1,354.0
MASSACHUSETTS MUTUAL LIFE INS CO	MA	189,173.1
MIDWESTERN UNITED LIFE INS CO	IN	237.0
MUTUAL OF AMERICA LIFE INS CO	NY	17,180.5
NEW YORK LIFE INS CO	NY	142,089.9
NIPPON LIFE INS CO OF AMERICA	IA	222.1
NORTHWESTERN MUTUAL LIFE INS CO	WI	222,040.6
OLD REPUBLIC INS CO	PA	2,591.0
PACIFIC GUARDIAN LIFE INS CO LTD	HI	518.1
PHYSICIANS LIFE INS CO	NE	1,406.1
PROTECTIVE INS CO	IN	770.4
SHELTER LIFE INS CO	MO	1,097.7
STANDARD LIFE & ACCIDENT INS CO	TX	525.1
Rating: B+		
AETNA HEALTH & LIFE INS CO	CT	2,193.0
AETNA LIFE INS CO	CT	22,226.6
AMERICAN FAMILY LIFE ASR CO OF COLUM	NE	111,249.2
AMERICAN FAMILY MUT INS CO	WI	13,709.4
AMERICAN FIDELITY ASR CO	OK	4,848.9
AMERICAN UNITED LIFE INS CO	IN	22,972.9
ASSURITY LIFE INS CO	NE	2,436.6
BOSTON MUTUAL LIFE INS CO	MA	1,222.3
CENTRAL STATES INDEMNITY CO OF OMAHA	NE	424.9
COLORADO BANKERS LIFE INS CO	CO	272.7
COVENTRY HEALTH & LIFE INS CO	MO	1,547.4
COVENTRY HEALTH CARE OF NEBRASKA INC	NE	142.3
FARM BUREAU LIFE INS CO	IA	7,987.7

INSURANCE COMPANY NAME	DOM. STATE	TOTAL ASSETS ($MIL)
FEDERAL INS CO	IN	32,182.2
GOVERNMENT EMPLOYEES INS CO	MD	21,998.7
GOVERNMENT PERSONNEL MUTUAL L I C	TX	833.6
GRANGE MUTUAL CAS CO	OH	2,061.4
JACKSON NATIONAL LIFE INS CO	MI	176,569.5
LINCOLN BENEFIT LIFE CO	NE	13,279.3
MEDCO CONTAINMENT LIFE INS CO	PA	507.6
MEDICO CORP LIFE INS CO	NE	25.7
MERIT LIFE INS CO	IN	560.2
MIDLAND NATIONAL LIFE INS CO	IA	39,622.6
MINNESOTA LIFE INS CO	MN	34,732.2
MUTUAL OF OMAHA INS CO	NE	6,375.2
NATIONAL BENEFIT LIFE INS CO	NY	475.2
NATIONAL CASUALTY CO	WI	287.3
NATIONAL WESTERN LIFE INS CO	CO	10,001.6
NATIONWIDE MUTUAL FIRE INS CO	OH	5,596.1
OHIO NATIONAL LIFE ASR CORP	OH	3,450.3
PIONEER MUTUAL LIFE INS CO	ND	507.2
PRINCIPAL LIFE INS CO	IA	150,015.7
SAVINGS BANK LIFE INS CO OF MA	MA	2,531.7
SENTRY SELECT INS CO	WI	672.6
STANDARD INS CO	OR	19,996.4
STATE FARM MUTUAL AUTOMOBILE INS CO	IL	135,478.4
SURETY LIFE INS CO	NE	14.3
SYMETRA LIFE INS CO	WA	28,322.5
THRIVENT LIFE INS CO	MN	3,560.4
TRUSTMARK INS CO	IL	1,404.7
TRUSTMARK LIFE INS CO	IL	380.8
UNITED HEALTHCARE OF THE MIDLANDS	NE	75.7
UNITED WORLD LIFE INS CO	NE	107.9
UNITEDHEALTHCARE PLAN RIVER VALLEY	IL	1,172.5
USABLE LIFE	AR	426.8
WELLMARK HEALTH PLAN OF IOWA	IA	233.7
WELLMARK INC	IA	2,143.2

Kansas

INSURANCE COMPANY NAME	DOM. STATE	TOTAL ASSETS ($MIL)	INSURANCE COMPANY NAME	DOM. STATE	TOTAL ASSETS ($MIL)
Rating: A+			FARM BUREAU LIFE INS CO	IA	7,987.7
COUNTRY LIFE INS CO	IL	10,519.0	FEDERAL INS CO	IN	32,182.2
PHYSICIANS MUTUAL INS CO	NE	1,968.0	GOVERNMENT EMPLOYEES INS CO	MD	21,998.7
TEACHERS INS & ANNUITY ASN OF AM	NY	256,932.8	GOVERNMENT PERSONNEL MUTUAL L I C	TX	833.6
Rating: A			GRANGE MUTUAL CAS CO	OH	2,061.4
4 EVER LIFE INS CO	IL	202.8	JACKSON NATIONAL LIFE INS CO	MI	176,569.5
AUTO-OWNERS LIFE INS CO	MI	3,557.4	KAISER PERMANENTE INS CO	CA	179.4
BERKSHIRE LIFE INS CO OF AMERICA	MA	3,589.9	LINCOLN BENEFIT LIFE CO	NE	13,279.3
CINCINNATI INS CO	OH	10,807.9	MEDCO CONTAINMENT LIFE INS CO	PA	507.6
FEDERATED LIFE INS CO	MN	1,483.1	MEDICO CORP LIFE INS CO	NE	25.7
GUARDIAN LIFE INS CO OF AMERICA	NY	44,344.6	MERIT LIFE INS CO	IN	560.2
LIFEWISE ASR CO	WA	129.7	MIDLAND NATIONAL LIFE INS CO	IA	39,622.6
RESERVE NATIONAL INS CO	OK	112.3	MINNESOTA LIFE INS CO	MN	34,732.2
SENTRY INS A MUTUAL CO	WI	6,832.1	MUTUAL OF OMAHA INS CO	NE	6,375.2
SENTRY LIFE INS CO	WI	5,167.7	NATIONAL BENEFIT LIFE INS CO	NY	475.2
USAA LIFE INS CO	TX	21,633.7	NATIONAL CASUALTY CO	WI	287.3
Rating: A-			NATIONAL WESTERN LIFE INS CO	CO	10,001.6
AMALGAMATED LIFE INS CO	NY	107.0	NATIONWIDE MUTUAL FIRE INS CO	OH	5,596.1
AMERICAN REPUBLIC INS CO	IA	799.7	OHIO NATIONAL LIFE ASR CORP	OH	3,450.3
ANTHEM LIFE INS CO	IN	571.2	PIONEER MUTUAL LIFE INS CO	ND	507.2
BALBOA LIFE INS CO	CA	58.9	PRINCIPAL LIFE INS CO	IA	150,015.7
CENTRAL STATES H & L CO OF OMAHA	NE	405.9	SAVINGS BANK LIFE INS CO OF MA	MA	2,531.7
COMPANION LIFE INS CO	SC	278.1	SENTRY SELECT INS CO	WI	672.6
COPIC INS CO	CO	523.3	STANDARD INS CO	OR	19,996.4
DEARBORN NATIONAL LIFE INS CO	IL	2,193.1	STATE FARM MUTUAL AUTOMOBILE INS CO	IL	135,478.4
FAMILY HERITAGE LIFE INS CO OF AMER	OH	706.7	SURETY LIFE INS CO	NE	14.3
FEDERATED MUTUAL INS CO	MN	4,667.2	SYMETRA LIFE INS CO	WA	28,322.5
GARDEN STATE LIFE INS CO	TX	120.1	THRIVENT LIFE INS CO	MN	3,560.4
GERBER LIFE INS CO	NY	2,680.4	TRUSTMARK INS CO	IL	1,404.7
HEALTHY ALLIANCE LIFE INS CO	MO	954.2	TRUSTMARK LIFE INS CO	IL	380.8
ILLINOIS MUTUAL LIFE INS CO	IL	1,354.0	UNITED WORLD LIFE INS CO	NE	107.9
MASSACHUSETTS MUTUAL LIFE INS CO	MA	189,173.1	USABLE LIFE	AR	426.8
MIDWESTERN UNITED LIFE INS CO	IN	237.0			
MUTUAL OF AMERICA LIFE INS CO	NY	17,180.5			
NEW YORK LIFE INS CO	NY	142,089.9			
NIPPON LIFE INS CO OF AMERICA	IA	222.1			
NORTHWESTERN MUTUAL LIFE INS CO	WI	222,040.6			
OLD REPUBLIC INS CO	PA	2,591.0			
PHYSICIANS LIFE INS CO	NE	1,406.1			
PROTECTIVE INS CO	IN	770.4			
SHELTER LIFE INS CO	MO	1,097.7			
STANDARD LIFE & ACCIDENT INS CO	TX	525.1			
Rating: B+					
ADVANCE INS CO OF KS	KS	52.2			
AETNA HEALTH & LIFE INS CO	CT	2,193.0			
AETNA LIFE INS CO	CT	22,226.6			
AMERICAN FAMILY LIFE ASR CO OF COLUM	NE	111,249.2			
AMERICAN FAMILY MUT INS CO	WI	13,709.4			
AMERICAN FIDELITY ASR CO	OK	4,848.9			
AMERICAN UNITED LIFE INS CO	IN	22,972.9			
ASSURITY LIFE INS CO	NE	2,436.6			
BOSTON MUTUAL LIFE INS CO	MA	1,222.3			
CENTRAL STATES INDEMNITY CO OF OMAHA	NE	424.9			
COLORADO BANKERS LIFE INS CO	CO	272.7			
COVENTRY HEALTH & LIFE INS CO	MO	1,547.4			

Kentucky

INSURANCE COMPANY NAME	DOM. STATE	TOTAL ASSETS ($MIL)
Rating: A+		
COUNTRY LIFE INS CO	IL	10,519.0
HEALTH CARE SVC CORP A MUT LEG RES	IL	18,206.4
PHYSICIANS MUTUAL INS CO	NE	1,968.0
TEACHERS INS & ANNUITY ASN OF AM	NY	256,932.8
Rating: A		
4 EVER LIFE INS CO	IL	202.8
AUTO-OWNERS LIFE INS CO	MI	3,557.4
BERKSHIRE LIFE INS CO OF AMERICA	MA	3,589.9
CINCINNATI INS CO	OH	10,807.9
FEDERATED LIFE INS CO	MN	1,483.1
GUARDIAN LIFE INS CO OF AMERICA	NY	44,344.6
RESERVE NATIONAL INS CO	OK	112.3
SENTRY INS A MUTUAL CO	WI	6,832.1
SENTRY LIFE INS CO	WI	5,167.7
SOUTHERN FARM BUREAU LIFE INS CO	MS	12,921.4
USAA LIFE INS CO	TX	21,633.7
Rating: A-		
AMALGAMATED LIFE INS CO	NY	107.0
AMERICAN REPUBLIC INS CO	IA	799.7
ANTHEM HEALTH PLANS OF KENTUCKY INC	KY	1,023.5
ANTHEM LIFE INS CO	IN	571.2
BALBOA LIFE INS CO	CA	58.9
CENTRAL STATES H & L CO OF OMAHA	NE	405.9
COMPANION LIFE INS CO	SC	278.1
COTTON STATES LIFE INS CO	GA	331.7
DEARBORN NATIONAL LIFE INS CO	IL	2,193.1
ERIE FAMILY LIFE INS CO	PA	2,058.7
FAMILY HERITAGE LIFE INS CO OF AMER	OH	706.7
FEDERATED MUTUAL INS CO	MN	4,667.2
GARDEN STATE LIFE INS CO	TX	120.1
GERBER LIFE INS CO	NY	2,680.4
ILLINOIS MUTUAL LIFE INS CO	IL	1,354.0
LIFE INS CO OF ALABAMA	AL	112.7
MASSACHUSETTS MUTUAL LIFE INS CO	MA	189,173.1
MIDWESTERN UNITED LIFE INS CO	IN	237.0
MUTUAL OF AMERICA LIFE INS CO	NY	17,180.5
NEW YORK LIFE INS CO	NY	142,089.9
NIPPON LIFE INS CO OF AMERICA	IA	222.1
NORTHWESTERN MUTUAL LIFE INS CO	WI	222,040.6
OLD REPUBLIC INS CO	PA	2,591.0
PHYSICIANS LIFE INS CO	NE	1,406.1
PROTECTIVE INS CO	IN	770.4
SHELTER LIFE INS CO	MO	1,097.7
STANDARD LIFE & ACCIDENT INS CO	TX	525.1
Rating: B+		
AETNA HEALTH & LIFE INS CO	CT	2,193.0
AETNA LIFE INS CO	CT	22,226.6
AMERICAN FAMILY LIFE ASR CO OF COLUM	NE	111,249.2
AMERICAN FIDELITY ASR CO	OK	4,848.9
AMERICAN UNITED LIFE INS CO	IN	22,972.9
ASSURITY LIFE INS CO	NE	2,436.6
BLUEGRASS FAMILY HEALTH INC	KY	105.4
BOSTON MUTUAL LIFE INS CO	MA	1,222.3
CENTRAL STATES INDEMNITY CO OF OMAHA	NE	424.9

INSURANCE COMPANY NAME	DOM. STATE	TOTAL ASSETS ($MIL)
COLORADO BANKERS LIFE INS CO	CO	272.7
COVENTRY HEALTH & LIFE INS CO	MO	1,547.4
FEDERAL INS CO	IN	32,182.2
GOVERNMENT EMPLOYEES INS CO	MD	21,998.7
GOVERNMENT PERSONNEL MUTUAL L I C	TX	833.6
GRANGE MUTUAL CAS CO	OH	2,061.4
JACKSON NATIONAL LIFE INS CO	MI	176,569.5
LINCOLN BENEFIT LIFE CO	NE	13,279.3
MEDCO CONTAINMENT LIFE INS CO	PA	507.6
MEDICO CORP LIFE INS CO	NE	25.7
MERIT LIFE INS CO	IN	560.2
MIDLAND NATIONAL LIFE INS CO	IA	39,622.6
MINNESOTA LIFE INS CO	MN	34,732.2
MUTUAL OF OMAHA INS CO	NE	6,375.2
NATIONAL BENEFIT LIFE INS CO	NY	475.2
NATIONAL CASUALTY CO	WI	287.3
NATIONAL WESTERN LIFE INS CO	CO	10,001.6
NATIONWIDE MUTUAL FIRE INS CO	OH	5,596.1
OHIO NATIONAL LIFE ASR CORP	OH	3,450.3
PIONEER MUTUAL LIFE INS CO	ND	507.2
PRINCIPAL LIFE INS CO	IA	150,015.7
SAVINGS BANK LIFE INS CO OF MA	MA	2,531.7
SENTRY SELECT INS CO	WI	672.6
STANDARD INS CO	OR	19,996.4
STATE FARM MUTUAL AUTOMOBILE INS CO	IL	135,478.4
SURETY LIFE INS CO	NE	14.3
SYMETRA LIFE INS CO	WA	28,322.5
THRIVENT LIFE INS CO	MN	3,560.4
TRUSTMARK INS CO	IL	1,404.7
TRUSTMARK LIFE INS CO	IL	380.8
UNITED WORLD LIFE INS CO	NE	107.9
UNIVERSITY HEALTH CARE INC	KY	261.3
USABLE LIFE	AR	426.8

Louisiana

INSURANCE COMPANY NAME	DOM. STATE	TOTAL ASSETS ($MIL)
Rating: A+		
COUNTRY LIFE INS CO	IL	10,519.0
HMO LOUISIANA INC	LA	497.8
LA HEALTH SERVICE & INDEMNITY CO	LA	1,813.5
PHYSICIANS MUTUAL INS CO	NE	1,968.0
TEACHERS INS & ANNUITY ASN OF AM	NY	256,932.8
Rating: A		
4 EVER LIFE INS CO	IL	202.8
BERKSHIRE LIFE INS CO OF AMERICA	MA	3,589.9
CINCINNATI INS CO	OH	10,807.9
FEDERATED LIFE INS CO	MN	1,483.1
GUARDIAN LIFE INS CO OF AMERICA	NY	44,344.6
RESERVE NATIONAL INS CO	OK	112.3
SENTRY INS A MUTUAL CO	WI	6,832.1
SENTRY LIFE INS CO	WI	5,167.7
SOUTHERN FARM BUREAU LIFE INS CO	MS	12,921.4
USAA LIFE INS CO	TX	21,633.7
Rating: A-		
AMALGAMATED LIFE INS CO	NY	107.0
AMERICAN REPUBLIC INS CO	IA	799.7
ANTHEM LIFE INS CO	IN	571.2
BALBOA LIFE INS CO	CA	58.9
CENTRAL STATES H & L CO OF OMAHA	NE	405.9
COMPANION LIFE INS CO	SC	278.1
COTTON STATES LIFE INS CO	GA	331.7
DEARBORN NATIONAL LIFE INS CO	IL	2,193.1
FAMILY HERITAGE LIFE INS CO OF AMER	OH	706.7
FEDERATED MUTUAL INS CO	MN	4,667.2
GARDEN STATE LIFE INS CO	TX	120.1
GERBER LIFE INS CO	NY	2,680.4
ILLINOIS MUTUAL LIFE INS CO	IL	1,354.0
LIFE INS CO OF ALABAMA	AL	112.7
MASSACHUSETTS MUTUAL LIFE INS CO	MA	189,173.1
MIDWESTERN UNITED LIFE INS CO	IN	237.0
MUTUAL OF AMERICA LIFE INS CO	NY	17,180.5
MUTUAL SAVINGS LIFE INS CO	AL	473.8
NEW YORK LIFE INS CO	NY	142,089.9
NIPPON LIFE INS CO OF AMERICA	IA	222.1
NORTHWESTERN MUTUAL LIFE INS CO	WI	222,040.6
OLD REPUBLIC INS CO	PA	2,591.0
PACIFIC GUARDIAN LIFE INS CO LTD	HI	518.1
PHYSICIANS LIFE INS CO	NE	1,406.1
PROTECTIVE INS CO	IN	770.4
SHELTER LIFE INS CO	MO	1,097.7
STANDARD LIFE & ACCIDENT INS CO	TX	525.1
Rating: B+		
AETNA HEALTH & LIFE INS CO	CT	2,193.0
AETNA LIFE INS CO	CT	22,226.6
AMERICAN FAMILY LIFE ASR CO OF COLUM	NE	111,249.2
AMERICAN FIDELITY ASR CO	OK	4,848.9
AMERICAN UNITED LIFE INS CO	IN	22,972.9
ASSURITY LIFE INS CO	NE	2,436.6
BLUEBONNET LIFE INS CO	MS	53.6
BOSTON MUTUAL LIFE INS CO	MA	1,222.3
CENTRAL STATES INDEMNITY CO OF OMAHA	NE	424.9

INSURANCE COMPANY NAME	DOM. STATE	TOTAL ASSETS ($MIL)
COLORADO BANKERS LIFE INS CO	CO	272.7
COVENTRY HEALTH & LIFE INS CO	MO	1,547.4
FEDERAL INS CO	IN	32,182.2
GOVERNMENT EMPLOYEES INS CO	MD	21,998.7
GOVERNMENT PERSONNEL MUTUAL L I C	TX	833.6
JACKSON NATIONAL LIFE INS CO	MI	176,569.5
LINCOLN BENEFIT LIFE CO	NE	13,279.3
MEDCO CONTAINMENT LIFE INS CO	PA	507.6
MEDICO CORP LIFE INS CO	NE	25.7
MERIT LIFE INS CO	IN	560.2
MIDLAND NATIONAL LIFE INS CO	IA	39,622.6
MINNESOTA LIFE INS CO	MN	34,732.2
MUTUAL OF OMAHA INS CO	NE	6,375.2
NATIONAL BENEFIT LIFE INS CO	NY	475.2
NATIONAL CASUALTY CO	WI	287.3
NATIONAL WESTERN LIFE INS CO	CO	10,001.6
NATIONWIDE MUTUAL FIRE INS CO	OH	5,596.1
OHIO NATIONAL LIFE ASR CORP	OH	3,450.3
PIONEER MUTUAL LIFE INS CO	ND	507.2
PRINCIPAL LIFE INS CO	IA	150,015.7
SAVINGS BANK LIFE INS CO OF MA	MA	2,531.7
SENTRY SELECT INS CO	WI	672.6
STANDARD INS CO	OR	19,996.4
STATE FARM MUTUAL AUTOMOBILE INS CO	IL	135,478.4
SURETY LIFE INS CO	NE	14.3
SYMETRA LIFE INS CO	WA	28,322.5
THRIVENT LIFE INS CO	MN	3,560.4
TRUSTMARK INS CO	IL	1,404.7
TRUSTMARK LIFE INS CO	IL	380.8
UNITED WORLD LIFE INS CO	NE	107.9
USABLE LIFE	AR	426.8

Maine

INSURANCE COMPANY NAME	DOM. STATE	TOTAL ASSETS ($MIL)
Rating:	**A+**	
COUNTRY LIFE INS CO	IL	10,519.0
HEALTH CARE SVC CORP A MUT LEG RES	IL	18,206.4
PHYSICIANS MUTUAL INS CO	NE	1,968.0
TEACHERS INS & ANNUITY ASN OF AM	NY	256,932.8
Rating:	**A**	
4 EVER LIFE INS CO	IL	202.8
BERKSHIRE LIFE INS CO OF AMERICA	MA	3,589.9
CINCINNATI INS CO	OH	10,807.9
FEDERATED LIFE INS CO	MN	1,483.1
GUARDIAN LIFE INS CO OF AMERICA	NY	44,344.6
RESERVE NATIONAL INS CO	OK	112.3
SENTRY INS A MUTUAL CO	WI	6,832.1
SENTRY LIFE INS CO	WI	5,167.7
USAA LIFE INS CO	TX	21,633.7
Rating:	**A-**	
AMALGAMATED LIFE INS CO	NY	107.0
AMERICAN REPUBLIC INS CO	IA	799.7
ANTHEM LIFE INS CO	IN	571.2
BALBOA LIFE INS CO	CA	58.9
CENTRAL STATES H & L CO OF OMAHA	NE	405.9
COMPANION LIFE INS CO	SC	278.1
DEARBORN NATIONAL LIFE INS CO	IL	2,193.1
FAMILY HERITAGE LIFE INS CO OF AMER	OH	706.7
FEDERATED MUTUAL INS CO	MN	4,667.2
GARDEN STATE LIFE INS CO	TX	120.1
GERBER LIFE INS CO	NY	2,680.4
ILLINOIS MUTUAL LIFE INS CO	IL	1,354.0
MASSACHUSETTS MUTUAL LIFE INS CO	MA	189,173.1
MIDWESTERN UNITED LIFE INS CO	IN	237.0
MUTUAL OF AMERICA LIFE INS CO	NY	17,180.5
NEW YORK LIFE INS CO	NY	142,089.9
NORTHWESTERN MUTUAL LIFE INS CO	WI	222,040.6
OLD REPUBLIC INS CO	PA	2,591.0
PHYSICIANS LIFE INS CO	NE	1,406.1
PROTECTIVE INS CO	IN	770.4
Rating:	**B+**	
AETNA HEALTH & LIFE INS CO	CT	2,193.0
AETNA LIFE INS CO	CT	22,226.6
AMERICAN FAMILY LIFE ASR CO OF COLUM	NE	111,249.2
AMERICAN FIDELITY ASR CO	OK	4,848.9
AMERICAN UNITED LIFE INS CO	IN	22,972.9
ASSURITY LIFE INS CO	NE	2,436.6
BOSTON MUTUAL LIFE INS CO	MA	1,222.3
CENTRAL STATES INDEMNITY CO OF OMAHA	NE	424.9
COLORADO BANKERS LIFE INS CO	CO	272.7
COVENTRY HEALTH & LIFE INS CO	MO	1,547.4
FEDERAL INS CO	IN	32,182.2
GOVERNMENT EMPLOYEES INS CO	MD	21,998.7
GOVERNMENT PERSONNEL MUTUAL L I C	TX	833.6
HARVARD PILGRIM HEALTH CARE INC	MA	837.3
JACKSON NATIONAL LIFE INS CO	MI	176,569.5
LINCOLN BENEFIT LIFE CO	NE	13,279.3
MEDCO CONTAINMENT LIFE INS CO	PA	507.6
MEDICO CORP LIFE INS CO	NE	25.7

INSURANCE COMPANY NAME	DOM. STATE	TOTAL ASSETS ($MIL)
MERIT LIFE INS CO	IN	560.2
MIDLAND NATIONAL LIFE INS CO	IA	39,622.6
MINNESOTA LIFE INS CO	MN	34,732.2
MUTUAL OF OMAHA INS CO	NE	6,375.2
NATIONAL BENEFIT LIFE INS CO	NY	475.2
NATIONAL CASUALTY CO	WI	287.3
NATIONAL WESTERN LIFE INS CO	CO	10,001.6
NATIONWIDE MUTUAL FIRE INS CO	OH	5,596.1
OHIO NATIONAL LIFE ASR CORP	OH	3,450.3
PIONEER MUTUAL LIFE INS CO	ND	507.2
PRINCIPAL LIFE INS CO	IA	150,015.7
SAVINGS BANK LIFE INS CO OF MA	MA	2,531.7
SENTRY SELECT INS CO	WI	672.6
STANDARD INS CO	OR	19,996.4
STATE FARM MUTUAL AUTOMOBILE INS CO	IL	135,478.4
SURETY LIFE INS CO	NE	14.3
SYMETRA LIFE INS CO	WA	28,322.5
TRUSTMARK INS CO	IL	1,404.7
TRUSTMARK LIFE INS CO	IL	380.8
UNITED WORLD LIFE INS CO	NE	107.9
USABLE LIFE	AR	426.8

Maryland

INSURANCE COMPANY NAME	DOM. STATE	TOTAL ASSETS ($MIL)
Rating: A+		
CAREFIRST BLUECHOICE INC	DC	1,140.8
COUNTRY LIFE INS CO	IL	10,519.0
HEALTH CARE SVC CORP A MUT LEG RES	IL	18,206.4
PHYSICIANS MUTUAL INS CO	NE	1,968.0
TEACHERS INS & ANNUITY ASN OF AM	NY	256,932.8
Rating: A		
4 EVER LIFE INS CO	IL	202.8
BERKSHIRE LIFE INS CO OF AMERICA	MA	3,589.9
CINCINNATI INS CO	OH	10,807.9
FEDERATED LIFE INS CO	MN	1,483.1
GUARDIAN LIFE INS CO OF AMERICA	NY	44,344.6
RESERVE NATIONAL INS CO	OK	112.3
SENTRY INS A MUTUAL CO	WI	6,832.1
SENTRY LIFE INS CO	WI	5,167.7
SHELTERPOINT LIFE INS CO	NY	103.8
UNITED FARM FAMILY LIFE INS CO	IN	2,116.5
USAA LIFE INS CO	TX	21,633.7
Rating: A-		
AMALGAMATED LIFE INS CO	NY	107.0
AMERICAN REPUBLIC INS CO	IA	799.7
ANTHEM LIFE INS CO	IN	571.2
BALBOA LIFE INS CO	CA	58.9
CENTRAL STATES H & L CO OF OMAHA	NE	405.9
COMPANION LIFE INS CO	SC	278.1
DEARBORN NATIONAL LIFE INS CO	IL	2,193.1
ERIE FAMILY LIFE INS CO	PA	2,058.7
FAMILY HERITAGE LIFE INS CO OF AMER	OH	706.7
FEDERATED MUTUAL INS CO	MN	4,667.2
GARDEN STATE LIFE INS CO	TX	120.1
GERBER LIFE INS CO	NY	2,680.4
HEALTHY ALLIANCE LIFE INS CO	MO	954.2
ILLINOIS MUTUAL LIFE INS CO	IL	1,354.0
MASSACHUSETTS MUTUAL LIFE INS CO	MA	189,173.1
MIDWESTERN UNITED LIFE INS CO	IN	237.0
MUTUAL OF AMERICA LIFE INS CO	NY	17,180.5
NEW YORK LIFE INS CO	NY	142,089.9
NIPPON LIFE INS CO OF AMERICA	IA	222.1
NORTHWESTERN MUTUAL LIFE INS CO	WI	222,040.6
OLD REPUBLIC INS CO	PA	2,591.0
PHYSICIANS LIFE INS CO	NE	1,406.1
PROTECTIVE INS CO	IN	770.4
STANDARD LIFE & ACCIDENT INS CO	TX	525.1
Rating: B+		
AETNA HEALTH & LIFE INS CO	CT	2,193.0
AETNA LIFE INS CO	CT	22,226.6
AMERICAN FAMILY LIFE ASR CO OF COLUM	NE	111,249.2
AMERICAN FIDELITY ASR CO	OK	4,848.9
AMERICAN UNITED LIFE INS CO	IN	22,972.9
ASSURITY LIFE INS CO	NE	2,436.6
BOSTON MUTUAL LIFE INS CO	MA	1,222.3
CENTRAL STATES INDEMNITY CO OF OMAHA	NE	424.9
COLORADO BANKERS LIFE INS CO	CO	272.7
COVENTRY HEALTH & LIFE INS CO	MO	1,547.4
FEDERAL INS CO	IN	32,182.2

INSURANCE COMPANY NAME	DOM. STATE	TOTAL ASSETS ($MIL)
GOVERNMENT EMPLOYEES INS CO	MD	21,998.7
GOVERNMENT PERSONNEL MUTUAL L I C	TX	833.6
JACKSON NATIONAL LIFE INS CO	MI	176,569.5
KAISER PERMANENTE INS CO	CA	179.4
LINCOLN BENEFIT LIFE CO	NE	13,279.3
MEDCO CONTAINMENT LIFE INS CO	PA	507.6
MEDICO CORP LIFE INS CO	NE	25.7
MERIT LIFE INS CO	IN	560.2
MIDLAND NATIONAL LIFE INS CO	IA	39,622.6
MINNESOTA LIFE INS CO	MN	34,732.2
MUTUAL OF OMAHA INS CO	NE	6,375.2
NATIONAL BENEFIT LIFE INS CO	NY	475.2
NATIONAL CASUALTY CO	WI	287.3
NATIONAL WESTERN LIFE INS CO	CO	10,001.6
NATIONWIDE MUTUAL FIRE INS CO	OH	5,596.1
OHIO NATIONAL LIFE ASR CORP	OH	3,450.3
PIONEER MUTUAL LIFE INS CO	ND	507.2
PRINCIPAL LIFE INS CO	IA	150,015.7
SAVINGS BANK LIFE INS CO OF MA	MA	2,531.7
SENTRY SELECT INS CO	WI	672.6
STANDARD INS CO	OR	19,996.4
STATE FARM MUTUAL AUTOMOBILE INS CO	IL	135,478.4
SURETY LIFE INS CO	NE	14.3
SYMETRA LIFE INS CO	WA	28,322.5
THRIVENT LIFE INS CO	MN	3,560.4
TRUSTMARK INS CO	IL	1,404.7
TRUSTMARK LIFE INS CO	IL	380.8
UNITED WORLD LIFE INS CO	NE	107.9
USABLE LIFE	AR	426.8

Massachusetts

INSURANCE COMPANY NAME	DOM. STATE	TOTAL ASSETS ($MIL)
Rating: A+		
COUNTRY LIFE INS CO	IL	10,519.0
HEALTH CARE SVC CORP A MUT LEG RES	IL	18,206.4
PHYSICIANS MUTUAL INS CO	NE	1,968.0
TEACHERS INS & ANNUITY ASN OF AM	NY	256,932.8
Rating: A		
4 EVER LIFE INS CO	IL	202.8
BERKSHIRE LIFE INS CO OF AMERICA	MA	3,589.9
CINCINNATI INS CO	OH	10,807.9
FEDERATED LIFE INS CO	MN	1,483.1
GUARDIAN LIFE INS CO OF AMERICA	NY	44,344.6
SENTRY INS A MUTUAL CO	WI	6,832.1
SENTRY LIFE INS CO	WI	5,167.7
SHELTERPOINT LIFE INS CO	NY	103.8
UNITED FARM FAMILY LIFE INS CO	IN	2,116.5
USAA LIFE INS CO	TX	21,633.7
Rating: A-		
AMALGAMATED LIFE INS CO	NY	107.0
AMERICAN FAMILY LIFE ASR CO OF NY	NY	706.5
AMERICAN REPUBLIC INS CO	IA	799.7
ANTHEM LIFE INS CO	IN	571.2
BALBOA LIFE INS CO	CA	58.9
CENTRAL STATES H & L CO OF OMAHA	NE	405.9
COMPANION LIFE INS CO	SC	278.1
DEARBORN NATIONAL LIFE INS CO	IL	2,193.1
FAMILY HERITAGE LIFE INS CO OF AMER	OH	706.7
FEDERATED MUTUAL INS CO	MN	4,667.2
GARDEN STATE LIFE INS CO	TX	120.1
GERBER LIFE INS CO	NY	2,680.4
ILLINOIS MUTUAL LIFE INS CO	IL	1,354.0
MASSACHUSETTS MUTUAL LIFE INS CO	MA	189,173.1
MIDWESTERN UNITED LIFE INS CO	IN	237.0
MUTUAL OF AMERICA LIFE INS CO	NY	17,180.5
NEW YORK LIFE INS CO	NY	142,089.9
NIPPON LIFE INS CO OF AMERICA	IA	222.1
NORTHWESTERN MUTUAL LIFE INS CO	WI	222,040.6
OLD REPUBLIC INS CO	PA	2,591.0
PHYSICIANS LIFE INS CO	NE	1,406.1
PROTECTIVE INS CO	IN	770.4
STANDARD LIFE & ACCIDENT INS CO	TX	525.1
Rating: B+		
AETNA HEALTH & LIFE INS CO	CT	2,193.0
AETNA LIFE INS CO	CT	22,226.6
AMERICAN FAMILY LIFE ASR CO OF COLUM	NE	111,249.2
AMERICAN FIDELITY ASR CO	OK	4,848.9
AMERICAN UNITED LIFE INS CO	IN	22,972.9
ASSURITY LIFE INS CO	NE	2,436.6
BOSTON MUTUAL LIFE INS CO	MA	1,222.3
CENTRAL STATES INDEMNITY CO OF OMAHA	NE	424.9
COLORADO BANKERS LIFE INS CO	CO	272.7
COVENTRY HEALTH & LIFE INS CO	MO	1,547.4
FEDERAL INS CO	IN	32,182.2
GOVERNMENT EMPLOYEES INS CO	MD	21,998.7
GOVERNMENT PERSONNEL MUTUAL L I C	TX	833.6
HARVARD PILGRIM HEALTH CARE INC	MA	837.3

INSURANCE COMPANY NAME	DOM. STATE	TOTAL ASSETS ($MIL)
JACKSON NATIONAL LIFE INS CO	MI	176,569.5
LINCOLN BENEFIT LIFE CO	NE	13,279.3
MEDCO CONTAINMENT LIFE INS CO	PA	507.6
MIDLAND NATIONAL LIFE INS CO	IA	39,622.6
MINNESOTA LIFE INS CO	MN	34,732.2
MUTUAL OF OMAHA INS CO	NE	6,375.2
NATIONAL BENEFIT LIFE INS CO	NY	475.2
NATIONAL CASUALTY CO	WI	287.3
NATIONAL WESTERN LIFE INS CO	CO	10,001.6
NATIONWIDE MUTUAL FIRE INS CO	OH	5,596.1
OHIO NATIONAL LIFE ASR CORP	OH	3,450.3
PIONEER MUTUAL LIFE INS CO	ND	507.2
PRINCIPAL LIFE INS CO	IA	150,015.7
SAVINGS BANK LIFE INS CO OF MA	MA	2,531.7
SENTRY SELECT INS CO	WI	672.6
STANDARD INS CO	OR	19,996.4
STATE FARM MUTUAL AUTOMOBILE INS CO	IL	135,478.4
SURETY LIFE INS CO	NE	14.3
SYMETRA LIFE INS CO	WA	28,322.5
TRUSTMARK INS CO	IL	1,404.7
TRUSTMARK LIFE INS CO	IL	380.8
UNITED WORLD LIFE INS CO	NE	107.9
USABLE LIFE	AR	426.8

Michigan

INSURANCE COMPANY NAME	DOM. STATE	TOTAL ASSETS ($MIL)
Rating: A+		
COUNTRY LIFE INS CO	IL	10,519.0
HEALTH CARE SVC CORP A MUT LEG RES	IL	18,206.4
PHYSICIANS MUTUAL INS CO	NE	1,968.0
TEACHERS INS & ANNUITY ASN OF AM	NY	256,932.8
Rating: A		
4 EVER LIFE INS CO	IL	202.8
AUTO-OWNERS LIFE INS CO	MI	3,557.4
BERKSHIRE LIFE INS CO OF AMERICA	MA	3,589.9
CINCINNATI INS CO	OH	10,807.9
FEDERATED LIFE INS CO	MN	1,483.1
GUARDIAN LIFE INS CO OF AMERICA	NY	44,344.6
RESERVE NATIONAL INS CO	OK	112.3
SENTRY INS A MUTUAL CO	WI	6,832.1
SENTRY LIFE INS CO	WI	5,167.7
SHELTERPOINT LIFE INS CO	NY	103.8
USAA LIFE INS CO	TX	21,633.7
Rating: A-		
AMALGAMATED LIFE INS CO	NY	107.0
AMERICAN REPUBLIC INS CO	IA	799.7
ANTHEM LIFE INS CO	IN	571.2
BALBOA LIFE INS CO	CA	58.9
CENTRAL STATES H & L CO OF OMAHA	NE	405.9
COMPANION LIFE INS CO	SC	278.1
DEARBORN NATIONAL LIFE INS CO	IL	2,193.1
FAMILY HERITAGE LIFE INS CO OF AMER	OH	706.7
FEDERATED MUTUAL INS CO	MN	4,667.2
GARDEN STATE LIFE INS CO	TX	120.1
GERBER LIFE INS CO	NY	2,680.4
ILLINOIS MUTUAL LIFE INS CO	IL	1,354.0
MASSACHUSETTS MUTUAL LIFE INS CO	MA	189,173.1
MEDICAL MUTUAL OF OHIO	OH	1,798.4
MIDWESTERN UNITED LIFE INS CO	IN	237.0
MUTUAL OF AMERICA LIFE INS CO	NY	17,180.5
NEW YORK LIFE INS CO	NY	142,089.9
NIPPON LIFE INS CO OF AMERICA	IA	222.1
NORTHWESTERN MUTUAL LIFE INS CO	WI	222,040.6
OLD REPUBLIC INS CO	PA	2,591.0
PHYSICIANS LIFE INS CO	NE	1,406.1
PROTECTIVE INS CO	IN	770.4
STANDARD LIFE & ACCIDENT INS CO	TX	525.1
Rating: B+		
AETNA HEALTH & LIFE INS CO	CT	2,193.0
AETNA LIFE INS CO	CT	22,226.6
ALLIANCE HEALTH & LIFE INS CO	MI	66.3
AMERICAN FAMILY LIFE ASR CO OF COLUM	NE	111,249.2
AMERICAN FIDELITY ASR CO	OK	4,848.9
AMERICAN UNITED LIFE INS CO	IN	22,972.9
ASSURITY LIFE INS CO	NE	2,436.6
BLUE CARE NETWORK OF MICHIGAN	MI	1,719.3
BOSTON MUTUAL LIFE INS CO	MA	1,222.3
CENTRAL STATES INDEMNITY CO OF OMAHA	NE	424.9
COLORADO BANKERS LIFE INS CO	CO	272.7
COVENTRY HEALTH & LIFE INS CO	MO	1,547.4
FEDERAL INS CO	IN	32,182.2

INSURANCE COMPANY NAME	DOM. STATE	TOTAL ASSETS ($MIL)
GOVERNMENT EMPLOYEES INS CO	MD	21,998.7
GOVERNMENT PERSONNEL MUTUAL L I C	TX	833.6
JACKSON NATIONAL LIFE INS CO	MI	176,569.5
LINCOLN BENEFIT LIFE CO	NE	13,279.3
MEDCO CONTAINMENT LIFE INS CO	PA	507.6
MEDICO CORP LIFE INS CO	NE	25.7
MERIDIAN HEALTH PLAN OF MICHIGAN INC	MI	263.1
MERIT LIFE INS CO	IN	560.2
MIDLAND NATIONAL LIFE INS CO	IA	39,622.6
MINNESOTA LIFE INS CO	MN	34,732.2
MUTUAL OF OMAHA INS CO	NE	6,375.2
NATIONAL BENEFIT LIFE INS CO	NY	475.2
NATIONAL CASUALTY CO	WI	287.3
NATIONAL WESTERN LIFE INS CO	CO	10,001.6
NATIONWIDE MUTUAL FIRE INS CO	OH	5,596.1
OHIO NATIONAL LIFE ASR CORP	OH	3,450.3
PIONEER MUTUAL LIFE INS CO	ND	507.2
PRINCIPAL LIFE INS CO	IA	150,015.7
PRIORITY HEALTH CHOICE INC	MI	76.2
SAVINGS BANK LIFE INS CO OF MA	MA	2,531.7
SENTRY SELECT INS CO	WI	672.6
STANDARD INS CO	OR	19,996.4
STATE FARM MUTUAL AUTOMOBILE INS CO	IL	135,478.4
SURETY LIFE INS CO	NE	14.3
SYMETRA LIFE INS CO	WA	28,322.5
THRIVENT LIFE INS CO	MN	3,560.4
TRUSTMARK INS CO	IL	1,404.7
TRUSTMARK LIFE INS CO	IL	380.8
UNITED WORLD LIFE INS CO	NE	107.9
USABLE LIFE	AR	426.8

Minnesota

INSURANCE COMPANY NAME	DOM. STATE	TOTAL ASSETS ($MIL)
Rating: A+		
COUNTRY LIFE INS CO	IL	10,519.0
GROUP HEALTH PLAN INC	MN	693.0
HEALTH CARE SVC CORP A MUT LEG RES	IL	18,206.4
PHYSICIANS MUTUAL INS CO	NE	1,968.0
TEACHERS INS & ANNUITY ASN OF AM	NY	256,932.8
Rating: A		
4 EVER LIFE INS CO	IL	202.8
AUTO-OWNERS LIFE INS CO	MI	3,557.4
BERKSHIRE LIFE INS CO OF AMERICA	MA	3,589.9
BLUE CROSS BLUE SHIELD OF MINNESOTA	MN	2,106.6
CINCINNATI INS CO	OH	10,807.9
FEDERATED LIFE INS CO	MN	1,483.1
GUARDIAN LIFE INS CO OF AMERICA	NY	44,344.6
SENTRY INS A MUTUAL CO	WI	6,832.1
SENTRY LIFE INS CO	WI	5,167.7
SHELTERPOINT LIFE INS CO	NY	103.8
USAA LIFE INS CO	TX	21,633.7
Rating: A-		
AMALGAMATED LIFE INS CO	NY	107.0
AMERICAN REPUBLIC INS CO	IA	799.7
ANTHEM LIFE INS CO	IN	571.2
BALBOA LIFE INS CO	CA	58.9
CENTRAL STATES H & L CO OF OMAHA	NE	405.9
COMPANION LIFE INS CO	SC	278.1
DEARBORN NATIONAL LIFE INS CO	IL	2,193.1
ERIE FAMILY LIFE INS CO	PA	2,058.7
FAMILY HERITAGE LIFE INS CO OF AMER	OH	706.7
FEDERATED MUTUAL INS CO	MN	4,667.2
GARDEN STATE LIFE INS CO	TX	120.1
GERBER LIFE INS CO	NY	2,680.4
HEALTHPARTNERS INS CO	MN	325.5
HMO MINNESOTA	MN	715.0
ILLINOIS MUTUAL LIFE INS CO	IL	1,354.0
MASSACHUSETTS MUTUAL LIFE INS CO	MA	189,173.1
MIDWESTERN UNITED LIFE INS CO	IN	237.0
MUTUAL OF AMERICA LIFE INS CO	NY	17,180.5
NEW YORK LIFE INS CO	NY	142,089.9
NIPPON LIFE INS CO OF AMERICA	IA	222.1
NORTHWESTERN MUTUAL LIFE INS CO	WI	222,040.6
OLD REPUBLIC INS CO	PA	2,591.0
PHYSICIANS LIFE INS CO	NE	1,406.1
PROTECTIVE INS CO	IN	770.4
STANDARD LIFE & ACCIDENT INS CO	TX	525.1
UCARE MINNESOTA	MN	969.6
Rating: B+		
AETNA HEALTH & LIFE INS CO	CT	2,193.0
AETNA LIFE INS CO	CT	22,226.6
AMERICAN FAMILY LIFE ASR CO OF COLUM	NE	111,249.2
AMERICAN FAMILY MUT INS CO	WI	13,709.4
AMERICAN FIDELITY ASR CO	OK	4,848.9
AMERICAN UNITED LIFE INS CO	IN	22,972.9
ASSURITY LIFE INS CO	NE	2,436.6
BOSTON MUTUAL LIFE INS CO	MA	1,222.3
CENTRAL STATES INDEMNITY CO OF OMAHA	NE	424.9

INSURANCE COMPANY NAME	DOM. STATE	TOTAL ASSETS ($MIL)
COLORADO BANKERS LIFE INS CO	CO	272.7
FARM BUREAU LIFE INS CO	IA	7,987.7
FEDERAL INS CO	IN	32,182.2
GOVERNMENT EMPLOYEES INS CO	MD	21,998.7
GOVERNMENT PERSONNEL MUTUAL L I C	TX	833.6
GRANGE MUTUAL CAS CO	OH	2,061.4
HEALTHPARTNERS	MN	1,138.9
JACKSON NATIONAL LIFE INS CO	MI	176,569.5
LINCOLN BENEFIT LIFE CO	NE	13,279.3
MEDCO CONTAINMENT LIFE INS CO	PA	507.6
MEDICA HEALTH PLANS	MN	760.3
MEDICO CORP LIFE INS CO	NE	25.7
MERIT LIFE INS CO	IN	560.2
MIDLAND NATIONAL LIFE INS CO	IA	39,622.6
MINNESOTA LIFE INS CO	MN	34,732.2
MUTUAL OF OMAHA INS CO	NE	6,375.2
NATIONAL BENEFIT LIFE INS CO	NY	475.2
NATIONAL CASUALTY CO	WI	287.3
NATIONAL WESTERN LIFE INS CO	CO	10,001.6
NATIONWIDE MUTUAL FIRE INS CO	OH	5,596.1
OHIO NATIONAL LIFE ASR CORP	OH	3,450.3
PIONEER MUTUAL LIFE INS CO	ND	507.2
PRINCIPAL LIFE INS CO	IA	150,015.7
SAVINGS BANK LIFE INS CO OF MA	MA	2,531.7
SENTRY LIFE INS CO OF NEW YORK	NY	77.0
SENTRY SELECT INS CO	WI	672.6
STANDARD INS CO	OR	19,996.4
STATE FARM MUTUAL AUTOMOBILE INS CO	IL	135,478.4
SURETY LIFE INS CO	NE	14.3
SYMETRA LIFE INS CO	WA	28,322.5
THRIVENT LIFE INS CO	MN	3,560.4
TRUSTMARK INS CO	IL	1,404.7
TRUSTMARK LIFE INS CO	IL	380.8
UNITED WORLD LIFE INS CO	NE	107.9
USABLE LIFE	AR	426.8

Mississippi

INSURANCE COMPANY NAME	DOM. STATE	TOTAL ASSETS ($MIL)
Rating: A+		
COUNTRY LIFE INS CO	IL	10,519.0
PHYSICIANS MUTUAL INS CO	NE	1,968.0
TEACHERS INS & ANNUITY ASN OF AM	NY	256,932.8
Rating: A		
4 EVER LIFE INS CO	IL	202.8
AUTO-OWNERS LIFE INS CO	MI	3,557.4
BERKSHIRE LIFE INS CO OF AMERICA	MA	3,589.9
CINCINNATI INS CO	OH	10,807.9
FEDERATED LIFE INS CO	MN	1,483.1
GUARDIAN LIFE INS CO OF AMERICA	NY	44,344.6
RESERVE NATIONAL INS CO	OK	112.3
SENTRY INS A MUTUAL CO	WI	6,832.1
SENTRY LIFE INS CO	WI	5,167.7
SOUTHERN FARM BUREAU LIFE INS CO	MS	12,921.4
USAA LIFE INS CO	TX	21,633.7
Rating: A-		
AMALGAMATED LIFE INS CO	NY	107.0
AMERICAN REPUBLIC INS CO	IA	799.7
ANTHEM LIFE INS CO	IN	571.2
BALBOA LIFE INS CO	CA	58.9
CENTRAL STATES H & L CO OF OMAHA	NE	405.9
COMPANION LIFE INS CO	SC	278.1
COTTON STATES LIFE INS CO	GA	331.7
DEARBORN NATIONAL LIFE INS CO	IL	2,193.1
FAMILY HERITAGE LIFE INS CO OF AMER	OH	706.7
FEDERATED MUTUAL INS CO	MN	4,667.2
GARDEN STATE LIFE INS CO	TX	120.1
GERBER LIFE INS CO	NY	2,680.4
HEALTHY ALLIANCE LIFE INS CO	MO	954.2
ILLINOIS MUTUAL LIFE INS CO	IL	1,354.0
LIFE INS CO OF ALABAMA	AL	112.7
MASSACHUSETTS MUTUAL LIFE INS CO	MA	189,173.1
MIDWESTERN UNITED LIFE INS CO	IN	237.0
MUTUAL OF AMERICA LIFE INS CO	NY	17,180.5
MUTUAL SAVINGS LIFE INS CO	AL	473.8
NEW YORK LIFE INS CO	NY	142,089.9
NIPPON LIFE INS CO OF AMERICA	IA	222.1
NORTHWESTERN MUTUAL LIFE INS CO	WI	222,040.6
OLD REPUBLIC INS CO	PA	2,591.0
PHYSICIANS LIFE INS CO	NE	1,406.1
PROTECTIVE INS CO	IN	770.4
SHELTER LIFE INS CO	MO	1,097.7
STANDARD LIFE & ACCIDENT INS CO	TX	525.1
Rating: B+		
AETNA HEALTH & LIFE INS CO	CT	2,193.0
AETNA LIFE INS CO	CT	22,226.6
AMERICAN FAMILY LIFE ASR CO OF COLUM	NE	111,249.2
AMERICAN FIDELITY ASR CO	OK	4,848.9
AMERICAN UNITED LIFE INS CO	IN	22,972.9
ASSURITY LIFE INS CO	NE	2,436.6
BLUE CROSS BLUE SHIELD OF MS, MUTUAL	MS	855.7
BLUEBONNET LIFE INS CO	MS	53.6
BOSTON MUTUAL LIFE INS CO	MA	1,222.3
CENTRAL STATES INDEMNITY CO OF OMAHA	NE	424.9

INSURANCE COMPANY NAME	DOM. STATE	TOTAL ASSETS ($MIL)
COLORADO BANKERS LIFE INS CO	CO	272.7
COVENTRY HEALTH & LIFE INS CO	MO	1,547.4
FEDERAL INS CO	IN	32,182.2
GOVERNMENT EMPLOYEES INS CO	MD	21,998.7
GOVERNMENT PERSONNEL MUTUAL L I C	TX	833.6
GREATER GEORGIA LIFE INS CO	GA	50.8
JACKSON NATIONAL LIFE INS CO	MI	176,569.5
LINCOLN BENEFIT LIFE CO	NE	13,279.3
MEDCO CONTAINMENT LIFE INS CO	PA	507.6
MEDICO CORP LIFE INS CO	NE	25.7
MERIT LIFE INS CO	IN	560.2
MIDLAND NATIONAL LIFE INS CO	IA	39,622.6
MINNESOTA LIFE INS CO	MN	34,732.2
MUTUAL OF OMAHA INS CO	NE	6,375.2
NATIONAL BENEFIT LIFE INS CO	NY	475.2
NATIONAL CASUALTY CO	WI	287.3
NATIONAL WESTERN LIFE INS CO	CO	10,001.6
NATIONWIDE MUTUAL FIRE INS CO	OH	5,596.1
OHIO NATIONAL LIFE ASR CORP	OH	3,450.3
PIONEER MUTUAL LIFE INS CO	ND	507.2
PRINCIPAL LIFE INS CO	IA	150,015.7
SAVINGS BANK LIFE INS CO OF MA	MA	2,531.7
SENTRY SELECT INS CO	WI	672.6
STANDARD INS CO	OR	19,996.4
STATE FARM MUTUAL AUTOMOBILE INS CO	IL	135,478.4
SURETY LIFE INS CO	NE	14.3
SYMETRA LIFE INS CO	WA	28,322.5
THRIVENT LIFE INS CO	MN	3,560.4
TRUSTMARK INS CO	IL	1,404.7
TRUSTMARK LIFE INS CO	IL	380.8
UNITED WORLD LIFE INS CO	NE	107.9
USABLE LIFE	AR	426.8

Missouri

INSURANCE COMPANY NAME	DOM. STATE	TOTAL ASSETS ($MIL)
Rating: A+		
COUNTRY LIFE INS CO	IL	10,519.0
HEALTH CARE SVC CORP A MUT LEG RES	IL	18,206.4
PHYSICIANS MUTUAL INS CO	NE	1,968.0
TEACHERS INS & ANNUITY ASN OF AM	NY	256,932.8
Rating: A		
4 EVER LIFE INS CO	IL	202.8
AUTO-OWNERS LIFE INS CO	MI	3,557.4
BERKSHIRE LIFE INS CO OF AMERICA	MA	3,589.9
CINCINNATI INS CO	OH	10,807.9
FEDERATED LIFE INS CO	MN	1,483.1
GUARDIAN LIFE INS CO OF AMERICA	NY	44,344.6
RESERVE NATIONAL INS CO	OK	112.3
SENTRY INS A MUTUAL CO	WI	6,832.1
SENTRY LIFE INS CO	WI	5,167.7
USAA LIFE INS CO	TX	21,633.7
Rating: A-		
AMALGAMATED LIFE INS CO	NY	107.0
AMERICAN REPUBLIC INS CO	IA	799.7
ANTHEM LIFE INS CO	IN	571.2
BALBOA LIFE INS CO	CA	58.9
CENTRAL STATES H & L CO OF OMAHA	NE	405.9
CIGNA LIFE INS CO OF NEW YORK	NY	376.2
COMPANION LIFE INS CO	SC	278.1
DEARBORN NATIONAL LIFE INS CO	IL	2,193.1
FAMILY HERITAGE LIFE INS CO OF AMER	OH	706.7
FARM BUREAU LIFE INS CO OF MISSOURI	MO	520.1
FEDERATED MUTUAL INS CO	MN	4,667.2
GARDEN STATE LIFE INS CO	TX	120.1
GERBER LIFE INS CO	NY	2,680.4
HEALTHCARE USA OF MISSOURI LLC	MO	203.4
HEALTHY ALLIANCE LIFE INS CO	MO	954.2
ILLINOIS MUTUAL LIFE INS CO	IL	1,354.0
MASSACHUSETTS MUTUAL LIFE INS CO	MA	189,173.1
MIDWESTERN UNITED LIFE INS CO	IN	237.0
MUTUAL OF AMERICA LIFE INS CO	NY	17,180.5
NEW YORK LIFE INS CO	NY	142,089.9
NIPPON LIFE INS CO OF AMERICA	IA	222.1
NORTHWESTERN MUTUAL LIFE INS CO	WI	222,040.6
OLD REPUBLIC INS CO	PA	2,591.0
PACIFIC GUARDIAN LIFE INS CO LTD	HI	518.1
PHYSICIANS LIFE INS CO	NE	1,406.1
PROTECTIVE INS CO	IN	770.4
SHELTER LIFE INS CO	MO	1,097.7
STANDARD LIFE & ACCIDENT INS CO	TX	525.1
Rating: B+		
AETNA LIFE INS CO	CT	22,226.6
AMERICAN FAMILY LIFE ASR CO OF COLUM	NE	111,249.2
AMERICAN FAMILY MUT INS CO	WI	13,709.4
AMERICAN FIDELITY ASR CO	OK	4,848.9
AMERICAN UNITED LIFE INS CO	IN	22,972.9
ASSURITY LIFE INS CO	NE	2,436.6
BOSTON MUTUAL LIFE INS CO	MA	1,222.3
CENTRAL STATES INDEMNITY CO OF OMAHA	NE	424.9
COLORADO BANKERS LIFE INS CO	CO	272.7

INSURANCE COMPANY NAME	DOM. STATE	TOTAL ASSETS ($MIL)
COVENTRY HEALTH & LIFE INS CO	MO	1,547.4
FEDERAL INS CO	IN	32,182.2
GOVERNMENT EMPLOYEES INS CO	MD	21,998.7
GOVERNMENT PERSONNEL MUTUAL L I C	TX	833.6
GRANGE MUTUAL CAS CO	OH	2,061.4
JACKSON NATIONAL LIFE INS CO	MI	176,569.5
KAISER PERMANENTE INS CO	CA	179.4
LINCOLN BENEFIT LIFE CO	NE	13,279.3
MEDCO CONTAINMENT LIFE INS CO	PA	507.6
MEDICO CORP LIFE INS CO	NE	25.7
MERIT LIFE INS CO	IN	560.2
MIDLAND NATIONAL LIFE INS CO	IA	39,622.6
MINNESOTA LIFE INS CO	MN	34,732.2
MUTUAL OF OMAHA INS CO	NE	6,375.2
NATIONAL BENEFIT LIFE INS CO	NY	475.2
NATIONAL CASUALTY CO	WI	287.3
NATIONAL WESTERN LIFE INS CO	CO	10,001.6
NATIONWIDE MUTUAL FIRE INS CO	OH	5,596.1
OHIO NATIONAL LIFE ASR CORP	OH	3,450.3
PIONEER MUTUAL LIFE INS CO	ND	507.2
PRINCIPAL LIFE INS CO	IA	150,015.7
SAVINGS BANK LIFE INS CO OF MA	MA	2,531.7
SENTRY SELECT INS CO	WI	672.6
STANDARD INS CO	OR	19,996.4
STATE FARM MUTUAL AUTOMOBILE INS CO	IL	135,478.4
SURETY LIFE INS CO	NE	14.3
SYMETRA LIFE INS CO	WA	28,322.5
THRIVENT LIFE INS CO	MN	3,560.4
TRUSTMARK INS CO	IL	1,404.7
TRUSTMARK LIFE INS CO	IL	380.8
UNITED WORLD LIFE INS CO	NE	107.9
USABLE LIFE	AR	426.8

Montana

INSURANCE COMPANY NAME	DOM. STATE	TOTAL ASSETS ($MIL)	INSURANCE COMPANY NAME	DOM. STATE	TOTAL ASSETS ($MIL)
Rating: **A+**			GOVERNMENT PERSONNEL MUTUAL L I C	TX	833.6
			JACKSON NATIONAL LIFE INS CO	MI	176,569.5
COUNTRY LIFE INS CO	IL	10,519.0	LINCOLN BENEFIT LIFE CO	NE	13,279.3
HEALTH CARE SVC CORP A MUT LEG RES	IL	18,206.4	MEDCO CONTAINMENT LIFE INS CO	PA	507.6
PHYSICIANS MUTUAL INS CO	NE	1,968.0	MEDICO CORP LIFE INS CO	NE	25.7
TEACHERS INS & ANNUITY ASN OF AM	NY	256,932.8	MERIT LIFE INS CO	IN	560.2
			MIDLAND NATIONAL LIFE INS CO	IA	39,622.6
Rating: **A**			MINNESOTA LIFE INS CO	MN	34,732.2
			MUTUAL OF OMAHA INS CO	NE	6,375.2
4 EVER LIFE INS CO	IL	202.8	NATIONAL BENEFIT LIFE INS CO	NY	475.2
BERKSHIRE LIFE INS CO OF AMERICA	MA	3,589.9	NATIONAL CASUALTY CO	WI	287.3
CINCINNATI INS CO	OH	10,807.9	NATIONAL WESTERN LIFE INS CO	CO	10,001.6
FEDERATED LIFE INS CO	MN	1,483.1	NATIONWIDE MUTUAL FIRE INS CO	OH	5,596.1
GUARDIAN LIFE INS CO OF AMERICA	NY	44,344.6	OHIO NATIONAL LIFE ASR CORP	OH	3,450.3
LIFEWISE ASR CO	WA	129.7	PIONEER MUTUAL LIFE INS CO	ND	507.2
RESERVE NATIONAL INS CO	OK	112.3	PRINCIPAL LIFE INS CO	IA	150,015.7
SENTRY INS A MUTUAL CO	WI	6,832.1	SAVINGS BANK LIFE INS CO OF MA	MA	2,531.7
SENTRY LIFE INS CO	WI	5,167.7	SENTRY SELECT INS CO	WI	672.6
USAA LIFE INS CO	TX	21,633.7	STANDARD INS CO	OR	19,996.4
			STATE FARM MUTUAL AUTOMOBILE INS CO	IL	135,478.4
Rating: **A-**			SURETY LIFE INS CO	NE	14.3
			SYMETRA LIFE INS CO	WA	28,322.5
AMALGAMATED LIFE INS CO	NY	107.0	THRIVENT LIFE INS CO	MN	3,560.4
AMERICAN REPUBLIC INS CO	IA	799.7	TRUSTMARK INS CO	IL	1,404.7
ANTHEM LIFE INS CO	IN	571.2	TRUSTMARK LIFE INS CO	IL	380.8
BALBOA LIFE INS CO	CA	58.9	UNITED WORLD LIFE INS CO	NE	107.9
CENTRAL STATES H & L CO OF OMAHA	NE	405.9	USABLE LIFE	AR	426.8
COMPANION LIFE INS CO	SC	278.1			
COPIC INS CO	CO	523.3			
DEARBORN NATIONAL LIFE INS CO	IL	2,193.1			
FAMILY HERITAGE LIFE INS CO OF AMER	OH	706.7			
FEDERATED MUTUAL INS CO	MN	4,667.2			
GARDEN STATE LIFE INS CO	TX	120.1			
GERBER LIFE INS CO	NY	2,680.4			
ILLINOIS MUTUAL LIFE INS CO	IL	1,354.0			
MASSACHUSETTS MUTUAL LIFE INS CO	MA	189,173.1			
MIDWESTERN UNITED LIFE INS CO	IN	237.0			
MUTUAL OF AMERICA LIFE INS CO	NY	17,180.5			
NEW YORK LIFE INS CO	NY	142,089.9			
NIPPON LIFE INS CO OF AMERICA	IA	222.1			
NORTHWESTERN MUTUAL LIFE INS CO	WI	222,040.6			
OLD REPUBLIC INS CO	PA	2,591.0			
PACIFIC GUARDIAN LIFE INS CO LTD	HI	518.1			
PHYSICIANS LIFE INS CO	NE	1,406.1			
PROTECTIVE INS CO	IN	770.4			
STANDARD LIFE & ACCIDENT INS CO	TX	525.1			
Rating: **B+**					
AETNA HEALTH & LIFE INS CO	CT	2,193.0			
AETNA LIFE INS CO	CT	22,226.6			
AMERICAN FAMILY LIFE ASR CO OF COLUM	NE	111,249.2			
AMERICAN FAMILY MUT INS CO	WI	13,709.4			
AMERICAN FIDELITY ASR CO	OK	4,848.9			
AMERICAN UNITED LIFE INS CO	IN	22,972.9			
ASSURITY LIFE INS CO	NE	2,436.6			
BOSTON MUTUAL LIFE INS CO	MA	1,222.3			
CENTRAL STATES INDEMNITY CO OF OMAHA	NE	424.9			
COLORADO BANKERS LIFE INS CO	CO	272.7			
FARM BUREAU LIFE INS CO	IA	7,987.7			
FEDERAL INS CO	IN	32,182.2			
GOVERNMENT EMPLOYEES INS CO	MD	21,998.7			

Nebraska

INSURANCE COMPANY NAME	DOM. STATE	TOTAL ASSETS ($MIL)
Rating: A+		
COUNTRY LIFE INS CO	IL	10,519.0
HEALTH CARE SVC CORP A MUT LEG RES	IL	18,206.4
PHYSICIANS MUTUAL INS CO	NE	1,968.0
TEACHERS INS & ANNUITY ASN OF AM	NY	256,932.8
Rating: A		
4 EVER LIFE INS CO	IL	202.8
AUTO-OWNERS LIFE INS CO	MI	3,557.4
BERKSHIRE LIFE INS CO OF AMERICA	MA	3,589.9
CINCINNATI INS CO	OH	10,807.9
FEDERATED LIFE INS CO	MN	1,483.1
GUARDIAN LIFE INS CO OF AMERICA	NY	44,344.6
RESERVE NATIONAL INS CO	OK	112.3
SENTRY INS A MUTUAL CO	WI	6,832.1
SENTRY LIFE INS CO	WI	5,167.7
USAA LIFE INS CO	TX	21,633.7
Rating: A-		
AMALGAMATED LIFE INS CO	NY	107.0
AMERICAN REPUBLIC INS CO	IA	799.7
ANTHEM LIFE INS CO	IN	571.2
BALBOA LIFE INS CO	CA	58.9
BLUE CROSS BLUE SHIELD OF NEBRASKA	NE	945.9
CENTRAL STATES H & L CO OF OMAHA	NE	405.9
COMPANION LIFE INS CO	SC	278.1
COPIC INS CO	CO	523.3
DEARBORN NATIONAL LIFE INS CO	IL	2,193.1
FAMILY HERITAGE LIFE INS CO OF AMER	OH	706.7
FEDERATED MUTUAL INS CO	MN	4,667.2
GARDEN STATE LIFE INS CO	TX	120.1
GERBER LIFE INS CO	NY	2,680.4
ILLINOIS MUTUAL LIFE INS CO	IL	1,354.0
MASSACHUSETTS MUTUAL LIFE INS CO	MA	189,173.1
MIDWESTERN UNITED LIFE INS CO	IN	237.0
MUTUAL OF AMERICA LIFE INS CO	NY	17,180.5
NEW YORK LIFE INS CO	NY	142,089.9
NIPPON LIFE INS CO OF AMERICA	IA	222.1
NORTHWESTERN MUTUAL LIFE INS CO	WI	222,040.6
OLD REPUBLIC INS CO	PA	2,591.0
PACIFIC GUARDIAN LIFE INS CO LTD	HI	518.1
PHYSICIANS LIFE INS CO	NE	1,406.1
PROTECTIVE INS CO	IN	770.4
SHELTER LIFE INS CO	MO	1,097.7
STANDARD LIFE & ACCIDENT INS CO	TX	525.1
Rating: B+		
AETNA HEALTH & LIFE INS CO	CT	2,193.0
AETNA LIFE INS CO	CT	22,226.6
AMERICAN FAMILY LIFE ASR CO OF COLUM	NE	111,249.2
AMERICAN FAMILY MUT INS CO	WI	13,709.4
AMERICAN FIDELITY ASR CO	OK	4,848.9
AMERICAN UNITED LIFE INS CO	IN	22,972.9
ASSURITY LIFE INS CO	NE	2,436.6
BOSTON MUTUAL LIFE INS CO	MA	1,222.3
CENTRAL STATES INDEMNITY CO OF OMAHA	NE	424.9
COLORADO BANKERS LIFE INS CO	CO	272.7
COVENTRY HEALTH & LIFE INS CO	MO	1,547.4

INSURANCE COMPANY NAME	DOM. STATE	TOTAL ASSETS ($MIL)
COVENTRY HEALTH CARE OF NEBRASKA INC	NE	142.3
FARM BUREAU LIFE INS CO	IA	7,987.7
FEDERAL INS CO	IN	32,182.2
GOVERNMENT EMPLOYEES INS CO	MD	21,998.7
GOVERNMENT PERSONNEL MUTUAL L I C	TX	833.6
JACKSON NATIONAL LIFE INS CO	MI	176,569.5
LINCOLN BENEFIT LIFE CO	NE	13,279.3
MEDCO CONTAINMENT LIFE INS CO	PA	507.6
MEDICO CORP LIFE INS CO	NE	25.7
MERIT LIFE INS CO	IN	560.2
MIDLAND NATIONAL LIFE INS CO	IA	39,622.6
MINNESOTA LIFE INS CO	MN	34,732.2
MUTUAL OF OMAHA INS CO	NE	6,375.2
NATIONAL BENEFIT LIFE INS CO	NY	475.2
NATIONAL CASUALTY CO	WI	287.3
NATIONAL WESTERN LIFE INS CO	CO	10,001.6
NATIONWIDE MUTUAL FIRE INS CO	OH	5,596.1
OHIO NATIONAL LIFE ASR CORP	OH	3,450.3
PIONEER MUTUAL LIFE INS CO	ND	507.2
PRINCIPAL LIFE INS CO	IA	150,015.7
SAVINGS BANK LIFE INS CO OF MA	MA	2,531.7
SENTRY SELECT INS CO	WI	672.6
STANDARD INS CO	OR	19,996.4
STATE FARM MUTUAL AUTOMOBILE INS CO	IL	135,478.4
SURETY LIFE INS CO	NE	14.3
SYMETRA LIFE INS CO	WA	28,322.5
THRIVENT LIFE INS CO	MN	3,560.4
TRUSTMARK INS CO	IL	1,404.7
TRUSTMARK LIFE INS CO	IL	380.8
UNITED HEALTHCARE OF THE MIDLANDS	NE	75.7
UNITED WORLD LIFE INS CO	NE	107.9
USABLE LIFE	AR	426.8

Nevada

INSURANCE COMPANY NAME	DOM. STATE	TOTAL ASSETS ($MIL)
Rating:	**A+**	
COUNTRY LIFE INS CO	IL	10,519.0
PHYSICIANS MUTUAL INS CO	NE	1,968.0
TEACHERS INS & ANNUITY ASN OF AM	NY	256,932.8
Rating:	**A**	
4 EVER LIFE INS CO	IL	202.8
AUTO-OWNERS LIFE INS CO	MI	3,557.4
BERKSHIRE LIFE INS CO OF AMERICA	MA	3,589.9
CINCINNATI INS CO	OH	10,807.9
FEDERATED LIFE INS CO	MN	1,483.1
GUARDIAN LIFE INS CO OF AMERICA	NY	44,344.6
LIFEWISE ASR CO	WA	129.7
RESERVE NATIONAL INS CO	OK	112.3
SENTRY INS A MUTUAL CO	WI	6,832.1
SENTRY LIFE INS CO	WI	5,167.7
USAA LIFE INS CO	TX	21,633.7
Rating:	**A-**	
AMALGAMATED LIFE INS CO	NY	107.0
AMERICAN REPUBLIC INS CO	IA	799.7
ANTHEM LIFE INS CO	IN	571.2
BALBOA LIFE INS CO	CA	58.9
CENTRAL STATES H & L CO OF OMAHA	NE	405.9
COMPANION LIFE INS CO	SC	278.1
CSAA INS EXCHANGE	CA	6,888.9
DEARBORN NATIONAL LIFE INS CO	IL	2,193.1
FAMILY HERITAGE LIFE INS CO OF AMER	OH	706.7
FEDERATED MUTUAL INS CO	MN	4,667.2
GARDEN STATE LIFE INS CO	TX	120.1
GERBER LIFE INS CO	NY	2,680.4
HEALTHY ALLIANCE LIFE INS CO	MO	954.2
ILLINOIS MUTUAL LIFE INS CO	IL	1,354.0
MASSACHUSETTS MUTUAL LIFE INS CO	MA	189,173.1
MIDWESTERN UNITED LIFE INS CO	IN	237.0
MUTUAL OF AMERICA LIFE INS CO	NY	17,180.5
NEW YORK LIFE INS CO	NY	142,089.9
NIPPON LIFE INS CO OF AMERICA	IA	222.1
NORTHWESTERN MUTUAL LIFE INS CO	WI	222,040.6
OLD REPUBLIC INS CO	PA	2,591.0
PACIFIC GUARDIAN LIFE INS CO LTD	HI	518.1
PHYSICIANS LIFE INS CO	NE	1,406.1
PROTECTIVE INS CO	IN	770.4
SHELTER LIFE INS CO	MO	1,097.7
STANDARD LIFE & ACCIDENT INS CO	TX	525.1
Rating:	**B+**	
AETNA HEALTH & LIFE INS CO	CT	2,193.0
AETNA LIFE INS CO	CT	22,226.6
AMERICAN FAMILY LIFE ASR CO OF COLUM	NE	111,249.2
AMERICAN FAMILY MUT INS CO	WI	13,709.4
AMERICAN FIDELITY ASR CO	OK	4,848.9
AMERICAN UNITED LIFE INS CO	IN	22,972.9
ASSURITY LIFE INS CO	NE	2,436.6
BOSTON MUTUAL LIFE INS CO	MA	1,222.3
CENTRAL STATES INDEMNITY CO OF OMAHA	NE	424.9
COLORADO BANKERS LIFE INS CO	CO	272.7
COVENTRY HEALTH & LIFE INS CO	MO	1,547.4

INSURANCE COMPANY NAME	DOM. STATE	TOTAL ASSETS ($MIL)
FARM BUREAU LIFE INS CO	IA	7,987.7
FEDERAL INS CO	IN	32,182.2
GOVERNMENT EMPLOYEES INS CO	MD	21,998.7
GOVERNMENT PERSONNEL MUTUAL L I C	TX	833.6
JACKSON NATIONAL LIFE INS CO	MI	176,569.5
LINCOLN BENEFIT LIFE CO	NE	13,279.3
MEDCO CONTAINMENT LIFE INS CO	PA	507.6
MEDICO CORP LIFE INS CO	NE	25.7
MERIT LIFE INS CO	IN	560.2
MIDLAND NATIONAL LIFE INS CO	IA	39,622.6
MINNESOTA LIFE INS CO	MN	34,732.2
MUTUAL OF OMAHA INS CO	NE	6,375.2
NATIONAL BENEFIT LIFE INS CO	NY	475.2
NATIONAL CASUALTY CO	WI	287.3
NATIONAL WESTERN LIFE INS CO	CO	10,001.6
NATIONWIDE MUTUAL FIRE INS CO	OH	5,596.1
OHIO NATIONAL LIFE ASR CORP	OH	3,450.3
PIONEER MUTUAL LIFE INS CO	ND	507.2
PRINCIPAL LIFE INS CO	IA	150,015.7
ROCKY MOUNTAIN HOSPITAL & MEDICAL	CO	889.3
SAVINGS BANK LIFE INS CO OF MA	MA	2,531.7
SENTRY SELECT INS CO	WI	672.6
STANDARD INS CO	OR	19,996.4
STATE FARM MUTUAL AUTOMOBILE INS CO	IL	135,478.4
SURETY LIFE INS CO	NE	14.3
SYMETRA LIFE INS CO	WA	28,322.5
THRIVENT LIFE INS CO	MN	3,560.4
TRUSTMARK INS CO	IL	1,404.7
TRUSTMARK LIFE INS CO	IL	380.8
UNITED WORLD LIFE INS CO	NE	107.9
USABLE LIFE	AR	426.8

New Hampshire

INSURANCE COMPANY NAME	DOM. STATE	TOTAL ASSETS ($MIL)
Rating:	**A+**	
PHYSICIANS MUTUAL INS CO	NE	1,968.0
TEACHERS INS & ANNUITY ASN OF AM	NY	256,932.8
Rating:	**A**	
4 EVER LIFE INS CO	IL	202.8
BERKSHIRE LIFE INS CO OF AMERICA	MA	3,589.9
CINCINNATI INS CO	OH	10,807.9
FEDERATED LIFE INS CO	MN	1,483.1
GUARDIAN LIFE INS CO OF AMERICA	NY	44,344.6
SENTRY INS A MUTUAL CO	WI	6,832.1
SENTRY LIFE INS CO	WI	5,167.7
UNITED FARM FAMILY LIFE INS CO	IN	2,116.5
USAA LIFE INS CO	TX	21,633.7
Rating:	**A-**	
AMALGAMATED LIFE INS CO	NY	107.0
AMERICAN REPUBLIC INS CO	IA	799.7
ANTHEM LIFE INS CO	IN	571.2
BALBOA LIFE INS CO	CA	58.9
CENTRAL STATES H & L CO OF OMAHA	NE	405.9
COMPANION LIFE INS CO	SC	278.1
DEARBORN NATIONAL LIFE INS CO	IL	2,193.1
FAMILY HERITAGE LIFE INS CO OF AMER	OH	706.7
FEDERATED MUTUAL INS CO	MN	4,667.2
GARDEN STATE LIFE INS CO	TX	120.1
GERBER LIFE INS CO	NY	2,680.4
ILLINOIS MUTUAL LIFE INS CO	IL	1,354.0
MASSACHUSETTS MUTUAL LIFE INS CO	MA	189,173.1
MATTHEW THORNTON HEALTH PLAN	NH	220.6
MIDWESTERN UNITED LIFE INS CO	IN	237.0
MUTUAL OF AMERICA LIFE INS CO	NY	17,180.5
NEW YORK LIFE INS CO	NY	142,089.9
NORTHWESTERN MUTUAL LIFE INS CO	WI	222,040.6
OLD REPUBLIC INS CO	PA	2,591.0
PHYSICIANS LIFE INS CO	NE	1,406.1
PROTECTIVE INS CO	IN	770.4
Rating:	**B+**	
AETNA LIFE INS CO	CT	22,226.6
AMERICAN FAMILY LIFE ASR CO OF COLUM	NE	111,249.2
AMERICAN FIDELITY ASR CO	OK	4,848.9
AMERICAN UNITED LIFE INS CO	IN	22,972.9
ANTHEM HEALTH PLANS OF NEW HAMPSHIRE	NH	343.1
ASSURITY LIFE INS CO	NE	2,436.6
BOSTON MUTUAL LIFE INS CO	MA	1,222.3
CENTRAL STATES INDEMNITY CO OF OMAHA	NE	424.9
COLORADO BANKERS LIFE INS CO	CO	272.7
FEDERAL INS CO	IN	32,182.2
GOVERNMENT EMPLOYEES INS CO	MD	21,998.7
GOVERNMENT PERSONNEL MUTUAL L I C	TX	833.6
JACKSON NATIONAL LIFE INS CO	MI	176,569.5
LINCOLN BENEFIT LIFE CO	NE	13,279.3
MEDCO CONTAINMENT LIFE INS CO	PA	507.6
MERIT LIFE INS CO	IN	560.2
MIDLAND NATIONAL LIFE INS CO	IA	39,622.6
MINNESOTA LIFE INS CO	MN	34,732.2
MUTUAL OF OMAHA INS CO	NE	6,375.2

INSURANCE COMPANY NAME	DOM. STATE	TOTAL ASSETS ($MIL)
NATIONAL BENEFIT LIFE INS CO	NY	475.2
NATIONAL CASUALTY CO	WI	287.3
NATIONAL WESTERN LIFE INS CO	CO	10,001.6
NATIONWIDE MUTUAL FIRE INS CO	OH	5,596.1
OHIO NATIONAL LIFE ASR CORP	OH	3,450.3
PIONEER MUTUAL LIFE INS CO	ND	507.2
PRINCIPAL LIFE INS CO	IA	150,015.7
SAVINGS BANK LIFE INS CO OF MA	MA	2,531.7
SENTRY SELECT INS CO	WI	672.6
STANDARD INS CO	OR	19,996.4
STATE FARM MUTUAL AUTOMOBILE INS CO	IL	135,478.4
SURETY LIFE INS CO	NE	14.3
SYMETRA LIFE INS CO	WA	28,322.5
TRUSTMARK INS CO	IL	1,404.7
TRUSTMARK LIFE INS CO	IL	380.8
UNITED WORLD LIFE INS CO	NE	107.9
USABLE LIFE	AR	426.8

New Jersey

INSURANCE COMPANY NAME	DOM. STATE	TOTAL ASSETS ($MIL)
Rating: A+		
HEALTH CARE SVC CORP A MUT LEG RES	IL	18,206.4
PHYSICIANS MUTUAL INS CO	NE	1,968.0
TEACHERS INS & ANNUITY ASN OF AM	NY	256,932.8
Rating: A		
4 EVER LIFE INS CO	IL	202.8
BERKSHIRE LIFE INS CO OF AMERICA	MA	3,589.9
CINCINNATI INS CO	OH	10,807.9
FEDERATED LIFE INS CO	MN	1,483.1
GUARDIAN LIFE INS CO OF AMERICA	NY	44,344.6
RESERVE NATIONAL INS CO	OK	112.3
SENTRY INS A MUTUAL CO	WI	6,832.1
SENTRY LIFE INS CO	WI	5,167.7
SHELTERPOINT LIFE INS CO	NY	103.8
UNITED FARM FAMILY LIFE INS CO	IN	2,116.5
USAA LIFE INS CO	TX	21,633.7
Rating: A-		
AMALGAMATED LIFE INS CO	NY	107.0
AMERICAN FAMILY LIFE ASR CO OF NY	NY	706.5
AMERICAN REPUBLIC INS CO	IA	799.7
AMERIGROUP NEW JERSEY INC	NJ	235.0
ANTHEM LIFE INS CO	IN	571.2
BALBOA LIFE INS CO	CA	58.9
CENTRAL STATES H & L CO OF OMAHA	NE	405.9
DEARBORN NATIONAL LIFE INS CO	IL	2,193.1
FAMILY HERITAGE LIFE INS CO OF AMER	OH	706.7
FEDERATED MUTUAL INS CO	MN	4,667.2
GARDEN STATE LIFE INS CO	TX	120.1
GERBER LIFE INS CO	NY	2,680.4
HORIZON HEALTHCARE OF NEW JERSEY INC	NJ	1,300.1
ILLINOIS MUTUAL LIFE INS CO	IL	1,354.0
MASSACHUSETTS MUTUAL LIFE INS CO	MA	189,173.1
MIDWESTERN UNITED LIFE INS CO	IN	237.0
MUTUAL OF AMERICA LIFE INS CO	NY	17,180.5
NEW YORK LIFE INS CO	NY	142,089.9
NIPPON LIFE INS CO OF AMERICA	IA	222.1
NORTHWESTERN MUTUAL LIFE INS CO	WI	222,040.6
OLD REPUBLIC INS CO	PA	2,591.0
PHYSICIANS LIFE INS CO	NE	1,406.1
PROTECTIVE INS CO	IN	770.4
Rating: B+		
AETNA HEALTH & LIFE INS CO	CT	2,193.0
AETNA LIFE INS CO	CT	22,226.6
AMERICAN FAMILY LIFE ASR CO OF COLUM	NE	111,249.2
AMERICAN FIDELITY ASR CO	OK	4,848.9
AMERICAN UNITED LIFE INS CO	IN	22,972.9
ASSURITY LIFE INS CO	NE	2,436.6
BOSTON MUTUAL LIFE INS CO	MA	1,222.3
CENTRAL STATES INDEMNITY CO OF OMAHA	NE	424.9
COLORADO BANKERS LIFE INS CO	CO	272.7
FEDERAL INS CO	IN	32,182.2
GOVERNMENT EMPLOYEES INS CO	MD	21,998.7
HORIZON HEALTHCARE SERVICES INC	NJ	3,679.0
JACKSON NATIONAL LIFE INS CO	MI	176,569.5
LINCOLN BENEFIT LIFE CO	NE	13,279.3

INSURANCE COMPANY NAME	DOM. STATE	TOTAL ASSETS ($MIL)
MEDCO CONTAINMENT LIFE INS CO	PA	507.6
MERIT LIFE INS CO	IN	560.2
MIDLAND NATIONAL LIFE INS CO	IA	39,622.6
MINNESOTA LIFE INS CO	MN	34,732.2
MUTUAL OF OMAHA INS CO	NE	6,375.2
NATIONAL BENEFIT LIFE INS CO	NY	475.2
NATIONAL CASUALTY CO	WI	287.3
NATIONAL WESTERN LIFE INS CO	CO	10,001.6
NATIONWIDE MUTUAL FIRE INS CO	OH	5,596.1
OHIO NATIONAL LIFE ASR CORP	OH	3,450.3
PIONEER MUTUAL LIFE INS CO	ND	507.2
PRINCIPAL LIFE INS CO	IA	150,015.7
SAVINGS BANK LIFE INS CO OF MA	MA	2,531.7
SENTRY SELECT INS CO	WI	672.6
STANDARD INS CO	OR	19,996.4
STATE FARM MUTUAL AUTOMOBILE INS CO	IL	135,478.4
SURETY LIFE INS CO	NE	14.3
SYMETRA LIFE INS CO	WA	28,322.5
THRIVENT LIFE INS CO	MN	3,560.4
TRUSTMARK INS CO	IL	1,404.7
TRUSTMARK LIFE INS CO	IL	380.8
UNITED WORLD LIFE INS CO	NE	107.9
USABLE LIFE	AR	426.8

New Mexico

INSURANCE COMPANY NAME	DOM. STATE	TOTAL ASSETS ($MIL)
Rating: A+		
COUNTRY LIFE INS CO	IL	10,519.0
HEALTH CARE SVC CORP A MUT LEG RES	IL	18,206.4
PHYSICIANS MUTUAL INS CO	NE	1,968.0
TEACHERS INS & ANNUITY ASN OF AM	NY	256,932.8
Rating: A		
4 EVER LIFE INS CO	IL	202.8
AUTO-OWNERS LIFE INS CO	MI	3,557.4
BERKSHIRE LIFE INS CO OF AMERICA	MA	3,589.9
CINCINNATI INS CO	OH	10,807.9
FEDERATED LIFE INS CO	MN	1,483.1
GUARDIAN LIFE INS CO OF AMERICA	NY	44,344.6
LIFEWISE ASR CO	WA	129.7
RESERVE NATIONAL INS CO	OK	112.3
SENTRY INS A MUTUAL CO	WI	6,832.1
SENTRY LIFE INS CO	WI	5,167.7
USAA LIFE INS CO	TX	21,633.7
Rating: A-		
AMALGAMATED LIFE INS CO	NY	107.0
AMERICAN REPUBLIC INS CO	IA	799.7
ANTHEM LIFE INS CO	IN	571.2
BALBOA LIFE INS CO	CA	58.9
CENTRAL STATES H & L CO OF OMAHA	NE	405.9
COMPANION LIFE INS CO	SC	278.1
DEARBORN NATIONAL LIFE INS CO	IL	2,193.1
FAMILY HERITAGE LIFE INS CO OF AMER	OH	706.7
FEDERATED MUTUAL INS CO	MN	4,667.2
GARDEN STATE LIFE INS CO	TX	120.1
GERBER LIFE INS CO	NY	2,680.4
ILLINOIS MUTUAL LIFE INS CO	IL	1,354.0
MASSACHUSETTS MUTUAL LIFE INS CO	MA	189,173.1
MIDWESTERN UNITED LIFE INS CO	IN	237.0
MUTUAL OF AMERICA LIFE INS CO	NY	17,180.5
NEW YORK LIFE INS CO	NY	142,089.9
NIPPON LIFE INS CO OF AMERICA	IA	222.1
NORTHWESTERN MUTUAL LIFE INS CO	WI	222,040.6
OLD REPUBLIC INS CO	PA	2,591.0
PACIFIC GUARDIAN LIFE INS CO LTD	HI	518.1
PHYSICIANS LIFE INS CO	NE	1,406.1
PROTECTIVE INS CO	IN	770.4
STANDARD LIFE & ACCIDENT INS CO	TX	525.1
Rating: B+		
AETNA HEALTH & LIFE INS CO	CT	2,193.0
AETNA LIFE INS CO	CT	22,226.6
AMERICAN FAMILY LIFE ASR CO OF COLUM	NE	111,249.2
AMERICAN FAMILY MUT INS CO	WI	13,709.4
AMERICAN FIDELITY ASR CO	OK	4,848.9
AMERICAN UNITED LIFE INS CO	IN	22,972.9
ASSURITY LIFE INS CO	NE	2,436.6
BOSTON MUTUAL LIFE INS CO	MA	1,222.3
CENTRAL STATES INDEMNITY CO OF OMAHA	NE	424.9
COLORADO BANKERS LIFE INS CO	CO	272.7
FARM BUREAU LIFE INS CO	IA	7,987.7
FEDERAL INS CO	IN	32,182.2
GOVERNMENT EMPLOYEES INS CO	MD	21,998.7

INSURANCE COMPANY NAME	DOM. STATE	TOTAL ASSETS ($MIL)
GOVERNMENT PERSONNEL MUTUAL L I C	TX	833.6
JACKSON NATIONAL LIFE INS CO	MI	176,569.5
LINCOLN BENEFIT LIFE CO	NE	13,279.3
MEDCO CONTAINMENT LIFE INS CO	PA	507.6
MEDICO CORP LIFE INS CO	NE	25.7
MERIT LIFE INS CO	IN	560.2
MIDLAND NATIONAL LIFE INS CO	IA	39,622.6
MINNESOTA LIFE INS CO	MN	34,732.2
MUTUAL OF OMAHA INS CO	NE	6,375.2
NATIONAL BENEFIT LIFE INS CO	NY	475.2
NATIONAL CASUALTY CO	WI	287.3
NATIONAL WESTERN LIFE INS CO	CO	10,001.6
NATIONWIDE MUTUAL FIRE INS CO	OH	5,596.1
OHIO NATIONAL LIFE ASR CORP	OH	3,450.3
PIONEER MUTUAL LIFE INS CO	ND	507.2
PRESBYTERIAN HEALTH PLAN INC	NM	415.3
PRINCIPAL LIFE INS CO	IA	150,015.7
SAVINGS BANK LIFE INS CO OF MA	MA	2,531.7
SENTRY SELECT INS CO	WI	672.6
STANDARD INS CO	OR	19,996.4
STATE FARM MUTUAL AUTOMOBILE INS CO	IL	135,478.4
SURETY LIFE INS CO	NE	14.3
SYMETRA LIFE INS CO	WA	28,322.5
THRIVENT LIFE INS CO	MN	3,560.4
TRUSTMARK INS CO	IL	1,404.7
TRUSTMARK LIFE INS CO	IL	380.8
UNITED WORLD LIFE INS CO	NE	107.9
USABLE LIFE	AR	426.8

New York

INSURANCE COMPANY NAME	DOM. STATE	TOTAL ASSETS ($MIL)
Rating: A+		
OXFORD HEALTH PLANS (NY) INC	NY	817.8
PHYSICIANS MUTUAL INS CO	NE	1,968.0
TEACHERS INS & ANNUITY ASN OF AM	NY	256,932.8
Rating: A		
4 EVER LIFE INS CO	IL	202.8
BERKSHIRE LIFE INS CO OF AMERICA	MA	3,589.9
CINCINNATI INS CO	OH	10,807.9
EXCELLUS HEALTH PLAN INC	NY	3,060.6
FEDERATED LIFE INS CO	MN	1,483.1
FIRST RELIANCE STANDARD LIFE INS CO	NY	188.3
GUARDIAN LIFE INS CO OF AMERICA	NY	44,344.6
SENTRY INS A MUTUAL CO	WI	6,832.1
SHELTERPOINT LIFE INS CO	NY	103.8
Rating: A-		
AMALGAMATED LIFE INS CO	NY	107.0
AMERICAN FAMILY LIFE ASR CO OF NY	NY	706.5
ANTHEM LIFE & DISABILITY INS CO	NY	23.0
BALBOA LIFE INS CO	CA	58.9
CIGNA LIFE INS CO OF NEW YORK	NY	376.2
CSAA INS EXCHANGE	CA	6,888.9
FEDERATED MUTUAL INS CO	MN	4,667.2
FIRST SYMETRA NATL LIFE INS CO OF NY	NY	869.5
GARDEN STATE LIFE INS CO	TX	120.1
GERBER LIFE INS CO	NY	2,680.4
JOHN HANCOCK LIFE INS CO OF NY	NY	17,549.0
LIFE INS CO OF BOSTON & NEW YORK	NY	120.6
MASSACHUSETTS MUTUAL LIFE INS CO	MA	189,173.1
MUTUAL OF AMERICA LIFE INS CO	NY	17,180.5
NEW YORK LIFE INS CO	NY	142,089.9
NIPPON LIFE INS CO OF AMERICA	IA	222.1
NORTHWESTERN MUTUAL LIFE INS CO	WI	222,040.6
OLD REPUBLIC INS CO	PA	2,591.0
PROTECTIVE INS CO	IN	770.4
STANDARD LIFE INS CO OF NY	NY	269.3
Rating: B+		
AETNA HEALTH & LIFE INS CO	CT	2,193.0
AETNA HEALTH INC (A NEW YORK CORP)	NY	377.2
AETNA LIFE INS CO	CT	22,226.6
AMERICAN UNITED LIFE INS CO	IN	22,972.9
BOSTON MUTUAL LIFE INS CO	MA	1,222.3
CENTRAL STATES INDEMNITY CO OF OMAHA	NE	424.9
DEARBORN NATIONAL LIFE INS CO OF NY	NY	41.2
FEDERAL INS CO	IN	32,182.2
FIRST UNITED AMERICAN LIFE INS CO	NY	187.3
GOVERNMENT EMPLOYEES INS CO	MD	21,998.7
HEALTHNOW NY INC	NY	1,063.7
HM LIFE INS CO OF NEW YORK	NY	72.5
MEDCO CONTAINMENT INS CO OF NY	NY	69.9
MERIT LIFE INS CO	IN	560.2
MINNESOTA LIFE INS CO	MN	34,732.2
MUTUAL OF OMAHA INS CO	NE	6,375.2
NATIONAL BENEFIT LIFE INS CO	NY	475.2
NATIONAL CASUALTY CO	WI	287.3
NATIONAL INCOME LIFE INS CO	NY	137.0

INSURANCE COMPANY NAME	DOM. STATE	TOTAL ASSETS ($MIL)
NATIONWIDE MUTUAL FIRE INS CO	OH	5,596.1
PRINCIPAL LIFE INS CO	IA	150,015.7
SENTRY LIFE INS CO OF NEW YORK	NY	77.0
SENTRY SELECT INS CO	WI	672.6
STATE FARM MUTUAL AUTOMOBILE INS CO	IL	135,478.4
TRUSTMARK INS CO	IL	1,404.7
TRUSTMARK LIFE INS CO	IL	380.8
UNION SECURITY LIFE INS CO OF NY	NY	142.5
UNITED HEALTHCARE OF NY INC	NY	564.2

North Carolina

INSURANCE COMPANY NAME	DOM. STATE	TOTAL ASSETS ($MIL)
Rating: **A+**		
COUNTRY LIFE INS CO	IL	10,519.0
PHYSICIANS MUTUAL INS CO	NE	1,968.0
TEACHERS INS & ANNUITY ASN OF AM	NY	256,932.8
Rating: **A**		
4 EVER LIFE INS CO	IL	202.8
AUTO-OWNERS LIFE INS CO	MI	3,557.4
BERKSHIRE LIFE INS CO OF AMERICA	MA	3,589.9
BLUE CROSS BLUE SHIELD OF NC	NC	4,159.1
CINCINNATI INS CO	OH	10,807.9
FEDERATED LIFE INS CO	MN	1,483.1
GUARDIAN LIFE INS CO OF AMERICA	NY	44,344.6
RESERVE NATIONAL INS CO	OK	112.3
SENTRY INS A MUTUAL CO	WI	6,832.1
SENTRY LIFE INS CO	WI	5,167.7
SHELTERPOINT LIFE INS CO	NY	103.8
SOUTHERN FARM BUREAU LIFE INS CO	MS	12,921.4
UNITED FARM FAMILY LIFE INS CO	IN	2,116.5
USAA LIFE INS CO	TX	21,633.7
Rating: **A-**		
AMALGAMATED LIFE INS CO	NY	107.0
AMERICAN REPUBLIC INS CO	IA	799.7
ANTHEM LIFE INS CO	IN	571.2
BALBOA LIFE INS CO	CA	58.9
CENTRAL STATES H & L CO OF OMAHA	NE	405.9
COMPANION LIFE INS CO	SC	278.1
COTTON STATES LIFE INS CO	GA	331.7
DEARBORN NATIONAL LIFE INS CO	IL	2,193.1
ERIE FAMILY LIFE INS CO	PA	2,058.7
FAMILY HERITAGE LIFE INS CO OF AMER	OH	706.7
FEDERATED MUTUAL INS CO	MN	4,667.2
GARDEN STATE LIFE INS CO	TX	120.1
GERBER LIFE INS CO	NY	2,680.4
ILLINOIS MUTUAL LIFE INS CO	IL	1,354.0
LIFE INS CO OF ALABAMA	AL	112.7
MASSACHUSETTS MUTUAL LIFE INS CO	MA	189,173.1
MEDICAL MUTUAL OF OHIO	OH	1,798.4
MIDWESTERN UNITED LIFE INS CO	IN	237.0
MUTUAL OF AMERICA LIFE INS CO	NY	17,180.5
NEW YORK LIFE INS CO	NY	142,089.9
NIPPON LIFE INS CO OF AMERICA	IA	222.1
NORTHWESTERN MUTUAL LIFE INS CO	WI	222,040.6
OLD REPUBLIC INS CO	PA	2,591.0
PHYSICIANS LIFE INS CO	NE	1,406.1
PROTECTIVE INS CO	IN	770.4
STANDARD LIFE & ACCIDENT INS CO	TX	525.1
Rating: **B+**		
AETNA HEALTH & LIFE INS CO	CT	2,193.0
AETNA LIFE INS CO	CT	22,226.6
AMERICAN FAMILY LIFE ASR CO OF COLUM	NE	111,249.2
AMERICAN FAMILY MUT INS CO	WI	13,709.4
AMERICAN FIDELITY ASR CO	OK	4,848.9
AMERICAN UNITED LIFE INS CO	IN	22,972.9
ASSURITY LIFE INS CO	NE	2,436.6
BOSTON MUTUAL LIFE INS CO	MA	1,222.3

INSURANCE COMPANY NAME	DOM. STATE	TOTAL ASSETS ($MIL)
CENTRAL STATES INDEMNITY CO OF OMAHA	NE	424.9
COLORADO BANKERS LIFE INS CO	CO	272.7
COVENTRY HEALTH & LIFE INS CO	MO	1,547.4
FEDERAL INS CO	IN	32,182.2
GOVERNMENT EMPLOYEES INS CO	MD	21,998.7
GOVERNMENT PERSONNEL MUTUAL L I C	TX	833.6
GREATER GEORGIA LIFE INS CO	GA	50.8
JACKSON NATIONAL LIFE INS CO	MI	176,569.5
LINCOLN BENEFIT LIFE CO	NE	13,279.3
MEDCO CONTAINMENT LIFE INS CO	PA	507.6
MEDICO CORP LIFE INS CO	NE	25.7
MERIT LIFE INS CO	IN	560.2
MIDLAND NATIONAL LIFE INS CO	IA	39,622.6
MINNESOTA LIFE INS CO	MN	34,732.2
MUTUAL OF OMAHA INS CO	NE	6,375.2
NATIONAL BENEFIT LIFE INS CO	NY	475.2
NATIONAL CASUALTY CO	WI	287.3
NATIONAL WESTERN LIFE INS CO	CO	10,001.6
NATIONWIDE MUTUAL FIRE INS CO	OH	5,596.1
OHIO NATIONAL LIFE ASR CORP	OH	3,450.3
PIONEER MUTUAL LIFE INS CO	ND	507.2
PRINCIPAL LIFE INS CO	IA	150,015.7
SAVINGS BANK LIFE INS CO OF MA	MA	2,531.7
SENTRY SELECT INS CO	WI	672.6
STANDARD INS CO	OR	19,996.4
STATE FARM MUTUAL AUTOMOBILE INS CO	IL	135,478.4
SURETY LIFE INS CO	NE	14.3
SYMETRA LIFE INS CO	WA	28,322.5
TRUSTMARK INS CO	IL	1,404.7
TRUSTMARK LIFE INS CO	IL	380.8
UNITED WORLD LIFE INS CO	NE	107.9
USABLE LIFE	AR	426.8

North Dakota

INSURANCE COMPANY NAME	DOM. STATE	TOTAL ASSETS ($MIL)
Rating: A+		
COUNTRY LIFE INS CO	IL	10,519.0
PHYSICIANS MUTUAL INS CO	NE	1,968.0
TEACHERS INS & ANNUITY ASN OF AM	NY	256,932.8
Rating: A		
4 EVER LIFE INS CO	IL	202.8
AUTO-OWNERS LIFE INS CO	MI	3,557.4
BERKSHIRE LIFE INS CO OF AMERICA	MA	3,589.9
CINCINNATI INS CO	OH	10,807.9
FEDERATED LIFE INS CO	MN	1,483.1
GUARDIAN LIFE INS CO OF AMERICA	NY	44,344.6
LIFEWISE ASR CO	WA	129.7
RESERVE NATIONAL INS CO	OK	112.3
SENTRY INS A MUTUAL CO	WI	6,832.1
SENTRY LIFE INS CO	WI	5,167.7
UNITED FARM FAMILY LIFE INS CO	IN	2,116.5
USAA LIFE INS CO	TX	21,633.7
Rating: A-		
AMALGAMATED LIFE INS CO	NY	107.0
AMERICAN FAMILY LIFE ASR CO OF NY	NY	706.5
AMERICAN REPUBLIC INS CO	IA	799.7
ANTHEM LIFE INS CO	IN	571.2
BALBOA LIFE INS CO	CA	58.9
CENTRAL STATES H & L CO OF OMAHA	NE	405.9
COMPANION LIFE INS CO	SC	278.1
DEARBORN NATIONAL LIFE INS CO	IL	2,193.1
FAMILY HERITAGE LIFE INS CO OF AMER	OH	706.7
FEDERATED MUTUAL INS CO	MN	4,667.2
GARDEN STATE LIFE INS CO	TX	120.1
GERBER LIFE INS CO	NY	2,680.4
ILLINOIS MUTUAL LIFE INS CO	IL	1,354.0
MASSACHUSETTS MUTUAL LIFE INS CO	MA	189,173.1
MIDWESTERN UNITED LIFE INS CO	IN	237.0
MUTUAL OF AMERICA LIFE INS CO	NY	17,180.5
NEW YORK LIFE INS CO	NY	142,089.9
NIPPON LIFE INS CO OF AMERICA	IA	222.1
NORTHWESTERN MUTUAL LIFE INS CO	WI	222,040.6
OLD REPUBLIC INS CO	PA	2,591.0
PHYSICIANS LIFE INS CO	NE	1,406.1
PROTECTIVE INS CO	IN	770.4
STANDARD LIFE & ACCIDENT INS CO	TX	525.1
Rating: B+		
AETNA HEALTH & LIFE INS CO	CT	2,193.0
AETNA LIFE INS CO	CT	22,226.6
AMERICAN FAMILY LIFE ASR CO OF COLUM	NE	111,249.2
AMERICAN FAMILY MUT INS CO	WI	13,709.4
AMERICAN FIDELITY ASR CO	OK	4,848.9
AMERICAN UNITED LIFE INS CO	IN	22,972.9
ASSURITY LIFE INS CO	NE	2,436.6
BOSTON MUTUAL LIFE INS CO	MA	1,222.3
CENTRAL STATES INDEMNITY CO OF OMAHA	NE	424.9
COLORADO BANKERS LIFE INS CO	CO	272.7
COVENTRY HEALTH & LIFE INS CO	MO	1,547.4
FARM BUREAU LIFE INS CO	IA	7,987.7
FEDERAL INS CO	IN	32,182.2

INSURANCE COMPANY NAME	DOM. STATE	TOTAL ASSETS ($MIL)
GOVERNMENT EMPLOYEES INS CO	MD	21,998.7
GOVERNMENT PERSONNEL MUTUAL L I C	TX	833.6
JACKSON NATIONAL LIFE INS CO	MI	176,569.5
LINCOLN BENEFIT LIFE CO	NE	13,279.3
MEDCO CONTAINMENT LIFE INS CO	PA	507.6
MEDICA HEALTH PLANS	MN	760.3
MEDICO CORP LIFE INS CO	NE	25.7
MERIT LIFE INS CO	IN	560.2
MIDLAND NATIONAL LIFE INS CO	IA	39,622.6
MINNESOTA LIFE INS CO	MN	34,732.2
MUTUAL OF OMAHA INS CO	NE	6,375.2
NATIONAL BENEFIT LIFE INS CO	NY	475.2
NATIONAL CASUALTY CO	WI	287.3
NATIONAL WESTERN LIFE INS CO	CO	10,001.6
NATIONWIDE MUTUAL FIRE INS CO	OH	5,596.1
OHIO NATIONAL LIFE ASR CORP	OH	3,450.3
PIONEER MUTUAL LIFE INS CO	ND	507.2
PRINCIPAL LIFE INS CO	IA	150,015.7
SAVINGS BANK LIFE INS CO OF MA	MA	2,531.7
SENTRY LIFE INS CO OF NEW YORK	NY	77.0
SENTRY SELECT INS CO	WI	672.6
STANDARD INS CO	OR	19,996.4
STATE FARM MUTUAL AUTOMOBILE INS CO	IL	135,478.4
SURETY LIFE INS CO	NE	14.3
SYMETRA LIFE INS CO	WA	28,322.5
THRIVENT LIFE INS CO	MN	3,560.4
TRUSTMARK INS CO	IL	1,404.7
TRUSTMARK LIFE INS CO	IL	380.8
UNITED WORLD LIFE INS CO	NE	107.9
USABLE LIFE	AR	426.8

Ohio

INSURANCE COMPANY NAME	DOM. STATE	TOTAL ASSETS ($MIL)
Rating:	**A+**	
COUNTRY LIFE INS CO	IL	10,519.0
HEALTH CARE SVC CORP A MUT LEG RES	IL	18,206.4
PHYSICIANS MUTUAL INS CO	NE	1,968.0
TEACHERS INS & ANNUITY ASN OF AM	NY	256,932.8
Rating:	**A**	
4 EVER LIFE INS CO	IL	202.8
AUTO-OWNERS LIFE INS CO	MI	3,557.4
BERKSHIRE LIFE INS CO OF AMERICA	MA	3,589.9
CARESOURCE	OH	1,491.7
CINCINNATI INS CO	OH	10,807.9
FEDERATED LIFE INS CO	MN	1,483.1
GUARDIAN LIFE INS CO OF AMERICA	NY	44,344.6
MOUNT CARMEL HEALTH PLAN INC	OH	336.9
RESERVE NATIONAL INS CO	OK	112.3
SENTRY INS A MUTUAL CO	WI	6,832.1
SENTRY LIFE INS CO	WI	5,167.7
UNITED FARM FAMILY LIFE INS CO	IN	2,116.5
USAA LIFE INS CO	TX	21,633.7
Rating:	**A-**	
AMALGAMATED LIFE INS CO	NY	107.0
AMERICAN REPUBLIC INS CO	IA	799.7
ANTHEM LIFE INS CO	IN	571.2
BALBOA LIFE INS CO	CA	58.9
CENTRAL STATES H & L CO OF OMAHA	NE	405.9
COMPANION LIFE INS CO	SC	278.1
DEARBORN NATIONAL LIFE INS CO	IL	2,193.1
ERIE FAMILY LIFE INS CO	PA	2,058.7
FAMILY HERITAGE LIFE INS CO OF AMER	OH	706.7
FEDERATED MUTUAL INS CO	MN	4,667.2
GARDEN STATE LIFE INS CO	TX	120.1
GERBER LIFE INS CO	NY	2,680.4
HEALTHY ALLIANCE LIFE INS CO	MO	954.2
ILLINOIS MUTUAL LIFE INS CO	IL	1,354.0
MASSACHUSETTS MUTUAL LIFE INS CO	MA	189,173.1
MEDICAL MUTUAL OF OHIO	OH	1,798.4
MIDWESTERN UNITED LIFE INS CO	IN	237.0
MUTUAL OF AMERICA LIFE INS CO	NY	17,180.5
NEW YORK LIFE INS CO	NY	142,089.9
NIPPON LIFE INS CO OF AMERICA	IA	222.1
NORTHWESTERN MUTUAL LIFE INS CO	WI	222,040.6
OLD REPUBLIC INS CO	PA	2,591.0
PARAMOUNT ADVANTAGE	OH	172.9
PHYSICIANS LIFE INS CO	NE	1,406.1
PROTECTIVE INS CO	IN	770.4
STANDARD LIFE & ACCIDENT INS CO	TX	525.1
Rating:	**B+**	
AETNA HEALTH & LIFE INS CO	CT	2,193.0
AETNA LIFE INS CO	CT	22,226.6
AMERICAN FAMILY LIFE ASR CO OF COLUM	NE	111,249.2
AMERICAN FAMILY MUT INS CO	WI	13,709.4
AMERICAN FIDELITY ASR CO	OK	4,848.9
AMERICAN UNITED LIFE INS CO	IN	22,972.9
ASSURITY LIFE INS CO	NE	2,436.6
BOSTON MUTUAL LIFE INS CO	MA	1,222.3

INSURANCE COMPANY NAME	DOM. STATE	TOTAL ASSETS ($MIL)
CENTRAL STATES INDEMNITY CO OF OMAHA	NE	424.9
COLORADO BANKERS LIFE INS CO	CO	272.7
COMMUNITY INS CO	OH	2,036.0
COVENTRY HEALTH & LIFE INS CO	MO	1,547.4
COVENTRY HEALTH CARE OF WEST VA INC	WV	90.8
FEDERAL INS CO	IN	32,182.2
GOVERNMENT EMPLOYEES INS CO	MD	21,998.7
GOVERNMENT PERSONNEL MUTUAL L I C	TX	833.6
GRANGE MUTUAL CAS CO	OH	2,061.4
HEALTH PLAN OF THE UPPER OHIO VALLEY	WV	253.1
JACKSON NATIONAL LIFE INS CO	MI	176,569.5
KAISER PERMANENTE INS CO	CA	179.4
LINCOLN BENEFIT LIFE CO	NE	13,279.3
MEDCO CONTAINMENT LIFE INS CO	PA	507.6
MEDICAL HEALTH INS CORP OF OHIO	OH	114.5
MEDICO CORP LIFE INS CO	NE	25.7
MERIT LIFE INS CO	IN	560.2
MIDLAND NATIONAL LIFE INS CO	IA	39,622.6
MINNESOTA LIFE INS CO	MN	34,732.2
MUTUAL OF OMAHA INS CO	NE	6,375.2
NATIONAL BENEFIT LIFE INS CO	NY	475.2
NATIONAL CASUALTY CO	WI	287.3
NATIONAL WESTERN LIFE INS CO	CO	10,001.6
NATIONWIDE MUTUAL FIRE INS CO	OH	5,596.1
OHIO NATIONAL LIFE ASR CORP	OH	3,450.3
PIONEER MUTUAL LIFE INS CO	ND	507.2
PRINCIPAL LIFE INS CO	IA	150,015.7
SAVINGS BANK LIFE INS CO OF MA	MA	2,531.7
SENTRY SELECT INS CO	WI	672.6
STANDARD INS CO	OR	19,996.4
STATE FARM MUTUAL AUTOMOBILE INS CO	IL	135,478.4
SURETY LIFE INS CO	NE	14.3
SYMETRA LIFE INS CO	WA	28,322.5
THRIVENT LIFE INS CO	MN	3,560.4
TRUSTMARK INS CO	IL	1,404.7
TRUSTMARK LIFE INS CO	IL	380.8
UNITED WORLD LIFE INS CO	NE	107.9
USABLE LIFE	AR	426.8

Oklahoma

INSURANCE COMPANY NAME	DOM. STATE	TOTAL ASSETS ($MIL)
Rating: A+		
COUNTRY LIFE INS CO	IL	10,519.0
HEALTH CARE SVC CORP A MUT LEG RES	IL	18,206.4
PHYSICIANS MUTUAL INS CO	NE	1,968.0
TEACHERS INS & ANNUITY ASN OF AM	NY	256,932.8
Rating: A		
4 EVER LIFE INS CO	IL	202.8
BERKSHIRE LIFE INS CO OF AMERICA	MA	3,589.9
CINCINNATI INS CO	OH	10,807.9
COMMUNITYCARE HMO INC	OK	207.2
FEDERATED LIFE INS CO	MN	1,483.1
GUARDIAN LIFE INS CO OF AMERICA	NY	44,344.6
LIFEWISE ASR CO	WA	129.7
RESERVE NATIONAL INS CO	OK	112.3
SENTRY INS A MUTUAL CO	WI	6,832.1
SENTRY LIFE INS CO	WI	5,167.7
USAA LIFE INS CO	TX	21,633.7
Rating: A-		
AMALGAMATED LIFE INS CO	NY	107.0
AMERICAN REPUBLIC INS CO	IA	799.7
ANTHEM LIFE INS CO	IN	571.2
BALBOA LIFE INS CO	CA	58.9
CENTRAL STATES H & L CO OF OMAHA	NE	405.9
COMPANION LIFE INS CO	SC	278.1
DEARBORN NATIONAL LIFE INS CO	IL	2,193.1
FAMILY HERITAGE LIFE INS CO OF AMER	OH	706.7
FEDERATED MUTUAL INS CO	MN	4,667.2
GARDEN STATE LIFE INS CO	TX	120.1
GERBER LIFE INS CO	NY	2,680.4
ILLINOIS MUTUAL LIFE INS CO	IL	1,354.0
LIFE INS CO OF ALABAMA	AL	112.7
MASSACHUSETTS MUTUAL LIFE INS CO	MA	189,173.1
MIDWESTERN UNITED LIFE INS CO	IN	237.0
MUTUAL OF AMERICA LIFE INS CO	NY	17,180.5
NEW YORK LIFE INS CO	NY	142,089.9
NIPPON LIFE INS CO OF AMERICA	IA	222.1
NORTHWESTERN MUTUAL LIFE INS CO	WI	222,040.6
OLD REPUBLIC INS CO	PA	2,591.0
PACIFIC GUARDIAN LIFE INS CO LTD	HI	518.1
PHYSICIANS LIFE INS CO	NE	1,406.1
PROTECTIVE INS CO	IN	770.4
SHELTER LIFE INS CO	MO	1,097.7
STANDARD LIFE & ACCIDENT INS CO	TX	525.1
Rating: B+		
AETNA HEALTH & LIFE INS CO	CT	2,193.0
AETNA LIFE INS CO	CT	22,226.6
AMERICAN FAMILY LIFE ASR CO OF COLUM	NE	111,249.2
AMERICAN FIDELITY ASR CO	OK	4,848.9
AMERICAN UNITED LIFE INS CO	IN	22,972.9
ASSURITY LIFE INS CO	NE	2,436.6
BOSTON MUTUAL LIFE INS CO	MA	1,222.3
CENTRAL STATES INDEMNITY CO OF OMAHA	NE	424.9
COLORADO BANKERS LIFE INS CO	CO	272.7
COVENTRY HEALTH & LIFE INS CO	MO	1,547.4
FARM BUREAU LIFE INS CO	IA	7,987.7

INSURANCE COMPANY NAME	DOM. STATE	TOTAL ASSETS ($MIL)
FEDERAL INS CO	IN	32,182.2
GOVERNMENT EMPLOYEES INS CO	MD	21,998.7
GOVERNMENT PERSONNEL MUTUAL L I C	TX	833.6
JACKSON NATIONAL LIFE INS CO	MI	176,569.5
LINCOLN BENEFIT LIFE CO	NE	13,279.3
MEDCO CONTAINMENT LIFE INS CO	PA	507.6
MEDICO CORP LIFE INS CO	NE	25.7
MERIT LIFE INS CO	IN	560.2
MIDLAND NATIONAL LIFE INS CO	IA	39,622.6
MINNESOTA LIFE INS CO	MN	34,732.2
MUTUAL OF OMAHA INS CO	NE	6,375.2
NATIONAL BENEFIT LIFE INS CO	NY	475.2
NATIONAL CASUALTY CO	WI	287.3
NATIONAL WESTERN LIFE INS CO	CO	10,001.6
NATIONWIDE MUTUAL FIRE INS CO	OH	5,596.1
OHIO NATIONAL LIFE ASR CORP	OH	3,450.3
PIONEER MUTUAL LIFE INS CO	ND	507.2
PRINCIPAL LIFE INS CO	IA	150,015.7
SAVINGS BANK LIFE INS CO OF MA	MA	2,531.7
SENTRY SELECT INS CO	WI	672.6
STANDARD INS CO	OR	19,996.4
STATE FARM MUTUAL AUTOMOBILE INS CO	IL	135,478.4
SURETY LIFE INS CO	NE	14.3
SYMETRA LIFE INS CO	WA	28,322.5
THRIVENT LIFE INS CO	MN	3,560.4
TRUSTMARK INS CO	IL	1,404.7
TRUSTMARK LIFE INS CO	IL	380.8
UNITED WORLD LIFE INS CO	NE	107.9
USABLE LIFE	AR	426.8

Oregon

INSURANCE COMPANY NAME	DOM. STATE	TOTAL ASSETS ($MIL)
Rating:	**A+**	
COUNTRY LIFE INS CO	IL	10,519.0
HEALTH CARE SVC CORP A MUT LEG RES	IL	18,206.4
PHYSICIANS MUTUAL INS CO	NE	1,968.0
PROVIDENCE HEALTH PLAN	OR	738.7
TEACHERS INS & ANNUITY ASN OF AM	NY	256,932.8
Rating:	**A**	
4 EVER LIFE INS CO	IL	202.8
AUTO-OWNERS LIFE INS CO	MI	3,557.4
BERKSHIRE LIFE INS CO OF AMERICA	MA	3,589.9
CINCINNATI INS CO	OH	10,807.9
FEDERATED LIFE INS CO	MN	1,483.1
GUARDIAN LIFE INS CO OF AMERICA	NY	44,344.6
LIFEWISE ASR CO	WA	129.7
RESERVE NATIONAL INS CO	OK	112.3
SENTRY INS A MUTUAL CO	WI	6,832.1
SENTRY LIFE INS CO	WI	5,167.7
USAA LIFE INS CO	TX	21,633.7
Rating:	**A-**	
AMALGAMATED LIFE INS CO	NY	107.0
AMERICAN REPUBLIC INS CO	IA	799.7
ANTHEM LIFE INS CO	IN	571.2
BALBOA LIFE INS CO	CA	58.9
CENTRAL STATES H & L CO OF OMAHA	NE	405.9
COMPANION LIFE INS CO	SC	278.1
DEARBORN NATIONAL LIFE INS CO	IL	2,193.1
FAMILY HERITAGE LIFE INS CO OF AMER	OH	706.7
FEDERATED MUTUAL INS CO	MN	4,667.2
GARDEN STATE LIFE INS CO	TX	120.1
GERBER LIFE INS CO	NY	2,680.4
ILLINOIS MUTUAL LIFE INS CO	IL	1,354.0
MASSACHUSETTS MUTUAL LIFE INS CO	MA	189,173.1
MIDWESTERN UNITED LIFE INS CO	IN	237.0
MUTUAL OF AMERICA LIFE INS CO	NY	17,180.5
NEW YORK LIFE INS CO	NY	142,089.9
NIPPON LIFE INS CO OF AMERICA	IA	222.1
NORTHWESTERN MUTUAL LIFE INS CO	WI	222,040.6
OLD REPUBLIC INS CO	PA	2,591.0
PACIFIC GUARDIAN LIFE INS CO LTD	HI	518.1
PHYSICIANS LIFE INS CO	NE	1,406.1
PROTECTIVE INS CO	IN	770.4
STANDARD LIFE & ACCIDENT INS CO	TX	525.1
Rating:	**B+**	
AETNA HEALTH & LIFE INS CO	CT	2,193.0
AETNA LIFE INS CO	CT	22,226.6
AMERICAN FAMILY LIFE ASR CO OF COLUM	NE	111,249.2
AMERICAN FAMILY MUT INS CO	WI	13,709.4
AMERICAN FIDELITY ASR CO	OK	4,848.9
AMERICAN UNITED LIFE INS CO	IN	22,972.9
ASSURITY LIFE INS CO	NE	2,436.6
BOSTON MUTUAL LIFE INS CO	MA	1,222.3
CENTRAL STATES INDEMNITY CO OF OMAHA	NE	424.9
COLORADO BANKERS LIFE INS CO	CO	272.7
FARM BUREAU LIFE INS CO	IA	7,987.7
FEDERAL INS CO	IN	32,182.2

INSURANCE COMPANY NAME	DOM. STATE	TOTAL ASSETS ($MIL)
GOVERNMENT EMPLOYEES INS CO	MD	21,998.7
GOVERNMENT PERSONNEL MUTUAL L I C	TX	833.6
JACKSON NATIONAL LIFE INS CO	MI	176,569.5
KAISER PERMANENTE INS CO	CA	179.4
LINCOLN BENEFIT LIFE CO	NE	13,279.3
MEDCO CONTAINMENT LIFE INS CO	PA	507.6
MEDICO CORP LIFE INS CO	NE	25.7
MERIT LIFE INS CO	IN	560.2
MIDLAND NATIONAL LIFE INS CO	IA	39,622.6
MINNESOTA LIFE INS CO	MN	34,732.2
MUTUAL OF OMAHA INS CO	NE	6,375.2
NATIONAL BENEFIT LIFE INS CO	NY	475.2
NATIONAL CASUALTY CO	WI	287.3
NATIONAL WESTERN LIFE INS CO	CO	10,001.6
NATIONWIDE MUTUAL FIRE INS CO	OH	5,596.1
OHIO NATIONAL LIFE ASR CORP	OH	3,450.3
PIONEER MUTUAL LIFE INS CO	ND	507.2
PRINCIPAL LIFE INS CO	IA	150,015.7
REGENCE BL CROSS BL SHIELD OREGON	OR	1,047.9
SAVINGS BANK LIFE INS CO OF MA	MA	2,531.7
SENTRY SELECT INS CO	WI	672.6
STANDARD INS CO	OR	19,996.4
STATE FARM MUTUAL AUTOMOBILE INS CO	IL	135,478.4
SURETY LIFE INS CO	NE	14.3
SYMETRA LIFE INS CO	WA	28,322.5
THRIVENT LIFE INS CO	MN	3,560.4
TRUSTMARK INS CO	IL	1,404.7
TRUSTMARK LIFE INS CO	IL	380.8
UNITED WORLD LIFE INS CO	NE	107.9
USABLE LIFE	AR	426.8

Pennsylvania

INSURANCE COMPANY NAME	DOM. STATE	TOTAL ASSETS ($MIL)
Rating: A+		
COUNTRY LIFE INS CO	IL	10,519.0
HEALTH CARE SVC CORP A MUT LEG RES	IL	18,206.4
PHYSICIANS MUTUAL INS CO	NE	1,968.0
TEACHERS INS & ANNUITY ASN OF AM	NY	256,932.8
Rating: A		
4 EVER LIFE INS CO	IL	202.8
AUTO-OWNERS LIFE INS CO	MI	3,557.4
BERKSHIRE LIFE INS CO OF AMERICA	MA	3,589.9
CINCINNATI INS CO	OH	10,807.9
FEDERATED LIFE INS CO	MN	1,483.1
GUARDIAN LIFE INS CO OF AMERICA	NY	44,344.6
RESERVE NATIONAL INS CO	OK	112.3
SENTRY INS A MUTUAL CO	WI	6,832.1
SENTRY LIFE INS CO	WI	5,167.7
SHELTERPOINT LIFE INS CO	NY	103.8
UNITED FARM FAMILY LIFE INS CO	IN	2,116.5
USAA LIFE INS CO	TX	21,633.7
Rating: A-		
AMALGAMATED LIFE INS CO	NY	107.0
AMERICAN REPUBLIC INS CO	IA	799.7
ANTHEM LIFE INS CO	IN	571.2
BALBOA LIFE INS CO	CA	58.9
CENTRAL STATES H & L CO OF OMAHA	NE	405.9
CIGNA LIFE INS CO OF NEW YORK	NY	376.2
COMPANION LIFE INS CO	SC	278.1
DEARBORN NATIONAL LIFE INS CO	IL	2,193.1
ERIE FAMILY LIFE INS CO	PA	2,058.7
FAMILY HERITAGE LIFE INS CO OF AMER	OH	706.7
FEDERATED MUTUAL INS CO	MN	4,667.2
GARDEN STATE LIFE INS CO	TX	120.1
GERBER LIFE INS CO	NY	2,680.4
ILLINOIS MUTUAL LIFE INS CO	IL	1,354.0
MASSACHUSETTS MUTUAL LIFE INS CO	MA	189,173.1
MEDICAL MUTUAL OF OHIO	OH	1,798.4
MIDWESTERN UNITED LIFE INS CO	IN	237.0
MUTUAL OF AMERICA LIFE INS CO	NY	17,180.5
NEW YORK LIFE INS CO	NY	142,089.9
NIPPON LIFE INS CO OF AMERICA	IA	222.1
NORTHWESTERN MUTUAL LIFE INS CO	WI	222,040.6
OLD REPUBLIC INS CO	PA	2,591.0
PHYSICIANS LIFE INS CO	NE	1,406.1
PROTECTIVE INS CO	IN	770.4
STANDARD LIFE & ACCIDENT INS CO	TX	525.1
Rating: B+		
AETNA HEALTH & LIFE INS CO	CT	2,193.0
AETNA LIFE INS CO	CT	22,226.6
AMERICAN FAMILY LIFE ASR CO OF COLUM	NE	111,249.2
AMERICAN FIDELITY ASR CO	OK	4,848.9
AMERICAN UNITED LIFE INS CO	IN	22,972.9
ASSURITY LIFE INS CO	NE	2,436.6
BOSTON MUTUAL LIFE INS CO	MA	1,222.3
CENTRAL STATES INDEMNITY CO OF OMAHA	NE	424.9
COLORADO BANKERS LIFE INS CO	CO	272.7
COVENTRY HEALTH & LIFE INS CO	MO	1,547.4

INSURANCE COMPANY NAME	DOM. STATE	TOTAL ASSETS ($MIL)
FEDERAL INS CO	IN	32,182.2
GOVERNMENT EMPLOYEES INS CO	MD	21,998.7
GOVERNMENT PERSONNEL MUTUAL L I C	TX	833.6
GRANGE MUTUAL CAS CO	OH	2,061.4
JACKSON NATIONAL LIFE INS CO	MI	176,569.5
KEYSTONE HEALTH PLAN EAST INC	PA	1,543.2
LINCOLN BENEFIT LIFE CO	NE	13,279.3
MEDCO CONTAINMENT LIFE INS CO	PA	507.6
MEDICO CORP LIFE INS CO	NE	25.7
MERIT LIFE INS CO	IN	560.2
MIDLAND NATIONAL LIFE INS CO	IA	39,622.6
MINNESOTA LIFE INS CO	MN	34,732.2
MUTUAL OF OMAHA INS CO	NE	6,375.2
NATIONAL BENEFIT LIFE INS CO	NY	475.2
NATIONAL CASUALTY CO	WI	287.3
NATIONAL WESTERN LIFE INS CO	CO	10,001.6
NATIONWIDE MUTUAL FIRE INS CO	OH	5,596.1
OHIO NATIONAL LIFE ASR CORP	OH	3,450.3
PIONEER MUTUAL LIFE INS CO	ND	507.2
PRINCIPAL LIFE INS CO	IA	150,015.7
SAVINGS BANK LIFE INS CO OF MA	MA	2,531.7
SENTRY SELECT INS CO	WI	672.6
STANDARD INS CO	OR	19,996.4
STATE FARM MUTUAL AUTOMOBILE INS CO	IL	135,478.4
SURETY LIFE INS CO	NE	14.3
SYMETRA LIFE INS CO	WA	28,322.5
THRIVENT LIFE INS CO	MN	3,560.4
TRUSTMARK INS CO	IL	1,404.7
TRUSTMARK LIFE INS CO	IL	380.8
UNITED WORLD LIFE INS CO	NE	107.9
UPMC FOR YOU INC	PA	421.0
USABLE LIFE	AR	426.8

Puerto Rico

INSURANCE COMPANY NAME	DOM. STATE	TOTAL ASSETS ($MIL)
Rating: **A+**		
TEACHERS INS & ANNUITY ASN OF AM	NY	256,932.8
Rating: **A**		
4 EVER LIFE INS CO	IL	202.8
CINCINNATI INS CO	OH	10,807.9
SENTRY INS A MUTUAL CO	WI	6,832.1
SOUTHERN FARM BUREAU LIFE INS CO	MS	12,921.4
TRANS OCEANIC LIFE INS CO	PR	61.6
Rating: **A-**		
CENTRAL STATES H & L CO OF OMAHA	NE	405.9
DEARBORN NATIONAL LIFE INS CO	IL	2,193.1
FAMILY HERITAGE LIFE INS CO OF AMER	OH	706.7
GERBER LIFE INS CO	NY	2,680.4
MASSACHUSETTS MUTUAL LIFE INS CO	MA	189,173.1
NEW YORK LIFE INS CO	NY	142,089.9
OLD REPUBLIC INS CO	PA	2,591.0
Rating: **B+**		
AETNA LIFE INS CO	CT	22,226.6
AMERICAN FAMILY LIFE ASR CO OF COLUM	NE	111,249.2
AMERICAN FIDELITY ASR CO	OK	4,848.9
BOSTON MUTUAL LIFE INS CO	MA	1,222.3
CENTRAL STATES INDEMNITY CO OF OMAHA	NE	424.9
FEDERAL INS CO	IN	32,182.2
MEDCO CONTAINMENT LIFE INS CO	PA	507.6
MERIT LIFE INS CO	IN	560.2
MIDLAND NATIONAL LIFE INS CO	IA	39,622.6
MINNESOTA LIFE INS CO	MN	34,732.2
MUTUAL OF OMAHA INS CO	NE	6,375.2
NATIONAL WESTERN LIFE INS CO	CO	10,001.6
OHIO NATIONAL LIFE ASR CORP	OH	3,450.3
PRINCIPAL LIFE INS CO	IA	150,015.7
TRIPLE-S SALUD INC	PR	713.6
TRUSTMARK INS CO	IL	1,404.7

Rhode Island

INSURANCE COMPANY NAME	DOM. STATE	TOTAL ASSETS ($MIL)
Rating: **A+**		
COUNTRY LIFE INS CO	IL	10,519.0
PHYSICIANS MUTUAL INS CO	NE	1,968.0
TEACHERS INS & ANNUITY ASN OF AM	NY	256,932.8
Rating: **A**		
4 EVER LIFE INS CO	IL	202.8
BERKSHIRE LIFE INS CO OF AMERICA	MA	3,589.9
CINCINNATI INS CO	OH	10,807.9
FEDERATED LIFE INS CO	MN	1,483.1
GUARDIAN LIFE INS CO OF AMERICA	NY	44,344.6
SENTRY INS A MUTUAL CO	WI	6,832.1
SENTRY LIFE INS CO	WI	5,167.7
SHELTERPOINT LIFE INS CO	NY	103.8
USAA LIFE INS CO	TX	21,633.7
Rating: **A-**		
AMALGAMATED LIFE INS CO	NY	107.0
AMERICAN REPUBLIC INS CO	IA	799.7
BALBOA LIFE INS CO	CA	58.9
CENTRAL STATES H & L CO OF OMAHA	NE	405.9
COMPANION LIFE INS CO	SC	278.1
DEARBORN NATIONAL LIFE INS CO	IL	2,193.1
FAMILY HERITAGE LIFE INS CO OF AMER	OH	706.7
FEDERATED MUTUAL INS CO	MN	4,667.2
GARDEN STATE LIFE INS CO	TX	120.1
GERBER LIFE INS CO	NY	2,680.4
ILLINOIS MUTUAL LIFE INS CO	IL	1,354.0
MASSACHUSETTS MUTUAL LIFE INS CO	MA	189,173.1
MIDWESTERN UNITED LIFE INS CO	IN	237.0
MUTUAL OF AMERICA LIFE INS CO	NY	17,180.5
NEW YORK LIFE INS CO	NY	142,089.9
NIPPON LIFE INS CO OF AMERICA	IA	222.1
NORTHWESTERN MUTUAL LIFE INS CO	WI	222,040.6
OLD REPUBLIC INS CO	PA	2,591.0
PHYSICIANS LIFE INS CO	NE	1,406.1
PROTECTIVE INS CO	IN	770.4
STANDARD LIFE & ACCIDENT INS CO	TX	525.1
Rating: **B+**		
AETNA HEALTH & LIFE INS CO	CT	2,193.0
AETNA LIFE INS CO	CT	22,226.6
AMERICAN FAMILY LIFE ASR CO OF COLUM	NE	111,249.2
AMERICAN FIDELITY ASR CO	OK	4,848.9
AMERICAN UNITED LIFE INS CO	IN	22,972.9
ASSURITY LIFE INS CO	NE	2,436.6
BOSTON MUTUAL LIFE INS CO	MA	1,222.3
CENTRAL STATES INDEMNITY CO OF OMAHA	NE	424.9
COLORADO BANKERS LIFE INS CO	CO	272.7
FEDERAL INS CO	IN	32,182.2
GOVERNMENT EMPLOYEES INS CO	MD	21,998.7
GOVERNMENT PERSONNEL MUTUAL L I C	TX	833.6
HM LIFE INS CO OF NEW YORK	NY	72.5
JACKSON NATIONAL LIFE INS CO	MI	176,569.5
LINCOLN BENEFIT LIFE CO	NE	13,279.3
MEDCO CONTAINMENT LIFE INS CO	PA	507.6
MERIT LIFE INS CO	IN	560.2
MIDLAND NATIONAL LIFE INS CO	IA	39,622.6

INSURANCE COMPANY NAME	DOM. STATE	TOTAL ASSETS ($MIL)
MINNESOTA LIFE INS CO	MN	34,732.2
MUTUAL OF OMAHA INS CO	NE	6,375.2
NATIONAL BENEFIT LIFE INS CO	NY	475.2
NATIONAL CASUALTY CO	WI	287.3
NATIONAL WESTERN LIFE INS CO	CO	10,001.6
NATIONWIDE MUTUAL FIRE INS CO	OH	5,596.1
OHIO NATIONAL LIFE ASR CORP	OH	3,450.3
PIONEER MUTUAL LIFE INS CO	ND	507.2
PRINCIPAL LIFE INS CO	IA	150,015.7
SAVINGS BANK LIFE INS CO OF MA	MA	2,531.7
SENTRY SELECT INS CO	WI	672.6
STANDARD INS CO	OR	19,996.4
STATE FARM MUTUAL AUTOMOBILE INS CO	IL	135,478.4
SURETY LIFE INS CO	NE	14.3
SYMETRA LIFE INS CO	WA	28,322.5
TRUSTMARK INS CO	IL	1,404.7
TRUSTMARK LIFE INS CO	IL	380.8
UNITED WORLD LIFE INS CO	NE	107.9
USABLE LIFE	AR	426.8

South Carolina

INSURANCE COMPANY NAME	DOM. STATE	TOTAL ASSETS ($MIL)
Rating:	**A+**	
COUNTRY LIFE INS CO	IL	10,519.0
HEALTH CARE SVC CORP A MUT LEG RES	IL	18,206.4
PHYSICIANS MUTUAL INS CO	NE	1,968.0
TEACHERS INS & ANNUITY ASN OF AM	NY	256,932.8
Rating:	**A**	
4 EVER LIFE INS CO	IL	202.8
AUTO-OWNERS LIFE INS CO	MI	3,557.4
BERKSHIRE LIFE INS CO OF AMERICA	MA	3,589.9
BLUECHOICE HEALTHPLAN OF SC INC	SC	309.1
CINCINNATI INS CO	OH	10,807.9
FEDERATED LIFE INS CO	MN	1,483.1
GUARDIAN LIFE INS CO OF AMERICA	NY	44,344.6
RESERVE NATIONAL INS CO	OK	112.3
SENTRY INS A MUTUAL CO	WI	6,832.1
SENTRY LIFE INS CO	WI	5,167.7
SHELTERPOINT LIFE INS CO	NY	103.8
SOUTHERN FARM BUREAU LIFE INS CO	MS	12,921.4
USAA LIFE INS CO	TX	21,633.7
Rating:	**A-**	
AMALGAMATED LIFE INS CO	NY	107.0
AMERICAN REPUBLIC INS CO	IA	799.7
ANTHEM LIFE INS CO	IN	571.2
BALBOA LIFE INS CO	CA	58.9
BLUE CROSS BLUE SHIELD OF SC INC	SC	3,141.3
CENTRAL STATES H & L CO OF OMAHA	NE	405.9
COMPANION LIFE INS CO	SC	278.1
COTTON STATES LIFE INS CO	GA	331.7
DEARBORN NATIONAL LIFE INS CO	IL	2,193.1
FAMILY HERITAGE LIFE INS CO OF AMER	OH	706.7
FEDERATED MUTUAL INS CO	MN	4,667.2
GARDEN STATE LIFE INS CO	TX	120.1
GERBER LIFE INS CO	NY	2,680.4
ILLINOIS MUTUAL LIFE INS CO	IL	1,354.0
LIFE INS CO OF ALABAMA	AL	112.7
MASSACHUSETTS MUTUAL LIFE INS CO	MA	189,173.1
MIDWESTERN UNITED LIFE INS CO	IN	237.0
MUTUAL OF AMERICA LIFE INS CO	NY	17,180.5
NEW YORK LIFE INS CO	NY	142,089.9
NIPPON LIFE INS CO OF AMERICA	IA	222.1
NORTHWESTERN MUTUAL LIFE INS CO	WI	222,040.6
OLD REPUBLIC INS CO	PA	2,591.0
PHYSICIANS LIFE INS CO	NE	1,406.1
PROTECTIVE INS CO	IN	770.4
STANDARD LIFE & ACCIDENT INS CO	TX	525.1
Rating:	**B+**	
AETNA HEALTH & LIFE INS CO	CT	2,193.0
AETNA LIFE INS CO	CT	22,226.6
AMERICAN FAMILY LIFE ASR CO OF COLUM	NE	111,249.2
AMERICAN FAMILY MUT INS CO	WI	13,709.4
AMERICAN FIDELITY ASR CO	OK	4,848.9
AMERICAN UNITED LIFE INS CO	IN	22,972.9
ASSURITY LIFE INS CO	NE	2,436.6
BOSTON MUTUAL LIFE INS CO	MA	1,222.3
CENTRAL STATES INDEMNITY CO OF OMAHA	NE	424.9

INSURANCE COMPANY NAME	DOM. STATE	TOTAL ASSETS ($MIL)
COLORADO BANKERS LIFE INS CO	CO	272.7
COVENTRY HEALTH & LIFE INS CO	MO	1,547.4
FEDERAL INS CO	IN	32,182.2
GOVERNMENT EMPLOYEES INS CO	MD	21,998.7
GOVERNMENT PERSONNEL MUTUAL L I C	TX	833.6
GRANGE MUTUAL CAS CO	OH	2,061.4
GREATER GEORGIA LIFE INS CO	GA	50.8
JACKSON NATIONAL LIFE INS CO	MI	176,569.5
KAISER PERMANENTE INS CO	CA	179.4
LINCOLN BENEFIT LIFE CO	NE	13,279.3
MEDCO CONTAINMENT LIFE INS CO	PA	507.6
MEDICO CORP LIFE INS CO	NE	25.7
MERIT LIFE INS CO	IN	560.2
MIDLAND NATIONAL LIFE INS CO	IA	39,622.6
MINNESOTA LIFE INS CO	MN	34,732.2
MUTUAL OF OMAHA INS CO	NE	6,375.2
NATIONAL BENEFIT LIFE INS CO	NY	475.2
NATIONAL CASUALTY CO	WI	287.3
NATIONAL WESTERN LIFE INS CO	CO	10,001.6
NATIONWIDE MUTUAL FIRE INS CO	OH	5,596.1
OHIO NATIONAL LIFE ASR CORP	OH	3,450.3
PIONEER MUTUAL LIFE INS CO	ND	507.2
PRINCIPAL LIFE INS CO	IA	150,015.7
SAVINGS BANK LIFE INS CO OF MA	MA	2,531.7
SENTRY SELECT INS CO	WI	672.6
STANDARD INS CO	OR	19,996.4
STATE FARM MUTUAL AUTOMOBILE INS CO	IL	135,478.4
SURETY LIFE INS CO	NE	14.3
SYMETRA LIFE INS CO	WA	28,322.5
THRIVENT LIFE INS CO	MN	3,560.4
TRUSTMARK INS CO	IL	1,404.7
TRUSTMARK LIFE INS CO	IL	380.8
UNITED WORLD LIFE INS CO	NE	107.9
USABLE LIFE	AR	426.8

South Dakota

INSURANCE COMPANY NAME	DOM. STATE	TOTAL ASSETS ($MIL)
Rating: A+		
COUNTRY LIFE INS CO	IL	10,519.0
PHYSICIANS MUTUAL INS CO	NE	1,968.0
TEACHERS INS & ANNUITY ASN OF AM	NY	256,932.8
Rating: A		
4 EVER LIFE INS CO	IL	202.8
AUTO-OWNERS LIFE INS CO	MI	3,557.4
BERKSHIRE LIFE INS CO OF AMERICA	MA	3,589.9
CINCINNATI INS CO	OH	10,807.9
FEDERATED LIFE INS CO	MN	1,483.1
GUARDIAN LIFE INS CO OF AMERICA	NY	44,344.6
RESERVE NATIONAL INS CO	OK	112.3
SENTRY INS A MUTUAL CO	WI	6,832.1
SENTRY LIFE INS CO	WI	5,167.7
USAA LIFE INS CO	TX	21,633.7
Rating: A-		
AMALGAMATED LIFE INS CO	NY	107.0
AMERICAN REPUBLIC INS CO	IA	799.7
ANTHEM LIFE INS CO	IN	571.2
BALBOA LIFE INS CO	CA	58.9
CENTRAL STATES H & L CO OF OMAHA	NE	405.9
COMPANION LIFE INS CO	SC	278.1
DEARBORN NATIONAL LIFE INS CO	IL	2,193.1
FAMILY HERITAGE LIFE INS CO OF AMER	OH	706.7
FEDERATED MUTUAL INS CO	MN	4,667.2
GARDEN STATE LIFE INS CO	TX	120.1
GERBER LIFE INS CO	NY	2,680.4
ILLINOIS MUTUAL LIFE INS CO	IL	1,354.0
MASSACHUSETTS MUTUAL LIFE INS CO	MA	189,173.1
MIDWESTERN UNITED LIFE INS CO	IN	237.0
MUTUAL OF AMERICA LIFE INS CO	NY	17,180.5
NEW YORK LIFE INS CO	NY	142,089.9
NIPPON LIFE INS CO OF AMERICA	IA	222.1
NORTHWESTERN MUTUAL LIFE INS CO	WI	222,040.6
OLD REPUBLIC INS CO	PA	2,591.0
PACIFIC GUARDIAN LIFE INS CO LTD	HI	518.1
PHYSICIANS LIFE INS CO	NE	1,406.1
PROTECTIVE INS CO	IN	770.4
STANDARD LIFE & ACCIDENT INS CO	TX	525.1
Rating: B+		
AETNA HEALTH & LIFE INS CO	CT	2,193.0
AETNA LIFE INS CO	CT	22,226.6
AMERICAN FAMILY LIFE ASR CO OF COLUM	NE	111,249.2
AMERICAN FAMILY MUT INS CO	WI	13,709.4
AMERICAN FIDELITY ASR CO	OK	4,848.9
AMERICAN UNITED LIFE INS CO	IN	22,972.9
ASSURITY LIFE INS CO	NE	2,436.6
BOSTON MUTUAL LIFE INS CO	MA	1,222.3
CENTRAL STATES INDEMNITY CO OF OMAHA	NE	424.9
COLORADO BANKERS LIFE INS CO	CO	272.7
COVENTRY HEALTH & LIFE INS CO	MO	1,547.4
FARM BUREAU LIFE INS CO	IA	7,987.7
FEDERAL INS CO	IN	32,182.2
GOVERNMENT EMPLOYEES INS CO	MD	21,998.7
GOVERNMENT PERSONNEL MUTUAL L I C	TX	833.6

INSURANCE COMPANY NAME	DOM. STATE	TOTAL ASSETS ($MIL)
JACKSON NATIONAL LIFE INS CO	MI	176,569.5
LINCOLN BENEFIT LIFE CO	NE	13,279.3
MEDCO CONTAINMENT LIFE INS CO	PA	507.6
MEDICA HEALTH PLANS	MN	760.3
MEDICO CORP LIFE INS CO	NE	25.7
MERIT LIFE INS CO	IN	560.2
MIDLAND NATIONAL LIFE INS CO	IA	39,622.6
MINNESOTA LIFE INS CO	MN	34,732.2
MUTUAL OF OMAHA INS CO	NE	6,375.2
NATIONAL BENEFIT LIFE INS CO	NY	475.2
NATIONAL CASUALTY CO	WI	287.3
NATIONAL WESTERN LIFE INS CO	CO	10,001.6
NATIONWIDE MUTUAL FIRE INS CO	OH	5,596.1
OHIO NATIONAL LIFE ASR CORP	OH	3,450.3
PIONEER MUTUAL LIFE INS CO	ND	507.2
PRINCIPAL LIFE INS CO	IA	150,015.7
SAVINGS BANK LIFE INS CO OF MA	MA	2,531.7
SENTRY SELECT INS CO	WI	672.6
STANDARD INS CO	OR	19,996.4
STATE FARM MUTUAL AUTOMOBILE INS CO	IL	135,478.4
SURETY LIFE INS CO	NE	14.3
SYMETRA LIFE INS CO	WA	28,322.5
THRIVENT LIFE INS CO	MN	3,560.4
TRUSTMARK INS CO	IL	1,404.7
TRUSTMARK LIFE INS CO	IL	380.8
UNITED WORLD LIFE INS CO	NE	107.9
USABLE LIFE	AR	426.8
WELLMARK INC	IA	2,143.2
WELLMARK OF SOUTH DAKOTA INC	SD	445.3

Tennessee

INSURANCE COMPANY NAME	DOM. STATE	TOTAL ASSETS ($MIL)
Rating:	**A+**	
COUNTRY LIFE INS CO	IL	10,519.0
PHYSICIANS MUTUAL INS CO	NE	1,968.0
TEACHERS INS & ANNUITY ASN OF AM	NY	256,932.8
Rating:	**A**	
4 EVER LIFE INS CO	IL	202.8
AUTO-OWNERS LIFE INS CO	MI	3,557.4
BERKSHIRE LIFE INS CO OF AMERICA	MA	3,589.9
BLUECROSS BLUESHIELD OF TENNESSEE	TN	2,450.7
CINCINNATI INS CO	OH	10,807.9
FEDERATED LIFE INS CO	MN	1,483.1
GUARDIAN LIFE INS CO OF AMERICA	NY	44,344.6
RESERVE NATIONAL INS CO	OK	112.3
SENTRY INS A MUTUAL CO	WI	6,832.1
SENTRY LIFE INS CO	WI	5,167.7
SHELTERPOINT LIFE INS CO	NY	103.8
SOUTHERN FARM BUREAU LIFE INS CO	MS	12,921.4
USAA LIFE INS CO	TX	21,633.7
Rating:	**A-**	
AMALGAMATED LIFE INS CO	NY	107.0
AMERICAN REPUBLIC INS CO	IA	799.7
ANTHEM LIFE INS CO	IN	571.2
BALBOA LIFE INS CO	CA	58.9
CENTRAL STATES H & L CO OF OMAHA	NE	405.9
CIGNA LIFE INS CO OF NEW YORK	NY	376.2
COMPANION LIFE INS CO	SC	278.1
COTTON STATES LIFE INS CO	GA	331.7
DEARBORN NATIONAL LIFE INS CO	IL	2,193.1
ERIE FAMILY LIFE INS CO	PA	2,058.7
FAMILY HERITAGE LIFE INS CO OF AMER	OH	706.7
FEDERATED MUTUAL INS CO	MN	4,667.2
GARDEN STATE LIFE INS CO	TX	120.1
GERBER LIFE INS CO	NY	2,680.4
ILLINOIS MUTUAL LIFE INS CO	IL	1,354.0
LIFE INS CO OF ALABAMA	AL	112.7
MASSACHUSETTS MUTUAL LIFE INS CO	MA	189,173.1
MIDWESTERN UNITED LIFE INS CO	IN	237.0
MUTUAL OF AMERICA LIFE INS CO	NY	17,180.5
MUTUAL SAVINGS LIFE INS CO	AL	473.8
NEW YORK LIFE INS CO	NY	142,089.9
NIPPON LIFE INS CO OF AMERICA	IA	222.1
NORTHWESTERN MUTUAL LIFE INS CO	WI	222,040.6
OLD REPUBLIC INS CO	PA	2,591.0
PHYSICIANS LIFE INS CO	NE	1,406.1
PROTECTIVE INS CO	IN	770.4
SHELTER LIFE INS CO	MO	1,097.7
STANDARD LIFE & ACCIDENT INS CO	TX	525.1
VOLUNTEER STATE HEALTH PLAN INC	TN	546.3
Rating:	**B+**	
AETNA HEALTH & LIFE INS CO	CT	2,193.0
AETNA LIFE INS CO	CT	22,226.6
AMERICAN FAMILY LIFE ASR CO OF COLUM	NE	111,249.2
AMERICAN FIDELITY ASR CO	OK	4,848.9
AMERICAN UNITED LIFE INS CO	IN	22,972.9
ASSURITY LIFE INS CO	NE	2,436.6

INSURANCE COMPANY NAME	DOM. STATE	TOTAL ASSETS ($MIL)
BLUEBONNET LIFE INS CO	MS	53.6
BLUEGRASS FAMILY HEALTH INC	KY	105.4
BOSTON MUTUAL LIFE INS CO	MA	1,222.3
CENTRAL STATES INDEMNITY CO OF OMAHA	NE	424.9
COLORADO BANKERS LIFE INS CO	CO	272.7
COVENTRY HEALTH & LIFE INS CO	MO	1,547.4
FEDERAL INS CO	IN	32,182.2
GOVERNMENT EMPLOYEES INS CO	MD	21,998.7
GOVERNMENT PERSONNEL MUTUAL L I C	TX	833.6
GRANGE MUTUAL CAS CO	OH	2,061.4
GREATER GEORGIA LIFE INS CO	GA	50.8
JACKSON NATIONAL LIFE INS CO	MI	176,569.5
LINCOLN BENEFIT LIFE CO	NE	13,279.3
MEDCO CONTAINMENT LIFE INS CO	PA	507.6
MEDICO CORP LIFE INS CO	NE	25.7
MERIT LIFE INS CO	IN	560.2
MIDLAND NATIONAL LIFE INS CO	IA	39,622.6
MINNESOTA LIFE INS CO	MN	34,732.2
MUTUAL OF OMAHA INS CO	NE	6,375.2
NATIONAL BENEFIT LIFE INS CO	NY	475.2
NATIONAL CASUALTY CO	WI	287.3
NATIONAL WESTERN LIFE INS CO	CO	10,001.6
NATIONWIDE MUTUAL FIRE INS CO	OH	5,596.1
OHIO NATIONAL LIFE ASR CORP	OH	3,450.3
PIONEER MUTUAL LIFE INS CO	ND	507.2
PRINCIPAL LIFE INS CO	IA	150,015.7
SAVINGS BANK LIFE INS CO OF MA	MA	2,531.7
SENTRY SELECT INS CO	WI	672.6
STANDARD INS CO	OR	19,996.4
STATE FARM MUTUAL AUTOMOBILE INS CO	IL	135,478.4
SURETY LIFE INS CO	NE	14.3
SYMETRA LIFE INS CO	WA	28,322.5
THRIVENT LIFE INS CO	MN	3,560.4
TRUSTMARK INS CO	IL	1,404.7
TRUSTMARK LIFE INS CO	IL	380.8
UNITED WORLD LIFE INS CO	NE	107.9
UNITEDHEALTHCARE PLAN RIVER VALLEY	IL	1,172.5
USABLE LIFE	AR	426.8

Texas

INSURANCE COMPANY NAME	DOM. STATE	TOTAL ASSETS ($MIL)
Rating:	**A+**	
COUNTRY LIFE INS CO	IL	10,519.0
HEALTH CARE SVC CORP A MUT LEG RES	IL	18,206.4
PHYSICIANS MUTUAL INS CO	NE	1,968.0
TEACHERS INS & ANNUITY ASN OF AM	NY	256,932.8
Rating:	**A**	
4 EVER LIFE INS CO	IL	202.8
BERKSHIRE LIFE INS CO OF AMERICA	MA	3,589.9
CINCINNATI INS CO	OH	10,807.9
FEDERATED LIFE INS CO	MN	1,483.1
GUARDIAN LIFE INS CO OF AMERICA	NY	44,344.6
LIFEWISE ASR CO	WA	129.7
RESERVE NATIONAL INS CO	OK	112.3
SENTRY INS A MUTUAL CO	WI	6,832.1
SENTRY LIFE INS CO	WI	5,167.7
SOUTHERN FARM BUREAU LIFE INS CO	MS	12,921.4
USAA LIFE INS CO	TX	21,633.7
Rating:	**A-**	
AMALGAMATED LIFE INS CO	NY	107.0
AMERICAN REPUBLIC INS CO	IA	799.7
ANTHEM LIFE INS CO	IN	571.2
BALBOA LIFE INS CO	CA	58.9
CENTRAL STATES H & L CO OF OMAHA	NE	405.9
COMPANION LIFE INS CO	SC	278.1
DEARBORN NATIONAL LIFE INS CO	IL	2,193.1
FAMILY HERITAGE LIFE INS CO OF AMER	OH	706.7
FEDERATED MUTUAL INS CO	MN	4,667.2
GARDEN STATE LIFE INS CO	TX	120.1
GERBER LIFE INS CO	NY	2,680.4
ILLINOIS MUTUAL LIFE INS CO	IL	1,354.0
MASSACHUSETTS MUTUAL LIFE INS CO	MA	189,173.1
MIDWESTERN UNITED LIFE INS CO	IN	237.0
MUTUAL OF AMERICA LIFE INS CO	NY	17,180.5
NEW YORK LIFE INS CO	NY	142,089.9
NIPPON LIFE INS CO OF AMERICA	IA	222.1
NORTHWESTERN MUTUAL LIFE INS CO	WI	222,040.6
OLD REPUBLIC INS CO	PA	2,591.0
PACIFIC GUARDIAN LIFE INS CO LTD	HI	518.1
PHYSICIANS LIFE INS CO	NE	1,406.1
PROTECTIVE INS CO	IN	770.4
STANDARD LIFE & ACCIDENT INS CO	TX	525.1
Rating:	**B+**	
AETNA HEALTH & LIFE INS CO	CT	2,193.0
AETNA LIFE INS CO	CT	22,226.6
AMERICAN FAMILY LIFE ASR CO OF COLUM	NE	111,249.2
AMERICAN FIDELITY ASR CO	OK	4,848.9
AMERICAN UNITED LIFE INS CO	IN	22,972.9
AMERIGROUP TEXAS INC	TX	645.6
ASSURITY LIFE INS CO	NE	2,436.6
BOSTON MUTUAL LIFE INS CO	MA	1,222.3
CENTRAL STATES INDEMNITY CO OF OMAHA	NE	424.9
COLORADO BANKERS LIFE INS CO	CO	272.7
COMMUNITY FIRST HEALTH PLANS INC	TX	85.9
COVENTRY HEALTH & LIFE INS CO	MO	1,547.4
FEDERAL INS CO	IN	32,182.2

INSURANCE COMPANY NAME	DOM. STATE	TOTAL ASSETS ($MIL)
GOVERNMENT EMPLOYEES INS CO	MD	21,998.7
GOVERNMENT PERSONNEL MUTUAL L I C	TX	833.6
JACKSON NATIONAL LIFE INS CO	MI	176,569.5
LINCOLN BENEFIT LIFE CO	NE	13,279.3
MEDCO CONTAINMENT LIFE INS CO	PA	507.6
MEDICO CORP LIFE INS CO	NE	25.7
MERIT LIFE INS CO	IN	560.2
MIDLAND NATIONAL LIFE INS CO	IA	39,622.6
MINNESOTA LIFE INS CO	MN	34,732.2
MUTUAL OF OMAHA INS CO	NE	6,375.2
NATIONAL BENEFIT LIFE INS CO	NY	475.2
NATIONAL CASUALTY CO	WI	287.3
NATIONAL WESTERN LIFE INS CO	CO	10,001.6
NATIONWIDE MUTUAL FIRE INS CO	OH	5,596.1
OHIO NATIONAL LIFE ASR CORP	OH	3,450.3
PIONEER MUTUAL LIFE INS CO	ND	507.2
PRINCIPAL LIFE INS CO	IA	150,015.7
SAVINGS BANK LIFE INS CO OF MA	MA	2,531.7
SENTRY SELECT INS CO	WI	672.6
STANDARD INS CO	OR	19,996.4
STATE FARM MUTUAL AUTOMOBILE INS CO	IL	135,478.4
SURETY LIFE INS CO	NE	14.3
SYMETRA LIFE INS CO	WA	28,322.5
THRIVENT LIFE INS CO	MN	3,560.4
TRUSTMARK INS CO	IL	1,404.7
TRUSTMARK LIFE INS CO	IL	380.8
UNITED WORLD LIFE INS CO	NE	107.9
UNITEDHEALTHCARE BENEFITS OF TEXAS	TX	703.3
UNITEDHEALTHCARE COMMUNITY PLAN TX	TX	394.8
USABLE LIFE	AR	426.8

Utah

INSURANCE COMPANY NAME	DOM. STATE	TOTAL ASSETS ($MIL)	INSURANCE COMPANY NAME	DOM. STATE	TOTAL ASSETS ($MIL)
Rating: A+			COLORADO BANKERS LIFE INS CO	CO	272.7
			COVENTRY HEALTH & LIFE INS CO	MO	1,547.4
COUNTRY LIFE INS CO	IL	10,519.0	FARM BUREAU LIFE INS CO	IA	7,987.7
HEALTH CARE SVC CORP A MUT LEG RES	IL	18,206.4	FEDERAL INS CO	IN	32,182.2
PHYSICIANS MUTUAL INS CO	NE	1,968.0	GOVERNMENT EMPLOYEES INS CO	MD	21,998.7
TEACHERS INS & ANNUITY ASN OF AM	NY	256,932.8	GOVERNMENT PERSONNEL MUTUAL L I C	TX	833.6
			JACKSON NATIONAL LIFE INS CO	MI	176,569.5
Rating: A			LINCOLN BENEFIT LIFE CO	NE	13,279.3
			MEDCO CONTAINMENT LIFE INS CO	PA	507.6
4 EVER LIFE INS CO	IL	202.8	MEDICO CORP LIFE INS CO	NE	25.7
AUTO-OWNERS LIFE INS CO	MI	3,557.4	MERIT LIFE INS CO	IN	560.2
BERKSHIRE LIFE INS CO OF AMERICA	MA	3,589.9	MIDLAND NATIONAL LIFE INS CO	IA	39,622.6
CINCINNATI INS CO	OH	10,807.9	MINNESOTA LIFE INS CO	MN	34,732.2
FEDERATED LIFE INS CO	MN	1,483.1	MUTUAL OF OMAHA INS CO	NE	6,375.2
GUARDIAN LIFE INS CO OF AMERICA	NY	44,344.6	NATIONAL BENEFIT LIFE INS CO	NY	475.2
LIFEWISE ASR CO	WA	129.7	NATIONAL CASUALTY CO	WI	287.3
RESERVE NATIONAL INS CO	OK	112.3	NATIONAL WESTERN LIFE INS CO	CO	10,001.6
SELECTHEALTH INC	UT	849.6	NATIONWIDE MUTUAL FIRE INS CO	OH	5,596.1
SENTRY INS A MUTUAL CO	WI	6,832.1	OHIO NATIONAL LIFE ASR CORP	OH	3,450.3
SENTRY LIFE INS CO	WI	5,167.7	PIONEER MUTUAL LIFE INS CO	ND	507.2
USAA LIFE INS CO	TX	21,633.7	PRINCIPAL LIFE INS CO	IA	150,015.7
			SAVINGS BANK LIFE INS CO OF MA	MA	2,531.7
Rating: A-			SENTRY SELECT INS CO	WI	672.6
			STANDARD INS CO	OR	19,996.4
AMALGAMATED LIFE INS CO	NY	107.0	STATE FARM MUTUAL AUTOMOBILE INS CO	IL	135,478.4
AMERICAN REPUBLIC INS CO	IA	799.7	SURETY LIFE INS CO	NE	14.3
ANTHEM LIFE INS CO	IN	571.2	SYMETRA LIFE INS CO	WA	28,322.5
BALBOA LIFE INS CO	CA	58.9	THRIVENT LIFE INS CO	MN	3,560.4
CENTRAL STATES H & L CO OF OMAHA	NE	405.9	TRUSTMARK INS CO	IL	1,404.7
COMPANION LIFE INS CO	SC	278.1	TRUSTMARK LIFE INS CO	IL	380.8
COPIC INS CO	CO	523.3	UNITED WORLD LIFE INS CO	NE	107.9
CSAA INS EXCHANGE	CA	6,888.9	USABLE LIFE	AR	426.8
DEARBORN NATIONAL LIFE INS CO	IL	2,193.1			
FAMILY HERITAGE LIFE INS CO OF AMER	OH	706.7			
FEDERATED MUTUAL INS CO	MN	4,667.2			
GARDEN STATE LIFE INS CO	TX	120.1			
GERBER LIFE INS CO	NY	2,680.4			
HEALTHY ALLIANCE LIFE INS CO	MO	954.2			
ILLINOIS MUTUAL LIFE INS CO	IL	1,354.0			
MASSACHUSETTS MUTUAL LIFE INS CO	MA	189,173.1			
MIDWESTERN UNITED LIFE INS CO	IN	237.0			
MUTUAL OF AMERICA LIFE INS CO	NY	17,180.5			
NEW YORK LIFE INS CO	NY	142,089.9			
NIPPON LIFE INS CO OF AMERICA	IA	222.1			
NORTHWESTERN MUTUAL LIFE INS CO	WI	222,040.6			
OLD REPUBLIC INS CO	PA	2,591.0			
PACIFIC GUARDIAN LIFE INS CO LTD	HI	518.1			
PHYSICIANS LIFE INS CO	NE	1,406.1			
PROTECTIVE INS CO	IN	770.4			
STANDARD LIFE & ACCIDENT INS CO	TX	525.1			
Rating: B+					
AETNA HEALTH & LIFE INS CO	CT	2,193.0			
AETNA LIFE INS CO	CT	22,226.6			
AMERICAN FAMILY LIFE ASR CO OF COLUM	NE	111,249.2			
AMERICAN FAMILY MUT INS CO	WI	13,709.4			
AMERICAN FIDELITY ASR CO	OK	4,848.9			
AMERICAN UNITED LIFE INS CO	IN	22,972.9			
ASSURITY LIFE INS CO	NE	2,436.6			
BOSTON MUTUAL LIFE INS CO	MA	1,222.3			
CENTRAL STATES INDEMNITY CO OF OMAHA	NE	424.9			

Vermont

INSURANCE COMPANY NAME	DOM. STATE	TOTAL ASSETS ($MIL)
Rating: A+		
PHYSICIANS MUTUAL INS CO	NE	1,968.0
TEACHERS INS & ANNUITY ASN OF AM	NY	256,932.8
Rating: A		
4 EVER LIFE INS CO	IL	202.8
BERKSHIRE LIFE INS CO OF AMERICA	MA	3,589.9
CINCINNATI INS CO	OH	10,807.9
FEDERATED LIFE INS CO	MN	1,483.1
GUARDIAN LIFE INS CO OF AMERICA	NY	44,344.6
RESERVE NATIONAL INS CO	OK	112.3
SENTRY INS A MUTUAL CO	WI	6,832.1
SENTRY LIFE INS CO	WI	5,167.7
USAA LIFE INS CO	TX	21,633.7
Rating: A-		
AMALGAMATED LIFE INS CO	NY	107.0
AMERICAN FAMILY LIFE ASR CO OF NY	NY	706.5
AMERICAN REPUBLIC INS CO	IA	799.7
BALBOA LIFE INS CO	CA	58.9
CENTRAL STATES H & L CO OF OMAHA	NE	405.9
COMPANION LIFE INS CO	SC	278.1
DEARBORN NATIONAL LIFE INS CO	IL	2,193.1
FAMILY HERITAGE LIFE INS CO OF AMER	OH	706.7
FEDERATED MUTUAL INS CO	MN	4,667.2
GARDEN STATE LIFE INS CO	TX	120.1
GERBER LIFE INS CO	NY	2,680.4
ILLINOIS MUTUAL LIFE INS CO	IL	1,354.0
MASSACHUSETTS MUTUAL LIFE INS CO	MA	189,173.1
MIDWESTERN UNITED LIFE INS CO	IN	237.0
MUTUAL OF AMERICA LIFE INS CO	NY	17,180.5
NEW YORK LIFE INS CO	NY	142,089.9
NIPPON LIFE INS CO OF AMERICA	IA	222.1
NORTHWESTERN MUTUAL LIFE INS CO	WI	222,040.6
OLD REPUBLIC INS CO	PA	2,591.0
PHYSICIANS LIFE INS CO	NE	1,406.1
PROTECTIVE INS CO	IN	770.4
STANDARD LIFE & ACCIDENT INS CO	TX	525.1
Rating: B+		
AETNA HEALTH & LIFE INS CO	CT	2,193.0
AETNA LIFE INS CO	CT	22,226.6
AMERICAN FAMILY LIFE ASR CO OF COLUM	NE	111,249.2
AMERICAN FIDELITY ASR CO	OK	4,848.9
AMERICAN UNITED LIFE INS CO	IN	22,972.9
ASSURITY LIFE INS CO	NE	2,436.6
BLUE CROSS BLUE SHIELD OF VERMONT	VT	248.8
BOSTON MUTUAL LIFE INS CO	MA	1,222.3
CENTRAL STATES INDEMNITY CO OF OMAHA	NE	424.9
COLORADO BANKERS LIFE INS CO	CO	272.7
FEDERAL INS CO	IN	32,182.2
GOVERNMENT EMPLOYEES INS CO	MD	21,998.7
GOVERNMENT PERSONNEL MUTUAL L I C	TX	833.6
JACKSON NATIONAL LIFE INS CO	MI	176,569.5
LINCOLN BENEFIT LIFE CO	NE	13,279.3
MEDCO CONTAINMENT LIFE INS CO	PA	507.6
MEDICO CORP LIFE INS CO	NE	25.7
MIDLAND NATIONAL LIFE INS CO	IA	39,622.6

INSURANCE COMPANY NAME	DOM. STATE	TOTAL ASSETS ($MIL)
MINNESOTA LIFE INS CO	MN	34,732.2
MUTUAL OF OMAHA INS CO	NE	6,375.2
NATIONAL BENEFIT LIFE INS CO	NY	475.2
NATIONAL CASUALTY CO	WI	287.3
NATIONAL WESTERN LIFE INS CO	CO	10,001.6
NATIONWIDE MUTUAL FIRE INS CO	OH	5,596.1
OHIO NATIONAL LIFE ASR CORP	OH	3,450.3
PIONEER MUTUAL LIFE INS CO	ND	507.2
PRINCIPAL LIFE INS CO	IA	150,015.7
SAVINGS BANK LIFE INS CO OF MA	MA	2,531.7
SENTRY SELECT INS CO	WI	672.6
STANDARD INS CO	OR	19,996.4
STATE FARM MUTUAL AUTOMOBILE INS CO	IL	135,478.4
SURETY LIFE INS CO	NE	14.3
SYMETRA LIFE INS CO	WA	28,322.5
TRUSTMARK INS CO	IL	1,404.7
TRUSTMARK LIFE INS CO	IL	380.8
UNITED WORLD LIFE INS CO	NE	107.9
USABLE LIFE	AR	426.8

Virginia

INSURANCE COMPANY NAME	DOM. STATE	TOTAL ASSETS ($MIL)
Rating: A+		
CAREFIRST BLUECHOICE INC	DC	1,140.8
COUNTRY LIFE INS CO	IL	10,519.0
HEALTH CARE SVC CORP A MUT LEG RES	IL	18,206.4
PHYSICIANS MUTUAL INS CO	NE	1,968.0
TEACHERS INS & ANNUITY ASN OF AM	NY	256,932.8
Rating: A		
4 EVER LIFE INS CO	IL	202.8
AUTO-OWNERS LIFE INS CO	MI	3,557.4
BERKSHIRE LIFE INS CO OF AMERICA	MA	3,589.9
CINCINNATI INS CO	OH	10,807.9
FEDERATED LIFE INS CO	MN	1,483.1
GUARDIAN LIFE INS CO OF AMERICA	NY	44,344.6
RESERVE NATIONAL INS CO	OK	112.3
SENTRY INS A MUTUAL CO	WI	6,832.1
SENTRY LIFE INS CO	WI	5,167.7
SOUTHERN FARM BUREAU LIFE INS CO	MS	12,921.4
USAA LIFE INS CO	TX	21,633.7
Rating: A-		
AMALGAMATED LIFE INS CO	NY	107.0
AMERICAN REPUBLIC INS CO	IA	799.7
ANTHEM LIFE INS CO	IN	571.2
BALBOA LIFE INS CO	CA	58.9
CENTRAL STATES H & L CO OF OMAHA	NE	405.9
COMPANION LIFE INS CO	SC	278.1
COTTON STATES LIFE INS CO	GA	331.7
DEARBORN NATIONAL LIFE INS CO	IL	2,193.1
ERIE FAMILY LIFE INS CO	PA	2,058.7
FAMILY HERITAGE LIFE INS CO OF AMER	OH	706.7
FEDERATED MUTUAL INS CO	MN	4,667.2
GARDEN STATE LIFE INS CO	TX	120.1
GERBER LIFE INS CO	NY	2,680.4
HEALTHKEEPERS INC	VA	650.1
ILLINOIS MUTUAL LIFE INS CO	IL	1,354.0
MASSACHUSETTS MUTUAL LIFE INS CO	MA	189,173.1
MIDWESTERN UNITED LIFE INS CO	IN	237.0
MUTUAL OF AMERICA LIFE INS CO	NY	17,180.5
NEW YORK LIFE INS CO	NY	142,089.9
NIPPON LIFE INS CO OF AMERICA	IA	222.1
NORTHWESTERN MUTUAL LIFE INS CO	WI	222,040.6
OLD REPUBLIC INS CO	PA	2,591.0
PHYSICIANS LIFE INS CO	NE	1,406.1
PROTECTIVE INS CO	IN	770.4
STANDARD LIFE & ACCIDENT INS CO	TX	525.1
VIRGINIA PREMIER HEALTH PLAN INC	VA	184.9
Rating: B+		
AETNA HEALTH & LIFE INS CO	CT	2,193.0
AETNA LIFE INS CO	CT	22,226.6
AMERICAN FAMILY LIFE ASR CO OF COLUM	NE	111,249.2
AMERICAN FIDELITY ASR CO	OK	4,848.9
AMERICAN UNITED LIFE INS CO	IN	22,972.9
ASSURITY LIFE INS CO	NE	2,436.6
BOSTON MUTUAL LIFE INS CO	MA	1,222.3
CENTRAL STATES INDEMNITY CO OF OMAHA	NE	424.9
COLORADO BANKERS LIFE INS CO	CO	272.7

INSURANCE COMPANY NAME	DOM. STATE	TOTAL ASSETS ($MIL)
COVENTRY HEALTH & LIFE INS CO	MO	1,547.4
FEDERAL INS CO	IN	32,182.2
GOVERNMENT EMPLOYEES INS CO	MD	21,998.7
GOVERNMENT PERSONNEL MUTUAL L I C	TX	833.6
GRANGE MUTUAL CAS CO	OH	2,061.4
GREATER GEORGIA LIFE INS CO	GA	50.8
INTOTAL HEALTH LLC	VA	55.3
JACKSON NATIONAL LIFE INS CO	MI	176,569.5
KAISER PERMANENTE INS CO	CA	179.4
LINCOLN BENEFIT LIFE CO	NE	13,279.3
MEDCO CONTAINMENT LIFE INS CO	PA	507.6
MEDICO CORP LIFE INS CO	NE	25.7
MERIT LIFE INS CO	IN	560.2
MIDLAND NATIONAL LIFE INS CO	IA	39,622.6
MINNESOTA LIFE INS CO	MN	34,732.2
MUTUAL OF OMAHA INS CO	NE	6,375.2
NATIONAL BENEFIT LIFE INS CO	NY	475.2
NATIONAL CASUALTY CO	WI	287.3
NATIONAL WESTERN LIFE INS CO	CO	10,001.6
NATIONWIDE MUTUAL FIRE INS CO	OH	5,596.1
OHIO NATIONAL LIFE ASR CORP	OH	3,450.3
OPTIMA HEALTH PLAN	VA	320.8
PIONEER MUTUAL LIFE INS CO	ND	507.2
PRINCIPAL LIFE INS CO	IA	150,015.7
SAVINGS BANK LIFE INS CO OF MA	MA	2,531.7
SENTRY SELECT INS CO	WI	672.6
STANDARD INS CO	OR	19,996.4
STATE FARM MUTUAL AUTOMOBILE INS CO	IL	135,478.4
SURETY LIFE INS CO	NE	14.3
SYMETRA LIFE INS CO	WA	28,322.5
THRIVENT LIFE INS CO	MN	3,560.4
TRUSTMARK INS CO	IL	1,404.7
TRUSTMARK LIFE INS CO	IL	380.8
UNITED WORLD LIFE INS CO	NE	107.9
UNITEDHEALTHCARE PLAN RIVER VALLEY	IL	1,172.5
USABLE LIFE	AR	426.8

Washington

INSURANCE COMPANY NAME	DOM. STATE	TOTAL ASSETS ($MIL)
Rating: A+		
COUNTRY LIFE INS CO	IL	10,519.0
PHYSICIANS MUTUAL INS CO	NE	1,968.0
PROVIDENCE HEALTH PLAN	OR	738.7
TEACHERS INS & ANNUITY ASN OF AM	NY	256,932.8
Rating: A		
4 EVER LIFE INS CO	IL	202.8
AUTO-OWNERS LIFE INS CO	MI	3,557.4
BERKSHIRE LIFE INS CO OF AMERICA	MA	3,589.9
CINCINNATI INS CO	OH	10,807.9
FEDERATED LIFE INS CO	MN	1,483.1
GUARDIAN LIFE INS CO OF AMERICA	NY	44,344.6
LIFEWISE ASR CO	WA	129.7
RESERVE NATIONAL INS CO	OK	112.3
SENTRY INS A MUTUAL CO	WI	6,832.1
SENTRY LIFE INS CO	WI	5,167.7
USAA LIFE INS CO	TX	21,633.7
Rating: A-		
AMALGAMATED LIFE INS CO	NY	107.0
AMERICAN REPUBLIC INS CO	IA	799.7
ANTHEM LIFE INS CO	IN	571.2
BALBOA LIFE INS CO	CA	58.9
CENTRAL STATES H & L CO OF OMAHA	NE	405.9
COMMUNITY HEALTH PLAN OF WASHINGTON	WA	363.5
COMPANION LIFE INS CO	SC	278.1
DEARBORN NATIONAL LIFE INS CO	IL	2,193.1
FAMILY HERITAGE LIFE INS CO OF AMER	OH	706.7
FEDERATED MUTUAL INS CO	MN	4,667.2
GARDEN STATE LIFE INS CO	TX	120.1
GERBER LIFE INS CO	NY	2,680.4
GROUP HEALTH COOPERATIVE	WA	1,617.8
ILLINOIS MUTUAL LIFE INS CO	IL	1,354.0
MASSACHUSETTS MUTUAL LIFE INS CO	MA	189,173.1
MIDWESTERN UNITED LIFE INS CO	IN	237.0
MUTUAL OF AMERICA LIFE INS CO	NY	17,180.5
NEW YORK LIFE INS CO	NY	142,089.9
NIPPON LIFE INS CO OF AMERICA	IA	222.1
NORTHWESTERN MUTUAL LIFE INS CO	WI	222,040.6
OLD REPUBLIC INS CO	PA	2,591.0
PACIFIC GUARDIAN LIFE INS CO LTD	HI	518.1
PHYSICIANS LIFE INS CO	NE	1,406.1
PREMERA BLUE CROSS	WA	2,178.3
PROTECTIVE INS CO	IN	770.4
STANDARD LIFE & ACCIDENT INS CO	TX	525.1
Rating: B+		
AETNA HEALTH & LIFE INS CO	CT	2,193.0
AETNA LIFE INS CO	CT	22,226.6
AMERICAN FAMILY LIFE ASR CO OF COLUM	NE	111,249.2
AMERICAN FAMILY MUT INS CO	WI	13,709.4
AMERICAN FIDELITY ASR CO	OK	4,848.9
AMERICAN UNITED LIFE INS CO	IN	22,972.9
ASSURITY LIFE INS CO	NE	2,436.6
BOSTON MUTUAL LIFE INS CO	MA	1,222.3
CENTRAL STATES INDEMNITY CO OF OMAHA	NE	424.9
COLORADO BANKERS LIFE INS CO	CO	272.7

INSURANCE COMPANY NAME	DOM. STATE	TOTAL ASSETS ($MIL)
COVENTRY HEALTH & LIFE INS CO	MO	1,547.4
FARM BUREAU LIFE INS CO	IA	7,987.7
FEDERAL INS CO	IN	32,182.2
GOVERNMENT EMPLOYEES INS CO	MD	21,998.7
GOVERNMENT PERSONNEL MUTUAL L I C	TX	833.6
JACKSON NATIONAL LIFE INS CO	MI	176,569.5
KAISER PERMANENTE INS CO	CA	179.4
LIFEWISE HEALTH PLAN OF WASHINGTON	WA	150.0
LINCOLN BENEFIT LIFE CO	NE	13,279.3
MEDCO CONTAINMENT LIFE INS CO	PA	507.6
MEDICO CORP LIFE INS CO	NE	25.7
MERIT LIFE INS CO	IN	560.2
MIDLAND NATIONAL LIFE INS CO	IA	39,622.6
MINNESOTA LIFE INS CO	MN	34,732.2
MOLINA HEALTHCARE OF WASHINGTON INC	WA	386.8
MUTUAL OF OMAHA INS CO	NE	6,375.2
NATIONAL BENEFIT LIFE INS CO	NY	475.2
NATIONAL CASUALTY CO	WI	287.3
NATIONAL WESTERN LIFE INS CO	CO	10,001.6
NATIONWIDE MUTUAL FIRE INS CO	OH	5,596.1
OHIO NATIONAL LIFE ASR CORP	OH	3,450.3
PIONEER MUTUAL LIFE INS CO	ND	507.2
PRINCIPAL LIFE INS CO	IA	150,015.7
REGENCE BL CROSS BL SHIELD OREGON	OR	1,047.9
SAVINGS BANK LIFE INS CO OF MA	MA	2,531.7
SENTRY SELECT INS CO	WI	672.6
STANDARD INS CO	OR	19,996.4
STATE FARM MUTUAL AUTOMOBILE INS CO	IL	135,478.4
SURETY LIFE INS CO	NE	14.3
SYMETRA LIFE INS CO	WA	28,322.5
THRIVENT LIFE INS CO	MN	3,560.4
TRUSTMARK INS CO	IL	1,404.7
TRUSTMARK LIFE INS CO	IL	380.8
UNITED WORLD LIFE INS CO	NE	107.9
USABLE LIFE	AR	426.8

West Virginia

INSURANCE COMPANY NAME	DOM. STATE	TOTAL ASSETS ($MIL)
Rating: A+		
COUNTRY LIFE INS CO	IL	10,519.0
HEALTH CARE SVC CORP A MUT LEG RES	IL	18,206.4
PHYSICIANS MUTUAL INS CO	NE	1,968.0
TEACHERS INS & ANNUITY ASN OF AM	NY	256,932.8
Rating: A		
4 EVER LIFE INS CO	IL	202.8
BERKSHIRE LIFE INS CO OF AMERICA	MA	3,589.9
CINCINNATI INS CO	OH	10,807.9
FEDERATED LIFE INS CO	MN	1,483.1
GUARDIAN LIFE INS CO OF AMERICA	NY	44,344.6
RESERVE NATIONAL INS CO	OK	112.3
SENTRY INS A MUTUAL CO	WI	6,832.1
SENTRY LIFE INS CO	WI	5,167.7
USAA LIFE INS CO	TX	21,633.7
Rating: A-		
AMALGAMATED LIFE INS CO	NY	107.0
AMERICAN REPUBLIC INS CO	IA	799.7
ANTHEM LIFE INS CO	IN	571.2
BALBOA LIFE INS CO	CA	58.9
CENTRAL STATES H & L CO OF OMAHA	NE	405.9
COMPANION LIFE INS CO	SC	278.1
DEARBORN NATIONAL LIFE INS CO	IL	2,193.1
ERIE FAMILY LIFE INS CO	PA	2,058.7
FAMILY HERITAGE LIFE INS CO OF AMER	OH	706.7
FEDERATED MUTUAL INS CO	MN	4,667.2
GARDEN STATE LIFE INS CO	TX	120.1
GERBER LIFE INS CO	NY	2,680.4
HEALTHY ALLIANCE LIFE INS CO	MO	954.2
ILLINOIS MUTUAL LIFE INS CO	IL	1,354.0
MASSACHUSETTS MUTUAL LIFE INS CO	MA	189,173.1
MEDICAL MUTUAL OF OHIO	OH	1,798.4
MIDWESTERN UNITED LIFE INS CO	IN	237.0
MUTUAL OF AMERICA LIFE INS CO	NY	17,180.5
NEW YORK LIFE INS CO	NY	142,089.9
NIPPON LIFE INS CO OF AMERICA	IA	222.1
NORTHWESTERN MUTUAL LIFE INS CO	WI	222,040.6
OLD REPUBLIC INS CO	PA	2,591.0
PHYSICIANS LIFE INS CO	NE	1,406.1
PROTECTIVE INS CO	IN	770.4
STANDARD LIFE & ACCIDENT INS CO	TX	525.1
Rating: B+		
AETNA HEALTH & LIFE INS CO	CT	2,193.0
AETNA LIFE INS CO	CT	22,226.6
AMERICAN FAMILY LIFE ASR CO OF COLUM	NE	111,249.2
AMERICAN FIDELITY ASR CO	OK	4,848.9
AMERICAN UNITED LIFE INS CO	IN	22,972.9
ASSURITY LIFE INS CO	NE	2,436.6
BOSTON MUTUAL LIFE INS CO	MA	1,222.3
CENTRAL STATES INDEMNITY CO OF OMAHA	NE	424.9
COLORADO BANKERS LIFE INS CO	CO	272.7
COVENTRY HEALTH & LIFE INS CO	MO	1,547.4
COVENTRY HEALTH CARE OF WEST VA INC	WV	90.8
FEDERAL INS CO	IN	32,182.2
GOVERNMENT EMPLOYEES INS CO	MD	21,998.7

INSURANCE COMPANY NAME	DOM. STATE	TOTAL ASSETS ($MIL)
GOVERNMENT PERSONNEL MUTUAL L I C	TX	833.6
HEALTH PLAN OF THE UPPER OHIO VALLEY	WV	253.1
HIGHMARK WEST VIRGINIA INC	WV	623.7
JACKSON NATIONAL LIFE INS CO	MI	176,569.5
LINCOLN BENEFIT LIFE CO	NE	13,279.3
MEDCO CONTAINMENT LIFE INS CO	PA	507.6
MEDICO CORP LIFE INS CO	NE	25.7
MERIT LIFE INS CO	IN	560.2
MIDLAND NATIONAL LIFE INS CO	IA	39,622.6
MINNESOTA LIFE INS CO	MN	34,732.2
MUTUAL OF OMAHA INS CO	NE	6,375.2
NATIONAL BENEFIT LIFE INS CO	NY	475.2
NATIONAL CASUALTY CO	WI	287.3
NATIONAL WESTERN LIFE INS CO	CO	10,001.6
NATIONWIDE MUTUAL FIRE INS CO	OH	5,596.1
OHIO NATIONAL LIFE ASR CORP	OH	3,450.3
PIONEER MUTUAL LIFE INS CO	ND	507.2
PRINCIPAL LIFE INS CO	IA	150,015.7
SAVINGS BANK LIFE INS CO OF MA	MA	2,531.7
SENTRY SELECT INS CO	WI	672.6
STANDARD INS CO	OR	19,996.4
STATE FARM MUTUAL AUTOMOBILE INS CO	IL	135,478.4
SURETY LIFE INS CO	NE	14.3
SYMETRA LIFE INS CO	WA	28,322.5
THRIVENT LIFE INS CO	MN	3,560.4
TRUSTMARK INS CO	IL	1,404.7
TRUSTMARK LIFE INS CO	IL	380.8
UNICARE HEALTH PLAN OF WEST VIRGINIA	WV	82.1
UNITED WORLD LIFE INS CO	NE	107.9
USABLE LIFE	AR	426.8

Wisconsin

INSURANCE COMPANY NAME	DOM. STATE	TOTAL ASSETS ($MIL)
Rating: A+		
COUNTRY LIFE INS CO	IL	10,519.0
HEALTH CARE SVC CORP A MUT LEG RES	IL	18,206.4
PHYSICIANS MUTUAL INS CO	NE	1,968.0
TEACHERS INS & ANNUITY ASN OF AM	NY	256,932.8
Rating: A		
4 EVER LIFE INS CO	IL	202.8
AUTO-OWNERS LIFE INS CO	MI	3,557.4
BERKSHIRE LIFE INS CO OF AMERICA	MA	3,589.9
CINCINNATI INS CO	OH	10,807.9
FEDERATED LIFE INS CO	MN	1,483.1
GUARDIAN LIFE INS CO OF AMERICA	NY	44,344.6
RESERVE NATIONAL INS CO	OK	112.3
SENTRY INS A MUTUAL CO	WI	6,832.1
SENTRY LIFE INS CO	WI	5,167.7
USAA LIFE INS CO	TX	21,633.7
Rating: A-		
AMALGAMATED LIFE INS CO	NY	107.0
AMERICAN REPUBLIC INS CO	IA	799.7
ANTHEM LIFE INS CO	IN	571.2
BALBOA LIFE INS CO	CA	58.9
CENTRAL STATES H & L CO OF OMAHA	NE	405.9
COMPANION LIFE INS CO	SC	278.1
COMPCARE HEALTH SERVICES INS CORP	WI	233.6
DEARBORN NATIONAL LIFE INS CO	IL	2,193.1
ERIE FAMILY LIFE INS CO	PA	2,058.7
FAMILY HERITAGE LIFE INS CO OF AMER	OH	706.7
FEDERATED MUTUAL INS CO	MN	4,667.2
GARDEN STATE LIFE INS CO	TX	120.1
GERBER LIFE INS CO	NY	2,680.4
HEALTHPARTNERS INS CO	MN	325.5
ILLINOIS MUTUAL LIFE INS CO	IL	1,354.0
MASSACHUSETTS MUTUAL LIFE INS CO	MA	189,173.1
MEDICAL MUTUAL OF OHIO	OH	1,798.4
MIDWESTERN UNITED LIFE INS CO	IN	237.0
MUTUAL OF AMERICA LIFE INS CO	NY	17,180.5
NEW YORK LIFE INS CO	NY	142,089.9
NIPPON LIFE INS CO OF AMERICA	IA	222.1
NORTHWESTERN MUTUAL LIFE INS CO	WI	222,040.6
OLD REPUBLIC INS CO	PA	2,591.0
PHYSICIANS LIFE INS CO	NE	1,406.1
PROTECTIVE INS CO	IN	770.4
SECURITY HEALTH PLAN OF WI INC	WI	322.0
STANDARD LIFE & ACCIDENT INS CO	TX	525.1
Rating: B+		
AETNA HEALTH & LIFE INS CO	CT	2,193.0
AETNA LIFE INS CO	CT	22,226.6
AMERICAN FAMILY LIFE ASR CO OF COLUM	NE	111,249.2
AMERICAN FAMILY MUT INS CO	WI	13,709.4
AMERICAN FIDELITY ASR CO	OK	4,848.9
AMERICAN UNITED LIFE INS CO	IN	22,972.9
ASSURITY LIFE INS CO	NE	2,436.6
BOSTON MUTUAL LIFE INS CO	MA	1,222.3
CENTRAL STATES INDEMNITY CO OF OMAHA	NE	424.9
COLORADO BANKERS LIFE INS CO	CO	272.7

INSURANCE COMPANY NAME	DOM. STATE	TOTAL ASSETS ($MIL)
COVENTRY HEALTH & LIFE INS CO	MO	1,547.4
FARM BUREAU LIFE INS CO	IA	7,987.7
FEDERAL INS CO	IN	32,182.2
GOVERNMENT EMPLOYEES INS CO	MD	21,998.7
GOVERNMENT PERSONNEL MUTUAL L I C	TX	833.6
GRANGE MUTUAL CAS CO	OH	2,061.4
JACKSON NATIONAL LIFE INS CO	MI	176,569.5
LINCOLN BENEFIT LIFE CO	NE	13,279.3
MEDCO CONTAINMENT LIFE INS CO	PA	507.6
MEDICO CORP LIFE INS CO	NE	25.7
MERIT LIFE INS CO	IN	560.2
MIDLAND NATIONAL LIFE INS CO	IA	39,622.6
MINNESOTA LIFE INS CO	MN	34,732.2
MUTUAL OF OMAHA INS CO	NE	6,375.2
NATIONAL BENEFIT LIFE INS CO	NY	475.2
NATIONAL CASUALTY CO	WI	287.3
NATIONAL WESTERN LIFE INS CO	CO	10,001.6
NATIONWIDE MUTUAL FIRE INS CO	OH	5,596.1
OHIO NATIONAL LIFE ASR CORP	OH	3,450.3
PIONEER MUTUAL LIFE INS CO	ND	507.2
PRINCIPAL LIFE INS CO	IA	150,015.7
SAVINGS BANK LIFE INS CO OF MA	MA	2,531.7
SENTRY SELECT INS CO	WI	672.6
STANDARD INS CO	OR	19,996.4
STATE FARM MUTUAL AUTOMOBILE INS CO	IL	135,478.4
SURETY LIFE INS CO	NE	14.3
SYMETRA LIFE INS CO	WA	28,322.5
THRIVENT LIFE INS CO	MN	3,560.4
TRUSTMARK INS CO	IL	1,404.7
TRUSTMARK LIFE INS CO	IL	380.8
UNITED WORLD LIFE INS CO	NE	107.9
USABLE LIFE	AR	426.8

Wyoming

INSURANCE COMPANY NAME	DOM. STATE	TOTAL ASSETS ($MIL)
Rating:	**A+**	
COUNTRY LIFE INS CO	IL	10,519.0
PHYSICIANS MUTUAL INS CO	NE	1,968.0
TEACHERS INS & ANNUITY ASN OF AM	NY	256,932.8
Rating:	**A**	
4 EVER LIFE INS CO	IL	202.8
BERKSHIRE LIFE INS CO OF AMERICA	MA	3,589.9
CINCINNATI INS CO	OH	10,807.9
FEDERATED LIFE INS CO	MN	1,483.1
GUARDIAN LIFE INS CO OF AMERICA	NY	44,344.6
LIFEWISE ASR CO	WA	129.7
RESERVE NATIONAL INS CO	OK	112.3
SENTRY INS A MUTUAL CO	WI	6,832.1
SENTRY LIFE INS CO	WI	5,167.7
USAA LIFE INS CO	TX	21,633.7
Rating:	**A-**	
AMALGAMATED LIFE INS CO	NY	107.0
AMERICAN REPUBLIC INS CO	IA	799.7
ANTHEM LIFE INS CO	IN	571.2
BALBOA LIFE INS CO	CA	58.9
CENTRAL STATES H & L CO OF OMAHA	NE	405.9
COMPANION LIFE INS CO	SC	278.1
COPIC INS CO	CO	523.3
CSAA INS EXCHANGE	CA	6,888.9
DEARBORN NATIONAL LIFE INS CO	IL	2,193.1
FAMILY HERITAGE LIFE INS CO OF AMER	OH	706.7
FEDERATED MUTUAL INS CO	MN	4,667.2
GARDEN STATE LIFE INS CO	TX	120.1
GERBER LIFE INS CO	NY	2,680.4
ILLINOIS MUTUAL LIFE INS CO	IL	1,354.0
MASSACHUSETTS MUTUAL LIFE INS CO	MA	189,173.1
MIDWESTERN UNITED LIFE INS CO	IN	237.0
MUTUAL OF AMERICA LIFE INS CO	NY	17,180.5
NEW YORK LIFE INS CO	NY	142,089.9
NORTHWESTERN MUTUAL LIFE INS CO	WI	222,040.6
OLD REPUBLIC INS CO	PA	2,591.0
PACIFIC GUARDIAN LIFE INS CO LTD	HI	518.1
PHYSICIANS LIFE INS CO	NE	1,406.1
PROTECTIVE INS CO	IN	770.4
ROCKY MOUNTAIN HEALTH MAINT ORG	CO	147.0
STANDARD LIFE & ACCIDENT INS CO	TX	525.1
Rating:	**B+**	
AETNA HEALTH & LIFE INS CO	CT	2,193.0
AETNA LIFE INS CO	CT	22,226.6
AMERICAN FAMILY LIFE ASR CO OF COLUM	NE	111,249.2
AMERICAN FAMILY MUT INS CO	WI	13,709.4
AMERICAN FIDELITY ASR CO	OK	4,848.9
AMERICAN UNITED LIFE INS CO	IN	22,972.9
ASSURITY LIFE INS CO	NE	2,436.6
BLUE CROSS BLUE SHIELD OF WYOMING	WY	406.0
BOSTON MUTUAL LIFE INS CO	MA	1,222.3
CENTRAL STATES INDEMNITY CO OF OMAHA	NE	424.9
COLORADO BANKERS LIFE INS CO	CO	272.7
COVENTRY HEALTH & LIFE INS CO	MO	1,547.4
FARM BUREAU LIFE INS CO	IA	7,987.7

INSURANCE COMPANY NAME	DOM. STATE	TOTAL ASSETS ($MIL)
FEDERAL INS CO	IN	32,182.2
GOVERNMENT EMPLOYEES INS CO	MD	21,998.7
GOVERNMENT PERSONNEL MUTUAL L I C	TX	833.6
JACKSON NATIONAL LIFE INS CO	MI	176,569.5
LINCOLN BENEFIT LIFE CO	NE	13,279.3
MEDCO CONTAINMENT LIFE INS CO	PA	507.6
MEDICO CORP LIFE INS CO	NE	25.7
MERIT LIFE INS CO	IN	560.2
MIDLAND NATIONAL LIFE INS CO	IA	39,622.6
MINNESOTA LIFE INS CO	MN	34,732.2
MUTUAL OF OMAHA INS CO	NE	6,375.2
NATIONAL BENEFIT LIFE INS CO	NY	475.2
NATIONAL CASUALTY CO	WI	287.3
NATIONAL WESTERN LIFE INS CO	CO	10,001.6
NATIONWIDE MUTUAL FIRE INS CO	OH	5,596.1
OHIO NATIONAL LIFE ASR CORP	OH	3,450.3
PIONEER MUTUAL LIFE INS CO	ND	507.2
PRINCIPAL LIFE INS CO	IA	150,015.7
SAVINGS BANK LIFE INS CO OF MA	MA	2,531.7
SENTRY SELECT INS CO	WI	672.6
STANDARD INS CO	OR	19,996.4
STATE FARM MUTUAL AUTOMOBILE INS CO	IL	135,478.4
SURETY LIFE INS CO	NE	14.3
SYMETRA LIFE INS CO	WA	28,322.5
TRUSTMARK INS CO	IL	1,404.7
TRUSTMARK LIFE INS CO	IL	380.8
UNITED WORLD LIFE INS CO	NE	107.9
USABLE LIFE	AR	426.8

Section V

Long-Term Care Insurers

A list of rated companies providing

Long-Term Care Insurance

Companies are listed in alphabetical order.

Section V Contents

This section provides contact addresses and phone numbers for all companies who sell long-term care insurance. The long-term care insurers in this section are listed in alphabetical order.

1. **Financial Strength Rating** — Our rating is measured on a scale from A to F and considers a wide range of factors. Highly-rated companies are, in our opinion, less likely to experience financial difficulties than lower-rated firms. See *About Weiss Financial Strength Ratings* for more information.

2. **Insurance Company Name** — The legally registered name, which can sometimes differ from the name that the company uses for advertising. An insurer's name can be very similar to the name of other companies, so make sure you note the exact name before contacting your agent.

3. **Address** — The address of the main office where you can contact the firm for additional financial data or for the location of local branches and/or registered agents.

4. **Telephone Number** — The number to call for additional financial data or for the phone numbers of local branches and/or registered agents.

To compare long-term care insurance policies and to walk through the maze of options, prices, and insurers, see the *Long-Term Care Insurance Planner*. It helps narrow down the choices available by addressing questions such as:

- What can you afford to pay for insurance?

- What type of care and living arrangement will suit your needs?

- When will you most likely need to utilize the insurance benefits?

- How much can you afford to pay from your own savings?

- Do you want a tax-qualified or non-qualified policy?

- What kind of insurance agent are you working with?

The planner offers an easy-to-use analysis tool to help identify the policy that best meets your needs. Based on information provided by insurance agents and literature from the provider, it addresses questions such as:

- How safe is the insurer?

- How are the coverage and facility options defined?

- What are the terms of coverage and reimbursement?

- How will the benefits be triggered?

- What other features are included in the policy?

RATING	INSURANCE COMPANY NAME	ADDRESS	CITY	STATE	ZIP	PHONE
B	AMERICAN FAMILY INS CO	6000 AMERICAN PARKWAY	MADISON	WI	53783	(608) 249-2111
B+	AMERICAN FAMILY MUT INS CO	6000 AMERICAN PKWY	MADISON	WI	53783	(608) 249-2111
B+	AMERICAN FIDELITY ASR CO	2000 N CLASSEN BLVD	OKLAHOMA CITY	OK	73106	(405) 523-2000
D+	BANKERS LIFE & CAS CO	222 MERCHANDISE MART PLAZA	CHICAGO	IL	60654	(312) 396-6000
A+	COUNTRY LIFE INS CO	1701 N TOWANDA AVE	BLOOMINGTON	IL	61701	(309) 821-3000
B-	GENWORTH LIFE INS CO	6604 WEST BROAD STREET	RICHMOND	VA	23230	(804) 662-2400
B	GENWORTH LIFE INS CO OF NEW YORK	125 PARK AVE 6TH FLOOR	NEW YORK	NY	10017	(212) 672-4299
B	JOHN HANCOCK LIFE & HEALTH INS CO	2711 CENTERVILLE RD STE 400	WILMINGTON	DE	19808	(617) 572-6000
B	JOHN HANCOCK LIFE INS CO (USA)	38500 WOODWARD AVE	BLOOMFIELD HILLS	MI	48304	(416) 926-0100
D-	LIFESECURE INS CO	1005 CONGRESS AVE, STE 825	AUSTIN	TX	78701	(847) 402-5000
A-	MASSACHUSETTS MUTUAL LIFE INS CO	1295 STATE ST	SPRINGFIELD	MA	01111	(413) 788-8411
B	MEDAMERICA INS CO	FOSTER PLAZA VIII 730 HOLIDAY	PITTSBURGH	PA	15220	(410) 684-3200
C+	MEDAMERICA INS CO OF FL	400 PARK AVE S SUITE 320	WINTER PARK	FL	32789	(585) 238-4659
B	MEDAMERICA INS CO OF NEW YORK	150 EAST MAIN ST	ROCHESTER	NY	14647	(716) 238-4456
B	MEDICO INS CO	1515 S 75TH ST	OMAHA	NE	68124	(402) 391-6900
B+	MUTUAL OF OMAHA INS CO	MUTUAL OF OMAHA PLAZA	OMAHA	NE	68175	(402) 342-7600
C	NATIONAL INS CO OF WISCONSIN INC	250 S EXECUTIVE DR	BROOKFIELD	WI	53005	(262) 785-9995
A-	NEW YORK LIFE INS CO	51 MADISON AVE	NEW YORK	NY	10010	(212) 576-7000
B	NORTHWESTERN LONG TERM CARE INS CO	720 E WISCONSIN AVE	MILWAUKEE	WI	53202	(414) 299-3136
A-	PREMERA BLUE CROSS	7001 220TH ST SW	MOUNTLAKE TERRACE	WA	98043	(425) 918-4000
B+	STATE FARM MUTUAL AUTOMOBILE INS CO	ONE STATE FARM PLAZA	BLOOMINGTON	IL	61710	(309) 766-2311
B-	TRANSAMERICA LIFE INS CO	4333 EDGEWOOD RD NE	CEDAR RAPIDS	IA	52499	(319) 398-8511
B+	TRUSTMARK INS CO	400 FIELD DR	LAKE FOREST	IL	60045	(847) 615-1500

Section VI

Medicare Supplement Insurance

Section VI Contents

Part I: Answers to Your Questions About Medigap

What Does Medicare Cover?

What are the Gaps in Medicare Coverage?

Medicare Prescription Drug Bill

Medicare, Medicare Advantage, Part D Sponsors, Medigap –
What Does It All Mean?

Part II: Steps to Follow When Selecting a Medigap Policy

How to Switch Medigap Policies

Part III: Medigap Premium Rates

Tables outlining the typical annual premiums charged for Plan A through

Plan N depending on age and gender.

Part IV: Medicare Supplement Insurers

Part I:
Answers to Your Questions About Medigap

The choices you make today about your health coverage – or the coverage of someone you care for – can have a major impact on both your health and your wealth. Since you are over 65, Medicare will provide you with a basic level of coverage, but there are many gaps in Medicare coverage that you will likely need to fill with a Medicare supplement insurance (Medigap) policy if you decide not to join a Medicare Advantage plan. The purpose of this report is to help you make coverage choices based on the most objective and broadest amount of information possible.

First, you want to understand what the federal Medicare program does and does not cover. We provide you with a clear layout starting on the following page.

Second, you will need to decide whether you want to fill the gaps in coverage by joining a Medicare Advantage plan or by combining Medicare supplement insurance with Medicare benefits. In Part 1 of this guide, we explain the differences between the two approaches.

Third, if you decide to use Medigap, your next step is to find out which plan best suits your needs. To help you figure this out, review Part II of this guide.

Fourth, check out the specific benefits for each plan along with the premium rates charged for those plans in Part III.

Finally, once you've found a couple of alternatives you like the best, call the companies to find the authorized agent nearest you. Phone numbers for the companies' main offices are listed in Part IV. If you need additional information on health insurance and related topics, call the agencies listed under Reference Organizations.

What Does Medicare Cover?

Table 1
MEDICARE (PART A): HOSPITAL INSURANCE-COVERED SERVICES FOR 2015

Service	Benefit	Medicare Pays	You Pay
HOSPITALIZATION			
Semiprivate room and board, general nursing and other hospital services and supplies. (Medicare coverage based on benefit periods). Up to 90 days inpatient healthcare in an approved psychiatric hospital.	First 60 days	All but $1,260	$1,260
	61st to 90th day	All but $315 a day	$315 a day
	91st to 150th day*	All but $630 a day	$630 a day
	Beyond 150 days	Nothing	All costs
SKILLED NURSING FACILITY CARE			
You must have been in a hospital for at least 3 days, enter a Medicare-approved facility generally within 30 days after hospital discharge, and meet other program requirements. ** (Medicare coverage based on benefit periods)	First 20 days	100% of approved amount	Nothing
	Additional 80 days	All but $157.50 a day	Up to $157.50 a day
	Beyond 100 days	Nothing	All costs
HOME HEALTH CARE			
Part-time or intermittent skilled care, home health services, physical and occupational therapy, durable medical equipment and supplies and other services	For as long as you meet Medicare requirements for home health care benefits	100% of approved amount; 80% of approved amount for durable medical equipment	Nothing for services; 20% of approved amount for durable medical equipment
HOSPICE CARE			
Includes drugs for symptom control and pain relief, medical and support services from a Medicare-approved hospice, and other services not otherwise covered by Medicare. Hospice care is usually given in your home.	For as long as doctor certifies need	All but limited costs for outpatient drugs and inpatient respite care	Limited cost sharing for outpatient drugs and inpatient respite care
BLOOD			
When furnished by a hospital or a skilled nursing facility during a covered stay	Unlimited during a benefit period if medically necessary	80% of the Medicare-approved after the first 3 pints per calendar year	***100% of the first 3 pints then 20% of the approved cost of additional pints.

*   60 reserve days may be used only once.

**   Neither Medicare nor Medicare supplement insurance will pay for most nursing home care.

*** To the extent the three pints of blood are paid for or replaced under one part of Medicare during the calendar year, they do not have to be paid for or replaced under the other part.

Table 2
MEDICARE (PART B): MEDICAL INSURANCE-COVERED SERVICES FOR 2015

Service	Benefit	Medicare Pays	You Pay
AMBULANCE SERVICES			
	Covers ground ambulance transportation when you need to be transported to a hospital, critical access hospital, or skilled nursing facility for medically necessary services, and transportation in any other vehicle could endanger your health	80% of approved amount (after deductible)	20% of the Medicare-approved amount, and the Part B deductible applies
AMBULATORY SURGICAL CENTERS			
	Covers the facility services fees related to approved surgical procedures in an ambulatory surgical center (facility where surgical procedures are performed, and the patient is expected to be released within 24 hours).	80% of the approved amount.	20% of the Medicare approved amount to both the ambulatory surgical center and the doctor who treats you, and Part B deductible applies. You pay for all of the facility service fees for procedures Medicare doesn't cover in ambulatory surgical centers
BLOOD			
		100% if the provider gets blood from a blood bank	A copayment for the blood processing and handling services for each unit of blood you get, and the Part B deductible applies. If the provider has to buy blood for you, you must either pay the provider costs for the first 3 units in a calendar year or have the blood donated by you or someone else.
CARDIAC REHABILITATION			
	Cover comprehensive programs that include exercise, education, and counseling for patients who meet certain conditions. Medicare also covers intensive cardiac rehabilitation programs that are typically more rigorous or more intense than regular cardiac rehabilitation programs.	80% of the approved amount.	20% of the Medicare-approved amount if you get the services in a doctor's office. In a hospital outpatient setting, you also pay the hospital a copayment. The Part B deductible applies.

Table 2
MEDICARE (PART B): MEDICAL INSURANCE-COVERED SERVICES FOR 2015

Service	Benefit	Medicare Pays	You Pay
CHEMOTHERAPY			
	Covers chemotherapy in a doctor's office, freestanding clinic, or hospital outpatient setting for people with cancer	80% of approved amount	20% of the Medicare-approved amount. If you get chemotherapy in a hospital outpatient setting, you pay a copayment for the treatment.
CHIROPRACTIC SERVICES (LIMITED COVERAGE)			
	Covers these services to help correct a subluxation (when one or more of the bones of your spine move out of position) using manipulation of the spine.	80% of the approved amount	20% of the Medicare-approved amount, and the Part B deductible applies. You pay all costs for any other services or tests ordered by a chiropractor (including X-rays and massage therapy)
CLINICAL RESEARCH STUDIES			
	Covers some costs, like office visits and tests, in qualifying clinical research studies.	80% of the approved amount	20% of the Medicare-approved amount, and the Part B deductible may apply
DEFIBRILLATOR (IMPLANTABLE AUTOMATIC)			
	Covers these devices for some people diagnosed with heart failure.	80% of the approved amount	20% of the Medicare-approved amount, if the surgery takes place in a outpatient setting. The doctor's services. If you get the device as a hospital outpatient, you also pay the hospital a copayment. The Part B deductible applies.

Table 2

MEDICARE (PART B): MEDICAL INSURANCE-COVERED SERVICES FOR 2015

Service	Benefit	Medicare Pays	You Pay
DIABETES SUPPLIES			
	Covers blood sugar testing monitors, test strips, lancet devices and lancets, blood sugar control solutions, and therapeutic shoes (in some cases). Covers insulin if it's medically necessary to use with an external insulin pump.	80% of the approved amount.	20% of the Medicare approved amount, the Part B deductible applies
DOCTOR AND OTHER HEALTH CARE PROVIDER SERVICES			
	Covers medically necessary doctor services (including outpatient services and some doctor services you get when you're a hospital inpatient) and covered preventive services. Medicare also covers services provided by other health care providers, like physician assistants, nurse practitioners, social workers, physical therapists, and psychologists.	80% of the approved amount.	20% of the Medicare approved amount, the Part B deductible applies
DURABLE MEDICAL EQUIPMENT (LIKE WALKERS)			
	Covers items like oxygen equipment and supplies, wheelchairs, walkers, and hospital beds ordered by a doctor or other health care provider enrolled in Medicare for use in the home	80% of the approved amount.	20% of the Medicare approved amount, the Part B deductible applies
EKG (ELECTROCARDIOGRAM) SCREENING			
	One time screening EKG/ECG if referred by your doctor or other health care provider as part of your one-time "Welcome to Medicare" preventive visit	80% of the approved amount.	20% of the Medicare approved amount, the Part B deductible applies. If you have the test at a hospital or a hospital-owned clinic, you also pay the hospital copayment

Table 2
MEDICARE (PART B): MEDICAL INSURANCE-COVERED SERVICES FOR 2015

Service	Benefit	Medicare Pays	You Pay
EMERGENCY DEPARTMENT SERVICES			
	When you have an injury, a sudden illness, or an illness that quickly gets much worse	80% of the approved amount.	A specified copayment for the hospital emergency department visit, and you pay 20% of the Medicare-approved amount for the doctor's or other health care provider's services. The Part B deductible applies. Cost may be different if you're admitted.
EYEGLASSES (LIMITED)			
	One pair of eyeglasses with standard frames (or one set of contact lenses) after cataract surgery that implants an intraocular lens.	80% of the approved amount. Medicare will only pay for contact lenses or eye glasses from a supplier enrolled in Medicare	20% of Medicare-approved amount, and the Part B deductible applies.
FEDERALLY-QUALIFIED HEALTH CENTER SERVICES			
	Covers many outpatient primary care and preventive services you get through certain community health centers	80% of the approved amount.	Generally, you're responsible for paying a federally-qualified health center 20% of its reasonable costs, but these health centers must offer you a discounted rate if your income is under a certain amount. The Part B deductible doesn't apply
FOOT EXAMS AND TREATMENT			
	Covers foot exams and treatment if you have diabetes-related nerve damage and/or meet certain conditions	80% of the approved amount.	20% of the Medicare-approved amount, and the Part B deductible applies.

Table 2
MEDICARE (PART B): MEDICAL INSURANCE-COVERED SERVICES FOR 2015

Service	Benefit	Medicare Pays	You Pay
HEARING AND BALANCE EXAMS			
	Covers these exams if your doctor or other health care provider orders them to see if your need medical treatment.	80% of the approved amount.	20% of the Medicare-approved amount, and the Part B deductible applies. In a hospital outpatient setting, you also pay the hospital a copayment.
HOME HEALTH SERVICES			
	Covers medically necessary part-time or intermittent skilled care, home-aid services, physical and occupational therapy, durable medical equipment and supplies, and other services	100% for services, 80% of approved amount for durable medical equipment	20% of approved amount for durable medical equipment
KIDNEY DIALYSIS SERVICES AND SUPPLIES			
	Covers 3 dialysis treatments per week if you have End-Stage Renal Disease (ESRD). This includes all ESRD-related drugs and biological, laboratory tests, home dialysis training, support services, equipment, and supplies	80% of the approved amount.	20% of approved Medicare-approved amount, and the Part B applies.
KIDNEY DISEASE EDUCATION SERVICES			
	Covers up to 6 sessions of kidney disease education services if you have Stage IV chronic kidney disease, and your doctor or other health care provider refers you for the service.	80% of the approved amount.	20% of approved Medicare-approved amount, and the Part B applies

Table 2
MEDICARE (PART B): MEDICAL INSURANCE-COVERED SERVICES FOR 2015

Service	Benefit	Medicare Pays	You Pay
LABORATORY SERVICES			
	Covers laboratory services including certain blood tests, urinalysis, and some screening tests.	Generally 100% of approved amount	Nothing for services
MENTAL HEALTH CARE (OUTPATIENT)			
	Covers mental health care services to help with conditions like depression or anxiety. Includes services generally provided in an outpatient setting (like a doctor's or other health care provider's office or hospital outpatient department).	100% of lab tests. 80% of the approved amount.	20% of the Medicare-approved amount and the Part B deductible applies for: • Visits to a doctor or other health care provider to diagnose your condition or monitor or change your prescriptions • Outpatient treatment of your condition (like counseling or psychotherapy)
OCCUPATIONAL THERAPY			
	Covers evaluation and treatment to help you perform activities of daily living (like dressing or bathing) when your doctor or other health care provider certifies you need it.	80% of the approved amount.	20% of the Medicare-approved amount and the Part B deductible applies.
OUTPATIENT HOSPITAL SERVICES			
	Covers many diagnostic and treatment services in participating hospital outpatient departments.	80% of the approved amount.	20% of the Medicare-approved amount and the Part B deductible applies.
OUTPATIENT MEDICAL AND SURGICAL SERVICES AND SUPPLIES			
	Covers approved procedures like X-rays, casts, stitches, or outpatient surgeries.	80% of the approved amount.	20% of the Medicare-approved amount, and the Part B deductible applies. In a hospital outpatient setting, you also pay the hospital a copayment.

Table 2

MEDICARE (PART B): MEDICAL INSURANCE-COVERED SERVICES FOR 2015

Service	Benefit	Medicare Pays	You Pay
PHYSICAL THERAPY			
	Covers evaluation and treatment for injuries and diseases that change your ability to function when your doctor or other health care provider certifies your need for it.	80% of the approved amount.	20% of the Medicare-approved amount, and the Part B deductible applies.
PRESCRIPTION DRUGS (LIMITED)			
	Covers a limited number of drugs like injections you get in a doctor's office, certain oral anti-cancer drugs, drugs used with some types of durable medical equipment (like a nebulizer or external infusion pump), immunosuppressant drugs and under very limited circumstances.	80% of the approved amount.	20% of the Medicare-approved amount, and the Part B deductible applies.
PROSTHETIC/ORTHOTIC ITEMS			
	Covers arm, leg, back, and neck braces; artificial eyes; artificial limbs (and their replacement parts); some types of breast prostheses (after mastectomy); and prosthetic devices needed to replace an internal body part or function.	80% of the approved amount.	20% of the Medicare-approved amount, and the Part B deductible applies.
PULMONARY REHABILITATION			
	Covers a comprehensive pulmonary rehabilitation program if you have moderate to very severe chronic obstructive pulmonary disease (COPD) and have a referral from the doctor treating this chronic respiratory disease.	80% of the approved amount.	20% of the Medicare-approved amount, and the Part B deductible applies. In a hospital outpatient setting, you also pay the hospital a copayment.

Table 2
MEDICARE (PART B): MEDICAL INSURANCE-COVERED SERVICES FOR 2015

Service	Benefit	Medicare Pays	You Pay
RURAL HEALTH CLINIC SERVICES			
	Covers many outpatient primary care and preventive services in rural health clinics.	80% of the approved amount. 100% for most preventive services.	20% of the Medicare-approved amount, and the Part B deductible applies.
SECOND SURGICAL OPINIONS			
	Covers second surgical opinions in some cases for surgery that isn't an emergency.	80% of the approved amount.	20% of the Medicare-approved amount, and the Part B deductible applies.
SPEECH-LANGUAGE PATHOLOGY SERVICES			
	Covers evaluation and treatment given to regain and strengthen speech and language skills, including cognitive and swallowing skills, when your doctor or other health care provider certifies you need it.	80% of the approved amount.	20% of the Medicare-approved amount, and the Part B deductible applies.
TELEHEALTH			
	Covers limited medical or other health services, like office visits and consultations provided using an interactive, two-way telecommunications system (like real-time audio and video) by an eligible provider who isn't at your location.	80% of the approved amount.	20% of the Medicare-approved amount, and the Part B deductible applies.
TESTS (OTHER THAN LAB TEST)			
	Covers X-rays, MRIs, CT scans, ECG/EKGs, and some other diagnostic tests.	80% of the approved amount.	20% of the Medicare-approved amount, and the Part B deductible applies. You also pay the hospital a copayment that may be more than 20% of the Medicare-approved amount, but in most cases this amount can't be more than the Part A hospital stay deductible.

Table 2
MEDICARE (PART B): MEDICAL INSURANCE-COVERED SERVICES FOR 2015

Service	Benefit	Medicare Pays	You Pay
TRANSPLANTS AND IMMUNOSUPPRESSIVE DRUGS			
	Covers doctor services for heart, lung, kidney, pancreas, intestine, and liver transplants under certain conditions and only in a Medicare-certified facility. Covers bone marrow and cornea transplants under certain conditions.	80% of the approved amount.	20% of the Medicare-approved amount for the drugs, and the Part B deductible applies.
TRAVEL (HEALTH CARE NEEDED WHEN TRAVELING OUTSIDE THE U.S.)			
	Generally doesn't cover health care while you're traveling outside the U.S., there are some exceptions, including cases where Medicare may pay for services that you get while on board a ship within the territorial waters adjoining the land areas of the U.S.	80% of the approved amount.	20% of the Medicare-approved amount, and the Part B deductible applies.
URGENTLY NEEDED CARE			
	Covers urgently needed care to treat a sudden illness or injury that isn't a medical emergency.	80% of the approved amount.	20% of the Medicare-approved amount for the doctor's or other health care provider's services and the Part B deductible applies.

Table 3
MEDICARE (PART B): PREVENTIVE SERVICES FOR 2015

Service	Benefit	Medicare Pays	You Pay
"WELCOME TO MEDICARE" PHYSICAL EXAM (ONE-TIME)			
	During the first 12 months that you have Part B, you can get a "Welcome to Medicare" preventive visit.	100% if provider accepts assignment.	If health care provider performs additional test or services during the same visit, you may have to pay coinsurance, and Part B deductible may apply
YEARLY "WELLNESS" VISIT			
	This visit is covered once every 12 months. If you've had Part B for longer than 12 months, you can get a yearly "Wellness" visit.	100% if provider accepts assignment.	If health care provider performs additional test or services during the same visit, you may have to pay coinsurance, and Part B deductible may apply
ABDOMINAL AORTIC ANEURYSM SCREENING			
	A one-time screening ultrasound for people at risk. You must get a referral for it as part of your one-time "Welcome to Medicare" preventive visit.	100% if provider accepts assignment	
ALCOHOL MISUSE SCREENING AND COUNSELING			
	Once every 12 months for adults with Medicare (including pregnant women) who use alcohol, but don't meet the medical criteria for alcohol dependency.	100% if provider accepts assignment	
BONE MASS MEASUREMENTS			
	Once every 24 months (more often if medically necessary) for people who have certain medical conditions or meet certain criteria.	100% if provider accepts assignment	
BREAST CANCER SCREENING (MAMMOGRAMS)			
	Once every 12 months for all women with Medicare who are 40 and older. Medicare covers one baseline mammogram for women between 35 - 39.	100% if provider accepts assignment	
CARDIOVASCULAR DISEASE (BEHAVIORAL THERAPY)			
	One visit per year with a primary care doctor in a primary care setting (like a doctor's office) to help lower your risk	100% if provider accepts assignment	

Table 3
MEDICARE (PART B): PREVENTIVE SERVICES FOR 2015 (cont'd.)

Service	Benefit	Medicare Pays	You Pay
CARDIOVASCULAR DISEASE SCREENINGS			
	Once every 5 years to test your cholesterol, lipid, lipoprotein, and triglyceride levels.	100% if provider accepts assignment	
CERVICAL AND VAGINAL CANCER SCREENING			
	Once every 24 months. Every 12 months if you're at high risk for cervical or vaginal cancer or child-bearing age and had an abnormal Pap test in the past 36 months	100% if the doctor or provider accepts assignment	
COLORECTAL CANCER SCREENING			
Fecal Occult Blood Test	Once every 12 months if you're 50 or older	100% if provider accepts assignment	
Flexible Sigmoidoscopy	Once every 48 months if you're 50 or older, or 120 months after a previous screening colonoscopy for those not at high risk.	100% if provider accepts assignment	
Colonoscopy	Once every 120 months (high risk every 24 months) or 48 months after a previous flexible sigmoidoscopy. There's no minimum age.	100% if provider accepts assignment	If a polyp or other tissue is found and removed during the colonoscopy, you may have to pay 20% of the Medicare-approved amount for the doctor's services and a copayment in a hospital outpatient setting.
Barium Enema	Once every 48 months if you're 50 or older (high risk every 24 months) when used instead of a sigmoidoscopy or colonoscopy.	80% of the approved amount	You pay 20% for the doctor's services. In a hospital outpatient setting, you also pay the hospital a copayment.
DERPRESSION SCREENING			
	One screening per year. The screening must be done in a primary care setting (like a doctor's office) that can provide follow-up treatment and referrals.	100% if provider accepts assignment	

Table 3
MEDICARE (PART B): PREVENTIVE SERVICES FOR 2015 (cont'd.)

Service	Benefit	Medicare Pays	You Pay
DIABETES SCREENING			
	Covers these screenings if your doctor determines you're at risk for diabetes. Up to 2 diabetes screenings each year.	100% if your doctor or provider accepts assignment	
DIABETES SELF-MANAGEMENT TRAINING			
	Covers diabetes outpatient self-management training to teach you to cope with and manage your diabetes.	80% of the approved amount	20% of the Medicare approved amount, and the Part B deductible applies
FLU SHOTS			
	Covers one flu shot per flu season	100% if the doctor or provider accepts assignment	
GLAUCOMA TESTING			
	Once every 12 months for those at high risk for glaucoma.	80% of approved amount	20% of the approved amount after the yearly Part B deductible. Copayment in a hospital outpatient setting
HEPATITIS B SHOTS			
	Covers these shots for people at medium or high risk for Hepatitis B	100% if the doctor or provider accepts assignment	
HIV SCREENING			
	Once per year for people at increased risk for HIV screenings for pregnant women up to 3 times during a pregnancy	100% if the doctor or provider accepts assignment	
MEDICAL NUTRITION THERAPY SERVICES			
	Covers medical nutrition therapy and certain related services if you have diabetes or kidney disease, or you have had a kidney transplant in the last 36 months or referred	100% if the doctor or provider accepts assignment	

Table 3
MEDICARE (PART B): PREVENTIVE SERVICES FOR 2015 (cont'd.)

Service	Benefit	Medicare Pays	You Pay
OBESITY SCREENING AND COUNSELING			
	Medicare may cover up to 22 face-to-face intensive counseling sessions over a 12 month period to help you lose weight. If you have a body mass index (BMI) of 30 or more.	100% if the primary care doctor or other qualified primary care practitioner accepts assignment	
PNEUMOCOCCAL SHOT			
	Covers pneumococcal shots to help prevent pneumococcal infections (like certain types of pneumonia). Most people only need a shot once in their lifetime.	100% if the doctor or provider accepts assignment	
PROSTATE CANCER SCREENING			
	Prostate Specific Antigen (PSA) and a digital rectal exam once every 12 months for men over 50 (beginning the day after your 50th birthday)	100% for the PSA test	20% of the Medicare-approved amount, and the Part B deductible applies for the digital rectal exam. In a hospital outpatient setting, you also pay the hospital a copayment.
SEXUALLY TRANSMITTED INFECTIONS SCREENING AND COUNSELING			
	Once every 12 months or at certain times during pregnancy. These screening are covered for people with Medicare who are pregnant and for certain people who are at increased risk for an STI	100% if the primary care doctor or other qualified primary care practitioner accepts assignment	
TOBACCO-USE CESSATION COUNSELING			
	Includes up to 8 face-to-face visits in a 12-month period	80% of the approved amount	20% of Medicare approved amount and the Part B deductible applies. In hospital outpatient setting, you also pay the hospital a copayment

In addition to the services listed, Medicare also helps cover the following: ambulance services, artificial eyes, artificial limbs (prosthetic devices and replacement parts), braces (arm, leg, back, and neck), chiropractic services (limited), eyeglasses (one pair of standard frames after cataract surgery with an intraocular lens), hearing and balance exams ordered by your doctor, kidney dialysis and prosthetic/orthodontic devices (including breast prosthesis after mastectomy).

In some cases and under certain conditions, Medicare may also cover these services: a second surgical opinion by a doctor, telemedicine services (in rural areas), and therapeutic shoes for people with diabetes, and transplants (heart, lung, kidney, pancreas, intestine, bone marrow, cornea, and liver).

Table 4
MEDICARE (PART D): PRESCRIPTION DRUG COVERAGE FOR 2015
Coverage is provided by private companies that have been approved by Medicare

Service	Costs	Medicare Provider Pays	You Pay
Medicare approved drug plans will cover generic and brand-name drugs. Most plans will have a formulary, which is a list of drugs covered by the plan. This list must always meet Medicare's requirements, including: - Inclusion of at least two drugs in every drug category. - Access to retail pharmacies. - For drugs not covered, a procedure must be in place to obtain, if medically necessary.	Premium	– – –	On average, $34.47 per month for basic coverage, and $68.63 per month for enhanced coverage
	First $320 in costs	Nothing	Up to $320 (this is the deductible)
	Costs between $320 and $2,960	$1,980	$660 (45% for branded companies, 55% for generic)
	Next $1,740 drug costs	Nothing	Until out of pocket spending, including drug company discount total $4,700
	All additional drug costs	All but co-pay	Co-pay $2.65 generic $6.60 all other drugs

Your plan must, at a minimum, offer this standard level of service and cost coverage outlined here, however, some plans may offer more coverage. Premiums will vary depending on any additional coverage provided by the plan.

What are the Gaps in Medicare Coverage?

Medicare has never covered all medical expenses and never will. The gap between what the doctors charge and the government pays is big and getting bigger. In fact, Medicare was never designed to cover chronic conditions or prolonged medical treatments. It was directed toward Americans age 65 or older who need minor or short-term care – little more. Be sure to understand where Medicare falls short. We can't list all the possible gaps, but here are the ones that affect almost everyone (see the tables on the previous pages for more details):

Gap #1: Deductibles

Medicare has two parts: **Part A** *acts as hospital insurance* and **Part B** *acts as medical insurance.* You are responsible for deductibles under both parts. Under Part A, for instance, you would be responsible for the $1,260 deductible for the first 60 days of a hospital stay. Plus, this $1,260 deductible applies each time you re-enter the hospital after a greater than 60-day span between admissions.

Under Part B, Medicare will pick up 80% of approved medical expenses after you pay a $147 deductible.

Gap #2: Co-Payments

You are responsible for a share of the daily costs if your hospital stay lasts more than 60 days. In 2015, you would be responsible for paying a $315 daily "coinsurance" fee if you stay in the hospital longer than 60 days but less than 90 days. Worse yet, Medicare Part A pays nothing after 90 days – unless you take advantage of the 60 "lifetime reserve days." The 60 reserve days can be used only once, and even then, you would still pay $630 daily for those 60 days.

Gap #3: Shortfalls

A national fee schedule established what physicians on Medicare assignment can charge for their services; Medicare will generally pay 80% of that amount. However, not all physicians are on Medicare assignment. Those who are not on assignment may charge more than the approved amount, leaving you responsible for the shortfall.

Gap #4: Nonpayment

The Original Medicare program does not directly provide any coverage whatsoever for certain services and expenses such as prescription drugs, hearing aids, treatment in foreign countries, and much more.

The bottom line: When all is said and done, the federal Medicare program will cover no more than half to three quarters of your medical expenses. That's why private Medicare supplement insurance, or Medigap, makes sense; its goal is to cover a portion of what Medicare doesn't. But in order for Medigap to make sense for you, you need to find the right policy, from the right company, for a reasonable price.

What about Medicare Prescription Drug Coverage?

The Medicare Prescription Drug, Improvement and Modernization (MMA) Act was passed in 2003. This legislation created Medicare Part D: Prescription Drug Coverage effective January 2006. Coverage is only available by private companies that have been approved by Medicare, not through the Medicare program directly. You can obtain coverage by either directly purchasing Part D coverage through a plan sponsor or in combination with enrollment in a Medicare Advantage health plan offering drug coverage. These drug plans are standardized across providers but they are required to offer a minimum level of coverage. Plans may vary in co-pays, premiums, deductibles, and drug coverage and pharmacy networks. (See Table 4 for an outline of the required coverage.)

You are no longer able to obtain drug coverage through Medicare Supplement policies. Policies H, I and J previously offered some coverage. This coverage will only remain available for those policyholders renewing an existing policy and that choose not to obtain drug coverage elsewhere. .

To assist you in the selection of a health benefit package complete with prescription drug coverage refer to our *Consumer Guide to Medicare Prescription Drug Coverage* that includes:

➢ Information on the Medicare prescription drug benefit.

➢ Help in making a choice about prescription drug coverage.

➢ What to consider once you enroll.

➢ An index of Medicare approved prescription drug plans.

Medicare, Medicare Advantage, Part D Sponsors, Medigap – What Does It All Mean?

The various terms used regarding coverage of health benefits for seniors is downright confusing. Let us take a moment here to review some of the terminology. The health insurance program for seniors managed by the federal government consists of the Original Medicare, Medicare Advantage, and Part D Prescription Drug Sponsors. Tables 1 through 3 on the preceding pages outline your coverage and coverage gaps under the Original Medicare plan. With this plan you seek services from Medicare providers who then receive payment from the government for the costs they incur for your care.

The Medicare Advantage program allows you to join a private health insurance plan that has contracted with Medicare to provide Part A and B coverage. The Medicare Advantage plans in turn receive funds from the government for providing you with benefits. These plans typically provide coverage beyond what Medicare offers, making supplemental policy unnecessary.

Medicare Part D will allow you to get prescription drug benefits in two ways. One option is to enroll with a Prescription Drug Plan sponsor in combination with your Original Medicare benefits. You will receive benefits from and pay a premium to the plan sponsor who then receives funds from the government. The second option is to enroll with a Medicare Advantage plan that is offering prescription drug coverage. Here you will receive all your benefits from the plan and pay only one premium. Refer to Table 4 for an outline of the minimum coverage that a plan sponsor must offer.

Medicare Supplement insurance, or Medigap as it is commonly referred to, is available through private insurers for those enrollees of the Original Medicare plan to fill the coverage 'gaps' in the Part A and B coverage. Basically, Medigap insurance will reimburse you for the out-of-pocket costs you incur that are not covered under Medicare. This insurance is completely optional.

Of course, if you're lucky, and your employer or union is continuing to cover your health benefits when you retire you won't need any of these types of insurance. But you want to stay educated because you never know when your old employer may discontinue retirement benefits.

Now let's take a closer look at the difference between Medicare supplement insurance policies and Medicare Advantage plans.

Medigap

To make comparing policies from one insurer to another easier Congress standardized and simplified Medigap plans so that there were just 10 to choose from – Plan 'A,' which is the bare bones, through Plan 'J,' the top of the line. This means that all Medigap insurers offer the same exact policy (though some companies may offer only a few of the plans). If you live in Wisconsin, Massachusetts, or Minnesota there are different types of Medigap plans that are sold in your state but are still standardized across insurers in each state.

Starting in 2006, two new plans, K and L, were introduced. These policies are structured to increase the portion of costs born by the policyholder while still providing the security of a cap on out-of-pocket expenses. These plans will be attractive to those individuals not able or willing to pay a higher premium for one of the other plans or expect to have minimal health expenses but still want the comfort of having costs capped. In June, 2010, plans E, H, I and J were discontinued and two new plans M and N were introduced. In Part II we provide you a table that outlines what each of the 10 plans cover.

You will have to pay a premium which can vary greatly, depending on the plan you choose and from which company you buy. Coverage is more expansive than through a Medicare Advantage plan but at a higher price. With a Medigap policy you have the freedom to choose your own doctors or specialists, and you will be covered regardless of which clinic or hospital you attend.

Medicare Select plans, a type of Medigap policy, are available in some areas which offer the same benefits but require you to use providers within the policy's network, similar to an HMO. These policies should be cheaper than non-Select plans since your choice of providers is restricted. Medigap plans do not cover long-term/custodial care at home or in a nursing home, hearing aids, vision care, private-duty nursing, dental care, or prescription medicine.

Even if you decide that you want a Medigap policy you may find that you will not be approved depending on your health, or you may not find an insurer in your area that sells these types of policies. However, once you do purchase a policy, Medigap policies are guaranteed renewable. This means that an insurance company cannot refuse to renew your policy unless you do not pay the premiums, or you made material misrepresentations on your application. You are typically able to obtain coverage each year once you are approved; however, the premium may change.

Prior to 2006, Medigap plans H, I, and J offered some prescription drug coverage. Effective in 2006 these plans were stripped of the prescription drug coverage benefit. If you purchased one of these plans prior to January 2006 and decided not to enroll in Medicare Part D, then you have been allowed to continue to renew the policy. If you decide to enroll in Part D, then you are allowed to switch to another Medigap plan (A, B, C, or F) without additional underwriting if one is offered by the insurer.

You are eligible to purchase a Medigap policy when you have enrolled in Medicare Parts A and B. In all states, there is an open enrollment period that lasts for six months and begins on the first day of the month in which you are both age 65 or older and enrolled in Part B. During this open enrollment period, the insurer cannot deny you coverage for any reason including pre-existing conditions. The insurer can, however, charge you a higher premium for the pre-existing condition or other health and lifestyle factors.

Medicare Advantage Plans

Under Medicare Part C, Medicare Advantage plans were introduced to offer seniors choices in coverage, more benefits at minimal cost, and to reduce the burden on the Medicare program. Insurers will often offer benefits not covered by Medicare, such as dental and vision services, at a lower price than a Medigap policy.

Prior to 2006 most offered some type of prescription drug coverage, but it varied from plan to plan. With the Medicare Prescription drug bill that took effect in 2006, health insurers may still offer prescription drug coverage but the benefits must match or exceed the requirements outlined in Medicare Part D (Refer Table). The insurers will then receive funding from the government for providing the benefits. All coverage is included in one premium charge.

With a Medicare Advantage plan you will not have to file any forms for reimbursement. You may or may not have to pay a premium and/or a co-pay for doctor's visits. In most cases you are restricted to the doctors in the plan's network, and you will need a referral before you see a specialist. Several new types of Medicare Advantage plans (PPOs, Special Need plans, Private Fee-for-Service plans, Medicare Medical Savings Account Plans, and Cost plans) have been introduced recently that vary from the current HMO plans offered including, in some cases, expanded options for accessing providers. Make sure to understand how these plans work before signing on.

There may be limited insurers offering a Medicare Advantage plan in your area and your benefits can be discontinued after the contract period (usually one year). At that time you would have to either choose a new insurer/plan or join the Original Medicare Plan.

Medigap Changes Effective June 1, 2010

In July 2008 the Medicare Improvements for Patients and Providers Act of 2008 (MIPPA) was approved by Congress. Part of the act covered Medigap and introduced some changes effective June 1, 2010.

One change affecting everyone is an additional benefit included with the basic coverage offered under all Medigap plans. If you purchased a Medigap policy on or after June 1, 2010 coverage includes the amount of cost sharing for all Part A Medicare eligible hospice care and respite care expenses. Prior to the implementation of the new coverage only those with the high deductible plans K and L received any benefit for this expense, with 50% and 75% coverage of the cost sharing amount respectively. The benefit for plans K and L will remain at the pre June 1, 2010 levels.

You will not gain this benefit if you choose to retain your current plan with the existing benefits.

Other changes were included that could affect your decisions about your choice of Medigap plan. As of June 1, 2010 four plans were discontinued, two plans had changes made to the coverage in addition to the hospice and respite care coverage already discussed, and two new plans were added.

Discontinued Plans

Plans E, H, I and J have been discontinued. This means that beginning June 1, 2010 these plans were no longer available for you to purchase. Existing holders of a policy with these plans will be able to renew the same policy when it falls due but only if the provider continues to offer the plan. If your provider decides not to continue to offer your plan you will not be able to obtain one of the discontinued plans from another provider.

Plan Changes

Plans D and G no longer offer at-home recovery as a benefit after June 1, 2010. This benefit was previously also available under plans I and J, and as they are discontinued the benefit will only continue to be available to holders of policies with plans D, G, I and J in effect prior to June 1, 2010.

Previously, Plan G offered coverage of 80% of the Part B excess. Beginning June 1, 2010 the coverage was increased to 100% of the Part B excess. If you currently hold a Plan G policy you will not be able to obtain the benefit of this change on renewal unless you give up the at-home recovery portion of your existing plan. Essentially you can either retain the benefits of the existing plan or you can accept the changes and have the benefits of the new Plan G. You can't have both.

New Plans

Two new plans, M and N were introduced on June 1, 2010.

Plan M is similar to Plan D except that only 50% of the Medicare Part A deductible is covered. In addition to 100% coverage of the Part B co-insurance, skilled nursing facility care and medically necessary emergency care in a foreign country are covered.

Plan N is also similar to Plan D, except that it requires co-payments of up to $20 for each covered health care provider office visit (including visits to medical specialists); and up to $50 for each covered emergency room visit. The ER co-payment is waived if you are admitted to the hospital.

If you are thinking about changing your plan you should consider doing it very carefully. Once you change your plan you cannot go back to your previous plan if it is not available to new policyholders.

See plan pages for further explanation of changes.

Part II:
Steps to Follow When Selecting
a Medigap Policy

Follow These Steps When Selecting a Medigap Policy

1. Determine what benefits you need. Consider the following:

- **Income.** If you are living on a **fixed income** and are able to afford only the most basic coverage, favor Plan A, the core plan. Among other things, you'll get an extra 30 days hospitalization per year beyond what Medicare pays. It also covers 100% of the Medicare Part B coinsurance for approved medical services, which is usually 20% of the approved amount.

  You may also want to consider plans, K or L, if they are available in your area. These policies help limit out-of-pocket costs for doctor's services and hospital care at a lower premium; however, you will have to pay more of Medicare's coinsurance and deductibles before the policy pays its share of the costs. These policies also do not cover 'excess' charges billed by your physician. Wisconsin, Massachusetts, and Minnesota also offer a core or basic plan to choose from.

- **Family History.** You or your family's medical history is such that you want to be prepared to pay for nursing care, consider Plan C. Your $157.50 per-day co-payment under Medicare would be covered up to 100 days for skilled nursing facility care.

- **Foreign Travel.** If you travel overseas extensively, you can get coverage for emergency care in a foreign country with Plan C through G, M and N. In Massachusetts and Minnesota foreign travel coverage can be found in the Supplement 1 and 2 Plans and to the Basic Medigap Coverage, respectively. In Wisconsin, a Foreign Travel rider can be added.

The chart below shows basic information about the different benefits Medigap policies cover.

X = the plan covers 100% of this benefit

Blank = the policy doesn't cover that benefit
% = the plan covers the percentage of this benefit
N/A = not applicable

Medigap Benefits	A	B	C	D	F *	G	K	L	M	N
Medigap Plans										
Part A coinsurance and hospital costs up to an additional 365 days after Medicare benefits are used up	X	X	X	X	X	X	X	X	X	X
Part B coinsurance or copayment	X	X	X	X	X	X	50%	75%	X	X***
Blood (first 3 pints)	X	X	X	X	X	X	50%	75%	X	X
Part A hospice care coinsurance or copayment	X	X	X	X	X	X	50%	75%	X	X
Skilled nursing facility care coinsurance			X	X	X	X	50%	75%	X	X
Part A deductible		X	X	X	X	X	50%	75%	50%	X
Part B deductible			X		X					
Part B excess charges					X	X				
Foreign travel exchange (up to plan limits)			X	X	X	X			X	X
Out-of-pocket limit**							$4,940	$2,740		

*Plan F also offers a high-deductible plan. If you choose this option, this means you must pay for Medicare-covered cost up to the deductible amount of $2,180 in 2015 before your Medigap plan pays anything.
**After you meet your out-of-pocket yearly limit and your yearly Part B deductible, the Medigap plan pays 100% of covered services for the rest of the calendar year.
***Plan N pays 100% of the Part B coinsurance, except for a copayment of up to $20 for some office visits and up to a $50 copayment for emergency room visits that don't result in inpatient admission.

2. Find out which policies are available to you.

- Not all insurers offer all plans in all areas.

- Will you be denied coverage by some insurers due to your health? Find out which ones and eliminate them from your choices.

- Does the insurer deny coverage for pre-existing conditions? If you are past the 6-month window following enrollment in Medicare Part B, companies most often deny you coverage for a specific period of time. However, some companies do not do this so their annual premium may be higher. You need to consider whether or not the higher premium is worth the coverage.

- Are you a member of AARP? If so, you may be able to obtain a policy through its sponsored insurer. Other affinity organizations also offer coverage through a Medigap insurer. Be sure to check with any groups of which you are a member.

- Do you want a Medicare Select plan? If you buy a Medicare Select policy, you are buying one of the 10 standardized Medigap plans A through N. With a Medicare Select plan, however, you must use the network providers to get full insurance benefits (except in an emergency). For this reason, Medicare Select policies generally cost less. If you don't use a Medicare Select hospital for non-emergency services, you will have to pay what a traditional Medicare plan doesn't pay. Medicare will pay its share of the approved charges no matter what hospital you choose.

3. **Compare the premiums.** Not only will you want to check out the premium you would be charged for different plans, but it is important to understand that there are three ways that insurance companies set the prices for policies. In order to compare the premium charged by two insurers for the same plan you need to make sure you are comparing apples to apples. No matter which type of pricing your Medigap insurer uses, the price of your policy will likely go up each year because of inflation and rising health care costs.

- **Attained-Age Rating.** With this type of policy the premium will rise as you age. For example: if you buy at 65, you pay what the company charges 65-year-old customers. Then at 66, you will pay whatever the company is charging a 66-year-old. The Medigap policy will go up in cost due to age, in addition to the increased cost of medical care.

- **Issue-Age Rating.** With this policy, the insurance company will charge you based on the age you were when you first signed up; you will always pay the same premium that someone that age pays. Unlike attained-age policies, issue-age policies do not go up because you are another year older. For example: if you first buy at 65, you will always pay the premium the company charges 65-year-old customers—no matter what your age. If you first buy at 70, you will always pay the premium the company charges 70-year-old customers. This is not to say that your premium won't go up. It will increase as the insurer raises rates for that particular age.

- **No-Age Rating or Community Rating.** This is the least common way that policies are priced. No matter how old you are, the policy costs the same. With this structure, younger people pay more than what they would pay for other polices and older people may pay less. The premium is the same for all people who buy this plan regardless of age. For example: XYZ Company will charge a 65-year-old $140, a 75-year-old $140 and an 85-year-old $140.

4. You may only be concerned with catastrophic illness. If so, you may not need to buy a Medigap policy at all, especially if you are relatively healthy, live a healthy lifestyle, and currently only incur routine medical expenses that would cost less than the premiums for a Medigap policy. You could purchase a catastrophic or high-deductible health insurance policy that would kick in when your medical bills exceeded a predetermined level, such as $5,000.

The Medigap K and L plans may also be a good choice. They should cost less than other Medigap plans but will provide a cap on out-of-pocket expenses.

5. What is the insurer's financial strength rating? If you were to experience the double misfortune of becoming seriously ill and having your insurer fail, you may be responsible for much of your unpaid claims, and it would be difficult to find replacement coverage. We recommend you choose a company with a B+ or higher Weiss Financial Strength Rating if you can. You should also consider an insurer's level of customer service and timeliness in reimbursing claims. Ask friends about their experiences and contact your state's insurance department or counsel for aging to find out if they keep public complaint records. As an industry, Medigap insurers have a good reputation for paying claims.

How to Switch Medigap Policies

If you are currently holding a Medigap policy and become uncomfortable with your company's financial stability, or if you find a cheaper policy at a stronger company, here are some steps to take before switching policies:

Step 1: Determine if your policy was issued prior to January 1, 1992. If it was, and if it was guaranteed renewable, you did not switch to one of the standard plans. This policy should be compared carefully to the newer standardized plans before switching. Remember: once you switch to one of the new standardized plans, you can never switch back to a non-standard plan.

Furthermore, you should know that if you already have a Medigap policy, it is against federal law for a company to sell you another one. When you buy another policy, you must sign a statement indicating that you are replacing your current policy and do not intend to keep both.

Step 2: Before switching policies, compare benefits and premiums. It is important to note that some of the older non-standard policies may provide superior coverage, and your increased age may make comparable coverage more expensive.

Step 3: Determine any impact on pre-existing conditions. Any portion of a pre-existing condition satisfied under the old policy will be credited to the new policy. Example: The old policy specified that it would not cover a pre-existing condition for the first six months. You switch policies after just two months. As a result, you only have four months to wait under the new policy to be covered for your pre-existing condition.
(Exception: If your new policy has a benefit that was not included in your old policy, a new six-month waiting period may be imposed on that particular benefit.)

Step 4: Use the "free-look" provision which allows you 30 days to review a Medigap policy once you've paid the first premium. If, during the first 30 days, you decide you don't want or need the policy you can return it to the company for a full refund.

Step 5: Do not cancel your old policy until your new policy is in force.

Part III:
Medigap Premium Rates

Basic Medigap Coverage
PLAN A

If you stay in the hospital for longer than 60 days, but less than 90 days, Plan A covers Medicare Part A coinsurance amount of $315 per day (in 2015) for each benefit period.

For each Medicare "hospital reserve day" you use, Plan A pays the $630 (in 2015) per day Medicare Part A coinsurance amount. "Hospital reserve days" are 60 nonrenewable hospital days that Medicare provides which can only be used once in a lifetime. After all Medicare hospital benefits are exhausted, Plan A will cover 100% of Medicare Part A eligible hospital expenses.

If the need arises, Plan A covers costs for the first three pints of blood or equivalent quantities of packed red blood cells received each year in connection with Medicare Parts A and B covered services. Once you have met this 3-pint blood deductible under Medicare Part A, it does not have to be met again under Part B.

After your $147 annual Medicare Part B deductible is met Plan A will cover the coinsurance amount for Medicare approved medical services, which is generally 20% of the approved amount.

Plan A now includes coverage of cost sharing for all Part A Medicare-eligible hospice care and respite care expenses.

If you feel that Plan A fits your needs, take a look at the two tables below to find out what price you should expect to be charged for this plan. The tables outline the typical annual premiums charged for Plan A depending on age and gender. These rates are based on our 2014 nationwide collection of insurance premiums.

PLAN A

Female

Age	Average Premium	Lowest Premium	Highest Premium	Median Premium
65	$1,456	$479	$7,275	$1,500
70	$1,673	$479	$7,275	$1,509
75	$1,893	$479	$7,275	$1,978
80	$2,058	$479	$7,275	$2,144
85	$2,204	$479	$7,275	$1,971
90	$2,273	$479	$25,602	$2,340
95	$2,329	$479	$25,602	$2,393

Male

Age	Average Premium	Lowest Premium	Highest Premium	Median Premium
65	$1,572	$479	$7,275	$1,500
70	$1,813	$479	$7,275	$1,735
75	$2,059	$479	$7,275	$1,978
80	$2,252	$479	$7,275	$2,144
85	$2,420	$479	$7,571	$2,268
90	$2,482	$479	$7,571	$2,340
95	$2,545	$479	$7,571	$2,393

Basic Medigap Coverage
PLAN B

If you stay in the hospital for longer than 60 days, but less than 90 days, Plan B covers Medicare Part A coinsurance amount of $315 per day (in 2015) for each benefit period.

For each Medicare "hospital reserve day" you use, Plan B pays the $630 (in 2015) per day Medicare Part A coinsurance amount. "Hospital reserve days" are 60 nonrenewable hospital days that Medicare provides which can only be used once in a lifetime. After all Medicare hospital benefits are exhausted, Plan B will cover 100% of Medicare Part A eligible hospital expenses.

If the need arises, Plan B covers costs for the first three pints of blood or equivalent quantities of packed red blood cells received each year in connection with Medicare Parts A and B covered services. Once you have met this 3-pint blood deductible under Medicare Part A, it does not have to be met again under Part B.

After your $147 annual Medicare Part B deductible is met Plan B will cover the coinsurance amount for Medicare approved medical services, which is generally 20% of the approved amount.

Plan B now includes coverage of cost sharing for all Part A Medicare-eligible hospice care and respite care expenses.

Additional Features
Plan B includes the core Medigap coverage PLUS one extra benefit:
- It will pay for the $1,260 Medicare Part A in-patient hospital deductible (per benefit period in 2015).

If you feel that Plan B fits your needs, take a look at the two tables below to find out what price you should expect to be charged for this plan. The tables outline the typical annual premiums charged for Plan B depending on age and gender. These rates are based on our 2014 nationwide collection of insurance premiums.

PLAN B

Female

Age	Average Premium	Lowest Premium	Highest Premium	Median Premium
65	$1,822	$834	$8,118	$1,589
70	$2,148	$1,050	$9,060	$2,132
75	$2,443	$1,219	$9,060	$2,287
80	$2,631	$1,371	$9,060	$2,367
85	$2,800	$1,371	$9,060	$2,522
90	$2,886	$1,371	$9,060	$2,960
95	$2,951	$1,371	$9,060	$2,618

Male

Age	Average Premium	Lowest Premium	Highest Premium	Median Premium
65	$1,959	$834	$8,118	$1,828
70	$2,313	$1,148	$9,060	$2,132
75	$2,631	$1,371	$9,060	$2,475
80	$2,850	$1,371	$9,060	$2,721
85	$3,046	$1,371	$9,060	$2,877
90	$3,140	$1,371	$9,060	$2,960
95	$3,211	$1,371	$9,060	$3,010

Basic Medigap Coverage
PLAN C

If you stay in the hospital for longer than 60 days, but less than 90 days, Plan C covers Medicare Part A coinsurance amount of $315 per day (in 2015) for each benefit period. For each Medicare "hospital reserve day" you use, Plan C pays the $630 (in 2015) per day Medicare Part A coinsurance amount. "Hospital reserve days" are 60 nonrenewable hospital days that Medicare provides you which can only be used once in a lifetime. After all Medicare hospital benefits are exhausted, Plan C will cover 100% of Medicare Part A eligible hospital expenses.

If the need arises, Plan C covers costs for the first three pints of blood or equivalent quantities of packed red blood cells received each year in connection with Medicare Parts A and B covered services. Once you have met this 3-pint blood deductible under Medicare Part A, it does not have to be met again under Part B.

After your $147 annual Medicare Part B deductible is met, Plan C will cover the coinsurance amount of Medicare approved medical services, which is generally 20% of the approved amount

Plan C now includes coverage of cost sharing for all Part A Medicare-eligible hospice care and respite care expenses.

Additional Features

Plan C includes the core Medigap coverage, plus four extra benefits.

- Your $1,260 Medicare Part A in-patient hospital deductible (per benefit period in 2015)
- Your coinsurance amount for skilled nursing facility care for the 21st through the 100th day of your stay (the amount is $157.50 per day in 2015).
- Your Medicare Part B deductible ($147 per calendar year in 2015).
- Any emergency care you may require when you are in a foreign country after a $250 deductible. This benefit pays 80% of the cost of your care for the first 60 days of each trip, up to $50,000 in your lifetime.

If you feel that Plan C fits your needs, take a look at the two tables below to find out what price you should expect to be charged for this plan. The tables outline the typical annual premiums charged for Plan C depending on age and gender. These rates are based on our 2014 nationwide collection of insurance premiums.

PLAN C

Female

Age	Average Premium	Lowest Premium	Highest Premium	Median Premium
65	$2,085	$1,010	$6,173	$2,054
70	$2,452	$1,159	$6,676	$2,439
75	$2,807	$1,319	$7,400	$2,549
80	$3,042	$1,380	$8,006	$3,108
85	$3,239	$1,380	$8,798	$3,316
90	$3,329	$1,380	$8,877	$3,433
95	$3,393	$1,380	$9,289	$3,060

Male

Age	Average Premium	Lowest Premium	Highest Premium	Median Premium
65	$2,224	$1,014	$7,095	$2,098
70	$2,616	$1,232	$7,673	$2,439
75	$2,993	$1,380	$8,505	$2,830
80	$3,262	$1,380	$9,203	$3,108
85	$3,487	$1,380	$10,644	$3,316
90	$3,584	$1,380	$10,644	$3,433
95	$3,656	$1,380	$10,677	$3,517

Basic Medigap Coverage
PLAN D

If you stay in the hospital for longer than 60 days, but less than 90 days, Plan D covers Medicare Part A coinsurance amount of $315 per day (in 2015) for each benefit period.

For each Medicare "hospital reserve day" you use, Plan D pays the $630 (in 2015) per day Medicare Part A coinsurance amount. "Hospital reserve days" are 60 nonrenewable hospital days that Medicare provides you which can only be used once in a lifetime. After all Medicare hospital benefits are exhausted, Plan D will cover 100% of Medicare Part A eligible hospital expenses.

If the need arises, Plan D covers costs for the first three pints of blood or equivalent quantities of packed red blood cells received each year in connection with Medicare Parts A and B covered services. Once you have met this 3-pint blood deductible under Medicare Part A, it does not have to be met again under Part B.

After your $147 annual Medicare Part B deductible is met, Plan D will cover the coinsurance amount of Medicare approved medical services, which is generally 20% of the approved amount

Plan D now includes coverage of cost sharing for all Part A Medicare-eligible hospice care and respite care expenses.

Additional Features

Plan D includes the core Medigap coverage, plus three extra benefits.

- Your $1,260 Medicare Part A in-patient hospital deductible (per benefit period in 2015).
- Your coinsurance amount for skilled nursing facility care for the 21st through the 100th day of your stay (the amount is $157.50 per day in 2015).
- Any emergency care you may require when you are in a foreign country after a $250 deductible. This benefit pays 80% of the cost of your care for the first 60 days of each trip, up to $50,000 in your lifetime.

If you feel that Plan D fits your needs, take a look at the two tables below to find out what price you should expect to be charged for this plan. The tables outline the typical annual premiums charged for Plan D depending on age and gender. These rates are based on our 2014 nationwide collection of insurance premiums.

PLAN D

Female

Age	Average Premium	Lowest Premium	Highest Premium	Median Premium
65	$1,787	$894	$4,617	$1,868
70	$2,065	$1,026	$4,981	$1,934
75	$2,359	$1,172	$5,564	$2,490
80	$2,630	$1,315	$6,126	$2,440
85	$2,857	$1,432	$6,535	$2,644
90	$2,968	$1,432	$6,867	$2,763
95	$3,057	$1,432	$7,115	$3,306

Male

Age	Average Premium	Lowest Premium	Highest Premium	Median Premium
65	$1,959	$1,027	$5,307	$1,868
70	$2,293	$1,179	$5,727	$2,157
75	$2,637	$1,347	$6,396	$2,490
80	$2,948	$1,432	$7,044	$2,806
85	$3,202	$1,432	$7,515	$3,041
90	$3,326	$1,432	$7,897	$3,193
95	$3,425	$1,432	$8,184	$3,306

Basic Medigap Coverage
PLAN F

If you stay in the hospital for longer than 60 days, but less than 90 days, Plan F covers Medicare Part A coinsurance amount of $315 per day (in 2015) for each benefit period.

For each Medicare "hospital reserve day" you use, Plan F pays the $630 (in 2015) per day Medicare Part A coinsurance amount. "Hospital reserve days" are 60 nonrenewable hospital days that Medicare provides you which can only be used once in a lifetime. After all Medicare hospital benefits are exhausted, Plan F will cover 100% of Medicare Part A eligible hospital expenses.

If the need arises, Plan F covers costs for the first three pints of blood or equivalent quantities of packed red blood cells received each year in connection with Medicare Parts A and B covered services. Once you have met this 3-pint blood deductible under Medicare Part A, it does not have to be met again under Part B.

After your $147 annual Medicare Part B deductible is met, Plan F will cover the coinsurance amount of Medicare approved medical services, which is generally 20% of the approved amount. A high deductible option is available, requiring you to pay the first $2,180 of Medicare covered costs before your Medigap policy pays anything.

Plan F now includes coverage of cost sharing for all Part A Medicare-eligible hospice care and respite care expenses.

Additional Features

Plan F includes all of the basic Medigap coverage plus five extra benefits.

- Your $1,260 Medicare Part A in-patient hospital deductible (per benefit period in 2015).
- Your coinsurance amount for skilled nursing facility care for the 21st through the 100th day of your stay (the amount is $157.50 per day in 2015).
- Any emergency care you may require when you are in a foreign country after a $250 deductible. This benefit pays 80% of the cost of your care for the first 60 days of each trip, up to $50,000 in your lifetime.
- Your deductible for Medicare Part B ($147 in 2015).
- 100% of any excess charges under Medicare Part B. This is the difference between the approved amount for Part B services and the actual charges (up to the charge limitations set by either Medicare or state law).

If you feel that Plan F fits your needs, take a look at the two tables below to find out what price you should expect to be charged for this plan. The tables outline the typical annual premiums charged for Plan F depending on age and gender. These rates are based on our 2014 nationwide collection of insurance premiums.

PLAN F

Female

Age	Average Premium	Lowest Premium	Highest Premium	Median Premium
65	$2,009	$976	$6,207	$1,797
70	$2,350	$1,188	$6,711	$2,206
75	$2,704	$1,352	$7,433	$2,788
80	$2,960	$1,467	$8,036	$3,088
85	$3,177	$1,467	$8,525	$3,020
90	$3,303	$1,467	$8,887	$3,023
95	$3,403	$1,467	$9,286	$3,115

Male

Age	Average Premium	Lowest Premium	Highest Premium	Median Premium
65	$2,173	$1,010	$7,134	$2,006
70	$2,540	$1,224	$7,714	$2,399
75	$2,925	$1,467	$8,544	$2,788
80	$3,219	$1,467	$9,237	$3,088
85	$3,466	$1,467	$9,799	$3,334
90	$3,592	$1,467	$10,215	$3,473
95	$3,703	$1,467	$10,673	$3,581

Basic Medigap Coverage
PLAN F with High Deductible

If you stay in the hospital for longer than 60 days, but less than 90 days, Plan F-High Deductible covers Medicare Part A coinsurance amount of $315 per day (in 2015) for each benefit period. For each Medicare "hospital reserve day" you use, Plan F-High Deductible pays the $630 (in 2015) per day Medicare Part A coinsurance amount. "Hospital reserve days" are 60 nonrenewable hospital days that Medicare provides you which can only be used once in a lifetime. After all Medicare hospital benefits are exhausted, Plan F – High Deductible will cover 100% of Medicare Part A eligible hospital expenses.

If the need arises, Plan F-High Deductible covers costs for the first three pints of blood or equivalent quantities of packed red blood cells received each year in connection with Medicare Parts A and B covered services. Once you have met this 3-pint blood deductible under Medicare Part A, it does not have to be met again under Part B.

After your $147 annual Medicare Part B deductible is met, Plan F-High Deductible will cover the coinsurance amount of Medicare approved medical services, which is generally 20% of the approved amount.

Plan F High Deductible includes coverage of cost sharing for all Part A Medicare-eligible hospice care and respite care expenses.

Additional Features

Plan F includes all of the basic Medigap coverage plus five extra benefits.

- Your $1,260 Medicare Part A in-patient hospital deductible (per benefit period in 2015).
- Your coinsurance amount for skilled nursing facility care for the 21st through the 100th day of your stay (the amount is $157.50 per day in 2015).
- Any emergency care you may require when you are in a foreign country after a $250 deductible. This benefit pays 80% of the cost of your care for the first 60 days of each trip, up to $50,000 in your lifetime.
- Your deductible for Medicare Part B ($147 in 2015).
- 100% of any excess charges under Medicare Part B. This is the difference between the approved amount for Part B services and the actual charges (up to the charge limitations set by either Medicare or state law).

Important Notice:

You must meet a $2,180 deductible of unpaid Medicare eligible expenses before benefits are paid by this plan.

If you feel that Plan F with High Deductible fits your needs, take a look at the two tables below to find out what price you should expect to be charged for this plan. The tables outline the typical annual premiums charged for Plan F depending on age and gender. These rates are based on our 2014 nationwide collection of insurance premiums.

PLAN F: with High Deductible

Female

Age	Average Premium	Lowest Premium	Highest Premium	Median Premium
65	$632	$250	$2,004	$648
70	$736	$258	$2,143	$666
75	$863	$298	$2,368	$832
80	$979	$350	$2,547	$1,008
85	$1,071	$350	$2,696	$1,090
90	$1,095	$350	$2,827	$1,120
95	$1,117	$350	$2,924	$987

Male

Age	Average Premium	Lowest Premium	Highest Premium	Median Premium
65	$677	$250	$2,323	$648
70	$794	$258	$2,814	$762
75	$940	$298	$3,415	$900
80	$1,073	$350	$4,074	$1,008
85	$1,180	$350	$4,792	$1,090
90	$1,188	$350	$5,637	$1,120
95	$1,211	$350	$6,118	$1,149

Basic Medigap Coverage
PLAN G

If you stay in the hospital for longer than 60 days, but less than 90 days, Plan G covers Medicare Part A coinsurance amount of $315 per day (in 2015) for each benefit period. For each Medicare "hospital reserve day" you use, Plan G pays the $630 (in 2015) per day Medicare Part A coinsurance amount. "Hospital reserve days" are 60 nonrenewable hospital days that Medicare provides you which can only be used once in a lifetime. After all Medicare hospital benefits are exhausted, Plan G will cover 100% of Medicare Part A eligible hospital expenses.

If the need arises, Plan G covers costs for the first three pints of blood or equivalent quantities of packed red blood cells received each year in connection with Medicare Parts A and B covered services. Once you have met this 3-pint blood deductible under Medicare Part A, it does not have to be met again under Part B.

After your $147 annual Medicare Part B deductible is met, Plan G will cover the coinsurance amount of Medicare approved medical services, which is generally 20% of the approved amount.

Plan G now includes coverage of cost sharing for all Part A Medicare-eligible hospice care and respite care

Additional Features

Plan G includes the core Medigap coverage plus four extra benefits.
- Your $1,260 Medicare Part A in-patient hospital deductible (per benefit period in 2015).
- Your coinsurance amount for skilled nursing care for the 21st through the 100th day of your stay (the amount is $157.50 per day in 2015).
- Any emergency care you may require when you are in a foreign country after a $250 deductible. This benefit pays 80% of the cost of your care for the first 60 days of each trip, up to $50,000 in your lifetime.
- 100% of any excess charges under Medicare Part B. Excess charges are the difference between the approved amount for Part B services and the actual charges (up to the charge limitations set by either Medicare or state law).

If you feel that Plan G fits your needs, take a look at the two tables below to find out what price you should expect to be charged for this plan. The tables outline the typical annual premiums charged for Plan G depending on age and gender. These rates are based on our 2014 nationwide collection of insurance premiums.

PLAN G

Female

Age	Average Premium	Lowest Premium	Highest Premium	Median Premium
65	$1,665	$807	$5,839	$1,734
70	$1,919	$926	$6,322	$2,023
75	$2,213	$1,056	$7,022	$2,055
80	$2,491	$1,181	$7,626	$2,315
85	$2,747	$1,287	$8,125	$2,456
90	$2,932	$1,336	$8,497	$2,629
95	$3,059	$1,336	$8,906	$2,831

Male

Age	Average Premium	Lowest Premium	Highest Premium	Median Premium
65	$1,819	$4927	$6,712	$1,734
70	$2,114	$1,064	$7,267	$2,023
75	$2,454	$1,213	$8,071	$2,362
80	$2,773	$1,336	$8,765	$2,665
85	$3,057	$1,336	$9,339	$2,930
90	$3,260	$1,336	$9,766	$3,118
95	$3,404	$1,336	$10,236	$3,255

Basic Medigap Coverage
PLAN K

If you stay in the hospital for longer than 60 days, but less than 90 days, Plan K covers Medicare Part A coinsurance amount of $315 per day (in 2015) for each benefit period.

For each Medicare "hospital reserve day" you use, Plan K pays the $630 (in 2015) per day Medicare Part A coinsurance amount. "Hospital reserve days" are 60 nonrenewable hospital days that Medicare provides you which can only be used once in a lifetime. After all Medicare hospital benefits are exhausted, Plan K will cover 100% of Medicare Part A eligible hospital expenses up to 365 days.

If the need arises, Plan K covers 50% of the costs for the first three pints of blood or equivalent quantities of packed red blood cells received each year in connection with Medicare Parts A and B covered services. Once you have met this 3-pint blood deductible under Medicare Part A, it does not have to be met again under Part B.

After your $147 annual Medicare Part B deductible is met, Plan K will cover 50% of the coinsurance amount of Medicare approved medical services, which is generally 20% of the approved amount.

Additional Features

Plan K includes four additional benefits.

- 50% of your $1,260 Medicare Part A in-patient hospital deductible (per benefit period in 2015).
- 50% of your coinsurance amount for skilled nursing facility care for the 21st through the 100th day of your stay (the amount is $157.50 per day in 2015).
- 100% coinsurance for medicare-covered preventive medical care. Preventive care would include physical examinations, flu shots, serum cholesterol screening, hearing tests, diabetes screening, and thyroid function tests.
- 50% of hospice cost-sharing for all Part A Medicare covered expenses and respite care.

Note: There is a $4,940 out-of-pocket annual limit. Once you meet the annual limit, the plans pays 100% of the Medicare Part A and Part B co-payments and coinsurance for the rest of the calendar year. "Excess charges" are not covered and do not count toward the out-of-pocket limit.

If you feel that Plan K fits your needs, take a look at the two tables below to find out what price you should expect to be charged for this plan. The tables outline the typical annual premiums charged for Plan K depending on age and gender. These rates are based on our 2014 nationwide collection of insurance premiums.

PLAN K

Female

Age	Average Premium	Lowest Premium	Highest Premium	Median Premium
65	$948	$456	$2,471	$964
70	$1,105	$538	$2,916	$1,125
75	$1,245	$546	$3,377	$1,272
80	$1,342	$546	$3,835	$1,225
85	$1,426	$546	$4,232	$1,496
90	$1,436	$546	$4,232	$1,342
95	$1,452	$546	$4,232	$1,494

Male

Age	Average Premium	Lowest Premium	Highest Premium	Median Premium
65	$1,003	$456	$2,477	$964
70	$1,168	$553	$3,008	$1,125
75	$1,317	$546	$3,655	$1,272
80	$1,435	$546	$4,315	$1,382
85	$1,538	$546	$4,999	$1,496
90	$1,525	$546	$4,999	$1,491
95	$1,544	$546	$4,999	$1,494

Basic Medigap Coverage
PLAN L

If you stay in the hospital for longer than 60 days, but less than 90 days, Plan L covers Medicare Part A coinsurance amount of $315 per day (in 2015) for each benefit period.

For each Medicare "hospital reserve day" you use, Plan L pays the $630 (in 2015) per day Medicare Part A coinsurance amount. "Hospital reserve days" are 60 nonrenewable hospital days that Medicare provides you which can only be used once in a lifetime. After all Medicare hospital benefits are exhausted, Plan L will cover 100% of Medicare Part A eligible hospital expenses up to 365 days.

If the need arises, Plan L covers 75% of the costs for the first three pints of blood or equivalent quantities of packed red blood cells received each year in connection with Medicare Parts A and B covered services. Once you have met this 3-pint blood deductible under Medicare Part A, it does not have to be met again under Part B.

After your $147 annual Medicare Part B deductible is met, Plan L will cover 75% of the coinsurance amount of Medicare approved medical services, which is generally 20% of the approved amount.

Additional Features

Plan L includes four additional benefits.

- 75% of your $1,260 Medicare Part A in-patient hospital deductible (per benefit period in 2015).
- 75% of your coinsurance amount for skilled nursing facility care for the 21st through the 100th day of your stay (the amount is $157.50 per day in 2015).
- 100% coinsurance for medicare-covered preventive medical care. Preventive care would include physical examinations, flu shots, serum cholesterol screening, hearing tests, diabetes screening, and thyroid function tests.
- 75% of hospice cost-sharing for all Part A Medicare covered expenses and respite care.

Note: There is a $2,470 out-of-pocket annual limit. Once you meet the annual limit, the plans pays 100% of the Medicare Part A and Part B co-payments and coinsurance for the rest of the calendar year. "Excess charges" are not covered and do not count toward the out-of-pocket limit.

If you feel that Plan L fits your needs, take a look at the two tables below to find out what price you should expect to be charged for this plan. The tables outline the typical annual premiums charged for Plan L depending on age and gender. These rates are based on our 2014 nationwide collection of insurance premiums.

PLAN L

Female

Age	Average Premium	Lowest Premium	Highest Premium	Median Premium
65	$1,385	$773	$3,158	$1,403
70	$1,635	$938	$3,728	$1,631
75	$1,852	$1,104	$4,318	$1,876
80	$1,995	$1,104	$4,905	$1,867
85	$2,115	$1,104	$5,414	$2,186
90	$2,158	$1,104	$5,414	$2,148
95	$2,190	$1,104	$5,414	$2,157

Male

Age	Average Premium	Lowest Premium	Highest Premium	Median Premium
65	$1,464	$773	$3,288	$1,403
70	$1,720	$938	$3,846	$1,631
75	$1,949	$1,104	$4,674	$1,876
80	$2,118	$1,104	$5,520	$1,056
85	$2,266	$1,104	$6,396	$2,186
90	$2,283	$1,104	$6,396	$2,148
95	$2,318	$1,104	$6,396	$2,157

Basic Medigap Coverage
PLAN M

If you stay in the hospital for longer than 60 days, but less than 90 days, Plan M covers the Medicare Part A coinsurance amount, $315 per day (in 2015) for each benefit period.

For each Medicare "hospital reserve day" you use, Plan M pays the Medicare Part A coinsurance amount, $630 (in 2015) per day. "Hospital reserve days" are 60 nonrenewable hospital days that Medicare provides you which can only be used once in a lifetime. After all Medicare hospital benefits are exhausted, Plan M will cover 100% of Medicare Part A eligible hospital expenses.

If the need arises, Plan M covers costs for the first three pints of blood or equivalent quantities of packed red blood cells received each year in connection with Medicare Parts A and B covered services. Once you have met this 3-pint blood deductible under Medicare Part A, it does not have to be met again under Part B.

After your $147 annual Medicare Part B deductible is met, Plan M will cover the coinsurance amount of Medicare approved medical services, which is generally 20% of the approved amount.

Coverage of cost sharing for all Part A Medicare eligible hospice care and respite care expense is included.

Additional Features

Plan M includes the core Medigap coverage, plus three extra benefits.

- 50% of your Medicare Part A in-patient hospital deductible ($1,260 per benefit period in 2015).
- Your coinsurance amount for skilled nursing facility care for the 21st through the 100th day of your stay (the amount is $157.50 per day in 2015).
- Any emergency care you may require when you are in a foreign country after a $250 deductible. This benefit pays 80% of the cost of your care for the first 60 days of each trip, up to $50,000 in your lifetime.

If you feel that Plan M fits your needs, take a look at the two tables below to find out what price you should expect to be charged for this plan. The tables outline the typical annual premiums charged for Plan M depending on age and gender. These rates are based on our 2014 nationwide collection of insurance premiums.

PLAN M

Female

Age	Average Premium	Lowest Premium	Highest Premium	Median Premium
65	$1,585	$810	$4,625	$1,634
70	$1,857	$992	$4,625	$1,731
75	$2,164	$1,177	$4,984	$2,033
80	$2,451	$1,337	$5,384	$2,573
85	$2,700	$1,453	$5,714	$2,814
90	$2,904	$1,532	$5,997	$2,822
95	$3,020	$1,542	$6,480	$2,657

Male

Age	Average Premium	Lowest Premium	Highest Premium	Median Premium
65	$1,714	$810	$4,777	$1,634
70	$2,016	$1,079	$5,155	$1,924
75	$2,361	$1,353	$5,732	$2,259
80	$2,681	$1,358	$6,194	$2,573
85	$2,954	$1,542	$6,567	$2,814
90	$3,175	$1,542	$6,895	$2,970
95	$3,302	$1,542	$7,200	$3,058

Basic Medigap Coverage
PLAN N

If you stay in the hospital for longer than 60 days, but less than 90 days, Plan N covers the Medicare Part A coinsurance amount, $315 per day (in 2015) for each benefit period.

For each Medicare "hospital reserve day" you use, Plan N pays the Medicare Part A coinsurance amount, $630 (in 2015) per day. "Hospital reserve days" are 60 nonrenewable hospital days that Medicare provides you which can only be used once in a lifetime. After all Medicare hospital benefits are exhausted, Plan N will cover 100% of Medicare Part A eligible hospital expenses.

If the need arises, Plan N covers costs for the first three pints of blood or equivalent quantities of packed red blood cells received each year in connection with Medicare Parts A and B covered services. Once you have met this 3-pint blood deductible under Medicare Part A, it does not have to be met again under Part B.

After your $147 annual Medicare Part B deductible is met, Plan N will cover the coinsurance amount of Medicare approved medical services, which is generally 20% of the approved amount.

Coverage of cost sharing for all Part A Medicare eligible hospice care and respite care expense is included.

Additional Features

Plan N includes the core Medigap coverage, plus four extra features and benefits.
- Your Medicare Part A in-patient hospital deductible ($1,260 per benefit period in 2015).
- You will have a co-payment of up to $20 per physician visit or $50 per Emergency Room visit under Part B. The ER co-pay will be waived if admitted.
- Your coinsurance amount for skilled nursing facility care for the 21st through the 100th day of your stay (the amount is $157.50 per day in 2015).
- Any emergency care you may require when you are in a foreign country after a $250 deductible. This benefit pays 80% of the cost of your care for the first 60 days of each trip, up to $50,000 in your lifetime.

If you feel that Plan N fits your needs, take a look at the two tables below to find out what price you should expect to be charged for this plan. The tables outline the typical annual premiums charged for Plan N depending on age and gender. These rates are based on our 2014 nationwide collection of insurance premiums.

PLAN N

Female

Age	Average Premium	Lowest Premium	Highest Premium	Median Premium
65	$1,379	$713	$5,318	$1,212
70	$1,644	$819	$5,770	$1,430
75	$1,913	$936	$6,436	$1,699
80	$2,116	$1,021	$7,026	$2,196
85	$2,286	$1,073	$7,528	$2,412
90	$2,400	$1,073	$7,935	$2,211
95	$2,481	$1,073	$8,384	$2,285

Male

Age	Average Premium	Lowest Premium	Highest Premium	Median Premium
65	$1,501	$808	$6,113	$1,394
70	$1,788	$941	$6,632	$1,645
75	$2,081	$1,073	$7,398	$1,951
80	$2,3315	$1,073	$8,076	$2,196
85	$2,506	$1,073	$8,653	$2,412
90	$2,632	$1,073	$9,121	$2,542
95	$2,723	$1,073	$9,636	$2,628

Part IV:
Index of Medigap Insurers

Following is a reference list of Medicare supplement insurers with their
Weiss Financial Strength Rating, corporate address, phone number,
and the states in which they are licensed to do business.

RATING	INSURANCE COMPANY NAME	ADDRESS	CITY	STATE	ZIP	PHONE
B+	AETNA LIFE INS CO	151 FARMINGTON AVE	HARTFORD	CT	06156	(860) 273-0123
B+	ALLIANCE HEALTH & LIFE INS CO	2850 W GRAND BLVD,5TH FLOOR	DETROIT	MI	48202	(313) 872-8100
C-	AMALGAMATED LIFE & HEALTH INS CO	333 SOUTH ASHLAND AVENUE	CHICAGO	IL	60607	(312) 738-6113
B	AMERICAN CONTINENTAL INS CO	800 CRESCENT CENTRE DR	FRANKLIN	TN	37067	(800) 264-4000
B+	AMERICAN FAMILY LIFE ASR CO OF COLUM	1932 WYNNTON RD	COLUMBUS	GA	31999	(706) 323-3431
B+	AMERICAN FAMILY MUT INS CO	6000 AMERICAN PKWY	MADISON	WI	53783	(608) 249-2111
B	AMERICAN GENERAL LIFE INS CO	2727-A ALLEN PARKWAY	HOUSTON	TX	77019	(713) 522-1111
B-	AMERICAN NATIONAL LIFE INS CO OF TX	ONE MOODY PLAZA	GALVESTON	TX	77550	(409) 763-4661
D+	AMERICAN PIONEER LIFE INS CO	600 COURTLAND ST	ORLANDO	FL	32804	(407) 628-1776
B	AMERICAN PROGRESSIVE L&H I C OF NY	6 INTERNATIONAL DR SUITE 190	RYE BROOK	NY	10573	(914) 934-8300
B	AMERICAN REPUBLIC CORP INS CO	237 WILLIAM HOWARD TAFT RD	CINCINNATI	OH	45219	(612) 628-1038
A-	AMERICAN REPUBLIC INS CO	601 SIXTH AVE	DES MOINES	IA	50309	(515) 245-2000
B-	AMERICAN RETIREMENT LIFE INS CO	1300 E NINTH ST	CLEVELAND	OH	44114	(512) 451-2224
B	ANTHEM HEALTH PLANS INC	108 LEIGUS RD	WALLINGFORD	CT	06492	(203) 677-4000
A-	ANTHEM HEALTH PLANS OF KENTUCKY INC	13550 TRITON PARK BLVD	LOUISVILLE	KY	40223	(888) 641-5224
B-	ANTHEM HEALTH PLANS OF MAINE INC	2 GANNETT DR	S PORTLAND	ME	04106	(207) 822-7000
B+	ANTHEM HEALTH PLANS OF NEW	3000 GOFFS FALLS RD	MANCHETER	NH	03111	(603) 695-7000
B	ANTHEM HEALTH PLANS OF VIRGINIA	2015 STAPLES MILL RD	RICHMOND	VA	23230	(804) 354-7000
B	ANTHEM INS COMPANIES INC	120 MONUMENT CIRCLE	INDIANAPOLIS	IN	46204	(317) 488-6000
B-	ASURIS NORTHWEST HEALTH	1800 9TH AVE	SEATTLE	WA	98101	(206) 464-3600
A	AUTO-OWNERS LIFE INS CO	6101 ANACAPRI BLVD	LANSING	MI	48917	(517) 323-1200
C	AVALON INS CO	2500 ELMERTON AVE	HARRISBURG	PA	17110	(717) 541-7000
C-	AVERA HEALTH PLANS INC	3816 S ELMWOOD AVE SUITE 100	SIOUX FALLS	SD	57105	(605) 322-4500
D	BANKERS CONSECO LIFE INS CO	11815 N PENNSYLVANIA STREET	CARMEL	IN	46032	(215) 244-1600
B	BANKERS FIDELITY LIFE INS CO	4370 PEACHTREE RD NE	ATLANTA	GA	30319	(404) 266-5500
D+	BANKERS LIFE & CAS CO	222 MERCHANDISE MART PLAZA	CHICAGO	IL	60654	(312) 396-6000
B+	BLUE CARE NETWORK OF MICHIGAN	20500 CIVIC CENTER DRIVE	SOUTHFIELD	MI	48076	(248) 799-6400
B	BLUE CROSS & BLUE SHIELD OF FLORIDA	4800 DEERWOOD CAMPUS PKWY	JACKSONVILLE	FL	32246	(904) 791-6111
A-	BLUE CROSS BLUE SHIELD OF ALABAMA	450 RIVERCHASE PARKWAY E	BIRMINGHAM	AL	35298	(205) 220-2100
A+	BLUE CROSS BLUE SHIELD OF ARIZONA	2444 W LAS PALMARITAS DR	PHOENIX	AZ	85021	(602) 864-4100
B	BLUE CROSS BLUE SHIELD OF GEORGIA	3350 PEACHTREE RD NE	ATLANTA	GA	30326	(404) 842-8000
B	BLUE CROSS BLUE SHIELD OF KANSAS INC	1133 SW TOPEKA BLVD	TOPEKA	KS	66629	(785) 291-7000
B-	BLUE CROSS BLUE SHIELD OF KC	2301 MAIN ST	KANSAS CITY	MO	64108	(816) 395-2222
B	BLUE CROSS BLUE SHIELD OF MA	401 PARK DR	BOSTON	MA	02215	(617) 246-5000
B	BLUE CROSS BLUE SHIELD OF MICHIGAN	600 LAFAYETTE EAST	DETROIT	MI	48226	(313) 225-9000
A	BLUE CROSS BLUE SHIELD OF MINNESOTA	3535 BLUE CROSS RD	EAGAN	MN	55122	(651) 662-8000
B+	BLUE CROSS BLUE SHIELD OF MS, MUTUAL	3545 LAKELAND DR	FLOWOOD	MS	39208	(601) 932-3704
A	BLUE CROSS BLUE SHIELD OF NC	5901 CHAPEL HILL BLVD	DURHAM	NC	27707	(919) 489-7431
A-	BLUE CROSS BLUE SHIELD OF NEBRASKA	1919 AKSARBEN DR	OMAHA	NE	68180	(402) 982-7000
C	BLUE CROSS BLUE SHIELD OF RI	444 WESTMINSTER ST	PROVIDENCE	RI	02903	(401) 459-1000
A-	BLUE CROSS BLUE SHIELD OF SC INC	2501 FARAWAY DR	COLUMBIA	SC	29219	(803) 788-3860
B+	BLUE CROSS BLUE SHIELD OF VERMONT	445 INDUSTRIAL LN	MONTPELIER	VT	05602	(802) 223-6131
B-	BLUE CROSS BLUE SHIELD OF WISCONSIN	6775 W WASHINGTON ST	MILWAUKEE	WI	53214	(414) 459-5000
B+	BLUE CROSS BLUE SHIELD OF WYOMING	4000 HOUSE AVE	CHEYENNE	WY	82001	(307) 634-1393
A-	BLUE CROSS OF IDAHO HEALTH SERVICE	3000 E PINE AVE	MERIDIAN	ID	83642	(208) 345-4550
A	BLUECROSS BLUESHIELD OF TENNESSEE	1 CAMERON HILL CIR	CHATTANOOGA	TN	37402	(423) 535-5600
C	CAPITAL ADVANTAGE INS CO	2500 ELMERTON AVENUE	HARRISBURG	PA	17110	(717) 541-7000
B-	CAPITAL BLUE CROSS	2500 ELMERTON AVE	HARRISBURG	PA	17110	(717) 541-7000
B	CAREFIRST OF MARYLAND INC	10455 MILL RUN CIRCLE	OWINGS MILLS	MD	21117	(410) 581-3000
E	CDPHP UNIVERSAL BENEFITS INC	500 PATROON CREEK BLVD	ALBANY	NY	12206	(518) 641-3000
C	CELTIC INS CO	233 S WACKER DR SUITE 700	CHICAGO	IL	60606	(312) 332-5401
C+	CENTRAL RESERVE LIFE INS CO	1300 E NINTH ST	CLEVELAND	OH	44114	(512) 451-2224

RATING	INSURANCE COMPANY NAME	ADDRESS	CITY	STATE	ZIP	PHONE
A-	CENTRAL STATES H & L CO OF OMAHA	1212 N 96TH ST	OMAHA	NE	68114	(402) 397-1111
B+	CENTRAL STATES INDEMNITY CO OF OMAHA	1212 N 96TH ST	OMAHA	NE	68114	(402) 997-8000
C	CENTRAL UNITED LIFE INS CO	2727 ALLEN PARKWAY,6TH FLOOR	HOUSTON	TX	77019	(713) 529-0045
B-	CHRISTIAN FIDELITY LIFE INS CO	2721 N CENTRAL AVE	PHOENIX	AZ	85004	(972) 937-4420
D+	COLONIAL PENN LIFE INS CO	399 MARKET ST	PHILADELPHIA	PA	19181	(215) 928-8000
B	COLUMBIAN MUTUAL LIFE INS CO	VESTAL PARKWAY EAST	BINGHAMTON	NY	13902	(607) 724-2472
C+	COMBINED INS CO OF AMERICA	1000 NORTH MILWAUKEE AVENUE	GLENVIEW	IL	60025	(312) 701-3000
B+	COMMUNITY INS CO	4361 IRWIN SIMPSON RD	MASON	OH	45040	(513) 872-8100
B-	CONNECTICUT GENERAL LIFE INS CO	900 COTTAGE GROVE RD,S-330	BLOOMFIELD	CT	06002	(860) 726-7234
D+	CONSECO LIFE INS CO	11825 N PENNSYLVANIA ST	CARMEL	IN	46032	(317) 817-6400
C+	CONSTITUTION LIFE INS CO	4211 NORBOURNE BLVD	LOUISVILLE	KY	40207	(214) 954-7111
C	CONTINENTAL GENERAL INS CO	8901 INDIAN HILLS DR	OMAHA	NE	68114	(402) 397-3200
B	CONTINENTAL LIFE INS CO OF BRENTWOOD	800 CRESCENT CENTRE DR	FRANKLIN	TN	37067	(800) 264-4000
A+	COUNTRY LIFE INS CO	1701 N TOWANDA AVE	BLOOMINGTON	IL	61701	(309) 821-3000
B+	COVENTRY HEALTH & LIFE INS CO	550 MARYVILLE CENTER DR #300	ST LOUIS	MO	63141	(800) 843-7421
B	DEAN HEALTH PLAN INC	1277 DEMING WAY	MADISON	WI	53717	(608) 836-1400
B-	EMI HEALTH	852 E ARROWHEAD LN	MURRAY	UT	84107	(801) 262-7476
B-	EMPIRE HEALTHCHOICE ASSURANCE INC	1 LIBERTY PLAZA 165 BROADWAY	NEW YORK	NY	10006	(212) 476-1000
C+	EQUITABLE LIFE & CASUALTY INS CO	3 TRIAD CENTER SUITE 200	SALT LAKE CITY	UT	84180	(801) 579-3400
A	EXCELLUS HEALTH PLAN INC	165 COURT ST	ROCHESTER	NY	14647	(585) 454-1700
E	FALLON HEALTH & LIFE ASR CO	10 CHESTNUT ST	WORCESTER	MA	01608	(508) 799-2100
C	FAMILY LIFE INS CO	1200 6TH AVE PARK PLACE BLDG	SEATTLE	WA	98101	(512) 404-5284
B	FIRST COMMUNITY HEALTH PLAN INC	699 GALLATIN ST STE A2	HUNTSVILLE	AL	35801	(256) 532-2780
B+	FIRST UNITED AMERICAN LIFE INS CO	1020 7TH NORTH ST	LIVERPOOL	NY	13088	(315) 451-2544
B-	FORETHOUGHT LIFE INS CO	FORETHOUGHT CENTER	BATESVILLE	IN	47006	(812) 933-6600
C	GEISINGER INDEMNITY INS CO	100 N ACADEMY AVE	DANVILLE	PA	17822	(570) 271-8777
B-	GENWORTH LIFE & ANNUITY INS CO	6610 W BROAD ST	RICHMOND	VA	23230	(804) 662-2400
B-	GENWORTH LIFE INS CO	6604 WEST BROAD STREET	RICHMOND	VA	23230	(804) 662-2400
A-	GERBER LIFE INS CO	1311 MAMARONECK AVE	WHITE PLAINS	NY	10605	(877) 778-0839
B	GLOBE LIFE & ACCIDENT INS CO	10306 REGENCY PARKWAY BLDG	OMAHA	NE	68114	(405) 270-1400
B	GOLDEN RULE INS CO	712 ELEVENTH ST	LAWRENCEVILLE	IL	62439	(618) 943-8000
B+	GOVERNMENT PERSONNEL MUTUAL L I C	2211 NE LOOP 410	SAN ANTONIO	TX	78217	(210) 357-2222
B-	GREAT AMERICAN LIFE INS CO	250 E FIFTH ST	CINCINNATI	OH	45202	(513) 357-3300
D+	GROUP HEALTH COOP OF S CENTRAL WI	1265 JOHN Q HAMMONS DR	MADISON	WI	53717	(608) 251-4156
D	GROUP HEALTH INCORPORATED	441 NINTH AVE	NEW YORK	NY	10001	(212) 615-0000
B-	GROUP HOSP & MEDICAL SERVICES INC	840 FIRST STREET NE	WASHINGTON	DC	20065	(410) 581-3000
B	GUARANTEE TRUST LIFE INS CO	1275 MILWAUKEE AVE	GLENVIEW	IL	60025	(847) 699-0600
C-	HARTFORD LIFE & ACCIDENT INS CO	200 HOPMEADOW ST	SIMSBURY	CT	06070	(860) 547-5000
C+	HARTFORD LIFE INS CO	200 HOPMEADOW ST	SIMSBURY	CT	06070	(860) 547-5000
A	HEALTH ALLIANCE MEDICAL PLANS	301 S VINE	URBANA	IL	61801	(217) 337-8406
A+	HEALTH CARE SVC CORP A MUT LEG RES	300 EAST RANDOLPH STREET	CHICAGO	IL	60601	(312) 653-6000
E	HEALTH NET HEALTH PLAN OF OREGON INC	13221 SW 68TH PKWY., STE 200	TIGARD	OR	97223	(888) 802-7001
B	HEALTH NET LIFE INS CO	225 N MAIN ST	PUEBLO	CO	81003	(719) 585-8017
B	HEALTH TRADITION HEALTH PLAN	1808 E MAIN ST	ONALASKA	WI	54650	(507) 538-5212
B+	HEALTHNOW NY INC	257 W GENESEE ST	BUFFALO	NY	14202	(716) 887-6900
A-	HEALTHY ALLIANCE LIFE INS CO	1831 CHESTNUT ST	ST LOUIS	MO	63103	(314) 923-4444
C	HEARTLAND NATIONAL LIFE INS CO	1060 E COUNTY LINE RD #3A-179	RIDGELAND	MS	39157	(816) 478-0120
B	HIGHMARK BCBSD INC	800 DELAWARE AVE	WILMINGTON	DE	19801	(800) 292-9525
B-	HIGHMARK INC	1800 CENTER ST	CAMP HILL	PA	17089	(412) 544-7000
B+	HIGHMARK WEST VIRGINIA INC	614 MARKET ST	PARKERSBURG	WV	26102	(304) 424-7700
B+	HORIZON HEALTHCARE SERVICES INC	3 PENN PLAZA EAST, PP-15D	NEWARK	NJ	07105	(973) 466-5607
B	HORIZON INS CO	3 PENN PLAZA EAST PP-15D	NEWARK	NJ	07105	(973) 466-5607

RATING	INSURANCE COMPANY NAME	ADDRESS	CITY	STATE	ZIP	PHONE
C	HOSPITAL SERV ASSN OF NORTH EAST PA	19 N MAIN ST	WILKES-BARRE	PA	18711	(800) 829-8599
B-	HPHC INS CO INC	93 WORCESTER ST	WELLESLEY	MA	02481	(781) 263-6000
B	HUMANA HEALTH BENEFIT PLAN LA	1 GALLERIA BLVD SUITE 850	METAIRIE	LA	70001	(504) 219-6600
C	HUMANA HEALTH INS CO OF FL INC	3501 SW 160TH AVENUE	MIRAMAR	FL	33027	(305) 626-5616
U	HUMANA INS CO					
B-	HUMANA INS CO OF KENTUCKY	500 W MAIN ST	LOUISVILLE	KY	40202	(502) 580-1000
B	HUMANA INS CO OF NEW YORK	125 WOLF RD	ALBANY	NY	12205	(518) 435-0459
C+	IDEALIFE INS CO	695 EAST MAIN STREET	STAMFORD	CT	06904	(203) 352-3000
C	INDEPENDENCE BLUE CROSS	1901 MARKET ST	PHILADELPHIA	PA	19103	(215) 241-2400
U	INTER-COUNTY HOSPITALIZATION PLAN	720 BLAIR MILL RD	HORSHAM	PA	19044	(215) 657-8900
C-	JEFFERSON NATIONAL LIFE INS CO	350 N ST PAUL ST	DALLAS	TX	75201	(502) 587-7626
C	KANAWHA INS CO	210 S WHITE ST	LANCASTER	SC	29721	(803) 283-5300
C	KPS HEALTH PLANS	400 WARREN AVE	BREMERTON	WA	98310	(360) 377-5576
A+	LA HEALTH SERVICE & INDEMNITY CO	5525 REITZ AVE	BATON ROUGE	LA	70809	(225) 295-3307
B	LIBERTY NATIONAL LIFE INS CO	10306 REGENCY PARKWAY DR	OMAHA	NE	68114	(205) 325-2722
B	LIFEWISE HEALTH PLAN OF OREGON	2020 SW 4TH ST SUITE 1000	PORTLAND	OR	97201	(503) 295-6707
B-	LINCOLN HERITAGE LIFE INS CO	GOVERNMENT CTR 200 PLEASANT	MALDEN	MA	02148	(602) 957-1650
C	LOYAL AMERICAN LIFE INS CO	525 VINE STREET,20TH FLOOR	CINCINNATI	OH	45202	(800) 633-6752
C	MARQUETTE NATIONAL LIFE INS CO	500 N AKARD	DALLAS	TX	75201	(214) 954-7111
A-	MEDICAL MUTUAL OF OHIO	2060 E NINTH ST	CLEVELAND	OH	44115	(216) 687-7000
B	MEDICO INS CO	1515 S 75TH ST	OMAHA	NE	68124	(402) 391-6900
B+	MUTUAL OF OMAHA INS CO	MUTUAL OF OMAHA PLAZA	OMAHA	NE	68175	(402) 342-7600
B	NATIONWIDE LIFE INS CO	ONE NATIONWIDE PLAZA	COLUMBUS	OH	43215	(800) 882-2822
C	NEW ERA LIFE INS CO	200 WESTLAKE PARK BLVD	HOUSTON	TX	77079	(713) 368-7200
C	NEW ERA LIFE INS CO OF THE MIDWEST	200 WESTLAKE PARK BLVD	HOUSTON	TX	77079	(713) 368-7200
A-	NEW YORK LIFE INS CO	51 MADISON AVE	NEW YORK	NY	10010	(212) 576-7000
C+	NORIDIAN MUTUAL INS CO	4510 13TH AVE S	FARGO	ND	58121	(701) 282-1100
C	NORTH AMERICAN INS CO	1232 FOURIER DRIVE	MADISON	WI	53717	(608) 662-1232
C	OLD SURETY LIFE INS CO	5235 N LINCOLN	OKLAHOMA CITY	OK	73105	(405) 523-2112
B-	OMAHA INS CO	MUTUAL OF OMAHA PLAZA	OMAHA	NE	68175	(402) 342-7600
B-	OXFORD LIFE INS CO	2721 N CENTRAL AVE	PHOENIX	AZ	85004	(602) 263-6666
C+	PACIFICARE LIFE & HEALTH INS CO	23046 AVENIDA DELA CARLOTA 700	LAGUNA HILLS	CA	92653	(714) 226-3321
B-	PARAMOUNT INS CO	1901 INDIAN WOOD CIR	MAUMEE	OH	43537	(419) 887-2500
B	PEKIN LIFE INS CO	2505 COURT ST	PEKIN	IL	61558	(309) 346-1161
C	PENNSYLVANIA LIFE INS CO	27 N FRONT ST	HARRISBURG	PA	17101	(401) 770-7699
B-	PHILADELPHIA AMERICAN LIFE INS CO	3121 BUFFALO SPEEDWAY	HOUSTON	TX	77098	(281) 368-7247
B-	PHYSICIANS BENEFITS TRUST LIFE INS	20 N MICHIGAN AVE STE 700	CHICAGO	IL	60602	(816) 395-2750
A-	PHYSICIANS LIFE INS CO	2600 DODGE ST	OMAHA	NE	68131	(402) 633-1000
A+	PHYSICIANS MUTUAL INS CO	2600 DODGE ST	OMAHA	NE	68131	(402) 633-1000
D	PHYSICIANS PLUS INS CORP	2650 NOVATION PARKWAY	MADISON	WI	53713	(608) 282-8900
A-	PREMERA BLUE CROSS	7001 220TH ST SW	MOUNTLAKE TERRACE	WA	98043	(425) 918-4000
B+	PRINCIPAL LIFE INS CO	711 HIGH ST	DES MOINES	IA	50392	(515) 247-5111
B	PRIORITY HEALTH	1231 E BELTLINE AVE NE	GRAND RAPIDS	MI	49525	(616) 942-0954
A+	PROVIDENCE HEALTH PLAN	4400 NE HALSEY BLDG 2 STE 690	PORTLAND	OR	97213	(503) 574-7500
B-	PROVIDENT AMER LIFE & HEALTH INS CO	250 E FIFTH ST	CINCINNATI	OH	45202	(913) 722-1110
D+	PURITAN LIFE INS CO OF AMERICA	8601 N SCOTTSDALE RD #300	SCOTTSDALE	AZ	85253	(800) 513-3243
C	PYRAMID LIFE INS CO	6201 JOHNSON DR	SHAWNEE MISSION	KS	66202	(913) 722-1110
B+	REGENCE BL CROSS BL SHIELD OREGON	100 SW MARKET ST	PORTLAND	OR	97201	(503) 225-5221
B	REGENCE BLUE CROSS BLUE SHIELD OF UT	2980 E COTTONWOOD PKWY	SALT LAKE CITY	UT	84109	(801) 333-2000
B	REGENCE BLUESHIELD	1800 9TH AVE	SEATTLE	WA	98101	(206) 464-3600
B	REGENCE BLUESHIELD OF IDAHO INC	1602 21ST AVE	LEWISTON	ID	83501	(208) 746-2671
A	RESERVE NATIONAL INS CO	601 E BRITTON RD	OKLAHOMA CITY	OK	73114	(405) 848-7931

RATING	INSURANCE COMPANY NAME	ADDRESS	CITY	STATE	ZIP	PHONE
E	ROCKY MOUNTAIN HEALTHCARE OPTIONS	2775 CROSSROADS BLVD	GRAND JUNCTION	CO	81506	(970) 244-7760
B+	ROCKY MOUNTAIN HOSPITAL & MEDICAL	700 BROADWAY	DENVER	CO	80273	(303) 831-2131
D	RYDER HEALTH PLAN INC	353 FONT MARTELO AVE SUITE 1	HUMACAO	PR	00791	(787) 852-0846
B	SANFORD HEALTH PLAN	300 CHERAPA PL SUITE 201	SIOUX FALLS	SD	57103	(605) 328-6868
A-	SECURITY HEALTH PLAN OF WI INC	1515 SAINT JOSEPH AVE	MARSHFIELD	WI	54449	(715) 221-9555
D	SENTINEL SECURITY LIFE INS CO	2121 S STATE ST	SALT LAKE CITY	UT	84115	(801) 484-8514
C	SHENANDOAH LIFE INS CO	2301 BRAMBLETON AVE SW	ROANOKE	VA	24015	(540) 985-4400
C+	SIERRA HEALTH AND LIFE INS CO INC	2720 N TENAYA WAY	LAS VEGAS	NV	89128	(702) 242-7732
A-	STANDARD LIFE & ACCIDENT INS CO	ONE MOODY PLAZA	GALVESTON	TX	77550	(409) 763-4661
B+	STATE FARM MUTUAL AUTOMOBILE INS CO	ONE STATE FARM PLAZA	BLOOMINGTON	IL	61710	(309) 766-2311
C	STATE MUTUAL INS CO	210 E SECOND AVE SUITE 301	ROME	GA	30161	(706) 291-1054
C-	STERLING INVESTORS LIFE INS CO	65 TECHNOLOGY PARKWAY	ROME	GA	30165	(813) 894-7978
D	STERLING LIFE INS CO	30 S WACKER DR	CHICAGO	IL	60025	(360) 647-9080
B-	STONEBRIDGE LIFE INS CO	187 WEST ST	RUTLAND	VT	05701	(319) 355-8511
B	TRANSAMERICA FINANCIAL LIFE INS CO	440 MAMARONECK AVE	HARRISON	NY	10528	(914) 697-8000
B-	TRANSAMERICA LIFE INS CO	4333 EDGEWOOD RD NE	CEDAR RAPIDS	IA	52499	(319) 398-8511
C+	TRANSAMERICA PREMIER LIFE INS CO	4333 EDGEWOOD RD NE	CEDAR RAPIDS	IA	52499	(319) 355-8511
B+	TRIPLE-S SALUD INC	F D ROOSEVELT AVE 1441	SAN JUAN	PR	00920	(787) 749-4949
D+	TUFTS INS CO	705 MOUNT AUBURN ST	WATERTOWN	MA	02472	(617) 972-9400
B	UNICARE LIFE & HEALTH INS CO	1209 ORANGE ST	WILMINGTON	DE	19801	(877) 864-2273
B	UNIFIED LIFE INS CO	7201 W 129TH ST SUITE 300	OVERLAND PARK	KS	66213	(913) 685-2233
D+	UNION FIDELITY LIFE INS CO	7101 COLLEGE BLVD SUITE 1400	OVERLAND PARK	KS	66210	(913) 982-3700
B	UNITED AMERICAN INS CO	10306 REGENCY PARKWAY DR	OMAHA	NE	68114	(972) 529-5085
C	UNITED HEALTHCARE INS CO	185 ASYLUM ST	HARTFORD	CT	06103	(877) 832-7734
B-	UNITED HEALTHCARE INS CO OF NY	2950 EXPRESSWAY DR S SUITE 240	ISLANDIA	NY	11749	(877) 832-7734
B	UNITED HEALTHCARE OF ALABAMA INC	33 INVERNESS CENTER PKWY	BIRMINGHAM	AL	35242	(205) 437-8500
C	UNITED NATIONAL LIFE INS CO OF AM	1275 MILWAUKEE AVE	GLENVIEW	IL	60025	(847) 803-5252
B	UNITED OF OMAHA LIFE INS CO	MUTUAL OF OMAHA PLAZA	OMAHA	NE	68175	(402) 342-7600
C	UNITED TEACHER ASSOCIATES INS CO	5508 PARKCREST DR	AUSTIN	TX	78731	(512) 451-2224
B+	UNITED WORLD LIFE INS CO	MUTUAL OF OMAHA PLAZA	OMAHA	NE	68175	(402) 342-7600
B-	UNITY HEALTH PLANS INS CORP	840 CAROLINA ST	SAUK CITY	WI	53583	(608) 643-2491
D	UNIVERSAL FIDELITY LIFE INS CO	2211 NORTH HIGHWAY 81	DUNCAN	OK	73533	(800) 366-8354
A	USAA LIFE INS CO	9800 FREDERICKSBURG RD	SAN ANTONIO	TX	78288	(210) 498-8000
A+	USABLE MUTUAL INS CO	601 S GAINES	LITTLE ROCK	AR	72201	(501) 378-2000
B	VERMONT HEALTH PLAN LLC	445 INDUSTRIAL LN	MONTPELIER	VT	05602	(802) 223-6131
D+	WASHINGTON NATIONAL INS CO	11825 N PENNSYLVANIA ST	CARMEL	I2	60069	(847) 793-3379
B+	WELLMARK INC	636 GRAND AVE	DES MOINES	IA	50309	(515) 376-4500
B+	WELLMARK OF SOUTH DAKOTA INC	1601 W MADISON STREET	SIOUX FALLS	SD	57104	(605) 373-7200
C+	WISCONSIN PHYSICIANS SERVICE INS	1717 WEST BROADWAY	MADISON	WI	53713	(608) 221-4711

Section VII

Analysis of
Medicare Managed
Care Complaints

An analysis of complaints filed against

U.S. Medicare Managed Care Plans

Companies are listed in alphabetical order.

Section VII Contents

As discussed in the previous section, no single measure is an end-all indicator of the quality of service provided by a health insurer. However, if you are a Medicare beneficiary, complaint information can give you a preliminary basis for informed shopping – especially for Medicare Managed Care plans. It will answer questions such as: Does the company have a high rate of enrollee complaints against it? Are most complaints upheld or overturned? Are many withdrawn before a decision is rendered?

The complaint information on the following pages will give you an indication of what beneficiaries, like yourself, have experienced with various Medicare insurers. This section is based on "reconsideration" data, reprinted from the Centers for Medicare and Medicaid Services (formerly known as Health Care Financing Administration) for providers with Medicare contracts.

"Reconsiderations" are complaints by members of Medicare Managed Care plans that have reached a federal review. Once they reach that stage, the complaints have already gone through at least two levels of internal appeals. Consequently, they are relatively serious and involve anywhere from several hundred dollars to many thousands of dollars of unpaid medical bills. In this section, all complaints cited are reconsiderations.

Complaints that were settled within the Plan's internal appeal process are not reflected. It is difficult to say what types of complaints these might be, but, in general, they are more likely to pertain to services of a lower dollar value.

We have made no attempt to render an opinion on the data contained in this section. Rather, we are reprinting the information strictly to help provide you with valuable information when shopping for a Medicare plan.

The Drawbacks of Complaint Data

One problem with the data is the time lag due to the lengthy reconsideration process. A company that has a high complaint rate in this section may have already begun to make improvements in its system to handle the types of issues that were raised in the complaints. Therefore, because it takes so long for a complaint to make it through the federal process, the company may appear to have worse service quality than it currently has.

Conversely, numerous companies that have obtained Medicare contracts very recently (within the past year), may show few or no complaints. But this may reflect merely the fact that the complaints filed against these companies have not yet reached the federal level. So before you make a final decision to select a company with a low level of complaints, find out how long it has had its Medicare contract. We estimate that the contract should be in force for about two years before these data reflect the complaints.

If you are interested in a company with a seemingly high complaint level, do take the time to ask the company what improvements, if any, it has made to correct the problems reflected in the complaint data. If a high rate of complaints against it have been upheld at the federal level, it will be far more difficult to explain away.

The plans included here are those from whom reconsiderations were received during 2013 or companies that had members enrolled in a specific Medicare contract as of July of that year. Not included are: 1) updates for later appeals of cases that have been decided and 2) companies whose contracts are so new that they don't have any current enrollment.

The plan name in this table represents one or more contracts with the Centers for Medicare and Medicaid Services (CMS). You may find some plans listed more than once; this is because they have contracts in different CMS-designated regions (see Column 3). If a plan has more than one contract in a particular region, the reconsideration data have been combined so that the company is only listed once for each region.

Three types of Medicare contracts are included here: risk, cost, and Health Care Prepayment Plans (HCPPs). A Medicare risk contract is one in which the CMS pays the plan a capitalization rate equal to a percentage of the average fee-for-service expense, in a given geographic area. A Medicare cost contract is one in which the CMS reimburses the plan for retroactively determined Part A and B costs. And an HCPP contract is similar to a cost contract but only Part B costs are paid by the CMS.

The following **BOLD** headings are the column reference guides for the tables

1. Insurance Company Name	The legally-registered name, which sometimes can differ from the name that the plan uses for advertising. If you cannot find the plan you are interested in, or if you have any doubts regarding the precise name, verify the information before looking it up in this Guide. Also, determine the domicile state for confirmation.
2. Domicile State	The state which has primary regulatory responsibility for the company. It may differ from the location of the company's corporate headquarters. You do not have to be living in the domicile state to purchase insurance from this firm, provided it is licensed to do business in your state.
	Also use this column to confirm that you have located the correct company. It is possible for two unrelated companies to have the same name if they are domiciled in different states.
3. Financial Strength Rating	Our rating is measured on a scale from A to F and considers a wide range of factors. Highly-rated companies are, in our opinion, less likely to experience financial difficulties than lower rated firms. See *About Weiss Financial Strength Ratings* for more information.

4. Region

The CMS region in which the complaint data applies for a particular company. The regions are as follows:

Boston: 1 (Connecticut, Maine, Massachusetts, New Hampshire, Rhode Island, Vermont), **New York: 2** (New Jersey, New York, Puerto Rico, Virgin Islands), **Philadelphia: 3** (Delaware, District of Columbia, Maryland, Pennsylvania, Virginia, West Virginia), **Atlanta: 4** (Alabama, Florida, Georgia, Kentucky, Mississippi, North Carolina, South Carolina, Tennessee), **Chicago: 5** (Illinois, Indiana, Michigan, Minnesota, Ohio, Wisconsin), **Dallas: 6** (Arkansas, Louisiana, Oklahoma, New Mexico, Texas), **Kansas City: 7** (Iowa, Kansas, Missouri, Nebraska), **Denver: 8** (Colorado, Montana, North Dakota, South Dakota, Utah, Wyoming), **San Francisco: 9** (Arizona, California, Guam, Hawaii, Nevada, Samoa), **Seattle: 10** (Alaska, Idaho, Oregon, Washington).

5. Rate

The rate of reconsiderations per 1,000 members, and is calculated as the sum of appeals received per year. Divided by the mid-year (July) enrollment, times 1,000.

"N/R" means that there were "no reconsiderations" for that particular plan's contract in that particular region. "N/E" means there was "no enrollment" during 2013. This happens when the complaints reflect prior enrollments in specific contracts, demonstrate the lag time between enrollment, and the complaint being represented in the reconsideration system.

6. Reconsiderations Received 2011

The number of reconsiderations received by the CMS from the health plan for the Medicare contract(s) only. Regardless of the number of complaints upheld or overturned (See columns 8 and 9), if this number is high relative to other Medicare plans, it signals that the plan has trouble satisfying its policyholders.

The health plan may have other business besides treating Medicare beneficiaries but this figure only pertains to enrollees that are served under a Medicare contract.

7. Reconsiderations Not Yet Decided

The number of reconsiderations received during 2013 that have not yet been settled.

8. Reconsiderations Upheld

The number of cases in which the CMS upheld the decision of the Medicare plan. This is the number of times CMS ruled against the policyholder in favor of the plan. If the number is high relative to the total number of reconsiderations received (Column 6), it is a sign that the firm's complaint process is somewhat ironclad and appeals beyond it are often futile. This, however, does not necessarily mean that the plan was not at fault.

9. **Reconsiderations Overturned**

The number of cases in which the CMS completely overturned the decision of the Medicare Managed Care plan. This is the number of times the CMS ruled in favor of the policyholder. If the number of complaints overturned is high, relative to the total number of reconsiderations received (Column 6), it is a sign that either the plan is falling short in meeting the needs of its policyholders; or, its complaint process is not streamlined enough to carry complaints to the appropriate conclusion.

10. **Reconsiderations Withdrawn**

The number of reconsiderations that were withdrawn from review.

The Regional CMS office will investigate the case and determine if the enrolee should revert back to fee-for-service (disenroll). If the CMS does not grant disenrollment, the case re-enters the reconsideration process and follows the same course as other complaints.

A high number of disenrollments may indicate that the plan has failed to clearly identify its coverage limitations at the time the policy is sold.

11. **Reconsiderations Dismissed**

The number of cases in which the CMS Regional Office decided the appeal is not valid or the CMS Regional Office does not have jurisdiction over the appeal.

INSURANCE COMPANY NAME	DOM. STATE	RATING	REGION	RATE	RECONS REC'VD	RECONS NOT YET DECIDED	RECONS UPHELD	RECONS OVER-TURNED	RECONS WITH-DRAWN	RECONS DISMISSED
ADVANTAGE HEALTH SOLUTIONS INC	IN	C	5	5.74	28	0	14	8	1	5
AETNA HEALTH INC (A CT CORP)	CT	C	8	2.26	29	0	12	3	1	11
AETNA HEALTH INC (A FLORIDA CORP)	FL	A-	8	3.70	25	0	6	2	1	16
AETNA HEALTH INC (A GEORGIA CORP)	GA	B	8	4.43	19	0	1	1	0	16
AETNA HEALTH INC (A MAINE CORP)	ME	B-	8	2.06	11	0	0	0	0	11
AETNA HEALTH INC (A NEW JERSEY CORP)	NJ	B	8	3.49	141	0	48	9	6	77
AETNA HEALTH INC (A NEW YORK CORP)	NY	B+	8	3.20	46	0	13	2	1	30
AETNA HEALTH INC (A PA CORP)	PA	B	8	51.48	180	0	88	6	11	74
AETNA HEALTH INC (A TEXAS CORP)	TX	B	8	4.46	70	0	18	0	3	49
AETNA HEALTH OF CALIFORNIA INC	CA	B	8	2.77	72	0	33	1	5	33
AETNA LIFE INS CO	CT	B+	1	N/E	--	--	--	--	--	--
AETNA LIFE INS CO	CT	B+	8	10.76	981	0	303	32	35	609
AIDS HEALTHCARE FOUNDATION MCO OF FL	FL	U	9	N/E	--	--	--	--	--	--
ALAMEDA ALLIANCE FOR HEALTH	CA	F	9	3.84	24	0	15	6	1	2
ALLIANCE HEALTH & LIFE INS CO	MI	B+	5	1.67	6	0	5	1	0	0
ALOHACARE	HI	B	9	0.59	1	0	1	0	0	0
ALTIUS HEALTH PLANS	UT	B	8	1.16	15	0	6	4	1	4
AMERICAN HEALTH INC	PR	B	2	2.31	103	0	47	11	1	44
AMERICAN PROGRESSIVE L&H I C OF NY	NY	B	6	119.97	871	0	343	101	23	394
AMERICAS 1ST CHOICE HEALTH PLANS INC	SC	E	4	0.74	6	0	4	0	0	2
AMERICAS 1ST CHOICE INS CO OF NC INC	NC	C	4	12.61	10	0	6	0	0	4
AMERICHOICE OF NEW JERSEY INC	NJ	B	9	21.27	216	0	63	8	26	119
AMERIGROUP COMMUNITY CARE NM	NM	B-	5	23.04	88	0	31	0	0	57
AMERIGROUP FLORIDA INC	FL	B	5	17.05	38	0	13	2	0	23
AMERIGROUP MARYLAND INC	MD	B	5	104.80	48	0	13	0	0	35
AMERIGROUP NEW JERSEY INC	NJ	A-	5	38.26	202	0	128	0	0	74
AMERIGROUP TENNESSEE INC	TN	B	5	19.95	85	0	17	1	1	66
AMERIGROUP TEXAS INC	TX	B+	5	13.01	311	0	109	5	2	195
AMERIHEALTH HMO INC	PA	B	3	6.84	8	0	6	2	0	0
AMGP GEORGIA MANAGED CARE CO INC	GA	B	5	60.98	5	0	1	0	0	4
ANTHEM BLUE CROSS LIFE & HEALTH INS	CA	B	5	5.29	233	0	101	13	7	110
ANTHEM HEALTH PLANS INC	CT	B	5	29.70	81	0	28	2	3	47
ANTHEM HEALTH PLANS OF KENTUCKY INC	KY	A-	5	5.22	40	0	20	2	3	14
ANTHEM HEALTH PLANS OF MAINE INC	ME	B-	5	1.07	3	0	2	0	0	1
ANTHEM HEALTH PLANS OF NEW HAMPSHIRE	NH	B+	5	N/E	--	--	--	--	--	--
ANTHEM HEALTH PLANS OF VIRGINIA	VA	B	5	14.59	55	0	13	3	6	33
ANTHEM INS COMPANIES INC	IN	B	5	23.32	533	0	183	30	52	267
ASURIS NORTHWEST HEALTH	WA	B-	10	0.89	2	0	1	0	0	0
ATLANTIS HEALTH PLAN	NY	E-	2	34.31	20	0	2	0	0	18
ATRIO HEALTH PLANS INC	OR	C-	10	39.14	116	0	67	22	8	18
AULTCARE INS CO	OH	C-	5	6.57	62	0	49	0	3	10
AVMED INC	FL	B+	4	1.09	33	0	27	1	4	1
BLUE CROSS & BLUE SHIELD MA HMO BLUE	MA	B	1	1.27	19	0	18	1	0	0
BLUE CROSS & BLUE SHIELD OF FLORIDA	FL	B	4	20.44	663	0	254	33	6	369
BLUE CROSS BLUE SHIELD HEALTHCARE GA	GA	A-	5	8.71	21	0	6	0	0	15
BLUE CROSS BLUE SHIELD OF ALABAMA	AL	A-	4	3.63	155	0	34	14	2	105
BLUE CROSS BLUE SHIELD OF GEORGIA	GA	B	5	4.72	29	0	13	0	1	14
BLUE CROSS BLUE SHIELD OF MICHIGAN	MI	B	5	1.31	187	0	131	20	21	14
BLUE CROSS BLUE SHIELD OF MINNESOTA	MN	A	5	2.46	234	0	128	40	3	61
BLUE CROSS BLUE SHIELD OF NC	NC	A	4	3.31	243	0	142	21	18	62
BLUE CROSS BLUE SHIELD OF RI	RI	C	1	2.00	64	0	40	2	3	19
BLUE CROSS BLUE SHIELD OF SC INC	SC	A-	4	8.62	108	0	79	8	0	21

INSURANCE COMPANY NAME	DOM. STATE	RATING	REGION	RATE	RECONS REC'VD	RECONS NOT YET DECIDED	RECONS UPHELD	RECONS OVER-TURNED	RECONS WITH-DRAWN	RECONS DISMISSED
BLUE CROSS OF CALIFORNIA	CA	A+	5	1.78	23	0	13	0	2	8
BLUE CROSS OF IDAHO HEALTH SERVICE	ID	A-	10	14.91	203	0	84	27	52	39
BLUECROSS BLUESHIELD OF TENNESSEE	TN	A	4	2.79	141	0	67	12	18	43
BRAVO HEALTH MID-ATLANTIC INC	MD	C	6	11.99	299	0	88	10	9	190
BRAVO HEALTH PENNSYLVANIA INC	PA	B	6	14.70	287	0	108	18	4	156
BUCKEYE COMMUNITY HEALTH PLAN INC	OH	C+	10	32.38	34	0	16	0	3	15
CALIFORNIA PHYSICIANS SERVICE	CA	A+	9	4.26	292	0	212	13	24	42
CAMBRIDGE LIFE INS CO	MO	B	8	N/E	--	--	--	--	--	--
CAPITAL ADVANTAGE INS CO	PA	C	3	3.79	72	0	48	8	0	14
CAPITAL DISTRICT PHYSICIANS HEALTH P	NY	B	2	4.02	119	0	93	15	1	8
CAPITAL HEALTH PLAN INC	FL	A-	4	2.40	35	0	27	2	3	3
CARE 1ST HEALTH PLAN	CA	D+	9	40.10	156	0	92	11	17	36
CARE IMPROVEMENT PLUS OF MARYLAND	MD	U	9	N/E	--	--	--	--	--	--
CARE IMPROVEMENT PLUS OF TEXAS INS	TX	B	9	13.74	617	0	206	44	4	362
CARE IMPROVEMENT PLUS SOUTH CENTRAL	AR	C	9	23.82	1655	0	786	147	5	710
CARE IMPROVEMENT PLUS WI INS	WI	C	9	0.94	3	0	3	0	0	0
CARE N CARE INS CO INC	TX	D	6	0.41	3	0	1	1	0	1
CARE WISCONSIN HEALTH PLAN INC	WI	B	5	N/E	--	--	--	--	--	--
CAREMORE HEALTH PLAN	CA	B+	5	7.46	389	0	215	25	6	141
CAREMORE HEALTH PLAN OF ARIZONA INC	AZ	B-	5	17.78	294	0	134	9	2	146
CAREMORE HEALTH PLAN OF NEVADA	NV	D	5	12.63	70	0	46	3	1	20
CAREPLUS HEALTH PLANS INC	FL	C	7	11.55	781	0	145	5	10	621
CAREPOINT INS CO	NJ	U	2	N/E	--	--	--	--	--	--
CARESOURCE	OH	A	5	1.60	2	0	1	0	0	1
CARILION CLINIC MEDICARE RESOURCES	VA	E+	3	6.21	20	0	10	3	0	7
CARITEN HEALTH PLAN INC	TN	B	7	8.09	743	0	60	4	9	668
CATHOLIC SPECIAL NEEDS PLAN LLC	NY	D	2	N/E	--	--	--	--	--	--
CDPHP UNIVERSAL BENEFITS INC	NY	E	2	2.10	12	0	8	2	0	2
CENTRAL HEALTH PLAN OF CALIFORNIA	CA	E+	10	14.21	177	0	66	8	1	102
CHA HMO INC	KY	C	7	9.96	35	0	2	0	0	33
CHINESE COMMUNITY HEALTH PLAN	CA	B-	9	1.38	12	0	7	3	1	1
CIGNA HEALTHCARE OF ARIZONA INC	AZ	C	6	5.82	223	0	152	13	6	51
CITRUS HEALTH CARE INC	FL	U	9	N/E	--	--	--	--	--	--
COLORADO ACCESS	CO	U	8	12.41	41	0	2	3	0	36
COLORADO CHOICE HEALTH PLANS	CO	C	8	1.27	1	0	1	0	0	0
COMMUNITY CARE HEALTH PLAN INC	WI	B-	5	14.67	4	0	3	0	0	1
COMMUNITY HEALTH GROUP	CA	C	9	0.79	1	0	1	0	0	0
COMMUNITY HEALTH PLAN OF WASHINGTON	WA	A-	10	17.17	307	0	97	40	3	165
COMMUNITY INS CO	OH	B+	5	6.33	336	0	141	22	24	148
COMMUNITYCARE HMO INC	OK	A	6	6.77	193	0	58	10	4	121
COMPCARE HEALTH SERVICES INS CORP	WI	A-	5	7.92	7	0	4	0	1	2
CONNECTICARE INC	CT	B	2	2.10	94	0	51	1	2	40
CONTRA COSTA HEALTH PLAN	CA	D	9	N/E	--	--	--	--	--	--
COVENTRY HEALTH & LIFE INS CO	MO	B+	8	12.54	132	0	84	13	10	24
COVENTRY HEALTH CARE OF GEORGIA	GA	B	8	8.43	26	0	8	5	2	11
COVENTRY HEALTH CARE OF ILLINOIS INC	IL	B+	8	3.19	19	0	6	3	0	9
COVENTRY HEALTH CARE OF IOWA INC	IA	B	8	3.70	14	0	6	3	3	2
COVENTRY HEALTH CARE OF KANSAS INC	KS	B	8	1.52	22	0	14	3	2	3
COVENTRY HEALTH CARE OF MISSOURI INC	MO	B	8	3.01	84	0	48	8	6	21
COVENTRY HEALTH CARE OF NEBRASKA INC	NE	B+	8	2.29	7	0	3	2	0	1
COVENTRY HEALTH PLAN OF FLORIDA INC	FL	A-	8	3.54	17	0	12	1	1	3
CRESTPOINT HEALTH INS CO	TN	D	4	N/E	--	--	--	--	--	--

INSURANCE COMPANY NAME	DOM. STATE	RATING	REGION	RATE	RECONS REC'VD	RECONS NOT YET DECIDED	RECONS UPHELD	RECONS OVER-TURNED	RECONS WITH-DRAWN	RECONS DISMISSED
CUATRO LLC	NY	E	2	3.38	9	0	5	4	0	0
DEAN HEALTH PLAN INC	WI	B	5	0.52	11	0	6	4	0	1
DENVER HEALTH MEDICAL PLAN INC	CO	B	8	N/E	--	--	--	--	--	--
EASY CHOICE HEALTH PLAN	CA	E+	4	2.51	139	0	88	11	7	29
ELDERPLAN INC	NY	C-	2	95.89	1298	0	396	21	9	871
EMPIRE HEALTHCHOICE ASSURANCE INC	NY	B-	5	7.99	380	0	160	16	22	179
EMPIRE HEALTHCHOICE HMO INC	NY	B	5	6.92	516	0	216	31	34	233
ESSENCE HEALTHCARE INC	MO	B	7	4.83	200	0	54	11	1	134
EXCELLUS HEALTH PLAN INC	NY	A	2	7.99	437	0	269	38	15	109
FALLON COMMUNITY HEALTH PLAN	MA	B-	1	24.35	187	0	143	15	1	28
FAMILYCARE HEALTH PLANS INC	OR	C-	10	12.39	32	0	6	3	0	21
FIDELIS SECURECARE OF MICHIGAN INC	MI	C	5	90.91	86	0	29	14	0	39
FIDELIS SECURECARE OF NORTH CAROLINA	NC	D+	5	72.07	8	0	1	1	0	6
FIDELIS SECURECARE OF TEXAS INC	TX	U	5	N/E	--	--	--	--	--	--
FIRST HEALTH LIFE & HEALTH INS CO	TX	B	8	7.20	16	0	7	1	2	5
FIRST MEDICAL HEALTH PLAN INC	PR	E	2	2.79	43	0	28	2	0	13
FIRSTCAROLINACARE INS CO INC	NC	B	4	N/E	--	--	--	--	--	--
FLORIDA HEALTHCARE PLUS INC	FL	U	4	1.21	10	0	6	1	0	3
FREEDOM HEALTH INC	FL	U	4	7.84	403	0	63	1	1	338
GATEWAY HEALTH PLAN INC	PA	B	3	5.03	175	0	121	14	7	33
GEISINGER HEALTH PLAN	PA	B	3	2.40	114	0	78	4	1	30
GEISINGER INDEMNITY INS CO	PA	C	3	1.37	20	0	13	3	0	4
GEISINGER INDEMNITY INS CO	PA	C	8	2.52	13	0	10	0	0	3
GEMCARE HEALTH PLAN INC	CA	E	9	8.73	70	0	58	3	3	5
GHS MANAGED HEALTH CARE PLANS INC	OK	B-	6	3.34	5	0	0	0	0	5
GLOBALHEALTH INC	OK	C+	6	N/E	--	--	--	--	--	--
GOLDEN STATE MEDICARE HEALTH PLAN	CA	C-	10	3.60	3	0	2	1	0	0
GROUP HEALTH COOPERATIVE	WA	A-	10	5.17	420	0	307	30	7	73
GROUP HEALTH INCORPORATED	NY	D	2	4.20	112	0	18	2	3	89
GROUP HEALTH OPTIONS INC	WA	B-	10	4.24	15	0	8	1	0	6
GROUP HEALTH PLAN INC	MN	A+	5	0.77	35	0	32	1	2	0
GUNDERSEN HEALTH PLAN INC	WI	B	5	4.53	62	0	48	11	2	0
GUNDERSEN HEALTH PLAN MN	MN	B-	5	N/E	--	--	--	--	--	--
HAP MIDWEST HEALTH PLAN INC	MI	B-	5	4.15	3	0	2	1	0	0
HARMONY HEALTH PLAN OF ILLINOIS INC	IL	B-	4	55.97	521	0	135	3	6	377
HAWAII MEDICAL SERVICE ASSOCIATION	HI	C	9	0.81	8	0	5	3	0	0
HCSC INS SERVICES CO	IL	B	6	6.28	4	0	1	0	1	2
HEALTH ALLIANCE MEDICAL PLANS	IL	A	5	8.56	52	0	32	19	0	1
HEALTH ALLIANCE PLAN OF MICHIGAN	MI	B	5	1.74	74	0	56	5	4	9
HEALTH CARE SVC CORP A MUT LEG RES	IL	A+	6	3.96	19	0	13	3	0	1
HEALTH FIRST HEALTH PLANS	FL	C-	4	14.02	333	0	137	7	2	187
HEALTH INSURANCE PLAN OF GREATER NY	NY	B	2	4.88	539	0	105	18	3	412
HEALTH NET HEALTH PLAN OF OREGON INC	OR	E	10	3.16	5	0	3	0	0	2
HEALTH NET LIFE INS CO	CA	B	10	156.97	814	0	194	39	12	567
HEALTH NET OF ARIZONA INC	AZ	D+	10	10.42	449	0	224	32	28	164
HEALTH NET OF CALIFORNIA INC	CA	C+	10	6.71	956	0	503	81	18	346
HEALTH NEW ENGLAND INC	MA	B	1	1.92	16	0	14	2	0	0
HEALTH OPTIONS INC	FL	U	4	21.37	318	0	79	6	4	229
HEALTH PLAN OF CAREOREGON INC	OR	B	10	7.53	69	0	38	7	1	20
HEALTH PLAN OF NEVADA INC	NV	B	9	3.07	161	0	125	5	8	23
HEALTH PLAN OF THE UPPER OHIO VALLEY	WV	B+	3	1.92	16	0	14	2	0	0
HEALTHAMERICA PENNSYLVANIA INC	PA	B	8	1.42	51	0	21	4	3	22

INSURANCE COMPANY NAME	DOM. STATE	RATING	REGION	RATE	RECONS REC'VD	RECONS NOT YET DECIDED	RECONS UPHELD	RECONS OVER-TURNED	RECONS WITH-DRAWN	RECONS DISMISSED
HEALTHASSURANCE PENNSYLVANIA INC	PA	B	8	1.61	75	0	37	3	9	24
HEALTHFIRST HEALTH PLAN NEW JERSEY	NJ	E	2	2.94	14	0	0	2	0	12
HEALTHKEEPERS INC	VA	A-	5	10.49	18	0	9	0	0	9
HEALTHNOW NY INC	NY	B+	2	2.16	65	0	47	10	3	5
HEALTHNOW NY INC	NY	B+	8	N/E	--	--	--	--	--	--
HEALTHPARTNERS	MN	B+	5	N/E	--	--	--	--	--	--
HEALTHPLUS INS CO	MI	C	5	1.42	2	0	0	0	0	2
HEALTHPLUS OF MICHIGAN	MI	B-	5	0.65	12	0	6	1	0	5
HEALTHSPRING LIFE & HLTH INS CO INC	TX	B-	6	38.50	355	0	68	5	3	278
HEALTHSPRING OF ALABAMA INC	AL	B	6	4.21	178	0	18	3	1	156
HEALTHSPRING OF FLORIDA INC	FL	B	6	5.85	255	0	103	8	6	138
HEALTHSPRING OF TENNESSEE INC	TN	C+	6	14.76	473	0	208	19	10	233
HEALTHSUN HEALTH PLANS	FL	C	4	19.83	368	0	42	1	1	323
HIGHMARK INC	PA	B-	3	3.95	816	0	612	83	14	94
HM HEALTH INS CO	PA	C-	3	3.07	33	0	22	1	0	9
HMO COLORADO	CO	B-	5	46.26	13	0	2	1	0	10
HMO MINNESOTA	MN	A-	5	3.09	62	0	44	10	0	5
HOMETOWN HEALTH PLAN	OH	U	3	1.34	6	0	6	0	0	0
HOMETOWN HEALTH PLAN INC	NV	C	10	4.39	37	0	11	2	1	22
HONORED CITIZENS CHOICE HEALTH PLAN	CA	E	10	9.14	135	0	96	23	2	12
HORIZON HEALTHCARE OF NEW JERSEY INC	NJ	A-	2	14.72	858	0	341	84	26	403
HUMANA BENEFIT PLAN OF ILLINOIS	IL	B	7	11.48	76	0	3	1	0	72
HUMANA EMPLOYERS HEALTH PLAN OF GA	GA	D	7	19.60	401	0	3	2	4	392
HUMANA HEALTH BENEFIT PLAN LA	LA	B	6	N/E	--	--	--	--	--	--
HUMANA HEALTH BENEFIT PLAN LA	LA	B	7	26.18	650	0	41	6	3	598
HUMANA HEALTH CO OF NEW YORK INC	NY	E	7	26.17	14	0	0	0	0	14
HUMANA HEALTH INS CO OF FL INC	FL	C	7	10.96	141	0	8	0	0	133
HUMANA HEALTH PLAN INC	KY	C	7	124.52	4083	0	82	6	16	3979
HUMANA HEALTH PLAN OF CALIFORNIA INC	CA	C-	7	8.56	182	0	11	1	2	168
HUMANA HEALTH PLAN OF OHIO INC	OH	C	7	27.78	535	0	8	0	2	524
HUMANA HEALTH PLAN OF TEXAS INC	TX	B	6	N/E	--	--	--	--	--	--
HUMANA HEALTH PLAN OF TEXAS INC	TX	B	7	22.78	1278	0	11	1	2	1264
HUMANA HEALTH PLANS OF PUERTO RICO	PR	B	7	2.02	64	0	15	2	1	46
HUMANA INS CO	WI	U	7	245.63	****	0	417	39	68	****
HUMANA INS CO OF NEW YORK	NY	B	7	35.54	145	0	5	0	1	139
HUMANA INS CO OF PUERTO RICO INC	PR	B-	7	8.54	24	0	2	0	0	22
HUMANA MEDICAL PLAN INC	FL	B	7	7.69	2336	0	46	8	10	2272
HUMANA MEDICAL PLAN OF MICHIGAN INC	MI	B	7	15.63	3	0	1	0	1	1
HUMANA MEDICAL PLAN OF UTAH INC	UT	D	7	12.41	55	0	2	0	0	53
HUMANA REGIONAL HEALTH PLAN INC	AR	U	7	N/E	--	--	--	--	--	--
HUMANA WISCONSIN HEALTH ORGANIZATION	WI	B	7	18.88	114	0	1	0	1	112
INDEPENDENT CARE HEALTH PLAN	WI	B	5	1.69	9	0	7	2	0	0
INDEPENDENT HEALTH ASSOC INC	NY	B	2	3.55	239	0	195	16	4	24
INDEPENDENT HEALTH BENEFITS CORP	NY	C+	2	6.91	26	0	21	3	0	1
INDIANA UNIVERSITY HEALTH PLANS INC	IN	D-	5	2.51	22	0	15	4	0	3
INTERVALLEY HEALTH PLAN	CA	D	10	3.10	63	0	57	2	3	1
K S PLAN ADMINISTRATORS LLC	TX	B	6	1.99	48	0	37	8	1	2
KAISER FOUNDATION HEALTH PLAN INC	CA	A	9	9.77	2284	0	1008	329	34	894
KAISER FOUNDATION HP MID-ATL STATES	MD	B	9	2.83	147	0	99	7	7	34
KAISER FOUNDATION HP NORTHWEST	OR	B	9	1.36	93	0	81	1	2	8
KAISER FOUNDATION HP OF CO	CO	B+	9	0.93	79	0	48	6	1	24
KAISER FOUNDATION HP OF GA	GA	D	9	2.14	41	0	22	4	1	14

INSURANCE COMPANY NAME	DOM. STATE	RATING	REGION	RATE	RECONS REC'VD	RECONS NOT YET DECIDED	RECONS UPHELD	RECONS OVER- TURNED	RECONS WITH- DRAWN	RECONS DISMISSED
KEYSTONE HEALTH PLAN CENTRAL INC	PA	B	3	4.45	55	0	38	10	0	6
KEYSTONE HEALTH PLAN EAST INC	PA	B+	3	3.71	287	0	194	36	1	56
KEYSTONE HEALTH PLAN WEST INC	PA	D+	3	3.71	461	0	342	47	9	60
LOCAL INITIATIVE HEALTH AUTH LA	CA	C	9	9.47	51	0	20	3	1	26
LOVELACE HEALTH SYSTEMS INC	NM	C+	6	1.13	32	0	15	0	1	16
MANAGED HEALTH INC	NY	B-	2	3.34	371	0	43	1	13	313
MANAGED HEALTH SERVICES INS CORP	WI	C+	10	25.35	27	0	4	1	1	21
MAPFRE LIFE INS CO OF PR	PR	C+	2	N/E	--	--	--	--	--	--
MARQUETTE NATIONAL LIFE INS CO	TX	C	6	N/E	--	--	--	--	--	--
MARTINS POINT GENERATIONS LLC	ME	D	1	5.49	46	0	19	4	2	21
MCLAREN HEALTH PLAN INC	MI	B-	5	1.88	1	0	1	0	0	0
MCS ADVANTAGE INC	PR	E	2	1.36	87	0	31	6	0	50
MD CARE INC	CA	C	7	N/E	--	--	--	--	--	--
MD INDIVIDUAL PRACTICE ASSOC INC	MD	B-	3	N/E	--	--	--	--	--	--
MEDICA HEALTH PLANS	MN	B+	5	0.41	5	0	5	0	0	0
MEDICA HEALTHCARE PLANS INC	FL	E-	9	57.10	1866	0	184	35	8	1639
MEDICA INS CO	MN	C+	5	0.47	67	0	61	2	1	3
MEDICAL ASSOC CLINIC HEALTH PLAN	WI	B-	7	N/E	--	--	--	--	--	--
MEDICAL ASSOCIATES HEALTH PLAN INC	IA	B	7	0.31	3	0	2	1	0	0
MEDISUN INC	AZ	B	9	4.94	115	0	84	6	8	15
MEDSTAR FAMILY CHOICE INC	MD	C-	3	25.97	2	0	2	0	0	0
MERCYCARE HMO	WI	C	5	10.75	4	0	4	0	0	0
MERIDIAN HEALTH PLAN OF MICHIGAN INC	MI	B+	5	8.60	3	0	2	1	0	0
METROPOLITAN HEALTH PLAN	MN	C-	5	N/E	--	--	--	--	--	--
MMM HEALTHCARE INC	PR	C	2	5.10	982	0	73	8	10	890
MODA HEALTH PLAN INC	OR	B-	10	2.20	20	0	9	5	1	4
MOLINA HEALTHCARE OF CALIFORNIA	CA	C-	10	62.97	515	0	135	37	10	330
MOLINA HEALTHCARE OF FLORIDA INC	FL	D	10	13.29	8	0	2	0	0	6
MOLINA HEALTHCARE OF MICHIGAN INC	MI	B	10	21.90	211	0	129	69	4	4
MOLINA HEALTHCARE OF NEW MEXICO	NM	B	10	14.59	13	0	4	1	1	7
MOLINA HEALTHCARE OF OHIO INC	OH	B	10	10.13	4	0	0	1	0	3
MOLINA HEALTHCARE OF TEXAS INC	TX	C	10	11.49	27	0	8	1	1	17
MOLINA HEALTHCARE OF UTAH INC	UT	B	10	16.73	132	0	64	18	4	41
MOLINA HEALTHCARE OF WASHINGTON INC	WA	B+	10	18.10	119	0	46	34	6	30
MOLINA HEALTHCARE OF WISCONSIN INC	WI	D	6	N/E	--	--	--	--	--	--
MOUNT CARMEL HEALTH INS CO	OH	D	5	1.16	1	0	1	0	0	0
MOUNT CARMEL HEALTH PLAN INC	OH	A	5	1.40	52	0	34	5	1	12
MVP HEALTH PLAN INC	NY	B-	2	6.49	190	0	144	30	5	11
NEW WEST HEALTH SERVICES	MT	E+	8	5.12	97	0	72	13	4	7
NHP OF INDIANA LLC	IN	U	5	N/E	--	--	--	--	--	--
ON LOK SENIOR HEALTH SERVICES	CA	B	9	N/E	--	--	--	--	--	--
OPTIMUM HEALTHCARE INC	FL	U	4	5.94	242	0	50	0	0	192
ORANGE PREVENTION & TREATMENT INTEGR	CA	B	9	13.24	204	0	146	23	5	27
OXFORD HEALTH PLANS (CT) INC	CT	B	9	37.89	1011	0	146	11	56	796
OXFORD HEALTH PLANS (NJ) INC	NJ	B	9	49.36	1842	0	207	10	81	1542
OXFORD HEALTH PLANS (NY) INC	NY	A+	9	21.62	1595	0	187	16	65	1327
PACIFICARE OF ARIZONA INC	AZ	B	9	6.15	592	0	208	15	57	309
PACIFICARE OF COLORADO INC	CO	B-	9	4.43	390	0	149	15	49	175
PACIFICARE OF NEVADA INC	NV	E	9	6.32	58	0	20	3	16	19
PACIFICARE OF OKLAHOMA INC	OK	B	9	3.73	119	0	36	2	8	73
PACIFICSOURCE COMMUNITY HEALTH PLANS	OR	C	10	18.29	287	0	97	13	53	124
PARAMOUNT HEALTH CARE	OH	C	5	0.94	13	0	8	1	2	2

INSURANCE COMPANY NAME	DOM. STATE	RATING	REGION	RATE	RECONS REC'VD	RECONS NOT YET DECIDED	RECONS UPHELD	RECONS OVER-TURNED	RECONS WITH-DRAWN	RECONS DISMISSED
PARTNERSHIP HEALTHPLAN OF CALIFORNIA	CA	A-	9	1.45	12	0	7	2	0	3
PEACH STATE HEALTH PLAN INC	GA	C	10	N/E	--	--	--	--	--	--
PEOPLES HEALTH INC	LA	D	6	3.36	184	0	110	3	1	70
PHOENIX HEALTH PLANS INC	AZ	D+	9	25.04	164	0	30	4	8	121
PHYSICIANS UNITED PLAN INC	FL	F	4	50.35	1849	0	174	43	53	1577
PIEDMONT COMMUNITY HEALTHCARE	VA	B	3	1.20	3	0	2	1	0	0
PMC MEDICARE CHOICE INC	PR	B-	2	6.28	264	0	14	5	2	243
PREFERRED CARE PARTNERS INC	FL	E-	9	24.70	1112	0	147	26	4	932
PREFERRED MEDICAL PLAN INC	FL	D+	4	N/E	--	--	--	--	--	--
PRESBYTERIAN INS CO INC	NM	B	6	8.89	89	0	39	4	0	46
PRIORITY HEALTH	MI	B	5	7.63	310	0	249	18	4	38
PROVIDENCE HEALTH PLAN	OR	A+	10	4.26	180	0	79	21	1	79
PUBLIC HEALTH TRUST OF DADE COUNTY	FL	U	4	0.96	2	0	0	0	0	2
PYRAMID LIFE INS CO	KS	C	6	123.17	1288	0	321	87	29	845
QCC INS CO	PA	B	3	3.22	16	0	13	1	0	2
QUALITY HEALTH PLANS OF NEW YORK INC	NY	E	4	47.62	6	0	0	1	1	4
REGENCE BL CROSS BL SHIELD OREGON	OR	B+	10	0.90	55	0	45	4	2	4
REGENCE BLUE CROSS BLUE SHIELD OF UT	UT	B	10	0.89	17	0	14	1	0	2
REGENCE BLUESHIELD	WA	B	10	1.05	32	0	25	1	3	3
REGENCE BLUESHIELD OF IDAHO INC	ID	B	10	1.02	7	0	5	2	0	0
ROCKY MOUNTAIN HEALTH MAINT ORG	CO	A-	8	4.42	108	0	53	6	6	42
ROCKY MOUNTAIN HOSPITAL & MEDICAL	CO	B+	5	17.52	27	0	7	1	0	19
SAMARITAN HEALTH PLANS INC	OR	B-	10	4.29	22	0	9	5	0	8
SAN MATEO HEALTH COMMISSION	CA	B+	9	6.64	58	0	5	1	0	52
SANFORD HEART OF AMERICA HEALTH PLAN	ND	D+	8	N/E	--	--	--	--	--	--
SCAN HEALTH PLAN	CA	C	9	32.00	1040	0	670	95	55	217
SCAN HEALTH PLAN ARIZONA	AZ	E	9	14.11	184	0	85	15	8	74
SCOTT & WHITE HEALTH PLAN	TX	B	6	3.41	86	0	51	8	1	26
SECURITY HEALTH PLAN OF WI INC	WI	A-	5	0.48	20	0	16	2	0	2
SELECT HEALTH OF SOUTH CAROLINA INC	SC	B	3	20.83	2	0	2	0	0	0
SELECTCARE HEALTH PLANS INC	TX	C	6	33.38	156	0	51	11	5	87
SELECTCARE OF OKLAHOMA INC	OK	B-	6	41.32	5	0	0	0	0	5
SELECTCARE OF TEXAS LLC	TX	C-	6	21.74	1083	0	529	71	34	444
SELECTHEALTH INC	UT	A	8	1.76	7	0	4	1	0	2
SENIOR WHOLE HEALTH OF NEW YORK INC	NY	E	1	34.48	1	0	1	0	0	0
SHA LLC	TX	E	6	3.63	13	0	7	1	0	5
SIDNEY HILLMAN HEALTH CENTRE	IL	U	5	N/E	--	--	--	--	--	--
SIERRA HEALTH AND LIFE INS CO INC	NV	C+	9	24.87	121	0	13	1	7	100
SIMPLY HEALTHCARE PLANS INC	FL	U	4	6.37	98	0	64	12	2	16
SOUNDPATH HEALTH	WA	C	10	7.21	120	0	104	4	0	11
STERLING LIFE INS CO	IL	D	8	3.57	2	0	0	0	0	2
STERLING LIFE INS CO	IL	D	10	N/E	--	--	--	--	--	--
SUMMACARE INC	OH	C-	5	1.46	41	0	29	0	11	1
SUPERIOR HEALTHPLAN INC	TX	C	10	40.74	101	0	13	4	7	77
SUTTER HEALTH PLAN	CA	U	9	N/E	--	--	--	--	--	--
THP INS CO	WV	D	3	2.93	3	0	3	0	0	0
TODAYS OPTIONS OF OKLAHOMA INC	OK	C	6	26.55	155	0	55	6	6	87
TOTAL HEALTH CARE INC	MI	D+	5	N/E	--	--	--	--	--	--
TOUCHSTONE HEALTH HMO INC	NY	E	2	29.97	386	0	188	103	2	87
TRILLIUM COMMUNITY HEALTH PLAN INC	OR	C+	10	6.97	24	0	18	3	1	2
TRIPLE-S SALUD INC	PR	B+	2	4.06	91	0	62	11	10	8
TUFTS ASSOCIATED HEALTH MAINT ORG	MA	B	1	4.08	376	0	304	14	12	46

INSURANCE COMPANY NAME	DOM. STATE	RATING	REGION	RATE	RECONS REC'VD	RECONS NOT YET DECIDED	RECONS UPHELD	RECONS OVER-TURNED	RECONS WITH-DRAWN	RECONS DISMISSED
UCARE HEALTH INC	WI	D	5	1.57	11	0	9	1	0	1
UCARE MINNESOTA	MN	A-	5	2.38	136	0	104	16	4	8
UHC OF CALIFORNIA INC	CA	C+	9	5.74	1915	0	993	105	323	484
UNICARE LIFE & HEALTH INS CO	IN	B	5	N/E	--	--	--	--	--	--
UNION HEALTH SERVICE INC	IL	B	5	N/E	--	--	--	--	--	--
UNITED HEALTHCARE INS CO	CT	C	9	982.67	****	0	1880	143	982	****
UNITED HEALTHCARE OF ALABAMA INC	AL	B	9	19.28	720	0	63	4	32	619
UNITED HEALTHCARE OF ARIZONA INC	AZ	B	9	20.38	566	0	51	4	25	484
UNITED HEALTHCARE OF ARKANSAS INC	AR	B	9	28.23	119	0	8	1	5	105
UNITED HEALTHCARE OF FLORIDA INC	FL	C	9	44.32	1127	0	124	3	66	934
UNITED HEALTHCARE OF GEORGIA INC	GA	B-	9	26.52	229	0	16	2	6	204
UNITED HEALTHCARE OF NC INC	NC	B	9	20.04	1674	0	118	5	86	1464
UNITED HEALTHCARE OF NEW ENGLAND INC	RI	B	9	9.42	306	0	58	5	19	224
UNITED HEALTHCARE OF NY INC	NY	B+	9	38.86	443	0	63	12	33	334
UNITED HEALTHCARE OF OHIO INC	OH	B	9	18.46	1886	0	147	10	114	1614
UNITED HEALTHCARE OF THE MIDLANDS	NE	B+	9	10.11	58	0	3	1	2	52
UNITED HEALTHCARE OF THE MIDWEST INC	MO	C+	9	16.08	811	0	53	0	34	724
UNITED HEALTHCARE OF UTAH	UT	B	9	9.88	450	0	43	1	31	375
UNITED HEALTHCARE OF WISCONSIN INC	WI	B	9	35.41	826	0	128	3	52	643
UNITEDHEALTHCARE BENEFITS OF TEXAS	TX	B+	9	3.54	608	0	198	16	85	307
UNITEDHEALTHCARE COMMUNITY PLAN INC	MI	B	9	59.98	315	0	107	20	9	175
UNITEDHEALTHCARE COMMUNITY PLAN TX	TX	B+	9	20.99	751	0	49	6	22	674
UNITEDHEALTHCARE OF OREGON	OR	B-	9	4.80	85	0	35	3	8	37
UNITEDHEALTHCARE OF PENNSYLVANIA INC	PA	B	9	24.64	462	0	90	16	14	339
UNITEDHEALTHCARE OF WASHINGTON INC	WA	B	9	4.53	295	0	108	12	31	142
UNITEDHEALTHCARE PLAN RIVER VALLEY	IL	B+	9	63.04	2179	0	277	43	158	1696
UNIVERSAL CARE	CA	E-	9	6.09	17	0	7	4	1	5
UPMC FOR YOU INC	PA	B+	3	2.50	38	0	21	4	1	12
UPMC HEALTH NETWORK INC	PA	D+	3	3.93	106	0	71	2	1	31
UPMC HEALTH PLAN INC	PA	B	3	4.68	374	0	235	11	5	121
UPPER PENINSULA HEALTH PLAN INC	MI	B-	5	N/E	--	--	--	--	--	--
USABLE MUTUAL INS CO	AR	A+	6	0.17	3	0	2	0	0	1
VANTAGE HEALTH PLAN INC	LA	B-	6	36.70	240	0	49	4	2	185
VISTA HEALTH PLAN INC	PA	B-	3	8.36	3	0	1	1	1	0
VIVA HEALTH INC	AL	B+	4	3.04	120	0	52	4	1	62
WELLCARE HEALTH INS OF ARIZONA INC	AZ	B-	4	7.09	56	0	6	0	0	50
WELLCARE HEALTH PLANS OF NEW JERSEY	NJ	C	4	51.30	77	0	15	0	3	59
WELLCARE OF CONNECTICUT INC	CT	C-	4	25.53	186	0	44	3	4	135
WELLCARE OF FLORIDA INC	FL	B	4	15.55	1230	0	268	11	41	906
WELLCARE OF GEORGIA INC	GA	B-	4	23.33	584	0	113	4	11	456
WELLCARE OF LOUISIANA INC	LA	B-	4	22.98	170	0	26	0	6	138
WELLCARE OF NEW YORK INC	NY	U	4	18.12	762	0	166	11	18	566
WELLCARE OF OHIO INC	OH	C	4	77.32	392	0	63	2	3	324
WELLCARE OF TEXAS INC	TX	B-	4	46.69	742	0	170	6	24	542
WINDSOR HEALTH PLAN OF TN INC	TN	D+	4	13.89	828	0	261	18	10	536

Section VIII

Rating Upgrades
and Downgrades

A list of all

U.S. Health Insurers

receiving a rating upgrade or downgrade
during the current quarter.

Section VIII Contents

This section identifies those companies receiving a rating change since the previous edition of this publication, whether it is a new rating to this guide, withdrawn rating, rating upgrade, rating downgrade or a, newly rated company. A rating may be withdrawn due to a merger, dissolution, or liquidation. A rating upgrade or downgrade may entail a change from one letter grade to another, or it may mean the addition or deletion of a plus or minus sign within the same letter grade previously assigned to the company. Ratings are normally updated once each quarter of the year. In some instances, however, a company's rating may be downgraded outside of the normal updates due to overriding circumstances.

1. **Insurance Company Name**   The legally-registered name, which can sometimes differ from the name that the company uses for advertising. An insurer's name can be very similar to that of another, so verify the company's exact name and state of domicile to make sure you are looking at the correct company.

2. **Domicile State**   The state which has primary regulatory responsibility for the company. It may differ from the location of the company's corporate headquarters. You do not have to be living in the domicile state to purchase insurance from this firm, provided it is licensed to do business in your state.

3. **Total Assets**   All assets admitted by state insurance regulators in millions of dollars as of the most recent year end. This includes investments and current business assets such as receivables from agents, reinsurers and subscribers.

4. **New or Current Financial Strength Rating**   The rating assigned to the company as of the date of this Guide's publication. Our rating is measured on a scale from A to F and considers a wide range of factors. Highly-rated companies are, in our opinion, less likely to experience financial difficulties than lower-rated firms. See *About Weiss Financial Strength Ratings* for more information.

5. **Previous Financial Strength Rating**   The rating assigned to the company prior to its most recent change.

6. **Date of Change**   The date on which the rating upgrade or downgrade officially occurred. Normally, all rating changes are put into effect on a single day each quarter of the year. In some instances, however, a rating may have been changed outside of this normal update.

Withdrawn Ratings

INSURANCE COMPANY NAME	DOM. STATE	TOTAL ASSETS ($MIL)	RATING	PRIOR FINANCIAL STRENGTH RATING	DATE
CARITEN INS CO	TN	20.4	U	A	11/05/14
COVENTRY SUMMIT HEALTH PLAN INC	FL	117.6	U	C+	11/05/14
HUMANA ADVANTAGECARE PLAN INC	FL	43.7	U	B-	11/05/14
MOLINA HEALTHCARE OF VIRGINIA INC	VA	0.0	U	U	11/05/14
UNICARE HEALTH INS OF THE MIDWEST	IL	44.1	U	C+	11/05/14

Rating Upgrades

AMERICAN HEALTH INC (PR) was upgraded to B from B- in November 2014 based on expansion in the profitability index, development in the stability index, and an increase in the capitalization index.

AMERICAN SPECIALTY HEALTH INS CO (IL) was upgraded to D- from E in November 2014 based on expansion in the profitability index.

AMERIGROUP WASHINGTON INC (WA) was upgraded to B from B- in November 2014 based on substantial expansion in the profitability index.

CALIFORNIA PHYSICIANS SERVICE (CA) was upgraded to A+ from A in November 2014 based on expansion in the profitability index.

CELTICARE HEALTH PLAN OF MA INC (MA) was upgraded to C+ from C in November 2014 based on substantial expansion in the profitability index, an increase in the capitalization index, and development in the stability index.

CIGNA WORLDWIDE INS CO was upgraded to B from B- in September 2014 based on a higher stability index. composite rating for affiliated CIGNA Corp Group rose to B from B-.

COMMONWEALTH ANNUITY & LIFE INS CO was upgraded to B- from C in September 2014 based on capitalization index and an improved five-year profitability index.

CUATRO LLC (NY) was upgraded to E from E- in November 2014 based on an increase in the capitalization index.

DESERET MUTUAL INS CO was upgraded to B from B- in September 2014 based on a markedly improved capitalization index, an improved investment safety index, a higher five-year profitability index and a markedly improved stability index.

EMI HEALTH was upgraded from C to B- in November 2014 based on overall strength of the index ratios.

ENVISION INS CO was upgraded from C- to C in November 2014 based on overall strength of the index ratios.

EQUITABLE LIFE & CASUALTY INS CO was upgraded to C+ from C in September 2014 based on a higher capitalization index and a markedly improved five-year profitability index.

FIRST ALLMERICA FINANCIAL LIFE INS was upgraded to C- from D+ in September 2014 based on capitalization index, a higher five-year profitability index and a markedly improved stability index. composite rating for affiliated Global Atlantic Financial Group rose to C from C-, as exemplified by recent upgrade of affiliates: COMMONWEALTH ANNUITY & LIFE INS CO to B- from C. ACCORDIA LIFE & ANNUITY CO to C- from D.

HEALTH NET COMMUNITY SOLUTIONS INC (CA) was upgraded to B- from C+ in November 2014 based on an increase in the capitalization index and expansion in the profitability index.

HEALTHSUN HEALTH PLANS (FL) was upgraded to C from D+ in November 2014 based on a substantial increase in the capitalization index.

HUMANA MEDICAL PLAN OF MICHIGAN INC (MI) was upgraded to B from C+ in November 2014 based on substantial expansion in the profitability index.

IA AMERICAN LIFE INS CO was upgraded to C from C- in September 2014 based on an improved capitalization index and a higher five-year profitability index.

INVESTORS LIFE INS CO NORTH AMERICA was upgraded to B from B- in September 2014 based on capitalization index and an improved investment safety index.

K S PLAN ADMINISTRATORS LLC was upgraded from B- to B in November 2014 based on overall strength of the index ratios.

LINCOLN LIFE & ANNUITY CO OF NY was upgraded to B from B- in September 2014 based on an improved investment safety index and an improved five-year profitability index. composite rating for affiliated Lincoln National Corp Group rose to B from B-.

MAGELLAN BEHAVIORAL HEALTH OF PA INC was upgraded from D to D+ in November 2014 based on overall strength of the index ratios

Rating Upgrades (Continued)

MCLAREN HEALTH PLAN INC (MI) was upgraded to B- from C in November 2014 based on an increase in the capitalization index.

MERIDIAN HEALTH PLAN OF ILLINOIS INC (IL) was upgraded to B from B- in November 2014 based on expansion in the profitability index and an increase in the capitalization index.

MERIDIAN HEALTH PLAN OF MICHIGAN INC (MI) was upgraded to B+ from B in November 2014 based on development in the stability index, expansion in the profitability index, and an increase in the capitalization index.

MOLINA HEALTHCARE OF TEXAS INS CO was upgraded to C from C- in September 2014 based on a greatly improved capitalization index and a markedly improved five-year profitability index.

MUTUAL SAVINGS LIFE INS CO was upgraded to A- from B+ in September 2014 based on an improved investment safety index.

PARAMOUNT ADVANTAGE was upgraded from B+ to A- in November 2014 based on overall strength of the index ratios

PARAMOUNT CARE OF MI INC was upgraded from C+ to B- in November 2014 based on overall strength of the index ratios.

PARAMOUNT INS CO (OH) was upgraded to B- from C+ in November 2014 based on expansion in the profitability index.

PROVIDENT AMERICAN INS CO was upgraded to D+ from D in September 2014 based on a higher capitalization index and a markedly improved stability index.

SCRIPPS CLINIC HEALTH PLAN SERVICES (CA) was upgraded to D from E+ in November 2014 based on a substantial increase in the capitalization index, expansion in the profitability index, and development in the stability index.

SELECTCARE OF OKLAHOMA INC (OK) was upgraded to B- from C in November 2014 based on expansion in the profitability index and an increase in the capitalization index.

STONEBRIDGE LIFE INS CO was upgraded to B- from C+ in September 2014 based on a markedly improved capitalization index and a markedly improved stability index.

TRILLIUM COMMUNITY HEALTH PLAN INC (OR) was upgraded to C+ from C in November 2014 based on a substantial increase in the capitalization index, expansion in the profitability index, and development in the stability index.

TRIPLE-S BLUE INC was upgraded to D- from E in September 2014 based on a markedly improved stability index.

TRUSTED HEALTH PLAN INC (DC) was upgraded to C- from D in November 2014 based on substantial expansion in the profitability index and an increase in the capitalization index.

UNITED HEALTHCARE OF ARIZONA INC (AZ) was upgraded to B from B- in November 2014 based on an increase in the capitalization index and expansion in the profitability index.

UNITED HEALTHCARE OF UTAH (UT) was upgraded to B from B- in November 2014 based on expansion in the profitability index.

VOLUNTEER STATE HEALTH PLAN INC (TN) was upgraded to A- from B+ in November 2014 based on expansion in the profitability index.

WELLCARE HEALTH INS OF KENTUCKY INC (KY) was upgraded to C+ from C in November 2014 based on substantial expansion in the profitability index and an increase in the capitalization index.

WILTON REASSURANCE LIFE CO OF NY was upgraded to B from B- in September 2014 based on a higher stability index.

Rating Downgrades

AMERICAN LIFE & SECURITY CORP was downgraded to E from D- in September 2014 due to a substantially lower capitalization index, a substantially lower investment safety index, a lower five-year profitability index and a substantially lower stability index.

AMERICAN MEDICAL & LIFE INS CO was downgraded to E- from D- in September 2014 due to a substantially lower capitalization index, a substantially lower investment safety index, a lower five-year profitability index and a substantially lower stability index.

AMERIGROUP FLORIDA INC (FL) was downgraded to B from B+ in November 2014 based on a substantial diminishment in the profitability index, a drop in the stability index, and a decrease in the capitalization index.

AMERIGROUP TEXAS INC (TX) was downgraded to B+ from A- in November 2014 based on a substantial drop in the stability index, a diminishment in the profitability index, and a decrease in the capitalization index.

ARCADIAN HEALTH PLAN INC (WA) was downgraded to C+ from B in November 2014 based on a substantial drop in the stability index, a diminishment in the profitability index, and contraction in the liquidity index.

ASURIS NORTHWEST HEALTH (WA) was downgraded to B- from B in November 2014 based on a diminishment in the profitability index and a drop in the stability index.

AVERA HEALTH PLANS INC (SD) was downgraded to C- from C in November 2014 based on a decrease in the capitalization index, contraction in the liquidity index, and a diminishment in the profitability index.

BLUE CROSS & BLUE SHIELD OF FLORIDA (FL) was downgraded to B from B+ in November 2014 based on a diminishment in the profitability index and a drop in the stability index.

BLUE CROSS BLUE SHIELD OF KC (MO) was downgraded to B- from B in November 2014 based on a diminishment in the profitability index.

CAPITAL DISTRICT PHYSICIANS HEALTH P (NY) was downgraded to B from B+ in November 2014 based on a diminishment in the profitability index, a drop in the stability index, and a decrease in the capitalization index.

CAREMORE HEALTH PLAN (CA) was downgraded to B+ from A- in November 2014 based on a drop in the stability index.

CIGNA HEALTHCARE OF SOUTH CAROLINA (SC) was downgraded to D+ from C in November 2014 based on a substantial diminishment in the profitability index, a substantial decline in the capitalization index, and a drop in the stability index.

CIGNA HEALTHCARE OF ST LOUIS (MO) was downgraded to D+ from C in November 2014 based on a substantial decline in the capitalization index and a diminishment in the profitability index.

COLUMBUS LIFE INS CO was downgraded to B- from B in September 2014 due to a declining five-year profitability index.

COMMUNITY CARE HEALTH PLAN INC (WI) was downgraded to B- from B in November 2014 based on a substantial diminishment in the profitability index, a drop in the stability index, and a decrease in the capitalization index.

CONNECTICARE INC (CT) was downgraded to B from B+ in November 2014 based on a diminishment in the profitability index.

COVENTRY HEALTH CARE OF WEST VA INC (WV) was downgraded to B+ from A- in November 2014 based on a substantial drop in the stability index, a diminishment in the profitability index, and a decrease in the capitalization index.

EMPIRE HEALTHCHOICE ASSURANCE INC (NY) was downgraded to B- from B in November 2014 based on a drop in the stability index and a diminishment in the profitability index.

EMPIRE HEALTHCHOICE HMO INC (NY) was downgraded to B from B+ in November 2014 based on a substantial drop in the stability index and a substantial diminishment in the profitability index.

EXCELLUS HEALTH PLAN INC (NY) was downgraded to A from A+ in November 2014 based on a diminishment in the profitability index.

Rating Downgrades (Continued)

EXPRESS SCRIPTS INS CO (AZ) was downgraded to B from B+ in November 2014 based on a drop in the stability index, a diminishment in the profitability index, and a decrease in the capitalization index.

FIRST PRIORITY LIFE INS CO (PA) was downgraded to C from B- in November 2014 based on a diminishment in the profitability index and a drop in the stability index.

FLORIDA COMBINED LIFE INS CO INC was downgraded to B from B+ in September 2014 due to a lower investment safety index and a substantially lower five-year profitability index. In addition, the financial strength of affiliates in Blue Cross Blue Shield of Florida is declining Group.

FORETHOUGHT LIFE INS CO was downgraded to B- from B in September 2014 due to a lower capitalization index and a substantially lower stability index. In addition, the composite rating for affiliated Global Atlantic Financial Group fell to C from B.

GLOBALHEALTH INC (OK) was downgraded to C+ from B in November 2014 based on a substantial diminishment in the profitability index.

GOOD HEALTH HMO INC (MO) was downgraded to C from C+ in November 2014 based on a diminishment in the profitability index.

GROUP HOSP & MEDICAL SERVICES INC (DC) was downgraded to B- from B in November 2014 based on a substantial diminishment in the profitability index.

HARMONY HEALTH PLAN OF ILLINOIS INC (IL) was downgraded to B- from B in November 2014 based on a diminishment in the profitability index.

HCSC INS SERVICES CO (IL) was downgraded to B from B+ in November 2014 based on a substantial diminishment in the profitability index and a drop in the stability index.

HEALTH INSURANCE PLAN OF GREATER NY (NY) was downgraded to B from B+ in November 2014 based on a drop in the stability index and a diminishment in the profitability index.

HEALTH NET OF ARIZONA INC (AZ) was downgraded to D+ from C- in November 2014 based on a substantial drop in the stability index, a decrease in the capitalization index, a diminishment in the profitability index, and contraction in the liquidity index.

HEALTHNOW NY INC (NY) was downgraded to B+ from A in November 2014 based on a diminishment in the profitability index.

HEALTHPLUS OF MICHIGAN (MI) was downgraded to B- from B in November 2014 based on a diminishment in the profitability index.

HEALTHSPRING LIFE & HLTH INS CO INC (TX) was downgraded to B- from B in November 2014 based on a substantial diminishment in the profitability index and a drop in the stability index.

HM HEALTH INS CO (PA) was downgraded to C- from C+ in November 2014 based on a substantial decline in the capitalization index, contraction in the liquidity index, and a diminishment in the profitability index.

HORIZON HEALTHCARE OF NEW JERSEY INC (NJ) was downgraded to A- from A in November 2014 based on a diminishment in the profitability index, a drop in the stability index, and a decrease in the capitalization index.

INDEPENDENT HEALTH ASSOC INC (NY) was downgraded to B from B+ in November 2014 based on a diminishment in the profitability index and a drop in the stability index.

INS CO OF SCOTT AND WHITE (TX) was downgraded to D+ from C+ in November 2014 based on a decrease in the capitalization index and a drop in the stability index.

KEYSTONE HEALTH PLAN WEST INC (PA) was downgraded to D+ from B- in November 2014 based on a substantial decline in the capitalization index, a diminishment in the profitability index, and a drop in the stability index.

Rating Downgrades (Continued)

LEADERS LIFE INS CO was downgraded to C+ from B- in September 2014 due to a lower capitalization index, a lower investment safety index and a declining five-year profitability index.

MANAGED HEALTH INC (NY) was downgraded to B- from B+ in November 2014 based on a substantial diminishment in the profitability index, a drop in the stability index, and a decrease in the capitalization index.

MCS LIFE INS CO was downgraded to E+ from D- in September 2014 due to a declining stability index. In addition, the composite rating for affiliated MCS Inc Group fell to E from D+.

MEDCO CONTAINMENT INS CO OF NY (NY) was downgraded to B+ from A- in November 2014 based on a diminishment in the profitability index and a drop in the stability index.

NETWORK HEALTH PLAN was downgraded from D+ to D in November 2014 based on overall strength of the index ratios.

OPTIMA HEALTH PLAN (VA) was downgraded to B+ from A- in November 2014 based on a drop in the stability index, a diminishment in the profitability index, and a decrease in the capitalization index.

OXFORD HEALTH PLANS (NJ) INC (NJ) was downgraded to B from B+ in November 2014 based on a drop in the stability index and a decrease in the capitalization index.

PACIFICARE OF COLORADO INC (CO) was downgraded to B- from B in November 2014 based on a drop in the stability index, a diminishment in the profitability index, and a decrease in the capitalization index.

PHOENIX HEALTH PLANS INC (AZ) was downgraded to D+ from C- in November 2014 based on a substantial decline in the capitalization index and a drop in the stability index.

PREFERREDONE INS CO (MN) was downgraded to B from B+ in November 2014 based on a substantial diminishment in the profitability index.

RED ROCK INS CO was downgraded to F having been placed into rehabilitation by the state insurance regulator in August 2014.

REGENCE BLUESHIELD (WA) was downgraded to B from B+ in November 2014 based on a diminishment in the profitability index and a drop in the stability index.

SELECTCARE OF TEXAS LLC was downgraded from C to C- in November 2014 based on overall strength of the index ratios.

SUMMACARE INC was downgraded from C to C- in November 2014 based on overall strength of the index ratios.

TRUASSURE INS CO was downgraded to C- from C in September 2014 due to a declining capitalization index, a significant decline in its five-year profitability index and a significant decline in its stability index.

UHC OF CALIFORNIA INC (CA) was downgraded to C+ from B- in November 2014 based on a drop in the stability index.

UNITED HEALTHCARE OF ILLINOIS INC (IL) was downgraded to C from B- in November 2014 based on a substantial drop in the stability index and a diminishment in the profitability index.

UNITED SECURITY ASR CO OF PA was downgraded to D+ from C- in September 2014 due to a declining capitalization index, a declining investment safety index and a declining five-year profitability index.

UPMC HEALTH NETWORK INC (PA) was downgraded to D+ from C+ in November 2014 based on a substantial drop in the stability index, a substantial decline in the capitalization index, and a diminishment in the profitability index.

VISTA HEALTH PLAN INC (PA) was downgraded to B- from B in November 2014 based on a substantial diminishment in the profitability index.

WELLCARE OF CONNECTICUT INC was downgraded from C to C- in November 2014 based on overall strength of the index ratios.

Rating Downgrades (Continued)

WELLCARE OF FLORIDA INC (FL) was downgraded to B from B+ in November 2014 based on a substantial diminishment in the profitability index, a substantial drop in the stability index, and a decrease in the capitalization index.

WELLCARE OF GEORGIA INC (GA) was downgraded to B- from B in November 2014 based on a diminishment in the profitability index.

WELLCARE OF LOUISIANA INC was downgraded from B to B- in November 2014 based on overall strength of the index ratios.

WELLCARE OF SOUTH CAROLINA INC (SC) was downgraded to B- from B in November 2014 based on a diminishment in the profitability index and a drop in the stability index.

WELLCARE OF TEXAS INC (TX) was downgraded to B- from B in November 2014 based on a substantial diminishment in the profitability index, a substantial drop in the stability index, and a decrease in the capitalization index.

Appendix

Risk-Adjusted Capital in Weiss Rating Models

There are three distinct rating models used to generate the ratings in this Guide. The first model is for companies that register with state insurance departments under the official classification of Life and Annuity Insurers. The second model is for companies that register under the official classification of Property and Casualty Insurers. The third is for Blue Cross/ Blue Shield plans, and other health insurers, that register as Health plans with the state insurance departments.

A key aspect of both models is the risk-adjusted capital calculations. Therefore, these are discussed in greater detail.

Risk-Adjusted Capital for Life and Annuity Insurers in Weiss Rating Model

Among the most important indicators used in the analysis of an individual company are our two risk-adjusted capital ratios, which are useful tools in determining exposure to investment, liquidity and insurance risk in relation to the capital the company has to cover those risks.

The first risk-adjusted capital ratio evaluates the company's ability to withstand a moderate loss scenario. The second ratio evaluates the company's ability to withstand a severe loss scenario.

In order to calculate these risk-adjusted capital ratios, we follow these steps:

1. Capital Resources
First, we add up all of the company's resources which could be used to cover losses. These include capital, surplus, the Asset Valuation Reserve (AVR), and a portion of the provision for future policyholders' dividends, where appropriate. Additional credit may also be given for the use of conservative reserving assumptions and other "hidden capital" when applicable.

2. Target Capital
Next, we determine the company's target capital. This answers the question: Based upon the company's level of risk in both its insurance business and its investment portfolio, how much capital would it need to cover potential losses during a moderate loss scenario? In other words, we determine how much capital we believe this company s*hould* have.

3. Risk-Adjusted Capital Ratio #1
We compare the results of step 1 with those of step 2. Specifically, we divide the "capital resources" by the "target capital" and express it in terms of a ratio. This ratio is called RACR #1. (See next page for more detail on methodology.)

If a company has a Risk-Adjusted Capital Ratio of 1.0 or more, it means the company has all of the capital we believe it requires to withstand potential losses which could be inflicted by a moderate loss scenario. If the company has less than 1.0, it does not currently have all of the basic capital resources we think it needs. During times of financial distress, companies often have access to additional capital through contributions from a parent company, current profits or reductions in policyholder dividends. Therefore, an allowance is made in our rating system for firms with somewhat less than 1.0 Risk-Adjusted Capital Ratios.

4. Risk-Adjusted Capital Ratio #2	We repeat steps 2 and 3, but now assuming a severe loss scenario. This ratio is called RACR #2.
5. Capitalization Index	We convert RACR #1 and #2 into an index. It is measured on a scale of zero to ten, with ten being the best and seven or better considered strong. A company whose capital, surplus and AVR equal its target capital will have a Risk-Adjusted Capital Ratio of 1.0 and a Risk-Adjusted Capital Index of 7.0.

How We Determine Target Capital

The basic procedure for determining target capital is to ask these questions:

1. What is the breakdown of the company's investment portfolio and types of business?

2. For each category, what are the potential losses which could be incurred in the loss scenario?

3. In order to cover those potential losses, how much in capital resources does the company need? It stands to reason that more capital is needed as a cushion for losses on high-risk investments, such as junk bonds, than would be necessary for low-risk investments, such as AAA-rated utility bonds.

   Unfortunately, the same questions we have raised about Wall Street rating systems with respect to how they rate insurance companies can be asked about the way they rate bonds. However, we do not rate bonds ourselves. Therefore, we must rely upon the bond ratings of other rating agencies. This is another reason why we have stricter capital requirements for the insurance companies. It accounts for the fact that they may need some extra protection in case an AAA-rated bond may not be quite as good as it appears to be.

   Finally, target capital is adjusted for the company's spread of risk in the diversification of its investment portfolio, the size and number of the policies it writes and the diversification of its business.

Table 1 on the next page shows target capital percentages used by the National Association of Insurance Commissioners (NAIC) in relation to Weiss Risk-Adjusted Capital Ratios #1 and #2 (RACR #1 and RACR #2).

The percentages shown in the table answer the question: How much should the firm hold in capital resources for every $100 it has committed to each category? Several of the items in Table 1 are expressed as ranges. The actual percentages used in the calculation of target capital for an individual company may vary due to the levels of risks in the operations, investments or policy obligations of that specific company.

Table 1. Target Capital Percentages

| Asset Risk | Weiss Ratings | | NAIC |
	RACR#1 (%)	RACR#2 (%)	
Bonds			
Government guaranteed bonds	0	0	0
Class 1	.5-.75	1-1.5	0.4
Class 2	2	5	1.3
Class 3	5	15	4.6
Class 4	10	30	10
Class 5	20	60	22
Class 6	20	60	15
Mortgages			
In good standing	0.5	1	0
90 days overdue	1.7-20	3.8-25	0.1-18
In process of foreclosure	25-33	33-50	1.4-23
Real Estate			
Class 1	20	50	15
Class 2	10	33	23
Preferred Stock			
Class 1	3	5	1.1
Class 2	4	6	3.0
Class 3	7	9	7.2
Class 4	12	15	15
Class 5	22	29	20
Class 6	30	39	15
Class 7	3-30	5-39	35
Common Stock			
Unaffiliated	25	33	35
Affiliated	25-100	33-100	35
Short-term investment	0.5	1	0.4
Premium notes	2	5	6.8
Collateral loans	2	5	6.8
Separate account equity	25	33	11 **
Other invested assets	5	10	6.8
Insurance Risk			
Individual life reserves*	.06-.15	.08-.21	.09-.23
Group life reserves*	.05-.12	.06-.16	.08-.18
Individual Health Premiums			
Class 1	12-20	15-25	15-25
Class 2	9.6	12	12
Class 3	6.4	8	8
Class 4	12-28	15-35	15-35
Class 5	12-20	15-25	15-25
Group Health Premiums			
Class 1	5.6-12	7-15	7-15
Class 2	20	25	25
Class 3	9.6	12	25
Class 4	6.4	8	8
Class 5	12-20	15-25	15-25
Managed care credit	5-40	6-50	NAIC calculation
Premiums subject to rate guarantees	100-209	120-250	2.4-6.4
Individual claim reserves	4	5	5-7
Group claim reserves	4	5	5-7
Reinsurance	0-2	0-5	0.8
Interest Rate Risk			
Policy loans	0-2	0-5	1.1
Life reserves	1-2	1-3	0.7-1.1
Individual annuity reserves	1-3	1-5	0.7-1.1
Group annuity reserves	1-2	1-3	0.7-1.1
Guaranteed interest contract reserves	1-2	1-3	0.7-1.1

All numbers are shown for illustrative purposes. Figures actually used in the formula vary annually based on industry experience.

*Based on net amount at risk.

**Risk-based capital for separate account assets that are not tied to an index = 100% of the risk-based capital of assets in the accounts.

Investment Class   Descriptions

Investment Class		Descriptions
Government guaranteed bonds		Guaranteed bonds issued by U.S. and other governments which receive the top rating of state insurance commissioners.
Bonds	Class 1	Investment grade bonds rated AAA, AA or A by Moody's or Standard & Poor's or deemed AAA - A equivalent by state insurance commissioners.
	Class 2	Investment grade bonds with some speculative elements, rated BBB or equivalent.
	Class 3	Noninvestment grade bonds, rated BB or equivalent.
	Class 4	Noninvestment grade bonds, rated B or equivalent.
	Class 5	Noninvestment grade bonds, rated CCC, CC or C or equivalent.
	Class 6	Noninvestment grade bonds, in or near default.
Mortgages		Mortgages in good standing
		Mortgages 90 days past due
		Mortgages in process of foreclosure
Real Estate	Class 1	Properties acquired in satisfaction of debt.
	Class 2	Company occupied and other investment properties.
Preferred stock	Class 1	Highest quality unaffiliated preferred stock.
	Class 2	High quality unaffiliated preferred stock.
	Class 3	Medium quality unaffiliated preferred stock.
	Class 4	Low quality unaffiliated preferred stock.
	Class 5	Lowest quality unaffiliated preferred stock.
	Class 6	Unaffiliated preferred stock, in or near default.
	Class 7	Affiliated preferred stock.
Common stock		Unaffiliated common stock.
		Affiliated common stock.
Short-term investments		All investments whose maturities at the time of acquisition were one year or less.
Premium Notes		Loans for payment of premiums.
Collateral loans		Loans made to a company or individual where the underlying security is in the form of bonds, stocks, or other marketable securities.
Separate account assets		Investments held in an account segregated from the general assets of the company, generally used to provide variable annuity benefits.
Other invested assets		Any invested assets that do not fit under the main categories above.
Individual life reserves		Funds set aside for payment of life insurance benefits under an individual contract rather than a company or group, underwriting based on individual profile.
Group life reserves		Funds set aside for payment of life insurance benefits under a contract with at least 10 people whereby all members have a common interest and are joined for a reason other than to obtain insurance.
Individual health premiums	Class 1	Usual and customary hospital and medical premiums which include traditional medical reimbursement plans that are subject to annual rate increases based on the company's claims experience.
	Class 2	Medicare supplement, dental, and other limited benefits anticipating rate increases.
	Class 3	Hospital indemnity plans, accidental death and dismemberment policies, and other limited benefits not anticipating rate increases.
	Class 4	Noncancellable disability income.
	Class 5	Guaranteed renewable disability income.

                www.weissratings.com

Group health premiums	Class 1	Usual and customary hospital and medical premiums which include traditional medical reimbursement plans that are subject to annual rate increases based on the company's claims experience.
	Class 2	Stop loss and minimum premium where a known claims liability is minimal or nonexistent.
	Class 3	Medicare supplement, dental, and other limited benefits anticipating rate increases.
	Class 4	Hospital indemnity plans, accidental death and dismemberment policies, and other limited benefits not anticipating rate increases.
	Class 5	Disability Income.
Managed care credit		Premiums for HMO and PPO business which carry less risk than traditional indemnity business. Included in this credit are provider compensation arrangements such as salary, capitation and fixed payment per service.
Premiums subject to rate guarantees		Health insurance premiums from policies where the rate paid by the policyholder is guaranteed for a period of time, such as one year, 15 months, 27 months or 37 months.
Individual claim reserves		Accident and health reserves for claims on individual policies.
Group claim reserves		Accident and health reserves for claims on group policies.
Reinsurance		Amounts recoverable on paid and unpaid losses for all reinsurance ceded; unearned premiums on accident and health reinsurance ceded; and funds held with unauthorized reinsurers.
Policy loans		Loans against the cash value of a life insurance policy.
Life reserves		Reserves for life insurance claims net of reinsurance and policy loans.
Individual annuity reserves		Reserves held in order to pay off maturing individual annuities or those surrendered before maturity.
Group annuity reserves		Reserves held in order to pay off maturing group annuities or those surrendered before maturity.
GIC reserves		Reserves held to pay off maturing guaranteed interest contracts.

Table 2. Bond Default Rates - potential losses as a percent of bond portfolio

	(1)	(2)	(3)	(4)	(5)	(6)	(7)	(8)
	Moody's	Moody's		3 Cum.	Weiss Ratings	Assumed	Losses	RACR
	15 Yr	12 Yr	Worst	Recession	15 Year	Loss	as % of	#2
Bond	Rate	Rate	Year	Years	Rate	Rate	Holdings	Rate
Rating	(%)	(%)	(%)	(%)	(%)	(%)	(%)	(%)
Aaa	2.80	1.60	0.10	0.30	1.89	50	0.95	1.00
Aa	2.00	1.60	0.20	0.60	2.19	50	1.09	1.00
A	3.30	2.50	0.40	1.20	3.67	55	2.02	1.00
Baa	7.20	5.50	1.10	3.26	8.58	60	5.15	5.00
Ba	20.10	17.90	8.40	23.08	36.47	65	23.71	15.00
B	33.70	32.50	21.60	50.80	62.24	70	43.57	30.00

Comments On Target Capital Percentages

The factors that are chiefly responsible for the conservative results of our Risk-Adjusted Capital Ratios are the investment risks of bond Classes 2 - 6, mortgages, real estate and affiliate common stock as well as the interest rate risk for annuities and GICs. Comments on the basis of these figures are found below. Additional comments address factors that vary based on particular performance or risk characteristics of the individual company.

Bonds   Target capital percentages for bonds are derived from a model that factors in historical cumulative bond default rates from the last 20 years and the additional loss potential during a prolonged economic decline. The continuance of post-World War II prosperity is by no means certain. Realistic analyses of potential losses must factor in the possibility of severe economic reversal. Table 2 shows how this was done for each bond rating classification. A 15-year cumulative default rate is used (column 1), due to the 15-year average maturity at issue of bonds held by life insurance companies. These are historical default rates for 1970-1990 for each bond class, taken from *Moody's Studies Loss Potential of Life Insurance Assets.*

To factor in the additional loss potential of a severe three-year-long economic decline, we reduced the base to Moody's 12-year rate (column 2), determined the worst single year experience (column 3), spread that experience over three years (column 4), and added the historical 12-year rate to the 3-year projection to derive Weiss Ratings 15-year default rate (column 5). Note: Due to the shrinking base of nondefaulted bonds in each year, column 4 may be somewhat less than three times column 3, and column 5 may be somewhat less than the sum of column 2 and column 4.

The next step was to determine the losses that could be expected from these defaults. This would be equivalent to the capital a company should have to cover those losses. Loss rates were assigned for each bond class (column 6), based on the fact that higher-rated issues generally carry less debt and the fact that the debt is also better secured, leading to higher recovery rates upon default. Column 7 shows losses as a percent of holdings for each bond class. Column 8 shows the target capital percentages that are used in RACR #2 (Table 1, RACR #2 column, Bonds – classes 1 to 6).

Regulations limiting junk bond holdings of insurers to a set percent of assets are a tacit acknowledgement that the 10% and 20% maximum reserve requirements used by State Insurance Commissioners (Table 1, NAIC column, Bonds-classes 4, 5, and 6) are inadequate. If the figure adequately represented full loss potential, there would be no need to limit holdings through legislation since an adequate loss reserve would provide sufficient capital to absorb potential losses.

Mortgages   Mortgage default rates for the Risk-Adjusted Capital Ratios are derived from historical studies of mortgage and real estate losses in selected depressed markets. The rate for RACR #2 (Table 1, RACR #2 column, Mortgages – 90 days overdue) will vary between 3.8% and 25%, based on the performance of the company's mortgage portfolio in terms of mortgage loans 90 days or more past due, in process of foreclosure and foreclosed during the previous year.

Real Estate   The 33% rate (Table 1, RACR #2 column, Real Estate - Class 2) used for potential real estate losses in Weiss Ratings ratios is based on historical losses in depressed markets. It avoids the commonly made assumption that the continuous appreciation of property values experienced since World War II must inevitably continue.

Affiliate Common Stock   The target capital rate on affiliate common stock for RACR #2 can vary between 33% and 100% (Table 1, RACR #2 column, Common stock – Affiliate), depending on the financial strength of the affiliate and the prospects for obtaining capital from the affiliate should the need arise.

Insurance Risk   Calculations of target capital for insurance risk vary according to categories. For individual and group life insurance, target capital is a percentage of net amount at risk (total amount of insurance in force less reserves). Individual and group health insurance risk is calculated as a percentage of premium. Categories vary from "usual and customary hospital and medical premiums" where risk is relatively low because losses from one year are recouped by annual rate increases, to "noncancellable disability income" where the risk of loss is greater because disability benefits are paid in future years without the possibility of recovery.

Reinsurance   This factor varies with the quality of the reinsuring companies and the type of reinsurance being used (e.g., co-insurance, modified co-insurance, yearly renewable term, etc.).

Interest Rate Risk On Annuities   The 1 - 5% rate on individual annuities as a percentage of reserves (Table 1, RACR #2 column 3, Individual annuity reserves), and the 1 - 3% rate for group annuities as a percentage of reserves (Table 1, RACR #2 column 3, Group annuity reserves and GICs), are derived from studies of potential losses that can occur when assets and liabilities are not properly matched.

Companies are especially prone to losses in this area for one of two reasons: (1) They promise high interest rates on their annuities and have not locked in corresponding yields on their investments. If interest rates fall, the company will have difficulties earning the promised rate. (2) They lock in high returns on their investments but allow policy surrenders without market value adjustments. If market values decline and surrenders increase, liquidity problems can result in substantial losses.

The target capital figure used for each company is based on the surrender characteristics of its policies, the interest rate used in calculating reserves and the actuarial analyses found in New York Regulation 126 filing, or similar studies where applicable.

Risk-Adjusted Capital for Property and Casualty Insurers

Over 100 companies that are registered with state insurance departments as property and casualty insurers offer health insurance policies. Included in this number are four Blue Cross/Blue Shield plans. Our ratings on these companies make use of the data in the Property and Casualty Statutory Statements that are required by state insurance departments. These financial statements employ a system of accounting that differs from that used by companies filing Life and Health Statutory Statements. Some of the chief distinguishing features of the Property and Casualty Statutory Accounting include:

- Life and health companies must hold reserves to protect specifically against investment losses. Property and casualty insurers keep no equivalent protection. One of the consequences of the lack of an investment loss reserve is that property and casualty companies, on the average, hold more nonaffiliated common stock than do life insurers. This factor is considered in our evaluation of capital adequacy.

- Policy reserves for life insurers are reduced to reflect investment income to be earned between the time premiums are received by the company, and the time when claims are to be paid. Property and casualty companies generally do not reduce or discount their reserves for the time value of money.

- Underwriting profits and losses for property and casualty insurers are calculated without reference to investment income.

Despite these factors, it is our goal to provide ratings that consumers can easily understand and to make technical differences as transparent to consumers as possible. The final ratings are intended to give the same message about our opinion of insurers financial strength.

As with the life and health companies, there are two risk-adjusted capital ratios, which measure whether the company has enough capital to cover unexpected losses.

However, unlike the life and health companies, the risks related to pricing and claims are more important, while the risks associated with investments are reduced because there is little exposure to risky investments such as junk bonds or mortgages.

Pricing Risk   The risk that premium levels are not sufficient to establish adequate reserves and/or pay claims and related expenses. Individual target capital percentages are used for each line of business based on the riskiness of the line and the company's own experience with underwriting losses and reserve shortfalls. Target capital requirements are reduced to account for the time value of money.

Risky Lines of Business and Catastrophic Losses

These include fire, earthquake, multiple peril (including storm damage), and similar personal and commercial property coverage. Even excluding Hurricane Andrew, the insured losses from natural disasters since 1989 have been far greater than in previous decades. Yet, too many insurance companies are basing their risk calculations on the assumption that losses will return to more normal levels. They are not ready for the possibility that the pattern of increasing disasters might be a real, continuing trend.

Also considered high-risk lines are medical malpractice, general liability, product liability, and other similar liability coverage. Court awards for damages often run into the millions. These settlement amounts can be very difficult to predict. This uncertainty hinders an insurer's ability to accurately assess how much to charge policyholders and how much to set aside to pay claims. Of special concern are large, unexpected liabilities related to environmental damages such as asbestos. Similar risk may lie hidden in coverage for medical equipment and procedures, industrial wastes, carcinogens, and other substances found in products previously viewed as benign. Companies that offer a variety of types of insurance in addition to health coverage can get into financial difficulties due to any of their lines of business. Accordingly, it is essential that the company's whole operation be strong. If the company is overrun with claims from an earthquake of hurricane, its ability to pay health claims will also be affected.

Risk-Adjusted Capital for Health Insurers

As with the other rating systems, the health insurance system includes two risk-adjusted capital ratios to measure a company's ability to withstand unexpected losses during moderate and severe loss scenarios. Health insurers are more likely exposed to risk from pricing and claims than from investments. They have no interest rate risk, in terms of potential policy surrenders, the way life insurance companies do.

Capital resources include the company's net worth adjusted for surplus notes; credit or penalty for overstating or understating reserves; and credit or penalty for the company's ability to spread risk based on overall net worth of the company's affiliate group.

These health plans file yet another type of statutory statement, different from life and health or property and casualty insurers. Weiss Rating System for health insurers addresses the unique business and accounting factors relevant to these firms. Among the many differences are the following:

- Rather than setting up reserves as a liability the way life insurance companies do, health insurer claims reserves are part of net worth.

- Investments are carried at book value, but market value is shown on Schedule B of the statutory statement. Market values are considered in the capitalization and liquidity indexes.

- Health insurers do not hold reserves to protect specifically against investment losses. This factor is considered in our evaluation of capital adequacy.

- Health insurers do not have long-term obligations like life insurance and annuities. Accordingly, reserves are not discounted for the time value of money. Our analysis examines reserve adequacy by comparing one year's reserve estimates with claims and medical expenses actually paid during the subsequent year, without factoring in investment income.

LONG-TERM CARE INSURANCE PLANNER

This planner is designed to help you decide what kind of long-term care insurance is best for you and help you shop for the policy that meets your needs. Many insurers charge a lot more – or less – for very similar policies. So there's a great benefit to shopping around. No policy is exactly alike. However, if you follow these steps, it will be easier to compare policies side by side:

Step 1: Try to determine, ahead of time, what type of care you think you will need from others beyond the assistance your own family members may be able to provide:

	Yes	No
Custodial Care	[ ]	[ ]
Intermediate Care	[ ]	[ ]
Skilled Care	[ ]	[ ]

This isn't easy, because it's often hard to anticipate your future needs, but try your best to decide if you're going to want access to one of the following. Custodial care is provided by someone without medical training who helps you with daily activities. Intermediate care includes occasional nursing and rehabilitative care supervised by skilled medical personnel. Skilled care includes 24-hour care provided by a skilled nurse or therapist.

Step 2: Decide where you would most likely be receiving the care?

	Yes	No
In-Home Care*	[ ]	[ ]
Nursing Home*	[ ]	[ ]
Adult Day Care	[ ]	[ ]
Assisted Living Facility	[ ]	[ ]
Other _____	[ ]	[ ]

*Typically available with all three levels of care – custodial, intermediate, and skilled.

Most people prefer in-home care. However, if you have no family members to help you at home, in-home care could be prohibitively expensive, especially if it requires skilled care. Nursing homes are designed for 24-hour care and are best utilized for short-term stays. Adult day care is an option, but will probably require someone, such as a family member, who can drop you off and pick you up daily. Assisted living facilities are increasingly popular, offering a good balance between independence and assistance. Other types of care could include hospice care (for the terminally ill) or respite care (temporary assistance to help relieve family members).

Step 3: Check out the facilities in the area in which you plan to live, make sure you're comfortable with them, and find out much how they cost:

	Estimated Costs
In-Home Care	_____
Nursing Home	_____
Assisted Living Facility	_____
Adult Day Care	_____
Other	_____

The insurance company is going to pay you a daily benefit that will be applied toward the cost of your care. Most of the costs above that daily benefit will have to come out of your own pocket. Therefore, find a facility that you'd be comfortable with, and then try to get a general idea of how much it would cost. Each facility may offer a different rate schedule for each level of care it provides, so make sure you understand the differences. For care within your home, contact a home care agency and ask them about the going rates for home nurses and therapists. Also consider costs associated with any modifications that may be needed for your home, such as wheelchair accessibility, handicap rails, etc.

Step 4: Try to estimate how much of the long-term care expenses you will be able to pay on your own: $_____ per month.

Your financial planner may be able to give you an estimate of your retirement income available for health care. However, even a good estimate can be off the mark, so make sure your policy covers enough to avoid being financially strapped by long-term care expenses. Later, make sure your agent takes this information into consideration when he works out the terms of your policy. He should limit your out-of-pocket expenses to what you have indicated here.

Step 5: Try to arrive at a reasonable guess regarding when you might start using the benefits.

_____

Again, it's hard to predict. But if you're in reasonably good health and you have a family history of longevity, that's something to consider. If you're already suffering from chronic health problems, you may need the benefits sooner rather than later. If it's more than 10 years from now, you can buy a long-term care policy with an optional inflation protection feature to help protect against the rising cost of health care. This can add significantly to the cost, but you get what you pay for. Typically, the insurance company will add an extra five percent to your daily benefit, compounded annually. Thus, if the policy provides a $100 daily benefit now, it would rise to $163 in 10 years.

Step 6: Determine whether you prefer a "tax-qualified" policy or a "non-qualified" policy:

	Yes	No
Tax-Qualified Policy	[ ]	[ ]
Non-Qualified Policy	[ ]	[ ]

If you buy a <u>tax-qualified</u> policy, you will be able to claim the policy premiums as itemized medical expenses on your tax return. Furthermore, the benefits you receive will <u>not</u> be subject to federal income taxation, up to a dollar cap. If you purchase a <u>non-qualified</u> policy, you will not be able to itemize the premiums. As to the benefits, the IRS has yet to clarify whether or not they will be subject to federal income taxation. Do not assume that a tax-qualified policy will automatically be more beneficial. Reason: Typically, a tax-qualified policy will have stricter guidelines as to when you can access the policy benefits. You also may not be able to take advantage of the tax benefits. You may want to consult with a tax advisor on this subject.

Step 7: Find insurance agents in your area that <u>specialize</u> in long-term care policies:

Agent Name	Phone Number	Specialization in LTC? (Y / N)	Name of insurance company
_____	_____	(Y / N)	_____
_____	_____	(Y / N)	_____
_____	_____	(Y / N)	_____
_____	_____	(Y / N)	_____

Long-term care insurance is very complex. Therefore, make sure you work with an agent who specializes in long-term care policies, and don't limit your choices to someone you know or who is associated with your broker. The agent should be able to help educate you and clarify any questions you have – not only on policies he or she sells, but on others as well. Try to avoid agents that work strictly with one insurance company. Complete the remaining steps with the direct assistance of the agent you choose.

Step 8: Ask your agent for the names of at least three different policies, from different insurers, that you can compare.

	Policy A	Policy B	Policy C
Insurance Company Name	_____	_____	_____
Policy Name/Number	_____	_____	_____

Step 9: Have your agent check the financial strength rating for each company.

Financial Strength Rating

Policy A: _____

Policy B: _____

Policy C: _____

It may be a long time before you begin to submit claims. Therefore, you will want to make sure your insurance company will still be viable at that time. If you use the Financial Strength Ratings, we recommend you favor companies with a rating of B+ (good) or higher, and we suggest you avoid companies with a rating of D+ (weak) or lower.

Step 10: Favor companies that have more experience with long-term care insurance.

	Years of experience with long-term care	Have they ever raised rates for existing policyholders?
Policy A:	_____	(Y / N)
Policy B:	_____	(Y / N)
Policy C:	_____	(Y / N)

This should not be a deal breaker. But you're better off with a company that has been offering long-term care policies for a while and has never raised rates for existing policyholders. In contrast, companies that are new in long-term care – or have a history of raising rates on existing policies – are more likely to raise your rates in the future.

Step 11: If you're considering buying a policy with your spouse, check how you qualify for a spousal discount.

Policy A: _____

Policy B: _____

Policy C: _____

In some cases, you may need to be married to qualify; in others you don't have to be formally married. Some insurers require that the policies be exactly the same, while others do not.

Step 12: Ask your agent for quotes on the monthly premiums. Make sure the quotes are based on the preferences and needs that you outlined in steps 1-6.

	Single Policy Premium	Combined Policy Premium	% Savings
Policy A:	_____	_____	_____
Policy B:	_____	_____	_____
Policy C:	_____	_____	_____

If you can buy your long-term care policy with a spouse or significant other, make sure you take advantage of spousal discounts, which can save you up to 20% on the combined premium.

Step 13: Find out exactly what each policy covers in addition to the basics that you require:

	Policy A	Policy B	Policy C
Custodial	(Y / N)	(Y / N)	(Y / N)
Intermediate	(Y / N)	(Y / N)	(Y / N)
Skilled	(Y / N)	(Y / N)	(Y / N)

The actual policies that your agent has suggested may differ somewhat from your wish list of benefits, including some that you did not ask for, or excluding others that you wanted. This may help explain some, but not all, of the price differences.

Step 14: Ask your agent to give you a list of the types of facilities that are included and how they are defined. Facilities may include nursing home care, in-home care, adult day care, hospice care, assisted living facilities, and other options.

Policy A
_____
_____
_____

Policy B
_____
_____

Policy C
_____
_____
_____

Step 15: Find out the basic terms of coverage and reimbursement, as follows:

Policy A: How the company calculates elimination period: _____

Facility of Care	Elimination Periods	Benefit Periods	Daily Benefit
In-home care:	_____	_____	_____
Nursing home	_____	_____	_____
Assisted living:	_____	_____	_____
Adult day care:	_____	_____	_____

Policy B: How the company calculates elimination period: _____

Facility of Care	Elimination Periods	Benefit Periods	Daily Benefit
In-home care:	_____	_____	_____
Nursing home	_____	_____	_____
Assisted living:	_____	_____	_____
Adult day care:	_____	_____	_____

Policy C: How the company calculates elimination period: _____

Facility of Care	Elimination Periods	Benefit Periods	Daily Benefit
In-home care:	_____	_____	_____
Nursing home	_____	_____	_____
Assisted living:	_____	_____	_____
Adult day care:	_____	_____	_____

Elimination Period: This is similar to a deductible. It is the amount of time you pay for services out of your own pocket <u>before</u> the insurance policy takes over. Typically, you can select elimination periods of 0, 30, 60, 90, or 180 days, depending on the policy and insurance company. But you must find out exactly how the elimination period is satisfied. Let's say, for example, you need care on days 1, 4 and 10. With some policies, that would be counted as only THREE days toward your elimination period. With other policies, it would be counted as TEN days, which would mean you'd start collecting the benefits much sooner.

Benefit Period (or maximum): Some companies tell you the length of time the policy will be paid; others just tell you the maximum value of benefits to be paid. The benefit period can typically range from 2 to 5 years, and some may even have an unlimited lifetime period.

Daily Benefit: The amount the policy will pay for each day of covered services. Some plans offer a daily benefit reimbursable on a weekly or monthly basis giving you more flexibility. For example, if you selected a daily benefit of $100 reimbursable on a weekly basis you would be reimbursed for up to $700 dollars per week in expenses no matter how much you incurred on any one day.

Step 16: Determine if the policy is "a pool of money" contract.

	Pool of money?
Policy A:	(Y / N)
Policy B:	(Y / N)
Policy C:	(Y / N)

Most current policies will actually give you more time to collect the benefits than indicated by the benefit period. For example, in a four-year policy, if you need care on and off, you may not use up all your benefits in that four-year period. So you could continue to collect those unused benefits in subsequent years as well. These are called "pool of money" contracts. (To calculate your pool, just multiple the total numbers of days by the daily benefit.) Other policies will actually end at the end of the four years, no matter what.

Step 17: Check into the requirements needed to activate the policy.

Policy A: _____

_____

Policy B: _____

_____

Policy C: _____

_____

You will need to meet what is referred to as "benefit triggers" before the policy can begin covering expenses and these can vary from policy to policy. Under most policies, you will be qualified for benefits when you meet certain conditions, such as: 1) The inability to perform activities of daily living ("ADLs"), which typically include bathing, dressing, transferring, toileting, eating, continence, and taking medication on your own; and 2) cognitive impairment. Some plans require you to satisfy either condition (1) or (2); some require that you satisfy both conditions. Still others also allow for a third trigger, often referred to as "medical necessity." This means that a doctor determines if you need care due to an injury or sickness. Make sure you find out the precise requirements of each policy.

Step 18: Find out what other features are included (or can be added by a "rider") to the policy.

Your agent should explain any additional features that may be included in the policies you are comparing including the following:

	Policy A	Policy B	Policy C
Waiver of Premium	(Y / N)	(Y / N)	(Y / N)
Nonforfeiture	(Y / N)	(Y / N)	(Y / N)
Restoration of Benefits	(Y / N)	(Y / N)	(Y / N)
Alternate Care Plan	(Y / N)	(Y / N)	(Y / N)
Bed Reservation	(Y / N)	(Y / N)	(Y / N)
Guaranteed Renewable	(Y / N)	(Y / N)	(Y / N)
Inflation Protection	(Y / N)	(Y / N)	(Y / N)

Your agent will explain the details. Just make sure that you actually need these additional benefits, because they can add substantially to your total costs.

Medicare Prescription Drug Planner

This planner is designed to help you compare the annual premium costs of a senior benefit package that includes prescription drug coverage. In conjunction with the worksheet attached, follow the steps for calculating the costs of prescription drug coverage options. Upon completion, you'll be able to compare the annual cost of each option. In addition to the cost, keep other out-of-pocket expenses, benefit coverage, and provider accessibility in mind, and then select the plan best suited to meet your needs.

STEP ONE: Review the cost of your current health care coverage.

Look up your current coverage and find the premium you pay, if any, for the coverage.

Original Medicare – Part A and Part B coverage

Do you receive benefits directly through the Original Medicare program? .... Y / N

If yes, you may be paying the Part B premium (there is no premium for Part A) yourself or perhaps you have an employer plan or a Medicare Supplement insurance policy that pays the premium.

▶ Record the annual amount, if any, you pay: **Part A and B: $**

Transfer this figure to the available lines under the Part A and B column on the worksheet. ✍

Employer Retirement Plan Coverage

Do you receive benefits through an Employer plan? .... Y / N

If yes, the coverage is most likely comprehensive and includes drug coverage.

▶ Record the annual amount, if any, you pay: **Employer Plan: $** _____

Transfer this figure to the available lines under the Employer Plan column on the worksheet. ✍

Medicare Supplement Insurance Policy ("Medigap")

Medigap policies are available through private insurers. Prior to 2006 there were 10 standardized plans that an insurer could offer. Three of those, H, I and J, offered some prescription drug coverage. This coverage will continue to be available to you if you already own one of these policies. Note: These policies were discontinued in June 2010 and are not available to new purchasers.

Medicare Supplement Insurance Policy ("Medigap") *continued*

Do you own a Medigap Plan H, I or J? .... Y / N

▶ If so, what do you pay in annual premiums?　　**Medigap Plan H, I or J:** $

_____

Transfer this figure to the available line under the Medigap Plan H, I or J column on the worksheet. 🖎

Do you own a different Medigap Plan? .... Y / N

▶ If so, what do you pay in annual premiums?　　**Medigap Plan A thru G :** $

_____

Transfer this figure to the available line under the Medigap Plan column on the worksheet. 🖎

Medicare Advantage Plan

Medicare Advantage policies are available through private insurers. You pay the insurer a premium and they provide coverage that is at least as good, if not better, than Medicare Part A and B. In turn, they receive reimbursement from the government. You are often restricted to a network of physicians with these plans.

Do you receive your benefits from a Medicare Advantage insurer? .... Y / N

▶ If so, what do you pay in annual premiums, if any? **Medicare Advantage Plan:** $ _____

Transfer this figure to the Annual Cost column in the Medicare Advantage row on the worksheet. 🖎

STEP TWO: Find the cost of your preferred Part D Prescription Drug Provider/Plan.

Part D is the new Prescription Drug component of the Medicare program. Under Part D you can obtain some coverage for your medications through a private provider. These plans will provide, at a minimum, the coverage mandated by the government. Otherwise each plan will vary depending on drugs covered, premiums, co-pays and participating pharmacies.

In this step we guide you through what you need to do in order to select a Part D provider. The average cost for Part D plans range from $34.47 to $68.63 per month. However, the range within each state can be significant. Your goal is to find the lowest cost plan that gives you the best price on the prescriptions you use and has convenient participating pharmacies.

Everything you need to do can be done on the Medicare website, however, you will need a computer and internet access. The site is loaded with information so we recommend that you first spend a few hours browsing the site to learn more. The site and process of selecting a provider can be overwhelming so you may want to have a family member or someone else to work with you through this process.

First: Gather critical information. Make sure to have the following:

✓ Medicare Number .... _____

✓ Effective Date of Medicare Part A or B coverage .... _____

✓ Birth Date .... _____

✓ Zip Code .... _____

✓ List of prescription drugs you use and their dosages.

Drug	**Dosage**
_____	_____
_____	_____
_____	_____
_____	_____
_____	_____
_____	_____

✓ Preferred pharmacies in your area.

Pharmacy Name

_____

_____

_____

Second: **Visit www.Medicare.gov.**

We can't list all of the website's steps here but to start out Click [*Compare Medicare Prescription Drug Plans*] and then Click [*Find a Medicare Prescription Drug Plan*]. You will then be asked to enter your personal information. The website will walk you through entering your prescription drugs and dosages so that you can get a list of Part D providers in your state that cover your drugs, the pharmacies and the contact information. You may select three plans to compare side by side at one time.

Third: **Narrow down your choices.**

Don't overburden yourself trying to compare all 40+ plans available in your state. Narrow your list down to the five or seven plans that cover your prescriptions and contract with local pharmacies. The premium cost of a plan for the minimum coverage will run you between $151.20 to $1,216.80 per year, in 2015, depending on where you live.

To narrow down your list further look for plans that reduce your out-of-pocket costs by covering the $320 deductible, the 25% co-payments and/or the $4,700 gap in coverage. After that, the government limits your co-payment to $2.65 for generic drugs and $6.60 all other drugs.

Use the lines below to enter the information to help you compare your choices. Enter the annual Premium charged by the plan and then under Deductible, Co-Pay and Gap enter the dollar amount <u>you would be responsible for</u> under each of the plan choices. Add these across to get an estimate of your total estimated costs under each plan.

Provider/Plan Name:	Premium	Annual Deductible (max $320)	Co-Pay Max (max $660)	Cost $1,740 Gap	Total Estimate
_____	_____ +	_____ +	_____ +	_____ =	_____
_____	_____ +	_____ +	_____ +	_____ =	_____
_____	_____ +	_____ +	_____ +	_____ =	_____
_____	_____ +	_____ +	_____ +	_____ =	_____
_____	_____ +	_____ +	_____ +	_____ =	_____

If you still need to narrow down your choices, then look for plans that either reduces your co-payment amount to less than $2.65 for generic drugs and $6.60 all other drugs and/or provide other benefits that you find attractive.

<u>**Final Part D Provider Selection**</u>

<u>Provider / Plan Name</u>   **<u>Total Cost Estimate</u>**

_____ $ _____

Transfer the total cost estimate of your final selection (above) to the available lines under the Part D column on the worksheet.

STEP THREE: Consider a Medicare Advantage Plan.

If you already have a Medicare Advantage plan that you are happy with, you may want to skip this step.

The Medicare Advantage program allows you to join a private plan that participates in the Medicare program. Medicare Advantage providers receive funds from the government for providing you benefits and often provides coverage beyond what Medicare offers.

Most of these plans provide prescription drug coverage at the same level or better than the requirements set by Medicare, either inclusive in their plan or in combination with a Medicare Part D provider. Either way you will only pay one premium to the Medicare Advantage insurer for all the coverage.

If you already belong to a Medicare Advantage plan they will send you information regarding their coverage for prescription drugs. Otherwise you can find information on the medicare.gov website or from the insurers through the mail, local kiosks or by calling their toll-free numbers. To narrow down your choices based on the prescription drug coverage use the following space to compare the different plans. Don't forget to check Weiss Financial Strength Rating to find out if the insurer is in good financial health.

Provider/Plan Name:	Premium	Annual Deductible (max $320)	Co-Pay Max (max $660)	Cost $1,740 Gap	Total Estimate
_____	_____ +	_____ +	_____ +	_____ =	_____
_____	_____ +	_____ +	_____ +	_____ =	_____
_____	_____ +	_____ +	_____ +	_____ =	_____
_____	_____ +	_____ +	_____ +	_____ =	_____
_____	_____ +	_____ +	_____ +	_____ =	_____

Final Medicare Advantage Provider Selection

Provider Plan Name   **Total Cost Estimate**

_____ $ _____

Once you have narrowed down your choices you will then want to consider other benefits that the Medicare Advantage plan offers.

When you have made a selection, transfer this figure to the Annual Cost column in the Medicare Advantage row on the worksheet.

STEP FOUR: Find the cost of your preferred Medicare Supplement Insurance ("Medigap") policy.

If you have a Medigap policy you want to keep, then you may want to skip this step.

Medigap policies are available through private insurers. Prior to 2006 there were 10 standardized plans (referred to as A through J) that an insurer could offer. Starting in 2006, two additional plans, K and L, became available. Medigap policies help to pay the expenses not paid under Medicare Part A and B. You cannot get any prescription drug coverage from these plans as a new policyholder after 2005.

The price of Medigap policies <u>can</u> differ dramatically even within the same city. You can learn more about the various Medigap plans available and the premium rates you would be charged based on your age, gender, and zip code by going to our website at http://www.weissmedigap.com. Once you have educated yourself and are leaning towards the purchase of a supplemental policy, you will need to meet with an insurance agent to further refine your selection and purchase a policy.

Make sure to check the financial stability of any insurer by using Weiss Financial Strength Rating.

Once you have selected a Medicare Supplement policy enter the annual cost under the Medigap Plan column on the worksheet. If you need an estimate to enter into the worksheet until an amount can be determined, use $2000 as a placeholder for the annual price.

STEP FIVE: Complete the worksheet.

If you haven't done so already, use the figures from Steps 1 through 4 to fill in the dollar amounts in the relevant parts of the worksheet to determine your total annual cost for every option you want to consider. Re-use the worksheet if you need to make adjustments.

STEP SIX: Narrow down your choices.

The worksheet helps you to narrow down your choices by providing a snapshot, based on cost, of the prescription drug benefit options available to you. Of course, premiums are only one of the components needed to make a final decision. You must also consider other out-of-pocket costs, completeness of coverage, accessibility, and insurer financial strength.

STEP SEVEN: More Information.

Educate yourself. The www.Medicare.gov website, Medicare & You 2015 Handbook, local workshops, and Medicare benefit agents on hand at 1-800-MEDICARE are available to assist in answering your questions. Take advantage of these resources to make sure you fully understand your options.

Medicare Prescription Drug Worksheet

	Part A and B	Employer Plan	Medigap Plan H, I or J	Medigap Plan	Part D	Annual Cost
Part A and B plus Employee Retirement Plan Coverage	$ ____ +	$ ____				$ ____ =
Part A and B plus existing Medigap H, I or J	$ ____		$ ____ +			$ ____ =
Part A, B and D	$ ____				$ ____ +	$ ____ =
Part A, B and D plus Medigap	$ ____			$ ____ +	$ ____ +	$ ____ =
Medicare Advantage (Private Medicare-Sponsored Provider) including prescription drug coverage						$ ____ =

Medicare

RECENT INDUSTRY FAILURES
2014

Institution	Headquarters	Industry	Date of Failure	At Date of Failure	
				Total Assets ($Mil)	Financial Strength Rating
Union Mutual Ins Co	Oklahoma	P&C	01/24/14	5.1	E+ (Very Weak)
Commonwealth Ins Co	Pennsylvania	P&C	03/20/14	1.1	E (Very Weak)
LEMIC Ins Co	Louisiana	P&C	03/31/14	51.6	D (Weak)
Interstate Bankers Casualty Co	Illinois	P&C	04/16/14	16.2	D+ (Weak)
Freestone Ins Co	Delaware	P&C	04/28/14	421.2	D- (Weak)
Alameda Alliance For Health	California	Health	05/05/14	176.3	D (Weak)
Sunshine State Ins Co	Florida	P&C	06/03/14	22.9	E+ (Very Weak)
Physicians United Plan Inc	Florida	Health	06/09/14	110.7	E (Very Weak)
Red Rock Ins Co	Oklahoma	P&C	08/01/14	28.5	E+ (Very Weak)
First Keystone RRG Inc	S. Carolina	P&C	10/21/14	13.6	E+ (Very Weak)

2013

Institution	Headquarters	Industry	Date of Failure	At Date of Failure	
				Total Assets ($Mil)	Financial Strength Rating
Partnership Health Plan Inc	Wisconsin	Health	01/18/13	27.1	D (Weak)
Driver's Insurance Co	Oklahoma	P&C	02/21/13	33.1	D+ (Weak)
Lewis & Clark LTC RRG	Nevada	P&C	02/28/13	16.4	E (Very Weak)
Pride National Ins Co	Oklahoma	P&C	03/08/13	17.1	E+ (Very Weak)
Santa Fe Auto	Texas	P&C	03/08/13	22.9	E (Very Weak)
Ullico Casualty Co	Delaware	P&C	03/11/13	327.7	D (Weak)
Builders Ins Co Inc	Nevada	P&C	03/15/13	15.0	U (Unrated)
Nevada Contractors Ins Co Inc	Nevada	P&C	03/15/13	49.0	U (Unrated)
Universal Health Care Ins Co Inc	Florida	Health	03/22/13	106.1	C (Fair)
Universal Health Care Inc	Florida	Health	03/25/13	109.0	D (Weak)
Universal HMO of Texas	Texas	Health	04/18/13	15.3	C- (Fair)
Universal Health Care of NV Inc	Nevada	Health	06/03/13	1.9	D+ (Weak)
Liberty First RRG Ins Co	Utah	P&C	08/06/13	2.5	E (Very Weak)
United Contractors Ins Co Inc, RRG	Delaware	P&C	08/22/13	17.0	E (Very Weak)
Georgia Mutual Ins Co	Georgia	P&C	09/10/13	3.3	D (Weak)
Ocean Risk Retention Group	D. C.	P&C	09/06/13	7.9	E (Very Weak)
Gertrude Geddes Willis L I C	Louisiana	L&H	10/24/13	4.9	U (Unrated)
San Antonio Indemnity Co	Texas	P&C	10/31/13	2.8	E+ (Very Weak)
Higginbotham Burial Ins Co	Arkansas	L&H	11/04/13	1.3	U (Unrated)
Indemnity Ins Corp RRG	Delaware	P&C	11/07/13	83.2	D- (Weak)
ICM Insurance Co	New York	P&C	12/23/13	5.0	E+ (Very Weak)

2012

Institution	Headquarters	Industry	Date of Failure	At Date of Failure	
				Total Assets ($Mil)	Financial Strength Rating
Autoglass Ins Co	New York	P&C	01/09/12	29.7	U (Unrated)
Health Facilities of CA Mutual	Nevada	P&C	01/10/12	1.9	U (Unrated)
Republic Mortgage Ins Co	North Carolina	P&C	01/19/12	1.4	E (Very Weak)
CAGC Ins Co	North Carolina	P&C	01/26/12	11.8	U (Unrated)
First Sealord Surety Inc	Pennsylvania	P&C	02/08/12	15.2	U (Unrated)
Scaffold Industry Ins Co RRG	D.C.	P&C	05/01/12	5.1	E+ (Very Weak)
Financial Guaranty Ins Co	New York	P&C	06/11/12	2,054.0	E- (Very Weak)
AvaHealth Inc	Florida	HMO	06/27/12	3.3	E (Very Weak)
American Manufacturers Mutual	Illinois	P&C	07/02/12	10.3	E+ (Very Weak)
Lumbermens Mutual Casualty	Illinois	P&C	07/02/12	789.4	E (Very Weak)
Millers First Ins Co	Illinois	P&C	07/24/12	23.0	E (Very Weak)
American Motorists Ins Co	Illinois	P&C	08/16/12	19.7	D (Weak)
Home Value Ins Co	Ohio	P&C	08/31/12	3.5	U (Unrated)
Northern Plains Ins Co	South Dakota	P&C	09/18/12	1.4	D (Weak)
Jamestown Ins Co RRG	South Carolina	P&C	09/24/12	5.9	E+ (Very Weak)
Interstate Auto Ins Co	Maryland	P&C	10/11/12	4.6	D (Weak)
DC Chartered Health Plan Inc	D.C.	HMO	10/19/12	65.4	E- (Very Weak)
American Fellowship Mut Ins Co	Michigan	P&C	10/29/12	50.0	D (Weak)
Gramercy Ins Co	Texas	P&C	12/04/12	41.8	D (Weak)
Triad Guaranty ASR Corp	Illinois	P&C	12/11/12	16.1	B (Good)
Triad Guaranty Ins Corp	Illinois	P&C	12/11/12	766.7	E (Very Weak)

2011

| Institution | Headquarters | Industry | Date of Failure | At Date of Failure | |
				Total Assets ($Mil)	Financial Strength Rating
Comm. Ins. Alliance Reciprocal	Florida	P&C	01/26/11	N/A	N/A
Aequicap Ins Co	Florida	P&C	02/28/11	29.7	E+ (Very Weak)
US Rail Ins Co a RRG	Vermont	P&C	03/04/11	3.2	E (Very Weak)
Seminole Casualty Ins Co	Florida	P&C	03/15/11	35.6	D (Weak)
Majestic Insurance Co	California	P&C	04/21/11	313.1	D+ (Weak)
Reinsurance Co of America Inc	Illinois	P&C	04/27/11	7.1	D (Weak)
National Insurance Co	Puerto Rico	P&C	05/24/11	79.4	D+ (Weak)
Argus Fire & Casualty Ins Co	Florida	P&C	05/27/11	33.8	D (Weak)
Great Republic Life Ins Co	Washington	L&H	07/07/11	16.9	E+ (Very Weak)
National Group Ins Co	Florida	P&C	08/01/11	9.53	E- (Very Weak)
Federal Motors Carriers RRG	Delaware	P&C	08/18/11	11.9	E (Very Weak)
PMI Insurance Co	Arizona	P&C	08/19/11	436.9	D (Weak)
PMI Mortgage Ins Co	Arizona	P&C	08/19/11	2,841.2	D (Weak)
Western Insurance Co	Utah	P&C	08/25/11	21.66	U (Unrated)
Homewise Preferred Ins Co	Florida	P&C	09/02/11	11.1	E (Very Weak)
American Sterling Ins Co	California	P&C	09/26/11	15.4	D (Weak)
Quality Health Plans Inc	Florida	HMO	10/17/11	45.0	E+ (Very Weak)
HomeWise Ins Co	Florida	P&C	11/18/11	84.7	D (Weak)
Minnesota Surety & Trust Co	Minnesota	P&C	12/02/11	1.5	E (Very Weak)
Southern Eagle Ins Co	Florida	P&C	12/06/11	18.6	D (Weak)

2010

| Institution | Headquarters | Industry | Date of Failure | At Date of Failure | |
				Total Assets ($Mil)	Financial Strength Rating
First American Life Ins Co	Texas	L&H	02/18/10	9.4	E- (Very Weak)
Colonial Cooperative Ins Co	New York	P&C	2/25/2010	7.0	E (Very Weak)
Northern Capital Ins Co	Florida	P&C	02/25/10	78.2	E+(Very Weak)
Gibraltar National Ins Co	Arkansas	P&C	3/11/2010	4.9	E+ (Very Weak)
Imperial Casualty & Indemnity Co	Oklahoma	P&C	03/18/10	39.6	C- (Fair)
National States Ins Co	Missouri	L&H	04/01/10	70.5	E (Very Weak)
American Comm. Mutual Ins Co	Michigan	L&H	04/08/10	128.7	B (Good)
Financial Advisors Assurance Select	Nevada	P&C	04/26/10	0.9	E (Very Weak)
Prof. Liability Ins Co of America	New York	P&C	04/28/10	39.5	D- (Weak)
Pegasus Insurance Co Inc	Oklahoma	P&C	06/18/10	9.9	C- (Fair)
Gulf Builders RRG, Inc	South Carolina	P&C	08/02/10	N/A	U (Unrated)
Carrier Solutions Risk Retention	Delaware	P&C	08/09/10	N/A	N/A
Georgia Restaurant Mutual Captive	Georgia	P&C	08/26/10	1.2	U (Unrated)
Atlantic Mutual Ins Co	New York	P&C	09/16/10	205.4	E- (Very Weak)
Centennial Ins Co	New York	P&C	09/16/10	74.9	E- (Very Weak)
Georgia Timber Harvesters' Mutual	Georgia	P&C	09/21/10	N/A	N/A
Peoples Assured Family Life Ins Co	Mississippi	L&H	09/21/10	N/A	N/A
Guardian Healthcare Inc	South Carolina	HMO	10/12/10	11.0	U (Unrated)
Long Island Insurance Co	New York	P&C	10/19/10	6.7	E-(Very Weak)
Constitutional Casualty Co	Illinois	P&C	11/04/10	15.6	E+ (Very Weak)

2009

Institution	Headquarters	Industry	Date of Failure	At Date of Failure	
				Total Assets ($Mil)	Financial Strength Rating
Scottish RE US Inc	Delaware	L&H	01/05/09	2950.6	D (Weak)
American Network Ins Co	Pennsylvania	L&H	01/06/09	125.8	D+ (Weak)
Penn Treaty Network Amer. Ins	Pennsylvania	L&H	01/06/09	1037.6	C- (Fair)
Shenandoah Life Ins Co	Virginia	L&H	02/12/09	1735.0	B (Good)
SDM HealthCare	Puerto Rico	HMO	02/17/09	N/A	U (Unrated)
NSA Rrg Inc	Vermont	P&C	03/09/09	23.4	N/A
The Transportation Liability Ins	South Carolina	P&C	03/16/09	0.8	E-(Very Weak)
Cosmopolitan Life Ins Co.	Arkansas	L&H	03/19/09	2.6	E+(Very Weak)
Wonder State Life Ins Co	Arkansas	L&H	03/23/09	N/A	U (Unrated)
Coral Ins Co	Florida	P&C	04/09/09	15.4	E+(Very Weak)
Consumer First Ins Co.	New Jersey	P&C	04/22/09	10.7	D- (Weak)
Universal Life Insurance Co	Alabama	L&H	04/24/09	13.1	E (Very Weak)
Continental Life Ins Co of SC	South Carolina	L&H	04/27/09	2.2	E(Very Weak)
Eastern Casualty Ins Co	Massachusetts	P&C	04/27/09	28.2	U (Unrated)
Escude Life Ins Co.	Louisiana	L&H	04/27/09	3.0	E- (Very Weak)
Texas Memorial Life Ins Co	Texas	L&H	06/10/09	3.80	E-(Very Weak)
Insurance Corp of New York	New York	P&C	06/29/09	87.3	E- (Very Weak)
Old American County Mutual Fire	Texas	P&C	07/02/09	82.8	E+(Very Weak)
First Commercial Insurance Co.	Florida	P&C	07/10/09	87.1	E+(Very Weak)
First Comm. Transp. & Prop. Ins	Florida	P&C	07/10/09	19.6	E+(Very Weak)
Medicore HP	California	HMO	07/30/09	5.5	D (Weak)
Preferred Health	Puerto Rico	HMO	07/30/09	16.2	D- (Weak)
Physicians Assurance Corp	Ohio	HMO	08/18/09	3.4	D+ (Weak)
Golden State Mutual Life Ins Co	California	L&H	09/30/09	90.0	D (Weak)
American Keystone Ins Co	Florida	P&C	10/09/09	24.1	C- (Fair)
Southeastern US Ins Co	Georgia	P&C	10/28/09	42.5	E (Very Weak)
Imerica Life & Health Ins Co	Arkansas	HMO	11/18/09	8.4	D(Weak)
Park Avenue Prop. & Casualty Ins	Oklahoma	P&C	11/18/09	92.0	C- (Fair)
Magnolia Ins	Florida	P&C	12/14/09	N/A	N/A
ProSalud HMO Care	Puerto Rico	HMO	12/21/09	N/A	U (Unrated)
Astraea Risk Retention Grp, Inc	Arizona	P&C	12/30/09	3.5	E+(Very Weak)

State Insurance Commissioners'
Departmental Contact Information

State	*Official's Title*	*Website Address*	*Phone Number*
Alabama	Commissioner	www.aldoi.org	(334) 269-3550
Alaska	Director	www.dced.state.ak.us/insurance/	(907) 465-2515
Arizona	Director	www.id.state.az.us	(800) 325-2548
Arkansas	Commissioner	www.insurance.arkansas.gov	(800) 282-9134
California	Commissioner	www.insurance.ca.gov	(800) 927-4357
Colorado	Commissioner	www.dora.state.co.us/insurance/	(800) 930-3745
Connecticut	Commissioner	www.ct.gov/cid/	(860) 297-3800
Delaware	Commissioner	www.state.de.us/inscom/	(302) 674-7300
Dist. of Columbia	Commissioner	disr.dc.gov/disr/	(202) 727-8000
Florida	Commissioner	www.fldfs.com	(800) 342-2762
Georgia	Commissioner	www.gainsurance.org	(800) 656-2298
Hawaii	Commissioner	www.hawaii.gov/dcca/areas/ins/	(808) 586-2790
Idaho	Director	www.doi.idaho.gov	(800) 721-3272
Illinois	Director	www.idfpr.com/doi/	(217) 782-4515
Indiana	Commissioner	www.ia.org/idoi/	(317) 232-2385
Iowa	Commissioner	www.iid.state.ia.us	(877) 955-1212
Kansas	Commissioner	www.ksinsurance.org	(800) 432-2484
Kentucky	Executive Director	www.doi.ppr.ky.gov/kentucky/	(800) 595-6053
Louisiana	Commissioner	www.ldi.state.la.us	(800) 259-5300
Maine	Superintendent	www.maine.gov/pfr/insurance/	(800) 300-5000
Maryland	Commissioner	www.mdinsurance.state.md.us	(800) 492-6116
Massachusetts	Commissioner	www.mass.gov/doi/	(617) 521-7794
Michigan	Commissioner	www.michigan.gov/cis/	(877) 999-6442
Minnesota	Commissioner	www.commerce.state.mn.us	(651) 296-4026
Mississippi	Commissioner	www.doi.state.ms.us	(800) 562-2957
Missouri	Director	www.insurance.mo.gov/	(800) 726-7390
Montana	Commissioner	www.sao.state.mt.us	(800) 332-6148
Nebraska	Director	www.nebraska.gov	(402) 471-2306
Nevada	Commissioner	doi.state.nv.us	(775) 687-4270
New Hampshire	Commissioner	www.nh.gov/insurance/	(800) 852-3416
New Jersey	Commissioner	www.state.nj.us/dobi/	(800) 446-7467
New Mexico	Superintendent	www.nmprc.state.nm.us/id.htm	(888) 427-5772
New York	Superintendent	www.ins.state.ny.us	(800) 342-3736
North Carolina	Commissioner	www.ncdoi.com	(800) 546-5664
North Dakota	Commissioner	www.nd.gov/ndins/	(800) 247-0560
Ohio	Director	www.ohioinsurance.gov	(800) 686-1526
Oklahoma	Commissioner	www.oid.state.ok.us	(800) 522-0071
Oregon	Insurance Administrator	www.cbs.state.or.us/ins/	(503) 947-7980
Pennsylvania	Commissioner	www.ins.state.pa.us/ins/	(877) 881-6388
Puerto Rico	Commissioner	www.ocs.gobierno.pr	(787) 722-8686
Rhode Island	Superintendent	www.dbr.state.ri.us	(401) 222-2223
South Carolina	Director	www.doi..sc.gov	(800) 768-3467
South Dakota	Director	www.state.sd.us/drr2/reg/insurance/	(605) 773-3563
Tennessee	Commissioner	www.state.tn.us/commerce/insurance/	(800) 342-4029
Texas	Commissioner	www.tdi.state.tx.us	(800) 252-3439
Utah	Commissioner	www.insurance.utah.gov	(800) 439-3805
Vermont	Commissioner	www.bishca.state.vt.us	(802) 828-3301
Virgin Islands	Lieutenant Governor	www.ltg.gov.vi	(340) 774-7166
Virginia	Commissioner	www.scc.virginia.gov/division/boi/	(877) 310-6560
Washington	Commissioner	www.insurance.wa.gov	(800) 562-6900
West Virginia	Commissioner	www.wvinsurance.gov	(304) 558-3386
Wisconsin	Commissioner	oci.wi.gov	(800) 236-8517
Wyoming	Commissioner	insurance.state.wy.us	(800) 438-5768

Glossary

This glossary contains the most important terms used in this publication.

Admitted Assets The total of all investments and business interests that are acceptable under statutory accounting rules.

Asset/Liability Matching The designation of particular investments (assets) to particular policy obligations (liabilities) so that investments mature at the appropriate times and with appropriate yields to meet policy obligations as they come due.

Asset Valuation Reserve (AVR) A liability established under statutory accounting rules whose purpose is to protect the company's surplus from the effects of defaults and market value fluctuation on stocks, bonds, mortgages, and real estate. This replaces the Mandatory Securities Valuation Reserve (MSVR) and is more comprehensive in that it includes a mortgage loss reserve, whereas the MSVR did not.

Average Recession A recession involving a decline in real GDP which is approximately equivalent to the average of the postwar recessions of 1957-58, 1960, 1970, 1974-75, 1980, and 1981-82. It is assumed, however, that in today's market, the financial losses suffered from a recession of that magnitude would be greater than those experienced in previous decades. (See also "Severe Recession.").

Capital Strictly speaking, capital refers to funds raised through the sale of common and preferred stock. Mutual companies have capital in the form of retained earnings. In a more general sense, the term capital is commonly used to refer to a company's equity or net worth, that is, the difference between assets and liabilities (i.e., capital and surplus as shown on the balance sheet).

Capital Resources The sum of various resources which serve as a capital cushion to losses, including capital, surplus, and Asset Valuation Reserve (AVR).

Capitalization Index An index, expressed on a scale of zero to ten, with seven or higher considered excellent, that measures the adequacy of the company's capital resources to deal with a variety of business and economic scenarios. It combines Risk-Adjusted Capital Ratios #1 and #2 as well as a leverage test that examines pricing risk.

Cash and Demand Deposits	Includes cash on hand and on deposit. A negative figure indicates that the company has more checks outstanding than current funds to cover those checks. This is not an unusual situation for an insurance company.
Collateralized Mortgage Obligation (CMO)	Mortgage-backed bond that splits the payments from mortgage pools into different classes, called tranches. The investor may purchase a bond or tranche that passes through to him or her the principal and interest payments made by the mortgage holders in that specific maturity class (usually two, five, 10, or 20 years). The risk associated with a CMO is in the variation of the payment speed on the mortgage pool which, if different than originally assumed, can cause the total return to vary greatly.
Common and Preferred Stocks	See "Stocks".
Deposit Funds	Accumulated contributions of a group out of which immediate annuities are purchased as the individual members of the group retire.
Direct Premiums Written	Total gross premiums derived from policies issued directly by the company. This figure excludes the impact of reinsurance.
Financial Strength Rating	Weiss Financial Strength Ratings grade insurers on a scale from A (Excellent) to F (Failed). Ratings are based on five major factors: investment safety, policy leverage, capitalization, profitability, and stability of operations.
Five-Year Profitability Index	See "Profitability Index."
Government Securities	Securities issued and/or guaranteed by U.S. and foreign governments which are rated as highest quality (Class 1) by state insurance commissioners. Included in this category are bonds issued by governmental agencies and guaranteed with the full faith and credit of the government. Regardless of the issuing entity, they are viewed as being relatively safer than the other investment categories. See "Investment Grade Bonds" to determine which items are excluded from this category.
Health Claims Reserve	Funds set aside from premiums for the eventual payment of health benefits after the end of the statement year.
Insurance Risk	The risk that the level of claims and related expenses will exceed current premiums plus reserves allocated for their payment.
Interest Rate Risk	The risk that, due to changes in interest rates, investment income will not meet the needs of policy commitments. This risk can be reduced by effective asset/liability matching.

Invested Assets	The total size of the firm's investment portfolio.
Investment Grade Bonds	This covers all investment grade bonds other than those listed in "Government Securities" (above). Specifically, this includes: (1) nonguaranteed obligations of governments, (2) obligations of governments rated as Class 2 by state insurance commissioners, (3) state and municipal bonds, plus (4) investment grade corporate bonds.
Investment Safety Index	Measured on a scale of zero to ten, with ten being the best and seven or better considered strong. Each investment area is rated as to quality and vulnerability during an unfavorable economic environment (updated using quarterly data when available).
Investments in Affiliates	Includes bonds, preferred stocks, and common stocks, as well as other vehicles which many insurance companies use to invest in—and establish a corporate link with—affiliated companies.
Life and Annuity Claims Reserve	Funds set aside from premiums for the eventual payment of life and annuity claims.
Liquidity Index	An index, expressed on a scale from zero to ten, with seven or higher considered excellent, which measures the company's ability to raise the necessary cash to meet policyholder obligations. This index includes a stress test which considers the consequences of a spike in claims or a run on policy surrenders. Sometimes a company may appear to have the necessary resources, but may be unable to sell its investments at the prices at which they are valued in the company's financial statements.
Mandatory Security Valuation Reserve (MSVR)	Reserve for investment losses and asset value fluctuation mandated by the state insurance commissioners for companies registered as life and health insurers. As of December 31, 1992, this was replaced by the Asset Valuation Reserve. HMDI companies are not required to establish such a reserve.
Moderate Loss Scenario	An economic decline from current levels approximately equivalent to that of the average postwar recession.
Mortgages in Good Standing	Mortgages which are current in their payments (excludes mortgage-backed securities).
Net Premiums Written	The total dollar volume of premiums retained by the company. This figure is equal to direct premiums written, plus reinsurance assumed less reinsurance ceded.
Noninvestment Grade Bonds	Low-rated issues, commonly known as "junk bonds," which carry a high risk as defined by the state insurance commissioners. These include bond Classes 3 - 6.
Nonperforming Mortgages	Mortgages which are (a) 90 days or more past due or (b) in process of foreclosure.
Other Investments	Items not included in any of the other categories such as contract loans (which include premium notes), receivables for securities, aggregate write-ins and other invested assets.

Other Structured Securities	Nonresidential-mortgage-related and other securitized loan-backed or asset-backed securities. This category also includes CMOs with noninvestment grade ratings.
Policy Leverage	A measure of insurance risk based on the relationship of net premiums to capital resources.
Policy Loans	Loans to policyholders under insurance contracts.
Profitability Index	Measured on a scale of zero to ten, with ten being the best and seven or better considered strong. A composite of five factors: (1) gain or loss on operations, (2) consistency of operating results, (3) impact of operating results on surplus, (4) adequacy of investment income as compared to the needs of policy reserves, and (5) expenses in relation to industry averages. Thus, the overall index is an indicator of the health of a company's current and past operations.
Purchase Money Mortgages	Mortgages written by an insurance company to facilitate the sale of property owned by the company.
Real Estate	Direct real estate investments including property (a) occupied by the company, (b) acquired through foreclosure and (c) purchased as an investment.
Reinsurance Assumed	Insurance risk acquired by taking on partial or full responsibility for claims on policies written by other companies. (See "Reinsurance Ceded.")
Reinsurance Ceded	Insurance risk sold to another company.
Risk-Adjusted Capital	The capital resources that would be needed in a worsening economic environment (same as "Target Capital").
Risk-Adjusted Capital Ratio #1	The capital resources which a company currently has, in relation to the resources that would be needed to deal with a moderate loss scenario. This scenario is based on historical experience during an average recession and adjusted to reflect current conditions and vulnerabilities (updated using quarterly data when available).
Risk-Adjusted Capital Ratio #2	The capital resources which a company currently has, in relation to the resources that would be needed to deal with a severe loss scenario. This scenario is based on historical experience of the postwar period and adjusted to reflect current conditions and the potential impact of a severe recession (updated using quarterly data when available).
Separate Accounts	Funds segregated from the general account and valued at market. Used to fund indexed products, such as variable life and variable annuity products.
Severe Loss Scenario	An economic decline from current levels in which the loss experience of the single worst year of the postwar period is extended for a period of three years. (See also "Moderate Loss Scenario" above.)
Severe Recession	A prolonged economic slowdown in which the single worst year of the postwar period is extended for a period of three years. (See also "Average Recession" above.)

Stability Index   Measured on a scale of zero to ten. This integrates a wide variety of factors that reflects the company's financial stability and diversification of risk.

State of Domicile   Although most insurance companies are licensed to do business in many states, they have only one state of domicile. This is the state that has primary regulatory responsibility for the company. Use the state of domicile to make absolutely sure that you have the correct company. Bear in mind, however, that this need not be the state where the company's main offices are located.

State Guaranty Funds   Funds that are designed to raise cash from existing insurance carriers to cover policy claims of bankrupt insurance companies.

Stocks   Common and preferred equities, including ownership in affiliates.

Surplus   The difference between assets and liabilities, including paid-in contributed surplus, plus the statutory equivalent of "retained earnings" in noninsurance business corporations.

Target Capital   See "Risk-Adjusted Capital."

Total Assets   Total admitted assets, including investments and other business assets. See "Admitted Assets."